Handbooks of Sociology and Social Research

Series editor
John DeLamater
University of Wisconsin, Madison, WI, USA

Each of these Handbooks survey the field in a critical manner, evaluating theoretical models in light of the best available empirical evidence. Distinctively sociological approaches are highlighted by means of explicit comparison to perspectives characterizing related disciplines such as psychology, psychiatry, and anthropology. These seminal works seek to record where the field has been, to identify its current location and to plot its course for the future. If you are interested in submitting a proposal for this series, please contact the series editor, John DeLamater: delamate@ssc.wisc.edu.

More information about this series at http://www.springer.com/series/6055

Barbara Schneider
Editor

Guan Kung Saw
Associate Editor
Michigan State University

Handbook of the Sociology of Education in the 21st Century

 Springer

Editor
Barbara Schneider
College of Education, Department of Sociology
Michigan State University
East Lansing, MI, USA

ISSN 1389-6903   ISSN 2542-839X   (electronic)
Handbooks of Sociology and Social Research
ISBN 978-3-319-76692-8   ISBN 978-3-319-76694-2   (eBook)
https://doi.org/10.1007/978-3-319-76694-2

Library of Congress Control Number: 2018944151

This Springer imprint is published by the registered company Springer International Publishing AG part of Springer Nature.
The registered company address is: Gewerbestrasse 11, 6330 Cham, Switzerland

Foreword

To the question, "Does the sociology of education matter in the 21st century?", this book provides a resounding "Yes!" It accomplishes this feat by vigorously pursuing pressing problems in the field, by examining feasible responses to those problems in theory, policy, and practice, and by considering new ways to increase the chances that evidence produced by sociologists will make a difference in the real world.

Enhancing opportunity and reducing inequality are at the heart of sociology as a discipline, and this is especially the case for the sociology of education, because education both reflects and contributes to stratification and inequality in the wider society. At a time of rising inequality in the United States, it is especially important that sociologists turn their attention not just to assessing the extent and sources of inequality, but to identifying effective responses to inequality (Gamoran 2014). It was heartening, therefore, to discover that access and opportunity constitute a unifying theme throughout this volume.

In December 2013, President Barack Obama called out "growing inequality and lack of upward mobility," which threaten the U.S. economy, social cohesion, and the practice of democracy, as "the defining challenge of our time." In the remaining three years of his term in office, some gaps began to narrow, most obviously in healthcare coverage but in the income distribution as well (Casselman 2016). In education, too, there were already signs that growing inequality may have been on the way toward reversing course (Reardon and Portilla 2016). Yet since the election of his successor and especially with the massive, partisan tax bill passed in late 2017 favoring high-income and wealthy Americans, recent gains may soon be lost. As a result, contributions from sociologists on access and opportunity in education are needed now more than ever.

This volume answers the call with timely reconsiderations of the familiar domain of the sociology of education. It is timely, first, because it emphasizes population groups that have not received enough attention in the past but which are crucial for addressing contemporary inequalities: immigrants, including undocumented young people; students who are the first-generation in their family to attend college; and sexual minority youth. Moreover, the familiar sociodemographic groups defined by gender, race, ethnicity, and social class are explored with greater attention to their intersectionality—the way these categorizations intersect and the special consequences for inequality of such dual or triple status distinctions—than in much of the past literature in sociology. The authors bring both theoretical and empirical aspects of intersectionality to bear on the challenge of understanding and addressing inequality.

Second, the work is both timely and needed because it recognizes the centrality of the opportunities young people have to experience rich, meaningful, and effective schooling. Whether the focus is on cognitive gains, social and emotional skills, or economic advances, productive opportunities for learning and interacting with others are at the core of the educational enterprise. Many of the chapters of this Handbook peer intently at how students' social and academic opportunities vary. To improve outcomes and reduce gaps, it is essential to consider, assess, and improve approaches to enrich young peoples' opportunities for learning and interaction.

Third, the chapters in this volume offer timely attention to the transition from schooling to the world of work. As technological developments have changed the nature of work and put a premium on skills as a determinant of economic rewards, schooling plays an increasing role, via both human and social capital development. Advancing equity in the twenty-first century requires that sociologists examine connections between access to schooling and workplace opportunities. Moreover, the last two decades have witnessed increasing attention to various forms of higher education within the sociology of education, and these developments are well represented in this Handbook.

Fourth, the volume is innovative in its attention to the challenges of getting evidence from research into the hands of policymakers and practitioners who will take the evidence into account when making decisions that affect young people. Typically, even the strongest contributions in the sociology of education have much more to say about the extent, sources, and consequences of inequality than about ways to *reduce* inequality. This volume, however, includes several chapters that focus on ways to reduce gaps. Even the most insightful research, moreover, will fail to contribute to equity if does not confront those making decisions. Research is more likely to influence policy and practice if it occurs within the context of ongoing relationships between producers and consumers of research, and the intermediary organizations that bring them together, as contrasted with the more typical approach of researchers acting on their own from within the metaphorical ivory tower (DuMont 2015). Consequently, this Handbook brings valuable attention to such relationships, in the form of teacher networks and research–practice partnerships, which may help turn research into action.

Why should sociologists of education focus on ways to *reduce* inequality (Gamoran 2014)? First, inequality in the United States is excessive, whether compared to other countries or our own past history. Second, excessive inequality is harmful, as it is socially divisive and a drag on economic productivity. Third, we are not paralyzed in the face of inequality; on the contrary, it is demonstrable that social programs can reduce inequality. The War on Poverty has not been won, for example, but there is less poverty today than there would be without the social programs enacted through this set of policies (Bailey and Danziger 2013). Fourth, we need research to identify which programs will be effective in reducing inequality, and that is the point of entry for sociologists of education.

Finally, the strength of this volume is that it examines specific strategies to improve access and opportunity in areas ranging from school–family relationships to charter schools to community colleges and alternative certification programs and other domains. Yet such interventions may be modest balms to heal major sores; that is, even the most effective programs may have little potency when larger social structural conditions preserve the deeply stratified foundations of society. Perhaps uniquely among the social science disciplines, sociologists have a role to play in exploring the structural foundations of inequality, demonstrating that reducing gaps is not merely a matter of providing equal access, but of dismantling and reconstructing the social structures that create unequal opportunities in the first place. Here, too, woven throughout many of its chapters, this Handbook provides the right place to start.

President, William T. Grant Foundation   Adam Gamoran

References

Bailey, M. J., & Danziger, S. (2013). *Legacies of the war on poverty*. New York: Russell Sage Foundation.

Casselman, B. (2016, September 26). The income gap began to narrow under Obama. *RealClearPolitics*. Available at https://fivethirtyeight.com/features/the-income-gap-began-to-narrow-under-obama/

DuMont, K. (2015). *Leveraging knowledge: Taking stock of the William T. Grant Foundation's use of research evidence grants portfolio*. New York: William T. Grant Foundation. Available at http://wtgrantfoundation.org/library/uploads/2015/09/Leveraging-Knowledge-Taking-Stock-of-URE.pdf

Gamoran, A. (2014). *Inequality is the problem: Prioritizing research on reducing inequality*. New York: William T. Grant Foundation. Available at http://wtgrantfoundation.org/library/uploads/2015/09/Inequality-is-the-Problem-Prioritizing-Research-on-Inequality.pdf

Obama, B. (2013, December 4). *Remarks by the President on economic mobility*. Washington, DC: The White House. Available at https://obamawhitehouse.archives.gov/the-press-office/2013/12/04/remarks-president-economic-mobility

Reardon, S. F., & Portilla, X. A. (2016). Recent trends in income, racial, and ethnic school readiness gaps at kindergarten entry. *AERA Open*, 2(3).

Preface

One of the major intellectual leaders in the discipline of sociology, and sociology of education in particular, was Professor Maureen Hallinan. Over her exceptional career in sociology, she conducted some of the most theoretically and empirically path-breaking studies on ability grouping; friendship ties; and the intersection between educational opportunities and race, ethnicities, and socioeconomic resources among students in public and private high schools. Her volume on the *Handbook of Sociology of Education* demonstrates the breadth of her vision and how she viewed the field of sociology of education at the beginning of the twenty-first century. Central to her vision was the idea that sociology of education is principally about the study of schools in three intersecting domains: (1) the formal organizational structure of schools and the interrelationships they have with other social systems such as the families and communities; (2) the internal function of schools that shape student and teacher social behaviors, attitudes, and performance; and (3) the estimation of schooling's impact on educational and occupational attainment. A volume on *Sociology of Education* should be about the study of schooling, as Hallinan elegantly describes in the introduction of her handbook, but the study of schooling has changed quite dramatically since 2000. This volume encompasses a new range of topics, methodological developments, and contributions sociology of education is making to educational practice and public policy.

Schooling careers begin in the family, and this volume is designed to be holistic in its coverage of the role of the family in their children's education from preschool through postsecondary education. The actions parents take with their children to advance their learning and how they vary by race, ethnicity, and social and economic circumstances are a critical aspect of sociology of education. Recognizing the importance of how families view education and the actions they take regarding their children's education, several chapters explore preschool education opportunities, homeschooling, school choice, and parent direct involvement in supplemental out-of-school activities which are of intellectual and political interest. The intent of many of the authors is to underscore how education norms—actions, interests, and sanctions—are developed and reinforced in the home, community, and school, rather than exclusively focusing on connections between the family and the school.

The outcomes of education are no longer measured strictly by academic achievement. Today, we increasingly recognize the interrelationships between academic performance and social and emotional learning that occurs throughout one's schooling career. Many of the chapters blend the relationship of these outcomes and their association with transitions into successful adulthood. Just as some of the authors examine the early beginnings of informal and formal schooling, several of the chapters move beyond the K–12 system to postsecondary education and beyond. The widening interest in higher education today needs a deeper and more comprehensive focus on the changing landscape of the variety of postsecondary institutions and the respective populations they serve. Several authors take up how labor market opportunities are enhanced or impeded by different postsecondary education, trainings, and occupational pathways.

Instead of placing a special section on inequality of educational opportunity, social justice, and questions of meritocracy and privilege, the authors take up these issues in the context of their work on such topics as school choice, accountability systems, teacher performance assessments, and special services for various populations including immigrants, undocumented students, and those with special needs. Several chapters are devoted to examining the continuing problems associated with race and social class, and more recently sexual orientation, all of which are discussed in relation to how larger educational social systems operate differentially and prejudicially for certain populations they serve.

There are a growing number of sociologists of education who are undertaking new methodological work for studying social systems, including network analyses, impact of household resources on educational mobility, and school and teacher effects on student performance. Some of these chapters are included in sections to demonstrate how context including communities, structure of the school year, and state policies mediate students' lives in and out of school. The work of these individuals is also included here in part to underscore how sociologists of education, who were among the first to model and estimate the nested structure of students within classrooms between schools, are now being followed by these authors and the contributions they are making for the study of education.

Moving away from standalone chapters on topics such as "the history of curricular tracking," all of the authors were asked to provide a historical theoretical overview to situate their topic and empirical work in the area. What this means is instead of a single theoretical section, each chapter has its own theoretical framing, including a major emphasis on the seminal empirical work in this area and a critique of its relevance to today. Additionally, the volume has a unifying theme, in that each of the chapters touches on the issues of institutional access and opportunity in the K–16 system for different groups of students (e.g., including race, ethnicity, socioeconomic class, ability, and special needs), taking into account immigration status and regional differences.

This book is not your traditional sociology of education volume; it is not narrow in its scope. It is forward-thinking and captures the issues that are now facing education, threading back to their provenance, and weaving them into a matrix that has cross-disciplinary interest for those in sociology, education, and other social science fields. Edited specifically for undergraduate,

graduate, and policy audiences, the message is one that reinforces why we need to be vigilant in addressing how inequities in schooling are manifested in the educational system. The major emphasis of all the chapters is that it is the social context of education that forms and shapes inequality of educational opportunities.

Perhaps the most unusual aspect of this volume is the authors themselves. Invitations for the chapters were sent to key senior authors in each of the chapters that constitute the five sections of the book. The invitations asked each to select their most promising graduate student(s) and/or newly minted colleague(s) to be a coauthor. The idea was not only to make the ideas fresh but to encourage the next generation of sociologists of education to take the reins on our future. I am thrilled that so many of my colleagues took up the offer and have produced some of the best chapters on the state of sociology of education today and where it needs to be for tomorrow.

I am very appreciative to all the authors and their dedication and commitment to the process and how quickly the book has come to fruition.

There is one person who truly made this book happen, and that is Guan Saw, the associate editor. His help has been invaluable in the development of this volume, and he is mainly the one who kept it on track. Like many of the authors in this volume, at the beginning of last year, he took his first academic position as an assistant professor at the University of Texas San Antonio, and kept the press on me and everyone else to bring the volume to completion. His ability to conquer multiple theories and methodologies is indeed remarkable. It is because of his contributions that the volume consists of a range of authors whose knowledge spans a diversity of emerging topics at the nexus of sociology of education.

And finally, we also contacted two blind senior scholars and those with specialized expertise as reviewers for each chapter. Their names are listed in the appendix. Thank you all.

East Lansing, MI, USA   Barbara Schneider
September 2017

Contents

**Part III The Social Organization of Schooling and Opportunities
         for Learning**

**Part IV Educational Opportunities and the Transition
into Adulthood**

Introduction

To achieve a more equitable, just, and functioning society, we need to pay attention to why some less-advantaged students receive a substantially lower quality of education than their more-advantaged peers. We need to understand why the educational needs of those with limited economic and social resources remain unheeded while the institutions that serve them remain woefully inadequate. This Handbook is not a well-rehearsed summary of the seminal work in the sociology of education—work that is often mired in debates of equity and barriers to social mobility. It is instead a compilation of 25 chapters that takes a contemporary sociological view of the issues facing education in the U.S. today, including the sources of many of these problems and what is needed to address them. Each chapter in this volume attends to the theoretical underpinnings of educational inequality while often turning them on their heads, questioning their relevance for today's varied educational landscape and the unforeseen—but now unfortunately real—social and economic consequences of inequality.

The sociology of education has long retained a central place in the field, as scholars recognize the importance of how families, communities, and schools shape individuals' actions and attitudes. It is not just the impact of social systems that continues to intrigue researchers but *how* these interdependent systems function as they interact both with the environments in which they exist and the smaller units within the systems themselves. A key objective of this volume is, therefore, to capture how social systems affect individuals and how social systems are shaped by their environments. To understand why some individuals succeed when the odds are clearly against them, or how some schools become sites of exemplary education in spite of limited resources, we need to investigate the interrelationships among individuals and their social systems. As a result, the chapters in this volume do not separate the individual or the institution from one another. Instead, the focus is on the actions and values embedded in each and how they relate to one another. The Handbook is organized into five major sections, each of which examines an interlocking theme that characterizes these interrelationships.

Part I. Families, Schools, and Educational Opportunity

Our volume begins with the family, which over the past 50 years has become a hallmark of the way values, resources, and subsequently social class are transferred from parents to children. The chapters in this section describe how this process is disrupted by social systems, such as schools and communities that interface with the family. Special attention is given to communities, which often receive limited consideration but can be powerful transmitters of the cultural values and attitudes that motivate actions by families, their children, and schools. Schools shoulder the primary responsibility for fostering successful academic performance—though they have the support of families and communities, schools cannot achieve this goal without society as a whole taking a major role in improving educational opportunities for all students.

Chapter 1, by George Farkas, bridges the relationship between parents' occupations and dispositions and their children's skills and habits, then examines how these characteristics influence teachers' judgments of student outcomes. Using the theoretical perspective of Pierre Bourdieu, Farkas describes how social class differences in parenting and parenting resources relate to school success and educational attainment. His comprehensive analysis of Bourdieu brings a clarity to how social class is reproduced, using an empirical analysis of middle school children through which he shows that the strongest determinants of grades are not cognitive skills but work habits demonstrated in school. Work habits include social learning behaviors such as "works well independently and with others," "is courteous," and "persists and completes tasks"; reviewing studies of these social behaviors, Farkas argues for their closer examination in relation to student performance, and cautions researchers against attributing differences in performance to broad distinctions of parents' social class activities (i.e., parent-organized activities and involvement in schools). This sociological emphasis on how students work in classrooms corresponds, in part, to many of the social behaviors that social psychologists have identified as fundamental to learning, such as a student's ability to persist at a task. The chapter concludes with policy prescriptions and suggested research studies showing how teachers' judgments of work habits can be used more effectively to lessen variation in academic performance.

Chapter 2, by Erin McNamara Horvat and Karen Pezzetti, extends traditional conceptions of family and provides an evidential voice to the importance of community for improving educational outcomes and reducing educational disparities. Reviewing work by James S. Coleman on social capital—the value of the relationships of an individual or a group—the authors argue that this perspective is critical for understanding school–home–community relations. They then highlight others who have stressed the significance of trustworthy connections for school success. This chapter describes how relationships are not composed of groups of "equal players" but commonly function through power and privilege across different racial, ethnic, and social classes, often forming unequal opportunities for parent participation and allocation of educational resources. These ideas have been incorporated into several new interventions that foster "grassroot" involvement to stimulate demand for parent and community organizing—not only for school reform, but in the neighborhoods where the schools and the students they serve are situated. There is substantial evidence about these types of parent and community initiatives, but the authors are cautious in explaining why reform requires serious study of the relationships across school, home, and community.

The last chapter in this section, by Douglas B. Downey, Aimee Yoon, and Elizabeth Martin, shifts our focus to the school. The authors' primary argument is that although schools start the formal educational process late in a child's development, they can (and have) made a difference in improving academic performance and social development, including schools attended by disadvantaged children. Beginning with the traditional narrative about schools and inequality—which posits that schools can only do so much to alter the huge variations in academic performance primarily due to disparate family, social, and economic resources—this chapter presents the alternative explanation that not all schools function in the same way: Some are more successful than others in producing positive academic outcomes. Neither of these explanations, the authors maintain, explain how schools can influence inequality. What, they ask, would inequality look like if schools did not exist? To answer this question, the chapter reviews several seminal studies of seasonal comparisons of schools—that is, comparing changes in achievement gaps when school is in session over a 9-month period, in contrast to the 3-month summer break. The authors provide several rationales for why this "seasonal approach," including its limitations, is particularly useful for overcoming problems with isolating school effects. They show that older studies suggest that summer can be a time when achievement gaps increase more than in the school year, while newer studies with larger samples show the opposite—that is, the Black–White achievement gap grows faster during the school year. Yet, when examining achievement by socioeconomic status, results show that the variation in children's skills grows about 50% faster when they are out of school than when school is in session. With the recognition that schools can only do so much, the authors nonetheless conclude by identifying several policy options that they suspect would likely benefit low-SES students and reduce inequality in mathematics and reading skills.

Part II. The Changing Demographics of Social Inequality

The landscape of the U.S. educational system has changed dramatically over the past several decades as the number of racial and ethnic minorities has continued to grow, eclipsing the White public elementary and secondary school population in 2014 (NCES 2017). The U.S. school population also serves increasing numbers of immigrants, whose resident status can limit access and persistence within the educational system; many are the first in their families to attend college, and face multiple obstacles as they try to navigate the increasingly complex postsecondary system while retaining a sense of belonging. Females now outnumber males in high school completion and higher education enrollment, but still fail to enter or advance in some occupations. Society's recognition of the multidimensionality of gender and sexuality—lesbian, gay, bisexual, transgender, or queer (LGBTQ)—has major implications for the educational system as it must now address the physical, social, and emotional needs of youths' gender and sexual identities. The six chapters in this section center around the ways in which the educational system has and has not assured equality of opportunity for these populations.

Samuel R. Lucas and Véronique Irwin begin Chap. 4 by presenting evidence of disparities in educational performance for students of different socioeconomic and racial backgrounds, and question why this is the case: What theories can explain why these patterns exist and have for multiple years? The authors describe their criteria for what constitutes a viable theory of inequality, separating theories into those that are *expansive* (generalizable, dynamic, and include processes or mechanisms) and those that are *narrow* (specific, static, and correlational). In either case, any claims made by these theories need to reference conceptual entities, be observable, map on to multiple patterns, be internally consistent rather than contradictory, and not be repetitive or redundant in their assertions. Focusing only on expansive theories of inequality, Lucas and Irwin identify ten such theories, highlighting their strengths and limitations for reducing inequality. The authors then engage in an in-depth assessment of combining theories, two of which they undertake empirically. Others—stereotype threat, the Wisconsin social-psychological model, and incorporation theory—have evidential claims and are presented as conceptually linked, though not empirically investigated by the authors. The chapter concludes with a message for why theories are important and need to be developed: If we are to remedy class- and racial/ethnic-linked educational inequality, there needs to be a justifiable explanation for its persistence that extends beyond singular theories that are fairly narrow in scope and difficult to reconcile.

In Chap. 5, Phoebe Ho and Grace Kao introduce their argument that contextual factors *beyond* family socioeconomic class distinctions account for significant differences in the education performance and attainment of racial/ethnic minority students by presenting evidence from the largest national educational survey of U.S. students: the National Assessment of Education Progress (NAEP). Using data from preschool enrollment through postsecondary completion that show differences in performance, the authors consistently highlight the process mechanisms (quality early childhood programs, coursework, college preparatory activities, and college access and affordability) that are often neglected in the allocation of education resources devoted to minority and immigrant children but that could be directed to them to promote educational success. An important contribution of this chapter is its examination of how students identify themselves, through a review of studies that debate the existence of a racial and ethnic hierarchical structure that reifies existing stereotypes, power structures, and intergenerational family conflict. The authors conclude with an in-depth discussion of the nonfamilial resources that are likely to matter, especially with respect to the educational success of minority and immigrant students; these include teacher expectations, straddling school and peer cultures, and neighborhood effects, particularly in areas with substantial increases in immigrant populations. In light of recent racist and anti-immigrant sentiment, how and why these education mechanisms affect the academic performance and social well-being of different groups takes on unprecedented immediacy and importance, both nationally and globally.

The intersectionality of gender, race, ethnic identity, and performance are the thematic conceptions that link the arguments and evidence Catherine Riegle-Crumb et al. present in Chap. 6, to show disparities in educational performance and identify considerations for future studies of education. Selecting grades, test scores, and course-taking—three observable measures that strongly predict students' postsecondary school success—and including factors linked to labor market participation, the authors demonstrate how these indicators sustain educational inequality and their impact on the labor force. The first part of the chapter examines gender differences in education, showing a female advantage with respect to grades and course-taking but a disadvantage with respect to enrollment in highly selective universities and some STEM fields. Theories attempting to validate these differences, the authors argue, are (1) too concentrated on a specific disparity; (2) contradictory to explanations regarding socialization; and (3) tautological, especially with respect to field of study (these criticisms reflect criteria identified by Lucas and Irwin in Chap. 4). Next, the authors concentrate on patterns of racial and ethnic differences in educational outcomes, arguing for the development of theories that target resource allocation and opportunities within school, and economic and social factors outside school, to understand inequities (points also made by Downy et al. in Chap. 3). The chapter concludes with an explicit agenda for future research that questions the reliance on standardized testing as an outcome measure; emphasizes more attention to school context and how it shapes inequality; and stresses the need for a clearer representation of the intersectionality of gender, race, ethnicity, and performance and its import in the social context of young people's lives.

In Chap. 7, Roberto G. Gonzales and Edelina M. Burciaga discuss research—theirs and others'—that describes the challenges undocumented youth experience growing up in the U.S., and how the youths' responses to these challenges relate to aspects of their schooling careers (i.e., enrolling in college versus leaving high school before completion) and location (i.e., living in urban versus rural environments, or in specific states). Although they lack legal citizenship, undocumented students can attend schools, which the authors label legally protected spaces. But these protected spaces are typically located in segregated, high-poverty neighborhoods, where schools are under-resourced and unapproachable for undocumented parents seeking additional educational services, such as for children with special needs. Recognizing the lack of large-scale data collections on undocumented students, the authors draw on their own intensive qualitative longitudinal studies in urban areas; these studies examine the values, social relations, and agency of undocumented youth, and the sense they make of their racial and ethnic identities. The chapter highlights the authors' individual research, specifically on the conflict regarding what it means to be undocumented and to claim one's country of origin; and how students grapple with what being undocumented means for their ability to, for instance, get a driver's license, apply to college, and access different sources of financial support. For these "exiters" (the authors' term), experiencing a lack of high-quality instruction, educational services, and meaningful connections in school often results in dead-end jobs and living in fear of deportation; these circumstances take their toll, with many exiters experiencing mental and physical problems. The college-goers are not without their own pressures and stresses that can derail persistence, whether over finances, the questionable future of Deferred Action for Childhood Arrivals (DACA), feelings of exclusion, or other college-related decisions (usually state-specific). Scholarly interest in undocumented students is likely to escalate in light of pending court cases that will determine not only these students' citizenship status, but what that status will mean for their future lives, both in the U.S. and their country of origin.

Chapter 8, by Irenee R. Beattie, delves deeper into the first-generation college students (FGS)—students whose parents did not complete their college degrees. Beattie argues that though sociologists have been relatively slow to study FGS, this population now constitutes a significant proportion of those attending college, especially among those in 2-year colleges (although, as she points out, these estimates are often inconsistent). As Riegle-Crumb and coauthors argue in Chap. 6, it is the intersectionality of FGS with gender, identity, and immigration status that can help isolate and track how institutional variation has interfered with students' transition to college, persistence, and completion. FGS, Beattie argues, represent a key population for understanding how and why social mobility functions differentially for some populations and not others. She suggests we examine more closely the ways in which social (e.g., living on campus, interacting with faculty and other students, developing friendship networks) as well as academic (e.g., academic and career advising, academic support programs) experiences shape their educational success. Recognizing that there are multiple transition problems for all groups entering postsecondary school, Beattie explains that her focus is on what happens to young people *after* they enter college, where the more obvious markers of institutional inequality can be observed and linked with individual experiences. She shows how traditional and newer sociological theories are useful but lacking in some respects, especially regarding the "messy" distinctions of social class, as these are often fine-grained; difficult to discern; and vary significantly by gender, race, immigration status, and parental economic resources. This chapter, together with the others in this section, underscores why sociological insights are important for understanding educational inequality, and that such insights need to be realized in useful educational policies across all levels.

The last chapter in this section, written by Jennifer Pearson and Lindsey Wilkinson, examines the experiences of LGBTQ students in educational contexts. Unquestionably, how to protect the civil rights of LGBTQ students has become one of the most prominent issues of this decade, from housing in postsecondary institutions and use of bathrooms/locker rooms to participation in extracurricular activities or registering for the armed services. What it means to refer to oneself or others as LGBTQ, and its significance with respect to educational opportunities, comprise some of the topics in this chapter, for which data and literature have thus far been sorely inadequate. Pearson and Wilkinson do not stop with identifying the problems often attached to labeling and insufficient data issues, but instead use their and others' work to highlight the types of abuse LGBTQ students are likely to encounter at school (such as bullying and harassment), how the abuse varies developmentally, and how it depends on school contexts (such as the demographics of the population the schools serve and if they are situated in urban, rural, or suburban areas). The ways in which these experiences affect students' academic engagement, academic success, and sense of self are also reviewed, including discussions of differences in social and emotional variation among racial and ethnic subgroups—although here again the research is limited. As schools and other social institutions struggle with legitimate and appropriate responses to the LGBTQ population, the authors offer recommendations for how schools can implement more supportive and effective practices, including curricular revisions, teacher training, and community responsiveness.

One has to ask the question, who is being left out? Most of the chapters in this section include references to *all* racial/ethnic minorities in the U.S. population. However, there is a dearth of research on Native American students, who comprise about 1% of the student body in public elementary and secondary schools (Fryberg 2013; NCES 2017) and whose population is diminishing, with limited access to high-quality schools. There are also growing numbers of certain religious populations, such as Muslims (Hossain 2017), who are not recent immigrants but also face severe discrimination in some schools. Hopefully, in future work, these populations will receive increased attention in both the research and policy arenas. The authors in this section are in agreement that reducing inequality remains a deep concern, both for the generations of racial and ethnic students who have repeatedly experienced a lack of educational opportunity, and for those who have recently found themselves in these situations.

Part III. The Social Organization of Schooling and Opportunities for Learning

In keeping with our intent for this volume to uphold a future perspective, the six chapters in this section take on several longstanding themes in the sociology of education—including public versus private schooling, curricular differentiation, teacher preparation, and the teaching profession—showing why they are in need of revision and how researchers are tackling these topics today. Incorporating a variety of data sources and methodologies, the authors frame their discussions by explaining how we need to conceptualize and measure the often-unpredictable boundaries that comprise the social context of schools and the diverse populations they serve. It is this uncertainty in the environment that places new demands and pressure on schools to create a more equitable educational system.

School choice, as Megan Austin and Mark Berends explain in Chap. 10, has become a primary organizing principle for the entire educational enterprise, from pre-kindergarten through postsecondary institutions, across the public and private sectors. Varied in its governance, economic support, and client base, controversies over school choice's effectiveness for improving student achievement and attainment and parent/student satisfaction continue. Most recently, these controversies have ushered in a political firestorm of debate on one of its dramatically expanding entities: charter schools. The authors review several major studies on charters, voucher programs, and Catholic schools, identifying explanations for their present varied achievement and attainment effects (charters and vouchers) and potential for producing sustained performance effects (Catholic schools).The second part of the chapter introduces several economic (market and competition) and sociological (institutional) theories to provide an underlying rationale for why choice should have positive effects on enhancing improvement across the whole enterprise. Summarizing these results, the authors conclude that, with respect to theories, small effects on achievement and attainment do not seem especially compelling for either economic or sociological theories. With respect to innovation, results again appear mixed, especially when taking into account reforms over time. The chapter next takes on the question of whether school choice enhances access to high-quality schools of varying types, drawing heavily on sociological research and theories and focusing on issues of parental school selection/preferences, segregation, information channels, social networks, and school organization—all of which point to persuasive reasons for the heterogeneity of school choice effects. Austin and Berends conclude by suggesting that we should consider these inconsistent results the "first wave" of how school choice affects students and schools, not as definitive evidence for a fundamental policy change.

Whether or not a student attends a school of choice or the local comprehensive public school, how the student's learning opportunities are organized, and the processes by which they occur, is undoubtedly one of the major factors contributing to differences in educational performance and occupational outcomes. Chapter 11, by Jamie M. Carroll and Chandra Muller, provides a rich history of curricular differentiation—the systematic, formal, and informal school curricular process that determines which courses students take; who takes them; when in the schooling trajectory they are taken; and what instructional goals and strategies teachers use. One description of curricular differentiation places it on an axis, with the vertical delineating what is taught at different grade levels and the horizontal delineating the variation in instruction taught at the same grade level (Sørensen 1970). It is the wide variation between what should be taught and what is actually taught that has resulted in a highly differentiated system in which more economically and socially advantaged students receive advanced coursework and often higher-quality instruction than students who are less-advantaged, including those with special needs and English Language learners (ELLs). The ways curricular differentiation occurs in the U.S. today (within and between schools), and how researchers measure student learning outcomes across the entire system (including the value of collecting and analyzing student course portfolios/transcripts), are discussed in the next section. The advent of these improved methods has produced a more transparent view of how curricular stratification occurs both within and across schools, especially for poor students, racial and ethnic minorities, and special needs students. Some of the more menacing problems with curricular differentiation, the authors explain, lie not just with content exposure but the fact that differentiation has been a major predictor of school attainment, postsecondary enrollment and completion, occupational status, and health. In other words, what is taught and learned in school has profound effects not only on the students but on the health and well-being of our society.

Chapter 12 by Sean Kelly et al. looks specifically at instruction, and begins with the following questions: Is there systematic variation in teaching quality across different populations of students that leads to gaps in student performance? If so, what efforts are needed to remediate this situation? The authors emphasize that to improve teacher quality it is critical to examine how teacher quality is identified and measured, what teaching practices are employed in classrooms, and what school social and organizational supports impact teacher effectiveness. This is not a trivial distinction: The literature (which the authors review) tends to measure teacher quality by attributes such as education level (e.g., baccalaureate versus master's degree), college selectivity, experience, test scores, and quality of degree-granting institution, and then relate these to student performance. The most consistent findings indicate that poor and low-performing students tend to have more inexperienced and less subject-matter qualified teachers than advantaged students. However, the authors argue, observed teacher characteristics seldom explain much of the variation in student achievement; if we are serious about improving teaching quality, we must examine what happens in different types of classrooms. The chapter turns to the Measures of Effective Teaching (MET) project, one of the largest randomized studies of teacher effectiveness in the U.S. which showed that some teachers are more effective than others in raising student achievement, and that students who were assigned to highly effective teachers experienced higher levels of achievement growth. Many of these highly effective teachers also scored higher on observations of best practices. These effects are not without critics, however, who raise concerns about the generalizability of teacher effects to other outcomes, and the stability of effectiveness over time. Reporting on several additional studies, the authors reinforce the idea that though high-quality teaching may occur with different types of students and in different subjects, this variability is more likely to be detectable with teachers ranked in the mid-range than those at the top or the bottom. Nevertheless, this chapter concludes with the assertion that to reduce educational inequality, it is imperative to identify gaps in teaching quality within and between schools, and teachers' relationships to the diverse students they serve.

The nature of social relationships among individuals and social systems has been, and continues to be, at the core of the sociology of education. In Chap. 13, Kenneth Frank et al. review how social networks among school personnel coordinate actions and allocate resources that influence opportunities for education. Social network theory and analysis has exploded within the last several decades, and Frank is one of the foremost researchers in this area; he has studied how the flow of information and other resources within formal and informal social groups oftentimes reifies group perceptions and behaviors that directly generate positive or negative learning opportunities. The role of these networks is dependent, in part, on the selectivity and perceived influence of the groups' position in the larger social system. This chapter briefly describes the basic structures and processes of these social networks based on existing studies, indicating how researchers using network methodology—particularly graphics—can extend these representations into formal models showing selection and influence effects on members' interactions. Formal selection and influence modeling specifications are presented, along with examples. With respect to questions of inequality of opportunity, Frank and coauthors underscore how some groups can either diffuse problems in a school or drive polarization; they then describe another scenario, where like-minded or high-quality teachers form tight networks that others cannot penetrate, furthering alienation and lack of access to valuable information by those most in need. We learn, however, that networks in schools can be shaped and redirected by formal leaders, such as administrators, especially when there is a need for local (and shared) knowledge on specific reforms. Networks also form outside the school, and the authors provide several examples of newer social networks organized across school districts that are drawing on dynamic relations to improve student outcomes. Another example of new social networks are those created through social media—such as Pinterest, which serves as an online discourse community for teachers. The potential for these social networks to change behaviors and/or to interact positively with their schools is just emerging, as are the challenges these social media networks pose for the schools (how well they meld with school, district, or state aims; their transparency regarding who is in the network; and confidentiality/privacy issues). This chapter argues that social networks (whether formed in-person or virtually) may be reorienting our understanding of how individuals select and are influenced by different groups; what impact that may ultimately have on access to information, and our ability to assess its veracity and usefulness for education reform, remains to be seen.

The concept of networks is also explored in Chap. 14, by Robert Crosnoe et al., but here the focus is on peer networks: how they are formed in school and their relationship to opportunities for learning. Paying tribute to sociologists who have been intellectual leaders in defining schools as social contexts, the authors extend these earlier conceptions by highlighting how the informal and formal social relationships in schools intersect with one another, influencing actions and values that shape individual and group behaviors. Covering school-wide peer cultures as well as smaller peer networks and cliques, Crosnoe et al. show how these relationships can positively or negatively affect engagement in school. The authors discuss three major books in the sociology of education, and explain that they were selected to illustrate how conceptualizations of schools as social contexts have developed over the last seventy years, drawing on different theories and methodologies. These books represent a progression of our understanding of peer groups: why and how they form both inside and outside of school; their connections with families, communities, and broad societal interventions (like social media); and methodologies used to analyze their influence on identity development, actions, attitudes, and norms. The authors then distinguish between collectivities of students and peer networks, which they label as "recurring and meaningful patterns of relationships and interactions" that exist over time. These networks can be characterized by the members' density of relationships; norms and values; influence on behaviors and attitudes; and racial, ethnic, and social class composition. Another set of distinctions are made between peer crowds: large groups of students that link smaller cliques and friendships, and tend to share a group identity and become more similar over time. These, in their most negative configurations, can be a source of conformity, bullying, and/or marginalization and exclusion. Peer crowds influence how student groups are conceptualized publicly and are often entangled with ideas about school climates that, in some instances, are racialized and/or profiled as low or high academic environments. Amidst efforts to identify how students relate to one another, the distinctions among peer networks, groups, cliques, and friendship are important, each operating in the social contexts of schools—supporting or deterring academic and health-related behaviors, belonging, and norms. In conclusion, the authors caution those working on interventions to alter certain student behaviors, they need to take into account the diversity of peer configurations: their presence, membership, and influence.

One aspect of teenage life that has consistently been a topic of interest among sociologists of education is the amount and type of work students pursue outside of school. This was more significant when many teenagers worked part-time in places where they could get full-time jobs after graduation. As desirable jobs increasingly began requiring more education, however, the lure of part-time work took on a different meaning, ranging from portfolio-building for college, and obtaining extra funds to supplement purchasing power for electronics and tickets to music events. Today, most teenagers are less likely to hold a part-time job during the school year than in earlier decades. One of the main themes of Chap. 15, by Jeremy Staff et al., is why there may be a decrease in the average number of hours teenagers work. The slide in numbers of 8th, 10th, and 12th grade students working intensively over 20 hours a week has dropped from 43% in 1994 to only 23% in 2014 (the decline in numbers of students working 1–20 hours among 8th and 10th graders has also declined, but not as significantly). Research on work hours remains curvilinear: Students with the least and the most economic resources work the least number of hours, with most students falling in the middle, working low or moderate hours. Most young people who work today report that their jobs do not match their career goals, and only a third believed their jobs are interesting and allow them to use their skills and abilities. Who works is likely to be related to gender, race/ethnicity, and family socioeconomic characteristics and, as expected, these factors are related to the type of work teenagers engage in and its effect on school outcomes. Recent work on teenage employment is relatively limited, which the authors believe is especially problematic for understanding differences in educational inequality. The following questions therefore arise: Is the type of work teenagers engage in (such as unpaid internships as a substitute for paid work) a pathway for school success? What groups of young people have access to these jobs? How does this access vary by race, ethnicity, and family income?

Additionally, how does summer work differ by social class, and, again, what are the effects of different types of this work on future school and employment? What groups today are involved in long hours of paid work, and what impact does that have on their lives in school and their path to a high school diploma? Paid work is certainly one of the mediating conditions that is likely to affect later school outcomes. We are therefore at a phase of research where it is imperative to learn what type of experiences young people are having out-of-school that help them build networks of support for future opportunities, and what groups of young people are being excluded. The questions raised in this chapter have become more salient than they might have been 20 years ago, before college competitiveness increased and the choice of college destination and college completion became major stratifiers in the labor market.

Part IV. Educational Opportunities and the Transition into Adulthood

Public perceptions of the high school-to-college transition often fail to acknowledge differences in social class, and the process of this transition, for whom it occurs, and where students enroll, often masks important differences in educational opportunities for disadvantaged youth. Due in part to poor preparation and a lack of guidance and counseling, many young people find navigating the complex college pathway very challenging. What makes the college transition so equitably problematic is that role high schools and postsecondary institutions play in the process, and the subsequent consequences it has for degree completion. Recognizing differences among students' college choices, this section describes the major destinations of most high school students as well as differences in applicants, programs, costs, and degree completion among the diverse institutions accepting these graduates (including both non- and for-profit). These chapters rely on multiple large-scale and smaller in-depth studies as well as diverse methodologies to describe the interlocking web of student and institutional responses to programmatic offerings, social activities, and policies regarding racial discrimination and sexual harassment.

Chapter 16, by Michal Kurlaender and Jacob Hibel, digs deep into the constrained choices that affect young people's postsecondary aspirations, beginning with activities and perceptions of family and teachers from early childhood through high school. Using longitudinal data from multiple sources, they highlight how ambitions have increased over time yet failed to result in higher college enrollment and completion for specific populations. Describing several theories for these uneven college trajectories, including theories from economics and social psychology, the chapter then turns to structural sociological explanations for gaps in enrollment and completion. Complementary to Chaps. 6 and 11, the authors focus on the problem of curricular exposure and participation, underscoring the impact of institutional structural barriers on college enrollment and introducing a number of new empirical studies and in-depth work from California. Reviewing social and cultural theories, they trace the unique informational barriers faced by nontraditional (i.e., older) students and those from low-income backgrounds, especially with respect to securing financial aid. Drawing attention to several new economic studies that address "under-matching" (i.e., students who attend institutions that are less competitive than their college preparation qualifications indicate), the authors create an important bridge between sociologists' understandings of structural constraints (particularly for low-income groups) and economists' interests in low-cost interventions that can be measured with results from randomized control trials. The inclusion of these studies underscores the importance of building intersections between multiple disciplines to address many of the pressing issues of educational inequality and their potential remediation.

The majority of high school seniors will enroll in 4-year colleges in the fall following their spring or summer graduation (McFarland et al. 2017). Richard Arum et al. construct Chap. 17 around two major themes: (1) the historical and institutional factors that have formed student life on college campuses; and (2) the variation in college experiences for students of different gender, socioeconomic, and racial/ethnic groups. Specific attention is also given to issues of sexuality and sexual violence, which is particularly relevant given the recent federal revisions of standards for sexual assault investigations (*New York Times* 2017; also see Department of Education's "Interim Guidance on Campus Sexual Misconduct" 2017). The first section of the chapter traces the history of higher education from the post-World War II period of rapid expansion coupled with increasing gaps in wealth inequality; the authors then explain how today's institutions are responding to rising student consumerism, and what that means for the accommodation of low-income and minority students' educational and financial needs. In the second section, the authors delve deeply into the experiences of college students, including their time studying, engagement with academics, and social participation in extracurricular activities, and how these vary both within and across institutions of differing selectivity. Rather than pointing out inequality variations in college enrollment by socioeconomic status, race/ethnicity, and gender, they focus on how college cultures formally and informally limit opportunities for minorities to feel a sense of belonging and receive services that support their persistence to graduation. The authors conclude by emphasizing the importance of attending to the range of student academic and social experiences in different institutions, as opposed to limiting studies of inequality to questions of access, if progress in persistence and degree completion is to be achieved.

Whereas Arum et al. concentrate on 4-year institutions, Lauren Schudde and Eric Grodsky in Chap. 18 examine the history of community colleges and their role in enhancing educational opportunities and social mobility for less economically advantaged students. The chapter opens with a historical overview of the aims of 2-year colleges, their exponential growth, academic preparation, and institutional differences between urban community colleges and private for-profit institutions (some of which also offer 4-year degrees). Compared to public 2-year colleges, students at private for-profit institutions are disproportionately Black or Hispanic, female, and single parents, and they encounter a more limited scope of degree programs and electives, accumulate more debt, and receive a lower cost return on employment possibilities. For an increasing number of students, beginning one's postsecondary education at community colleges with the expectation of transferring to a 4-year college or earning a postsecondary credential has become an inexpensive alternative. Public 2-year colleges, compared to 4-year institutions, enroll more minorities and more first-time college students, and proportionately fewer students ultimately receive their degrees. Addressing the incongruent issues of access and opportunity in community colleges, the authors point out the "democratic" value of community colleges and their increased access to students from diverse backgrounds, while highlighting their limited educational opportunities—as evidenced by low degree completion rates, relative costs for degree completion, and labor market opportunities. Schudde and Grodsky, drawing on other scholars, discuss why community colleges may have "diversionary" (i.e., a pathway that diverts students away from receiving a baccalaureate degree) rather than democratic outcomes. They then turn to new studies to assess the actual impact of diversionary effects, contrasting these studies with others that have examined democratic effects, to suggest that these distinctions vary considerably by subgroups. Complexity appears to be an overriding theme of the pathway to degree, and this chapter thoughtfully summarizes problems of high school preparation and their relationship to community college remediation, dual enrollment opportunities for high school students seeking more-advanced college work, transfer policies for students leaving 2-year institutions for 4-year ones, and the reversal process of students at 4-year institutions who transfer to 2-year institutions to receive a degree. This chapter provides an important, and timely, spotlight on issues of educational inequality that are not easily resolved—especially when trying to understand the mechanisms of social stratification at the institutional level.

In Chap. 19, James E. Rosenbaum—whose name is synonymous with the critique of the commonly used phrase "college-for-all"—and colleagues Caitlin Ahearn and Jennifer Lansing move beyond who attends what types of colleges and which students fail to reach degree completion, to identify the *strategies* disadvantaged youth undertake when confronting major institutional obstacles. Recognizing the many challenges that students face in college, the authors raise the question: How do these students survive and complete their degrees? Creating an alternative to traditional models that predict who attends college and the sequential challenges that lie along their path to degree completion, the authors focus instead on students' success, drawing on evidence from an in-depth study of low-income, nontraditional students. Three alternative strategies were observed among study participants (here and in other work on nontraditional students), which could be traced to the following: unconventional high school-to-college trajectories; the value and flexibility offered by open-access institutions; and the ability to build a portfolio of incremental degree attainment (beginning with a certificate or associate degree, moving on to a higher degree, and allowing for periods of "intermission"). One of the draws of open-access institutions for this population, as the authors explain, is that many of the programs are designed for specific occupations, which corresponded to respondent goals and financial needs. Further, experiencing success at school served as a motivator for continued education experiences, especially as students discovered new abilities that were not disrupted by intermission and incremental degree attainment. Turning to the institutions, the authors argue that the success of nontraditional students is aided by colleges that provide procedural structures that help keep students on track, offer support (including peer groups), and form career direction with information and appreciative reflection of prior work-related experiences. The authors remind us that there are multiple deviations from the conventional model of degree attainment, and that studying these will likely provide a clearer path to helping students achieve their educational goals.

Richard A. Settersten, Jr. and Barbara Schneider, in Chap. 20, critique the conventional high school-to-college degree path by focusing on the changing characterization of who is a college student and how 4-year institutions are dealing with chronologically older students. The intent of this chapter is to broaden the sociology of education's focus from K–12 to include students we typically refer to as "midlife and beyond" (also see Pallas 2016 on this point). As Rosenbaum et al. argue in the preceding chapter, the conventional degree path from high school to college has changed, and the prototypical model of a college student has been substantially transformed. Reviewing the misconceptions of the conventional tripartite model of frontloaded education, which is followed by work and then retirement, the authors discuss the disconnection between today's diverse life course paths and the constraints institutions and policies face as they try to adapt to this change in clientele and meet their educational needs. The authors provide several examples of how businesses have attempted to remediate the pressing financial problems of some students by offering repayment of student loans as part of hiring practices or working collaboratively with colleges to develop specific job programs to accelerate the transition to subsequent employment. The second part of the chapter discusses some of the normative developmental expectations of higher education institutions that are inconsistent with the needs of young and older adults alike, such as independence, autonomy, and residential living. The authors conclude by identifying the goals—often referred to as noncognitive or soft skills—that universities might adopt to assist both young and older students in leading more successful lives.

Part V. Sociological Perspectives on Accountability and Evaluation

The last section of the volume takes a bold step, highlighting new methodological work being conducted by sociologists of education and identifying the policy topics sociologists must pay closer attention to if they are to understand how to measure and lessen inequities in education. Two statistically analytic chapters focus on measuring academic growth with young children and another focuses on measuring school effects, followed by a review and discussion of the authors' work using incentivized randomized control trials in higher education to improve education persistence and completion. This section concludes with a chapter detailing an innovative researcher–practitioner model and how it negotiates the challenges of working collaboratively to solve pressing education problems in schools. The overarching theme of these chapters is a focus on the intensity of the education experiences young people encounter in schools and in society. The authors do not simply review the characteristics associated with inequality—instead, they explore *how* inequality is perpetuated through actions and values within specific environments (even those viewed as being in the service of the public good), and propose approaches for embarking on researchable solutions for reform.

Chapter 21, by Joel Mittleman and Jennifer L. Jennings, links the development of recent federal education policies and their impact on three domains: instruction, student outcomes, and refitted policies. The chapter begins by charting the history of formal accountability in education—from A Nation at Risk through No Child Left Behind and, most recently, the Every Student Succeeds Act—and how these were implemented at the federal and state level. The authors then link accountability policies using student test scores with their impact on teachers, students, school systems, and public opinion. For example, one instructional consequence of federal legislation is the larger proportion of time spent on mathematics and reading at the expense of other academic subjects, the arts, and physical education. The more schools face sanctions for poor performance, the more likely "teaching to the test" will occur, particularly in schools that serve lower-income and non-Asian minority students. Aided by technology and data systems, however, research indicates that students tend to have better test gains on low-stakes tests than ones directly tied to punitive sanctions. Testing accountability pressures have also created gaps between students, with some receiving more instruction and resources under the assumption that they will be the most likely to benefit from these allocations; other inequitable effects of this testing, outcome, and accountability push include a negative long-term impact on poorly performing students, who are sometimes funneled into special education classes unnecessarily. The last part of the chapter takes up the question of the relationship between school quality indicators and public support for public education, suggesting that negative ratings result in decreased support for school tax referenda, principal and teacher school employment instability, and an erosion of professional communities at the school and district levels. The authors conclude by identifying other types of accountability systems that show promise for public schooling. What is particularly novel about this work is the intensive examination of the impacts of accountability systems and their relationship not only to students, teachers, and administrators, but to the public, who ultimately decides the extent of actual dollar support for education. This chapter raises important questions about our commitment to endorsing policies seemingly for advancing education as a public good, even when this is not necessarily the case.

One of the newest sources of data comes from states that have allowed researchers to access the rich longitudinal databases that states collect for the federal government and their own purposes. These states' administrative databases provide unprecedented opportunities to analyze education data, not only within state but between participating states, federal sources, and smaller scale studies. In Chap. 22, Douglas Lee Lauen et al. describe their study of a state's administrative longitudinal database of third graders (and, if promoted, their school performance in fourth and fifth grade). With a final sample of over two hundred thousand student observations, Lauen et al. examine the relationship between school poverty and achievement to determine the effects of the social context of schools on student test scores, over and above individual student characteristics. The chapter begins with several caveats that form the crux of sociological studies focused on untangling the effects of poverty at the individual and school level on changes in student achievement. The authors suggest researchers to use *longitudinal* data for when estimating causal inferences in order to disentangle time variant from time-invariant conditions on performance. The second is the *measurement of poverty* itself, and the authors emphasize the importance of acknowledging its limitations when employing different types of models. The main body of the chapter statistically demonstrates the problems that arise when using cross-national data sets and two- and three-level longitudinal models to measure contextual factors (mainly the poverty gap) between and within schools on changes in student test scores. The underlying purpose here is to show multiple ways to measure the pathway through which school poverty affects outcomes, in addition to highlighting the strengths and weaknesses of each of the models used in many of today's empirical studies. The primary takeaway from the authors' argument and analysis is that three-level models are the most robust when pursuing this question with these data. One of the most important contributions of this chapter is its assertion that it is easier to ascertain *school* correlates of change in test scores than *student* correlates of change in test scores. While the authors were unable to detect a relationship between school poverty and achievement with their models, they did find greater variation in test score growth across schools than across students. Their results suggest that we need to rethink what it is about today's schools that are creating this variation.

Chapter 23, by Stephen L. Morgan and Daniel T. Shackelford, makes the case that the relationship between effective teaching and school effects should be taken up more seriously by sociologists of education as a topic of study. This chapter (as with the preceding one) is somewhat unusual in the tradition of Handbooks, which tend to be substantive; what is refreshing about these chapters is how they situate the purpose of their work on issues of inequality in education, explain why social context plays a fundamental role in shaping and measuring student and teacher performance, and illustrate this conception with various statistical models. Most contemporary research on teacher effectiveness has been dominated by economists and policy analysts, many of whom pay little attention to the social context in which teachers work (i.e., their motivations, and pressures and strains from parents and administrators). To advance the work of sociologists, Morgan and Shackelford begin by summarizing some of the older sociological studies of education, including work by Willard Waller (1932) and Coleman et al. (1966), that emphasize the training and professional lives of teachers, their commitment and dedication, and the challenges they were likely to confront with their students. Pushing through the research on teacher effectiveness to today's educational landscape, the goal of this review is to spotlight that which researchers tend to minimize or ignore: "...the characterizations of teachers as professionals embedded in communities, struggling to navigate institutional rules and social relations while working with heterogeneous populations of students" (p. 516). The sociological research is then followed by a capstone of economic work, which examines the distribution of teachers across and within schools—referred to as "teacher sorting"—to suggest that this literature, and that of earlier sociologists, points to more heterogeneity within the teaching force than assumed, and that the social context of schools may be more homogeneous than previously thought. To test this assumption, the authors employ the latest national longitudinal survey of high school students (the High School Longitudinal Study of 2009, or HSLS:09) and the Common Core of Data, showing first that the relationships between resource expenditures and problems attributed to them are smaller than some might expect, and that when looking between schools the differences in teacher effects appear smaller, but trend in the same direction when using large state administrative data. Schools with the highest performing students appear to benefit from having the strongest teachers. The chapter concludes with a call for an increase in measures of student, teacher, and school activities that can capture more discrete information on the pedagogy and expertise of teachers, as well as the learning climates in which they work. Arguing that these smaller grain size measures are likely to result in a clearer understanding of teacher effects on student performance, the authors assert that these ideas are deeply rooted in the theoretical and empirical provenance of sociology of education.

Complementing an earlier section of this volume, where there are a number of reviews of studies on community colleges, Chap. 24—by David Monaghan et al.—presents some of the most rigorous work on this topic that employs interventions and measures their effectiveness with experimental randomized control trial designs (RCTs). While the Handbook does not specifically address the statistical considerations one must take into account when estimating causal effects, given the increasing import of interventions (both quasi- and RCT-experiments) and their potential for scale-up, we wanted to include a chapter by one of the strongest evidential sociological voices on the community college experience: that of Sara Goldrick-Rab, who has studied the effects of interventions designed to affect community college access, persistence, and completion. The chapter begins by highlighting the levers in the community college landscape that would benefit from intervention work, such as course counseling, financial resource constraints, and quality of instructors. Describing these interventions, the authors begin with those that are school-focused, such as providing assistance with counseling services (improving student–counselor ratios and assignment to counselors), course redesign, and structuring support services. They then move to system-level interventions and the financial structures that provide them with operating resources (including state allocations). Although not a meta-analysis, the authors review and critique the work of studies that used random assignment, where subjects were entering or enrolled at a community college, and whose purpose was to improve retention, credit accumulation, grades, and degree completion. Using these criteria, they identify: interventions that augmented the resources and behaviors of the students; studies with eligibility and support for financial aid; financial aid information interventions; material resources, such as free computers; college skill classes (some of which are commonly assumed to be remedial but are often lower-stakes, with pass/fail options); social and psychological interventions that motivate students to believe they can succeed; and incentivizing academic credit accumulation. At the school level were interventions that enhance student services (such as counseling, mentoring, summer bridge programs, and testing and remediation), and learning communities similar to cohort approaches (where students are assigned to an academic advisor and group). One of the largest and arguably most successful system-level interventions, the City University of New York's Center for Economic Opportunity, is the last of the interventions discussed. What is truly critical, in terms of this chapter's importance, are why we need interventions, what we are learning, and where gaps in our knowledge remain.

The final chapter of the volume, by Paula Arce-Trigatti et al., focuses on one of the newest forms of infrastructure, research–practice partnerships (RPPs), which have multiple purposes but share one goal: improving the effectiveness of school systems through collaborative research, dissemination, and professional learning community development. As the authors state, these relatively new RPPs exemplify several tenets of organizational sociology literature, and open a door to the execution of potentially more authentic research that is designed not for practice but for direct involvement with the practice community. The authors begin by examining the growth of RPPs, identifying some of the most successful partnerships, such as the UChicago Consortium on School Research, founded in 1990 and largely perceived as ushering in this new model of collaboration. Acceptance of the RPP was slow going initially because, the authors claim, the traditional bureaucratic organizational structures of universities and schools—with their privilege of status, isolationism, financial pressures, and normative and reward cultures—hindered their development. While this model did not have much traction, with the passage of No Child Left Behind and the efforts of the National Research Council, the idea resurfaced as a constructive mechanism for helping schools adopt research findings to avoid sanctions and other penalties for poor performance. Soon, research partnerships sprang up all over the country, now funded by government and philanthropic endeavors. Varying in organizational models and goals, the authors categorize these entities as research alliances, design-based partnerships (typically narrower in scope than the research alliances), or networked improvement communities that tend to focus on a single problem. The reasons these types of RPPs have pursued such distinct pathways form the second part of the chapter, underscoring differences in social, political, and institutional conditions that account for their heterogeneity. Bringing us full circle to the beginning of this volume, the authors raise three institutional theories of sociology—imitative, normative, and coercive—to explain the social construction of these variations. Still a relatively new collaborative form of work between research and practice, the authors conclude by hypothesizing about the sustainability of current models and what types of newer organizations may yet arise. In sociology of education, when we think about institutions, RPPs have not yet taken their place next to intermediary school district organizations and federal- and state-supported research education laboratories. Yet these organizations—how they function and their impact—need further study, alongside virtual networks and other configurations of socially purposeful organizations that, with the instigation of technological change, are likely to materialize in the near future.

Concluding Caveats

Two important topics are missing from this volume. The first is an in-depth examination of affirmative action policies and court cases that address debates regarding race/class considerations for postsecondary admission and the evidence for why such indicators should or should not be used. We refer readers to Sigal Alon's (2015) book, *Race, Class and Affirmative Action*. This is an issue that is unlikely to be resolved, even in light of the most recent Supreme Court decision (*Fisher v. University of Texas at Austin,* 2016). Second, this volume is nation-centric and does not cover how sociologists are studying global issues in education. This was a decision based on major projects underway that are designed to address the international scope of many of the themes presented here. There is a rich tradition of international sociological work in education, with such major figures as David Baker (2014), John Meyer (Krucken and Drori 2009), Francisco Ramirez (2016), and rising stars like Anna K. Chmielewski (2017). Their work and that of their colleagues is part of another Handbook series, soon to be released. Nonetheless, issues in the U.S. educational system are decidedly problematic and profoundly negative in their impact on the academic performance, social and emotional development, and social mobility of low-income and minority students living in the wealthiest country in the world. The reasons for these problems provided the motivation for this volume; its most important contribution is the strength of evidence each chapter provides for what we need to learn and change.

East Lansing, MI, USA   Barbara Schneider

References

Alon, S. (2015). *Race, class and affirmative action*. New York: Russell Sage.

Baker, D. P. (2014). *The schooled society: The educational transformation of global culture*. Stanford: Stanford University Press.

Chmielewski, A. K. (2017). Social inequality in educational transitions under different types of secondary school curricular differentiation. In I. Schoon & R. Silbereisen (Eds.), *Pathways to adulthood: Educational opportunities, motivation and attainment in times of social change*. London: UCL IOE Press.

Coleman, J. S., Campbell, E. Q., Hobson, C. J., McPartland, J., Mood, A. M., Weinfeld, F. D. York, R. L. (1966). *Equality of educational opportunity*. Washington, DC: U.S. Department of Health, Education, and Welfare, Office of Education. Retrieved from https://eric.ed.gov/?id=ED)12275

Fisher v. University of Texas at Austin. (2016). No 14-981 (U.S. Ct. App. 5th Ct. 2016).

Fryberg, S., Covarrubias, R. & Burack, J. (2013). Cultural models of education and academic performance for Native American and European American students. *School Psychology International, 34*(4), 439–452.

Hossain, S. (2017). Understanding the legal landscape of discrimination against Muslim students in public elementary and secondary schools: A guide for lawyers. *Duke Forum for Law and Social Change, 9*, 81–104.

Krucken, G. & Drori, G. S. (Eds.). (2009). *World society: The writings of John Meyer*. Oxford: Oxford University Press.

McFarland, J., Hussar, B., de Brey, C., Snyder, T., Wang, X., Wilkinson-Flicker, S., Gebrekristos, S., Zhang, J., Rathbun, A., Barner, A., Bullock Mann, F. & Hinz, S. (2017). *The condition of education*. Washington, DC: National Center for Education Statistics. Retrieved from https://nces.ed.gov/pubsearch/pubsinfo.asp?pubid=2017144

Ninneman, A. M., Deaton, J. & Francis-Begay, K. (2017). *National Indian Education Study 2015* (NCES 2017-161). Washington, DC: Institute of Education Sciences, U. S. Department of Education. Retrieved from https://nces.ed.gov/nationsreportcard/pdf/studies/2017161.pdf

Pallas, A. (2016). Schooling, learning, and the life course. In R. Scott & S. Kosslyn (Eds.), *Emerging trends in the social and behavioral sciences: An interdisciplinary, searchable and linkable resource*. Retrieved from http://onlinelibrary.wiley.com/book/10.1002/9781118900772

Ramirez, F., Meyer, J., & Lerch, J. (2016). World society and the globalization of educational policy. In K. Mundy, A. Green, & R. Lingard (Eds.), *Handbook on Global Policy and Policy Making in Education* (pp. 43–63). Hoboken: Wiley Blackwell.

Sørensen, A. B. (1970). Organizational differentiation of students and educational opportunity. *Sociology of Education, 43*(4), 355–376.

U.S. Department of Education. (2017). Racial/ethnic enrollment in public schools. *The condition of education*. Washington, DC: National Center for Education Statistics. Retrieved from https://nces.ed.gov/programs/coe/indicator_cge.asp

U.S. Department of Education. (2017, September 22). Department of Education issues new interim guidance on campus sexual misconduct. Retrieved from https://www.ed.gov/news/press-releases/department-education-issues-new-interim-guidance-campus-sexual-misconduct

Waller, W. (1932). *The sociology of teaching*. New York: Wiley.

Part I

Families, Schools, and Educational Opportunity

Family, Schooling, and Cultural Capital

1

George Farkas

Abstract

School-related cultural capital refers to the skills, habits, identities, worldviews, preferences or values that students enact in schools and that affect their school success. This chapter describes how Pierre Bourdieu's theory of cultural capital explains social reproduction—the fact that, as adults, children tend to replicate the social class status of their parents. This is largely because academic performance and school success are strongly and positively correlated with parental social class. I examine social class differences in parenting and how these affect the habitus, or underlying skills and dispositions toward schooling of children from different social classes. These differential skills and dispositions in turn give rise to differential academic skills, work habits, and related school behaviors which are judged by teachers when they assign course grades on the report cards of students. As students move up through the levels of schooling, social class differences in course grades lead to social class differences in curriculum selection and high school graduation. Then, high school grades, teacher's recommendations,

and standardized test scores affect postsecondary enrollment and degree attainment. These in turn lead to differences in occupational employment and earnings favoring children from higher social class backgrounds.

Bourdieu writes extensively about effects of social class background, arguing that early socialization, combined with later experiences, lead to personal characteristics that lessen the odds of upward or downward class mobility...By personal characteristics I refer to things individuals carry across situations, such as skills, habits, identities, worldviews, preferences or values. (England 2016, p. 6)

1.1 Introduction

Social reproduction—the fact that, as adults, children tend to replicate the social class status of their parents—is one of the central empirical findings in the sociology of inequality. A primary determinant of this outcome is that, beginning in kindergarten, children's academic performance is strongly and positively related to the social class background of their parents. One result of this is the existence of a strong positive relationship between parental socioeconomic status (SES) and the years of school completed by their children. Since, in modern industrialized societies, educational attainment determines occupational attainment, which in turn is strongly related to earnings, the sequence of events leading to social reproduction is relatively

I am grateful for comments on an earlier draft by Katerina Bodovski, Susan Dumais, Greg Duncan, Paula England, and Jacob Hibel, but I alone am responsible for any errors.

G. Farkas (✉)
School of Education, University of California,
Irvine, CA, USA
e-mail: gfarkas@uci.edu

clear. But what causal mechanisms underlie and determine these events? In particular, what determines the strong relationship between parental social class background and the academic performance of their children, beginning as early as kindergarten?

Two proximal social institutions are likely to play important roles—the family and the school. We know that children from lower social class backgrounds tend to have less salutary family situations (more single parents, fewer resources, less preparation for school, greater interpersonal conflict, lesser parental involvement with the child's schooling), as well as attend lower-quality schools (less experienced teachers, lower performing peers, greater disorder). But what is the relative influence of these two institutions—family and school—in social reproduction? Since the Coleman Report (1966) we have known that variation in children's academic performance is most strongly associated with variation in the characteristics of their families, rather than in the schools they attend. Only approximately 20% of the variance in test scores occurs between schools; fully 80% is within schools (Rumberger and Palardy 2004), a finding that has been replicated countless times.

How does the family do it? How is it that at kindergarten entry, only 5 years after birth, children from families in the bottom quintile of the SES distribution score 1.3 standard deviations lower in early math knowledge than those from families in the top quintile of the SES distribution, a social class achievement gap that persists relatively unchanged to 5th grade, and continues to be observed in 8th and 12th grade (Duncan and Magnuson 2011; Farkas 2011)? To examine this seriously, one must consider theories and findings from the nature/nurture debate. Certainly the evidence suggests that there is a significant positive heritability for cognitive skills (Duncan et al. 2005), which may explain about half or more of the variance in these skills, and cognitive skill differences no doubt play a role in the higher academic performance of children from higher-SES families. However, although genetic effects may limit the residual role of family and school influences, they are not our concern here. Instead, we are concerned with social class differences in parenting and parenting resources, and the role these differences play in the differential academic performance and school success of students from different SES backgrounds.

The theory of *cultural capital*, developed by French sociologist Pierre Bourdieu and employed by researchers throughout the world (although with the greatest energy and impact by American[1] sociologists), is the leading explanation of how middle-class parents provide schooling advantages to their children, advantages that are not provided by working-class parents. But explicating and correctly operationalizing this theory is not a simple matter, since Bourdieu was not clear or explicit about how this should be done, leading to significant controversy and much variation in the studies that have been undertaken. As a result, the research literature in this area is a tangled web, with many competing claims, critiques, and confusion. However, in this chapter I present a clear pathway through this literature, leading to a consensus view that is both faithful to Bourdieu's intentions and offers the greatest opportunity to explain (be a mediator for) the strong relationship between parental social class background and both school success and educational attainment. As shown below, Bourdieu explicitly states that he invented the cultural capital concept *in order* to explain social class reproduction. With an appropriate understanding of how the concept should be operationalized and measured, I will be able to review those empirical studies that estimate the theory's success in explaining how families and schools combine to reproduce the social class structure.

This chapter is organized as follows. Section 1.2 briefly situates cultural capital theory alongside human and social capital theories, which it was designed to either complement or replace. Then I trace a series of descriptions by different

---

[1] Over time, sociologists in many additional countries, notably England, the Netherlands, and France, have contributed to the literature on cultural capital. However, the U.S. has dominated, not only in the quantity of publications, but also because the most influential researchers, including Paul DiMaggio, Annette Lareau, Ann Swidler, and Loic Wacquant, are based at American universities.

authors who focused on differences in class cultures and how these differences explain the differential educational success of students from the working and middle classes. In this section I show that a variety of sociologists have come up with similar notions of the cultural capital that students from different social classes are provided with by their families, and that lead to their differential school success. Bourdieu referred to these as *long lasting dispositions of the mind and body*, which these scholars have taken, and in some cases expanded to include the *skills, habits, and styles* that children in different social classes are socialized into and learn from their families and peer groups. Other names for these dispositions and skills include *informal know-how, cultured capacities, practices, repertoires, orientations, tools,* and *procedural knowledge.* Bourdieu's theory posits that socialization in the family leads a child to possess an underlying habitus, which differs across social classes. When these habitus, or dispositions and skills,[2] are called upon for school-related decision-making,

they cause students from different social classes to enact the possession of differential cultural capital (behaviors and performance) with regard to their schoolwork, both inside and outside the classroom. These are in turn judged by the teacher, who is likely to give more positive feedback to behaviors typical of middle-class rather than working-class youth.

With this relatively unambiguous understanding of the cultural capital concept, Sect. 1.3 summarizes three prominent critiques of the empirical work on cultural capital. I find that much of the problem with prior research and these critiques is that they employed an overly narrow notion of cultural capital, one restricted to elite, "highbrow" beaux-arts activities (e.g., classical music, fine arts). Not surprisingly, these are typically found to be incapable of explaining the relative schooling success and attainment of children from working- and middle-class families. By contrast, the broader category of more general skills, habits, and styles, where teachers report their judgment of these on the report cards sent home to parents, are more likely than elite cultural activities to be able to explain a significant portion of the greater school success of middle-class than working-class children.

Section 1.4 brings together the discussion in the previous two sections to present a theory of cultural capital that is consistent with the themes and approaches that have guided this theory since its inception; is integrative of a wide range of studies by sociologists, psychologists, and economists; and, while being consistent with the work of qualitative researchers, can also be operationalized and tested with quantitative data. Central to this theory are the actions of teacher-gatekeepers in judging student skills and behaviors. These judgments are transmitted to parents on report cards, so that by examining the skills and behaviors listed there, we can infer the cultural capital items determining school success. These tend to be the same items focused on by earlier schooling researchers, the sociologists Jencks et al. (1979) and the economists Bowles and Gintis (1976), as well as by more recent cultural capital researchers such as Farkas et al. (1990): namely reading, math, and other subject

---

[2]Like many of Bourdieu's concepts, the precise meaning of habitus has been much debated. Bourdieu often referred to it as an individual's "dispositions," so that many researchers concluded that it encompasses tastes, preferences, attitudes, and related characteristics, but does not include skills. However, Loic Wacquant, a student and coauthor of Bourdieu, has forcefully argued that it does include skills, since it is often created in apprentice-like situations in which an individual is learning, through iterative engagement with others, practical knowledge that can be deployed within a particular "field" or setting of action. Thus, in a debate on the meaning of habitus, Wacquant cites Bourdieu to argue that "settings that inculcate, cultivate, and reward distinct but transposable sets of categories, *skills*, and desires among their participants can be fruitfully analyzed as sites of production and operation of habitus" (Wacquant 2014, p. 120, emphasis added). It is this understanding of habitus, including both skills and dispositions, which I employ in this chapter. This logic, in which an individual's position within a field of action leads to her habitus, which in turn leads to the cultural capital she enacts within this field of action, is central to cultural capital theory, and will be discussed at greater length later in the chapter. Economists may say, "skills are just human capital." But their discussions of the determinants and consequences of skill development do not typically include the complex social psychological issues examined by Wacquant and others working in the cultural capital tradition.

proficiencies, as well as behaviors including following rules, working independently, showing effort, and not disturbing other students—behaviors that can be summarized by the word "conscientiousness." Schematically, this leads to the following causal chain to explain social class reproduction: Differences in family social class status lead to differences in parenting, which lead to differences in school-related habitus, which lead to differences in the cultural capital skills and behaviors manifested by students which are then judged and graded by teacher-gatekeepers. The over-time trajectory of these grades powerfully affects the student's educational attainment, which in turn determines occupational employment and earnings.

Section 1.5 reviews the empirical studies that have tested portions of this model. I begin with the evidence for the positive relationship between parental social class and student school-related cultural capital represented by academic skills and work habits at kindergarten entry. Studies repeatedly show very large social class gaps in these skills and work habits at this time point. Comparing students from the highest and lowest SES quintiles, the cognitive gap is about 1.3 standard deviations (SD), and the academic work habits gap is about 0.6 SD. These school readiness gaps appear to be the central mechanism underlying the correlation between parental social class and student educational success. Section 1.5.2 examines the evidence on the extent to which cognitive skills and academic work habits determine course grades. Perhaps the most convincing correlational evidence comes from a study (Farkas 1996) estimating a model in which basic cognitive skills and academic work habits determine students' performance in learning the course material, after which all three of these variables affect the course grade. As we shall see, Fig. 1.1 shows the estimated model in schematic form, while Fig. 1.2 shows the results of this model when applied to predicting 7th and 8th grade social studies grades in one large, diverse school district. The strongest determinants of grades are the student's academic work habits, followed in importance by the student's basic cognitive skills. Each of these predicts the student's mastery of the course material, which in turn predicts the teacher-assigned grade they receive in the course, but additionally, each has an independent direct effect on the student's grade. These independent associations are relatively large, particularly that of work habits on the course grade. It is this large standardized coefficient (0.53 SD for the direct effect of work habits on the course grade) that suggests the importance of student cultural capital in influencing the decision-making of teacher-gatekeepers within the educational stratification system.

Fig. 1.1 Cultural capital conceptual model

SES → Parenting → Student Habitus → Student Skills, Habits → Student Course Grades

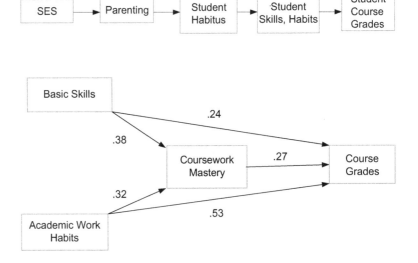

Fig. 1.2 Effect sizes in a simplified model of course grade determination, 7th and 8th grade social studies classes. (Source: Farkas 1996)

Section 1.5.3 examines empirical studies of the role of parenting as a mediator of the relationship between family social class background and the course grades received by students. Results show that family SES is positively associated with parenting quality, and that parenting quality partially mediates the relationship between family SES and students' school-related work habits and cognitive skills. Overall, parenting mediates a portion of the relationship between family SES and both students' cultural capital and course grades.

The family is not the only aspect of social organization shaping the habitus and cultural capital of children. Preschool attendance, the child's peer group, and the child's biological endowment and health also play significant roles. However, because of space limitations, Sects. 1.5.4, 1.5.5 and 1.5.6 provide only brief introductions to the extensive and growing research literature on these topics.

Section 1.6 examines overlap and similarities between the student behaviors we have included under cultural capital and a new synthesis of psychology and economics that has been promoted by James Heckman and colleagues (Borghans et al. 2008). We see that a focus on these student behaviors not only continues the research tradition begun by Bowles and Gintis (1976) and Jencks et al. (1979), but also provides a unifying umbrella over research occurring in disparate social science disciplines.

Section 1.7 concludes the chapter with a discussion of policy implications. The central importance of cultural capital to stratification outcomes is shown by the fact that the Knowledge is Power Program (KIPP), the charter school network showing the best documented success in raising the school performance of low-income children, is largely based on a "contract" with students and their parents to act in ways that maximize the positive cultural capital behaviors discussed here. Focus on these behaviors is likely to play a central role in future efforts to improve educational outcomes for disadvantaged children.

1.2 Human, Social, and Cultural Capital

Note: Because there has been extensive criticism of the notions of social and cultural capital as being vaguely defined and widely misunderstood, and because there is continuing controversy over variable definitions and operationalization, I make unusually extensive use of direct quotations to reduce ambiguity in this section.

1.2.1 Human Capital

Three theoretical perspectives have been advanced to describe and explain social reproduction. Economists Mincer (1958, 1974), Becker (1964), and Schultz (1960, 1981) introduced the first of these—human capital (productive human skills and abilities)—in order to better understand how human labor and physical capital are combined in the economic production process. Their ideas extended economists' long-standing focus on physical capital (land, factories, machines), which combines with the efforts of workers to produce market goods and services. Human capital was conceived as the skills, knowledge, experience, and other characteristics that workers come to possess which allow them to be productive and add economic value. The analogy with physical capital was purposeful since both share the following characteristics—they are created through investment, they are relatively durable and long-lasting, and their creation involves forgoing other investments which might have been made instead (opportunity cost).

This economic viewpoint sees individuals, families and other groups making decisions regarding human capital investment after considering the benefits and costs of alternative lines of action, thereby seeking to achieve optimization of outcomes under resource and other constraints. Defined broadly to include every possible mode of learning and education, as well as mental and physical health, abilities, and habits, the human capital concept has encouraged the application of economic analysis to essentially every area of human behavior. It has also come to be one of the most widely used concepts in all of social science, as well as throughout government and the economy.[3]

Human capital theory explains social reproduction as a natural consequence of the fact that higher social class parents decide, and, with their greater resources, are enabled, to make greater investments in the human capital (cognitive and behavioral skills) of their children, leading to the higher academic performance of these children. Of course, this "rational" explanation of social reproduction is far from the causal explanation accepted by most sociologists. Nor were sociologists happy with the encroachment of economic reasoning into so many other areas of sociological study. Thus, it is not surprising that sociologists sought to develop analogous concepts that could be deployed alongside or in place of the human capital concept to explain social reproduction as well as to enable the continued importance of sociological analysis to areas such as the family, organizations, occupations, earnings, law, crime, sex, religion, immigration, and many other topics. Two prominent sociologists of education—James Coleman and Pierre Bourdieu—independently rose to the challenge by creating, respectively, the concepts of social and cultural capital.

1.2.2   Social Capital

Coleman contrasted human and social capital as follows.

> If physical capital is wholly tangible, being embodied in observable material form, and human capital is less tangible, being embodied in the skills and knowledge acquired by an individual, social capital is less tangible yet, for it exists in the *relations* between persons. Just as physical capital and human capital facilitate productive activity, social capital does as well. For example, trust is a form of social capital. A group within which there is extensive trustworthiness and extensive trust is able to

accomplish much more than a comparable group without that trustworthiness and trust. (Coleman and Hoffer 1987, p. 221)

Coleman goes on to define the social capital of the family as the "relations between children and parents (and when families include other members, relationships with them as well)," but notes that this will benefit the children only if parents employ it for this purpose. Coleman extends the social capital concept beyond the family to religious and other private schools where the parents have strong social relationships among themselves and with the institution (Coleman and Hoffer 1987). An important concept here is intergenerational closure, defined as the extent to which meaningful social relationships exist between children and their friends' parents and among parents whose children are friends.

1.2.3   Cultural Capital

French sociologist Pierre Bourdieu also posited that social capital consists of resources available to an individual as a result of their social ties and/or group memberships. But Bourdieu offered a third form of capital that he believed to be particularly valuable for explaining social reproduction.

> The notion of cultural capital initially presented itself to me…as a theoretical hypothesis which made it possible to explain the unequal scholastic achievement of children originating from the different social classes. (Bourdieu 1986, p. 243)

As was the case with social capital, Bourdieu introduced the concept of cultural capital to refer to sociological mechanisms existing alongside human capital theory as explanations of human skill and behavioral development. Indeed, he insisted that family cultural capital is essential to the development of children's human capital (Bourdieu 1986, p. 244). However, by contrast with Coleman, who believed in the economists' view of free markets modified by social structure, Bourdieu was influenced by the Marxian view of class conflict, with the upper-class always in an advantaged position.

---

[3] *Human Capital* was even the title of a movie released in 2013.

But what is cultural capital? Bourdieu (1986, p. 243) suggested that cultural capital exists in three forms: "in the *embodied* state, i.e., in the form of long-lasting dispositions of the mind and body; in the *objectified* state, in the form of cultural goods…and in the *institutionalized* state." While an individual's ownership of status-conferring cultural goods such as expensive automobiles as well as particular styles of speech, dress, and home décor will be easily understood by others operating within the same cultural milieu (whether that be the subculture of corporate executives, university faculty, hip hop music performers, or other subgroups), and "institutionalized" employment-related credentials and certificates confer obvious advantages, attempts to utilize the cultural capital concept in empirical work have struggled to specify exactly which "long-lasting dispositions of the mind and body" Bourdieu was referring to. However, one particular formulation has been most successful. This is cultural sociologist Anne Swidler's (1986) discussion of a "toolkit of skills" employed in the furtherance of individual strategies of action.

Culture…is more like a style or a set of skills and habits than a set of preferences or wants. If one asked a slum youth why he did not take steps to pursue a middle-class path to success… the answer might well be not 'I don't want that life,' but instead, 'Who, me?' One can hardly pursue success in a world where the accepted skills, styles and informal know-how are unfamiliar. One does better to look for a line of action for which one already has the cultural equipment. (Swidler 1986)

Or, as Swidler stated more recently:

"skills" (or, more subtly, skills, habits, practices, and other "cultured capacities," such as intuitive capacities for perception and judgment, that have to be learned and that people can't perform with confidence unless they get reasonably good at them) provide the major link between culture and action. Whether, like Bourdieu, one sees those skills as a more or less unitary "habitus," or whether one sees them as part of a repertoire, the causal claim is that people are more likely to act in ways that utilize their skills than in ways that enhance their values. (Swidler 2008, pp. 615–616)

Bourdieu uses "habitus" to refer to the underlying dispositions possessed (he says "embodied") in an individual, which in turn lead to the cultural capital (skills, habits, and styles) visibly enacted by this individual. This habitus is created, exists, and may evolve within a "field" or "social arena within which struggles or manoeuvres take place over specific resources or stakes and access to them" (Jenkins 1992, p. 84). The individual's structural position within the field helps determine her habitus, which in turn helps determine the cultural capital she can deploy within this field. Thus, for example, the social class status of a student's family helps determine her school-related habitus, which in turn helps determine the cultural capital she can deploy within the field defined by her classroom, teacher, other students, school, and the larger structures of formal education.

A field, therefore, is a structured system of social positions—occupied either by individuals or institutions—the nature of which defines the situation for their occupants…a field is structured internally in terms of power relations. Positions stand in relationships of domination, subordination or equivalence. (Jenkins 1992, p. 85)

We cannot, in general, directly observe the habitus. Rather, we observe the student's enacted cultural capital, the actions resulting from the individual's habitus and in particular the characteristics of these actions. As judged by the teacher, do the student's actions demonstrate high (or perhaps low) cognitive skill in speech, writing, and on tests? Do these actions disrupt the daily work of the classroom? Does the student display work-related discipline and a positive attitude toward schoolwork? As explained by Jenkins (p. 78):

The habitus disposes actors to do certain things, it provides a basis for the generation of practices. Practices are produced in and by the encounter between the habitus and its dispositions, on the one hand, and the constraints, demands, and opportunities of the social field or market to which the habitus is appropriate or within which the actor is moving, on the other. This is achieved by a less than conscious process of adjustment of the habitus and practices of individuals to the objective and external constraints of the social world.

Jenkins (p. 72) summarizes Bourdieu's theory of action as follows:

> He [Bourdieu] describes the interplay of culturally "given" dispositions, interests and ways of proceeding, on the one hand, and, on the other, individual skills and social competences, the constraints of resource limitations, the unintended consequences which intrude into any ongoing chain of transactions, personal idiosyncrasies and failings, and the weight of the history of relationships between the individuals concerned and the groups in which they claim membership.
>
> In postulating this model of strategy and strategizing, Bourdieu hopes to move away from two separate, if intimately related dualisms. In the first place he is attempting adequately to communicate the mixture of freedom *and* constraint which characterizes social interaction. In the second, he presents practice as the product of processes which are neither wholly conscious nor wholly unconscious, rooted in an ongoing process of learning which begins in childhood, and through which actors know—without knowing—the right thing to do. Taking these two points together, Bourdieu describes the practical accomplishment of successful interaction as 'second nature.'

This is a theory of iterative individual action with feedback, where the individual pursues strategies within a social structural field of opportunities and constraints, based on the resources she possesses. Wacquant (2004, 2011, 2014) conducted participant observation within a boxing gym and based his analysis on how the habitus of a boxer is developed through apprenticeship in this activity. He explains his study as seeking to answer the following questions:

> What is it that thrills boxers? Why do they commit themselves to this harshest and most destructive of all trades? How do they acquire the desire and the skills necessary to last in it? What is the role of the gym, the street, the surrounding violence and racial contempt, of self-interest and pleasure, and of the collective belief in personal transcendence in all this? How does one create a social competency that is an embodied competency, transmitted through a silent pedagogy of organisms in action? In short, how is the *pugilistic habitus* fabricated and deployed? (Wacquant 2011, p. 85)

These same questions could be asked about the process of becoming an "A" student, a cheerleader, a gang member, a homeless person, a steelworker, a mental patient,[4] a union organizer, or a stay-at-home mother. Within a field of social play, skills (or their absence) and dispositions (or their absence) affect the individual's actions, which, in interaction with other individuals within this social field, lead to the individual's upward, downward, or static trajectory of positions as well as the evolution of her habitus. A generalized notion of apprenticeship often applies to these occurrences, and their trajectory bears a resemblance to the economist's notion of "learning by doing."

This theory of individual action seems to naturally include elements of rational choice strategizing, but always within the constraints imposed by the social structural location the individual is born into and/or occupies as a result of her personal history. The theory thus permits an extension of human capital reasoning, where rationality is not denied, but is realistically complicated with cultural, social, and psychological capacities and processes. This formulation of subgroup culture focused on the concepts of "repertoires of behavior" and "habitual behavior" instead of differential values appears to have been first suggested by Ulf Hannerz (1969), based on his fieldwork in an African-American area of Washington, D.C.

> When people draw on their *repertoires* to establish idioms for interaction with more or less specified others, they enter to some extent into the control of these others as they orient their behavior toward that of the others. This is not a case of explicitly recognized norms and sanctions. The basic fact is simply that in order to achieve efficient and satisfying interaction with significant others one is constrained not to deviate too far from the culture one shares with them, as imputed from their *habitual overt behavior*. (p. 194, emphases added)

Greenstone (1991) expanded on the notion that tools and repertoires useful for rational and purposive behavior are central to a correct understanding of "culture":

> Among the many aspects of "culture" are a community's fundamental beliefs, ethical and esthetic values, revered rituals, and material preferences.

---

[4] See Erving Goffman's "The Moral Career of the Mental Patient" (Goffman 1961, chapter 2).

But culture also includes the tools—material and linguistic, practical and theoretical—that people employ in their purposive and reflective activities. Again, the instrumental side of "rationality" specifies those actions, techniques, and skills necessary to achieve specific goals, but rationality also includes the capacity to make human experience bearable by rendering it intelligible. Once these more complex meanings are recognized, a sharp distinction between culture and rationality becomes untenable.

Similarly, in a chapter on "ghetto related behavior and the structure of opportunity," Wilson (1996) pointed out that individual behaviors, habits, skills, and styles exist within the structural constraints and opportunities experienced by the people living within the culture:

> The social action—including behavior, habits, skills, styles, orientations, attitudes—discussed in this chapter and in the next chapter ought not to be analyzed as if it were unrelated to the broader structure of opportunities and constraints that have evolved over time. This is not to argue that individuals and groups lack the freedom to make their own choices, engage in certain conduct, and develop certain styles and orientations, but it is to say that these decisions and actions occur within a context of constraints and opportunities that are drastically different from those present in middle-class society.

Wilson goes on to discuss causal mechanisms in which the social capital arising from neighborhood social controls interacts with the cultural capital—skills, styles, orientations, and habits—of adults and youngsters in the neighborhood:

> In such areas, not only are children at risk because of the lack of informal social controls, they are also disadvantaged because the social interaction among neighbors tends to be confined to those whose skills, styles, orientations, and habits are not as conducive to promoting positive social outcomes (academic success, pro-social behavior, etc.) as are those in more stable neighborhoods. Although the close interaction among neighbors in such areas may be useful in devising strategies, disseminating information, and developing styles of behavior that are helpful in a ghetto milieu… they may be less effective in promoting the welfare of children in the society at large.

Patterson (2015) references the same idea when he talks about the importance of *procedural knowledge* in cultural processes:

> Bourdieu's widely acclaimed concepts of "habitus" and "cultural capital" are grounded on the principle of procedural knowledge acquisition, as he himself recognizes. "The essential part of the modus operandi which defines practical mastery is transmitted in practice, in its practical state, without attaining the level of discourse." (p. 29)

Patterson observes that procedural knowledge is acquired primarily through interaction, observation, and practice. He describes groups and their situations, for example Black middle-class parents, in which the procedural knowledge valued by their children's peer group competes with that valued by the school and the parents themselves. Thus, the peer group can also function as a gatekeeper, competing with the teacher in placing a value on and providing a reward for the behaviors flowing from an individual's habitus. Patterson says that when the peer group wins, the child is likely to fall to a social class that is lower than that of his parents. A similar point was made by Anderson (1999) in his discussion of the "code of the street" and its potential to penetrate and dominate the classroom in ghetto communities. In other words, different fields of social activity may have different habitus and cultural capital needed to succeed within them, and when their actors inhabit the same physical space the fields may compete for allegiance and dominance.

A related description of social class differences in the creation and enactment of repertoires of skills, habits, and styles has been presented in an influential book by Lareau (2011). Here she distinguishes between the child rearing styles of working-class parents, which she calls "the accomplishment of natural growth," and that of middle-class parents, which she refers to as "concerted cultivation." According to Lareau, middle-class parents work hard, albeit often unconsciously, to give their children the tools needed to maintain their social class status, thereby helping to reproduce the social class structure. In a follow-up study, Lareau found that these social class differences extended far beyond childhood, and continued even as children reached adulthood.

> The results of the follow-up study provide further support for the argument that a pattern of social inequality is being reproduced. Parents' cultural practices play a role. The commitment to concerted cultivation, whereby parents actively fostered and developed children's talents and skills did not, it turns out, wane over time. Even as children became autonomous adolescents with driver's licenses, jobs, and dorm rooms, the middle-class parents closely monitored and intervened in their lives. (p. 305)

In an appendix, Lareau explicitly ties her observations to Bourdieu's theory.

> To make this book more readable, I refrained from burdening it with Bourdieu's terminology. Still, the book is a reasonably straightforward, if *partial*, empirical application of Bourdieu's broader theoretical model. For example, in *Distinction: A Social Critique on the Judgment of Taste*, as well as other works, Bourdieu clearly intends for habitus to be a set of internalized dispositions that operate in a large number of social spheres. In his discussion of habitus, Bourdieu includes the preferences in food, furniture, music, makeup, books, and movies. The focus of *Unequal Childhoods* is much narrower, looking primarily at time use for children's leisure activities, language use in the home, and interventions of adults in children's institutional lives. Still, it is reasonable to assert that the elements discussed in this book, taken together, do constitute a set of dispositions that children learn, or habitus. Concerted cultivation and the accomplishment of natural growth are aspects of the habitus of the families discussed in this book. (p. 362)

As pointed out by Lareau and Weininger (2003), there is another aspect of Bourdieu's theory that is often neglected. This is the role of institutional gatekeepers in judging and valuing the cultural capital (skills, habits, and styles) of the individuals who appear before them. An example is found in the play Pygmalion, where Liza could not enter upper-class society until Henry Higgins had taught her to speak "properly," and importantly, her speech patterns had passed the tests informally administered by the members of this society as they conversed with her. It is in the judgment conferred by gatekeepers on the skills, habits, and styles of those

appearing before them that stratification outcomes are determined. Thus, Lareau and Weininger (2003, p. 568) argue that the most accurate theory of the role of cultural capital in status attainment "stresses the micro-interactional processes through which individuals comply (or fail to comply) with the evaluative standards of dominant institutions such as schools."

Teachers are the school's primary gatekeepers.[5] They express their judgments in the grades they assign, which are sent home to parents in a report card so that they can see how their child is doing. In elementary school these report cards typically provide a grade (e.g., outstanding, satisfactory or needs improvement) in reading, math, and other academic skills, as well as in behaviors, including examples such as the following (taken from the form used by one district): completes homework on time, effort, makes good use of time, is cooperative and gets along with peers, is courteous in speech and actions, controls unnecessary talking, listens and follows directions, respects personal and school property, seeks help when needed. These elementary school reports transform into letter grades in each subject as the student moves up through middle and high school. A sequence of high grades typically leads to enrollment in more advanced courses, and eventually college attendance and graduation. A sequence of low grades and poor behavior typically leads to dropout, or perhaps a terminal high school diploma or GED.

Farkas et al. (1990) and Farkas (1996) applied the cultural capital framework to this situation by positing that the student's school-related habitus was best defined by the skills and behaviors that are rated by teachers on the report card. As noted in the paragraph above, these importantly include academic performance and academic-related work habits. Using data from the Dallas School

---

[5]This is an important point, which is often missed by cultural capital researchers who use standardized test scores rather than course grades as outcome variables. Central to cultural capital theory is the interaction between individuals and gatekeepers, and the judgment that the latter render on the former's suitability and standing in the field of play. In K–12 education this interaction is largely between students and their teachers. Course grades are the result.

District, Farkas and colleagues empirically estimated a causal flow model in which student and teacher sociodemographic background characteristics lead to student skills, habits, and styles, which lead to student coursework mastery, which lead to the teacher-assigned course grade. Indirect effects in which, for example, student background characteristics lead to student academic work habits which directly affect the course grade (after controlling the effect via coursework mastery) were also estimated. The resulting calculations appear to be one of the few times that teacher's grading responses to students' skills, habits, and styles have been empirically evaluated. (For other examples see Bodovski and Farkas 2008 and Dumais et al. 2012.) The findings from this and related research will be examined in a later section of this chapter. For now, we turn to the extensive controversies that have surrounded the cultural capital concept and its empirical implementation.

1.3   Critiques of Cultural Capital

As noted above, Bourdieu's writings on cultural capital are often vague and suggestive rather than clear and explicit. This has led to a number of critiques of the concept and how it has been used in empirical research. Three of these critiques have received the most attention—those by Kingston (2001), Lareau and Weininger (2003), and Goldthorpe (2007).

1.3.1   Critique by Kingston

Kingston sets out to review empirical studies that have used the cultural capital concept to explain why children from more socially privileged homes typically receive higher grades in school and have greater educational attainment. He sets the stage for this review by following Lamont and Lareau (1988) in defining cultural capital as "institutionalized, i.e., widely shared, high status cultural signals (attitudes, preferences, formal knowledge, behaviors, goals, and credentials) used for social and cultural exclusion." The claim

is that high status knowledge and activities—fine arts knowledge and museum attendance, classical musical knowledge and attendance at concerts, knowledge of literature and visits to the library or bookstores—are the elements of the enacted student's cultural capital that are rewarded by teachers and that explain the greater schooling success of children from higher social classes. Teachers supposedly favor these students by the use of "exclusionary practices" that enable the children to attain greater school success.

That teachers favor children who are knowledgeable about "highbrow" aesthetic culture (e.g., classical music and art), and do so pervasively enough to account for the reproduction of social classes in America, may seem unlikely. Yet it is exactly such high status activities indulged in by the parents and children of higher social classes that have been widely used to operationalize cultural capital in empirical work.[6]

Why this particular operationalization of cultural capital? DiMaggio (1982) first used this definition of cultural capital in empirical work, and his operationalization of cultural capital has been enormously influential. This usage was further supported in the paper by Lamont and Lareau (1988). Since Bourdieu's own writings lack clarity on the subject, it is not surprising that subsequent researchers have followed the path marked out by these American scholars.

Kingston is aware that teacher discrimination in favor of children involved in elite cultural activities seems unlikely by itself to explain the society-wide reproduction of the social class structure. Indeed, he attacks this notion both with evidence showing that elite cultural activities are not that widely engaged in by an upper class defined by professionals and managers, as well as with findings by Lamont herself that Americans strongly oppose giving social preferment to individuals engaged in elite activities. Nevertheless,

---

[6]Of course, exposure to highbrow culture may result in improved language use and presentation of self which might positively impress teachers. However empirical estimates of this effect including a full range of controls including test scores have typically found at best a very weak relationship between elite cultural activities and course grades. For example, see Dumais et al. (2012).

we should look at the empirical evidence. He does so, reviewing a number of papers providing estimates of the effects of elite culture participation on student educational outcomes. Overall, he finds these to be modest in magnitude. (I will review the detailed findings on the effects of cultural capital in the following section.) He then repeats his argument that because elite culture is not widely distributed among the professional and managerial classes, even should it have an effect on school success, this mechanism would not meet what he regards as Bourdieu's theoretical claim that cultural capital can only be gained in upper-class homes, and thus represents "exclusionary practices that are valued for their connection to a social group." Instead, he says, elite cultural activities are available in the homes of some working-class students and not in the homes of some middle- and upper-class students, so they don't meet the test of "exclusionary practices." Further, he says, any positive effects of these variables on school success may be due not to exclusionary practices, but instead simply that such participation is associated with other variables such as intellectual curiosity and perseverance which themselves aid school success.

1.3.2 Critique by Lareau and Weininger

A second critique was published by Lareau and Weininger (2003). These authors seek to understand how the concept of cultural capital has been employed by English language sociologists of education. In the first part of their paper they do so by reviewing 15 papers that used the concept in empirical work. They conclude that almost all of these papers follow DiMaggio (1982) in measuring cultural capital by participation in and knowledge of elite ("highbrow") arts activities. They also note that most of these papers make a point of differentiating the cultural capital concept from that of skills or technical ability (typically measured by test scores).

The second part of the paper by Lareau and Weininger closely examines Bourdieu's writings on this subject. They demonstrate that he did not intend the cultural capital concept to be confined to "highbrow" cultural activities, although he may have thought that it played an important role within the French educational system. Instead, he states "in highly generic terms, that any given 'competence' functions as cultural capital if it enables appropriation 'of the cultural heritage' of a society, but is unequally distributed among its members, thereby engendering the possibility of 'exclusive advantages'" (p. 579).

Further, Lareau and Weininger report that nowhere in Bourdieu's writing does he imply a distinction between cultural capital on the one hand, and technical knowledge or ability on the other. Indeed, as I have quoted earlier, Bourdieu invented the cultural capital concept in response to economists' concept of human capital, and asserted that family cultural capital was essential to the creation of human capital conceived as ability or talent. Thus, as stated by Lareau and Weininger, the "effects of 'status,' for Bourdieu, are not distinct from those of 'skill' (or by extension, 'ability'). Cultural capital amounts to an irreducible amalgamation of the two."

Thus, in place of elite, "highbrow" culture, Lareau and Weininger offer their own definition of cultural capital. As applied to schooling it has two parts.

> First, studies of cultural capital in school settings must identify the particular expectations—both formal and, especially, informal—by means of which school personnel appraise students. Secondly, as a result of their location in the stratification system, students and their parents enter the educational system with dispositional skills and knowledge that differentially facilitate or impede their ability to conform to institutionalized expectations. ...In addition...we believe that technical skills, including academic skills, should not be excluded from any discussion of cultural capital. (p. 588)

Teachers' appraisals of their students are recorded on the students' report cards. As we shall see, they are largely based on the teacher's judgments of her students' academic skills and work habits. *These* appear to constitute the observable indicators of a student's cultural capital that teachers are judging in a form that is consequential for the student's later educational trajectory.

1.3.3 Critique by Goldthorpe

Goldthorpe (2007) presents a very negative view of cultural capital theory. To begin with, he denies the fundamental claim of social reproduction theory, that working-class children are constrained to remain in their class, and that middle-class children do not suffer downward mobility into the working class. He instead references empirical studies showing that during the twentieth-century expansion of secondary education in Britain, "substantial and primarily upward educational mobility did in fact occur between generations" (p. 8). He then cites additional studies finding that, for example, "as of the early 1970s, over two-thirds of the individuals surveyed who had attended a selective secondary school were 'first generation'—i.e., their parents had not received any education at this level; and while children of working-class background were underrepresented in this group, they were far from being excluded."

Goldthorpe then cites more recent findings that the same pattern has occurred with the expansion of higher education. He notes that children from all social classes have taken up the expanded opportunities for a university education, so that the *relative* chances of such attainment from different social class origins is a debated issue. However, he cites evidence that among those French children born into the working class in the 1960s and early 1970s, 40% of the children of skilled workers and 25% of the children of unskilled workers gained the baccalaureat or a higher qualification. Thus, says Goldthorpe, Bourdieu's claim of social reproduction just doesn't fit the facts. Instead, there has been widespread upward social mobility for the working-class children.[7]

Goldthorpe, like Lareau and Weininger, argues that defining cultural capital as elite cultural activities, totally separate from cognitive skills, was never intended by Bourdieu. Thus, he follows Lareau and Weininger in judging all the empirical literature that followed DiMaggio by operationalizing cultural capital as high culture to be misguided. Instead, he argues for a more inclusive definition of "cultural resources," including such mundane activities as reading to the child, and notes that, not surprisingly, family reading behavior is more predictive of student educational success than is beaux-arts involvement. He goes on to state that as an empirical matter, Bourdieu's cultural capital theory is simply wrong. Facts contradict the theory, Goldthorpe (p. 14) says, because

> differing class conditions do not give rise to such distinctive and abiding forms of *habitus* as Bourdieu would suppose; because even within more disadvantaged classes, with little access to high culture, values favoring education may still prevail and perhaps some relevant cultural resources exist; and because, therefore, schools and other educational institutions can function as important agencies of re-socialisation—that is, can not only underwrite but also in various respects, *compensate for or indeed counter* family influences in the creation and transmission of "cultural capital."

Goldthorpe follows these arguments with a more general attack on the premises of cultural capital theory. He asserts that the student's habitus is not formed once and for all in the family, subsequently remaining immutable. Rather, he suggests that the school also molds the student's habitus, which can evolve during an individual's educational career. He asserts that there is little empirical support for social reproduction (because there has been so much upward educational mobility out of the working class) or for a set of dispositions that upper-class parents transmit to their children, that are immutable, that lower-class children are unable to attain, and that the schools employ as an exclusionary device to keep lower-class children in their place.

Instead, Goldthorpe advises rejecting cultural capital theory and replacing it with a more eclectic notion of cultural resources that can be

---

[7]Of course, institutions of higher learning themselves have a prestige hierarchy, and doubtless the children of unskilled workers were more likely to attend the less prestigious institutions. For theories of "maximally maintained inequality" and "effectively maintained inequality" arguing that upper-class parents strive to and will always manage to maintain their children's advantages over those of children from lower classes, see Raftery and Hout (1993) and Lucas (2001).

acquired from the family and the school, as well as other sources (such as peers and neighborhoods). His emphasis is more on those variables that can be empirically demonstrated to affect educational attainment than on a theory that says that such attainment by working-class youth is improbable.

County, Maryland. All of the report cards have a place for the teacher to mark the student's grade on each of the academic subjects—math, language arts, science, social studies, art, music, and physical education. However, there is also a place for the teachers to grade the behaviors and attitudes described below.

1.4 An Approach That Works

A viable empirical approach to these issues has long been available, but little taken advantage of.[8] Central to Bourdieu's theory, and recommended as the key to the cultural capital concept by Lareau and Weininger (2003), is the idea of teachers as gatekeepers, judging the outward behavioral manifestations of each student's habitus, that is, the student's enacted cultural capital in school, with these judgments favoring children from middle- and upper-class homes. So what is the mechanism through which these judgments are made known and recorded in K–12 education? The answer is simple—the report card. *This* is where teachers report their judgments of each student, on both academics and behavior; these are the judgments that become part of the student's record; and *this* is the mechanism by which these judgments affect student educational careers. Students with strong positive report cards on both academics and behavior are likely to attend college and perhaps go further; those with constantly failing report cards are likely to never complete high school.[9]

What academics and behaviors are graded on these cards? Using the internet, I selected grade 2–5 report cards from three randomly chosen school districts, in, respectively, Sarasota, Florida; Richland, Washington; and Montgomery

1.4.1 Items Graded on Elementary School Report Cards in Three Districts

Sarasota, Florida: For each academic subject, the teacher can select from a list of 18 possible comments. These basically fall into two sets. The first involves student behavior and includes

- Works well in class, is courteous, respectful and cooperative
- Interacts well with peers
- Works independently, without disturbing others, and with little assistance from the teacher
- Has made good overall improvement in his/her effort this quarter
- Has difficulty following school/classroom rules and/or directions
- Needs frequent assistance from the teacher
- Often disturbs others during class
- Has difficulty completing classwork
- Has difficulty playing with others

A second set involves actions that involve parents, including

- Would benefit from additional reading practice at home
- Would benefit from additional writing practice at home
- Would benefit from additional math practice at home
- Would benefit from having homework reviewed at home
- Would benefit from attending school regularly as frequent absences have a negative impact on his/her academic performance

---

[8]This may be partly because some researchers misunderstand the theory. But it is also the case that access to students' records is often difficult to obtain.

[9]In addition, course grades are not the only determinant of school success. Standardized test scores also play an important role in college access. *Why* colleges place such great weight on test scores is a subject worthy of additional investigation.

Montgomery County, Maryland: The report card has separate sections for grading each of the academic subjects, plus one for grading what are called *Learning Skills*. This is divided into two sets of items. The first, called Work Habits, contains the following:

- Rules and Procedures
- Task Completion

The second, called Thinking and Academic Success Skills, contains the following:

- Analysis
- Collaboration
- Effort/Motivation/Persistence
- Fluency
- Intellectual Risk Taking
- Metacognition
- Originality
- Synthesis

Richland, Washington: The report card, in addition to grades for the separate academic subjects, also has grades for what are called *Social and Learning Skills*. These are the following:

- Engages effectively with others
- Understands effort and perseverance directly impact learning
- Listens attentively in different learning situations
- Respects individual differences/rights of others
- Takes responsibility for choices and actions
- Manages materials and time
- Advocates for self

All of these districts give grades in each of the academic subjects. But what sets of behaviors, explicitly identified for grading, do these districts have in common? The answer is—*habitual behaviors that facilitate learning in the American classroom*. In Sarasota these include "works well in class, is courteous, respectful and cooperative; works independently, without disturbing others." In Montgomery County these include "rules and procedures, task completion, and

effort/motivation/persistence." In Richland they include that the student "understands effort and perseverance directly impact learning, listens attentively in different learning situations, and manages materials and time." What these have in common is that they all describe aspects of *good academic work habits*. They are the traits needed to be academically successful while not reducing the success of the other students in the class. *These* are the behaviors that teachers are most focused on rewarding, not knowledge of classical music or fine arts. Teacher "gatekeeping" rewards effective and cooperative[10] academic work habits, and punishes their opposite—low effort, poor organization, inattention, sloppiness, disrespect, and disruptiveness. A quick perusal of a larger number of district report card formats available online suggests that teacher judgment of these aspects of students' academic work habits is widespread.[11]

1.4.2 Putting It All Together

A focus on academic skills and work habits was the basis for the empirical study of cultural capital undertaken by Farkas and colleagues more than 25 years ago (Farkas et al. 1990; Farkas 1996). In this work, a representative sample of Dallas Independent School District (DISD) 7th and 8th grade social studies teachers responded to a "student work-ethic characteristics questionnaire" regarding up to six of their students selected by stratified random sampling. The teachers rated the students on homework, class participation, effort, organization, disruptiveness, assertiveness, and appearance and dress. The first four of these had correlations between 0.80 and 0.95, and were combined into a scale of work habits. One of the variables—assertiveness—showed little relationship with the other (independent or dependent) variables and was omitted from the study. A student's days absent as

---

[10] But note that Richland also judges whether the student "advocates for self."

[11] And these teachers' values likely benefit females more than males. See Dumais (2002), Morris (2008).

recorded by the district was also included as a behavioral variable, as were disruptiveness and appearance and dress. Basic skills were measured by student scores on the Iowa Test of Basic Skills (ITBS), which includes both Language and Mathematics totals, as well as subskill scores for each of these variables. Farkas and colleagues operationalized student skills, habits, and styles as the student's ITBS score, work habits, days absent, disruptiveness, and appearance and dress.

This research was also able to profit from an unusual initiative undertaken by the DISD in response to the Texas Education Reform Act of 1984. Groups of teachers in each of the subject-matter areas were assembled over the summer to create test items representative of the course subject matter. These curriculum-referenced tests were then administered uniformly to DISD students at the end of the appropriate semester. The resulting scores provide an objective measure of each student's coursework mastery in the subject.

The authors then estimated a causal model in which student and teacher sociodemographics are regarded as determining the student's basic skills and the teacher's judgment of the student's habits and styles, and these in turn are related to the student's actual coursework mastery. All of these variables together are then related to the teacher-assigned course grade. This model is summarized in Fig. 1.1. It shows the key relationships involved as students from different social backgrounds interact with teachers from different social backgrounds, resulting in the teacher-gatekeeper's final judgment on the student for the semester—the course grade. This is the closest that empirical research has come to implementing a quantitative and testable version of Lareau and Weininger's (2003) suggestion that cultural capital studies focus on the interaction of students with their teacher-gatekeepers, and how this interaction results in different schooling outcomes for students from different social backgrounds.

I will defer discussion of the empirical findings from this work until the following section, where the detailed findings from prior empirical work are reviewed. However, the question arises, what has been done since this work by Farkas and colleagues to implement and test this version of cultural capital theory, in which the student's habitus, strongly influenced by parents and peers in the home and neighborhood, and by the child's preschool experiences before kindergarten entry, then evolves via the student's interaction with family, peers, and teachers as the student moves up the grade-levels?

Farkas (2003) reviewed the literature on cognitive and noncognitive skills developed by economists and sociologists and related it to the "skills, habits, and styles" version of cultural capital theory discussed above. Economists' research in this area can be traced back to the work of Bowles and Gintis (1976), whereas related work by sociologists dates from the book by Jencks and colleagues (Jencks et al. 1979).

Bowles and Gintis argued that "in capitalist America," variation in the design and management of schools exists to create those worker personality traits needed by different jobs in the industrial system, largely based on the jobs held by the student's parents, thereby leading to social reproduction. Thus, the children of working-class parents typically obtained no more than a high school degree, perhaps with an emphasis on vocational training, and became factory workers whose obedience to authority was their most desired trait. Accordingly, such obedience was emphasized by K–12 teachers. By comparison, the children of middle- and upper-class parents went on to college, where creativity and independence received greater rewards, since these are the skills needed for middle-class management and professional employment.

To provide evidence for these assertions, Bowles and Gintis empirically tested their assertion that the personality trait they labeled "submission to authority" was, along with cognitive skills, the principal determinant of course grades in high school. Their empirical work supported this assertion, but crucially, they defined such submission as including the following characteristics of a student's academic work habits: perseverance, dependability, consistency, identifies with school, empathizes orders, punctuality, and defers gratification. As we shall see throughout this review, these are indeed the habits and behaviors graded positively by K–12 teachers.

However, for most teachers and many other researchers, myself included, these traits do not deserve the pejorative label "submission to authority." Instead, they simply constitute "good work habits" whose effects are to be measured empirically, and which may be desirable at all levels of the occupational structure.

This is the approach taken by Jencks et al. (1979), who conducted extensive analyses of the roles played by individual cognitive skills and non-cognitive (personality) traits on school and employment success. Using multiple data sets they measured the effects of self-assessed personality traits as well as what they considered to be indirect personality measures involving self-reports of various behaviors possibly reflecting underlying personality. A principle components analysis of 14 questions identified a construct they referred to as "study habits." They also analyzed data in which teachers rated students on each of nine personality traits. Results of these analyses are summarized in the following section.

Other researchers continued the analysis of the effects of cognitive and noncognitive skills on school success. Within sociology, Lareau (2011) echoed the distinction between working-class and middle-class parenting orientations discussed by Bowles and Gintis, referring to the working-class style as "the accomplishment of natural growth" and the middle-class style as "concerted cultivation." She repeats the Bowles and Gintis observation that working-class parents tend to want their children to follow directives, while middle-class parents tend to encourage their children to ask questions and to reason. Rather than emphasizing the social class differences in academic work habits likely resulting from these parenting differences, Lareau instead emphasized that the middle-class parenting style teaches the child to develop an individualized sense of self, including a sense of comfort, entitlement, and agency when dealing with adult organizations such as the school, where they learn to present themselves and perform (Lareau 2011, pp. 242–243). Lareau asserts that, by contrast, the working-class parenting style leaves children feeling uncomfortable and constrained when dealing with these same institutions. These social class differences are replicated, says Lareau, when parents interact with teachers. In such situations she describes working-class and poor parents as "baffled, intimidated, and subdued."

Other sociologists have undertaken related analyses, both quantitative and qualitative, seeking to discover which parent and student behaviors are most strongly associated with student success. At the same time, economists have produced a quantitative literature on the effects of cognitive and non-cognitive skills on school and employment success. Prominent here is a paper by Heckman and Kautz (2014) seeking to estimate the empirical importance of cognitive skills and non-cognitive traits in determining schooling outcomes. Findings from these literatures will be reviewed in the following section.

To summarize, the "skills, habits, and styles" paradigm has been widely used to investigate how the actions of parents, children, and teachers lead to the differential school success of children from middle- and upper-class children, compared to those from the working class. It seems to reasonably capture Bourdieu's intentions for the habitus (underlying) and cultural capital (enacted) concepts to serve as mediators between family background and schooling success. Indeed, after the dominance of this research area by cultural sociologists focused on elite cultural activities, this research approach brings back an emphasis on the daily actions and interactions involving students and teachers that ultimately determine the schooling and social class attainment of the students. It also brings back the concern with finding a sociological equivalent of the human capital paradigm advanced by economists, and employed so successfully to apply economic reasoning to almost every field of human endeavor. Both James Coleman and Pierre Bourdieu were explicitly in interaction with economists, and were inspired to create their formulations by the world-wide success of the human capital paradigm. Bringing this research area back to a place where economists and sociologists speak to one another, and empirically test their theories, simply puts this research area back on a developmental trajectory consistent with its beginning.

1.5   Empirical Findings

A schematic model of cultural capital's causal effects was presented in Fig. 1.1. This is a mediation model, in which parenting, habitus, and academic skills and habits mediate the relationship between SES and course grades. The SES of each student implies the parenting they receive. This parenting helps determine the student's habitus, his/her disposition (including skills) toward various behaviors and strategies of action. These dispositions then lead to the academic skills and work habits that the student presents to the teacher in the classroom. These skills and habits are then employed by the teacher to assign a course grade to the student. Where quantitative empirical work is concerned, researchers are able to find measures of SES, parenting, academic skills, work habits, and course grades (or teachers' judgements of students' skills) on many of the large, nationally representative data sets collected by the National Center for Education Statistics and that are widely available to researchers (these include the ECLS-K, the ECLS: 2011, the NELS, and ELS). Other data sets, including the 28-nation PISA, have also been used in empirical studies.

The habitus, conceived as a collection of underlying dispositions, including skills, habits, identities, worldviews, preferences, or values, can typically not be measured directly, so that its characteristics are inferred by the academic skills and habits it gives rise to. (However, as we shall see, Gaddis (2013) seeks to measure it by using two attitudinal scales.) Thus, empirical work has typically included some subset (or all) of the variables SES, parenting, academic skills and work habits, and course grades shown in Fig. 1.1. The result has been empirical studies in which parenting is regressed on SES, skills and work habits are regressed on SES and parenting, and course grades are regressed on some or all of SES, parenting, and skills and work habits. Empirical studies of these types are the ones reviewed here.[12]

1.5.1   Social Class Differences in Parenting and Their Consequences

Duncan and Magnuson (2011, Fig. 3.1) provide a schematic model of how genes, families, schools, and peer groups combine to determine the trajectories of children's cognitive skills and behaviors from birth to grade 12, which in turn determine the individual's subsequent educational and labor market attainment. For a variable to play a role in creating social class differences in children's school success, two conditions must be met. First, it must significantly differ across social class groupings. And second, it must significantly affect schooling outcomes, such that when it is controlled, the relationship between parental social class and student success in school is reduced or eliminated. In this section we examine empirical tests of the extent to which parenting meets these conditions.

1.5.1.1 Measuring Parenting: The HOME Score

That working-class parents have different parenting styles from middle- and upper-class parents is a perennial finding of sociologists, psychologists, and economists. These differences have been conceptualized and measured in a number of ways.

Particularly widely used is the Home Observation for Measurement of the Environment (HOME). Separate versions of this measurement instrument have been created to measure parenting quality for children of different ages, but all versions are similarly structured. As modified for use in the National Longitudinal Survey of Youth (NLSY), the HOME produces two parenting measures—one for cognitive stimulation and the other for emotional support. It is useful to examine the behavioral items typically included

---

[12]A subset of studies use standardized test scores as their ultimate outcome measures. But it would be more appro-

priate to use teacher-assigned course grades, because only these represent the teacher-gatekeeper judgments that are so central to cultural capital theory. (Of course standardized test scores should be one of the predictors of the teacher-assigned course grade, since test scores measure the academic knowledge and skills that the student displays to the teacher.)

in these scales in order to understand which parental behaviors researchers consider most important for children's development. To take one example, for children aged 3–5, the following items are used to measure parental cognitive stimulation and emotional support:

Cognitive Stimulation Scale:

– How often read stories to child?
– How many children's books does child have?
– How many magazines family gets regularly?
– Child has use of CD player?
– Do you help child with numbers?
– Do you help child with alphabet?
– Do you help child with colors?
– Do you help with shapes and sizes?
– How often is child taken on any kind of outing?
– How often is child taken to museum?
– Child's play environment is safe?
– Interior of the home is dark or perceptually monotonous?
– All visible rooms of the home are reasonably clean?
– All visible rooms of the home are minimally cluttered?

Emotional Support Scale:

– If child got so angry that s/he hit you, what would you do? Respondent is offered multiple responses. If either "hit him/her back" or "spank child," item is scored "not emotionally supportive."
– How much choice is child allowed in deciding foods s/he eats at breakfast & lunch?
– About how many hours is the TV on in your home each day? >4 is scored "not emotionally supportive."
– How often does child eat a meal with you and his/her father/stepfather/father-figure?
– About how many times, if any, have you had to spank child in the past week? >1 is scored "not emotionally supportive."

Interviewer observed:

– Mother conversed w/child >1 time (no scolding or suspicious comments)?

– Mother caressed, kissed, or hugged child at least once?
– Mother introduced interviewer to child by name?
– Mother physically restricted or (shook/grabbed) child? Coded non-supportive
– Mother slapped or spanked child at least once? Coded non-supportive
– Mother's voice conveyed positive feeling about child?

We see that the cognitive stimulation scale is focused on direct parental instruction and the materials useful for learning. That is, this scale emphasizes parental actions that foster cognitive readiness for school. The emotional responsiveness scale focuses on warm, positive parent–child interaction, and gives a lower score when the parent employs physical punishment. The elements of the HOME score listed above encompass many of the items that quantitative studies have used to measure parenting. However, some studies, particularly those associated with the original notion of cultural capital defined as knowledge of and participation in high (elite) cultural activities (e.g., classical music and museum quality art) advanced by DiMaggio (1982) and of "concerted cultivation" (e.g., scheduled activities including sports, music and dance classes) advanced by Lareau (2011) have added or substituted these activities for the items in the HOME above.

1.5.1.2 Social Class Differences in HOME Parenting Measures

Reeves and Howard (2003) used longitudinal HOME scores from the Children of the NLSY to create measures of "strong versus weak parenting." That is, for each child they measured whether the HOME score was in the bottom or top 25% of parents at each of the three stages— infancy (age 0–2), early childhood (age 3–5), and middle childhood (age 10–15). Parents scoring in the bottom 25% during at least two of these stages were considered to be the weakest parents; those scoring in the top 25% during at least two of these stages were considered to be the strongest parents. (This resulted in 20.9% of parents being categorized as weakest and 17.6% as strongest.) The researchers then computed the percent of each type of parent among families in either the bottom or the top quintile on family income. They found that, for families in the bottom income quintile, almost 50% were among the weakest parents whereas fewer than 5% were among the strongest parents. By contrast, for families in the top income quintile, about 35% were among the strongest parents, whereas only about 5% were among the weakest. Thus, parenting quality as measured by the HOME scale varies strongly and significantly across social classes. But to what extent do these social class differences in parenting quality account for social class differences in children's cognitive and behavioral outcomes?

1.5.1.3 HOME Parenting Affects Cognitive and Behavioral Outcomes

This question has been addressed by a number of empirical studies. Morgan et al. (2009) replicated the findings of Reeves and Howard, reporting that mothers in the lowest educational quintile displayed HOME scores approximately one standard deviation lower than those in the highest educational quintile. They also found that these parenting scores significantly affected children's learning-related behaviors, and explained a significant portion of the social class differences in these behaviors. Hoff (2003) followed up on work by Hart and Risley (1995), showing that social class differences in mothers' speech to their 2-year-olds fully explained social class differences in these children's vocabularies. Farkas and Beron (2004) found that parenting measures partially explained social class differences in the oral language skills of children. Bradley et al. (2001) showed the significant effects of HOME parenting scores on children's cognitive and behavioral development. Smith et al. (2006) showed that maternal responsiveness to the child positively affected cognitive development. In sum, the cognitive stimulation and emotional support activities measured by the HOME are significantly and positively associated with the skills and habits of children, and explain a portion, but not all, of the social class differences in

these skills and habits when children enter kindergarten.[13]

1.5.1.4 Concerted Cultivation

In a widely discussed study, Lareau (2011) focused on a somewhat different set of parenting behaviors on which working-class and middle-class parents differ. These are the formalized out-of-home activities that middle-class parents typically schedule for their children, contrasted with the more around the home and neighborhood, self-organized activities of working-class children. Lareau referred to the latter as "the accomplishment of natural growth" and the former as "concerted cultivation." As described by Lareau (2011, pp. 238–239), in middle-class families

> parents actively fostered and assessed their children's talents, opinions, and skills. They scheduled their children for activities. They reasoned with them. They hovered over them and outside the home they did not hesitate to intervene on the children's behalf. They made a deliberate and sustained effort to stimulate children's development and cultivate their cognitive and social skills.

By contrast, Lareau says,

> working-class and poor parents viewed children's development as unfolding spontaneously, as long as they were provided with comfort, food, shelter, and other basic support...Parents who relied on natural growth generally organized their children's lives so they spent time in and around home, in informal play with peers, siblings, and cousins... Instead of the relentless focus on reasoning and negotiation that took place in middle-class families, there was less speech (including less whining and badgering) in working-class and poor homes... Directives were common. In their institutional encounters, working-class and poor parents turned over responsibility to professionals; when they did try to intervene, they felt they were less capable and less efficacious than they would have liked.

Lareau's mention of middle-class parents actively fostering their children's "talents, opinions, and skills" is reminiscent of Swidler's

---

[13] There is a large literature on parental involvement with their child's school work, teacher, and school activities more generally, and how this involvement is related to student achievement. For examples, see Van Voorhis et al. (2013) and Nunez et al. (2015).

"skills, habits, and styles." Yet in Lareau's discussion of the consequences of these social class differences in parenting, she emphasizes the organized activities that middle-class children experience—for example, sports and summer camps—and the way these help the child to develop an "individualized sense of self." She goes on to describe these experiences as assisting middle-class children to develop a sense of entitlement and agency when dealing with adults and their institutions, such as teachers and schools. By contrast, she says, the working-class child rearing style does not foster such a sense of self (Lareau 2011, pp. 241–43). Lareau's emphasis on scheduled activities and the development of a sense of entitlement in middle-class children tends to de-emphasize the importance of those direct, academic skill building activities that middle-class parents also devote time to fostering (although she does mention language use as a key component of concerted cultivation). While it is no doubt true that middle- and upper-class parents provide their children with both a sense of entitlement and agency and with the concrete skills and behaviors needed to succeed in school, it is important to know which of these plays the larger role in the greater school success of middle-class students compared with those from the working class. Thus, although the report cards I sampled emphasized academic work habits, at least one, from Richland WA, included an item about the student's agency, namely "advocates effectively for self."

1.5.1.5 Determinants and Consequences of Concerted Cultivation

Quantitative studies of the determinants and consequences of concerted cultivation have yielded mixed results. Roscigno and Ainsworth-Darnell (1999) found a relatively strong positive relationship between SES and each of cultural trips, cultural classes, and household educational resources. However, when they employed these parenting variables to predict course grades, either with or without controlling prior grades and test scores, they found insignificant or small effects. By contrast, they found much larger

effects for student academic work habits and prior achievement. Sticking relatively closely with Lareau's definition of concerted cultivation, Dumais et al. (2012) found no positive significant relationship between (a) parents' cultural activities with their child and/or parents' school involvement and (b) teachers' evaluations of students' language and literacy skills, academic work habits, or interpersonal skills. Similar results were reported by De Graaf et al. (2000). They used both elite cultural activities and parental reading to their children to predict the child's ultimate educational attainment. They found that reading to the child, but not elite cultural activities, significantly predicted educational attainment.

Bodovski and Farkas (2008) used ECLS-K data for first grade to estimate the association between both social class and parenting quality (with an emphasis on the concerted cultivation parenting style) on the one hand and students' academic work habits, academic performance, and the teacher's judgment of the student's performance on the other. The authors employed a more general definition of concerted cultivation that added parental instructional and interactional activities to the measures of participation in organized activities and parental involvement with the schools. The result was three dimensions of parental activities for first graders, measured in three separate scales and then combined into a single scale. The first dimension is *parental perceptions of their responsibilities towards their child*, with a particular focus on instruction and interaction. The following variables were used to construct this scale: tell a child stories, sing songs, do art, play games, teach about nature, build blocks, do sports, practice numbers and letters, read to a child, listen to a child even if busy, foster the child's opinion, help with homework.

The second dimension is how children spend their *leisure time, particularly their participation in organized activities*. These were measured as music, arts and crafts, dance lessons, clubs, organized performing arts and athletic activities, educational trips to the library, museum, zoo, concert, or live show.

The third dimension was conceptualized as *parents' relationships with social institutions, particularly schools.* This was measured as participation in parent–teacher conferences, attending an open house or back-to-school night, participating in PTA, attending a school event, volunteering at school, and participating in fundraising. The authors also added another variable—number of children's books in the home—providing an additional measure of parental efforts to enrich their children's lives and understanding, as well as assist with pre-reading and reading skills.

Bodovski and Farkas restricted their analysis sample to White children in order to avoid controversies regarding whether or not race functions as a stratifying factor in addition to SES. They first ran regressions using SES and other demographics to predict the concerted cultivation measure. They found a medium standardized coefficient of 0.40 for the path from SES to concerted cultivation. This validates the observations of Lareau and others regarding strong social class differentials in the parenting activities measured by this variable.

Next, Bodovski and Farkas used SES and concerted cultivation in sequential regressions to predict the student's teacher-judged academic work habits—persistence at tasks, eagerness to learn, attentiveness, learning independence, flexibility, and organization. With only SES and demographics as predictors, the authors found that SES had a standardized coefficient of 0.19 with academic work habits. When parental expectations for the child's educational attainment and concerted cultivation were added to the equation, the coefficient of SES declined 26% to 0.14; the direct effect of concerted cultivation was 0.07. This shows once again that direct measures of parenting activities are able to explain a portion, but only a portion, of the effect of SES on the child's academic work habits.

Following this, Bodovski and Farkas used SES, demographics, parental educational expectations for the child, concerted cultivation, and academic work habits in sequential regressions to predict the student's reading test score. With only demographics controlled, the standardized coef-

ficient of SES on reading test scores was 0.31. Adding parental expectations and concerted cultivation reduced this by 26% to 0.23, showing that concerted cultivation can explain at most a portion of SES differentials in cognitive performance. The direct effect of concerted cultivation on reading test scores was 0.09. Finally, academic work habits were added to the equation. This reduced the SES effect to 0.18, slightly more than half of its total effect. The direct effect of academic work habits on reading test scores was a very substantial 0.38, showing once again that these behaviors appear to strongly affect learning.

Finally, these variables were used in sequential regressions to predict the teacher's judgment of the student's language and literacy skills. In the first regression, with only SES and demographics controlled, the total effect of SES was 0.24. As the variables were added sequentially, by far the strongest predictors of the teacher's judgment were academic work habits and reading test scores. By the final regression, with all predictors in the equation, the effect of the reading test score was 0.62, that of academic work habits was 0.32, and the SES effect on the teacher's judgment of the student's language and literacy skills had been fully explained. I conclude that, at least in this nationally representative data set of first grade students, the teacher-assigned course grade is determined about 2/3 by actual performance and 1/3 by student work habits. This gives a smaller role to work habits than was found by Farkas (1996) for the Dallas schools (see Fig. 1.2). However, this may be accounted for by differences in the subjects examined and the available data. In particular, the 1996 Farkas study predicted the actual grade assigned for 7th and 8th grade social studies, whereas the 2008 Bodovski and Farkas study predicted the teacher's judgment of first grade student's language and literacy skills. The latter study likely showed a stronger effect of test scores since it was the skills tested that the teacher was asked to judge. The fact that even in this case, with standardized test scores controlled, student work habits had an effect size as large as 0.32 in predicting student skills demonstrates the importance of these work habits in the teacher's judgment of student performance.

Several additional studies have employed quantitative measures of concerted cultivation, typically testing for its role as a mediator in explaining the relationship between SES and achievement measured by test scores, but without attention to either the academic work habits of students or to teacher's judgment of these and the role of this judgment in the assignment of a grade for the course. An example is Cheadle (2008), who uses ECLS-K data to test the role of concerted cultivation as a mediator between SES and math and reading test score trajectories from kindergarten through third grade. Cheadle uses many of the same variables as Bodovski and Farkas to measure concerted cultivation. These comprised elite cultural activities, participation in school activities such as parent–teacher conferences, and the number of the child's books, but omitted the direct instructional activities included by Bodovski and Farkas, such as time spent reading to a child or helping with homework. Cheadle finds that concerted cultivation explains about 20% of the effect of SES on test scores. He also finds that concerted cultivation is most strongly associated with race gaps in achievement at kindergarten entry, and appears to play a smaller role in achievement growth as children move up to first and third grade. Overall, the conclusion is that the concerted cultivation parenting style plays a modest role in mediating the effect of SES on achievement. Cheadle might have found larger effects if he had included direct instructional activities in his measure of concerted cultivation. However, since this study employs test scores rather than course grades as the outcome, it does not test for the determinants of teacher judgments which are so central to cultural capital theory.

Other studies have used concerted cultivation measures that partially overlap with those used by Bodovski/Farkas and Cheadle. Bodovski (2010) found that, contrary to Lareau, even after controlling SES, Black parents were less supportive of their children's school success than Whites. Lee and Bowen (2006) used measures of the parent physically visiting the school, discussing educational topics with the child, helping with homework, managing the child's time on literacy and nonliteracy activities, and the parent's educational expectations for the child. (Note that Bodovski and Farkas included this last measure in their analyses, but did not consider it to be part of concerted cultivation.) The dependent variable was academic achievement, measured as a composite including the teacher-assigned grades in reading and math as well as teacher reports of whether the child was above or below grade level in reading and math. This use of grades and teacher judgments as outcomes puts the study more directly in the cultural capital field.

The authors found a positive relationship between parental social class and concerted cultivation. Lee and Bowen also found that parental involvement at school and expectations for the child's educational attainment were positively associated with achievement, and partially mediated the effect of social class on this outcome. These findings are generally consistent with those of other researchers. This study also found some significant interactions (moderation) between elements of their measure of concerted cultivation and some of the demographic measures. However, these did not follow any meaningful pattern.

Gaddis (2013) uses data from youth who participated in the Big Brothers/Big Sisters of America program to test whether a measure of habitus mediates the relationship between a concerted cultivation parenting style and course grades. He operationalizes cultural capital using three measures of elite cultural participation plus weekly hours spent reading. This paper is one of the few to claim to quantitatively measure habitus, which Gaddis does using two scales—a youth's belief that she/he can succeed in school and a scale measuring the youth's belief that education is valuable to her/his success in life. Using first difference models, he first regresses change in grades on change in each of his four elements of cultural capital (museum visits, play attendance, cultural lessons, and time spent reading). Two of these (museum visits and time spent reading) show significant positive effects on GPA. Second, he adds change in the habitus variables (the two attitude measures) to the equation. They are both significantly associated with GPA, and with these variables controlled the effects of the cultural capital variables become smaller and lose significance. Gaddis concludes that habitus mediates the effect of cultural capital on GPA. He finds that museum visits and reading both have effect sizes of 0.05; the habitus attitude variables both have effect sizes of 0.15. These are small to modest in size.

How can we compare Gaddis' work where habitus is measured by two schooling attitude scales with that of Farkas (1996) or Bodovski and Farkas (2008) where habitus is not explicitly measured, but academic work habits and test scores measuring cultural capital are taken to be the variables that teachers consider when assigning course grades? Clarification is attained by looking at the items comprising each of Gaddis' scales. The "I can succeed at school" scale may measure habitus, since it shows how the student sees herself in the school setting. But it is likely also measuring the student's actual success at schoolwork. It is not surprising that positive changes in school performance would be associated with positive changes in the student's reports of her school performance. However there is a danger of reverse causality, where school performance is driving attitudes rather than the other way around.

As for the second scale, described by Gaddis as a measure of "the youth's belief that education is valuable to her success in life," it *does* contain items such as "How valuable do you think your education will be in getting the job you want?" However, it also contains items such as the following: Do you think your school work is boring? Do you think your homework is fun to do? Do you think the things you learn in school are worthless? Do you care about doing your best in school? How upset would you be if you got a low grade for one of your subjects? Change in these items could also be expected to be positively correlated with changes in grades, but once again, there may be reverse causality, where positive change in grades leads to positive change in these measures of feelings toward school. Further, these items are likely correlated

with the academic work habits that teachers use in determining course grades. Indeed, when assigning course grades, teachers had no knowledge of the student's scores on these attitude scales. Their only opportunity to observe differences in these attitudes across students was due to their observation of the student's academic work habits.

Comparing the way Gaddis operationalized the cultural capital theory with the way it was operationalized by Farkas (1996) and Bodovski and Farkas (2008) is instructive. Gaddis operationalized the habitus with two attitudinal scales closely related to the student's positive feelings about her/his schoolwork, and used these as mediators between concerted cultivation and course grades. He did not use a measure of actual student academic performance. Farkas (1996) did not seek to measure the habitus, which is theorized to be dispositions and skills internal to the student. Instead, he measured the academic work habits partially determined by the student's habitus, and estimated how the teacher-assigned course grade was affected by the student's academic performance (measured by both basic skills and curriculum referenced tests) and the student's academic work habits. Similarly, Bodovski and Farkas (2008) did not attempt to measure the habitus, but again tested the extent to which academic work habits and test score performance affected the teacher's assessment of the student's competency at the subject. They also tested the extent to which these work habits and test scores mediated the relationship between concerted cultivation and the teacher's judgment of the student. Gaddis used many of the same parenting variables used by others, but chose to refer to these as "cultural capital." Bodovski and Farkas employed similar variables (although containing more about the parent's direct instruction of the child) and, instead of viewing these as measures of habitus, tested for the effects of work habits and test scores as mediators between parenting and the teacher's judgment of the child. The largest difference between the two research approaches is that Gaddis uses survey questions about attitudes toward school to measure habitus and tests for it as a mediator without controlling test scores. By contrast, Bodovski and Farkas use academic work habits as expressions of the student's cultural capital, and employ both work habits and test scores as mediators. Since Gaddis' survey questions appear to be closely related to work habits, the most consequential difference between the two studies may be that Gaddis does not control test scores.

Using ECLS-K data, Bodovski (2014) operationalized students' emerging habitus using 8th grade students' educational expectations, internal locus of control, and general and area-specific self-concepts. She examined how early parental practices and educational expectations (measured during kindergarten and first-grade years) affect students' emerging habitus and academic achievement when they reach adolescence (measured in eighth grade). The findings revealed that students from higher-SES families had more positive general and area-specific self-concepts, higher educational expectations, internal locus of control, and higher academic achievement. Higher parental educational expectations were positively associated with all studied outcomes. The findings provided only partial support for the effects of early parental practices and highlighted the role of gender and race/ethnicity in shaping adolescents' habitus.

Potter and Roksa (2013) also analyzed the ECLS-K, emphasizing the over-time nature of concerted cultivation, and the effects of contemporaneous and cumulative concerted cultivation on student test scores in reading and math, estimated with growth curve models. Their measure of concerted cultivation combines child activities (e.g., dance, music, athletics), parental school involvement, parental educational expectations, the number of books in the household, and parent-to-parent contact. They find that the mother's education is positively associated with each of these parenting behaviors, and that, with the exception of parent-to-parent contact, cumulative measures of each of these behaviors are positively associated with increasing social class gaps in both reading and math test scores as children move up the grade levels. When entered as controls, these behaviors explain about 23% of the effect of mother's education on reading test scores, and about 18% of the mother's education effect on math test scores. This is generally consistent with prior work, although the use of test scores rather than grades makes these results less of a true test of the cultural capital theory. It appears that, in general, explicitly measured parenting activities of the type available on large nationally representative data sets can explain about 1/4 of the relationship between parental social class and student grades or test scores. This estimate is quite similar to the findings reported by Bodovski and Farkas (2008) and Cheadle (2008).

Tramonte and Willms (2010) take a similar approach, but analyze PISA data containing information on more than 200,000 students across 28 OECD countries. They operationalize cultural capital along two dimensions. They measure "static cultural capital" by combining responses to nine questions about elite ("highbrow") cultural activities. They measure "relational cultural capital" by responses to six items concerning conversations between parents and the child covering topics such as social issues, books, films, television programs, how well the child is doing at school, as well as whether the child herself enjoys talking with other people about books or going to the bookstore or library. The authors run regressions, separately for each country, estimating the effects of relational and cultural capital on the student's reading test score and sense of belonging at school, controlling parental education, occupation, and sex. They find that both cultural capital measures are positively and significantly associated with reading test scores for each of the 28 countries, with the relational measure association slightly stronger than that of the static measure for a majority of the countries. The associations of these variables with sense of belonging is also generally positive, more consistently so for the relational cultural capital measure. However, once again, this study used test scores rather than grades as the outcome. For a related study focused on the countries of Eastern Europe see Bodovski et al. (2016).

1.5.2 Social Class Differences in Cognitive Skills and Academic Work Habits

Studies reviewed in the previous section focused on the role of parenting as a mediator of the relationship between SES and educational outcomes, perhaps involving cognitive skills and work habits as additional mediators. In this section we focus on studies that do not consider parenting, but simply consider cognitive skills and work habits as mediators between social class background and schooling success.

If cognitive skills and academic work habits are to mediate the relationship between SES and course grades, they must first be shown to differ across social classes, with middle- and upper-class students showing greater cognitive skills and academic work habits than students from the working and lower classes. I now turn to the empirical evidence on these issues.

Cognitive Skills A relatively large body of empirical research has demonstrated that social class differences in cognitive skills begin very early in life, are of relatively large magnitudes at kindergarten entry and are, in general, maintained through to high school education. Fernald et al. (2013) found that significant disparities in vocabulary and language processing efficiency were already evident at 18 months between infants from higher- and lower-SES families, and that by 24 months there was a 6-month gap between SES groups in processing skills critical to language development. That is, it was not until 24 months of age that the less advantaged children reached the same level of processing speed and accuracy displayed by the more advantaged children at 18 months. Hart and Risley (1995) and Hoff (2003) showed that higher social class parents speak a very much greater number and variety of words to their infants and toddlers than do working-class parents, and these differences partially explain the larger vocabularies of middle and upper-class children. Farkas and Beron (2004) found large SES oral vocabulary gaps at 36 months of age, and subsequent vocabulary growth rates that were similar across different

SES groups, so that the magnitude of the 36-month SES gap persists at least through to 13 years of age. As discussed earlier, large social class gaps in cognitive performance are found at kindergarten entry, and persist as children move up through the grades. These school readiness and persistent social class differences in children's cognitive performance are likely due to combinations of parenting, environmental, and biological differences between children from lower- and higher-SES families.

1.5.2.1 Academic Work Habits

As with cognitive skills, social class differences in task-related work habits are observed very early in children's development. Morgan et al. (2009) estimated SES differences in behaviors at 24 months of age, using data collected from administration of the Bayley Scales of Infant Development. They found that when mother and child were given simple tasks to do, children from mothers in the lowest education quintile were more than twice as likely as those from mothers in the highest education quintile to not persist at tasks, to be inattentive, to show no interest, to be uncooperative, and to be frustrated. Since mother and child performed as a dyad, these outcomes are suggestive of mother–child interaction differences across social classes.

By kindergarten entry, the academic work habits of children in the top SES quintile are 0.6 standard deviation above those of children from the bottom SES quintile (Duncan and Magnuson 2011, p. 56). By 5th grade this behavior gap has widened slightly. By 8th grade these gaps have decreased to about 0.4 standard deviation, and by 12th grade to 0.3 standard deviation (Farkas 2011, p. 79) In kindergarten, children from the lowest SES quintile show antisocial behaviors (externalizing problem behaviors) that are 0.3 standard deviation worse than those from the highest SES quintile. By 5th grade this gap has increased to 0.5 standard deviation but it decreases thereafter, to 0.3 SD in 12th grade. However, this may be at least partly due to the higher school dropout rate among students with the worst behaviors, particularly those from lower- and working-class homes.

In sum, there is ample evidence showing that family social class background is a powerful determinant of academic skills and work habits. If these are found to strongly determine the course grades a student receives, then the basic tenets of the cultural capital theory presented here will have been supported.

1.5.3 Skills and Habits Determine Course Grades

Farkas et al. (1990) and Farkas (1996) used data collected from the Dallas School District to estimate portions of the model presented in Fig. 1.1. These studies contained measures of poverty, academic skills and work habits, and course grades. They lacked measures of parenting, but they did have separate measures of basic academic skills (measured by the Iowa Test of Basic Skills) and of the actual coursework mastery of the students in the 7th and 8th grade social studies classes from which the study sample was drawn (this measure is drawn from a curriculum referenced test administered uniformly within the Dallas schools).

These researchers found that when it comes to predicting social studies course grades assigned in 7th and 8th grade, the direct effect of coursework mastery had an effect size of 0.27, and the direct effect of basic skills (measured by language arts and math scores from the Iowa Test of Basic Skills) was 0.22. The largest direct effect was that of academic work habits, with a standardized coefficient of 0.53. Absenteeism, disruptiveness, and appearance and dress also had significant direct effects, but of much smaller magnitude. The striking finding is that despite controls for two types of cognitive skills, work habits still had such a large effect size, even as late as middle school, when one might expect cognitive performance to have become much more important than the student's work habits.

These are direct effects, with all variables controlled. But in addition, there are indirect effects in which causally prior variables affect course grades through their effects on mediators. One such mediator is coursework mastery. This is most strongly determined by Basic Skills and Work Habits. The path model in Fig. 1.2 shows the results of putting these effect estimates together into a single model. Basic skills has a direct effect of 0.22 on course grades plus an indirect effect of $0.38 \times 0.27 = 0.10$ via coursework mastery, for a total effect of 0.32. Work habits has a direct effect of 0.53 on course grades plus an indirect effect $0.32 \times 0.27 = 0.09$, for a total effect of 0.62. Coursework mastery itself has a direct effect of 0.27. Other effects are much smaller, with the largest of these being days absent, with a direct effect of -0.15. In sum, academic work habits exert the strongest effect on teacher-assigned course grades in 7th and 8th grade social studies, with a total effect size of 0.62. That is, increasing these work habits by 1 standard deviation would lead to a course grade increase of 0.62 of a standard deviation. By contrast, basic skills have an effect only about half this size, and the effect of coursework mastery is smaller still.

Group differences in work habits also accounted for large portions of race gaps in academic achievement. For example, other findings included the fact that Asian children, scoring high on academic work habits, received a double benefit from these behaviors. First, these work habits strongly and positively affected coursework mastery, which raised their grades. However, over and above this effect via coursework mastery, Asians' good work habits earn an extra reward by further raising their grades.

These are striking findings. It has been widely believed that during the early elementary grades, when children are being trained to have good academic learning habits, these habits form a significant portion of the teacher-assigned course grade. But it has also been believed that in middle and high school, where students have different teachers for different academic subjects, and the focus is on learning the assigned material, tests and other objective measures of such learning play the largest role in course grade assignment. Yet, this is not what we have found for 7th and 8th grade social studies. Of course these data are from the late 1980s, in only one city. It would be valuable to have research updating these findings to a more recent time period and to the nation as a whole. More generally, a structural equation model could be estimated in which the habitus is a latent variable, with test scores and academic work habits as indicators. Or, perhaps a better model would involve two latent habitus variables, one for cognitive ability and the other for habits and behaviors. Then test scores would be the indicators of cognitive skills, and teacher reported judgments of student work habits and other behaviors as the indicators of the latent habits and behaviors variable. This would seem to be the appropriate operationalization of a model in which the student's habitus is not directly observed.

Research by Blanchard and Muller (2015) further supports the importance of academic work habits in determining the teacher-assigned course grade. This study analyzes ELS:2002 data to test whether teacher-perceived student work habits mediate the relationship between being an immigrant student and the course grade received in 10th grade math. The authors find that the teacher's perception that the student "works hard" is positively related to the student's course grade, with (after controls) an effect size of 0.62 SD. This is a very strong effect, which is likely at least partly inflated by the authors' failure to control test scores in the analysis.

1.5.4   Child Care

Parenting activities are not the only way that children's school-related habitus and cultural capital may be shaped. Federal and state preschool programs for low-income children were designed to compensate for SES differences in the stimulating, nurturing, and healthful aspects of home environments. Head Start, and most recently state-run preschool programs, serve many, but not all, low-income children, since Head Start is not fully funded. The best of these programs operate in child care centers utilizing a "whole child" model of comprehensive service provision, including health- and family-related services. Research has shown that these programs do increase cognitive performance, although

unfortunately the effect sizes are small, and fade out by second grade (Puma et al. 2010). In addition, many higher-income families also send their children to child care centers, which are often of higher quality than those utilized by low-income families, thereby exacerbating rather than reducing SES differentials in the cognitive stimulation and support provided to preschoolers. Further, research has shown that longer time periods in out-of-home child care tend to be associated with more conflictual relationships between the child and both teachers and the child's mother, although this effect is reduced when the care is of higher quality (Early Child Care Research Network 2005). Overall, and particularly for cognitive skills, preschool programs can play a role in complementing or even substituting for the efforts of parents to prepare children for kindergarten entry. There is a very large research literature on this, which I do not have the space to consider here. For a useful starting point, see the meta-analysis by Duncan and Magnuson (2013).

1.5.5   Peer Effects

In addition to the family and teachers, the peer group has been found to exert significant effects on the educational success of students. That working- and lower-class peer groups, particularly among males, can create a culture antithetical to school achievement has long been reported by ethnographic studies. This has been reported within both White and Black low-income peer groups (Ogbu 1978, 2003; Willis 1977; Macleod 1995; Anderson 1999; Tyson et al. 2005) and has led to a spirited controversy regarding the existence of an "oppositional culture," in which, among both male and female Black students, striving for academic achievement is denigrated as "acting White" (Fordham and Ogbu 1986; Ainsworth-Darnell and Downey 1998; Downey and Ainsworth-Darnell 2002; Farkas et al. 2002; Carter 2005; Fryer and Torelli 2010). The reality of this effect may be inferred from the well-established finding that, all other things equal, the higher the percentage of Black students in a school, the lower the average academic achievement of students in the school (Mickelson et al. 2013). Of course other explanations, including lower-quality teachers, are also possible.

But what about peer effects of having a high percentage of working- and lower-class students in a school? Palardy (2013) found that even among otherwise similar students, attending a school where the average student comes from a high-SES family significantly increases the probability of high school graduation and college enrollment. He concludes that these effects are largely explained by peer effects, which tend to be negative in low-SES schools. Once again, the likely mediating mechanism is lower levels of academic work habits where the student peer group comes largely from working- and lower-class homes. Similar findings have been reported by Anderson (1999), Carrell and Hoekstra (2010), Hanushek et al. (2003), Morris (2008), and Willis (1977) among others.

1.5.6 Biological Make-Up and Health

Beginning even before birth, children from low-SES households experience lower-quality health than higher-SES children. Low-SES children are more likely to experience growth retardation and inadequate neurobehavioral development in utero. These children are also more likely to be born prematurely, at low birth weight, with a disability, or with fetal alcohol syndrome or AIDS. These outcomes are typically due to poor prenatal care, poor nutrition and maternal substance use during pregnancy, and living in an environment where violence is common and containing toxins such as lead and airborne pollutants. Further, when low-income children experience a health problem or disability they are less likely than higher-SES children to receive adequate health care (Bradley and Corwyn 2002). There is insufficient space here to review this very large literature. But there is little doubt that the biological and health differences between children from low and middle social class backgrounds play a significant role in the development of social class differences in the school-related habitus of these children. (For additional reading see Currie and Reichman (2015), and the literature cited there.)

1.6 Academic Work Habits as Personality Traits

Once we moved past studies restricting cultural capital to behaviors and skills associated with elite "high culture" we found a great commonality among the skills and habits reported by ethnographers as being central to different subcultural repertoires, those included by psychologists in scales of quality parenting such as the HOME, those explicitly listed on report cards to be graded by teachers, and those work habits that are empirically found to join cognitive performance as being most predictive of the grades assigned by teachers. As noted by Farkas (2003), these are the same characteristics included in the concept of "conscientiousness" that industrial psychologists find to be the only one of the "big five" personality characteristics to predict job performance and wages. These are the same characteristics that the Knowledge is Power Program (KIPP n.d.) schools, the charter school network with the most well-documented positive effects, uses as the basis of their "contract" with students.

These conscientious academic work habits have been somewhat neglected by sociologists of education, even as economists and psychologists have concentrated on them, in some cases claiming that they hold the key to improving the schooling and life outcomes of children from low-income households. Thus, Borghans et al. (2008) and Heckman and Kautz (2014) emphasize personality traits, particularly conscientiousness, as the key to success in school and life. These authors refer to the work of psychologist Roberts (2009), who states that "conscientiousness is a personality trait, which is defined as a 'tendency to respond in certain ways under certain circumstances,'…the tendency to think, feel, and behave in a relatively enduring and consistent fashion across time in trait-affording situations."

Note that this is very close to the definition of habitus discussed earlier. Heckman and Kautz go on to list the American Psychology Dictionary description of conscientiousness, its facets, related skills, and analogous childhood temperament skills. The word is defined as the tendency to be organized, responsible, and hardworking. It includes competence (efficient), order (organized), dutifulness (not careless), achievement striving (ambitious), self-discipline (not lazy), and deliberation (not impulsive). Related skills are grit, perseverance, delay of gratification, impulse control, achievement striving, ambition, and work ethic. Analogous childhood temperament skills are attention/(lack of) distractibility, effortful control, impulse control/delay of gratification, persistence, and activity.

These traits and behaviors are similar to the academic work habits we have emphasized throughout this chapter. Almlund et al. (2011) report effect sizes for intelligence and each of the big five personality traits in their effects on years of education attained. The largest effect is for conscientiousness, with an effect size of 0.25. The next largest effect is for intelligence. The other personality traits either have no or much smaller effects. This finding, in which academic work habits have even stronger effects on educational attainment than test scores, is reminiscent of Farkas' (1996) findings on the relative strength of effect of test scores and work habits on course grades. For a wide-ranging discussion of the importance of grit in life success see Duckworth (2016). Here we see another example of the convergence of viewpoints in sociology, economics, and psychology.

1.7   Policy Implications

What are the policy implications of the finding that teacher-judged academic work habits are a major mediating factor for the strong positive relationship between family social class background and student success in school? Can this finding be employed to increase the school success of children from lower- and working-class families?

The Knowledge is Power (KIPP n.d.) charter schools appear to have done just that. First developed by two Teach for America teachers in 1994, this network of charter schools now numbers more than 180 schools across the country. Their highly structured program for children from low-income households includes commitment statements that must be agreed to by teachers, parents, and students. That for students reads as follows:

- I will always work, think, and behave in the best way I know how, and I will do whatever it takes for me and my fellow students to learn. This also means that I will complete all my homework every night, I will call my teachers if I have a problem with the homework or a problem with coming to school, and I will raise my hand and ask questions in class if I do not understand something.
- I will always behave so as to protect the safety, interests, and rights of all individuals in the classroom. This also means that I will always listen to all my KIPP teammates and give everyone my respect.
- I am responsible for my own behavior, and I will follow the teachers' directions.

This is nothing other than the academic work habits discussed throughout this chapter. Similarly, the pledge that must be signed by parents reads as follows:

We will make sure our child arrives at KIPP every day by 7:25 a.m. (Monday–Friday) or boards a KIPP bus at the scheduled time. We will always help our child in the best way we know how and we will do whatever it takes for him/her to learn. This also means that we will check our child's homework every night, let him/her call the teacher if there is a problem with the homework, and try to read with him/her every night. We will always make ourselves available to our children and the school, and address any concerns they might have. This also means that if our child is going to miss school, we will notify the teacher as soon as possible, and we will carefully read any and all papers that the school sends home to us.

Here the emphasis on checking homework and reading with the student every night reflects the kinds of good parenting behaviors embodied in the HOME score instrument.

What has been the impact of KIPP schools on the students attending them? The answer is that they have shown significant positive effects on reading and math achievement at elementary, middle and high school levels (Angrist et al. 2010, 2012; Nichols-Barrer et al. 2015; Tuttle et al. 2015). These results appear to be the brightest spot in a great variety of school structure experiments that have been unleashed by the charter schools movement. This is perhaps the strongest evidence yet for the overwhelming importance of student skills, habits, and styles in the determination of student outcomes, and the possibility of fostering increased school success for students from low-income and working-class families by creating a schooling environment within which these students can improve these skills, habits, and styles.

1.8   Summary and Discussion

I began this chapter by discussing social reproduction, arguably the most important empirical finding in the sociology of education. Seeking to understand the mechanisms by which the children of middle- and upper-class parents attain greater school success than lower- and working-class children, I explicated Bourdieu's theory of cultural capital, which supposes that parents from different social classes imbue children with different sorts of habitus, or dispositions (including skills) toward action. The resulting habitus differs across social classes, so that children from middle and higher social class families tend to present the cultural capital (cognitive skills and academic work habits enacted in the classroom and homework) that are pleasing to, and rewarded by, teachers, whereas this is less common among children from lower- and working-class families. Teachers respond by giving higher report card grades to the middle- and upper-class students, leading them to experience more successful academic trajectories and to attain greater academic skills and knowledge as they progress up through the elementary, middle, and high school grade levels. These more successful K–12 trajectories then translate into more successful postsecondary

enrollment and completion, leading to more rewarding (in both the pecuniary and non-pecuniary sense) employment careers.

I consider this narrative to be consistent with the work of economist Gary Becker, who brought great attention to the development and output from human skills, and of sociologist James Coleman, who emphasized the importance of social networks, trust, and the individual's position within a social structure as determinants of human capital development and deployment. Sociologist Pierre Bourdieu added a focus on how the individual's position in the social structure affects her habitus, which helps determine the individual's enacted educational cultural capital (skills and behaviors) that are judged by teacher-gatekeepers whose feedback and assigned grades help determine the student's educational attainment and thus subsequent occupational employment and earnings. In this chapter I have tried to show that cultural capital theory, by introducing student strategies of action constrained by their habitus, producing classroom cultural capital (skills and work habits) judged by teachers, offers an integrative focus in which the study of educational stratification can be advanced in a way consistent with the visions of Becker, Coleman, and Bourdieu, as well as many other sociologists, economists, and psychologists working on these issues today.

The epigraph was a quotation from Paula England's ASA Presidential Address (2016), where she defined personal characteristics as "things individuals carry across situations, such as skills, habits, identities, worldviews, preferences or values." England is a gender scholar, and does not generally undertake research in the sociology of education. She writes about skills and habits because she is treating them as central to the "social structure and personality" theorizing that, she argues, offers an important vantage point for understanding a very wide variety of outcomes across the social world. She concentrates on two examples. One is the finding that more women than men report being bisexual. The second is that disadvantaged women use contraception less consistently than more advantaged women, even when they do not want to get pregnant. She argues that in each case, the structurally disadvantaged position of the members of a group, gay men in the first case, disadvantaged women in the second, has caused them to internalize particular skills, habits, identities, worldviews, preferences, or values. For a gay man, this is a straight identity, which he feels constrained to present because of the stigma attached to gayness. For the disadvantaged woman, this is a lesser sense of efficacy—the ability to align your identity with your goals—which is the result of the constrained resources available at her place in the social structure. A principal point of England's paper is to argue against the long held view that any study involving the personal characteristics of a group that is disadvantaged by the social structure involves "blaming the victim" (Ryan 1971), a point of view arguing that focusing on the personal characteristics of disadvantaged groups shifts the discussion away from the social structure and instead makes the individual's situation "their own fault." But instead, England argues, examining the personal characteristics of disadvantaged groups needn't direct attention away from the social structure. Instead, it merely shifts the social structure one step back in the causal chain, from which it leads to the creation of the personal characteristics (habitus) which in turn lead to less than desirable (constrained) behaviors. That is, the social structure constrains the individual to become a person who produces less than desirable behaviors. As England quotes Wacquant (2005, p. 316), "the society becomes deposited in persons in the form of lasting dispositions, or trained capacities and structured propensities to think, feel and act in determinant ways, which then guide them." Thus, the vision of cultural capital theory presented here is built upon the now well-demonstrated notion that to understand the lower academic performance of working- and lower-class students we need to understand the social psychology of both the academic performance and the academic work habits they bring to the school, as well as the student–teacher interactions and course grades that result from these interactions.

There are many promising directions for future research in these areas. One is to seek improved understanding of those portions of working- and lower-class family and neighborhood life that are most determinative of student academic skills and work habits. We have already seen that the hypothesis that elite cultural activities are central to the school success of middle-class children has been empirically rejected. We have also seen that the parenting activities measured by instruments such as the HOME explain only a modest portion of the better academic skills and work habits of middle- and upper-class children. We expect that children's academic work habits evolve continuously over time, so that behavior in kindergarten likely reflects preschool behavior. And we have also learned that greater time in lower-quality preschool is associated with lower attention skills and greater externalizing behavior (McCartney et al. 2010). Yet research is only beginning on how parenting, social structure, and peers shape preschool behavior, and the four together shape student behaviors in kindergarten. (For examples of this work see Henry and Rickman 2007; Neidell and Waldfogel 2010.) This is just one of many areas where it would be useful to learn more about parenting, peers, skills, and behaviors and their joint variation across the social structure. In this regard, recent research has suggested that the test score achievement gap between children from families in the top and bottom income quintile increased significantly in the 1970s and 1980s (Reardon 2011), but appears to have modestly narrowed between 1998 and 2010 (Reardon and Portilla 2015), and these most recent changes may be at least partly due to narrowing of the income–parenting gap (Bassok et al. 2016). Such over-time change in social class differences in parenting and test scores indicate that social reproduction is dynamic rather than static, and should be studied as a dynamic system subject to a wide variety of forces, importantly including government policy and public media dissemination of information about families and parenting.

Another area ripe for investigation is social class differences in the detailed patterns of academic work habits within each grade level, and as students move up the grade levels. Our current measures of student academic work habits are typically restricted to a few questions asked of the teacher at a single point in time. More detailed data might provide insights that could be used to develop interventions, programs, or policies to improve the academic work habits of working- and lower-class children. Other promising research areas include greater attention to how student course grades evolve over time, and how these are related to outcomes such as dropout, high school graduation, college enrollment, and employment. To the greatest extent possible these studies should attempt to move beyond merely correlational evidence, and incorporate evidence from experimental or quasi-experimental research designs. If non-experimental data (e.g., those in large national data sets like the ECLS-K) are used, researchers should at least attempt to use methods such as teacher fixed effects that at least partially control for possible selection bias.

Also worthy of investigation is the way that cognitive skills and academic work habits provide an advantage to children from higher social class backgrounds in higher education and the labor market. Empirical research has established that positive attitudinal/behavioral traits have effects on wages that are at least as large as those of cognitive skills (see Hall and Farkas (2011) and the studies cited there). But the detailed mechanisms of these effects across varied occupations and industries are unknown. There is much to study here.

I began with the question, what are the mechanisms by which children from middle- and higher social class parents tend to achieve greater school success than those from lower- and working-class parents? The evidence shows that the greater school success of middle- and upper-class children is due to their stronger cognitive skills and academic work habits. These are in turn strongly affected by parenting, peers, and genetics, as well as teachers and school climate. Fortunately, schools such as KIPP have demonstrated that by creating a culture focused on developing positive academic work habits and related values, with buy-in from both teachers and parents, children from lower- and working-class schools can succeed at school to a greater

extent than has heretofore been demonstrated by other programs, policies, or interventions. Efforts to better understand the detailed mechanisms by which student skills and habits determine educational attainment, and how schools can be managed so as to increase all three for children from working- and lower-class households, should be high on the research agenda of sociologists of education for many years to come.

References

Ainsworth-Darnell, J. W., & Downey, D. B. (1998). Assessing the oppositional culture explanation for racial/ethnic differences in school performance. *American Sociological Review, 63*, 536–553.

Almlund, M., Duckworth, A., Heckman, J. J., & Kautz, T. (2011). Personality psychology and economics. In E. A. Hanushek, S. Machin, & L. Wofsmann (Eds.), *Handbook of the economics of education*, (Vol. 4, pp. 1–181). Amsterdam: Elsevier.

Anderson, E. (1999). *Code of the street: Decency, violence, and the moral life of the inner city*. New York: Norton.

Angrist, J. D., Dynarski, S. M., Kane, T. J., Pathak, P. A., & Walters, C. R. (2010). Inputs and impacts in charter schools: KIPP Lynn. *American Economic Review: Papers & Proceedings* 100 (May). http://www.aeaweb.org/articles.php?doi=10.1257/aer.100.2.1

Angrist, J. D., et al. (2012). Who benefits from KIPP? *Journal of Policy Analysis and Management, 31*(4), 837–860.

Bassok, D., Finch, J. E., Lee, R., Reardon, S., & Waldfogel, J. (2016). Socioeconomic gaps in early childhood experiences, 1998 to 2010. *AERA Open, 2*(3), 1–22.

Becker, G. (1964). *Human capital*. New York: National Bureau of Economic Research.

Blanchard, S., & Muller, C. (2015). Gatekeepers of the American Dream: How teachers' perceptions shape the academic outcomes of immigrant and language-minority students. *Social Science Research, 51*, 262–275.

Bodovski, K. (2010). Parental practices and educational achievement: Social class, race, and *habitus*. *British Journal of Sociology of Education, 31*(2), 139–156.

Bodovski, K. (2014). Adolescents' emerging habitus: The role of early parental expectations and practices. *British Journal of Sociology of Education, 35*(3), 389–412.

Bodovski, K., & Farkas, G. (2008). "Concerted cultivation" and unequal achievement in elementary school. *Social Science Research, 37*, 903–919.

Bodovski, K., Jeon, H., & Byun, S. Y. (2016). Cultural capital and academic achievement in post-socialist Eastern Europe. *British Journal of Sociology of Education, 38*(6), 1–18.

Borghans, L., Duckworth, A. L., Heckman, J. J., & ter Weel, B. (2008). The economics and psychology of personality traits. *Journal of Human Resources, XLIII*(4), 972–1059.

Bourdieu, P. (1986). The forms of capital. In J. E. Richardson (Ed.), *Handbook of theory and research for the sociology of education* (pp. 241–258). Westport: Greenwood.

Bowles, S., & Gintis, H. (1976). *Schooling in capitalist America*. New York: Basic Books.

Bradley, R. H., & Corwyn, R. F. (2002). Socioeconomic status and child development. *Annual Review of Psychology, 53*, 371–399.

Bradley, R. H., Corwyn, R. F., Burchinal, M., McAdoo, H. P., & Coll, C. G. (2001). The home environments of children in the United States Part II: Relations with behavioral development through age thirteen. *Child Development, 72*(6), 1868–1886.

Carrell, S., & Hoekstra, M. (2010). Externalities in the classroom: How children exposed to domestic violence affect everyone's kids. *American Economic Journal: Applied Economics, 2*(1), 211–228.

Carter, P. L. (2005). *Keepin' it real: School success beyond Black and White*. New York: Oxford University Press.

Cheadle, J. (2008). Educational investment, family context, and children's math and reading growth from kindergarten through third grade. *Sociology of Education, 81*, 1–31.

Coleman, J., & Hoffer, T. (1987). *Public and private high schools: The impact of communities*. New York: Basic Books.

Coleman, J., et al. (1966). *Equality of educational opportunity*. Washington, DC: U.S. Government Printing Office.

Currie, J. & Reichman, N., (Eds.), (2015). Policies to promote child health. In *The future of children*. Washington, DC: Princeton-Brookings.

De Graaf, N. D., De Graaf, P. M., & Kraaykamp, G. (2000). Parental cultural capital and educational attainment in the Netherlands: A refinement of the cultural capital perspective. *Sociology of Education, 73*, 92–111.

DiMaggio, P. (1982). Cultural capital and school success: The impact of status culture participation on the grades of U.S. high school students. *American Sociological Review, 47*, 189–201.

Downey, D., & Ainsworth-Darnell, J. (2002). The search for oppositional culture among Black students. *American Sociological Review, 67*, 156–164.

Duckworth, A. (2016). *Grit: The power of passion and perseverance*. New York: Scribner.

Dumais, S. (2002). Cultural capital, gender, and school success: The role of habitus. *Sociology of Education, 75*(1), 44–68.

Dumais, S., Kessinger, R. J., & Ghosh, B. (2012). Concerted cultivation and teachers' evaluations of students: Exploring the intersection of race and parents' educational attainment. *Sociological Perspectives, 55*(1), 17–42.

Duncan, G. J., & Magnuson, K. (2011). The nature and impact of early achievement skills, attention skills, and behavior problems. In G. J. Duncan & R. J. Murnane (Eds.), *Whither opportunity? Rising inequality, schools, and children's life chances* (pp. 47–70). New York: Russell Sage.

Duncan, G. J., & Magnuson, K. (2013). Investing in preschool programs. *The Journal of Economic Perspectives, 27*(2), 109–132. https://doi.org/10.1257/jep.27.2.109.PMC.

Duncan, G. J., et al. (2005). The apple does not fall far from the tree. In S. Bowles, H. Gintis, & M. E. Groves (Eds.), *Unequal chances: Family background and economic success* (pp. 23–79). New York: Russell Sage.

England, P. (2016). Sometimes the social becomes personal: Gender, class, and sexualities. *American Sociological Review, 81*, 4–28.

Farkas, G. (1996). *Human capital or cultural capital? Ethnicity and poverty groups in an urban school district*. New York: Aldine de Gruyter.

Farkas, G. (2003). Cognitive skills and noncognitive traits and behaviors in stratification processes. *Annual Review of Sociology, 29*, 541–562.

Farkas, G. (2011). Middle and high school skills, behaviors, attitudes, and curriculum enrollment, and their consequences. In G. J. Duncan & R. J. Murnane (Eds.), *Whither opportunity? Rising inequality, schools, and children's life chances* (pp. 71–90). New York: Russell Sage.

Farkas, G., & Beron, K. (2004). The detailed age trajectory of oral vocabulary knowledge: Differences by class and race. *Social Science Research, 33*, 464–497.

Farkas, G., Grobe, R., Sheehan, D., & Shuan, Y. (1990). Cultural resources and school success: Gender, ethnicity, and poverty groups within an urban school district. *American Sociological Review, 55*, 127–142.

Farkas, G., Lleras, C., & Maczuga, S. (2002). Does oppositional culture exist in minority and poverty peer groups? *American Sociological Review, 67*, 148–155.

Fernald, A., Marchman, V. A., & Weisleder, A. (2013). SES differences in language processing skill and vocabulary are evident at 18 months. *Developmental Science, 16*, 234–248. https://doi.org/10.1111/desc.12019.

Fordham, S., & Ogbu, J. (1986). Black students' school success: Coping with the "burden of 'acting White'". *Urban Review, 18*, 176–206.

Fryer, R. G., & Torelli, P. (2010). An empirical analysis of "acting White". *Journal of Public Economics, 94*, 380–396. https://doi.org/10.1016/j.jpubeco.2009.10.011.

Gaddis, M. (2013). The influence of habitus in the relationship between cultural capital and academic achievement. *Social Science Research, 42*, 1–13.

Goffman, E. (1961). *Asylums: Essays on the condition of the social situation of mental patients and other inmates*. New York: Doubleday.

Goldthorpe, J. H. (2007). "Cultural capital": Some critical observations. *Sociologica, 2*, 1–22.

Greenstone, D. (1991). Culture, rationality, and the underclass. In C. Jencks & P. Peterson (Eds.), *The urban underclass* (pp. 399–408). Washington, DC: Brookings Institution.

Hall, M., & Farkas, G. (2011). Adolescent cognitive skills, attitudinal/behavioral traits and career wages. *Social Forces, 89*, 1261–1285.

Hannerz, U. (1969). *Soulside: Inquiries into ghetto culture and community*. New York: Columbia University Press.

Hanushek, E., Kain, J., Markman, J., & Rivkin, S. (2003). Does peer ability affect student achievement? *Journal of Applied Econometrics, 18*, 527–544.

Hart, B., & Risley, T. (1995). *Meaningful differences in everyday experiences of young American children*. Baltimore: Brookes.

Heckman, J., & Kautz, T. (2014). Achievement tests and the role of character in American life. In J. J. Heckman, J. E. Humphries, & T. Kautz (Eds.), *The myth of achievement tests: The GED and the role of character in American life* (pp. 1–56). Chicago: University of Chicago Press.

Henry, G. T., & Rickman, D. K. (2007). Do peers influence children's skill development in preschool? *Economics of Education Review, 26*(1), 100–112.

Hoff, E. (2003). The specificity of environmental influence: Socioeconomic status affects early vocabulary development via maternal speech. *Child Development, 74*, 1368–1378.

Jencks, C., Bartlett, S., Corcoran, M., Crouse, J., Eaglesfield, D., et al. (1979). *Who gets ahead? The determinants of economic success in America*. New York: Basic Books.

Jenkins, R. (1992). *Pierre Bourdieu*. New York: Routledge.

Kingston, P. (2001). The unfulfilled promise of cultural capital theory. *Sociology of Education, 74*(Extra Issue), 88–99.

KIPP. (n.d.). http://www.kipp.org/our-approach/five-pillars#sthash.xvyNMjIm.dpuf. Accessed on 28 Jan 2016.

Lamont, M., & Lareau, A. (1988). Cultural capital. *Sociological Theory, 6*, 153–168.

Lareau, A. (2011). *Unequal childhoods. Class, race, and family life* (2nd ed., with an update a decade later). Berkeley: University of California Press.

Lareau, A., & Weininger, E. B. (2003). Cultural capital in educational research: A critical assessment. *Theory and Society, 32*(5), 567–606.

Lee, J., & Bowen, N. (2006). Parent involvement, cultural capital, and the achievement gap among elementary school children. *American Educational Research Journal, 43*(2), 193–218.

Lucas, S. (2001). Effectively maintained inequality: Educational transitions and social background. *American Journal of Sociology, 106*, 1642–1690.

Macleod, J. (1995). *Ain't no makin' it: Leveled aspirations in a low-income neighborhood* (2nd ed.). Boulder: Westview.

McCartney, K., Burchinal, M., Clarke-Stewart, A., Bub, K. L., Owen, M. T., & Belsky, J. (2010). Testing a series of causal propositions relating time in child care to children's externalizing behavior. *Developmental Psychology, 46*, 1–17. https://doi.org/10.1037/a0017886.

Mickelson, R. A., Bottia, M. C., & Lambert, R. (2013). Effects of school racial composition on K–12 mathematics outcomes: A metaregression analysis. *Review of Educational Research, 83*, 121–158. https://doi.org/10.31102/0034654312475322.

Mincer, J. (1958). Investment in human capital and personal income distribution. *Journal of Political Economy, 66*, 281–302.

Mincer, J. (1974). *Schooling, experience, and earnings*. New York: National Bureau of Economic Research.

Morgan, P., Farkas, G., Hillemeier, M., & Maczuga, S. (2009). Risk factors for learning-related behavior problems at 24 months of age: Population-based estimates. *Journal of Abnormal Child Psychology, 37*, 401–413.

Morris, E. W. (2008). "Rednecks," "Rutters," and 'Rithmetic: Social class, masculinity, and schooling in a rural context. *Gender and Society, 22*, 728–751.

Neidell, M., & Waldfogel, J. (2010). Cognitive and non-cognitive peer effects in early education. *Review of Economics & Statistics, 92*(3), 562–576.

NICHD Early Child Care Research Network. (2005). Early child care and children's development in the primary grades: Follow-up results from the NICHD Study of Early Child Care. *American Educational Research Journal, 42*(3), 537–570.

Nichols-Barrer, I., Gleason, P., Gill, B., & Tuttle, C. C. (2015). Student selection, attrition, and replacement in KIPP middle schools. *Educational Evaluation and Policy Analysis, 38*, 5–20. https://doi.org/10.3102/0162373714564215.

Nunez, J. C., Suarez, N., Rosario, P., Vallejo, G., Valle, A., & Epstein, J. L. (2015). Relationships between perceived parental involvement in homework, student homework behaviors, and academic achievement: Differences among elementary, junior high, and high school students. *Metacognition and Learning, 10*, 375–406.

Ogbu, J. (1978). *Minority education and caste: The American system in cross-cultural perspective*. Orlando: Academic.

Ogbu, J. (2003). *Black American students in an American suburb: A study of academic disengagement*. Mahwah: Erlbaum.

Palardy, G. J. (2013). High school socioeconomic segregation and student attainment. *American Educational Research Journal, 50*, 714–754. https://doi.org/10.3102/0002831213481240.

Patterson, O. (Ed.). (2015). *The cultural matrix: Understanding Black youth*. Cambridge, MA: Harvard University Press.

Potter, D., & Roksa, J. (2013). Accumulating advantages over time: Family experiences and social class inequality in academic achievement. *Social Science Research, 42*, 1018–1032.

Puma, M., Bell, S., Cook, R., & Heid, C. (2010). *Head Start Impact Study: Final Report*. Washington, DC: U.S. Department of Health and Human Services.

Raftery, A. E., & Hout, M. (1993). Maximally maintained inequality: Expansion, reform, and opportunity in Irish education. *Sociology of Education, 66*, 41–62.

Reardon, S. F. (2011). The widening socioeconomic status achievement gap: New evidence and possible explanations. In R. J. Murnane & G. J. Duncan (Eds.), *Whither opportunity? Rising inequality and the uncertain life chances of low-income children*. New York: Russell Sage Foundation.

Reardon, S. F., & Portilla, X. A. (2015, September). *Recent trends in socioeconomic and racial school readiness gaps at kindergarten entry* (Working Paper). Stanford University.

Reeves, R. V., & Howard, K. (2003). *The parenting gap*. Washington, DC: Center on Children and Families, Brookings Institution.

Roberts, B. W., Jackson, J. J., Fayard, J. V., Edmonds, G., & Meints, J. (2009). Conscientiousness. In M. R. Leary & H. Hoyle (Eds.), *Handbook of individual differences in social behavior* (pp. 369–381). New York: Guilford Press.

Roscigno, V. T., & Ainsworth-Darnell, J. W. (1999). Race, cultural capital, and educational resources: Persistent inequalities and achievement returns. *Sociology of Education, 72*, 158–178.

Rumberger, R. W., & Palardy, G. J. (2004). Multilevel models for school effectiveness research. In D. Kaplan (Ed.), *The SAGE handbook of quantitative methodology for the social sciences* (pp. 235–258). Thousand Oaks: SAGE Publications.

Ryan, W. (1971). *Blaming the victim*. New York: Vintage.

Schultz, T. W. (1960). Capital formation by education. *Journal of Political Economy, 68*, 571–583.

Schultz, T. W. (1981). *Investing in people*. Berkeley: University of California Press.

Smith, K. E., Landry, S. H., & Swank, P. R. (2006). The role of early maternal responsiveness in supporting school-aged cognitive development for children who vary in birth status. *Pediatrics, 117*, 1608–1617. https://doi.org/10.1542/peds2005-1284.

Swidler, A. (1986). Culture in action: Symbols and strategies. *American Sociological Review, 51*, 273–286.

Swidler, A. (2008). Comment on Stephen Vaisey's "Socrates, Skinner, and Aristotle: Three ways of thinking about culture in action". *Sociological Forum, 23*, 614–618. https://doi.org/10.1111/j.1573-7861.2008.00080.x.

Tramonte, L., & Willms, J. D. (2010). Cultural capital and its effects on education outcomes. *Economics of Education Review, 29*, 200–213.

Tuttle, C. C., Booker, K., Gleason, G., Chojnacki, G., Knechtel, V. et al. (2015). *Understanding the effect of KIPP as it scales: Volume I, impacts on achievement and other outcomes*. Final report of KIPP's investing in innovation grant evaluation. Princeton: Mathematica Policy Research.

Tyson, K., Darity, W., & Castellino, D. R. (2005). It's not "a Black thing": Understanding the burden of acting White and other dilemmas of high achievement. *American Sociological Review, 70*(4), 582–605.

Van Voorhis, F. L., Maier, M. F., Epstein, J. L., & Lloyd, C. M. (2013, October). *The impact of family involvement on the education of children ages 3 to 8*. MDRC report.

Wacquant, L. (2004). *Body and soul: Notebooks of an apprentice boxer*. New York: Oxford University Press.

Wacquant, L. (2005). Habitus. In J. Becket & M. Zafirovski (Eds.), *International encyclopedia of economic sociology* (pp. 315–319). London: Routledge.

Wacquant, L. (2011). Habitus as topic and tool: Reflections on becoming a prizefighter. *Qualitative Research in Psychology, 8*, 81–92.

Wacquant, L. (2014). Putting habitus in its place: Rejoinder to the symposium. *Body and Society, 20*(2), 118–139.

Willis, P. (1977). *Learning to labor*. London: Gower.

Wilson, W. J. (1996). *When work disappears*. New York: Knopf.

Erin McNamara Horvat and Karen Pezzetti

Now more than ever, the world needs research that sheds light on how social contexts matter in learning, teaching, student achievement, and in the development of equitable and just forms and systems of education.

Elizabeth Birr Moje (2016)

Abstract

This chapter offers a critical perspective on sociological research exploring the interactions among students' homes, schools and communities. We conceptualize each of these spaces as a unique context that influences students and, as such, must be attended to both on its own terms but also especially where each context meets, conflicts with, or exerts power over the others. We highlight three major areas of promising research in this field: first, research that attends to the tensions inherent to the struggle for power among and between these contexts; second, research that explores the foundations and practice of creating equal, communicative relationships between stakeholders from each context; and third, research that can account for the presence, absence, or impact of trust in these relationships.

E. M. Horvat (✉)
Drexel University, Philadelphia, PA, USA
e-mail: emh@drexel.edu

K. Pezzetti
Grand Valley State University, Allendale, MI, USA
e-mail: pezzetka@gvsu.edu

2.1 Introduction

Above, Moje acknowledges that the social contexts that sociologists of education need to "shed light on" are *multiple*. This multiplicity means not only that each student lives in a unique social context, but further, that each young person grows up negotiating multiple social contexts; it is the interactions and relationships among and between these contexts that we must explore.

Children's educational experiences are influenced by the various cultures and expectations of their home lives, schools, and communities. It is important to keep in mind that while there are many differences across race, class, and culture, all families want children to do well in school. However, for some children, the specific cultures and expectations across home, school, and community align, working together to nurture and support the academic and social development of these young people. The educational experiences of other children, in contrast, are characterized by imbalances in power or incongruities in the realities across these three contexts. Too often, schools expect racially, linguistically, and culturally diverse families to adopt the White, middle-class, Eurocentric norms and values of schools, reinforc-

B. Schneider (ed.), *Handbook of the Sociology of Education in the 21st Century*, Handbooks of Sociology and Social Research, https://doi.org/10.1007/978-3-319-76694-2_2

ing a power imbalance between home and school. The contested interactions between families, schools, and communities have roots in deep tensions about how various stakeholders understand the role of schools in our society. These stakeholders have engaged repeatedly over questions such as: How, when, and where should we educate our children? For what purpose are we educating our children? What are the impacts on children when different families, schools, and communities answer these questions in different ways? And, most importantly for this chapter, how do researchers approach the study of the ways that interactions among home, school, and community influence students' experiences and achievement?

This chapter offers our perspective on some current trends in sociological research, focusing on the interactions and relationships among three different contexts: home, school, and community. Below, we offer a brief historical and theoretical overview of the literature. Rather than provide an exhaustive review, we explore the gains that have been made and the areas that have been neglected by particular perspectives. We focus on approaches that allow researchers to explore and understand the complex power dynamics and tensions that are interwoven throughout research in this area. We conclude the chapter with a review of the most recent scholarship and policy and discuss directions for future work.

2.2 Definitional Considerations

In the last 60 years, researchers, practitioners, and policy-makers have used different and evolving terms to refer to the relationship between the home and school. Cutler (2000, p. 5) described the home–school relationship at its best as a "marriage between distinct but reciprocal institutions," yet parents and teachers have more frequently been characterized as "natural enemies" (Lightfoot 2004; Waller 1932). Perhaps influenced by underlying assumptions about the parties involved, some scholars have studied *parental involvement*, while others have focused on "family–school interactions" or "home–school relationship." In the field of educational psychology, the theoretical construct *parental involvement* has been the focus of a considerable body of research in the last 30 years. This literature tends to focus on the activities and behaviors that parents do at home (like help with homework) or at school (like attend a parent–teacher conference) that may correlate positively with student academic achievement. Many studies have sought to discover what factors mediate whether or not—or how—parents engage in activities like these (i.e., Cardona et al. 2012; Davis-Kean 2005; Hoover-Dempsey and Sandler 1997; Lendrum et al. 2015; Schneider and Coleman 1993; Smith et al. 1997; Spera 2005; Wanat 2012; Widding 2012).

Some researchers have critiqued the construct of parental involvement as limited to specific forms of engagement dictated by schools. From this perspective, parents who do not show up for parent–teacher conferences or school events risk being labeled as ineffective, uncaring, uninvolved parents. These critics have proposed a different framing of the term: *family engagement* (Epstein and Sheldon 2002; Ferlazzo and Hammond 2009). In contrast with parental involvement, which focuses on what parents do (or do not do), family engagement foregrounds the responsibility of schools to nurture trusting, two-way relationships with all parents (Yull et al. 2014).

The particular framing of the research term is not just rhetoric. Whether researchers choose to study "parents" or "families" or "home" matters; just as whether they focus on "parenting style" (i.e., Darling and Steinberg 1993), "involvement" or "interaction" or "engagement" or "relationship" or "participation" (Lewis and Forman 2002). For instance, Mallett (2004) explored the ways that sociologists conceptualize "home." She points out that both the use of "home" and "family" as sociological terms and the relationship between them are "keenly contested" (p. 73). She argues that researchers who use "home" and "family" interchangeably are usually drawing on a Eurocentric, middle-class, heteronormative conceptualization of a home as a particular kind of house a person was born in, inhabited by a nuclear family.

In this chapter, we have deliberately used the word *home* because it can encompass all individuals who support a student in the space, including parents, grandparents, siblings, extended family, and non-related caregivers. This more expansive view of the home–school relationship embedded in a community context is drawn from a collective orientation towards education. As we will see, over time, schooling and the act of providing for the education of children and youth have been at times the purview of the family, at times the school, and at other times the community. Each stakeholder has fought for the responsibility and right to make decisions that impact the education of children and youth.

2.3 Historical Antecedents

The relationship between home and school has been contested for centuries. Over the past 150 years, there have been numerous shifts in the distribution of power between these two stakeholders. Before the existence of widespread public schools, White American parents had extensive control of what their children learned and how and when they learned it. Before the mid-1800s, most children were primarily educated in the home by family members, or, for wealthier families, by tutors. Some children went to nearby neighbors' homes or dame schools for lessons. With the advent of widespread public schools in the nineteenth century, however, control over education generally shifted from the home to the school (Cutler 2000). As teachers and administrators worked to professionalize and bureaucratize schooling systems, education came to be seen as a scientific enterprise that was best left in the hands of experts. As school systems grew in scale in the nineteenth century, some educators and reformers made efforts to formalize contact between families and schools. For example, in the 1840s, report cards began to replace face-to-face communication (Cutler 2000). Parents' groups (or PTAs) first appeared in the 1880s and contributed to the institutionalization of further aspects of the family–school relationship. In the Progressive Era and then again after World War I,

control and power shifted so far into the hands of the professionals that some educators began to scrutinize parenting practices and eventually to recommend "modifications in the behavior of families" through parental education programs (Cutler 2000, p. 8).

In the twentieth century, however, schools relinquished some of their power and control to parents. In the 1960s and 1970s, for example, Parents Rights Movements advocated for increased decision-making power in public schools. In 1997, the National Parent Teacher Association adopted a set of standards or guidelines for the home–school relationship based primarily on the work of Joyce Epstein. The standards highlight the importance of communication between schools and families, but make it clear that schools should initiate that communication. In 2001, No Child Left Behind stipulated parental involvement as a condition for receiving federal funding (Reynolds et al. 2015).

Today, most educators and researchers acknowledge both that children's first teachers are their families and that families should be involved in their children's academic lives. Still, despite this more welcoming attitude toward family involvement in schools, issues of power and control remain endemic to this relationship. (Henderson 2007; Lareau and Muñoz 2012). Henderson delineates four different kinds of power stances and practices that schools adopt toward families: the *Partnership School*, the *Open-Door School*, the *Come-if-We-Call School* and the *Fortress School* (p. 14). While any typology can over-simplify complex relationships, Henderson's work ably captures the different approaches taken to working with students' home spaces and the people in them. It also acknowledges the imbalance of power wielded by educators in defining these relationships. More recently, Lareau and Muñoz (2012) document the tussles over control in middle-class schools where parents are organized, engaged, and want to share control with classroom teachers and administration.

Historically, researchers studying parents and schools tended not to adopt a critical stance. What this means is that the context, power structures, and roles that shaped parental involvement or family involvement in schools were accepted without critique or question. As Baquedano-López et al. (2013) note, normative White middle-class norms have been the default expectations for family involvement. These expectations often translated directly into differential treatment of students. There is a fair amount of recent research that explores the ways that these normative expectations for family involvement shape educational experiences and outcomes (i.e., Auerbach 2012; Cardona et al. 2012; Reynolds et al. 2015). Rist's classic (1970) study regarding teacher expectations and the way that these expectations played into academic placement as well as long-term achievement and outcomes provides an illustrative case. This seminal article marked a turning point in thinking about the impact of home influences on academic outcomes for sociologists of education. While interpretations of this article often rightly focus on the class background of the families and the impact of social class background on the teacher's placement of students, this article also illustrates the powerful role of family background and context in shaping how teachers and school agents interpret family involvement in education.

There are a few relevant points here for our analysis of research on the family–school interaction. Rist argues that the teacher placement of students in ability groups was based on attributes rooted in family background. Thus, the home–school or family–school connection extends far beyond the notion of the PTA or report card conferences. Students are in large part products of their environment, and the most formative environmental factor in their lives is the home. There is power in teachers' perceptions of students. As this classic article illustrates, these perceptions are rooted in familial or home influences on students that are often generated in relation to a hypothetical "ideal type" of successful student, illustrating the pervasive presence and power of normative expectations for students and families (see also Rose 2016 for an extension of this argument). As Baquedano-López et al. (2013) note, these early studies—as well as later formulations

that treated parent or family involvement as a one size fits all enterprise—miss an essential piece of the puzzle in understanding how families and communities' reciprocal relations with schools are shaped. They do not take into account the social context and power dynamics that surround these relationships. And while some studies in the last 20 years have begun to address power differentials, Baquedano-López, Alexander, and Hernandez contend that much of this work is still rooted in a deficit narrative about racially, culturally, and linguistically diverse parents.

Further straining the power dynamics between families and schools is the fact that each year, fewer American students are taught by teachers who share their cultural background. As the teaching force continues to be predominantly White and middle-class while the American public school student body diversifies, the power differential between home and school takes on added dimensions of race and class. While the politics of who should decide what and how students should learn in school have always been influenced by issues of race and class, we believe that these tensions are exacerbated in the present context in which parents and families are experiencing tremendous pressure to advantage their children by performing in a variety of ways dictated by White, middle- and upper-class policy-makers and educators (Baquedano-López et al. 2013; Horvat and Baugh 2015; Oakes et al. 2015).

Although a handful of recent studies question this assumption (i.e., Robinson and Harris 2014), most of the literature we reviewed for this chapter accepted as a point of departure the premise that parental involvement and a positive home–school relationship boosts students' academic achievement (i.e., Dusi 2012; Hoover-Dempsey and Sandler 1997). Epstein and Sanders (2000, p. 287) summarize this consensus: "It is now generally agreed that school, family, and community partnerships are needed in order to improve the children's chances for success in school." Generally speaking, researchers tend to study the relationships between parents and schools from either the parent side of the question or the school side. From the parent side, researchers theorize that parental involvement helps students in the following ways: Involved parents model their value for education, which their children then adopt; involved parents better understand schools' expectations for their children, so they can help their children meet those expectations; and involved parents provide their children with extracurricular and academic opportunities that support in-school learning outside of school (Crosnoe 2015). Studies on the school side include research on the efficacy of interventions designed to reduce inequities in family and community engagement. A strong home–school relationship allows schools to better understand the particular strengths, needs and goals of children and their families. In addition, researchers have found that schools favor children whose parents are involved (Crosnoe 2015).

It is also important to note that the debate about whether parents or teachers are to blame when children or schools perform poorly on standardized tests obscures other possible responsible parties. As the government has withdrawn resources from public schooling, teachers have borne the primary heft of responsibility (and blame) for educating (and failing to educate) children. In a situation in which they have challenging jobs and limited resources, teachers look for someone else to shift the responsibility to— and parents are the available suspects. This increasing tension, aided by the implementation of high-stakes accountability measures in an environment of decreasing resources, again draws our attention to the contested nature of the home–school–community relationship.

In 2016, we believe it is important to note that schools' expectations for parents have increased in the last 20 years. In order to ensure that their children receive a quality education, parents must do more now. Cutler summarized the current state of the home–school relationship in the following way: "Today it would be unusual for parents to believe that they should not be active at their children's school. Educators, reformers, and even politicians have made such an issue of parental involvement that many well-meaning mothers and fathers probably feel guilty about not being more active than they already are"

(Cutler 2000, p. 207). As we discuss below, this has important consequences. In particular, we fear that this trend may increase educational inequity if parents' differential capacities to meet those expectations exacerbate entrenched class and race patterns of inequality.

2.4 Theoretical Frameworks

Many theoretical perspectives have been employed in research and policy related to the interactions between family and school. In understanding the research and past practice and exploring future directions for research and policy, it is important to understand both these perspectives and the strengths and limitations they bring. Historically, there has been a separation between home and school in both policy and research. In other words, researchers who studied schools rarely explored the influences of family, and, likewise, family researchers rarely explored the powerful effects of school on family (Epstein and Sanders 2000). Often, explorations of the wider community—including the neighborhood, after-school issues and care and other community organizations and resources such as churches, recreation centers, and libraries—have been completely excluded in discussions of the home–school relationship.

More recently, researchers have expanded their lenses to include a more holistic view of home and school that, for the most part, acknowledges the overlapping influences present as well as the important role played by the wider communities in which families and schools are situated (Epstein 1987; Epstein and Sheldon 2002; Epstein 2013; Epstein et al. 2013; Smith et al.1997). Below, we review some of the significant theoretical perspectives that have informed sociological research on the relationships and interactions between schools and families. In doing so, we highlight the contributions of some scholars and inevitably miss others. As noted previously, researchers operating from a psychological perspective have produced a rich literature on the role of parent involvement in student achievement (see, for example, Hoover-Dempsey and Sandler 1997; Hoover-Dempsey et al. 2001). A thorough review of this body of literature is outside the scope of this chapter (see Kim and Sheridan 2015 for an excellent foundational overview of this work). In contrast, our goal in this chapter is to shine a light on some of the seminal ideas that have informed sociological research in this area.

2.4.1 Social Capital

Without question, one of the concepts most central to any understanding of communities and schools is social capital. Mentioned by almost all of the major researchers in the field, social capital refers to the value of the relationships of an individual or group. James Coleman (1987) explored the social capital found within and surrounding families, as well as in the relationships between families, communities, and schools. His work with Thomas Hoffer and Sally Kilgore (1982) on social capital in Catholic schools found that the community support and shared values that inhered in these environments were critical to their success. Coleman's work is foundational to the understanding of school–home–community relations, as it brought significant national attention to the role of culture in both schools and in families as an important variable. Though the findings of the Coleman Report are often misunderstood, and his work was often over-simplified to be understood as simply finding that family background matters more than money in achieving school success, a more careful reading of Coleman's work finds a groundbreaking focus on the relationships among family background, community resources, the effects of social class, and school success.

Coleman and his colleagues' focus on the role of social capital in understanding school success highlighted the relationship between the family and school as a key variable in understanding schooling outcomes. Others in the field drew on this foundational work. James Comer (1995, 2015), who came to work in school improvement from a background in psychiatry in the early 1960s, adopted a developmental whole-child approach. Comer and his team at the Yale Child Study Center were asked to work with high-poverty low-performing schools in New Haven, CT. They adopted what we might now call a strengths-based approach that emphasized the role of social capital in school improvement (Comer 1995). Comer notes, "the social capital needed for school and life success is not provided in most public schools serving non-mainstream families" (2015). Moreover, Comer acknowledged not only the importance of connections as an aspect of social capital but also the trust embedded in these relationships. Comer's School Development Model thus included a strong emphasis on the construction of trusting relationships across and among students, parents, teachers, and a wide array of actors in the surrounding community. Comer's training was in psychiatry and his model, therefore, logically focuses on the importance of attending to the psychological and individual developmental needs and safety of children as they proceed through school. However, unlike his predecessors from the field of psychology, Comer emphasized the development of trusting relationships—social capital—in his model for school improvement.

Like Coleman's school improvement model, Epstein's (Epstein and Sanders 2000; Epstein et al. 2013) far more recent work on school, family, and community partnerships draws on the concept of social capital. Epstein's "theory of overlapping spheres of influence" highlights the capacity of educators, parents, and community members to work together in the service of students. Epstein's description of "school-like" homes (p. 36) in which a family's expectations of children at home are similar to the expectations of teachers in schools acknowledges the importance of consistent values and expectations across these spheres.

While both Comer and Epstein acknowledge the power of social capital in their models, neither takes a particularly sociological view. What we mean by this is that the work does not focus on what some see as the inherent conflict between schools and families, nor does it provide an analysis that accounts for the differential amounts of power that people from different social classes and positions in society can wield. As some scholars have noted, the work often downplays the role of conflict or tension between parents and schools (Lareau and Horvat 1999; Lareau and Muñoz 2012; Lewis and Forman 2002). In addition, we argue that this work does not sufficiently account for the importance of particularly class but also cultural, racial, and ethnic differences in shaping home–school–community relationships.

In our view, this theoretical difference stems from fundamentally different theoretical formulations of social and cultural capital. Comer, Epstein, Coleman, Putnam, and others view social capital as a readily shared commodity within families and communities. Bourdieu's conceptualization (Bourdieu 1986; Bourdieu and Wacquant 1992), which provides the foundation for Lareau (2000, 2003) and her followers' work, takes a more critical stance. In Bourdieu's formulation, all forms of capital (social, cultural, symbolic) are not created equal. They are the product of the family social class background and are—and this is the important point—differentially valued by dominant societal institutions, including schools. As Lareau (2014) notes in explaining the central finding of her seminal 2003 work, "the key issue was not the intrinsic nature of parenting itself, but rather the uneven rewards dominant institutions bestowed on different types of strategies." Research like Lareau's represents a move away from simply examining best practices or from attempting to build relationships across overlapping spheres of influence in a child's life to include a focus on the powerful ways in which some displays and activities are accorded value by dominant and powerful institutions, most notably schools, and others are not. This acknowledgement of the differential power accorded forms of social and cultural capital by dominant institutions lays the groundwork for a more critical

approach (i.e., Auerbach 2012; Baquedano-López et al. 2013; Reay 1999; Reynolds et al. 2015; Williams and Sanchez 2012).

Central to the critical work investigating the relations between home, school, and community is a deeper and more nuanced exploration into the factors that promote strong relationships across these stakeholders using this concept of social capital. The work of the Consortium on Chicago School Research (Bryk and Schneider 2002, 2003; Bryk et al. 2010) explored the important role of trust in these social relationships. We review the practical implications of this work in subsequent sections, however, here we note the theoretical sophistication of this work that focused explicitly on the notion of relational trust as a key variable in promoting positive relationships across stakeholders. This work both valued the resources that promoted trust and school success that reside in low-income communities and implicitly recognized the power of parents and communities in advancing school reform in relationship with school agents. With careful, detailed and extensive data collection, Bryk and Schneider identified the components of relational trust: respect, personal regard, competence in core role responsibilities, and personal integrity. They show that the benefits of developing trust across these domains are vast. This work illustrated that trust is the "connective tissue that binds individuals together to advance the education and welfare of students" (Bryk and Schneider 2003) and provided a theoretical and empirical base for further development of critical research and practices to bridge the divides across home, school, and community.

These more recent theoretical developments that place power at the heart of the analysis and use a more contextualized and inclusive notion of "family" that includes relevant actors from the home and community provide a theoretical foundation for understanding collective parental and community engagement in schooling. We hope that future research continues to shift away from an "all players are equal" over-generalization and toward a stance that recognizes the power inherent in institutions and takes seriously the unequal distribution of power across race and social class.

2.4.2 The Importance of Power: A Critical Approach to Family–School Relations

Recent scholarship has translated these theoretical notions into a reconceptualization of the home–school–community relationship incorporating notions of power and privilege into the analysis. In an excellent critical review of the literature on parent involvement in schools, Baquedano-López et al. (2013) identify and describe five ways that academic discourse and public policy have framed the relationship between parents and schools. Baquedano-López and her colleagues contend that although several of these tropes seem like common sense, each also is drawn from a White middle-class American worldview and hides a deficit view of nondominant parents and families, specifically low-income families, families of color, and families who are immigrants. We understand Baquedano-López, Alexander, and Hernandez' use of the term *trope* as a deliberate choice meant to signal the accepted, common, and often overused nature of the stories or narratives employed to explain the relationship between parents and schools. Instead of the term *narrative*, which could also signal an agreed-upon point of view or story that gives meaning to a particular set of circumstances, the authors use *trope* to indicate that these viewpoints are widely held, often unquestioned, and embedded into the shorthand of the lexicon. In this context, the use of the term trope implies a cynical and critical approach to the narratives used to explain family–school relationships that highlights the taken-for-granted nature of these viewpoints. Because so much of the research and practice on parent involvement in schools takes as an underlying assumption one or more of these tropes, we briefly review them here.

Several of the tropes discussed below fall into the first and largest discursive frame: *Parents as Problems*. Although current programs and policies are eager to avoid deficit discourses, under-lying much of the new rhetoric remains a view of families, particularly nondominant families, as ineffective at preparing their children for school and life. From this perspective, poor child-rearing practices and so-called "broken homes" are responsible for national and international achievement gaps and the perceived decline of American public schools.

Second, Baquedano-López and her colleagues identify the trope *Parents as First Teachers*: The literature and policy on early childhood education takes as a beginning point that parents are their children's first teachers. The creation of federally-funded programs intended to close the "school readiness gap" often begins with the assumption that nondominant parents are failing at this role, and therefore require training and intervention to perform the "right" (i.e., middle-class, White, Eurocentric) kinds of behaviors and interactions with their children.

A related trope is *Parents as Learners*. Baquedano-López and her colleagues argue that many family literacy programs sponsored by programs like the Workforce Investment Act, ESEA, and the Head Start Act draw on a decontextual-ized understanding of literacy that assumes that some parents need support in gaining fundamental tools and understandings so that they can assist their children in school. This perspective ignores the home literacy practices that families may already be engaging in and prioritizes those practices valued by the dominant culture.

Increasingly prominent in the legislation and literature is the frame of *Parents as Partners*. While the rhetoric of partnership implies equal footing, a closer look at legislation like Title I reveals that while the term "partner" is used, the mandated parent's role is passive and relegated to surveillance activities such as "monitoring attendance, homework completion, and TV watching" (Baquedano-López et al. 2013, p. 155). The limits of these prescribed activities suggest that, from this perspective, the ideal parent's role may be more like that of a "compliance officer" or "watchdog" rather than a partner (Baquedano-López et al. 2013, p. 155).

The final trope, *Parents as Choosers and Consumers*, highlights the role of parents in an increasingly privatized, market-based model of education wherein parents are expected to make decisions like choosing which school their children will attend. Baquedano-López and her colleagues argue that this frame is limiting in that it relegates parental involvement to the act of choosing from a limited set of options. Furthermore, the discourse of choice often hides underlying structural inequalities. As Baquedano-López et al. contend, "the mechanisms of choice create a hierarchical system of inequitable distribution that harms nondominant families when that choice does not contest neighborhood segregation, racialized tracking, or inequitable resource/opportunity provisions, and existing systems of power harmful to nondominant peoples" (2013, p. 156).

Many other recent empirical studies have brought a critical lens to the study of home–community–school relationships that questions the assumption that families must always adapt to schools' values and expectations. For instance, a recent study focused on a course that preservice teachers take that is intended to help them develop family-centered involvement practices, re-framing the issue of creating positive home–school–community relationships as at least partly the responsibility of teacher education programs (Amatea et al. 2012). Evans (2014) explored the ways that diverse parents made use of a community-based organization, instead of the local school, in order to meet some of their children's educational needs, highlighting parents' commitments to their children's education as well as the important role of community-based organizations in furthering those commitments. Jefferson (2015) studied the administrative and institutional barriers that prevented parents from fully participating in a school-turnaround process, even when some of these practices and policies were intended to foster parent participation. Jefferson's work highlights the complexities of enacting policies that are, at least superficially, designed to support home–school relationships.

As another example of recent critical work, Yull et al. (2014) used Critical Race Theory as a conceptual framework as they conducted focus group interviews with middle-class parents of color in a Northeastern urban school district. In conversation with the parents, Yull and her colleagues discovered that the parents saw the racism and the cultural incompetence of the school staff as a barrier to their effective engagement with the school. As the study was conducted as part of a larger community-based participatory action research approach project, the team of university-based researchers shared the parents' concerns with the school district administrators and collaborated to revise the district's strategic plan. We find research like this to be exciting for several reasons: First, it genuinely takes up the concerns of parents of color, and second, the collaborative, action research design means that not only does this study contribute to the research literature, it also seeks to immediately improve the conditions for home–school interactions in this community. Indeed, universities ought to consider themselves part of the communities that can contribute both to individual student academic success and the creation of positive learning environments and school cultures (McAlister 2013).

2.5 New Developments in School, Home, and Community Connection Research: Escalating Demands on Parents and Community Organizing

In recent years a growing body of research on school choice (Buckley and Schneider 2003; Henig 1995; Goyette 2008, 2014; Kisida and Wolf 2010; Ravitch 2010, 2013) has demonstrated the escalating demands on parents. As school choice options increase, so, too, do parents' responsibilities. For most of the twentieth century, the only real public school choice that families had was the choice they could make through moving neighborhoods. Many families who could afford to do so moved to areas with schools with better reputations (Coons and Sugarman 1978). In the twenty-first century, however, with the rapid expansion of charter schools, magnet schools, citywide admission schools, themed schools, and others, the number of schooling choices families must make for their children has increased dramatically. While some families still live in districts where the only cost-free option is to send children to the local neighborhood school, a growing number of American parents—including White, middle-class suburban parents—must use their social networks and "do their research" (Altenhofen et al. 2016) in order to ascertain which schools to apply to.

Previous research has found that parents consider a number of criteria when deciding which school to send their children to, including the following factors: academics (Schneider et al. 1996), extracurricular activities (Harris and Larsen 2014), social networks (Schneider et al. 1996; Cucchiara 2013a, b), safety (Stewart and Wolf 2014), location (Goyette 2008, 2014), and the racial demographics of the school (Altenhofen et al. 2016). In weighing these factors, it appears that parents engage in a multi-step decision-making process that involves steps such as consulting with friends who are parents and/or education professionals, researching prospective schools on the internet, and visiting prospective schools (Altenhofen et al. 2016; Harris and Larsen 2014). This growing list of activities engaged in by parents in selecting a school are part of an ever escalating constellation of activities that are increasingly expected of parents.

Horvat and Baugh (2015) divide these escalating pressures related to school choice into three inter-related categories. First, parents are experiencing increased pressure "to secure a viable educational setting for their child." Horvat and Baugh explain that in previous iterations of our schooling system, schools and teachers have been the first to blame when children are not learning. Increasingly, however, parents are seen as the responsible parties for sending their children to "failing" schools. Second, Horvat and Baugh describe the increased competition to secure a seat in a high-performing school. Researchers have documented phenomena such as parents camping out in front of schools in order to register their children, engaging in schemes to demonstrate that they are residents in the catchments of desired schools, putting chil-

dren on waitlists years before they enter a particular school/grade, and becoming intensely emotionally invested in charter school lotteries. Finally, many of these non-traditional public schools require parents to be involved in particular ways that schools specify, such as volunteering a certain number of hours per year, or becoming organizers, fundraisers, or activists in the service of the school. Perhaps ironically, many of the proponents of school choice programs use as their most formidable argument the desire to increase family engagement in the education system, to make public education more accessible and democratic (Coons and Sugarman 1978). Research has also examined the nature of parental involvement.

Some scholars (Lareau and Muñoz 2012; Horvat et al. 2003) have noted the individualistic nature of most research and policy related to parental involvement. These scholars find that most research has examined the effect of individual parents on their child's educational experiences and has largely ignored the collective nature of some parental involvement in schools. Other work has explored the tension between the individual aims of parents to advance their own child's educational success and taking actions that benefit children collectively (Cucchiara and Horvat 2009). In this era of increasing demands on parents and a political climate that calls for parents to advocate for their children, a broader approach that includes the study of parents working together collectively to effect education reform is vitally important. In addition, we have seen a rise in the incidence of community organizing for educational reform. This collective approach and efforts to document and promote community organizing as a strategy for reform are most effectively captured by the work of Mark Warren and Jeannie Oakes and their colleagues (Oakes and Rogers 2006; Warren and Mapp 2011).

Building on the early seminal work in this area by Dennis Shirley (1997), Warren and Mapp (2011, p. 5) note: "Community organizing offers a fresh approach to addressing educational failure as a part of a larger effort to build power for marginalized communities and tackle issues associated with poverty and racism inside and outside of schools." The perspective offered by community organizing builds on many of the theoretical notions discussed earlier, namely social capital—the paramount importance of power and trust in relationships—as well as a contextual strengths-based approach to school improvement. Warren and Mapp's book provides powerful examples of community organizing to improve schools from around the country. The authors find that community organizing is a relational process that "brings a powerful bottom-up thrust to education reform efforts" (p. 251). This approach not only focuses on schools but also on the communities in which schools reside, and works to address "educational failure as a part of a larger effort to build power for marginalized communities and tackle issues associated with poverty and racism inside and outside of schools" (p. 5).

The community organizing paradigm brings a strengths-based approach to school reform and community involvement by recognizing and valuing the assets to be found in all communities, including low-income communities. The approach "takes power seriously" (p. 251), attending to historic mistrust in the building of relationships in the community and clearly recognizing the differential power accorded to institutions and individuals. Lastly, this approach is community- rather than parent-focused. Providing for the effective education of children and youth is a collective community endeavor, at times requiring professional facilitation to build the capacity for collaboration. As Oakes and her colleagues (2015) note, it takes the investment of time to build the required relationships and develop common understandings so that effective collective action can be taken.

This approach has implications for leadership and teaching. While community organizing is not usually led by teachers, teachers and school leaders can be powerful allies in this work. As Oakes and her colleagues argue, the strategies of community organizing—"building relationships, forging common meanings about teaching and learning and taking action together" (p. 349)—are key elements to creating strong ties to students' homes and communities. Cooper et al. (2011) argue that leaders must enter these relationships

with a "spirit of humility and an openness to the full emotional presence" of the families. In addition, leaders and teachers must adopt a Freirian stance that positions them as "no longer the sole possessors of knowledge and power" (p. 781). This practical advice to teachers and leaders from a community organizing perspective clearly has roots in the sociological tradition that acknowledges the power at work in institutions and individuals that shapes educational outcomes. The focus on the importance of building trusting relationships to advance educational aims draws on the key tenets of social capital.

2.6 Directions for Future Research: Relationships and Context

We see potential for future work in further exploring the relationships between and among schools, homes and communities. Indeed, we must redefine the way in which research is conducted and policy is drafted to acknowledge the differences inherent across geographical contexts as well as expand our work to cross the boundaries of homes, schools, and communities. With federally funded programs such as Promise Neighborhoods, modeled on the Harlem Children's Zone, there is wide acknowledgement that improving the educational outcomes of children and youth must be a multifaceted and inclusive endeavor that cannot be confined to particular spheres—home, school, or community. Both the Harlem Children's Zone, a groundbreaking approach begun in 1997 to end the cycle of poverty in New York City that provides comprehensive services for an entire neighborhood, and the Promise Neighborhoods that have followed in its wake, take as gospel that the needs of communities, families, parents, children, and students must be addressed in a seamless fashion to provide every child the opportunity to thrive.

In order to improve educational outcomes for all students, we must find ways to promote productive relationships across homes, schools, and communities. Here, we use the word relationship—as opposed to "interaction" or "involvement"—purposefully. As Crosnoe (2015) and

Pomerantz et al. (2007) note, there is growing evidence that all home–school connections and interactions are not, in fact, positive. Greater attention needs to be paid to developing an understanding of the important nuances that influence the effectiveness of these relationships. In addition, as Crosnoe contends, relationships and "congruence" across these contexts do not necessarily need to be a function of direct interaction. Congruence between what is done at home and what is done at school matters. Ideally each of these spaces reinforce and build on what is done in the other. As a goal, Crosnoe introduces the concept of "mutual engagement" in which families and schools mutually reach out to one another. How and under what conditions this relationship of mutual engagement can be built are critical research and policy questions. Such investigations must recognize as a starting point that communities, homes, and schools vary. Context matters. Determining how to build relationships across these varying contexts is another area worthy of the attention of researchers, policymakers, and practitioners.

Increasingly, building these relationships means expanding beyond the traditional boundaries of home, school, and community. Efforts in Philadelphia, currently the poorest major city in the nation, provides a case in point. In an effort to create opportunities for children to thrive in the city, Philadelphia local government has passed a beverage tax to fund quality Pre-K education across the city, has funded community schools that provide wraparound services to students, families, and communities, and has partnered with local industry and higher education partners to advance career and technical education and career access. Each of these core initiatives spans across school, home, and community. None are targeting a single sphere alone. This approach acknowledges the strength in a concerted strategy across these spheres to improve outcomes for children and moves beyond stand-alone efforts to move the dial on educational outcomes or career competence simply by "engaging parents." Like efforts at the national level such as Promise Neighborhoods, these signature programs of the

city's mayor are multi-faceted and address the needs of children from a combined school, home, and community perspective.

The capacity of Philadelphia and other urban centers to improve the opportunity for children to thrive depends on increasing our capacity to work seamlessly across these spheres without becoming mired in dated debates about control while providing educators, families, and activists with the cultural and educational training and tools to work effectively across disparate cultural contexts. We see the potential for work in the area of educator training and development. As we have illustrated, educators are a powerful presence in the lives of students and their families. Recognizing the power they wield, we advocate for research and training for our predominantly White and female teaching force that makes clear to teachers the power that they hold and provides multiple pathways for working to create trusting relationships across the race, class, and ethnic differences. As many others (Oakes et al. 2015; Crosnoe 2015; Kim and Sheridan 2015) have noted, intentions matter. Adopting an open, curious, and respectful stance to the development of these relationships is a significant first step. Articulating the need to work across traditionally separate spheres of influence (home, school, community) affecting children and young people and providing pathways for seamless support across these spheres so children can thrive must become the work of educators, researchers, and policy advocates.

References

Altenhofen, S., Berends, M., & White, T. G. (2016). School choice decision making among suburban, high-income parents. *AERA Open, 2*(1), 1–14.

Amatea, E. S., Cholewa, B., & Mixon, K. A. (2012). Influencing preservice teachers' attitudes about working with low-income and/or ethnic minority families. *Urban Education, 47*(4), 801–834.

Auerbach, S. (Ed.). (2012). *School leadership for authentic family and community partnerships: Research perspectives for transforming practice.* New York: Routledge.

Baquedano-López, P., Alexander, R. A., & Hernández, S. J. (2013). Equity issues in parental and community involvement in schools: What teacher educators need to know. *Review of Research in Education, 37*(1), 149–182.

Bourdieu, P. (1986). The forms of capital. In J. Richardson (Ed.), *Handbook of theory and research for the sociology of education* (pp. 241–258). New York: Greenwood.

Bourdieu, P., & Wacquant, L. J. (1992). *An invitation to reflexive sociology*. Chicago: University of Chicago Press.

Bryk, A., & Schneider, B. (2002). *Trust in schools: A core resource for improvement*. New York: Russell Sage Foundation.

Bryk, A. S., & Schneider, B. (2003). Trust in schools: A core resource for school reform. *Educational Leadership, 60*(6), 40–45.

Bryk, A. S., Sebring, P. B., Allensworth, E., Easton, J. Q., & Luppescu, S. (2010). *Organizing schools for improvement: Lessons from Chicago*. Chicago: University of Chicago Press.

Buckley, J., & Schneider, M. (2003). Shopping for schools: How do marginal consumers gather information about schools? *Policy Studies Journal, 31*(2), 121–145.

Cardona, B., Jain, S., & Canfield-Davis, K. (2012). Home–school relationships: A qualitative study with diverse families. *The Qualitative Report, 17*(35), 1.

Coleman, J. S. (1987). Families and schools. *Educational Researcher, 16*(6), 32–38.

Coleman, J. S., Hoffer, T., & Kilgore, S. (1982). *High school achievement: Public, Catholic, and private schools compared*. New York: Basic Books.

Comer, J. P. (1995). *School power*. New York: Free Press.

Comer, J. P. (2015). Developing social capital in schools. *Society, 52*(3), 225–231.

Coons, J. E., & Sugarman, S. D. (1978). *Education by choice: The case for family control*. Berkeley: University of California Press.

Copper, C., Riehl, C., & Hasan, A. (2011). Leading and learning with diverse families in schools: Critical epistemology amid communities of practice. *Journal of School Leadership, 20*(6), 758–788.

Crosnoe, R. (2015). Continuities and consistencies across home and school systems. In S. M. Sheridan & E. M. Kim (Eds.), *Processes and pathways of family–school partnerships across development* (pp. 61–80). Cham: Springer.

Cucchiara, M. (2013a). "Are we doing damage?" Choosing an urban public school in an era of parental anxiety. *Anthropology & Education Quarterly, 44*(1), 75–93.

Cucchiara, M. B. (2013b). *Marketing schools, marketing cities: Who wins and who loses when schools become urban amenities*. Chicago: University of Chicago Press.

Cucchiara, M. B., & Horvat, E. M. (2009). Perils and promises: Middle-class parental involvement in urban schools. *American Education Research Journal, 46*(4), 974–1004.

Cutler, W. W. (2000). *Parents and schools: The 150-year struggle for control in American education*. Chicago: University of Chicago Press.

Darling, N., & Steinberg, L. (1993). Parenting style as context: An integrative model. *Psychological Bulletin, 113*(3), 487.

Davis-Kean, P. E. (2005). The influence of parent education and family income on child achievement: The indirect role of parental expectations and the home environment. *Journal of Family Psychology, 19*(2), 294.

Dusi, P. (2012). The family–school relationships in Europe: A research review. *CEPS Journal: Center for Educational Policy Studies Journal, 2*(1), 13–33.

Epstein, J. L. (1987). Toward a theory of family–school connections. In K. Hurrelmann, F. Kaufmann, & F. Losel (Eds.), *Social intervention: Potential and constraints* (pp. 121–136). New York: DeGruyter.

Epstein, J. L. (2013). Ready or not? Preparing future educators for school, family, and community partnerships. *Teaching Education, 24*(2), 115–118.

Epstein, J. L., & Sanders, M. G. (2000). Connecting home, school, and community. In M. T. Hallanan (Ed.), *Handbook of the sociology of education* (pp. 285–306). New York: Springer US.

Epstein, J. L., & Sheldon, S. B. (2002). Present and accounted for: Improving student attendance through family and community involvement. *Journal of Educational Research, 95*, 308–318.

Epstein, J. L., Sanders, M., Simon, B., Salinas, K., Jansorn, N., & Van Voorhis, F. (2013). *School, family, and community partnerships: Your handbook for action*. Thousand Oaks: Corwin.

Evans, M. (2014). Natural allies or natural enemies? The evolution of participant self-interest in community-based organizations. *Journal of Family Diversity in Education, 1*(1), 21–39.

Ferlazzo, L., & Hammond, L. A. (2009). *Building parent engagement in schools*. Santa Barbara: Linworth.

Goyette, K. (2008). Race, social background, and school choice options. *Equity & Excellence in Education, 41*(1), 114–129.

Goyette, K. (2014). Setting the context. In A. Lareau & K. Goyette (Eds.), *Choosing homes, choosing schools* (pp. 1–24). New York: Russell Sage Foundation.

Harris, D. N., & Larsen, M. F. (2014). *What schools do families want (and why)? School demand and information before and after the New Orleans post-Katrina school reforms*. New Orleans: Education Research Alliance for New Orleans, Tulane University.

Henderson, A. T. (2007). *Beyond the bake sale: The essential guide to family–school partnerships*. New York: The New Press.

Henig, J. R. (1995). *Rethinking school choice: Limits of the market metaphor*. Princeton: Princeton University Press.

Hoover-Dempsey, K. V., & Sandler, H. M. (1997). Why do parents become involved in their children's education? *Review of Educational Research, 67*(1), 3–42.

Hoover-Dempsey, K. V., Battiato, A. C., Walker, J. M., Reed, R. P., DeJong, J. M., & Jones, K. P. (2001). Parental involvement in homework. *Educational Psychologist, 36*(3), 195–209.

Horvat, E. M., & Baugh, D. E. (2015). Not all parents make the grade in today's schools. *Phi Delta Kappan, 96*(7), 8–13.

Horvat, E. M., Weininger, E. B., & Lareau, A. (2003). From social ties to social capital: Class differences in the relations between schools and parent networks. *American Educational Research Journal, 40*(2), 319–351.

Jefferson, A. (2015). Examining barriers to equity: School policies and practices prohibiting interaction of families and schools. *The Urban Review, 47*(1), 67–83.

Kim, E. M., & Sheridan, S. M. (2015). *Foundational aspects of family–school partnership research* (Vol. 1). Cham: Springer.

Kisida, B., & Wolf, P. J. (2010). School governance and information: Does choice lead to better-informed parents? *American Politics Research, 38*, 783–805.

Lareau, A. (2000). *Home advantage: Social class and parental intervention in elementary education*. Lanham: Rowman & Littlefield Publishers.

Lareau, A. (2003). *Unequal childhoods*. Berkeley: UC Press.

Lareau, A. (2014). Cultural knowledge and social inequality. *American Sociological Review, 80*(1), 1–27.

Lareau, A., & Horvat, E. M. (1999). Moments of social inclusion and exclusion: Race, class, and cultural capital in family–school relationships. *Sociology of Education, 72*(1), 37–53.

Lareau, A., & Muñoz, V. L. (2012). "You're not going to call the shots": Structural conflicts between the principal and the PTO at a suburban public elementary school. *Sociology of Education, 85*(3), 201–218.

Lendrum, A., Barlow, A., & Humphrey, N. (2015). Developing positive school–home relationships through structured conversations with parents of learners with special educational needs and disabilities (SEND). *Journal of Research in Special Educational Needs, 15*(2), 87–96.

Lewis, A. E., & Forman, T. A. (2002). Contestation or collaboration? A comparative study of home–school relations. *Anthropology & Education Quarterly, 33*(1), 60–89.

Lightfoot, S. L. (2004). *The essential conversation: What parents and teachers can learn from each other*. New York: Ballantine Books.

Mallett, S. (2004). Understanding home: A critical review of the literature. *The Sociological Review, 52*(1), 62–89.

McAlister, S. (2013). Why community engagement matters in school turnaround. *The Next Four Years: Recommendations for Federal Education Policy, 36*, 35–42.

Moje, E. (2016). *Message from division VP*. Retrieved from http://www.aera.net/Division-G/Social-Context-of-Education-G

Oakes, J., & Rogers, J. (2006). *Learning power: Organizing for education and justice*. New York: Teachers College Press.

Oakes, J., Lipton, M., Anderson, L., & Stillman, J. (2015). *Teaching to change the world*. London: Routledge.

Pomerantz, E. M., Moorman, E. A., & Litwack, S. D. (2007). The how, whom, and why of parents' involvement in children's academic lives: More is not always better. *Review of Educational Research, 77*(3), 373–410.

Ravitch, D. (2010). *The life and death of the great American school system: How testing and choice are undermining education*. New York: Perseus.

Ravitch, D. (2013). *Reign of error: The hoax of the privatization movement and the danger to America's public schools*. New York: Vintage.

Reay, D. (1999). Linguistic capital and home–school relationships: Mothers' interactions with their children's primary school teachers. *Acta Sociologica, 42*(2), 159–168.

Reynolds, R. E., Howard, T. C., & Jones, T. K. (2015). Is this what educators really want? Transforming the discourse on Black fathers and their participation in schools. *Race Ethnicity and Education, 18*(1), 89–107.

Rist, R. (1970). Student social class and teacher expectations: The self-fulfilling prophecy in ghetto education. *Harvard Educational Review, 40*(3), 411–451.

Robinson, K., & Harris, A. L. (2014). *The broken compass: Parental involvement with children's education*. Cambridge, MA: Harvard University Press.

Rose, T. (2016). *The end of average: How we succeed in a world that values sameness*. New York: Harper One.

Schneider, B., & Coleman, J. S. (1993). *Parents, their children, and schools*. Boulder: Westview Press, Inc.

Schneider, B., Schiller, K. S., & Coleman, J. S. (1996). Public school choice: Some evidence from the National Education Longitudinal Study of 1988. *Educational Evaluation and Policy Analysis, 18*(1), 19–29.

Shirley, D. (1997). *Community organizing for urban school reform*. Austin: University of Texas Press.

Smith, E. P., Connell, C. M., Wright, G., Sizer, M., Norman, J. M., Hurley, A., & Walker, S. N. (1997). An ecological model of home, school, and community partnerships: Implications for research and practice. *Journal of Educational and Psychological Consultation, 8*(4), 339–360.

Spera, C. (2005). A review of the relationship among parenting practices, parenting styles, and adolescent school achievement. *Educational Psychology Review, 17*(2), 125–146.

Stewart, T., & Wolf, P. (2014). *The school choice journey: School vouchers and the empowerment of urban families*. New York: Palgrave.

Waller, W. (1932). *The sociology of teaching*. New York: Wiley.

Wanat, C. L. (2012). Home–school relationships: Networking in one district. *Leadership and Policy in Schools, 11*(3), 275–295.

Warren, M. R., & Mapp, K. L. (2011). *A match on dry grass: Community organizing as a catalyst for school reform*. Oxford: Oxford University Press.

Widding, G. (2012). What's gender got to do with it?: Gender and diversity in research on home and school relationships. *International Journal about Parents in Education, 6*(1), 57–68.

Williams, T. T., & Sánchez, B. (2012). Parental involvement (and uninvolvement) at an inner-city high school. *Urban Education, 47*(3), 625–652.

Yull, D., Blitz, L. V., Thompson, T., & Murray, C. (2014). Can we talk? Using community-based participatory action research to build family and school partnerships with families of color. *School Community Journal, 24*(2), 9.

Douglas B. Downey, Aimee Yoon,
and Elizabeth Martin

Abstract

The traditional narrative posits that differences in school quality are an important source of inequality in the stratification system. Improving the schools attended by disadvantaged children, therefore, is key to reducing inequality. But what if this view is wrong? We discuss the results of seasonal comparison studies that analyze how achievement gaps change when school is in versus out. Contrary to most education research, these studies suggest that the traditional narrative may be partly wrong in some cases and entirely misplaced in others. Indeed, when it comes to understanding socioeconomic-based gaps in math and reading skills, the evidence indicates that achievement gaps are mostly formed prior to formal schooling and that schools probably reduce the growth in gaps that we would observe in their absence. If this is correct, then the implications for battling inequality are profound. School reform efforts are likely to have limited influence; the primary source of the problem is the level of inequality in broader society.

D. B. Downey (✉) · A. Yoon · E. Martin
Ohio State University, Columbus, OH, USA
e-mail: downey.32@osu.edu

3.1 Introduction

How do schools influence inequality? This is a big question, and it is fundamental to our understanding of stratification. We consider what we learn about this question by looking at the magnitude of achievement gaps across socioeconomic status, race, and gender in cognitive skills at kindergarten entry, along with how those gaps change over the next several years of schooling. Once children are in school, we emphasize seasonal comparison studies (observing how achievement gaps change when school is in versus out of session) because they provide an attractive way of separating school from non-school effects. Of course, this approach falls short of a comprehensive analysis of the relationship between schools and inequality, but we believe it provides important insight regarding how schools influence achievement gaps in cognitive skills during the first few years of school. Our review helps us understand whether schools tend to make achievement gaps worse, leave them largely the same, or reduce them.

In this chapter, we discuss the traditional narrative about schools and inequality and then contrast it with our newer perspective shaped by seasonal comparison studies. We then discuss the methodological advantages of seasonal comparison studies, along with their implications for understanding the relationship between schools and inequality. We conclude that schools, at least

© Springer International Publishing AG, part of Springer Nature 2018
B. Schneider (ed.), *Handbook of the Sociology of Education in the 21st Century*, Handbooks of Sociology and Social Research, https://doi.org/10.1007/978-3-319-76694-2_3

under some conditions, play a more positive role than previously thought and significantly reduce the kind of inequality we would observe in their absence.

3.2 Schools and Inequality: The Traditional Narrative

The 1966 Coleman Report has shaped scholarly discussion of schools and inequality for the last half century (Coleman et al. 1966). The massive study of over 650,000 American children famously concluded that variations in children's math and reading skills were only weakly related to variation in school resources (e.g., per pupil expenditures, class size). Instead, Coleman and colleagues found that inequality in skills was mostly associated with inequalities in families, a pattern echoed by Jencks (1972). This message represented a serious challenge to those who believed that unequal schools were key to inequality and so, not surprisingly, it prompted an energetic response. For the last 50 years we have been trying to sort things out.

Critics of the Coleman Report have produced a large body of scholarship outlining the ways that schools increase inequality. Bowles and Gintis (1976) posited that schools provide the capitalist economy with workers who know their place and are prepared for their roles. Schools contribute to the reproduction of stratification, therefore, by promoting skills congruent with the students' backgrounds. As a result, schools serving elite students prepare them for jobs as managers while schools serving poor students prepare them to be workers. Bourdieu (1977) also sees schools as a culprit but via a different mechanism. He notes that students from elite backgrounds signify their advantage by exhibiting "cultural capital" (styles, habits, tastes) that allows them to affiliate with elite groups. School officials and teachers recognize and reward the arbitrary cultural capital of the elite, advantaging them unfairly and reproducing inequality (DiMaggio 1982).

Pushing the critical perspective of schools even further, other scholars contend that schools do more than just reproduce inequality; they increase it. School funding schemes, for example, result in vastly different resources for children from advantaged versus disadvantaged backgrounds (Kozol 1991). Moreover, within-school processes such as ability grouping and tracking exacerbate skill differences because advantaged children enjoy better learning environments than their disadvantaged counterparts (Condron 2008; Gamoran and Mare 1989; Oakes 1985).

This traditional view, largely a response to the Coleman Report, has created a dominant and largely critical narrative about schools and inequality: Schools serving advantaged children are better equipped, safer, produce more college-going graduates, attract better teachers, and provide more Advanced Placement classes, college test preparation courses, and extra-curricular opportunities. This well-known understanding of schools in American society is why high-income parents are willing to pay more for homes in neighborhoods with "good" schools and low-income parents push for more equitable funding formulas and enter their children into lotteries for a chance to attend a high-prestige charter school. The critical narrative is the driving force behind much of the education research aimed at identifying school practices that might reduce achievement gaps and it continues to dominate sociological research on schools. To fix inequality, the story goes, America needs to improve the schools serving disadvantaged children.

A newer line of research consistent with the notion that schools are the problem interprets "between-school" variance as evidence of school effects. For example, Borman and Dowling (2010) reanalyzed Coleman's data and concluded that "[f]ormal decomposition of the variance attributable to individual background and the social composition of the schools suggest that going to a high-poverty school or a highly segregated African-American school has a profound effect on a student's achievement outcomes, above and beyond the effect of individual poverty or minority status" (p. 1202). Similarly, Jennings et al. (2015) demonstrate that, if the focus is on college attendance rather than test scores, there is greater unexplained between-school variance, a pattern that could be attributable to schools. These studies demonstrate the possibility of school effects, but it is unclear whether between-school variation really does reflect differences in schools rather than the kinds of students who happen to attend them. For example, there is substantial between-school variance in children's skills at kindergarten entry, before schools have a chance to matter. Between-school variance observed at later stages of schooling may also represent significant differences in non-school factors that typically go unmeasured.

Others have pushed further the notion that schools are the key to inequality and have made the case that school reform itself is enough to eliminate achievement gaps. For example, Abigail and Stephan Thernstrom made this idea popular in their book, *No Excuses: Closing the Gap in Learning* (Thernstrom and Thernstrom 2003). They applauded those who have: (1) implemented policies aimed at changing school cultures, and (2) refused to blame family background disadvantage as the reason for the Black–White gap. And in an article testing the effectiveness of the Harlem Children's Zone, Dobbie and Fryer (2011) concluded that school reforms themselves had substantial effects on achievement gaps and that school effects were not improved by the addition of broader community reforms.[1]

Rothstein (2004) notes, however, that the evidence for these "high-flying" schools is substantially weaker when examined closely. For example, among schools that managed to severely reduce achievement gaps, the majority of them served a select group of children (e.g., children whose parents were motivated enough to join the program). In addition, although some schools have managed impressive learning gains in a particular grade for a particular subject, there are virtually no schools that produce impressive gains across many grades and subjects over many

years. But most importantly, even if it is possible to reduce some achievement gaps via school reform alone, it may be more efficient to support social reform that prevents these large gaps from emerging in the first place. As we discuss later, socioeconomic and racial achievement gaps are largely formed *prior* to kindergarten.

To date, the debate about schools and inequality has largely been framed as between those who think schools play a big role (critics of Coleman) versus those who believe schools play a modest role (supporters of Coleman). We believe that this discussion needs to expand to include the possibility that schools do not increase some achievement gaps at all, but rather are a meaningful compensatory institution. This more favorable view of schools has played a minimal role in academic or policy discussions. It merits greater attention, however, because important evidence (discussed in detail below) suggests that some achievement gaps would be larger if not for schools.

3.3   Schools and Inequality: An Alternative Perspective

Our alternative perspective is motivated by a desire to understand schools' *overall* role in the stratification system. Traditional approaches are limited because they tend to be school-centric and therefore focus on variation within school systems. This approach may reflect scholars' beliefs that schools are mostly responsible for achievement gaps, or that even if schools are not mostly responsible, they are the primary policy lever available for reducing achievement gaps. Indeed, many education researchers admit that they focus on schools, in part, for political reasons—they view schools as the most politically viable mechanism by which to influence the opportunity structure.[2] In contrast, we see schools

---

[1] We are not persuaded by this conclusion because in their study children in the "school-only" condition enjoyed many benefits typically not available to children at school, such as free medical, dental, and mental health services.

[2] Economist Eric Hanushek (1992, p. 106) explains the focus on schools: "While family inputs to education are indeed extremely important, the differential impacts of schools and teachers receive more attention when viewed from a policy viewpoint. This reflects simply that the characteristics of schools are generally more easily manipulated than what goes on in the family."

as just one institution affecting the opportunity structure and so its role should be understood within the broader context of other societal institutions and other social forces. For us, concentrating on variation within school systems alone runs the risk of distorting how schools really matter. Our goal is to identify the kinds of social conditions *in general* (school or non-school) that influence inequality.

And while we are interested broadly in the relationship between schooling and inequality, we limit our focus here to the formal schooling opportunities readily available to all children (kindergarten through twelfth grade in the United States) because our primary interest is in whether publicly provided mass education really does serve as a "great equalizer." Of course, there exist other kinds of "schooling" that are not provided publicly (or are only partly subsidized) and therefore depend more heavily on parents' resources, such as preschool, shadow education, private schools, summer programs, and higher education. At times, it is difficult to separate the schooling that is provided publicly from the schooling that is provided privately. For example, achievement gaps at kindergarten entry are probably influenced to some degree by school exposure (e.g., preschool), and so do not strictly represent "non-school" factors. But for our purposes, they represent the magnitude of the gap prior to the onset of widely available publicly funded schooling. What happens after that is our primary interest in this chapter.

3.3.1 The Seasonal Comparison Method

Traditional research frames the question as "How well would a particular student perform if they attended school A versus school B?" This framing promotes research aimed at determining whether children would have learned more had they experienced a different school or particular school practice. Many scholars and policymakers are attracted to this counterfactual because they assume that schools are the primary problem and/ or lever by which to shape inequality. But the value of this counterfactual approach is contingent on whether schools really are a primary source of inequality. If this assumption is wrong then the school-centric approach has considerably less value.

We recommend a different counterfactual— "What would inequality look like if children's exposure to school changed?"—because it provides a view of schools' *overall* role in the stratification system (Raudenbush and Eschmann 2015). The traditional approach, focusing on variation among schools, lacks the breadth necessary to allow us to see the big picture. It is difficult to assess whether schools increase or decrease inequality, for example, simply by documenting variations among schools.

One problem is that schools might provide advantages to high-socioeconomic children, yet still be an equalizing force (Downey et al. 2004), as presented in Fig. 3.1. This could occur if unequal schools are *more equal* than the conditions children experience when they are not in school. In this way schools could be an equalizing force by reducing the level of inequality we would observe in their absence. Importantly, we would not be able to identify this pattern if we focused on the traditional counterfactual.

In addition, the traditional approach struggles to isolate school from non-school effects. The 800-pound gorilla problem education scholars face is that children are not randomly assigned to schools and so differences in how children learn in one school versus another could represent either school or non-school factors. The "measurement-based" approach to this challenge is to isolate school "effects" by identifying all relevant non-school factors and statistically controlling for them in a regression model. This is common practice but it is also insufficient because scholars cannot identify and measure perfectly all of the relevant factors that influence children's development. In a sobering example of the limitations of this method, Burkam et al. (2004) note that, even in models including an impressive array of measures of the non-school environment, they were unable to explain more

Fig. 3.1 School as equalizers. (Source: Adapted from Downey et al. (2004))

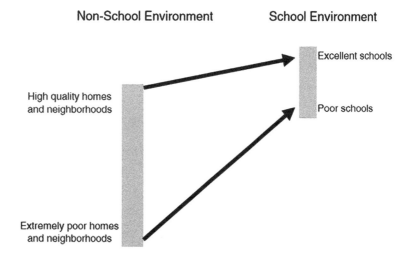

than 15% of the variation in summer learning among children in the Early Childhood Longitudinal Study—Kindergarten Cohort of 1998.[3] As a result, even in models with what seems like a comprehensive set of statistical controls, students at two different schools may learn at different rates during the year because of "unknown differences" in their non-school environments that go unmeasured. These "unknown differences" in non-school environments distort estimates of school effects in a predictable way, making them appear larger than they really are.

Seasonal comparison scholars approach the problem from a different angle. They leverage the seasonal nature of the American school calendar—9 months of school followed by a 3-month summer break—which provides a natural experiment for understanding how schools matter (Gangl 2010). Scholars compare how achievement gaps change when school is in versus out, thereby gaining leverage on the schools' role in producing these gaps. Note the similarity

between the seasonal comparison method and the cross-over designs employed by medical researchers. Medical researchers testing the effectiveness of a drug may observe patients off treatment for a period, and then observe how they change when on treatment (von Hippel et al. 2007). The difference between the two periods provides an estimate of the treatment effect. Similarly, comparing how achievement gaps change when school (treatment) is in versus out provides leverage for understanding how schools matter.

While not a randomized experiment, the seasonal design is a powerful method for separating the effects of the school and non-school environment because there are no differences between subjects receiving the treatment and those receiving the control—each subject is observed under both conditions and serves as his or her own control. This means that there is no need to identify all the various school and non-school processes at stake because the overall consequence of all mechanisms (both exacerbatory and compensatory) is observable in how inequality changes when school is in session versus out of session.

The advantages of seasonal comparisons over more traditional education scholarship are multiple. First, they provide a better method for overcoming the formidable obstacle of isolating school effects. Second, most traditional scholars target a specific school process thought to increase achievement gaps (e.g., class size), which represents just one of the many school processes that

---

[3]Burkam et al. (2004) predicted summer learning (fall first grade score minus spring kindergarten score) with socioeconomic status, race, gender, age, repeat kindergarten status, family structure, home language (English or not), summer trips, summer literacy activities, computer for educational use, and summer school attendance. They explained 0.079%, 0.136%, and 0.131% of the variation in literacy, math, and general knowledge learning respectively. Clearly, the vast majority of why some children learn faster than others during the summer is not captured by the information typically available in large data sets.

shape inequality in schools. These studies are not without value—we can learn something about whether a particular school practice increases inequality—but they tell us little about how all exacerbatory and compensatory school processes stack up against each other. If we want to understand schools' overall effect we need to identify all processes at stake (exacerbatory and compensatory) and compare their *relative* strength.[4] Seasonal comparison studies achieve that goal. Finally, traditional education scholarship lacks the scope to assess whether schools, as a whole, do more to reduce or increase inequality. The problem is that the school-centric approach merely looks at variations in school conditions without considering the bigger question, how do schools matter overall? The possibility that unequal schools might still be an equalizing force (Fig. 3.1) goes overlooked with traditional methods.

Of course, the seasonal comparison approach requires assumptions and these have yet to be scrutinized in the way that they should. Perhaps the most critical assumption is that reading and math skills are measured on interval-level scales, and so gains at the bottom of the scale are assumed to be comparable to those at the top. If it is easier to register gains at the bottom of the scale than the top, then it is hard to interpret the seasonal patterns.[5] Early seasonal studies, some

of our own included, relied on scales that were later found to fall short of this interval-level requirement. More recent scales appear to approximate interval-level characteristics more closely, but the field would still benefit from greater use of non-parametric methods (Ho and Reardon 2011) that would be less dependent on this assumption and allow researchers to use seasonal methods across a broader range of dependent variables. Some scholars have observed changes in gaps across scales that may be interval level, like theta scores, and those that are clearly not, like standardized versions of theta scores. The first approach gauges whether a gap in skills changed over time and depends on interval level assumptions. The second approach considers whether a group's relative position in the distribution changed over time (Quinn 2015; Quinn et al. 2016).

In addition, it is important that nothing else of consequence change across the summer and school year other than children's exposure to schooling. Similar to the cross-over designs in medical research, we need to be confident that exposure to the "treatment" is the only thing different between treatment and non-treatment periods. One can imagine ways in which this assumption might be violated in seasonal comparison studies. For example, when children are in school, we would expect parents' time with children to decline relative to the summer periods. When focusing on achievement gaps, this could be problematic if non-school factors change across seasons *and* they do so differently across groups. For example, suppose high-SES parents out-invest their low-SES counterparts during the summer and that this advantage *increases* during school periods. If this is the case, then seasonal comparisons underestimate how good schools are for low-SES children because they might misattribute, for example, an increase in SES-based achievement gaps observed during the school year, to school rather than non-school factors. Or, alternatively, if high-SES parents out-invest low-SES parents during the summer, but this pattern reverses during school periods, then seasonal comparison patterns might underestimate the extent to which

---

[4] It is important to recognize that with this kind of study design we do not look to the treatment period alone for our estimate of the treatment effect. We should not make the mistake, therefore, of simply observing the school-year patterns as a way of understanding how schools matter. If we just focus on the school year we would mistakenly conclude that high- and low-SES children learn at roughly the same rate, and so schools play a mostly neutral role. But the proper way to understand how schools matter is to compare the treatment (school year) period to the control period (summer). When we make that proper comparison, we learn that schools are compensatory with respect to SES-based gaps in math and reading because they reduce the magnitude of the gaps we would observe in their absence (Downey et al. 2004; Entwisle and Alexander 1992). See Downey and Condron (2016) for further discussion on this point.

[5] We would note, however, that this issue is an awkward explanation for seasonal patterns because it needs to be applied selectively—the problem exists during the school year but not the summers.

schools advantage high-SES children. This assumption is especially difficult to assess, but relevant work fails to find much evidence that SES-based patterns in parental investments change systematically across seasons. For example, high-SES parents are more likely than low-SES parents to enroll their children in dance and music classes during the summer, and both groups increase the likelihood of enrolling their child in dance and music during the school year, but the direction and magnitude of this advantage is roughly similar across seasons (Downey et al. 2017).

Finally, seasonal comparisons assume that summers represent "non-school" periods of learning, but in reality school processes likely contaminate most summer estimates. One problem is that students are typically not assessed on the very first and last days of school, and so when scholars estimate summer learning between the spring of one academic year and the fall of the next, there are usually several days of schooling on each end. Scholars attempt to reduce the severity of this problem by modeling the learning that occurs during these school days and removing it from the estimate of summer learning, but this is an imperfect approach.

These assumptions should give scholars pause regarding seasonal results, but we posit that they are significantly more palatable than the assumptions required for more traditional approaches. For example, the notion that scholars can isolate school effects by statistically controlling for observables of the family environment (e.g., socioeconomic status, family structure, race) available in surveys or by estimating school year learning gains with covariates is most certainly in error and, as a result, produces patterns that consistently overestimate the negative effects of schools. Given that our conclusions about how schools matter for socioeconomic achievement gaps change dramatically based on which approach we use—schools increase inequality (traditional method) versus schools reduce inequality (seasonal comparison method)—we think the results from seasonal comparison research merit special attention.

So what do we learn about schools and inequality if we employ the seasonal method? Below we describe patterns for achievement gaps across socioeconomic status, race, and gender. We emphasize the magnitude of achievement gaps at kindergarten entry, along with how school exposure modifies the trajectory of those gaps during 9-month school sessions versus summer periods. We start by recalling the patterns from early seasonal comparison studies before discussing more recent studies.

3.3.2 Early Seasonal Comparison Studies

Seasonal studies go back nearly a half century. One of the earliest seasonal studies was of over 600 children in New York City elementary schools from 1965 to 1967. Researchers reported that the gap in reading skills between high-income White and low-income minority schools grew at a faster rate during the summer than during the school year (Hayes and Grether 1983). This same pattern was replicated in New Haven (Murnane 1975) and in Atlanta (Heyns 1978).

Perhaps most widely-known, however, is Entwisle and Alexander's Beginning School Study (BSS) of nearly 800 first graders who were followed seasonally until sixth grade and then into adulthood. In a series of widely-cited publications, Entwisle and Alexander demonstrated that gaps in math and reading skills grew faster in the summer than the school year (Alexander et al. 2007, 2014; Entwisle and Alexander 1992; Entwisle et al. 1994). Indeed, among ninth graders, the authors found that one-third of the reading gap between high- and low-socioeconomic children could be traced to the gap that was already present at the beginning of first grade, and two-thirds of the gap was due to the summers in between the school years (Alexander et al. 2007). The entire gap, therefore, was a product of non-school forces. From the BSS comes the term "summer setback," widely used to explain the loss of skills observed among low-income children during the summer. The studies' patterns were popularized in a *Time* magazine article, and

have motivated the proliferation of summer programs designed to prevent setback among disadvantaged children (Von Drehle 2010).

Perhaps more important than these empirical
patterns, however, was the insight the authors
provided in terms of framing the question. Rather
than merely focusing on the summer patterns as
the period when gaps grow, Alexander (1997)
pointed out that the summer and school-year patterns in combination suggest that, when it comes
to inequality, schools are "more part of the solution than the problem."

3.4   A Review of Recent Seasonal Comparison Studies

In this next section, we focus on what the more
recent data sets reveal about the first few years of
schooling. We are especially interested in the
magnitude of achievement gaps at kindergarten
entry because, if they are large relative to changes
in the gap, then most of the "action" generating
inequality occurs prior to formal schooling.[6]

Our review draws on several studies that have
employed different seasonal data sets, but we end
up emphasizing patterns from the ECLS-K: 1998
and the more recent ECLS-K: 2010 for several
reasons. Both ECLS-K data sets are nationally

representative of American children, were collected on a seasonal schedule, include scales of
cognitive skills that approach interval level, and
have individual-level measures of socioeconomic
status. Of course, a limitation is that the ECLS-K
studies only follow children seasonally until the
end of first grade (1998) and second grade (2010).

To estimate seasonal patterns beyond second
grade researchers must revert to small-scale local
studies or they can employ an extract of data
from the Growth Research Database collected by
the Northwest Evaluation Association (NWEA).
The NWEA is a private non-profit organization
that partners with school districts to assess children's math, reading, and science skills and then
provides schools with reports of children's progress. The NWEA assesses children both at the
beginning and end of the school year (and sometimes winter), producing a rich seasonally-
collected database of over ten million American
children from kindergarten through twelfth
grade. These advantages are countered, however,
by the fact that the NWEA data are not nationally
representative and each researcher tends to analyze their own unique extract of the overall database, making it a challenge to compare results
from different NWEA-based studies. In addition,
the NWEA data lack individual-level information
on children's socioeconomic status. Finally, children in each school are not necessarily representative of the students in that school. Some
districts, for example, may have tested all students while others may have tested a subset.

3.4.1   Socioeconomic Gaps in Cognitive Skills

There is growing consensus that socioeconomic
(SES) achievement gaps are developed predominantly prior to kindergarten entry (Duncan and
Magnuson 2011; Reardon 2011a). Analyzing the
ECLS-K: 1998, Duncan and Magnuson (2011)
estimate that children from families in the top
SES quintile begin school, on average, 1.26 standard deviation (SD) units ahead in reading and
1.34 standard deviation units ahead in math compared to children from families in the bottom

---

[6]Studying the kindergarten and elementary school years
may offer an additional methodological advantage. Some
evidence suggests that children learn more rapidly during
these early years, about four times faster than during high
school (LoGerfo et al. 2006). It is hard to know if young
children actually learn faster or if this pattern is merely an
artifact of the tests—early tests focus on more basic skills
while later tests focus on the development of subject-specific course knowledge. Regardless of whether these patterns are real or an artifact, they have consequences for
our ability to distinguish the learning "signal" from the
"noise" produced by test measurement error. This issue
becomes especially important when we estimate children's summer learning rates that rely on test scores only
a few months apart. Given the tests that are currently
available, high school students only demonstrate modest
learning gains, making it difficult to estimate learning
accurately during the 9-month school year and even more
difficult to confidently estimate summer patterns. In contrast, young children demonstrate much faster learning
growth on currently available tests, producing a clearer
picture of schools' role.

SES quintile. Moreover, these gaps remain relatively stable throughout the first few years of school, growing only slightly larger to 1.43 SD in reading and 1.38 SD in math by the end of fifth grade. That means that 90% or more of the fifth grade gaps are already in place at kindergarten entry. When it comes to understanding SES-based gaps in math and reading, the early childhood years prior to kindergarten entry are the dominant force.

The fact that the SES gaps grow little once school starts is the major story, but we also learn something by observing whether the gaps grow faster when school is in versus out. Analyzing the ECLS-K: 1998, Downey et al. (2004) clarify that the SES gaps grow faster during the summer months between kindergarten and first grade than the school periods, suggesting that even the modest growth in the SES gap that occurs during the school years is driven primarily by the non-school environment. These findings support previous seasonal research from Baltimore (Alexander et al. 2007; Entwisle and Alexander 1992) and Atlanta (Heyns 1978). The more recent ECLS-K data, collected beginning in 2010, produce a somewhat mixed picture. Schools look compensatory across kindergarten, more neutral during first grade, and may even play a pernicious role during second grade, at least for reading skills (Quinn et al. 2016), raising the possibility that compensatory school effects for socioeconomic status are strongest during kindergarten.[7]

3.4.2 Racial/Ethnic Gaps in Cognitive Skills

Seasonal comparison patterns also can shed light on the role that schools play generating or maintaining racial/ethnic achievement gaps. The Black–White gaps at kindergarten entry are substantial. For the ECLS-K: 1998 cohort, Fryer and Levitt (2004) estimate the gaps to be at 0.64 SD in math and 0.40 SD in reading. Using the more recent 2010 cohort, Quinn (2015) estimates slightly smaller gaps at 0.54 SD in math and 0.32 SD in reading. And compared to the SES gaps, the Black–White gaps increase more as children progress through school (Condron 2009; Fryer and Levitt 2004; Quinn 2015; Reardon et al. 2009), although this growth is modest. Von Hippel and Hamrock (2016) find that, in the ECLS-K: 1998 data, between first and eighth grades, unstandardized Black–White gaps increase by 22% in reading and 6% in math.[8] The majority of the Black–White gap is largely formed before formal schooling begins—highlighting how the early childhood environment plays a critical role in generating the gap.

Once school begins, there is mixed evidence regarding whether the Black–White gap grows faster when school is in versus out. Some scholars find that schools play a role reducing the gap. Heyns' study of sixth and seventh graders in Atlanta noted that the Black–White gap grew faster during the summer than school year (Heyns 1978). However, studies relying on broader samples reach the opposite conclusion. Analyzing kindergartners through eighth graders in 14 states

---

[7]One caveat to the general SES pattern is that NWEA extracts do not always produce consistent results. In the most extensive analysis of seasonal data sets to date, von Hippel and Hamrock (2016) compared patterns across the BSS, ECLS-K: 1998, and an NWEA extract covering 14 states and concluded that "The preschool years are the period of fastest gap growth; after school starts, it is hard to say unequivocally whether gaps grow faster during school or during summer." This impressive analysis reinforces previous findings that most of the gap develops during the early childhood years, but raises questions about whether the SES gaps grow faster during the summers or school periods, once schooling begins. In von Hippel and Hamrock's (2016) study, ECLS-K patterns were consistent with the notion that SES gaps grow fastest when school is out, but the patterns from the NWEA extract were at times contradictory. There are challenges interpreting the NWEA patterns, however. For example, the NWEA lacks an individual-level socioeconomic indicator, and so von Hippel and Hamrock (2016) had to compare school-level gaps across Title 1 and non-Title 1 schools. Another challenge interpreting the NWEA patterns is that various scholars typically analyze unique subsets of the larger Research Growth Database, making replication difficult.

[8]For our purposes, it would be better if this study had estimated how the gaps increase from the beginning of kindergarten rather than first grade, but we know from other studies that the Black–White gap increases only slightly during kindergarten, and so these estimates would only increase slightly.

from the NWEA, von Hippel and Hamrock (2016) report that the Black–White gap tends to grow faster during the 9-month school periods than during the summers. And using the ECLS-K: 1998 data set, Downey et al. (2004) also found that Black students exhibited a similar rate of learning (relative to White students) during the summer after kindergarten, but fell behind during kindergarten and first grade, even after controlling for SES.[9] The more recent ECLS-K: 2010 also suggests that the Black–White gap grows larger during the school years but either stabilizes or narrows during the summer months (Quinn et al. 2016).

The evidence regarding the Black–White gap is mixed, but we think it leans more in one direction—that schools play a pernicious role. We say this because the studies that have found that the Black–White gap grows faster during the school year than summer have relied on broader, more generalizable data than the studies that have found the opposite pattern.

There is also a growing group of studies focusing on the Asian–White gap. These studies provide provocative evidence from the ECLS-K and NWEA surveys that schools may undermine the performance of Asian-American students (Downey et al. 2004; Quinn et al. 2016; Yoon and Merry 2015). In 1998, Asian-Americans began kindergarten with a 0.11 SD advantage in math and a 0.31 SD in reading relative to White students. Nevertheless, the Asian-American advantage begins to fade with the onset of formal schooling, and completely disappears by the end of third grade (Fryer and Levitt 2006). In their seasonal analysis using the ECLS-K: 1998,

Downey et al. (2004) clarify that the decline in the Asian-American advantage occurs during the school year. They found that Asian-American students had higher academic achievement than White students in the first two years of school, but that these advantages were primarily maintained through faster rates of learning during the summer months. Similar patterns are found in the ECLS-K: 2010 for reading, but not for math (Quinn et al. 2016). Asian-American students begin kindergarten with significant advantages in both subjects. Nevertheless, the Asian–White gap in math does not change, while the gap in reading begins to narrow. Furthermore, the seasonal patterns reveal that the reading gap specifically declines during the kindergarten and first grade school years, while Asian students learn at similar or even faster rates than White students during the summer months (Quinn et al. 2016). Beyond second grade, Yoon and Merry (2015) analyzed second to seventh graders in the NWEA data and noted that the decline in the Asian-American advantage mainly occurred during the school year, and Asian-American students recuperated their loss during the summer periods. Although the evidence is still accumulating, there is reason to worry that schools may play a role reducing the educational progress of Asian-American students compared to White students.

The seasonal findings for the Latino–White gap are the most limited and inconsistent. Latino/a students begin school the furthest behind White students. Once schooling begins, however, it is unclear what happens to the gaps; some studies find that gaps begin to close (Fryer and Levitt 2004; Han 2008; Reardon and Galindo 2009), while others find that only the gap in math shrinks while the reading gap remains the same (von Hippel and Hamrock 2016), and some studies find that both gaps remain unchanged (Quinn et al. 2016) Overall, the limited seasonal comparison studies on Latino/a students suggest that schools are compensatory for math, but results for reading are inconsistent. In both ECLS-K data sets and the NWEA, scholars note that the standardized Latino–White gap in math narrows during the school year and grows faster in the summer months, suggesting that schools promote

---

[9]Confusingly, utilizing the same ECLS-K: 1998 data set, one study finds that Black students experience summer setbacks in math (Burkam et al. 2004). Nevertheless, Quinn (2015) clarifies that these contradictory findings result from variation in modeling strategy, test metric, and assumptions about measurement error. Burkam et al. (2004) explored conditional growth and found that Black students who had the same spring scores as White students made slower math gains during the summer, but overall, Black and White students learn at similar rates during the summer and there is little evidence to show that the summer period contributes to the growing Black–White gaps (Quinn 2015).

the educational progress of Latino/a students (relative to White students) (Quinn et al. 2016; von Hippel and Hamrock 2016). On the other hand, these same studies find mixed results for reading, with ECLS-K: 1998 and the NWEA suggesting that summers are responsible for gap growth while the ECSL-K: 2010 indicates that schools are responsible. These divergent findings may be due to the vast heterogeneity within the Latino/a group. For example, one study that disaggregated the group by country of origin reported that certain Latino/a groups (i.e., Central American and Cubans) reach equivalent achievement levels as White students by third grade despite their disadvantaged beginnings (Han 2008).

3.4.3 Gender Gaps in Cognitive Skills

How do schools shape gender gaps in cognitive skills? With respect to math, girls exhibit a modest advantage before kindergarten but then lose that advantage after school starts (Gibbs 2010). Gibbs (2010) differentiates between types of mathematical content to better understand the so-called "reversal of fortunes" that girls experience in terms of math achievement. Using ECLS-B and ECLS-K: 1998 data, he found that girls excelled at less complex math skills throughout childhood, but experienced disadvantages when the content became more complex. These patterns direct our attention to schools as a potential source of the gender gap in math skills.

Patterns for reading skills are different. Girls tend to begin kindergarten with better reading scores than boys and their advantage increases throughout kindergarten. Controlling for ethnicity and poverty, boys are behind girls in reading by 0.17 standard deviation units at the time of kindergarten entry and the gap increases to 0.31 at the end of grade one (Chatterji 2006; Ready et al. 2005). So before turning to seasonal studies, these studies focusing on the growth in the gaps during the first few years suggest that schools may disadvantage girls with respect to math and boys with respect to reading.

Of course, if schools play a unique role in promoting gender gaps, one way or the other, we would expect that gender-based gaps would grow faster when school is in versus out. Notably, seasonal comparison studies have tended to focus their attention on SES gaps, and to a lesser extent, racial/ethnic gaps, while gender gaps have received little attention. Still, in some of the tables from seasonal comparison research we can glean the necessary patterns. In Downey et al. (2004) the authors combined the school period learning rates (kindergarten and first grade) for reading and math and found that, overall, gender gaps operated similarly during the school periods and the summer (Downey et al. 2004, pp. 628–629, Table 4). Similarly, Entwisle and Alexander 1992) analyzed the Baltimore data and reported that seasonal patterns of growth did not vary by child's gender. These two patterns are consistent with the view that schools are not the driving force behind the changes in the gender gap during the first few years of schooling. We are unaware of other seasonal comparison research that compares how the gender gap in skills changes when school is in versus out and so we urge scholars to build greater empirical knowledge in this area.

3.4.4 Overall Variation in Cognitive Skills

An additional way of considering how schools matter is to ask—How does *overall* variation in skills (among all children) change when school is in versus out (Meyer 2016)? As Downey et al. (2004) pointed out, SES, race, and gender explain only a small fraction of the variation in children's skills—less than 10%. Of course, achievement gaps across social groups are of interest, but by analyzing overall variation, we may produce a more comprehensive understanding of how schools influence inequality. Few scholars have considered whether overall variation in skills grows faster when school is in versus out, but the exceptions are revealing. Analyzing the ECLS-K: 1998, Downey et al. (2004) found that variation in cognitive skills grew much faster during the summer versus school year—58% faster for reading and 40% faster for math, patterns replicated in more recent work with the ECLS-K: 2010 (Downey et al. 2017).

3.5 Conclusion

We reviewed studies revealing the magnitude of achievement gaps at kindergarten entry, along with how those gaps change over the next few years, when school is in versus out. The value in this analytic approach is that it more confidently separates school from non-school influences, a major stumbling block for most research designs attempting to understand how schools matter. We acknowledge that this strategy falls short of a comprehensive analysis of the relationship between schools and inequality because we restrict our discussion to children's cognitive skills, and then restrict our focus even further to the first few years of schooling.[10] A broader review would consider a wider range of outcomes and extend into later stages of education.[11] Nevertheless, the patterns from this exercise tell us quite a bit about how large achievement gaps are prior to kindergarten, and what schools tend to do those gaps over the next few years.

The main message from our review is that achievement gaps are well-established prior to kindergarten entry. This pattern highlights how early childhood experiences prepare children unequally and send them on different learning trajectories. Studying achievement gaps in schools has value, of course, but if we want to understand why gaps emerge in the first place, we need to focus more attention on early childhood. With respect to socioeconomic gaps in cognitive skills, the time prior to kindergarten explains the vast majority of why high-SES children outperform low-SES children during the elementary school years. The race and gender gaps are smaller in magnitude than the SES-based gap, but they are also significantly formed prior to the onset of formal schooling. Achievement gaps are often observed in schools, but they are primarily formed by early childhood processes that have little to do with schools (defined by formal schooling available to all).

Another conclusion from this work is that schools do not consistently advantage the already socioeconomically advantaged. There is very little evidence that schools increase SES-based achievement gaps; in fact, they are probably an important compensatory force, especially during kindergarten. We say this because the SES gaps grow when school is out, and are mostly unchanged when school is in. The more children are exposed to schools, the smaller the socioeconomic gaps in skills. Schools, therefore, are probably compensatory, reducing the magnitude of the SES gap we would otherwise observe in their absence. And, when we expand our focus to consider how overall variation in children's skills, schools' compensatory power is even clearer—variation in children's skills grows about 50% faster when out of school versus in.

Our inferences regarding racial achievement gaps are more mixed. There are some indications that schools play a pernicious role. The Black–White gap, for example, grows faster during the first three years of school than during the summers in between, a pattern implicating schools (Downey et al. 2017; Quinn et al. 2016). The strongest evidence that schools undermine the educational achievement of Black students is the

---

[10] It is possible that the patterns we report here, emphasizing kindergarten and the next couple years, are unique and do not apply to later stages of the educational career. Some scholars have questioned whether seasonal patterns persist into high school, for example, where tracking mechanisms may produce greater school-based inequality (Gamoran 2016). It is worth noting, however, that prior to seasonal comparison analysis, most scholars assumed that schools increase achievement gaps, even among young children. Given that seasonal analysis reversed this view, we think it is important to refrain from making a similar mistake before we have seasonal analysis of high schoolers.

[11] It is worth noting that when seasonal comparisons are applied to other dependent variables we also tend to come away with more favorable views of schools. For example, children's body mass index tends to grow about twice as fast during the summer versus school year (von Hippel et al. 2007), and there does not seem to be any consistent pattern to how SES, racial/ethnic, and gender gaps in social-behavioral skills change when school is in versus out (Downey et al. 2016b).

seasonal patterns for the standardized Black–White reading gap using the ECLS-K: 2010. Quinn et al. (2016) finds that while the reading gap grows during kindergarten, first, and second grade, the gap significantly narrows in the two summers in between. In other words, Black students fall behind White students during the school years, but learn at a significantly faster rate than White students during the summer months when they are no longer exposed to schools. There is also evidence that schools reduce the Asian–White gap, which may simply be a product of schools' overall compensatory power, or it may reflect a race-based process within schools that has been inadequately studied.

We also applied our method to gender differences in cognitive skills. There has been considerable discussion about how girls have surpassed boys in school on a wide range of educational outcomes and the role that schools might play in that process (Diprete and Buchmann 2013). Some have suggested that classrooms have become a feminized environment, more conducive to girls' ways of learning. If it were true, we would expect that girls' advantage would grow faster when school is in session than during the summer, but we rarely observe that pattern. Although schools may influence gendered outcomes in later grades, the seasonal patterns during the early grades produce no "school reason" for the gaps.[12]

What does all this mean for how we understand the relationship between schools and inequality? Seasonal comparison methods provide a different, and we believe valuable, way of understanding how schools matter. This window into the relationship between schools and inequality ends up producing a more positive view of

schools than the more traditional methods. This is noteworthy and should cause scholars employing the more traditional methods to reconsider whether schools really exacerbate inequality in the way many have argued. This is not to say that seasonal comparison methods provide the definitive word on how schools matter, but rather that their methodological advantages should prompt a renewed discussion about why some studies tend to describe schools as exacerbatory, while seasonal comparison studies produce a different conclusion.

Of course, if schools play a more favorable role in the stratification system than they are generally given credit for, by what processes are they actually reducing inequality? Sociology of education scholars have created a wide range of plausible mechanisms by which schools might exacerbate inequality, but considerably less theoretical effort has gone into understanding how schools might be compensatory (Downey and Condron 2016). It is difficult to know what these mechanisms might be because seasonal comparison studies do not provide that insight, but we can speculate. We suspect that schools may reduce SES achievement gaps and overall variance in skill because they consolidate children's curriculum experiences (by organizing children by chronological age) more than they differentiate curriculum via ability grouping and tracking. In addition, despite the discriminatory processes uncovered in some research, it may be that teachers generally operate in an egalitarian manner, helping disadvantaged children the most. For example, a national survey of teachers found that, when asked who was most likely to receive one-on-one attention, 80% of teachers said "academically struggling students" while just 5% said "academically advanced" students (Duffett et al. 2008).

Finally, the seasonal results prompt us to reconsider what the most effective school policies might be for reducing achievement gaps. We would support increasing the amount of schooling available to all children because exposure to public schooling appears to reduce socioeconomic achievement gaps and the growth in overall variation in skills. If the U.S. expanded the

---

[12]The three demographic characteristics studied here (socioeconomic status, race/ethnicity, and gender) all produced different seasonal patterns. It is worth noting that socioeconomic status is an indicator of diverse home and neighborhood resources while gender is a socially constructed status largely uncorrelated with these non-school conditions and race/ethnicity has characteristics of both. This distinction may explain why we see the clearest seasonal patterns for socioeconomic status, the weakest for gender, and patterns somewhat in between for race/ethnicity.

number of days children went to school, we would expect that change to benefit low-SES students the most and reduce overall inequality in math and reading skills.[13]

Relatedly, seasonal results have implications for school accountability systems. It is likely that current attempts to isolate teacher or school effects based on student growth from one year to the next are producing biased information. If summer learning loss is variable, then differences in teachers' "effectiveness" gleaned from value-added models partially reflect the families and neighborhoods in which their students live, which are unlikely to be fully accounted for by statistical controls in value-added models.[14] We are unaware of any state that currently employs a value-added accountability method that sufficiently accounts for children's non-school environments. The result is predictable—the real performance of teachers and schools serving disadvantaged children is underestimated. Rather than pressuring the schools that are actually performing poorly to improve, therefore, the information produced by these accountability schemes is as likely to mislead parents as it is to properly inform them about the best-performing schools (Downey et al. 2008).

But our primary message with respect to policy is this: There is only so much schools can do. To make substantial changes to societal-level achievement gaps will require reducing the level of inequality that exists in the non-school environment. We do not share the view of some education scholars that reforms aimed at ameliorating inequality outside of schools are too politically difficult to confront. Instead, we view these broader non-school issues as education policies and we encourage education scholars to start talking about them in this way. For example, decisions regarding access to health care, income inequality, racial and income-based housing seg-

regation, the strength of organized labor, tax policy, immigrant status, mass incarceration, the real value of the minimum wage, unemployment benefits, and family leave options, all have implications for the kind of inequality we have outside of schools (Fischer et al. 1996) and they likely shape the size and malleability of the achievement gaps observed in them (Morsy and Rothstein 2016; Reardon 2011b). It may turn out that broader reform is also a less expensive way to reduce inequality than is school reform. For example, Whitehurst (2016) reports that, for every $1000 in public expenditures, programs aimed at providing poor families with more money (e.g., Earned Income Tax Credit) were six to eight times more effective in promoting disadvantaged children's cognitive skills than were preschool or Head Start programs.

To be clear, we do not suggest that scholars discontinue studying school mechanisms that harm the disadvantaged. This research continues to have value and there are indications that some school reforms would reduce achievement gaps. But when the focus on inequality is overly school-centric, which we believe it currently is, we run the risk of misallocating resources toward school reform while the fundamental source of the problem continues unaddressed. The problem is that school-based solutions to achievement gaps run the risk of distracting us from the kind of broader social reform really needed to reduce inequality.

---

[13]We would worry, of course, about whether racial gaps would increase.

[14]Growth models constructed with 9-month data remove summer noise and correlate only around 0.50 with traditional growth models using 12-month data, demonstrating that summer noise is a nontrivial problem (Atteberry 2011).

References

Alexander, K. L. (1997). Public schools and the public good. *Social Forces, 76*(1), 1–30.

Alexander, K. L., Entwisle, D. R., & Olson, L. S. (2007). Lasting consequences of the summer learning gap. *American Sociological Review, 72*(2), 167–180.

Alexander, K. L., Entwisle, D. R., & Olson, L. S. (2014). *The long shadow: Family background, disadvantaged urban youth, and the transition to adulthood.* New York: Russell Sage Foundation.

Atteberry, A. (2011). *Defining school value-added: Do schools that appear strong on one measure appear strong on another?* Evanston: Society for Research on Educational Effectiveness.

Borman, G., & Dowling, M. (2010). Schools and inequality: A multilevel analysis of Coleman's equality of educational opportunity data. *Teachers College Record, 112*(5), 1201–1246.

Bourdieu, P. (1977). Cultural reproduction and social reproduction. In J. Karabel & A. H. Halsey (Eds.), *Power and ideology in education* (pp. 487–511). New York: Oxford University Press.

Bowles, S., & Gintis, H. (1976). *Schooling in capitalist America: Educational reform and the contradictions of economic life*. New York: Basic Books.

Burkam, D. T., Ready, D. D., Lee, V. E., & LoGerfo, L. F. (2004). Social-class differences in summer learning between kindergarten and first grade: Model specification and estimation. *Sociology of Education, 77*(1), 1–31. Retrieved http://www.jstor.org.proxy.lib.ohio-state.edu/stable/3649401

Chatterji, M. (2006). Reading achievement gaps, correlates and moderators of early reading achievement: Evidence from the Early Childhood Longitudinal Study (ECLS) kindergarten to first grade sample. *Journal of Educational Psychology, 98*(3), 489–507.

Coleman, J. S., et al. (1966). *Equality of educational opportunity*. Washington, DC: Department of Health, Education and Welfare.

Condron, D. J. (2008). An early start: Skill grouping and unequal reading gains in the elementary years. *The Sociological Quarterly, 49*, 363–394.

Condron, D. J. (2009). Social class, school and non-school environments, and Black/White inequalities in children's learning. *American Sociological Review, 74*(5), 685–708. Retrieved http://asr.sagepub.com/content/74/5/685

DiMaggio, P. (1982). Cultural capital and school success: The impact of status culture participation on the grades of U.S. high school students. *American Sociological Review, 47*(2), 189–201.

Diprete, T. A., & Buchmann, C. (2013). *The rise of women: The growing gender gap in education and what it means for American schools*. CUP Services. Retrieved http://www.amazon.com/The-Rise-Women-Education-American/dp/0871540517/ref=sr_1_1?ie=UTF8&qid=1373561211&sr=8-1&keywords=the+rise+of+women

Dobbie, W., & Fryer, R. G. (2011). Are high quality schools enough to close the achievement gap? Evidence from a social experiment in Harlem. *American Economic Journal: Applied Economics, 3*(3), 158–187.

Downey, D. B., & Pribesh, S. (2004). When race matters: Teachers' evaluations of students' classroom behavior. *Sociology of Education, 77*(4), 267–282.

Downey, D. B., & Condron, D. J. (2016). Fifty years since the Coleman report: Rethinking the relationship between schools and inequality. *Sociology of Education, 89*(3), 207–220.

Downey, D. B., von Hippel, P. T., & Broh, B. A. (2004). Are schools the great equalizer? Cognitive inequality during the summer months and the school year. *American Sociological Review, 69*(5), 613–635.

Downey, D. B., von Hippel, P. T., & Hughes, M. (2008, July). Are "failing" schools really failing? *Sociology of Education, 81*, 242–270.

Downey, D. B., Workman, J., & von Hippel, P. (2017, August 15). *Socioeconomic, racial, and gender gaps in children's social/behavioral skills: Do they grow faster in school or out?* Available at SSRN: https://ssrn.com/abstract=3044923 or https://doi.org/10.2139/ssrn.3044923

Downey, D. B., Quinn, D., & Alcaraz, M. (2017). *The distribution of school quality* (Working Paper).

Duffett, A., Farkas, S., & Loveless, T. (2008). *High-achieving students in the era of No Child Left Behind*. Washington, DC. Retrieved http://www.edexcellence.net/detail/news.cfm?news_id=732&id=92

Duncan, G. J., & Magnuson, K. (2011). The nature and impact of early achievement skills, attention skills, and behavior problems. In G. J. Duncan & R. J. Murnane (Eds.), *Whither opportunity: Rising inequality, schools, and children's life chances* (pp. 47–69). New York: The Russell Sage Foundation.

Entwisle, D. R., & Alexander, K. L. (1992). Summer setback: Race, poverty, school composition, and mathematics achievement in the first two years of school. *American Sociological Review, 57*(1), 72–84.

Entwisle, D. R., Alexander, K. L., & Olson, L. S. (1994). The gender gap in math: Its possible origins in neighborhood effects. *American Sociological Review, 59*(6), 822–838.

Fischer, C. S., et al. (1996). *Inequality by design: Cracking the bell curve myth* (1st ed.). Princeton University Press. Retrieved http://www.amazon.com/dp/0691028982

Fryer, R. G., & Levitt, S. D. (2004). Understanding the Black–White test score gap in the first two years of school. *The Review of Economics and Statistics, 86*(2), 447–464. Retrieved http://www.jstor.org/stable/3211640

Fryer, R. G., & Levitt, S. D. (2006). Testing for racial differences in the mental ability of young children. *National Bureau of Economic Research* (Working Paper). http://www.nber.org/papers/w12066

Gamoran, A. (2016). Gamoran comment on Downey and Condron. *Sociology of Education, 89*(3), 231–233. Retrieved December 21, 2016, http://soe.sagepub.com/cgi/doi/10.1177/0038040716651931

Gamoran, A., & Mare, R. D. (1989). Secondary school tracking and educational inequality: Compensation, reinforcement, or neutrality? *American Journal of Sociology, 94*(5), 1146–1183.

Gangl, M. (2010). Causal inference in sociological research. *Annual Review of Sociology, 36*, 21–47.

Gibbs, B. (2010). Reversing fortunes or content change? Gender gaps in math-related skill throughout childhood. *Social Science Research, 39*(4), 540–569.

Han, W.-J. (2008). The academic trajectories of children of immigrants and their school environments. *Developmental Psychology, 44*(6), 1572–1590.

Hanushek, E. A. (1992). The trade-off between child quantity and quality. *Journal of Political Economy, 100*(1), 84–117. Retrieved January 31, 2013. http://www.jstor.org/stable/2138807.

Hayes, D. P., & Grether, J. (1983). The school year and vacations: When do students learn? *Cornell Journal of Social Relations, 17,* 56–71. New York City.

Heyns, B. (1978). *Summer learning and the effects of schooling.* New York: Academic.

Ho, A. D., & Reardon, S. F. (2011). Estimating achievement gaps from test scores reported in ordinal "proficiency" categories. *Journal of Educational and Behavioral Statistics, 37*(4), 489–517. Retrieved April 19, 2014, http://jeb.sagepub.com/cgi/doi/10.3102/1076998611411918

Jencks, C. S. (1972). The Coleman report and the conventional wisdom. In Mosteller, F. & Moynihan, D. P. (Eds.), *On equality of educational opportunity* (pp. 69–115). New York: Vintage. Retrieved https://courses.utexas.edu/bbcswebdav/pid-2031893-dt-content-rid-2384509_1/xid-2384509_1

Jennings, J. L., Deming, D., Jencks, C., Lopuch, M., & Schueler, B. E. (2015). Do differences in school quality matter more than we thought? New evidence on educational opportunity in the twenty-first century. *Sociology of Education, 88*(1), 56–82.

Kozol, J. (1991). *Savage inequalities: Children in America's schools* (1st ptg). New York: Harper Perennial.

LoGerfo, L. F., Nichols, A., & Reardon, S. F. (2006). *Achievement gains in elementary and high school.* Washington, DC: Urban Institute.

Meyer, J. W. (2016). Meyer comment on Downey and Condron. *Sociology of Education, 89*(3), 227–228. Retrieved December 21, 2016, http://soe.sagepub.com/cgi/doi/10.1177/0038040716651679

Morsy, L., & Rothstein, R. (2016). *Mass incarceration and children's outcomes.* Washington, DC: Economic Policy Institute.

Murnane, R. J. (1975). *The impact of school resources on the learning of inner city children.* Cambridge, MA: Ballinger Publishing Company.

Oakes, J. (1985). *Keeping track: How schools structure inequality* (1st ed.). New Haven: Yale University Press.

Quinn, D. (2015). Kindergarten Black–White test score gaps: Re-examining the roles of socioeconomic status and school quality with new data. *Sociology of Education, 88*(2), 120–139.

Quinn, D. M., Cooc, N., McIntyre, J., & Gomez, C. J. (2016). Seasonal dynamics of academic achievement inequality by socioeconomic status and race/ethnicity. *Educational Researcher, 45*(8), 443–453.

Raudenbush, S. W., & Eschmann, R. D. (2015). Does schooling increase or reduce social inequality? *Annual Review of Sociology, 41,* 443–470.

Ready, D. D., LoGerfo, L. F., Burkam, D. T., & Lee, V. E. (2005). Explaining girls' advantage in kindergarten literacy learning: Do classroom behaviors make a difference? *The Elementary School Journal, 106*(1), 21–38.

Reardon, S. F. (2011a). *The widening academic achievement gap between the rich and the poor: New evidence and possible explanations* (pp. 91–116). New York: Russell Sage Foundation.

Reardon, S. F. (2011b). The widening socioeconomic status achievement gap: New evidence and possible explanations. In *Whither opportunity: Rising inequality, schools, and children's life chances* (pp. 91–115). Washington, DC: Brookings Institution.

Reardon, S. F., & Galindo, C. (2009). The Hispanic–White achievement gap in math and reading in the elementary grades. *American Educational Research Journal, 46*(3), 853–891.

Reardon, S. F., Cheadle, J. E., & Robinson, J. P. (2009). The effect of Catholic schooling on math and reading development in kindergarten through fifth grade. *Journal of Research on Educational Effectiveness, 2*(1), 45–87. Retrieved http://www.tandfonline.com/doi/abs/10.1080/19345740802539267

Rothstein, R. (2004). *Class and schools: Using social, economic, and educational reform to close the Black–White achievement gap.* Washington, DC/New York: Economic Policy Institute/Teachers College.

Thernstrom, A. M., & Thernstrom, S. (2003). *No excuses: Closing the racial gap in learning.* New York: Simon & Schuster.

Von Drehle, D. (2010). The case against summer vacation. *Time.*

von Hippel, P. T., & Hamrock, C. (2016). Do test score gaps grow before, during, or between the school years? Measurement artifacts and what we can know in spite of them. *Educational Researcher, 45*(8), 443–453.

von Hippel, P. T., Powell, B., Downey, D. B., & Rowland, N. J. (2007). The effect of school on overweight in childhood: Gain in body mass index during the school year and during summer vacation. *American Journal of Public Health, 97*(4), 696–702. Retrieved November 30, 2014, http://www.pubmedcentral.nih.gov/articlerender.fcgi?artid=1829359&tool=pmcentrez&rendertype=abstract

Whitehurst, G. J. (2016). *Family support of school readiness? Contrasting models of public spending on children's early care and learning.* Evidence Speaks Reports, Vol 1.

Yoon, A., & Merry, J. J. (2015). Understanding the role of schools in the Asian–White gap: A seasonal comparison approach. In *American Sociological Association,* Chicago, IL.

Part II

The Changing Demographics of Social Inequality

Race, Class, and Theories of Inequality in the Sociology of Education

Samuel R. Lucas and Véronique Irwin

Abstract

After explaining a focus on race and class inequality, we briefly sketch contemporary racial and socioeconomic inequality in education. Then, we convey key criteria used to select which of the many theories to consider. We then describe ten theories of racial/ethnic- and class-linked inequality in education. After the last theory has been described, we identify selected points of contact across the theories. We then discuss three examples of existing research to demonstrate how research may be used to assess the theories. We conclude by offering suggestions for next steps.

We thank Jan Jacobs, Susan Schacht (posthumously), H. Sorayya Carr, Aimée Dechter, and Olivia Garcia for many helpful conversations. This research has been supported by funding from the NSF-GRFP (Grant No. DGE 1106400). All errors and omissions are the fault of the authors. Please direct correspondence to Samuel R. Lucas / Sociology Department / University of California-Berkeley / 410 Barrows Hall #1980 / Berkeley, CA 94720-1980 or by e-mail to lucas@berkeley.edu

S. R. Lucas (✉) · V. Irwin
Department of Sociology, University of California-Berkeley, Berkeley, CA, USA
e-mail: lucas@berkeley.edu; virwin@berkeley.edu

4.1 Introduction

Multiple analysts have documented a relation between educational outcomes and students' socioeconomic (e.g., Blau and Duncan 1967; Featherman and Hauser 1978; Sewell and Hauser 1980) and racial/ethnic (e.g., Featherman and Hauser 1978; Jaynes and Williams 1989; Jencks and Phillips 1998) origins. Such works have documented the changing power of class and race/ethnicity, but none have documented the eradication of either effect. Additional research indicates powerful education associations with and effects on multiple individually and societally consequential outcomes, from matters as material as health (e.g., Kimbro et al. 2008) and mortality (e.g., Kitagawa and Hauser 1968) to matters as ideological as political efficacy (e.g., Paulsen 1991) and prejudice attitudes on grounds of sex (e.g., Cherlin and Walters 1981), race (e.g., Bobo and Licari 1989), and anti-semitism (in liberal democracies) (Weil 1985). Because effects of education are wide-ranging, class and racial/ethnic inequalities in education ramify far beyond the realm of schooling. Perhaps owing to the importance of education in individuals' well-being and thus society's capacities, the intransigence of class and race effects on educational outcomes has motivated many analysts to attempt explanations. In the pages below we attend to some of the most widely-researched and/or promising explanations at present.

One could take one of two vantage points for considering the relation between class and education. One approach considers how the socioeconomic position of children's, adolescents', and young adults' families of origin affect children's, adolescents' or young adults' educational trajectories and outcomes. A second approach studies how young adults' education matters for their own placement in the labor force, occupational distribution, and earnings distribution. Both approaches are important, but we will focus on the former because the research claiming racial fluidity (e.g., Saperstein and Penner 2010, 2012) is seriously flawed in the U.S. context (Lucas and Beresford 2010, pp. 32–37; Defina and Hannon 2016; Kramer et al. 2016), making it more correct to consider a persons' race as a factor in their educational trajectories, not as a result thereof. To make our focus consistent, we will address race and class effects on education, not education effects on class or race.

Even so, some theories explain race and/or class effects on education by considering how education affects later class position. Thus, our stark division, while empirically possible, is not necessarily always recognized in the literature. Where necessary, we will follow the theoretical claims, and not enforce an arbitrary narrowing of focus.

We begin by justifying our joint focus on race and class inequality and by providing a brief sketch of contemporary racial and socioeconomic inequality in education. Afterwards, we introduce key criteria used in selecting which of the many theories to consider. Then, ten theories are conveyed. After the last theory has been described, we identify selected points of contact across the theories. In our next-to-final section, we draw on empirical research to show how the theories might be assessed in an effort to trim the list of viable theories. We conclude by offering suggestions for next steps.

4.2 Race and Socioeconomic Status: Processes and Inequalities

Across developed nations, inequalities exist between more and less advantaged students in opportunities (e.g., gifted and talented education (GATE), special education assignments), treatment (e.g., suspensions, expulsions), academic performance (e.g., grades, test scores) and attainments (e.g., years of school completed, college degree attainment, advanced degree attainment). Inequalities can exist along lines of class, race, gender, sexual orientation, disability status, and more. This chapter focuses specifically on the inequalities between students from different socioeconomic and racial/ethnic backgrounds. In this section, we first explain our focus on race/ethnicity and class; afterwards, we convey a snapshot of class and racial/ethnic inequality in education.

4.2.1 Why Race and Class?

The decision to focus on race and class necessarily omits many other factors of great importance. One could justify the decision by noting that it reflects a widespread emphasis on these ascribed characteristics as bases of stratification beyond the school. For social reproduction in education, however, the interest in race and class is more than a historical artifact of the discipline. Particularly in the United States, where public schools are funded through property taxes and students are generally allocated to schools based on the neighborhood in which they live, generations-long patterns of the geographic concentration of disadvantage are amplified in education. Because neighborhoods are segregated along race and class lines rather than along other very important axes of stratification, such as gender, and because construction of school catchment areas can result and has resulted in even more racial/ethnic and class segregation than neighborhoods would actually have (Saporito and Sohoni 2006, 2007), it is especially important to understand how education is implicated in these inequalities.

Race and class, for better or worse, are also key sites of struggle in educational policy reform in the United States. This is especially apparent in postsecondary education, likely because bachelor's degrees long ago replaced high school diplomas as the prerequisite for good jobs (Jencks et al. 1988) while access to the institutions that award those degrees remains more a privilege than a right. Most visibly, race-based affirmative action remains a hotly contested issue. At the same time, reproduction of stratification at these institutions through legacy admissions policies (Howell and Turner 2004), which function as affirmative action for wealthy Whites, occurs almost completely without protest. Therefore, among other reasons, understanding how inequalities along race and class lines play out in education, both before and after matriculation to college, is essential to better inform policy decisions.

4.2.2 Inequalities in Education by Race and Socioeconomic Class: A Snapshot

Every 3 years, the Program for International Student Assessment (PISA) tests the reading, math, and science literacy of 15-year-old students in the 34 nations from the Organization for Economic Cooperation and Development (OECD), along with 31 partner nations/economies. Students' report of their parents' education, occupation, and "classical" cultural material in the home are used to construct an index of economic, social, and cultural status (ESCS). National Center for Education Statistics (NCES) data allow comparison of PISA scores by students' national quartile rank on the ESCS index. With only one exception (students in the second ESCS quartile in Liechtenstein outperform their third quartile peers by a statistically non-significant margin), students from higher-ESCS quartiles perform better in math and reading than their (adjacent quartile) lower-ESCS compatriots in every participating country. Over 90% of country-quartile differences were statistically significant.[1] Carnoy and Rothstein (2013) simi-

Table 4.1 Average scores of U.S. 15-year-old students on 2012 PISA assessments[a]

	Reading		Math		Science	
	Avg.	s.e.	Avg.	s.e.	Avg.	s.e.
OECD Average	496[†]	0.5	494[†]	0.5	501[†]	0.5
U.S. Average[b]	498	3.7	481*	3.6	497	3.8
Percent of students in school receiving free or reduced price lunch[c]						
Less than 10%	559[†]	8.6	540[†]	7.8	556[†]	7
10–24%	524*	5.3	513*	5.7	528*	6.5
25–49.9%	519	6.7	506	6.4	523	5.6
50–74.9%	479*	4.7	464*	4.6	483*	5.0
75% or more	452*	8.5	432*	7.2	442*	8.1
Student race/ethnicity[d]						
White	519[†]	4.1	506[†]	3.7	528[†]	3.7
Black	443*	8.3	421*	6.2	439*	6.8
Hispanic	478*	4.5	455*	4.8	462*	4.7
Asian	550*	8.1	549*	9.0	546*	8.6
Multiracial	517	7.6	492*	7.4	511	7.8

† reference group, * $p < 0.05$
[a]Source: National Center for Education Statistics, Archived International Data Table Library
[b]Significance stars are relative to OECD average
[c]Includes only students in public schools. Significance stars in this portion of the table refer to the difference relative to the FRL group in the immediately preceding row
[d]Significance stars in this portion of the table are relative to White students

larly find that students from higher socioeconomic backgrounds perform better on international assessments in all OECD countries. Thus, while the remainder of the chapter focuses heavily on evidence from the United States, we treat socioeconomic inequalities in education as a universal dilemma.

Table 4.1 demonstrates strong socioeconomic and racial patterns in test performance in the United States. Across all subjects, scores decline steadily as one moves from students who attend schools with the fewest socioeconomically disadvantaged peers to those who attend schools with the most socioeconomically disadvantaged peers. Moreover, because socioeconomic disadvantage

---

[1]Three comparisons were made in each of 65 countries (2nd-1st quartile, 3rd-2nd, and 4th-3rd), for a possible 195 significant within-country quartile gaps in each subject. Non-significant differences were found in only 17 countries for math and 21 countries for reading and generally only in 1 of the 3 comparisons. In all other instances, students in higher quartiles performed statistically significantly better than their adjacent lower-quartile peers on

average. Data from the National Center for Education Statistics International Data Table Library: Table B.1.119 (PISA 2012 Results Table M8) and Table B.1.95 (PISA 2012 Results Table R8).

is measured at the school level, rather than the student level, these figures may underestimate the achievement gap between the most advantaged (wealthy students attending wealthy schools) and most disadvantaged (poor students attending poor schools) students. Black and Hispanic students also underperform relative to their White and Asian peers. Given the relative concentration of Black and Hispanic students in the most socioeconomically disadvantaged schools, these achievement gaps reflect compound disadvantages.

The test scores summarize socioeconomic and racial/ethnic differences in performance, but may not make it clear what differences in test scores mean for differences in students' capabilities. PISA reports also indicate students of different socioeconomic contexts and racial/ethnic backgrounds' distribution along benchmarks of mathematics literacy. Abstracting from the NCES report on PISA (NCES 2013, p. 3), one can summarize the levels as in Table 4.2.

Considering these capability thresholds, Fig. 4.1 sketches the distribution of U.S. 15-year-old students by the proportion of schoolmates eligible for free or reduced price lunch. In Fig. 4.1 (and Fig. 4.2, below), the marks are connected with lines to facilitate recognition of the patterns. Considering the patterns, slightly less than 59% of the students attending schools with one-quarter

Table 4.2 Proficiency levels in mathematics, PISA 15-year-olds

Level	Students are able to
1	"answer clearly defined questions with routine procedures"
2	"make direct inferences and provide literal interpretations"
3	"execute sequential procedures with basic reasoning"
4	"integrate assumptions and connect to real-world arguments"
5	"compare and select strategies to develop complex models"
6	"develop and communicate complex models for novel contexts"

to one-half of students qualifying for free or reduced price lunch exceed performance level 2.

In comparison, nearly 75% of students attending schools with no more than 1 in 10 students in poverty exceed performance level 2. In contrast in hyperpoverty schools, schools with three-quarters or more students in poverty, barely 25% of students exceed level 2. For race/ethnicity, shown in Fig. 4.2, similar disparities are evident.

It is difficult to see how a nation can maintain a productive economy if large numbers of its adolescents do not have the mathematics literacy to execute sequential procedures with basic reasoning. It is difficult to see how future citizens will make well-informed decisions in a democracy if substantial proportions of its adolescents cannot integrate assumptions and connect them to real-world arguments. Thus, failure to reach noted benchmarks, and the race- and class-linked nature of the shortfall, is consequential not only for individuals, but also (perhaps) for society.

Educational stratification occurs not only in performance at a given grade or level of schooling, but in the highest level of education that individuals pursue and complete. While the expansion of the community college in the United States has opened the door to postsecondary education for many low-SES and underrepresented minority students, both enrollment and persistence in college continue to lag for these groups. The first panel of Table 4.3 presents the college enrollment rates of recent high school completers over three decades, with the most recent year chosen to align with the PISA assessments from Table 4.1.[2] The second panel presents degree attainment after 6 years for students who enrolled full-time for the first time in a bachelor's degree program in the 2003–2004 school year. These data, taken from the Current Population Survey (CPS) and Beginning Postsecondary Study (BPS), respectively, show that Black, Hispanic, and lower-income students are not only less likely to enroll in college than their White and higher-SES peers, they are less likely to complete a degree if they do.[3] As with their performance on

---

[2]Recent high school completers are 16- to 24-year-olds who completed high school during the calendar year.

[3]By reporting enrollment and persistence only for *recent* high school completers (CPS) these figures overlook the

Fig. 4.1 Math distribution by school poverty, U.S. 15-year-olds, 2012

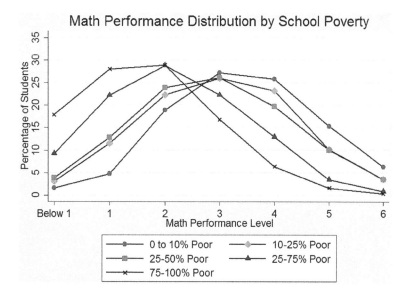

Fig. 4.2 Math distribution by race/ethnicity, U.S. 15-year-olds, 2012

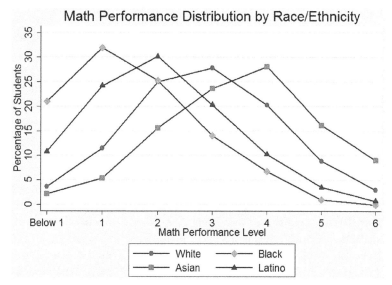

important increase in "non-traditional" college students (CITE). Thus, enrollment rates are likely understated because of the omission of older students, while persistence rates are likely overstated because of the omission of students who begin postsecondary education part-time.

Because percentages have a ceiling of 100% and a floor of 0%, assessing change through percentages is often misleading. Odds ratios provide a better indicator. Odds ratios between High/Mid SES are 2.75, 2.76, and 2.22 across cohorts respectively. Mid/Low SES odds ratios are 1.74, 1.35, and 1.83, and High/Low SES odds ratios are 4.81, 3.74, and 4.05 across the cohorts, respectively. The advantage of High SES students compared to Mid and Low SES students is extremely large.

the PISA assessments, Asian American students outperform White students, both attending and completing college at higher rates.[4]

The tables above report the connection between socioeconomic position and racial/ethnic category on the one hand, and achievement or attainment outcomes on the other. Yet, these outcomes are produced by opportunity and treatment

[4]Degree completion rates may not differ significantly. NCES QuickStats does not provide standard errors for BPS.

Table 4.3 College enrollment and persistence (%)

	Recent high school completers enrolled in 2- or 4-year college[a] (standard errors in parentheses)						Attainment by 08–09 for students starting bachelor's in 03–04[b]		
	1992		2002		2012		BA	AA	Neither
Total	63.2	(0.92)	63.7	(0.78)	66.8	(0.94)	63.2	2.9	33.9
Socioeconomic status[c]									
Low	43.6	(2.60)	50.9	(2.14)	50.3	(2.63)	51.7	2.7	45.6
Middle	57.4	(1.26)	58.4	(1.08)	64.9	(1.26)	64.3	3.6	32.1
High	78.8	(1.38)	79.5	(1.20)	80.4	(1.59)	77.7	1.7	20.6
Race/ethnicity									
White	64.2	(1.06)	66.5	(0.97)	67.6	(1.12)	67.4	3.3	29.3
Black	50.0	(2.98)	57.3	(2.33)	60.5	(2.64)	47.6	2.2	50.2
Hispanic	58.2	(5.04)	54.8	(2.75)	65.9	(1.99)	47.5	2.5	49.9
Asian	–		–		82.3	(3.59)	73.0	0.4	26.6
Other	–		–		–		56.6	2.6	40.8

[a]Source: NCES tabulations from Current Population Survey (CPS)
[b]Source: BPS:2009 Beginning Postsecondary Students, NCES QuickStats
[c]SES for enrollment rates is provided by the CPS simply as "low," "middle," and "high." From BPS these groups are based on dependent students' parental income in 2003–2004 (lowest 25%, middle 50%, highest 25%)

processes within education. If there are class and/or racial/ethnic inequalities in in-school opportunity and treatment, then observed class- and racial/ethnic-linked differences in outcomes are at least somewhat to be expected. Are there opportunity and treatment differences by race and class?

Table 4.4 addresses opportunity, and indicates that White and Asian students are two to three times as likely to enter gifted and talented education (GATE) than are Black students. At the same time, Black students are more likely than White students, and four times more likely than Asian students, to be assigned to special education. And, while in 2009 nearly two-thirds of Asian students enrolled in Advanced Placement courses, less than a quarter of Black students enrolled in Advanced Placement courses. Advanced Placement also tracked with school poverty, as the poorer the school, the less likely students were to enroll in Advanced Placement courses.

Table 4.5 continues the documentation of difference. In 2007, Black students were over 2.5 times more likely to be suspended than were Whites, and over 9 times more likely to be expelled than were Whites, even though research shows Blacks have infraction rates comparable to (e.g., McNulty and Bellair 2003) or lower than (e.g., Bachman et al. 1991) Whites. Poorer

schools also had higher police presence than did wealthier schools, suggesting students in poorer schools engage their learning under the watchful, possibly intimidating, and potentially anxiety-inducing gaze of state surveillance officers. These differences in students' experience of schooling certainly contextualize achievement and attainment differences analysts have documented. Taken together, the information provided in Tables 4.1, 4.3, 4.4, and 4.5 indicate that both processes and outcomes are unequal, and connect in multifaceted and intertwining ways.

Many theories have been advanced to explain the race and class achievement gaps described above. The remainder of the chapter focuses on ten key theories of racial/ethnic and class inequality. We select these theories based on criteria we establish in the next section.

4.3 Theories of Inequality

We focus on theories because they are the tools by which we can interpret the changing facts of inequality. We first convey criteria that all theories of inequality must meet. Then, we describe the characteristics of expansive and narrow theories of inequality.

Table 4.4 Inequalities in opportunity: special education, GATE, and College prep.

	Percent in SPED[a]	Percent in GATE program[b]		Percent of graduates who earned dual credit or AP credit[c]			
				Dual credit		AP courses	
	2007	2004	2006	2005	2009	2005	2009
Total	**4.55**	**6.70**	**6.70**	**8.9**	**9.3**	**28.8**	**36.3**
		(0.05)	**(0.04)**	**(0.60)**	**(0.76)**	**(0.68)**	**(0.94)**
Race/ethnicity							
White	4.03	7.90	8.00	10.0	9.7	29.8	37.3
		(0.07)	(0.07)	(0.73)	(1.00)	(0.86)	(0.95)
Black	6.59	3.50	3.60	4.7	6.4	18.3	22.2
		(0.05)	(0.05)	(0.80)	(0.99)	(0.97)	(1.00)
Hispanic	4.95	4.30	4.20	7.7	10.8	28.5	33.8
		(0.05)	(0.04)	(1.10)	(1.18)	(1.29)	(1.30)
Asian	1.78	11.90	13.10	9.2	9.2	47.2	66.3
		(0.20)	(0.29)	(1.25)	(1.46)	(2.25)	(2.56)
Percent of students in school eligible for free or reduced-price lunch							
Less than 25%	–	–	–	9.8	9.3	32.9	44.9
				(1.32)	(1.56)	(1.27)	(1.72)
25–49.9%	–	–	–	9.6	9.2	24.9	31.3
				(1.31)	(1.25)	(1.16)	(1.40)
More than 50%	–	–	–	5.9	9.1	24.5	28.6
				(1.32)	(1.33)	(1.46)	(1.64)

[a]Figures refer to students of all ages receiving Special Education due to a "specific learning disability" or being "emotionally disturbed" (these subgroups were chosen because they are likely more discretionary than physical disabilities, autism, or "mental retardation"). Source: U.S. Department of Education, Office of Special Education Programs (OSEP), 2007 [NCES Table 8.1b]
[b]Figures refer to elementary and high school public school students in Gifted and Talented Education programs. Source: U.S. Department of Education, National Center for Education Statistics, High School and Beyond Longitudinal Study of 1980 Sophomores (HS&B-So:80/82), "High School Transcript Study"; and 1990, 1994, 1998, 2000, 2005, and 2009 High School Transcript Study (HSTS) [NCES Table 225.30]
[c]Number and percentage of public high school graduates taking dual credit (courses that earn both high school and college-level credit), Advanced Placement (AP), and International Baccalaureate (IB) courses in high school. Source: U.S. Department of Education, National Center for Education Statistics, 2000, 2005, and 2009 High School Transcript Study (HSTS) [Table 225.60]

4.3.1   Theoretical Criteria

We agree with Silberberg (1990, p. 10) that "A theory, in an empirical science, is a set of explanations or predictions about various objects in the real world." For claims to coalesce into a theory five criteria must be met. First, the claims must reference *conceptual* entities (e.g., classes, ethnic groups). These entities are conceptual in that no pure example of the entity may exist. For example, essentialists notwithstanding, no member of an ethnic group is *only* a member of an ethnic group. Consequently, one can never attain the *pure* form of the conceptual entity. Even so, to be a theory one or more claims must reference conceptual entities.

Second, it must be possible to map the conceptual entities to observable entities or phenomena. Were this not possible evaluation of the theory would also be impossible. Indeed, if one cannot map conceptual entities to observed entities, doubt arises as to whether the statements are relevant for the real social world.

Third, the claims, once mapped onto real entities, must imply some observable patterns, events, outcomes that may or may not pertain. That is, there must be multiple possible states of affairs, and the claims and the mapping must imply at least one fewer state of affairs than is otherwise possible. In other words, the implications must be falsifiable.

Fourth, the postulates cannot be internally contradictory. One cannot claim, for example, that $A = B$, $B = C$, and $C \neq A$. If a set of claims are internally contradictory it is impossible to assess the veracity of the claims.

Table 4.5 Inequalities in treatment: discipline and indicators of potential discipline[a]

	Suspended		Expelled	
	2003	2007	2003	2007
Total[b]	**20.4**	**24.5**	**3.9**	**3.2**
White	18.1	17.7	3.2	1.1
Black	30.2	49.0	8.5	10.3
Hispanic !	21.9	26.5	3.6	4.1
Asian/Pacific Islander !!	11.6	12.8		
	2011–2012			
	Random metal detector checks		Daily presence of police or security	
	(%)	se	(%)	se
Total (public schools)[c]	**5.0**	**(0.32)**	**28.1**	**(0.51)**
Less than 25%	1.9	(0.45)	26.3	(1.39)
26–50%	2.2	(0.40)	24.1	(0.99)
51–75%	5.3	(0.65)	25.8	(1.21)
76 or More	9.5	(0.88)	36.2	(1.52)

! Interpret "expelled" data with caution. The coefficient of variation (CV) for this estimate is 30% or greater
!! Interpret "suspended" and "expelled" data with caution. The coefficient of variation (CV) for this estimate is 30% or greater
[a]Tables included both discipline and potential indicators because statistics (from public-use data) were available only broken down by either race or class for each
[b]Total includes other racial/ethnic groups not shown separately. Source: U.S. Department of Education, National Center for Education Statistics, Parent and Family Involvement in Education Survey of the National Household Education Surveys Program (PFI-NHES), 2003 and 2007
[c]Source: U.S. Department of Education, National Center for Education Statistics, Schools and Staffing Survey (SASS), "Public School Principal Data File" and "Private School Principal Data File," 2011–2012

Fifth, the postulates cannot be tautological. One cannot claim, for example, that A = B, and B = A. If a set of claims are tautological, nothing is gained by assessing the claims.

Sociological theories are usually conveyed informally, in words alone. Formalization of theories—often their translation from words to mathematical relations—can make it easier to see and root out tautologies and contradictions. The dearth of formalization means that it is possible that some claims offered as a theory may someday be shown to fail to satisfy one or more of the criteria above. However, without formalizing the theories, we use these criteria to select theories for attention.

4.3.2 Characteristics of Expansive and Narrow Theories

The most expansive theories of inequality are general, dynamic, and identify mechanisms. The narrowest theories of inequality are specific, static, and merely correlational.

Generality What we call *specific* theories apply to only one outcome and/or apply to only one categorical system. In contrast, general theories of inequality apply to multiple outcomes and multiple categorical systems. So, for example, a specific theory might explain only class inequality in test scores, which is less general than a theory that explains inequality with respect to both class and race in test scores and college entrance. Parsimony is a valued criterion for theories to satisfy and, all else equal, a general theory that explains multiple outcomes for multiple social divisions is more parsimonious than is the sum of specific theories needed to explain each single outcome for each social division.

Dynamics All theories of inequality focus on some form of the XY relation in Fig. 4.3. The

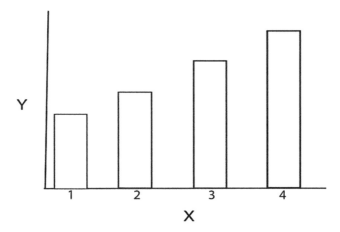

Fig. 4.3 Re-labeling positions in a less than fully enlightening way
A: X = Class categories, 1 = underclass, 2 = working class, 3 = small proprietor, 4 = capitalist
B: X = Racial/ethnic groups, 1 = Blacks, 2 = Latino/as, 3 = Whites, 4 = Asians
C: X = Amount of financial resources, 1 = None, 2 = A little, 3 = Some, 4 = A lot
D: X = Enjoys school, 1 = None, 2 = A little, 3 = Some, 4 = A lot
E: X = Number of teachers certified, 1 = None, 2 = A few, 3 = About half, 4 = Almost all

relation may be linear or curvilinear; positive or negative; and reflected in a bar graph as in Fig. 4.3 (for categorical X variables), in a line-graph (for continuous X-variables), or in other ways. Given our focus, in Fig. 4.3 X might indicate parents' class category, and Y might be measured achievement (e.g., test scores). Note, before we proceed, that the bars *summarize* the relationship. Surely, some persons in category 1 on X obtain higher Y than the bar indicates. Some persons in category 1 on X obtain lower Y than the bar indicates, too. The claim is not that every person is right at the level of the bar; the claim is that the bars summarize differences in the averages for persons located in different positions on X. If there were no average differences, all the bars would be the same height, and Y would be mean independent of X (Goldberger 1991, pp. 61–63), suggesting no causal effect of X on Y.

The differences in the heights of the bars reflect the relationship between X and Y, and that relationship is the fundamental matter to be explained. Many claims focus so much on the specific relationship in the data that the explanations threaten to provide mere substitute labels for the observed relation. So, for example, notes A and B in Fig. 4.3 reflect two variables known to be associated with education outcomes. Note C makes the very plausible claim that financial resources are associated with education outcomes. However, as an explanation of the XY relation, the claim in note C simply replaces 1, 2, 3, and 4 class categories with labels for financial resources: None, A little, Some, and A lot.

The explanation that children who attend schools that match their culture do better may be offered to explain racial differences in achievement. But, again, this threatens to simply substitute note D for note B. A similar substitution—for notes A and/or B—is offered by note E.

True though the claims expressed in notes C, D, and E may be, the simple re-labeling does not take us very far or, rather, it takes us in one possibly helpful direction, but not in another one. A simplistic example may make the point. The re-labeling may take us to an assessment of what an individual student with a given value of X might do to perhaps change their prospects on Y. If students in category two average lower achievement than their category three peers, the re-labeling by note D suggests that category two students might deepen their familiarity and understanding of the culture of the school, and then their performance on Y might improve. Or, if one is uncomfortable with a blaming the victim approach, one could use the re-labeling of note D to claim that schools attended by mostly category two students should become more culturally matched to that specific population of students. Note that both counsels *leave the relation intact; both simply change the score on "cultural match" for some students in some schools.*

The direction the re-labeling does not go is toward telling us why the heights of the bars are sloped as they are, and not more equal (flatter sloped) or less equal (steeper sloped). To determine what makes slopes steepen or flatten is a complex matter, but one essential part of the task requires embedding any single claim in a coherent web of claims. Together such a web would provide resources to aid us in understanding the *dynamics of inequality*, not simply offer a possibly tautological, often highly individualistic re-labeling of observed patterns.

To clarify, there are, of course, multiple kinds of change. Claims about inequality necessarily address at least one. Panel 1 of Fig. 4.4 traces the most common kind of change claim-sets reference. The variable X represents the variable along which inequality is a concern; for example, in our work the X-dimension could be socioeconomic status/class. The Y-variable, therefore, would be the outcome that is distributed unequally—in our case it may be measures of educational attainment (years of schooling, proportion obtaining a bachelor's degree), cognitive achievement, or some other education treatment or outcome. In Panel 1 entities at point A on X have certain values on Y; moving an entity from point A to point B will give them higher (expected) values on Y. This is the most common kind of change inequality analysts address. We term this kind of change *cross-sectional change*, which should signify that difference between persons at points A and B, *not* change (i.e., *not* movement from point A to point B), has actually been studied.

In Panel 2 entities at point A move to point A′, while entities at point B move to point B′. Both moves in Panel 2 constitute change, but obviously the order of the entities on Y remains *un*changed, and, indeed, the amount of inequality

Fig. 4.4 Types of change

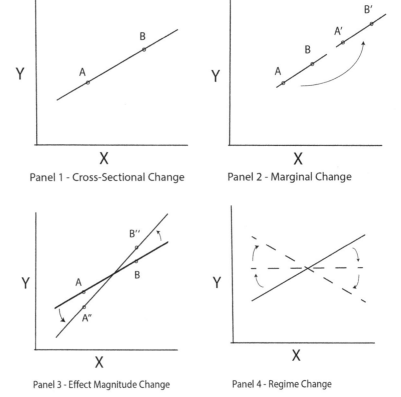

Panel 1 - Cross-Sectional Change

Panel 2 - Marginal Change

Panel 3 - Effect Magnitude Change

Panel 4 - Regime Change

is also unchanged. Essentially, what changes in Panel 2 is the marginal distributions of X and Y. Both X and Y are higher after the change. However, the relation between them is unchanged. We term this kind of change *marginal change* because all that has changed is the marginal (i.e., univariate) distributions of X and Y.

An example of marginal change might be helpful. If all prices, including the price of labor (i.e., wages) and capital, doubled, everyone would receive 100% more for any sale and everyone would have to pay 100% more for anything they buy. Everyone would have twice as much money as now, but no one would be richer or poorer, as the relation between all prices (as well as everyone's ability to pay) would be unchanged.

Panels 1 and 2 do not contain the kind of change we mean when we indicate that a theory will be dynamic. A dynamic theory is one that can account for possible shifts in the structure of inequality. Panels 3 and 4 more accurately reflect the criterion. In Panel 3, the slope of line AB shifts, which is reflected in line A″B″. We term this kind of change *effect magnitude change*. And, in Panel 4, the slope of the line shifts so much as to reverse the relationship between X and Y, from positive to negative. Such shifts are rare and momentous. For example, the Russian revolutions of 1917 altered the relationship between support for the czar and attainment of cushy occupational positions, taking it from positive to negative. In this sense, such shifts often reflect regime changes; thus, we term this kind of change *regime change*. We present both Panels 3 and 4 to convey that deciding whether a regime has changed is not always straightforward, for it raises the question—how much change in quantity can occur before a change in quality pertains?

The answer to that question must be specific to the issue in question and the theories under consideration. For example, a Marxist could claim that a regime change has occurred if the relationship between capitalist class origins and outcomes moves from above zero (positive) to below zero (negative).[5] But, there is nothing

magical about *zero*; it only appears to be the magic number for three chained reasons. First, few social theories calibrate their claims precisely. Second, this means that most theories cannot attach numeric values that will signal important thresholds of change. Third, because of this, most theories are stated in terms or translated into terms of whether statistical relations are positive or negative, thus institutionalizing zero as the key criterion for extracting conclusions concerning a theory. This is clear in that if there were a theory of the nation-state which, once traced precisely, implied that the simple regression coefficient summarizing the XY relation will fall between 1 and 1.5 in "true" welfare state economies, but be higher in laissez-faire economies, observing the coefficient shift over a decade from 1.2 to 1.8 would signify a regime change, from welfare state to laissez-faire. Consequently, just as dynamic theories address changes *within* a regime, more fully dynamic theories also address regime change—they identify thresholds of regime change, and they identify the mechanisms that cause or prevent the crossing of those thresholds. Thus, both Panels 3 and 4 indicate that expansive theories will address the causes of the direction and size of the slope and its change over time, and, given the tenets of the theory and their precision, some more fully dynamic theories can signify regime change.

Microfoundational Mechanisms Relatedly, expansive theories will identify the specific microfoundational mechanisms underlying the XY relation. Inequality is produced and/or maintained by humans acting consciously or unconsciously. Expansive theories are not satisfied with simply observing a correlation between X and Y, nor with simply substituting other terms for the value labels of X. Expansive theories seek to explicitly state the desires, beliefs, opportunities, and actions (Hedström 2005) that coalesce to constitute the microfoundations upon and through which all social entities—institutions, norms, extraindividual structures—are ground, the mechanisms through which they activate their complex, often nonlinear effects. The task is tricky, because the theory must attend to the real

---

[5]The Marxist might also say that the relationship will be below zero for some specified time, then return to zero.

motivations of real persons even as the theory itself constitutes an abstracted model of the processes at issue. The difficulty of this task may partly explain why the number of expansive theories is dwarfed by the number of narrow theories.

4.3.3   Theories Expansive and Narrow

An expansive theory of inequality will explain multiple outcomes, will explain those outcomes for multiple categorical systems, will explain stasis and change in the XY relation, and will identify the microfoundational mechanisms underlying both static and dynamic relations of interest. The fewer of those features a theory has, the narrower it is.

Certainly, narrow theories have their value. First, a narrow theory is more finely focused, easing empirical assessment. Second, being more focused, a narrow theory is likely to more closely match empirical observation than will an expansive theory. Third, narrow theories can be used as building blocks for more expansive theories.

However, the focus of narrow theories means that one requires many such theories to explain broad phenomena such as inequality in education. As education involves many outcomes, there is insufficient space to survey the set of narrow theories applicable to important outcomes, much less do so for both race- and class-based inequality. Consequently, our review attends only to major expansive theories of inequality. We treat genetics/epigenetics, human capital theory, the Wisconsin social-psychological model, credentialism, structural Marxism, cultural capital theory, (what we label) incorporation theory, oppositional culture theory, relative risk aversion, and effectively maintained inequality. We begin with genetics/epigenetics.

4.4   From Incoherent Genetics to Epigenetics

Old-style biogenetic theorists see educational attainment and achievement as driven by ability, see ability as driven by genes, and see genes as determined by one's parents (e.g., Jensen 1969; Herrnstein and Murray 1994). To complete the circle, assortative mating, the tendency of mating pairs to contain people of similar levels of education (Kalmijn 2001; Schwartz and Mare 2005), occupation (Kalmijn 1994), and earnings (Sweeney and Cancian 2004), reinforce genetics-based ability differences by race and class (Herrnstein and Murray 1994).

Such old-school views have not been informed by more recent genetic research. Geneticists have long seen DNA as the basic building block of life. However, for DNA (a genotype-level phenomenon) to matter in a living organism (a phenotype) it must be expressed. How DNA is expressed and what determines its expression is a cutting edge area of early twenty-first century research. Notably, epigeneticists have found that determinants of gene expression are directly affected by the environment. An important, crucial finding of this research is that organisms pass not just the DNA, but *the proclivity for expression* to the next generation. Far from deepening the determinism of DNA, this new evidence explains the crucial importance of environment while providing a more precise specification of the mechanisms underlying evolution.

What is meant by *gene expression*? Analogically, imagine one has one blueprint for a 3-bedroom house. One builds two houses in different environments. One house is built on flat terrain in an earthquake zone, while the other is built on sloped terrain in a seismically stable zone. To express the 3-bedroom house blueprint in the former environment one will have to bolt the house to the foundation, while in the latter terrain one may have to sink stilts into the hill on which part of the house may rest. The blueprint, by itself, is insufficient to determine the actual realization of the house in any environment. But the differing elements of each realized house— bolted foundation or stilts—are intrinsic elements without which the house would not be viable for the length of its otherwise designed life. Similarly, DNA, by itself, does not fully determine the actual realization of the living being in any environment. The blueprint analogy is clarifying in that it shows that DNA is insufficient to describe a particular living organism. Yet, the blueprint analogy is incomplete in that it misses an important implication—epigeneticists are finding that humans, other mammals, and insects experience certain environments that, through identifiable hormonal pathways, affect DNA expression, such that the resulting phenotypes are visible in multiple later generations even after the environment changes (e.g., Lumey 1992).

This epigenetics research means that the nature–nurture dichotomy at the center of the effort to emphasize biological rather than social factors is even more unsustainable than critics have usually maintained. Analysts have already established that the statistical separation of outcomes into that owing to genes and that owing to environment is impossible because genes and environment intertwine to produce observed outcomes (e.g., Daniels et al. 1997). New findings from epigenetics go farther, suggesting that the very expression of an organism's DNA is affected by environment, and thus the environment fundamentally produces the way in which the very genetic code of the organism is translated into material existence and, in this way, produces the biological endowment of the progeny of that organism (e.g., Meaney 2010). Such research implies that the claim that genes set a limit on the power of social factors will finally be revealed to have been as fundamentally mistaken as opponents (e.g., Fischer et al. 1996) of that view have oft maintained. Indeed, it appears that social factors, including education, not only may nurture native ability, but they may cause the very "native" ability they later nurture.

The old genetics literature made many assertions about education, often calling for the sad but sober acceptance that nothing could be done in the face of the alleged overwhelming power of genetics. The literature on epigenetics has yet to address inequality in education. But the evidence on other issues suggests a much more hopeful posture is warranted. Indeed, such evidence suggests that a society's level of cognitive performance, as well as inequality in that performance, is a direct function of the society's tolerance for substandard and unequal environments. The theory identifies a key mechanism, hormonal pathways involving gene expression, and how change can occur through those mechanisms. And, because epigenetically-informed genetic theories of education potentially address all outcomes, the theory promises to be general. But, to date, the research steps needed to realize the theory's promise has not commenced for education.

4.5 Human Capital Theory

Human capital theory makes sense of race and class inequality in education, the role of class in inequality in education, and the intergenerational transmission of inequality. The theory posits the following relations. First, adults' ability and prior investment drive adults' productivity (e.g., output per unit of time, quality of product per unit of inputs). Investment thus generates a later income stream. Although some versions of the theory focus solely on education and material earnings, the broader version Becker (1962) offers considers multiple kinds of human capital investment (e.g., migration, health care) as well as both material and psychic income. The broader Becker definition is the one we consider here.

Human capital exists along a continuum anchored at one point by general human capital and at the other by specific human capital. In the extreme general human capital raises persons' productivity in all firms, while at the other extreme specific human capital raises persons' productivity in one firm, only. Reading provides an example of a skill closer to the general human capital pole, while the Byzantine procedures for requesting a blackboard for a classroom at the University of California-Berkeley provide an example of a skill closer to the specific human capital pole, i.e., of arguably absolutely no value outside the specific campus. Firms are unlikely to pay for general human capital acquisition (e.g., literacy) because if the person so-aided quits the job, some other firm would recoup the returns to the first firm's investment. But, the closer the training is to the specific (i.e., firm-specific) pole, the fewer firms can gain from the investment, and thus the more likely a firm will pay at least some part of the cost of the human capital investment. Thus, in the face of temporary downturns in firm performance, firms are less likely to temporarily lay-off those with specific human capital, because once the downturn ends the firm might be unable to rehire the laid-off workers, for many may have found other employment, thereby forcing the firm to pay to assess and hire new employees and then bring new hires up to the same level of specific human capital attainment the laid-off workers had formerly reached. Instead, firms are likely to lay-off those with general human capital. One way that these relations explain the positive association between education and employment is that specific human capital typically builds on general human capital, such that those with specific human capital typically have higher overall education.

Human capital resembles other investments in that the longer persons have to accrue income from the investment, the more likely they are to make the investment. To make an investment the investor must have resources sufficient to pay the costs of the investment. The costs are both direct (e.g., tuition) and indirect (e.g., time). The latter is interesting in reference to human capital because in order to make the investment the investor must spend the time in the activities that embody the investment, and thus must forego any gains that would accrue to spending time in some other activity. The theory phrases this claim in terms of foregone income; the classic example is that in order to attend school full-time a college student must forego the earnings they would have obtained had they taken a paying full-time job. The foregone earnings are added to the cost of tuition and fees to produce the total cost of college attendance. Notably, the above explains why younger persons are more likely to invest in education, for older workers have average higher earnings than younger workers and thus foregone earnings costs are lower for younger persons.

Human capital theory contends that if persons lack money or credit (i.e., loans) to enable them to pay the direct and indirect (i.e., opportunity) costs of an investment, they may fail to make investments they otherwise might make. In this way human capital theory has direct implications for class inequality. First, and most notably, persons with insufficient resources face financial (or credit) constraints that prevent investment and thereby reduce their later productivity. This challenge becomes an intergenerational one in that children's credit constraint or lack thereof is a downstream implication of the resource limitations or non-limitations of their parents (Tomes 1981; Becker and Tomes 1986). Becker and Tomes (1986) show that only children of wealthy parents do not face credit constraints; children of middle-income and poor parents do face credit constraints that hinder their ability to make optimal human capital investments. In this way human capital theory suggests and explains a high association between parent and child educational attainment. Indeed, as ability is a realized phenomenon partly produced by early childhood socialization, part of the inequality generated by differences in ability are also arguably produced through family differences in human capital, such that even the ability pathway is partly a function of inequality in human capital.

Human capital theory offers many ways to explain racial/ethnic inequality in education. First, if racial/ethnic groups differ in wealth, credit constraints may produce lower investment for members of poorer racial/ethnic groups independent of their ability. Second, if members of a racial/ethnic group are more likely to doubt access to the occupational positions that would allow them to reap the returns of additional investment, perhaps owing to current or historic discrimination (Loury 1992), then the average human capital investment of members of that racial/ethnic group would be expected to be lower than that for others. Third, if different racial/ethnic groups have different health profiles and life expectancies, members of groups with worse health and/or shorter life expectancies should be expected to invest less in education because they will have less time to accrue the benefits of that education.

This third pathway may seem odd to some who doubt that children look into the future, see dim life expectancy prospects, and then reduce their investment in education. But such a criticism caricatures the human capital logic while ignoring the literature on children's decision-making. Recall that human capital investment imposes opportunity costs in the form of other activities in which one cannot engage while making the investment. Those opportunity costs could entail foregone leisure. Seen in this way, a key reason to forego a benefit in the short term is to obtain a larger benefit in the long-term. Given that some communities may have higher than average doubt there will be sufficient time to obtain later long-term benefits (owing, perhaps, to long-running poor access to or experience with the health care system (e.g., Jones 1981; McBean and Gornick 1994)), the theory suggests that people in those communities will invest less in human capital, on average.

Intriguingly, the empirical evidence is consistent with this third pathway. Research indicates that not only are adolescents who doubt they will live to age 35 more likely to begin selling drugs, but also, the higher the proportion of schoolmates who doubt reaching age 35, the more likely the adolescent is to begin selling drugs (Harris et al. 2002). These findings are consistent with the third pathway above.

The clear generality of human capital theory does not imply only as grim conclusions as the above empirical relations may suggest, for the theory contains the possibility of change. If investment returns and/or financial constraints change, inequality will likely change, too. With respect to the role of race and class inequality in education outcomes, changing the financial constraints to investment can alter the role of race and class in educational attainment and achievement. And, with respect to the role of education in producing class inequality, changing the returns to education can, by definition, alter the role of education in class inequality. However, the direction of any change in either case depends on implementation and other factors beyond (but perhaps related to) human capital theory. For example, whether reducing financial constraints on early childhood education will raise or lower race and/or class inequality may depend on the means by which the financial constraints are reduced, how widespread the reduction is, and how childcare and education providers respond to the reduction.

4.6   Wisconsin Social-Psychological Model

The Wisconsin Social-Psychological Model of Status Attainment (aka the Wisconsin model) addresses race and class inequality in educational attainment, placing a social-psychological factor at the center of the process of educational attainment, occupational success, and earnings (e.g., Sewell and Hauser 1980; Hauser et al. 1983). The *key* factor in the Wisconsin model is significant others' influence, for the theory asserts that a primary conduit of social background factors' (e.g., parents' earnings) causal effect on later outcomes works through this chokepoint.

Figure 4.5 reveals the structure of the claims at the conceptual level. Both academic performance and family socioeconomic position—measured by parents' education, father's occupation, and family income—cause significant others' influence, which is measured via students' report of their parents' and teachers' encouragement for college and peers' plans for college. Significant others provide the main conduit through which social background has its effects on adult outcomes, and the effect runs through children's educational aspiration, occupational aspiration, and educational attainment.

Class inequality in producing educational attainment is referenced in the models' relating parent status characteristics to the encouragement of parents, teachers, and peers. But the relation can be explained in one of two ways. One view claims the theory asserts that socioeconomically advantaged parents socialize their children to succeed in school and this leads teachers and peers to encourage those children to seek higher levels of education and occupational success (Kerckhoff 1976). An alternative view claims that teachers respond more positively to socioeconomically advantaged students and that parents select socioeconomically advantaged contexts (e.g., neighborhoods) such that their children's peers will also be encouraging in a matter-of-fact manner. In such neighborhoods it is as obvious that college entry follows high school completion as it is that

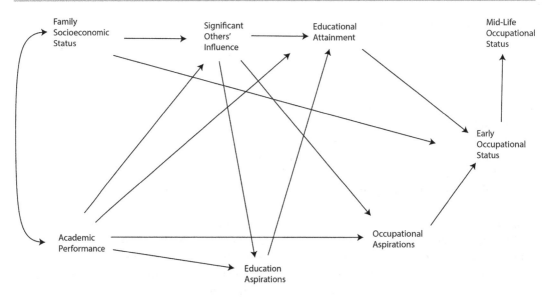

Fig. 4.5 Wisconsin model, trimmed structural version. (Adapted from Table 1, Hauser et al. 1983)

February follows January—for children with such peers, both "truths" are so true that comment on their truth is almost non-existent. The theory, thus, identifies social-psychological connections that link parental sociodemographic characteristics to children's educational and occupational expectations and outcomes. But the explanatory basis of the linkage remains under study.

With respect to race, a key question the theory poses is whether the process works the same for different racial groups—where to work the "same" is reasonably interpreted as structural coefficients being equal across groups. The evidence of whether the process works the same across races is unclear, however. Some research finds similarity (e.g., Wolfle 1985); some does not (e.g., Kerckhoff and Campbell 1977); and some claims the highly variable statistical methods, sample designs, and populations studied undermine any general answer to the question (e.g., Gottfredson 1981), a conclusion that unfortunately has not changed in the intervening decades (e.g., Morgan 2004). What can be noted is that the Wisconsin model provides an encompassing perspective within which one may assess racial inequality, socioeconomic inequality, and other sociodemographic grounds for inequality (e.g., gender).

4.7 Credentialism

Credential theory comes in two variants. One perspective, which we term the *non-linear effects* version, simply highlights the empirical evidence that the earning gains are boosted for obtaining a credential over and above the gain persons accrue owing to the completion of an additional year of schooling. At major credential-completion years, such as college graduation (e.g., Goodman 1979; Grubb 1992, 2002), analysts have observed such non-linearities.

Collins (1974, 1977, 1979) offers what we term a *monopolization process* version, which is a more complex version of the theory that subsumes the possible non-linear effects of credentials into a wider discussion of the genesis of specific credentials as markers of earnings-enhancement. Collins (1979) argues that credentials are the result of and resource for a joint, complex process of ethnic status competition and occupational professionalization.

It is well-known that members of a field that successfully secures the designation "professional" obtain earnings and other advantages (Klegon 1978). One mechanism that can increase earnings is professionals' control of certification to practice the profession, as professions generally obtain largely independent control of certification (Greenwood 1957) on the argument that only they, guided by a code of ethics, have sufficient expertise to evaluate competence and recognize appropriate conduct of the discipline (Mitchell and Kerchner 1983).

In a context of ethnic competition, in which ethnic groups attempt to dominate particular occupational niches, the resources of professionalization are quite useful. The ability of professions to certify practitioners facilitates reducing competition between co-ethnic peers, just as the same resource facilitates reducing competition between professional colleagues. Notably, controlling the certification process facilitates maintaining scarcity as well as barring persons whose sociodemographic category will lower the status of the profession. Maintaining scarcity and the social status of practitioners can help erect a floor beneath earnings for the profession.

Schools enter this process as a cite for certification, but schools are not independent because for a field designated as a profession the faculty involved in teaching the material will themselves tend to be certified practitioners. Consequently, professions and would-be-professions turn to the school—first the high school, then the colleges, and later (perhaps) post-graduate institutions—to certify at least some stages of the training deemed necessary. This position becomes clearer upon noting that the placement of occupational training inside schools is a historically recent phenomenon (Benavot 1983, p. 64; Jacoby 1991).

This variant of credentialing theory identifies the role of signaling amongst firms as key to explaining why firms make college (for example) a prerequisite even for jobs whose tasks (e.g., filing, keyboarding, simple mathematics) do not require college training. Basically, firms signal their quality to important others (e.g., clients, regulators) by requiring high levels of education for even many rudimentary jobs.

The stark nonlinear effects version of credentialism theory is more directly focused on how education affects class (e.g., earnings, wealth). But, because the broader monopolization process variant highlights class- and ethnic-based efforts to erect barriers to entry and monopolize occupa-

tional niches, it focuses on both race/class effects on education and later education effects on class. Because monopolizers can extract rents (Sørensen 2000)—payment over and above the level of productivity—and non-monopolizers cannot, credential theory implies an increase in inequality along lines of race and class. Notably, by linking processes assigning earnings to occupations (e.g., firms' reward structures), prerequisites (e.g., education credentials) to positions (e.g., jobs), and racial/ethnic closure, this more complex version of credentialism theory becomes potentially relevant for the intergenerational transmission of inequality.

4.8 Structural Marxism

In *Schooling in Capitalist America*, Bowles and Gintis (1976) investigate the function of education in social reproduction. They argue that, rather than developing cognitive skills that foster meritocratic social mobility, the primary function of the school is to prepare students for work in (their ascribed status in) the capitalist labor market. They support this argument in three ways. First, although cognitive skills are important in the labor market, they show that this only partly explains the advantage attributed to more years of education, with personality traits signaling conformity having notable additional effects (Bowles and Gintis 1976, pp. 137–139). Second, children reproduce their parents' socioeconomic status at rates that could not be fully explained by either their inherited cognitive advantage or by the elite educational opportunities they are afforded. Finally, the authors argue that historically in the United States, periods of school reform have tracked periods of change in the structure of labor.

Based on these patterns, Bowles and Gintis argue that education prepares students for the stratified labor market through what they call the *correspondence principle*. The correspondence principle refers to the parallel between the social relations of labor and the social relations of education. In the capitalist context the correspondence principle implies that schools inure students to the types of hierarchical relationships that are characteristic of corporations. Rather than cooperation, students are encouraged to compete—or, more accurately, made to believe they are engaged in meritocratic competition—for the few spots at the top, and only those who secure these school positions are given the tools for autonomy and advanced critical thinking reserved for the capitalist elite. Rather than fostering an actual meritocracy, schools reinforce students' place in the educational hierarchy beginning at a very young age and, by "correspondence," cultivate the impression that workers arrive in the only position in the hierarchy of production for which they are inherently qualified.

Melvin Kohn and colleagues (e.g., Kohn and Schooler 1969) highlight a similar correspondence between men's occupation and the values they hold for their children, such that upper-class men value self-direction, a useful orientation in jobs that, within circumscribed limits, require creativity. In contrast, working-class men value conformity and rule-following, an essential orientation given the much more constraining coercion of the shop floor. Kohn implicates education in the formation and maintenance of these values insofar as it provides the space for intellectual flexibility for some students and fails to provide it for others, foreshadowing Bowles and Gintis' correspondence principle. Put together, these theories suggest that working-class students are not only less likely to be given the opportunity in school to engage and enhance their critical and creative thinking skills, but they are also less likely to have parents who emphasize the fostering of critical and creative orientations as the purpose of education.

The correspondence principle offers a grim perspective on the role of education in the potential for social mobility of lower-income and minority students. By beginning from disadvantaged positions, these students are nearly guaranteed to be placed low in the initial educational hierarchy and, if the correspondence principle holds, are unlikely to be given the tools to struggle their way out of this position. Moreover, once in the labor force, Kohn argues that the stratification of job-relevant skills and behaviors cements the correspondence between education and class-specific values. Not only this, but because the meritocratic ideal of education persists, the failure of members of disadvantaged groups to achieve social mobility is understood to result from their own failures.

The structural Marxist theory of class inequality in education, particularly as exemplified by Bowles and Gintis, differs importantly from some theories in that the reproduction mechanism it proposes is institutional rather than individual. It is not the students' resources or aspirations that primarily drive inequality, but rather how the stratified school system shapes and realizes them. Yet, while structural Marxism is generally interpreted as one of rigid reproduction, with schools populated by passive, non-agentic students (e.g., Giroux 1981; McNeil 1981), the theory *actually* relies on individual variation and student action. It is the few working-class kids who succeed in attaining middle-class positions, after working hard in school of course, who are truly indispensable to the perception of a meritocratic competition, a perception that is necessary to maintain capitalism. However, because the mechanism is at the institutional level, altering this mechanism (the correspondence between the social relations of education and the social relations of labor) could potentially change not only the distribution of outcomes and thus inequality, but also the relationship between origin and destination class. The theory is therefore dynamic. Finally, the theory is general because, as we see with Kohn, the concept of "correspondence" can be applied to institutions beyond the school.

4.9   Cultural Capital Theory

In *Reproduction in Education, Society, and Culture*, Pierre Bourdieu and Jean-Claude Passeron (1977) explain inequality, among other phenomena, by contending that schools reward behavior that complies with the norms and standards of the dominant group in a society. Inequality follows because, try as they might, outsiders cannot fully adopt the norms and standards of the dominant group because one's core, one's *habitus*, develops in the family, is impossible to change, and directly affects one's behavior despite one's efforts. Consequently, one's likelihood of educational success is constrained by one's earliest formative experiences, sedimented into one's habitus.

Bourdieu (1986) describes cultural capital—of which habitus is one type—as a resource one may use to navigate various *fields*. Success in the schooling process and the many labor markets depends on one's deployment of cultural capital in such fields. One does not deploy cultural capital in a neutral arena because there are no neutral arenas, for all arenas have differing mixtures of material and symbolic criteria for success and any criterion inescapably advantages some and disadvantages others. Yet, Bourdieu highlights gatekeeper exclusion on the basis of arbitrarily selected criteria of evaluation that advantage the previously advantaged.

Some readings of Bourdieu assert that markers and mechanisms of success are selected *because* of their ability to legitimate social closure for the advantaged (e.g., Lareau and Weininger 2003). In this view, much that schools' value has no intrinsic utility, but rather serves to distinguish (upper-) middle-class children from their lower-class peers. Others see exclusion via a symbolic as opposed to material dimension as the key theoretical contribution of the concept of cultural capital (Lamont and Lareau 1988), regardless of how the symbols are selected.

If the content and character of childhood socialization depend on parents' cultural repertoire, and cultural repertoires are associated with class location and race/ethnicity, then childrens' developing habitus will differ by class and race. Consequently, cultural capital theory implies that intergenerational transmission of socioeconomic and racial inequality occurs partly through the intergenerational transmission of culturally distinct repertoires along lines of race and class that do not match socially-constructed definitions of merit. Further, intragenerational inequality—the association between early and later placements of a person in various educational and/or occupational positions—is explained by virtue of habitus.

Cultural capital theory attempts to be nothing short of a complete theory of attainment, and thus is extremely general. The mechanism of attainment is capital, in both material and symbolic forms. The theory is dynamic, but its conclusion is that, alas, *plus ça change, plus c'est la même chose*.

4.10   Incorporation Theory

Ogbu (1987) articulates a theory of immigrant incorporation. He maintains that the posture native-born minority students strike with respect to school depends upon the predominant historical pattern of incorporation of their racial/ethnic group. Ogbu conceives of minority incorporation as either *voluntary* or *involuntary*. Voluntary minorities are those who have entered the U.S. primarily through immigration. The theory suggests that voluntary minorities continue to view their opportunity structure in relation to that of peers in their ancestral country. Further, voluntary minorities can explain difficulties, inequalities, and poor treatment by their lack of knowledge of their newfound land. Thus, they view the returns to education favorably even though they may be lower than for natives, because voluntary immigrants anticipate better returns for later generations. With this posture, voluntary minorities engage school in ways that can facilitate successful performance.

In contrast, involuntary minority groups are those who "were *originally brought into United States society involuntarily* through slavery, conquest, or colonization" (Ogbu 1987, p. 321, emphasis in original). Native Americans, Native Hawaiians, and African Americans are primary examples in the United States. The phenomenon is not confined to the United States, as many examples exist, including the Burakumin in Japan, the Maori in New Zealand (Ogbu 1987, p. 321), travelers in Eastern Europe, and more (Fischer et al. 1996, p. 192, Table 8.1). Involuntary minorities and their children cannot explain difficulties, inequalities, and poor treatment by lack of knowledge of their homeland. Historical enslavement, conquest, or colonization echoes in contemporary poor treatment, creating a clanging inconsistency with any expectation of fair returns now or better returns for later generations. This history of unfairness makes education a poor investment.

Some analysts point to an "immigrant paradox," in which children of some immigrant groups attain higher levels of education than their native-born peers on average, an advantage that tends to dissipate or even reverse by the third generation (Rumbaut 1999; Perreira et al. 2006). The "immigrant paradox" basically compares better than expected performance of the first and second generation with worse than expected performance for later generations. Evidence suggests the "paradox" may be explained by considering the educational context of immigrant-sending countries (e.g., Feliciano and Lanuza 2017). But even if the paradox were to hold, it suggests that incorporation into a society where racial stereotypes and White advantage are pervasive may produce sustained disadvantage relative to native-born Whites, unravelling initial voluntary immigrant optimism and fostering disengagement among some immigrant groups.

According to incorporation theory minorities' initial reception is critical, as history cannot be re-run. Thus, incorporation theory implies strong inertia in the inequality between groups. By explicitly theorizing stasis even as conditions may change, their theory satisfies our criteria for dynamic theories of inequality.

4.11 Oppositional Culture

In *Learning to Labour*, Willis (1977) studies "the lads," a White, male working-class peer group at a single school in England. Resigned to their fate as manual laborers, in a town where there are virtually no available alternatives, these young men develop a hypermasculine counter-school ethos that values common sense over book knowledge and measures worth through physical and sexual prowess. Yet, Willis also studies the "ear'oles" who, despite sharing job prospects similar to the lads, uphold the meritocratic ideal of education. Although it is the "lads" who are typically considered the noteworthy case because they reject school authorities' orientation towards educa-

tion, it is at least as important to keep the ear'oles in mind as we consider race and class inequalities in education. Their existence raises important questions about whether peer subcultures offer an adequate means of explaining variation in the correspondence between school and work.

Although Willis's theory is based on class—and the White male subculture he describes is propped up by rampant racism and sexism—the most famous school subculture theory, oppositional culture, aims instead to explain racial inequality in education. From this theory, the "burden of acting White" hypothesis (Fordham and Ogbu 1986; Ogbu 2003) states that Black students view academic achievement as a "White" enterprise and therefore resist this path so as not to be labeled a traitor to their race. According to this theory, minority students perceive that their efforts and achievement in school will result in fewer career opportunities than that same effort or achievement would produce for White students. As a result, involuntary minority students, particularly Blacks, demonstrate resistance to school and negatively sanction their high-performing co-ethnic peers. Ogbu hypothesizes that it is this racialized rejection of education that best accounts for the persistence of the achievement gap between Black and White students.

However, Fordham and Ogbu's (1986) original research that proposed the theory used a poor sample design (Lucas 2016) that prohibited the drawing of *any* conclusions beyond the specific students studied, while at the same time conflating labels such as "brainiac" with Whiteness. Similarly, the premise that involuntary minority students (Ogbu 1987) reject education or view achievement as White has been largely discredited (e.g., Ainsworth-Darnell and Downey 1998; Downey et al. 2009; Harris 2006). Other work, including Willis's, also clearly demonstrates that disengagement from schooling is not exclusively a minority phenomenon (Willis 1977; MacLeod 1987; Tyson et al. 2005). Yet, the legacy of understanding some students' underperformance in terms of a conflict between their racial/ethnic identity and dominant cultural values endures.

Notably, Prudence Carter (2005) finds that students do not interpret academic success as a White trait, but identifies the importance of "keepin' it real," or being authentic, to students' evaluations of their peers (Carter 2003, 2005, 2006). Carter does not suggest that students are never negatively sanctioned by their peers for "acting White," but rather that this epithet was used on students regarded as snobs, not on students regarded as pursuing academic excellence. Thus, the epithet's use is distinct from students' opinions about the institution of education, which she finds to be uniformly positive among her sample of Black and Latino/a adolescents in Yonkers, New York. Rather, educational achievement is associated with their ability or willingness to enact the behaviors and competencies valued by the school. Students who straddled school (i.e., dominant) and nonschool (i.e., non-dominant) competencies were the most socially successful and also performed well academically. Flores-Gonzàlez (2002) similarly finds that the ability to maintain and meld diverse identities is also key to persistence in high school in her sample of Puerto Rican adolescents.

While Carter does identify a group of students who behave in a manner that echoes Ogbu's "opposition"—using "Black English Vernacular," putting forth minimal effort in school, and demonstrating high ethnic-centrality—and the hegemonic masculinity of "the lads," she finds that these students regard education as important and do not view achievement as White. Rather, the seemingly oppositional cultural codes employed by many minority youths were simply intended "to create a coherent, positive self-image (or set of images) in the face of hardship or subjugation" (Carter 2005, p. 57). Thus, although student subcultures arguably exist, evidence does not support the notion that noncompliance is synonymous with rejection of education. Carter identifies students' ability to negotiate competing sets of values as the operative mechanism in social and academic school success. Understood this way, the theory is general—not only can it be applied to different minority groups, but the reward structure of the school has also been shown to conflict with class-identity expression (e.g., Willis 1977).

The theory is also dynamic because if schools were to change their reward structure to value students' adaptability (an arguably important life skill), then Carter's typology could accommodate a different pattern of inequality (e.g., where only the ability to "straddle," not dominant competencies alone, would predict greater school success).

4.12 Relative Risk Aversion

Relative Risk Aversion (RRA) is offered by Breen and Goldthorpe (1997) to contest cultural theories of inequality while explaining stable class differentials across cohorts, declining class effects across education transitions, and rapidly changing gender effects. RRA accepts that educational opportunities require both financial and cognitive resources. Conditional on those constraints, RRA posits that students (and families) make decisions based on students' understanding of their likelihood of success were they to follow specific educational paths and their estimation of the probability of attaining sought occupational positions via those paths. The core of the theory rests on three key theorems: (1) Adolescents seek to avoid downward socioeconomic mobility, (2) each educational path entails some risk that students will seek to avoid if possible, and (3) cultural differences are not necessary to explain inequality (Breen and Goldthorpe 1997, p. 238).

With respect to the first theorem, assume the socioeconomic distribution is divided into thirds—top, middle, and underclass. Those hailing from the middle can avoid downward mobility by obtaining middle or top occupations, but those at the top can only avoid downward mobility by reaching a top occupational destination. The theory states that this difference produces different incentives for the level and kind of educational attainment pursued.

With respect to the second theorem, the theory posits that paths that entail demanding educational opportunities are great for those who succeed, but those who follow that path yet fail will encounter worse outcomes than they would have encountered had they succeeded in a less demanding curriculum path. This assumption is the source of the theory's name, relative risk aversion; specifying costs to failure makes it possible for some students to expect to do better by taking less than the most demanding curriculum available. Thus, such students will engage as if risk averse.

With respect to the third theorem, their rejection of the subcultural thesis, Breen and Goldthorpe (1997) posit a society-wide consensus that certain educational pathways are more likely to lead to occupational success. Although students' assessment of their likelihood of *educational* success will depend in part on what they see as their ability, it will not depend on subcultural values, norms, or behaviors.

The theory, thus, explains class and race inequality in education with the same mechanism—socioeconomically disadvantaged students and students from racially and/or ethnically disempowered communities are likely to have parents with lower occupational attainments. Children whose parents have lower occupational attainments have a lower floor their own educational attainments must reach to avoid downward mobility. Although the theory posits lower cognitive ability for students from poor (and racially disempowered) families, the difference in floors for success is sufficient to create educational inequality.

4.13   Effectively Maintained Inequality

Lucas (2001) proposes Effectively Maintained Inequality (EMI), a general theory of inequality. EMI claims that socioeconomically advantaged actors secure for themselves and their children advantage wherever advantages are commonly possible. The theory further contends that all goods have both qualitative and quantitative dimensions. This multi-dimensional nature of goods facilitates the intransigence of inequality, for the theory claims that if quantitative differences are common, the socioeconomically advantaged obtain quantitative advantage. But, if qualitative differences are common, the socioeconomically advantaged obtain qualitative advantage. If this is true, consid-

ering only one dimension may lead analysts to presume a decline in inequality when, in actuality, for example, all that has happened is that the locus of consequential inequality shifted from the quantitative to the qualitative dimension.

EMI has been applied to education almost exclusively (e.g., Esping-Anderson and Wagner 2012). Further, most applications focus on only one aspect of the theory, its assertion that all goods have both qualitative and quantitative dimensions, to highlight inequality in qualitative dimensions of education.

Applying this general theory of inequality to education, EMI explained socioeconomic effects on education in one of at least two ways. When some attain a particular level of schooling whereas many others do not (e.g., high school completion throughout the first half of the twentieth century in the United States), the socioeconomically advantaged use their advantages to secure that level of schooling. However, if that level of schooling becomes widely or perhaps even universally attained, the socioeconomically advantaged seek out whatever qualitative differences there are *at that level*, using their advantages to secure quantitatively similar but qualitatively better education (e.g., qualitatively better, more challenging curricular tracks). Thus, EMI notes that actors' foci may shift as qualitative differences supplant quantitative differences in importance. Alternatively, actors may reference qualitative differences even when quantitative differences are common. Either way, EMI claims that the socioeconomically advantaged will use their advantages to secure both quantitatively and qualitatively better outcomes.

Aspects beyond the qualitative/quantitative distinction have not received much attention, even though they are constitutive aspects of EMI. The theory articulated its decomposition of goods into qualitative and quantitative dimensions while also identifying an important role for (student) myopia [aka nearsightedness], inequality (amongst students) in access to information that could dispel the myopia, the discretionary power of (school personnel) gatekeepers, and the possibility of *class-based* (parental) collective action to maintain advantage. School-related

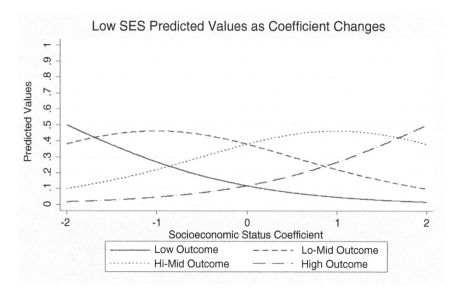

Fig. 4.6 Low SES predicted values as socioeconomic background coefficient changes

labels are placed in parentheses because they translate the general theoretical postulates into the realm of education.

One important feature of EMI is illustrated across Figs. 4.6, 4.7, and 4.8. To test for the qualitative hypothesis of EMI, one must use a categorical dependent variable (e.g., dropout, no academic course, academic low-track course, academic high-track course) and calculate and compare predicted outcome category probabilities for those of low and high socioeconomic background. Figures 4.6 and 4.7, for low and high socioeconomic background students respectively, trace the predicted probability of entering each of four categories of an outcome variable as the socioeconomic background coefficient changes.[6] EMI is supported if the category with the highest predicted probability differs for those of high and low socioeconomic background. Intriguingly, this means that EMI implies bounds on the socioeconomic background coefficient, for only some coefficients make the predicted outcome category for those of high socioeconomic background exceed the predicted outcome category for those of low socioeconomic background. Given the illustrative

results plotted in Figs. 4.6 and 4.7, Fig. 4.8 sketches the range of coefficients that satisfy EMI.

Most theories of inequality would be satisfied if the coefficient on social background is positive. EMI, however, has a more constrained prediction, for it asserts that myopia, differential information to dispel myopia, gatekeeper discretion, and class-based collective action all work to keep the social background coefficient within a smaller band of values. EMI implies that efforts to move the coefficient outside of that band will encounter serious resistance (Lucas 2017). Thus, for EMI, most positive coefficients would be inconsistent with EMI, making it possible for the association between the outcome and socioeconomic background to be statistically significant but still not support EMI (Lucas 2009), rendering EMI falsifiable even amidst ubiquitous findings showing a positive association between socioeconomic background and education outcomes. Or, in other words, EMI theory identifies the thresholds at which a society shifts from an Effectively Maintained Inequality regime to something else.

The theory specifically addresses change within an EMI regime by denying its consequentiality. In a sense, EMI posits a basic cause à la Lieberson (1985, pp. 185–195)—the aim of advantaged actors to maintain their advantage.

---

[6]Three thresholds divide the four categories: −2, 0, and 2.

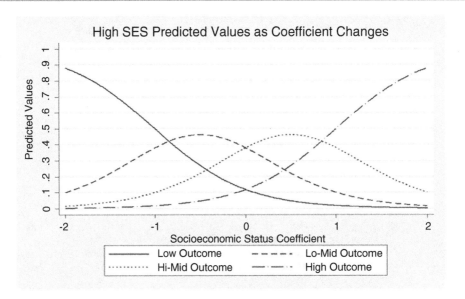

Fig. 4.7 High SES predicted values as socioeconomic background coefficient changes

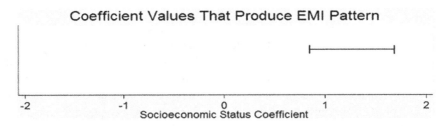

Fig. 4.8 Coefficient values that produce EMI pattern

That cause creates (and thus explains) a diverging trajectories pattern such that children of socioeconomic advantage transition into occupations and earnings niches of socioeconomic advantage while their poor peers tend to make other transitions. However, the process by which these transitions are produced change over time; the stable pattern exists amidst a plethora of superficial causes/pathways through which the basic cause maintains consistent force. In the sphere of education, the superficial causes include the various levels and kinds of education—high school graduation, Advanced Placement courses, honors, International Baccalaureate, 4-year college, small liberal arts college, community college,

professional school, vocational training program, R1 research university, and more. Amidst this plethora of possibilities, the basic cause remains operative—advantaged people secure for themselves advantage wherever advantage is (commonly) possible.

Despite its doubt about overall societal change, EMI posits that some individuals will be able to follow more advantaged trajectories than their disadvantaged origins might suggest. The theory claims that our predictions for disadvantaged students, however, will diverge from those we make for advantaged students, even after we control for academic achievement. Such patterns reflect the intransigence of inequality and its intergenerational transmission.

4.14   Points of Contact Between and Challenges of Expansive Theories

4.14.1   Selected Points of Contact Across the Theories

Expansive theories might be arrayed as if each offers an entirely separable understanding of the phenomena at issue. Yet, these theories work the same intellectual terrain, so it should come as no surprise that they connect and reinforce each other at some points. To correct the possible tendency of seeing each theory in isolation, we note a few points of contact across the theories.

First, epigenetics can be interpreted as suggesting that educational success partly flows from a genetic basis, but a key part of that basis is etched through environmental pathways. That is, the provision of encouraging environments can create hormonal responses that coax gene expressions conducive to better cognitive performance. Seen in this way, epigenetics implies an important role for encouraging environments, at the molecular level and above. In a way, epigenetics deepens the importance of the environment, for environmental effects are insinuated into the organism in a constitutive way. Epigenetics thus deepens the implications of the Wisconsin model, with its emphasis on significant others' (i.e., parents', teachers', and peers') encouragement, structural Marxism, with its identification of economic and education structures that squelch human potential, incorporation theory, with its distinction between immigrants facing hostile, exclusionary or non-hostile inclusionary responses from natives, and EMI, with its emphasis on gatekeeper ability to encourage (open) or discourage (block) student access to environments that encourage increasing performance. Each of these theories identifies a mechanism that may involve an undiscussed epigenetic pathway through which intergenerational effects of

the mechanisms they highlight can escalate and rigidify.

Human capital theory highlights persons' decisions to invest (in education), accepting such decisions occur under constraint. Both RRA and EMI also prioritize persons' decisions to invest under constraint—RRA with unequal cost constraints, EMI with unequal information constraints and unequal discretionary gatekeeper support.

The Wisconsin model's emphasis on encouragement by others resonates with the social-psychological aspects of incorporation theory, which can be seen as generalizing the set of significant others, with oppositional culture, which suggests that peer evaluations are an import factor in students' attitudes toward and behavior in school, and with RRA, which implies a social-psychological process through its assertion of a role for students' assessment of their likelihood of success along various paths.

Credentialism, in referencing the qualitative category of *professional*, highlights ethnic competition and professionalization as a resource for exclusion, in affinity with structural Marxism's recognition of elites' monopolization of well-remunerated positions, cultural capital theory's notice of elites' erection of arbitrary barriers to their advantage, and EMI's reference to a qualitative dimension and class-based collective action in the allocation of advantaged positions on that dimension.

Structural Marxism, privileging distinctions between categorically differentiated economic positions and identifying stratified pathways to those positions, resonates with incorporation theory's reference to legally-defined distinctions of immigrant incorporation.

Cultural capital theory, with its emphasis on translating capital from one field to another, is consistent with incorporation theory's understanding of the differential valuation of immigrants from different origin countries and with oppositional culture's understanding of differential cultural markets.

Finally, incorporation theory's reference to the differential reception of different immigrants not only may provide the context within which oppositional cultures may arise and take root, but also may matter for EMI's suggested differential discretionary response of gatekeepers (i.e., gatekeepers may respond differently to voluntary and involuntary immigrants).

The listed points of contact do not exhaust the possible connections between the theories. But, they are enough to draw two conclusions. First, even disparate theories may not deny every aspect of each other, suggesting that if high levels of hostility are observed in scholars' debates, those emotions have more to do with the discussants than with the material for discussion. Perhaps recognizing theories' shared elements may reduce the heat, and increase the light, that dialogue can provide.

Second, because many theories share some elements, adjudicating between theories can be challenging, because shared elements—when confirmed—contribute to concluding in favor of each theory that shares the element. Consequently, one should expect adjudication to require intense study and to be difficult. Difficult though it is, adjudication is an important task. It is to the important task of adjudication to which the penultimate section turns. But first we must consider, why adjudicate? Why not simply accept each theory singly, or see each as contributing one piece to our understanding of racial/ethnic and class inequality in education?

4.14.2 Challenges of the Theories

It may be heartening to observe multiple points of contact across theories, for their existence may suggest some degree of consensus, at least within subsets of similar theories. If consensus is emerging, this may suggest that all is well with each theory, and the task now is to simply see how they fit together. Alas, such an impression is misleading. The collective points of contact are important, but they exist alongside another set of important observations: Although each theory may appear internally consistent initially, closer scrutiny reveals nagging issues with each.

With epigenetics, one challenge is that geneticists have established that many complex tasks require multiple genes acting in concert (Marsh 1997). To discover a genetic connection for such a complex process as learning and/or education seems a daunting task. Thus, at present, epigenetics is a tantalizingly promising theory, its possibility revealed more in our imaginations than in even the beginnings of research.

Human capital theory would seem to require a coherent understanding of productivity, but empirical analysts usually simply assume or assert that earnings track productivity (e.g., Byrus and Stone 1984), a view falsified by decades of sociological research (e.g., Wright and Perrone 1977; Kalleberg and Griffin 1980; Spaeth 1985; Halaby and Weakliem 1993). Once one realizes the uncertainty plaguing the operationalization of productivity, the theory's mechanism is no longer clear and the theory's elegance is seriously endangered.

The Wisconsin model foregrounds significant others' influence, making it the chokepoint of intergenerational status transmission. Teachers are key significant others, and teachers could encourage all students. If teachers encourage all students enough but in patterns that lead to the equalization of overall encouragement across students, downstream outcomes should alter such that *every* child would have and reach high occupational aspirations. Yet, occupational distributions are not only a function of young adult demand for jobs, they also are a function of larger macroeconomic features (e.g., trade surpluses and deficits) as well as employers' supply of occupational positions, such that it is unlikely that every child, no matter how encouraged, will attain high status occupations and earnings. One response is to interpret the Wisconsin model as a static summary of relations for a cohort, but such an interpretation undermines the view of the model as reflecting a causal theory.

Bourdieu has been viewed as identifying the process by which oppression is constructed and maintained by arbitrarily-selected criteria of merit. Yet, because the theory offers no criteria for what is and is not or can be and cannot be cultural capital, *anything* can be cultural capital, and *all* criteria are arbitrary. While this may make cultural capital theory seem to be incredibly broad, the result is to leave only *political* grounds for contesting criteria of merit, i.e., the only way to contest a theory with integrity is to claim one is disadvantaged by the criteria. But, as someone must always be disadvantaged (e.g., someone must be last in line), any given person's being in the set of disadvantaged persons on the basis of some criterion is hardly good reason to change the criteria. Indeed, even if criteria were to greatly change, the new criteria would still be arbitrary, and thus as susceptible to Bourdieusian critique as former criteria. Thus, cultural capital theory is now and will always be a critique of the status quo, no matter what that status quo is. If the theory cannot extricate itself from this conclusion, it is revealed to be tautological and thus, ultimately, unilluminating.

Credentialism is articulated in line with professional occupations, but very few credentials are actually about traditional or powerful professions. It remains to be seen whether the theory's social closure mechanism is truly class- and racial/ethnic-specific, or even operational, once one broadens the understanding of *credential* to include the burgeoning number of non-professional certificates so as to reflect the experience of the bulk of any cohort.

Structural Marxism is often vilified for an alleged lack of agency (e.g., Giroux 1981), but the actual foundational text rebuts this criticism (e.g., Bowles and Gintis 1976, pp. 143–144). Far more questionable, however, is whether the theory allows non-class-based forms of oppression to matter for education (Davies 1995). It would be difficult to maintain a structural Marxist position while considering the history of Little Rock and Birmingham, or the way in which post-World War II economic structure first rejected than embraced women's paid labor force participation. And, if one makes space for non-class-based grounds for economic action, the theory's understanding of schools is undermined.[7]

Incorporation theory implies that the conditions under which immigrant groups entered the country matter. But, research also shows that changing demographics and policy can greatly reduce the impact of the history of incorporation (Lieberson 1980). This raises the question of whether the apparent power of incorporation is real or, instead, epiphenomenal, apparent only because many (most?) groups' treatment does not change as their incorporation recedes into the past (e.g., Cubans welcomed, Mexicans vilified).

Oppositional culture is based in a claim that communities hold antagonistic views toward mainstream success. Yet, research shows late twentieth-century minority elementary school children seeking to succeed in school (e.g., Tyson 2002), and mid-twentieth-century mainstream adolescents rejecting school (e.g., Coleman 1961). Faced with such findings, the origin of students' alleged opposition in *communities* presents a serious puzzle for oppositional culture theory for, if opposition does not originate in disenfranchised communities and only in disenfranchised communities, how can it explain long-standing group-linked differences in education?

Relative risk aversion asserts the existence of a society-wide consensus as to which positions are better, but immigration and concomitant increasing diversity makes the assertion less and less secure. The assertion is important because without it empirical study of RRA mechanisms becomes increasingly difficult, or perhaps even impossible, owing to challenges of statistical identification (i.e., too many parameters to estimate).

Effectively maintained inequality has been found in every nation for which studies assessing it exist (e.g., Lucas 2001 for the United States; Byrne and McCoy 2017 for Ireland; Byun and Park 2017 for Korea; McKeever 2017 for South Africa; Weiss and Schindler 2017 for Germany).

---

[7] Self-described resistance theorists of a post-Marxist bent claim to resolve this problem, but, as Davies (1995) shows, their efforts grow increasingly aspirational and decreasingly tied to empirical evidence, such that, in the main, they fail to satisfy the coherence and falsifiability criteria noted earlier. Thus, we do not include them.

Yet, no research assessing EMI has interrogated EMI's claim of class-based collective action. While the widespread confirmatory research may seem to reflect a powerful theory, failure to assess its collective action assertion raises questions about the mechanisms the theory identifies.

Given the existence of such critical observations for each theory, it appears it would be worthwhile to assess, and even adjudicate, the theories.

4.15   Assessing the Theories

We have offered 10 theories of socioeconomic and racial inequality in education. The large number of theories may reflect real complexity in the phenomenon. In contrast, however, it may instead be a result of sociology's insufficient attention to the task of critically assessing or adjudicating theories. Or, a third option may be more appropriate—it may be that some theories can be combined, ultimately leading to far fewer than 10 theories of class and racial/ethnic inequality in education.

There are at least two ways to proceed. One way is to conduct empirical analyses designed to assess two or more theories simultaneously. A second way is to conduct purely theoretical comparative analyses. Both approaches can reveal whether a theory is viable and/or whether a combination of two theories is worth pursuing.

Alas, purely theoretical assessments of theories are rare in the sociology of education. And, while empirical research is dominant, unfortunately, most contemporary empirical research in the sociology of education focuses on establishing a given theory, rather than critically adjudicating multiple theories. Thus, to illustrate the potential power of work geared to comparing and adjudicating theories, we provide three examples, one purely theoretical and two empirical. The purely theoretical work assesses three theories of inequality, of which we will discuss only two. The empirical studies can be used to consider multiple theories as well, even if the original paper did not.

4.15.1   Example 1: "Stratification Theory, Socioeconomic Background, and Educational Attainment: A Formal Analysis"

Lucas (2009) formally translated EMI and Maximally Maintained Inequality (MMI) (Raftery and Hout 1993) into mathematical equations and then considered those theories in concert with RRA, a theory that had already been expressed mathematically. Working through the equations of these three theories revealed several useful insights. One important finding is that MMI is internally contradictory and tautologous, making it unfalsifiable and thus unworthy of consideration. For this reason, we did not discuss MMI here. Lucas (2009, pp. 491–498) also established that EMI is not a tautology, showing that it is possible to have outcome inequality associated with origins yet reject EMI.

Lucas (2009) also found intriguing yet formerly unrecognized implications of RRA equations, and intriguing possible connections between RRA and EMI. First, the analysis revealed that RRA implies the existence of a phenomenon Lucas (2009) labelled the *Gates Gambit*. Essentially, RRA implies that the only socioeconomically advantaged students who will exit advanced programs are those who believe their chances of matching or exceeding their parents' socioeconomic attainments are better if they drop out. This pattern was named after Bill Gates, an adolescent of high socioeconomic status who, despite scoring 1590 on the pre-renormed SAT, dropped out of Harvard to pursue a career in computers, a decision that appears to have worked for him (Lucas 2009, p. 508, note 5). At the same time, by simplifying RRA equations it was shown that RRA implies that all other high socioeconomic background students will stay in school and enter demanding programs, and they will do so *without* considering their subjective likelihood of succeeding in school. This implication tumbles directly out of the equations specifying RRA (Lucas 2009, pp. 482–483). Thus, despite the summary claims of the non-mathematical summary of RRA, which state that students consider their likelihood of success in school as they make rational choice decisions of whether to continue, the actual equations of the theory imply otherwise for particular classes of students.

Notably, this RRA claim is consistent with EMI's claim that academically mediocre high socioeconomic background students enter demanding programs while their equally adept low-socioeconomic background peers do not. EMI highlights the use of non-academic resources (e.g., pressure well-off parents apply to school gatekeepers to secure their children' admission to demanding programs) to predict and explain this pattern. Thus, the theories are complementary as follows.

RRA equations imply a pattern of behavior—the entry of mediocre, well-off students into programs for high achievers—but because RRA allows entry to demanding programs only on the basis of merit (e.g., prior achievement) and ability to pay, RRA processes of entry deny the possibility of mediocre well-off students entering demanding educational programs. Thus, RRA equations imply a behavior, but RRA relations offer no means for the behavior to be enacted. EMI, however, by noting the role of gatekeepers holding discretionary power, provides a way for the implications embedded in RRA equations to be realized. Thus, EMI complements RRA by providing a pathway for the outcome RRA equations predict—mediocre high status students' entry to demanding programs. The pathway is gatekeeper discretion.

This is not the only example of how RRA and EMI may be complementary. Another example flows from EMI's effort to rebut the neo-classical economic position that students act with foresight. EMI contended that myopia is differentially distributed, and that it is a feature of the process. It turns out that once one works through the equations of RRA, one finds that RRA implies decision processes consistent with differential myopia. This possible complementarity is powerful because, as a rational choice theory, RRA might be expected to deny myopia. Yet, simplifying the equations reveals that RRA indicates that students of well-off parents utilize a subjective estimate of their likelihood of attaining various occupational positions given a par-

ticular level of success in school, but students of lower socioeconomic status act as if they have no such estimate, i.e., *they do not reference estimates of future occupational success*. This differential is consistent with differential myopia.

Such findings provide new, more focused grounds for empirical research, and, thus, promising opportunities for theory adjudication and/or synthesis. For example, the results imply that analysts interested in adjudicating between RRA and EMI should not devote time to assessing the existence of student myopia, for doing so will not adjudicate between EMI and RRA because both theories predict myopia for some students. Thus, it appears that assessing the coherence of multiple theories can pay large dividends.

4.15.2 Example 2: "A Threat in the Air: How Stereotypes Shape Intellectual Identity and Performance"

Stereotype threat (Steele 1997) occurs when a negative stereotype becomes self-relevant and fear of fulfilling this stereotype actually impedes performance. Stereotype threat has generally been studied in relation to race and gender stereotypes in academic performance, but can be applied to any group, including low-income students, who face negative stereotypes about their performance. Studies have triggered stereotype threat both through the labeling of tests as diagnostic of ability (e.g., Steele and Aronson 1995) and through the presence of a White examiner (e.g., Huang 2009); neither of these designs stipulates the presence of a prejudiced observer or evaluator (e.g., teacher). Thus, the threat is particularly insidious, because it does not require the gatekeeper with which the person interacts to hold the stereotype, it is only necessary that a student be conscious of the stereotype. Opportunities for stereotype threat to occur are many, extending far beyond the school to experiences with family, friends, co-workers, employers, and more.

The implications for class and racial/ethnic inequalities in education flow from the flood of stereotypes students encounter daily regarding the abilities and relative rankings of different groups of students. It is possible that a constant low level of threat underlies some poor and racial/ethnic minority students' entire school experience.

Stereotype threat resonates with theories that explain educational inequality through expectations. For example, social-psychological processes are the *key* mechanism of the Wisconsin model; the model argues that students' aspirations are shaped by the influence of significant others, with teachers being an important such other. Yet, stereotype threat evidence both intensifies the potential role of teachers, while *broadening* the sources of *influence* by noting that expectations of generalized (i.e., nonsignificant) others can also matter for students' later attainments. Thus, existence of stereotype threat is not only consistent with the Wisconsin Model, it suggests an intriguing elaboration of the model; it is an elaboration because it, too, emphasizes *social*-psychological processes at its core.

Stereotypes develop in historical context, and education-related racial stereotypes tend to track with Ogbu's involuntary (e.g., Black students are less motivated and able than White students) and voluntary (e.g., "Asian" students are model minorities) immigrant designations. In that sense, there is a parallel between the phenomena to which students are responding vis à vis stereotype threat and according to incorporation theory. However, *why* involuntary/stereotyped students underperform differs. Thus, while stereotype threat is consistent with incorporation theory, it is not evidence of the reduced school engagement that the theory suggests. Indeed, a scope condition for stereotype threat to occur is that the person must care about the domain at issue (Aronson et al. 1999), and empirical evidence indicates the strongest, not the weakest, students are affected by it (e.g., Steele 1999). It is only because the student cares about success in the domain at issue that anxiety associated with confirming a negative stereotype rises enough to lower performance quality.

4.15.3 Example 3: Unequal Childhoods

Schools expect (and generally require) that students will interact with teachers and other authorities in certain ways, but students may not arrive at school equally prepared to do so. Lareau (2003) suggests that this is related to the way that parents employ language and discipline with their children. Lareau identifies two different parenting strategies: *concerted cultivation* and the *accomplishment of natural growth*. Concerted cultivation, the child-rearing strategy associated with the middle-class, is characterized by highly structured time, and eventual conversation and negotiation in the practice of discipline. Lareau argues that such practices reflect and facilitate the skills, knowledge, and interpersonal postures rewarded by the school. In contrast, the accomplishment of natural growth, the parenting style more commonly adopted by working-class and poor families, is characterized by unstructured time, more directive language use, and authoritarian discipline. Importantly, Lareau argues that these different patterns of socialization are associated with different levels of comfort and ability in interacting with authority.

These findings parallel those of Kohn (e.g., 1969) and of Bernstein (e.g., 1971), and contribute to research traditions on language use in communities and its impact on schooling. For example, Nystrand and Gamoran (1988, 1991) distinguish authentic and inauthentic questions. Authentic questions are questions to which the asker does not know the answer. Inauthentic questions are questions to which the asker does know the answer. Nystrand and Gamoran (1991) find that authentic questions are associated with greater learning.

Research indicates that middle-class and White communities tend to use inauthentic questions in early childhood language training, whereas other communities use authentic questions (e.g., Heath

1983). When students arrive at school, an institution with a predominance of inauthentic questions, some students, unfamiliar with such an odd language situation—Why would someone ask me a question to which I know they know I know they know the answer?—are more likely to be made uncomfortable or unsure. The resulting befuddlement and hesitation can quickly set students on a path to failure.

Lareau's findings would appear to parallel the correspondence principal and Kohn's work in particular. While Bowles and Gintis focus on the socialization that happens within the school, the contrast between concerted cultivation and the accomplishment of natural growth suggests that the divergence in training for class-stratified positions in adulthood begins before children enter school. Thus, the predicted reproduction is even more rigid, because working-class students are not only more likely to be placed in substandard academic settings, but Lareau's findings suggest that working-class and poor children will be less likely to strike the posture that their schools value. In this way, we can see how divergent child-rearing and language acquisition strategies might promote the kind of disjuncture between community and school reflected in Ogbu's and Carter's discussions of oppositional culture.

However, arbitrariness of school procedures, not correspondence, is also evident in such analyses. Heath (1983) documented the rich language use and talent of children raised in homes that use authentic questions, and how changes in school practice made their school achievements improve. For every class difference one could consider the question of "Which is better?" For example, Lucas asks:

> Are inauthentic questions "better" for teaching children? Most analyses say no; although inauthentic questions have their place, they are overused in U.S. education (Newmann et al. 1996). Further, they fail to match the aim of education in a globalizing, highly competitive, neoliberal, take-no-prisoners economy, and they do not match the aim of many parents to empower their children in the social, political, and economic arenas. (Lucas 2013, p. 71)

Newmann, Marks, and Gamoran highlight the mismatch, contending that:

> Scientists, jurists, artists, journalists, designers, engineers, and other accomplished adults rely on complex forms of communication both to conduct their work and to express their conclusions. The language they use—verbal, symbolic, and visual—includes qualifications, nuances, elaborations, details, and analogues woven into extended expositions, narratives, explanations, justifications, and dialogue. In contrast, much of the communication demanded in school requires only brief answers: true or false, multiple choice, fill in the blank, or short sentences (e.g., "Prices increase when demand exceeds supply"). (1996, pp. 283–284)

One implication of the middle-class use of inauthentic questions in child development is that in order for middle-class children to attain their parent's occupational positions, their inauthentic-question-based childhood communication patterns must someday be undone. In contrast, many Black children engage authentic questions at an early age, meaning that they enter school ready and able to engage in complex communication forms, in a sense ahead of the game. But, after intense involvement with a school communicative environment that re-labels their creativity as deficiency, their linguistic advantage is lost.

Seen in this way, at least some notable non-correspondences are evident, a fact quite consistent with Bourdieu's perspective on cultural capital, especially the variant highlighting the social construction of skill.

Lareau (2003) does not support the "burden of acting White" hypothesis, as the findings connect child-rearing strategies to class, rather than race, and also offer no suggestion that either the children or their parents devalue education, only that they interact differently with school authority.

Lareau's work also demonstrates the importance of significant others' influence. In concerted cultivation and the accomplishment of natural growth, parents set implicit expectations for the manner in which children will structure and orient their time. Because the former is in line with the expectations of education authorities (e.g., college admissions officers), middle-class students can be expected to attain higher levels of education. Moreover, while parents' encouragement of certain styles of interaction with authority is important, the effect escalates to the extent that middle-class children are also given greater *access* to authority figures at younger ages. Middle-class parents accomplish this by enrolling their children in all kinds of organized activities, like sports and music lessons. This gives middle-class children many more opportunities to build their comfort with authority figures.

4.16 Concluding Remarks

Evidence indicates that class and racial/ethnic inequality in education is ubiquitous or perhaps even universal. Analysts have proposed multiple theories to explain the documented inequalities and their intransigence. Even so, many theories suggest mechanisms that might be manipulable enough to reduce, or even eliminate, class- and racial/ethnic-linked educational inequality. Yet, prior to the challenge of constructing the political will to engage such mechanisms, analysts must intensify their efforts to assess the theories through which those potential mechanisms are identified. As analysts deepen their engagement with this task, it is likely that some theories will be found wanting. At the same time, new, more, full comprehension of the maintenance of inequality may come within reach. In this way, sociologists may contribute to closing the gap not only between classes and racial/ethnic groups in achievement and attainment but, also, to reducing the gap between humans' cognitive potential and realized cognitive achievement. Perhaps the possible gains to such a closure, and the prospect of sociologists contributing to such an enterprise, will spur the next adjudicatory steps in the research agenda of sociologists of education.

References

Ainsworth-Darnell, J. W., & Downey, D. B. (1998). Assessing the oppositional culture explanation for racial/ethnic differences in school performance. *American Sociological Review, 63*, 536–553.

Aronson, J., Lustina, M. J., Good, C., Keough, K., Steele, C. M., & Brown, J. (1999). When White men can't do math: Necessary and sufficient factors in stereotype threat. *Journal of Experimental Social Psychology, 35*, 29–46.

Bachman, J. G., Wallace, J. M., Jr, O'Malley P. M., Johnston, L. D., Kurth, C. L., & Neighbors, H. W. (1991). Racial/ethnic differences in smoking, drinking, and illicit drug use among American high school seniors, 1976–89. *American Journal of Public Health, 81*, 372–377.

Becker, G. S. (1962). Investment in human capital: A theoretical analysis. *Journal of Political Economy, 70*, S9–S49.

Becker, G. S., & Tomes, N. (1986). Human capital and the rise and fall of families. *Journal of Labor Economics, 4*, S1–S39.

Benavot, A. (1983). The rise and decline of vocational education. *Sociology of Education, 56*, 63–76.

Bernstein, B. (1971). *Class, codes and control. Volume 1: Theoretical studies towards a sociology of language*. Boston: Routledge/Kegan Paul.

Blau, Peter M., & Duncan, O. D., with the collaboration of Andrea Tyree. (1967). *The American occupational structure*. New York: The Free Press.

Bobo, L., & Licari, F. C. (1989). Education and political tolerance: Testing the effects of cognitive sophistication and target group affect. *Public Opinion Quarterly, 53*, 285–308.

Bourdieu, P. (1986). The forms of capital. In J. Richardson (Ed.), *Handbook of theory and research for the sociology of education* (pp. 241–258). New York: Greenwood Press.

Bourdieu, P., & Passeron, J.-C. (1977). *Reproduction in education, society, and culture* (2nd ed.). London: SAGE Publications.

Bowles, S., & Gintis, H. (1976). *Schooling in capitalist America*. New York: Basic Books.

Breen, R., & Goldthorpe, J. H. (1997). Explaining educational differentials: Towards a formal rational action theory. *Rationality and Society, 9*, 275–305.

Byrne, D., & McCoy, S. (2017). Effectively maintained inequality in compulsory and post-compulsory education in the Republic of Ireland. *American Behavioral Scientist, 64*, 49–73.

Byrus, R. T., & Stone, G. W. (1984). *Microeconomics* (2nd ed.). Glenview: Scott Foresman.

Byun, S.-y., & Park, H. (2017). When different types of education matter: Effectively maintained inequality of educational opportunity in Korea. *American Behavioral Scientist, 64*, 94–113.

Carnoy, M., & Rothstein, R. (2013). *What do international tests really show about U.S. student performance?* Washington, DC: Economic Policy Institute.

Carter, P. L. (2003). "Black" cultural capital, status positioning, and schooling conflicts for low-income African American youth. *Social Problems, 50*, 136–155.

Carter, P. L. (2005). *Keepin' it real: School success beyond Black and White*. New York: Oxford University Press.

Carter, P. L. (2006). Straddling boundaries: Identity, culture, and school. *Sociology of Education, 79*, 304–328.

Cherlin, A., & Walters, P. B. (1981). Trends in United States men's and women's sex-role attitudes: 1972 to 1978. *American Sociological Review, 46*, 453–460.

Coleman, J. S., with the assistance of Johnstone, J. W. C, & Jonassohn, K. (1961). *The adolescent society: The social life of the teenager and its impact on education.* New York: The Free Press.

Collins, R. (1974). Where are educational requirements for employment highest? *Sociology of Education, 47,* 419–442.

Collins, R. (1977). Some comparative principles of educational stratification. *Harvard Educational Review, 47,* 1–27.

Collins, R. (1979). *The credential society: An historical sociology of education and stratification.* San Diego: Academic.

Daniels, M., Devlin, B., & Roeder, K. (1997). Of genes and IQ. In B. Devlin, S. E. Fienberg, D. P. Resnick, & K. Roeder (Eds.), *Intelligence, genes, & success: Scientists respond to the bell curve* (pp. 45–70). New York: Springer.

Davies, S. (1995). Leaps of faith: Shifting currents in critical sociology of education. *American Journal of Sociology, 100,* 1448–1478.

Defina, R., & Hannon, L. (2016). Social status attainment and racial category selection in the contemporary United States. *Research in Social Stratification and Mobility, 44,* 91–97.

Downey, D. B., Ainsworth-Darnell, J. W., & Qian, Z. (2009). Rethinking the attitude–achievement paradox among Blacks. *Sociology of Education, 82,* 1–19.

Esping-Anderson, G., & Wagner, S. (2012). Asymmetries in the opportunity structure: Intergenerational mobility trends in Europe. *Research in Social Stratification and Mobility, 30,* 473–487.

Featherman, D. L., & Hauser, R. M. (1978). *Opportunity and change.* New York: Academic.

Feliciano, C., & Lanuza, Y. R. (2017). An immigrant paradox? Contextual attainment and intergenerational educational mobility. *American Sociological Review, 82,* 211–241.

Fischer, C., Hout, M., Jankowski, M. S., Lucas, S. R., Swidler, A., & Voss, K. (1996). *Inequality by design: Cracking the bell curve myth.* Princeton: Princeton University Press.

Flores-Gonzàlez, N. (2002). *School kids/street kids: Identity development in Latino students.* New York: Teachers College Press.

Fordham, S., & Ogbu, J. U. (1986). Black students' school success: Coping with the burden of acting White. *Urban Review, 18*(3), 176–206.

Giroux, H. A. (1981). Hegemony, resistance, and the paradox of educational reform. *Interchange, 12*(2), 3–26.

Goldberger, A. S. (1991). *A course in econometrics.* Cambridge, MA: Harvard University Press.

Goodman, J. D. (1979). The economic returns of education: An assessment of alternative models. *Social Science Quarterly, 60,* 269–283.

Gottfredson, D. C. (1981). Black–White differences in the educational attainment process: What have we learned? *American Sociological Review, 46,* 542–557.

Greenwood, E. (1957). Attributes of a profession. *Social Work, 2*(3), 45–55.

Grubb, W. N. (1992). The economic returns to baccalaureate degrees: New evidence from the class of 1972. *Review of Higher Education, 15,* 213–231.

Grubb, W. N. (2002). Learning and earning in the middle, part I: National studies of pre-baccalaureate education. *Economics of Education Review, 21,* 299–321.

Halaby, C. N., & Weakliem, D. L. (1993). Ownership and authority in the earnings function: Nonnested tests of alternative specifications. *American Sociological Review, 58,* 16–30.

Harris, A. L. (2006). I (Don't) hate school: Revisiting oppositional culture theory of Blacks' resistance to schooling. *Social Forces, 85,* 797–834.

Harris, K. M., Duncan, G. J., & Boisjoly, J. (2002). Evaluating the role of "nothing to lose" attitudes on risky behavior in adolescence. *Social Forces, 80,* 1005–1039.

Hauser, R. M., Tsai, S.-L., & Sewell, W. H. (1983). A model of stratification with response error in social and psychological variables. *Sociology of Education, 56,* 20–46.

Heath, S. B. (1983). *Ways with words: Language, life, and work in communities and classrooms.* New York: Cambridge University Press.

Hedström, P. (2005). *Dissecting the social: On the principles of analytic sociology.* New York: Cambridge University Press.

Herrnstein, R. J., & Murray, C. (1994). *The bell curve: Intelligence and class structure in American life.* New York: Free Press.

Howell, C., & Turner, S. E. (2004). Legacies in Black and White: The racial composition of the legacy pool. *Research in Higher Education, 45*(4), 325–351.

Huang, M.-H. (2009). Race of the interviewer and the Black–White test score gap. *Social Science Research, 38,* 29–38.

Jacoby, D. (1991). The transformation of industrial apprenticeship in the United States. *Journal of Economic History, 51,* 887–910.

Jaynes, G. D., & Williams, R. M., Jr. (1989). *A common destiny: Blacks and American society.* Washington, DC: National Academy Press.

Jencks, C., & Phillips, M. (1998). *The Black–White test score gap.* Washington, DC: Brookings Institution Press.

Jencks, C., Perman, L., & Rainwater, L. (1988). What is a good job? A new measure of labor-market success. *American Journal of Sociology, 93,* 1322–1357.

Jensen, A. (1969). How much can we boost IQ and scholastic achievement? *Harvard Educational Review, 39,* 1–123.

Jones, J. H. (1981). *Bad blood: The Tuskegee syphilis experiment: A tragedy of race and medicine.* Washington, DC: The Free Press.

Kalleberg, A., & Griffin, L. (1980). Class, occupation, and inequality in job rewards. *American Journal of Sociology, 85,* 731–768.

Kalmijn, M. (1994). Assortative mating by cultural and economic occupational status. *American Journal of Sociology, 100,* 422–452.

Kalmijn, M. (2001). Assortative meeting and mating: Unintended consequences of organized settings for partner choices. *Social Forces, 79*, 1289–1312.

Kerckhoff, A. C. (1976). The status attainment process: Socialization or allocation? *Social Forces, 55*, 368–381.

Kerckhoff, A. C., & Campbell, R. T. (1977). Black–White differences in the educational attainment process. *Sociology of Education, 50*, 15–27.

Kimbro, R. T., Bzostek, S., Goldman, N., & Rodríguez, G. (2008). Race, ethnicity, and the education gradient in health. *Health Affairs, 27*, 361–372.

Kitagawa, E. M., & Hauser, P. M. (1968). Education differentials in mortality by cause of death: United States 1960. *Demography, 5*, 318–354.

Klegon, D. (1978). The sociology of professions: An emerging perspective. *Work & Occupations, 5*, 259–283.

Kohn, M. (1969). *Class and conformity: A study in values*. Homewood: Dorsey Press.

Kohn, M., & Schooler, C. (1969). Class, occupation, and orientation. *American Sociological Review, 34*, 659–678.

Kramer, R., DeFina, R., & Hannon, L. (2016). Racial rigidity in the United States: Comment on Saperstein and Penner. *American Journal of Sociology, 122*, 233–246.

Lamont, M., & Lareau, A. (1988). Cultural capital: Allusions, gaps, and glissandos in recent theoretical developments. *Sociological Theory, 6*, 153–168.

Lareau, A. (2003). *Unequal childhoods: Class, race, and family life*. Berkeley: University of California Press.

Lareau, A., & Weininger, E. B. (2003). Cultural capital in educational research: A critical assessment. *Theory and Society, 32*, 567–606.

Lieberson, S. (1980). *A piece of the pie: Blacks and White immigrants since 1880*. Berkeley: University of California Press.

Lieberson, S. (1985). *Making it count: The improvement of social research and theory*. Berkeley: University of California Press.

Loury, G. C. (1992). Incentive effects of affirmative action. *Annals of the American Academy of Political and Social Science, 523*, 19–29.

Lucas, S. R. (2001). Effectively maintained inequality: Education transitions, track mobility, and social background effects. *American Journal of Sociology, 106*, 1642–1690.

Lucas, S. R. (2009). Stratification theory, socioeconomic background, and educational attainment: A formal analysis. *Rationality & Society, 21*, 459–511.

Lucas, S. R. (2013). *Just who loses? Discrimination in the United States* (Vol. 2). Philadelphia: Temple University Press.

Lucas, S. R. (2016). Where the rubber meets the road: Probability and non-probability moments in experiment, interview, archival, administrative, and ethnographic data collection. *Socius: Sociological Research for a Dynamic World, 2*. https://doi.org/10.1177/2378023116634709.

Lucas, S. R. (2017). An archaeology of effectively maintained inequality. *American Behavioral Scientist, 61*, 8–29.

Lucas, S. R., & Beresford, L. (2010). Naming and classifying: Theory, evidence, and equity in education. *Review of Research in Education, 34*, 25–85.

Lumey, L. H. (1992). Decreased birthweights in infants after maternal in utero exposure to the Dutch famine of 1944–1945. *Paediatric and Perinatal Epidemiology, 6*, 240–253.

MacLeod, J. (1987). *Ain't no makin' it: Aspirations and attainment in a low-income neighborhood*. Boulder: Westview Press.

Marsh, D. G. (1997). Approaches toward the genetic analysis of complex traits: Asthma and atopy. *American Journal of Respiratory and Critical Care Medicine, 156*, S133–S138.

McBean, A. M., & Gornick, M. (1994). Differences by race in the rates of procedures performed in hospitals for Medicare beneficiaries. *Health Care Financing Review, 15*(4), 77–90.

McKeever, M. (2017). Educational inequality in apartheid South Africa. *American Behavioral Scientist, 64*, 114–131.

McNeil, L. M. (1981). Negotiating classroom knowledge: Beyond achievement and socialization. *Journal of Curriculum Studies, 13*, 313–328.

McNulty, T. L., & Bellair, P. E. (2003). Explaining racial and ethnic differences in adolescent violence: Structural disadvantage, family well-being, and social capital. *Justice Quarterly, 20*, 1–31.

Meaney, M. (2010). Epigenetics and the biological definition of gene × environment interactions. *Child Development, 81*, 41–79.

Mitchell, D. E., & Kerchner, C. T. (1983). Labor relations and teacher policy. In L. S. Shulman & G. Sykes (Eds.), *Handbook of teaching and policy* (pp. 214–238). New York: Longman Publishing Group.

Morgan, S. L. (2004). Methodologist as arbitrator: Five models for Black–White differences in the causal effect of expectations on attainment. *Sociological Methods and Research, 33*, 3–53.

NCES. (2013). *Performance of U.S. 15-year-old students in mathematics, science, and reading literacy in an international context: First look at PISA 2012*. Washington, DC: U.S. Department of Education.

Newmann, F. M., Marks, H. M., & Gamoran, A. (1996). Authentic pedagogy and student performance. *American Journal of Education, 104*, 280–312.

Nystrand, M., & Gamoran, A. (1988). *A Study of instruction as discourse*. Washington, DC: U.S. Department of Education, Office of Educational Research and Improvement. Education Resources Information Center ED328516.

Nystrand, M., & Gamoran, A. (1991). Instructional discourse, student engagement, and literature achievement. *Research in the Teaching of English, 25*, 261–290.

Ogbu, J. U. (1978). *Minority education and caste* (Vol. 581). New York: Academic Press.

Ogbu, J. U. (1987). Variability in minority school performance: A problem in search of an explanation. *Anthropology & Education Quarterly, 18*, 312–334.

Ogbu, J. U. (2003). *Black American students in an affluent suburb: A study of academic disengagement*. Mahwah: Erlbaum Associates.

Paulsen, R. (1991). Education, social class, and participation in collective action. *Sociology of Education, 64*, 96–110.

Perreira, K. M., Harris, K. M., & Lee, D. (2006). Making it in America: High school completion by immigrant and native youth. *Demography, 43*, 511–536.

Raftery, A. E., & Hout, M. (1993). Maximally maintained inequality: Expansion, reform, and opportunity in Irish education, 1921–75. *Sociology of Education, 66*, 41–62.

Rumbaut, R. G. (1999). Assimilation and its discontents: Ironies and paradoxes. In C. Hirschman, P. Kasinitz, & J. DeWind (Eds.), *The handbook of international migration: The American experience* (pp. 172–195). New York: Russell Sage Foundation.

Saperstein, A., & Penner, A. M. (2010). The race of a criminal record: How incarceration colors racial perceptions. *Social Problems, 57*, 92–113.

Saperstein, A., & Penner, A. M. (2012). Racial fluidity and inequality in the United States. *American Journal of Sociology, 118*, 676–727.

Saporito, S., & Sohoni, D. (2006). Coloring outside the lines: Racial segregation in public schools and their attendance boundaries. *Sociology of Education, 79*, 81–105.

Saporito, S., & Sohoni, D. (2007). Mapping educational inequality: Concentrations of poverty among poor and minority students in public schools. *Social Forces, 85*, 1227–1253.

Schwartz, C. R., & Mare, R. D. (2005). Trends in educational assortative marriage from 1940 to 2003. *Demography, 42*, 621–646.

Sewell, W. H., & Hauser, R. M. (1980). The Wisconsin Longitudinal Study of social and psychological factors in aspirations and achievement. *Research in Sociology of Education and Socialization, 1*, 59–99.

Silberberg, E. (1990). *The structure of economics: A mathematical analysis* (2nd ed.). San Francisco: McGraw-Hill.

Sørensen, A. B. (2000). Toward a sounder basis for class analysis. *American Journal of Sociology, 105*, 1523–1558.

Spaeth, J. (1985). Job power and earnings. *American Sociological Review, 50*, 603–617.

Steele, C. M. (1997). A threat in the air: How stereotypes shape intellectual identity and performance. *American Psychologist, 52*, 613–629.

Steele, C. M. (1999). Thin ice: Stereotype threat and Black college students. *The Atlantic, 284*, 44–54.

Steele, C. M., & Aronson, J. (1995). Stereotype threat and the intellectual test performance of African Americans. *Journal of Personality and Social Psychology, 69*, 797–811.

Sweeney, M., & Cancian, M. (2004). The changing importance of White women's economic prospects for assortative mating. *Journal of Marriage and the Family, 66*, 1015–1028.

Tomes, N. (1981). The family, inheritance, and the intergenerational transmission of inequality. *Journal of political Economy, 89*, 928–958.

Tyson, K. (2002). Weighing in: Elementary-age students and the debate on attitudes toward school among Black students. *Social Forces, 80*, 1157–1189.

Tyson, K., Darity, W., Jr., & Castellino, D. R. (2005). It's not "a Black thing": Understanding the burden of acting White and other dilemmas of high achievement. *American Sociological Review, 70*, 582–605.

Useem, E. (1992). Middle schools and math groups: Parents' involvement in children's placement. *Sociology of Education, 65*, 263–279.

Weil, F. D. (1985). The variable effects of education on liberal attitudes: A comparative-historical analysis of anti-semitism using public opinion survey data. *American Sociological Review, 50*, 458–474.

Weiss, F., & Schindler, S. (2017). EMI in Germany—Qualitative differentiation in a tracked education system. *American Behavioral Scientist, 64*, 74–93.

Willis, P. (1977). *Learning to labour*. Farnborough: Saxon House.

Wolfle, L. M. (1985). Postsecondary educational attainment among Whites and Blacks. *American Educational Research Journal, 22*, 501–525.

Wright, E. O., & Perrone, L. (1977). Marxist class categories and income inequality. *American Sociological Review, 42*, 32–55.

Educational Achievement and Attainment Differences Among Minorities and Immigrants

5

Phoebe Ho and Grace Kao

Abstract

The U.S. student population is increasingly comprised of racial/ethnic minority and immigrant students. Drawing on national-level data, we document the gaps in educational achievement and attainment for minority and immigrant students that are apparent at all levels of education, from early education through postsecondary schooling. These achievement gaps reflect, in part, the broader racial and ethnic hierarchy of the U.S., but the experiences of immigrant-origin minority students additionally contribute to the complexity of racial and ethnic stratification in education. Though research shows that socioeconomic status accounts for much of the differences in achievement, factors such as schools and teachers, peer relationships, and neighborhoods and communities may also contribute to the variation in academic outcomes.

5.1 Introduction

Recent estimates show that nearly half of the 50 million students enrolled in public elementary and secondary schools in the U.S. are racial and ethnic minorities. Specifically, the student population in public schools is 51% White, 16% Black, 24% Hispanic, 5% Asian/Pacific Islander, and 1% American Indian/Alaska Native.[1] In some of the largest urban school districts in the U.S., the student population is already "majority minority" (Aud et al. 2010). Moreover, racial and ethnic differences in academic achievement and attainment are longstanding and continue to be the subject of much research and debate (Kao and Thompson 2003; Noguera 2008). The U.S. student population also includes a significant number of children of immigrants. Nearly one in four children have at least one immigrant parent (Fortuny et al. 2009), and by 2050, an estimated one in three children will come from immigrant families (Passel 2011). Further, the children of immigrants are highly diverse—about 58% are Hispanic, 19% are Asian, 16% are White, and 9% are Black (The Urban Institute n.d.).

P. Ho (✉)
Department of Sociology, University of Pennsylvania, Philadelphia, PA, USA
e-mail: phoebeho@sas.upenn.edu

G. Kao
Department of Sociology, Yale University, New Haven, CT, USA
e-mail: g.kao@yale.edu

[1]The U.S. Department of Education is the source for much of the data presented in this chapter and typically combines Asian and Pacific Islander populations into one category. We recognize that this broad category masks considerable diversity and, where possible, we present data for sub-groups.

© Springer International Publishing AG, part of Springer Nature 2018
B. Schneider (ed.), *Handbook of the Sociology of Education in the 21st Century*, Handbooks of Sociology and Social Research, https://doi.org/10.1007/978-3-319-76694-2_5

Scholars have proposed various scenarios for how the U.S. racial and ethnic hierarchy might change due to the diversity of immigrants, and how such changes are likely to affect different groups (Lee and Bean 2010). However, the recent rise of anti-immigrant rhetoric and a new political administration that favors restrictive immigration policies have arguably made the U.S. less welcoming of immigrants more generally. As a result, immigrant children may face greater obstacles in the near future. While some cities such as San Francisco, Seattle, and Philadelphia and a number of college campuses have declared themselves as sanctuary sites, proposed policies that target individuals from specific countries and undocumented individuals threaten educational opportunities. Elsewhere, this volume examines undocumented children, who will suffer the greatest impact of the current administration's focus on the deportation of undocumented adults. A non-trivial share of native-born children from immigrant families come from families with mixed legal statuses (Fix and Zimmermann 2001). In such families, children with legal status may have a parent, sibling, or other close relative who is undocumented. Such families are at risk of being separated and face significant challenges that will likely affect their children's educational achievement.

Researchers commonly use educational achievement and attainment measures to gauge the integration of minorities and immigrants. It is critical to understand the educational outcomes of children of minority native-born and foreign-born parents, especially in the context of growing racial tensions. In this chapter, we compile data from U.S. Department of Education reports and studies to present an overview of racial, ethnic, and immigrant differences in achievement and attainment from early education to postsecondary completion. We then place educational outcomes in context by drawing upon prior reviews of literature and highlighting illustrative examples of current empirical research. We do not focus on gender differences or the experiences of undocumented youth because other chapters in this volume do so.

5.2 Early Education

Enrollment in early education helps children prepare academically for entry into formal schooling. In the fall of 2014, about 41% of White 3- to 5-year-olds were enrolled in preschool, followed by 40% of Asians, 39% of Blacks, 32% of Hispanics, and 31% of American Indians/Alaska Natives. Among children attending preschools, greater proportions of minority children did so for the full day compared to White children (Kena et al. 2016). Immigrant parents are less likely to enroll their children in center-based care (Karoly and Gonzalez 2011). For minority and immigrant children, access to early education may help them adapt to the "middle-class mainstream" norms expected by schools (Entwisle and Alexander 1993). Access to early education can strengthen the English language skills of children with immigrant parents (Karoly and Gonzalez 2011). Moreover, early childcare centers serve as important facilitators of social capital, providing mothers with access to a broader network of parents and resources (Small 2009). There is some evidence that Black children receive lower-quality care than White children in early education programs and that providing universal, quality early childhood education would substantially reduce early achievement gaps for both Black and Hispanic students (Magnuson and Waldfogel 2005).

The Early Childhood Longitudinal Study Birth Cohort of 2001 (ECLS-B 2001) is a nationally representative study conducted by the Department of Education that administered tests of letter and number and shape recognition to a sample of children who were about 4 years of age in 2005–06. Overall, about 33% of children were proficient in letter recognition and 65% were proficient in number and shape recognition. Race and ethnic differences are already apparent at this early age. Asian children had the highest rates of proficiency in both letter (49%) and number and shape recognition (81%), followed by White children (37% and 73%, respectively). In letter recognition, Black children had a proficiency rate of 28%, followed by 23% for Hispanic children, and

19% for American Indian/Alaska Native children. For number and shape recognition, Black children had a proficiency rate of 55%, followed by 51% for Hispanic children, and 40% for American Indian/Alaska Native children (Aud et al. 2010).

Studies have linked parenting behaviors and infant health to racial and ethnic differences in early cognitive ability using ECLS-B data (Gibbs et al. 2016; Lynch 2011). Lynch (2011) found that Black infants had poorer health (e.g., premature birth, lower birth weight) than White infants. Asian infants had better health and Hispanic infants did not differ from White infants. Accounting for infant health explained a large portion of the Black, but not Hispanic, disadvantage in early educational outcomes and some of the Asian advantage. Other studies have found that when socioeconomic factors, such as family income and parents' education are taken into account, much of the gap in early educational outcomes for minority and immigrant children is accounted for (Entwisle and Alexander 1993; Glick and Bates 2010). Understanding early differences in child developmental outcomes has implications for achievement gaps that are found later in life, when children enter schools (Torche 2016).

5.3 Primary and Secondary Education

5.3.1 Test Scores

Trends in reading and math performance of 4th-graders in the main National Assessment of Educational Progress (NAEP) show persistent differences by race/ethnicity (Fig. 5.1). In 2015, Asian/Pacific Islander 4th-graders had the highest achievement, with an average NAEP reading score of 239 and an average NAEP math score of 257, followed by White students (232 and 248, respectively). In reading/math, Black (206/224), Hispanic (208/230), and American Indian/Alaska Native (205/227) 4th-graders scored similarly, but below their White and Asian/Pacific Islander

peers. These differences have remained largely unchanged over the past decade.

There are also stark differences in NAEP scores by English language learner (ELL) status (Fig. 5.2).[2] On average, non-ELL 4th-graders outperform their ELL peers in both reading and math, though differences are larger in reading scores. In reading, non-ELL 4th-graders scored an average of 226 compared to 189 for their ELL peers. In math, non-ELL students had an average score of 243 while ELL students had an average score of 218. The ELL disadvantage is present across racial/ethnic groups. Further, racial/ethnic differences in ELL student performance mirror those of non-ELL students, with Asian/Pacific Islander and White ELL 4th-graders outperforming their Black and Hispanic ELL peers.

Similar racial and ethnic patterns are seen in NAEP 8th-grade reading and math assessment trends (Fig. 5.1). Results from the 2015 assessment show that Asian/Pacific Islander students have the highest average reading and math scores (280/306), followed by White students (274/292). Hispanic and American Indian/Alaska Native students had similar reading and math scores (253/270 and 252/267, respectively) while Black students had the overall lowest scores (248/260). These racial/ethnic differences in reading and math achievement are also found among high schoolers (Fig. 5.1). In the 2013 NAEP reading assessment of 12th-graders, White students had the highest average score (297), followed by Asian/Pacific Islander (296), American Indian/Alaska Native (277), Hispanic students (276), and Black (268) students. In math, Asian/Pacific Islander students had the highest average score (172), followed by Whites (162), American

---

[2]We acknowledge that the term English language learner (ELL) is an imprecise measure of students' immigrant status. Unfortunately, the federal data used in this chapter do not provide measures of student or parent place of birth. There may be immigrant students who are fluent in English and thus not classified as ELL and native-born students who are classified as ELL. An ELL student, as defined by the National Center for Education Statistics (NCES), is one who has "sufficient difficulty speaking, reading, writing, or understanding the English language."

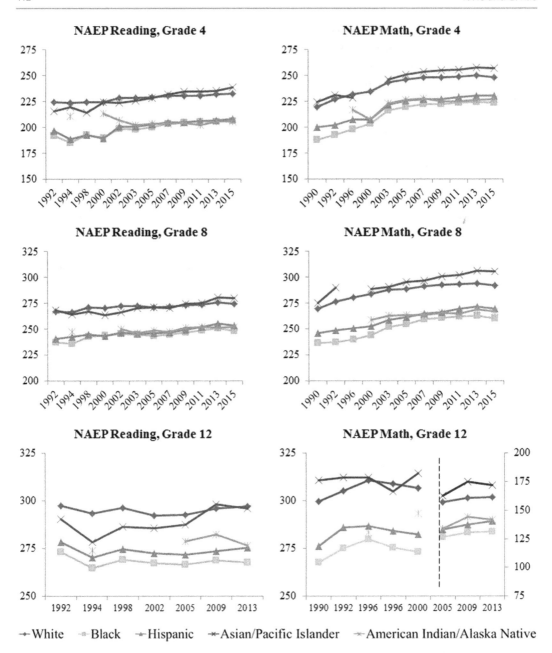

Fig. 5.1 Trends in NAEP reading and math scores by race/ethnicity. (*Broken lines* are due to lack of data for that year. In 2005, the math portion of the NAEP for 12th-graders was redesigned with a new scoring scale—scores from 2005 onwards are graphed on the secondary axis to the right. Authors' compilation of data from the NAEP Data Explorer (NDE), U.S. Department of Education, Institute of Education Sciences, National Center for Education Statistics (https://nces.ed.gov/nationsreport-card/naepdata/))

Indian/Alaska Native (142), Hispanic students (141), and Black students (132).

There are large differences in both reading and math scores between non-ELL students and their ELL peers in both 8th and 12th grade, on average and across racial/ethnic groups (Fig. 5.2). Among 8th-graders, non-ELL students had an average reading score of 268 compared to a score of 223

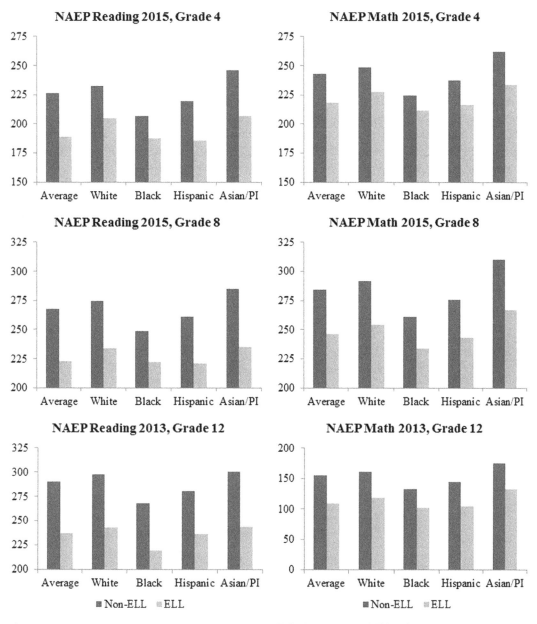

Fig. 5.2 Average NAEP reading and math scores in 2015 by ELL status and race/ethnicity. (Authors' compilation of data from the NAEP Data Explorer (NDE), U.S. Department of Education, Institute of Education Sciences, National Center for Education Statistics (https://nces.ed.gov/nationsreportcard/naepdata/))

for ELL students. In math, non-ELL students had a score of 284 compared to 246 for their ELL peers. Among 12th graders, non-ELL students had an average reading score of 290 compared to 237 for their ELL peers. In math, non-ELL students scored an average of 155 compared to 109 for ELL students. This pattern of ELL disadvantage holds across racial and ethnic groups in both 8th and 12th grade. However, racial and ethnic gaps among ELL students are generally smaller than those found among non-ELL students.

5.3.2 High School Grades and Coursework

The NAEP High School Transcript Study (HSTS) collects transcript data on a nationally representative sample of graduating U.S. high school students. Data from HSTS show that the racial and ethnic and immigrant differences in test scores are mirrored in students' grades and coursework as well. Between 1990 and 2009, the average GPA of all students increased slightly, but racial/ethnic differences persist (Fig. 5.3). Asian/Pacific Islander students maintain the highest GPAs (3.26 in 2009), followed by White (3.09), American Indian/Alaska Native (2.87), and

Hispanic (2.84) students, while Black students, on average, have the lowest GPAs (2.69).

ELL students earn somewhat lower grades than their non-ELL peers (Fig. 5.4). The average GPA for ELL students in 2009 was 2.75, 0.25 points lower than that of non-ELL students. For some racial/ethnic groups, ELL students earn comparable or even higher grades than their non-ELL peers. For example, Black ELL students have an average GPA of 2.75, higher than the 2.69 average for non-ELL Black students. Hispanic ELL students have an average GPA that is 0.18 points lower than their non-ELL counterparts, smaller than the average non-ELL/ELL difference, and much smaller than the 0.30 point

Fig. 5.3 Trends in high school achievement by race/ethnicity. (Authors' compilation of data from the NAEP Data Explorer (NDE), U.S. Department of Education, Institute of Education Sciences, National Center for Education Statistics (https://nces.ed.gov/nationsreportcard/naepdata/))

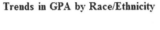
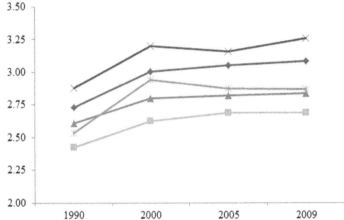
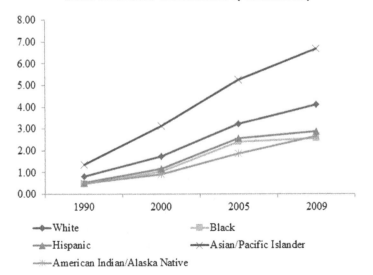

Fig. 5.4 High school achievement in 2009 by ELL status and race/ethnicity. (Authors' compilation of data from the NAEP Data Explorer (NDE), U.S. Department of Education, Institute of Education Sciences, National Center for Education Statistics. Data for White students did not meet reporting standards and are thus not shown (https://nces.ed.gov/nationsreportcard/naepdata/))

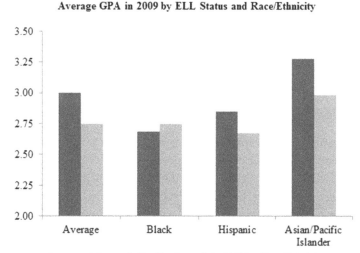

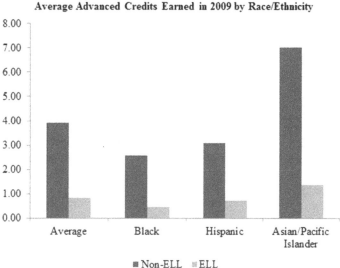

difference between Asian/Pacific Islander ELL and non-ELL students. Moreover, among ELL students, racial/ethnic differences in grades are less pronounced. Black ELL students have an average GPA comparable to the ELL student average while Hispanic ELL students have an average GPA just 0.08 points lower than the ELL average. In contrast, among non-ELL students, Black and Hispanic students have average GPAs that are 0.31 and 0.15 points lower than the non-ELL average, respectively.

Because students are likely to encounter some form of tracking once they enter formal schooling, it is important to examine differences in coursework. For high school students, enrolling in honors, Advanced Placement (AP), and International Baccalaureate (IB) courses can give them access to higher-quality instruction and indicate their college readiness to postsecondary institutions. The increasing relevance of advanced coursework for high school students is evident in the steep growth over the past two decades in the average number of advanced credits earned by students (Fig. 5.3). In 1990, with the exception of Asian/Pacific Islander students who earned slightly less than 1.5 credits, all student groups accumulated on average less than one advanced course credit, defined as an honors, pre-AP/AP, or pre-IB/IB course. By 2009, all racial and ethnic groups of students on average had more advanced course credits. However, the gaps between racial/ethnic groups also sharply increased. Asian/Pacific Islander students earned an average of nearly seven advanced course credits, while White students earned an average of just over four credits. Black, Hispanic, and American Indian/Alaskan Native students all accumulated on average between 2.5 and 3 advanced course credits, less than half that of Asian/Pacific Islander students.

The gap in advanced course credits between non-ELL and ELL students is also substantial (Fig. 5.4). On average, non-ELL students had about four advanced course credits, compared to less than one credit for ELL students. Black and Hispanic ELL students earned an average of less than one advanced course credit, while their non-ELL counterparts accumulated an average of between 2.5 to 3 credits, respectively. The ELL to non-ELL gap in credits earned is especially large among Asian/Pacific Islander students—non-ELL students earned about seven credits compared to fewer than two for ELL students. Thus, though ELL students had GPAs that were fairly comparable to their non-ELL peers, they are less likely to accumulate advanced credits.

5.4 High School Completion and College Readiness

The Averaged Freshman Graduation Rate (AFGR) is a measure used by the Department of Education that estimates on-time high school graduation with a regular diploma. In 2013–14, the overall AFGR was estimated to be 82%. Asian/Pacific Islander students had the highest AFGR—89%—followed by White students, at 87%. Hispanic students had an AFGR of 76%, followed by Black (73%) and American Indian/ Alaska Native (70%) students (Kena et al. 2016).

Another measure of high school completion is the "status dropout rate" (SDR) which relies on census data to estimate the percentage of 16- to 24-year-olds who are not enrolled in school and who have not received either a regular high school diploma or an equivalent credential, such

as a GED certificate. In 2014, the average SDR was about 7%, but this varied significantly by race, ethnicity, and nativity. Overall, Asian youths had the lowest average SDR (3%), followed by Whites (5%), Blacks (7%), and Hispanics (11%). However, among Hispanic and Asian subgroups, average SDRs varied considerably. Among Hispanics, Central American groups, such as Guatemalans (29%) and Hondurans (20%), generally had average SDRs higher than the Hispanic average while South Americans, such as Colombians and Peruvians (both 3%), generally had lower average SDRs. The average SDR for Mexicans (11%) was similar to the Hispanic average. Among Asians, average SDRs for Nepalese (20%) and Burmese (28%) were much higher than the average Asian SDR. Hmong (6%), Cambodian (8%), and Laotian (9%) youth also had average SDRs higher than the Asian average (Kena et al. 2016). These widely varying estimates highlight the limitations of broad racial/ ethnic categories such as Hispanic and Asian when analyzing educational outcomes, although data limitations often preclude disaggregation by subgroups.

Among U.S.-born youth, Asians had the lowest average SDR (2%), followed by Whites (4%), Blacks and Pacific Islanders (both 7%), Hispanics (8%), and American Indians/Alaska Natives (11%). Among foreign-born youth, Asians and Whites had average SDRs comparable to their U.S.-born counterparts (3% and 4%, respectively). Black immigrant youth had a slightly lower average SDR (6%) than their U.S.-born peers while immigrant Hispanics and Pacific Islanders had much higher average SDRs (21% and 23%, respectively) (Kena et al. 2016). However, because the SDR measure is population-based and includes a broad age range, it likely includes many immigrants who never attended schools in the U.S. (Aud et al. 2010; Oropesa and Landale 2009).

Students who intend to enter postsecondary schooling usually have to take the SAT and/or the ACT. Across SAT test subjects, White and Asian/ Pacific Islander students have higher average scores than Black, Hispanic, and American Indian/Alaska Native students (The College

Board 2015). For the ACT, the percentage of 2015 high school graduates who met ACT college readiness benchmarks also varied by race/ethnicity, with a higher percentage of White and Asian students meeting benchmarks than other racial/ethnic minority students (ACT, Inc. 2015). Factors such as high school coursework and track placement likely shape students' preparedness for college entrance tests.

Researchers have also examined access to resources such as SAT/ACT test preparation courses and private tutors. Some studies have shown that minority students are more likely than their White peers to use such strategies to improve their performance (Alon 2010; Buchmann et al. 2010; Byun and Park 2012; Espenshade and Radford 2009). However, studies of low-income urban Black and Hispanic youth show that such students generally report limited knowledge about college entrance exams and their importance in college admissions and have less access to test preparation resources (Deil-Amen and Tevis 2010; Walpole et al. 2005). While special programs that seek to improve the college readiness of underrepresented minority students may be helpful, they likely offer fewer resources than what is available to students in high academic tracks (Ochoa 2013). Cram schools often found in Chinese and Korean ethnic communities may offer even less wealthy Asian American students access to supplementary education services (Byun and Park 2012; Lee and Zhou 2015), but these resources are less readily available to other minority students (Zhou and Kim 2006).

5.5 Postsecondary Enrollment and Completion

5.5.1 Postsecondary Enrollment

The immediate college enrollment rate, or the percentage of graduating high school students enrolled in 2- or 4-year colleges the following fall, was approximately 68% in 2014. Asian students had the highest immediate enrollment rate (85%), followed by Whites (68%), Blacks (63%), and Hispanics (62%). The college participation rate is

an estimate of the percentage of 18- to 24-year-olds enrolled in college. In 2014, the average college participation rate was about 40%. Asians had the highest college participation rate (65%), followed by Whites (42%), Pacific Islanders (41%), Hispanics and American Indians/Alaska Natives (both 35%), and Blacks (33%) (Kena et al. 2016). Studies using nationally representative longitudinal data find that differences in college enrollment between White and minority students are largely explained by differences in socioeconomic status and family background (Bennett and Xie 2003; Charles et al. 2007).

Among White students enrolled in college in 2013, about 35% attended a 2-year public institution. This is in contrast to 49% of all Hispanic students enrolled in college who attended 2-year public institutions. About 45% of American Indian/Alaska Native college students, 39% of Black students, and 38% of both Asian and Pacific Islander students attended public 2-year colleges. About 40% of White and 44% of Asian college students were enrolled in 4-year public institutions compared to 31% of both Pacific Islander and Black students and 34% of both Hispanic and American Indian/Alaska Native students. About 18% of White college students enrolled in private, not-for-profit 4-year institutions, followed by 14% of Asian students, 13% of both Black and Pacific Islander students, 11% of American Indian/Alaska Native students, and 10% of Hispanic students. Pacific Islander students had the highest rate of enrollment in private, for-profit schools (19%), followed by Black students (15%), American Indian/Alaska Native students (10%), Hispanic students (9%), White students (6%), and Asian students (4%) (Musu-Gillette et al. 2016).

In 2007–08, nearly one quarter of undergraduates had at least one immigrant parent. For some groups, immigrant generational status is especially salient to their postsecondary experiences. For example, among Asian college students, more than half (55%) were foreign-born and another 38% had at least one immigrant parent. Among Hispanic college students, 21% were foreign-born and 45% had at least one immigrant parent. Enrollment patterns among first and second generation immigrant Hispanic college students were comparable—for both groups, 51% were enrolled in community college, 36% in nonprofit 4-year schools, and 12% in for-profit schools. Among foreign-born Asian college students, 54% were enrolled in community colleges and 38% in nonprofit 4-year schools, compared to 40% and 55%, respectively, of second generation Asian college students. About 7% of foreign-born and 5% of U.S.-born Asian college students were enrolled in for-profit schools (Staklis and Horn 2012).

The type of institution students attend matters for their graduation rates—when comparing similar students attending differently selective institutions, researchers found that minority students have a higher likelihood of graduating if they attend a more selective institution (Alon and Tienda 2005). Some research has shown that Black and Hispanic applicants to highly selective schools receive an admissions advantage in terms of their ACT/SAT scores (though Asians do not) (Espenshade and Radford 2009). However, high schools vary in the amount of support they provide to students to help them navigate the transition to postsecondary schooling, which may result in underrepresented minority students applying to less selective schools than they are actually qualified for (Roderick et al. 2011). The concentration of immigrant students in community colleges is also an area of ongoing research concern, including issues of access, affordability, and language learning (Teranishi et al. 2011).

5.5.2   Postsecondary Completion

For students attending a 4-year college full-time for the first time in 2006, the average graduation rate after 4 years was 39%. About 46% of Asian students and 43% of White students graduated within 4 years. Hispanic students had an average 4-year graduation rate of 29%, and for Pacific Islander, American Indian/Alaska Native, and Black students, the corresponding rates were 24%, 22%, and 21%. Not surprisingly, 6-year graduation rates are higher overall (60%) and for all racial/ethnic groups compared to 4-year grad-

uation rates. Asian students had the highest 6-year graduation rate (71%), followed by Whites (63%), Hispanics (53%), Pacific Islanders (50%), Blacks (41%), and American Indian/Alaska Native students (41%) (Snyder et al. 2016). Another measure of college attainment is the percentage of adults over the age of 25 who have a postsecondary degree. In 2013, about 30% of adults had a bachelor's degree or higher. Among Asians, 52% earned a bachelor's or higher, followed by Whites (33%), Blacks (19%), Pacific Islanders (16%), American Indian/Alaska Natives (15%), and Hispanics (14%). The broad categories of Hispanic and Asian mask considerable variation by sub-groups. For example, 32% of South Americans and 25% of Cubans are college graduates compared to 10% of Mexicans and 8% of Salvadorans. Among Asian sub-groups, 73% of Asian Indian and 52% of Chinese adults have a college degree compared to 28% of Vietnamese adults (Musu-Gillette et al. 2016).

In 2008, the percentage of U.S.-born adults over the age of 25 with at least a bachelor's degree was about 28% and 24% for the foreign-born. Among Hispanics, about 13% of the U.S.-born and 12% of the foreign-born earned a college degree. U.S.- and foreign-born Asians students also had comparable rates of college degree attainment overall (50% and 49%, respectively). Though there are considerable variations in college degree attainment among both U.S.-born and foreign-born Hispanic and Asian sub-groups, within sub-groups rates of college degree attainment by nativity are similar. For example, 10% of U.S.-born and 9% of foreign-born Hondurans earned a college degree, and about 50% of U.S.-born and 51% of foreign-born Korean adults are college graduates (Kao et al. 2013).

5.6   The Importance of Race, Ethnicity, and Nativity

At every level of education and across multiple educational outcomes, patterns of racial and ethnic stratification are apparent. In general, Black, Hispanic, and American Indian/Alaska Native students experience poorer educational outcomes relative to more advantaged groups such as White and Asian students. Students identified as English Language Learners (ELL) on average also fare worse than non-ELL students, although racial and ethnic differences among ELL students typically, though not always, mirror those found among non-ELL students. In this section, we describe how these racial, ethnic, and immigrant differences in educational outcomes fit into the larger debates around racial relations in the U.S. We also highlight some of the issues that set children of immigrants apart from their peers with native-born parents.

Scholars envision various ways in which the U.S. racial and ethnic hierarchy may shift due to demographic changes, including the growing size and diversity of the immigrant population. Some scholars believe that "[c]hildren of Asian, black, mulatto, and mestizo immigrants cannot escape their ethnicity and race, as defined by the mainstream" and that discrimination will likely affect these students' academic performance (Portes et al. 2005). Others argue that boundaries between Whites and Asian and Latino groups are more likely to erode over time than Black–White lines (Lee and Bean 2010), suggesting more positive outcomes for non-Black minorities. Still others believe that a tri-racial hierarchy is more likely—with lighter-skinned minorities (such as East Asians and White Latinos) earning "honorary White" status and darker-skinned minorities forming a disadvantaged "collective Black" group (Bonilla-Silva 2004).

How the minority children of immigrant parents adapt to the U.S. racial and ethnic hierarchy is important for understanding their educational outcomes (Kao et al. 2013). Some research suggests that academically successful first and second generation minority youth assert a more "traditional" identity that they contrast with the "Americanized" values of their less successful co-ethnics (Lee 2005; Louie 2012; Matute-Bianchi 1986; Waters 1994). In interviews with West Indian and Haitian youths in New York, Waters (1994) found that although second generation youth all realized they were likely to be perceived as native Blacks by others, those from middle-class backgrounds tended to emphasize

their ethnic identity and immigrant origins, distancing themselves from native Blacks. These students believed that doing well in school would pay off. Poorer second generation youths tended to identify with native Black peers and believed they would have limited opportunities for upward mobility and did not do as well in school. Matute-Bianchi (1986) found similar patterns among Mexican-descent students in central California—academically successful first and second generation students used their immigrant and ethnic culture to distinguish themselves from less academically successful Chicanos and "cholos." In contrast to the negative stereotypes about Black and Hispanic students' academic abilities, the general academic success of Asian students has led to the "model minority" stereotype that paints all Asian students as naturally high-achieving. However, the stereotype can be harmful to Asian groups that do not fare as well academically because their struggles may be overlooked in schools (Lee 2005; Ngo and Lee 2007; Teranishi 2010), and also contributes to perceptions of Asian students as overly competitive academically and less well-rounded (Jiménez and Horowitz 2013; Kao 1995; Oakes and Guiton 1995; Ochoa 2013).

In addition to their experiences with the racial and ethnic hierarchy of the U.S., children of immigrants are also affected by generational status. The proportions of first, second, and third generation and higher varies considerably across groups. Among Hispanic youth, about 6% are first-generation, 51% second generation, and 42% third generation or higher. For Asian youth, the corresponding estimates are 13%, 65%, and 20%; for Black youth 2%, 12%, and 86%; for White youth less than 1%, 7%, and 92%. These generational differences matter for student outcomes. Among first-generation youth, the age of arrival matters for language acquisition and socialization (Rumbaut 2004). Research is mixed on whether the first or second generation immigrants experience better educational outcomes (Baum and Flores 2011; Coll and Marks 2012; Crosnoe and Turley 2011; Duong et al. 2015; Kao and Tienda 1995; White and Glick 2009). An ongoing research concern is the notion of "immigrant paradox," where greater acculturation is associated with poorer health, behavioral, and educational outcomes, and the mechanisms behind the paradox (Coll and Marks 2012; Crosnoe and Turley 2011). Evidence of the paradox often depends on the population studied and how researchers define and measure acculturation. Some scholars argue that immigrant parents and their children experience assimilation differently and that when children acculturate to American norms and lack ties to their ethnic communities, "dissonant" acculturation may result, leading to conflicts with parents and lower achievement. Dissonant acculturation, such scholars argue, is more likely among immigrant groups that arrive with fewer socioeconomic resources and who perceive little chance of upward mobility (Portes and Rumbaut 2001).

5.7 Academic Outcomes in Context

Prior reviews of research have concluded that family socioeconomic status (SES) accounts for a significant portion of differences in educational outcomes for racial/ethnic minority students (Kao and Thompson 2003; Lee 2002; Magnuson and Duncan 2006; Sakamoto et al. 2009; Sewell et al. 1969). However, an ongoing research concern is to understand what factors beyond SES contribute to remaining academic gaps (Hallinan 1988). Below, we review several bodies of literature on non-familial resources that may influence educational outcomes, and focus on how these factors might matter in particular for minority and immigrant students.

5.7.1 Schools and Teachers

The role schools play in minority student outcomes is an area of ongoing research. Researchers have used seasonal comparison studies—in which student achievement is measured when schools are in session and out of session—to try to isolate the effects of schooling on student outcomes. Such studies have shown that while schools help "equalize" class differences in educational outcomes (Downey and Condron 2016), Black–White achievement gaps actually grow during the school year (Condron 2009; Downey et al. 2004). Using data from the nationally representative Early Childhood Longitudinal Study, Kindergarten Class of 1998–99 (ECLS-K), Downey et al. (2004) measured kindergarten, summer, and first-grade learning rates. After accounting for socioeconomic status, the authors found that Black and Hispanic students learned at similar rates to White students, and Asian students at a faster rate, during the summer between kindergarten and first grade. However, during the kindergarten and first-grade school years, Black students learned at slower rates than White students, and Asian students lost their advantage, suggesting that early schooling experiences are a source of racial/ethnic inequality. In another seasonal study using ECLS-K data, Condron (2009) found that school characteristics, such as having a predominantly minority student population and using ability grouping, explained more of the Black–White achievement gap in first grade than non-school factors, although the exact mechanisms through which these school factors impact minority students is less clear.

In a review of research on school segregation and its effects on students, Reardon and Owens (2014) argue that while much research has focused on the extent of school racial segregation, which has remained largely unchanged for the past 25 years, research has not yet provided solid theoretical models for how segregation affects educational outcomes. While studies on the effects of early desegregation policies showed improvements for Black students, and no harmful effects for White students, more contemporary studies have yielded mixed findings on the link between segregation and achievement. For example, Black high school students in predominantly White schools are less likely to take higher-level math courses than Black students in predominantly Black schools (Kelly 2009), but racially balanced schools appear to provide more equitable access to higher-level English courses than schools that are predominantly White or Black (Southworth and Mickelson 2007). Reardon and

Owens (2014) suggest that the mechanisms through which racial segregation affects student achievement may have changed over time—for example, differences in school resources might have been a primary reason for Black–White educational inequality in the past but such a mechanism might not be as applicable today if school resources are distributed more evenly. They argue that to better understand how segregation affects student outcomes, researchers should examine the links between segregation and the availability, distribution, and impact of various school resources.

School policies such as ability grouping and tracking may contribute to racial and ethnic differences in educational outcomes. Studies have shown that Black and Hispanic students are less likely to be placed in higher-level academic tracks compared to Asian and White students (Dauber et al. 1996; Oakes et al. 1990; Oakes and Guiton 1995; Ochoa 2013) and that ELL students may be isolated from mainstream courses while they gain English fluency, preventing them from participating in higher-level coursework in other subjects (Callahan 2005). While there are mixed findings on whether minority students remain at a disadvantage in course placement once prior achievement is accounted for (Van de Werfhorst and Mijs 2010), it is important to note that racial and ethnic differences in academic outcomes are present from an early age and can grow over time due to a variety of both school and non-school factors. These early differences likely shape students' track placements, which can be based on a variety of subjective criteria, including teacher beliefs about student abilities—beliefs that may be influenced by students' race/ethnicity (Gamoran 1992; Oakes and Guiton 1995). Studies have shown that generally there are few opportunities for students to move into higher-level tracks once placed into low-level tracks (Dauber et al. 1996; Hallinan 1996). Access to advanced coursework is associated with higher achievement (Gamoran 1987) and being in a higher-level track can benefit students through greater access to school resources, such as regular meetings with counselors (Oakes and Guiton 1995; Ochoa 2013).

Research also points to the important role teachers' expectations can play in shaping student outcomes. In their influential model of the educational and occupational attainment process, Sewell et al. (1969) included teachers alongside parents and peers as "significant others" whose expectations are likely to influence students' own aspirations and attainment. Their model suggested that students' prior academic achievement would be a strong influence on teacher expectations, but other researchers have since pointed out the importance of race. Alexander et al. (1987) found that White and Black teachers from higher-SES backgrounds tended to rate Black first-graders more negatively than White children, while student race did not seem to matter for ratings among teachers from lower-SES backgrounds. These ratings mattered for students' grades, with Black children performing worse than White children in the classrooms of high-SES teachers but not in the classrooms of low-SES teachers. Some research suggests that once family background and academic performance is controlled for, there are no racial differences in how high school students perceive teacher expectations (Cheng and Starks 2002), although Alexander et al. (1987) suggest that differences in teacher expectations may be most apparent at earlier stages of schooling, when expectations and academic trajectories are first formed.

One of the mechanisms through which teacher expectations may influence student performance on tests is "stereotype threat"—the theory that negative stereotypes, such as those about the academic abilities of minority groups, can cause students to feel threatened, out of fear of being judged by that stereotype or conforming to it, and hamper performance (Steele 1997). Another perspective is that "positive" stereotypes can cause students to "choke under pressure." In an experimental study, researchers primed some Asian American female students, a group that would fall under the "model minority" stereotype, about their ethnic identity prior to a math test and found this group performed lower than the control group (Cheryan and Bodenhausen 2000). Most studies of the stereotype threat have been done in lab settings (Spencer et al. 2016), so it is not always clear how it would operate in classroom settings.

5.7.2 Peer Relationships

Research has shown that adolescents' friendships are important for their emotional well-being (Giordano 2003) and educational outcomes (Cherng et al. 2013; Hallinan and Williams 1990). Using data from the National Longitudinal Study of Adolescent Health, which followed a nationally representative sample of middle and high school students, Cherng et al. (2013) found that students benefitted academically in terms of college completion from having best friends with college-educated mothers, above and beyond their own family resources. The authors suggested that friendships are an "underrecognized" resource for students. In an earlier study using different nationally representative data, Hallinan and Williams (1990) found evidence that interracial friendships between Black and White students were related to positive outcomes, such as higher educational aspirations. However, the influence of peers on students' educational outcomes remains understudied, particularly the roles of "structuring" variables such as race/ethnicity (Giordano 2003) and nativity (Cherng 2015).

One of the most prominent theories about the importance of student attitudes and peer groups is Ogbu's cultural-ecological theory (Ogbu 2004; Ogbu and Simons 1998). Though Ogbu took into account the broader context or "ecology" of education for minority students—including educational policies and practices, societal rewards for educational achievement, and the treatment of minorities in school—it is the "cultural" component of his theory that has received the most attention. Ogbu argued that because they have experienced discrimination, Black students (as well as other "involuntary minorities" such as Puerto Ricans and Mexicans in the Southwest) do not believe education will help them achieve upward mobility. As a result, these students embrace an "oppositional culture" that hinders academic achievement because high achievement is considered "acting White" (Downey 2008; Ogbu 2004; Ogbu and Simons 1998; Warikoo and Carter 2009).

More recent work has argued that what is considered an "oppositional" attitude in minority students is actually a more general youth culture concerned with not appearing to be too overly studious, and that minority students do strongly believe in the value of education (Carter 2005; Goldsmith 2004; Harris 2011; Tyson et al. 2005; Warikoo 2011). Harris (2011) used survey data collected from Black and White families in Maryland and found that Black students are not embedded in peer groups that engage in negative behaviors or that hold negative academic attitudes. After accounting for SES, Black students' friends actually hold more positive attitudes toward school than White students' peer groups, a finding consistent with earlier research (Ainsworth-Darnell and Downey 1998; Hallinan and Williams 1990). Carter (2005) found that minority students who culturally "straddle" school and peer culture are successful academically and socially, offering a different approach to understanding minority youth culture.

5.7.3 Neighborhoods and Communities

More recently, there has been an increase in research on the role of neighborhoods in shaping educational outcomes. Broadly, neighborhoods are theorized to influence children's outcomes through both structural (e.g., unemployment, racial segregation, poverty rates) and social processes (e.g., social disorganization, social networks). Poorer neighborhoods might lack community institutions that provide extracurricular and enrichment activities for children (Bennett et al. 2012) and can be more "culturally heterogeneous" in regards to youth's educational goals, which plays a role in college enrollment patterns (Harding 2011). A number of studies have found the prolonged exposure to poorer neighborhoods, both across generations and within a child's own lifetime, is associated with lower academic performance and greater risk of dropping out of high school (Sharkey and Elwert 2011; Wodtke et al. 2011). However, on the whole, neighborhood effects literature has yielded mixed findings regarding children's academic outcomes, in part because it is challenging to separate neighborhood effects from important factors, such as family background and school characteristics, and because of inconsistencies in how researchers define and measure neighborhood characteristics (Arum 2000; DeLuca and Dayton 2009; Johnson 2010; Robert J. Sampson et al. 2002; Small and Newman 2001).

One of the ways researchers have sought to measure neighborhood effects is through housing mobility programs, which offer low-income, usually minority families the opportunity to move into neighborhoods with less poverty. Studies of the Gautreaux program, an early housing mobility program in Chicago, found benefits for children in families who moved to suburban areas through the program, including lower school dropout and higher college enrollment rates, compared to students whose families moved but stayed in urban neighborhoods. However, studies of later programs such as the Yonkers Family and Community Project in New York and the multi-city Moving to Opportunity (MTO) program have shown mixed results or even negative outcomes stemming from children changing neighborhoods (DeLuca and Dayton 2009; Johnson 2010). Researchers continue to debate outcomes from MTO, such as the relative importance of racial and social class segregation and the best way to measure individual-level outcomes (Clampet-Lundquist and Massey 2008; Ludwig et al. 2008; Sampson 2008), with some researchers arguing that the age at which children change neighborhoods and the length of exposure to different types of neighborhoods matter for educational outcomes (Chetty et al. 2016; Clampet-Lundquist and Massey 2008).

In studies of immigrant families and schooling, researchers have emphasized the role of ethnic communities for some immigrant groups. Segmented assimilation theory posits that assimilation paths are influenced in part by the strength of co-ethnic communities. Depending on their context, immigrant youth might assimilate into under-achieving minority communities, high-achieving mainstream communities, or they may selectively assimilate by maintaining ties to their ethnic community while striving for high educational achievement (Portes and Rumbaut 2001, 2006; Portes and Zhou 1993). Research has found that the average level of education of immigrant groups prior to migrating influenced immigrant children's educational expectations independent of their parents' own level of education, suggesting the importance of ethnic communities (Feliciano 2006). Ethnic communities can be useful resources for members, by providing access to information and resources for navigating school systems (Kasinitz et al. 2008). Ethnic communities can also define and enforce social norms in ways that both help and hinder academic achievement (Lee and Zhou 2015; Portes 1998; Zhou and Bankston 1994). Portes (1998) suggests that group solidarity might lead to "negative social capital" in the form of "downward leveling norms"—similar to "oppositional culture" arguments. Jennifer Lee and Min Zhou (2015) suggest that the ethnic communities of more highly selective immigrant groups, such as those of East Asians, are characterized by narrow definitions of success that emphasize high achievement, while less selective immigrant groups, such as Mexicans, define success more broadly. However, it can be difficult to measure individuals' embeddedness in ethnic communities, and measures are not always consistent across studies.

An emerging area of research for immigrant scholars has been the growth of immigrant populations in areas that previously experienced little immigration, particularly in parts of the South and Midwest (Massey 2008; Singer 2013; Tienda and Fuentes 2014; Waters and Jiménez 2005). Many of these new immigrant destinations are in rural and suburban areas, contexts that differ from the urban environments on which much of our theoretical understanding of immigrant assimilation is based. While there has been some research into the integration of immigrant families in these new destinations (Marschall et al.

2012; Massey 2008; Winders 2013), more research is needed to understand how communities and schools respond to new and growing immigrant populations and how immigrant children fare in these environments. Of course, what may matter most moving forward is the impact of anti-immigrant sentiments and policies in the U.S. on these vulnerable populations.

5.8   Conclusion

Growing far-right movements and anti-immigrant sentiments have imperiled many minority and immigrant families worldwide. A recent report from the United Nations notes that, globally, more than half of the nearly six million school-aged refugee children are not in school (United Nations High Commissioner for Refugees 2016). In the U.S., the changing demographics of the student population and the continued salience of race, ethnicity, and immigrant status for social stratification underscore the need for continued research on persistent racial, ethnic, and immigrant differences in educational achievement and attainment. At all levels of education, Black, Latino, and American Indian students experience poorer outcomes than their White and Asian peers. However, broad racial categories mask considerable variations by ethnicity and nativity, especially among Asian and Latino students. Moreover, how the racial and ethnic hierarchy both influences and is influenced by minority immigrant-origin youth has implications for students' educational outcomes.

Socioeconomic status consistently accounts for a sizeable share of the academic gap for minority and immigrant students but researchers are also interested in the ways other factors, such as schools and teachers, peer relationships, and neighborhoods and communities, influence student achievement. Research in these areas is important, particularly research focusing on how and why the effects of these factors vary across racial/ethnic and immigrant groups.

Though beyond the scope of this review, we note that how education pays off for different racial/ethnic and immigrant groups is an impor-

tant area of research. Among young adults with a bachelor's degree or higher, racial/ethnic minorities and immigrants have lower rates of employment than Whites and the native-born (Snyder et al. 2016). A recent audit study of job applications found that Black graduates of elite institutions receive fewer responses than Whites and the responses they do receive are for lower pay and less prestigious positions (Gaddis 2015). Some research finds that at all levels of higher education White males receive higher returns than Asian, Hispanic, and Black males (Hout 2012). Sakamoto et al. (2010) found that first and second generation immigrant Black males earn less than similarly educated White males, but more than non-immigrant-origin Black men. Zeng and Xie (2004) compared the earnings of U.S.- and foreign-educated Asian males to those of Whites, and found no earnings disadvantage among the former but a significant disadvantage among the latter. While a college education seems to protect Whites and Asians from economic downturns, it does not seem to do so for Blacks and Hispanics (Emmons and Noeth 2015). Future research should seek to connect earlier schooling experiences to later outcomes, with particular attention to how outcomes vary among individuals with similar educational levels.

References

ACT, Inc. (2015). *The condition of college & career readiness 2015*. https://www.act.org/content/dam/act/unsecured/documents/CCCR15-NationalReadinessRpt.pdf

Ainsworth-Darnell, J. W., & Downey, D. B. (1998). Assessing the oppositional culture explanation for racial/ethnic differences in school performance. *American Sociological Review, 63*(4), 536–553. https://doi.org/10.2307/2657266.

Alexander, K. L., Entwisle, D. R., & Thompson, M. S. (1987). School performance, status relations, and the structure of sentiment: Bringing the teacher back in. *American Sociological Review, 52*(5), 665–682. https://doi.org/10.2307/2095602.

Alon, S. (2010). Racial differences in test preparation strategies: A commentary on shadow education, American style: Test preparation, the SAT and college enrollment. *Social Forces, 89*(2), 463–474. https://doi.org/10.1353/sof.2010.0053.

Alon, S., & Tienda, M. (2005). Assessing the "mismatch" hypothesis: Differences in college graduation rates by institutional selectivity. *Sociology of Education, 78*(4), 294–315. https://doi.org/10.1177/003804070507800402.

Arum, R. (2000). Schools and communities: Ecological and institutional dimensions. *Annual Review of Sociology, 26*(1), 395–418. https://doi.org/10.1146/annurev.soc.26.1.395.

Aud, S., Fox, M. A., & KewalRemani, A. (2010). *Status and trends in the education of racial and ethnic groups* (NCES 2010–15). Washington, DC: U.S. Department of Education, National Center for Education Statistics. http://nces.ed.gov/pubsearch/pubsinfo.asp?pubid=2010015. Accessed 10 Nov 2015.

Baum, S., & Flores, S. M. (2011). Higher education and children in immigrant families. *The Future of Children, 21*(1), 171–193. https://doi.org/10.1353/foc.2011.0000.

Bennett, P. R., & Xie, Y. (2003). Revisiting racial differences in college attendance: The role of historically Black colleges and universities. *American Sociological Review, 68*(4), 567–580. https://doi.org/10.2307/1519739.

Bennett, P. R., Lutz, A. C., & Jayaram, L. (2012). Beyond the schoolyard: The role of parenting logics, financial resources, and social institutions in the social class gap in structured activity participation. *Sociology of Education, 85*(2), 131–157. https://doi.org/10.1177/0038040711431585.

Bonilla-Silva, E. (2004). From bi-racial to tri-racial: Towards a new system of racial stratification in the USA. *Ethnic and Racial Studies, 27*(6), 931–950. https://doi.org/10.1080/0141987042000268530.

Buchmann, C., Condron, D. J., & Roscigno, V. J. (2010). Shadow education, American style: Test preparation, the SAT and college enrollment. *Social Forces, 89*(2), 435–461.

Byun, S., & Park, H. (2012). The academic success of East Asian American youth: The role of shadow education. *Sociology of Education, 85*(1), 40–60.

Callahan, R. M. (2005). Tracking and high school English learners: Limiting opportunity to learn. *American Educational Research Journal, 42*(2), 305–328. https://doi.org/10.3102/00028312042002305.

Carter, P. L. (2005). *Keepin' it real: School success beyond Black and White*. Oxford: Oxford University Press.

Charles, C. Z., Roscigno, V. J., & Torres, K. C. (2007). Racial inequality and college attendance: The mediating role of parental investments. *Social Science Research, 36*(1), 329–352. https://doi.org/10.1016/j.ssresearch.2006.02.004.

Cheng, S., & Starks, B. (2002). Racial differences in the effects of significant others on students' educational expectations. *Sociology of Education, 75*(4), 306–327. https://doi.org/10.2307/3090281.

Cherng, H.-Y. S. (2015). Social isolation among racial/ethnic minority immigrant youth. *Sociology Compass, 9*(6), 509–518. https://doi.org/10.1111/soc4.12276.

Cherng, H.-Y. S., Calarco, J. M., & Kao, G. (2013). Along for the ride: Best friends' resources and adolescents' college completion. *American Educational Research Journal, 50*(1), 76–106. https://doi.org/10.3102/0002831212466689.

Cheryan, S., & Bodenhausen, G. V. (2000). When positive stereotypes threaten intellectual performance: The psychological hazards of "model minority" status. *Psychological Science, 11*(5), 399–402. https://doi.org/10.1111/1467-9280.00277.

Chetty, R., Hendren, N., & Katz, L. F. (2016). The effects of exposure to better neighborhoods on children: New evidence from the Moving to Opportunity experiment. *American Economic Review, 106*(4), 855–902. https://doi.org/10.1257/aer.20150572.

Clampet-Lundquist, S., & Massey, D. S. (2008). Neighborhood effects on economic self-sufficiency: A reconsideration of the Moving to Opportunity experiment. *American Journal of Sociology, 114*(1), 107–143. https://doi.org/10.1086/588740.

Coll, C. G., & Marks, A. K. E. (Eds.). (2012). *The immigrant paradox in children and adolescents: Is becoming American a developmental risk?* Washington, DC: American Psychological Association. Accessed 12 July 2013.

College Board. (2015). *2015 College-bound seniors: Total group profile report*. New York: College Board. https://secure-media.collegeboard.org/digitalServices/pdf/sat/total-group-2015.pdf

Condron, D. J. (2009). Social class, school and non-school environments, and Black/White inequalities in children's learning. *American Sociological Review, 74*(5), 685–708. https://doi.org/10.1177/000312240907400501.

Crosnoe, R., & Turley, R. N. L. (2011). K–12 educational outcomes of immigrant youth. *The Future of Children, 21*(1), 129–152. https://doi.org/10.1353/foc.2011.0008.

Dauber, S. L., Alexander, K. L., & Entwisle, D. R. (1996). Tracking and transitions through the middle grades: Channeling educational trajectories. *Sociology of Education, 69*(4), 290–307. https://doi.org/10.2307/2112716.

Deil-Amen, R., & Tevis, T. L. (2010). Circumscribed agency: The relevance of standardized college entrance exams for low SES high school students. *The Review of Higher Education, 33*(2), 141–175. https://doi.org/10.1353/rhe.0.0125.

DeLuca, S., & Dayton, E. (2009). Switching social contexts: The effects of housing mobility and school choice programs on youth outcomes. *Annual Review of Sociology, 35*(1), 457–491. https://doi.org/10.1146/annurev-soc-070308-120032.

Downey, D. B. (2008). Black/White differences in school performance: The oppositional culture explanation. *Annual Review of Sociology, 34*(1), 107–126. https://doi.org/10.1146/annurev.soc.34.040507.134635.

Downey, D. B., & Condron, D. J. (2016). Fifty years since the Coleman report: Rethinking the relationship between schools and inequality. *Sociology of Education, 89*(3), 207–220. https://doi.org/10.1177/0038040716651676.

Downey, D. B., von Hippel, P. T., & Broh, B. A. (2004). Are schools the great equalizer? Cognitive inequality during the summer months and the school year. *American Sociological Review, 69*(5), 613–635. https://doi.org/10.2307/3593031.

Duong, M. T., Badaly, D., Liu, F. F., Schwartz, D., & McCarty, C. A. (2015). Generational differences in academic achievement among immigrant youths: A meta-analytic review. *Review of Educational Research.* https://doi.org/10.3102/0034654315577680.

Emmons, W. R., & Noeth, B. J. (2015). *Why didn't higher education protect Hispanic and Black wealth?* (No. 12). St. Louis: Center for Household Financial Stability, Federal Reserve Bank of St. Louis. https://www.stlouisfed.org/publications/in-the-balance/issue12-2015/why-didnt-higher-education-protect-hispanic-and-black-wealth. Accessed 6 Feb 2015.

Entwisle, D. R., & Alexander, K. L. (1993). Entry into school: The beginning school transition and educational stratification in the United States. *Annual Review of Sociology, 19*, 401–423. https://doi.org/10.2307/2083394.

Espenshade, T. J., & Radford, A. W. (2009). *No longer separate, not yet equal: Race and class in elite college admission and campus life.* Princeton: Princeton University Press.

Feliciano, C. (2006). Beyond the family: The influence of premigration group status on the educational expectations of immigrants' children. *Sociology of Education, 79*(4), 281–303. https://doi.org/10.1177/003804070607900401.

Fix, M., & Zimmermann, W. (2001). All under one roof: Mixed-status families in an era of reform. *International Migration Review, 35*(2), 397–419. https://doi.org/10.1111/j.1747-7379.2001.tb00023.x.

Fortuny, K., Capps, R., Simms, M., & Chaudry, A. (2009). *Children of immigrants: National and state characteristics* (No. 9). Washington, DC: The Urban Institute. http://www.urban.org/publications/411939.html. Accessed 2 Sept 2015.

Gaddis, S. M. (2015). Discrimination in the credential society: An audit study of race and college selectivity in the labor market. *Social Forces, 93*(4), 1451–1479. https://doi.org/10.1093/sf/sou111.

Gamoran, A. (1987). The stratification of high school learning opportunities. *Sociology of Education, 60*(3), 135–155. https://doi.org/10.2307/2112271.

Gamoran, A. (1992). Access to excellence: Assignment to honors English classes in the transition from middle to high school. *Educational Evaluation and Policy Analysis, 14*(3), 185–204. https://doi.org/10.3102/01623737014003185.

Gibbs, B. G., Shah, P. G., Downey, D. B., & Jarvis, J. A. (2016). The Asian American advantage in math among young children: The complex role of parenting. *Sociological Perspectives.* https://doi.org/10.1177/0731121416641676.

Giordano, P. C. (2003). Relationships in adolescence. *Annual Review of Sociology, 29*(1), 257–281. https://doi.org/10.1146/annurev.soc.29.010202.100047.

Glick, J. E., & Bates, L. (2010). Diversity in academic achievement: Children of immigrants in U.S. schools. In E. L. Grigorenko & R. Takanishi (Eds.), *Immigration, diversity, and education.* New York: Routledge.

Goldsmith, P. A. (2004). Schools' racial mix, students' optimism, and the Black–White and Latino–White achievement gaps. *Sociology of Education, 77*(2), 121–147. https://doi.org/10.1177/003804070407700202.

Hallinan, M. T. (1988). Equality of educational opportunity. *Annual Review of Sociology, 14*(1), 249–268. https://doi.org/10.1146/annurev.so.14.080188.001341.

Hallinan, M. T. (1996). Race effects on students' track mobility in high school. *Social Psychology of Education, 1*(1), 1–24. https://doi.org/10.1007/BF02333403.

Hallinan, M. T., & Williams, R. A. (1990). Students' characteristics and the peer-influence process. *Sociology of Education, 63*(2), 122–132. https://doi.org/10.2307/2112858.

Harding, D. J. (2011). Rethinking the cultural context of schooling decisions in disadvantaged neighborhoods: From deviant subculture to cultural heterogeneity. *Sociology of Education, 84*(4), 322–339. https://doi.org/10.1177/0038040711417008.

Harris, A. L. (2011). *Kids don't want to fail: Oppositional culture and the Black–White achievement gap.* Cambridge, MA: Harvard University Press.

Hout, M. (2012). Social and economic returns to college education in the United States. *Annual Review of Sociology, 38*(1), 379–400. https://doi.org/10.1146/annurev.soc.012809.102503.

Jiménez, T. R., & Horowitz, A. L. (2013). When White is just alright: How immigrants redefine achievement and reconfigure the ethnoracial hierarchy. *American Sociological Review, 78*(5), 849–871. https://doi.org/10.1177/0003122413497012.

Johnson, O. (2010). Assessing neighborhood racial segregation and macroeconomic effects in the education of African Americans. *Review of Educational Research, 80*(4), 527–575. https://doi.org/10.3102/0034654310377210.

Kao, G. (1995). Asian Americans as model minorities? A look at their academic performance. *American Journal of Education, 103*(2), 121–159. https://doi.org/10.1086/444094.

Kao, G., & Thompson, J. S. (2003). Racial and ethnic stratification in educational achievement and attainment. *Annual Review of Sociology, 29*(1), 417–442. https://doi.org/10.1146/annurev.soc.29.010202.100019.

Kao, G., & Tienda, M. (1995). Optimism and achievement: The educational performance of immigrant youth. *Social Science Quarterly, 76*(1), 1–19.

Kao, G., Vaquera, E., & Goyette, K. (2013). *Education and immigration.* Cambridge: Polity Press.

Karoly, L. A., & Gonzalez, G. C. (2011). Early care and education for children in immigrant families. *The Future of Children, 21*(1), 71–101. https://doi.org/10.1353/foc.2011.0005.

Kasinitz, P., Mollenkopf, J. H., Waters, M. C., & Holdaway, J. (2008). *Inheriting the city: The children of immigrants come of age*. New York: Russell Sage Foundation.

Kelly, S. (2009). The Black–White gap in mathematics course taking. *Sociology of Education, 82*(1), 47–69. https://doi.org/10.1177/003804070908200103.

Kena, G., Hussar, W., McFarland, J., de Brey, C., Musu-Gillette, L., Wang, X., et al. (2016). *The condition of education 2016* (NCES 2016-144). Washington, DC: U.S. Department of Education, National Center for Education Statistics. http://nces.ed.gov/pubsearch/pubsinfo.asp?pubid=2016144. Accessed 7 July 2016.

Lee, J. (2002). Racial and ethnic achievement gap trends: Reversing the progress toward equity? *Educational Researcher, 31*(1), 3–12. https://doi.org/10.3102/0013189X031001003.

Lee, S. J. (2005). *Up against Whiteness: Race, school, and immigrant youth*. New York: Teachers College Press.

Lee, J., & Bean, F. D. (2010). *The diversity paradox: Immigration and the color line in twenty-first century America*. New York: Russell Sage Foundation.

Lee, J., & Zhou, M. (2015). *The Asian American achievement paradox*. New York: Russell Sage Foundation.

Louie, V. (2012). *Keeping the immigrant bargain: The costs and rewards of success in America*. New York: Russell Sage Foundation Publications.

Ludwig, J., Liebman, J. B., Kling, J. R., Duncan, G. J., Katz, L. F., Kessler, R. C., & Sanbonmatsu, L. (2008). What can we learn about neighborhood effects from the Moving to Opportunity experiment? *American Journal of Sociology, 114*(1), 144–188. https://doi.org/10.1086/588741.

Lynch, J. L. (2011). Infant health, race/ethnicity, and early educational outcomes using the ECLS-B. *Sociological Inquiry, 81*(4), 499–526. https://doi.org/10.1111/j.1475-682X.2011.00390.x.

Magnuson, K. A., & Duncan, G. J. (2006). The role of family socioeconomic resources in the Black–White test score gap among young children. *Developmental Review, 26*(4), 365–399. https://doi.org/10.1016/j.dr.2006.06.004.

Magnuson, K. A., & Waldfogel, J. (2005). Early childhood care and education: Effects on ethnic and racial gaps in school readiness. *The Future of Children, 15*(1), 169–196. https://doi.org/10.1353/foc.2005.0005.

Marschall, M. J., Shah, P. R., & Donato, K. (2012). Parent involvement policy in established and new immigrant destinations. *Social Science Quarterly, 93*(1), 130–151. https://doi.org/10.1111/j.1540-6237.2011.00833.x.

Massey, D. S. (Ed.). (2008). *New faces in new places: The changing geography of American immigration*. New York: Russell Sage Foundation.

Matute-Bianchi, M. E. (1986). Ethnic identities and patterns of school success and failure among Mexican-descent and Japanese-American students in a California high school: An ethnographic analysis. *American Journal of Education, 95*(1), 233–255. https://doi.org/10.1086/444298.

Musu-Gillette, L., Robinson, J., McFarland, J., KewalRamani, A., Zhang, A., & Wilkinson-Flicker, S. (2016). *Status and Trends in the Education of Racial and Ethnic Groups 2016* (NCES 2016-007). Washington, DC: U.S. Department of Education, National Center for Education Statistics. http://nces.ed.gov/pubsearch/pubsinfo.asp?pubid=2016007. Accessed 11 Aug 2016.

Ngo, B., & Lee, S. J. (2007). Complicating the image of model minority success: A review of Southeast Asian American education. *Review of Educational Research, 77*(4), 415–453. https://doi.org/10.3102/0034654307309918.

Noguera, P. A. (2008). Creating schools where race does not predict achievement: The role and significance of race in the racial achievement gap. *The Journal of Negro Education, 77*(2), 90–103.

Oakes, J., & Guiton, G. (1995). Matchmaking: The dynamics of high school tracking decisions. *American Educational Research Journal, 32*(1), 3–33. https://doi.org/10.3102/00028312032001003.

Oakes, J., Ormseth, T., Bell, R., & Camp, P. (1990). *Multiplying inequalities: The effects of race, social class, and tracking on opportunities to learn mathematics and science* (No. NSF-R-3928). Santa Monica: RAND Corporation. http://eric.ed.gov/?id=ED329615. Accessed 15 Dec 2015.

Ochoa, G. L. (2013). *Academic profiling: Latinos, Asian Americans, and the achievement gap*. Minneapolis: University of Minnesota Press.

Ogbu, J. U. (2004). Collective identity and the burden of "acting White" in Black history, community, and education. *The Urban Review, 36*(1), 1–35. https://doi.org/10.1023/B:URRE.0000042734.83194.f6.

Ogbu, J. U., & Simons, H. D. (1998). Voluntary and involuntary minorities: A cultural-ecological theory of school performance with some implications for education. *Anthropology & Education Quarterly, 29*(2), 155–188. https://doi.org/10.1525/aeq.1998.29.2.155.

Oropesa, R. S., & Landale, N. S. (2009). Why do immigrant youths who never enroll in U.S. schools matter? School enrollment among Mexicans and non-Hispanic Whites. *Sociology of Education, 82*(3), 240–266. https://doi.org/10.1177/003804070908200303.

Passel, J. S. (2011). Demography of immigrant youth: Past, present, and future. *The Future of Children, 21*(1), 19–41. https://doi.org/10.1353/foc.2011.0001.

Portes, A. (1998). Social capital: Its origins and applications in modern sociology. *Annual Review of Sociology, 24*(1), 1–24. https://doi.org/10.1146/annurev.soc.24.1.1.

Portes, A., & Rumbaut, R. G. (2001). *Legacies: The story of the immigrant second generation*. Berkeley: University of California Press.

Portes, A., & Rumbaut, R. G. (2006). *Immigrant America: A portrait*. Berkeley: University of California Press.

Portes, A., & Zhou, M. (1993). The new second generation: Segmented assimilation and its variants. *The Annals of the American Academy of Political and Social Science, 530*(1), 74–96. https://doi.org/10.1177/0002716293530001006.

Portes, A., Fernández-Kelly, P., & Haller, W. (2005). Segmented assimilation on the ground: The new second generation in early adulthood. *Ethnic and Racial Studies, 28*(6), 1000–1040. https://doi.org/10.1080/01419870500224117.

Reardon, S. F., & Owens, A. (2014). 60 years after Brown: Trends and consequences of school segregation. *Annual Review of Sociology, 40*(1), 199–218. https://doi.org/10.1146/annurev-soc-071913-043152.

Roderick, M., Coca, V., & Nagaoka, J. (2011). Potholes on the road to college: High school effects in shaping urban students' participation in college application, four-year college enrollment, and college match. *Sociology of Education, 84*(3), 178–211. https://doi.org/10.1177/0038040711411280.

Rumbaut, R. G. (2004). Ages, life stages, and generational cohorts: Decomposing the immigrant first and second generations in the United States. *International Migration Review, 38*(3), 1160–1205. https://doi.org/10.1111/j.1747-7379.2004.tb00232.x.

Sakamoto, A., Goyette, K. A., & Kim, C. (2009). Socioeconomic attainments of Asian Americans. *Annual Review of Sociology, 35*(1), 255–276.

Sakamoto, A., Woo, H., & Kim, C. (2010). Does an immigrant background ameliorate racial disadvantage? The socioeconomic attainments of second-generation African Americans. *Sociological Forum, 25*(1), 123–146. https://doi.org/10.1111/j.1573-7861.2009.01160.x.

Sampson, R. J. (2008). Moving to inequality: Neighborhood effects and experiments meet social structure. *American Journal of Sociology, 114*(1), 189–231. https://doi.org/10.1086/589843.

Sampson, R. J., Morenoff, J. D., & Gannon-Rowley, T. (2002). Assessing "neighborhood effects": Social processes and new directions in research. *Annual Review of Sociology, 28*(1), 443–478. https://doi.org/10.1146/annurev.soc.28.110601.141114.

Sewell, W. H., Haller, A. O., & Portes, A. (1969). The educational and early occupational attainment process. *American Sociological Review, 34*(1), 82–92. https://doi.org/10.2307/2092789.

Sharkey, P., & Elwert, F. (2011). The legacy of disadvantage: Multigenerational neighborhood effects on cognitive ability. *American Journal of Sociology, 116*(6), 1934–1981. https://doi.org/10.1086/660009.

Singer, A. (2013). Contemporary immigrant gateways in historical perspective. *Daedalus, 142*(3), 76–91. https://doi.org/10.1162/DAED_a_00220.

Small, M. L. (2009). *Unanticipated gains: Origins of network inequality in everyday life.* New York: Oxford University Press.

Small, M. L., & Newman, K. (2001). Urban poverty after the truly disadvantaged: The rediscovery of the family, the neighborhood, and culture. *Annual Review of Sociology, 27*(1), 23–45. https://doi.org/10.1146/annurev.soc.27.1.23.

Snyder, T. D., de Brey, C., & Dillow, S. A. (2016). *Digest of education statistics, 2014* (NCES 2016–6). Washington, DC: National Center for Education Statistics, Institute of Education Sciences, U.S. Department of Education. http://nces.ed.gov/pubsearch/pubsinfo.asp?pubid=2016006. Accessed 28 Apr 2016.

Southworth, S., & Mickelson, R. A. (2007). The interactive effects of race, gender and school composition on college track placement. *Social Forces, 86*(2), 497–523. https://doi.org/10.2307/20430751.

Spencer, S. J., Logel, C., & Davies, P. G. (2016). Stereotype threat. *Annual Review of Psychology, 67*(1), 415–437. https://doi.org/10.1146/annurev-psych-073115-103235.

Staklis, S., & Horn, L. (2012). *New Americans in postsecondary education: A profile of immigrant and second-generation American undergraduates.* National Center for Education Statistics, Institute of Education Sciences, U.S. Department of Education. https://nces.ed.gov/pubsearch/pubsinfo.asp?pubid=2012213. Accessed 17 Apr 2014.

Steele, C. M. (1997). A threat in the air: How stereotypes shape intellectual identity and performance. *American Psychologist, 52*(6), 613–629. https://doi.org/10.1037/0003-066X.52.6.613.

Teranishi, R. T. (2010). *Asians in the ivory tower: Dilemmas of racial inequality in American higher education.* New York: Teachers College Press.

Teranishi, R. T., Suárez-Orozco, C., & Suárez-Orozco, M. (2011). Immigrants in community colleges. *The Future of Children, 21*(1), 153–169. https://doi.org/10.1353/foc.2011.0009.

The Urban Institute. (n.d.). The Urban Institute Children of Immigrants Data Tool: Data from the integrated public use microdata series datasets drawn from the 2012 and 2013 American Community Survey. http://datatool.urban.org/charts/datatool/pages.cfm. Accessed 17 May 2016.

Tienda, M., & Fuentes, N. (2014). Hispanics in metropolitan America: New realities and old debates. *Annual Review of Sociology, 40*, 499–520.

Torche, F. (2016). Torche comment on Downey and Condron. *Sociology of Education, 89*(3), 229–230. https://doi.org/10.1177/0038040716651680.

Tyson, K., Darity, W., & Castellino, D. R. (2005). It's not "a Black thing": Understanding the burden of acting White and other dilemmas of high achievement. *American Sociological Review, 70*(4), 582–605. https://doi.org/10.1177/000312240507000403.

United Nations High Commissioner for Refugees. (2016). *Missing out: Refugee education in crisis.* Geneva. http://www.unhcr.org/57d9d01d0. Accessed 22 Feb 2017.

Van de Werfhorst, H. G., & Mijs, J. J. B. (2010). Achievement inequality and the institutional structure of educational systems: A comparative perspective. *Annual Review of Sociology, 36*(1), 407–428. https://doi.org/10.1146/annurev.soc.012809.102538.

Walpole, M., McDonough, P. M., Bauer, C. J., Gibson, C., Kanyi, K., & Toliver, R. (2005). This test is unfair: Urban African American and Latino high school students' perceptions of standardized college admission tests. *Urban Education, 40*(3), 321–349. https://doi.org/10.1177/0042085905274536.

Warikoo, N. (2011). *Balancing acts: Youth culture in the global city*. Berkeley: University of California Press. Accessed 13 Jan 2016.

Warikoo, N., & Carter, P. (2009). Cultural explanations for racial and ethnic stratification in academic achievement: A call for a new and improved theory. *Review of Educational Research, 79*(1), 366–394. https://doi.org/10.3102/0034654308326162.

Waters, M. C. (1994). Ethnic and racial identities of second-generation Black immigrants in New York City. *The International Migration Review, 28*(4), 795–820. https://doi.org/10.2307/2547158.

Waters, M. C., & Jiménez, T. R. (2005). Assessing immigrant assimilation: New empirical and theoretical challenges. *Annual Review of Sociology, 31*(1), 105–125.

White, M. J., & Glick, J. E. (2009). *Achieving anew: How new immigrants do in American schools, jobs, and neighborhoods*. New York: Russell Sage Foundation.

Winders, J. (2013). *Nashville in the new millennium: Immigrant settlement, urban transformation, and social belonging*. New York: Russell Sage Foundation.

Wodtke, G. T., Harding, D. J., & Elwert, F. (2011). Neighborhood effects in temporal perspective: The impact of long-term exposure to concentrated disadvantage on high school graduation. *American Sociological Review, 76*(5), 713–736. https://doi.org/10.1177/0003122411420816.

Zeng, Z., & Xie, Y. (2004). Asian-Americans' earnings disadvantage reexamined: The role of place of education. *American Journal of Sociology, 109*(5), 1075–1108. https://doi.org/10.1086/381914.

Zhou, M., & Bankston, C. L. (1994). Social capital and the adaptation of the second generation: The case of Vietnamese youth in New Orleans. *International Migration Review, 28*(4), 821–845. https://doi.org/10.2307/2547159.

Zhou, M., & Kim, S. S. (2006). Community forces, social capital, and educational achievement: The case of supplementary education in the Chinese and Korean immigrant communities. *Harvard Educational Review, 76*(1), 1–29. https://doi.org/10.17763/haer.76.1.u08t548554882477.

Gender and Racial/Ethnic Differences in Educational Outcomes: Examining Patterns, Explanations, and New Directions for Research

6

Catherine Riegle-Crumb, Sarah Blanchard Kyte, and Karisma Morton

Abstract

Gender and race/ethnicity function as major axes of social stratification in the United States, and males and those from White backgrounds have historically occupied a position of advantage within the educational system. Although there has been progress towards decreasing inequality in recent decades, gender disparities and, to a much greater extent, racial/ethnic disparities remain in educational outcomes. This chapter reviews the empirical patterns and discusses the major theoretical explanations behind these patterns, focusing on K–16 education within the U.S. Additionally, some of the limitations of prior research are discussed. In closing, the authors also outline three key areas where more empirical sociological research is needed, and highlight recent research that provides compelling examples of where the field of sociology of education should be headed in order to better understand and disrupt educational inequality.

6.1 Introduction

As gender and race/ethnicity function as major axes of social stratification in the United States, males and those from White backgrounds have historically occupied a position of advantage within the educational system, with females and those from certain racial/ethnic minority groups (Black and Hispanic youth in particular) occupying positions of less advantage. Consequently, educational outcomes are not distributed equally across groups, which sets the stage for the creation and maintenance of inequality in the labor force, in the home, and in society at large.

In the first two parts of this chapter, we review the recent patterns of gender (Part 1) and racial/ethnic (Part 2) disparities in educational outcomes, and discuss the major theoretical explanations behind these patterns. We limit our focus to K–16 education within the United States, as an examination of comparative patterns across different countries is beyond the scope of this chapter. Within the K–12 realm, we focus on three different educational outcomes that are observable to others and serve as tangible representations of cognitive achievement: grades, test scores, and course-taking. These outcomes also capture, to some extent, students' mastery of the demands that schools place on students, both academic and social/behavioral. Additionally, these three outcomes strongly predict students' subse-

C. Riegle-Crumb (✉) · S. B. Kyte · K. Morton
The University of Texas at Austin, Austin, TX, USA
e-mail: riegle@austin.utexas.edu

© Springer International Publishing AG, part of Springer Nature 2018
B. Schneider (ed.), *Handbook of the Sociology of Education in the 21st Century*, Handbooks of Sociology and Social Research, https://doi.org/10.1007/978-3-319-76694-2_6

quent success in postsecondary education. For this next educational stage we focus on matriculation, attainment, and field of study. Again, these are observable outcomes that are believed to represent both the acquisition of knowledge as well as perseverance, and have important implications for whether and how individuals fare in the labor market and beyond. Our focus on these tangible outcomes leads us to discuss mostly quantitative literature in the sociology of education, although we discuss key contributions of qualitative research at several points.

We note that the organization of the chapter into separate sections focusing on gender and race/ethnicity follows the partitioned nature of research on inequality, as studies tend to focus on one axis of stratification but rarely consider both simultaneously. Subsequently, in the third part of this chapter, we discuss this and related limitations of prior research and outline key areas where we think more empirical sociological research is needed. In doing so, we also highlight recent studies that we think provide compelling examples of where the field of sociology of education should be headed. Overall, we argue that research needs to move towards an intersectional approach that brings a critical eye to average differences on particular outcomes and more fully considers the social construction of both identity and inequality.

6.2 Examining Patterns and Explanations for Gender Differences in Educational Outcomes

Although historically males in the U.S. have outpaced their female peers across a range of outcomes, an overall pattern of male advantage no longer applies. Instead, females now hold an advantage on many indicators, though males maintain an advantage in others. The fact that gender patterns vary across different outcomes has led to some confusion and seemingly contradictory accounts in the popular press and public discourse. Specifically, while some proclaim a "boy crisis" in schools, still others argue that girls remain strongly disadvantaged in an educational system rooted in patriarchy (Corbett et al. 2008; Sommers 2000).

From a theoretical standpoint, research within the sociology of education has done relatively little to help make sense of these complex patterns of gender inequality. Rather, studies tend to focus on examining a particular instance of inequality (e.g., boys' higher scores on a math test) and providing a relevant yet narrow explanation for its existence. While this specificity has certainly contributed to our collective knowledge of gender inequality, nevertheless there is a relative shortage of larger theoretical explanations that effectively encompass the broad constellation of gender differences—and gender similarities—in educational outcomes. To better orient the reader, we turn first to a brief overview of empirical research on gender differences in grades, test scores, and course-taking in K–12 education, and then disparities at the college level, before returning to a discussion of the theories that have been offered to explain these patterns, the limitations of such theories, and the need for more work in this area.

6.2.1 Gender Differences in Educational Outcomes in K–12 Education

6.2.1.1 Grades

The grades teachers give to students are both a measure of students' academic success and part of the educational process. Grades signal students' mastery of course content and in doing so provide positive or negative feedback that may guide students' future behaviors (Kelly 2008). For decades, gender differences in students' grades have favored girls (Buchmann et al. 2008; Entwisle et al. 1994; Mickelson 1989). In a meta-analysis of the female advantage in school grades from kindergarten through high school, Voyer and Voyer (2014) find that girls' grades are consistently higher than boys' across all academic subjects, with the largest gaps in language courses and the smallest gaps in math courses. Furthermore, they find no evidence for an increasing female advantage over time, discrediting arguments that boys today are in a new school achievement crisis (Sommers 2000). Although teachers do reward students' non-cognitive characteristics, such as effort and engagement, with higher grades (Farkas et al. 1990), recent empirical evidence finds that only substantive engagement leads to higher grades, as opposed to less academically-relevant forms of positive classroom behavior (Kelly 2008).

6.2.1.2 Course-Taking

The courses students take as they move through the K–12 pipeline towards postsecondary enrollment indicate their exposure to challenging curriculum across subjects. Following the transition from formal tracking to de facto tracking of academic subjects (Lucas 1999), scholars have paid attention to gender gaps in subject-specific course-taking. This focus is partly due to concerns that gender gaps in course-taking could contribute to gender disparities in college-going and to horizontal gender segregation in postsecondary education and the labor force (Buchmann and DiPrete 2006; Xie and Shauman 2003). Although math course-taking continues to powerfully shape students' preparation for and access to college (Adelman 1999; Bozick et al. 2007; Gamoran and Hannigan 2000; Riegle-Crumb 2006), gender gaps in math course-taking have long been closed (Catsambis 2005; Lee et al. 2007), even at the most advanced levels (Hyde et al. 2008). Gender gaps in science course-taking depend on the academic subject, with girls taking more biology and chemistry classes (Xie and Shauman 2003) but fewer courses in physics (Riegle-Crumb and Moore 2014). In terms of advanced placement (AP) course-taking, girls comprised 62% of AP English students,[1] 60% of AP biology students, and 48% of AP chemistry students, but only 35% of AP physics students and

22% of AP computer science students (College Board 2015 (author's calculations)). Thus, gender differences in course-taking only persist in the most advanced course offerings of the K–12 curriculum and are characterized by male and female advantages in different subjects.

6.2.1.3 Test Scores

Achievement tests—including those used by states to measure academic progress, assessments used in educational studies to measure cognitive skills, and college entrance exams such as the SAT and ACT—offer varied and sometimes conflicting views of gender disparities in educational success. These gaps have changed over time, and vary between academic subjects and across early and later grades. The most recent studies of gender differences in achievement in the early grades show strong similarities in girls' and boys' achievement, with some suggesting greater gains for boys in math achievement (Penner and Paret 2008), and others emphasizing a lack of differences in achievement across reading and math (DiPrete and Jennings 2012). Hyde et al. (2008) found no evidence of a gender difference in math skills as measured by the National Assessment of Educational Progress (NAEP) and only slightly greater variability in test scores among males among students in grades 2 through 11. Using nationally representative data from the Early Childhood Longitudinal Study, Robinson and Lubienski (2011) identify a slight male advantage in math test scores that emerges during elementary school (0.24 standard deviations (SD)) but disappears by the end of middle school. The authors also identify a widening female advantage in reading, particularly among the lowest achieving students; for example, the gap in eighth grade among the highest achievers (90th percentile) is 0.10 SD but about 0.25 for the lowest achievers (10th percentile) (ibid.). Digging deeper into a potential male advantage in math, Gibbs (2010) finds evidence in ECLS for gender gaps favoring boys in math as test items increase in complexity. For example, by third grade girls outperform boys by about 0.05 SD in items pertaining to relative size and ordinality and

---

[1] The College Board reports annually on the AP program in its *Report to the Nation*. Note that this report includes the number of students taking exams in subject fields rather than the number of students enrolled in courses designated as AP.

sequences but boys outperform girls by about 0.15 SD in place values and rate and measurement. By contrast, analysis of NAEP science test scores reveals a declining male advantage between third (0.23 SD) and eighth grade (0.19 SD) (Quinn and Cooc 2015). Finally, boys taking the ACT or SAT tend to slightly outscore girls taking these exams, a disparity often attributed to gender differences in selectivity, as more girls take these college entrance exams (Corbett et al. 2008; McNeish et al. 2015). These differences are also driven by boys' relatively higher scores on quantitative reasoning sections. For example, girls' average math scores on the 2014 SAT were 0.26 SD lower than boys' average scores (College Board 2014, Table 1 (author's calculation)).

Taken together, gender gaps in K–12 education that disadvantage girls are limited to course-taking in physics (as well as engineering and computer science, courses only rarely offered in high schools nationwide), and small differences on some (but not all) standardized tests in math and science. Yet at the same time, girls exhibit advantages in grades in all subjects across all years, and outperform boys in several subjects in both standardized exams and rates of advanced course-taking. Thus the weight of disparities in educational outcomes observed during the K–12 years arguably favors girls more than boys.

6.2.2 Gender Differences in College Outcomes

The general pattern of high female academic achievement in K–12 foreshadows contemporary gender gaps in higher education. Since the mid-1980s, women have outpaced men in terms of college attendance and graduation rates, with experts anticipating that the gender gap in college completion will continue to grow over the next decade (Buchmann and DiPrete 2006). However, notable areas of gender disparities persist, namely in matriculation to elite colleges and universities and in the horizontal gender segregation of students into majors. We now unpack gender disparities in each of these areas in turn.

6.2.2.1 College Matriculation and Persistence

As a college degree becomes ever more crucial to getting ahead in an increasingly competitive economy, rates of matriculation in colleges and universities have been rising. In the 2000s, men's rates of postsecondary enrollment increased by 36% compared with a 63% increase among women, a trend attributed to increased rates of postsecondary participation among low-income women and women of color (Buchmann 2009; Buchmann and DiPrete 2006; Savas 2016; Snyder and Dillow 2011). Among 2013 high school graduates, 68% of women enrolled in any college compared to only 63% of men (NCES 2014). This female advantage is evident in 4-year college attendance as well as 2-year college attendance. Additionally, unequal rates of persistence also contribute to widening gender disparities in attainment. In a recent study, Ewert (2010) found that a third of women, but only a quarter of men, aged 25–30 have completed a bachelor's degree (Ewert 2010). The gender gap in college persistence can be attributed to both weaker academic preparation for college and to poorer performance in college following enrollment among males (Buchmann and DiPrete 2006; Ewert 2010).

Despite a decades-long advantage in overall enrollment, women remain underrepresented at the most elite postsecondary institutions. Among this same ELS cohort, women comprised about 55% of enrollment in non-selective to highly-competitive 4-year colleges; yet, they comprised only 47% of those enrolled at the most selective institutions (Bielby et al. 2014). The authors note that women and men have comparable rates of application to such institutions, indicating that differences in matriculation rates are not the result of women being less likely to apply.

6.2.2.2 Field of Study

Despite this reversal in gender disparities in educational attainment over the past several decades, horizontal gender segregation—or gender gaps in the majors chosen by students—persists (Morgan et al. 2013; Riegle-Crumb et al. 2012). Earlier decreases in horizontal desegregation have been driven by women's increased entry into business-related fields and declining overrepresentation in fields like education and English (England and Li 2006). By contrast, men's choices of major have remained more constant and more concentrated in fields related to science, technology, engineering, and math (STEM) (England and Li 2006). Reports of aggregate disparities across STEM fields mask variation in the representation of women between STEM fields. Although women comprise roughly 40% of STEM majors, women outnumber men in the biological sciences but remain underrepresented in some STEM fields such as engineering and computer science (Mann and DiPrete 2013; Riegle-Crumb et al. 2012). Very little of the aggregate difference in STEM participation has been explained by students' prior achievement in science and math (which makes sense given the small scale of gender differences discussed in the previous section), nor by students' goals in work–family balance; rather, students' expected college majors and future careers as measured during their high school years are the single most powerful predictor of the gap in undergraduate STEM majors (Mann and DiPrete 2013; Morgan et al. 2013; Riegle-Crumb et al. 2012).

6.2.3 Theoretical Perspectives on Gender Differences in Educational Outcomes

Taken together, patterns of gender disparities in education appear complex. From kindergarten through twelfth grade, girls outperform boys in grades in all subjects. Differences in test scores are generally small and are subject-specific, with girls scoring higher on reading/writing tests and boys scoring higher on math or science tests. Similarly, gender differences in course-taking are small and yet also subject-specific, with boys taking physics and girls taking advanced placement courses in the humanities at higher rates. In postsecondary education, women have surpassed men in matriculation and completion of 4-year degrees, but men maintain higher rates of entry into the most selective colleges and universities

and into engineering and tech-driven fields, which are linked to highly in-demand sectors of the labor market (Xue and Larson 2015).

In terms of trying to explain gender inequality, studies within the sociology of education have tended to focus specifically on explaining or understanding a particular disparity. For example, studies that have focused on girls' higher academic performance as measured by grades earned in school have pointed to gender socialization, arguing that girls are raised to conform to the expectations dictated by adults and authorities, including following the academic "rules" of schools and conforming to teacher requests and expectations (Kaufman and Richardson 1982; Mickelson 1989). Some more recent research in this area refers to this as a female advantage in non-cognitive or social-behavioral skills, such as doing homework, studying for tests, and getting along with other students and their teachers, all of which lead to higher performance in school (DiPrete and Jennings 2012; Owens 2016).[2]

Explanations for boys' higher scores on math and science tests, on the other hand, have included several different theories. First, biological/genetic arguments have been offered by some to explain why boys score higher on tests of advanced math content in particular (Baron-Cohen 2003; Maccoby and Jacklin 1974; Spelke 2005). Such arguments fall short of explaining girls' relative advantage on tests of reading, and have been largely discredited on a variety of grounds (Ceci et al. 2009; Halpern 2013; Hyde and Mertz 2009). Instead, broad theories of gender socialization have argued that the girls are raised to think of math and science as masculine domains, which leads to doubt and a lack of self-confidence in these areas (Correll 2001; Eccles 2011; Riegle-Crumb et al. 2006). These approaches acknowledge the importance of gender stereotypes and norms, yet do not explicitly address how girls nevertheless earn higher grades

---

[2] We note here that while research typically views females' higher social-behavioral skills as a mediating variable to explain higher performance, it is arguable that such skills are an important educational outcome in their own right. We return to this point in Part 3 of this chapter.

than boys on these subjects. More recently, theories of stereotype threat offered primarily by social psychologists argue that stereotyped expectations become salient specifically in testing situations, where individuals feel that their performance has high stakes for representing their group (McGlone and Aronson 2006; Schmader 2002).

Arguments for disparities in course-taking have echoed some of the same explanations for test scores. When gaps were bigger (e.g., when girls did not take as much math and science as boys), explanations regarding presumed "natural abilities" were often offered, yet again, notably, focused on girls' disadvantage without simultaneously considering their advantage in reading. As these gaps have shrunk in recent decades to be very small and only present in a few classes, socialization arguments have become more prevalent, namely that girls and boys are raised to think of some subjects as masculine and others as feminine (Cheryan 2012; Cheryan et al. 2011; Steele 2003; Wang and Degol 2013). Note that such explanations are inadequate to explain why some classes have reached equity (calculus) while others have not (physics).

With regard to gender inequalities in college, different explanations are offered for different dimensions. Arguments for females' greater rates of matriculation have included utilitarian and rational actor models, such that as returns to college-going increased, girls' decisions to attend college responded accordingly (Charles and Luoh 2003; DiPrete and Buchmann 2006). This is typically coupled with an acknowledgement that gender norms had to shift to encourage girls to pursue higher education (Golden 2006; Reynolds and Burge 2008), as well as changes in family composition and the growth of single-mother families that encouraged educational investments in girls relative to boys (Buchmann and Diprete 2006; Doherty et al. 2015). Explanations for girls' greater persistence after matriculation tend to recall the same explanations offered for girls' greater grades, namely that they are socialized to do what is expected by those in authority positions, and that their better social-behavioral skills, such as engagement and effort, lead to greater educational attainment (Conger and Long 2010; Jacob 2002; Owens 2016).

These explanations are distinct from those offered to explain differences in choice of major, which instead echo aspects of gender socialization arguments offered for gender differences in high school course-taking (Gerber and Cheung 2008; Wang and Degol 2013). In addition to arguments that young people are raised to like different subjects and think of them as more or less appropriate for their gender, arguments about girls' relative absence from STEM majors also posit that girls are turned off by the high demands of such majors and perceive them to be incompatible with future desires for family and children (Eccles 2011; Williams and Ceci 2012). Despite the logical appeal of such arguments, they fall short of explaining why females are well-represented in some STEM fields (math, biology) and not others (engineering, computer science), as well as why women have entered business, pre-med, and pre-law majors at similar or higher rates than men (England 2010; Mann and Diprete 2013; Xie and Shauman 2003).

Thus, within the field of sociology of education we have a myriad of explanations tailored to explain specific instances of gender inequality. While helpful, these explanations may be more useful if situated within a broader theoretical framework of gender that can help us to understand the creation, maintenance, and (sometimes) changes in this overall constellation of differences. In this regard, sociologists of education have argued for the relevance of two major theories that help to explain why there is gender equity (or even a female advantage) in some areas, while there are male advantages in others.

First, as argued by Charles and Bradley (2002), in advanced industrial societies there is an increased cultural emphasis on egalitarianism ideals as well as self-expression; yet this coexists with gender essentialism, the notion that men and women are fundamentally different. Thus, on the one hand, girls do as well (or better) than boys in school (and the general sentiment is that they should be offered the same resources and opportunities to pursue their education). And yet at the same time, choices related to subject area specialization are an ideal arena in which to maintain gender differences. Thus, egalitarian and essentialist ideologies co-exist. Under this framework, there does not necessarily have to be a logical explanation for why some fields are defined as masculine or feminine, and indeed the assignment could be quite arbitrary.

Coupled with this perspective, England and Li (2006) argue that the theory of gender devaluation must also be considered. Specifically, within our culture, men and women are not just assumed to be fundamentally different, but men and masculinity in society are also viewed as superior. Therefore, things associated with females and femininity are *ceteris paribus*, considered socially inferior. This explains why the change in the segregation of college majors that has occurred over the last several decades is limited to the movement of women into male-dominated majors and not the other way around. It also perhaps explains why the areas where females outperform males (subjects like reading and outcomes such as grades) are generally considered to be less interesting and important than the areas where males outperform females. Further, we note here that as a field, the sociology of education pays less attention to these instances of female advantage, and instead focuses much more on the male advantage in some STEM fields. While this is certainly due in part to the higher social and economic status of those fields, it nevertheless seems likely that researchers contribute to downplaying female achievement by focusing comparatively less attention on those areas where they excel.

In closing, we suggest that theories of gender essentialism and gender devaluation offer compelling explanations for the sometimes contradictory patterns of gender inequality in educational outcomes, and should continue to be developed and extended. Yet we also suggest that research in this area should do more to consider the insights of Black feminist scholarship, particularly that which employs an intersectional perspective and calls needed attention to the continued power of a White patriarchal system (Hill Collins 2000; hooks 1984). At the end of this chapter, we will return to the theme of the need for future research to push forward in accounting (both theoretically and empirically) for the complexity of patterns in gender disparities that exist in our current time.

6.3 Examining Patterns and Explanations for Racial/Ethnic Differences in Educational Outcomes

Race/ethnicity is another main axis of social stratification in our contemporary society. Yet unlike gender, where females often reach comparable or higher levels of educational outcomes than males, patterns by race/ethnicity are extremely consistent across a range of outcomes. Specifically, within the U.S., Whites exceed the educational outcomes of Black and Hispanic youth. At a time when the demographics of the country are drastically changing and becoming much more diversified, an examination into continued disparities is critical. According to the U.S. Department of Education, the combined percentage of Black and Hispanic students has grown from 29% of the student population nationally in 1997 to 39% in 2014, and that percentage is projected to grow to 44% by 2022 (Hussar and Bailey 2014).

Consistent with the focus of the majority of research on racial/ethnic gaps within the sociology of education, we primarily discuss gaps between Whites and their Black and Hispanic peers, the two largest racial/ethnic minorities in U.S. schools with persistent disparities in educational outcomes. However, in doing so, it is not our intent to in any way minimize the importance of examining disparities between Whites and other minority groups (e.g., Asians), but rather to limit our focus to a finite and relatively manageable scope for this chapter.[3] Again, as with our discussion of gender differences in educational

---

[3]As space constraints limit us from including a thorough review of disparities between Asian students and their White peers, as well as their Black and Hispanic peers, we recommend that readers see recent work by Pang et al. (2011), Pong et al. (2005), and Lee and Kumashiro (2005) among others.

outcomes, we concentrate on results of quantitative research. However, due to the generally consistent patterns of White advantage across a range of educational outcomes, we choose to begin with a discussion of the major theoretical explanations behind them, before then turning to a review of specific instances of inequality.

6.3.1 Theoretical Explanations for Racial/Ethnic Disparities in Educational Outcomes

The theoretical rationales offered for differences in educational outcomes between majority and minority youth can be categorized into two strands: those that argue that the educational system is an agent in the social reproduction of inequality, and those that argue that schools in fact serve to minimize or decrease inequality. Both camps acknowledge the critical role of social class, as Black and Hispanic youth are disproportionately likely to come from families with relatively fewer economic resources, and also recognize the importance of factors that occur outside of school but nevertheless have strong implications for the outcomes that occur within school. Yet they differ in their accounting of the role that schools play in contributing to inequitable outcomes in grades, course-taking, test scores, and college matriculation and attainment.

Theories of social reproduction are the ones most commonly invoked within the sociology of education. Put briefly, such theories argue that schools serve a vital function of reproducing and maintaining inequality by sorting and socializing students within school walls in ways that lead to disparate outcomes by student background (Apple 1978; Bourdieu and Passeron 1977; Bowles and Gintis 2002; Lucas 2001). The end result is that those that come from disadvantaged minority backgrounds accrue far fewer favorable educational outcomes, and thus are far less likely to achieve economic and social success later in life. Within this literature on social reproduction, researchers may disagree about the extent to which educational agents such as teachers are

intentional or more accidental agents in this process. Additionally, there are also diverging opinions about the extent to which inequality is produced via the separation of youth into different schools (e.g., school segregation) versus the inequality that is produced via the differential sorting of students into different classrooms within schools (Kelly 2009; Mickelson and Heath 1999; Oakes 2005). Research arguing for the former points to increasing patterns of school segregation in recent years, and the fact that teachers from high minority schools relative to those in low minority schools have fewer years of experience, lower likelihood of certification in the subject they are teaching, and higher likelihood of teaching out of their field of specialization (Clotfelter et al. 2005; Darling-Hammond 2001). Those that argue for the greater role that sorting within schools plays in reproducing inequality point to the importance of the differential allocation of resources and opportunities, such that Blacks and Hispanics attending integrated schools are often in less rigorous courses taught by teachers with low expectations (Lucas and Berends 2002; Oakes 2005). In our review of the empirical literature below, we call attention to when different aspects of this argument are implicated.

In contrast to major theories of social reproduction, another major theoretical strand argues that racial/ethnic disparities in educational outcomes are primarily the result of factors that happen outside of school, and that schools are either neutral in this process or perhaps even decrease inequality (Downey et al. 2004). According to this line of reasoning, the larger processes of stratification in society are linked to economic and social factors that impact the families and communities of different groups, and schools are either powerless to stop this, or sometimes manage to even help alleviate some problems by providing minority youth with the chance to break the cycle. As we will discuss below, the empirical literature in support of this theory is comparatively limited. Yet it is nevertheless important to consider those instances where such a theory might explain inequality in outcomes.

6.3.2 Racial/Ethnic Disparities in K–12 Education Outcomes

6.3.2.1 Test Scores

The largest body of extant research on educational inequality by race/ethnicity focuses on differences in test scores; this research indicates that Blacks and Hispanics continue to lag behind their White peers on standardized exams across different subjects and different grade levels. While there has been some change over time, such that gaps have modestly decreased, disparities remain and are generally found to grow larger throughout the K–12 years and to be slightly larger in math than in reading (Hemphill and Vanneman 2011; Vanneman et al. 2009). For instance, Cheadle (2008), using data from ECLS-K found that among kindergarteners in math, Blacks and Hispanics scored 0.34 SD and 0.45 SD lower than Whites, respectively. From 1st through 3rd grade the Black–White gap grows slowly while the Hispanic–White gap remained relatively constant. Further, data on a national sample of high school seniors from the Education Longitudinal Study (ELS), find test score gaps close to one standard deviation in scope (Riegle-Crumb and Grodsky 2010). Results from NAEP assessments reveal similar patterns (NCES 2015). Scores on college admission tests such as the SAT also indicate gaps of a large magnitude. For example 2012–2013 math test scores show Whites surpassing minority groups by at least 0.8 SD (NCES 2015).

Research on the test score gap has provided strong evidence that social class disparities greatly contribute to inequality, but the estimates of the extent of the gap that can be explained vary considerably across studies. For example, Quinn (2015) summarizes the literature on the Black–White gap in particular and finds that "depending on the sample, year of data collection, and assessment …various SES measures have explained from 12 to 100 percent of these gaps." In his own analyses of recent kindergarten data from the ECLS-K, Quinn (2015) found that while Blacks entered kindergarten with lower reading test scores than their White peers, controlling for SES resulted in an advantage for Blacks relative to their White peers at the beginning of the year. SES also reduced the Hispanic–White reading gap, but did not eliminate it or reverse the direction of advantage. His findings also show that net of SES, the Black–White math and reading gaps actually increased over the kindergarten year suggesting that school factors, not SES, may exacerbate test score disparities between these groups. Such findings are also echoed by Condron (2009), as well as by Downey et al. (2004) who found that while test score gaps between some groups were smaller during the school year than during the summer, gaps between Black and White students did in fact grow stronger during the academic calendar year. While factors outside of school certainly continue to play a contributing role to test score gaps, contemporary research offers strong evidence that schools strengthen rather than lessen racial/ethnic inequality.

6.3.2.2 Grades

Compared to the vast body of research examining racial/ethnic differences in test scores, research on disparities in the grades earned in school in K–12 is much more sparse but nevertheless reveals strong evidence of disparities. Among high school graduates in 2009, the grade point averages of all students were higher in 2009 than they were in 1990; yet across years consistent gaps existed between groups. The GPA of Whites exceeded those of Hispanics and Blacks, with Blacks having the lowest GPA (Nord et al. 2011). As with test scores, there is evidence that such gaps are at least partly explained by differences in students' social class background. For instance, Roscigno and Ainsworth-Darnell (1999), using data of 10th graders from the National Educational Longitudinal Study (NELS), found that over half of the Black–White gaps in student GPAs were explained by family social class. Similarly, Kao et al. (1996) used data from NELS and found that while the gap between Hispanics and Whites was completely explained by family factors, the Black–White gap in GPA remained statistically significant.

6.3.2.3 Course-Taking

Research on racial/ethnic disparities in course-taking has its roots in concern for the differentiated curricular practices of school officials at the turn of the twentieth century, who designated those students with darker skin and foreign-sounding names as most-suited for coursework with low cognitive demands but a high emphasis on behavior and hygiene (Kliebard 2004; Oakes 2005), as well as the disparate opportunities available to Blacks in predominantly Black schools vis-à-vis Whites in all-White schools in the early to mid-twentieth century. While school desegregation efforts, following the seminal *Brown v. Board of Education* ruling, resulted in more integrated schools, within-school sorting practices are robust and ever-present, in spite of the attempts of the anti-tracking movement (Lucas 2001; Mickelson 2001).

Much of the research on course-taking disparities has focused on what happens in secondary schools and primarily in the area of mathematics. The sequential and hierarchical nature of mathematics, starting in middle school, affords a ripe area for examining issues of access to advanced course-taking. Although mathematics course-taking is a key area of study, researchers have highlighted the symbiotic relationship between course types on the secondary level, such that students taking advanced courses in mathematics are likely to be engaged in advanced course-taking in other subjects as well (Lucas and Berends 2002), providing even more of an advantage for students who are enrolled in these courses. Data on course-taking trends have revealed that the number of Blacks and Hispanics taking more advanced math courses has increased, however, the minority–White gap in advanced course-taking has actually been increasing over time. For instance, a recent NCES report reveals that while Black and Hispanic high school graduates have seen a 4% and 8% increase, respectively, in the number of rigorous courses taken between 1990 and 2009, the Black–White and Hispanic–White gap in rigorous course-taking increased from 3 percentage points each, to 8 and 6 percentage points, respectively, over the same period (Nord et al. 2011). Also, while the number

of students taking 8th grade algebra, a course identified as the gatekeeper to favorable outcomes in high school and beyond (Gamoran and Hannigan 2000; Newton et al. 2008; Spielhagen 2006), has increased over the years (Loveless 2008; Rampey et al. 2008), students from disadvantaged minority groups are still not enrolling in this course at the same rates as their White peers. For instance, Walston and McCarroll (2010) using 8th grade data from the Early Childhood Longitudinal Study—Kindergarten class of 1998–1999 (ECLS-K) determined that the percentages of Whites enrolled in algebra was 37%, compared to 34% and 17% for Hispanics and Blacks, respectively.

Some research on gaps in course-taking suggests the presence of less rigorous academic courses being offered in high minority schools compared to integrated or predominantly White schools (Mickelson 2001; Riegle-Crumb and Grodsky 2010). For example, approximately 60% of White students enrolled in AP courses score a 3 or higher on the AP exam, compared to approximately 26% for Blacks and 43% for Hispanics (Aud et al. 2010). While not conclusive, such patterns hint at the possibility that the AP courses taken by minority students are not of the same caliber in terms of preparing students to be successful on the exam. Nevertheless, the bulk of the research on course-taking disparities strongly implicates within-school sorting processes, such that Black and Hispanic youth are less likely to be enrolled in advanced courses compared to their White peers, even net of social class (Kelly 2009; Mickelson 2001).

6.3.2.4 High School Completion

Student high school completion and dropout rates are another indicator where racial/ethnic disparities exist. In 2010, the percentage of White high school students attending public school who graduate within 4 years was 83%. For Hispanics and Blacks, those percentages were 71.4% and 69.1%, respectively (Stillwell and Sable 2013). A recent study by Bradley and Renzulli (2011) using data from the Educational Longitudinal Study (ELS) investigated the extent to which such disparities were associated with social class differences, as well as other economic reasons such as family responsibilities. Their results revealed that there were no differences between the likelihood of dropping out for Blacks compared to Whites once SES was controlled. In addition, they found that while SES explained much of the Hispanic–White gap in high school completion, the remaining gap was explained by students' economic responsibilities to their families. Importantly, the authors found no evidence that disparities in completion rates were the result of a lack of engagement or negative school attitudes on the part of minority youth.

6.3.3 Racial/Ethnic Disparities in College Outcomes

6.3.3.1 College Matriculation and Persistence

Whites have, for the most part, consistently exceeded non-Asian minorities in rates of matriculation into college. However, this advantage is more apparent for 4-year colleges as opposed to 2-year colleges. For example, among initial college-goers from the high school sophomore class of 2002 of ELS, 46.4% of Whites attended a 4-year college compared to 32.7% of Blacks and 22.2% of Hispanics. However, for 2-year colleges, 26.9% of Whites matriculated versus 25.4% of Blacks and 31.8% of Hispanics. So particularly for Hispanics, while more than 50% of students are attending college, the majority are attending 2-year institutions (Bozick et al. 2007). Rates of attainment tend to follow group patterns in matriculation. Recent national data reveal that the percentages of Black (51%) and Hispanic (52%) full-time students at 4-year institutions who attained bachelor's degrees were lower than the percentage of White students (73%) (NCES 2012).

Not surprisingly, researchers have found that disparities in college attendance are greatly explained by differences in social class background. For example, using data from the NELS, Charles et al. (2007) investigated racial/ethnic disparities in both 2- and 4-year college attendance. They found that Hispanics, particularly those with immigrant mothers, were in fact more likely than Whites to attend a 2- or 4-year college once family background is taken into account. Additionally, they also found that net of family background, the Black–White gap in 2-year college attendance narrows but still favors Whites, while the gap for 4-year college attendance reverses. Consistent with this pattern, other studies have also found evidence of a "net Black advantage" (Merolla 2013) for both immigrant and U.S. Blacks (Bennett and Lutz 2009).

Disparities in college graduation have been explained by differences in social background as well as test scores. For instance, Alon (2007) examined the effects of "overlapping (dis)advantages," namely socioeconomic status, high school academic preparation (i.e., SAT scores), and parental education, on the likelihood of obtaining a bachelor's degree from a selective university and found that Blacks and Hispanics are more likely to have overlapping disadvantages than their White peers. While the Hispanic–White gap in graduation was mostly explained by Hispanics' overlapping disadvantages, for Blacks only 30% of the Black–White gap was explained by such disadvantages (particularly those including academic preparation).

Within the 4-year college sector, variation in the selectivity of institutions that students attend represents an additional marker of inequality. Using data from the ELS, Bozick and others (2007) documented substantial racial/ethnic disparities in elite college attendance, such that while about 17% of White students attended such a school, only about 5% of Hispanic and Black students did. Beyond these basic numbers, research shows evidence of under-matching, such that highly academically qualified Hispanic and Black youth are more likely than their White peers to attend a school that is less selective or academically rigorous (Bowen et al. 2009; Roderick et al. 2011). This trend is particularly problematic since the practice of undermatching has been linked to decreased likelihood of graduating from college (Bowen et al. 2009). Similarly, Alon and Tienda (2005) investigated the legitimacy of the mismatching hypothesis, that is, that Hispanics and Blacks at more selective institutions were less likely than their demo-graphically and academically similar counter-parts at less selective institutions to graduate from college. Their analyses refuted this hypoth-esis and concluded that Blacks and Hispanics are more likely to graduate from college as the selec-tivity of the college increases, suggesting the benefit of affirmative action policies that are designed to increase the numbers of minority stu-dents gaining college degrees.

6.3.3.2 Field of Study

Finally, we note that in contrast to the sharp racial/ethnic disparities discussed above on other educa-tional outcomes, there are few major differences in terms of the field of study that students choose to pursue. Across racial/ethnic groups, the highest concentration of bachelor's degrees earned in 2009 were in science and engineering, followed by either arts and humanities or business, then educa-tion, and finally, science and engineering-related fields (Siebens and Ryan 2012). Additionally, researchers have found evidence that, contingent on college matriculation, Black and Hispanic youth are as likely as White students to pursue degrees in STEM fields (Chen 2009; Riegle-Crumb and King 2010). While the persistence rates of these minority youth are lower than their White peers, this is not particular to STEM fields, but rather a trend found across fields of study, such that minority youth are less likely to attain a col-lege degree than their White peers (Chen 2009).

6.3.4 Examining Disparities in Outcomes at the Intersection of Gender and Race/Ethnicity

While investigating race/ethnic disparities in educational outcomes is imperative, it is equally important to consider gender differences within and across race/ethnic groups. Feminist scholars have long called attention to the need to critically explore the intersection of race/ethnicity and gender, with the recognition that different racial/ethnic-gender groups have unique educational experiences that cannot be captured by looking at either axis of stratification alone (Browne and Misra 2003; Hill Collins 2000; hooks 1984). Yet the quantitative literature within the sociology of education has to date done little to explore how gaps on the educational outcomes discussed in this chapter vary across subgroups.

Within the limited extant literature there is evidence that while general patterns of inequality by gender are consistent across racial/ethnic gaps (and vice versa), nevertheless the magnitude of such gaps varies in ways that may be important to consider. For instance, while across racial/ethnic groups, females surpassed their male counter-parts on high school regular diploma attainment rates, immediate postsecondary enrollment, and bachelor's degree completion within 6 years, nevertheless this pattern of female advantage is more pronounced among Blacks and Hispanics than it is among Whites (Aud et al. 2013; Buchmann et al. 2008). Additionally, while the higher representation of males in STEM degrees persists across racial/ethnic groups, the gaps are largest among Hispanic youth and smallest among Black youth (Ross et al. 2012).

Additionally, in an examination of gender gaps in test scores, Hyde et al. (2008) reported that math test score gaps were non-existent or even favored girls for some minority groups. More research attention should be directed to such patterns, in part to understand when and where the evidence of smaller gender gaps for some minority groups is the result of minority females doing comparatively better, or minority males doing comparatively worse. In part three of this chapter we further discuss the need for an intersectional approach that goes beyond a focus on examining average differences in outcomes and instead more fully considers the differenti-ated school experiences of young people from different gender and racial/ethnic subgroups.

6.4 Outlining Future Directions for Research

We now turn to a discussion of some potential future directions for research that may help us to better understand and ultimately disrupt patterns of inequality in educational outcomes. Specifically, we argue that as a field, sociology of education should: (1) bring more of a critical eye towards research on standardized testing, (2) place more attention on how school contexts shape different forms of inequality, and (3) think more critically about definitions of gender and race/ethnicity and the ways in which a more fluid or contextual emphasis is needed to better reflect the reality of young people's lives.

6.4.1 Moving Beyond Test Scores

Although our review focused attention on patterns of inequality across a range of educational outcomes in an effort to be relatively comprehensive and in-depth, we note that the bulk of the research literature on educational gaps, particularly regarding racial/ethnic gaps, has focused on test scores. Studies have utilized test scores from a plethora of sources, including high school exit exams (Grodsky et al. 2009) and college entrance exams (Buchmann et al. 2010), as well as those available through NCES (Gamoran and Hannigan 2000; Kelly 2009), a very common source of data for sociologists of education. As a field, interest in the use of achievement test scores as a valid measure of academic achievement has even recently been extended to the postsecondary level (Arum and Roksa 2014). Yet there are some potentially serious problems with such a strong reliance on test scores to measure inequality.

The most obvious concern is whether tests are biased towards certain groups, and therefore whether standardized tests fairly assess all students (see Grodsky et al. 2008 for a review). For example, Freedle (2003) asserts that the SAT is culturally biased, as indicated by Black and Hispanic students' consistent underperformance relative to Whites, likely due to the two groups' (i.e., minority vs non-minority) differing interpretations of test items. Accountability policies also bring to light the pressures that teachers have to "teach to the test," therefore calling into question whether tests actually measure cognitive growth and the mastery of conceptual knowledge, or more simply capture students' adeptness

at answering an array of finite questions posed in a particular format (Linn 2013). However, studies such as these are relatively few in number and, as such, do not provide a very strong base of evidence for arguments against the validity of achievement tests, and their subsequent use in research studies on achievement disparities.

Perhaps what is more compelling are arguments that standardized tests privilege certain kinds of knowledge, and that as a field we should think more critically about the implications of this. For example, Sternberg (2007) points out variation in the cultural definitions of intelligence here in the U.S. between different racial/ethnic groups, and the invalidation of the types of student knowledge that diverge from the mainstream culture's definition of intelligence. He further argues that this type of knowledge is vastly different from that assessed in achievement tests. Critical race theorists also emphasize the mismatch between what students (particularly those from marginalized groups) know and what is tested on exams, such that the former is not given consideration when schooling (and test development) is taking place (Ladson-Billings 1998).

Furthermore, research primarily from the field of psychology offers evidence of the fragility and variability of student performance in testing environments, and thus calls into question how accurately both researchers and educators are measuring student knowledge in many circumstances. Research on stereotype threat finds that environmental/contextual factors such as the racial/ethnic or gender composition of the classroom or the cueing of stereotypes can lead students within stereotyped groups to severely underperform, thus creating biased results and misleading conclusions about groups' differences in ability (Good et al. 2003; Steele and Aronson 1995). Yet, sociologists of education have spent little attention considering the implications of such findings for research on gender and racial/ethnic inequality in educational outcomes (one notable exception includes a study by Hanselman et al. (2014), discussed later in this chapter).

Stepping back, it is also important to ask whether researchers' well-intentioned aims to highlight inequalities by repeatedly pointing to test score gaps have reified the current system instead of interrogating or disrupting it. While researchers typically focus on gaps in achievement test scores because of the belief that they are emblematic of differential access to curriculum, teachers, and pedagogy, perhaps there is too much time and energy spent working within this paradigm that privileges the importance of testing, at the expense of critically questioning it. Our recommendation is not that we eliminate the examination of test score gaps; simply doing away with tests altogether is likely to reproduce stratification, perhaps by reassigning importance to other outcomes that more privileged groups have greater access to (Belasco et al. 2014). Notably, others (e.g., Haut and Elliott 2011; Kane and Staiger 2012) have considered the need for a more comprehensive way to assess student learning, but perhaps more needs to be done to challenge the status quo in order to effectively move forward towards equitable educational experiences for all students. In this vein, we propose that more of a dialogue is needed not only on the impact that achievement tests have on social stratification, but also on the types of outcomes (both cognitive and non-cognitive) that could meaningfully serve as measures of achievement (e.g., college matriculation, postsecondary job attainment, self-confidence, perseverance).

6.4.2 Considering School Context

In this chapter, we also argue that future research needs to pay more attention to the critical role of school contexts in shaping inequality. While there is a large literature on school effects on gaps in educational outcomes, it has primarily considered demographic characteristics of schools (e.g., racial/ethnic or social class composition) as independent variables of interest, and gaps in test scores (such as Black–White differences) as dependent variables of interest. As mentioned earlier, this research tradition has produced somewhat mixed results. Advances in statistical methods as well as the growing availability of rich administrative state data sets have come together to allow researchers to estimate better

causal models, and thus this research tradition is likely to continue. Yet as we argued above, test scores are certainly not the only worthy outcome of interest that should be investigated, and schools likely shape inequality on a range of different kinds of outcomes. Additionally, moving beyond measuring racial/ethnic composition (or other compositional variables) to measure the influence of school contexts also holds much promise.

There are several recent studies that highlight the powerful implications of such a research focus. Regarding studies on race/ethnicity, Jennings et al. (2015) focused on how gaps in college attendance varied across students' high school contexts. The authors also argue persuasively that we need to consider how the same schools could lessen racial/ethnic gaps but increase SES gaps, for example, as they find in their sample from Texas and Tennessee. Jennings and her colleagues (2015) suggest that researchers should avoid the inclination to characterize some schools as uniformly "good" and others as "bad," and instead focus on understanding why and how schools produce some equitable outcomes while simultaneously producing inequality in others. A recent study by Hanselman et al. (2014) also moves beyond a singular focus on racial/ethnic gaps in test scores, and focuses on how schools contribute to gaps in grades. Additionally, the authors conceptualize school context in a novel way, distinguishing between schools in terms of their likelihood of creating a high-risk environment for social identity or stereotype threat to impact minority students.

Additionally, a qualitative study by Ispa-Landa and Conwell (2015) suggests the intriguing idea that students' identification of a school as a racialized institution is a meaningful outcome to consider in its own right. Specifically, the authors find that urban minority students who attended affluent, White-dominated, suburban schools began to classify schools as "White" or "Black" based on their academic quality. Ispa-Landa and Conwell (2015) argue that the school culture reinforced harmful racial stereotypes and produced antagonism between Black students attending "White" schools vs "Black" schools.

Such qualitative studies should motivate future quantitative research that considers how schools themselves influence students' definitions of race and racial differences.

In contrast to the large extant literature on school effects on racial/ethnic gaps in educational outcomes (predominantly test scores), the literature that considers how variation in school contexts might shape gender inequality is currently quite sparse. Yet a small emerging body of literature provides exciting new ground on which the field should start to build. For example, a recent study by Legewie and Diprete (2015) used data from the National Educational Longitudinal Study (NELS) to examine how high school academic cultures and gender norms shaped gender disparities in students' intentions to major in STEM fields. The authors found that schools that had more academically rigorous STEM curricula, as well as less gender segregated extra-curricular activities, produced more gender equitable patterns of intended college major. Other studies consider how the academic norms of peers within a school (both friends and coursemates) contribute to gender gaps in course-taking (Frank et al. 2008; Riegle-Crumb et al. 2006), as well as how the communities in which schools are embedded may also shape gender inequalities in course-taking (Riegle-Crumb and Moore 2014). Such studies offer evidence that is consistent with theorists who argue that gender is socially constructed at the local level through interactions and experiences in the school, home, etc., and that to better understand inequality we need to consider variation in such contexts (Ridgeway and Correll 2004; Risman 2004). We suggest the need for more research in this vein to advance our understanding of how gender inequality is reproduced, or alternatively in some contexts, interrupted.

6.4.3 Considering Alternative Definitions of Gender and Race/Ethnicity

As a field, sociology of education has showed only limited innovation in how it both conceptualizes and operationalizes individuals as gendered or as a member of a particular racial/ethnic group. We argue that two pervasive habits in particular are especially restricting. Specifically, the overwhelming majority of theoretical and empirical models rely on mutually exclusive definitions of race/ethnicity and/or gender that are limited to a small or even binary choice set, and furthermore seldom allow for individuals to self-identify in more complex and fluid ways, including acknowledging students' identities at the intersection of gender and race/ethnicity. We unpack each of these issues in turn and in doing so, advocate for future work that pushes the field forward.

6.4.3.1 Multi-racial Youth

A common refrain in the literature examining how racial and ethnic minorities are faring within the U.S. educational system is that America is becoming increasingly diverse. Less often mentioned, however, is the fact that the multiracial population within the U.S. is growing at a rate three times faster than the general population (Pew Research Center 2015). Currently, 7% of American adults could be considered multiracial and the percentage of U.S. born infants in this group has risen from 1% in 1970 to 10% today (ibid.). Lee and Bean (2004) attribute this growth to immigration and increased rates of ethnic/racial inter-marriage and anticipate that 1 in 5 Americans may be multiracial in their self-identification by 2050. They argue that these population trends are not necessarily indicative of a declining significance of race/ethnicity in social inequality. Instead, following their analysis of social indicators of status among multiracial and immigrant Americans—including patterns of intermarriage and identification—they conclude that "America's changing color lines could involve a new racial/ethnic divide that may consign many blacks to disadvantaged positions qualitatively similar to those perpetuated by the traditional black/white divide" (2004, p. 238). Further, Black immigrants and interracial Black students are typically advantaged over other Black students by socioeconomic indicators including family resources and residential segregation (Cokley et al. 2016). Thus changing patterns of immigration and interracial family formation continue to increase the numbers of multiracial Americans and may be shaping inequalities between and among ethnic/racial groups in important ways.

Despite these trends, empirical research within sociology of education rarely considers multiracial statuses in analyses of racial/ethnic disparities in educational outcomes. Instead, analyses typically rely on mutually exclusive categories into which students are assigned as either White, Black, Hispanic or Latino, Asian, and Native American, with many studies focused only on contrasting a smaller subset of groups against one another. There are a few notable exceptions, however. Using nationally representative data from Add Health, Campbell (2009) demonstrates that disparities in academic achievement vary between mono- and multiracial students such that monoracial young adults' outcomes—including Hispanics'—are empirically associated with their perceived race/ethnicity but for multiracial students, parental education and income are the most influential in explaining disparities. Additionally, a recent study by Irizarry (2015) argued for the importance of considering multi-dimensional measures of race in quantitative studies on inequality. The author examined teacher ratings of 14 subgroups characterized by race, ethnicity, and immigrant status, and found substantial variation in how teachers rated students' behavior that would have been masked by using conventional categories.

Taken together, these studies underscore the importance of taking multiracial backgrounds seriously in specifying students' race/ethnicity to better understand processes related to gaps in educational outcomes. Nevertheless, studies like this are the exception rather than the norm within the sociology of education and much more work is needed in this area. In her critique of past literature, Irizarry (2015) notes that quantitative researchers are often hampered by their use of large data sets and surveys that do not allow students to self-identify as belonging to more than one racial/ethnic category. We point out that this is even more true of gender, as the convention in survey research is to ask students to choose

between one of two mutually exclusive categories of "male" or "female." Thus there is arguably a whole new body of research that could be generated on what we might learn about inequality in educational outcomes if we moved away from a strict binary definition of gender.

6.4.3.2 Racial/Ethnic and Gender Identity

Furthermore, we argue that more empirical research on educational inequality needs to consider the importance of gender and racial/ethnic identity, or how individuals perceive their own membership in certain categories and the importance they place on such membership. Gender theorists point out that while binary beliefs about gender continue to underlie social dynamics, nevertheless the salience of individuals' gender membership and the way in which they define their gender varies widely (Ridgeway and Correll 2004). For example, research by social psychologists demonstrates that the importance individuals place on their gender identity can moderate differences in performance in gendered arenas. Results of a quasi-experimental study by Schmader (2002) showed that women who placed greater importance on their gender identity performed worse to men when exposed to stereotype threat, but women who placed less importance on their gender identity performed equally to men. Furthermore, research in this area also highlights the reality that individuals have multiple identities that are important to defining their sense of self, and that this can have implications (either positive or negative) for education-related outcomes. For example, an experiment by McGlone and Aronson (2006) showed that women primed to think about their academic identity as high-performing students at an elite college performed better in a spatial reasoning test than women primed to think about their gender identity.

Other studies highlight the complexity of students' racial/ethnic identification. A study by Herman (2009) collected data at several high schools in California and the Midwest using surveys that collected information about the race/ethnicity of students' biological parents, and also asked students to pick the racial/ethnic category with which they most identified. She found that among multi-racial youth, the choice of which category best captured their identity significantly predicted their academic performance in school. Additionally, Herman (2009) found that about 30% of the multi-racial youth changed their identification over the 3 years of study, suggesting some fluidity over time. This is consistent with findings of a national study where students' self-reports of their (single) racial/ethnic identity varied over time for about 12% of those in the sample (Harris and Sim 2002). Awareness of such issues have prompted some to call for more studies that attempt to understand how race and ethnicity may be contextually determined, and how this has likely implications for educational inequality (Warikoo and Carter 2009).

6.4.3.3 Intersectionality in Context

Finally, as we discussed earlier, there is a need for more research that considers the intersection of gender and race/ethnicity with regard to students' educational experiences, as these are likely to have implications for educational outcomes. The limited literature in this area is mostly qualitative and highlights how the meanings of gender and race/ethnicity come together in particular ways. For example, a recent study by Ovink (2013) highlights how gendered dynamics within Hispanic families are linked to both high academic expectations and "traditional roles" which in some ways advantages and in some ways strains Hispanic girls in comparison to their brothers. By contrast, a study by Morris (2007) finds that pressure from teachers for Black girls to conform to expectations of lady-like behavior may undermine their independence, confidence, and ultimately their academic performance. These studies echo earlier work by Carter (2005), who found that differentiated gender expectations in low-income urban communities resulted in Black and Hispanic males developing a "hard" posture that was sometimes at odds with social and academic expectations within their schools.

Furthermore, we argue that the most powerful new studies are those that not only take the intersection of gender and race/ethnicity seriously, yet also consider how young people's multiple identities may be fluid and vary across context (Warikoo and Carter 2009). A recent qualitative study by Holland (2012) exemplifies this approach. Specifically, she examines the experiences of male and female minority students in a very particular context, a predominantly White school that is part of a voluntary desegregation program, and finds that this context strongly shapes gender differences in students' experiences. While minority female students are primarily excluded by both the academic and social culture of the school, minority males were given more opportunities for interracial contact and integration into the school through participation in sports. This was further facilitated by what White students perceived as minority males' physical embodiment of a desirable, hip urban culture. Another study by Ispa-Landa (2013) also considers how race and gender intersect in an affluent White high school, and finds similar evidence of the greater social integration of minority males compared to their minority female peers. Yet a study by Wilkins (2014) examines the transition to college and finds that the cultural expectations of Black masculinity that young men confronted in college were much more restrictive than those they experienced as younger men in high school, further underlining how school contexts shape differentiated social experiences for minority males and females.

Together, these qualitative studies offer compelling evidence of the need to consider how the very meanings assigned to the categories of gender and race/ethnicity, and how young people choose to self-identify and make sense of such meanings, varies by both time and place. We suggest that the fluidity of individuals' multiple gender and racial/ethnic identities has likely implications for inequality in educational outcomes. The empirical literature within the sociology of education should move forward to shed light on such issues.

6.5　　Concluding Remarks

In closing, we see many promising new areas that can advance the field to better understand the creation, maintenance, and disruption of gender and racial/ethnic inequality. As discussed earlier, we note that many existing large-scale longitudinal surveys are quite limited in their treatment of critical issues pertaining to gender and racial/ethnic identity, both in terms of how individuals choose to identify themselves and in terms of the centrality or saliency of these identities. Aiming to capture these dimensions through innovative survey items, for example, would be a welcome direction, as would research designs that sample entire classrooms and/or schools and thus better enable researchers to construct measures of students' local contexts. Finally, research designs that better capture students' thoughts and experiences within the different contexts they occupy (e.g., science classroom, English classroom, after-school activity, home environment) would provide rich data to explore the complex ways in which race/ethnicity and gender work to shape young people's educational outcomes.

References

Adelman, C. (1999). *Answers in the toolbox: Academic intensity, attendance patterns, and bachelor's degree attainment*. Washington, DC: U.S. Department of Education.

Alon, S. (2007). The effect of overlapping disadvantages on the racial/ethnic graduation gap among students attending selective institutions. *Social Science Research, 36*(4), 1475–1499.

Alon, S., & Tienda, M. (2005). Assessing the "mismatch" hypothesis: Differences in college graduation rates by institutional selectivity. *Sociology of Education, 78*(4), 294–315.

Apple, M. W. (1978). Ideology, reproduction, and educational reform. *Comparative Education Review, 22*(3), 367–387.

Arum, R., & Roksa, J. (2014). *Aspiring adults adrift: Tentative transitions of college graduates*. Chicago: University of Chicago Press.

Aud, S., Fox, M., & KewalRamani, A. (2010). *Status and trends in the education of racial and ethnic groups* (NCES 2010-015). National Center for Education Statistics. Retrieved from U.S. Department of Education. http://nces.ed.gov/pubs2010/2010015. pdf.

Aud, S., Wilkinson-Flicker, S., Kristapovich, P., Rathbun, A., Wang, X., & Zhang, J. (2013). *The condition of education 2013* (NCES 2013-037). Washington, DC: U.S. Department of Education, National Center for Education Statistics. http://nces.ed.gov/pubsearch. Accessed 22 Feb 2016.

Baron-Cohen, S. (2003). *Essential difference: Male and female brains and the truth about autism*. New York: Basic Books.

Belasco, A. S., Rosinger, K. O., & Hearn, J. C. (2014). The test-optional movement at America's selective liberal arts colleges: A boon for equity or something else? *Educational Evaluation and Policy Analysis, 37*(2), 206–223.

Bennett, P. R., & Lutz, A. (2009). How African American is the net Black advantage? Differences in college attendance among immigrant Blacks, native Blacks, and Whites. *Sociology of Education, 82*(1), 70–100.

Bielby, R., Posselt, J., Jaquette, O., & Bastedo, M. (2014). Why are women underrepresented in elite colleges and universities? A non-linear decomposition analysis. *Research in Higher Education, 55*(8), 735–760.

Bourdieu, P., & Passeron, J. C. (1977). *Reproduction in education, culture and society* (R. Nice, Trans.). London: Sage.

Bowen, W. G., Chingos, M. M., & McPherson, M. S. (2009). *Crossing the finish line: Completing college at America's public universities*. Princeton: Princeton University Press.

Bowles, S., & Gintis, H. (2002). Schooling in capitalist American revisited. *Sociology of Education, 75*(1), 1–18.

Bozick, R., Lauff, E., & Wirt, J. (2007). *Education longitudinal study of 2002 (ELS:2002): A first look at the initial postsecondary experiences of the sophomore class of 2002* (NCES 2008-308). Washington, DC: National Center for Education Statistics, Institute of Education Sciences, U.S. Department of Education.

Bradley, C. L., & Renzulli, L. A. (2011). The complexity of non-completion: Being pushed or pulled to drop out of high school. *Social Forces, 90*(2), 521–545.

Browne, I., & Misra, J. (2003). The intersection of gender and race in the labor market. *Annual Review of Sociology, 29*, 487–513.

Buchmann, C. (2009). Gender inequalities in the transition to college. *Teachers College Record, 111*, 2320–2346.

Buchmann, C., & DiPrete, T. (2006). The growing female advantage in college completion: The role of family background and academic achievement. *American Sociological Review, 71*, 515–541.

Buchmann, C., DiPrete, T., & McDaniel, A. (2008). Gender inequalities in education. *Annual Review of Sociology, 34*, 319–337.

Buchmann, C., Condron, D. J., & Roscigno, V. J. (2010). Shadow education, American style: Test preparation, the SAT and college enrollment. *Social Forces, 89*(2), 435–461.

Campbell, M. (2009). Multiracial groups and educational inequality: A rainbow or a divide? *Social Problems, 56*(3), 425–446.

Carter, P. L. (2005). *Keepin' it real: School success beyond Black and White*. Oxford: Oxford University Press.

Catsambis, S. (2005). The gender gap in mathematics: Merely a step function? In A. M. Gallager & J. C. Kaufman (Eds.), *Gender differences in mathematics: An integrative psychological approach*. Cambridge: Cambridge University Press.

Ceci, S., Williams, W., & Barnett, S. (2009). Women's underrepresentation in science: Sociocultural and biological considerations. *Psychological Bulletin, 135*, 218–261.

Charles, M., & Bradley, K. (2002). Equal but separate? A cross-national study of sex segregation in higher education. *American Sociological Review, 67*, 573–599.

Charles, K., & Luoh, M. (2003). Gender differences in completed schooling. *Review of Economics and Statistics, 85*, 559–577.

Charles, C. Z., Roscigno, V. J., & Torres, K. C. (2007). Racial inequality and college attendance: The mediating role of parental investments. *Social Science Research, 36*(1), 329–352.

Cheadle, J. E. (2008). Educational investment, family context, and children's math and reading growth from kindergarten through the third grade. *Sociology of Education, 81*(1), 1–31.

Chen, X. (2009). *Students who study science, technology, engineering, and mathematics (STEM) in postsecondary education* (Stats in Brief, NCES 2009-161). Washington, DC: National Center for Education Statistics.

Cheryan, S. (2012). Understanding the paradox in math-related fields: Why do some gender gaps remain while others do not? *Sex Roles, 66*, 184–190.

Cheryan, S., Meltzoff, A. N., & Kim, S. (2011). Classrooms matter: The design of virtual classrooms' influences gender disparities in computer science classes. *Computers and Education, 57*, 1825–1835.

Clotfelter, C. T., Ladd, H. F., & Vigdor, J. (2005). Who teaches whom? Race and the distribution of novice teachers. *Economics of Education Review, 24*(4), 377–392.

Cokley, K., Obaseki, V., Moran-Jackson, K., Jones, L., & Vohra-Gupta, S. (2016). College access improves for Black students but which ones? *Kappan Magazine, 97*(5), 43–48.

College Board. (2014). *Total group profile report*. https://secure-media.collegeboard.org/digitalServices/pdf/sat/TotalGroup-2014.pdf. Accessed 22 Feb. 2016.

College Board. (2015). *Program summary report 2015*. http://research.collegeboard.org/programs/ap/data/participation/ap-2015. Accessed 22 Feb 2016.

Condron, D. J. (2009). Social class, school and non-school environments, and Black/White inequalities in children's learning. *American Sociological Review, 74*(5), 685–708.

Conger, D., & Long, M. (2010). Why are men falling behind? Gender gaps in college performance and persistence. *The Annals of the American Academy of Political and Social Science, 627*(1), 184–214.

Corbett, C., Hill, C., & St Rose, A. (2008). *Where the girls are: The facts about gender equity in education*. Washington, DC: American Association of University Women Educational Foundation.

Correll, S. J. (2001). Gender and the career choice process: The role of biased self-assessments. *American Journal of Sociology, 106*(6), 1691–1730.

Darling-Hammond, L. (2001). The challenge of staffing our schools. *Educational Leadership, 58*(8), 12–17.

DiPrete, T., & Buchmann, C. (2006). Gender-specific trends in the value of education and the emerging gender gap in college completion. *Demography, 43*, 1–24.

DiPrete, T., & Jennings, J. (2012). Social and behavior skills and the gender gap in early educational achievement. *Social Science Research, 41*, 1–15.

Doherty, W., Willoughby, B., & Wilde, J. (2015). Is the gender gap in college enrollment influenced by non-marital birth rates and father absence? *Family Relations, 65*(2), 663–275.

Downey, D. B., Von Hippel, P. T., & Broh, B. A. (2004). Are schools the great equalizer? Cognitive inequality during the summer months and the school year. *American Sociological Review, 69*(5), 613–635.

Eccles, J. (2011). Gendered educational and occupational choices: Applying the Eccles et al. model of achievement-related choices. *International Journal of Behavioral Development, 35*, 195–201.

England, P. (2010). The gender revolution: Uneven and stalled. *Gender & Society, 24*, 149–166.

England, P., & Li, S. (2006). Desegregation stalled: The changing gender composition of college majors, 1971–2002. *Gender & Society, 20*, 657–577.

Entwisle, D. R., Alexander, K., & Olson, L. S. (1994). The gender gap in math: Its possible origins in neighborhood effects. *American Sociological Review, 59*, 822–838.

Ewert, S. (2010). Male and female pathways through four-year colleges: Disruption and sex stratification in higher education. *American Educational Research Journal, 47*, 744–773.

Farkas, G., Sheehan, D., & Grobe, R. (1990). Coursework mastery and school success: Gender, ethnicity, and poverty groups within an urban school district. *American Educational Research Journal, 27*, 807–827.

Frank, K., Muller, C., Schiller, K., Riegle-Crumb, C., Mueller, A., Crosnoe, R., & Pearson, J. (2008). The social dynamics of mathematics course-taking in high school. *American Journal of Sociology, 113*(6), 1645–1696.

Freedle, R. (2003). Correcting the SAT's ethnic and social-class bias: A method for reestimating SAT scores. *Harvard Educational Review, 73*(1), 1–43.

Gamoran, A., & Hannigan, E. C. (2000). Algebra for everyone? Benefits of college-preparatory mathematics for students with diverse abilities in early secondary school. *Educational Evaluation and Policy Analysis, 22*(3), 241–254.

Gerber, T. P., & Cheung, S. Y. (2008). Horizontal stratification in postsecondary education: Forms, explanations, and implications. *Annual Review of Sociology, 34*, 299–318.

Gibbs, B. G. (2010). Reversing fortunes or content change? Gender gaps in math-related skill throughout childhood. *Social Science Research, 39*, 540–569.

Golden, C. (2006). The quiet revolution that transformed women's employment, education, and family. *American Economic Review, 96*, 1–21.

Good, C., Aronson, J., & Inzlicht, M. (2003). Improving adolescents' standardized test performance: An intervention to reduce the effects of stereotype threat. *Journal of Applied Developmental Psychology, 24*(6), 645–662.

Grodsky, E., Warren, J. R., & Felts, E. (2008). Testing and social stratification in American education. *Annual Review of Sociology, 34*, 385–404.

Grodsky, E., Warren, J. R., & Kalogrides, D. (2009). State high school exit examinations and NAEP long-term trends in reading and mathematics, 1971–2004. *Educational Policy, 23*(4), 589–614.

Halpern, D. F. (2013). *Sex differences in cognitive abilities*. New York: Psychology Press.

Hanselman, P., Bruch, S., Gamoran, A., & Borman, G. (2014). Threat in context: School moderation of the impact of social identity threat on racial/ethnic achievement gaps. *Sociology of Education, 87*(2), 106–124.

Harris, D. R., & Sim, J. J. (2002). Who is multiracial? Assessing the complexity of lived race. *American Sociological Review, 67*, 614–627.

Haut, M., & Elliott, S. W. (Eds.). (2011). *Incentives and test-based accountability in education*. Washington, DC: National Academies Press.

Hemphill, F. C., & Vanneman, A. (2011). *Achievement gaps: How Hispanic and White students in public schools perform in mathematics and reading on the National Assessment of Educational Progress* (NCES 2011-459). Washington, DC: National Center for Education Statistics, Institute of Education Sciences, U.S. Department of Education.

Herman, M. (2009). The Black–White–Other achievement gap: Testing theories of academic performance among multiracial and monoracial adolescents. *Sociology of Education, 82*, 20–46.

Hill Collins, P. (2000). *Black feminist thought: Knowledge, consciousness, and the politics of empowerment*. New York: Routledge.

Holland, M. (2012). Only here for the day: The social integration of minority students at a majority White high school. *Sociology of Education, 85*(2), 101–120.

hooks, b. (1984). *Feminist theory: From margin to center*. Cambridge, MA: South End Press.

Hussar, W. J., & Bailey, T. M. (2014). *Projections of education statistics to 2022* (NCES 2014-051). National Center for Education Statistics.

Hyde, J., Lindberg, S., Linn, M., Ellis, A., & Williams, C. (2008). Gender similarities characterize math performance. *Science, 321*, 494–495.

Hyde, J. S., & Mertz, J. E. (2009). Gender, culture, and mathematics performance. *Proceedings of the National Academy of Sciences, 106*(22), 8801–8807.

Irizarry, Y. (2015). Utilizing multidimensional measures of race in education research: The case of teacher perceptions. *Sociology of Race and Ethnicity, 1*(4), 1–20.

Ispa-Landa, S. (2013). Gender, race and justifications for group exclusion: Urban Black students bussed to affluent suburban schools. *Sociology of Education, 86*(3), 218–233.

Ispa-Landa, S., & Conwell, J. (2015). "Once you go to a White school, you kind of adapt": Black adolescents and the racial classification of schools. *Sociology of Education, 88*(1), 1–19.

Jacob, B. (2002). Where the boys aren't: Non-cognitive skills, returns to school and the gender gap in higher education. *Economics of Education Review, 21*, 589–598.

Jennings, J., Deming, D., Jencks, C., Lopuch, M., & Schueler, B. (2015). Do differences in school quality matter more than we thought? New evidence on educational opportunity in the 21st century. *Sociology of Education, 88*(1), 56–82.

Kane, T. J. & Staiger, D. O. (2012). *Gathering feedback for teaching: Combining high quality observations with student surveys and achievement gains* (MET Project Research Paper). Seattle: Bill and Melinda Gates Foundation.

Kao, G., Tienda, M., & Schneider, B. (1996). Racial and ethnic variation in educational outcomes. *Research in Sociology of Education and Socialization, 11*, 263–297.

Kaufman, D., & Richardson, B. (1982). *Achievement and women: Challenging the assumptions*. New York: Free Press.

Kelly, S. (2008). What types of students' effort are rewarded with high marks? *Sociology of Education, 81*, 32–52.

Kelly, S. (2009). The Black–White gap in mathematics course taking. *Sociology of Education, 82*, 47–69.

Kliebard, H. M. (2004). *The struggle for the American curriculum, 1893–1958*. New York: Routledge.

Ladson-Billings, G. (1998). Just what is critical race theory and what's it doing in a nice field like education? *International Journal of Qualitative Studies in Education, 11*(1), 7–24.

Lee, J., & Bean, F. D. (2004). America's changing color lines: Immigration, race/ethnicity, and multiracial identification. *Annual Review of Sociology, 30*, 221–242.

Lee, S. J., & Kumashiro, K. (2005). *A report on the status of Asian Americans and Pacific Islanders in education: Beyond the "model minority" stereotype*. Washington, DC: National Education Association.

Lee, J., Grigg, W., & Dion, G. (2007). *The nation's report card*. Washington, DC: National Center for Education Statistics, Institute of Education Sciences, U.S. Department of Education.

Legewie, J., & DiPrete, T. (2015). The high school environment and the gender gap in science and engineering. *Sociology of Education, 87*(4), 259–280.

Linn, R. L. (2013). *Test-based accountability*. The Gordon Commission on the Future of Assessment in Education. http://www.gordoncommission.org/publications_reports/assessment_education.html

Loveless, T. (2008). *The misplaced math student: Lost in eighth-grade algebra*. Washington, DC: Brookings Institution, Brown Center on Education Policy.

Lucas, S. R. (1999). *Tracking inequality: Stratification and mobility in American high schools*. New York: Teachers College Press.

Lucas, S. R. (2001). Effectively maintained inequality: Education transitions, track mobility, and social background effects. *American Journal of Sociology, 106*(6), 1642–1690.

Lucas, S. R., & Berends, M. (2002). Sociodemographic diversity, correlated achievement, and de facto tracking. *Sociology of Education, 75*(4), 328–348.

Maccoby, E., & Jacklin, C. (1974). *The psychology of sex differences*. Stanford: Stanford University Press.

Mann, A., & DiPrete, T. (2013). Trends in gender segregation in the choice of science and engineering majors. *Social Science Research, 42*, 1519–1541.

McGlone, M. S., & Aronson, J. (2006). Stereotype threat, identity salience, and spatial reasoning. *Journal of Applied Developmental Psychology, 27*, 486–493.

McNeish, D., Radunzel, J., & Sanchez, E. (2015). *A multidimensional perspective of college readiness: Relating student and school characteristics to performance on the ACT*. Iowa City: ACT, Inc. http://www.act.org/research/researchers/reports/pdf/ACT_RR2015-6.pdf.

Merolla, D. M. (2013). The net Black advantage in educational transitions: An education careers approach. *American Educational Research Journal, 50*(5), 895–924.

Mickelson, R. A. (1989). Why does Jane read and write so well? The anomaly of women's achievement. *Sociology of Education, 62*, 47–63.

Mickelson, R. A. (2001). Subverting Swann: First-and second-generation segregation in the Charlotte-Mecklenburg schools. *American Educational Research Journal, 38*(2), 215–252.

Mickelson, R. A., & Heath, D. (1999). The effects of segregation on African American high school seniors' academic achievement. *Journal of Negro Education, 68*(4), 566–586.

Morgan, S., Gelbgiser, D., & Weeden, K. (2013). Feeding the pipeline: Gender, occupational plans, and college major selection. *Social Science Research, 42*, 989–1005.

Morris, E. W. (2007). "Ladies" or "loudies"? Perceptions and experiences of Black girls in classrooms. *Youth & Society, 38*(4), 490–515.

NCES. (2012). *The condition of education 2012* (NCES 2012-045). Washington, DC: National Center for Education Statistics, U.S. Department of Education.

NCES. (2014). *Digest of education statistics*. Washington, DC: National Center for Education Statistics, U.S. Department of Education. https://nces.ed.gov/programs/digest/d14/tables/dt14_302.10.asp

NCES. (2015). *Digest of education statistics, 2013* (NCES 2015-011). Washington, DC: National Center for Education Statistics, U.S. Department of Education.

Newton, X. A., Torres, D., & Rivero, R. (2008). Making the connection: Timing of taking algebra in secondary schools and future college STEM participation. *Journal of Women and Minorities in Science and Engineering, 17*(2), 111–128.

Nord, C., Roey, S., Perkins, R., Lyons, M., Lemanski, N., Brown, J., & Schuknecht, J. (2011). *The nation's report card: America's high school graduates* (NCES 2011-462). Washington, DC: U.S. Department of Education, National Center for Education Statistics.

Oakes, J. (2005). *Keeping track: How schools structure inequality*. New Haven: Yale University Press.

Ovink, S. M. (2013). "They always call me an investment": Gendered familism and Latino/a college pathways. *Gender & Society, 28*(2), 265–288.

Owens, J. (2016). Early childhood behavior problems and the gender gap in educational attainment in the United States. *Sociology of Education, 89*(3), 236–258.

Pang, V. O., Han, P. P., & Pang, J. M. (2011). Asian American and Pacific Islander students: Equity and the achievement gap. *Educational Researcher, 40*(8), 378–389.

Penner, A. M., & Paret, M. (2008). Gender differences in mathematics achievement: Exploring the early grades and the extremes. *Social Science Research, 37*, 239–253.

Pew Research Center. (2015). *Multiracial in America: Proud, diverse and growing in numbers*. Washington, DC: Pew Research Center.

Pong, S. L., Hao, L., & Gardner, E. (2005). The roles of parenting styles and social capital in the school performance of immigrant Asian and Hispanic adolescents. *Social Science Quarterly, 86*(4), 928–950.

Quinn, D. M. (2015). Black–White summer learning gaps: Interpreting the variability of estimates across representations. *Educational Evaluation and Policy Analysis, 37*(1), 50–69.

Quinn, D., & Cooc, N. (2015). Science achievement gaps by gender and race/ethnicity in elementary and middle school trends and predictors. *Educational Researcher, 44*, 336–346.

Rampey, B. D., Dion, G. S., & Donahue, P. L. (2008). *The nation's report card: Trends in academic progress in reading and mathematics*. Washington, DC: National Center for Education Statistics.

Reynolds, J., & Burge, S. (2008). Educational expectations and the rise in women's post-secondary attainments. *Social Science Research, 37*, 485.

Ridgeway, C. L., & Correll, S. J. (2004). Unpacking the gender system: A theoretical perspective on gender beliefs and social relations. *Gender & Society, 18*(4), 510–531.

Riegle-Crumb, C. (2006). The path through math: Course sequences and academic performance at the intersection of math course-taking and achievement. *Sociology of Education, 83*, 248–270.

Riegle-Crumb, C., & Grodsky, E. (2010). Racial-ethnic differences at the intersection of math course-taking and achievement. *Sociology of Education, 83*(3), 248–270.

Riegle-Crumb, C., & King, B. (2010). Questioning a White male advantage in STEM: Examining disparities in college major by gender and race/ethnicity. *Educational Researcher, 39*(9), 656–664.

Riegle-Crumb, C., & Moore, C. (2014). The gender gap in high school physics: Considering the context of local communities. *Social Science Quarterly, 95*, 253–268.

Riegle-Crumb, C., Farkas, G., & Muller, C. (2006). The role of gender and friendship in advanced course-taking. *Sociology of Education, 79*(3), 206–228.

Riegle-Crumb, C., King, B., Grodsky, E., & Muller, C. (2012). The more things change, the more they stay the same? Prior achievement fails to explain gender inequality in entry to STEM college majors over time. *American Educational Research Journal, 49*, 1048–1073.

Risman, B. (2004). Gender as a social structure: Theory wrestling with activism. *Gender & Society, 18*, 429–450.

Robinson, J., & Lubienski, S. (2011). The development of gender gaps in mathematics and reading during elementary and middle school: Examining direct cognitive assessments and teacher ratings. *American Educational Research Journal, 48*, 268–302.

Roderick, M., Coca, V., & Nagaoka, J. (2011). Potholes on the road to college: High school effects in shaping urban students' participation in college application, four-year college enrollment, and college match. *Sociology of Education, 84*, 178–211.

Roscigno, V. J., & Ainsworth-Darnell, J. W. (1999). Race, cultural capital, and educational resources: Persistent inequalities and achievement returns. *Sociology of Education, 72*, 158–178.

Ross, T., Kena, G., Rathbun, A., KewalRamani, A., Zhang, J., Kristapovich, P., & Manning, E. (2012). *Higher education: Gaps in access and persistence study* (NCES 2012-046). Washington, DC: U.S. Department of Education, National Center for Education Statistics, Government Printing Office.

Savas, G. (2016). Gender and race differences in American college enrollment: Evidence from the Education Longitudinal Study of 2002. *American Journal of Education Research, 4*, 64–75.

Schmader, T. (2002). Gender identification moderates stereotype threat effects on women's math performance. *Journal of Experimental Social Psychology, 38*, 194–201.

Siebens, J., & Ryan, C. L. (2012). *Field of bachelor's degree in the United States: 2009* (American Community Survey Reports. ACS-18). US Census Bureau.

Snyder, T. D., & Dillow, S. A. (2011). *Digest of education statistics 2010*. Washington, DC: National Center for Education Statistics.

Sommers, C. (2000). *The war against boys: How misguided feminism is harming our young men.* New York: Simon and Schuster.

Spelke, E. S. (2005). Sex differences in intrinsic aptitude for mathematics and science? A critical review. *American Psychologist, 60*, 950–958.

Spielhagen, F. R. (2006). Closing the achievement gap in math: The long-term effects of eighth-grade algebra. *Journal of Advanced Academics, 18*(1), 34–59.

Steele, J. (2003). Children's gender stereotypes about math: The role of stereotype stratification. *Journal of Applied Social Psychology, 33*, 2587–2606.

Steele, C. M., & Aronson, J. (1995). Stereotype threat and the intellectual test performance of African Americans. *Journal of Personality and Social Psychology, 69*(5), 797.

Sternberg, R. J. (2007). Who are the bright children? The cultural context of being and acting intelligent. *Educational Researcher, 36*(3), 148–155.

Stillwell, R., & Sable, J. (2013). *Public school graduates and dropouts from the common core of data: School year 2009–10. First look* (Provisional Data, NCES 2013-309). National Center for Education Statistics.

Vanneman, A., Hamilton, L., Anderson, J. B., & Rahman, T. (2009). *Achievement gaps: How Black and White students in public schools perform in mathematics and reading on the National Assessment of Educational Progress* (Statistical Analysis Report, NCES 2009455). National Center for Education Statistics.

Voyer, D., & Voyer, S. (2014). Gender differences in scholastic achievement: A meta-analysis. *Psychological Bulletin, 140*, 1174–1204.

Walston, J., & McCarroll, J. (2010). *Eighth-grade algebra: Findings from the eighth grade round of the early childhood longitudinal study, kindergarten class of 1998–99* (NCES-2010-016). Washington, DC: U.S. Department of Education.

Wang, M., & Degol, J. (2013). Motivational pathways to STEM career choices: Using expectancy-value perspective to understand individual and gender differences in STEM fields. *Developmental Review, 33*, 304–340.

Warikoo, N., & Carter, P. (2009). Cultural explanations for racial and ethnic stratification in academic achievement: A call for a new and improved theory. *Review of Educational Research, 79*(1), 366–394.

Wilkins, A. C. (2014). Race, age and identity transformations in the transition from high school to college for Black and first-generation White men. *Sociology of Education, 87*(3), 171–187.

Williams, W. M., & Ceci, S. (2012). When scientists choose motherhood. *American Scientist, 100*, 138–146.

Xie, Y., & Shauman, K. (2003). *Women in science: Career processes and outcomes.* Cambridge, MA: Harvard University Press.

Xue, Y., & Larson, R. (2015). STEM crisis or STEM surplus? Yes and yes. *Monthly Labor Review, 138*, 1–9.

Undocumented Youth and Local Contours of Inequality

Roberto G. Gonzales and Edelina M. Burciaga

Abstract

About 2.1 million undocumented immigrants are members of the 1.5-generation, meaning they arrived in the United States as children and remain without legal permission. The experiences of the undocumented 1.5-generation have captured the sociological imagination, and research about undocumented immigrant youth is a burgeoning and exciting field of study. This research captures both the challenges that immigrant youth face growing up undocumented in the United States, and also how they are responding to these challenges. This chapter draws from two different studies examining the experiences of undocumented youth in the United States, in order to understand this group's conflicting experiences of illegality and belonging. The data presented in this chapter suggests that there are two key axes of educational stratification *within* the undocumented youth community. The first is among those who complete high school and attend college vs those who are considered early exiters, young people who leave K–12 schools at or before high school

graduation. Relatedly, the second axis of stratification is connected to *where* undocumented youth grow up and live. Ultimately, we show that as undocumented young people make critical transitions from childhood to adolescence and young adulthood, their immigration status is a central impediment to their hopes and dreams. Almost as consequential, the resources and practices of their school districts and the policies of their states condition their post high school lives.

Approximately 11.1 million undocumented immigrants, largely from Mexico and Central America, currently live in the United States, the result of decades of unauthorized migration and settlement and increasingly restrictive immigration laws and policies (Passel and Cohn 2011; Massey et al. 2002). About 2.1 million are members of the undocumented 1.5-generation (Batalova and McHugh 2010), meaning they arrived in the United States as children and remain without legal permission. Unlike the first-generation who migrated as adults and the second generation, who are similarly children of immigrants but are born in the United States, undocumented youth and young adults have developed values, identities, and aspirations that are influenced by growing up American. But their lives are also deeply impacted by the practical reality of living "illegally" in the United States.

R. G. Gonzales (✉)
Harvard University, Cambridge, MA, USA
e-mail: roberto_gonzales@gse.harvard.edu

E. M. Burciaga
University of Colorado Denver, Denver, CO, USA
e-mail: EDELINA.BURCIAGA@ucdenver.edu

© Springer International Publishing AG, part of Springer Nature 2018
B. Schneider (ed.), *Handbook of the Sociology of Education in the 21st Century*, Handbooks of Sociology and Social Research, https://doi.org/10.1007/978-3-319-76694-2_7

The experiences of the undocumented 1.5-generation have captured the sociological imagination, and research about undocumented immigrant youth is a burgeoning and exciting field of study (Gonzales 2015).

Over the last 10 years, researchers have examined a diversity of issues pertaining to undocumented young people, including the high school experiences of undocumented immigrant youth (Gonzales 2010a; Gonzales and Ruiz 2014; Jefferies 2014); the effects of in-state tuition policies on these young people (Conger and Chellman 2013; Diaz-Strong et al. 2011; Dougherty et al. 2010; Flores 2010; Flores and Horn 2009; Kaushal 2008; Olivas 2004, 2009); efforts of higher education institutions and their staff to integrate undocumented students (Gildersleeve and Ranero 2010; Gildersleeve et al. 2010; Gonzales 2010b), the identity development and relationships among undocumented young people (Abrego 2008; Chang 2010; Ellis and Chen 2013; Mangual Figueroa 2012; Munoz and Maldonado 2012); the transitions undocumented young people experience after high school (Abrego 2006; Abrego and Gonzales 2010; Enriquez 2011; Gonzales 2011; Gonzales and Bautista-Chavez 2012; Terriquez 2014); and their civic and political participation (Enriquez 2014; Galindo 2012; Gonzales 2008; Negrón-Gonzales 2013, 2014; Nicholls 2013; Patler and Gonzales 2015; Perez et al. 2009; Rincon 2008; Rogers et al. 2008; Seif 2004; Zimmerman 2012).

This growing body of research expands understandings of the immigrant experience by highlighting the profound impact of undocumented immigration status on the incorporation and mobility prospects of the undocumented 1.5-generation (Abrego 2006; Gonzales 2007, 2009, 2011). Beyond understanding the impact of immigration status for social mobility and access, research about the experiences of undocumented youth has also addressed fundamental questions about membership and exclusion.

Because undocumented 1.5-generation young adults arrive as children, often before the age of 14, primary and secondary schools are a key socializing force (Gonzales 2010a; Gonzales et al. 2015a). In 1982, the United States Supreme Court held in *Plyler v. Doe* that undocumented immigrant youth had a right to a public education through high school (Olivas 2011). After high school, though, undocumented youth face more uncertain futures (Abrego 2006; Gonzales 2011; Enriquez 2011). In addition, research suggests that making it through high school, and to college, is no easy feat for undocumented immigrant youth, as they face the same challenges that many low-income students of color must also overcome on the road to and through college (Abrego 2006; Gonzales 2010b; Enriquez 2011; Gonzales and Ruiz 2014). A well-established body of research, however, captures the unique role that an undocumented immigration status plays in shaping the lives and the futures of undocumented immigrant youth (Abrego and Gonzales 2010; Enriquez 2011; Gonzales and Ruiz 2014). In this chapter, drawing from our own research and the vibrant field of studies about the experiences of undocumented immigrant youth, we examine how laws and policies have created conflicting experiences of illegality and belonging for undocumented young people living in the United States.

7.1 Growing Up Undocumented in the United States

Sociological inquiries into the immigrant experience have long sought to understand and explain immigrant incorporation, largely around the questions of how immigrants and their children are becoming a part of the United States. While there is lively debate about how contemporary processes of incorporation are taking place (Alba and Nee 2003; Bean and Stevens 2003; Kasinitz et al. 2008; Portes and Rumbaut 2001; Portes and Zhou 1993), these different theoretical approaches to immigrant integration share a central concern, that of membership. And while formal citizenship and the legal conferring of rights have been historically defined by immigration status, many immigration scholars have argued for a broader view of citizenship that recognizes community and cultural participation as forms of membership (Bosniak 2008; Nakano Glenn 2011; Blooemraad et al. 2008; Soysal 1994). Sometimes referred to as cultural citizenship (Rosaldo 1994; Rosaldo and Flores 1997) or substantive citizenship (Brubaker 1992; Marshall 1950), or a sense of belonging (Yuval-Davis 2006), these notions of citizenship are meant to capture feelings of membership that cannot be defined by the nation-state (Nakano Glenn 2011; Blooemraad et al. 2008). Developing in concert with this expanded view of citizenship, has been a close examination of the ways in which policies and enforcement practices frame the everyday lives of undocumented immigrants (Coutin 1999; DeGenova 2002; Ngai 2004; Willen 2007). The concept of "migrant illegality" emerges from this research, which is rooted in the everyday experiences of undocumented immigrants, and captures a "social relation that is fundamentally inseparable from citizenship" (DeGenova 2002, p. 422). Like expanded notions of citizenship, the theoretical construct of "illegality" simultaneously encompasses a relationship between the individual and the nation-state *and* the social and cultural realities of undocumented immigrants as members of their communities. In this vein, the experiences of undocumented immigrant youth who were raised in the United States and yet face significant constraints as they age because of their formal legal status, have provided unique insight into the contradictions of U.S. immigration law and policy (Gonzales 2016).

For nearly a decade, scholars have made incredible strides in gathering systematic, empirical research about the constraints facing undocumented immigrant youth. This research captures both the challenges that immigrant youth face growing up undocumented in the United States, and also how they are responding to these challenges. The social, political, and educational integration of undocumented immigrant youth has been profoundly shaped by the aforementioned 1982 *Plyler v. Doe* decision. In *Plyler* the Supreme Court argued that denying undocumented immigrant children a public education based on their immigration status would create an educational underclass, and that this was not in the best interest of undocumented children and society. This decision highlighted the key role that schools play in socializing children and in

shaping their social and educational opportunities. Perhaps more importantly, the Supreme Court's decision was also an implicit acknowledgement of the settled lives that undocumented immigrant children and their families were living in the United States. In fact, just 4 years later in 1986, the Immigration Reform and Control Act (IRCA) was passed, granting citizenship to nearly 3 million undocumented immigrants living in the United States.

In the years since the *Plyler v. Doe* decision and the passage of IRCA, the undocumented immigrant population has grown dramatically. During the 1990s the number of people living in an unauthorized residency status increased by 3.5 million, and between 2000 and 2013, it increased by 4 million (Rosenblum and Ruiz Soto 2015). However, IRCA was the last major comprehensive immigration reform to offer a pathway to citizenship, and the law ushered in an era of increased immigration enforcement (Golash-Boza 2015; Kanstroom 2012). Nevertheless, undocumented immigrant families have become a part of the fabric of American life, settling into everyday patterns of living, working, and attending schools in their local communities (Chavez 1991, 1994). Still, they struggle to achieve full social incorporation precisely because their undocumented status narrowly circumscribes their possibilities. This paradox is most acutely experienced by undocumented immigrant children, many of whom have spent most of their lives in the United States and have grown up with "American" values, identities, and aspirations.

Previous research finds that because school is the major socializing institution for undocumented immigrant children, their experience of "growing up undocumented" is complicated by the fact that for most of their lives they inhabit a legally protected space, the educational system. While public schools, writ large, are legally protected spaces, undocumented immigrant children participate in an educational system that is stratified (Gonzales 2010a; Gonzales et al. 2015a). Because immigration status and poverty are intimately connected for this group, undocumented immigrant children often grow up in segregated neighborhoods and attend high-poverty, low-achieving schools (Gonzales 2016, Gonzales and Ruiz 2014; Abrego 2006). These schools are often under-resourced, experience high teacher turnover, and have inadequate facilities and learning materials. While these structural disadvantages impact the whole student body, the implications may be greater for undocumented children precisely because of the additional layer of vulnerability due to their undocumented status. As previous research suggests, being undocumented increases children's chances of "living in the shadows"—as undocumented parents may be less likely to access an array of services that have traditionally benefitted immigrant families (Yoshikawa and Kalil 2011; Menjívar and Abrego 2009; Fortuny et al. 2007)—and negatively impacts school outcomes (Bean et al. 2011). For this group, conflicting experiences of illegality and belonging start very early, as they often experience integration in their schools but also witness their parents' legal exclusion (Dreby 2015).

This chapter draws from two different studies examining the experiences of undocumented youth in the United States, in order to understand this group's conflicting experiences of illegality and belonging. Between 2003 and 2015, Roberto G. Gonzales carried out longitudinal research in the five-county Los Angeles metropolitan area. This chapter draws from his extensive fieldwork and interviews with 150 Mexican young adults who came to the United States before the age of 12. Edelina Burciaga conducted ethnographic research between 2009 and 2011 that consisted of 20 interviews with undocumented youth activists involved in the Development Relief and Education for Alien Minors (DREAM) Act campaign in Los Angeles and Orange County, California. This chapter also draws from her comparative qualitative research conducted between 2014 and 2015, including 70 interviews with undocumented young people growing up and living in metropolitan Los Angeles, CA, a traditional immigrant gateway, and Atlanta, GA, a new immigrant destination.

The data presented in this chapter suggests that there are two key axes of educational stratification *within* the undocumented youth community. The first is among those who complete high school and attend college vs those who are considered early exiters, young people who leave K–12 schools at or before high school graduation (Gonzales 2011, 2016). Relatedly, the second axis of stratification is connected to *where* undocumented youth grow up and live. Previous research about the undocumented 1.5-generation has focused primarily on undocumented youth living in California, arguably one of the most welcoming regions in terms of postsecondary access (Gonzales 2015; Gonzales et al. 2015a; Enriquez and Saguy 2016; Terriquez 2014; Abrego 2006). While there is emergent research about the educational experiences of undocumented immigrant youth in regions other than California, (see for example Cebulko 2014; Gonzales and Ruiz 2014; Martinez 2014; Silver 2012), the comparative data presented in this chapter suggests that state and local contexts matter for the educational trajectories as well as the experiences of illegality and belonging for undocumented youth.

7.2 Studying Undocumented Youth

Until recently, there was scant available evidence from which to understand the lives of undocumented youth. Part of the difficulty inherent in such an endeavor is the lack of reliable demographic and empirical data. It is difficult to obtain survey data about undocumented immigrants because they comprise a small share of the U.S. population. In addition, large-scale surveys generally do not include questions about immigration status, so we do not have sufficient data from which to develop a clear statistical portrait. And, surveying them through random dialing methods, respondent driven sampling, or other similar approaches can be costly and cost prohibitive, especially when trying to generate a national sample.

To move beyond conjecture requires a methodological approach that yields deep familiarity with the lives of the undocumented young people and their families. Foner (2003) makes a persuasive case for ethnography as a central method to engage and understand hard-to-reach populations. While this approach has its downside in that it limits the number of people a researcher can study and the ability to make generalizations for broad populations, in-depth study of a small number of people over time provides insights into their beliefs, values, and social relations, as well as the complex ways they construct their identities in specific contexts (Foner 2003, p. 26). Relying on large-scale surveys may mean missing some of this important nuance or even getting it wrong. As Kubal (2013, p. 20) notes, inquiry into the power of the state is most fertile at "the level of lived experience, where power is exercised, understood, and sometimes resisted." Understanding how young adults experience and push back against power requires a methodology deeply rooted in their lives.

As such, qualitative inquiry has provided valuable insight into how undocumented youth make meaning of their experiences of illegality. Ethnography and in-depth interviews, the most widely employed methods of data collection with undocumented youth, are able to uncover how these young adults navigate the transition to and through adulthood, including their educational trajectories. It is through ethnographic research that we have learned that the transition to illegality is a complex process. Because undocumented youth experience both social inclusion and legal exclusion (Gonzales 2011, 2016), sociologists employing qualitative methods have learned that illegality shapes processes of incorporation differently for undocumented youth than for other immigrant youth. Ethnography and interview based research has documented the differences in participation in education and the labor market, hallmarks of immigrant incorporation, as well as the symbolic and emotional implications of incomplete inclusion. Capturing the affective component of the undocumented youth experience has been a key strength of the body of qualitative studies in this area. While immigration scholars have been long concerned with sense of belonging, qualitative research about undocumented youth has significantly extended sociological understandings of this complex process.

Another strength of qualitative work about undocumented immigrant youth is that it is rooted in the everyday lived experience of this group. Distinct from quantitative research, these studies reveal how undocumented youth negotiate and manage their legal status in multiple facets of their lives. While most of this research focuses on educational access, amongst the most formative experiences for undocumented young adults, this research also has revealed how undocumented youth make sense of their racial and ethnic identity, their mental health and well-being, and their own articulation of what it means to be an American (Patler and Pirtle 2018; Aranda et al. 2015). A key strength of the qualitative approach in this field has been that it centers the voices and experiences of undocumented young adults. In doing so, it has highlighted the challenges that undocumented youth face, but also their agency and power in the face of significant structural barriers. In contrast to public perceptions of undocumented young people as vulnerable because of their legal status and age, qualitative studies have shown that undocumented youth activism is a vibrant aspect of the undocumented youth experience in the United States. To date, qualitative research about undocumented youth has made significant strides in building theory about how legal status shapes immigrant integration, especially in the area of educational access, but the field remains open to new lines of inquiry.

Research on undocumented young people must continue to be methodologically rigorous and address the multi-layered complexities that exist within this diverse population. Much of the current research has focused its attention on high academic achievers and a small group of undocumented youth who are connected to immigrant rights organizations or who are politically active. Indeed, high-achieving undocumented college student activists are an attractive convenience sample for university researchers, politicians, and journalists. And they are also much easier to locate and with whom to gain cooperation. But this group is not representative of the undocumented population as a whole. And if we limit our scope of inquiry to the most talented, resourced, and connected among a particular community, what we know is inherently skewed. Efforts to study inequality must seek to fully understand a range of experiences, not merely those of the most successful. We know very little about undocumented young people who do not make the successful transition from high school to postsecondary education, and even less about those with little to no K–12 experiences in the United States.

In addition, this research has focused primarily on undocumented young people living in urban areas in states with a significant portion of the undocumented immigrant population, including California, New York, and Illinois. We are just beginning to understand the consequences of different state and local-level policies for undocumented youth living in new immigrant destinations. We still know very little about how undocumented youth living in rural areas of the United States are faring (for an exception see, Gonzales and Ruiz 2014). Given the racial and ethnic makeup of the undocumented immigrant population more generally, much of the research has captured the experiences of Latina/o undocumented youth. There is still more to learn about the experiences of undocumented youth from other racial and ethnic groups (for exceptions see, Cebulko 2014; Buenavista 2012). To be sure, studying hard-to-reach populations can be difficult, time consuming, and expensive, but scholars employing qualitative methods are uniquely positioned to continue gathering data that highlight the contours of how undocumented immigrant youth experience both exclusion and belonging, which we address in the sections that follow.

7.3   Formative Experiences of Illegality and Belonging

As undocumented children grow up, they continue to face barriers and challenges on the road to and through adulthood, as their family responsibilities increase but their opportunities for social and economic mobility become more limited. Previous research finds that as undocu-

mented immigrant youth transition into adulthood, there is a pattern of defining moments that shape their educational and social mobility, as well as their sense of belonging (Gonzales 2011). Recent administrative action through the introduction of the Deferred Action for Childhood Arrivals (DACA) program has opened some short-term opportunities for undocumented young adults as they transition to adulthood (Gonzales et al. 2014). The long-term benefits, however, are still being understood.[1] Announced in 2012, DACA offers a stay of deportation and a work permit for eligible undocumented young people. While DACA has shifted the experiences of undocumented young people in some ways for better, the transition to adulthood is still significantly shaped by their undocumented status. Many undocumented young people grow up aware of their undocumented status, as some of their parents openly discuss and share with them their efforts to fix their status. In addition, parents often offer advice about how to handle questions about their undocumented status. Dolores, a 22-year-old college student who migrated to the United States with her mother at just 2 months old, was encouraged to have an alternate story about where she was born,

> In elementary school, my dad used to always tell me, "Don't say that you were born in Mexico. Tell them that you were born in Texas and that you're from Texas. Whatever you say, don't tell them that you're Mexican, and that you don't have papers or anything like that."

During our interview, Dolores, who had since "come out" as an undocumented youth activist, shared that she and her mother had recently come across an elementary school art project where Dolores had drawn the state of Texas as the place she was born. While she and her mother could laugh about the art project 15 years later, Dolores' experience reflects how early the conflicting experience of illegality and belonging starts for undocumented immigrant youth.

---

[1] Efforts such as the National UnDACAmented Research Project, headed by Roberto G. Gonzales at Harvard University, are collecting multi-sited, longitudinal data on the impacts of DACA.

Victoria, who also lived in Orange County, and migrated from Mexico at the age of 13, was explicitly advised by her parents not to tell anyone that she "didn't have papers." Instead when asked if she was born in the United States, she would say, "'No, I was born in Mexico.' But I would leave it up them. I wouldn't say, 'Oh, I don't have papers.'" Other undocumented youth learn about their status through their parents' unsuccessful attempts to adjust their immigration status. Jennifer, whose family overstayed their visa, shared that she grew up under the impression that she, her sister, and her parents were going to be a "hundred percent and be legal soon." She shared, "That was the goal that—we always talked about it, with our family, that by now—like by college, I would have a green card. I would be legalized." While Jennifer did not grow up with explicit advice from her parents to hide her immigration status, Jennifer's sense of belonging was informed in part by her parents' assurances that someday she would be a legal resident and have a green card. Like Jennifer, Yadira, who immigrated on a 6-month visa with her mother and brother, watched her mother spend over ten thousand dollars to "fix their status." After September 11, 2001, when Yadira was in the third grade, her mother's attorney informed her that, "there wasn't anything to do," leaving Yadira's family without any hope of adjusting their status.

These early experiences of knowing and yet hiding their immigration status socialize undocumented young people to understand to some degree that it is shameful to be undocumented. Andrea, who lived in Orange County and would return to Mexico during the summers before 2001, shared,

> Yeah, I definitely knew I was undocumented. Just because you had to hide—you had to lie. I remember that I had this bracelet that had my initials and every time I would cross, I would have to take it off. When it came to school or those kinds of things, I myself was ashamed to say it because I thought I was wrong.

At the same time that undocumented youth internalize the stigma of being undocumented, they also form a sense of belonging through experiences in school and in their communities. Jennifer, who is 19 years old, migrated to Los Angeles when she was 7 years old. She described her transition as less shocking than she expected, primarily because she migrated to a predominantly Latino neighborhood, or as she described it,

> I would like to say [my neighborhood was] one hundred percent Latino. I mean when we got there I was like, "Why is everyone speaking Spanish?" I was surprised because I was like, "Okay." It was comforting to go to a city where at least other people knew the language that I spoke. I didn't feel too out of place.

While Jennifer later described facing challenges in school because she didn't know English, like many undocumented youth, she eventually transitioned out of English as a Second Language classes into mainstream classes. Like Jennifer, Edith and her family also migrated to Los Angeles and she lived there until she was 12 years old. Edith recalled her earliest memories of living in the greater Los Angeles area as happy. She shared,

> I have really looked back at my childhood experiences, and I started reflecting and I started thinking, there were so many signs [that I was undocumented], but I did not put them together. I think that is because I was, I had a really happy childhood in Los Angeles, I sincerely mean that.

While Edith attributed her happy childhood to the simple needs of a child, her experience reflects how during elementary and middle school, for undocumented youth a sense of belonging is cultivated in part by just being able to be children.

Between the ages of 16 and 18, undocumented youth begin to wrestle with the full impact of their undocumented status in their day-to-day lives. During this discovery stage (Gonzales 2011), undocumented young people begin to negotiate access to rites of passage such as getting their first job, a driver's license, and considering the college application process. As Dolores, who we introduced earlier, shared during our interview,

> I always knew [that I was undocumented] but it didn't start to affect me until high school, like senior year. When everybody was applying to

college. I thought maybe we had the money so that I could go to school. And that's when reality hit. Like, I can't. My parents can't afford it, I can't get financial aid because I don't have documentation. I thought that was like, the end of my world. Because I couldn't go to college.

Dolores—like many undocumented young adults who attended college before California passed the state Dream Act which expanded access to state and institutional financial aid—faced significant financial barriers to college access.[2] Despite the passage of the California Dream Act, which in some ways has eased the transition to college, undocumented youth still navigate an array of confusing systems. Yesenia, who was 20 years old at the time of our interview and had enrolled in a 4-year college in Southern California, shared that when it was time to apply for financial aid, her high school guidance counselor was not able to help her. Instead her counselor focused on helping citizen students navigate the financial aid process. During our interview, she shared,

> Then the day before I told her that I still needed help with my Dream Act [application] and she just told me there was nothing she could do about it because she was helping the FAFSA students…it made me feel like I didn't belong, like I was just another random student nobody cared about. So I got mad [laughs] and I went to the library and I just did my application on my own.

While in some states laws like the California Dream Act are easing the transition to college in practical ways by providing financial support, Yesenia's experience shows that legal reforms are incomplete without training and preparation for school agents who are most likely to interact with undocumented students. For many undocumented youth, who do attend college, the need for informed and trained staff does not end in high school, as exemplified by Kelvin, who grew up in the Pomona Valley and attended community college for 4 years before applying to transfer to

a 4-year university. Kelvin shared that after being accepted to his dream college, the University of California, Berkeley, he still did not know whether and if he would be able to attend because his financial aid offer was confusing. He shared,

> I was finally able to get on the [online financial aid] portal. Then I saw the numbers. It was really confusing. I just remember seeing like, "I need $5000 by the time I get there and to attend UC Berkeley." I was like, "Whoa, I need to come up with $5000 in 2 or 3 months" so I was working almost 3 jobs because I wasn't sure if it was going to be covered.

Kelvin, like many other undocumented young adults, lives in a financially vulnerable family. To cover the $5000 he thought he would have to pay, he continued working his retail job and started to work a second job at a warehouse. He said, "I was basically on my feet all day, just running around." After several phone calls to the university's financial aid office, Kelvin learned that he would be responsible for $2500 of his educational costs that year, an amount that was still steep but more manageable.

In addition to state laws expanding or constricting higher education access, DACA has shaped the transition out of high school as eligible undocumented young people are able to get driver's licenses and can legally work, mitigating some of the isolation of the discovery stage. Yet, research continues to show that undocumented young people still begin to feel the profound personal effects of living without "papers" in the United States as they transition out of the K–12 system (Gonzales and Bautista-Chavez 2012; Gonzales et al. 2016; Teranishi et al. 2015). Thus, even with a provisional status, the post-DACA period continues to be a critical moment in the lives of undocumented young people. Estimates on high school to postsecondary transitions prior to DACA suggest that about only 5–10% of undocumented students attend college, with an even smaller number actually graduating from college (Passel 2003). While DACA has opened up some important avenues that support a smoother college transition, it does not address exclusions from financial aid. Moreover, in the absence of federal immigration reform, immigra-

---

[2]The California DREAM Act refers to two state laws, California Assembly Bill 130 and Assembly Bill 131, that allow eligible undocumented students to apply for certain state public financial aid benefits.

tion action at the state, county, and municipal levels ensures that now, more so than ever before, where one lives is consequential for experiences of integration and incorporation. Therefore, the "transition to illegality" is also critically shaped by K–12 experiences and increasingly by which region of the country they grow up in.

7.4 Divergent Experiences of Illegality and Belonging After High School

7.4.1 College-Goers and Early Exiters

The transition to illegality does not play out in a singular manner among all undocumented adolescents. As immigration scholars have noted, local institutions mediate immigrants' incorporation prospects. While adult immigrants typically become incorporated into the U.S. economy through the labor market, children are woven into the country's social and cultural fabric through schools (Gleeson and Gonzales 2012). Schools provide immigrant students opportunities to learn the language, customs, and culture of their new country and to integrate into a peer group that will experience common milestones together (Rumbaut 1997; Suárez-Orozco et al. 2009).

Participation in K–12 schools is undoubtedly a defining and integrative experience. However, undocumented students, like their peers, are educated in a stratified public educational system (Gonzales et al. 2015a) that structures opportunities for its pupils. Increasingly, poor, minority, and immigrant students attend high-poverty, low-achieving school districts with fewer resources (Miller and Brown 2011). Operating with limited resources, schools often make decisions regarding how students are integrated into the larger curriculum and they determine student access to scarce resources. These decisions benefit a small portion of students while disadvantaging large segments.

While access to school resources has an important bearing on the success of all students, decisions that negatively affect a larger student body can be especially detrimental to undocumented students (Gonzales 2010a). Due to barriers related to legal exclusions and limited family finances, undocumented students confront several barriers. Their parents often lack knowledge of the U.S. education system, and their own unauthorized status keeps them in the shadows. This can have a direct effect on children, as it limits their access to critically needed services (Hagan et al. 2011; Menjívar and Abrego 2012; Rodriguez and Hagan 2004) and leaves them without the guidance and advocacy needed to persist, graduate, and advance to college. Undocumented students are also ineligible for federal financial aid, limiting their pathways to college. While DACA has bridged some of the financial gap, by providing work authorization to its beneficiaries, it does not address financial aid exclusions (Gonzales and Bautista-Chavez 2012). And for those without work authorization, once they leave school they exit a legally protected space and enter a world of low-wage work and legal exclusions (Gonzales 2016).

In his longitudinal work on undocumented immigrant youth, Gonzales (2010a, 2011, 2016) has examined the diverging experiences of two groups of differently achieving young people, the college-goers and the early exiters. The college-goers benefited from positive school-based networks, nurturing relationships, and avenues of access to academic counseling and advanced curricula. The early-exiters, on the other hand, did not make meaningful social connections in high school, followed trajectories that ended in dead-end jobs, and exposed them repeatedly to a harsher world of legal exclusions. During high school, extra-familial mentors, access to information about postsecondary options, and financial support for college helped college-goers to bypass some of the negative effects of undocumented status. These benefits enabled them to make transitions from high school to college and to continue membership in an institution for which participation was legally permissible. They also allowed them to engage in meaningfully productive activities and to maintain positive aspirations about the future.

For those unable to make transitions to post-secondary education, the onset of adult responsibilities coupled with legal exclusions dramatically shrunk their worlds. Limited to low-wage employment and driven deeply into the shadows by legal exclusions and fear of deportation, early exiters settled into lives of limitation and struggle. As a result, their future aspirations flattened and stress and worry developed into mental and physical ailments.

Undocumented youth enter the transition to adulthood with varying resources. Public schools offer them access and inclusion. The school is arguably the single most important institution in their education and integration. However, as decades of research suggest, schools are not meritocracies, and stratification within and across school districts detours the postsecondary trajectories of many undocumented students. As such, the futures of undocumented students are tied to school reform efforts. Similarly, state and local contexts have a great bearing on their futures.

7.4.2   The Influence of State Laws and Policies on Educational Trajectories and Belonging

As previously mentioned, much of what sociologists know about the undocumented 1.5-generation has been based on research about immigrants living in California, arguably an ideal locale to study this group because of the long history of immigrant flows to the state and the large size of the undocumented immigrant population (Gonzales 2016; Rumbaut 2012). In recent years, undocumented immigrants have dispersed to new destinations, including the Midwest and the South (Marrow 2011; Massey 2008; Waters and Jiménez 2005; Singer 2004; Zuniga and Hernandez-Leon 2009). In the absence of a national comprehensive immigration reform, states and localities have enacted a number of laws and policies that impact the day-to-day lives and incorporation of undocumented immigrants, resulting in a variegated legal climate (Olivas 2008; Walker and Leitner 2011). Some states have broadened access to the polity—offering

undocumented immigrants the ability to apply for driver's licenses and in-state tuition at public universities. Others have taken a more restrictive approach—for example, by attempting to criminalize unauthorized presence and exclude undocumented immigrants from public universities.

Neither undocumented nor DACAmented students are eligible for federal financial aid. However, opportunities for postsecondary education still vary widely by state. In states with the most inclusive policies, undocumented and DACAmented students receive in-state tuition rates and qualify for state-based financial aid. Currently, 20 states offer in-state tuition to undocumented immigrant students, 16 by state legislative action (California, Colorado, Connecticut, Florida, Illinois, Kansas, Maryland, Minnesota, Nebraska, New Jersey, New Mexico, New York, Oregon, Texas, Utah, and Washington) and 4 by state university systems (the University of Hawaii Board of Regents, University of Michigan Board of Regents, Oklahoma State Regents for Higher Education and Rhode Island's Board of Governors for Higher Education established policies to offer in-state tuition rates to undocumented immigrants). In addition, 5 states (California, New Mexico, Minnesota, Texas, and Washington) offer state financial assistance to undocumented students. In states with the most exclusionary policies, these students may be barred from in-state tuition rates and scholarships, be excluded from state-based financial aid and scholarships, or be banned from public universities and colleges entirely (e.g., Georgia and South Carolina). Presently, 6 states (Alabama, Arizona, Georgia, Indiana, Missouri, and South Carolina) bar undocumented students from in-state tuition benefits, while public university systems in Alabama, South Carolina, and Georgia bar undocumented students from admission.

In addition, several states have passed laws providing additional access to DACA beneficiaries, otherwise unavailable to undocumented immigrants without DACA. While state governments cannot directly alter DACA itself, they can control the state benefits available to individuals receiving deferred action. The driver's license is an important example. Rules for governing eligibility for driver's licenses vary by state, and currently, only 12 states plus the District of Columbia offer undocumented immigrants eligibility for driver's licenses.[3] However, otherwise-eligible DACA recipients who obtain an employment authorization document and a Social Security number are now able to obtain a license in every state. This benefit provides DACA holders the ability to travel freely and safely to school or work, a significant form of relief for DACA beneficiaries and their families.

Higher education is an important area where DACA beneficiaries have added layers of access. In addition to being able to legally work to help pay for college, DACA beneficiaries in certain states now have significant advantages over those without DACA. For example, several states, including Arizona, have passed state legislation allowing eligible DACA beneficiaries to pay tuition at in-state residency rates. Also, South Carolina, which otherwise bans undocumented students from enrolling in its public higher education systems, allows DACA beneficiaries to enroll. In addition, certain postsecondary institutions offer scholarships to DACA beneficiaries that are not open to other undocumented immigrants. DACA has also opened up possibilities for beneficiaries to pursue graduate studies. Many graduate programs offer funding packages to their graduate students that include teaching or research assistantships and fellowships; each are considered a form of university employment. And, many medical schools have opened up opportunities to DACA beneficiaries. But university employment and participation in residency programs is tied to the ability to lawfully work. Without work authorization, many of these opportunities would not be available and, as such, a range of graduate programs would not be an option for DACA beneficiaries.

Saul, a lanky 20-year-old, was in the 11th grade when Policies 4.1.6 and 4.3.4, collectively known as "the Georgia ban," took effect. During our interview, which we conducted at the dining table of his parents' home, he shared that it was during 10th grade that he became serious about attending college. He was looking forward to starting the college application process, but after learning that the ban would prevent him from attending college in Georgia, he fell into a depression. He stopped doing his homework and he let his grades slip. Despite this setback, in his senior year, with prodding from a good friend, Saul decided to explore community college as an option. He visited the admissions office of Southern Crescent, the closest 2-year college, and learned the following:

> So we went there and like asked about the like applications, and then that's when I found out again, they were like "Well, these are the in-state tuition rates, but this is what you have to pay, out-of-state tuition, which is like 3 or 4 times more," and I was like "Wow, this is ridiculous"…I was like, I'm not paying this, especially for a technical school.

Several of the respondents in Georgia echoed Saul's statement that the financial challenge of paying out-of-state tuition prevented them from attending even 2-year colleges. For example, Georgia Perimeter College, the 2-year university in the Atlanta area, would cost an undocumented immigrant $21,000 for 2 years versus the $7600 in-state tuition rate.

At the time of his interview, Omar had been out of high school for 2 years. While he attended the University of North Georgia directly after high school, he was not able to continue because he could not meet the costs of tuition, fees, and books. When we spoke, he was taking a year off from the University of North Georgia, and was planning to work while he attended the less expensive technical college in his community:

> It's hard for me to pay for college. Last year I attended University of North Georgia, and it was hard cuz I was paying out of state tuition. I paid five grand for twelve credits…and here in Tech I tried to apply earlier to enter spring semester but apparently their policies have changed and now even for [DACA] students from the beginning, they're charging them as international. So that's three to four times.

---

[3]These states are: California, Colorado, Connecticut, Delaware, Hawaii, Illinois, Maryland, New Mexico, Nevada, Utah, Vermont, and Washington.

As Omar emphasized, even attending Athens Tech was out of his financial reach. As such, he was actively saving to return to college. He managed to save about $150 from each paycheck for college, but could not maintain the level of savings because his father, also an undocumented immigrant, was out of work. So Omar contributed a portion of his weekly earnings to his family for food and bills, reducing the amount of money he could save in order to return to UNG.

In addition to the policies explicitly excluding undocumented immigrants from Georgia public universities, the Board of Regents announced in 2015 that some smaller colleges would merge with larger colleges in order to streamline administrative costs. Two of the colleges that merged were Georgia Perimeter College, the 2-year college in the Atlanta area, and Georgia State University, one of the five colleges included in the ban. The announcement created uncertainty about whether or not undocumented young adults would also be banned from Georgia Perimeter College. Jovan, a 23-year-old DACA beneficiary was working in retail and not enrolled in college although he hoped to be. During our interview, he shared that the merger created uncertainty for him and other students who might consider attending Georgia Perimeter,

> ...There is Georgia Perimeter, but, it's soon merging with Georgia State University, and that's one of the schools where I'm banned from, so I don't know if they are going to continue the same policies of banning us from that. So it's in a limbo altogether, and I don't really want to put up a fight with that...

The consolidation of several campuses across the state created a sense of anxiety about narrowing educational opportunities. While Policy 4.3.4 (out-of-state tuition) made the cost of attending 2- and 4-year colleges nearly impossible for undocumented young adults, Policy 4.1.6 (ban from top five colleges and universities) heightened the negative impact of seemingly neutral policies like the consolidation of smaller colleges and universities with larger ones. Participants shared that like most of their citizen classmates, they preferred to stay in the state of Georgia to attend college. This was due in part to their desire

to be close to their parents, of whom many were also undocumented.

While the Board of Regents policies presented structural barriers to college completion and entry for undocumented young adults, these policies also had symbolic implications. During interviews many undocumented young adults expressed feelings of rejection, disappointment and frustration over these policies. Like Saul, who fell into a depression upon learning that his legal status would make it difficult for him to attend college, other undocumented young adults described similar instances of depression both during and after high school (Gonzales et al. 2013). Jovan, for example, shared that at a party during his senior year of high school,

> I do remember this one time I went to a party, my friends and me were drinking, and you know having fun, and, I just broke down crying in front of them because I told them, you know I couldn't go to school, you know I couldn't do the military, I couldn't do all of this, and I felt just stuck...

For Jovan, who went to a predominantly White high school in a suburb of Atlanta, this incident was one of the first times he disclosed his immigration status to his friends, many of whom were not undocumented. While most of his friends planned to attend technical or state colleges, Jovan felt stuck and excluded from the opportunity to "go off and leave this small town to find something...figure out life." Similarly, both Diana and her younger sister, who was also undocumented, worked hard in high school to take full advantage of the educational opportunities that were available to them, including taking Advanced Placement courses. Diana who described herself as a "very hard worker," shared that she regularly worked 50–60 h a week as a server at a local restaurant, both to contribute to her family's household income and to be able to save enough to eventually go to college. Because of her full-time work schedule, her interview took place on her one day off. During our interview she shared,

> It's just the limitation of what I can do frustrates me. It's frustrating. That's how I feel. I feel frustrated. I know for a fact that my parents do too. They want us to go to school. They came here to

give us a better life, to get a better education. The fact that I can't get it frustrates me. It makes me angry. I can't do anything about it. I don't have a say in the government. I can't vote. I can't. It's my country, too. This is all I know. The fact that they're limiting me to not only my potential, my success, my education, my right as a human being to get that education frustrates me.

During our interview, it was clear that Diana was proud of her work ethic and her contribution to her family's economic well-being. But like many of the undocumented young adult respondents in Georgia, she was frustrated that her intellect and her work ethic were not being used to improve her own and her family's life. In short, Diana and other undocumented youth felt that they were failing not only themselves, but also their parents. Like Diana, Ines worked between 60 and 70 h per week as a manager at a pizzeria. Her work schedule was demanding and unpredictable, and because of this, her interview took place at the restaurant when her shift was over. Ines, who shared that she had done very well in high school, wanted to attend a culinary arts program to become a pastry chef. While she knew that there were different routes she could take to achieve her goals, she wanted to attend a culinary arts program to give herself the best chance of securing a good job in a competitive industry. Nevertheless, attending a culinary arts program at a technical college or a culinary school was impossible because of the cost. During our interview, it became apparent that being prevented from attending school not only meant that she felt stuck but it was also taking an emotional toll on Ines. Through tears, she said, "I always get teary, because it means a lot to me. It means a lot to me to be able to go to school. I felt like, in a way, I felt like I had let my parents down, because I wasn't able to do more. But [my mom] was like, 'You don't have to go to school to be good.'" For Ines and many of the other undocumented young adults interviewed in Georgia, the Board of Regents policies not only created a structural barrier to upward mobility but also had significant implications for their sense of belonging.

7.5 Educational Exclusion and Belonging

This chapter captures the varied educational experiences of undocumented immigrant youth as they navigate the transition out of the legally protected spaces of the K–12 system and into adulthood. As this chapter shows, schools are not only crucial for undocumented immigrant youth's educational mobility, but they are also a significant socializing institution. It is in America's public schools where undocumented immigrant youth learn and begin to internalize both a sense of belonging *and* exclusion. In addition, schools are nested within a broader web of immigration laws and policies that have become increasingly hostile. These laws and policies, in conjunction with the complete absence of a comprehensive immigration reform for the nearly 11 million undocumented immigrants living in the United States, has created a variegated landscape of belonging and exclusion for undocumented immigrants broadly, and more specifically for undocumented immigrant youth. Despite the *Plyler v. Doe* holding in which the Supreme Court explicitly sought to avoid creating an educational underclass, many undocumented immigrant youths find it difficult to realize the promise of *Plyler*. The temporary relief provide by DACA has in some ways eased the transition to adulthood for this group. However, their long-term futures are still uncertain.

And while there have been considerable strides in gathering systematic, empirical research on the contradictory circumstances that frame the lives of undocumented immigrant youth, there has been considerable focus on the experiences of college-bound and high-achieving youth. In this chapter, we draw from our own work to introduce additional axes of stratification and show how they play out differently across educational attainment and place. Highlighting the experiences of differently achieving young people is key to painting a more complete picture of the educational trajectories and experiences of undocumented immigrant youth.

As data collected by both authors show, experiences of illegality and belonging are profoundly shaped by whether or not undocumented young people successfully complete high school and/or make it to college, and increasingly by which area of the country they grow up in. Hostile educational access policies, like those enacted in Georgia, not only create educational exclusion that has long-term implications for undocumented youth's structural incorporation, but also has socio-emotional implications, as Latino undocumented youth in hostile states must negotiate the emotional ups and downs of feeling educationally untethered. During our interview with Saul, he shared that he felt like Georgia, a place he considered "home," no longer cared about what happened to him and his future after high school. He said that he believed that through hostile policies, like those enacted in Georgia, states were effectively sending the message, "Okay, thanks for coming…good luck."

Despite the layers of inequality we have uncovered, the young people we met shared more similarities than differences. They grew up in neighborhoods across the United States where they were encouraged to work hard to achieve their dreams. During their integrated childhoods they had as much in common with their peers as they did with their parents. However, as they made critical transitions from childhood to adolescence and young adulthood, their immigration status became a central impediment to their hopes and dreams. Almost as consequential, the resources and practices of their school districts and the policies of their states conditioned their post high school lives.

References

Abrego, L. J. (2006). "I can't go to college because I don't have papers": Incorporation patterns of Latino undocumented youth. *Latino Studies, 4*(3), 212–231.

Abrego, L. J. (2008). Legitimacy, social identity, and the mobilization of the law: The effects of Assembly Bill 540 on undocumented students in California. *Law and Social Inquiry, 33*(3), 709–734.

Abrego, L. J., & Gonzales, R. G. (2010). Blocked paths, uncertain futures: The postsecondary education and labor market prospects of undocumented Latino youth. *Journal of Education for Students Placed at Risk, 15*(1–2), 144–157.

Alba, R. D., & Nee, V. (2003). *Remaking the American mainstream: Assimilation and contemporary immigration*. Cambridge, MA: Harvard University Press.

Aranda, E., Vaquera, E., & Sousa-Rodriguez, I. (2015). Personal and cultural trauma and the ambivalent national identities of undocumented young adults in the USA. *Journal of Intercultural Studies, 36*(5), 600–619.

Batalova, J., & McHugh, M. (2010). *DREAM vs reality: An analysis of potential Dream Act beneficiaries*. Washington, DC: Migration Policy Institute.

Bean, F. D., & Stevens, G. (2003). *America's newcomers and the dynamics of diversity*. New York: Russell Sage Foundation.

Bean, F. D., Leach, M. A., Brown, S. K., Bachmeier, J. D., & Hipp, J. R. (2011). The educational legacy of unauthorized migration: Comparisons across U.S.-immigrant groups in how parents' status affects their offspring. *International Migration Review, 45*(2), 348–385.

Bloeemraad, I., Korteweg, A., & Yurkadal, G. (2008). Citizenship and immigration: Multiculturalism, assimilation, and challenges to the nation-state. *Annual Review of Sociology, 34*, 153–179.

Bosniak, L. (2008). *The citizen and the alien: Dilemmas of contemporary membership*. Princeton: Princeton University Press.

Brubaker, R. (1992). Citizenship struggles in Soviet successor states. *International Migration Review, 26*(2), 269–291.

Buenavista, T. L. (2012). Citizenship at a cost: Undocumented Asian youth perceptions and the militarization of immigration. *Asian American and Pacific Islander Nexus, 10*(1), 101–124.

Cebulko, K. (2014). Documented, undocumented, and liminally legal: Legal status during the transition to adulthood for 1.5-generation Brazilian immigrants. *The Sociological Quarterly, 55*(1), 143–167.

Chang, A. (2010). Undocumented to hyperdocumented: A jornada of protection, papers, and PhD status. *Harvard Educational Review, 81*(3), 508–520.

Chavez, L. R. (1991). Outside the imagined community: Undocumented settlers and experiences of incorporation. *American Ethnologist, 18*(2), 257–278.

Chavez, L. R. (1994). The power of imagined community: The settlement of undocumented Mexicans and Central Americans in the United States. *American Anthropologist, 96*(1), 52–73.

Conger, D., & Chellman, C. C. (2013). *Undocumented college students in the United States: In-state tuition not enough to ensure four-year degree completion* (Institute for Education and Social Policy Brief, brief no. 01-13).

Coutin, S. B. (1999). Denationalization, inclusion, and exclusion: Negotiating the boundaries of belonging. *Indiana Journal of Global Legal Studies, 7*, 585–593.

DeGenova, N. P. (2002). Migrant illegality and deportability in everyday life. *Annual Review of Anthropology, 31*, 419–437.

Diaz-Strong, D., Gomez, C., Luna-Duarte, M. E., & Meiners, E. R. (2011). Purged: Undocumented students, financial aid policies, and access to higher education. *Journal of Hispanic Higher Education, 10*(2), 107–119.

Dougherty, K. J., Nienhusser, H. K., & Vega, B. E. (2010). Undocumented immigrants and state higher education policy: The politics of in-state tuition eligibility in Texas and Arizona. *The Review of Higher Education, 34*(1), 123–173.

Dreby, J. (2015). *Everyday illegal: When policies undermine immigrant families*. Berkeley: University of California Press.

Ellis, L. M., & Chen, E. C. (2013). Negotiating identity development among undocumented immigrant college students: A grounded theory study. *Journal of Counseling Psychology, 60*(2), 251–264.

Enriquez, L. E. (2011). Because we feel the pressure and we also feel the support: Examining the educational success of Latina/o students. *Harvard Educational Review, 81*(3), 476–500.

Enriquez, L. E. (2014). Undocumented and citizen students unite: Building a cross-status coalition through shared ideology. *Social Problems, 61*(2), 155–174.

Enriquez, L. E., & Saguy, A. (2016). Coming out of the shadows: Harnessing a cultural schema to advance the undocumented immigrant youth movement. *American Journal of Cultural Sociology, 4*(1), 107–130.

Flores, S. M. (2010). State dream acts: The effect of in-state resident tuition policies and undocumented Latino students. *The Review of Higher Education, 33*(2), 239–283.

Flores, S. M., & Horn, C. L. (2009). College persistence among undocumented students at a selective public university: A quantitative case study analysis. *Journal of College Student Retention, 11*(1), 57–76.

Foner, N. (2003). *American arrivals: Anthropology engages the new immigration*. Santa Fe: School of American Research Press.

Fortuny, K., Capps, R., & Passel, J. (2007). *The characteristics of unauthorized immigrants in California, Los Angeles County, and the United States*. Washington, DC: Urban Institute. Retrieved from http://www.urban.org/UploadedPDF/411425_Characteristics_Immigrants.pdf

Galindo, R. (2012). Undocumented and unafraid: The DREAM Act 5 and the public disclosure of undocumented status as a political act. *Urban Review, 44*, 589–611.

Gildersleeve, R. E., & Ranero, J. J. (2010). Precollege contexts of undocumented students: Implications for student affairs professionals. *New Directions for Student Services, 2010*(131), 19–33.

Gildersleeve, R. E., Rumann, C., & Mondragon, R. (2010). Serving undocumented students: Current law and policy. *New Directions for Student Services, 2010*(131), 5–18.

Gleeson, S., & Gonzales, R. G. (2012). When do papers matter? An institutional analysis of undocumented life in the United States. *International Migration, 50*(4), 1–19.

Golash-Boza, T. M. (2015). *Immigration nation: Raids, detentions, and deportations in post-9/11 America*. New York: Routledge.

Gonzales, R. G. (2007). Wasted talent and broken dreams: The lost potential of undocumented students. *Immigration Policy in Focus, 5*, 1–11. Washington, DC: Immigration Policy Center.

Gonzales, R. G. (2008). Left out but not shut down: Political activism and the undocumented student movement. *Northwestern Journal of Law and Social Policy, 3*(2), 219–239.

Gonzales, R. G. (2009). *Young lives on hold: The college dreams of undocumented students*. New York: College Board Advocacy & Policy Center.

Gonzales, R. G. (2010a). On the wrong side of the tracks: Understanding the effects of school structure and social capital in the educational pursuits of undocumented immigrant students. *Peabody Journal of Education, 85*(4), 469–485.

Gonzales, R. G. (2010b). More than just access: Undocumented students navigating the post-secondary terrain. *Journal of College Admissions, 206*, 48–52.

Gonzales, R. G. (2011). Learning to be illegal: Undocumented youth and shifting legal contexts in the transition to adulthood. *American Sociological Review, 76*(4), 602–619.

Gonzales, R. G. (2015). Imagined futures: Thoughts on the state of policy and research concerning undocumented immigrant youth and young adults. *Harvard Educational Review, 85*(3), 518–524.

Gonzales, R. G. (2016). *Lives in limbo: Undocumented and coming of age in America*. Oakland: University of California Press.

Gonzales, R. G., & Bautista-Chavez, A. M. (2012). *Two years and counting: Assessing the growing power of DACA* (American Immigration Council special report).

Gonzales, R. G., & Ruiz, A. G. (2014). Dreaming beyond the fields: Undocumented youth, rural realities, and a constellation of disadvantage. *Latino Studies, 12*, 194–216.

Gonzales, R. G., Suárez-Orozco, C., & Dedios-Sanguineti, M. C. (2013). No place to belong: Contextualizing concepts of mental health among undocumented immigrant youth in the United States. *American Behavioral Scientist, 57*(8), 1174–1199.

Gonzales, R. G., Terriquez, V., & Ruszcxyk, S. (2014). Becoming DACAmented: Assessing the short-term benefits of deferred action for childhood arrivals (DACA). *American Behavioral Scientist, 58*(14), 1852–1872.

Gonzales, R. G., Heredia, L. L., & Negrón-Gonzales, G. (2015a). Untangling Plyler's legacy: Undocumented students, schools, and citizenship. *Harvard Educational Review, 85*(3), 318–341.

Gonzales, R. G., Roth, B., Brant, K., Lee, J., & Valdivia, C. (2016). *DACA at year three: Challenges and opportunities in assessing education and employment, new evidence from the UnDACAmented Research Project.* Washington, DC: American Immigration Council.

Hagan, J. M., Rodriguez, N., & Castro, B. (2011). Social effects of mass deportations by the United States government, 2000–10. *Ethnic and Racial Studies, 34*(8), 1374–1391.

Jefferies, J. (2014). The production of "illegal" subjects in Massachusetts and high school enrollment for undocumented youth. *Latino Studies, 12*(1), 65–87.

Kanstroom, D. (2012). *Aftermath: Deportation law and the new American diaspora.* Oxford: Oxford University Press.

Kasinitz, P., Mollenkopf, J. H., Waters, M. C., & Holdaway, J. (2008). *Inheriting the city: The children of immigrants come of age.* New York: Russell Sage Foundation.

Kaushal, N. (2008). In-state tuition for the undocumented: Education effects on Mexican young adults. *Journal of Policy Analysis and Management, 27*(4), 771–792.

Kubal, A. (2013). Conceptualizing semi-legality in migration research. *Law and Society Review, 47*(3), 555–587.

Mangual Figueroa, A. (2012). "I have papers so I can go anywhere!": Everyday talk about citizenship in a mixed-status family. *Journal of Language, Identity, and Education, 11*(5), 291–311.

Marrow, H. (2011). *New destination dreaming: Immigration, race, and legal status in the rural American South.* Stanford: Stanford University Press.

Marshall, T. H. (1950). *Citizenship and social class: And other essays.* Cambridge: University Press.

Martinez, L. M. (2014). Dreams deferred: The impact of legal reforms on undocumented Latino youth. *American Behavioral Scientist, 58*(14), 1873–1890.

Massey, D. S. (2008). *New faces in new places: The changing geography of American immigration.* New York: Russell Sage Foundation Publications.

Massey, D., Durand, J., & Malone, N. J. (2002). *Beyond smoke and mirrors: Mexican immigration in an era of economic integration.* New York: Russell Sage Foundation.

Menjívar, C., & Abrego, L. (2009). Parents and children across borders: Legal instability and intergenerational relations in Guatemalan and Salvadoran families. In N. Foner (Ed.), *Across generations: Immigrant families in America* (pp. 160–189). New York: New York University Press.

Menjívar, C., & Abrego, L. (2012). Legal violence: Immigration law and the lives of central American immigrants. *American Journal of Sociology, 117*(5), 1380–1421.

Miller, R., & Brown, C. (2011). *The persistence of inequality: Newly released data confirms our nation needs educational funding reform.* Washington, DC: Center for American Progress.

Munoz, S. M., & Maldonado, M. M. (2012). Counterstories of college persistence by undocumented Mexicana students: Navigating race, class, gender, and legal status. *International Journal of Qualitative Studies, 25*(3), 293–315.

Nakano Glenn, E. (2011). Constructing citizenship: Exclusion, subordination, and resistance. *American Sociological Review, 76*(1), 1–24.

Negrón-Gonzales, G. (2013). Navigating "illegality": Undocumented youth and oppositional consciousness. *Children and Youth Services Review, 35*(8), 1284–1290.

Negrón-Gonzales, G. (2014). Undocumented, unafraid, and unapologetic: Re-articulatory practices and migrant youth "illegality". *Latino Studies, 12*(2), 259–278.

Ngai, M. (2004). *Impossible subjects: Illegal aliens and the making of modern America.* Princeton: Princeton University Press.

Nicholls, W. J. (2013). *The DREAMers: How the undocumented youth movement transformed the immigrant rights debate.* Stanford: Stanford University Press.

Olivas, M. A. (2004). IIRIRA, the DREAM Act, and undocumented college student residency. *Immigration and Nationality Law Review, 30*(2), 435–464.

Olivas, M. A. (2008). Lawmakers gone wild—College residency and the response to Professor Kobach. *SMU Law Review, 61*, 99–132.

Olivas, M. A. (2009). The political economy of the DREAM Act and the legislative process: A case study of comprehensive immigration reform. *The Wayne Law Review, 55*, 1759–1802.

Olivas, M. A. (2011). *No undocumented child left behind: Plyler v. Doe and the education of undocumented school children.* New York: New York University Press.

Passel, J. (2003). *Further information relating to the DREAM Act.* Washington, DC: The Urban Institute. Retrieved May 1, 2016. http://cccie.org/images/stories/pdf/ui_dream_demographics.pdf

Passel, J. S., & Cohn, D. (2011). *Unauthorized immigrant population: National and state trends.* Washington, DC: Pew Hispanic Center.

Patler, C., & Gonzales, R. G. (2015). Framing citizenship: Media coverage of anti-deportation cases led by undocumented youth organizations. *Journal of Ethnic and Migration Studies, 41*(9), 1453–1474.

Patler, C., & Pirtle, W. L. (2018). From undocumented to lawfully present: Do changes to legal status impact psychological wellbeing among Latino immigrant young adults? *Social Science & Medicine, 199*, 39–48. https://doi.org/10.1016/j.socscimed.2017.03.009.

Perez, W., Espinoza, R., Ramos, K., Coronado, H. M., & Cortes, R. (2009). Academic resilience among undocumented students. *Hispanic Journal of Behavioral Sciences, 31*(2), 149–181.

Portes, A., & Rumbaut, R. (2001). *Legacies: The story of the immigrant second generation.* Berkeley/New York: University of California Press and Russell Sage Foundation.

Portes, A., & Zhou, M. (1993). The new second generation: Segmented assimilation and its variants. *Annals of the American Academy of Political and Social Sciences, 530*, 74–96.

Rincon, A. (2008). *Undocumented immigrants and higher education: ¡Sí se puede!* New York: LFB Scholarly Publications.

Rodriguez, N., & Hagan, J. M. (2004). Fractured families and communities: Effects of immigration reform in Texas, Mexico, and El Salvador. *Latino Studies, 2*(3), 328–351.

Rogers, J., Saunders, M., Terriquez, V., & Velez, V. (2008). Civic lessons: Public schools and the civic development of undocumented students and parents. *Northwestern Journal of Law and Social Policy, 3*(2), 201–218.

Rosaldo, R. (1994). Cultural citizenship and educational democracy. *Cultural Anthropology, 9*(3), 402–411.

Rosaldo, R., & Flores, W. V. (1997). Identity, conflict, and evolving Latino communities: Cultural citizenship in San Jose, California. In W. V. Flores & R. Benmayor (Eds.), *Latino cultural citizenship: Claiming identity, space, and rights* (pp. 57–96). Boston: Beacon Press.

Rosenblum, M. R., & Ruiz-Soto, A. G. (2015). *An analysis of unauthorized immigrants in the United States by country and region of birth.* Washington, DC: Migration Policy Institute.

Rumbaut, R. (1997). Assimilation and its discontents: Between rhetoric and reality. *International Migration Review, 31*(4), 923–960.

Rumbaut, R. (2012). *Paradise shift: Immigration, mobility, and inequality in Southern California* (KMI Working Paper Series). Commission for Migration and Integration Research.

Seif, H. (2004). "Wise up!" Undocumented Latino youth, Mexican-American legislators, and the struggle for higher education access. *Latino Studies, 2*(2), 210–230.

Silver, A. (2012). Aging into exclusion and social transparency: Undocumented immigrant youth and the transition to adulthood. *Latino Studies, 10*(4), 499–522.

Singer, A. (2004). *The rise of new immigrant gateways.* Washington, DC: Brookings Institution.

Soysal, Y. (1994). *Limits of citizenship: Migrants and postnational membership in Europe.* Chicago: University of Chicago Press.

Suárez-Orozco, C., Suárez-Orozco, M. M., & Todorova, I. (2009). *Learning a new land.* Harvard: Harvard University Press.

Teranishi, R. T., Suárez-Orozco, C., & Suárez-Orozco, M. (2015). *In the shadows of the ivory tower: Undocumented undergraduates in the uncertain era of immigration reform.* Los Angeles: Institute for Immigration, Globalization, and Education, UCLA.

Terriquez, V. (2014). Trapped in the working class? Prospects for the intergenerational (im)mobility of Latino youth. *Sociological Inquiry, 84*(3), 382–411.

Walker, K. E., & Leitner, H. (2011). The variegated landscape of local immigration policies in the United States. *Urban Geography, 32*(2), 156–178.

Waters, M. C., & Jiménez, T. (2005). Assessing immigrant assimilation: New empirical and theoretical challenges. *Annual Review of Sociology, 31,* 105–125.

Willen, S. S. (2007). Towards a critical phenomenology of "illegality": State power, criminality, and abjectivity among undocumented migrant workers in Tel Aviv, Israel. *International Migration, 45,* 7–38.

Yoshikawa, H., & Kalil, A. (2011). The effects of parental undocumented status on the developmental contexts of young children in immigrant families. *Child Development Perspectives, 5*(4), 291–297.

Yuval-Davis, N. (2006). Belonging and the politics of belonging. *Patterns of Prejudice, 40*(3), 197–214.

Zimmerman, A. (2012). *Documenting DREAMS: New media, undocumented youth and the immigrant rights movement* (Media Activism and Participatory Politics Project Case Study Working Paper). University of Southern California. https://ypp.dmlcentral.net/sites/default/files/publications/Documenting_DREAMs.pdf.

Zuniga, V., & Hernandez-Leon, R. (2009). The Dalton story: Mexican immigration and social transformation in the carpet capital of the world. In M. E. Odem & E. Lacy (Eds.), *Latino immigrants and the transformation of the U.S. South* (pp. 34–50). Athens: University of Georgia Press.

Sociological Perspectives on First-Generation College Students

8

Irenee R. Beattie

Abstract

First-generation college students (FGS)—postsecondary students whose parents did not complete college degrees—are a theoretically critical group for understanding social inequality in higher education and processes of social mobility. They are successful in navigating into higher education institutions in spite of a lack of parental experience, and may derive particular benefits from their social origins in terms of motivation and novel sources of support. However, college experiences can prove challenging for FGS due to more limited social and cultural capital. Sociologists have arrived relatively late to the study of this group. I argue that sociological perspectives can add to our understanding of FGS by investigating the ways that first-generation status intersects with other dimensions of identity and experience (race/ethnicity, gender, social class, sexuality, immigration status, etc.). Sociological insight can also further develop understandings of how institutional variation as well as institutional neglect and abuse shape FGS experiences and outcomes.

Being the first-generation in my family to go to college is amazing. It means a lot to me because I make my family proud and also because I am proving to my family and everyone else that I can reach my goals and dreams that I work so hard to achieve. My mom has helped me so much along the way because she teaches me valuable lessons and makes me believe more in myself.
—Odalize from Garland, TX

...I'm [a first generation high school senior] from a low-income area, and my mom knows little about college. So, I had to do my college research on my own. I go to an underfunded public school, so my guidance counselor isn't very helpful. I've struggled a ton during high school, with issues such as bullying and homelessness. Today, I'm a happy, successful student with a 90 GPA. I've been accepted into two schools so far, and I'm waiting on four more... Being a first generation student is difficult... But, it also gives us motivation to continue our education, so we're able to have easier lives than our parents.
—Nina from Garfield, NJ[1]

As these quotes from first-generation college students illustrate, young adults who are the first in their families to attend college experience both barriers and benefits from their situations. On one hand, they often attend more poorly

I. R. Beattie (✉)
Department of Sociology, University of California, Merced, CA, USA
e-mail: ibeattie@ucmerced.edu

---

[1]Quotes from: More Stories | I'm First. (n.d.). Retrieved January 20, 2016, from http://www.imfirst.org/more/

funded elementary and secondary schools and have less access to familial financial resources or knowledge about the college-going process. On the other hand, they can have particularly strong motivation to succeed and may draw on important sources of support and inspiration from their families and communities. First-generation college students (FGS)—students enrolled in 4-year colleges with neither parent holding a bachelor's degree or higher—have grown into an increasingly salient social group on college campuses.[2] It is important to distinguish the term "first-generation" in this chapter from its use in the discussion of immigration. In this chapter, it refers to the student's status as a member of the first-generation in their family *to attend college,* but says nothing about their immigrant status. While estimates of the share of FGS enrolled in colleges and universities vary, as I discuss more below, just over half of all students attending 4-year colleges and universities come from families where neither parent earned a bachelor's degree, as do over 90% of the students who enter community colleges (Núñez and Cuccaro-Alamin 1998).

Understanding student experiences among those who are the first in their families to attend college is important because FGS have more difficult transitions to college and lower levels of engagement, persistence, and post-graduate degree attainment than their peers with a college-educated parent (Choy 2001; Ishitani 2006; Pike and Kuh 2005; Terenzini et al. 1996; Warburton et al. 2001). For example, while 88% of continuing-generation college students (CGS) persist from the first to the second year of college, only 73% of FGS do (Warburton et al. 2001). FGS are also an increasingly salient socially constructed group that is targeted by specialized federal, state, and campus programs (Wildhagen 2015). Theoretically, first-generation college students

represent an important group for understanding the role of education in social mobility processes at the individual level, as well as the ways social and cultural capital shape life outcomes (Beattie and Thiele 2016; Jack 2014, 2016). Studying FGS can also help us more thoroughly understand institutional influences on student experiences, as well as how intersections of race, class, gender play out in educational settings.

In this chapter, I provide a theoretical overview on the study of first-generation college students and review the prior research, noting some key gaps in our understanding that would benefit from a greater incorporation of sociological perspectives. I also discuss the implications for policy and practice. Sociological theories and concepts—particularly social and cultural capital theories—have often guided the study of FGS among scholars in schools of education. However, sociologists have arrived relatively late to the study of this population—largely within the past decade—with only a handful of exceptions (e.g., London 1989). This may stem from a resistance to eschewing the discipline's more complex conceptualization of social class in favor of a relatively simplistic one based solely on parental educational attainment. Nonetheless, I argue that sociological theories and related approaches are central to understanding inequalities between first-generation college students and their peers, but that these perspectives have been underutilized. In particular, sociological theories can help illuminate the ways first-generation status *intersects with other dimensions of inequality*, including race/ethnicity, gender, sexuality, disability, social class, immigrant status, and age, as well as how variation within and between *institutional contexts* matters for FGS experiences and outcomes. Further, while much of the research highlights the *deficits* individual FGS face relative to CGS, I encourage greater attention to the particular *benefits* FGS bring to college with them, as well as the ways that institutions may themselves have "deficits" for serving FGS population, in the form of correctible practices of institutional abuse and neglect (González et al. 2003).

---

[2] Although there are a variety of ways to define first-generation status, I follow Davis (2010) in including in my definition students whose parents attended no college, some college, or earned an associate degree while excluding those with either parent who earned a bachelor's degree. I note when research cited uses different criteria to identify FGS.

There is evidence that first-generation and continuing generation students have divergent experiences along the college-going pipeline long before they step foot on college campuses (Warburton et al. 2001; Deil-Amen 2015). For example, disadvantaged and first-generation students attend less rigorous and more poorly funded high schools than CGS, take less challenging high school courses, and are less likely to be minimally qualified to attend college (Warburton et al. 2001). FGS are also more likely than CGS to begin their postsecondary attendance at public 2-year colleges or private for-profit colleges, but less likely to ultimately transfer to 4-year colleges (Goldrick-Rab 2016; Warburton et al. 2001). FGS that do enroll in 4-year colleges are less academically prepared for college work than their CGS peers (Choy 2001). For example, only 20% of FGS had completed calculus in high school, compared to 31% of CGS (Warburton et al. 2001). Demographically, first-generation students who enroll in 4-year colleges significantly differ from CGS in some important ways. FGS are more likely to be Hispanic, older, and married (Warburton et al. 2001). FGS are also significantly more likely to come from families that speak a language other than English in the home and are low income (Choy 2001). FGS are also more likely than CGS to have been born in another country (Warburton et al. 2001).[3] The high schools attended by FGS are more likely to be public and/or located in small towns and rural areas instead of private schools or those located in urban areas (Warburton et al. 2001).

While the experiences of FGS prior to entering 4-year colleges are important, this chapter focuses primarily on the role of sociological analysis for understanding the experiences of FGS after entering a 4-year college. This decision is largely driven by the relative dearth of existing research on FGS that focuses on their pre-college

experiences.[4] Further, it is in line with a broader trend among sociologists to increasingly focus on the "experiential core" of college life in the wake of Stevens et al.'s (2008) call for greater attention to this key educational sector. Further, prior research has demonstrated that experiences during college are more consequential for college outcomes among FGS than are pre-college characteristics (Pascarella et al. 2004; Lundberg et al. 2007), making what happens in college especially important to understand.

8.1 Sociological Understandings of First-Generation Students

8.1.1 Theoretical Relevance

The phrase "first-generation college students" was not yet in vogue when scholars of social mobility began examining the critical role education plays in the intergenerational transmission of inequality. Nonetheless, those who achieve more education than their parents are key to understanding societal mobility patterns—long central to sociological inquiry (Sorokin 1959; Weber 2015 [1841]). First-generation college students are at the nexus of what Weber (2015 [1841]) characterized as the dual character of education: While educational institutions support meritocratic advancement in social status from one generation to the next, they are also central to processes of social closure that limit advancement for many.

Status attainment models, developed in the 1960s and 1970s to extend earlier theoretical work, further established the importance of educational attainment for social mobility. Blau and Duncan (1967) examined the social processes that led men to attain higher occupational prestige than their fathers, and found that the primary

---

[3]To further highlight the importance of distinguishing between first-generation college students and first-generation immigrants, it is worth noting that only 11% of FGS were immigrants, compared to 6% of CGS (Warburton et al. 2001). However, intersections of immigration and first-generation college attendance should be examined more closely, as I discuss below.

[4]Given that students are not analytically defined as FGS until after they enter college (with some researchers even withholding the designation until students reach a 4-year college), this focus is understandable. Nonetheless, future research should harness the power of longitudinal data sets collected by the U.S. Department of Education to better delineate the pre-college and 2- to 4-year college transfer experiences among FGS and investigate how they shape experiences and outcomes in 4-year colleges.

effects of social origins on destinations operate indirectly through their influence on educational attainment. The Wisconsin model revised the original status attainment model to incorporate the interpersonal influences (e.g., parents, teachers, and peers) and social psychological factors (such as future aspirations) that affect educational attitudes and behaviors (Haller and Portes 1973; Sewell et al. 1970; Sewell et al. 1969). More recently, Buchmann and DiPrete (2006) found that the declining rate of college completion among White boys whose fathers were not college educated (or were absent) is largely responsible for the growing female advantage in college completion since the 1980s among Whites.

Torche (2011) recently confirmed that even in the wake of increasing differentiation in higher education (both in terms of institutional selectivity and choice of majors), colleges and universities continue to play a role in social mobility processes. Importantly, her careful analysis of longitudinal data sources confirms that earning a college degree erases the intergenerational transmission of socioeconomic status—showing that "the chances of achieving economic success are independent of social background among those who attain a BA" (Torche 2011, p. 798). This affirms the importance of studying FGS in college to understand the mechanisms that contribute to broad-scale trends toward educational equality.

At the same time as these patterns of social mobility hold true, research on individual student learning, occupational preparation, and extracurricular engagement during college shows continuing gaps by social origins (Armstrong and Hamilton 2013; Arum and Roksa 2011; Mullen 2010; Stuber 2011a). Students with less educated parents begin their college careers with lower critical thinking, analytic reasoning, and problem solving skills than their peers with highly educated parents, and these gaps persist into the sophomore year of college (Arum and Roksa 2011). Thus, FGS are also central to developing social reproduction theory, which examines the ways institutions reproduce social class variation across generations (Bowles and Gintis 1976;

McDonough 1997). In this view, schools can be a hindrance to social mobility by providing the illusion of opportunity ensconced in a structure that allows only very limited advancement for those from the least advantaged backgrounds. Bowles and Gintis (1976) argued that educational institutions socialize working-class youth to accept their lower levels of attainment as resulting from their individual failure. Social reproduction theory emphasizes the important role of the intergenerational transfer of social and cultural capital for facilitating educational success among those from lower social origins (Bourdieu 1977). Research shows that parenting practices in middle- and upper-class families facilitate greater comfort interacting with authority figures, such as teachers and professors, giving children who grow up in more advantaged settings greater interactional resources for succeeding in educational settings (Lareau 2011, 1989). However, social reproduction processes are not automatic and can be challenged and disrupted, allowing FGS and other relatively disadvantaged groups to draw from alternative individual, family, peer, and/or community/institutional resources to succeed (McCabe 2016; Muñoz and Maldonado 2012; Stuber 2011a). In spite of the theoretical relevance to FGS for many core sociological ideas, sociologists have not been at the forefront of examining this population.

Wildhagen (2015) illustrates the dramatic increase in scholarly attention to first-generation college students since the 1970s: Between 1970 and 1999 only a very small number of publications each year included the phrases "first-generation college student(s)" or "first-generation student(s)" in their titles. However, "the number of studies with those terms in the title increased by 606% between 1999 and 2013" (Wildhagen 2015, p. 287). Still, few scholars have published research on first-generation students in key sociological journals. For example, to date not a single article has been published referencing FGS in the title in the top general-interest sociology journals such as *American Sociological Review, American Journal of Sociology, Social Problems,* or *Social Forces.* Even *Sociology of Education*, considered the top sub-area journal, has only published one article that references first-generation students in the title (Amy Wilkins' 2014 article, "Race, Age, and Identity Transformations in the Transition from High School to College for Black and First-generation White Men," discussed below).

Of course, in spite of relatively limited attention to FGS, sociologists have published influential books and articles in recent years that include implicit or explicit analyses of FGS college experiences and outcomes (which I discuss in more detail below). For example, two recent sociological books, Stuber's *Inside the College Gates* (2011a) and Mullen's *Degrees of Inequality* (2010) centrally examine FGS, and two others— *Academically Adrift* (Arum and Roksa 2011) and *Paying for the Party* (Armstrong and Hamilton 2013)—include attention to the role of family background and social class in shaping student experiences, although they are not centrally focused on FGS. I discuss some compelling recent research on FGS using sociological perspectives (e.g., Beattie and Thiele 2016; McCabe 2016; McCabe and Jackson 2016; Jack 2016, 2014; Wildhagen 2015) that helps lay the groundwork for future sociological work in this area. Before discussing the research on FGS, I briefly discuss the relationship of first-generation status to broader conceptualizations of social class.

8.1.2   First-Generation Status and Social Class

One reason that sociologists may hesitate to focus on FGS as an analytical category may be the centrality of more complex conceptualizations of social class to the discipline. Social mobility and status attainment scholars focus on complex formulations of occupational status to capture social origins (Blau and Duncan 1967; Torche 2011). A Marxist definition of social class involves not only measuring the categories of occupations, but also capturing the social relations of control over resources, decision-making, and others' work (Wright et al. 1982). Typically, in quantitative studies by sociologists of education, socioeconomic status (SES) is used as a proxy for social class. Measures of SES are often

composite measures that include parent's educational attainment, parent's occupational status, and family income (e.g., Beattie 2002; Goldrick-Rab 2016). Other research on SES and college outcomes uses disaggregated measures of parental education and income, along with measures of sources of college financing (Fischer 2007). Examining FGS requires boiling down the multifaceted notion of social origins into a single feature: parental educational attainment. Focusing solely on the possession of a credential by one's parents overlooks the social class implications of family income, occupational prestige, wealth, and the relationship to the means of production. However, it provides a meaningful measure of social origins that is linked with college outcomes.

Social class and family background have been conceptualized many ways in recent sociological analysis of students in higher education. For example, in their influential book, *Paying for the Party*, Armstrong and Hamilton (2013) examine how public universities structure pathways through college that have disparate influences on women undergraduates based on their social class origins. Consistent with the complexity with which sociologists typically measure social class, an entire appendix (Appendix B) is devoted to exploring the authors' thinking in developing class categories using their extensive interview and observational data—acknowledging that defining social class is "messy" (Armstrong and Hamilton 2013, p. 264). They measure student social class using five categories based on parental education, occupation, economic resources (Upper; Upper-middle; Middle; Lower-middle; and Working). The latter two of these categories include women who are nearly all FGS, while the first three categories are all CGS. Yet they mention "first-generation students" just a handful of times. For their study, the distinction between FGS and CGS is not the most important one they observed. As a result of their analysis, they primarily group together the first two categories (Upper and Upper-middle class), referring to them as "more privileged" and compare them to the latter three (Middle, Lower-middle, and Working), which include some FGS and some

CGS and are considered "less privileged" based on their parents' occupation and income. Their approach highlights the limits of always using a binary definition of social class among college students—some aspects of class distinction are fine-grained and require more nuance to discern. In advocating for the study of FGS by sociologists, I am mindful that other dimensions of social class differ among these groups and sometimes demand in-depth analysis. Nonetheless, there are reasons to believe that the distinction between FGS and CGS is an important one for scholarly attention.

In their groundbreaking book, *Academically Adrift: Limited Learning on College Campuses*, Arum and Roksa (2011) use longitudinal survey data to consider the role of college experiences in shaping student learning during the first 2 years of college, with an eye toward variation by institution type and family background. Like much sociological work that is relevant to understanding FGS, their book does not mention first-generation students by name, but uses parental educational attainment throughout as its key measure of family background after determining that it is more significantly linked to student learning and other college experiences than parental occupational attainment. Like theirs, numerous studies highlight the importance of parental educational attainment for student college attainment (e.g., Kim and Schneider 2005). Thus, if studies of college students are to select a key aspect of social class to examine for understanding social mobility processes, there is evidence that parental education is of central importance.

First-generation students are also an important group to study because they are being actively socially constructed by high schools, colleges, governments, the media, and others. Thus, first-generation status is becoming an increasingly salient element of college students' subjective understanding of their social class location. Prevailing societal images of FGS also influence perceptions among professors, parents, and CGS. In 2015, UC Berkeley's alumni association published an article, "The Struggle to be First: First-Gen Students May Be Torn Between College and Home" (Tugend 2015), and the American Sociological Association published a research brief titled, "First-Generation Sociology Majors Overcome Deficits" (Spalter-Roth et al. 2015). Although both of these publications actually present evidence of successful outcomes among FGS, the titles highlight a dominant social construction of FGS as somehow "misfits" with the college student role due to their lack of college resources and greater connections to home.

There is experimental evidence showing that making social class differences salient during student orientation and tying them to resources to navigate through college can benefit FGS in terms of college GPA without disadvantaging CGS (Stephens et al. 2014). However, others argue that the discursive construction of FGS, especially in elite institutions, is negative for student experiences and identities because it obscures class conflict on campus and leads to distancing from one's origins (Wildhagen 2015). Nonetheless, this category continues to be actively socially constructed, so it deserves critical examination. Because of the resonance of this category with the broader population, first-generation college students offer a way for sociologists to talk about social class (especially in the U.S., where class-based discourse is lacking) that may be more accessible to a broader audience than more typical complex conceptualizations.

8.2 Defining and Measuring First-Generation Status

While scholarly and policy attention to FGS attending 4-year colleges has exploded in recent decades, it is not clear that actual increases in the share of FGS in college are driving this trend. To my knowledge, the National Center for Education Statistics of the U.S. Department of Education has not produced a report that uses nationally representative data and a common definition of FGS to illustrate trends over time in the share of all college students who are FGS. As such, rather than a detailed picture of the long-term patterns in college attendance among FGS we are left with more of an impressionistic collage based on different data sources that use different definitions of FGS. According to data from the National Center for Education Statistics (NCES) that tracks enrollment in 2- or 4-year colleges, 43% of the sample of Beginning Postsecondary School Survey (BPS) students in 1989–1990 were categorized as FGS (neither parent *attended* any college), while an additional 23% had at least one parent with some college but no degree, resulting in 66% of the sample fitting our definition of FGS (Núñez and Cuccaro-Alamin 1998). Using another NCES data set, the National Postsecondary Student Aid Study data from the 1995 to 1996 cohort, Kojaku and Núñez (1998) show that there was little change during these 5 years: 47% of college enrollees had parents with a high school diploma or less, while 19% of enrollees had parents with some college, for a total of 66% matching our definition of FGS.

Analyses that include only students enrolled in 4-year colleges result in different estimates. For example, Saenz et al. (2007) argue that the proportion of students who were the first in their families to attend college steadily declined from 1971 to 2005 (from 39% to 16%) in 4-year colleges. The authors attribute this trend to increases in the overall educational attainment levels of the U.S. population over time. Highlighting the importance of examining intersectional influences on FGS, this decline in the share of students who are FGS was steeper for African Americans than other racial/ethnic groups, and went down "faster than the relative proportion of African American adults without a college education" (Saenz et al. 2007). Further, there are persistent institutional differences: Only 13% of students attending private colleges were FGS in their definition, compared to 18% at public universities. Notably, this report defined FGS more conservatively than many studies, in that it only examined students enrolled in 4-year universities and categorized them as FGS only if neither parent had *ever attended* a postsecondary institution.

Research estimating the share of the high school population that is potentially first generation based on different definitions of FGS using Educational Longitudinal Study data finds that the proportion varies from 22%–77% of high school students depending on how the group is defined (Toutkoushian et al. 2015). In particular, the definition varied by whether it used information from one or both parents, as well as whether FGS included students whose parents had no exposure to college versus some exposure (either through attending but not earning a degree, or by earning an associate degree). Nonetheless, regardless of which criteria the researchers used to define first generation high school students, FGS were less likely than CGS to take SAT/ACT exams, apply to college, and ultimately enroll in college.

Just as national patterns of FGS enrollment over time and across locations are challenging to discern, international trends are likewise difficult to track. In their effort to conduct an international review of the literature on FGS, Spiegler and Bednarek (2013, p. 321) highlight three key challenges in providing even the most basic comparative cross-national statistics:

> Firstly, different definitions of FGS status lead to remarkable variations in their proportional share. Secondly, even if the same definition is applied, non-academic vocational training systems have developed differently [cross-nationally]. Professions which require at least some college education in a specific country can be obtained in others at practice-oriented institutions. And thirdly, even if we apply the same definition in comparable education systems, the data do not serve as direct and comparable measurements for educational equity. A high share of FGS indicates a phase of educational expansion. The higher share of academic-educated parents becomes over time, the less likely it will be to find a high percentage of FGS.

Nonetheless, they draw from the Eurostudent IV data (Orr et al. 2011, cited in Spiegler and Bednarek 2013) to show that estimates of the proportion of FGS (defined as no parental college experience) enrolled in college in European countries range from 21% to 76%. They divide European countries into three groups indicating a lower share of FGS, less than 40% (e.g., Denmark and Germany), a middle share, 40–60% (e.g., France and England/Wales), and a higher share of FGS, more than 60% (e.g., Poland, Italy, Turkey). Using a comparable definition of FGS, the United States and Canada would be in the lower share group, with 35% and 30% respectively (Organization for Economic Cooperation and Development [OECD] Report 2012). The challenges in pinpointing longitudinal and cross-national trends in college attendance among first-generation students highlight the need for standardized measures to document variation.

8.3 Understanding First-Generation Student Experiences

Education scholars first began examining first-generation college students in the 1990s, producing several important descriptive studies aimed at painting a picture of FGS for higher education administrators and other higher education scholars (Terenzini et al. 1994, 1996). In the last decade or so, sociologists have joined in the effort to build upon this work, especially deepening the application of social and cultural capital theories and institutional analysis, particularly, to enhance understanding of variation in FGS college experiences. I begin this section with a general overview of the research on FGS, and then focus in more depth on some recent studies that draw from cultural and social capital theories, respectively.

FGS and CGS who enter 4-year colleges have different pre-college characteristics, including lower family incomes, lower standardized test scores, less effective high school preparation, and less engagement with peers and teachers in high school (Kojaku and Núñez 1998; Terenzini et al. 1996; Warburton et al. 2001). FGS are also significantly more likely to be older, married, Hispanic, and to have dependent children than are CGS (Choy 2001). Largely due to these differences, they can have more difficult transitions from high school to college (Ostrove and Long 2007; Terenzini et al. 1994, 1996). Once they arrive on college campuses, FGS continue to lag behind CGS peers on several outcomes. In longitudinal analysis, FGS are more likely than CGS to drop out of college during their first semester, and continue to have a greater risk of leaving college before completing their degree, even net of pre-college characteristics (Ishitani 2003). They also earn fewer credit hours, lower grades, and work significantly more hours per week than CGS (Pascarella et al. 2004; Warburton et al. 2001).

Scholars of higher education have long highlighted the importance of college student engagement (Kuh et al. 1991) and integration (Tinto 1987) for student success. This work shows that students who are involved in campus activities and interact with faculty and peers on campus are more likely to persist. First-generation students are less likely to be involved in campus activities and have fewer interactions with peers (Pascarella et al. 2004; Terenzini et al. 1996). They also have less social and academic engagement on campus than CGS, which is largely due to lower educational aspirations and a greater likelihood of living off campus (Pike and Kuh 2005). There is some debate in the literature as to whether college experiences are equally or more consequential for FGS outcomes compared to their CGS peers. Pike and Kuh (2005) found equivalent effects, while Terenzini et al. (1996) found that FGS benefitted more from experiences during college than CGS. It is not clear whether these differences are artifacts of sample differences (e.g., Terenzini et al. include community college students in their sample, while Pike and Kuh do not), suggesting the need for additional research.

Research on variation in college adjustment has criticized theories of engagement and integration for overlooking the perspectives of marginalized students, who are less likely to feel like they belong on campus (Hurtado and Carter 1997; Ostrove and Long 2007). Hurtado and Carter (1997) point out that "integration" on campus holds a different meaning for traditionally marginalized groups than it does for groups that are dominant among college students. They demonstrate that students' sense of belonging, not only their engagement behaviors, is important to assessing their adjustment to campus life. Ostrove and Long (2007) empirically demonstrate that lower social class is linked to diminished sense of belonging on college campuses, and that this in turn influences students' academic and social adjustment to college.

Rather than leveling the playing field, variation in college experiences often widens the gap between FGS and their CGS peers. For example, FGS see their faculty as less concerned with teaching and student development than do CGS. They also report more experiences with racial/ethnic and gender discrimination during the first year of college than CGS do (Terenzini et al. 1996). Further, FGS have fewer academically oriented interactions with faculty than do CGS (Kim and Sax 2009). Interacting with faculty is beneficial for all students, but FGS and students of color may especially benefit (Lundberg and Schreiner 2004). This suggests the importance of examining the ways that race/ethnicity, social class (captured by income, wealth, and occupational prestige rather than parental education), and gender intersect with FG status.

8.3.1 Cultural Capital Theory

Cultural capital theory is clearly the dominant sociological perspective guiding the study of FGS. Bourdieu (1997) defines cultural capital as a resource that can help provide access to social and economic rewards and that can be passed from one generation to another. Upper-class families, especially those with more educated parents, teach skills to and provide opportunities for their children that facilitate social and economic success by leading to behaviors and habits that are then unequally rewarded by educational institutions (Bourdieu 1977; Lareau 1989). As Lareau and Weininger (2003) have argued, much of the early empirical work on cultural capital focused on Bourdieu's original conceptualizations of "highbrow aesthetic culture" (such as opera or impressionist art). They suggest (2003, p. 569) that examining "micro-interactional processes whereby individual's strategic use of knowledge, skills, and competence comes into contact with institutionalized standards of evaluation" is more in line with Bourdieu's conceptualization of cultural capital. The study of FGS has largely adopted this approach, but has focused primarily on the individual's behaviors and attitudes and less on institutionalized standards of evaluation.

Central to understanding the role of cultural capital in shaping class differences in college outcomes and experiences are the class dispositions, or *habitus*, that young adults develop in their families and communities that they bring with them to college (Lareau and Weininger 2003; Lee and Kramer 2013; Lehmann 2013). Habitus includes the largely unconscious and internalized cultural styles, tastes, and signals that emerge from one's biography and class position, and is a key cultural resource which can facilitate or hinder success in educational institutions (Bourdieu 1977). This cultural capital is not static, but can be transformed throughout the lifetime through experiencing new interactions and institutions.

Habitus influenced the majors FGS selected in Mullen's (2010) study of class inequality at an elite private and broader-access public institution. FGS and CGS had competing narratives about the meaning of education: FGS largely viewed education as job preparation, while CGS primarily saw it as self-cultivation. Thus, FGS sought more practical and applied majors that would lead to specific occupations, while majors aligned with intellectual or personal interests were more common among CGS. However, because the more elite campus offered fewer applied majors, FGS were sometimes funneled into less practical fields (which also had the benefit of providing better routes to graduate school than applied majors). As FGS move through college, a lower- or working-class habitus is often altered through interaction with the middle-class culture that dominates college campuses. Lehmann (2013) conducted longitudinal interviews with working-class students at a Canadian university to understand how successful students' cultural capital changes over the course of their college careers. He found that the students felt that they grew personally through expanded cultural capital and developed new outlooks on various issues, such as food, future careers, and politics. However, they were conflicted about eschewing their working-class roots, which created challenges for their relationships with families and friends from home. Likewise, Lee and Kramer (2013) refer to the experience of possessing two different habitus simultaneously using Bourdieu's (2004) concept of *cleft habitus*. They consider how upward mobility among FGS shapes their interactions with nonmobile family and friends. FGS tend to cut off or diminish their interactions with nonmobile friends and family as they develop a cleft habitus, while CGS do not.

Likewise, students who arrive at college without the cultural capital expected of them by the institution can become newly aware of social class, which can affect their identity. Aries and Seider (2005) studied White lower-income students, most of whom were FGS, at both an elite college and a state college. The low-income students attending the elite college experienced a greater awareness of social class, recognizing that their advantaged peers possessed forms of cultural capital valued by the institution while they did not. These differences were less prevalent at the state school where there was more similarity in class backgrounds among the students. Other research argues that institutional agents at elite colleges actively construct the FGS category and encourage FGS to distance themselves from their families and communities (Wildhagen 2015). Regardless of their campus, all low-income students "struggled with class-based discontinuities between their pre-college identities and their evolving identities" (Aries and Seider 2005, p. 439). The students adopted new cultural styles, including their dress, speech, and behaviors, which they believed could distance them from their families and friends from home. Low-income students sought to cope with the discontinuities they experienced, and some thought being in college allowed them to explore new aspects of their identities. Low-income students in elite colleges, in particular, developed greater appreciation for the character traits they attributed to their class background that they possessed which their affluent peers lacked, including self-reliance, empathy, and independence. There is additional evidence that adolescent cultural capital acquired from family sources is less consequential as FGS move through the higher

education pipeline: It may matter for initial entry into higher education, but less for outcomes like GPA and completion (Dumais and Ward 2010).

Collier and Morgan (2008) argue that mastering the role of "college student" is a form of cultural capital. Following Lareau and Weininger (2003), they highlight the importance of moments when instructors evaluate student performance and the criteria they use in relation to student's resources for understanding and responding to faculty expectations. FGS have less inside knowledge than CGS about how to perform the college student role, making it challenging to respond to faculty expectations, regardless of the student's actual understanding of course material. FGS were less likely to understand professors' expectations about things like the amount of time they should study to succeed in their classes, how to complete writing assignments, and the purpose of office hours. This lack of understanding contributed to their lower levels of classroom achievement. This study also points to the importance of considering not only student perspectives, but also those of institutional actors, such as professors (see also Wildhagen 2015). The faculty participating in the study believed they had communicated expectations and opportunities for support clearly, but FGS disagreed. Misunderstanding the student role may be an important mechanism driving the lower levels of student–faculty interaction among FGS compared to CGS also found in quantitative analyses, net of controls for student background (Kim and Sax 2009).

In *Paying for the Party*, Armstrong and Hamilton (2013) look at the ways that institutional actions matter differently for women's pathways through college depending on their social class. They find that many working-class and low-income students, who aren't always identified by their campus as FGS due to their parents having some college experience, "fall through the cracks" at the large public university they studied. The programs targeting FGS were too small to serve all eligible students, and were generally targeted, ironically, toward those with higher academic achievement. The standard academic advising did not offer sufficient information to make up for the limited cultural capital lower-SES students brought with them to college for navigating college life.

Stuber (2011b) finds that FGS who persist through college fall into three distinct categories: (1) Integrated persisters who are actively involved in campus life and don't perceive deficiencies relative to CGS peers; (2) Alienated persisters who felt different than others on campus and opted out of campus extracurricular and social domains; and (3) Resilient and motivated persisters who previously felt alienated by campus life, but dealt with their feelings and became more engaged. The public flagship campus that Armstrong and Hamilton (2013) studied structured academic and social experiences to accommodate a "party pathway" through college. This pathway can especially derail less privileged women from successful academic and career outcomes because of the different cultural resources they had compared to more privileged women.

Newer work drawing on cultural capital theory explicitly demonstrates how cultural capital that facilitates college success can be developed outside the family. Jack (2016, 2014) interviewed Black and Latino undergraduates attending elite universities to identify how divergent high school opportunities shape cultural resources that support successful college experiences. He contrasts the experiences of the "doubly disadvantaged"— low-income, first-generation students who attended under-resourced schools in their home community with the "privileged poor"—also low-income, FGS, but who attended college preparatory boarding and day schools. Developing this kind of "acquired" cultural capital may be important for disrupting processes of social inequality in higher education. Institutions outside the family—especially college preparatory boarding and day schools—can provide some FGS (the "privileged poor") with the cultural tools to navigate more successful college pathways than their peers who are not exposed to these opportunities (Jack 2016, 2014). Knowledge about financing a college education is another form of cultural capital that varies by first-generation status and race and can be influenced by non-familial sources (McCabe and Jackson

2016). High school counselors can especially help students who have limited parental and financial capital, but they are too scarce and overburdened in poor high schools to help all students who would benefit (McDonough 1997; McCabe and Jackson 2016).

Some scholars argue that rather than focusing on perceived "deficits" of cultural capital among marginalized and underrepresented college populations, we should instead revise our theories to recognize the unique forms of capital that FGS and other marginalized groups have developed through their experiences with marginalization. While FGS have less access to some forms of knowledge that are rewarded by colleges and universities, research is increasingly examining alternative forms of cultural capital that facilitate college success. In multiple studies of Black and Latino adolescents, Carter (2003, 2006) delineated the importance of non-dominant forms of cultural capital for social relations within low-income minority communities and demonstrated that the value of cultural capital is context specific. Further, some adolescents adopt either dominant or non-dominant forms of capital, while others are "cultural straddlers" who switch between the two forms depending on the setting (Carter 2006). Scholars drawing from critical race theory have criticized cultural capital theory for ignoring the ways that experiencing marginalization by race and class help underrepresented groups develop valuable skills and knowledge that facilitate success (Yosso 2005; Muñoz and Maldonado 2012). Asking, "Whose culture has capital?", Yosso (2005) outlines six important forms of cultural capital that marginalized groups develop which are typically overlooked: (1) *Aspirational capital* is "the ability to maintain hopes and dreams for the future, even in the face of real and perceived barriers" (p. 77); (2) *Linguistic capital* consists of the intellectual and social skills derived from communicating in multiple languages or dialects; (3) *Familial capital* refers to forms of cultural knowledge developed through kinship ties "that carry a sense of community history, memory, and cultural intuition" (p. 78); (4) *Social capital* includes network connections and community resources that provide both instrumental and emotional support to survive in dominant social institutions; (5) *Navigational capital* involves "skills for maneuvering through social institutions" that were not created with marginalized groups in mind, such as resilience (p. 80); and (6) *Resistant capital* includes the skills and knowledge that individuals develop "through oppositional behavior that challenges inequality" (p. 80). Although Yosso (2005) is explicitly theorizing about the assets students of color carry with them from their homes and communities into the elementary and secondary school classrooms, I argue that these alternative forms of capital (and likely others) are also central for understanding college success among FGS. The various forms of dominant and non-dominant cultural capital, and how they intersect with varied institutional norms, need to be more fully examined in college settings.

To date, there are only a handful of studies that consider the beneficial types of capital that may uniquely benefit FGS in college. For example, building on Yosso's (2005) work, Muñoz and Maldonado (2012) show that the undocumented, first generation Mexicana students they interviewed drew upon unique forms of "navigational capital" that helped them succeed in a predominantly White, middle-class institution. Future work should build upon these studies to further specify the kinds of capital FGS use to succeed in and transform colleges.

8.3.2   Social Capital Theory

Social capital theory has also helped shape scholarly understanding of social class differences, including those between FGS and their CGS counterparts. Social capital is a resource that one gains through relationships and interactions with others in one's social network, which helps subsequent social and economic action (Coleman 1988). Social capital acquisition is often embedded within institutional contexts, which provide both a setting for developing social relationships and can structure variation in the amount, quality, and transferability of resources in one's network (Bourdieu 1997). Social and cultural capital are

related to one another since access to cultural resources is often transmitted through social network ties. Social capital during high school is important for helping marginalized youth navigate institutional barriers, enhancing their college-going behaviors and identities (Stanton-Salazar 1997).

Prior research shows that once they arrive on campus, students are more successful when they are both academically and socially engaged (Astin 1985; Kuh et al. 2005; Pascarella and Terenzini 2005; Tinto 1993). The types of engagement and networking these studies discuss can be considered forms of social capital. In particular, talking to professors and peers outside of class about academic matters benefits student outcomes, but first-generation students have fewer of these interactions (Beattie and Thiele 2016). There is suggestive evidence that social capital with family members, peers, STEM programs, and university personnel is important to the selection of and persistence in engineering majors among FGS (Pfirman et al. 2014). Thus, in addition to helping FGS compete in college overall, it may help them persist in fields in which they are underrepresented.

As with cultural capital theory, the majority of existing studies using social capital theory focus on student "deficits." While the parents of FGS have not completed college degrees, they nonetheless provide important resources to their children as they transition to college. In her study of how FGS realize social mobility in Israel, Gofen (2009) argues that "family capital" is especially important for supporting college attendance and completion among FGS. She argues that this form of capital includes elements of social capital and cultural capital, as well as other experiences in the context of family life, that help young adults have "breakthrough" moments that undergird college success. Specifically, she highlights the importance of familial attitudes toward education, interpersonal family relationships (with parents and siblings), and family values (solidarity, respect, and ambition) for facilitating college success. Puquirre (2015) likewise points to the particular importance of older siblings who have attended college as a key resource for helping students from underrepresented groups succeed in college.

Recent research also considers the dynamic forces that help FGS develop new social capital during college that can facilitate positive outcomes. Birani and Lehmann (2013) show that "bonding social capital" developed among Asian students at a Canadian university helps ease their transition to college. Connections with families and one's home community help provide this beneficial capital, but so do ethnic student organizations on campus that cement student ties. Likewise, in their study of first-generation Latino students, Saunders and Serna (2004) highlight the importance of both "old" (at home) and "new" (on campus) networks, finding that those who had both earned higher GPAs and were more comfortable in the college environment. This is in contrast to Tinto's influential theory of college student persistence which posited that students needed to separate from their home communities and integrate into campus life in order to be successful in college (Tinto 1987). Scholars have criticized this perspective for particularly ignoring the importance of family and community support and resources for racial/ethnic minority students—many of whom are FGS (Rendón et al. 2000; Tierney 1992). This criticism likely also applies to FGS, since many report that their families and communities offer important motivation and support for success. FGS are also more likely than CGS to say they want to help their families—69% vs 49%—and give back to their communities—63% vs 43% (Stephens et al. 2014).

McCabe (2016) demonstrates that variation in friendship network structures can amplify or diminish the effects of family background on student GPA and college completion. FGS in her study fared better academically if they had friendship networks that provided "academic multiplex ties," or two out of three of the following: emotional support, instrumental help, and intellectual engagement. Black and Latino FGS were more likely than other students to be "tight-knitters," with friendship networks that provided emotional support and feelings of belonging, but fewer academic ties. White FGS and CGS who were more often "samplers" (numerous disparate friendship groups) or "compartmentalizers" (at least two distinct friendship groups) had more variety in their networks and were more likely to have multiple academic ties, which helped them academically. Future research should further explore how different friendship network structures intersect with race and first-generation status to shape student outcomes.

Recent research also demonstrates the key importance of interactions with professors and peers during college for shaping student outcomes (Chambliss and Takacs 2014). These kinds of interactions are especially beneficial for FGS and other economically disadvantaged groups (Lundberg and Schreiner 2004; Pascarella et al. 2004). Building on this work, Beattie and Thiele (2016) consider how the campus environment—specifically class size—shapes variation by first-generation status (and race) in access to what they term *academic social capital*—frequent conversations about current and future academic and career matters with professors, teaching assistants, and peers. Using survey and institutional data, they demonstrate that all students are negatively affected by larger classes with respect to two forms of academic social capital (discussing course material with professors and ideas from class with peers). Importantly, larger classes had a significantly more negative effect on FGS than their CGS peers with respect to discussing ideas from classes with professors and TAs (and Black and Latino/a students were more sensitive to the effects of class size for interactions with professors and peers, respectively, about future careers). This suggests that future research should consider how the organization of instruction and other features of campus institutional environments may have unique effects on students whose parents have not completed college.

Other recent research on the role of social capital in the transition to college offers suggestive avenues for future examination. Although they don't explicitly mention first-generation students, Kim and Schneider (2005) use National Educational Longitudinal data to show that the effect of parental education on the selectivity of the college their child attended is mediated by aligned ambitions and aligned actions between parents and young adults. In particular, young adults whose parents have lower educational attainment levels benefit more than those with highly educated parents from parental participation in college guidance programs (Kim and Schneider 2005). This study shows the importance of examining continued activation of social capital from parents while students are in college, and how its effects vary by first-generation status. Few studies have examined this, largely because early conceptualizations of college success have downplayed the value of family ties, suggesting that students—especially disadvantaged ones—should instead forge ties on campus to be successful (Tinto 1987).

8.4 Emerging Trends and New Directions

8.4.1 Intersectionality and First-Generation Students

Sociological research in education and other sub-fields is increasingly recognizing the intersectional nature of social inequalities (O'Connor 2001). Race, class, gender, sexuality, (dis)ability, age, immigrant generation, language status, and other dimensions of social identity do not operate separately to affect college students, but rather intersect in myriad ways to shape outlooks, experiences, and outcomes. A lens of intersectionality encourages recognition that these kinds of ascribed statuses are lived simultaneously and cannot be considered distinct categories (Collins 1991). Further, an intersectionality framework is most effective when it moves beyond examining individual identities and helps reveal the importance of domains of power that shape individual experience in higher education differently depending on ascribed characteristics (Núñez 2014). Because FGS are more likely to be students of color, female, low-income, immigrant, and of non-traditional college age than are CGS, it is especially important to consider intersections across different dimensions of inequality (Choy 2001). Middle-income first-generation students

who are of average college age are likely to have different experiences than those who are low-income and non-traditional age, for example.

Studies of FGS provide evidence of intersectional variation that deserves further investigation. For example, there is evidence that FGS who are female, Hispanic, and/or low-income have especially low rates of college persistence, while CGS who are members of these groups do not face particular difficulties with persisting to their degrees (Lohfink and Paulsen 2005). Examining a sample of students attending elite colleges and universities, Fischer (2007) found that being a first-generation student had negative effects on cumulative college GPA, but only among White and Hispanic students. Stuber (2011b) shows that for some of the White FGS she studied, their Whiteness helped them fit in, yet for others, it made them feel invisible as an FGS since others assumed White students were advantaged.

In contrast, Wilkins (2014) uses an intersectional framework to understand identity transformations as Black and first-generation White men transition to college. She finds that the FGS White men developed identity strategies of "being normal guys" in high school that continued to help them successfully transition to college. This approach allowed them to find common interests with other academically oriented friends and perform adult-like behaviors linked to school success. The Black men in her study, however, were from more advantaged backgrounds than the White FGS—their parents had professional occupations and some were college educated and they attended predominantly White, advantaged high schools. In spite of this, they had more difficult identity adjustments in college. Wilkins argues that the Black men were not able to draw upon scripts about middle-class masculinity, since others imposed scripts linked to adolescence and the Black lower-class on them. This negatively affected their friendships and their self-images as they were expected to perform counter-school actions. Further, Mullen (2010) found evidence that habitus was gendered in her sample, with FGS and CGS women exhibiting important differences from men. In other research, scholars have highlighted the importance of parental educational attainment for shaping the college trajectories of youth who are immigrants or the children of immigrants (Baum and Flores 2011). Not only are the children of immigrants more likely than those with U.S.-born parents to have parents with no college experience (8% versus 26%), families from some countries of origin have extremely low parental educational attainment. For example, nearly half of Mexican-origin youth have parents without a high school diploma while those whose families hail from South Asia, the Middle East, and East Asia are more likely than the U.S.-born population to have parents who hold college degrees (Baum and Flores 2011). Prior work has not fully considered the ways that immigrant generation and country of origin intersect with first-generation student status to shape college trajectories. These findings highlight the need to consider intersections of race, gender, immigration, and income with first-generation status.

Sociologists should develop greater insight into the intersectional influences that shape FGS and CGS college experiences and outcomes. In particular, this area of research would benefit from systematic methods using comparison groups to help understand intersectional inequalities among FGS, as some recent studies have done (Wilkins 2014; McCabe and Jackson 2016). We can also look to work on patterns of broad-scale stratification processes in sociology (even those not directly examining FGS) to consider fruitful avenues for future analyses of intersectional processes. For example, Torche (2011) shows that as attainment of post-baccalaureate degrees has expanded for more recent cohorts, intergenerational transmission of social class standing among advanced-degree holders has grown stronger than for other levels of educational attainment, particularly among men. This suggests that future research should examine how first-generation status relates to patterns of graduate degree attainment, with a focus on intersectional differences by gender (and race, which was not a focus of this earlier research).

8.4.2 Variation in Institutional Contexts

To date, with a handful of exceptions, the literature on FGS has largely focused on how *students* should adapt to the largely middle-class setting endemic at 4-year campuses instead of on how *colleges* can adapt their approaches to meet the needs of students from lower- and working-class backgrounds. FGS and their families are framed as lacking key aspects of cultural and social capital that are known to be beneficial for college persistence, satisfaction, and completion. Instead of focusing on individual "deficits," I suggest that future research consider how systematic *institutional neglect and abuse* of marginalized students can undermine the academic and social success of FGS on campus (González et al. 2003). In their study of Latino/a high school students' pathways to college attendance, González et al. (2003, p. 153) define institutional neglect as "the inability or unwillingness of schools or its personnel to prepare students for postsecondary education, particularly 4-year universities" and institutional abuse as "actions by institutional agents that discourage or produce barriers for college attendance."

In addition to more thoroughly examining how first-generation status intersects with other dimensions of inequality, future sociological research on FGS should give greater consideration to how variation in institutional contexts shape student experiences. A handful of excellent studies have taken some initial steps in revealing that different institution types (e.g., public vs private; highly selective vs less selective) have differential effects on students (Arum and Roksa, 2011; Stuber 2011a). Many studies focus on FGS at elite institutions, where the experience of cultural mismatch is greatest (Lee and Kramer 2013; Wildhagen 2015), but comparative studies offer important insights (Mullen 2010; Stuber 2011a). Further, institutional practices and programs (e.g., class sizes; summer bridge programs) can have differential effects by first-generation status and/or ameliorate differences in resources (Armstrong and Hamilton 2013; Beattie and Thiele 2016; Jack 2014; Stuber 2011a).

McDonough (1997) identifies the importance of "organizational habitus" for understanding how educational institutions mediate the effects of social class origins on student outcomes. Her study showed that high schools had different types of college-going cultures which caused guidance counselors to channel students of different social origins to divergent colleges and universities. Stuber (2011a) shows that such a form of habitus also operates on college campuses. Student involvement was institutionalized at Benton, the private liberal arts campus she studied, which helped erase differences between FGS and CGS in campus engagement since the policies and programs in place made it nearly impossible to avoid becoming engaged. At Big State, the public state university, there was less organizational commitment and fewer resources directed toward student engagement, so only the handful of FGS who were involved in specialized programs directed at FGS were involved in extracurricular activities. Thus, ironically, the cultural mismatch experienced by FGS on more elite campuses may be especially pronounced (Aries and Seider 2005), but such environments can also provide greater access to resources to support student success (Stuber 2011a). Research should investigate these paradoxical differences across different types of institutions using both qualitative and quantitative methods to understand patterns of organizational habitus.

Also consistent with the notion of organizational habitus (McDonough 1997), there is evidence that apparently similar universities can have different orientations toward diversity and inclusion that influence student outcomes. Warikoo and Deckman (2014) show that "Powers University's" diversity programming based on a critical framework that recognized individual experiences as socially situated within unequal institutional structures was beneficial for students of color. However, White students at the campus were sometimes alienated by this approach. In contrast, "Harmony University"—demographically similar to Powers—adopted an integration and celebration model for diversity conversations on campus. This approach was more inclusive of all students, but was linked with less pronounced

changes in student perspectives on diversity and multiculturalism than the power approach. Similarly, different organizational approaches to socioeconomic diversity on campus likely play a role in FGS identities and experiences across campuses, which should be explored in future research.

Psychologists Stephens et al. (2012) demonstrate through a series of linked studies that one challenge faced by FGS is the cultural mismatch between the cultural ideals of college campuses—especially elite ones—which stress middle-class notions of independence, and working-class values that prioritize interdependence. Using administrator reports on institutional expectations, they demonstrate that college campuses are more likely to prioritize values of independence than interdependence. However, top-tier campuses were significantly more likely to value independence than second-tier campuses were. This provides suggestive evidence that college campuses are not a monolithic group and provide different contexts that may have important implications for FGS college student experiences. Cultural mismatches experienced by FGS are likely to vary by institutional characteristics. As Spiegler and Bednarek (2013, p. 331) suggest, "Ultimately, structural problems inherent in the organization of education are camouflaged as cultural deficits of individuals." Future research should consider how different organizational approaches to addressing (or ignoring) cultural mismatch can shape the ways college campuses engage in institutional neglect and abuse instead of institutional support for FGS and other marginalized students.

FGS who attended larger institutions were more likely to persist to a degree than those who attended smaller ones (Lohfink and Paulsen 2005). Identity challenges based on social class were less pronounced at a public institution then an elite private one (Aries and Seider 2005).

Arum and Roksa (2011) found that CGS enroll in highly selective universities at much higher rates than FGS. Forty-four percent of students with a parent who had earned graduate or professional degrees and 20% of those with a parent who had earned a bachelor's degree enrolled in such schools. In contrast, only 8% of those whose parents had earned a high school diploma and 10% of those whose parents had attended some college enrolled in highly selective colleges and universities. First-generation students at selective schools, therefore, encounter environments where they are scarcer than their peers who attend less selective schools. Research should investigate these institutional differences in greater depth, again with an eye toward how the composition of the student body relates to the institutional neglect and abuse.

Institutional variation between high schools also may influence college trajectories, and there may be variation in these effects by first-generation status. In her compelling study of first year persistence among Latino college students, Deil-Amen (2015) shows that students' high school curricular track, school SES, and the associated messages students received about college in these tracks had an effect on their self-perceptions about their abilities to successfully persist in college. Importantly, however, she noted that it was continuing generation Latino students who attended high-SES schools (often in the general rather than the college preparatory track) that were the most likely to be negatively affected. This highlights the importance of not just looking at barriers and benefits experienced by FGS, but also among CGS. Just as the study of gender must include men and the study of race must include Whites, the study of first-generation students must also consider continuing generation students, especially those who are otherwise underrepresented or marginalized. Further, this study illustrates the importance of considering variation in institutional neglect and abuse of FGS (and marginalized CGS) at both the high school and college levels.

8.4.3 Implications for Policy and Practice

Although inequalities between FGS and their CGS counterparts emerge largely from differential social, cultural, and financial resources in their family and school environments, the body of evidence suggests that policies and practices at the institutional, state, and federal levels can help level the playing field for FGS to disrupt the intergenerational transmission of inequality. High school programs and school cultures that provide adolescents with skills and knowledge as well as teachers who provide consistent and accurate messages about college readiness facilitate college success (Jack 2014, 2016; Deil-Amen 2015). In addition to policies and practices at the high school level, there is substantial evidence that colleges can take actions to avoid institutional neglect and abuse, and thus ameliorate inequalities between FGS and CGS.

Research illustrates the value—yet often limited reach—of academic support programs for FGS in college that facilitate the development of institutionally valued forms of social and cultural capital which facilitate student success (Armstrong and Hamilton 2013; McCabe 2016; Stuber 2011a). Such programs should be expanded, but targeted to the students who are not the "privileged poor" (Jack 2016) who have already developed these forms of capital. In particular, academic bridge programs over the summer before the first year of college, which provide underrepresented and disadvantaged students with opportunities to settle into college and gain access to institutional and interpersonal resources, can be especially beneficial (Deil-Amen 2015). Student orientation should also acknowledge the ways that social background can shape college experiences, and point students toward particular campus resources that can help students with less ready access to important information in their social networks (Stephens et al. 2014).

There is suggestive evidence that college classroom experiences that provide critical analysis of social inequality can help improve the self-image, feelings of belonging, and student–faculty relationships among FGS, especially students of color (Núñez 2011). Further, maintaining smaller class sizes is particularly beneficial to FGS's development of academic social capital in terms of their likelihood of having beneficial interactions about course-related issues with their professors and TAs (Beattie and Thiele 2016). In addition, multicultural student clubs and organizations can offer important sources of support and places to "belong," and provide access to beneficial knowledge for first-generation students of color (Birani and Lehmann 2013). However, campuses should support student development of broad social networks, not limited to a single club or organization (McCabe 2016). Stuber (2011a) identifies numerous policies and programs that help institutionalize campus involvement, erasing differences between FGS and CGS in rates of extracurricular engagement. Programs that target FGS and provide them with information and social connections are important, as are financial aid and work opportunities that enable access to internships and study abroad experiences. Mentoring programs can also benefit students by connecting them to resources. Housing and residential life policies can also influence social inequality on campus (Armstrong and Hamilton 2013; Stuber 2011a). In sum, rather than assuming differential social and cultural capital between FGS and CGS is immutable, campuses need to recognize how institutional neglect and abuse of marginalized students hinders their full incorporation into campus life and take steps to address these institutional problems, rather than blaming students' origins.

8.5 Conclusion

First-generation college students represent a theoretically critical group for understanding social inequality in higher education and processes of social mobility. They are successful in navigating into higher education institutions in spite of a lack of parental experience, and may derive particular benefits from their social origins in terms of motivation and novel sources of support. Their experiences can thus shed light on the mechanisms of social mobility processes. However, college experiences can prove challenging for FGS due to their more limited social, cultural, and financial capital that is valued by institutions of higher education.

Sociologists have arrived relatively late to the study of this group, and sometimes conduct research relevant to describing their experiences and outcomes without mentioning them at all. I argue that sociological perspectives can add to our understanding of FGS, and that sociologists should not let our disciplinary preference for a more complex conceptualization of social class keep us from contributing to understandings of the complex realities of being a first-generation student. In particular, sociological methods and theories can improve understandings of the ways that first-generation status intersects with other dimensions of identity and experience (race/ethnicity, gender, social class, sexuality, immigration status, etc). Sociological insight can also help illustrate how institutional variation and institutional neglect and abuse shape FGS experiences and outcomes. Such insights can help institutions of higher education refrain from blaming FGS and instead develop programs and policies that better support success for all students, regardless of parental educational attainment.

References

Aries, E., & Seider, M. (2005). The interactive relationship between class identity and the college experience: The case of lower income students. *Qualitative Sociology, 28*(4), 419–443.

Armstrong, E. A., & Hamilton, L. T. (2013). *Paying for the party*. Cambridge: Harvard University Press.

Arum, R., & Roksa, J. (2011). *Academically adrift: Limited learning on college campuses*. Chicago: University of Chicago Press.

Astin, A. (1985). *Achieving educational excellence*. San Francisco: Jossey-Bass.

Baum, S., & Flores, S. M. (2011). Higher education and children in immigrant families. *The Future of Children, 21*(1), 171–193.

Beattie, I. R. (2002). Are all "adolescent econometricians" created equal? Racial, class, and gender differences in college enrollment. *Sociology of Education, 75*(1), 19–43.

Beattie, I. R., & Thiele, M. (2016). Connecting in class? College class size and inequality in academic social capital. *The Journal of Higher Education, 87*(3), 332–362.

Birani, A., & Lehmann, W. (2013). Ethnicity as social capital: An examination of first-generation, ethnic-minority students at a Canadian university. *International Studies in Sociology of Education, 23*(4), 281–297.

Blau, P. M., & Duncan, O. D. (1967). *The American occupational structure*. New York: Wiley.

Bourdieu, P. (1977). Cultural reproduction and social reproduction. In J. Karabel & A. H. Halsey (Eds.), *Power and ideology in education* (pp. 487–511). New York: Oxford University Press.

Bourdieu, P. (1997). The forms of capital. In A. H. Halsey, H. Lauder, P. Brown, & A. S. Wells (Eds.), *Education: culture, economy, and society* (pp. 46–58). Oxford: Oxford University Press.

Bourdieu, P. (2004). *Science of science and reflexivity*. Chicago: University of Chicago Press.

Bowles, S., & Gintis, H. (1976). *Schooling in capitalist America*. New York: Basic Books.

Buchmann, C., & DiPrete, T. A. (2006). The growing female advantage in college completion: The role of family background and academic achievement. *American Sociological Review, 71*(4), 515–541.

Carter, P. L. (2003). "Black" cultural capital, status positioning, and schooling conflicts for low-income African American youth. *Social Problems, 50*(1), 136–155.

Carter, P. L. (2006). Straddling boundaries: Identity, culture, and school. *Sociology of Education, 79*(4), 304–328.

Chambliss, D. F., & Takacs, C. G. (2014). *How college works*. Cambridge, MA: Harvard University Press.

Choy, S. (2001). *Students whose parents did not go to college: Postsecondary access, persistence, and attainment* (Findings from the condition of education). Washington, DC: NCES, U.S. Department of Education.

Coleman, J. S. (1988). Social capital in the creation of human capital. *American Journal of Sociology*, 94, S95–S120.

Collier, P. J., & Morgan, D. L. (2008). "Is that paper really due today?": Differences in first-generation and traditional college students' understandings of faculty expectations. *Higher Education, 55*(4), 425–446.

Collins, P. H. (1991). *Black feminist thought: knowledge, consciousness, and the politics of empowerment*. New York: Routledge.

Davis, J. (2010). *The first-generation student experience: Implications for campus practice, and strategies for improving persistence and success*. Sterling: Stylus.

Deil-Amen, R. J. (2015). College for all Latinos? The role of high school messages in facing college challenges. *Teachers College Record, 117*(3), 1–50.

Dumais, S. A., & Ward, A. (2010). Cultural capital and first-generation college success. *Poetics, 38*(3), 245–265.

Fischer, M. (2007). Settling into campus life: Differences by race/ethnicity in college involvement and outcomes. *The Journal of Higher Education, 78*(2), 125–161.

Gofen, A. (2009). Family capital: How first-generation higher education students break the intergenerational cycle. *Family Relations, 58*(1), 104–120.

Goldrick-Rab, S. (2016). Following their every move: An investigation of social-class differences in college pathways. *Sociology of Education, 79*(1), 67–79.

González, K. P., Stoner, C., & Jovel, J. E. (2003). Examining the role of social capital in access to college for Latinas: Toward a college opportunity framework. *Journal of Hispanic Higher Education, 2*(2), 146–170.

Haller, A. O., & Portes, A. (1973). Status attainment processes. *Sociology of Education, 46*(1), 51–91.

Hurtado, S., & Carter, D. F. (1997). Effects of college transition and perceptions of the campus racial climate on Latino college students' sense of belonging. *Sociology of Education, 70*, 324–345.

Ishitani, T. T. (2003). A longitudinal approach to assessing attrition behavior among first-generation students: Time-varying effects of pre-college characteristics. *Research in Higher Education, 44*(4), 433–449.

Ishitani, T. T. (2006). Studying attrition and degree completion behavior among first-generation college students in the United States. *Journal of Higher Education, 77*(5), 861–885.

Jack, A. A. (2014). Culture shock revisited: The social and cultural contingencies to class marginality. *Sociological Forum, 29*(2), 453–475.

Jack, A. A. (2016). (No) harm in asking: Class, acquired cultural capital, and academic engagement at an elite university. *Sociology of Education, 89*(1), 1–19.

Kim, Y. K., & Sax, L. J. (2009). Student–faculty interaction in research universities: Differences by student gender, race, social class, and first-generation status. *Research in Higher Education, 50*(5), 437–459.

Kim, D. H., & Schneider, B. (2005). Social capital in action: Alignment of parental support in adolescents' transition to postsecondary education. *Social Forces, 84*(2), 1181–1206.

Kojaku, L. K., & Núñez, A. M. (1998). *Descriptive summary of 1995–96 beginning postsecondary students, with profiles of students entering 2-and 4-year institutions. National postsecondary student aid study: 1995–96. Statistical analysis report*. Washington, DC: US Government Printing Office.

Kuh, G. D., Schuh, J. H., Whitt, E., Andreas, R. E., Lyons, J. W., Strange, C. C., Krehbiel, L. E., & MacKay, K. A. (1991). *Involving colleges*. San Francisco: Jossey Bass.

Kuh, G. D., Kinzie, J., Schuh, J. H., Whitt, E. J., & Associates. (2005). *Student success in college: Creating conditions that matter*. Jossey-Bass: San Francisco.

Lareau, A. (1989). *Home advantage: Social class and parental involvement in elementary education*. London: Falmer.

Lareau, A. (2011). *Unequal childhoods: Class, race, and family life*. Berkeley: University of California Press.

Lareau, A., & Weininger, E. B. (2003). Cultural capital in educational research: A critical assessment. *Theory and society, 32*(5–6), 567–606.

Lee, E. M., & Kramer, R. (2013). Out with the old, in with the new? Habitus and social mobility at selective colleges. *Sociology of Education, 86*(1), 18–35.

Lehmann, W. (2013). Habitus transformation and hidden injuries: Successful working-class university students. *Sociology of Education, 87*(1), 1–15.

Lohfink, M. M., & Paulsen, M. B. (2005). Comparing the determinants of persistence for first-generation and continuing-generation students. *Journal of College Student Development, 46*(4), 409–428.

London, H. B. (1989). Breaking away: A study of first-generation college students and their families. *American Journal of Education, 97,* 144–170.

Lundberg, C. A., & Schreiner, L. A. (2004). Quality and frequency of faculty–student interaction as predictors of learning: An analysis by student race/ethnicity. *Journal of College Student Development, 45*(5), 549–565.

Lundberg, C. A., Schreiner, L. A., Hovaguimian, L. D., & Miller, S. S. (2007). First-generation status and student race/ethnicity as distinct predictors of student involvement and learning. *NASPA Journal, 44*(1), 57–83.

McCabe, J. (2016). *Connecting in college: How friendship networks matter for academic and social success.* Chicago: University of Chicago Press.

McCabe, J., & Jackson, B. A. (2016). Pathways to financing college: Race and class in students' narratives of paying for school. *Social Currents.* https://doi.org/10.1177/2329496516636404.

McDonough, P. M. (1997). *Choosing colleges: How social class and schools structure opportunity.* Albany: SUNY Press.

Mullen, A. L. (2010). *Degrees of inequality: Culture, class, and gender in American higher education.* Baltimore: Johns Hopkins University Press.

Muñoz, S. M., & Maldonado, M. M. (2012). Counterstories of college persistence by undocumented Mexicana students: Navigating race, class, gender, and legal status. *International Journal of Qualitative Studies in Education, 25*(3), 293–315.

Núñez, A. M. (2011). Counterspaces and connections in college transitions: First-generation Latino students' perspectives on Chicano studies. *Journal of College Student Development, 52*(6), 639–655.

Núñez, A. M. (2014). Advancing an intersectionality framework in higher education: Power and Latino postsecondary opportunity. In *Higher education: Handbook of theory and research* (pp. 33–92). Dordrecht: Springer Netherlands.

Núñez, A. M., & Cuccaro-Alamin, S. (1998). *First-generation students: Undergraduates whose parents never enrolled in postsecondary education* (NCES statistical analysis report 98-082). Washington, DC: U.S. Department of Education.

O'Connor, C. (2001). Comment: Making sense of the complexity of social identity in relation to achievement: A sociological challenge in the new millennium. *Sociology of Education, 74,* 159–168.

OECD. (2012). *Education at a glance 2012: OECD indicators.* Paris: OECD Publishing.

Orr, D., Gwosc, C., & Netz, N. (2011). *Social and economic conditions of student life in Europe. Synopsis of Indicators. Final report. Eurostudent IV 2008–2011.* Bielefeld: W. Bertelsmann Verlag. [Cited in Spiegler & Bednarek, 2013].

Ostrove, J. M., & Long, S. M. (2007). Social class and belonging: Implications for college adjustment. *Review of Higher Education, 30*(4), 363–389.

Pascarella, E. T., & Terenzini, P. T. (2005). *How college affects students: A third decade of research.* San Francisco: Jossey-Bass.

Pascarella, E. T., Pierson, C. T., Wolniak, G. C., & Terenzini, P. T. (2004). First-generation college students: Additional evidence on college experiences and outcomes. *Journal of Higher Education, 75*(3), 249–284.

Pfirman, A. L., Miller, M. K., Alvarez, G. A. S., & Martin, J. P. (2014, October). First generation college students' access to engineering social capital: Towards developing a richer understanding of important alters. In *2014 IEEE Frontiers in Education Conference (FIE) Proceedings* (pp. 1–7). IEEE.

Pike, G., & Kuh, G. (2005). First-and second-generation college students: A comparison of their engagement and intellectual development. *Journal of Higher Education, 76*(3), 276–300.

Puquirre, W. V. (2015). *Sibling social capital and college success among underrepresented students.* MA thesis, Department of Sociology, University of California, Merced.

Rendón, L. I., Jalomo, R. E., & Nora, A. (2000). Theoretical considerations in the study of minority student retention in higher education. In J. M. Braxton (Ed.), *Reworking the student departure puzzle* (pp. 127–156). Nashville: Vanderbilt University Press.

Saenz, V. B., Hurtado, S., Barrera, D., Wolf, D., & Yeung, F. (2007). *First in my family: A profile of first-generation college students at four-year institutions since 1971.* Los Angeles: Higher Education Research Institute, UCLA.

Saunders, M., & Serna, I. (2004). Making college happen: The college experiences of first-generation Latino students. *Journal of Hispanic Higher Education, 3*(2), 146–163.

Sewell, W. H., Haller, A. O., & Portes, A. (1969, February). The educational and early occupational attainment process. *American Sociological Review, 34,* 82–92.

Sewell, W. H., Haller, A. O., & Ohlendorf, G. W. (1970, December). The educational and early occupational attainment process: Replications and revisions. *American Sociological Review, 35,* 1014–1027.

Sorokin, P. A. (1959). *Social and cultural mobility.* New York: The Free Press.

Spalter-Roth, R., Van Vooren, N., & Senter, M. S. (2015, May). First generation sociology majors overcome deficits. *Research brief from the American Sociological Association's Bachelor's and Beyond series.* Washington, DC: American Sociological Association.

Spiegler, T., & Bednarek, A. (2013). First-generation students: what we ask, what we know and what it means: An international review of the state of research. *International Studies in Sociology of Education, 23*(4), 318–337.

Stanton-Salazar, R. (1997). A social capital framework for understanding the socialization of racial minority children and youths. *Harvard Educational Review, 67*(1), 1–41.

Stephens, N. M., Fryberg, S. A., Markus, H. R., Johnson, C. S., & Covarrubias, R. (2012). Unseen disadvantage: How American universities' focus on independence undermines the academic performance of first-generation college students. *Journal of Personality and Social Psychology, 102*(6), 1178.

Stephens, N. M., Hamedani, M. G., & Destin, M. (2014). Closing the social-class achievement gap: A difference-education intervention improves first-generation students' academic performance and all students' college transition. *Psychological Science, 25*(4), 943–953.

Stevens, M. L., Armstrong, E. A., & Arum, R. (2008). Sieve, incubator, temple, hub: Empirical and theoretical advances in the sociology of higher education. *Annual Review of Sociology, 34*, 127–151.

Stuber, J. M. (2011a). *Inside the college gates: How class and culture matter in higher education*. Lanham: Lexington Books.

Stuber, J. M. (2011b). Integrated, marginal, and resilient: Race, class, and the diverse experiences of White first-generation college students. *International Journal of Qualitative Studies in Education, 24*(1), 117–136.

Terenzini, P. T., Rendón, L. I., Upcraft, M. L., Millar, S. B., Allison, K. W., Gregg, P. L., & Jalomo, R. (1994). The transition to college: Diverse students, diverse stories. *Research in Higher Education, 35*(1), 57–73.

Terenzini, P. T., Springer, L., Yaeger, P. M., Pascarella, E. T., & Nora, A. (1996). First-generation college students: Characteristics, experiences, and cognitive development. *Research in Higher Education, 37*(1), 1–22.

Tierney, W. G. (1992). An anthropological analysis of student participation in college. *The Journal of Higher Education, 63*(6), 603–618.

Tinto, V. (1987). *Leaving college: Rethinking the causes and cures of student attrition*. Chicago: University of Chicago Press.

Torche, F. (2011). Is a college degree still the great equalizer? Intergenerational mobility across levels of schooling in the United States. *American Journal of Sociology, 117*(3), 763–807.

Toutkoushian, R. K., Stollberg, R. S., & Slaton, K. A. (2015, November). *Talking 'bout my generation: Defining "first generation students" in higher education research*. Paper presented at the Association for the Study of Higher Education Meeting, Denver, CO.

Tugend, A. (2015, Spring). The struggle to be first: First-gen students may be torn between college and home. *California Magazine*. Berkeley: University of California, Berkeley.

Warburton, E. C., Bugarin, R., & Núñez, A.M. (2001). *Bridging the gap: Academic preparation and post-secondary success of first-generation students* (NCES statistical analysis report 2001-153). Washington, DC: U.S. Department of Education.

Warikoo, N. K., & Deckman, S. L. (2014). Beyond the numbers: Institutional influences on experiences with diversity on elite college campuses. *Sociological Forum, 29*(4), 959–981.

Weber, M. (2015). Rationalization of education and training. In R. Arum, I. R. Beattie, & K. Ford (Eds.), *The Structure of Schooling: Readings in the sociology of education* (3rd ed., pp. 14–16). Thousand Oaks: SAGE Publications.

Wildhagen, T. (2015). "Not your typical student": The social construction of the "first-generation" college student. *Qualitative Sociology, 38*(3), 285–303.

Wilkins, A. C. (2014). Race, age, and identity transformations in the transition from high school to college for Black and first-generation White men. *Sociology of Education, 87*(3), 171–187.

Wright, E. O., Costello, C., Hachen, D., & Sprague, J. (1982). The American class structure. *American Sociological Review, 47*(6), 709–726.

Yosso, T. J. (2005). Whose culture has capital? A critical race theory discussion of community cultural wealth. *Race Ethnicity and Education, 8*(1), 69–91.

School Experiences and Educational Opportunities for LGBTQ Students

Jennifer Pearson and Lindsey Wilkinson

Abstract

This chapter provides an overview of empirical research on the educational experiences and opportunities of LGBTQ students in U.S. K–12 and postsecondary institutions, situating this research within theoretical frameworks that emphasize heteronormativity, gendered sexual socialization, and minority stress. We begin with a historical overview of research on LGBTQ students in U.S. schools and discuss conceptualization and measurement issues inherent in studying sexual orientation and gender identity. After reviewing the educational experiences and outcomes of LGBTQ students and the consequences of heteronormative school contexts, we discuss policies, programs, and supportive school environments associated with greater well-being and academic success among LGBTQ youth. Throughout the chapter, we emphasize the unique experiences of gender minority students, relative to sexual minority students, as well as the complex interplay of sexuality and gender identity. We conclude with a discussion of remaining barriers to equal educational opportunity for LGBTQ students and provide suggestions for future research.

9.1 Introduction

Over the past three decades, research on the school experiences and educational opportunities of lesbian, gay, bisexual, transgender, and queer (LGBTQ) students has grown exponentially. In 1988, the National Education Association added sexual orientation to those groups protected from discrimination in its code of ethics, and the following year, the U.S. Department of Health and Human Services released a report noting high suicide rates among gay and lesbian youth. Though very little empirical or peer-reviewed research on LGBTQ youth existed prior to the 1990s, these two events motivated greater attention to the experiences and needs of this population (Meyer 2015). The Gay, Lesbian, and Straight Education Network (GLSEN) was founded in 1990 by Kevin Jennings and a group of educators in Massachusetts with a mission to improve educational experiences for LGBTQ youth, and GLSEN released the National School Climate Study in 1999, the first national study to document the school experiences of sexual minority youth.

The 1990s are considered a transitional decade that led to increasing awareness of and resources

J. Pearson (✉)
Wichita State University, Wichita, KS, USA
e-mail: Jennifer.Pearson@wichita.edu

L. Wilkinson
Portland State University, Portland, OR, USA
e-mail: lindsw@pdx.edu

© Springer International Publishing AG, part of Springer Nature 2018
B. Schneider (ed.), *Handbook of the Sociology of Education in the 21st Century*, Handbooks of Sociology and Social Research, https://doi.org/10.1007/978-3-319-76694-2_9

for LGBTQ students. Before the 1990s, Gay–Straight Alliances (GSAs) and other supportive clubs were almost nonexistent, but a decade later more than 1200 GSAs had been formed (Fetner and Kush 2008). The availability of GSAs has continued to grow, with 60% of students in the most recent National School Climate Study reporting that they had a GSA at their school, up from 40% in 2007 (Kosciw et al. 2016). In addition, the first state anti-bullying law enumerating sexual orientation as a protected category was adopted in Vermont in 1992, yet by 2014, 18 states and the District of Columbia had adopted anti-bullying laws that protected both LGB and transgender students, with the biggest increase in state anti-bullying laws occurring in the 2000s. As of 2011, 1 in 10 U.S. school districts had an anti-bullying policy that enumerated both sexual orientation and gender identity/expression (Kull et al. 2015).

Despite the growing attention to LGBTQ student experiences, this population remains relatively understudied within the Sociology of Education. A search of articles in our flagship journal, *Sociology of Education*, reveals only two related articles, both of which address heteronormativity in schools but not LGBTQ youth directly (Gansen 2017; Ripley et al. 2012). Given the focus within our subfield on gendered socialization and educational inequalities, the lack of research on inequalities based on sexual orientation or the experiences of transgender students is puzzling. Importantly, this chapter is not intended to be a comprehensive review of research on LGBTQ students. Rather, our goals are to introduce some of the empirical research on the educational experiences, opportunities, and outcomes of sexual and gender minority youth and to situate these using theoretical frameworks that emphasize the importance of context. We focus on students in U.S. schools given both the scope of the literature on this population as well as cultural variation in the meaning and consequences of gender and sexual identities in schools (for an introduction to international perspectives of LGBTQ youth, see a recent special issue in the *Journal of LGBT Youth*, Kosciw and Pizmony-Levy 2016). Finally, we summarize what is

known about inclusive and effective policies, programs, and environments in schools, and provide some aims for future research.

9.1.1 Who Is LGBTQ? Conceptualization and Measurement Issues

The acronym LGBTQ refers to lesbian, gay, bisexual, transgender, or queer identified individuals, but is assumed to include a range of other sexual and gender identities (e.g., intersex, asexual, two-spirit, etc.) as well as individuals who are questioning or unsure of their sexual or gender identities. Given the complexity and multi-dimensionality of gender and sexuality, identifying who falls within the population of LGBTQ youth can be challenging. Our understanding of youth identities and experiences are shaped by existing data and the limitations of that data. In fact, as empirical research on LGBTQ youth has grown, particularly research using population-based samples of youth, the issue of identifying these youth has become even more complicated (Wagaman 2016).

Sexual orientation encompasses multiple dimensions, including sexual or romantic attraction, behaviors, relationships, and identities (Savin-Williams 2006). This multidimensionality makes it difficult to define groups or to compare the numbers and outcomes of "LGBQ" individuals across studies. Many individuals who experience same-sex attraction or have relationships or sexual encounters with someone of the same sex never identify as LGBQ (Friedman et al. 2004). This is a particularly important consideration for school-aged youth, as adolescence is a key period for identity development. In addition, LGB-identified women and men report feeling same-sex attractions at different developmental stages (Diamond 2003), and a majority of lesbian and gay identified adults have engaged in heterosexual sex at some point during their lives (Cochran et al. 1996; Einhorn and Polgar 1994; Saewyc 2011), often within a dating relationship (Baumeister 2000; Diamond 2003). Thus the number of youth we might categorize as LGBQ

Table 9.1 Mean age respondents first experienced transgender identity milestones by birth cohort

	Full sample	Millennials	Gen Xers	Baby Boomers	Silent Generation
Recognized difference due to gender	8.18	8.63	7.92	7.95	9.58
Identified as transgender or gender non-conforming	17.50	14.99	16.98	19.74	26.80
Began living as transgender or gender non-conforming	26.68	17.41	23.75	37.53	50.67
N	5162	1428	2145	1417	172

Source: Data from 2010 National Transgender Discrimination Survey

depends on which dimension of sexuality is considered, and these dimensions may have different impacts on the outcome being examined. Recent data from the Youth Risk Behavior Survey (one of the few nationally representative surveys of youth to include sexual orientation information) estimate that 2% of youth in grades 9 through 12 identify as gay or lesbian, 6% identify as bisexual, and 3.2% are unsure of their sexual identity. Of those youth who reported having had sexual contact, 3.6% had contact with same-sex partners only and 9.1% had contact with partners of both sexes (Kann et al. 2016). However, research using nationally representative data collected in the mid-1990s suggests that a much greater proportion of adolescents and young adults experience romantic or sexual attractions to others of their same-sex (Pearson and Wilkinson 2013), and these youth may or may not identify as LGBQ or engage in same-sex contact in adolescence. In addition, these different dimensions of same-sex sexuality as well as the timing of these experiences may have different implications for outcomes such as emotional well-being (Ueno 2010) and educational achievement and attainment (Pearson and Wilkinson 2017).

Similarly, transgender is an umbrella term that is often used to include numerous different gender identities and expressions. Transgender youth may identify as a gender different from that assigned to them at birth, whether in terms of a binary understanding of gender (e.g., a child assigned female at birth who identifies as a boy and/or expresses themselves in more masculine terms) or in non-binary ways (e.g., identifies as both masculine and feminine, as androgynous, as gender queer, or moves back and forth between masculine and feminine identities and expres-

sions). Importantly, not all youth who express gender variance in childhood or adolescence identify as transgender (Bartlett et al. 2000; Menvielle 2012). Transgender identities and gender variance have gained more visibility and understanding in recent years (Menvielle 2012; Schilt and Lagos 2017), with more awareness of transgender and gender variant students in schools (Case and Meier 2014; Schulman 2013). Transgender individuals are identifying and coming out as transgender at younger ages today compared to the past (Beemyn and Rankin 2011a; Hendricks and Testa 2012; Zucker et al. 2008). Table 9.1 presents the mean age at which individuals experience transgender identity milestones using data from the 2010 National Transgender Discrimination Survey. Note that the age at which individuals first felt different due to gender has not changed much across birth cohorts, with a mean age around 8 years old. However, the age at which individuals first identify or first begin living as transgender has changed dramatically, with Millennials first identifying around the age of 15, compared to Baby Boomers who first identified around the age of 20. Recent estimates suggest that about 0.7% of youth aged 13–17 identify as transgender (Herman et al. 2017). Translating to about 150,000 youth nationwide, such findings underscore the importance of understanding the experiences and opportunities of this population of students.

In this chapter, we use the terms *sexual and gender minority (SGM) youth* to include children, adolescents, and young adults with a range of sexual and gender identities, expressions, and behaviors. Given the importance of adolescence and emerging adulthood in identity development, we recognize that many youth who experience non-heterosexual desires, relationships, or contact may not yet or not ever identify as LGBQ. This may be particularly true of younger generations, as research finds some resistance by youth to identify with older sexual identity labels (Savin-Williams 2005), and Millennials (those born after 1981) are more likely than older generations to describe their gender and sexual identities in fluid and complex terms (Beemyn and Rankin 2011a; Vaccaro 2009; Wilkinson et al. 2016). Importantly, these identities and expressions intersect with youth's other social identities in ways that shape not only their experiences in schools but also the language they use to describe their identities. For example, communities of color may associate the identity labels gay and lesbian with Whiteness (DeBlaere et al. 2010), and may thus create new identity labels (such as "same gender loving") (Parks 2001; Wagaman 2016). SGM youth with disabilities experience discrimination based on gender, sexuality, and disability (Duke 2011). For example, youth with disabilities are often assumed to be asexual, so SGM youth with disabilities may be marginalized in or excluded from LGBTQ communities or spaces.

Both sexual and gender minority youth are impacted by gendered structures and gendered socialization that can create stigma and minority stress. SGM youth often face harassment and discrimination based on both their sexual orientation and gender expression, yet may also find strength and support through LGBTQ identities and supportive policies, programs, and environments. Below we identify key theoretical concepts for understanding how school cultures shape SGM youth's educational experiences and opportunities, focusing on the risk and resilience experienced by SGM youth in schools and the policies, programs, and supportive environments schools can provide.

9.1.2 Conceptualizing School Cultures: Heteronormativity and Minority Stress

9.1.2.1 Heteronormativity

In the United States, as in most other Western societies, heterosexism and transphobia are per-
vasive, resulting in a school culture dominated by heteronormativity. Within such a cultural landscape, heterosexuality is "produced as a natural, unproblematic, taken-for-granted, ordinary phenomenon" that is privileged relative to other deviant sexualities or sexual behaviors (Kitzinger 2005, p. 478). At the same time, the binary division of sex/gender and the social construction of gender difference is deeply entrenched, resulting in the construction and enforcement of hegemonic masculinities and emphasized femininities and the sanctioning of gender transgressions that deviate from normative forms of doing gender, including same-sex sexuality (Connell 1995; Pascoe 2007; West and Zimmerman 1987). Importantly, doing gender appropriately is premised on cisnormativity, or a binary division of gender that assumes an alignment between assigned sex at birth and personal gender identity and expression (Schilt and Westbrook 2009), leaving little room for transgender or gender nonconforming identities or expressions. We use the term *heteronormativity* to describe a hierarchical system in which heterosexual identities and expressions are privileged above nonheterosexual identities and expressions, where cisgender identities are privileged above noncisgender identities, where heterosexuality and cisgenderism are assumed and celebrated, and where anyone perceived as gender nonconforming, noncisgender, or nonheterosexual is stigmatized (Worthen 2016). Given the dominance of heteronormativity in our culture and thus within schools, SGM students, including those who are or are perceived to be transgender, gender nonconforming, or nonheterosexual, are often stigmatized, encountering additional stressors and fewer opportunities for educational success.

9.1.2.2 Gendered Sexual Socialization

It is often within schools that gender and sexual socialization, or "the process[es] through which individuals…come to understand rules, beliefs, meanings, and gender-specific codes of conduct associated with conducting oneself as 'proper' for girls and boys" (Gansen 2017, p. 256) occurs. Importantly, gender and sexual socialization are intersecting phenomena that happen simultaneously as teachers and peers conflate gender and sexuality, leading to gendered sexual socialization and sexualized gender socialization (Pascoe 2007). For example, preschool teachers often respond more positively to children's heterosexual (opposite-gender) romantic play than to children's same-gender romantic play (Gansen 2017). In secondary schools, heterosexual boys are often targets of "anti-gay" bullying when peers assess their behavior as deviating from expectations of hegemonic masculinity (Pascoe 2007; Swearer et al. 2008), and the "dyke" label is often assigned to girls who do not enact normative gender scripts assigned to women (Neilson et al. 2000). Given teachers' influence in the socialization of school-aged youth, LGBTQ educators have historically been targets of employment discrimination (Blount 2005; Graves 2015; Lugg and Adelman 2015), and heterosexism and cisgenderism remain pervasive in the field of education and teacher training (Elia and Eliason 2010; Graves 2015; Luker 2006).

SGM youth experience gender and sexual socialization from teachers and peers within a heteronormative culture during critical developmental periods. Transgender individuals first report feeling different due to their gender before the age of 12 (Beemyn and Rankin 2011a), suggesting that elementary school cultures are critical to the educational opportunities and experiences of transgender students. SGM students are also beginning to identify and to first live as transgender and LGBQ in adolescence more frequently today than in the past (Savin-Williams 2005; Vanderburgh 2009; Zucker et al. 2008), during a critical period in the life course when levels of school bullying and harassment are at their highest (Horn 2006; Poteat et al. 2009; Unnever and Cornell 2004), when bodily changes due to puberty may exacerbate experiences of gender dysphoria (Vanderburgh 2007), when the need to "fit in" among peers is heightened (Crosnoe 2011; Eccles and Roeser 2011), and when adaptive coping strategies are likely underdeveloped (Andersen and Teicher 2008). In many secondary schools status hierarchies are formed around heteronormativity, where popularity requires demonstrating heterosexuality and

appropriate gendered behaviors that match assigned sex/gender as well as the policing of peers' gender and sexuality (Bortolin 2010; Connell 2000; Kehily 2001; Martino 2000). It is important to consider the impact of gender and sexual socialization within school contexts, as stressors associated with an LGBTQ identity do not result from these identities themselves but from heteronormative contexts and ensuing minority stressors.

9.1.2.3 Minority Stress and Ecological Systems Theory

A minority stress framework helps explain the experience and potential consequences of stressors that accrue to sexual and gender minorities due to higher rates of stigma and discrimination in a society dominated by heteronormativity (Hendricks and Testa 2012; Lick et al. 2013; Meyer 2003, 2015). According to the minority stress theory, sexual minority and transgender identities are socially stigmatized statuses associated with greater exposure to prejudice and discrimination (Meyer 2003) through external processes, including actual experiences of rejection and discrimination, and through internal processes, such as perceived rejection and expectations of being stereotyped or discriminated against (Bockting et al. 2013; Goffman 1963; Herek 2007). Importantly, one's gender or sexual identity does not need to be known to others for one to experience minority stress (Goffman 1963; Herek 2007). In addition, stigmatized identities can also provide access to identity-based resources used to combat such risks, such as coping and social support that buffer the negative effects of stressors (Meyer 2015). A minority stress approach is inherently ecological (Bronfenbrenner 1977, 1986) as it focuses on environments rather than on individuals as the cause of stress (Meyer 1995). Thus, gender and sexual minority identities are not in themselves stressful, rather it is heteronormative contexts that create stress for gender and sexual minorities, and not all contexts are equally heteronormative (Chesir-Teran 2003). From an ecological systems perspective, it is important to consider the contexts in which SGM students are embedded, including the larger community, families, and the school context, and the minority stressors students are exposed to within each. Similarly, it is important to recognize potential resources available to SGM youth to combat stressors (Meyer 2015).

9.1.3 Variation in School Heteronormativity

Research suggests that gendered sexual socialization, minority stressors, and access to LGBTQ resources can vary dramatically from school to school. Below we identify the ways in which heteronormativity manifests itself within schools, how it varies across schools, and how heteronormative school culture is associated with the educational experiences and opportunities of SGM students. We focus on programs, policies, and supportive environments and discuss how each encompasses various features of heteronormative school cultures: physical-architectural, program-policy, suprapersonal, and social features (Chesir-Teran 2003; Moos and Lemke 1983). While we generally limit our discussion to schools, avoiding national politics and policies, it is important to recognize school contexts as microsystems embedded within a larger cultural context. Legal changes associated with same-sex marriage, LGBTQ persons in the military, and employment discrimination, for example, trickle down and impact school cultures (Bronfenbrenner 1986; Chesir-Teran 2003).

Programs are a nebulous feature of schools, including "official and unofficial…curricula as well as special programs, services, and resources such as assemblies, student clubs, counseling or health services, and library holdings" (Chesir-Teran 2003, p. 269). Programs can include those that actively resist heteronormativity, such as Gay–Straight Alliances (GSAs) and similar student clubs, teacher/counselor diversity training programs (Case and Meier 2014; Szalacha 2003), Safe Zone and ally programs (Finkel et al. 2003), inclusive school-based sexuality education (Black et al. 2012; Elia and Eliason 2010), and LGBTQ-inclusive curriculum and library

resources (Friend 1998; Kielwasser and Wolf 1994; Lipkin 1995; Rofes 1989). Such programs may reduce levels of victimization experienced by SGM youth by providing safe spaces and resources and creating a greater sense of belonging (Kosciw et al. 2010; Toomey et al. 2011), resulting in more positive school experiences. Programs relevant to SGM youth can also include, however, those that reinforce heteronormativity, such as non-inclusive curricula and the organization of classes and activities around the gender binary that assume heterosexuality (Castro and Sujak 2014; Elia and Eliason 2010; Mandel and Shakeshaft 2000; Wilkinson and Pearson 2009).

Policies include both official and unofficial policies that press against heteronormativity, such as formal anti-discrimination and anti-harassment policies, and those that reflect a press toward heteronormativity, such as policies reinforcing the gendered organization of pep rallies or prom, for example (Chesir-Teran 2003). While many districts in the U.S. have developed anti-harassment policies to address student bullying, many of these polices fail to adequately protect gender and sexual minority students, particularly transgender students, or do not actively prevent victimization (Kull et al. 2015). Beyond students, few states have adopted anti-discrimination policies to protect LGBTQ school workers (Lugg and Adelman 2015), yet policies impacting school workers have implications for students. New policy initiatives aimed at protecting the privacy and safety of transgender students are emerging at both the K–12 and postsecondary levels, through policies addressing restroom, locker room, and student housing access, for example. At the same time, heteronormative policies are emerging in response to such inclusive policies (Glenza 2015), and many policies aimed at subverting heteronormativity within schools do not have adequate support from administrators, staff, and communities (Kull et al. 2015).

Supportive Environments. While inclusive programs and policies are important for reducing heteronormativity within schools, these policies are unlikely to emerge without supportive administrators, staff, and parents, and existing programs and policies are more effective when developed within a supportive environment (Chesir-Teran and Hughes 2009; Evans 2002; Hatzenbuehler 2011; Kosciw et al. 2010). These findings highlight the importance of suprapersonal and social features of schools, which may represent more fundamental aspects of local cultures and present stumbling blocks to changes initiated through inclusive programs and policies. Suprapersonal features of schools represent the "average personal characteristics of a setting's members," which often shape the social features of schools, or the "behavioral or social regularities that reflect a press toward heterosexuality" and cis-normativity (Chesir-Teran 2003, p. 270). Variation in heteronormativity is "created and reinforced in part through the aggregation of staff and students' cultural schemas or habitus, which include taken-for-granted outlooks, beliefs, and experiences that are carried into and developed within schools" (Wilkinson and Pearson 2009, p. 547). Such cultural schemas are strongly influenced by the communities students and school personnel live within (e.g., region and locale), as well as by their individual characteristics such as religiosity, political orientation, race, gender, and social class (Barron and Bradford 2007; Eder and Parker 1987; Heath 2009; Messner 1992; Olson et al. 2006; Rostosky et al. 2004; Rubin 1999; Stein 2001; Wilson 1995).

In this chapter we highlight aspects of heteronormativity receiving the most attention in the literature, particularly the impact of program-policy features on SGM youth. When relevant we distinguish between levels of schooling, particularly K–12 and postsecondary contexts, but also between elementary education and secondary education, given developmental differences of students. Finally, we integrate throughout a discussion of the unique ways in which heteronormativity impacts transgender and gender variant students relative to sexual minority students and highlight best practices for addressing the needs of all SGM students. Before identifying the various ways programs and policies impact SGM students, we first review what we know about the educational experiences and outcomes of these youth.

9.2 Educational Experiences of Sexual and Gender Minority Youth

Research continues to document that SGM youth experience significantly more bullying and victimization than their heterosexual or cisgender peers (see Fedewa and Ahn 2011 for a meta-analysis; Greytak et al. 2009; Kosciw et al. 2015). GLSEN's National School Climate Study (NSCS) has been conducted every other year since 1999 and remains the primary data for information on national trends in SGM youth's experiences with bullying and harassment at school. The most recent data were collected in 2015 and provide reports from 10,528 students between the ages of 13 and 21 from all 50 states and the District of Columbia (Kosciw et al. 2016). The encouraging news is that results from the NSCS indicate that over the past 15 years there has been a decrease in the incidence of homophobic remarks and negative comments about gender expression as well as in verbal and physical harassment, as seen in Figs. 9.1 and 9.2. For example, the number of students reporting physical harassment based on sexual orientation has decreased from 41.9% in 2001 to 27% in 2015. However, as also reflected in this figure, SGM youth still report high rates of verbal and physical harassment at school.

The 2015 NSCS data demonstrate that a heteronormative discourse is common in schools and creates an unwelcoming environment. Two thirds (67%) of students in the NSCS reported hearing homophobic remarks at school frequently or often, 63% reported hearing negative comments about gender expression frequently or often, and 41% reported hearing negative comments about transgender people specifically frequently or often. Even more concerning was how frequently these comments came from adults in schools: Over half of students surveyed reported hearing negative comments about sexual orientation or gender expression from teachers and staff (Kosciw et al. 2016). More directed experiences of harassment are also common: A majority of SGM students (85%) reported experiencing verbal harassment at school, with 71% reporting the

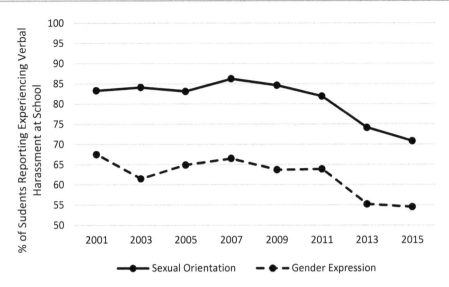

Fig. 9.1 Changes in rates of verbal harassment based on sexual orientation or gender expression, 2001–2015. (Source: Data from the National School Climate Survey, years 2001–2015. GLSEN)

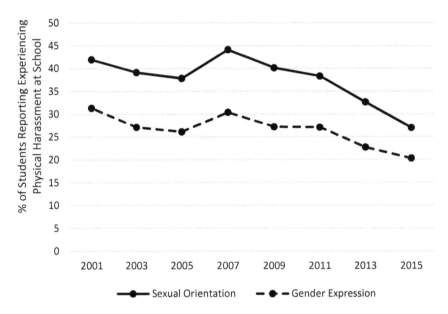

Fig. 9.2 Changes in rates of physical harassment based on sexual orientation or gender expression, 2001–2015. (Source: Data from the National School Climate Survey, years 2001–2015. GLSEN)

harassment was due to sexual orientation and 55% reporting it was due to gender expression (Fig. 9.1). Not surprisingly, many SGM students report feeling unsafe at school, with 58% feeling unsafe due to sexual orientation and 43% feeling unsafe due to their gender expression. These students' reports of specific types of harassment provide a clear picture of why they feel unsafe: About 1 in 4 students reported physical harassment (e.g., being pushed or shoved) due to sexual orientation, and 1 in 5 due to gender expression (Fig. 9.2). Even physical assault (being punched, kicked, or injured with a weapon) is not a rare occurrence for SGM youth: 13% reported being physically assaulted due to sexual orientation and 9% report being assaulted due to their gender expression. Heteronormative school contexts do not only impact SGM youth: Students from LGBTQ families may also experience stigma and discrimination (Russell et al. 2008; Van Gelderen et al. 2012).

Experiences of social exclusion and being targeted by peers impact SGM youth across the early life course. While elementary-age children may be allowed more flexibility in their gender expressions and engaging in "cross-gender" activities compared to older students, the physical and social world of elementary school is largely segregated by gender (Thorne 1993; Payne and Smith 2012). Parents of gender-variant children report that their children experience teasing and bullying at school (Riley et al. 2011) and at times fear for their safety (Hill and Menvielle 2009). Bullying and harassment is more prevalent in middle school (Kosciw et al. 2016; Nansel et al. 2001; Unnever and Cornell 2004), and older SGM youth report hearing fewer homophobic epithets and are less likely to be victimized in school (Kosciw et al. 2009). In addition, these experiences are not limited to primary and secondary schools: SGM college students are more likely than their heterosexual cisgender peers to rate their college campus climates as hostile, and they are more likely to experience discrimination and harassment (Rankin et al. 2010).

Faculty and staff also contribute to the heteronormative culture of a school, through their own language and behavior toward SGM students as well as their response to bullying and harassment taking place in the school. According to the 2015 NSCS, 64% of students who had reported incidents of harassment to school staff said that staff took no action or simply told the student to ignore the victimization. Only about 1 in 5 students reported that the perpetrator was disciplined, and in about 10% of incidents, the respondent was disciplined when reporting the harassment. One important consequence of this lack of action is its impact on reports of victimization: Over half of SGM students surveyed said they never reported an incident of harassment or assault to school

staff. Students also report being treated differently by faculty and staff because of their sexual orientation or gender expression; for example, 1 in 5 students were prevented from attending a school dance with a same-sex partner (Kosciw et al. 2016).

While hostile school environments are common for all SGM youth, transgender and gender non-conforming students report more harassment and victimization than their cisgender LGBQ peers (Greytak et al. 2009; Kosciw et al. 2008) and face the most hostile climates (Kosciw et al. 2016). Faculty and school administrators often directly contribute to this hostile climate by preventing students from expressing an authentic gender identity. For example, the NSCS study found that 42% of transgender students were prevented from using their preferred name at school, 59% had to use the bathroom associated with their legal sex, and 32% were prevented from wearing clothing consistent with their identity (because it was considered inappropriate for their legal sex) (Greytak et al. 2009). Gender minority students report frequently hearing homophobic language and derogatory comments about gender expression from both students and staff (Clements-Nolle et al. 2006; Greytak et al. 2009; Grossman and D'Augelli 2007). In the 2015 NSCS, 75% of transgender students reported feeling unsafe at school because of their gender expression, and they were more likely to be targeted for physical harassment and physical assault (Movement Advancement Project & GLSEN 2017). In fact, transgender students have described their experiences at school as among the most traumatic experiences of growing up (Grossman and D'Augelli 2006). This harassment often continues in college, with many transgender college students also reporting harassment, derogatory remarks, exclusion, and violence based on their gender identity (Griner et al. 2017; Rankin et al. 2010). The largest national study of LGBTQ college students to date, the 2010 National College Climate Survey, found that over 60% of LGB and transgender respondents reported being the target of derogatory remarks on campus. Such experiences take place within the classroom as well, with 42% of LGB students and 55% of transgender students reporting that they experienced harassment in the classroom (either from students or faculty) (Rankin et al. 2010).

Importantly, however, not all SGM youth confront a hostile school environment, and levels of heteronormativity differ across local schools and communities. Indeed, research finds that rates of victimization vary according to school context and school characteristics. Sexual minority youth report lower levels of victimization in large, more diverse urban schools compared to those with less economic or racial diversity (Goodenow et al. 2006). Conversely, SGM students in rural schools and schools in high-poverty communities report more victimization (Kosciw et al. 2009). Schools with greater numbers of college-bound students are associated with more tolerance of SGM students (Szalacha 2003), as are schools in communities with more college graduates (Kosciw et al. 2009). Regional differences emerge as well, with increased reports of homophobic remarks, harassment, and victimization among SGM students in the South and Midwest (Kosciw et al. 2009, 2016).

9.3 Consequences of Stigma and Discrimination for Educational Success

The stigma, marginalization, and discrimination faced in heteronormative school environments interact with SGM youths' experiences in their families and communities to shape their well-being, engagement in school, and ultimately their educational success. On average, SGM youth report lower levels of well-being and higher levels of emotional distress than their heterosexual, cisgender peers (Almeida et al. 2009; Grossman and D'Augelli 2007; Russell and Toomey 2012), with increased distress and lower self-esteem among those who experience more harassment at school (Kosciw et al. 2014). SGM youth are also more likely to run away from home, be thrown out by their parents, and experience homelessness (Corliss et al. 2011; Pearson et al. 2017; Waller and Sanchez 2011), all of which have

implications for their educational success (Edidin et al. 2012; Whitbeck 2009). Hostile school environments and experiences of victimization lead SGM youth to miss more days of school (Robinson and Espelage 2011, 2012). For example, almost one third of students in the 2015 NSCS report missing at least one day of school in the past month because they felt unsafe or uncomfortable, and 10% reported missing four days or more (Kosciw et al. 2016). SGM youth may also respond to hostile classrooms or school climates by disengaging from school, their teachers, and their coursework (Pearson et al. 2007; Poteat and Espelage 2007; Rostosky et al. 2003; Russell et al. 2001) or from extracurricular activities (Kosciw et al. 2014).

As a result of these minority stress processes, SGM youth's academic performance may suffer (Aragon et al. 2014; Pearson et al. 2007; Watson and Russell 2016). Same-sex attracted students, particularly boys, leave high school with lower grades and are more likely to fail a course (Pearson et al. 2007). Sexual minority students also complete less advanced coursework in math and science (Pearson and Wilkinson 2017; Pearson et al. 2007), which is linked to college admission and success. While some research suggests this may be due in part to different occupational interests or expectations (Badgett and King 1997; Blandford 2003; Hewitt 1995), research suggests an important link to experiences of stigma and discrimination: More in-school victimization is associated with more truancy, lower grades, and lower educational expectations (Aragon et al. 2014; Kosciw et al. 2013), both directly and through its association with well-being (Kosciw et al. 2015).

At the same time, SGM youth demonstrate resilience in the face of heteronormativity and minority stress, carving out safe spaces and seeking out resources within their schools and communities in order to get the support they need to succeed in school. For example, SGM students describe forming and participating in GSAs and similar clubs as empowering (Russell et al. 2009), and some may find a home in extracurricular activities (Toomey and Russell 2013). A majority of SGM students plan to attend college (Kosciw et al. 2014) and may migrate to cities and college towns in search of more tolerant and diverse environments (Annes and Redlin 2012). Certainly many SGM students emerge from high school with high grades, expectations, and attainment (Ueno et al. 2013; Watson and Russell 2016). One way in which SGM students may demonstrate resilience within heteronormative environments is by being "out" to their families, peers, and teachers. While being out to more individuals may make an SGM student more vulnerable to victimization, particularly in rural schools, it is also associated with higher self-esteem and lower levels of depressive symptoms (Kosciw et al. 2015). SGM students who were out to friends, family, and others at school reported lower rates of harassment and higher grades than those who were only out to some groups or individuals (Watson et al. 2015).

Research is less consistent when it comes to SGM college students. While research on campus climates and the experiences of LGBTQ college students demonstrate that they face similar concerns as SGM students in secondary schools, data on the academic performance and engagement of SGM students is less clear. A study using the National Survey of Student Engagement (NSSE) found no differences between LGBTQ-identified and non-LGBTQ students in self-reported grades (Gonyea and Moore 2007), and other research has found *higher* grades among male college students with same-sex sexual partners (Carpenter 2009). However, research using campus climate surveys indicate that LGBTQ-identified respondents are more likely than their heterosexual, cisgender peers to consider leaving their institution, and this difference increased with each year of study (Rankin et al. 2010). Colleges offer a site for identity exploration for SGM students that may provide them with important resources and supports to resist heteronormativity and buffer against minority stressors. Increased advocacy on college campuses has led to a growth in supportive spaces and policies (Beemyn 2015; Beemyn and Rankin 2011b), which allow SGM college students increased opportunities to participate in social, academic, and leadership activities related to LGBTQ issues

(Longerbeam et al. 2007; Renn and Bilodeau 2005) that may promote positive identity development (Annes and Redlin 2012; Zemsky 2004).

The association between SGM identity and long-term educational attainment is also unclear. Though research on K–12 students finds lower levels of academic engagement and performance on average among SGM youth compared to their heterosexual, cisgender peers, research on the educational attainment of SGM adults is less consistent. For example, research using census data finds *higher* levels of education among men and women in same-sex cohabiting partnerships (Antecol et al. 2008; Black et al. 2000; Clain and Leppel 2001; Elmslie and Tebaldi 2007; Jepsen 2007). Similarly, research using nonprobability samples finds *higher* levels of education among lesbian women and gay-identified men compared to their heterosexual peers (Carpenter 2005; Rothblum et al. 2004), and similar (Black et al. 2003) or higher (Carpenter 2007) levels of education among men and women with same-sex sexual partners. And while the 2015 U.S. Transgender Survey was not a probability sample, respondents had an average level of education higher than that of the general U.S. population (38% of respondents had a four-year degree or higher) (James et al. 2016). These patterns appear to depend on timing of identity development, gender, and context, which may explain differences between youth and adult samples. Research suggests that the age at which men identify as gay is positively associated with attainment (Barrett et al. 2002), and the experience of same-sex sexuality in *adulthood* is associated with increased educational attainment among men but not women (Fine 2014; Ueno et al. 2013, Pearson and Wilkinson 2017). Sexual minority men who experienced same-sex sexuality only in adolescence struggled in high school, and sexual minority women are less likely to complete college due to their high school performance and transition into college (Pearson and Wilkinson 2017).

Just as SGM student experiences vary by school context, so too does their academic performance and long-term educational attainment depend on the type of school they attend. For example, previous research suggests that sexual minority youth may have poorer academic outcomes in rural communities compared to their counterparts in urban areas (Wilkinson and Pearson 2009). Rural communities are often characterized by a lack of visibility of LGBTQ people and spaces (Paceley 2016) and higher levels of homophobic or heterosexist attitudes among residents (Dillon and Savage 2006; Herek 2002; Sherkat et al. 2011). Similarly, SGM youth in schools with lower levels of religiosity and less emphasis on hyper-masculine sports such as football, two aspects of school culture linked to heteronormativity, perform better than those in more religious and more football-dominant school environments (Wilkinson and Pearson 2009). As discussed in more detail below, school programs, policies, and the presence of supportive school staff also moderate the association between SGM status and educational success. Students in schools with more supportive teachers and staff reported less victimization, fewer missed days of school, and higher grades (Diaz et al. 2010; Goodenow et al. 2006; Kosciw et al. 2013), and more inclusive curriculum (i.e., positive representations of LGBTQ people and history) is associated with higher educational expectations (Kosciw et al. 2016) and higher grades among SGM students (Kosciw et al. 2013). These findings demonstrate that academic risks do not stem directly from the experience of same-sex sexuality or diverse gender identities, but are a result of a heteronormative and cisnormative culture that leads to feelings of difference, discrimination, and a lack of social support for SGM youth (Eisenberg and Resnick 2006; Hatzenbuehler et al. 2014; Meyer 2003). Moreover, the benefits of a positive school climate for SGM youth extends beyond educational success, with implications for depressive symptoms and suicidal ideation (Birkett et al. 2009); for example, sexual minority youth who live in areas with more protective school climates reported fewer suicidal thoughts than those in less protective climates (Hatzenbuehler et al. 2014). Climate studies on college campuses also find that a more positive climate improves SGM students' well-being and academic achievement (Rankin et al. 2010).

9.4 Creating Supportive School Environments for Sexual and Gender Minority Youth

Research on the educational experiences and outcomes of SGM youth demonstrate the importance of providing SGM youth with inclusive programs, policies, and supportive environments that reduce minority stressors and increase access to resilience-promoting resources. Research on supportive schools emphasizes the following: (1) provision of resources and curricula covering the history and experiences of LGBTQ people, (2) support for student clubs such as GSAs, (3) creation of professional development opportunities for school staff, (4) ensuring school practices do not discriminate against SGM students, and (4) adoption and implementation of comprehensive anti-harassment policies that include protections based on sexual orientation and gender identity/ expression (Kosciw et al. 2016). Importantly, these inclusive programs and policies are less effective when deployed in environments that are not supportive, highlighting the importance of community context and the social characteristics of school administrators, staff, and parents. Some aspects of school context, particularly formal programs and policies such as GSAs and anti-harassment/anti-bullying policies, have received a great deal of attention and empirical support in studies of SGM students. Other aspects of school contexts have been understudied. Further, we know little about the mechanisms through which these school features impact SGM youth well-being and educational success; therefore, we end by highlighting important areas for future research.

9.4.1 Programs

Gay–Straight Alliances (GSAs) are perhaps the most well-known and most frequently assessed form of inclusive programming. GSAs are "extra-curricular groups in high schools that support and advocate for lesbian, gay, bisexual, transgender, and queer students…[and] include students of any sexual orientation, including heterosexual"

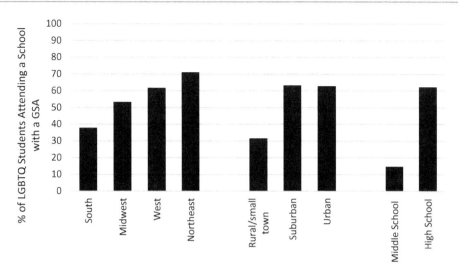

Fig. 9.3 Prevalence of Gay–Straight Alliances by region, locale, and level of schooling. (Source: Data from Kosciw et al. (2016). The 2015 National School Climate Survey. GLSEN)

(Fetner and Kush 2008, p. 1). GSAs serve a variety of functions, including awareness, advocacy, and provision of safe and affirming spaces for SGM students (Griffin et al. 2004). These clubs emerged in the late 1980s and 1990s, and exploded in the 2000s (Fetner and Kush 2008; Meyer 2015), with more than 4,000 GSAs in U.S. schools today (Poteat et al. 2012). Yet many SGM youth still lack access to GSAs (Kosciw et al. 2016), particularly SGM students of color, those in the South and in rural areas, and students in middle schools (Fetner and Kush 2008; Kosciw et al. 2016), as seen in Fig. 9.3. For example, while 63% of SGM students in urban and suburban schools reported having a GSA at their school, only 31.4% of SGM students in small towns/rural areas reported having a GSA at their school (Kosciw et al. 2016). And while 62% of high school SGM students surveyed in the 2015 NSCS reported having a GSA at their school, only 14.5% of LGBTQ middle school students surveyed reported having a GSA at their school. This is significant given GSAs play an important role in reducing heteronormativity within schools by signaling to students and staff that heterosexism and transphobia are not tolerated (Kosciw et al. 2008; Russell et al. 2009), making schools safer for SGM students (Lee 2002; Russell et al. 2010), and creating a greater sense of belonging

(Kosciw et al. 2008; Greytak et al. 2013b; Kosciw et al. 2010). SGM students in schools with GSAs are more often able to identity and access supportive staff (Kosciw et al. 2016) in part because GSAs require a faculty advisor. The presence of GSAs is also associated with better educational outcomes among SGM youth (Kosciw et al. 2010; Kosciw et al. 2008) as well as with less heterosexism and transphobia expressed by non-SGM students (Miceli 2005; Worthen 2016). Importantly, GSAs have been found to have a positive impact on transgender students, even though many GSAs and other LGBTQ programs are often not explicitly inclusive of transgender students and transgender issues (Greytak et al. 2013b).

Another important aspect of LGBTQ-inclusive programming is counseling and teacher training programs. Historically, counseling and teacher education programs have not adequately prepared school personnel to serve the needs of SGM youth, often excluding training on transgender youth (Carroll 2010; Cole et al. 2000). Given gender identity development begins prior to kindergarten (Beemyn and Rankin 2011a; Menvielle 2012), this is a critical oversight on the part of teacher training programs, suggesting the need for schools to provide continuing education on LGBTQ issues. Continuing education through diversity and ally training programs are thus critical aspects of inclusive programs aimed at reducing heteronormativity within schools (Szalacha 2003; Payne and Smith 2012). Research on educator training suggests that school personnel may be resistant to learning about or supporting inclusive LGBTQ programs and policies (Payne and Smith 2012), highlighting the importance of educator-to-educator training models that are school specific. Such resistance on the part of school workers also highlights the role of suprapersonal features of schools, including individuals' attitudes toward and acceptance of SGM youth.

Other aspects of school programming may work in tandem with LGBTQ-inclusive training for school personnel. As an example, research suggests schools that create visible safe spaces and identify particular staff as allies increase feelings of belonging and connectedness among SGM students (Finkel et al. 2003). In schools with teachers trained on LGBTQ issues, formal and informal school-based sexuality education may be more inclusive and less likely to be taught from a heterosexual perspective that excludes LGBTQ people and experiences (Elia and Eliason 2010; Black et al. 2012). Beyond formal programs such as GSAs and Safe Zones that focus on creating "safe" spaces for SGM students, inclusive programs need to go further to address and disrupt the underlying heteronormative organization of schools such as gendered spaces and activities (Blackburn and Pascoe 2015; Worthen 2014). Additionally, inclusive programs need to ensure they are accessible to all students, including students who have been historically marginalized in the LGBTQ community, such as youth of color and those attending smaller high schools (McCready 2004; Miceli 2005; Worthen 2011) and who may live in communities that are less tolerant and supportive of inclusive school programming, such as those in small towns, rural areas, and in the South (Fetner and Kush 2008).

At the postsecondary level, LGBTQ resource centers and safe-space programs are becoming common (Beemyn 2015; Poynter and Tubbs 2008; Rankin 2005), yet these programs may be inadequate in challenging heteronormativity on college campuses and providing equal opportunity for SGM students, particularly transgender students (Singh et al. 2013). Transgender students and students of color are less likely to access designated LGBTQ centers and student groups, relative to LGBQ students and White students (Seelman 2016). And while many LGBTQ centers have added a "T" to their names as a token response, many are unable to provide proper training on transgender issues and lack adequate resources for serving transgender students (Beemyn 2005; Nicolazzo and Marine 2015). The extent to which postsecondary institutions adequately address the needs of their SGM student population varies dramatically, with groups like Campus Pride providing ratings and ranking of campus climates for SGM students based on institutional supports, protective policies, and LGBTQ programming (Campus Pride Index 2017). However, similar to K–12 schools, postsecondary institutions should consider the subtle and explicit ways in which everyday programs stigmatize gender variance and nonheterosexuality, as not all SGM students identify as LGBTQ or are able to access formal programs developed for LGBTQ students.

9.4.2 Policies

A key element of inclusive policies are district and school-level anti-harassment policies that specifically protect SGM students. As of 2011, nearly 30% of U.S. school districts did not have any type of anti-harassment policy (Kull et al. 2015). Of those districts that did have a policy, less than half enumerated protections for students based on sexual orientation, and very few (14%) enumerated protections for students based on gender identity and/or expression. Even districts that have formal anti-harassment policies often lack broad anti-discrimination policies that go beyond bullying or harassment. This is particularly relevant for transgender students who are more often excluded from school anti-harassment policies. GLSEN recommends covering the following in anti-discrimination policies in order to make schools safe and welcoming for transgender students: protect the privacy and confidentiality of transgender students; provide training on the use of preferred pronouns and names; provide access to safe restrooms and other physical features by allowing gender-neutral facilities or use of facilities that match a student's preferred gender identity; provide flexibility with gender-specific dress codes; and have counselors and nurses who are able to support the social or medical transitioning of transgender students (National Center for Transgender Equality & GLSEN 2016).

Yet it is not enough to have an enumerated policy if school administrators and staff do not support it and if systems of accountability are not in place (Kull et al. 2015). GLSEN recommends district anti-harassment policies include the following elements: enumerated protection for sexual orientation and gender identity/expression, professional development requirements for staff, and accountability; yet, as of 2011 only 4% of school district policies included all three of these elements (Kull et al. 2015). The extent to which anti-harassment policies reduce levels of SGM student victimization remains unclear given most school policies focus on reporting, investigation, and sanctioning, rather than on prevention, and may not adequately train staff on how to intervene (Kosciw et al. 2010; Greytak et al. 2013a). Research suggests comprehensive anti-harassment policies that enumerate gender identity/expression and sexual orientation are associated with feelings of greater safety, less absenteeism (Greytak et al. 2013b), and more positive psychological outcomes (Span 2011) among SGM youth, and heteronormativity is often less visible in schools with inclusive anti-harassment policies (Chesir-Teran and Hughes 2009). It is important, however, to consider issues of selection and causality given many schools that develop inclusive policies (and programs) are likely already less heteronormative than are schools that do not develop inclusive policies. Students, staff, and parents in schools with LGBTQ-inclusive policies are likely more supportive of SGM students, which could lead simultaneously to both adoption of inclusive policies and better outcomes for SGM students in these schools.

Importantly, the existence of and inclusiveness of anti-harassment policies varies by school district characteristics, highlighting the influence of suprapersonal features of schools, or the aggregate characteristics of students and staff (Chesir-Teran 2003), and systems beyond the microsystem of the school (Bronfenbrenner 1977, 1986): Districts in the Northeast are most likely to have any anti-harassment policy, while those in the South and in rural districts are least likely to have any anti-harassment policy, to have LGBTQ-inclusive policies, or to require professional development related to LGBTQ issues. Districts with inclusive policies that require professional development, which is a best practice, are more likely to be in districts with higher student populations and higher socioeconomic status (Kosciw et al. 2016). As seen in Fig. 9.4, while nearly 17% of SGM students in the Northeast attended a school with a comprehensive anti-harassment policy, only 5% of SGM students in the South attended such a school. SGM students attending schools in a rural area or small town were also less likely to attend schools with comprehensive anti-harassment policies, relative to SGM students attending urban or suburban schools (Kosciw et al. 2016).

Research and practice tends to emphasize anti-harassment policies impacting students, failing to address protections for school personnel. Faculty and staff fearful about their own identities and expressions are less likely to advocate on behalf of SGM students, with implications for the school environments of SGM students. As of 2017, 50% of the LGBTQ population was living in states that did not prohibit employment discrimination based on sexual orientation or gender identity (ACLU 2017; Movement Advancement Project 2017), and teacher training programs continue to be influenced by heteronormativity with a focus on gender as natural and binary and heterosexuality as normative (Gunn 2011). In the U.S., there is a storied history of discrimination against school workers based on assumed or actual nonheterosexuality and gender nonconformity (Blount 2005; Graves 2015; Griffin and

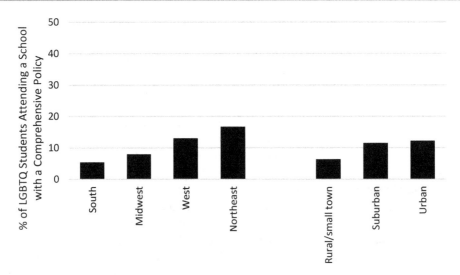

Fig. 9.4 Prevalence of comprehensive anti-bullying/harassment policies, by region and locale. (Source: Data from Kosciw et al. (2016). The 2015 National School Climate Survey. GLSEN)

Ouellett 2003). Research at the postsecondary level indicates that students' evaluate their professors in part based on professors' sexual and gender identities (Anderson and Kanner 2011; Russ et al. 2002), with implications for educators revealing their identities to students. Creating less heteronormative environments for SGM students requires providing SGM school staff and educators greater protections through workplace anti-discrimination policies.

Another important component of inclusive policies are those related to physical-architectural features of schools, including the design of and access to restrooms, locker rooms, and student housing (Chesir-Teran 2003; Healy and Perez-Pena 2016; Schilt and Westbrook 2015). The layout of restrooms, locker rooms, and showers may reinforce the gender binary and increase levels of stress and victimization of SGM students. It is important that youth have access to privacy when changing and showering and access to safe restrooms that match their gender identity, preferably multiple-occupancy gender-neutral restrooms with lockable single-occupancy stalls (zamantakis et al. 2017). During the Obama Administration, Title IX protections were extended to include (trans)gender identity, requiring schools receiving federal funding to allow transgender students to access bathrooms and locker rooms that matched their gender identity, regardless of assigned birth sex. Yet this change unleashed backlash in the form of proposed "bathroom bills" in many state legislatures, and the Trump administration quickly rescinded Title IX protections for transgender students (Kreighbaum 2017). Transgender students often identity bathroom access as one of the most difficult aspects of navigating campus life (Bilodeau 2007), and while colleges and universities are beginning to become aware of and address the need for gender-neutral restrooms across campus (Seelman 2016; zamantakis et al. 2017; Zippin 2015), progress is slow, and less change has occurred at the elementary and secondary levels. Not surprisingly, resistance has been stronger in rural districts, districts located in the South, or in otherwise socially conservative areas (Zippin 2015). Housing policies and those associated with the healthcare of transgender students become more relevant at the postsecondary level, as institutions must address the on-campus housing and medical needs of gender minority students. This includes providing options for gender-congruent or gender-neutral/inclusive housing, giving students the ability to make their own choices about where they can and cannot live, and considering the unique physical and mental health needs of transgender students.

9.4.3 Supportive Environments

Supportive school environments are crucial for the development and implementation of inclusive programs and policies; LGBTQ-inclusive policies and programs are less effective when not supported by staff and the larger school community. While schools may adopt anti-harassment policies and provide space for GSAs, school staff may vary in the extent to which they value and support such policies and programs (Evans 2002; Steck and Perry 2016; Swanson and Gettinger 2016), integrate LGBTQ issues into the formal or informal curriculum (Russell et al. 2006; Kosciw et al. 2010; Greytak et al. 2013b), intervene in anti-LGBTQ harassment, or advocate for SGM students (Gonzalez and McNulty 2010; Goodenow et al. 2006; Toomey et al. 2010). Supportive school staff, committed leadership, and staff that intervene when harassment occurs are also independently associated with the well-being of SGM students (Elze 2003; Evans 2002; Kosciw et al. 2010; Russell et al. 2010), highlighting the importance of suprapersonal and social features of schools in creating educational opportunities for SGM students and reducing heteronormativity.

A supportive environment may be particularly important for transgender and gender variant youth, given transgender students are more often excluded from anti-harassment policies (Kosciw et al. 2016), anti-bullying education (GLSEN and Harris Interactive 2008), and from formal programs such as GSAs (Kosciw et al. 2016). Educators are often less educated on issues relevant to transgender students and may themselves engage in harassment of transgender youth (Grossman and D'Augelli 2006; McGuire et al. 2010; Sausa 2005). Parents who identify their children as gender nonconforming at a young age often have concerns about their child's transition into elementary school, including whether the elementary school is safe and if staff are adequately trained to meet the needs of gender variant children (Slesaransky-Poe 2013). Best practices recommend parents take an active role by communicating early with the school principal, counselors, and teachers, yet this places the burden on parents, and research suggests that it is children from two-parent, higher-SES families who are more likely to have parents advocate on their behalf (Vanderburgh 2007). In order to more equitably address the needs of SGM children and youth, schools should be proactive by providing staff training, collaborating with community resources, and integrating discussion of gender variance into classrooms.

While supportive environments are critical for the development and effectiveness of inclusive programs and policies, the extent to which environments are supportive is more difficult to measure, relative to measuring if a school has or has not adopted a particular policy or program, for example. Creating a supportive environment is also more challenging: Positive attitudes toward SGM youth and the acceptance of "alternative" lifestyles cannot be mandated, and creating changes at the suprapersonal and social levels, particularly in communities historically intolerant of gender variance and nonheterosexuality, requires continued change at the larger cultural level. Yet history has shown that legal changes, particularly at the federal level, force program-policy changes that often lead to attitudinal and cultural changes (Lugg and Adelman 2015). Advocates for SGM students continue to urge more action at the federal level through passage of legislation that would, for example, require all districts to include sexual orientation and gender identity/expression as protected categories in anti-harassment policies (Russell et al. 2010). It is also important to recognize the power of grassroots movements such as those that led to the creation of GLSEN and the emergence of GSAs and other LGBTQ-inclusive policies and programs (Graves 2015).

9.5 Conclusions and Implications for Future Research

In this chapter, we considered how heteronormativity in schools creates contexts in which SGM youth are stigmatized and exposed to minority stressors that have consequences for their mental and physical health, academic engagement, and long-term educational opportunities. Existing research has also explored how particular programs and policies can help to disrupt heteronormativity in schools and provide resources and support for SGM students. Importantly, SGM youth also demonstrate a great deal of resilience in the face of hostile environments, finding a sense of empowerment from their identities, seeking out or creating safe spaces such as GSAs or LGBTQ resource centers, and earning high grades and college degrees despite experiences of harassment and exclusion.

Previous research also demonstrates the complexity and dynamic nature of youth gender and sexual identities: SGM youth today do not fall neatly into categories marked "gay" and "straight" or "male" and "female," and many are seeking to actively disrupt these binary understandings of gender and sexuality. This has important implications for researchers studying SGM youth and those who want to advocate for safer, more inclusive schools. Rather than using methods better suited for older generations, we need to attend to the ways in which youth themselves understand their gender and sexuality in order to develop measures that will accurately identify this population and adequately describe their educational experiences and opportunities.

A lack of high-quality, longitudinal data limits our understanding of the mechanisms through which heteronormativity impacts SGM youths' well-being, academic engagement and performance, and long-term educational attainment. At the middle and high school level, widely used data sets from the National Center for Education Statistics continue to omit questions for identifying sexual and gender minority youth. The National Longitudinal Study of Adolescent to Adult Health (Add Health) remains the only longitudinal data that includes information about sexual orientation in addition to educational experiences and outcomes, and the respondents in that study attended school over 20 years ago. While GLSEN continues to provide extensive data about school experiences of sexual and gender minority youth, heterosexual, cisgender youth are not surveyed; thus, there is no compari-

son group from which to document inequalities and explore differences. The Youth Risk Behavior Survey (YRBS) now includes sexual orientation and sexual contact (but not sexual attraction) in both the national, state, and local questionnaires for high school students (but not middle school students), and can now be used to compare SGM youth to their heterosexual, cisgender peers on a range of healthy behaviors and outcomes. However, YRBS provides little information about school experiences or outcomes, and still does not contain inclusive measures of gender identity that could be used to identify gender minority youth. National data on college students is also lacking. Data from the American Freshman Survey (Cooperative Institutional Research Program 2016) and the National Survey of Student Engagement (NSSE) data (Indiana University Center for Postsecondary Research 2017) now ask about both sexual orientation and gender identity and allow researchers to explore the academic attitudes, behaviors, and outcomes of SGM college students at the national level. However, these studies do not provide data on experiences of sexual or gender identity-related stigma, discrimination, or supports.

Research reviewed in this chapter also underscores the importance of school context for SGM well-being and educational success. Previous studies document extensive variation across schools and districts in the policies and programs offered within schools, the prevalence of bullying and harassment of SGM youth, and the short- and long-term educational outcomes of SGM youth. On average, SGM youth tend to fare worse in rural schools, high-poverty schools, smaller schools, and schools in the South. Conversely, SGM youth have better outcomes when their schools have a GSA, inclusive curriculum, and supportive staff. Qualitative studies of SGM students provide important examples of how school context can shape the meanings attached to same-sex sexuality and diverse gender expressions as well as how this may impact the daily experiences of SGM youth. However, given the lack of longitudinal data with rich contextual information, we know less about how these characteristics translate to better educational outcomes and what the long-term consequences of particular programs and policies may be. Moreover, we have less understanding of how these features of schools interact with individual characteristics or with overlapping contexts of families and communities.

There is clearly a need for nationally representative, longitudinal data tracking the educational trajectories and contexts of SGM students at both the K–12 and postsecondary levels. First, longitudinal data would help researchers address issues of selection and better assess causal relationships. For example, previous research finds higher educational attainment among men who first experience same-sex sexuality or first identify as gay in adulthood (Pearson and Wilkinson 2017; Ueno et al. 2013); however, the direction of this association is unclear, as it is possible that the experience of attending college shapes how men recognize, interpret, and respond to feelings toward other men (Barrett and Pollack, 2005; Evans and Herriott 2004). In addition, research is not able to discern whether the effectiveness of particular programs and policies such as GSAs and anti-bullying policies are a result of the program or policy itself or of a less heteronormative school culture that both reduces minority stressors for SGM youth and leads to the creation of such programs and policies. Second, more research is needed to create age-appropriate programs and policies for elementary and middle schools, given that gender and sexual socialization begin so early (Gansen 2017; Martin 1998; Martin and Kazyak 2009). GLSEN notes that only 14% of middle school students have access to a GSA, but research finds that SGM youth are exploring their identities at that age and earlier (Beemyn and Rankin 2011a; Savin-Williams 2005). Finally, research on school programs, policies, and cultures should be accompanied by information about the larger cultural context and overlapping systems of families and communities. While schools may have more difficulty implementing programs and policies when surrounded by more heteronormative communities and resistant families, such programs and policies are likely even more essential in such contexts, not only because they offer protection and safe spaces for students within hostile environments but they may lead to cultural shifts in local contexts as well. Given the tremendous changes over the past 20 years in the school experiences and opportunities of SGM youth, research should continue to explore the most needed and most influential practices that will improve the success of SGM students.

References

ACLU. (2017). Past LGBT nondiscrimination and anti-LGBT bills across the country. https://www.aclu.org/other/past-lgbt-nondiscrimination-and-anti-lgbt-bills-across-country#affirmnondisc. Accessed 28 Sept 2017.

Almeida, J., Johnson, R. M., Corliss, H. L., Molnar, B. E., & Azrael, D. (2009). Emotional distress among LGBT youth: The influence of perceived discrimination based on sexual orientation. *Journal of Youth and Adolescence, 38*, 1001–1014.

Andersen, S. L., & Teicher, M. H. (2008). Stress, sensitive periods and maturational events in adolescent depression. *Trends in Neurosciences, 31*, 183–191.

Anderson, K. J., & Kanner, M. (2011). Inventing a gay agenda: Students' perceptions of lesbian and gay professors. *Journal of Applied Social Psychology, 41*(6), 1538–1564. https://doi.org/10.1111/j.1559-1816.2011.00757.x.

Annes, A., & Redlin, M. (2012). Coming out and coming back: Rural gay migration and the city. *Journal of Rural Studies, 28*, 56–68.

Antecol, H., Jong, A., & Steinberger, M. (2008). The sexual orientation wage gap: The role of occupational sorting and human capital. *Industrial and Labor Relations Review, 61*, 518–543. https://doi.org/10.2307/25249171.

Aragon, S. R., Poteat, V. P., Espelage, D. L., & Koenig, B. W. (2014). The influence of peer victimization on educational outcomes for LGBTQ and non-LGBTQ high school students. *Journal of LGBT Youth, 11*(1), 1–19. https://doi.org/10.1080/19361653.2014.840761.

Badgett, M. V. L., & King, M. (1997). Lesbian and gay occupational strategies. In A. Gluckman & B. Reed (Eds.), *Capitalism, community, and lesbian and gay life*. New York: Routledge.

Barrett, D. C., & Pollack, L. M. (2005). Whose gay community? Social class, sexual self-expression, and gay community involvement. *Sociological Quarterly, 46*, 437–456. https://doi.org/10.1111/j.1533-8525.2005.00021.x.

Barrett, D. C., Pollack, L. M., & Tilden, M. L. (2002). Teenage sexual orientation, adult openness, and status attainment in gay males. *Sociological Perspectives, 45*(2), 163–182. https://doi.org/10.1525/sop.2002.45.2.163.

Barron, M., & Bradford, S. (2007). Corporeal controls: Violence, bodies, and young gay men's identities. *Youth & Society, 39*, 232–261.

Bartlett, N. H., Vasey, P. L., & Bukowski, W. M. (2000). Is gender identity disorder in children a mental disorder? *Sex Roles, 43*(11/12), 753–785.

Baumeister, R. F. (2000). Gender differences in erotic plasticity: The female sex drive as socially flexible and responsive. *Psychological Bulletin, 126*, 347–374.

Beemyn, B. G. (2005). Trans on campus: Measuring and improving the climate for transgender students. *On Campus with Women, 34*(3), 77–87.

Beemyn, G. (2015). Campus Pride Trans Policy Clearinghouse. http://www.campuspride.org/tpc. Accessed 29 Sept 2017.

Beemyn, G., & Rankin, S. (2011a). *The lives of transgender people.* New York: Columbia University Press.

Beemyn, G., & Rankin, S. (2011b). Introduction to the special issue on "LGBTQ campus experiences". *Journal of Homosexuality, 58*, 1159–1164. https://doi.org/10.1080/00918369.2011.605728.

Bilodeau, B. L. (2007). *Genderism: Transgender students, binary systems and higher education.* Doctoral dissertation, ProQuest Dissertations and Theses Database (UMI No. 3264140).

Birkett, M., Espelage, D. L., & Koenig, B. (2009). LGB and questioning students in schools: The moderating effects of homophobic bullying and school climate on negative outcomes. *Journal of Youth and Adolescence, 38*(7), 989–1000.

Black, D., Gates, G., Sanders, S., & Taylor, L. (2000). Demographics of the gay and lesbian population in the United States: Evidence from available systematic data sources. *Demography, 37*, 139–154. https://doi.org/10.2307/2648117.

Black, D., Makar, H. R., Sanders, S. G., & Taylor, L. J. (2003). The earnings effects of sexual orientation. *Industrial & Labor Relations Review, 56*, 449–469. https://doi.org/10.1177/001979390305600305.

Black, W. W., Fedewa, A. L., & Gonzalez, K. A. (2012). Effects of "Safe School" programs and policies on the social climate for sexual-minority youth: A review of the literature. *Journal of LGBT Youth, 9*(4), 321–339. https://doi.org/10.1080/19361653.2012.714343.

Blackburn, M., & Pascoe, C. J. (2015). K–12 students in schools. In G. L. Wimberly (Ed.), *LGBTQ issues in education: Advancing a research agenda* (pp. 89–104). Washington, DC: AERA.

Blandford, J. M. (2003). The nexus of sexual orientation and gender in the determination of earnings. *ILR Review, 56*(4), 622–642.

Blount, J. M. (2005). *Fit to teach: Same-sex desire, gender, and schoolwork in the twentieth century.* Albany: State University of New York Press.

Bockting, W. O., Miner, M. H., Swinburne Romine, R. E., Hamilton, A., & Coleman, E. (2013). Stigma, mental health, and resilience in an online sample of the U.S. transgender population. *American Journal of Public Health, 103*, 943–951. https://doi.org/10.2105/AJPH.2013.301241.

Bortolin, S. (2010). "I don't want him hitting on me": The role of masculinities in creating a chilly high school climate. *Journal of LGBT Youth, 7*(3), 200–223. https://doi.org/10.1080/19361653.2010.486116.

Bronfenbrenner, U. (1977). *The ecology of human development: Experiments by nature and design.* Cambridge, MA: Harvard University Press.

Bronfenbrenner, U. (1986). Recent advances in research on the ecology of human development. In R. K. Silbereisen, K. Eyferth, & G. Rudinger (Eds.), *Development as action in context: Problem behavior and normal youth development* (pp. 287–309). Heidelberg/New York: Springer.

Campus Pride Index. (2017). *National listing of LGBTQ-friendly colleges and universities.* Campus Pride. https://www.campusprideindex.org/. Accessed 28 Sept 2017.

Carpenter, C. S. (2005). Self-reported sexual orientation and earnings: Evidence from California. *Industrial & Labor Relations Review, 58*, 258–273. https://doi.org/10.1177/001979390505800205.

Carpenter, C. (2007). Revisiting the income penalty for behaviorally gay men: Evidence from NHANES III. *Labour Economics, 14*, 25–34. https://doi.org/10.1016/j.labeco.2005.06.001.

Carpenter, C. S. (2009). Sexual orientation and outcomes in college. *Economics of Education Review, 28*(6), 693–703.

Carroll, L. (2010). *Counseling sexual and gender minorities.* Upper Saddle: Pearson Education.

Case, K. A., & Meier, S. C. (2014). Developing allies to transgender and gender-nonconforming youth: Training for counselors and educators. *Journal of LGBT Youth, 11*(1), 62–82.

Castro, I., & Sujak, M. C. (2014). "Why can't we learn about this?" Sexual minority students navigate the official and hidden curricular spaces of high school. *Education and Urban Society, 46*(4), 450–473. https://doi.org/10.1177/0013124512458117.

Chesir-Teran, D. (2003). Conceptualizing and assessing heterosexism in high schools: A setting-level approach. *American Journal of Community Psychology, 31*(3–4), 267–279.

Chesir-Teran, D., & Hughes, D. (2009). Heterosexism in high school and victimization among lesbian, gay, bisexual, and questioning students. *Journal of Youth and Adolescence, 38*, 963–975. https://doi.org/10.1007/s10964-008-9364-x.

Clain, S. H., & Leppel, K. (2001). An investigation into sexual orientation discrimination as an explanation for wage differences. *Applied Economics, 33*, 37–47. https://doi.org/10.1080/00036840122961.

Clements-Nolle, K., Marx, K. R., & Katz, M. (2006). Attempted suicide among transgender persons. *Journal of Homosexuality, 51*(3), 53–69. https://doi.org/10.1300/J082v51n03_04.

Cochran, S. D., Bybee, D., Gage, S., & Mays, V. M. (1996). Prevalence of HIV-related self-reported sexual behaviors, sexually transmitted diseases, and problems with drugs and alcohol in 3 large surveys of lesbian and bisexual women: A look into a segment of the community. *Women's Health: Research on Gender, Behavior, and Policy, 2*(1–2), 11–33.

Cole, S. S., Denny, D., Eyler, A. E., & Samons, S. L. (2000). Issues of transgender. In L. T. Szuchman & F. Muscarella (Eds.), *Psychological perspectives on human sexuality* (pp. 149–195). New York: Wiley.

Connell, R. W. (1995). *Masculinities*. Cambridge: Polity Press.

Connell, R. W. (2000). *The men and the boys*. Berkeley: University of California Press.

Cooperative Institutional Research Program. (2016). CIRP Freshman Survey. https://heri.ucla.edu/cirp-freshman-survey/. Accessed 29 Sept 2017.

Corliss, H. L., Goodenow, C. S., Nichols, L., & Austin, B. (2011). High burden of homelessness among sexual-minority adolescents: Findings from a representative Massachusetts high school sample. *American Journal of Public Health, 101*(9), 1683–1689.

Crosnoe, R. (2011). *Fitting in, standing out: Navigating the social challenges of high school to get an education*. New York: Cambridge University Press.

DeBlaere, C., Brewster, M. E., Sarkees, A., & Moradi, B. (2010). Conducting research with LGB people of color: Methodological challenges and strategies. *The Counseling Psychologist, 38*(3), 331–362.

Diamond, L. (2003). New paradigms for research on heterosexual and sexual-minority development. *Journal of Clinical Child and Adolescent Psychology, 32*(4), 490–498.

Diaz, E. M., Kosciw, J. G., & Greytak, E. A. (2010). School connectedness for lesbian, gay, bisexual, and transgender youth: In-school victimization and institutional supports. *The Prevention Researcher, 17*(3), 15–18.

Dillon, M., & Savage, S. (2006). *Values and religion in rural America: Attitudes toward abortion and same-sex relations* (Carsey Institute, Issue Brief, No. 1).

Duke, T. S. (2011). Lesbian, gay, bisexual, and transgender youth with disabilities: A meta-synthesis. *Journal of LGBT Youth, 8*(1), 1–52. https://doi.org/10.1080/19361653.2011.519181.

Eccles, J. S., & Roeser, R. W. (2011). School and community influences on human development. In M. H. Bornstein & M. E. Lamb (Eds.), *Developmental sciences: An advanced textbook* (6th ed., pp. 571–644). New York: Psychology Press.

Eder, D., & Parker, S. (1987). The cultural production and reproduction of gender: The effect of extracurricular activities on peer-group culture. *Sociology of Education, 60*, 200–213.

Edidin, J. P., Ganim, Z., Hunter, S. J., & Karnik, N. S. (2012). The mental and physical health of homeless youth: A literature review. *Child Psychiatry and Human Development, 43*(3), 354–375.

Einhorn, L., & Polgar, M. (1994). HIV-risk behavior among lesbians and bisexual women. *AIDS Education and Prevention, 6*(6), 514–523.

Eisenberg, M. E., & Resnick, M. D. (2006). Suicidality among gay, lesbian and bisexual youth: The role of protective factors. *Journal of Adolescent Health, 39*(5), 662–668. https://doi.org/10.1016/j.jadohealth.2006.04.024.

Elia, J. P., & Eliason, M. (2010). Discourse of exclusion: Sexuality education's silencing of sexual others. *Journal of LGBT Youth, 7*(1), 29–48. https://doi.org/10.1080/19361650903507791.

Elmslie, B., & Tebaldi, E. (2007). Sexual orientation and labor market discrimination. *Journal of Labor Research, 28*, 436–453. https://doi.org/10.1007/s12122-007-9006-1.

Elze, D. (2003). Gay, lesbian, and bisexual youths' perceptions of their high school environments and comfort in school. *Children & Schools, 25*(4), 225–239. https://doi.org/10.1093/cs/25.4.225.

Evans, N. (2002). The impact of an LGBT Safe Zone Project on campus climate. *Journal of College Student Development, 43*, 522–539.

Evans, N., & Herriott, T. K. (2004). Freshmen impressions: How investigating the campus climate for LGBT students affected four freshmen students. *Journal of College Student Development, 45*, 316–332. https://doi.org/10.1353/csd.2004.0034.

Fedewa, A. L., & Ahn, S. (2011). The effects of bullying and peer victimization on sexual-minority and heterosexual youths: A quantitative meta-analysis of the literature. *Journal of GLBT Family Studies, 7*(4), 398–418. https://doi.org/10.1080/1550428X.2011.592968.

Fetner, T., & Kush, K. (2008). Gay–Straight Alliances in high schools: Social predictors of early adoption. *Youth & Society, 40*(1), 114–130. https://doi.org/10.1177/0044118X07308073.

Fine, L. E. (2014). Penalized or privileged? Sexual identity, gender, and postsecondary educational attainment. *American Journal of Education, 121*(2), 271–297.

Finkel, M. J., Storaasli, R. D., Bandele, A., & Schaefer, V. (2003). Diversity training in graduate school: An exploratory evaluation of the Safe Zone project. *Professional Psychology: Research and Practice, 34*(5), 555–561. https://doi.org/10.1037/0735-7028.34.5.55.

Friedman, M. S., Silvestre, A. J., Gold, M. A., Markovic, N., Savin-Williams, R. C., Huggins, J., et al. (2004). Adolescents define sexual orientation and suggest ways to measure it. *Journal of Adolescence, 27*, 303–317.

Friend, R. (1998). Heterosexism, homophobia, and the culture of schooling. In S. Books (Ed.), *Invisible children in the society and its schools* (pp. 137–166). Mahwah: Lawrence Erlbaum.

Gansen, H. M. (2017). Reproducing (and disrupting) heteronormativity: Gendered sexual socialization in preschool classrooms. *Sociology of Education, 90*(3), 255–227. https://doi.org/10.1177/0038040717720981.

Glenza, J. (2015, January 15) Mississippi schools under fire over efforts to curb gay–straight alliance. *The Guardian*. https://www.theguardian.com/us-news/2015/jan/15/mississippi-schoolsefforts-gay-straight-alliance-membership. Accessed 28 Sept 2017.

GLSEN, & Harris Interactive. (2008). *The principal's perspective: School safety, bullying and harassment, a survey of public school principals*. New York: GLSEN.

Goffman, E. (1963). *Stigma: Notes on the management of spoiled identity*. Englewood Cliffs: Prentice Hall.

Gonyea, R. M., & Moore, J. V. (2007). Gay, lesbian, bisexual, and transgender students and their engagement in educationally purposeful activities in college. In *Association for the Study of Higher Education Annual Conference*.

Gonzalez, M., & McNulty, J. (2010). Achieving competency with transgender youth: School counselors as collaborative advocates. *Journal of LGBT Issues in Counseling, 4*, 176–186. https://doi.org/10.1080/15538605.2010.524841.

Goodenow, C., Szalacha, L., & Westheimer, K. (2006). School support groups, other school factors, and the safety of sexual minority adolescents. *Psychology in the Schools, 43*(5), 573–589. https://doi.org/10.1002/pits.20173.

Graves, K. (2015). LGBTQ education research in historical context. In G. L. Wimberly (Ed.), *LGBTQ issues in education: Advancing a research agenda* (pp. 23–42). Washington, DC: AERA.

Greytak, E. A., Kosciw, J. G., & Diaz, E. M. (2009). *Harsh realities: The experiences of transgender youth in our nation's schools*. New York: GLSEN.

Greytak, E. A., Kosciw, J. G., & Boesen, M. J. (2013a). Educating the educator: Creating supportive school personnel through professional development. *Journal of School Violence, 12*(1), 80–97.

Greytak, E. A., Kosciw, J. G., & Boesen, M. J. (2013b). Putting the "T" in "resource": The benefits of LGBT-related school resources for transgender youth. *Journal of LGBT Youth, 10*(1–2), 45–63. https://doi.org/10.1080/19361653.2012.718522.

Griffin, P., & Ouellett, M. (2003). From silence to safety and beyond: Historical trends in addressing lesbian, gay, bisexual, transgender issues in K–12 schools. *Equity & Excellence in Education, 36*(2), 106–114. https://doi.org/10.1080/10665680303508.

Griffin, P., Lee, C., Waugh, J., & Beyer, C. (2004). Describing roles that Gay–Straight Alliances play in schools: From individual support to social change. *Journal of Gay and Lesbian Issues in Education, 1*, 7–22.

Griner, S. B., Vamos, C. A., Thompson, E. L., Logan, R., Vázquez-Otero, C., & Daley, E. M. (2017). The intersection of gender identity and violence: Victimization experienced by transgender college students. *Journal of Interpersonal Violence*. https://doi.org/10.1177/0886260517723743.

Grossman, A. H., & D'Augelli, A. R. (2006). Transgender youth: Invisible and vulnerable. *Journal of Homosexuality, 51*, 111–128.

Grossman, A. H., & D'Augelli, A. R. (2007). Transgender youth and life-threatening behaviors. *Suicide and Life-Threatening Behavior, 37*, 527–537.

Gunn, A. C. (2011). Even if you say it three ways, it still doesn't mean it's true: The pervasiveness of heteronormativity in early childhood education. *Journal of Early Childhood Research, 9*(3), 280–290. https://doi.org/10.1177/1476718X11398567.

Hatzenbuehler, M. L. (2011). The social environment and suicide attempts in lesbian, gay, and bisexual youth. *Pediatrics, 127*(5), 896–903.

Hatzenbuehler, M. L., Birkett, M., Van Wagenen, A., & Meyer, I. H. (2014). Protective school climates and reduced risk for suicide ideation in sexual minority youths. *American Journal of Public Health, 104*, 279–286.

Healy, J., & Perez-Pena, R. (2016, May 13). Solace and fury as schools react to transgender policy. *The New York Times*. https://www.nytimes.com/2016/05/14/us/transgender-bathrooms.html?mcubz=3&_r=0. Accessed 28 Sept 2017.

Heath, M. (2009). State of our unions: Marriage promotion and the contested power of heterosexuality. *Gender & Society, 23*, 27–48.

Hendricks, M. L., & Testa, R. L. (2012). A conceptual framework for clinical work with transgender and gender nonconforming clients: An adaptation of the minority stress model. *Professional Psychology: Research and Practice, 43*(5), 460–467.

Herek, G. M. (2002). Heterosexuals' attitudes toward bisexual men and women in the United States. *Journal of Sex Research, 39*(4), 264–274.

Herek, G. M. (2007). Confronting sexual stigma and prejudice: Theory and practice. *Journal of Social Issues, 63*(4), 905–925.

Herman, J. L., Flores, A. R., Brown, T. N. T., Wilson, B. D. M., & Conron, K. J. (2017). *Age of individuals who identify as transgender in the United States*. Los Angeles: The Williams Institute.

Hewitt, C. (1995). The socioeconomic position of gay men: A review of the evidence. *American Journal of Economics and Sociology, 54*, 461–479. https://doi.org/10.1111/ajes.1995.54.

Hill, D. B., & Menvielle, E. (2009). "You have to give them a place where they feel protected and safe and loved": The views of parents who have gender-variant children and adolescents. *Journal of LGBT Youth, 6*(2–3), 243–271.

Horn, S. S. (2006). Heterosexual students' attitudes and beliefs about same-sex sexuality and the treatment of gay, lesbian, and gender non-conforming youth. *Cognitive Development, 21*, 420–440.

Indiana University Center for Postsecondary Research. (2017). National Survey of Student Engagement. http://nsse.indiana.edu/. Accessed 29 Sept 2017.

James, S. E., Herman, J. L., Rankin, S., Keisling, M., Mottet, L., & Anafi, M. (2016). *The report of the 2015 U.S. Transgender Survey*. Washington, DC: National Center for Transgender Equality.

Jepsen, L. K. (2007). Comparing the earnings of cohabiting lesbians, cohabiting heterosexual women, and married women: Evidence from the 2000 census. *Industrial Relations: A Journal of Economy and Society, 46*, 699–727.

Kann, L., O'Malley Olsen, E., McManus, T., et al. (2016). Sexual identity, sex of sexual contacts, and health-related behaviors among students in grades 9–12—United States and selected sites, 2015. *MMWR Surveillance Summaries, 65*, 1–202.

Kehily, M. J. (2001). Understanding heterosexualities: Masculinities, embodiment and schooling. *Men and Masculinities, 4*(2), 173–185.

Kielwasser, A., & Wolf, M. (1994). Silence, difference, and annihilation: Understanding the impact of mediated heterosexism on high school students. *The High School Journal, 77*(1/2), 58–79.

Kitzinger, C. (2005). Heteronormativity in action: Reproducing the heterosexual nuclear family in after-hours medical calls. *Social Problems, 52*, 477–498.

Kosciw, J. G., & Pizmony-Levy, O. (2016). International perspectives on homophobic and transphobic bullying in schools. *Journal of LGBT Youth, 13*(1–2), 1–5.

Kosciw, J. G., Diaz, E. M., & Greytak, E. A. (2008). *The 2007 National School Climate Survey: The experiences of lesbian, gay, bisexual and transgender youth in our nation's schools*. New York: Gay, Lesbian and Straight Education Network.

Kosciw, J. G., Greytak, E. A., & Diaz, E. M. (2009). Who, what, where, when, and why: Demographic and ecological factors contributing to hostile school climate for lesbian, gay, bisexual, and transgender youth. *Journal of Youth and Adolescence, 38*(7), 976–988.

Kosciw, J. G., Greytak, E. A., Diaz, E. M., & Bartkiewicz, M. J. (2010). *The 2009 National School Climate Survey: The experiences of lesbian, gay, bisexual, and transgender youth in our nation's schools*. New York: GLSEN.

Kosciw, J. G., Palmer, N. A., Kull, R. M., & Greytak, E. A. (2013). The effect of negative school climate on academic outcomes for LGBT youth and the role of in-school supports. *Journal of School Violence, 12*(1), 45–63.

Kosciw, J. G., Greytak, E. A., Palmer, N. A., & Boesen, M. J. (2014). *The 2013 National School Climate Survey: The experiences of lesbian, gay, bisexual and transgender youth in our nation's schools*. New York: GLSEN.

Kosciw, J. G., Palmer, N. A., & Kull, R. M. (2015). Reflecting resiliency: Openness about sexual orientation and/or gender identity and its relationship to well-being and educational outcomes for LGBT students. *American Journal of Community Psychology, 55*, 167–178.

Kosciw, J. G., Greytak, E. A., Giga, N. M., Villenas, C., & Danischewski, D. J. (2016). *The 2015 National School Climate Survey: The experiences of lesbian, gay, bisexual, transgender, and queer youth in our nation's schools*. New York: GLSEN.

Kreighbaum, A. (2017, February 23). Transgender protections withdrawn. *Inside Higher Ed*. https://www.insidehighered.com/news/2017/02/23/trump-administration-reverses-title-ix-guidance-transgender-protections. Accessed 28 Sept 2017.

Kull, R. M., Kosciw, J. G., & Greytak, E. A. (2015). *From statehouse to schoolhouse: Anti-bullying policy efforts in U.S. States and school districts*. New York: Gay, Lesbian and Straight Education Network (GLSEN).

Lee, C. (2002). The impact of belonging to a high school gay/straight alliance. *The High School Journal, 85*(3), 13–26.

Lick, D. J., Durso, L. E., & Johnson, K. L. (2013). Minority stress and physical health among sexual minorities. *Perspectives on Psychological Science, 8*, 521–548.

Lipkin, A. (1995). The case for a gay and lesbian curriculum. In G. Unks (Ed.), *The gay teen: Educational practice and theory for lesbian gay and bisexual adolescents* (pp. 31–52). New York: Routledge.

Longerbeam, S. D., Inkelas, K. K., Johnson, D. R., & Lee, Z. S. (2007). Lesbian, gay, and bisexual college student experiences: An exploratory study. *Journal of College Student Development, 48*(2), 215–230.

Lugg, C. A., & Adelman, M. (2015). Sociolegal contexts of LGBTQ issues in education. In G. L. Winberly (Ed.), *LGBTQ issues in education: Advancing a research agenda* (pp. 23–42). Washington, DC: AERA.

Luker, K. (2006). *When sex goes to school: Warring views on sex and sex education since the sixties*. New York: Norton.

Mandel, L., & Shakeshaft, C. (2000). Heterosexism in middle schools. In N. Lesko (Ed.), *Masculinities at school: Research on men and masculinities* (pp. 75–103). Thousand Oaks: Sage.

Martin, K. A. (1998). Becoming a gendered body: Practices of preschools. *American Sociological Review, 63*, 494–511.

Martin, K. A., & Kazyak, E. (2009). Hetero-romantic love and heterosexiness in children's G-rated films. *Gender & Society, 23*(3), 315–336.

Martino, W. (2000). Mucking around in class, giving crap, and acting cool: Adolescent boys enacting masculinities at school. *Canadian Journal of Education, 25*, 102–112.

McCready, L. T. (2004). Some challenges facing queer youth programs in urban high schools: Racial segregation and de-normalizing Whiteness. *Journal of Gay and Lesbian Issues in Education, 1*(3), 37–51.

McGuire, J. K., Anderson, C. R., Toomey, R. B., & Russell, S. T. (2010). School climate for transgender youth: A mixed method investigation of student experiences and school responses. *Journal of Youth and Adolescence, 39*(10), 1175–1188. https://doi.org/10.1007/s10964-010-9540-7.

Menvielle, E. (2012). A comprehensive program for children with gender variant behaviors and gender identity disorders. *Journal of Homosexuality, 59*(3), 357–368.

Messner, M. A. (1992). *Power at play: Sports and the problem of masculinity*. Boston: Beacon.

Meyer, I. H. (1995). Minority stress and mental health in gay men. *Journal of Health and Social Behavior, 36*(1), 38–56.

Meyer, I. H. (2003). Prejudice, social stress, and mental health in lesbian, gay, and bisexual populations: Conceptual issues and research evidence. *Psychological Bulletin, 129*, 674–697.

Meyer, E. J. (2015a). The personal is political: LGBTQ education research and policy since 1993. *The Educational Forum, 79*, 347–352.

Meyer, I. H. (2015b). Resilience in the study of minority stress and health of sexual and gender minorities. *Psychology of Sexual Orientation and Gender Diversity, 2*(3), 209–213.

Miceli, M. (2005). *Standing out, standing together: The social and political impact of Gay–Straight Alliances.* New York: Routledge.

Moos, R., & Lemke, S. (1983). Assessing and improving social and ecological settings. In E. Seidman (Ed.), *Handbook of social intervention* (pp. 143–162). Beverly Hills: Sage.

Movement Advancement Project. (2017). Non-discrimination laws. http://www.lgbtmap.org/equality-maps/non_discrimination_laws. Accessed 28 Sept 2017.

Movement Advancement Project & GLSEN. (2017) Separation and stigma: Transgender youth & school facilities. http://lgbtmap.org/transgender-youth-school. Accessed 29 Sept 2017.

National Center for Transgender Equality & GLSEN. (2016). Transgender model district policy. https://www.glsen.org/sites/default/files/Trans%20Model%20Policy.pdf. Accessed 28 Sept 2017.

Nansel, T. R., Overpeck, M., Pilla, R. S., Ruan, W. J., Simons-Morton, B., & Scheidt, P. (2001). Bullying behaviors among U.S. youth: Prevalence and association with psychosocial adjustment. *JAMA: The Journal of the American Medical Association, 285*(16), 2094–2100.

Neilson, J. M., Walden, G., & Kunkel, C. A. (2000). Gendered heteronormativity: Empirical illustrations in everyday life. *Sociological Quarterly, 41*(2), 283–296.

Nicolazzo, Z., & Marine, S. B. (2015). "It will change if people keep talking": Trans* students in college and university housing. *Journal of College and University Student Housing, 42*(1), 160–177.

Olson, L. R., Cadge, W., & Harrison, J. T. (2006). Religion and public opinion about same-sex marriage. *Social Science Quarterly, 87*(2), 340–360.

Paceley, M. S. (2016). Gender and sexual minority youth in nonmetropolitan communities: Individual- and community-level needs for support. *Families in Society: The Journal of Contemporary Social Services, 97*(2), 77–85.

Parks, C. W. (2001). African-American same-gender-loving youths and families in urban schools. *Journal of Gay & Lesbian Social Services, 13*(3), 41–56.

Pascoe, C. J. (2007). *Dude, you're a fag: Masculinity and sexuality in high school.* Berkeley: University of California Press.

Payne, E., & Smith, M. (2012). Rethinking safe schools approaches for LGBTQ students: Changing the questions we ask. *Multicultural Perspectives, 14*(4), 187–193.

Pearson, J., & Wilkinson, L. (2013). Adolescent sexual experiences. In A. Baumle (Ed.), *International handbook on the demography of sexuality* (pp. 167–193). Dordrecht: Springer Netherlands.

Pearson, J., & Wilkinson, L. (2017). Same-sex sexuality and educational attainment: The pathway to college. *Journal of Homosexuality, 64*(4), 538–576.

Pearson, J., Muller, C., & Wilkinson, L. (2007). Adolescent same-sex attraction and academic outcomes: The role of school attachment and engagement. *Social Problems, 54*(4), 523–542.

Pearson, J., Thrane, L., & Wilkinson, L. (2017). Consequences of runaway and thrownaway experiences for sexual minority health during the transition to adulthood. *Journal of LGBT Youth, 14*(2), 145–171.

Poteat, V. P., & Espelage, D. L. (2007). Predicting psychosocial consequences of homophobic victimization in middle school students. *Journal of Early Adolescence, 27*, 175–191. https://doi.org/10.1177/0272431606294839.

Poteat, V. P., Espelage, D. L., & Koenig, B. W. (2009). Willingness to remain friends and attend school with lesbian and gay peers: Relational expressions of prejudice among heterosexual youth. *Journal of Youth and Adolescence, 38*, 952–962.

Poteat, V. P., Sinclair, K. O., DiGiovanni, C. D., Koenig, B., & Russell, S. T. (2012). Gay–Straight Alliances are associated with student health: A multischool comparison of LGBTQ and heterosexual youth. *Journal of Research on Adolescence, 23*(2), 319–330.

Poynter, K., & Tubbs, N. J. (2008). Safe zones: Creating LGBT safe space ally programs. *Journal of LGBT Youth, 5*, 121–132.

Rankin, S. (2005). Campus climates for sexual minorities. *New Directions for Student Services, 111*, 17–23. https://doi.org/10.1002/ss.170.

Rankin, S., Weber, G. N., Blumenfeld, W. J., & Frazer, S. (2010). *2010 state of higher education for lesbian, gay, bisexual and transgender people.* Charlotte: Campus Pride. https://www.campuspride.org/wp-content/uploads/campuspride2010lgbtreportssummary.pdf. Accessed 29 Sept 2017.

Renn, K. A., & Bilodeau, B. (2005). Queer student leaders: An exploratory case study of identity development and LGBT student involvement at a Midwestern research university. *Journal of Gay & Lesbian Issues in Education, 2*(4), 49–71.

Riley, E. A., et al. (2011). The needs of gender-variant children and their parents: A parent survey. *International Journal of Sexual Health, 23*(3), 181–195.

Ripley, M., Anderson, E., McCormack, M., & Rockett, B. (2012). Heteronormativity in the university classroom: Novelty attachment and content substitution among gay-friendly students. *Sociology of Education, 85*(2), 121–130.

Robinson, J. P., & Espelage, D. L. (2011). Inequities in educational and psychological outcomes between LGBTQ and straight students in middle and high school. *Educational Researcher, 40*(7), 315–330. https://doi.org/10.3102/0013189x11422112.

Robinson, J. P., & Espelage, D. L. (2012). Bullying explains only part of LGBTQ–heterosexual risk disparities: Implications for policy and practice. *Educational Researcher, 41*(8), 309–319. https://doi.org/10.3102/0013189x12457023.

Rofes, E. (1989). Opening up the classroom closet: Responding to the educational needs of gay and lesbian youth. *Harvard Educational Review, 59*, 444–453.

Rostosky, S. S., Owens, G. P., Zimmerman, R. S., & Riggle, E. D. B. (2003). Associations among sexual attraction status, school belonging, and alcohol and marijuana use in rural high school students. *Journal of Adolescence, 26*, 741–751. https://doi.org/10.1016/jadolescence.2003.09.002.

Rostosky, S. S., Wilcox, B. L., Comer Wright, M. L., & Randall, B. A. (2004). The impact of religiosity on adolescent sexual behavior: A review of the evidence. *Journal of Adolescent Research, 19*(6), 677–697.

Rothblum, E. D., Balsam, K. F., & Mickey, R. M. (2004). Brothers and sisters of lesbians, gay men, and bisexuals as a demographic comparison group: An innovative research methodology to examine social change. *Journal of Applied Behavioral Science, 40*, 283–301. https://doi.org/10.1177/0021886304266877.

Rubin, G. (1999). Thinking sex: Notes for a radical theory of the politics of sexuality. In R. Parker & P. Aggleton (Eds.), *Culture, society and sexuality*. London: UCL Press.

Russ, T., Simonds, C., & Hunt, S. (2002). Coming out in the classroom … an occupational hazard? The influence of sexual orientation on teacher credibility and perceived student learning. *Communication Education, 51*, 311–324.

Russell, S. T., & Toomey, R. B. (2012). Men's sexual orientation and suicide: Evidence for U.S. adolescent-specific risk. *Social Science & Medicine, 74*, 523–529.

Russell, S. T., Seif, H., & Truong, N. L. (2001). School outcomes of sexual minority youth in the United States: Evidence from a national study. *Journal of Adolescence, 24*, 111–127. https://doi.org/10.1006/jado.2000.0365.

Russell, S. T., Kostroski, O., McGuire, J. K., Laub, C., & Manke, E. (2006). *LGBT issues in the curriculum promotes school safety* (California Safe Schools Coalition Research Brief No. 4). San Francisco: California Safe School Coalition. http://www.casafeschools.org/FactSheet-curriculum.pdf. Accessed 28 Sept 2017.

Russell, S. T., McGuire, J. K., Lee, S. A., Larriva, J. C., & Laub, C. (2008). Adolescent perceptions of school safety for students with lesbian, gay, bisexual, and transgender parents. *Journal of LGBT Youth, 5*(4), 11–27. https://doi.org/10.1080/19361650802222880.

Russell, S. T., Muraco, A., Subramaniam, A., & Laub, C. (2009). Youth empowerment and high school Gay–Straight Alliances. *Journal of Youth and Adolescence, 38*(7), 891–903.

Russell, S. T., Kosciw, J., Horn, S., & Saewyc, E. (2010). Safe schools policy for LGBTQ students. *Social Policy Report, 24*(2.) Society for Research in Child Development. https://eric.ed.gov/?id=ED519243. Accessed 28 Sept 2017.

Saewyc, E. (2011). Research on adolescent sexual orientation: Development, health disparities, stigma, and resilience. *Journal of Research on Adolescence, 21*(1), 256–272.

Sausa, L. A. (2005). Translating research into practice: Trans youth recommendations for improving school systems. *Journal of Gay & Lesbian Issues in Education, 3*(1), 15–28. https://doi.org/10.1300/J367v03n01_04.

Savin-Williams, R. C. (2005). *The new gay teenager*. Cambridge, MA: Harvard University Press.

Savin-Williams, R. C. (2006). Who's gay? Does it matter? *Current Directions in Psychological Science, 15*(1), 40–44.

Schilt, K., & Lagos, D. (2017). The development of transgender studies in sociology. *Annual Review of Sociology, 43*(1), 425–443.

Schilt, K., & Westbrook, L. (2009). "Gender normal," transgender people, and the social maintenance of heterosexuality. *Gender & Society, 23*(4), 440–464. https://doi.org/10.1177/0891243209340034.

Schilt, K., & Westbrook, L. (2015). Bathroom battlegrounds and penis panics. *Contexts, 14*, 26–31.

Schulman, M. (2013, January 9). Generation LGBTQIA. *The New York Times*.

Seelman, K. L. (2016). Transgender adults' access to college bathrooms and housing in relationship to suicidality. *Journal of Homosexuality, 63*(10), 1378–1399.

Sherkat, D. E., Powell-Williams, M., Maddox, G., & de Vries, K. M. (2011). Religion, politics, and support for same-sex marriage in the United States, 1988–2008. *Social Science Research, 40*(1), 167–180. https://doi.org/10.1016/j.ssresearch.2010.08.009.

Singh, A., Meng, S., & Hansen, A. (2013). "It's already hard enough being a student": Developing affirming college environments for trans youth. *Journal of LGBT Youth, 10*(3), 2080223. https://doi.org/10.1080/19361653.2013.800770.

Slesaransky-Poe, G. (2013). Adults set the tone for welcoming all students. *Phi Delta Kappan, 94*(5), 40–44. https://doi.org/10.1177/003172171309400509.

Span, S. A. (2011). Addressing university students' anti-gay bias: An extension of the contact hypothesis. *American Journal of Sexuality Education, 6*(2), 192–205. https://doi.org/10.1080/15546128.2011.571957.

Steck, A. K., & Perry, D. R. (2016). Fostering safe and inclusive spaces for LGBTQ students: Phenomenographic exploration of high school administrators' perceptions about GSAs. *Journal of LGBT Youth, 13*(4), 352–377. https://doi.org/10.1080/19361653.2016.1185759.

Stein, A. (2001). *The stranger next door*. Boston: Beacon.

Swanson, K., & Gettinger, M. (2016). Teachers' knowledge, attitudes, and supportive behaviors toward LGBT students: Relationship to Gay–Straight Alliances, anti-bullying policy, and teacher training. *Journal of LGBT Youth, 13*(4), 326–351. https://doi.org/10.1080/19361653.2016.1185765.

Swearer, S. M., Turner, R. K., Givens, J. E., & Pollack, W. S. (2008). "You're so gay!": Do different forms of bullying matter for adolescent males? *School Psychology Review, 37*(2), 160–173.

Szalacha, L. A. (2003). Safer sexual diversity climates: Lessons learned from an evaluation of Massachusetts' Safe Schools Program for gay and lesbian students. *American Journal of Education, 110*, 58–88.

Thorne, B. (1993). *Gender play: Girls and boys in school.* New Brunswick: Rutgers University Press.

Toomey, R. B., & Russell, S. T. (2013). An initial investigation of sexual minority youth involvement in school-based extracurricular activities. *Journal of Research on Adolescence, 23*(2), 304–318.

Toomey, R., Ryan, C., Diaz, R., Card, N., & Russell, S. (2010). Gender-nonconforming lesbian, gay, bisexual, and transgender youth: School victimization and young adult psychosocial adjustment. *Developmental Psychology, 46*(6), 1580–1589. https://doi.org/10.1037/a0020705.

Toomey, R. B., Ryan, C., Diaz, R. M., & Russell, S. T. (2011). High school Gay–Straight Alliances (GSAs) and young adult well-being: An examination of GSA presence, participation, and perceived effectiveness. *Applied Developmental Science, 15*(4), 175–185.

Ueno, K. (2010). Same-sex experience and mental health during the transition between adolescence and young adulthood. *Sociological Quarterly, 51*, 484–510. https://doi.org/10.1111/(ISSN)1533-8525.

Ueno, K., Roach, T. A., & Pena-Talamantes, A. E. (2013). The dynamic association between same-sex contact and educational attainment. *Advances in Life Course Research, 18*, 127–140.

Unnever, J. D., & Cornell, D. G. (2004). Middle school victims of bullying: Who reports being bullied? *Aggressive Behavior, 30*(5), 373–388.

Vaccaro, A. (2009). Intergenerational perceptions, similarities and differences: A comparative analysis of lesbian, gay, and bisexual Millennial youth with Generation X and Baby Boomers. *Journal of LGBT Youth, 6*(2–3), 113–134. https://doi.org/10.1080/19361650902899124.

Van Gelderen, L., Gartrell, N., Bos, H. M., van Rooij, F. B., & Hermanns, J. M. (2012). Stigmatization associated with growing up in a lesbian-parented family: What do adolescents experience and how do they deal with it? *Children and Youth Services Review, 34*(5), 999–1006.

Vanderburgh, R. (2007). *Transition and beyond: Observations on gender identity.* Portland: Q Press.

Vanderburgh, R. (2009). Appropriate therapeutic care for families with pre-pubescent transgender/gender-dissonant children. *Child and Adolescent Social Work Journal, 26*, 135–154.

Wagaman, A. M. (2016). Self-definition as resistance: Understanding identities among LGBTQ emerging adults. *Journal of LGBT Youth, 13*(3), 207–230. https://doi.org/10.1080/19361653.2016.1185760.

Waller, M., & Sanchez, R. (2011). The association between same-sex romantic attractions and relationships and running away among a nationally representative sample of adolescents. *Child & Adolescent Social Work Journal, 28*(6), 475–493.

Watson, R. J., & Russell, S. T. (2016). Disengaged or bookworm: Academics, mental health, and success for sexual minority youth. *Journal of Research on Adolescence, 26*(1), 159–165.

Watson, R. J., Wheldon, C. W., & Russell, S. T. (2015). How does sexual identity disclosure impact school experiences? *Journal of LGBT Youth, 12*(4), 385–396.

West, C., & Zimmerman, D. H. (1987). Doing gender. *Gender & Society, 1*(2), 125–151.

Whitbeck, L. B. (2009). *Mental health and emerging adulthood among homeless young people.* New York: Psychology Press.

Wilkinson, L., & Pearson, J. (2009). School culture and the well-being of same-sex attracted youth. *Gender & Society, 23*(4), 542–568. https://doi.org/10.1177/0891243209339913.

Wilkinson, L., Pearson, J., & Liu, H. (2016). Educational attainment of transgender adults: Does the timing of transgender identity development matter? In *Annual meeting of the American Sociological Association*, Seattle.

Wilson, T. C. (1995). Urbanism and unconventionality. *Social Science Quarterly, 76*(2), 346–363.

Worthen, M. G. F. (2011). College student experiences with an LGBTQ ally training program: A mixed methods study at a university in the southern United States. *Journal of LGBT Youth, 8*, 332–377.

Worthen, M. G. F. (2014). The interactive impacts of high school Gay–Straight Alliances (GSAs) on college student attitudes toward LGBT individuals: An investigation of high school characteristics. *Journal of Homosexuality, 61*(2), 217–250. https://doi.org/10.1080/00918369.2013.839906.

Worthen, M. G. F. (2016). Hetero-cis-normativity and the gendering of transphobia. *International Journal of Transgenderism, 17*(1), 31–57. https://doi.org/10.1080/15532739.2016.1149538.

zamantakis, a., Miller, J. F., & Chace, A. (2017, Spring). TRANSforming higher education. *NASPA Gender & Sexuality Knowledge Community White Paper* (pp. 7–10).

Zemsky, B. (2004). Coming out of the ivy closet: Improving campus climate for LGBT students, staff, and faculty. In W. Swan (Ed.), *Handbook of gay, lesbian, and transgender administration and policy.* New York: Marcel Dekker.

Zippin, A. (2015, April 8). LGBTQ issues on campus: What's changing? *NASPA GLBT KC Blog Series.* https://www.naspa.org/constituent-groups/posts/lgbtq-issues-on-campus-whats-changing. Accessed 28 Sept 2017.

Zucker, K. J., Bradley, S. J., Owen-Anderson, A., Kibblewhite, S. J., & Cantor, J. M. (2008). Is gender identity disorder in adolescents coming out of the closet? *Journal of Sex & Marital Therapy, 34*, 287–290. https://doi.org/10.1080/00926230802096192.

The Social Organization of Schooling and Opportunities for Learning

School Choice and Learning Opportunities

Megan Austin and Mark Berends

Abstract

School choice has expanded significantly in the past couple of decades and is likely to continue doing so. Rigorous research has informed our understanding of the impact of school choice options on student achievement, attainment, and family satisfaction. It has also shed light on the effects of different school governance structures, residential location and access, segregation patterns, parents' stated and actual preferences, information flows, and the attributes of effective choice schools. Further research is needed to address the variability in effects of school choice options, both between and within sectors (e.g., charter, voucher, and private schools). Such research will allow sociologists to broaden their focus from the "horse race" of comparing one school sector to another (e.g., public and private, charter, and traditional public) to considering new waves of questions that can benefit today's increasing number of partnerships between researchers, policymakers, and practitioners. This in turn will lead researchers to additional theorizing, moving them beyond market and institutional theories to developing new ones that depict current empirical conditions.

M. Austin (✉) · M. Berends
University of Notre Dame, Notre Dame, IN, USA
e-mail: maustin@air.org

10.1 Background on School Choice

School choice is growing in the United States and as it does so, the research evidence has expanded as well. School choice comes in many forms—including charter schools, private schools, magnet schools, vouchers, tuition tax credits, inter- and intra-district public school choice, virtual schools, and homeschooling. And the idea that parents should have some choice in the education of their children is deeply ingrained in U.S. culture (Berends et al. 2009, 2011). Nonetheless, there has been a great deal of controversy around school choice and its impact on research, policy, and public perceptions (Henig 2008). Debates about its various effects are likely to continue, which we hope the growing body of research will continue to inform as we assess whether and how school choice policies affect the learning opportunities of our nation's youth.

We are especially interested in the following questions: What does the research to date say about the effects of school choice on academic outcomes, educational attainment, and parent satisfaction? And, is school choice operating in a manner consistent with market theory or institutional theory? We begin with a review of the empirical literature on what we call the "first wave" of rigorous studies—primarily on charter schools, voucher programs, and private (Catholic) school effects—that tend to make school choice a

© Springer International Publishing AG, part of Springer Nature 2018
B. Schneider (ed.), *Handbook of the Sociology of Education in the 21st Century*, Handbooks of Sociology and Social Research, https://doi.org/10.1007/978-3-319-76694-2_10

horse race that pits public against private schools or charter against traditional public schools. Then we discuss whether the literature is consistent with market theory or institutional theory. We go on to review a second wave of research that moves toward new questions within the context of research–practice partnerships, in which researchers and practitioners work together to form a research agenda that practitioners can use in actionable ways for improving schools. Finally, we argue that sociologists need to play a key role in these partnerships to address broader sociological questions whose answers can further inform the debates about school choice. These questions include access to schools, inequalities among socioeconomic and racial/ethnic groups in accessing schools, why these inequalities exist and what processes are driving them, and the organizational and instructional conditions in different schools of choice compared with traditional public schools. By forming research–practice partnerships, sociologists can address these issues, which may have a significant impact on improving practice, informing market and institutional theories, and moving toward new theoretical perspectives.

10.1.1 School Choice and Academic Achievement

The major question in research on school choice has been, what are the effects of school choice on academic achievement? Are students learning more in schools of choice as measured by their test score gains compared with students in traditional public schools? In what follows we focus on studies that rigorously assess the effects of charter schools, voucher programs, and private schools more generally. (We point to additional reviews in each section.)

10.1.1.1 Charter Schools and Achievement

As the fastest growing sector of school choice, charter schools have received a great deal of attention over the past 10–15 years. Some studies using randomized designs show positive effects on academic achievement gains for students in charter schools compared with those students who are not so enrolled (Abdulkadiroglu et al. 2009; Angrist et al. 2011; Dobbie and Fryer 2011; Hoxby and Murarka 2008; Hoxby et al. 2009). Other experimental studies relying on broader samples of schools (Gleason et al. 2010) and those using quasi-experimental methods show mixed results for charter school effects on achievement—some positive, some negative, and some null (for a review see Berends 2015; Betts and Tang 2014; CREDO 2009; Epple et al. 2016; Imberman 2011; Teasley 2009).

Although the bulk of the charter school studies reveal mixed results, it is noteworthy that some studies have found significant and substantial positive effects of charter schools, particularly in urban areas where it has been difficult to implement meaningful educational reforms. For example, in New York City, some charter schools are significantly narrowing the achievement gaps between racial/ethnic groups (Dobbie and Fryer 2011; Hoxby et al. 2009). Dobbie and Fryer (2011) studied students who won and lost the charter school lotteries in the Harlem Children's Zone, and they found that the effects of charter elementary schools were large enough to close the racial achievement gap across subjects—i.e., students gained about 0.20 of a standard deviation a year in both mathematics and English/language arts. Similar large effects of charter schools have also been shown in Boston (Angrist et al. 2011).

Studies of school choice shed some light on the main effects in different locales, but they provide limited information about the schools as organizations and the conditions within them that may promote student achievement, particularly the curriculum and instruction that is most likely to affect student learning (see Berends 2015). Although some researchers have started to examine features of effective charter schools (Berends et al. 2010; Dobbie and Fryer 2013), future research needs to better attend to the organization of schooling within the charter and traditional public school sectors. Moreover, researchers should gather additional measures for student outcomes, such as measures of social-emotional learning, engagement, and motivation.

10.1.1.2 Research on School Vouchers

With the expansion in the number of voucher programs, the research addressing the effects of these programs has increased as well. Overall, the research portrays a mixed view of voucher impacts (Berends 2014; Epple et al. 2015; Figlio 2009; Shakeel et al. 2016; Zimmer and Bettinger 2015).

The first voucher program was the Milwaukee Parental Choice Program, which began in 1990, provided scholarships to students from low- and modest-income families to attend private schools, and included an external evaluation (see Witte 2000). Others have also analyzed Milwaukee evaluation data (Greene et al. 1999a; Rouse 1998). These studies were different from Witte in their methodological approaches and the selection of the data analyzed, so the findings differed. Witte's research found generally no systematic academic achievement differences between voucher and public school students based on regression models that used Heckman selection corrections. Greene et al. (1999a), analyzing a subset of voucher participants who had won their voucher via a lottery system to a small number of oversubscribed private schools, found positive achievement impacts associated with participation. Rouse employed a series of quasi-experimental approaches from student fixed effects and instrumental variable designs, finding no effect in reading but positive achievement impacts in math.

These differences between findings have since been reflected in other studies of voucher programs. For example, Greene (2001) found positive achievement impacts from an experimental analysis of the privately-funded voucher program in Charlotte, a result generally supported by Cowen (2008) using more sophisticated statistical models. Howell et al.'s (2002) analysis of lottery-based privately funded programs in New York City, Washington, DC, and Dayton, Ohio revealed positive student achievement outcomes for Black students, but not for the overall sample, a finding subsequent analysts of the

New York data both confirmed (Barnard et al. 2003) and questioned (Krueger and Zhu 2004).

Studies of the Cleveland Scholarship Program similarly found both positive impacts for voucher students (Greene et al. 1999b) and no significant differences (Metcalf et al. 2003)—findings that differed due to study design and sample. Using a regression discontinuity approach on the state-wide voucher system in Florida, Figlio and Hart (2014) found that the program generated statistically significant positive impacts on student reading achievement, at least for students near the income-eligibility ceiling. Witte et al. (2012) reported that Milwaukee voucher students on average gained more than a matched sample of public school students in reading but not in math in the final year of that four-year evaluation. They noted that a new high-stakes testing policy may have been partly or wholly responsible for the voucher gains (Witte et al. 2014).

The evaluation of the first federally funded voucher program in Washington, DC, relied on an experimental design based on scholarship lotteries (Wolf et al. 2010, 2011). The series of reports described significant achievement gains in reading in the third year of the evaluation but no significant reading impacts in other years, including the fourth and final year, or in math in any year.

There are a few studies of statewide voucher programs in Louisiana, Ohio, and Indiana that have shown negative effects on student achievement growth. Examining the experimental effects of using a Louisiana voucher to enroll in a private school, Abdulkdiroglu et al. (2015) analyzed data between 2008 and 2012—covering the first year of the Louisiana Scholarship Program. Following students who won and lost the lottery for a scholarship, Abdulkdiroglu et al. found significant and large negative effects for students who participated in the first year of the voucher program—with declines of 16 percentile points in math and 14 percentile points in reading. The effects were consistent across income groups, geographic areas, and private school characteristics (higher and lower proportion of White students, enrollment, achievement scores, and whether the private school was Catholic). Investigating experimental effects through the second year of the program, Mills and Wolf (2017) reported negative effects in both math and reading in year one, but less negative effects in year two. Only the effects for mathematics were statistically significant. In mathematics in year two of the program, they found that students who won the voucher lottery and transferred to a public school scored 0.34 of a standard deviation below those students who lost the voucher lottery. They state that "the magnitude of these negative estimates is unprecedented in the literature of random assignment evaluations of school voucher programs" (p. 2). These findings are consistent with what Figlio and Karbownik (2016) found in their evaluation of the Ohio EdChoice Scholarship Program, a study that used student matching estimation techniques because the program did not rely on a lottery to provide scholarships. Negative effects were also found in a study by Waddington and Berends (2017) of the Indiana Choice Scholarship program. Examining students who switched from a public to a private school with a voucher, the authors found a negative effect in mathematics (about 0.10 of a standard deviation) and no statistically meaningful overall effect in English/language arts. The largest math losses occurred during the first and second year that voucher students attended a private school; students recouped their initial math loss after four years of attending a private school with a voucher.

In a recent review of nineteen voucher studies in the U.S. and other countries that relied on randomized controlled trials (RCTs), Shakeel et al. (2016) found overall positive effects of school vouchers. The impacts were larger in reading than mathematics, for programs outside the U.S. compared with those within the U.S., and for publically funded programs compared with privately funded programs. In the U.S., the RCT locales included Charlotte, NC, Dayton, OH, the state of Louisiana, Milwaukee, WI, New York City, Toledo, OH, and Washington, DC. RCTs in locales outside the U.S. included Andhra Pradesh and Delhi, India, and Bogota, Colombia.

Similar to the research on charters, few studies have examined the specific learning conditions that students experienced in their voucher schools vis-à-vis comparable students in traditional public schools (Figlio et al. 2013; Zimmer and Bettinger 2015). Although such studies are difficult to design and implement, more research is needed on school and classroom experiences to understand the conditions under which voucher programs provide more meaningful and substantive learning opportunities (or not).

10.1.1.3 Private and Catholic School Effects

Several researchers argue that private schools (especially Catholic) outperform public schools (Chubb and Moe 1990; Coleman and Hoffer 1987; Coleman et al. 1982), but not all researchers hold this view (see Lubienski and Lubienski 2013). The size of these private and Catholic school effects and their implications for educational policy are often the center of heated debate (see Lee and Bryk 1993). Do students who attend Catholic schools score higher on academic achievement tests than their peers in traditional public schools? Although a straightforward question, it is difficult to examine empirically because, when comparing school types, there is a continuing concern about selection bias. Students who attend private or Catholic schools may differ from those who attend public schools according to social background, motivation, values and beliefs, and other factors; thus there may be selection bias that makes the measurement of school effects difficult (Berends and Waddington 2018; Goldberger and Cain 1982).

Research has shown that the effects of Catholic schools differ when one is considering high school effects versus those at lower grade levels (elementary or middle school). There is evidence that the effect of attending a Catholic high school on students' mathematics achievement is consistently positive. In a nationally representative sample, Coleman and Hoffer (1987) found that between grades 10 and 12, students in Catholic schools outperformed public school students by about one grade level equivalent in both mathematics and reading, controlling for other relevant factors. With more sophisticated multivariate models in more recent nationally representative data (2002–2004), Carbonaro and Covay (2010) found that Catholic school students had higher mathematics achievement than their peers in public schools. In Hoffer's (2009) review of the achievement effects of Catholic schools in nationally representative cohorts of high school students between the early 1980s and 2000s, he found the average Catholic–public differences ranged from 0.37 to 0.50 of a standard deviation.

On the other hand, a growing number of studies that have focused on grades K–8 in Catholic schools show that Catholic school effects are less robust than at the high school level. For example, Carbonaro (2006) found that kindergarten students in public and Catholic schools experienced similar achievement gains in mathematics and general knowledge, net of other characteristics, in the nationally representative Early Childhood Longitudinal Study (ECLS-K). Also analyzing the ECLS-K data and the gains of students between 3rd and 5th grades, Reardon et al. (2009) found that public school students outperformed their Catholic school peers in math but experienced similar gains in reading. Using an approach to assess the degree of selection bias (Altonji et al. 2005), Elder and Jepsen's (2014) analysis of the ECLS-K data found no evidence of Catholic school effects on elementary and middle school students' test scores, with many of their estimates pointing toward sizeable negative effects. The authors argue that the Catholic school advantage existing in the raw data is a result of the general selection of higher ability students into Catholic schools.

In addition to the average effects of Catholic schools on students, some research shows that Catholic schools benefit historically disadvantaged students (Bryk et al. 1993; Coleman and Hoffer 1987; Coleman et al. 1982; Grogger and Neal 2000; Lee and Bryk 1989; Neal 1997; Sander 1996). However, other researchers argue that "the evidence that Catholic schools are especially helpful for initially disadvantaged students is quite suggestive, but not conclusive" (Jencks 1985, p. 134).

Unfortunately, the research on school choice options is not definitive, which allows for continued debate at different levels of policy about whether or not to scale up various school choice options. Future research can help clarify the debate by examining the educational trajectories of students in choice and non-choice schools with data, not only on test score gains and graduation rates, but other measures of student outcomes (e.g., behavior, engagement, motivation, educational, and occupational expectations). In addition, scholars must gather more systematic information from the choice and non-choice learning environments, including not only instructional conditions but also differences in the social organization of schools (see Berends 2015; Berends et al. 2010).

10.1.2 School Choice and Educational Attainment

In addition to the studies that have examined achievement effects of charter schools, voucher programs, and Catholic schools, a smaller number of studies have examined the effects of school choice on educational attainment. The accumulated knowledge regarding educational attainment is more robust in some areas of school choice (e.g., Catholic schools) than other areas (e.g., charter schools and voucher programs).

10.1.2.1 Charter Schools

As mentioned, research that has examined the impact of charter schools on educational attainment is somewhat limited compared to the charter school research on academic achievement (Angrist et al. 2013a, b; Dobbie and Fryer 2013; Furgeson et al. 2012; Sass et al. 2016). Booker et al. (2011) analyzed whether attendance in charter high schools was related to educational attainment. For schools in Florida and Chicago, they found substantial positive effects on both high school completion and college attendance, estimating univariate and bivariate probit models that controlled for student characteristics and test scores. If students attended a charter middle school and then went on to a charter high school, they were 7–15 percentage points more likely to earn a high school diploma compared with students who attended a traditional public high school. In addition, students who attended a charter high school were 8–10 percentage points more likely to attend college than their peers in traditional public high schools.

10.1.2.2 Voucher Programs

Several studies of voucher programs have examined not only achievement effects but also effects on educational attainment. The Wolf et al. (2010, 2011) longitudinal randomized study of the voucher program in Washington, DC, revealed significant gains in voucher students' high school graduation rates. They found that the DC Scholarship Program raised the high school graduation rate by 21 percentage points compared with students in the control group (i.e., 91% of the treatment group graduated compared with 70% of the control group). In addition, the voucher program increased four-year college enrollment and persistence by 4–7 percentage points (Cowen et al. 2013).

In New York City, Chingos and Peterson (2012) found that Blacks who participated in the privately funded voucher experiment enrolled in college at higher rates than the experimental control group, though there were no significant attainment effects of the program on the entire sample of students. The New York City scholarship program increased the rate of attending a four-year college by 8 percentage points for Black students.

10.1.2.3 Private/Catholic Schools

A number of studies have also focused on the educational attainment outcomes of students attending Catholic high schools (Evans and Schwab 1995; Grogger and Neal 2000; Neal 1997). Using instrumental variables to account for selection effects, these studies collectively find that students attending Catholic high schools are more likely than their public school counterparts to graduate from high school and attend college. For example, analyzing nationally representative data from the early 1990s, Evans and Schwab (1995) found that students who attended a Catholic high school were about 10–13% more likely to attend college compared with their public school peers. In a novel approach that addresses selection bias through accounting for

the ratio of selection on observables to selection on the unobservables, Altonji et al. (2005) analyzed the same data as Evans and Schwab and showed that Catholic school students were more likely to graduate from high school and attend college even though they found little evidence of a Catholic school effect on student achievement.

Relying on propensity score models in the longitudinal, nationally representative data from the National Study of Youth and Religion (NSYR), which started in 2001 (see Smith 2005, 2009, 2011), Freeman and Berends (2016) found that students who attended a Catholic high school were more likely to continue their education, other factors being equal. They also found that, in most cases, students from Catholic high schools were not enrolling in more selective institutions than their peers who attended public schools. Comparing their results to the previous studies mentioned above, many of which use data that are 20 years old or older, Freeman and Berends suggest that the effect of Catholic schools on educational attainment may be decreasing over time—a reduction of about one-fifth to one-third in the effect size. They go on to hypothesize that the changing demographic patterns and the political restructuring of the Catholic Church may be contributing to the declining effects.

10.1.3 School Choice and Satisfaction

In addition to school choice effects on achievement and attainment, an important question is whether or not parents and students are satisfied with their choices. As Buckley and Schneider state: "Parental satisfaction is critical to the politics of school reform" (2006, p. 58). Existing research has found that parents of children in schools of choice are more satisfied than parents of children in traditional public schools. Specifically, parents who choose charter schools or select private schools with a voucher tend to be more satisfied than parents in traditional public schools (e.g., Gleason et al. 2010; Greene 2001; Grady and Bielick 2010; Howell and Peterson

2006; McArthur et al. 1995; Schneider and Buckley 2003; Teske and Schneider 2001; Tuttle et al. 2013; Wolf et al. 2010).

Analyzing randomized designs with charter school lotteries to understand the outcomes of lottery winners compared to lottery losers, Gleason et al. (2010) and Tuttle et al. (2013) show that charter school parents are more satisfied than traditional public school parents. Although these studies do not reveal *why* charter parents are more satisfied, one explanation is that greater satisfaction reflects real differences between the school types in terms of positive student outcomes. That said, we need to be cautious about this explanation because Gleason et al. (2010) and Tuttle et al. (2013) show that parent satisfaction with charter schools may be independent from school quality. For example, although Gleason et al. found strong effects on parent satisfaction, they also found no effects on student achievement or other student outcomes, such as parent- and student-reported effort in school, misbehavior in school, and student well being. When examining KIPP charter schools, Tuttle et al. (2013) found positive impacts on student achievement and parent satisfaction, but no positive effects on student engagement, educational aspirations, and student behavior.

Another explanation for why parents are more satisfied in schools of choice is that parents have invested time and energy into making the choice, so they view the schools through "rose colored glasses" (Schneider and Buckley 2003; Teske et al. 2007). This makes sense since it is likely that, when making difficult schooling decisions for their children, families will view the chosen school more favorably than the rejected alternative. Choosing a school may be intrinsically satisfying because it allows parents to match what they want for their children with what they believe a particular school offers (Goldring and Shapira 1993). This is consistent with the social science perspective that states that parents are rational consumers (see Berends and Zottola 2009).

However, schools of choice may be what economists call an "experience good," meaning that parents cannot observe the value of the chosen school at the time of selection but only after

their children start attending. This suggests that parent satisfaction may change over time, an issue that Buckley and Schneider (2006) analyzed using up to five years of survey data from parents with children attending charter and traditional public schools in Washington, DC. Parents assigned "A–F" grades to the school and its principal, teachers, disciplinary policies, school and class size, facility, and general values. They found that, except for facilities, charter parents' satisfaction declined across all these school factors.

Based on Buckley and Schneider's (2006) findings, future research should measure parent satisfaction over time and pay attention to the social context of the schools. Such research should measure satisfaction at different time points as well as gather information to see what may explain changes over time. It should also address the schools' social context (to date, most studies of parent satisfaction have not), which may be important in explaining both parent satisfaction and student outcomes. For instance, some evidence shows that charter schools attract families with higher socioeconomic status compared with traditional public schools (Butler et al. 2013). Other evidence from charter school studies suggests that urban and suburban charters may differ. Existing achievement evidence suggests that students in suburban charter schools do not perform as well as students in urban charters (Angrist et al. 2013a, b; Betts and Tang 2014). Moreover, suburban parents with high educational attainment may be more difficult to satisfy (Goldring and Shapira 1993; Lareau and Goyette 2014) or they may place less value on achievement test scores than urban economically disadvantaged parents do (Angrist et al. 2013a, b).

10.2 Theories of School Choice

When addressing differences among school choice options, economists tend to draw on market theory for predicting effects on student outcomes and competition among schools, while sociologists tend to focus on the social context of school choice, examining the social organization of schools and drawing on institutional theory as a counterpoint to market theory (see Berends 2015).

10.2.1 Market Theory

The theory behind market-based choice programs predicts that expanding choice options and competition will benefit students because their families will seek out high-quality schools and schools that fit particular student needs (Chubb and Moe 1990; Friedman 1955, 1962). Such processes will results in a "rising tide" of improving all schools (Hoxby 2001, 2003). Friedman argued for giving parents government vouchers as a way to accomplish his vision of a system of education that was publicly financed but delivered both privately and publicly. Many reformers have expanded on Friedman's arguments beyond vouchers to school choice more generally, arguing that consumer choice and competition among schools will encourage innovative approaches to schooling that will in turn positively affect student outcomes (e.g., Betts 2005; Chubb and Moe 1990; Walberg and Bast 2003).

10.2.2 Institutional Theory

As one alternative to a market-based theory of choice, sociologists have pointed to institutional theory, which characterizes schools as institutions with persistent patterns of social action that individuals take for granted (Meyer 1977; Meyer and Rowan 1977, 1978; Powell and DiMaggio 1991; Scott and Meyer 1994; Scott and Davis 2007). Institutional theorists agree with market theorists that school bureaucracies dominate the public education sector, but they point more to the sociological environment. Institutional theory argues that schools operate in uncertain and highly institutionalized environments that define what counts as legitimate schooling, and because schools need to establish legitimacy, they will look more alike than different (Meyer and Ramirez 2000; Bidwell and Dreeben 2006). Even schools of choice pay attention to institutional

rules such as teacher certification, curricular subject matter, instructional time, reasonable class size, and mostly age-based grade organization, so choice schools may not end up differing that much from traditional public schools (Berends et al. 2010).

Thus, on the one hand, market theory predicts that students attending schools of choice will experience more positive student outcomes because of parents' freedom to choose and the resulting competition that holds all schools to a higher level. On the other hand, institutional theorists predict that students who choose schools of choice over traditional public schools are not likely to experience more positive outcomes because schools are more similar than different in terms of their organizational structure and processes.[1]

What does the evidence show regarding theoretical predictions that competition will raise the achievement not only of choice schools but the public school system as a whole? What is the evidence for increased innovation as theory predicts? We review the research addressing these questions in the sections that follow.

10.2.3 Competition

Analyzing state-level data from the Census and the U.S. Department of Education, Arum (1996) examined measures of the size of the private school sector, student/teacher ratio, income per student, and percent of the population in a metropolitan area. In addition, he analyzed student-level data in the nationally representative High School and Beyond to examine whether measures of school competition were related to student achievement in the public sector. Arum found that the private school market share was significantly related to the performance of public schools, which is consistent with market theory. However, improved performance was not due to

---

[1] These competing theories provide a helpful framework to assess school choice, but it should be noted that sociologists are also interested in additional theories related to school choice, such as sense making and social network theories (Jennings 2010), some of which we address later in this chapter.

greater efficiency. Rather, in states with large private school sectors, it was due to increased resources provided to public schools. In short, "increased resources at the school level, not organizational changes caused by increased competition, affect student outcomes" (Arum 1996, p. 29). Thus, the findings do not clearly support market theory or institutional theory; we will need further theorizing to inform school choice.

10.2.3.1   Charter Schools and Competition

Scholars have studied charter schools and their competitive effects in California (Buddin and Zimmer 2009), Florida (Sass 2006), Michigan (Arsen and Ni 2011; Bettinger 2005; Ni 2009), North Carolina (Bifulco and Ladd 2006a), and Texas (Booker et al. 2008). Most of these studies have relied on geographic proximity to measure competition—counting the number of charter schools within a given distance of a traditional public school (for a review see Betts 2009). It is assumed that charter schools close to other public schools present greater competitive pressures on the public schools to perform. Generally, the competitive effects of charter schools are mixed, either showing no effects or some positive effects (Betts 2009).

For example, in California, Buddin and Zimmer (2009) analyzed competitive effects in six districts using distance to the nearest charter school, the presence of *any* charter school within 2.5 miles, the *number* of charters within 2.5 miles, and the *proportion* of charter school enrollment within 2.5 miles. They found little evidence that greater competition is associated with achievement gains of students in public schools. As part of this study, Buddin and Zimmer administered a principal survey to a representative sample of California schools; between 80% and 90% of principals reported that the presence of charter schools in their district had "no effect" on their school's ability to attract and recruit students, the school's financial security, and teacher recruitment and retention.

In Florida, Sass (2006) analyzed longitudinal student records and found that the presence of charter schools within 2.5 and 5 miles of traditional public schools is associated with mathematics achievement gains for students in traditional public schools. Using a similar approach in North Carolina, Bifulco and Ladd (2006a) found no evidence that the presence of charter schools near traditional public schools improves the test score gains of public school students.

In her qualitative study, Jabbar (2015a, b, 2016) found that whether charter school principals perceive and respond to competition depended not simply on the number of schools of choice or competitor schools in the vicinity of a school but on a number of other factors: the skill, experience, and social networks of a school's principal, how the principal defines competitors, and whether a school belongs to a Charter Management Organization (CMO). She also found that schools' responses to perceived competition varied; some made academic changes in response to competition while others engaged in more superficial changes, such as marketing or cream-skimming students.

10.2.3.2   Voucher Programs and Competition

In Milwaukee, with the oldest voucher program in the U.S., Chakrabarti (2013) relied on a difference-in-differences approach and found that competitive effects were mixed; there was a positive significant effect in reading in the second year, but no other competitive effects of the program.

In Florida, researchers have examined a few voucher programs for competitive effects: (1) the Florida Opportunity Scholarship Program (FOS), which existed between 1999 and 2006 and provided vouchers to students attending public schools that were in need of improvement twice in a four-year period; (2) the Florida Tax Credit Scholarship Program (FTC), which began in 2001 and provides vouchers to students from low-income families; and (3) the McKay Scholarships for Student with Disabilities Program, which began in 1999 and continues today. Several studies examined whether the FOS led to competitive effects, and all of them found positive effects on traditional public schools (Chakrabarti 2013;

Figlio and Rouse 2006; Greene and Winters 2004; Rouse et al. 2013; West and Peterson 2006). Examining the means-tested Florida Tax Credit Scholarship Program (FTC), Figlio and Hart (2014) relied on the difference-in-differences strategy to address the endogeneity of public school test scores and private school competition. The scholars surmised that because the FTC introduced a shock to the system—in that students could move from public to private schools—there might be the opportunity to observe the public schools experiencing increased competition. The study found that public schools subjected to more competitive pressures from private schools increased students' test scores, although the effect sizes were small (i.e., a one standard deviation increase in competition improves test scores by 1/20th of a standard deviation when comparing high-competition to low-competition areas of Florida). Moreover, they found that schools facing the greatest financial incentive to keep low-income students increased test scores the most. Finally, Greene and Winters (2008) examined the McKay program and found that the test scores of students with disabilities improved significantly for those students who remained in traditional public schools.

Egalite (2016) examined competitive effects of the first year of the Louisiana Scholarship Program (LSP) with school fixed effects and a regression discontinuity framework. The school fixed effects model used competition information based on (1) a distance measure between a public school and the nearest private school, a shorter distance between schools indicating a greater number of school choice options; (2) a density measure of the number of private schools (the competitors) within a 5 and 10 mile radius; (3) a diversity measure of the different types of private schools near a public school, which indicates the number of choice alternatives that families have in a given area; and (4) a market concentration measure, which is a modified Herfindahl Index that sums the squared market shares of each type of private school within a given public school radius (e.g., 10 miles). The regression discontinuity design analyzed whether students in lower performing schools experience greater test score gains compared with students in higher performing schools. In the fixed effects strategy, Egalite found statistically significant impacts for mathematics with the density and diversity measures and no effects in English Language Arts. There were no significant test score results based on the regression discontinuity approach.

Examining the competitive effects of Ohio's EdChoice Scholarship Program, Figlio and Karbownik (2016) relied on a regression-discontinuity design by comparing schools that were just above the cut to be eligible for the voucher program to those schools just below the cut to be eligible—the idea being that these sets of schools have very similar observable and unobservable characteristics, allowing for enlightening insights into competitive effects of the voucher program. They find that mathematics and reading achievement increased modestly as a result of voucher competition.

In a review of the competitive effects of voucher programs, Figlio (2009, p. 336) states that "there are no definitive studies of the effects of school vouchers on voucher users' performance or on the overall education system. The weight of the evidence indicates that vouchers lead to… some positive spillovers to the overall public school population."

Thus, generally across the studies of charter schools and voucher programs the evidence of small effects does not robustly support market theory. However, with neutral to positive effects found in most studies, the evidence may be more consistent with market theory than institutional theory.

10.2.4 Innovation

Some researchers have attempted to address whether school choice leads to greater innovation. This would be consistent with market theory, which holds that school choice (particularly charter school choice) will result in greater school autonomy that will produce organizational innovations promoting structures and processes that lead to changes in instructional practices, which in turn will lead to better student outcomes

(Chubb and Moe 1990; Walberg and Bast 2003). As Lubienski (2003) states, "choice, competition, and innovation are cast as the necessary vehicles for advancing academic outcomes" (p. 397).

Defining innovation is important when conducting research on school choice (Berends 2015), and the definitions vary widely. For example, the very existence of charter schools and their differing governance structures may be considered innovation (Center for Education Reform 2008; U.S. Department of Education 2004, 2008). However, innovation may also mean the implementation of instructional designs that change schools on every level—teaching and learning; the organization of time, curriculum, and instruction; a governance partnership with a non-profit charter management organization (CMO) or a for-profit educational management organization (EMO) (e.g., KIPP, Expeditionary Learning, Green Dot, National Heritage Academies).

Lubienski (2003) looks at innovation at the teaching and learning as well as the administrative levels. He distinguishes between "*educational* changes (practices regarding curricular content and instructional strategies with immediate impact at the classroom-level) and *administrative* changes (organizational-level practices and structural designs that do not directly affect classroom techniques or content)" (pp. 404–5, emphasis in original). Reviewing the empirical studies on innovation (i.e., 56 studies on charter schools), Lubienski (2003) found that although some charter schools were organizationally innovative, classroom practices were quite similar in charter and traditional public schools.

Others have relied on state charter school laws to help define what school choice innovation means. Wohlstetter et al. (2013) examined charter school laws across the United States, which aim their directives toward *classrooms* (providing teachers with new professional opportunities, implementing innovative programs and practices, and improving student performance), the *school community* (increased autonomy, parent involvement, and accountability), and the *school system* (increased public school competition, increased

capacity of the K–12 system, and improved student achievement district-wide). They found that most of the state charter laws (over 90%) encouraged schools to use their autonomy to experiment with new educational practices for students.

Examining innovation through school mission statements, Renzulli et al. (2015) focused on the growth and decline of specialist charter school mission statements, which address particular goals such as serving at-risk populations, emphasizing certain values (e.g., citizenship, civic responsibility), teaching in a language other than English, or providing a virtual school for home-schooled students. Coding these mission statements between 1992 and 2005 in the Center for Education Reform database (2006) and analyzing growth curves over time, Renzulli et al. found that specialist mission statements of charter schools became more diverse over time but comprised a smaller proportion of charter schools overall. Moreover, charter schools' mission statements came to resemble those of traditional public schools over time rather than something more innovative.

Other researchers have defined innovation within the local context, meaning whether charter schools implement organization and instructional practices in a way that differs from the surrounding traditional public school district. Analyzing the nationally representative Schools and Staffing Survey, Preston et al. (2012) investigated whether charter schools implement innovations more than their traditional public school neighbors. Specifically, the researchers examined differences in staffing practices (teacher compensation and tenure not governed by unions); academic support services (after school tutoring or extended day instruction); school organizational structures (year round schools, block scheduling, looping, houses or families of classrooms, and multi-grade or mixed-age classrooms); and governance (stakeholder involvement). They found that charter schools did not differ from traditional public schools on any of these dimensions.

Thus, the research on whether school choice leads to innovation is mixed and does not definitively support either market theory or institutional theory. While some charter schools are more innovative organizationally (Lubienski 2003) and charter school laws in states aim to promote educational innovation and experimentation (Wohlstetter et al. 2013), practices closest to students in classrooms tend toward the ordinary (Preston et al. 2013; Berends et al. 2010) as do charter school mission statements (Renzulli et al. 2015).

The research and theory discussed above represent what might be called a "first wave" of rigorous research that aims to understand how school choice affects students and schools. Moving forward, researchers have additional questions that will require longitudinal student- and school-level data. Gaining access to such data may be difficult, although with federal laws, it should be readily available. The emergence of research–practice partnerships provides an avenue to gain access to data, conduct rigorous analyses, and offer feedback to policymakers and practitioners. In what follows, we describe some examples of research–practice partnerships and discuss the research that such partnerships might allow.

10.3 The Prospects of Research–Practice Partnerships

Research–practice partnerships are becoming more common throughout the U.S. in order to facilitate better educational policies, programs, and practices. Such partnerships establish "relationships between researchers and practitioners (in states, districts, or schools) to learn from each other when implementing interventions and to modify and improve them based on researchers' expert knowledge and practitioners' local expertise and experiences" (Berends and Austin 2017). Establishing these relationships is important for building capacity within the system (at state or local levels), allowing researchers and practitioners to focus on the core practices and processes in schools when various educational reforms are implemented (Roderick, Easton, and Sebring 2009; Sebring and Allensworth 2012).

A model for research–practice partnerships is the Consortium on Chicago School Research (CCSR) at the University of Chicago Urban Education Institute. Beginning over twenty-five years ago, the CCSR aims to further the relationships and communication among researchers, policymakers, and practitioners so that research can better inform policy and practice. CCSR focuses on the core problems facing practitioners and decision makers and requires changing the researcher's role from outside expert to an active, knowledge-building partner with practitioners and policy makers (Roderick et al. 2009). To accomplish its goals, CCSR has focused on (1) developing a data system that allows researchers to monitor key education reforms; (2) engaging key stakeholders in ongoing relationships; (3) conducting rigorous studies to inform both research and practice; (4) cumulating knowledge over time by conducting coherent and connected studies; and (5) disseminating research findings and implications to the public (Roderick et al. 2009).

Because of CCSR's efforts and because there are a number of charter schools in Chicago, there is great potential in examining not only whether charter schools have effects on achievement and attainment, but also the conditions under which charter schools may be having effects on student outcomes. Recently, for instance, some researchers worked with CCSR to examine school choice and racial segregation patterns (Burdick-Will 2017; Logan and Burdick-Will 2015).

With the support of the federal government, several other research–practice partnerships have been established. Since 2014, the Institute of Education Sciences (IES), the wing of the U.S. Department of Education that funds research, has funded twenty-eight different projects at about $400,000 each (over $11 million total) to help create and sustain such partnerships across the U.S. Examples include the Houston Education Research Consortium (HERC) led by Ruth López Turley at Rice University and Carla Stevens of the Houston Independent School District (see López Turley and Stevens 2015); the Baltimore Education Research Consortium (BERC), a partnership between researchers at Johns Hopkins University and Morgan State University in Baltimore and Baltimore City

Public Schools (Durham et al. 2015); the Minority Student Achievement Network (MSAN), a self-organized network of twenty-nine suburban and small urban districts focused on addressing Asian–White, Latino–White, and Black–White achievement gaps (Booth et al. 2015); and the Michigan Consortium for Education Research (MCER), a partnership involving the Michigan Department of Education, the Center for Education Performance and Information, Michigan State University, and the University of Michigan to engage stakeholders and experts in rigorous research to benefit public education (see Dynarski and Berends 2015).

A partnership that specifically examines school choice along with other educational issues is the Education Research Alliance for New Orleans (ERA), which specifically focuses on the post-Katrina school reforms in New Orleans. For example, because New Orleans relies on CMOs more than any other city in the U.S., the ERA research examines CMO policies and practices and their impact on schools, teachers, and students. In addition, the research considers New Orleans' OneApp system of choice (parents can apply to multiple schools on one application) and its impact on families and their choice among schools.

Yet another partnership with a goal to examine school choice is between the University of Notre Dame's Center for Research on Educational Opportunity (CREO) and the Indiana Department of Education. The partnership's guiding mission is to conduct independent, rigorous research to inform educational policy and decision making in Indiana. Beginning in 2011, the partnership has made transitions from a Republican State Superintendent of Public Instruction to a Democratic one and back to a Republican. Throughout administrations, the partnership has focused on school choice, teacher effectiveness, students' transitions into higher education, student mobility, and the teacher labor market and shortages.

With the growth of these partnerships, there is now a National Network of Education Research–Practice Partnerships housed at the Kinder Institute for Urban Research at Rice University, which supports and develops the relationships between research institutions and education agencies to improve the connections among research, policy, and practice. Toward that end this network convenes leaders from various research–practice partnerships across the country to learn from each other, share best practices, synthesize research findings, facilitate cross-partnership collaborations, and advance educational policies and system reforms.

Despite the opportunities that research–practice partnerships have to further influential research, they face many obstacles (Dynarski and Berends 2015; Roderick et al. 2009; Sebring and Allensworth 2012). Building trust and collaboration among the partners poses a significant challenge (Roderick et al. 2009; Turley and Stevens 2015; Coburn and Penuel 2016; Coburn et al. 2013). It takes a great deal of time and effort to agree on a common mission, arrive at research priorities, and conduct feasible research projects completed within a reasonable time frame.

An example of the challenge of sustaining trust is the partnership between the Indiana Department of Education and Notre Dame. The transition from the Republican Superintendent Bennett to the Democratic Ritz administration was fraught with conflict and contentiousness, which had significant implications for the partnership. Because the Republican administration established school choice as a research priority, the newly elected Democratic staff was skeptical about the partnership with Notre Dame. Could the researchers be objective? Were they advocates of school choice? Would their work be informative? Over time, the new staff came to appreciate the Notre Dame research team and its commitment not only to doing independent, objective research but to keeping the research out of the public eye until it passed peer review. To further trust in the partnership, Notre Dame also committed to sharing its research findings with the Indiana Department of Education well before the research was published. In addition, Notre Dame expanded the research priorities that were consistent with those of the superintendent.

In addition to building trust in a research–practice partnership, other challenges include the time and effort needed to nurture the relationship, difficulty in finding a common language between researchers and practitioners, building longitudinal data systems that allow for rigorous research, and communicating effectively with stakeholders (see Berends and Austin 2017).

10.4 Sociology and School Choice

The growth of research–practice partnerships creates the potential for researchers to examine additional questions about school choice, especially for those who take a sociological approach. Such questions can build on the "horse race" comparisons of which sector performs better and on the broad market and institutional theories.

Sociologists' major contribution to research on school choice is to highlight conditions—both within schools and in the social contexts surrounding them—that affect whether (and how well) different racial/ethnic and socioeconomic groups can benefit from school choice. We identify two broad categories into which this information falls: (1) accessing schools of choice, including parents' choices of neighborhoods and schools, and availability of choice; and (2) experiences within schools of choice. Within each category, we review recent literature and highlight opportunities for future research.

10.4.1 Access to School Choice

10.4.1.1 Theory and Early Research

The primary means of school choice available to families historically has been neighborhood selection (Holme 2002; Lareau and Goyette 2014). Students were assigned to schools based on where they lived. More affluent families were able to choose their children's schools by selecting homes in neighborhoods associated with strong schools. Low-income and minority students, however, often were trapped in neighborhoods associated with lower-performing schools. Racial residential segregation and financial barriers limited their families' ability to choose where their homes were located (Bischoff 2008;

Jargowsky 2014; Reardon et al. 2008; Reardon and Bischoff 2011).

One idea behind school choice that could theoretically increase student access to better schools is to change the governance structure of schools. Unlike traditional public schools, which follow district, state, and federal policies, schools of choice have governance structures that have fewer bureaucratic layers. For example, charter public schools are publicly funded but run under a charter by parents, educators, community groups, universities, or private organizations. As such, they are given independence and flexibility in order to encourage school autonomy, innovation, and accessibility. Although some charter schools are part of a CMO or EMO network, over two-thirds are free-standing, self-regulating schools (National Alliance for Public Charter Schools 2016).

Catholic schools provide another example of promoting accessibility through a differing governance structure. Specifically, they often are part of a diocese (which may or may not set school policies) and thus follow the tenets of the Catholic Church, which emphasize the Catholic identity of schools, development of students' faith, and social justice. Although, as noted above, the research on Catholic school effects differs by level of schooling, proponents of Catholic schools have theorized that the positive effects are due to the schools' governance structure, which embraces the "common school ideal" of educating students from all social backgrounds and providing them with equal access to learning opportunities (Hallinan and Kubitschek 2012).

A second idea behind school choice to promote accessibility is to unlink residential location and school assignment. This idea, sometimes called the "liberation model" (Archbald 2004; Denice and Gross 2016), is a common argument in support of school choice. If school attendance could be disconnected from residential location, the racial segregation in neighborhoods would no longer lead to racially segregated schools. Instead, by enabling low-income and minority families to choose a school outside their neighborhood, school choice would decrease school segregation and allow these students to attend higher-quality schools than would otherwise be available to them.

The liberation model assumes that school choice operates according to market principles. That is, it assumes that parents choose the best school for their children based on full knowledge and consideration of three primary elements of choice—availability of information, availability of opportunities, and cost/benefit analysis (Bast and Walberg 2004; Lubienski and Lubienski 2013). It further assumes that they do so in a schooling market that is "open, fair, and unbiased" (Berends and Zottola 2009).

A large body of research has tested these assumptions by examining which parents make use of school choice and how they choose (e.g., Lareau and Goyette 2014; Schneider et al. 2000; Teske and Schneider 2001). Other studies have examined the characteristics of the schooling market and the extent to which schooling choices are accessible to different groups of students and families. We take up each of these in turn.

10.4.1.2 Patterns of Access to School Choice

Racial residential segregation remains pervasive, especially in metropolitan areas (Jargowsky 2014; Reardon and Bischoff 2011). Traditional school assignment based on residential location reproduces this segregation within public schools (Fiel 2013; Logan et al. 2012; Logan and Burdick-Will 2015; Saporito and Sohoni 2006). In theory, school choice breaks this association and thereby decreases school segregation (Orfield and Frankenberg 2013; Schneider et al. 2000). Egalite et al. (2016), for instance, found that Louisiana's voucher program facilitated student transfers that substantially reduced segregation in the public schools they left, but slightly increased segregation in the private schools they entered. However, other studies have shown that school choice most often produces greater segregation than would be present without it. Saporito (2003) found that in Philadelphia, lower-income families applied to predominantly non-White magnet schools, and higher-income families applied to schools with lower poverty rates, increasing segregation in the traditional public schools that the students left.

These preferences are net of other factors, such as school test performance or school and neighborhood violence. Saporito and Sohoni compared the racial (2006) and socioeconomic (2007) compositions of traditional public schools with those of the schools' attendance areas. They found that the public schools were more segregated both racially and socioeconomically than their attendance zones, indicating that White and high-income students' enrollment in private, charter, and magnet schools increased segregation in the traditional public schools they left behind.

School choice may affect segregation patterns if students who applied to and/or ultimately made use of voucher programs or charter schools differ significantly from those who did not (Teske and Schneider 2001). Several studies have tested for such differences by comparing the two groups on individual characteristics (e.g., race, ability, prior academic performance) as well as family characteristics (e.g., parents' education, income, and involvement in schooling) (Cullen et al. 2005, 2006; Greene et al. 1996; Howell and Peterson 2006; Krueger and Zhu 2004; Lauen 2009; Rouse 1998; Schneider et al. 2000; Witte 2000). Much of this work was developed in response to concerns about whether differences in achievement between students who exercise choice and those who stay in public schools are due to the effects of choice programs or simply reflect selection into choice programs. Researchers have also compared students who do and do not use choice to determine the extent to which school choice programs "cream-skim," or pull more advantaged students away from traditional public schools, leaving behind less advantaged students and thereby increasing segregation by academic performance if not race and income (Lacireno-Paquet et al. 2002; Zimmer et al. 2011).

In general, White and higher-SES families are more likely to participate in school choice than are minority and lower-SES families (Bifulco et al. 2009; Lauen 2007; Saporito 2003; Saporito and Sohoni 2007). However, patterns of participation differ somewhat by type of school choice. Nationally, White students have been somewhat more likely to enroll in charter schools, but the overall composition has shifted over time; the proportion of White and Black students has declined and that of Latino/a students has increased (Berends 2015; Gill et al. 2007). Specifically, charter school enrollment was disproportionately Black and Latino/a in 2010–11, partly because charter schools tend to be located in urban areas and because they have expanded in states with large Latino/a populations, such as California and Florida (Berends 2015). The proportion of low-income students in charter schools has also increased, from 27% eligible for free and reduced-price lunch in 1999–2000 to 53% in 2010–2011 (compared to 50% of public school students; Berends 2015). Differences between students and families who apply to and/or attend charter schools tend to vary more by state. In some states charter schools enroll a higher proportion of minority, low-income students and in other states, schools enroll a higher proportion of White, higher-income students. Thus, relative to public schools, segregation increases in some locations and decreases in others (Zimmer et al. 2009).

Other research has discovered that charter schools are associated with racial isolation, especially for Black students (Bifulco and Ladd 2006b; Frankenberg et al. 2010; Garcia 2007; Logan and Burdick-Will 2015; Siegel-Hawley and Frankenberg 2013; Renzulli and Evans 2005). Bifulco and Ladd (2006b) found that Black students in North Carolina entered charter schools that were even more racially segregated than the public schools they left. Using national survey data on charter schools in 338 districts, Renzulli and Evans (2005) found that charter schools facilitated White flight out of school districts in which there were higher levels of racial integration, and that even when Whites made up the majority in integrated schools, they sought out schools with even higher proportions of White students. In Arizona, Garcia (2007) showed that both White flight and minority self-segregation into charter schools led to greater segregation in charter schools than the traditional public schools students left.

Often by design of the educational policy, school voucher programs are more likely to serve lower-income and minority students (Berends

and Waddington 2018; Greene et al. 1999b; Witte 2000). This pattern is driven by voucher programs' tendency to target low-income families through restrictions that limit eligibility to families below a certain income threshold (Howell 2004; Peterson et al. 2002). Even where racial and socioeconomic differences between choosers and non-choosers are minimized, other differences emerge in parents' education level. In Detroit, low-income parents with higher levels of education were more likely to use choice than less-educated low-income parents (Lee et al. 1996). Witte (2000) found that students whose parents applied to the Milwaukee Parental Choice Program were lower performing, lower income, and more likely to be Black or Latino/a than their public school peers who did not apply, but that they had mothers with somewhat higher relative levels (but still low absolute levels) of education than their peers. Similar patterns were found in other voucher programs, such as those in New York, Washington, DC, Cleveland, Dayton, Ohio, and Indiana (Berends and Waddington 2018; Gill et al. 2007; Howell and Peterson 2006).

10.4.1.3   Processes of Access to School Choice

The research described above provides broad information on whether differences exist between parents who do and do not make use of school choice options, and whether these differences increase or decrease school segregation. However, it generally provides less information on why these differences exist and what processes are driving them. More recent research has begun to focus on the *processes* by which students end up in schools of choice, looking especially at the role of parents, including which school characteristics were important to parents' decisions and how they became informed about their choice options.

10.4.1.4   Parental Preferences

To understand parental preferences in school choice, researchers traditionally have relied on surveys that ask parents to list or rank the factors that are most important to them when choosing a school (Billingham and Hunt 2016; Kimelberg and Billingham 2013; Stein et al. 2011; Teske and Schneider 2001). Results overwhelmingly show that, no matter their racial or socioeconomic background, parents' strongest preference is for academic quality (Bell 2009a; Billingham and Hunt 2016; Denice and Gross 2016; Harris and Larsen 2015; Kleitz et al. 2000; Phillips et al. 2012; Schneider et al. 2000; Weiher and Tedin 2002; Witte 2000).

However, researchers have consistently shown that what parents *say* they want is not necessarily what they actually want or ultimately choose. In Chicago, for instance, the majority of students whose parents chose a non-neighborhood school moved into schools with higher test scores (79%) and higher graduation rates (87%) than their neighborhood school; White and Asian students moved into higher-performing schools than did Black and Latino/a students (Stevens et al. 2011). In other locations, far fewer students ended up in better schools. Bell (2009a) found that despite stating strong preferences for academic quality, only 53% of middle-class parents and only 36% of working-class and poor parents chose a non-failing school. This discrepancy could be due to nuances in how parents define academic quality or weigh academic quality with other priorities, or differences between true preferences and stated preferences. They could also be due to structural constraints that prevent parents, especially minority and low-income parents, from acting on their preferences.

Some research has examined the relative significance of academics with other factors (e.g., school safety, discipline, racial or socioeconomic composition), and whether the importance of these factors differs by race or socioeconomic status. Findings suggest that academic quality means different things to different parents, ranging from "decent" to "excellent" (Altenhofen et al. 2016). Other academic factors, such as teacher effectiveness and academic rigor, are also frequently mentioned.

Several studies have found class differences in how academic quality is assessed (Harris and Larsen 2015; Horvat et al. 2003; Rhodes and DeLuca 2014; Schneider et al. 2000). Among

low-income parents in particular, safety and discipline are major concerns (Kleitz et al. 2000). These factors weigh especially heavily for parents in neighborhoods whose schools are less safe, but they also often serve as a signal of academic quality. Other factors that concern low-income families include extracurricular activities (Harris and Larsen 2015) and distance from home to school (Kleitz et al. 2000), indicating a structural barrier to use of school choice. These findings highlight that school choice is not a single decision-making process that is uniform for all parents, but rather that there are different processes for parents of different backgrounds (Saporito and Lareau 1999).

The quality of parents' responses to survey questions about their preferences may be limited by social desirability bias. This creates pressure to provide socially acceptable responses (e.g., desire for academic quality) while avoiding socially sanctioned responses (e.g., racial preferences) (Billingham and Hunt 2016; Stein et al. 2011; Teske and Schneider 2001). Despite this pressure, some survey and interview evidence shows that White parents admit to make schooling choices based on racial preferences (Goyette et al. 2012; Henig 1996; Johnson and Shapiro 2003; Saporito and Lareau 1999). Evidence also shows that, when evaluating a school's status, middle- and upper-middle-class parents use schools' race and socioeconomic composition as a proxy for school quality (Goyette 2008; Henig 1996; Holme 2002; Saporito and Lareau 1999).

In other cases, racial preferences are explicit. Saporito and Lareau (1999), for example, found that White and Black families showed different sensitivities to the racial composition of a school. Using quantitative and interview data from eighth-graders in a Northeastern school district, they discovered that White parents took a multistep approach to choosing a school: First, they eliminated schools with a high percentage of Black students. Then, they chose from among the remaining "White" schools, many of which were in fact lower quality in terms of test scores, safety, and poverty rates. Black parents do not take race into account to the same extent as White parents, but there is some evidence that they choose schools with lower poverty rates (Saporito and Lareau 1999). There also is some evidence that minority parents prioritize schools in which their child would be in the racial majority (Dougherty et al. 2013; Henig 1990).

In addition to problems of social desirability bias, differences in the way parents are asked to identify their preferences can cause confusion or differing results from survey to survey (Stein et al. 2011). For example, some surveys ask parents to list their preferences, others ask them to choose preferences from a list or to rank a given set of preferences from most to least important. The same factors are often defined differently: Educational quality, academic quality, good teachers, high test scores, or taking a lot of classes in core subjects may all be used as indicators of academic quality in different surveys (Kleitz et al. 2000; Schneider et al. 2000; Teske et al. 2007; Weiher and Tedin 2002).

A few recent studies have attempted to distinguish between parents' stated preferences (as indicated in surveys and interviews) and their actual preferences (as indicated by the school into which they ultimately move their children) (Phillips et al. 2015). Others have examined parents' actual choosing behaviors by using, for example, survey-based experiments (Billingham and Hunt 2016) or tracking their online searches for schools (Buckley and Schneider 2003; Schneider and Buckley 2002). Schneider and colleagues found that in New York City, parents' stated preferences correlated highly with the characteristics of the schools they chose (Buckley and Schneider 2003; Schneider et al. 1998). Comparing parents' stated preferences on surveys with patterns of student movement into charter schools, Stein et al. (2011) found that although many Indianapolis students moving into charter schools were leaving failing schools, only a small percentage moved into a school that was making adequate yearly progress—and nearly 41% moved into another failing school. Billingham and Hunt (2016) asked White parents to respond to experimental vignettes that prompted them to choose a school based on characteristics such as safety, facilities, academic performance, and racial composition; they found

strong preferences among White families for schools that were predominantly White.

10.4.1.5 Constraints Limiting Access to School Choice: Structural Inequalities

Systemic inequalities in access to information about choice options, school practices that target or exclude particular populations, and the structure of neighborhoods and schooling options also may limit the extent to which parents' preferences are realized in their choice of school. A growing body of research seeks to understand what information is available to parents, whether it is equitably distributed, and how parents make use of it (Fuller and Elmore 1996; Lareau and Goyette 2014; Rich and Jennings 2015; Schneider et al. 2000). School choice systems are often complex and difficult to navigate (Archbald 2004; Bell 2009b; Mickelson and Southworth 2005; Roda and Wells 2013; Sattin-Bajaj 2011); how schools, districts, and choice programs provide information and structure access influences parents' ability to identify their options, select among them, and successfully enroll in a choice school.

The market model of school choice assumes that parents have access to the information they need to make informed, rational choices for their children. However, research indicates that there is often too little or too much information on schooling options, that it is not effectively or equitably communicated, or that application processes are prohibitively complex. Schneider and colleagues (Schneider and Buckley 2003; Schneider et al. 2000) found that information was simply not available on characteristics of choice schools, including test scores, student retention rates, and graduation rates. Weininger (2014) found that, where information was available, parents needed "spreadsheets and Web bookmarks and priority rankings to organize and process [it]" (Pattillo et al. 2014, p. 262). Pattillo et al. (2014) found that Chicago Public Schools—which allow students to attend schools outside of their neighborhood attendance zone—did not make information readily available to families. Official sources of information, including a handbook and a high school fair, were overwhelming for parents to navigate. Most Washington, DC, parents knew little about schools' academic performance, school safety, or school racial composition, but parents who had utilized school choice knew more about their children's schools than those who had not (Buckley and Schneider 2003; Schneider et al. 1998).

The process of applying to schools of choice is also often complicated. Stevens et al. (2011) found that although most Chicago students in their study wanted to attend a high school other than their neighborhood school, fewer than half actually succeeded in gaining admission, largely because they could not navigate the application process. Guidance from adults—teachers, counselors, other staff—increases students' success but varies widely in accuracy and usefulness (Pattillo et al. 2014; Stevens et al. 2011). Pattillo and colleagues also found that applications for certain Chicago schools were not widely available.

These difficulties may account for findings that, when making decisions, relatively few parents consider the available information on school characteristics, and many parents fail to consider all the options available to them (Buckley and Schneider 2003; Schneider et al. 2000). Instead, their scrutiny of schools tends to be fairly superficial. Altenhofen et al. (2016) found that just under one in five upper-middle-class parents reported having done some research before selecting a school for their child(ren), whether "visiting schools, talking with principals and teachers, attending school information meetings, looking at school websites, or examining school information provided by the [...] Department of Education." Holme (2002) found that 34 of 42 parents interviewed had not looked at test scores for the schools in their previous neighborhoods; only one parent had visited the neighborhood school before determining that it was a "bad" school; less than a quarter of parents who moved to a new area "for the schools" visited the school associated with their residential choice; and only about 30% looked at test score achievement before moving (Holme 2002).

Lareau (2014) discovered through interviews with middle- and upper-middle-class parents that, despite their vigilant involvement in many aspects of their children's upbringing (from choosing formal extracurricular activities to volunteering in their children's classrooms), this same vigilance did not apply to choosing a school. Instead, they rely on relatively vague information focused on the reputations of various schools from members of their social networks. Within middle-class informal social networks, evaluations are often based on the perceived status of the school rather than on objective information about academic quality (Bell 2009a; Holme 2002; Weininger 2014).

Some research suggests that middle- and upper-middle-class parents are more likely to use performance data than working-class and poor parents, but other research finds that lower-income parents rely more heavily on administrative and school performance information because their social networks provide more limited information about schooling options (Schneider et al. 2000). Weininger (2014) found that Black parents place greater emphasis on performance data than Whites, while White parents tend to use school test scores to screen for a basic level of performance and then turn to networks for recommendations among acceptable schools. He also found that working-class parents had little knowledge of publicly available information on school performance. Some evidence shows that when parents are given detailed information on school performance, they are more likely to choose higher-performing schools than parents who must do the research themselves (Dougherty et al. 2013; Hastings and Weinstein 2008; Kisida and Wolf 2010).

Getting good information on schooling options can be particularly difficult and stressful for low-income families (Hastings and Weinstein 2008; Pattillo et al. 2014; Sattin-Bajaj 2011). They must gather information and make choices while juggling everyday challenges such as transportation and childcare without the safety net from which middle- and upper-middle-class families benefit. Although low-income families make use of informal social networks to gather information, that information is less likely to be concrete (Hastings and Weinstein 2008; Pattillo et al. 2014; Weininger 2014).

To address the issue of providing useful information to parents interested in charter schools, some cities have moved toward a common application to facilitate the process. Typically, in the charter sector parents go to an individual school to fill out an application. With the common application, parents can apply online to a number of schools at the same time. Denver and New Orleans now offer this option, and researchers find that it results in less confusion among parents because it provides a standardized process of learning about and applying to the available schools (Gross et al. 2015). Yet, even with this process, minority and low-income parents participate in school choice at lower rates than White and higher-income families.

Several studies find that parents of all social class backgrounds rely more on their social networks than on other sources of school data as their primary source of information for deciding which schools to consider and for evaluating the quality of each school (Holme 2002; Lareau 2014; Schneider et al. 2000; Weininger 2014). As economic stratification and segregation increase, social networks also become increasingly homogenous (Reardon and Bischoff 2011). To the extent that social networks help parents choose schools, therefore, parent reliance on informal sources of information may perpetuate inequality. Holme (2002) argued that "the reputations of 'good' schools were not simply passed through the networks of high-status parents, but were actually constructed through such networks" (p. 180). The result is a relatively narrow set of "acceptable" schools into which middle-class parents place their children, either by using their social and financial capital to move into a reputable school district or by exercising policy-based choice options.

In contrast, more disadvantaged families consider a wider set of schools to be acceptable than advantaged families (Bell 2009a), and choose from an entirely different set of schools. Not unlike the way various network sharing shapes parents' considerations, the geography of school choice often leaves minority and low-income parents with different schooling options than White and high-income parents within the same city. Kimelberg (2014) emphasized that parents' ability to exercise choice is a function of both their individual financial, social, and cultural capital and the legal, geographic, and financial characteristics of the local school environment. Similarly, Rich and Jennings (2015) showed that "family resources and structural constraints" intersect to reduce the likelihood that low-income students would leave failing schools compared to their more affluent peers—and limit their options if they do leave. In other words, whereas higher-income students are more likely to leave probationary schools and enroll in high-performing ones, lower-income students have less access to high-quality schools, leading those who leave probationary schools to transfer into similarly low-performing ones.

Recent research has returned to the role of residential segregation in shaping schooling options and indicates that it continues to influence school choice programs. Studies on the "unofficial choice market" (Holme 2002; Kimelberg 2014; Lareau and Goyette 2014)—the schools families opt into through residential moves—show that residential segregation affects schooling opportunities. Parents' choice of a neighborhood is still a major form of school choice, which is most available to families with the financial means to purchase homes in areas with desirable schools or districts (Kimelberg 2014). In contrast, low-income and minority families still find themselves constrained to poorer neighborhoods with lower-quality neighborhood schools. This recent research examines more complex patterns of residential choice and mobility in an effort to understand how the residential-school choice connection differs for different race and socioeconomic groups (Lareau and Goyette 2014).

The lower quality of schools in poor urban neighborhoods can lead to higher rates of school choice—but lower-quality options—among low-income and minority students (Burdick-Will 2017; Lauen 2007). Denice and Gross (2016) showed that, despite having similar strong preferences for high academic performance, Latino/a and Black families in Denver chose from a different set of schools than did White families because quality choice options are not evenly distributed across the city. For many low-income families, access to transportation is a major limiting factor that exacerbates the unequal distribution of choice options across a city or metropolitan area (Hastings and Weinstein 2008; Lubienski and Dougherty 2009; Nathanson et al. 2013; Weininger 2014). Lack of transportation combined with unstable housing and an inability to escape disadvantaged neighborhoods with few schooling options means poor families' choices are often limited by default to a narrow set of low-quality schools (Rhodes and DeLuca 2014).

Black and Latino/a families who do attend higher-performing schools generally travel farther to do so (Denice and Gross 2016), which makes utilizing school choice a greater burden for these students. Burdick-Will (2017) found that the costs of using school choice were greater for students from high-poverty neighborhoods. In contrast to their more affluent peers (whose neighborhood schools provided a quality education or who attended non-neighborhood schools closer to their homes and with students like themselves), poor and minority students who attended non-neighborhood schools traveled farther and were more likely to be the only ones from their neighborhood attending that school.

10.5 School Choice and School Organization

Whereas research on parental choice focuses on the demand side of school choice, another recently expanding set of studies focuses on the supply side. The relationship between public school characteristics and student outcomes—particularly between school characteristics and the equitable distribution of opportunities to learn—has long been a focus for sociologists of education, dating back to the Coleman Report (Coleman et al. 1966). Identifying the conditions within schools of choice that facilitate opportunities to learn is an important extension of this line

of research. Compared to research on parental choices, however, this area remains relatively underdeveloped. Emphasizing the need for more research on the social organization of schooling within schools of choice, Schneider (2003, p. 12) wrote:

> Studies of school choice have also not yet overcome the inadequacies we find in studies of the social organization of public schools. One reason may be that the pressure to link school choice with gains in student achievement has placed issues of selection bias and test score differences at the forefront, thus overshadowing serious efforts to examine qualitative differences in the learning opportunities experienced in choice versus other types of school settings.

Some research has looked at the academic and administrative practices in schools of choice (e.g., Berends et al. 2010; Dobbie and Fryer 2013; Preston et al. 2012). The goal has been to determine whether schools of choice perform as theory predicts, providing an innovative alternative to traditional public schools, or whether they do not differ significantly from public school practices. Recent research has also taken a closer look at within-school practices that may produce positive test score gains but have other negative outcomes. For example, Golann (2015) found that practices focused on raising test scores in a no-excuses charter school produce "worker-learners" focused on rule following and deference to authority instead of "lifelong learners" who are self-directed and develop skills for success later in life.

10.5.1 Characteristics of Effective Choice Schools

Some studies on charter and Catholic schools have looked at school characteristics that are associated with positive effects on student outcomes. In charter schools, these characteristics include *longer school days* (Angrist et al. 2013a, b; Dobbie and Fryer 2013; Furgeson et al. 2012; Gleason et al. 2010; Hoxby et al. 2009; Tuttle et al. 2013), *school-wide focus on achievement* (Berends et al. 2010; Dobbie and Fryer 2013; Furgeson et al. 2012), *school behavioral policy*

(Angrist et al. 2013a, b; Hoxby et al. 2009), *coaching and feedback to teachers* (Dobbie and Fryer 2013; Furgeson et al. 2012), and *data-based decision-making* (Angrist et al. 2013a, b; Dobbie and Fryer 2013; Furgeson et al. 2012; Hoxby et al. 2009). Although these studies have pointed to these attributes as effective charter school characteristics, these are characteristics of effective schools more generally, and the autonomy that charter schools have in certain contexts may facilitate the implementation of effective structures and processes (Goldring and Berends 2009; Bryk et al. 2010).

Researchers examining Catholic school effects have focused on the explanatory mechanisms for these effects. These include stronger *ties between stakeholders* invested in Catholic schools (Coleman and Hoffer 1987), a more *explicit curriculum aimed at college attendance* (Carbonaro and Covay 2010; Hoffer 2009), a *skimming effect* whereby Catholic schools in underserved areas recruit students with strong academic backgrounds to their schools (Altonji et al. 2010; Epple and Romano 1998), an educational *environment inspiring hard work and internal motivation* (Jeynes 2008), a *caring community* (Bryk et al. 1993) and *disciplinary climate* (Coleman et al. 1982).

10.5.2 Environmental Conditions Related to School Choice

Other research considers how broader influences shape the effectiveness and supply of schools available to students. The broader educational landscape into which choice is introduced (e.g., New Orleans, Indianapolis) is related to the programs' efficacy (Jabbar 2015b). So, too, can the way schools perceive and respond to competitive pressure. Recent research examined those factors, testing the assumption that school choice generates productive competition among schools. It found that perceived competition does not affect how principals spend their time or how districts allocate their resources (Arsen and Ni 2011; Cannata 2011).

In terms of supply, principals' perceptions and interpretations of choice policies—and how those policies would affect the school's academics, school climate, and administrative functioning—influence their decisions to participate or not in voucher programs (Austin 2015; Stuit and Doan 2013). School practices also shape the set of schools available to different groups of students. Some schools make decisions about both where to locate and who to admit that are "focused on maintaining an advantageous market position" and therefore exclude or limit access for the highest-need populations (Jennings 2010; Lubienski et al. 2009). Other schools may create barriers to entry for all but a select group of applicants through enactment of admissions standards, behind-the-scenes exclusionary practices (Jennings 2010), or activities that appear to be neutral but impose a burden on certain types of families, such as requiring attendance at an evening open house, when transportation options are limited and low-income parents are working extra hours (Jennings et al. 2016; Pattillo et al. 2014). Sometimes information schools provide is not communicated effectively or is not equally available to all parents. For example, low-income parents in Chicago reported that communications from the schools they were trying to access were often erratic or nonexistent, and in some cases prevented them from enrolling their children in the school of their choice (Pattillo et al. 2014; Stevens et al. 2011). In other cases, district-wide school choice handbooks or individual schools' marketing materials are presented only in English, disadvantaging parents whose first language is not English (Jennings 2010; Sattin-Bajaj 2011). Jennings (2010) found that for some schools, printing materials only in English was an intentional strategy to avoid attracting "the wrong kind of student."

10.6 Conclusion

In the past couple of decades, we have learned a great deal about the choice options that parents have for their children. In particular, the comparative perspective that examines public and private schools and charter and traditional public schools have revealed a great deal about the consequences of choice for student achievement and educational attainment as well as family satisfaction. Research has also contributed to our understanding of how school choice is related to different school governance structures, residential location and access, segregation patterns, parents' stated and actual preferences, information flows, and the organization of schools. Yet, on many of these issues there needs to be additional research to address the heterogeneity of school choice effects.

Despite its critics, school choice is likely to expand in the near future with the bipartisan support of charter schools that currently exists at the federal level and the expansion of scholarship and voucher programs in many states. With such expansion, additional research opportunities exist for sociologists to examine new waves of questions that can be addressed within the increasing number of research–practice partnerships. New analysis and syntheses of research findings will likely push sociologists to develop new theories that depict current empirical conditions and suggest hypotheses to investigate in different locales in the U.S. and other countries.

References

Abdulkadiroglu, A., Angrist, J. D., Cohodes, S. R., Dynarski, S. M., Fullerton, J. B., Kane, T. J., & Pathak, P. A. (2009). *Informing the debate: Comparing Boston's charter, pilot and traditional schools*. Boston: The Boston Found.

Abdulkadiroglu, A., Pathak, P. A., & Walters, C. R. (2015). *School vouchers and student achievement: Evidence from the Louisiana Scholarship Program* (Working Paper No. 21839). Cambridge, MA: National Bureau of Economic Research.

Altenhofen, S., Berends, M., & White, T. G. (2016). School choice decision making among suburban, high-income parents. *AERA Open, 2*(1), 1–14.

Altonji, J. G., Elder, T. E., & Taber, C. R. (2005). An evaluation of instrumental variable strategies for estimating the effects of Catholic schooling. *Journal of Human Resources, 15*(4), 791–821.

Altonji, J. G., Huang, C., & Taber, C. R. (2010). *Estimating the cream skimming effect of school choice*. (NBER Working Paper No. 16579).

Angrist, J. D., Cohodes, S. R., Dynarski, S. M., Fullerton, J. B., Kane, T. J., Pathak, P. A., & Walters, C. R. (2011). *Student achievement in Massachusetts' charter schools*. Boston: Center for Education Policy Research at Harvard University.

Angrist, J. D., Pathak, P. A., & Walters, C. R. (2013a). Explaining charter school effectiveness. *American Economic Journal: Applied Economics, 5*(4), 1–27.

Angrist, J. D., Cohodes, S. R., Dynarski, S. M., Pathak, P. A., & Walters, C. D. (2013b). *Charter schools and the road to college readiness: The effects on college preparation, attendance and choice*. Boston: Boston Foundation and New Schools Venture Fund.

Archbald, D. A. (2004). School choice, magnet schools, and the liberation model: An empirical study. *Sociology of Education, 77*, 283–310.

Arsen, D., & Ni, Y. (2011). Shaking up public schools with competition: Are they changing the way they spend money? In M. Berends, M. Cannata, & E. B. Goldring (Eds.), *School choice and school improvement* (pp. 193–214). Cambridge, MA: Harvard Education Press.

Arum, R. (1996). Do private schools force public schools to compete? *American Sociological Review, 61*, 29–46.

Austin, M. J. (2015). Schools' responses to voucher policy: Participation decisions and early implementation experiences in the Indiana Choice Scholarship Program. *Journal of School Choice, 9*(3), 354–379.

Barnard, J., Frangakis, C. E., Hill, J. L., & Rubin, D. B. (2003). Principal stratification approach to broken randomized experiments: A case study of school choice vouchers in New York City. *Journal of the American Statistical Association, 97*(457), 284–292.

Bast, J. L., & Walberg, H. J. (2004). Can parents choose the best schools for their children? *Economics of Education Review, 23*(4), 431–440.

Bell, C. (2009a). All choices created equal? The role of choice sets in the selection of schools. *Peabody Journal of Education, 84*(2), 191–208.

Bell, C. (2009b). Geography in parental choice. *American Journal of Education, 115*, 493–521.

Berends, M. (2014). The evolving landscape of school choice in the United States. In H. R. Milner IV & K. Lomotey (Eds.), *Handbook of urban education* (pp. 451–473). New York: Routledge.

Berends, M. (2015). Sociology and school choice: What we know after two decades of charter schools. *Annual Review of Sociology, 41*, 159–180.

Berends, M., & Austin, M. (2017). The promises and pitfalls of research–practice partnerships. In M. C. Makel & J. Plucker (Eds.), *Toward a more perfect psychology: Improving trust, accuracy, and transparency in research* (pp. 153–170). Washington, DC: American Psychological Association.

Berends, M., & Waddington, R. J. (2018). School choice in Indianapolis: Effects of charter, magnet, private, and traditional public schools. *Education Finance and Policy, 13*(2), 210–239.

Berends, M., & Zottola, G. C. (2009). Social perspectives on school choice. In M. Berends, M. G. Springer, D. Ballou, & H. J. Walberg (Eds.), *Handbook of research on school choice* (pp. 35–54). New York: Routledge.

Berends, M., Springer, M. G., Ballou, D., & Walberg, H. J. (Eds.). (2009). *Handbook of research on school choice*. New York: Routledge.

Berends, M., Goldring, E. B., Stein, M., & Cravens, X. (2010). Instructional conditions in charter schools and students' mathematics achievement gains. *American Journal of Education, 116*(3), 303–335.

Berends, M., Cannata, M., & Goldring, E. B. (Eds.). (2011). *School choice and school improvement*. Cambridge, MA: Harvard Education Press.

Bettinger, E. P. (2005). The effect of charter schools on charter students and public schools. *Economics of Education Review, 24*(2), 133–147.

Betts, J. R. (2005). The economic theory of school choice. In J. R. Betts & T. Loveless (Eds.), *Getting choice right: Ensuring equity and efficiency in education policy* (pp. 14–39). Washington, DC: Brookings Institution Press.

Betts, J. R. (2009). The competitive effects of charter schools on traditional public schools. In M. Berends, M. G. Springer, D. Ballou, & H. J. Walberg (Eds.), *Handbook of research on school choice* (pp. 195–208). New York: Routledge.

Betts, J. R., & Tang, Y. E. (2014). *A meta-analysis of the literature on the effect of charter schools on student achievement*. Bothel: National Charter Schools Research Project, Center on Reinventing Public Education, University of Washington.

Bidwell, C. E., & Dreeben, R. (2006). Public and private education: Conceptualizing the distinction. In M. T. Hallinan (Ed.), *School sector and student outcomes* (pp. 9–37). Notre Dame: University of Notre Dame Press.

Bifulco, R., & Ladd, H. (2006a). The impacts of charter schools on student achievement: Evidence from North Carolina. *Education Finance and Policy, 1*(1), 50–90.

Bifulco, R., & Ladd, H. (2006b). School choice, racial segregation, and test score gaps: Evidence from North Carolina's charter school program. *Journal of Policy Analysis and Management, 26*, 31–56.

Bifulco, R., Ladd, H. F., & Ross, S. L. (2009). Public school choice and integration evidence from Durham, North Carolina. *Social Science Research, 38*(1), 71–85.

Billingham, C. M., & Hunt, M. O. (2016). School racial composition and parental choice: New evidence on the preferences of White parents in the United States. *Sociology of Education, 89*(2), 99–117.

Bischoff, K. (2008). School district fragmentation and racial residential segregation: How do boundaries matter? *Urban Affairs Review, 44*(2), 182–217.

Booker, K., Gilpatric, S. M., Gronberg, T., & Jansen, D. (2008). The effect of charter competition on traditional public school students in Texas: Are children who stay behind left behind? *Journal of Urban Economics, 64*, 123–145.

Booker, K., Sass, T., Gill, B., & Zimmer, R. (2011). The effects of charter high schools on educational attainment. *Economics of Education Review, 31*(2), 209–212.

Booth, J. L., Cooper, L. A., Donovan, M. S., Huyghe, A., Koedinger, K. R., & Paré-Blagoev, E. J. (2015). Design-based research within the constraints of practice: Algebra by example. *Journal of Education for Students Placed at Risk, 20*(1–2), 79–100.

Bryk, A. S., Lee, V., & Holland, P. (1993). *Catholic schools and the common good*. Cambridge, MA: Harvard University Press.

Bryk, A., Sebring, P. B., Allensworth, E., Luppescu, S., & Easton, J. Q. (2010). *Organizing schools for improvement: Lessons from Chicago*. Chicago: University of Chicago Press.

Buckley, J., & Schneider, M. (2003). Shopping for schools: How do marginal consumers gather information about schools? *Policy Studies Journal, 31*(2), 121–145.

Buckley, J., & Schneider, M. (2006). Are charter school parents more satisfied with schools? Evidence from Washington, DC. *Peabody Journal of Education, 81*(1), 57–78.

Buddin, R., & Zimmer, R. (2009). Is charter school competition in California improving the performance of traditional public schools? *Public Administration Review, 69*(5), 831–845.

Burdick-Will, J. (2017). Neighbors, but not classmates: School choice, neighborhood disadvantage, local violent crime, and the heterogeneity of educational experiences in Chicago. *American Journal of Education, 124*(1), 37–65.

Butler, J. S., Carr, D., Toma, E. F., & Zimmer, R. (2013). School attributes and distance: Tradeoffs in the school choice decision. *Journal of Policy Analysis and Management, 32*(4), 785–806.

Cannata, M. (2011). How do principals respond to charter school competition? Understanding the mechanisms of the competitive effects of choice. In M. Berends, M. Cannata, & E. B. Goldring (Eds.), *School choice and school improvement* (pp. 177–192). Cambridge, MA: Harvard Education Press.

Carbonaro, W. (2006). Public–private differences in achievement among kindergarten students: Differences in learning opportunities and student outcomes. *American Journal of Education, 113*(1), 31–65.

Carbonaro, W., & Covay, E. (2010). School sector and student achievement in the era of standards based reforms. *Sociology of Education, 83*(2), 160–182.

Center for Education Reform. (2006). *1994–2006 national charter school directory*. Washington, DC: Center for Education Reform.

Center for Education Reform. (2008). *America's attitudes toward charter schools*. Washington, DC: Center for Education Reform.

Chakrabarti, R. (2013). Impact of voucher design on public school performance: Evidence from Florida and

Milwaukee voucher programs. *The B.E. Journal of Economic Analysis & Policy, 13*(1), 349–394.

Chingos, M. M., & Peterson, P. E. (2012). *The effects of school vouchers on college enrollment: Experimental evidence from New York City.* Washington, DC: Brookings Press.

Chubb, J. E., & Moe, T. M. (1990). *Politics, markets, and America's schools.* Washington, DC: Brookings Institution.

Coburn, C. E., & Penuel, W. R. (2016). Research–practice partnerships in education: Outcomes, dynamics, and open questions. *Educational Researcher, 45*(1), 48–54.

Coburn, C. E., Penuel, W. R., & Geil, K. E. (2013). *Research–practice partnerships: A strategy for leveraging research for educational improvement in school districts.* New York: William T. Grant Foundation.

Coleman, J. S., & Hoffer, T. (1987). *Public and private high schools: The impact of communities.* New York: Basic Books.

Coleman, J. S., Campbell, E. Q., Hobson, C. J., McPartland, J., Mood, A. M., Weinfeld, F. D., & York, R. L. (1966). *Equality of educational opportunity.* Washington, DC: U.S. Government Print Office.

Coleman, J. S., Hoffer, T., & Kilgore, S. (1982). *High school achievement: Public, Catholic, and private schools compared.* New York: Basic Books.

Cowen, J. (2008). School choice as a latent variable: Estimating the "complier average causal effect" of vouchers in Charlotte. *Policy Studies Journal, 36*(2), 301–315.

Cowen, J. M., Fleming, D. J., Witte, J. F., Wolf, P. J., & Kisida, B. (2013). School vouchers and student attainment: Evidence from a state-mandated study of Milwaukee's Parental Choice Program. *Policy Studies Journal, 41*(1), 147–167.

CREDO. (2009). *National charter school study.* http://credo.stanford.edu/documents/NCSS%202013%20Final%20Draft.pdf

Cullen, J. B., Jacob, B. A., & Levitt, S. D. (2005). The impact of school choice on student outcomes: An analysis of the Chicago Public Schools. *Journal of Public Economics, 89*, 729–760.

Cullen, J. B., Jacob, B. A., & Levitt, S. D. (2006). The effect of school choice on student outcomes: Evidence from randomized lotteries. *Econometrics, 74*, 1191–1230.

Denice, P., & Gross, B. (2016). Choice, preferences, and constraints: Evidence from public school applications in Denver. *Sociology of Education, 89*(4), 300–320.

Dobbie, W., & Fryer, R. G. (2011). Are high-quality schools enough to increase achievement among the poor? Evidence from the Harlem Children's Zone. *American Economic Journal: Applied Economics, 3*(3), 158–187.

Dobbie, W., & Fryer, R. G. (2013). Getting beneath the veil of effective schools: Evidence from New York City. *American Economic Journal: Applied Economics, 5*(4), 28–60.

Dougherty, J., Zamboni, D., Chowhan, M., Coyne, C., Dawson, B., Guruge, T., & Nukic, B. (2013). School information, parental decisions, and the digital divide: The SmartChoices project in Hartford, Connecticut. In G. Orfield & E. Frankenberg (Eds.), *Educational delusions? Why choice can deepen inequality and how to make schools fair.* Berkeley: University of California Press.

Durham, R. E., Bell-Ellwanger, J., Connolly, F., Robinson, H. R., Olson, L. S., & Rone, R. (2015). University–district partnership research to understand college readiness among Baltimore city students. *Journal of Education for Students Placed at Risk, 20*(1–2), 120–140.

Dynarski, S., & Berends, M. (2015). Special issue introduction: Research using longitudinal student data systems: Findings, lessons, and prospects. *Educational Evaluation and Policy Analysis, 37*(1S), 3S–5S.

Egalite, A. J. (2016). *The competitive effects of the Louisiana Scholarship Program on public school performance.* Fayetteville: University of Arkansas, School Choice Demonstration Project.

Egalite, A. J., Mills, J. N., & Wolf, P. J. (2016). The impact of targeted school vouchers on racial stratification in Louisiana schools. *Education and Urban Society.* https://doi.org/10.1177/0013124516643760.

Elder, T., & Jepsen, C. (2014). Are Catholic primary schools more effective than public primary schools? *Journal of Urban Economics, 80*(1), 28–38.

Epple, D., & Romano, R. E. (1998). Competition between private and public schools, vouchers, and peer-group effects. *American Economic Review, 88*(1), 33–62.

Epple, D., Romano, R. E., & Urquiola, M. (2015). *School vouchers: A survey of the economics literature* (Working Paper No. 21523). Cambridge, MA: National Bureau of Economic Research.

Epple, D., Romano, R., & Zimmer, R. (2016). *Charter schools: A survey of research on their characteristics and effectiveness* (Working Paper No. 21256). Cambridge, MA: National Bureau of Economic Research.

Evans, W. N., & Schwab, R. M. (1995). Finishing high school and starting college: Do Catholic schools make a difference? *The Quarterly Journal of Economics, 110*, 941–974.

Fiel, J. E. (2013). Decomposing school resegregation: Social closure, racial imbalance, and racial isolation. *American Sociological Review, 78*(5), 828–848.

Figlio, D. N. (2009). Voucher outcomes. In M. Berends, M. G. Springer, D. Ballou, & H. J. Walberg (Eds.), *Handbook of research on school choice* (pp. 321–337). New York: Routledge.

Figlio, D. N., & Hart, C. M. D. (2014). Completive effect of means-tested school vouchers. *American Economic Journal: Applied Economics, 6*(1), 133–156.

Figlio, D., & Karbownik, K. (2016). *Evaluation of Ohio's EdChoice Scholarship Program: Selection, competition, and performance effects.* Columbus: Thomas B. Fordham Foundation.

Figlio, D., & Rouse, C. E. (2006). Do accountability and voucher threats improve low-performing schools? *Journal of Public Economics, 92*(1–2), 239–255.

Figlio, D., Goldhaber, D., Hannaway, J., & Rouse, C. (2013). Feeling the Florida heat? How low-performing schools respond to voucher and accountability pressure. *American Economic Journal: Economic Policy, 5*(2), 251–281.

Frankenberg, E., Siegel-Hawley, G., & Wang, J. (2010). *Choice without equity: Charter school segregation and the need for civil rights standards.* Los Angeles: Civil Rights Project/Proyecto Derechos Civiles.

Freeman, K. J., & Berends, M. (2016). The Catholic school advantage in a changing social landscape: Consistency or increasing fragility? *Journal of School Choice, 10*(1), 22–47.

Friedman, M. (1955). The role of government in education. In R. A. Solo (Ed.), *Economics and the public interest* (pp. 123–144). New Brunswick: Rutgers University Press.

Friedman, M. (1962). *Capitalism and freedom.* Chicago: Chicago University Press.

Fuller, B. F., & Elmore, R. (1996). *Who chooses? Who loses? Culture, institutions, and the unequal effects of school choice.* New York: Teachers College Press.

Furgeson, J., Gill, B., Haimson, J., Killewald, A., McCullough, M., Nichols-Barrer, I., The, B., Verbitsky-Savitz, N., Bowen, M., Demeritt, Al, Hill, P., & Lake, R. (2012). *Charter-school management organizations: Diverse strategies and diverse student impacts* (Updated ed.). Princeton: Mathematica Policy Research.

Garcia, D. R. (2007). The impact of school choice on racial segregation in charter schools. *Educational Policy, 22*(6), 805–829.

Gill, B., Timpani, P. M., Ross, K. E., Brewer, D. J., & Booker, K. (2007). *Rhetoric vs reality: What we know and what we need to know about vouchers and charter schools.* Santa Monica: Rand Education.

Gleason, P., Clark, M., Tuttle, C., & Dwoyer, E. (2010). *The evaluation of charter school impacts: Final report* (NCEE 2010–4029). Washington, DC: National Center for Education Evaluation and Regional Assistance, Institute of Education Sciences, U.S. Department of Education.

Golann, J. W. (2015). The paradox of success at a no-excuses school. *Sociology of Education, 88*(2), 103–119.

Goldberger, A. S., & Cain, G. C. (1982). The causal analysis of cognitive outcomes in the Coleman, Hoffer, and Kilgore Report. *Sociology of Education, 55*(2/3), 103–122.

Goldring, E. B., & Shapira, R. (1993). Choice, empowerment, and involvement: What satisfies parents? *Educational Evaluation and Policy Analysis, 15*(4), 396–409.

Goyette, K. A. (2008). Race, social background, and school choice options. *Equity and Excellence in Education, 41*(1), 114–129.

Goldring, E., & Berends, M. (2009). *Leading with data: Pathways to improve your school.* Thousand Oaks: Corwin Press.

Goyette, K. A., Farrie, D., & Freely, J. (2012). This school's gone downhill: Racial change and perceived school quality among Whites. *Social Problems, 59*(2), 155–176.

Grady, S., & Bielick, S. (2010). *Trends in the use of school choice: 1993 to 2007* (NCES 2010–004). Washington, DC: National Center for Education Statistics, Institute of Education Sciences, U.S. Department of Education.

Greene, J. P. (2001). Vouchers in Charlotte. *Education Matters, 1*(2), 55–60.

Greene, J. P., & Winters, M. A. (2004). Competition passes the test. *Education Next, 4*(3), 66–71.

Greene, J. P., & Winters, M. A. (2008). *The effect of special education vouchers on public school achievement: Evidence from Florida's McKay Scholarship Program.* New York City: The Manhattan Institute for Policy Research.

Greene, J. P., Peterson, P. E., Du, J., Boeger, L., Frazier, C. L. (1996). The effectiveness of school choice in Milwaukee: A secondary analysis of data from the program's evaluation. *Harvard University Occasional Paper* 96-3.

Greene, J. P., Peterson, P. E., & Du, J. (1999a). Effectiveness of school choice: The Milwaukee voucher experiment. *Education and Urban Society, 31*(2), 190–213.

Greene, J. P., Howell, W. G., & Peterson, P. E. (1999b). *An evaluation of the Cleveland Scholarship Program.* Cambridge, MA: Harvard University Program on Education Policy and Governance.

Grogger, J., & Neal, D. (2000). *Further evidence on the effects of Catholic secondary schooling* (pp. 151–193). Washington, DC: Brookings-Wharton Papers on Urban Affairs.

Gross, B., DeArmond, M., & Denice, P. (2015). *Common enrollment, parents, and school choice: Early evidence from Denver and New Orleans.* Seattle: Center for Reinventing Public Education.

Hallinan, M., & Kubitschek, W. N. (2012). A comparison of academic achievement and adherence to the common school ideal in public and Catholic schools. *Sociology of Education, 85*(1), 1–22.

Harris, D. N., & Larsen, M. F. (2015). *What schools do families want (and why)? School demand and information before and after the New Orleans post-Katrina school reforms.* New Orleans: Education Research Alliance for New Orleans.

Hastings, J. S., & Weinstein, J. M. (2008). Information, school choice, and academic achievement: Evidence from two experiments. *The Quarterly Journal of Economics, 123*(4), 1373–1414.

Henig, J. R. (1990). Choice in public schools: An analysis of transfer requests among magnet schools. *Social Science Quarterly, 71*(1), 69–82.

Henig, J. R. (1996). The local dynamics of choice: Ethnic preferences and institutional responses. In B. Fuller &

R. F. Elmore (Eds.), *Who chooses? Who loses? Culture, institutions, and the unequal effects of school choice* (pp. 95–117). New York: Teachers College Press.

Henig, J. R. (2008). *Spin cycle: How research is used in policy debates, The case of charter schools*. New York: Russell Sage Foundation/The Century Foundation.

Hoffer, T. B. (2009). Perspectives on private schools. In M. Berends, M. G. Springer, D. Ballou, & H. J. Walberg (Eds.), *Handbook of research on school choice* (pp. 429–446). New York: Routledge.

Holme, J. J. (2002). Buying homes, buying schools: School choice and the social construction of school quality. *Harvard Educational Review, 72*(2), 177–205.

Horvat, E. M., Weininger, E. B., & Lareau, A. (2003). From social ties to social capital: Class differences in the relations between schools and parent networks. *American Educational Research Journal, 40*(2), 319–351.

Howell, W. G. (2004). Dynamic selection effects in means-tested, urban school voucher programs. *Journal of Policy Analysis and Management, 23*(2), 225–250.

Howell, W. G., & Peterson, P. E. (2006). *The education gap: Vouchers and urban Schools*. Washington, DC: Brookings Institution Press.

Howell, W. G., Wolf, P. J., Campbell, D. E., & Peterson, P. E. (2002). School vouchers and academic performance: results from three randomized field trials. *Journal of Policy Analysis and Management, 21*(2), 191–217.

Hoxby, C. M. (2001). Rising tide. *Education Next, 1*(4), 68–74.

Hoxby, C. M. (2003). School choice and school productivity (or, could school choice be a tide that lifts all boats?). In C. M. Hoxby (Ed.), *The economics of school choice* (pp. 287–341). Chicago: University of Chicago Press.

Hoxby, C. M., & Murarka, S. (2008). Methods of assessing achievement of students in charter schools. In M. Berends, M. G. Springer, & H. J. Walberg (Eds.), *Charter school outcomes* (pp. 7–37). Mahweh: Taylor & Francis Group.

Hoxby, C. M., Murarka, S., & Kang, J. (2009). *How New York City's charter schools affect achievement*. Cambridge, MA: New York City Charter Schools Evaluation Project.

Imberman, S. A. (2011). Achievement and behavior in charter schools: Drawing a more complete picture. *The Review of Economics and Statistics, 93*(2), 416–435.

Jabbar, H. (2015a). Competitive networks and school leaders' perceptions: The formation of an education marketplace in post-Katrina New Orleans. *American Educational Research Journal, 52*(6), 1093–1131.

Jabbar, H. (2015b). "Every kid is money": Market-like competition and school leader strategies in New Orleans. *Educational Evaluation and Policy Analysis, 34*(4), 638–659.

Jabbar, H. (2016). Selling schools: Marketing and recruitment strategies in New Orleans. *Peabody Journal of Education, 91*(1), 4–23.

Jargowsky, P. A. (2014). Segregation, neighborhoods, and schools. In A. Lareau & K. Goyette (Eds.), *Choosing homes, choosing schools* (pp. 97–136). New York: Russell Sage Foundation.

Jencks, C. (1985). How much do high school students learn? *Sociology of Education, 58*(2), 128–135.

Jennings, J. L. (2010). School choice or schools' choice? Managing in an era of accountability. *Sociology of Education, 83*(3), 227–247.

Jennings, J. L., Corcoran, S. P., Dinger, S., Sattin-Bajaj, C., Cohodes, S., & Baker-Smith, C. (2016). *Administrative complexity as a barrier to school choice: Evidence from New York City*. Paper presented at the annual meeting of the Sociology of Education Association, Asilomar, CA.

Jeynes, W. H. (2008). The effects of Catholic and Protestant schools: A meta-analysis. *Catholic Education: A Journal of Inquiry and Practice, 12*(2), 255–275.

Johnson, H. B., & Shapiro, T. M. (2003). Good neighborhoods, good schools: Race and the "good choices" of White families. In A. W. Doane & E. Bonilla-Silva (Eds.), *White out: The continuing significance of racism*. New York: Routledge.

Kimelberg, S. M. (2014). Middle-class parents, risk, and urban public schools. In A. Lareau & K. Goyette (Eds.), *Choosing homes, choosing schools* (pp. 207–236). New York: Russell Sage Foundation.

Kimelberg, S. M., & Billingham, C. M. (2013). Attitudes toward diversity and the school choice process: Middle-class parents in a segregated urban public school district. *Urban Education, 48*(2), 198–231.

Kisida, B., & Wolf, P. (2010). School governance and information: Does choice lead to better-informed parents? *American Politics Research, 38*(5), 783–805.

Kleitz, B., Weiher, G. R., Tedin, K., & Matland, R. (2000). Choice, charter schools, and household preferences. *Social Science Quarterly, 81*(3), 846–854.

Krueger, A. B., & Zhu, P. (2004). Another look at the New York City school voucher experiment. *American Behavioral Scientist, 47*(5), 658–698.

Lacireno-Paquet, N., Holyoke, T. T., Moser, M., & Henig, J. R. (2002). Creaming versus cropping: Charter school enrollment practices in response to market incentives. *Educational Evaluation and Policy Analysis, 24*(2), 145–158.

Lareau, A. (2014). Schools, housing, and the reproduction of inequality. In A. Lareau & K. Goyette (Eds.), *Choosing homes, choosing schools* (pp. 169–206). New York: Russell Sage Foundation.

Lareau, A., & Goyette, K. (Eds.). (2014). *Choosing homes, choosing schools*. New York: Russell Sage Foundation.

Lauen, D. L. (2007). Contextual explanations of school choice. *Sociology of Education, 80*(3), 179–209.

Lauen, D. L. (2009). To choose or not to choose: High school choice and graduation in Chicago. *Educational Evaluation and Policy Analysis, 31*(3), 179–199.

Lee, V. E., & Bryk, A. S. (1989). A multilevel model of the social distribution of high school achievement. *Sociology of Education, 62*(3), 172–192.

Lee, V. E., & Bryk, A. S. (1993). The organization of effective secondary schools. *Review of Research in Education, 19*, 171–267.

Lee, V. E., Croninger, R. G., & Smith, J. B. (1996). Equity and choice in Detroit. In B. Fuller & R. F. Elmore (Eds.), *Who chooses? Who loses? Culture, institutions, and the unequal effects of school choice* (pp. 70–91). New York: Teachers College Press.

Logan, J. R., & Burdick-Will, J. (2015). School segregation, charter schools, and access to quality education. *Journal of Urban Affairs, 38*(3), 323–343.

Logan, J. R., Minca, E., & Adar, S. (2012). The geography of inequality: Why separate means unequal in American public schools. *Sociology of Education, 85*(3), 287–301.

López Turley, R. N., & Stevens, C. (2015). Lessons from a school district–university research partnership: The Houston Education Research Consortium. *Educational Evaluation and Policy Analysis, 37*(S), 6S–15S.

Lubienski, C. (2003). Innovation in education markets: Theory and evidence on the impact of competition and choice in charter schools. *American Educational Research Journal, 40*(2), 395–443.

Lubienski, C., & Dougherty, J. (2009). Mapping educational opportunity: Spatial analysis and school choices. *American Journal of Education, 115*(4), 485–491.

Lubienski, C., & Lubienski, S. T. (2013). *The public school advantage: Why public schools outperform private schools*. Chicago: University of Chicago Press.

Lubienski, C., Gulosino, C., & Weitzel, P. (2009). School choice and competitive incentives: Mapping the distribution of educational opportunities across local education markets. *American Journal of Education, 115*(4), 601–647.

McArthur, E., Colopy, K. W., & Schlaline, B. (1995). *Use of school choice educational policy issues. Statistical perspectives* (NCES-95-724R). Washington, DC: National Center for Education Statistics.

Metcalf, K. K., West, S. D., Legan, N. A., Paul, K. M., & Boone, W. J. (2003). *Evaluation of the Cleveland Scholarship and Tutoring Program: 1998–2001*. Bloomington: Indiana Center for Evaluation.

Meyer, J. W. (1977). The effects of education as an institution. *American Journal of Sociology, 83*(1), 55–77.

Meyer, J. W., & Ramirez, F. (2000). The world institutionalization of education. In J. Schriewer (Ed.), *Discourse formation in comparative education* (pp. 111–132). Frankfurt: Peter Lang.

Meyer, J. W., & Rowan, B. (1977). Institutionalized organizations: Formal structure as myth and ceremony. *American Journal of Sociology, 83*, 340–363.

Meyer, J. W., & Rowan, B. (1978). The structure of educational organizations. In M. W. Meyer and Associates (Ed.), *Environments and organizations* (pp. 78–109). San Francisco: Jossey-Bass.

Mickelson, R. A., & Southworth, S. (2005). When opting out is not a choice: Implications for NCLB's transfer option from Charlotte, North Carolina. *Equity and Excellence in Education, 38*(3), 249–263.

Mills, J. N., & Wolf, P. J. (2017). Vouchers in the Bayou: The effects of the Louisiana Scholarship Program on student achievement after two years. *Educational Evaluation and Policy Analysis, 39*(3), 464–484.

Nathanson, L., Corcoran, S. P., & Baker-Smith, C. (2013). *High school choice in New York City: A report on the school choices and placements of low-achieving students*. New York: Research Alliance for New York City Schools.

Neal, D. (1997). The effects of Catholic secondary schooling on educational achievement. *Journal of Labor Economics, 15*(1), 98–123.

Ni, Y. (2009). The impact of charter school on the efficiency of traditional public schools: Evidence from Michigan. *Economics of Education Review, 28*(5), 571–584.

Orfield, G., & Frankenberg, E. (2013). *Educational delusions? Why choice can deepen inequality and how to make schools fair*. Berkeley: University of California Press.

Pattillo, M., Delale-O'Connor, L., & Butts, F. (2014). High-stakes choosing. In A. Lareau & K. Goyette (Eds.), *Choosing homes, choosing schools* (pp. 237–267). New York: Russell Sage Foundation.

Peterson, P., Campbell, D., & West, M. (2002). Who chooses? Who uses? Participation in a national school voucher program. In P. Hill (Ed.), *Choice with equity* (pp. 51–84). Stanford: Hoover Institution Press.

Phillips, K. J. R., Hausman, C., & Larsen, E. S. (2012). Students who choose and the schools they leave: Examining participation in intradistrict transfers. *The Sociological Quarterly, 53*(2), 264–294.

Phillips, K. J. R., Larsen, E. S., & Hausman, C. (2015). School choice & social stratification: How intra-district transfers shift the racial/ethnic and economic composition of schools. *Social Science Research, 51*, 30–50.

Powell, W. W., & DiMaggio, P. J. (1991). *The new institutionalism in organizational analysis*. Chicago: The University of Chicago Press.

Preston, C., Goldring, E., Berends, M., & Cannata, M. (2012). School innovation in district context: Comparing traditional public schools and charter schools. *Economics of Education Review, 31*, 318–330.

Preston, C., Goldring, E., Berends, M., & Cannata, M. (2013). School innovation in district context: Comparing traditional public schools and charter schools. *Economics of Education Review, 31*(2), 318–330.

Reardon, S. F., & Bischoff, K. (2011). Income inequality and income segregation. *American Journal of Sociology, 116*(4), 1092–1153.

Reardon, S. F., Matthews, S. A., O'Sullivan, D., Lee, B. A., Firebaugh, G., Farrell, C. R., & Bischoff, K. (2008). The geographic scale of metropolitan racial segregation. *Demography, 45*(3), 489–514.

Reardon, S. F., Cheadle, J., & Robinson, J. (2009). The effect of Catholic schooling on math and reading development in kindergarten through fifth grade. *Journal of Research on Educational Effectiveness, 2*(1), 45–87.

Renzulli, L. A., & Evans, L. (2005). School choice, charter schools, and White flight. *Social Problems, 52*(3), 344–365.

Renzulli, L. A., Barr, A. B., & Paino, M. (2015). Innovative education? A test of specialist mimicry or generalist assimilation in trends in charter school specialization over time. *Sociology of Education, 88*(1), 83–102.

Rhodes, A., & DeLuca, S. (2014). Residential mobility and school choice among poor families. In A. Lareau & K. Goyette (Eds.), *Choosing homes, choosing schools* (pp. 137–166). New York: Russell Sage Foundation.

Rich, P., & Jennings, J. L. (2015). Choice, information, and constrained options: School transfers in a stratified educational system. *American Sociological Review, 80*(5), 1069–1098.

Roda, A., & Wells, A. S. (2013). School choice policies and racial segregation: Where White parents' good intentions, anxiety, and privilege collide. *American Journal of Education, 119*(2), 261–293.

Roderick, M., Easton, J. Q., & Sebring, P. B. (2009). *The Consortium on Chicago School Research: A new model for the role of research in supporting urban school reform*. Chicago: The University of Chicago Urban Education Institute.

Rouse, C. E. (1998). Private school vouchers and student achievement: An evaluation of the Milwaukee Parental Choice Program. *Quarterly Journal of Economics, 113*, 553–602.

Rouse, C., Hannaway, J., Goldhaber, D., & Figlio, D. (2013). Feeling the Florida heat: How low-performing schools respond to voucher and accountability pressure. *American Economic Journal: Economic Policy, 5*(2), 251–281.

Sander, W. (1996). Catholic grade schools and academic achievement. *The Journal of Human Resources, 31*(3), 540–548.

Saporito, S. (2003). Private choices, public consequences: Magnet school choice and segregation by race and poverty. *Social Problems, 50*(2), 181–203.

Saporito, S., & Lareau, A. (1999). School selection as a process: The multiple dimensions of race in framing educational choice. *Social Problems, 46*(3), 418–439.

Saporito, S., & Sohoni, D. (2006). Coloring outside the lines: Racial segregation in public schools and their attendance boundaries. *Sociology of Education, 79*(2), 81–105.

Saporito, S., & Sohoni, D. (2007). Mapping educational inequality: Concentrations of poverty among poor and minority students in public schools. *Social Forces, 85*(3), 1227–1253.

Sass, T. (2006). Charter schools and student achievement in Florida. *Education Finance and Policy, 1*(1), 91–122.

Sass, T., Zimmer, R., Gill, B., & Booker, K. (2016). Charter high school's effect on educational attainment and earnings. *Journal of Policy Analysis and Management, 35*(3), 683–706.

Sattin-Bajaj, C. (2011). Communication breakdown: Informing immigrant families about high school choice in New York City. In M. Berends, M. Cannata, & E. B. Goldring (Eds.), *School choice and school improvement* (pp. 147–176). Cambridge, MA: Harvard Education Press.

Schneider, B. (2003). Sociology of education: An overview of the field at the turn of the twenty-first century. In M. Hallinan, A. Gamoran, W. Kubitscheck, & T. Loveless (Eds.), *Stability and change in American education: Structure, process, and outcomes*. Clinton Corners: Eliot Werner.

Schneider, M., & Buckley, J. (2002). What do parents want from schools? Evidence from the Internet. *Educational Evaluation and Policy Analysis, 24*(2), 133–144.

Schneider, M., & Buckley, J. (2003). Making the grade: Comparing DC charter schools to other DC public schools. *Educational Evaluation and Policy Analysis, 25*(2), 203–215.

Schneider, M., Marschall, M., Teske, P., & Roch, C. (1998). School choice and culture wars in the classroom: What different parents seek from education. *Social Science Quarterly, 79*(3), 489–501.

Schneider, M., Teske, P., & Marschall, M. (2000). *Choosing schools: Consumer choice and the quality of American schools*. Princeton: Princeton University Press.

Scott, W. R., & Davis, G. F. (2007). *Organizations & organizing: Rational, natural and open system perspectives*. Englewood Cliffs: Prentice Hall.

Scott, W. R., & Meyer, J. W. (1994). *Institutional environments and organizations: Structural complexity and individualism*. Thousand Oaks: Sage.

Sebring, P. B., & Allensworth, E. (2012). *The development, challenges and lessons of the consortium on Chicago school research*. Paper presented at the annual meeting of the American Educational Research Association, Vancouver, British Columbia, Canada.

Shakeel, M. D., Anderson, K. P., & Wolf, P. J. (2016). *The participation effects of private school vouchers across the globe: A meta-analytic and systematic review*. Fayetteville: University of Arkansas.

Siegel-Hawley, G., & Frankenberg, E. (2013). A segregating choice? An overview of charter school policy, enrollment trends, and segregation. In G. Orfield & E. Frankenberg (Eds.), *Educational delusions? Why choice can deepen inequality and how to make schools fair* (pp. 129–144). Berkeley: University of California Press.

Smith, C. (2005). *Soul searching: The religious and spiritual lives of American teenagers*. New York: Oxford University Press.

Smith, C. (2009). *Souls in transition: The religion and spiritual lives of young adults*. New York: Oxford University Press.

Smith, C. (2011). *Lost in transition: The dark side of emerging adulthood*. Oxford: Oxford University Press.

Stein, M. L., Goldring, E. B., & Cravens, X. (2011). Do parents do as they say? Choosing Indianapolis charter schools. In M. Berends, M. Cannata, & E. B. Goldring (Eds.), *School choice and school improvement* (pp. 105–123). Cambridge, MA: Harvard Education Press.

Stevens, W. D., de la Torre, M., & Johnson, D. W. (2011). Barriers to access: High school choice processes and outcomes in Chicago. In M. Berends, M. Cannata, & E. B. Goldring (Eds.), *School choice and school improvement* (pp. 125–146). Cambridge, MA: Harvard Education Press.

Stuit, D., & Doan, S. (2013). *School choice regulations: Red tape or red herring?* Washington, DC: The Thomas B. Fordham Institute.

Teasley, B. (2009). Charter school outcomes. In M. Berends, M. G. Springer, D. Ballou, & H. J. Walberg (Eds.), *Handbook of research on school choice* (pp. 209–225). New York: Routledge.

Teske, P., & Schneider, M. (2001). What research can tell policymakers about school choice. *Journal of Policy Analysis and Management, 20*(4), 609–631.

Teske, P., Fitzpatrick, J., & Kaplan, G. (2007). *Opening doors: How low-income parents search for the right school.* Seattle: Center on Reinventing Public Education.

Tuttle, C. C., Gill, B., Gleason, P., Knechtel, V., Nichols-Barrer, I., & Resch, A. (2013). *KIPP middle schools: Impacts on achievement and other outcomes.* Washington, DC: Mathematica Policy Research.

Waddington, R. J., & Berends, M. (2017). *Impact of the Indiana Choice Scholarship Program: Achievement effects for students in upper elementary and middle school.* Paper presented at the annual meeting of the Society For Research on Educational Effectiveness, Washington, DC.

U.S. Department of Education. (2004). *Successful charter schools.* Washington, DC: U.S. Department of Education, Office of Innovation and Improvement.

U.S. Department of Education. (2008). *A commitment to quality: National charter school policy forum report.* Washington, DC: U.S. Department of Education, Office of Innovation and Improvement.

Walberg, H. J., & Bast, J. (2003). *Education and capitalism: How overcoming our fear of markets and economics can improve America's schools.* Stanford: Hoover Institution Press.

Weiher, G. R., & Tedin, K. L. (2002). Does choice lead to racially distinctive schools? Charter schools and household preferences. *Journal of Policy Analysis and Management, 21*(1), 79–92.

Weininger, E. B. (2014). School choice in an urban setting. In A. Lareau & K. Goyette (Eds.), *Choosing homes, choosing schools* (pp. 268–294). New York: Russell Sage Foundation.

West, M. R., & Peterson, P. E. (2006). The efficacy of choice threats within school accountability systems. *The Economic Journal, 116*(510), 48–62.

Witte, J. F. (2000). *The market approach to education: An analysis of America's first voucher program.* Princeton: Princeton University Press.

Witte, J. F., Carlson, D., Cowen, J. M., Fleming, D. J., & Wolf, P. J. (2012). *MPCP longitudinal education growth study: Fifth year report.* Fayetteville: University of Arkansas.

Witte, J. F., Wolf, P. J., Cowen, J. M., Carlson, D. E., & Fleming, D. J. (2014). High stakes choice: achievement and accountability in the nation's oldest urban voucher program. *Educational Evaluation and Policy Analysis, 36*(4), 437–456.

Wohlstetter, P., Smith, J., & Farrell, C. C. (2013). *Choices and challenges: Charter school performance in perspective.* Harvard: Harvard Education Press.

Wolf, P., Gutmann, B., Puma, M., Kisida, B., Rizzo, L., Eissa, N., & Carr, M. (2010). *Evaluation of the DC opportunity scholarship program: Final report.* Washington, DC: U.S. Government Printing Office: U.S. Department of Education, Institute for Education Sciences, National Center for Education Evaluation and Regional Assistance.

Wolf, P. J., Kisida, B., Gutmann, B., Puma, M., Rizzo, L., & Eissa, N. (2011). School vouchers in the nation's capital: Summary of experimental impacts. In M. Berends, M. Cannata, & E. B. Goldring (Eds.), *School choice and school improvement* (pp. 17–34). Cambridge, MA: Harvard Education Press.

Zimmer, R., & Bettinger, E. P. (2015). Beyond the rhetoric: Surveying the evidence on vouchers and tax credits. In H. F. Ladd & M. E. Goertz (Eds.), *Handbook of research in education finance and policy* (2nd ed., pp. 447–467). New York: Routledge.

Zimmer, R., Gill, B., Booker, K., Lavertu, S., Sass, T. R., & Witte, J. (2009). *Charter schools in eight states: Effects on achievement, attainment, integration, and competition.* Santa Monica: RAND.

Zimmer, R., Gill, B., Booker, K., Lavertu, S., & Witte, J. (2011). Charter schools: Do they cream skim, increasing student segregation? In M. Berends, M. Cannata, & E. B. Goldring (Eds.), *School choice and school improvement* (pp. 215–232). Cambridge, MA: Harvard Education Press.

Curricular Differentiation and Its Impact on Different Status Groups Including Immigrants and Students with Disabilities

11

Jamie M. Carroll and Chandra Muller

Abstract

Schools organize students' learning through informal and formal curricular differentiation, which refers to systematic differences in the experiences, processes, and exposure of curricular content. Research has long found that students have unequal access to learning opportunities based on status group factors, and that these inequalities lead to gaps in educational, occupational, and health outcomes. This chapter outlines the history of curricular differentiation in U.S. schools, key findings on disparities in course-taking by race/ethnicity, family background, gender, disability status and immigrant status, and the effects of curricular differentiation on school and non-school outcomes. We additionally note measurement issues within curriculum research and implications for policy, practice, and social inequality.

11.1 Introduction

School curriculum refers to the structure of school processes and materials that contribute to students' learning and other education outcomes.

It includes the formal, administrative, and official aspects of organization—such as which subjects students take, who takes them, and when they take them—as well as the informal, hidden and social organization of experiences—such as the types of instructional strategies used, the goals teachers have for their students, and the peer composition of the classroom—that combine to form the curricular content to which students are exposed in school (Jackson 1992). Curricular differentiation refers to systematic differences in the experiences, processes, and exposure (Oakes et al. 1992). The basis of differentiation and its role in producing and reproducing social inequality is a major concern of research because of the primary role of education in determining social mobility, economic opportunity, and participation in political and civic institutions in modern life. In advanced economies, and especially in the U.S., education and academic success is a preferred pathway to social mobility, or enhancing one's socioeconomic status. The American Dream idealizes this process, suggesting that academic accomplishments are rooted in individuals' achievements based on what they do—the merit of their accomplishments—rather than who they are or what family they grew up in. The ideal is that education will produce a society in which every person has an equal opportunity to succeed if they work hard and are deserving.

Sociologists recognize a core tension between individual agency—or the return to an individual's

J. M. Carroll (✉) · C. Muller
University of Texas, Austin, TX, USA
e-mail: jmcarroll@utexas.edu

© Springer International Publishing AG, part of Springer Nature 2018
B. Schneider (ed.), *Handbook of the Sociology of Education in the 21st Century*, Handbooks of Sociology and Social Research, https://doi.org/10.1007/978-3-319-76694-2_11

personal initiative, hard work, and achievement—versus the social structure of a system that may limit some individuals' opportunities more than others. Both individual agency and social structure are relevant for understanding who gets ahead and who is left behind. Curricular differentiation is one aspect of the social structure inherent in schools that limits individual agency. Curricular differentiation on the basis of status group characteristics like race and ethnicity, gender, parents' social status (e.g., parents' education or occupation), immigrant status, or disability status are of particular concern because they represent a lack of equality of educational opportunity to succeed. These unequal opportunities can turn into a lifetime of inequality in work, health, and well-being. This chapter provides a brief historical and theoretical overview of curricular differentiation, describes key empirical research on the topic in general and on status group disparities, considers the effects of curricular differentiation, discusses measurement of curriculum and curricular differentiation, and concludes with implications for policy, practice, and social inequality.

11.2 Historical and Theoretical Overview

Major debates in education have been focused on what students should learn, who should have the opportunity to learn what, and who has the capacity to learn what (Lee and Ready 2009; Lucas 1999; Oakes 2005; Labaree 1997). The content of education—what students should learn—reflects two seemingly contradictory purposes for education. According to John Dewey, one of the main functions of schools is to create productive citizens who can question and change the status quo (Dewey 1916). To achieve this goal of education, students certainly need to learn basic literacy skills to understand information, but they also need to learn critical thinking skills to analyze and question information and advance society. The underlying theme behind this goal of schooling is that *all* citizens require certain analytic and critical thinking skills to help sustain

our democracy. The other purpose of education, which has garnered much more theoretical and empirical attention, is to prepare students to enter the stratified labor force (Oakes 2005; Spring 1976; Bowles and Gintis 1976). In this view, the content of schools depends on the type of occupation for which students are preparing. Some students will have professional occupations that require higher-level, analytic thinking, while others might do better to learn how to follow rules and complete tasks that require little or no creative thought (such as many manual labor jobs). Throughout the history of schooling in the U.S., both of these goals of education have driven educational policy and processes with implications for curricular differentiation.

Curricular differentiation occurs in a number of complex ways that have important consequences for who gets ahead (Sørensen 1970). First, the *vertical* organization of schools limits the scope of learning experiences students have the capacity to learn, grouping students according to their age and developmental stage, which results in differences in curriculum content taught at different grade levels. The second form of curricular stratification is a *horizontal* organization that results in curricular differentiation at the same grade level. Combined, the vertical and horizontal organization of exposure to curriculum results in a highly differentiated system that can limit opportunities, even for students who are highly motivated and invested in school (Sørensen 1970).

The early history of the U.S. school system used vertical curricular differentiation to stratify students; only some students made it to secondary and postsecondary schools, while most students entered the labor force. Typically, the students who stayed in school longer were from more socioeconomically advantaged families who could afford to have their children out of the labor force. Secondary schools were viewed as elite institutions that focused on a narrow curriculum to prepare all the students who reached that level for college and high status occupations (Goldin and Katz 1999; Oakes et al. 1992). The United States led the rest of the world in the expansion of mass education at the secondary level. Between 1910 and 1940, during the "high school movement," the rates of high school attendance in the U.S. increased from 18% to 71% of adolescents (Goldin and Katz 2003). A number of factors contributed to this large increase in the importance of high school. First, compulsory schooling laws increased the grade level and age needed to be exempt from education. By 1950, all states required students to stay in school until age 16 (Black et al. 2008). Second, child labor laws, in conjunction with these compulsory schooling laws, placed more restrictions on youth labor, increasing the costs of working for youth and of employing youth (Goldin and Katz 2003). At the same time, employment opportunities increased for those with a high school diploma. Previously, the benefits of the terminal high school diploma were limited because most students who received this credential continued to postsecondary education. After the high school movement, only about one quarter of students with high school diplomas continued their education into college (Goldin and Katz 1999). High schools started focusing more on training students for their future lives than just for college.

The increase in high school attendance meant that schools were faced with teaching students from diverse backgrounds with diverse educational needs within the same grade. Students from socioeconomically advantaged backgrounds were mixed with the increasing immigrant population, students with disabilities and, after *Brown v. Board of Education*, Black students. In response, schools organized the curriculum to horizontally stratify content and learning opportunities (Lucas 1999). Some scholars argued that schools became the social machines used to prepare all students for their projected unequal future adult roles (Lucas 1999; Oakes et al. 1992; Spring 1976). As future workers, students were separated into those who would enter manual, low-status jobs directly after high school and those who would become managers and supervisors and continue their education after high school (Spring 1976). As future citizens, students were separated into the followers who are educated just enough to follow and the leaders who will be able to make the country a better place (Lucas 1999; Oakes 2005). To some, this

differentiation was necessary in order to accommodate the disparate needs of students from different backgrounds and ability levels. Others argued that curricular differentiation emerged to ensure high status students would always remain at the top of the academic hierarchy, purposefully limiting the educational opportunities of low status individuals (Oakes et al. 1992).

The origin of curricular differentiation was rooted in beliefs about intelligence: Some individuals just have higher intellectual capacity than others. According to this paradigm, it would be pointless to give those with perceived low intelligence, such as women, immigrants, minority students, and students with disabilities, access to advanced coursework, because they do not have the capacity to learn at high levels (Lucas 1999; Mehan et al. 1986; Oakes et al. 1992). Students were thus placed in rigid curricular pathways in schools, called "tracks," to prepare them for their future roles, both for the betterment of the individual and the country. The tracks labeled students according to their perceived ability and future role: "learning disabled," "general," "vocational," and "college preparatory," for example.

One example of early horizontal stratification is in the education of immigrant students in elementary schools. Students were "Americanized," forced to learn English and to understand their role as citizens—to follow the leaders and do as they are told (Olsen 1997). Often, learning English was a priority, so immigrant students were excluded from subject-based instruction and classrooms with native English speakers (Olneck 1989). The goal of this separation was to eventually train immigrant students to be able to join their American classmates, having learned both the language and behavioral skills necessary to be an "American student" (Olneck 1989).

Rigid tracking structures restrained students' choices of courses, but not all students within the same track took the same courses. During the 1960s, allowing for individual choice became more important in schools. Referred to as the "shopping mall high school" or "cafeteria curriculum," the diverse course options during this time made students active consumers of their education (Powell et al. 1985; Labaree 1997). Students could choose courses that provided rigorous preparation for college or courses that might be less demanding and more entertaining. There still were limitations on course choices. Some of the more academically rigorous and demanding courses required preparation or prerequisites that restricted access for unprepared students. These prerequisites served to segregate students according to their background preparation, often because poor students or students of color in the post-segregation era had attended lower-quality schools. Additionally, teachers and administrators, who formally and informally "sold" courses to students, served as gatekeepers, suggesting specific course pathways related to students' perceived skills (Powell et al. 1985). Course-taking decisions were based on these structural and individual factors, but ultimately students had to make decisions about what to take, generally uninformed about the implications of their choices for their futures.

After World War II, scientists and policy makers recognized the value of science for medicine and addressing disease, national security, and public welfare (Bush 1945). A push for improving education in science and mathematics to build an innovative workforce came with this more general prioritization of a national investment in science. This sense of urgency heightened after the Soviet launch of Sputnik. Universities and high schools expanded their mathematics and science programs and invested in advanced coursework as part of this national priority. Training to build this specialized workforce meant that some students would take advanced curriculum in which knowledge was sequenced across years, stratifying talented students (Tyack and Cuban 1995).

Prior to the early 1980s, there were no federal guidelines or requirements about the curricular content of courses that students should take. In 1983, *A Nation at Risk* sounded an alarm and criticized schools for not preparing students sufficiently for the technical skills needed to progress the scientific goals of our country (Gardner et al. 1983). The report called for implementation of a "New Basics Curriculum," which suggested

all students should graduate from high school only after completing 4 years of English, 3 years of mathematics, 3 years of science, 3 years of social studies, and half a year in computer science (Alexander and Pallas 1984). Even though these reforms did improve student academic performance (Alexander and Pallas 1984), what is largely missing is any stipulation of course content or level. Students on the college preparatory track had opportunities to complete advanced coursework, whereas lower-level students completed their years of math and science instruction without reaching advanced levels. During the late 1970s and 1980s, school systems underwent the "unremarked revolution," dismantling the overarching tracking systems—sometimes referred to as "detracking"—that had determined students' opportunities to learn (Lucas 1999; Oakes et al. 1997). Yet differentiation between course levels still occurred; the stratification was just subject specific. School segregation and stratification was still alive, just in a more covert form.

With the decline of manufacturing and the increase in analytic skills demanded for many occupations in the 1990s (Autor et al. 2003), the curriculum to prepare students for their future adult roles adapted. There were fewer opportunities for students to take vocational coursework that prepared students for the routine, manual jobs that were being replaced by computers. Students needed more academic training in advanced math, science, and computers to be successful. More generally, the returns to a college degree compared to only graduating from high school have increased, and an increasing share of high school graduates have been enrolling in postsecondary institutions. In other words, in today's economy a college degree is more essential than ever for access to good jobs. Vertical differentiation that stratifies people according to the number of years of schooling they get, or when they exit the educational system, has extended to the early adult years—now everyone attends high school but only some complete college or an advanced degree. Horizontal differentiation is also apparent in higher education, with curricular differences between 2-year and 4-year institutions, and 4-year institutions that are non-selective and selective.

High school curriculum that prepares young people for college is key to postsecondary success and the curricular differentiation that occurs in high school has potential long run consequences for inequality.

The U.S. educational system differs from European systems in some important respects that have implications for students' social mobility. In a classic article, Ralph Turner (1960) contrasted the American and English education systems in regards to norms of social mobility. The British education system follows the ideal of a sponsored mobility system, where only elite members of society can recognize and reward students who have the characteristics to be allowed into the elite. Individuals are thus sorted at an early age to ensure that only those who are deemed deserving have access to higher levels of education. The American education system follows the ideal of contest mobility, where students compete for elite status through their skills and effort. In this meritocratic system, students can receive rewards for hard work and effort throughout their education, delaying the sorting of futures until later in their lives (Turner 1960). Effectively, in the American system, students are given a second, third, or more chances to get ahead in the contest. Rosenbaum (1978) added the concept of tournament mobility as another ideal type after studying a school tracking system in the U.S. in the 1970s. In the reality of tracked schools, he argued, meritocracy has its limits. The tournament mobility ideal claims that students "win" access to advanced coursework, and stay in these advanced courses regardless of performance. But, students who "lose" and end up in lower courses are not given opportunities to compete again for more advanced slots (Rosenbaum 1978).

In all Western countries, there is a point where all students select and/or are selected into formal educational pathways. In Switzerland, Germany, the Netherlands, and Great Britain, curricular differentiation begins between ages 10 and 12, with students being placed into vocational or academic pathways through their performance on entrance exams (Lucas 1999). Although informal curricular differentiation persists throughout schooling in the U.S., the formal separation into specialized coursework occurs at a relatively late stage. For example, it is only in the last two years of high school that most U.S. students choose whether or not to take advanced science and mathematics coursework that can lead to science, technology, engineering, and mathematics (STEM) fields. A small share of students concentrate on career and technical courses that prepare them for work rather than a 4-year college degree; fewer than 20% of high school graduates in 2009 took more than two specialized career and technical courses (U.S. Department of Education 2014). In contrast, in many European systems students are streamed into courses that lead directly to specific careers as early as middle school. Consequently, the connection between coursework and occupations in the U.S. system is weaker, and what constitutes preparation for twenty-first century careers and best prepares young people for the future labor market is debated (Rosenbaum 2001; Symonds et al. 2011).

11.3 Curriculum in Contemporary United States

11.3.1 The Organization of Curricular Differentiation

Vertical curricular differentiation according to age and grade level—from preschool, elementary, middle, and high schools, to college—is a basic feature of how most U.S. schools are organized today. The exposure to learning opportunities that students have in one year of school contributes to their preparation for learning in the following year and results in an accumulation of skills and knowledge that opens or closes future opportunities to learn. For example, the level of content taught in elementary schools prepares students for different levels of instruction in middle and secondary schools, and high school instruction can prepare students for college. In the U.S. today, compulsory school laws pertain to elementary school through high school; preschool preparation and postsecondary education are optional, bookending the years that students are required to attend school. Although some cost-subsidized school choices may be available for the optional years of school, free public school options for all students, including students with disabilities, are mandated nationwide for elementary through high schools. Nonetheless, the context for teaching and learning varies considerably across schools and classrooms and the differences have major implications for curricular differentiation (Gamoran et al. 2000).

Elementary schools generally focus on a restricted curriculum for all students, but curricular differentiation still exists between schools, between classrooms, and within classrooms (Oakes et al. 1992). The skills students have upon entry to elementary school can vary substantially. Access to preschool can greatly enhance a student's preparation to transition into schooling at this critical stage (Entwisle and Alexander 1993). School readiness in mathematics and reading ability is predictive of students' advancing mathematics and reading skills through elementary school and beyond (Duncan et al. 2007). Elementary schools tend to focus on the development of basic skills needed by every student, but the quality of instruction varies across classrooms and is linked to school resources (Gamoran et al. 2000) and students' race and class background (Pianta et al. 2007).

The experiences students have in school during the first few years can determine their curricular placements and opportunities through secondary schooling and higher education. Students can be organized into within-class ability groups, especially in reading. The reading group level is determined in part by reading ability upon school entry, but also students' abilities to work with others and follow the rules (Entwisle and Alexander 1993). Students placed in high-ability groups at this life stage are better situated to remain in advanced groupings through middle and high school because learning opportunities and outcomes differ by ability group (Slavin 1987; Steenbergen-Hu et al. 2016). For example, Gamoran (1986) found that students in high-ability reading groups in first grade on average learn more words because they are given more words to learn. Additionally, elementary school

students who are perceived to have very low academic aptitude and high behavioral problems may be placed in special education programs, which will change the curriculum they have access to throughout their schooling experiences.

Middle schools introduce more horizontal differentiation through placing students in different levels of coursework. How the transition to middle school occurs can impact success through upper grade levels. Students who transition early, for sixth instead of seventh grade, exhibit lower academic achievement and motivation, potentially because they are not developmentally prepared for the shift in environment (Eccles and Midgely 1989). Middle schools also expand the geographic areas students come from, bringing in more students from diverse backgrounds with different skill levels. Students who were at the top of their elementary school class may be relegated to lower-level coursework if placed in schools with more advantaged students (Dauber et al. 1996). Mathematics preparation is particularly important in middle schools; students who are not prepared to take Algebra 1 upon high school entry are less likely to take advanced mathematics later in high school and to continue to college (Gamoran and Hannigan 2000; Long et al. 2012). Course-taking experiences in middle school shape the options for course-taking once students get to high school.

High school curricular differentiation can be characterized along three dimensions for understanding who has access to what learning opportunities: inclusivity, electivity, and scope (Gamoran 1992; Sørensen 1970). Inclusivity is the share of the student body that takes the highest levels of curriculum. Part of the positive effects of Catholic schools on learning are due to high inclusivity; most Catholic school students take advanced coursework to prepare for college (Coleman et al. 1982). The next characteristic, electivity, has to do with how students' individual agency impacts the level and academic rigor of coursework that they take. Whether or not students can choose certain courses is usually constrained by their prior academic ability and teacher recommendations, but some schools allow for more choice than others. The last element, scope, concerns whether the curriculum level is consistent across all subject areas and grade levels. Some subject areas, such as math, are ordered in such a way that certain courses must be completed before students have access to more advanced courses. Other courses, such as English, are generally only separated by offering some students access to an honors-level course. In some schools, students may be in different levels of courses in different subject areas. In other schools, students may be in the same level of course for all subjects.

Schools also vary considerably in the content of courses that they offer even within a level (Frank et al. 2008). Although some coursework, such as state history or U.S. history, may be mandated by state law and taken by all students, the content focus of other courses may differ depending on the school. A school's course offerings can uniquely define each school. Schools organize their resources and schedules—such as their teachers, classroom spaces, and number of seats—according to a master schedule (Riehl et al. 1999). Practical constraints such as the master schedule and students' preferences will shape course-taking patterns within a school. Certainly, the courses students take prepare them differentially for postsecondary opportunity over the long run. In addition, the sets of courses students take define their social world and peer interactions that also have long-term academic and social consequences (Frank et al. 2013; Frank et al. 2008). These informal social and peer contexts defined by the formal structuring of curricular offerings are a good example of why curricular differentiation is important for understanding educational stratification.

Many factors shape the curricular offerings and differentiation in U.S. schools today. Just as the geographic regions and rural, urban, and suburban areas in the U.S. differ economically, socially, and politically, school curricular differentiation also occurs along spatial lines. Both urban and rural schools suffer from a lack of resources for the school itself and within the community, which shapes the schools' course offerings and the decisions that students make

about course-taking. For example, a lower proportion of residents of rural and urban areas have a college degree than in suburban areas, and schools in these areas offer fewer Advanced Placement courses that can be used as college credit (Roscigno et al. 2006). The local labor market of a school can also shape students' curricular opportunities; blue collar communities are more likely to have schools that offer specific vocational training than non-blue collar parts of the country (Sutton 2017). Urban schools are generally larger than rural and suburban schools and offer a wider number of courses. However, some of these courses may lean more vocational than advanced academic (Monk and Haller 1993). Racial and economic segregation also increases differences in course offerings between schools in urban areas (Oakes et al. 1990). "White flight" from the cities to the suburbs left many urban schools drained of resources and educational opportunities.

11.3.2 Equality of Opportunity and Curricular Differentiation

As is apparent from the above discussion, the U.S. education system has a highly complex structure that provides curriculum to students. It is important to recognize that schools structure curricular offerings, but individual students also exercise agency in how they engage with and take advantage of the school curriculum (Tyler 1976). Considerable attention in the sociology of education is devoted to questions about whether or not the structure provides equality of opportunities for all people who are motivated and meritorious to succeed. In other words, does the system allow for individual agency to determine who succeeds?

Ever since the passages of the Civil Rights Act in 1957, it has been the duty of the U.S. Commission on Civil Rights to discover, research and eradicate any discrimination in citizen's rights based on race, religion, or national origin (U.S. Commission on Civil Rights 2016). Over the years the Commission has been reauthorized to include discrimination based on age, sex or disability status. There has been documented inequality in educational opportunities and outcomes for all of these groups, which can be traced to discrimination based on perceptions of intelligence, motivation, or worthiness (Wiggan 2007; Jacobs 1996; Suárez-Orozco et al. 2008). Students from these status groups, as well as students growing up in poverty and members of the LGBTQ community, may experience inequalities in the type of curriculum they have access to (Crosnoe 2011; Conger et al. 2009). A dimension of educational opportunity that is currently monitored by the Office of Civil Rights is enrollment in various advanced academic courses, such as Advanced Placement and International Baccalaureate courses (U.S. Department of Education 2016). Research on unequal access to advanced coursework by race and ethnicity has showcased how schools resegregated their students through within-school tracking systems (Oakes et al. 1997; Mickelson 2001; Welner 2001). These findings led to litigation within states to try to minimize discrimination in course-taking within schools by race/ethnicity (Welner 2001).

It is important to recognize that these population subgroups may be vulnerable to discrimination in different ways, which may impact students' access to curriculum. One important dimension of social stratification has to do with the students' family. Families differ in level of socioeconomic status (SES), generally characterized by levels of parents' education, family income, and parents' occupation. These factors can determine certain resources—from food security and nutrition to the quality of schools and safety of neighborhoods—that are available to all children in the family (Milner 2013). Family resources are especially important in shaping educational opportunities in the preschool and postsecondary years when school is not uniformly available to all students (Jencks et al. 1979). Generally, parents' race and ethnicity and sometimes the language spoken within a home is shared within a family, making the effects of socioeconomic factors and racial, ethnic, or language factors on education outcomes potentially difficult to disentangle. Other population sub-

groups, notably female students and students with disabilities, may have very different levels of resources available as they are growing up, even within the same families as male students or students without disabilities. Even so, the family resources determined by SES and race and ethnicity can be important factors that determine education outcomes for female students or persons with disabilities. For these reasons, sociologists recognize the value of intersectional approaches that take into account more than one attribute or axis of discrimination (e.g., boys and girls of color).

Scholars debate how to determine whether students have fair and equal access to curriculum, and in part the approach depends on the type of curricular differentiation under scrutiny. One of the most vexing general problems is sorting out the effects of family resources as compared to school effects. Untangling these effects is important for identifying the source of inequality and when and where policy can be most effective to correct the inequality. A clever approach used by researchers is to gauge the differences between children's change in test scores during the months that they are attending school compared with the summer months when they are not in school. Findings show that students from poorer families suffer a larger "summer setback" in test scores. In other words, the gaps that develop during the summer are larger than those that develop during the school year (Heyns 1978). This approach provides evidence that schools contribute to equalizing the academic outcomes of students rather than exacerbating them. Indeed, schools can be an equalizer in our otherwise unequal society. However, considerable evidence also suggests that schools have a long way to go to provide a level playing field for all students from all backgrounds.

11.3.2.1 Curricular Differentiation Between Schools

An advance in our understanding of curricular differentiation has come from studies on school curricular effects. The research on Catholic schools, conducted about 35 years ago, showed that students who attend Catholic high schools generally have superior academic outcomes because of their more rigorous course-taking, and that this effect is strongest among students from lower-SES families least likely to attend private schools (Coleman and Hoffer 1987). Magnet schools, charter schools, and other non-comprehensive schools may specialize in particular subject matter and skill-building, for example a curriculum in science, technology, engineering and mathematics (STEM), humanities, foreign languages, or training for a vocation. In general, these schools are held to the same state standards of graduation and test scores, but they have more autonomy in deciding how to reach these standards and students have additional opportunities to pursue their intended specialty (Berends 2015). Specialty schools can be magnet schools, which typically require an application, portfolio, or test for admissions, charter schools, which are generally open to any students and often employ lottery systems to fill their seats, or a school within a regular public school. For example, schools that focus on STEM education vary from selective to non-selective, charter to public, and college preparatory to career and technical, but they all offer more instruction in mathematics and science than schools without this curricular focus (Means et al. 2008). The push for school choice recently has provided parents with more opportunities to send their kids to these specialized schools, but the extent to which they improve access to advanced curriculum for underrepresented groups and provide more innovative curriculum offerings compared to comprehensive public schools is debated (Renzulli and Evans 2005; Lubienski 2003).

Schools may also serve special populations and concentrate curriculum on special needs. Single-sex schools can provide unique learning opportunities and settings geared toward the needs of female students, or of male students, though whether single sex schools promote academic success is unclear (Marsh 1989). There is some evidence that both sexes in single-sex schools take more mathematics courses than those in coeducational schools, but the effect is larger for male students (Lee and Bryk 1986). Some all-female schools encourage advanced

mathematics and science course-taking and leadership opportunities, which may be more restricted in schools where they compete with male students. Until fairly recently, students with disabilities often attended schools dedicated to educating and serving the special needs of this population subgroup (Mehan et al. 1986; Martin et al. 1996). It wasn't until 1975 that a policy, which would become the Individuals with Disabilities Education Act (IDEA), ensured that all students with disabilities were granted access to free and appropriate education. This education should be in the least restrictive environment, meaning students with disabilities should be included in classrooms with students without disabilities, when appropriate (Martin et al. 1996). Yet, even within the same school, students with disabilities can be separated into self-contained classrooms with only other students with disabilities and a lower-level curriculum (Martin et al. 1996; Mehan et al. 1986).

11.3.2.2 Curricular Differentiation Within Schools

Inequality in curricular exposure starts in elementary schools and progresses throughout education. Although gaps in curricular exposure are related to school readiness differences by race and social class before entering school and during summer breaks (Alexander et al. 2001; Entwisle and Alexander 1993; Quinn et al. 2016), these gaps are exacerbated by stratification within schools. Students from low-income families and students of color are more often placed in low-level reading groups, where they are exposed to fewer words, and have lower skill gains during elementary school (Gamoran 1986; Lleras and Rangel 2009). Students who enter school with lower-level mathematics readiness are more likely to experience lower-quality teaching and student engagement, which is related to lower mathematics skill gains during elementary school (Bodovski and Farkas 2007). These gaps in learning experiences may be within the same class for elementary school, and can vary across subject area. The inequality of access to high-quality instruction, engaging material, and high-level curriculum from elementary schools feeds into the courses students take in middle school and beyond.

Formal within-school stratification generally begins in middle school, where students can take different levels of courses in academic subject areas. High school students enrolled in advanced courses, especially mathematics, often already took middle school courses like Algebra 1 that prepared them for advanced mathematics throughout high school (Catsambis 1994; Oakes et al. 1990). Recent studies have found that Black students are less likely to take middle school courses that prepare them for college preparatory high school instruction than White students with similar levels of skills (Mickelson 2015). Students carry these outcomes of inequality of course placement in middle school through their high school years and beyond.

Inequality in access to advanced coursework in high school has long been a barrier for students of color and those from lower-income families. Research on course tracking systems from the 80s and early 90s pinpointed the stark differences in enrollment rates in vocational, general and college preparatory tracks by race and class, feeding into debates about the effectiveness and fairness of tracking. The intended purpose of tracking was to include students with similar skill levels in the same classroom, to allow for ease of instruction and appropriate level of content for students' skills (Hallinan 1994). Track assignment was guided by students' academic preparation in middle school or early high school, usually indicated by scores on assessment tests (which signals their cognitive skills), grades (which reflect teachers' perceptions of students' ability, effort, and satisfactory completion of a course), and noncognitive abilities, such as a student's desire to tackle challenges and take risks. Although some research finds that gaps in track placement are accounted for by differences in prior skills (Lucas and Berends 2007), other research shows that track disparities remain or even widen over time even when accounting for prior skill differences (Lucas 2001; Mickelson 2001). These findings suggest that track assignment is driven by factors other than skills (Rubin 2008), and calls into

question whether the tracking system is effective for teaching and instruction (Hallinan 1994).

Evidence also suggests that what is taught and how it is taught differs according to a student's track. Instruction in vocational, general, and college preparatory tracks consisted of more than just differences in content and curriculum level. Oakes' (2005) study of high school classrooms found a hidden curriculum that taught advanced students to be leaders, be creative, ask questions and question authority, and lower-level students to be disciplined, listen to authority, and conform to others. The low-income students and students of color relegated to these lower tracks were thus not only given instruction in lower-level academic content; they were also taught that their opinions, questions, and aspirations didn't matter as much as their advantaged peers in advanced tracks. Most researchers thus called for "detracking" to get rid of these rigid curriculum structures in favor of more flexible course placement across grade levels and subjects (Oakes 1994; Burris et al. 2008). Yet, gaps in course-taking levels remained. Now, stratification in course-taking tends to be subject and course specific.

Certain courses, including advanced mathematics, advanced science, honors and foreign language, provide important college preparation for students. Racial minority students and students from low-SES families are less likely to complete these courses than their advantaged peers. Black and Latino students are less likely to begin high school having taken advanced mathematics (Oakes et al. 1990); even if they do and even when they have higher test scores, they are less likely to progress to higher levels of mathematics than their White peers (Riegle-Crumb 2006). These disparities in high school course-taking can lead to disparities in test scores, graduation rates, college attendance, college completion, employment, and health by race and class.

Language minority students are less likely to take courses that teach a curriculum to prepare for college. Language minority students often begin school in English as a Second Language (ESL) classes, and transition out when their

English skills improve. States have different regulations about how much time should be spent in these segregated classrooms, but by the middle and high school years students still in those courses may have fewer advanced learning opportunities (Callahan 2005; Kanno and Kangas 2014). High school students who are in ESL courses are less likely to take college preparatory courses, especially in science and social science, than students not in ESL coursework (Callahan et al. 2010). The story is similar for students enrolled in special education courses. Historically, students with disabilities were excluded from general education, either because they were in special schools or segregated classrooms. The recent push for including students with disabilities in classrooms with their nondisabled peers may have resulted in access to an academic curriculum. Yet, students with disabilities are less likely to take college preparatory courses, even when conditioning on their prior skills (Shifrer et al. 2013). Status group factors other than disability status, including race, gender, and social status, can also impact placement into special education (Morgan et al. 2015; O'Connor and Fernandez 2006). Special education and ESL courses in high school can limit the course-taking opportunities for students with disabilities and language minority students, further limiting their educational opportunities in the future.

11.3.3 Trends in End of High School Course Portfolio

By the end of high school, each student has a portfolio of courses taken during their years in high school that represents his or her curricular exposure. High school coursework signals preparation for adolescents' transitions to postsecondary school or work. Next, we discuss how U.S. students' high school course-taking portfolios have changed over the past four decades, when data collection has made it possible to monitor the trends.

One way to think about a high school course portfolio is as signaling a level of academic rigor. The National Assessment of Academic Progress (NAEP) High School Transcript Studies (HSTS) has been tracking curricular levels of students from the early 1990s through 2009 (Nord et al. 2011). We used the High School & Beyond (HS&B) high school transcripts to compute similar statistics on curriculum levels of students who graduated from high school in 1982.

Figure 11.1 shows the trends in academic rigor of students' course-taking from 1982 through 2009. As is apparent, the overall levels of high school students' academic course-taking has been increasing during the past three and a half decades. Only 2% of the Class of 1982 had taken a rigorous curriculum, compared to 13% for the Class of 2009. A rigorous curriculum includes 4 years of English, 3 years of Social Studies, 4 years of mathematics (including precalculus or higher), 3 years of science (including biology, chemistry, and physics), and 3 years of foreign language (Nord et al. 2011, p. 7). The majority of high school students today complete at least a standard level of curriculum; in 1990 and before, the majority of high school graduates did not complete even a standard high school curriculum. Although many more students are leaving high school with coursework to prepare them for postsecondary education, strikingly few American high school students today are completing a rigorous level of coursework.

The NAEP report also describes substantial disparities in the level of coursework according to parents' level of education, race and ethnicity, students' disability and English language learner status. About two-thirds (68%) of students in the Class of 2009 whose parents graduated from college completed either a midlevel or rigorous level of curriculum. In contrast, fewer than half (48%) of students in the Class of 2009 whose parents did not finish high school completed a midlevel or rigorous curriculum. Gaps exist by race as well; 14% of White students completed a rigorous curriculum compared to only 6% of Black students and 8% of Hispanic students. Students with disabilities and English language learners are at very high risk of not completing a standard curriculum; 45% and 63%, respectively, were below standard (Nord et al. 2011). This is consistent with findings that show that students with

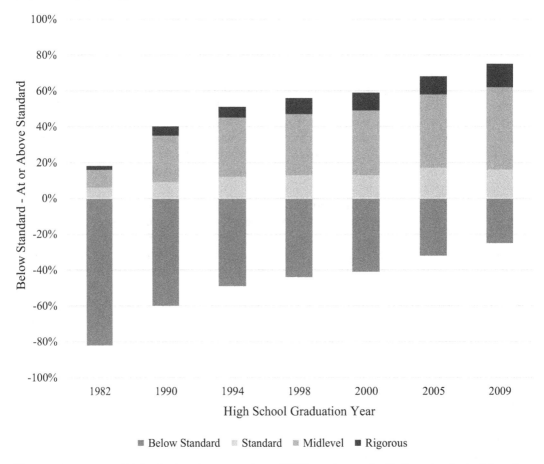

Fig. 11.1 Percentage of high school graduates completing below standard through rigorous curriculum levels, 1982 to 2009. (Source: NCES's *The Nation's Report Card* (2011) supplemented with the authors' calculations from the High School & Beyond Sophomore Cohort)

disabilities (Shifrer et al. 2013) and English language learners (Callahan et al. 2010) do not complete basic college preparatory coursework, even when they have the skills and preparation to do so.

The two trends we observe in Fig. 11.1 and the NAEP report—that levels of course-taking are rising and that there are disparities in those levels—are important dual considerations in understanding curricular differentiation. A key question is whether the subgroup disparities increase or close as the curriculum levels rise. Figure 11.2 shows the curricular levels for 1982 and 2009 high school graduates, by parents' highest level of education. In 2009, 20% of high school graduates whose parents had a bachelor's degree graduated with a rigorous curriculum level, compared to only 6% of graduates whose parents had not graduated from high school. In 1982, those percentages were 5% and 1%, respectively, and illustrate how the relative disparity in curricular differentiation between students based on SES is maintained even as curriculum levels improve. Similarly, Fig. 11.3 shows that the racial and ethnic disparities in rigorous level course-taking have been maintained as well.

These trends in disparities have theoretical significance for sociologists. Two different but related theories address how inequality manifests in curricular differentiation. First, according to the theory of maximally maintained inequality, students from advantaged families will always upgrade their level of education to stay at the top (Raftery and Hout 1993). Once one level of edu-

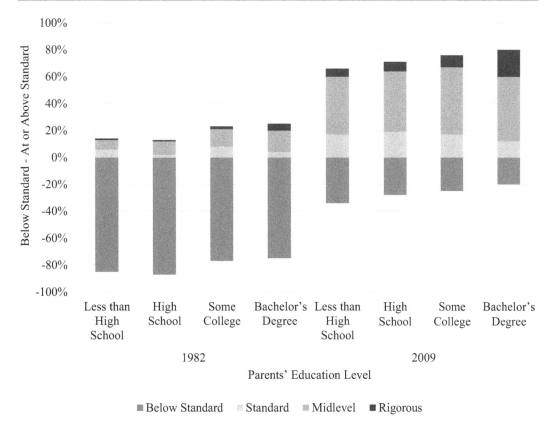

Fig. 11.2 Percentage of high school graduates completing below standard through rigorous curriculum levels, by parents' highest level of education, 1982 and 2009.

(Source: NCES's *The Nation's Report Card* (2011) supplemented with the authors' calculations from the High School & Beyond Sophomore Cohort)

cation becomes saturated, advantaged individuals will secure higher levels. As more students started graduating from high school, advantaged students continued into college. Now that college degrees are becoming more essential, more advantaged individuals are pursuing graduate degrees (Gamoran 2001). This theory of inequality addresses vertical curriculum differentiation. A second theoretical perspective about stratification, effectively maintained inequality, addresses horizontal curricular differentiation. According to this theory, once a level of education becomes nearly universal, advantaged individuals will secure qualitatively better educational experiences within the same level (Lucas 2001). With the vast majority of students enrolling in high school today, advantaged individuals secure positions in advanced and college preparatory courses, with more advanced levels of instruction

and learning opportunities. As more low-income students gained access to Algebra 1 in eighth grade, advantaged students started taking geometry in eighth grade (Domina et al. 2016). Even after there have been strides to improve the curricular opportunities for low-income and minority students, Figs. 11.2 and 11.3 show that advantaged students remain on the top.

Another way to think about trends in high school course portfolios is with the total numbers of credits students earned by the time that they graduated. Generally, one course credit is earned for a course that meets for an hour per school day for an academic year. According to a 2011 report of the NAEP HSTS, on average, students who graduated in 2009 had earned about 27.2 credits across subjects, compared to 23.6 credits in 1990. More summer school, more online courses, and more high school credit courses taken in middle

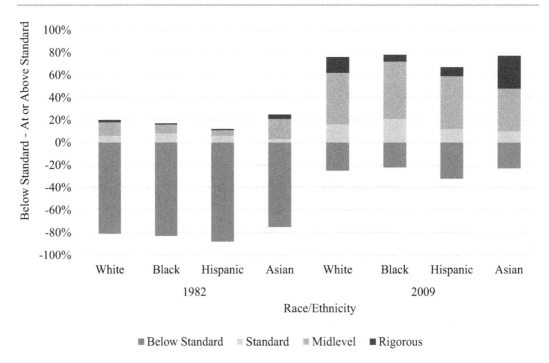

Fig. 11.3 Percentage of high school graduates completing below standard through rigorous curriculum levels, by race/ethnicity, 1982 and 2009. (Source: U.S. Department of Education, Institute of Education Sciences, National Center for Education Statistics, High School Transcript Study (HSTS) 2009 and authors' calculations from the High School & Beyond Sophomore Cohort)

school account for a substantial share of the increase in 400 h more instructional time that young people spend in high school credit courses today (Nord et al. 2011).

Students' credit accumulation has increased in most academic subjects, including mathematics, science, and social studies. Domina and Saldana (2012) show this change for the Classes of 1982, 1992, and 2004. For example, between 1982 and 2004 students took on average one more year of mathematics, one more year of science, and half a year more of social studies. This represents an intensification of students' high school academic curriculum. The increase was triggered by policy responses to the *A Nation at Risk* report that recommended that states implement curriculum standards and requirements for high school graduation (Muller and Schiller 2000; Schiller and Muller 2003). Generally, the policies have raised the levels of academic course-taking for most subgroups of students, and in this way there has been a trend toward equality in high school aca-

demic preparation. However, Domina and Saldana (2012) also show that at the highest level of high school mathematics, calculus, low-SES students and students of color have been left behind and inequality has been maintained. Consistent with the theory of effectively maintained inequality, there is essentially no change in calculus course-taking disparities between 1982 through 2004, even though the overall shares of graduates taking calculus has risen and students are taking more academic coursework.

Students often opt out of mathematics courses in the last two years of high school. Opting out may result in completing less advanced and college preparatory mathematics, possibly reducing students' academic preparation for college. Figure 11.4 shows trends in who did not take mathematics coursework in junior and/or senior years of high school. In 1982, fully two-thirds of high school seniors did not take a mathematics course, and over one-quarter (27%) did not take a mathematics course in junior or senior years. The

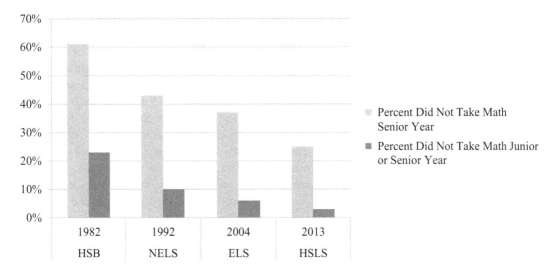

Fig. 11.4 Percentages of high school graduates who did not take a mathematics course (1) in senior year of high school and (2) in junior or senior year of high school, 1982 through 2013. (Source: Authors' calculations from the following data sets: High School & Beyond of 1980 Sophomore Cohort (HS&B), National Education Longitudinal Study of 1988 (NELS), Educational Longitudinal Study of 2002 (ELS) and High School Longitudinal Study of 2009 (HSLS))

Class of 2013 cut those rates substantially: 34% did not complete mathematics in their last year of high school, and only 6% did not take mathematics in their last 2 years of high school. Although we observe that more students who are graduating from high school have been exposed to more advanced mathematics curriculum, many students opt to not take advanced mathematics even when they can fit it in their schedule.

11.3.4 Curricular Content

The actual curriculum that is taught in classrooms with the same course title may be different for different students. In fact, the tracking literature, described above, debated whether the informal or "hidden" curriculum taught some students critical thinking skills and other students how to follow rules and defer to authority (Oakes 2005). Researchers today also ask about whether the concepts and substantive academic material that is taught in classes with the same title is equitable. Perhaps the best studied example is algebra. Algebra 1 is an important building block course for more advanced mathematics; abstract and

more complex reasoning skills are generally introduced. The state of California took progressive steps to mandate that all students take algebra in the eighth grade instead of waiting until high school. Domina and his colleagues (2015) found that when more students take algebra before high school, test scores go down on average rather than up, as policy makers expected. High-achieving students learn more when they take algebra early (Heppen et al. 2012). Others without adequate preparation or skills may learn less (Clotfelter et al. 2012), possibly because the course may cover less rigorous academic content when students in the class are not adequately prepared. Either way, it appears that students may learn a different amount of algebra depending on the course that they take.

Differences in course content may also explain why U.S. middle and high school students perform lower on mathematics and science achievement tests than students in most Organization for Economic Co-operation and Development (OECD) countries, and they have trailed since 1995 (Schmidt 2012). Schmidt and his colleagues (Schmidt et al. 1999) studied the curricular content in the textbooks used in mathematics and science courses to determine the level of challenge and rigor. They asked teachers and administrators how much of the textbook was covered in a particular class. In some courses, much of the material was at an elementary level, and in other courses the level of challenge ranged from elementary to very challenging, but the teacher only used part of the textbook. The researchers found that students in U.S. schools typically take courses with less rigorous curricular content compared with students in other OECD countries. For example, students in U.S. algebra classes are more likely to cover pre-algebra concepts like fractions and other elementary concepts rather than more advanced and rigorous topics covered in countries with higher performing students. A more recent study found that gaps in math literacy by SES across countries is related to the subject areas within mathematics that students are differentially exposed to within schools and between countries (Schmidt et al. 2015). In the U.S., a special NAEP study of curricular content found curricular differentiation in algebra and geometry courses along the lines of exposure to challenge and rigor. On average, students of color took courses with lower levels of rigor than White students, which predicted gaps in achievement on math assessments (Brown et al. 2013).

Providing textbooks and rigorous curricular materials in U.S. schools is an essential first step for ensuring that students learn abstract and complex concepts, but will not completely close gaps. More generally, researchers distinguish between "intended" and "enacted" curriculum (Porter et al. 2011; Schmidt 2012). Textbook studies tend to focus on the intended curriculum, although this may not reflect what actually takes place in classrooms. The enacted curriculum depends on many factors ranging from teacher knowledge and quality to the social and peer environment in the classroom, resulting in substantial differentiation across classes and schools.

11.3.5 Measuring Curriculum

As we have seen, curriculum and curricular differentiation are concepts that can be measured with many different indicators. The indicators

use different data sources—notably school transcripts that are coded for uniformity across schools, textbooks that are coded for curricular content, or student, teacher, or administrator reports of curricular track. Even a single data source can provide a range of indicators. For example, Arum and Savit (1995) found that transcript-based indicators of track differ substantially from student self-reports of their track location in HS&B. Only about half of the students who claimed to be in the academic track took courses that signal being in the academic track. The definitions of college preparatory track or general track can differ across schools, including the scope and selectivity (Gamoran et al. 2000; Oakes et al. 1992; Sørensen 1970), thus researchers must be aware of the implications of their findings when choosing single indictors of curricular differentiation (Lucas 1999). Perhaps the clearest example is students' high school transcripts, which show the level of academic rigor of the students' course portfolio, the number of credits earned, as well as students' performance in each course (indicated by their grades), the timing of when the course was taken (e.g., freshman, sophomore, junior year), and other aspects of students' course-taking. An advantage of high school (and college) transcripts is that they are held by schools indefinitely because they serve as an official record of students' academic progress. Even with the rich range of indicators that can be constructed from transcripts, the high school transcript is limited in the information that it provides. Notably, curricular differentiation in schools begins long before high school, and transcript records are held less reliably before grade nine.

With the introduction of computers to maintain administrative records online in nearly all schools today, researchers are increasingly using administrative data systems (e.g., Domina et al. 2015) to measure curricular differentiation. Depending on the state data system, these records may extend from early elementary school through graduate school, and also include indicators of workforce participation. In addition, data sources compile records from multiple schools to link the course-taking records of an individual across institutions such as high schools (as with

Advanced Placement course-taking) and postsecondary institutions at the National Student Clearinghouse (Muller 2015). These records are valuable because they are generally available for entire populations, for example all students in schools in a state. They are limited in the level of detail available about the curriculum, especially the enacted curriculum. Some states may only include course-taking information, requiring the researcher to define what taking different course levels may mean for stratification within that school system. No single source of measurement will give a complete picture of curricular differentiation, yet used together multiple sources may provide rich information about inequality in curriculum.

11.4 Effects of Curricular Differentiation

Why do sociologists care about inequality in course-taking? Research on curricular differentiation and tracking has consistently found both short- and long-run effects. First, skill development during high school differs according to the level of coursework taken. For example, Gamoran (1992) found that students who took an academic curriculum on average answered about 1.5 more questions correctly on a mathematics test and one more question correctly on a verbal test in between their sophomore and senior years than students in a general curriculum. Carbonaro (2005) assessed changes in effort after transitioning to high school and found that students in honors or academic courses had higher levels of effort in tenth grade than students in general courses, even controlling on their effort prior to entering high school. Students' opinions about their skills can also be impacted by tracking. Karlson (2015) found that students adjust their educational expectations according to their track placement; students in advanced or honors courses in tenth grade are more likely to increase their educational expectations than students in general academic courses. These findings suggest that gaps in both cognitive and noncognitive skills at the beginning of high school are exacerbated by curricular differentiation.

The effects of curricular differentiation can persist even after leaving high school. The learning opportunities granted to students in different levels of courses make certain adulthood destinations more or less probable (Ferrare 2013). Students in advanced coursework are more likely to enter college within 4 years of high school (Arum and Shavit 1995). Most recent research has focused on the effects taking advanced mathematics courses for preparation for college. Students who took Algebra II or higher in high school are more likely to go to college, persist through the first and second years of college, and earn a college degree than students who only completed lower levels of mathematics (Adelman 1999; Gaertner et al. 2014). Taking more mathematics and science coursework in high school is also predictive of selecting a STEM major once in college (Wang 2013). Students at the top of the academic hierarchy in high school are thus more likely to continue their education after high school and complete bachelor's degrees, but course-taking effects persist into the labor market as well.

The research on labor market effects of curricular differentiation is mixed depending on the measures of course-taking used and the time frame. Studies that only look at the number of courses students took in different subject areas have found negligible returns to taking more years of coursework (Altonji et al. 2012; Altonji 1995). Studies that investigate the level of coursework, not just the subject, have found that students who take more advanced mathematics courses on average have higher earnings, even when considering their educational attainment (Gaertner et al. 2014; Rose and Betts 2004). Taking vocational coursework can increase earnings and protect individuals from unemployment in the short-term (Arum and Shavit 1995), but the returns decrease in the long-run (Bishop and Mane 2004). Students who took higher-level courses in high school are more likely to have professional and managerial jobs in early adulthood than those in vocational or general courses (Arum and Shavit 1995). Taking advanced math courses additionally supports better labor market outcomes in midlife (Black et al. 2015). The curricular pathways students enter in high school can be predictive of their labor market success over the life course.

One relatively new area of research on the effects of course-taking is on health outcomes. Research has long noted that individuals with higher-level academic degrees and more years of schooling have longer life expectancy, better physical functioning, and higher self-reported health than those with less education (Montez et al. 2012; Ross and Wu 1995). The pathways students take to get to college, including high school course-taking, may also impact health outcomes. One study that looked at educational advantages during high school, including taking college preparatory courses, found that these advantages in progress toward college predict health limitations later in life, whether or not the individual actually went to college (Walsemann et al. 2008). Other studies have found that skills during adolescence are predictive of self-reported health status and healthy lifestyle behaviors in midlife (Clouston et al. 2015; Herd 2010). Over the long run, taking more advanced high school coursework is associated with lower mortality and obesity and better physical functiong and self-reported health status in midlife (Carroll et al. 2017; Warren et al. 2015). Curricular differentiation places students on different paths into adulthood and throughout their lives, which can impact skills, labor market outcomes, educational attainment, and health over the life course. Effectively, course-taking represents an important aspect of education that may impact how much individuals are able to pursue their own American dreams.

11.5   Implications for Policy, Practice, and Social Inequality

The curriculum to which students are exposed during the many years that they spend in school has profound implications for their own futures and for society (Goldin and Katz 2008). Over the past half century we have observed an increase in students' exposure to curriculum and, in particular, exposure to advanced curriculum in schools. Evidence suggests that this may have positive consequences for students over their lifetimes. However, curricular differentiation pertains to inequalities and systematic differences among students. Even as levels of curricular exposure at the bottom and in the middle rise, with fewer students exposed to low levels of curriculum, inequalities may be maintained or even exacerbated at the more advanced or elite areas of the spectrum, where access to advanced courses and learning opportunities are located.

During the past 50 years or more, since the high school movement and the Civil Rights Movement, and especially since the release of *A Nation at Risk*, attention has turned to policies geared toward increasing the advanced curriculum that students are exposed to, and to structuring equality of access to advanced curriculum. Although students may take different courses, differentiation based on ability versus on status group classifications, such as those monitored by the Office of Civil Rights, represent very important distinctions for understanding curricular differentiation and social inequality. Pinpointing inequalities in course-taking by status groups is an avenue for policy and litigation to ensure all students have access to courses that benefit their future outcomes (Welner and Oakes 1996; Welner 2001).

Today, states vary in the requirements for students to graduate from high school and in what teachers are expected to teach at each grade level. The Common Core (Porter et al. 2011) is an effort to reduce the differentiation at each grade level across states and to provide recommendations for curriculum throughout the U.S. Adopting the standards is voluntary and not mandated by the federal government. Many states have adopted the standards because they provide carefully crafted guidelines to reduce curricular differentiation and inequality (Porter et al. 2011; Schmidt 2012). Yet, as the skills required to advance our economy change, policies, states, schools, students, and parents will have to continuously question whether the level of coursework offered and taken in schools is equitable and will prepare all students to be successful in the future.

References

Adelman, C. (1999). *Answers in the tool box: Academic intensity, attendance patterns, and bachelor's degree attainment*. Washington, DC: U.S. Department of Education.

Alexander, K. L., & Pallas, A. M. (1984). Curriculum reform and school performance: An evaluation of the "new basics". *American Journal of Education, 92*(4), 391–420.

Alexander, K. L., Entwisle, D. R., & Olson, L. S. (2001). Schools, achievement, and inequality: A seasonal perspective. *Educational Evaluation and Policy Analysis, 23*(2), 171–191. https://doi.org/10.3102/01623737023002171.

Altonji, J. G. (1995). The effects of high school curriculum on education and labor market outcomes. *Journal of Human Resources, 30*(3), 409–438. https://doi.org/10.2307/146029.

Altonji, J. G., Blom, E., & Meghir, C. (2012). *Heterogeneity in human capital investments: High school curriculum, college major, and careers* (NBER Working Paper No. 17985). Cambridge, MA: National Bureau of Economic Research.

Arum, R., & Shavit, Y. (1995). Secondary vocational education and the transition from school to work. *Sociology of Education, 68*(3), 187–204.

Autor, D. H., Levy, F., & Murnane, R. J. (2003). The skill content of recent technological change: An empirical exploration. *Quarterly Journal of Economics, 118*(4), 1279–1333. https://doi.org/10.1162/003355303322552801.

Berends, M. (2015). Sociology and school choice: What we know after two decades of charter schools. *Annual Review of Sociology, 41*(1), 159–180. https://doi.org/10.1146/annurev-soc-073014-112340.

Bishop, J. H., & Mane, F. (2004). The impacts of career-technical education on high school labor market success. *Economics of Education Review, 23*(4), 381–402. https://doi.org/10.1016/j.econedurev.2004.04.001.

Black, S. E., Devereux, P. J., & Salvanes, K. G. (2008). Staying in the classroom and out of the maternity ward? The effect of compulsory schooling laws on teenage births. *The Economic Journal, 118*(530), 1025–1054. https://doi.org/10.1111/j.1468-0297.2008.02159.x.

Black, S. E., He, Z., Muller, C., & Spitz-Oener, A. (2015). *On the origins of STEM: The role of high school STEM coursework in occupational determination and labor market success in mid-life*. Unpublished Manuscript.

Bodovski, K., & Farkas, G. (2007). Mathematics growth in early elementary school: The roles of beginning knowledge, student engagement, and instruction. *Elementary School Journal, 108*(2), 115–130. https://doi.org/10.1086/525550.

Bowles, S., & Gintis, H. (1976). *Schooling in capitalist America: Educational reform and the contradictions of economic life*. New York: Basic Books.

Brown, J., Schiller, K., Roey, S., Perkins, R., Schmidt, W., & Houang, R. (2013). *The nation's report card: Algebra I and geometry curricula: Results from the 2005 High School Transcript Mathematics Curriculum Study (NCES 2013-451)* (The Nation's ReportCard, Vol. NCES 2013-451). Washington, DC: U.S. Department of Education, National Center for Education Statistics.

Burris, C. C., Wiley, E., Welner, K. G., & Murphy, J. (2008). Accountability, rigor, and detracking: Achievement effects of embracing a challenging curriculum as a universal good for all students. *Teachers College Record, 110*(3), 571–607.

Bush, V. (1945). *Science, the endless frontier: A report to the President*. Washington, DC: US Government Printing Office.

Callahan, R. M. (2005). Tracking and high school English learners: Limiting opportunity to learn. *American Educational Research Journal, 42*(2), 305–328.

Callahan, R. M., Wilkinson, L., & Muller, C. (2010). Academic achievement and course taking among language minority youth in U.S. schools: Effects of ESL placement. *Educational Evaluation & Policy Analysis, 32*(1), 84–117. https://doi.org/10.3102/0162373709359805.

Carbonaro, W. (2005). Tracking, students' effort, and academic achievement. *Sociology of Education, 78*(1), 27–49. https://doi.org/10.1177/003804070507800102.

Carroll, J. M., Muller, C., Grodsky, E., & Warren, J. R. (2017). Tracking health inequalities from high school to midlife. *Social Forces, 96*(2), 591–628.

Catsambis, S. (1994). The path to math: Gender and racial-ethnic differences in mathematics participation from middle school to high school. *Sociology of Education, 67*(3), 199–215.

Clotfelter, C. T., Ladd, H. F., & Vigdor, J. L. (2012). *Algebra for 8th graders: Evidence on its effects from 10 North Carolina districts* (NBER Working Paper No. 18649). Cambridge, MA: National Bureau of Economic Research.

Clouston, S. A. P., Richards, M., Cadar, D., & Hofer, S. M. (2015). Educational inequalities in health behaviors at midlife: Is there a role for early-life cognition? *Journal of Health and Social Behavior, 56*(3), 323–340. https://doi.org/10.1177/0022146515594188.

Coleman, J. S., & Hoffer, T. (1987). *Public and private high schools: The impact of communities*. New York: Basic Books.

Coleman, J. S., Hoffer, T., & Kilgore, S. (1982). *High school achievement: Public, Catholic, and private schools compared*. New York: Basic Books.

Conger, D., Long, M. C., & Iatarola, P. (2009). Explaining race, poverty, and gender disparities in advanced course-taking. *Journal of Policy Analysis and Management, 28*(4), 555–576. https://doi.org/10.1002/pam.20455.

Crosnoe, R. (2011). *Fitting in, standing out: Navigating the social challenges of high school to get an education.* New York: Cambridge University Press.

Dauber, S. L., Alexander, K. L., & Entwisle, D. R. (1996). Tracking and transitions through the middle grades: Channeling educational trajectories. *Sociology of Education, 69*(4), 290–307. https://doi.org/10.2307/2112716.

Dewey, J. (1916). *Democracy and education: An introduction to the philosophy of education.* New York: The Macmillan Company.

Domina, T., & Saldana, J. (2012). Does raising the bar level the playing field? Mathematics curricular intensification and inequality in American high schools, 1982–2004. *American Educational Research Journal, 49*(4), 685–708. https://doi.org/10.3102/0002831211426347.

Domina, T., McEachin, A., Penner, A., & Penner, E. (2015). Aiming high and falling short: California's eighth-grade algebra-for-all effort. *Educational Evaluation and Policy Analysis, 37*(3), 275–295. https://doi.org/10.3102/0162373714543685.

Domina, T., Hanselman, P., Hwang, N., & McEachin, A. (2016). Detracking and tracking up: Mathematics course placements in California middle schools, 2003–2013. *American Educational Research Journal, 53*(4), 1229–1266. https://doi.org/10.3102/0002831216650405.

Duncan, G. J., Dowsett, C. J., Claessens, A., Magnuson, K., Huston, A. C., Klebanov, P., et al. (2007). School readiness and later achievement. *Developmental Psychology, 43*(6), 1428–1446. https://doi.org/10.1037/0012-1649.43.6.1428.

Eccles, J. S., & Midgely, C. (1989). Stage/environment fit: Developmentally appropriate classrooms for early adolescents. In R. Ames & C. Ames (Eds.), *Research in Motivation in Education* (Vol. 3). New York: Academic Press.

Entwisle, D. R., & Alexander, K. L. (1993). Entry into school: The beginning school transition and educational stratification in the United States. *Annual Review of Sociology, 19*, 401–423.

Ferrare, J. J. (2013). The duality of courses and students: A field-theoretic analysis of secondary school coursetaking. *Sociology of Education, 86*(2), 139–157. https://doi.org/10.1177/0038040712456557.

Frank, K. A., Muller, C., Schiller, K. S., Riegle-Crumb, C., Mueller, A. S., Crosnoe, R., et al. (2008). The social dynamics of mathematics coursetaking in high school. *American Journal of Sociology, 113*(6), 1645–1696. https://doi.org/10.1086/587153.

Frank, K. A., Muller, C., & Mueller, A. S. (2013). The embeddedness of adolescent friendship nominations: The formation of social capital in emergent network structures. *American Journal of Sociology, 119*(1), 216–253. https://doi.org/10.1086/672081.

Gaertner, M. N., Kim, J., DesJardins, S. L., & McClarty, K. L. (2014). Preparing students for college and careers: The causal role of Algebra II. *Research in Higher Education, 55*(2), 143–165. https://doi.org/10.1007/s11162-013-9322-7.

Gamoran, A. (1986). Instructional and institutional effects of ability grouping. *Sociology of Education, 59*(4), 185–198. https://doi.org/10.2307/2112346.

Gamoran, A. (1992). The variable effects of high school tracking. *American Sociological Review, 57*(6), 812–828. https://doi.org/10.2307/2096125.

Gamoran, A. (2001). American schooling and educational inequality: A forecast for the 21st century. *Sociology of Education, 74*(Extra Issue), 135–153. https://doi.org/10.2307/2673258.

Gamoran, A., & Hannigan, E. C. (2000). Algebra for everyone? Benefits of college-preparatory mathematics for students with diverse abilities in early secondary school. *Educational Evaluation and Policy Analysis, 22*(3), 241–254. https://doi.org/10.3102/01623737022003241.

Gamoran, A., Secada, W. G., & Marrett, C. B. (2000). The organizational context of teaching and learning: Changing theoretical perspectives. In M. T. Hallinan (Ed.), *Handbook of the sociology of education* (pp. 37–63). Boston: Springer.

Gardner, D. P., Larsen, Y. W., Baker, W. O., & Campbell, A. (1983). *A nation at risk: The imperative for educational reform: A report to the nation and the Secretary of Education, United States Department of Education.* Washington, DC: U.S. National Commission on Excellence in Education.

Goldin, C., & Katz, L. F. (1999). Human capital and social capital: The rise of secondary schooling in America, 1910–1940. *The Journal of Interdisciplinary History, 29*(4), 683–723.

Goldin, C., & Katz, L. F. (2003). Mass secondary schooling and the state: The role of state compulsion in the high school movement (NBER Working Paper No. 10075). Cambridge, MA: National Bureau of Economic Research.

Goldin, C., & Katz, L. F. (2008). *The race between education and technology.* Cambridge, MA: Harvard University Press.

Hallinan, M. T. (1994). Tracking: From theory to practice. *Sociology of Education, 67*(2), 79–84.

Heppen, J. B., Walters, K., Clements, M., Faria, A.-M., Tobey, C., Sorensen, N., et al. (2012). *Access to Algebra I: The effects of online mathematics for grade 8 students* (NCEE 2012-4021). Washington, DC: National Center for Education Evaluation and Regional Assistance.

Herd, P. (2010). Education and health in late-life among high school graduates: Cognitive versus psychological aspects of human capital. *Journal of Health & Social Behavior, 51*(4), 478–496. https://doi.org/10.1177/0022146510386796.

Heyns, B. (1978). *Summer learning and the effects of schooling.* New York: Academic.

Jackson, P. W. (1992). Conceptions of curriculum and curriculum specialists. In P. W. Jackson (Ed.), *Handbook of research on curriculum.* New York: Macmillan Publishing Company.

Jacobs, J. A. (1996). Gender inequality and higher education. *Annual Review of Sociology, 22*, 153. https://doi.org/10.1146/annurev.soc.22.1.153.

Jencks, C., Bartlett, S., Corcoran, M., Crouse, J., Eaglesfield, D., Jackson, G., et al. (1979). *Who gets ahead? The determinants of economic success in America*. New York: Basic Books.

Kanno, Y., & Kangas, S. E. N. (2014). "I'm not going to be, like, for the AP": English language learners' limited access to advanced college-preparatory courses in high school. *American Educational Research Journal, 51*(5), 848–878. https://doi.org/10.3102/0002831214544716.

Karlson, K. B. (2015). Expectations on track? High school tracking and adolescent educational expectations. *Social Forces, 94*(1), 115–141. https://doi.org/10.1093/sf/sov006.

Labaree, D. F. (1997). Public goods, private goods: The American struggle over educational goals. *American Educational Research Journal, 34*(1), 39–81. https://doi.org/10.2307/1163342.

Lee, V. E., & Bryk, A. S. (1986). Effects of single-sex secondary schools on student achievement and attitudes. *Journal of Educational Psychology, 78*(5), 381–395. https://doi.org/10.1037//0022-0663.78.5.381.

Lee, V. E., & Ready, D. D. (2009). U.S. high school curriculum: Three phases of contemporary research and reform. *The Future of Children, 19*(1), 135–156.

Lleras, C., & Rangel, C. (2009). Ability grouping practices in elementary school and African American/Hispanic achievement. *American Journal of Education, 115*(2), 279–304. https://doi.org/10.1086/595667.

Long, M. C., Conger, D., & Iatarola, P. (2012). Effects of high school course-taking on secondary and postsecondary success. *American Educational Research Journal, 49*(2), 285–322. https://doi.org/10.2307/41419458.

Lubienski, C. (2003). Innovation in education markets: Theory and evidence on the impact of competition and choice in charter schools. *American Educational Research Journal, 40*(2), 395–443. https://doi.org/10.3102/00028312040002395.

Lucas, S. R. (1999). *Tracking inequality: Stratification and mobility in American high schools*. New York: Teachers College Press.

Lucas, S. R. (2001). Effectively maintained inequality: Education transitions, track mobility, and social background effects. *American Journal of Sociology, 106*(6), 1642–1690. https://doi.org/10.1086/321300.

Lucas, S. R., & Berends, M. (2007). Race and track location in U.S. public schools. *Research in Social Stratification and Mobility, 25*(3), 169–187. https://doi.org/10.1016/j.rssm.2006.12.002.

Marsh, H. W. (1989). Effects of attending single-sex and coeducational high schools on achievement, attitudes, behaviors, and sex differences. *Journal of Educational Psychology, 81*(1), 70–85. https://doi.org/10.1037//0022-0663.81.1.70.

Martin, E. W., Martin, R., & Terman, D. L. (1996). The legislative and litigation history of special education. *The Future of Children, 6*(1), 25–39. https://doi.org/10.2307/1602492.

Means, B., Confrey, J., House, A., & Bhanot, R. (2008). *STEM high schools: Specialized science technology engineering and mathematics secondary schools in the U.S.* (SRI Project P17858). Menlo Park: SRI International.

Mehan, H., Hertweck, A., & Meihls, J. L. (1986). *Handicapping and handicapped: Decision making in students' educational careers*. Stanford: Stanford University Press.

Mickelson, R. A. (2001). Subverting Swann: First- and second-generation segregation in the Charlotte-Mecklenburg schools. *American Educational Research Journal, 38*(2), 215–252. https://doi.org/10.3102/00028312038002215.

Mickelson, R. A. (2015). The cumulative disadvantages of first- and second-generation segregation for middle school achievement. *American Educational Research Journal, 52*, 657. https://doi.org/10.3102/0002831215587933.

Milner, H. R. I. (2013). Analyzing poverty, learning, and teaching through a critical race theory lens. *Review of Research in Education, 37*, 1–53. https://doi.org/10.3102/0091732X12459720.

Monk, D. H., & Haller, E. J. (1993). Predictors of high school academic course offerings: The role of school size. *American Educational Research Journal, 30*(1), 3–21. https://doi.org/10.3102/00028312030001003.

Montez, J. K., Hummer, R. A., & Hayward, M. D. (2012). Educational attainment and adult mortality in the United States: A systematic analysis of functional form. *Demography, 49*(1), 315–336. https://doi.org/10.1007/s13524-011-0082-8.

Morgan, P. L., Farkas, G., Hillemeier, M. M., Mattison, R., Maczuga, S., Li, H., et al. (2015). Minorities are disproportionately underrepresented in special education. *Educational Researcher, 44*(5), 278–292. https://doi.org/10.3102/0013189X15591157.

Muller, C. (2015). Measuring education and skill. *The Annals of the American Academy of Political and Social Science, 657*(1), 136–148. https://doi.org/10.1177/0002716214550586.

Muller, C., & Schiller, K. (2000). Leveling the playing field? Students' educational attainment and states' performance testing. *Sociology of Education, 73*(3), 196–218. https://doi.org/10.2307/2673216.

Nord, C., Roey, S., Perkins, R., Lyons, M., Lemanski, N., Brown, J., et al. (2011). *The nation's report card: America's high school graduates (NCES 2011-462)*. Washington, DC: U.S. Department of Education. National Center for Education Statistics.

O'Connor, C., & Fernandez, S. D. (2006). Race, class, and disproportionality: Reevaluating the relationship between poverty and special education placement. *Educational Researcher, 35*(6), 6–11. https://doi.org/10.3102/0013189X035006006.

Oakes, J. (1994). More than misapplied technology: A normative and political response to Hallinan on tracking. *Sociology of Education, 67*(2), 84–91. https://doi.org/10.2307/2112698.

Oakes, J. (2005). *Keeping track: How schools structure inequality* (2nd ed.). New Haven: Yale University Press.

Oakes, J., Ormseth, T., Bell, R. M., & Camp, P. (1990). *Multiplying inequalities: The effects of race, social class, and tracking on opportunities to learn mathematics and science* (Vol. R-3928-NSF). Santa Monica: RAND Corporation.

Oakes, J., Gamoran, A., & Page, R. N. (1992). Curriculum differentiation: Opportunities, outcomes, and meanings. In P. W. Jackson (Ed.), *Handbook of research on curriculum*. New York: Macmillan Publishing Company.

Oakes, J., Wells, A. S., & Jones, M. (1997). Detracking: The social construction of ability, cultural politics, and resistance to reform. *Teachers College Record, 94*(3), 482–510.

Olneck, M. R. (1989). Americanization and the education of immigrants, 1900–1925: An analysis of symbolic action. *American Journal of Education, 97*(4), 398–423.

Olsen, L. (1997). *Made in America: Immigrant students in our public schools*. New York: The New Press.

Pianta, R. C., Belsky, J., Houts, R., & Morrison, F. (2007). Opportunities to learn in America's elementary classrooms. *Science, 315*(5820), 1795–1796. https://doi.org/10.1126/science.1139719.

Porter, A., McMaken, J., Hwang, J., & Yang, R. (2011). Common core standards: The new U.S. intended curriculum. *Educational Researcher, 40*(3), 103–116. https://doi.org/10.3102/0013189X11405038.

Powell, A. G., Farrar, E., & Cohen, D. K. (1985). *The shopping mall high school: Winners and losers in the educational marketplace*. Boston: Houghton Mifflin.

Quinn, D. M., Cooc, N., McIntyre, J., & Gomez, C. J. (2016). Seasonal dynamics of academic achievement inequality by socioeconomic status and race/ethnicity. *Educational Researcher, 45*(8), 443–453. https://doi.org/10.3102/0013189X16677965.

Raftery, A. E., & Hout, M. (1993). Maximally maintained inequality: Expansion, reform, and opportunity in Irish education, 1921–75. *Sociology of Education, 66*(1), 41–62.

Renzulli, L. A., & Evans, L. (2005). School choice, charter schools, and White flight. *Social Problems, 52*(3), 398–418. https://doi.org/10.1525/sp.2005.52.3.398.

Riegle-Crumb, C. (2006). The path through math: Course sequences and academic performance at the intersection of race-ethnicity and gender. *American Journal of Education, 113*(1), 101–122. https://doi.org/10.1086/506495.

Riehl, C., Pallas, A. M., & Natriello, G. (1999). Rites and wrongs: Institutional explanations for the student course-scheduling process in urban high schools. *American Journal of Education, 107*(2), 116–154. https://doi.org/10.1086/444209.

Roscigno, V. J., Tomaskovic-Devey, D., & Crowley, M. (2006). Education and the inequalities of place. *Social Forces, 84*(4), 2121–2145. https://doi.org/10.1353/sof.2006.0108.

Rose, H., & Betts, J. R. (2004). The effect of high school courses on earnings. *Review of Economics & Statistics, 86*(2), 497–513. https://doi.org/10.1162/003465304323031076.

Rosenbaum, J. E. (1978). The structure of opportunity in school. *Social Forces, 57*(1), 236–256. https://doi.org/10.2307/2577636.

Rosenbaum, J. E. (2001). *Beyond college for all: Career paths for the forgotten half*. New York: Russell Sage.

Ross, C. E., & Wu, C.-I. (1995). The links between education and health. *American Sociological Review, 60*(5), 719–745. https://doi.org/10.2307/2096319.

Rubin, B. C. (2008). Detracking in context: How local constructions of ability complicate equity-geared reform. *Teachers College Record, 110*(3), 646–699.

Schiller, K. S., & Muller, C. (2003). Raising the bar and equity? Effects of state high school graduation requirements and accountability policies on students' mathematics course taking. *Educational Evaluation and Policy Analysis, 25*(3), 299–318. https://doi.org/10.3102/01623737025003299.

Schmidt, W. H. (2012). At the precipice: The story of mathematics education in the United States. *Peabody Journal of Education, 87*(1), 133–156. https://doi.org/10.1080/0161956x.2012.642280.

Schmidt, W. H., McKnight, C. C., Cogan, L. S., Jakwerth, P. M., & Houang, R. T. (1999). *Facing the consequences: Using TIMSS for a closer look at U.S. mathematics*. Dordrecht/Boston: Kluwer Academic Publishers.

Schmidt, W. H., Burroughs, N. A., Zoido, P., & Houang, R. T. (2015). The role of schooling in perpetuating educational inequality: An international perspective. *Educational Researcher, 44*(7), 371–386. https://doi.org/10.3102/0013189x15603982.

Shifrer, D., Callahan, R. M., & Muller, C. (2013). Equity or marginalization? The high school course-taking of students labeled with a learning disability. *American Education Research Journal, 50*(4), 656–682. https://doi.org/10.3102/0002831213479439.

Slavin, R. E. (1987). Ability grouping and student achievement in elementary schools: A best-evidence synthesis. *Review of Educational Research, 57*, 293–350. https://doi.org/10.2307/1170460.

Sørensen, A. B. (1970). Organizational differentiation of students and educational opportunity. *Sociology of Education, 43*(4), 355–376. https://doi.org/10.2307/2111838.

Spring, J. H. (1976). *The sorting machine: National educational policy since 1945*. New York: David McKay.

Steenbergen-Hu, S., Makel, M. C., & Olszewski-Kubilius, P. (2016). What one hundred years of research says about the effects of ability grouping and acceleration on K–12 students' academic achievement. *Review of Educational Research, 86*(4), 849–899. https://doi.org/10.3102/0034654316675417.

Suárez-Orozco, C., Suárez-Orozco, M. M., & Todorova, I. (2008). *Learning a new land: Immigrant students in American society*. Cambridge, MA: Harvard University Press.

Sutton, A. (2017). Preparing for local labor: Curricular stratification across local economies in the United States. *Sociology of Education, 90*(2), 172–196.

Symonds, W. C., Schwartz, R., & Ferguson, R. F. (2011). *Pathways to prosperity: Meeting the challenge of preparing young Americans for the 21st century*. Cambridge, MA: Pathways to Prosperity Project, Harvard University Graduate School of Education.

Turner, R. H. (1960). Sponsored and contest mobility and the school system. *American Sociological Review, 25*(6), 855–867. https://doi.org/10.2307/2089982.

Tyack, D. B., & Cuban, L. (1995). *Tinkering toward utopia: A century of public school reform*. Cambridge, MA: Harvard University Press.

Tyler, R. W. (1976). Two new emphases in curriculum development. *Educational Leadership, 34*(1), 61.

U.S. Commission on Civil Rights (2016). *U.S. Commission on Civil Rights mission webpage*. http://www.usccr.gov/about/index.php. Accessed 5 Dec 2016.

U.S. Department of Education. (2014). *National assessment of career and technical education: Final report to congress*. Washington, DC: U.S. Department of Education. Office of Planning, Evaluation and Policy Development.

U.S. Department of Education (2016). *2015–15 civil rights data collection: List of CRDC data elements for school year 2015–16*. http://www2.ed.gov/about/offices/list/ocr/docs/2015-16-crdc-data-elements.pdf

Walsemann, K. M., Geronimus, A. T., & Gee, G. C. (2008). Accumulating disadvantage over the life course: Evidence from a longitudinal study investigating the relationship between educational advantage in youth and health in middle age. *Research on Aging, 30*(2), 169–199. https://doi.org/10.1177/0164027507311149.

Wang, X. (2013). Why students choose STEM majors: Motivation, high school learning, and postsecondary context of support. *American Education Research Journal, 50*(5), 1081–1121. https://doi.org/10.3102/0002831213488622.

Warren, J. R., Muller, C., Hummer, R. A., Grodsky, E., & Humphries, M. (2015). *What aspect of "education" matters to early mortality? Evidence from the high school and beyond cohort*. Paper presented at the Annual Meeting of the Society for Longitudinal and Life Course Studies (SLLS), October 18–22, Dublin.

Welner, K. G. (2001). *Legal rights, local wrongs: When community control collides with educational equity*. Albany: SUNY Press.

Welner, K. G., & Oakes, J. (1996). (Li)ability grouping: The new susceptibility of school tracking systems to legal challenges. *Harvard Educational Review, 66*(3), 451–470. https://doi.org/10.17763/haer.66.3.p92775298646n342.

Wiggan, G. (2007). Race, school achievement, and educational inequality: Toward a student-based inquiry perspective. *Review of Educational Research, 77*(3), 310–333. https://doi.org/10.3102/003465430303947.

Sean Kelly, Ben Pogodzinski, and Yuan Zhang

Abstract

Sociological research has often focused on teaching practices, and features of the teaching profession, in search of mechanisms that explain disparate schooling outcomes. Yet, the study of teachers and teaching practices is complicated by the fact that students' themselves influence classroom instruction. To what extent is systematic variation in teaching quality responsible for persistent and sometimes widening gaps in educational outcomes among social groups in the United States? The evidence summarized in this chapter reveals that most teachers in the United States are both well-qualified and skilled at increasing student achievement. This is true even in schools that serve students facing serious social problems associated with poverty. At the same time, close studies of the teaching process reveal room for improvement, and we conclude that raising the aggregate quality of teaching, and making sure that all students have access to high-quality instruction, will indeed help address persistent gaps in educational outcomes. To improve teaching quality, research, policy initiatives, and future investments must treat teachers' work as an integrated whole, supporting the professional socialization, ongoing development, and learning of teachers, and the organizational climate in which they work.

Popular conceptions of the teaching profession often depict the quality of instruction in teachers' classrooms as highly variable: An entire year's worth of learning experiences, perhaps even an entire educational career, are thought to hang in the balance each fall when classroom assignments are made. For example, blockbuster Hollywood teacher narratives, from *Up the Down Stair Case* (1967) to *Dangerous Minds* (1989) to *Freedom Writers* (2007), have long depicted the lone "teacher hero," struggling to make a difference amongst a sea of ineffectual colleagues (Kelly and Caughlan 2011; Bulman 2005). Is the quality of instruction in different classrooms really so widely disparate? And if so, what are the sources of this variation? To what extent does systematic variation in teaching quality explain persistent gaps in educational outcomes among social groups in the United States (see e.g., Reardon 2011 and chapter 3 in this handbook)? What essential principles should guide efforts to improve teaching quality?

To answer these questions, we begin by considering variability between poor and non-poor

S. Kelly (✉) · Y. Zhang
University of Pittsburgh, Pittsburgh, PA, USA
e-mail: spkelly@pitt.edu; yuz55@pitt.edu

B. Pogodzinski
Wayne State University, Detroit, MI, USA
e-mail: Ben.pogodzinski@wayne.edu

© Springer International Publishing AG, part of Springer Nature 2018
B. Schneider (ed.), *Handbook of the Sociology of Education in the 21st Century*, Handbooks of Sociology and Social Research, https://doi.org/10.1007/978-3-319-76694-2_12

schools in the teacher qualifications and background characteristics thought to produce high-quality instruction and student learning outcomes. Next, we review the literature examining the effect of basic teacher qualifications on student learning outcomes. We find that while access to qualified teachers is unevenly distributed across schools and student groups, most teachers in the United States are well-qualified, and existing variation in basic qualifications is not responsible to any great extent for high levels of educational inequality. In Sects. 12.2 and 12.3 we consider studies that focus on observed teaching practices and student learning outcomes associated with specific teachers. This "teacher effects" research shows both pronounced variability in teaching quality and that teachers' use of known best practices do correlate with improved student outcomes. However, as with research on teacher qualifications, these studies speak more to the possibilities for improving teaching quality—what we might hope to ultimately achieve from the right mix of educational reforms—than to shortcomings of the teaching workforce in low-SES schools. In Sect. 12.4 we discuss seminal studies of teaching in the sociology of education which demonstrate the difficulty and uncertainty of teaching and the impact of social context on teachers' work. Building on these insights, we conclude by discussing the school organizational supports that show the most promise in improving teaching quality.

Consistent with an emphasis on social context supports for teaching, throughout this chapter we employ the term *teaching* quality, rather than *teacher* quality, in order to emphasize that effective instruction is not primarily a product of immutable attributes that characterize individual teachers, but rather occurs at the intersection of the teacher, the classroom context, and the social and organizational supports that are in place. In addition, the term "teacher quality" seems to imply a stability in the quality and impact of instruction that is not always present (Darling-Hammond et al. 2012). However, we begin by reviewing research concerning teacher qualifications, as well as estimates of effectiveness associated with specific teachers because these studies

are an important component of an overall understanding of teaching quality (see also Hamilton 2012 or Kennedy 2010 for discussions of this distinction in terminology).

12.1 Variation in Teacher Qualifications Between and Within Schools

One common explanation for educational inequality is that achievement gaps are produced by differences in access to highly-qualified teachers; some students, even entire schools, have well-trained, effective teachers, while other students and schools have poorly-qualified teachers. Potentially important teacher qualifications and background variables that might exist between students and schools include: the selectivity of the universities teachers attended, their measured test scores, graduate training and practice-teaching experiences, a priori motivations, personality traits, and experience. While it is not possible in large-scale research to fully measure all aspects of teacher qualifications and background that might be important to successful teaching, studies of the teacher labor market across schools and districts reveal an uneven distribution of several basic teacher characteristics.

At the national level, data from the federally-sponsored Schools and Staffing Survey (SASS) provide evidence on the qualifications of the teaching workforce. Table 12.1 provides estimates of differences across poor and non-poor schools in three qualifications, years of teaching experience, master's degree (or higher) attainment, and certification status, compiled from fives waves of SASS beginning with the 1987–1988 school year. Students who attend a high-poverty school are more likely to have a teacher with three years or less of experience, and less likely to have a teacher with a full state certification or an advanced degree. In earlier waves of SASS the reported results focused on teacher qualifications in urban schools, and disparities exist between urban and suburban schools as well, although the differences are less substantial in this case.

Table 12.1 Disparities in teacher qualifications among full-time public secondary school teachers: findings from five waves of the schools and staffing survey

	Three Years or less Teaching Experience		Regular (full) Certification		Degree Attained (MA or higher)	
	Low-poverty (0–25%)	High-poverty (76–100%)	Low-poverty (0–25%)	High-poverty (76–100%)	Low-poverty (0–25%)	High-poverty (76–100%)
2011–2012[a]	9.3%	13.9%	92.6%	87.8%	63.2%	53.6%
2007–2008[b]	15.3%	21.9%	88.8%	81.7%	59.9%	46.5%
1999–2000	15.3%	16.5%	90.8%	87.3%	52.0%	44.7%
	Low-poverty (0–5%)	High-poverty (40–100%)	Suburban	Urban	Suburban	Urban
1990–1991[c]	–	–	95.5%	94.6%	59.6%	56.2%
1987–1988	7.1%	12.2%	95.3%	91.8%	59.1%	57%

Note: This table relies primarily on results reported in official publications from the National Center for Education Statistics, and thus there are some differences in reporting categories, and which teachers are considered
[a]In 2011–2012, statistics are for both part- and full-time teachers, and include both primary and secondary school teachers. In addition, poverty categories used are 0–34% vs 75% or more. Certification statistics are from author's calculation. Other statistics are from Goldring et al. (2013)
[b]Statistics for 2007–2008 and 1999–2000 are reported in Aud et al. (2010)
[c]Certification statistics for 1987–1988 and 1990–1991 refer to within-field certification (i.e., specifically in the teacher's main assignment field). Comparison of teaching experience in 1987–1988 is for both primary and secondary school teachers. Statistics reported in Smith et al. (1994) and Lippman et al. (1996)

The nationally-representative data from SASS reveal a situation of uneven teacher qualifications across poor and non-poor schools (and relatedly in urban vs suburban schools, and in minority vs predominantly White schools). However, it is also true that most teachers are highly qualified even in poor schools. For example, in the most recent wave of the SASS data, almost 90% of teachers are fully certified even in schools with a high-poverty concentration (although they may be teaching out-of-field, see Hill and Stearns 2015). Importantly, states have raised certification requirements in recent decades; such that today's fully certified teacher is more highly trained than ever before (Darling-Hammond et al. 2009a, b). This phenomenon is partially reflected in the increasing percentage of teachers with advanced degrees in the most recent waves of SASS. Yet, SASS provides a limited portrait of school-to-school variation in teacher qualifications on a few rough indicators. Studies using state-level administrative data in some cases find starker differences than reported in SASS, and also help

explain how labor-market sorting processes produce uneven access to highly qualified teachers.

Lankford et al. (2002) examined the uneven distribution of teachers across schools using a comprehensive database of teachers in New York State during the 1999–2000 school year. In some cases, comparisons among different types of schools revealed pronounced differences in teacher qualifications. For example, Lankford et al. found that the relative risk of having a teacher who failed the state's general knowledge exam was approximately 38% higher for the average poor student than the average non-poor student (a probability of .279 vs .202). Among the state's non-White students, the relative risk of having a teacher who failed the state exam was almost three times higher than among White students (a probability of .212 vs .071), while the risk of having a teacher with a bachelor's degree from a least competitive college (as measured by the Barron's ranking of selectivity) was more than twice as high for non-White students (a probability of .214 vs .102).

More recent data from New York show that teacher qualifications in high-poverty schools are improving (Lankford et al. 2014), but the findings from 1999–2000 continue to serve as an example of the kinds of disparities that can occur across school, district, and regional boundaries, and that have been found in other state data (Adamson and Darling-Hammond 2012; Clotfelter et al. 2005; Goldhaber et al. 2015; Schultz 2014). Indeed, gaps in teacher qualifications are likely to continue to exist, as long as high levels of school segregation, particularly segregation across district boundaries (Clotfelter 2004; Vigdor 2011), create incentives in the teacher labor market for the most highly qualified teachers to move to higher socioeconomic status schools, where they find more favorable behavioral climates and higher salaries (Kelly 2004; Guarino et al. 2006; Ingersoll 2001). For example, in the New York data, Lankford et al. (2002) found that when teachers moved from one district to another they moved to schools with 50% fewer poor students (19.2% on average in the receiving school vs 38.1% in the originating school), and enjoyed a non-trivial increase in salary and a decline in class size. Relatedly, school administrators in high-poverty, high-minority schools (as well as schools with a larger student body enrollment), report greater difficulty in filling vacant teaching positions (Malkus et al. 2015; Jacob 2007). When staffing difficulties do occur, some school administrators must reluctantly rely on long-term substitutes or less than fully qualified applicants to fill positions (Jacob 2007).

12.1.1 Variation in Teacher Qualifications Within Schools

In addition to the possibility of an uneven distribution of teachers across schools, within schools there is great potential for uneven access to teachers with expert qualifications (Kalogrides et al. 2013). In secondary schools in particular (middle and high schools), the curriculum differentiation of students into high- and low-track classrooms creates the potential for "teacher tracking." For example, in the ninth grade, teachers assigned to teach honors geometry may have, on average, more substantial mathematical content knowledge than teachers assigned to teach a 2-year Algebra 1 sequence starting in ninth grade. Indeed, studies of the allocation of teachers to tracked classrooms show that such differences are widespread (Kelly 2004; Raudenbush et al. 1992; Riehl and Sipple 1996; Talbert 1992). Talbert (1992) estimated that approximately 34% of teachers are assigned to teach predominately high-or-low track classrooms, while Kelly (2004) reported that over 90% of secondary schools engage in some amount of teacher tracking (where an imbalance in teaching assignments was found among sampled teachers). In addition to differences in rates of master's degree attainment and subject-matter coursework, Kelly found several potential indicators of greater motivation among teachers with high-track assignments, including higher rates of participation in professional organizations and lower earnings from part-time work outside of teaching. Finally, low-track teachers report lower levels of efficacy than high-track teachers, and relatedly, lower career satisfaction (see Kelly 2009 for a summary of this research).

Clotfelter et al. (2005) analyzed differences in exposure to experienced teachers among Black and White seventh grade students using administrative data from North Carolina, and found that a substantial proportion of the total gap occurs within schools. In the state as a whole, approximately 8.3% of White students are taught by a novice math teacher (with no prior experience), while 12.8% of Black students have a novice math teacher, a 54% difference. Approximately 1/4 of the total gap among all students in the entire state (which captures differences across districts and schools, as well as within schools) was due to differences between classrooms within the same school. Moreover, in some districts racial gaps in access to experienced teachers occurred almost entirely within schools. In the NC analysis, the total effect of gaps in teacher qualifications on educational inequality is likely small because the absolute rates on this indicator are low (most teachers are not novice teachers). However, the implication from the teacher tracking literature is that observable indicators of teacher qualifications between tracks probably underestimate the true differences between teachers because assignment to high-track classes serves as an informal career ladder for the most motivated teachers.

12.2 Teacher Qualifications and Student Outcomes

The research reviewed in Sect. 12.1 showed systematic variation in access to highly-qualified teachers, for example in poor students' access to experienced teachers, and in low-track students' access to teachers with the strongest subject-matter training. To what extent are basic teacher qualifications related to student learning outcomes? Answers to this question are important both for understanding how the gaps in Sect. 12.1 might translate into differences in opportunity to learn, but also in informing policy efforts to improve teaching quality. For example, if teacher experience is strongly related to achievement outcomes, then targeted efforts to recruit experienced teachers to teach in low-performing schools, along with a concerted effort to retain them, might be a particularly effective reform strategy.

Although the 1966 Coleman report is best known for its implications in the study of school effects, it was also one of the first large-scale studies to produce estimates of how teacher qualifications affect student achievement, controlling for the effects of student family background. Coleman and his research team considered a number of teacher variables including: years of experience, teachers' educational attainment, and teachers' tested vocabulary. These variables were aggregated to the school level, along with student background variables, such that differences in achievement across schools might be identified statistically, free from student background effects. The results showed that teacher characteristics were more strongly related to school-to-school variation in achievement than all other measured attributes of schools (e.g., per pupil expenditures, physical resources, curricular attributes), apart from the aggregate effects of student

background. Yet, in terms of the total variability in student achievement, the effects of teacher variables were small in Coleman's Equality of Educational Opportunity (EEO) study data, explaining at most 1–2% of the total variance among White students for example. Jencks et al. (1972) and colleagues reanalyzed the EEO data, along with other large educational databases of the era, and described the effects of teacher characteristics as having "small and inconsistent effects" on achievement (p. 96).

Since the early work by Coleman, Jencks, and others, researchers have continued to study the effects of teacher qualifications for three reasons: First, improved data have shown more consistent effects of certain teacher variables; second, some qualifications can be directly improved through policy mechanisms; third, the talent and capacity of the teaching workforce is a prerequisite to engaging in school improvement efforts. Even if the direct effect of a given teacher attribute on student achievement growth is small, effective reform to improve teaching practices hinges on having adequate human and social (as well as material/financial) resources in the form of a well-trained teaching workforce (Gamoran et al. 2000).

Table 12.2 presents evidence on the relationship between four major qualifications and teacher quality as measured by student achievement outcomes. Each of the three studies in Table 12.2 used large-scale state administrative data to explore teacher effects in public schools. We showcase these findings from North Carolina, Texas, and Florida in Table form for two main reasons. First, the data used in each study are representative of all public school students in particular grades/subject areas, constituting especially substantial populations of learners. Second, while other studies are available that use high-quality state or national data sets to examine teacher qualifications (e.g., Darling-Hammond 2000; Jepsen 2005; Kane et al. 2008), the three studies in Table 12.2 are indicative of the kind of divergent findings on the relationship between teacher qualifications and student achievement outcomes found throughout the literature. Additional evidence, including major reviews of

Table 12.2 Divergent findings on the relationship between teacher characteristics and student achievement

Studies (Data source)	Subjects	Teacher qualifications			
		Education	Experience	Test scores	College selectivity
Clotfelter, Ladd, & Vigdor, 2007 (North Carolina)	Math	Negative	Positive	Positive	Null
	Reading	Negative	Positive	Positive	Null
Rivkin, Hanushek, & Kain, 2005 (Texas)	Math	Null	Null		
	Reading	Null	Null		
Harris & Sass 2011 (Florida)	Math	Positive	Positive		
	Reading	Negative	Positive		

the literature by Wayne and Youngs (2003) and Greenwald et al. (1996), is also considered.

Teachers vary in the educational degrees they obtain in subject-matter areas, as well as in pedagogy, leadership, educational psychology, and related educational studies, with formal training occurring both before and after they enter teaching. While some research has shown positive effects of degree attainment (Wilson et al. 2001), other studies find no significant impact (e.g., Adams 2012; Jepsen 2005). Indeed, as revealed in Table 12.2, some studies even show a *negative* impact of master's degree attainment (e.g., Clotfelter et al. 2007). One explanation for negative effects of degree attainment in some states is that pursuing a master's degree may be part of preparation for a future administrative position, or otherwise signal a de-prioritization of the teacher's current classroom teaching assignment (Ladd and Sorensen 2015). In synthesizing results from studies on teacher qualifications, Wayne and Youngs (2003) concluded that overall, positive relationships between teacher education and student achievement could only be detected in mathematics, and only for high school students, suggesting that teacher education is not one of the most consistent or strongest predictors across educational settings. In contrast, instead of emphasizing teachers' basic educational attainment, efforts to specifically measure teachers' pedagogical content knowledge (i.e., content knowledge for teaching certain subjects) have found effects on student outcomes net of other teacher variables (e.g., Hill et al. 2005). These results suggest that *rigorous* degree attainment is in fact likely to improve teacher effectiveness.

In addition to educational attainment, teacher experience in the classroom is another well-researched measure of teacher qualifications. Similar to the findings on teachers' educational attainment, the evidence concerning years of teaching experience is somewhat conflicting. In their review of the literature, Greenwald et al. (1996) present both positive and negative findings on teacher experience, with the effect size varying substantially across studies. Wayne and Youngs (2003) argue that across a given sample of teachers, "years of experience" captures multiple underlying processes beyond experience itself (e.g., hiring conditions in the job market when teachers entered the profession), which may account for the inconclusive findings in the research literature. However, studies have shown consistent evidence of a positive association between teaching experience and student achievement during the earliest years of the teaching career (e.g., Clotfelter et al. 2006; Clotfelter et al. 2007). Teachers do become more effective as they accumulate real-world teaching experience in the first few years (see also Sect. 12.5 or more specifically Sect. 12.5.1 below).

Measures of teacher selectivity, including test scores on licensure exams, as well as the selectivity of the teachers' undergraduate institution, are generally positively related to student achievement outcomes (Wayne and Youngs 2003). Teachers' tested achievement may be particularly important in mathematics (Clotfelter et al. 2006; Kukla-Acevedo 2009). For example, estimates from Clotfelter et al. (2007) suggest that teachers with mathematics test scores two or more standard deviations above the average (as might be found among STEM-focused graduates from top universities) could increase student gains on mathematics tests by 0.068 of a standard deviation, while teachers who scored two or more standard deviations below the average would reduce student gains by 0.062 standard deviations, an overall difference of 0.130 standard deviations. While such an effect size is non-trivial and important, given the sheer size of the teaching workforce, we are unlikely to realize such gains on a large scale. Moreover, as is evinced in Table 12.2, even these teacher qualifications have null effects on achievement in some cases (e.g., the effect of college selectivity in the NC data).

An additional factor not shown in Table 12.2 but relevant to state policy decisions is the effect of teacher certification, including the prestigious National Board for Professional Teaching Standards (NBPTS) certification. As of 2011–2012, less than half of secondary school teachers held both a subject-matter major and full state certification in their main teaching assignment (Baldi et al. 2015; Hill and Stearns 2015). Although requirements for certification vary across states, by 2012, many states required substantial formal coursework in the subject matter taught, evidence of mastery of basic skills and subject-specific knowledge on written tests, and 10 or more weeks of student teaching experience (Quality Counts 2012). Overall, the effects of teacher certification appear to be important. For instance, state-certified mathematics teachers in North Carolina have mathematics achievement gains that are 0.03 to 0.06 standard deviations higher than teachers on provisional/emergency certification, while NBPTS certified teachers show gains 0.02 to 0.06 standard deviations higher than remaining teachers (Clotfelter et al. 2007). Currently however, NBPTS certification remains a rare and prestigious accomplishment; as of 2015, only 40,033 teachers nationwide were NBPTS certified (Quality Counts 2015).

Considering the findings in Sect. 12.1 and 12.2 on the distribution of teacher qualifications and their effects on student outcomes, uneven access to high-quality teachers does not appear to be the main driver of educational inequality in the U.S. There is, on balance, evidence that teacher preparation, experience, and selectivity are related to teacher effectiveness, *but the lack of consistency across studies and the modest effect sizes mean that observed teacher characteristics* *seldom explain much of the variation in student achievement* (Aaronson et al. 2007; Hanushek and Rivkin 2004; Konstantopoulos 2012; Rivkin et al. 2005). When comparing a teacher with a set of very weak credentials to very strong credentials, the effect on student achievement growth can be quite large relative to established reform benchmarks (Clotfelter et al. 2007), but such comparisons apply to relatively small percentages of students. Thus, considering specific student groups including poor vs non-poor students, or White vs non-White students, gaps in basic teacher qualifications among student groups appear to be only minimally responsible for disparate learning rates among those students (see e.g., Desimone and Long 2010; Guarino et al. 2006). One implication from existing literature then might be that in school improvement efforts focus should be shifted from teacher characteristics to observed teacher behaviors and student outcomes (Gamoran 2012; Kane and Staiger 2012). For example, teacher staffing reforms that use student test scores and other measures to identify the most effective teachers, and then provide these effective teachers with incentives to teach in low-performing schools, might be a promising reform strategy. We consider literature that speaks to teacher-to-teacher variability in observed practices and student outcomes in the next section.

12.3 Teacher-to-Teacher Differences in Instructional Practice and Student Achievement Growth

Studies of teaching quality that link student achievement growth to specific teachers (i.e., "teacher effects" research), consistently reveals significant variability in teacher effects on student achievement outcomes (Sanders and Horn 1998). Early efforts to quantify teacher effects were confounded by the non-random assignment of students to teachers; the teachers that appear most effective may just be the teachers who happened to be assigned the most effortful students. Studies in which students have been randomly assigned to teachers have overcome this challenge, providing an especially robust portrait of teacher effectiveness. Project STAR (Student–Teacher Achievement Ratio) was a randomized experiment commissioned in 1985 by the Tennessee state legislature. The experiment sites included 79 elementary schools in 42 school districts, where kindergarten students were randomly assigned into small classes (13–17 students), large classes (22–26 students), or large classes with a full-time classroom aide; teachers were also randomly assigned to classes. The random assignments of students and teachers were maintained through the third grade (Nye et al. 2000). While the original goal was to shed light on the possible effect of class-size reduction policies, educational researchers realized that the STAR data addressed an even more fundamental educational question—just how strong an impact on achievement does an especially effective teacher have? Although not nationally representative, the overall design and quality of the data collection have made STAR "one of the great experiments in education in U.S. history" (Mosteller et al. 1996, p. 814).

Konstantopoulos and colleagues have used data from Project STAR and its follow-up study, the Lasting Benefits Study, to investigate the size and persistence of teacher effects from kindergarten through sixth grade. For example, Konstantopoulos and Chung (2011) used advanced statistical models to estimate teacher effects in grades K-6 for mathematics, reading, and science. Konstantopoulos and Chung found that students who had a highly effective teacher in fifth grade increased their achievement in mathematics by more than one quarter of a standard deviation in sixth grade; the results for reading and science were comparable. In addition, the findings indicate that kindergarten teacher effects persisted; students who had an effective teacher in kindergarten were still benefiting through sixth grade, although less so than from exposure to effective teachers in, say, fourth or fifth grade (see also Sanders and Horn 1998). Teacher effectiveness also appears to be cumulative. Konstantopoulos (2011) found that students assigned to teachers ranked at the 85th percentile of the teacher effectiveness distribution for three

consecutive grades (from kindergarten through second grade) experienced an achievement increase of about one-third of a standard deviation in reading. Such effects are substantial and represent nearly one-third of a year's growth in achievement (see for example the discussion of empirical benchmarks for interpreting effect sizes in Hill et al. 2008). In addition to demonstrating the considerable magnitude and persistence of teacher effects, other Project STAR studies show that students, regardless of their race/ethnic or socioeconomic background characteristics, benefit from having effective teachers (Konstantopoulos 2009; Konstantopoulos and Chung 2011; Konstantopoulos and Sun 2012). For additional research on the variability and durability of teacher effects see Fan and Bains (2008) and Stigler and Hiebert (1999).

The Measures of Effective Teaching (MET) project was another large-scale experimental study that provided insight into teachers' impact on student achievement outcomes. During Year 1 (2009–2010), teachers' impact on student achievement growth was assessed using statistical controls for prior achievement; during Year 2 (2010–2011), teachers signed up as groups of three or more colleagues working in the same school and were randomly assigned to students in their grades and subjects. Researchers then studied the differences in student achievement gains within each of the Year 2 groupings to see if the students assigned to the teachers identified as "more effective" in Year 1 actually outperformed the students assigned to the "less effective" teachers. In addition to estimating teachers' impact on student achievement, the MET project observed and video-taped classroom sessions, such that the quality of teachers' instruction could be directly assessed using generic frameworks for the evaluation of effective teaching (e.g., CLASS, PLATO, FFT). Student and teacher surveys of instructional practice, as well as tests of teachers' pedagogical content knowledge, were also administered for the MET project. One aim of the project was an applied research goal, to provide information on how educational professionals might simultaneously draw on multiple measures in assessing teachers' work (e.g., for accountability purposes).

As with Project STAR though, the design and high quality of the measures in the MET study gave educational researchers new insight into basic teacher-to-teacher differences in classroom processes and outcomes.

Findings from MET confirm that some teachers are more effective at raising student achievement than others; the differences in learning between students assigned to teachers from the top quartile (top 25%) on the effectiveness distribution and students assigned to teachers from the bottom quartile ranged from 2.8 months (estimates based on state ELA test) to 10.8 months (estimates based on SAT9/Open-Ended Reading) (Bill and Melinda Gates Foundation 2010). Moreover, while there was not complete overlap, the most effective teachers also scored well on observations of best practices (Kane et al. 2013; Mihaly et al. 2013). For example, correlations between teacher scores on the Framework for Teaching (Danielson 2011) classroom observational protocol scores and the state value-added achievement measures ranged from .17 to .41 depending on the grade level and subject matter (see Mihaly et al. 2013, Table 3). Schacter and Thum (2004) provide additional evidence on the relationship between the quality of observed instruction and student achievement growth; in data from five elementary schools in Arizona, teachers who scored high on 12 research-based teaching performance standards produced about one full standard deviation gain above lower-scoring teachers.

12.3.1 Teacher Effectiveness Across Domains and Over Time

While the MET study was successful in confirming the variability in teacher effectiveness found in prior research, and in showcasing the relationship between high-quality instruction and student outcomes, other research raises questions about the generalizability of teacher effects to other important student outcomes and about the stability of teacher effectiveness over time (see Rothstein and Mathis 2013 for a critical review of the MET findings in particular and their application to teacher evaluation and other policy decisions).

Jennifer Jennings and colleagues have examined teacher-to-teacher variability in effectiveness as measured by specific, alternative student outcomes, which reinforces a multidimensional definition of high-quality teaching and shows that individual teachers may be more competent or focused on some dimensions than others. In the Early Childhood Longitudinal Study data, elementary school teachers who are effective at raising achievement in mathematics also tend to be effective at raising reading scores; correlations on reading and math gains ranged from .42–.48 (Jennings and Diprete 2010). In contrast, many teachers who were generally strong at promoting academic achievement had more difficulty cultivating desirable "approaches to learning" in students, the learning behaviors like task persistence, attentiveness, etc. that predict school success over the long-run (correlations between academic and behavioral outcomes ranged from .13 to .17).

Similar findings arose in the MET data; teacher effectiveness seemed to generalize, at least moderately so, across subject-matter tests with differing items and learning domains, and to student enjoyment of class, but not to other important motivation and engagement outcomes (Kane et al. 2013). In a study of mathematics learning and instruction in four districts, Blazer et al. 2016 found a significant relationship on average between value-added effectiveness ratings and observational measures of high-quality instruction, but the relationship was much stronger in some districts than in others. It can be difficult to predict, on the basis of a single measure, how effective any given teacher might be on a different measure or broader domain (see also Berliner 1976; Chaplin et al. 2014; Jennings and Corcoran 2012; Strunk et al. 2014).

An additional concern is the stability or consistency of teacher effects over time and/or with a different set of students. Early studies primarily focused on the stability of teacher effects across instructional periods during a single school year, finding relatively low stability of teacher effects from class to class (Rosenshine 1970; Emmer et al. 1979). The increasing policy emphasis on teacher accountability in the 2000s has generated renewed interest in investigating the stability of teacher effectiveness. In a study of teacher performance rankings, Darling-Hammond et al. (2012) report that nearly 50% of the teachers changed rankings by at least two deciles from one year to the next. Other research confirms that, overall, teachers frequently move between adjacent performance rankings from year-to-year (e.g., second-quintile to median), but that teachers in the top- and bottom-performing categories often exhibit higher levels of stability (Aaronson et al. 2007; Ballou 2005; Goldhaber and Hanson 2010; Koedel and Betts 2007). In the MET data, the state value-added achievement measures had reliabilities (factoring in both the aggregation error and section-to-section stability) ranging from .32 in elementary English and language arts to .85 in middle school mathematics (Mihaly et al. 2013).

12.3.2 Implications of Teacher Effects Research

Despite the multidimensional nature of high-quality teaching and the difficulty of measuring instruction and student outcomes, the teacher effects research discussed in this section shows substantial variability in teaching quality. In addition, studies that include well-developed measures of teaching practice as well as student achievement growth find a correspondence between process and outcomes. More so than the research on teacher qualifications alone then, teacher effects studies suggest the possibility of a substantially uneven distribution of access to high-quality instruction.

However, it is important to stress that even if teacher effectiveness was highly stable and generalized to multiple domains, much of the variability in teacher effectiveness found in the studies discussed here occurs *within* schools and

across rather than between student groups. In other words, it's not clear that large proportions of students are consistently exposed to ineffective teachers. Indeed, a long history of school effects research suggests that it is rare for entire schools to have a uniformly high or low level of teaching effectiveness of the magnitude used to illustrate variation in the studies above (Coleman et al. 1966; Scheerens and Bosker 1997). Even many high-poverty, chronically low-performing schools have admirable rates of achievement growth during the school year comparable to low-poverty schools (Entwisle et al. 1997; Downey et al. 2008). Unequal access to highly effective teachers is surely one source of educational inequality (see e.g., Isenberg et al. 2013; Sass et al. 2010), but the large and persistent educational gaps in the U.S. (and elsewhere) cannot be easily explained by any one factor. Rather, educational inequality is the result of a complex set of interrelated social conditions in families, schools, neighborhoods, and society at large (see Chap. 2).

Nevertheless, future research in the teacher effects tradition might inform our understanding of educational inequality and prospects for reform in (at least) two ways. First, studies should be designed to develop understandings of the systematic gaps in teaching quality that *do* exist between schools and social groups. Such studies will be most useful when they identify specific elements of instruction and teacher capacity for improvement. Hill and Lubienski's (2007) study identifying limitations in teachers' mathematical knowledge for teaching in urban schools is an example of such a study. Second, research on teacher effectiveness can speak to the possible effects of instructional improvement efforts by studying change in effectiveness within the same teachers over time. For example, what conditions of teacher training and support allow beginning teachers to make the most progress in challenging educational contexts? What conditions renew experienced teachers' motivation and effort?

12.4 The Influence of Social and Organizational Contexts on Teaching Quality

The work of teachers is complex and is heavily influenced by aspects of the profession itself, as well as social and organizational features of the school environment. Moreover, aspects of the profession interact with the school environment to influence norms and expectations for teachers' work. Teachers' work is highly regulated and standardized in many respects, but this does not eliminate the fundamental complexity of teaching. For example, teacher certification and licensure requirements structure entry into the profession and increasingly curricular choices have been removed from teachers in part as a response to increased school accountability pressures (Wills and Sandholtz 2009). At the same time, a myriad of decisions about the teaching and learning process at the classroom level remain, and consistent achievement growth for all students is often elusive.

One of the most important early works to further our understanding of the social and organizational contexts affecting teachers' work was Dan Lortie's (1975) *School Teacher*. In teaching, or indeed in most complex and difficult career endeavors, success hinges on having the personal skill and psychological resources to excel in uncertain or changing environments. The sociological analysis in *School Teacher* revealed the fragile nature of teachers' motivation and commitment, and the extent to which fundamental elements of the profession itself and the organization of schools shape teachers' work.

For his study, Lortie interviewed 94 teachers in 5 New England Towns in the summer of 1963, and relied on survey data from thousands of teachers in Dade County Florida in 1964. At that time, Lortie noted several structural features of the profession that make it different from medicine, law, engineering, and other professions. The large size of the teaching workforce, low pay, and other recruitment forces mean that the teaching profession has difficulty recruiting the most selective college graduates or attaining the prestige of other professions. These recruitment features are important, but Lortie argued that the most salient forces affecting teachers' work are two other structural aspects of the profession. First, compared to other professions, Lortie showed that teachers experience relatively weak professional socialization. Although teachers receive special schooling and a program of practice teaching, these experiences are often not robust enough to fully support the difficult work of teaching. As a result, many teachers lack the kind of "reassurance capital" that is found in other professions. Whereas a doctor is daily reassured that they are capable by having survived the arduous experience of medical school and residency, many teachers are left with a more personal burden of success or failure.

Second, Lortie emphasized that teaching is a mostly "unstaged" career. The pay-scale in teaching is front-loaded; pay does not rise dramatically over the course of a teacher's career. Nor does the nature of teacher's work itself change dramatically, the veteran teacher engages in much the same day-to-day tasks as the beginning teacher. In contrast, other professions are marked by career ladders with more sharply rising pay, and greater opportunity for transition to more complex tasks and supervisory roles. This structural feature has a profound effect on teachers. Staged careers produce cycles of effort, attainment, and renewed ambition. Teachers are left without the career staging that signals success. They are thus left to define success on their own terms, and to find renewed ambition in their interpersonal work with students.

The overall portrait of teachers' work that emerged for Lortie was one of "endemic uncertainty." Teachers are charged with diffuse and difficult goals, to not only promote achievement growth on tests, but ideally, to instill students with a love of learning, to not only be expert in the pedagogy of their subject matter, but to relate well to students. Moreover, they must accomplish all this in the turbulent social setting of a school full of developing, some might say, not yet "wholly-formed," persons. The teachers Lortie interviewed expressed a great deal of uncertainty about how best to accomplish all of this or even to know when they have been successful. Teaching is difficult and uncertain work, and features of the profession itself, quite apart from the inherent proficiency of any given teacher, exacerbate these challenges.

However, there was also a silver-lining in *School Teacher*. Due to the lack of career-staging, to recruitment forces, and to the interpersonal nature of the work itself, many teachers Lortie interviewed were heavily focused precisely on the work rewards that were within their grasp, the psychic rewards that stem from reaching students:

> It is of great importance to teachers to feel that they have "reached" their students…We would therefore expect that much of a teachers' work motivation will rotate around the conduct of daily tasks—the actual instruction of students. In that regard, exertion of effort and the earning of important rewards are congruent; they are not in the position of those who must trade away psychic rewards in order to make a living.

The overall portrait of the teaching profession and the preoccupations, beliefs, and preferences of teachers in *School Teacher* has had an enduring effect on the study of teaching and remains relevant to contemporary efforts to reform the profession. For example, contemporary pay-for-performance reforms (Yuan et al. 2013) are precisely an effort to address the structural features outlined by Lortie. Yet, an important unit of analysis is unseen in *School Teacher*, the school itself as an organizational context that constrains or supports teachers' work. Subsequent research by Dworkin (1987, 2009), Rosenholtz (1989), Ingersoll (2003) and others examines school-building differences in the context of teachers' work.

It is critical to consider how the social and organizational context (e.g., levels of *relational trust* and *collective responsibility* amongst teachers and between teachers and administrators) influences the work of teachers (Bryk and Schneider 2002). Aspects of a school's formal and informal organization shape the norms and

expectations for teachers' work, and affect the level of resources and support that teachers have access to within their school communities (Coburn and Russell 2008). Therefore, to understand and improve the work of teachers, continued attention should be given to the relationships among individuals within a school (Kardos et al. 2001; Penuel et al. 2010).

Susan Rosenholtz's (1989) study of 78 elementary schools in Tennessee was a landmark study in demonstrating how the organizational context of schools affects teachers' work. Rosenholtz identified a variety of important school organizational features which shaped teachers' work experiences including: the extent to which teachers (and the principal) shared common goals, the extent of teacher collaboration, teacher learning opportunities, participation in school-wide decision-making, task autonomy and discretion, evaluation practices and positive feedback, and school behavioral climate. Her work identified important links between organizational variables and teacher outcomes related to efficacy (labeled certainty in her analysis) and commitment. For example, Rosenholtz and colleagues found that about 76% of the teacher-to-teacher differences in commitment they observed could be traced to three organizational factors: task autonomy and discretion, positive feedback and evaluative practices, and the provision of teacher learning opportunities. Committed faculty respond affirmatively to question like, "In general, I really enjoy my students" while uncommitted faculty are prone to feelings like "By the middle of the day, I can't wait for my students to go home." An especially salient outcome related to low levels of commitment was the negative effect it had on constructive efforts to improve their teaching. In schools marked with high levels of teacher commitment, 73% of teachers had specific plans for new academic activities or content, while in schools with low levels of teacher commitment only 4% of teachers had academic plans.

More recent work has focused on the role that relational trust and collective responsibility have in shaping the work of teachers (e.g., Bryk and Schneider 2002; Bryk et al. 2010). For example, Bryk and Schneider (2002) defined relational trust as encompassing four elements: (a) respect, (b) competence, (c) personal regard for others, and (d) integrity. Relational trust among teachers and between teachers and administrators is hypothesized to affect the quality of interactions among individuals within a school, which in turn influence individuals' beliefs and behavior. Through analyzing data collected in Chicago Public Schools, Bryk and Schneider (2002) reported that schools marked by high levels of relational trust were much more likely to see improvements in students' math and reading scores.

Along with relational trust, collective responsibility among individuals within a school has emerged as a strong predictor of teacher and school effectiveness. At its core, the concept of collective responsibility places emphasis on the extent to which individuals take shared responsibility for improvement (particularly related to student outcomes) and work together to move towards organizational improvement (Bryk and Schneider 2002; Bryk et al. 2010; Penuel et al. 2009). Thus collective responsibility goes beyond making an individual contribution (i.e., by being effective in your own classroom), to participating in relationships within the school that support organizational goals. For example, research has shown that teachers who identify with the collective are more likely to provide support and resources to others within a school regardless of the strength of individual ties (Frank 2009).

An important take-away from the research of Rosenholtz, Bryk and Schneider, and others focusing on the social organization of schools, is that the work of teachers is often not as isolated as oft depicted (e.g., Lortie's "egg-crate school" metaphor for teacher isolation). Rather, teachers operate within social networks that shape the experiences of teachers in many ways. Within a school, these relationships manifest social capital, or resources that are linked to a network of individuals (Bidwell 2000; Bourdieu 1986; Coleman 1988). Therefore, levels of social capital within a school are dependent upon attributes of individuals (e.g., levels of content or pedagogical expertise) and the quality and extent of relationships among individuals. For example, teachers in schools marked by high levels of relational trust

and collective responsibility are more likely to have frequent interactions around instruction, curriculum, and assessments (Bryk and Schneider 2002; Bryk et al. 2010; Coburn and Russell 2008; Kardos et al. 2001; Youngs 2007). These high-quality social networks produce high levels of social capital, and such interactions have been shown to improve teacher and organizational effectiveness (Ingersoll and Strong 2011).

The social organizational context of schools also directly affects the implementation of external and internal policies and reforms. In an era of increased governmental accountability at the school and teacher level, it is critical that we develop better understandings of the ways in which social networks mediate policies which impact teachers' work. Researchers have continually found evidence that the social organizational context of a school influences policy implementation (e.g., Coburn 2001; Coburn and Russell 2008; Frank et al. 2004; Penuel et al. 2009). Policy sense-making occurs in the collective as groups share information and generate common interpretations of policy expectations and goals. This collective sense-making can emerge from deliberate activities (e.g., planning committees), but it also emerges from informal social networks within a school (Coburn 2001; Weick and Roberts 1993). For example, in an in-depth case study of an elementary school implementing reading instruction reform, Coburn (2001) found that teachers turned to colleagues to make sense of the policy reforms, and that "patterns of interaction and the conditions of conversation in formal and informal settings influence the process by which teachers adopt, adapt, combine, and ignore messages from the environment, mediating the way messages from the environment shape classroom practice" (p. 162).

In addition to aspects of policy sense-making at the individual and collective level, often times the actual nuts and bolts of policy implementation relies upon the diffusion of information and resources among individuals (Coburn and Russell 2008; Frank et al. 2004; Penuel et al. 2009, 2010). As such, a teacher's own social network (i.e., access to information, resources, and support) mediates her ability to effectively implement reforms at the classroom level (Penuel et al. 2009). For example, in a case study of two schools implementing literacy instruction reforms, Penuel et al. (2009) found that the structure of the internal social organization of the two schools impacted teachers' access to expertise and the distribution of resources among teachers which in turn impacted changes in teachers' instructional practices. More specifically, one school relied on outside resources to provide expertise and foster collaboration among teachers, which ultimately was less effective than in the other school where the leadership sought to draw upon internal strengths and relationships to foster reform.

Overall, the research reviewed in this section emphasizes that teachers' work occurs within the dynamic social environment of particular schools. Teachers' work therefore centers on the interplay between their own background and characteristics, the constraints of the profession itself, and the social organization of the school environment. These elements define the norms and expectations for teachers' work and directly influence teachers' instructional practice and effectiveness. Therefore, sociological research on teachers' work and effectiveness should attend to these important and dynamic elements of the profession.

12.5 Improving Teaching Quality

This chapter began by referencing Hollywood depictions of schooling, which often show the work of an exceptional teacher who rises above her incompetent colleagues in a low-performing school. Such depictions make for compelling narratives, but they are a substantial exaggeration of reality. The research discussed in this chapter, which includes classic works in the sociology of education but also the economics of education and subject-matter disciplines in education, finds that teachers do indeed vary substantially in their effects on student achievement. Yet, most teachers in the United States are not only well-qualified (see Table 12.1), but even teachers in so-called "low-performing schools" are effective at raising

achievement growth. In our view, given the social challenges facing schools in many communities, *the vast majority of teachers are generally competent at increasing student achievement.*

At the same time, there is clearly room for improvement in teaching quality, which is particularly evident in close studies of the teaching process (e.g., Hiebert et al. 2005; Weiss et al. 2003). Raising the aggregate quality of teaching, and making sure that all students have access to high-quality instruction will help address persistent gaps in educational outcomes. In order to do so, multiple reforms and initiatives must be pursued simultaneously, because effective teaching is the product of a complex set of factors at the teacher- and school-level. The many specific state policies that impact teacher quality (including teacher licensure, standards for accrediting teacher preparation programs, teacher evaluation and accountability, teacher compensation, and policies affecting working conditions, etc.) are too numerous to be considered in detail here. Instead, we conclude by emphasizing three general principles of reform for teaching quality consistent with the research discussed in this chapter. In all of the principles, we stress that reforms targeting improvements in teacher effectiveness should encompass the social organizational factors of a school that influence teachers' work and effectiveness.

12.5.1 Teacher Socialization

First, in both the recruitment of teachers into the profession as well as initial training in teacher education programs, reforms must stress rich socialization into the profession, such that teachers are equipped to deal with the inherent challenge and uncertainty of teaching. The socialization of teachers into the profession occurs through different phases over time, beginning with preservice training through teacher preparation programs and in-service training in the early years of a teacher's career (Lortie 1975; Staton and Hunt 1992). Early effective socialization of novice teachers into the profession, including socialization into their own specific school context, is critical for promoting effective teacher practices and reducing teacher attrition (Jones et al. 2013; Pogodzinski et al. 2013; Ingersoll and Strong 2011).

Teacher socialization relays the behaviors, knowledge, and attributes that are needed to flourish as a teacher in a particular school context (Feiman-Nemser 2010; Staton and Hunt, 1992). Additionally, socialization efforts help build relationships among novice teachers and their more senior colleagues through which novice teachers access information, resources, and support as they navigate their early years in the profession (Coleman 1988; Frank et al. 2004). Across numerous organizational contexts, socialization efforts have been associated with worker outcomes such as turnover, satisfaction, stress, and performance (Feldman 1981; Van Maanen and Schein 1979).

Teachers are socialized through both formal and informal mechanisms. Formally, many teachers experience some type of district or school sponsored induction, most often including formal mentoring (Ingersoll and Strong 2011). Mentoring can provide rich opportunities for novice teachers to engage in meaningful learning activities and influence practice (Youngs 2007). Novice teachers are also socialized through their day-to-day interactions with their colleagues which provide opportunities to access varying information, resources, and support and can lead to changes in teachers' beliefs and practice and influence their career decisions (Kapadia et al. 2007; Pogodzinski et al. 2013).

Whether formal or informal in nature, the quality of socialization and the impact it has on teachers' beliefs and practices largely depends on whom novices interact with and what they talk about (Kardos et al. 2001; Smith and Ingersoll 2004). Therefore, it is essential that efforts are made by school leaders to ensure that novice teachers are engaged in high-quality interactions with colleagues around the technical core of teaching and learning. For example, research has shown that having a mentor in the same field as the novice teacher has a positive association with the frequency and quality of interactions (Pogodzinski 2012), and ultimately, retention

(Smith and Ingersoll 2004). Additionally, steps should be made to increase the likelihood that novice teachers are interacting with teachers across the school who have the knowledge, skills, and dispositions which are more likely to elicit growth among novice teachers (Crow and Pounder 2000; Penuel et al. 2010).

12.5.2 Professional Development

Second, ongoing efforts must be made to renew experienced teachers' enthusiasm and expertise with rich, content-oriented professional development. Professional development (PD) for teachers includes a wide range of activities, from stand-alone conferences and workshops, to internships in degree programs, to collaborative curriculum development with colleagues. By 2006, teachers were averaging up to 100 h of professional development, all inclusive, per year (Birman et al. 2009). Yet, the typical activities offered by states and districts have been criticized for being intellectually superficial (Ball and Cohen 1999). Currently, it is difficult to know how many teachers receive professional development that supports their work in a meaningful way, or themselves generate active learning opportunities for their colleagues. Much of the research literature on teacher professional development itself lacks sufficient rigor to inform program adoption efforts, but the limited existing findings show that high-quality professional development, when available, improves teacher effectiveness (Yoon et al. 2007). In all, we suspect that far too few teachers have regular access to transformative and sustaining learning opportunities.

To address shortcomings in professional development, there have been increased calls for job-embedded professional learning opportunities for teachers. The term job-embedded refers to learning opportunities that are situated in the immediate context within which individuals and groups of teachers operate, and thus, are relevant to teachers' day-to-day practices and experiences (Croft et al. 2010). One reason that job-embedded professional development may be more effective than traditional "conference style" PD, is that it better encourages reflective practice (Camburn 2010; Camburn and Han 2015; Putnam and Borko 2000). Reflective practice refers to thoughtfully considering one's own actions and experiences to refine a set of disciplinary or professional skills (Schon 1987). Professional development to enhance reflective practice might include: engaging teachers in analyzing student work, conducting peer-observations, sharing and discussing lesson plans with mentors or colleagues, or even carrying out "action research"-type studies of alternative pedagogical approaches.

However, to date, the large-scale implementation of job-embedded professional development has been challenging due to the difficulties and costs associated with rigorous in-class observations of teaching, which form the basis of evidence-based reflection. Indeed, even under a relatively minimal schedule of observation, administrators and curriculum support personnel have difficulty providing high-quality, in-depth feedback to teachers (Kraft and Gilmour 2016). One solution to this challenge is to use technology to automate the process of observation and feedback, giving teachers themselves flexibility and agency in analyzing their own teaching.

Research is currently underway by a team of computer scientists (in collaboration with the first author of this chapter and other educational researchers) to develop an automated observational system to measure dimensions of teaching effectiveness associated with student engagement and achievement growth that are exhibited/expressed in classroom discourse (Olney et al. 2017). This work uses digital signal processing, natural language processing, and machine learning to record and analyze classroom audio. The system is designed to meet the technical requirements and constraints of real-world classrooms and school budgets (D'Mello et al. 2015). To date, analyses of transcript data from tens of thousands of questions in 418 class sessions show that it is possible to automatically detect dialogic question properties (e.g., "authentic" questions vs test questions) at an accuracy level that rivals human coding of questions with simi-

lar contextual information (Samei et al. 2014). We have also succeeded in the automatic identification of teachers' basic instructional time use; for example, lecture vs question and answer sessions vs small group work (Donnelly et al. 2016). We are currently refining approaches to speech recognition, which is difficult in the complex, noisy environment of the classroom, to further improve automation. While much work remains to achieve a fully-functioning, closed-loop technology for use by teachers, the initial results are promising.

In addition to stressing reflective practice among individual teachers, research on professional learning opportunities emphasizes the importance of explicitly cultivating a shared vision for school improvement and values among teachers, in order to promote collective efforts towards goal-oriented improvement (Darling-Hammond and McLaughlin 1995; DuFour and Eaker 1998; Levine and Shapiro 2004). In addition, Darling-Hammond and colleagues (2009a, b) argue that effective professional development should be focused on the technical core of teaching and learning and do so in a way that strengthens ties among teachers within the school. As previously illustrated, the work life of teachers does not occur in total isolation from other adults within the school. This is particularly true in an era of heightened school accountability and whole-school reform efforts.

Overall, the concept of collective responsibility conveys that relationships among individuals within a school have the potential to mediate professional development efforts, and in some circumstances relationships themselves are impacted by such efforts (Coburn and Russell 2008; Penuel et al. 2009). For example, professional learning communities (PLC) can be purposefully created to strengthen ties among teachers within a school and facilitate the sharing of information, resources, and expertise. This is particularly useful when experts are embedded within a PLC to help diffuse knowledge. Such efforts also draw from naturally occurring ties related to personal and professional interests, as well as common areas of teaching (e.g., grade level or content areas) which strengthen ties and increase the opportunities for enhancement of social capital. Additionally, professional development centered on relationships within a school are by default "job embedded," thus relating to the shared realities of the local school context (Croft et al. 2010).

12.5.3 Organizational Climate

Third, teaching quality is strongly affected by the context of teachers' work, so reforms that improve the overall climate of the school and students' opportunity to learn also improve the work of individual teachers. Research in the sociology of education has long shown that the organizational functioning of schools is impacted by the social context in which they are embedded (see Schneider, Introduction). We have already touched upon this in relation to the need to develop relational trust and collective responsibility among teachers and between teachers and administrators as one important aspect of organizational climate (e.g., Bryk and Schneider 2002; Bryk et al. 2010), but organizational climate relates more broadly to all stakeholders within a school community. Specifically, climate relates to the enduring aspects of an organization such as routines, practices, policies, and beliefs among stakeholders which define an organization (Halpin and Croft 1963; Tagiuri 1968). For example, even within a single school district, elementary schools which serve similarly situated students can operate very differently based on the organizational climate and the perceptions of students, teachers, administrators, and parents which emerge.

Therefore, organizational climate does not just define the organization in structural terms (e.g., formal policies related to student attendance); rather, how members of a school community perceive the routines, practices, and policies influences their beliefs and practices (Halpin and Croft 1963; Pogodzinski et al. 2013; Tagiuri 1968). It is essential then that school communities forge ties among all members of the school community to ensure healthy engagement, resource flow, and common efforts towards realizing shared goals. For example, the presence or absence of social networks and other mechanisms connecting schooling with job placements affects students' understanding of how their own educational efforts matter, especially for students who do not immediately apply to college (Rosenbaum 2001). When students perceive strong school-to-work connections, and thus have an incentive to be engaged, this strengthens the individual teacher's ability to work with students. Likewise, the behavioral climate of a school, which every teacher contributes to but does not alone control, has a profound impact on teachers' work lives (Ingersoll 2001; Kelly 2004). Clearly then, beyond the teacher herself, improving teaching quality requires strengthening social supports for schooling related to students directly.

References

Aaronson, D., Barrow, L., & Sander, W. (2007). Teachers and student achievement in the Chicago public high schools. *Journal of Labor Economics, 25*, 95–135.

Adams, J. (2012). *Identifying the attributes of effective rural teachers: Teacher attributes and mathematics achievement among rural primary school students in Northwest China* (Working Paper). Gansu Survey of Children and Families.

Adamson, F., & Darling-Hammond, L. (2012). Funding disparities and the inequitable distribution of teachers: Evaluating sources and solutions. *Education Policy Analysis Archives, 20*, 1–46.

Aud, S., Hussar, W., Planty, M., Snyder, T., Bianco, K., Fox, M., et al. (2010). *The condition of education 2010*. Washington, DC: National Center for Education Statistics.

Baldi, S., Warner-Griffin, C., & Tadler, C. (2015). *Education and certification qualifications of public middle grades teachers of selected subjects: Evidence from the 2011–12 Schools and Staffing Survey* (NCES 2015-815). U.S. Department of Education, National Center for Education Statistics. Washington, DC: U.S. Government Printing Office.

Ball, D. L., & Cohen, D. K. (1999). Developing practices, developing practitioners: Toward a practice-based theory of professional development. In G. Sykes & L. Darling-Hammond (Eds.), *Teaching as the learning profession: Handbook of policy and practice* (pp. 30–32). San Francisco: Jossy-Bass.

Ballou, D. (2005). Value-added assessment: Lessons from Tennessee. In R. Lissitz (Ed.), *Value-added models in education: Theory and application* (pp. 1–26). Maple Grove, JAM Press.

Berliner, D. (1976). A status report on the study of teacher effectiveness. *Journal of Research in Science Teaching, 13*, 369–382.

Bidwell, C. E. (2000). School as context and construction: A social psychological approach to the study of schooling. In M. T. Hallinan (Ed.), *Handbook of sociology in education* (pp. 15–36). New York: Kluwer Academic.

Bill & Melinda Gates Foundation. (2010). *Learning about teaching: Initial findings from the Measures of Effective Teaching project.* https://docs.gatesfoundation.org/documents/preliminary-findings-research-paper.pdf

Birman, B. F., Boyle, A., Le Floch, K. C., Elledge, A., Holtzman, D., Song, M., et al. (2009). *State and local implementation of the No Child Left Behind act, Volume VIII—Teacher quality under NCLB: Final report.* Washington, DC: U.S. Department of Education.

Blazer, D., Litke, E., & Barmore, J. (2016). What does it mean to be ranked a "high" or "low" value-added teacher? Observing differences in instructional quality across districts. *American Educational Research Journal, 53*, 324–359.

Bourdieu, P. (1986). The forms of capital. In J. G. Richardson (Ed.), *International handbook of theory & research for sociology of education* (pp. 241–258). New York: Greenwood.

Bryk, A., & Schneider, B. (2002). *Trust in schools: A core resource for improvement.* New York: Russell Sage Foundation.

Bryk, A. S., Sebring, P. B., Allensworth, E., Easton, J. Q., & Luppescu, S. (2010). *Organizing schools for improvement: Lessons from Chicago.* Chicago: University of Chicago Press.

Bulman, R. C. (2005). *Hollywood goes to high school: Cinema, schools, and American culture.* New York: Worth.

Camburn, E. M. (2010). Embedded teacher learning opportunities as a site for reflective practice: An exploratory study. *American Journal of Education, 116*, 463–489.

Camburn, E. M., & Han, S. W. (2015). Infrastructure for teacher reflection and instructional change: An exploratory study. *Journal of Educational Change, 16*, 511–533.

Chaplin, D., Gill, B,. Thompkins, A., & Miller, H. (2014). *Professional practice, student surveys, and value-added: Multiple measures of teacher effectiveness in the Pittsburgh Public Schools* (REL 2014–024). Washington, DC: U.S. Department of Education, Institute of Education Sciences, National Center for Education Evaluation and Regional Assistance, Regional Educational Laboratory Mid-Atlantic.

Clotfelter, C. T. (2004). *After Brown: The rise and retreat of school desegregation.* Princeton: Princeton University Press.

Clotfelter, C. T., Ladd, H. F., & Vigdor, J. L. (2005). Who teaches whom? Race and the distribution of novice teachers. *Economics of Education Review, 24*, 377–392.

Clotfelter, C. T., Ladd, H. F., & Vigdor, J. L. (2006). Teacher–student matching and the assessment of teacher effectiveness. *The Journal of Human Resources, 41*, 778–820.

Clotfelter, C. T., Ladd, H. F., & Vigdor, J. L. (2007). Teacher credentials and student achievement: Longitudinal analysis with student fixed effects. *Economics of Education Review, 26*, 673–682.

Coburn, C. E. (2001). Collective sensemaking about reading: How teachers mediate reading policy in their professional communities. *Educational Evaluation and Policy Analysis, 23*, 145–170.

Coburn, C. E., & Russell, J. L. (2008). District policy and teachers' social networks. *Educational Evaluation and Policy Analysis, 30*, 203–235.

Coleman, J. S. (1988). Social capital in the creation of human capital. *American Journal of Sociology, 94* (Supplement 1988), S95–S120.

Coleman, J. S., Campbell, E. Q., Hobson, C. J., McPartland, J., Mood, A. M., Weinfeld, F. D., & York, R. L. (1966). *Equality of educational opportunity.* Washington, DC: U.S. Government Printing Office.

Croft, A., Coggshall, J. G., Dolan, M., & Powers, E. (2010). *Job-embedded professional development: What it is, who is responsible, and how to get it done well* (Issue Brief). Washington, DC: National Comprehensive Center for Teacher Quality. Retrieved from http://files.eric.ed.gov/fulltext/ED520830.pdf

Crow, G. M., & Pounder, D. G. (2000). Interdisciplinary teacher teams: Context, design, and process. *Educational Administration Quarterly, 36*, 216–254.

Danielson, C. (2011). *The framework for teaching evaluation instrument, 2011 edition.* Princeton: The Danielson Group.

Darling-Hammond, L. (2000). Teacher quality and student achievement: A review of state policy evidence. *Education Policy Analysis Archives, 8*(1).

Darling-Hammond, L., & McLaughlin, M. W. (1995). Policies that support professional development in an era of reform. *Phi Delta Kappan, 76*, 597–604.

Darling-Hammond, L., Wei, R. C., & Johnson, C. M. (2009a). Teacher preparation and teacher learning. In G. Sykes, B. Schneider, & D. L. Plank (Eds.), *Handbook of education policy research* (pp. 613–636). New York: Routledge.

Darling-Hammond, L., Wei, R. C., Andree, A., Richardson, N., & Orphanos, S. (2009b). *Professional learning in the learning profession.* Washington, DC: National Staff Development Council.

Darling-Hammond, L., Amrein-Beardsley, A., Haertel, E., & Rothstein, S. (2012). Evaluating teacher evaluation. *Phi Delta Kappan, 93*, 8–15.

Desimone, L. M., & Long, D. (2010). Teacher effects and the achievement gap: Do teacher and teaching quality influence the achievement gap between Black and White and high- and low-SES students in the early grades? *Teachers College Record, 112*, 3024–3073.

D'Mello, S. K., Olney, A. M., Blanchard, N., Samei, B., Sun, X., Ward, B., & Kelly, S. (2015). Multimodal capture of teacher–student interactions for automated dialogic analysis in live classrooms. *Proceedings* of the 2015 ACM on International Conference on Multimodal Interaction (ICMI 2015) (pp. 557–566). New York: ACM.

Donnelly, P., Blanchard, N., Samei, B., Olney, A. M., Sun, X., Ward, B., Kelly, S., Nystrand, M., & D'Mello, S. K. (2016). Automatic teacher modeling from live classroom audio. In L. Aroyo, S. D'Mello, J. Vassileva, & J. Blustein (Eds.), Proceedings of the 2016 ACM on International Conference on User Modeling, Adaptation, & Personalization (ACM UMAP 2016) (pp. 45–53). New York: ACM.

Downey, D. B., Von Hippel, P. T., & Hughes, M. (2008). Are "failing" schools really failing? Removing the influence of nonschool factors from measures of school quality. Sociology of Education, 81, 242–270.

DuFour, R., & Eaker, R. (1998). Professional learning communities at work: Best practices for enhancing student achievement. Bloomington: Solution Tree Press.

Dworkin, A. G. (1987). Teacher burnout in the public school: Structural causes and consequences for children. Albany: State University of New York Press.

Dworkin, A. G. (2009). Teacher burnout and teacher resilience: Assessing the impact of the school accountability movement. In L. J. Saha & A. G. Dworkin (Eds.), International handbook of research on teachers and teaching (pp. 491–510). New York: Springer.

Emmer, E. T., Evertson, C. M., & Brophy, J. E. (1979). Stability of teacher effects in junior high classrooms. American Educational Research Journal, 16, 71–75.

Entwisle, D. R., Alexander, K. L., & Olson, L. S. (1997). Children, schools, and inequality. Boulder: Westview Press.

Fan, W., & Bains, L. (2008). The effects of teacher instructional practice on kindergarten mathematics achievement: A multi-level national investigation. International Journal of Applied Educational Studies, 3, 1–17.

Feiman-Nemser, S. (2010). Multiple means of new teacher induction. In J. Wang, S. J. Odell, & R. T. Clift (Eds.), Past, present, and future research on teacher induction: An anthology for researchers, policy makers, and practitioners (pp. 15–30). Lanham: Rowman and Littlefield Education and the Association of Teacher Educators.

Feldman, D. C. (1981). The multiple socialization of organization members. Academy of Management Review, 6, 309–318.

Frank, K. A. (2009). Quasi-ties: Directing resources to members of a collective. American Behavioral Scientist, 52, 1613–1645.

Frank, K. A., Zhao, Y., & Borman, K. (2004). Social capital and the diffusion of innovations within organizations: The case of computer technology in schools. Sociology of Education, 77, 148–171.

Gamoran, A. (2012). Improving teacher quality: Incentives are not enough. In S. Kelly (Ed.), Assessing teacher quality: Understanding teacher effects on instruction and achievement (pp. 201–214). New York: Teachers College Press.

Gamoran, A., Secada, W. G., & Marrett, C. B. (2000). The organizational context of teaching and learning: Changing theoretical perspectives. In M. T. Hallinan (Ed.), Handbook of the sociology of education (pp. 37–64). New York: Kluwer.

Goldhaber, D., & Hanson, M. (2010). Is it just a bad class? Assessing the stability of measured teacher performance (CEDR Working Paper 3). University of Washington, Seattle.

Goldhaber, D., Lavery, L., & Theobald, R. (2015). Uneven playing field? Assessing the teacher quality gap between advantaged and disadvantaged students. Educational Researcher, 44, 293–307.

Goldring, R., Gray, L., & Bitterman, A. (2013). Characteristics of public and private elementary and secondary school teachers in the United States: Results from the 2011–12 schools and staffing survey. Washington, DC: National Center for Education Statistics.

Greenwald, R., Hedges, L. V., & Laine, R. D. (1996). The effect of school resources on student achievement. Review of Educational Research, 66, 361–396.

Guarino, C. M., SantiBanez, L., & Daley, G. A. (2006). Teacher recruitment and retention: A review of the recent empirical literature. Review of Educational Research, 76, 173–208.

Halpin, A. W., & Croft, D. B. (1963). The organizational climate of schools. Chicago: Midwest Administration Center of the University of Chicago.

Hamilton, L. (2012). Measuring teaching quality using student achievement tests: Lessons from educators' responses to No Child Left Behind. In S. Kelly (Ed.), Assessing teacher quality: Understanding teacher effects on instruction and achievement (pp. 49–76). New York: Teachers College Press.

Hanushek, E. A., & Rivkin, S. G. (2004). How to improve the supply of high-quality teachers. Brookings Papers on Education Policy, 2004(1), 7–25.

Harris, D. N., & Sass, T. R. (2011). Teacher training, teacher quality and student achievement. Journal of Public Economics, 95, 798–812.

Hiebert, J., Stigler, J. W., Jacobs, J. K., Givvin, K. B., Garnier, H., Smith, M., Hollingsworth, H., Manaster, A., Wearne, D., & Gallimore, R. (2005). Mathematics teaching in the United States today (and tomorrow): Results from the TIMSS 1999 video study. Educational Evaluation and Policy Analysis, 27, 111–132.

Hill, H. C., & Lubienski, S. T. (2007). Teachers' mathematics knowledge for teaching and school context: A study of California teachers. Educational Policy, 21, 747–768.

Hill, J., & Stearns, C. (2015). Education and certification qualifications of departmentalized public high school-level teachers of selected subjects: Evidence from the 2011–12 Schools and Staffing Survey. (NCES 2015-814). U.S. Department of Education, National Center for Education Statistics. Washington, DC: U.S. Government Printing Office.

Hill, H. C., Rowan, B., & Ball, D. L. (2005). Effects of teachers' mathematical knowledge for teaching on student achievement. *American Educational Research Journal, 42*, 371–406.

Hill, C. J., Bloom, H. S., Black, A. R., & Lipsey, M. W. (2008). Empirical benchmarks for interpreting effect sizes in research. *Child Development Perspectives, 2*, 172–177.

Ingersoll, R. M. (2001). Teacher turnover and teacher shortages: An organizational analysis. *American Educational Research Journal, 38*, 499–534.

Ingersoll, R. M. (2003). *Who controls teachers' work? Power and accountability in America's schools.* Cambridge, MA: Harvard University Press.

Ingersoll, R. M., & Strong, M. (2011). The impact of induction and mentoring programs for beginning teachers: A critical review of the research. *Review of Educational Research, 81*, 201–233.

Isenberg, E., Max, J., Gleason, P., Potamites, L., Santillano, R., Hock, H., & Hansen, M. (2013). *Access to effective teaching for disadvantaged students.* Washington, DC: National Center for Education Evaluation and Regional Assistance, U.S. Department of Education.

Jacob, B. A. (2007). The challenges of staffing urban schools with effective teachers. *The Future of Children, 17*, 129–153.

Jencks, C., Smith, M., Acland, H., Bane, M. J., Cohen, D., Gintis, H., Heyns, B., & Michelson, S. (1972). *Inequality: A reassessment of family and schooling in America.* New York: Basic Books.

Jennings, J. L., & Corcoran, S. P. (2012). Beyond high stakes tests: Teacher effects on other educational outcomes. In S. Kelly (Ed.), *Assessing teacher quality: Understanding teacher effects on instruction and achievement* (pp. 77–96). New York: Teachers College Press.

Jennings, J. L., & Diprete, T. A. (2010). Teacher effects on social and behavioral skills in elementary school. *Sociology of Education, 83*, 135–159.

Jepsen, C. (2005). Teacher characteristics and student achievement: Evidence from teacher surveys. *Journal of Urban Economics, 57*, 302–319.

Jones, N., Youngs, P., & Frank, K. (2013). The role of school-based colleagues in shaping the commitment of novice special and general education teachers. *Exceptional Children, 79*, 365–383.

Kalogrides, D., Loeb, S., & Beteille, T. (2013). Systematic sorting: Teacher characteristics and class assignments. *Sociology of Education, 86*, 103–123.

Kane, T. J., & Staiger, D. O. (2012). *Gathering feedback for teaching: Combining high-quality observations with student surveys and achievement gains.* Seattle: Bill & Melinda Gates Foundation.

Kane, T. J., Rockoff, J. E., & Staiger, D. O. (2008). What does certification tell us about teacher effectiveness? Evidence from New York City. *Economics of Education Review, 27*, 615–631.

Kane, T. J., McCaffrey, D. F., Miller, T., & Staiger, D. O. (2013). *Have we identified effective teachers? Validating measures of effective teaching using random assignment.* Seattle: Bill and Melinda Gates Foundation.

Kapadia, K., Coca, V., & Easton, J. Q. (2007). *Keeping new teachers: A first look at the influences of induction in the Chicago Public Schools.* Chicago: Consortium on Chicago School Research, University of Chicago.

Kardos, S. M., Johnson, S. M., Peske, H. G., Kauffman, D., & Liu, E. (2001). Counting on colleagues: New teachers encounter the professional cultures of their schools. *Educational Administration Quarterly, 37*, 250–290.

Kelly, S. (2004). An event history analysis of teacher attrition: Salary, teacher tracking, and socially disadvantaged schools. *Journal of Experimental Education, 72*, 195–220.

Kelly, S. (2009). Tracking teachers. In L. J. Saha & A. G. Dworkin (Eds.), *The new international handbook of teachers and teaching* (pp. 451–461). New York: Springer.

Kelly, S., & Caughlan, S. (2011). The Hollywood teachers' perspective on authority. *Pedagogies, 6*, 46–65.

Kennedy, M. M. (2010). The uncertain relationship between teacher assessment and teacher quality. In M. M. Kennedy (Ed.), *Teacher assessment and the quest for teacher quality: A handbook* (pp. 1–6). San Francisco: Jossey-Bass.

Koedel, C., & Betts, J. R. (2007). *Re-examining the role of teacher quality in the educational production function* (Working Paper). University of Missouri, Columbia.

Konstantopoulos, S. (2009). Effects of teachers on minority and disadvantaged students' achievement in the early grades. *The Elementary School Journal, 110*, 92–113.

Konstantopoulos, S. (2011). Teacher effects in early grades: Evidence from a randomized study. *Teachers College Record, 113*, 1541–1565.

Konstantopoulos, S. (2012). Teacher effects: Past, present, and future. In S. Kelly (Ed.), *Assessing teacher quality: Understanding teacher effects on instruction and achievement* (pp. 33–48). New York: Teachers College Press.

Konstantopoulos, S., & Chung, V. (2011). The persistence of teacher effects in elementary grades. *American Educational Research Journal, 48*, 361–386.

Konstantopoulos, S., & Sun, M. (2012). Is the persistence of teacher effects in early grades larger for lower-performing students? *American Journal of Education, 118*, 309–339.

Kraft, M. A., & Gilmour, A. F. (2016). Can principals promote teacher development as evaluators? A case study of principals' views and experiences. *Educational Administration Quarterly, 52*, 711–753.

Kukla-Acevedo, S. (2009). Do teacher characteristics matter? New results on the effects of teacher preparation on student achievement. *Economics of Education Review, 28*, 49–57.

Ladd, H. F., & Sorensen, L. C. (2015). *Do master's degrees matter? Advanced degrees, career paths, and the effectiveness of teachers* (CALDER Working Paper No. 136).

Lankford, H., Loeb, S., & Wyckoff, J. (2002). Teacher sorting and the plight of urban schools: A descriptive analysis. *Educational Evaluation and Policy Analysis, 24*, 37–62.

Lankford, H., Loeb, S., McEachin, A., Miller, L. C., & Wyckoff, J. (2014). Who enters teaching? Encouraging evidence that the status of teaching is improving. *Educational Researcher, 43*, 444–453.

Levine, J., & Shapiro, N. S. (2004). *Sustaining and improving learning communities*. San Francisco: Jossey-Bass.

Lippman, L., Burns, S., & McArthur, E. (1996). *Urban schools: The challenge of location and poverty*. Washington, DC: National Center for Education Statistics.

Lortie, D. C. (1975). *School teacher: A sociological study*. Chicago: University of Chicago Press.

Malkus, N., Ralph, J., Hoyer, K. M., & Sparks, D. (2015). *Teaching vacancies and difficult-to-staff teaching positions in public schools*. Washington DC: National Center for Education Statistics.

Mihaly, K., McCaffrey, D. F., Staiger, D. O., & Lockwood, J. R. (2013). *A composite estimator of effective teaching*. Seattle: Bill and Melinda Gates Foundation.

Mosteller, F., Light, R. J., & Sachs, J. A. (1996). Sustained inquiry in education: Lessons learned from skill grouping and class size. *Harvard Educational Review, 66*, 797–842.

Nye, B., Hedges, L. V., & Konstantopoulos, S. (2000). The effects of small classes on academic achievement: The results of the Tennessee class size experiment. *American Educational Research Journal, 37*, 123–151.

Olney, A. M., Kelly, S., Samei, B., Donnelly, P., & D'Mello, S. K. (2017). Assessing teacher questions in classrooms. In R. Sottilare, A. Graesser, X. Hu, & G. Goodwin (Eds.), *Design recommendations for intelligent tutoring systems: Assessment* (Vol. 5). Orlando: Army Research Laboratory. 261–274.

Penuel, W. R., Riel, M., Krause, A., & Frank, K. A. (2009). Analyzing teachers' professional interactions in a school as social capital: A social network approach. *Teachers College Record, 11*, 124–163.

Penuel, W. R., Riel, M., Joshi, A., Pearlman, L., Kim, C. M., & Frank, K. A. (2010). The alignment of the informal and formal organizational supports for reform: Implications for improving teaching in schools. *Educational Administration Quarterly, 46*, 57–95.

Pogodzinski, B. (2012). Socialization of novice teachers. *Journal of School Leadership, 22*, 982–1023.

Pogodzinski, B., Youngs, P., & Frank, K. A. (2013). Collegial climate and novice teachers' intent to remain teaching. *American Journal of Education, 120*, 27–54.

Putnam, R. T., & Borko, H. (2000). What do new views of knowledge and thinking have to say about research on teacher learning? *Educational Researcher, 29*, 4–15.

Quality Counts: Preparing to launch: Early childhood's academic countdown. [Special Issue]. (2015). *Education Week, 34*(16).

Quality Counts: The global challenge. [Special Issue]. (2012). *Education Week, 31*(16).

Raudenbush, S. W., Rowan, B., & Cheong, Y. F. (1992). Contextual effects on the self perceived efficacy of high school teachers. *Sociology of Education, 65*, 150–167.

Reardon, S. F. (2011). The widening academic achievement gap between the rich and poor: New evidence and possible explanations. In G. J. Duncan & R. J. Murnane (Eds.), *Whither opportunity: Rising inequality, schools, and children's life chances* (pp. 91–116). New York: Russell Sage Foundation.

Riehl, C., & Sipple, J. W. (1996). Making the most of time and talent: Secondary school organizational climates, teaching task environments, and teacher commitment. *American Educational Research Journal, 33*, 873–901.

Rivkin, S. G., Hanushek, E. A., & Kain, J. F. (2005). Teachers, schools, and academic achievement. *Econometrica, 73*, 417–458.

Rosenbaum, J. (2001). *Beyond college for all: Career paths for the forgotten half*. New York: Russell Sage Foundation.

Rosenholtz, S. J. (1989). *Teachers' workplace: The social organization of schools*. New York: Longman.

Rosenshine, B. (1970). The stability of teacher effects upon student achievement. *Review of Educational Research, 40*, 647–662.

Rothstein, J., & Mathis, W. (2013). Review of "*have we identified effective teachers?*" and "*A composite estimator of effective teaching: Culminating findings from the Measures of Effective Teaching project*". Boulder: National Education Policy Center.

Samei, B., Olney, A., Kelly, S., Nystrand, M., D'Mello, S., Blanchard, N., Sun, X., Glaus, M., & Graesser, A. (2014). Domain independent assessment of dialogic properties of classroom discourse. In J. Stamper, Z. Pardos, M. Mavrikis & B. M. McLaren (Eds.), *Proceedings of the 7th international conference on Educational Data Mining (EDM 2014)* (pp. 233–236). International Educational Data Mining Society.

Sanders, W. L., & Horn, S. P. (1998). Research findings from the Tennessee value-added assessment system (TVAAS) database: Implications for educational evaluation and research. *Journal of Personnel Evaluation in Education, 12*, 247–256.

Sass, T. R., Hannaway, J., Xu, Z., Figlio, D. N., & Feng, L. (2010). Value added of teachers in high-poverty schools and lower poverty schools. *Journal of Urban Economics, 72*, 104–122.

Schacter, J., & Thum, Y. M. (2004). Paying for high- and low-quality teaching. *Economics of Education Review, 23*, 411–430.

Scheerens, J., & Bosker, R. J. (1997). *The foundations of educational effectiveness*. New York: Pergamon.

Schon, D. A. (1987). *Educating the reflective practitioner: Toward a new design for teaching and learning the professions*. San Francisco: Jossey-Bass.

Schultz, L. M. (2014). Inequitable dispersion: Mapping the distribution of highly qualified teachers in St. Louis metropolitan elementary schools. *Education Policy Analysis Archives, 22*(90), 1–24.

Smith, T. M., & Ingersoll, R. M. (2004). Reducing teacher turnover: What are the components of effective induction? *American Educational Research Journal, 41*, 681–714.

Smith, T. M., Rogers, G. T., Alsalam, N., Perie, M., Mahoney, R. P., & Martin, V. (1994). *The condition of education 1994*. Washington, DC: National Center for Education Statistics.

Staton, A. Q., & Hunt, S. L. (1992). Teacher socialization: Review and conceptualization. *Communication Education, 41*(2), 109–137.

Stigler, J. W., & Hiebert, J. (1999). *The teaching gap*. New York: Free Press.

Strunk, K. O., Weinstein, T. L., & Makkonen, R. (2014). Sorting out the signal: Do multiple measures of teachers' effectiveness provide consistent information to teachers and principals? *Education Policy Analysis Archives, 22*(100), 1–41.

Tagiuri, R. (1968). The concept of organizational climate. In R. Tagiuri & G. H. Litwin (Eds.), *Organizational climate* (pp. 11–32). Boston: Harvard University Press.

Talbert, J. (1992). *Teacher tracking: Exacerbating inequalities in the high school*. Revision of a paper presented at the meeting of the American Educational Research Association, Boston, April 16–20, 1990.

Van Maanen, J., & Schein, E. H. (1979). Toward a theory of organizational socialization. In B. Staw (Ed.), *Research in organizational behavior* (Vol. 1, pp. 209–264). Greenwich: JAI Press.

Vigdor, J. L. (2011). School desegregation and the Black–White test score gap. In G. J. Duncan & R. J. Murnane (Eds.), *Whither opportunity: Rising inequality, schools, and children's life chances* (pp. 443–464). New York: Russell Sage Foundation.

Wayne, A. J., & Youngs, P. (2003). Teacher characteristics and student achievement gains: A review. *Review of Educational Research, 73*, 89–122.

Weick, K. E., & Roberts, K. H. (1993). Collective mind in organizations: Heedful interrelating on flight decks. *Administrative Science Quarterly, 38*, 357–381.

Weiss, I. R., Pasley, J. D., Smith, P. S., Banilower, E. R., & Heck, D. J. (2003). *Looking inside the classroom: A study of K–12 mathematics and science education in the United States*. Chapel Hill: Horizon Research.

Wills, J. S., & Sandholtz, J. H. (2009). Constrained professionalism: Dilemmas of teaching in the face of test-based accountability. *Teachers College Record, 111*, 1065–1114.

Wilson, S. M., Floden, R. E., & Ferrini-Mundy, J. (2001). *Teacher preparation research: Current knowledge, gaps, and recommendations*. University of Washington: Center for the Study of Teaching and Policy.

Yoon, K. S., Duncan, T., Lee, S. W.-Y., Scarloss, B., & Shapley, K. L. (2007). *Reviewing the evidence on how teacher professional development affects student achievement*. Washington, DC: U.S. Department of Education.

Youngs, P. (2007). District induction policy and new teachers' experiences: An examination of local policy implementation in Connecticut. *Teachers College Record, 109*, 797–837.

Yuan, K., Le, V.-N., McCaffrey, D. F., Marsh, J. A., Hamilton, L. S., Stecher, B. M., & Springer, M. G. (2013). Incentive pay programs do not affect teacher motivation or reported practices: Results from three randomized studies. *Educational Evaluation and Policy Analysis, 35*, 3–22.

Social Networks and Educational Opportunity

Kenneth Frank, Yun-jia Lo, Kaitlin Torphy, and Jihyun Kim

Abstract

This chapter reviews the basic structures of social networks and how they have been used to study interrelationships in schools, most prominently those among teachers and students. Part of this discussion includes how network structures are visualized, with multiple examples. These graphic representations demonstrate how information flows in social organizations and is influenced by interactions with colleagues and personalized selections. One of the most important contributions of network analysis is the ability to visualize influence and how inferences of influence can be determined. Influence modeling shows how actors change behaviors in response to others. Selection models show how actors choose with whom they wish to interact and allocate their resources. Finally, this work shows how network forces can facilitate learning by creating opportunities and regulating specific practices. This is particularly beneficial for modeling interactions of teachers within schools and understanding how interactions among teachers and administrators create
norms and conditions that can promote or impede reforms within schools. Teacher networks can be especially useful in the formation of learning communities and can enhance effective teaching. But networks also exist outside of school, and the final section of the chapter discusses the emergence of virtual social networks and how professionals are interacting and using them.

In this chapter we review how social networks have been studied to inform our understanding of how schools allocate opportunities for education. In particular, we focus on the role of the school as a social organization that facilitates coordinated action and allocates resources to students through informal networks and formal structures involving teachers and administrators.[1] In turn,

---

[1] For a complete review of social networks in educational research, see Frank (1998); on teacher networks and the implementation of innovations, see Carolan (2013), Daly (2010), Yoon and Baker-Doyle (2018) and Frank et al. (2014); on teacher networks and collaboration, see Moolenaar (2012); and on network formation see

With contribution from Kim Jansen.

K. Frank (✉) · Y.-j. Lo · K. Torphy
Michigan State University, East Lansing, MI, USA
e-mail: kenfrank@msu.edu; loyunjia@msu.edu;
torphyka@msu.edu

J. Kim
Lehigh University, Bethlehem, PA, USA
e-mail: jik317@lehigh.edu

© Springer International Publishing AG, part of Springer Nature 2018
B. Schneider (ed.), *Handbook of the Sociology of Education in the 21st Century*, Handbooks of Sociology and Social Research, https://doi.org/10.1007/978-3-319-76694-2_13

coordination and resource flows affect the equity of educational opportunities.

Given our attention to coordination and resource flows, processes of social capital drive much of what we will explore below. As we use it here, social capital represents the potential for individuals to access resources through social relationships (Lin 2002; Portes 1998; see Carolan 2013, chapter 10).[2] In particular, this applies to how teachers access information or support from other teachers (Frank et al. 2004; Penuel et al. 2009), or how administrators use their informal relations to influence teaching (Coburn 2005; Coburn and Woulfin 2012; Daly et al. 2010, p. 375; Moolenaar and Sleegers 2015; Sun et al. 2013a; Hopkins and Spillane 2014). In fact, the social capital on which teachers draw may be more important for implementing innovations than narrowly focused human capital (Yoon et al. in press). The flows of such resources can improve teachers' capacity to teach, innovate, and coordinate with one another. Correspondingly, such flows of resources conveyed by informal networks are critical to how schools as social organizations distribute educational opportunity.

In the next section, we begin with a general introduction to social network analysis in terms of the structure and function of networks. This includes graphical visualizations of networks as well as the fundamental models of how actors influence one another through networks and how they select with whom to form network ties. While the models have many applications, the typical drivers of influence and selection can accentuate existing differences among teachers as teachers tend to interact with similar others (e.g., of the same grade) and are influenced by those with whom they interact. In turn, these differences among teachers generate differential

learning opportunities that can lead to stratification.

We then turn to the network forces that can counteract the polarizing tendencies of influence and selection. These forces include the actions of formal administrators who might facilitate certain interactions among teachers or professional learning communities that provide opportunities for interaction. Formal administrators must also consider how their mediation of external forces affects the internal social dynamics of the school. Thus our chapter is partly an analysis of how informal networks complement or hybridize (e.g., teacher professional learning communities) with the formal organization. Such complementarities should contribute to higher quality, and more uniform teaching, and, ultimately, to the equity of educational opportunity.

We also recognize networks that transcend the school boundary, such as networked improvement communities and networks on social media such as Pinterest and Twitter. These forms challenge conventional conceptualizations of the school boundary as they are supported by infrastructures not defined by the formal organization of the school. As such, they can mitigate tendencies for inequitable opportunities, but only if carefully cultivated. We discuss that the ultimate challenge for any network form is how well it supports the primary process of teaching. As these forms may provide unique resources and potential for diffusion, they can contribute to higher levels and more uniform teaching that can mitigate otherwise unequal educational opportunities.

13.1 The Basic Structures and Processes of Social Networks[3,4]

At its most basic level, a social network consists of a set of nodes and edges connecting the nodes. For example, the nodes might be teachers in a

McPherson et al. (2001). For a motivation of network analysis from utility theory and a guide to the application of social network analysis see Frank et al. (2010).

[2]The social capital paradigm may also include factors such as norms that facilitate the flow of resources (Coleman, 1988). See Adler and Kwon (2002) and Kwon and Adler (2014) for reviews.

[3]Adapted from Frank et al. (2014).

[4]See Lima (2010) or Carolan (2013, chapter 4) for a description of methods for collecting and managing

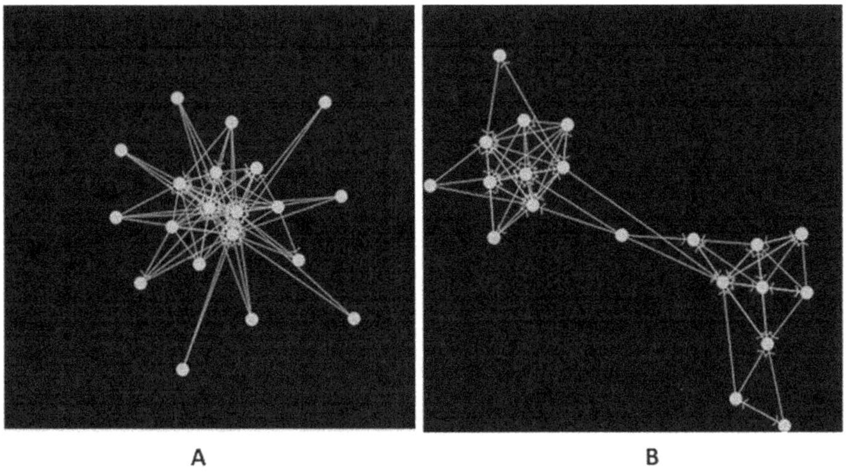

Fig. 13.1 Examples of network structures. (**a**) Core periphery structure in which a small number of actors engage in a large percentage of the edges. (**b**) Network clustering featuring regions of sparse and dense edges

single school and the edges might represent those teachers who are close colleagues. In this sense the edges represent a stable relation between the pair of actors/nodes.

13.1.1 Visualization of Networks

The structure of a network might then be defined in terms of the distribution of the edges between the nodes. For example, in Fig. 13.1 each dot represents a hypothetical actor (e.g., a teacher) and lines between dots represent actors connected to one another (e.g., teachers who are close colleagues or who share information with each other). A network might exhibit a core-periphery structure in which a small number of actors are engaged in a disproportionate number of edges (see Fig. 13.1a). Other networks might exhibit clustering defined by regions of dense and sparse concentrations of edges (see Fig. 13.1b).

These different structures will have implications for function. Informally defined cohesive subgroups can be critical for knowledge generation (Coburn et al. 2012; Bidwell and Yasumoto

1999) and the diffusion of innovations. For example, Penuel et al. (2009) compared two case studies, finding that the school that more successfully implemented a reform had better flows of expertise between subgroups. Subgroups also can constrain the ultimate diffusion of an innovation, as an innovation can become contained within the boundaries of a given subgroup. In such cases the diffusion ultimately depends on the action of those who bridge between clusters. More generally, core-periphery networks can diffuse innovations more rapidly and thoroughly than networks in which there are strong cliques, referred to as modularity (e.g., Csermely et al. 2013).

To give a sense of how the rate of diffusion is affected by the structure of a network, consider Figs. 13.2 and 13.3, originally used to study diffusion of technology into instruction in Westville High School (Frank and Zhao 2005). In the mid-1990s, the district central administration forced Westville to switch from Macintosh computers to Windows. To illustrate how the informal network shaped the organizational response, Frank and Zhao (2005) first used Fig. 13.2 to illustrate the informal structure of collegial ties among the teachers in Westville. Each teacher is represented by a number, and the lines indicate close collegial relationships obtained from the survey question, "Who are your closest colleagues in the school?" Frank's *KliqueFinder* algorithm identified the

---

high-quality data. For a review of reliability and validity of network measures see Marsden (2011), with improvement offered from Brewer (2000) and Henry et al. (2012), and specific to teachers in Pitts and Spillane (2009).

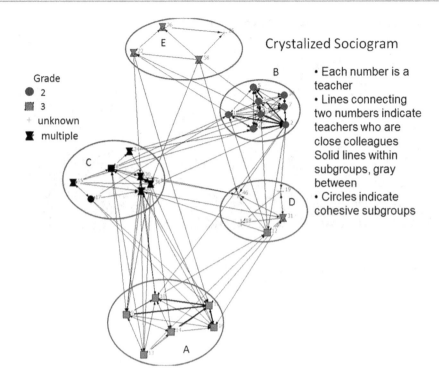

Fig. 13.2 Crystalized sociogram

subgroup boundaries in the image by maximizing the concentration of ties within subgroups versus between subgroups (see Frank 1995, 1996, for more details of the algorithm).[5] The black lines indicate within-subgroup (or cluster) interactions, while gray lines indicate between-subgroup interactions.[6]

The shape associated with each node in Fig. 13.2 indicates the grade in which the teacher taught. This information reveals an alignment of grade and subgroup boundaries. Subgroup A consists mostly of third grade teachers and subgroup B mostly of second grade teachers. But the subgroup structure also characterizes those faculty, administrators, and staff who do not neatly fit into the categories of the formal organization. For example, subgroup C contains the physical edu-

cation teacher, a special education teacher, the principal, and two teachers who did not have extensive ties with others in their grades.

To relate the social structure in Fig. 13.2 to the flow of expertise about Windows and ultimately to changes in teachers' computer use, Fig. 13.3 represents interactions concerning use of technology (in response to the question: "Who in the last year has helped you use technology in the classroom?") with the location of the teachers still determined by the close collegial relations in Fig. 13.2. Generally the provision of technology support was concentrated within subgroups, especially the grade-based subgroups A and B. To represent the flow of knowledge or expertise, each teacher's identification number was replaced with a dot proportional to his or her use of technology at time 1 (a + indicates no information available). The larger the dot, the more the teacher used technology as reported at time 1. The ripples indicate increases in the use of technology from time 1 to time 2.[7]

---

[5]Available at https://msu.edu/~kenfrank/resources. htm#KliqueFinder.

[6]Directionality is not represented in Fig. 13.2 because close collegial relationships are used only to establish the underlying social structure. Arrowheads are used in Fig. 13.3 to show the flow of resources.

---

[7]Because the metrics varied slightly between administrations of the instrument, each measure of use was standardized

Fig. 13.3 Ripple plot

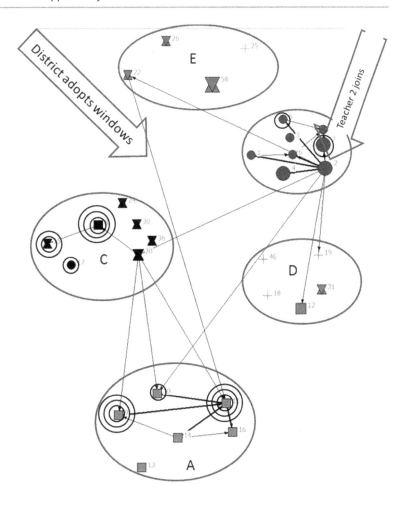

Ultimately, the story of Figs. 13.2 and 13.3 is one of the forms and distribution of social capital. In Fig. 13.3, intra-organizational diffusion essentially began when teacher 2 was assigned to Westville because of her expertise with the Windows platform. Teacher 2 immediately became a close colleague of other teachers in subgroup B, generating bonding social capital as she helped others in subgroup B with computer technology, resulting in some increments in technology use.

The key to extending teacher 2's knowledge beyond her subgroup was the bridging social capital (Atteberry and Bryk 2010; Daly et al. 2010; Penuel et al. 2009, 2010) between 2 and teacher

20, a veteran teacher in the school. Through teacher 20, the expertise of teacher 2 was disseminated to both subgroups C and B, resulting in substantial changes in use (e.g., as can be observed in the ripples around school actors in subgroup C). Without this bridging tie, teacher 2's expertise would likely have been confined to subgroup B, limiting the capacity of the school to implement technology, and potentially creating a cleavage in the social structure between subgroup B and the other subgroups.

Building on the results in Figs. 13.2 and 13.3, Frank et al. (2015) found in a longitudinal study across 21 schools that the distribution of resource flows between subgroups ultimately predicted a school's capacity to diffuse new teaching practices. In particular, schools that successfully cultivated expertise within a small number of

---

and then the difference was taken from the standardized measures. Each ring represents an increase of .2 standardized units.

subgroups (Nonaka 1994; Yasumoto et al. 2001), and then facilitated the flow of expertise from those subgroups throughout the school, more successfully implemented reforms than those in which expertise could emanate from almost any subgroup. That is, schools which manifest a cacophony of expert voices may find it difficult to implement and coordinate new practices, ultimately compromising educational opportunities for their students.

Graphical representations can intuitively demonstrate the information flow in a social organization and illustrate the process of change. But the application of social network analysis to educational research can extend these graphical representations by formally modeling the extent to which teachers are influenced through interactions with colleagues and what factors affect the ways in which teachers select with whom to interact.

13.1.2 The Influence Model

We begin the discussion of statistical modeling of teacher networks with the influence model (Friedkin and Marsden 1994), which can be used to estimate a teacher's implementation of specific teaching practices as a function of the prior behaviors of others around her (as a norm), and her own prior behaviors. For example, Frank et al. (2013b) modeled a teacher's implementation of skills-based reading instruction[8] as a function of her previous implementation as well as the behaviors of those with whom she frequently interacted regarding professional matters. Formally, let skills-based instruction$_i$ represent

the extent to which teacher i implemented skills-based instruction. This is modeled as

$$
\begin{aligned}
Skills-based\ instruction_i = {} & \beta_0 \\
& + \beta_1 previous\ skills-based\ instructional \\
& \quad of\ others\ in\ the\ network\ of\ i_i \\
& + \beta_2 previous\ skills-based\ instruction\ of\ i_i + e_i,
\end{aligned}
$$

(13.1)

where the error terms (e_i) are assumed independently distributed, $N(0,\sigma^2)$. The term *previous skills-based instructional of others in the network of i* can simply be the mean or sum of the behaviors of those with whom teacher i interacted (e.g., as indicated in response to a question about from whom a teacher has received help with instruction). Using the mean as an example, if teacher Ashley indicated interacting with Kim and Sam who previously implemented skills-based instruction at levels of 25 and 30 respectively (representing the number of times per month the teachers used skills-based instruction for the core tasks of teaching), then Ashley is exposed to a norm of 27.5 (=[25+30]/2) through her network.[9] Correspondingly, the term β_1 indicates the normative influence of others on teacher i. If β_1 is positive, the more the members of Ashley's network use skills-based instruction, the more she increases her use of skills-based instruction. Corresponding to Fig. 13.3, if β_1 is large, then one would observe many ripples associated with teachers who interacted with others who had previously implemented skills-based instruction into their instruction.

Note that the inference of influence is indirect—Frank et al. (2013b) did not directly ask people who influenced them. Instead, influence is assumed if teachers change their behaviors in the direction of the average behavior of those in their network. Behaviors such as teaching practices and interactions can be more reliably and objectively reported than influence. A positive coefficient of β_1 indicates that the higher the level

---

[8]The skilled-based instructional practices include that teachers read stories or other imaginative texts; practice dictation (teacher reads and students write down words) about something the students are interested in; use context and pictures to read words; blend sounds to make words or segment the sounds in words; clap or sound out syllables of words; drill and practice sight words (e.g., as part of a competition); use phonics-based or letter-sound relationships to read words in sentences; use sentence meaning and structure to read words; and practice letter-sound associations (see Frank et al. 2013b, pp. 318–319 for details).

---

[9]In this sense, the exposure term extends basic conceptualizations of centrality (e.g., Freeman 1978) because the exposure term is a function of the characteristics of members of a network, whereas centrality is a function only of the structure of the network.

of average implementation of a set of practices of those in one's network, the greater the likelihood of increasing one's own implementation. Furthermore, one may include covariates such as a teacher's attitude toward instructional practices representing a key predictor from the diffusion of innovation literature (Frank et al. 2013a, b, 2004; Rogers 2010). Frank et al. (2011; Penuel et al. 2012) also find that network effects are stronger for those who already have high levels of implementation.

Note the use of timing to identify the effects in model (1). The individual's outcome is modeled as a function of her peers' *prior* characteristics. This would be natural if one were to model contagion. For example, whether A gets a cold from B is a function of A's exposure to B over the last week and whether B had a cold *last week*. We would not argue that contagion occurs if A and B interacted in the last 24 h and both A and B got sick today (see Lyons 2011 and Cohen-Cole and Fletcher's 2008a, b critique of Christakis and Fowler's 2007, 2008 contemporaneous models of the contagion of obesity; see also Leenders 1995). Given longitudinal data, the influence model can be estimated with ordinary software once one has constructed the network term and controlled for prior engagement in the practice (see Frank and Xu 2018).[10]

Frank et al.'s (2013a, b) estimates of model (1) showed that teacher's teaching practices were influenced by those of her colleagues. Consistent with several other studies, teachers' influences tend to be small to moderate, but persistent across domains (e.g., Baker-Doyle 2015; Bidwell and Yasumoto 1999; Cole and Weinbaum 2010; Frank et al. 2004; Moolenaar 2010; Penuel et al. 2012; Spillane et al. 2001; Spillane and Kim 2012; Schneider 2015; Supovitz et al. 2010). Correspondingly, when networks are weak or sparse, innovations are unlikely to diffuse (Finnigan et al. 2013).

13.1.3 The Selection Model

While the influence model represents how actors change behaviors or beliefs in response to others around them, the selection model represents how actors choose with whom to interact or to whom to allocate resources. For example, the choices a teacher makes in helping others can be modeled as:

$$\log\left[\frac{p\left(help_{ii'}\right)}{1 - p\left(help_{ii'}\right)}\right] = \theta_0 + \theta_1 samegrade_{ii'},$$

(13.2)

where p (help$_{ii'}$) represents the probability that actor i' provides help to actor i (similar to the influence model, these data can be obtained in response to a question about from whom teacher i received helped with instruction) and θ_1 represents the effect of teaching in the same grade on the provision of help.[11] As in the influence model, other terms could be included such as common grade taught, level of knowledge, etc. (e.g., Frank 2009; Frank and Zhao 2005; Spillane et al. 2012; Wilhelm et al. 2016).

Using this type of selection model, several studies have found that teachers receive help from close colleagues as well as others who teach the same grade (e.g., Frank and Zhao 2005; Gamoran et al. 2005; Penuel et al. 2010; Spillane et al. 2012; Wilhelm et al. 2016). Help also tends to flow from experts to novices (Coburn et al. 2010; Frank and Zhao 2005; Penuel et al. 2009), although the transaction costs of locating and engaging expertise are not trivial (Baker-Doyle and Yoon 2010; Spillane et al. 2017), and can be extreme when schools are under scrutiny for performance (Finnigan and Daly 2012).

---

[10]See https://www.msu.edu/~kenfrank/resources.htm: influence models for SPSS, SAS, and STATA modules and PowerPoint demonstrations that calculate a network effect and include it in a regression model.

[11]Estimation of model (2) can be challenging because of dependencies among the network ties. Techniques that control for dependencies through random effects (Baerveldt et al. 2004; Hoff, 2005; Lazega and Van Duijn, 1997) as well as latent spaces (Hoff et al. 2002; Sweet et al. 2013) have encouraging potential, although we note the focus of Exponential Random Graph Models on a relatively small number of geometrically weighted terms may address some previous concerns about degeneracies in estimation (Hunter et al. 2008). See Frank and Xu (2018), for more discussion.

13.1.4 Influence and Selection: Social Capital and Educational Opportunity

The processes of influence and selection complement each other in a social capital exchange (Blau 1968). In the social capital exchange between teachers (Frank et al. 2004), teachers trade their conformity (i.e., accepting influence) for access to knowledge, expertise, and support in a form of social capital exchange (i.e., selection of the provision of help). As a result, those teachers less in need of local knowledge, support, and expertise will be less compelled to conform to the norms of their colleagues. This might apply to a veteran teacher who already has extensive local knowledge and whose employment and success do not depend on conformity. It might also apply to a participant in alternative certification such as Teach for America who does not intend to remain in a school for more than a few years. On the other hand, novice teachers who have extensive need for local support and knowledge may find the norms of their colleagues compelling.

Ultimately, the processes of influence and selection work in tandem to distribute the key resource of expertise and provide organizational coordination through conformity. But unchecked, the processes of influence and selection can contribute to inequitable opportunities for education. To begin, if teachers are organized into clusters or subgroups (e.g., Fig. 13.1b; Frank and Zhao 2005; Frank et al. 2015), and teachers are influenced by their colleagues early in reform implementation (Camburn et al. 2003; Coburn 2005; Coburn et al. 2012), then reforms will not diffuse evenly and can even polarize a school (Frank et al. 2013a, b). More generally, processes of influence may exacerbate initial differences in teaching quality if high-quality teachers select to interact with other high-quality teachers with equal status or with whom there is an equal exchange.

Differences in the quality of teaching create a situation in which more advantaged students can leverage their backgrounds to navigate to higher-quality teachers, creating a mechanism through which initial advantages accumulate through intra-school dynamics. Furthermore, even if all teaching is of equally high quality, differences in the type of teaching can create learning challenges as students transition from one classroom to another from one year to the next (as in an elementary school) or 1 h to the next (as in a high school). The more support a child has in the home (in terms of parental education or capacity to navigate to teachers with good fit) the better the child will be able to adapt. Although there is great value in teachers learning from each other, if the learning is concentrated within specific pockets the attendant social dynamics may contribute to differences among teachers that may not be benign.

13.2 Network Forces That May Mitigate Inequities of Educational Opportunity

We now represent network forces that contribute to and may mitigate inequitable educational opportunities. Consider Fig. 13.4 in which we depict 3 teachers and 3 students within a single school. The black lines represent the assignment of students to teachers, one of the fundamental functions of a school (Dreeben and Barr 1988; Bidwell and Kasarda 1980). We represent potential stratification in a laissez faire system with the less eager (or less advantaged) student in the middle assigned to the less knowledgeable and less effective teacher on the left. On the bottom, the student might draw on his student network (blue line) for support or to gain assignment to a different teacher. While this may be an effective adaptation for the particular student, it does not mitigate the underlying inequities among the teachers which generally contribute to the conditions for inequitable opportunity. As we have presented above, differences among teachers can be reduced if teachers of different style and levels of expertise interact with one another, as shown by the blue arcs in Fig. 13.4.

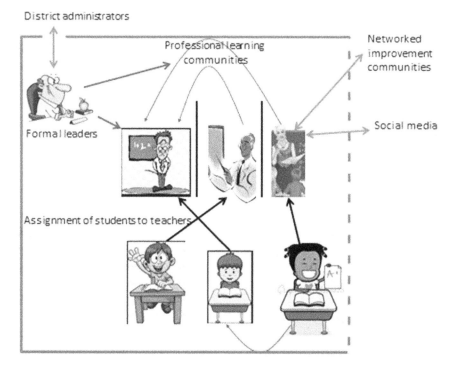

Fig. 13.4 Teacher networks and equity of opportunity

13.2.1 Effects of Formal Networks and Formal Leaders on Teachers

As shown on the left of Fig. 13.4, the school may organize network flows through the designation of formal assignments. For example, because teachers typically seek advice from others in the same grade or subject, as administrators make instructional assignments they shape teacher networks. Correspondingly administrators should consider the attendant diffusion of expertise in making those assignments.

Formal leaders may also directly affect teacher's networks through brokering advice-seeking networks (Spillane and Kim 2012). Differences among teachers may be further mitigated through interactions outside the gray dashed line of the school boundary such as with networked improvement communities or social media. Critically, these supports and knowledge must be adapted and reconciled with the intra-school network (Coburn and Russell 2008; Daly, Moolenaar, Bolivar et al. 2010; Frank et al. 2011; Frank et al.

2013b). In the sections below we elaborate on each of these processes.

Administrators may also affect professional networks by designating certain teachers for formal roles. For example, Coburn and Woulfin (2012) found that coaches were some of the strongest influences on changes in teachers' instructional practice when a new policy message was introduced. Interestingly, some of the stronger effects of coaches may be in promoting knowledge flows among others in the school (Coburn and Woulfin 2012; Sun et al. 2013a, b; Sun et al. 2014). Ultimately, the strength of a teacher's informal connection to formal leaders predicts student achievement (Friedkin and Slater 1994; Pil and Leana 2009), possibly mediated by sense of efficacy (Moolenaar et al. 2012), use of data (Daly 2012), and commitment (Thomas 2007).

Formal leaders may also facilitate teachers' instructional learning by creating opportunities and regulating general instructional practices (Coburn et al. 2013; Daly et al. 2010, p. 375; Sun et al. 2013a; Hopkins and Spillane 2014; Supovitz et al. 2010). For example, principals and coaches can influence the social process of understanding reform by framing the meaning of the reform (Coburn 2005; Sun et al. 2014). Formal leaders may also be critical to maintaining existing network ties (Spillane and Shirrell 2017). In this sense, formal leaders create the norms and conditions that support the flow of social capital (Bryk and Schneider 2002; Coleman 1988). As they do so, formal leaders may indirectly affect the networks through which teachers interact, creating a potential counterbalance to any tendencies for polarization in teachers' networks.

Of course, the external contexts of schools can exert polarizing forces within schools as schools react to competing external demands (e.g., Coleman 1961; Powell et al. 1985). Leaders can be a conduit or buffer for external pressures, partly depending on their networks (Daly et al. 2010; Rigby 2016). For example, principals who were central in both intra- and inter-school networks played critical roles in diffusing innovations from outside the school to the school, and then within the school (Moolenaar et al. 2010b; Moolenaar and Sleegers 2015; Hopkins et al. 2013). Furthermore, Leana and Pil (2006) found that administrators' ties to the external environment predicted student achievement, possibly because poor network ties impede the formation of trust and exchange of critical support (Daly and Finnigan 2010).[12] Of course given the demands of engaging in in-depth interactions (Coburn and Russell 2008) it may be difficult for formal leaders to maintain high centrality within and outside of a school (Moolenaar and Sleegers 2015; Atteberry and Bryk 2010; Coburn and Russell 2008; Cole and Weiss 2009; Frank et al. 2013b; Spillane and Kim 2012; Spillane and Healey 2010).

The interplay of formal and informal processes raises an interesting proposition about the primacy of either (Selznick 1948; Sun et al. 2013a). On one hand, informal interactions among teachers can affect teachers' commitment and sense of efficacy (Hong et al. 2013;

Pogodzinski et al. 2013; Pogodzinski et al. 2012). On the other hand, implementation of reforms certainly depends on the direct support of formal leaders (Daly and Finnigan 2016). Ultimately, schools are likely more effective when formal and informal are aligned (Penuel et al. 2010; Spillane et al. 2010). But our analysis would suggest that principals would want to carefully guide the intra-organizational diffusion process so as not to exacerbate existing differences in expertise or teaching style among teachers.

13.2.2 Teacher Professional Learning Communities: Mid-Ground Between Formal and Informal

While the school formally shapes teachers partly through professional development (Garet et al. 2001; Desimon et al. 2002), the school also shapes teachers through informal networks of teachers. As shown at the top of Fig. 13.4, teacher professional learning communities (PLCs) occupy a mid-ground between the formal and informal organizations (Gamoran et al. 2005; Hord 1997; Resnick and Scherrer 2012; Wood 2007). PLCs are established by the formal organization and leaders, with designated membership and venues for interaction (Achinstein 2002; Fullan 1993; Lave and Wenger 1991). But once established, the interactions within the PLC may be wide-ranging and informal as teachers explore ways to learn from each other and improve instructional practices.

The informal processes in PLCs offer opportunities for teachers to develop norms and trust in one another so they may have frank professional exchanges that lead to learning (Stoll and Louis 2007; Bryk et al. 1999; Daly et al. 2010; Moolenaar et al. 2012). Ultimately these norms can have far-reaching effects into the culture of a school, affecting the capacity of the school to implement effective teaching (Bidwell and Yasumoto 1999; Leana and Pil 2006) and innovations (Moolenaar et al. 2010a, b) creating educational opportunities for students attending the school (Bryk and Schneider 2002).

---

[12]Although formal ties tend to be weakly related to use of evidence (Daly et al. 2014a, b).

The importance of the norms highlights the location of the PLC in the mid-ground between the formal and informal organization. To build trust and develop a norm of learning means that vulnerabilities will not be exploited or sanctioned. Consequently, formal leaders must support informal, deep conversations without exploiting such conversations for the purposes of evaluation (Coburn and Russell 2008). This may be especially challenging in schools that face extreme accountability pressures (Rigby et al. under review), potentially introducing norms counter to those that cultivate sharing and trust (Bryk and Schneider 2002; Frank et al. 2008).

As PLCs occupy a mid-ground between the formal and informal organization, the study of PLCs partly engages conventional network analysis of interactions among teachers. But within the context of a PLC it is difficult to know the directionality of interaction. Typically all who are present are exposed to the member who speaks at any given time. This is in contrast to typical network analysis focused on one-to-one professional conversations, advice seeking, or knowledge sharing. Correspondingly, studies of PLCs often focus on the relationship of members to the collective of the PLC (Goddard et al. 2007; Louis et al. 1996; Ronfeldt et al. 2015), whereas studies of teacher networks typically focus on resources that flow through specific relationships to specific teachers.

Frank (2009) offers a potential synthesis of the one-to-many (e.g., PLC) and one-to-one (e.g., conventional teacher network) paradigms, arguing that a relationship with a group of people as a collective generates quasi-ties. Quasi-ties between a person and a group can direct the flow of resources evenly throughout the group, overcoming the tendency for people to favor allocations of resources (e.g., expertise) to specific others with whom they have a direct personal relationship. In this sense, PLCs can contribute to the even distribution of resources throughout a school, overcoming the tendency for resources such as expertise to become concentrated in specific pockets or teacher cliques. As a result, the PLC can contribute to more coordinated and even teaching, and thus to more equitable educational opportunities.

The study of PLCs can also offer potential insight into the substance of professional interactions. It is rare for those who study teacher networks to directly observe and record conversations among teachers which may be very intimate from a professional standpoint. But researchers have gained access to PLC meetings in their slightly more open venues. In one such study Horn and Kane (2015) showed not all PLCs are equally conducive to teachers' learning. The richer PLCs had more conversations, featured richer conceptualizations and specific future work (Horn and Kane 2015). Recent work also suggests that PLCs with deeper interactions are more likely to foster one-to-one professional interactions outside of the PLC than are PLCs with lower quality of interaction (Horn et al. 2017). This demonstrates the complex social position of the PLC, with the substance and process determined in part by formal leaders, and in turn affecting the informal networks that reside outside the PLC.

13.3 Crossing the School Boundary

13.3.1 Effects of External Institutions on Teacher Networks

Following the long history of the study of schools relative to their environments (Bidwell and Kasarda 1987; Callahan 1962; Greenfield 1975; Meyer and Rowan 1977; Rowan 1995), the intra-organizational networks of schools can be affected by forces external to the school. Daly and Finnigan (2010, 2011) and Wilhelm et al. (2016) found that in schools facing accountability pressures teachers sought math-related expertise from those with high value-added scores over those whose practices featured ambitious math instruction or who possessed high levels of mathematics content knowledge (Rigby et al. 2014). Coburn et al. (2010) found teachers sought others with specific expertise related to the implementation of a new reform, while Supovitz et al. (2014) found that teachers sought expertise from colleagues and administrators about the common core.

Examining the implications of external institutions on school networks, Frank et al. (2013b) identified subgroups or cliques of teachers at the onset of institutional pressures associated with NCLB (e.g., emphasis on skills-based instruction). As teachers responded to the practices of others in their cliques the cliques became more differentiated. Thus, the pressures of "No Child Left Behind" ultimately contributed to polarization among teachers within their schools. Such polarization can create immediate challenges to the coordination of teaching, which can then affect educational opportunities within schools as well each school's capacity to implement future reforms. Bridwell-Mitchell and Sherer (2017) extend this to the development of institutional logics within subgroups that then shapes teachers' reactions to external institutions.

13.3.2 District Administrators as Bridgers

In general, district administrators (shown at the top left of Fig. 13.4) span the boundary between schools, outside institutional forces and the community (Daly et al. 2014; Honig 2003, 2006; Hite et al. 2005). Critically, when a school or district leader holds a more central position in the social network, he or she has more influence in the organization as well as increased access to resources (Daly et al. 2014b). But district administrators must carefully manage their position in informal networks, which can be quite fluid (Daly and Finnigan 2011; Honig 2003, 2006) and in which churn can create challenges for developing trusting or deep relationships.

Michigan offers a particularly interesting case of the administrator as boundary spanner (Spillane 1996). Beginning in the 1980s Michigan expanded state-level testing (MEAP test), and state-level legislation revised the state's learning standards and tied financial sanctions to district failure to align their curriculum to the state model. The district's response to such policies depended heavily on the district administrators (Spillane 1996). For example, one district used

district policies to buffer teachers from state policy by preserving more skills-based reading instruction, while another mobilized resources to promote more ambitious reading instruction aligned to the new state policy (Spillane 1996).

There is an important tension between forcing immediate responses versus buffering teachers to provide opportunities and a culture for teachers to interact, share knowledge and coordinate contributing to equitable opportunities. For example, Daly and Finnigan (2011, 2010) found that in schools under accountability policy sanctions, school leaders' interactions tended to focus mainly on reform strategies over innovative practices. As a result, newcomers to the network who could bring innovative knowledge were kept on the periphery. Also, school leaders remained on the periphery, while central office staff held more central positions, resulting in most knowledge flowing within and throughout the central office rather than to the school sites. Thus, administrators' decisions can accumulate to limit other informal networks and resource flows within the district. Ultimately, these limitations restrict the flow of knowledge, contributing to differences in expertise that can affect educational opportunities.

13.4 New Network Forms That Transcend School Boundaries

13.4.1 Networked Improvement Communities

Recently administrators and policymakers have begun to attend to inter-district entities that draw on network dynamics to improve schooling outcomes—Lieberman (2000) (e.g., the green lines at the top left and top right of Fig. 13.4). For example, the National Writing Project (NWP) organizes summer institutes in which teachers from different schools share their best lessons and teaching strategies, engage in the writing process, participate in writing groups, and receive peer feedback (Lieberman and Wood 2002; Little 2006; National Writing Project 2016). After a teacher successfully finishes the summer institute, he or she becomes a teacher consultant, bridging between the NWP and local school communities. Some lead professional development in their schools, while others join local leadership teams to help create special interest groups relevant to teaching writing (Lieberman and Wood 2004). In fact the spillover effects of the NWP on others in a participant's school may be as great as the direct effects on the teachers who participate in professional development (Penuel et al. 2012; Sun et al. 2013b).

Recently Bryk et al. (2015) have extended models such as NWP to propose a general model of Networked Improvement Communities (NIC). Analogous to the PLCs within a school, NICs between schools carefully cultivate the types of interactions that support collective learning and knowledge sharing. In particular, the NIC process consists of a series of cycles of Plan-Do-Study-Act (PDSA). Explicitly stating the need to cycle through PDSA lays the foundation for teachers to share their vulnerabilities and invest in one another. Furthermore, over multiple PDA cycles networks can be expanded to include new school staff. For example, in the later PDSA cycles of the BTEN NIC, members of a principal group began their own cycles of PDSA (Bryk et al. 2015).

While the PDSA of NICs holds great potential for generating and diffusing knowledge about teaching practices, teaching practices advocated in inter-school networks may conflict with the norms of a particular school as on the right hand side of Fig. 13.4. Part of the test of the NICs is how they can systemically support the integration of knowledge into the school. Indeed, design based research attends to networks partly to facilitate this transfer (Cobb and Jackson 2011; Russell et al. 2013). Furthermore, the knowledge itself may be transformed as it permeates the school boundary (Frank et al. 2011). Critically, failure to meld extra-school knowledge with intra-school norms can create coordination challenges and unequal instruction within schools that can lead to inequitable opportunities to learn.

13.4.2 Social Media: The Case of Pinterest

The evolution of educator networks now includes entities formed on social media (e.g., see http://www.hashtagcommoncore.com/; Noble et al. 2016; see Macià and García 2016 for a review of online professional communities). These entities challenge standard distinctions between formal versus informal networks because they may be formed deliberately, may emerge organically, or may be facilitated through data mining algorithms, programmed to connect a set of participants with shared interests. Similarly, social media networks challenge standard distinctions between intra- and inter-school networks as participation is not easily defined by the school boundary.

While teachers may use various social media (Facebook, Twitter), a set of recent studies has focused on Pinterest, a personalized social media platform, because it is one of the most frequently used social media platforms by teachers (Kaufman et al. 2016). Pinterest allows users to "pin" pictures or videos (posted by others or found by themselves) to organize and save for future reference. Evidence from a recent study focusing on early career teachers (ECTS) suggests that the Pinterest platform creates a discourse community for teachers that is different from the traditional face-to-face interactions ECTs have with their colleagues or in PLCs (Torphy et al. 2016a). A second study shows how ECTs purposely choose worthwhile sources of information (Torphy et al. 2016b). In particular, entrepreneurial teachers (called teacherpreneurs), seek out other teacher practitioners in the pursuit of exemplary teaching resources, practices, and pedagogy. Furthermore, data from Pinterest can provide valuable insights into what teachers are thinking, how they change their practices, and who they learn from as they do so (Hu and Torphy 2016; Torphy and Hu 2016).[13]

---

[13] Given the recent emergence of the phenomenon, many of the studies we report on here are in early stages, such as conference presentations, but not yet published in peer review journals.

There are three fundamental challenges to the realization of the potential of social media networks. First, as with the challenge for other extra-school networks, the challenge for teachers' use of social media will be in how interactions through social media meld with professional interactions within the school (Cho et al. 2013; Cho 2016). For example, materials and resources accessed on Pinterest may not conform to state or district adopted standards, or with teaching norms within a school. The teacher must then navigate the use of the resources given her local context. This is not an insurmountable challenge, but requires teachers' professional judgment.

Second, one must consider the motivation for teachers to provide their expertise and help to others via online social media. A small number of teachers may do so for remuneration (e.g., https://www.teacherspayteachers.com/). Others may do so for status as in traditional social exchange (Blau 1968). But social exchange depends on the visibility of the exchange and the extent to which the provider values status as part of her identity. Currently, sites like Pinterest make exchanges known in the form of publicizing followers. How much teachers identify with these sites is less known. As social media become increasingly salient with each new cohort of teachers social media identities may increase. Nonetheless, a social media identity must compete with identification with the school organization with whose members a teacher shares students, common evaluation, and therefore the form of social capital known as bounded solidarity (Portes and Sensenbrenner 1993).

Third, there is the concern regarding educational opportunity and online networks. On one hand, online networks may provide teachers in disadvantaged settings or teachers with relatively less training or skill access to critical resources that can make them better teachers. This can contribute to more equitable educational opportunities. On the other hand, if existing advantages in skill or resources make it easier for teachers to access online resources and integrate them in their classrooms, then the diffusion of online resources can contribute to stratification just as any other resource can.

13.5 Discussion

Most sociology of education has focused on the resources to which students have access and the equitable distribution of those resources. To be sure, such resources as family education and income contribute directly to the opportunities students have to learn in the home and school. But a key aspect of the family resource determines the school the children attend. And a critical resource of the school is the quality of the teaching (e.g., Nye et al. 2004). As a direct result, differences among teachers within and between schools contribute to inequities in opportunities within and between schools.

There are various policies and practices that can reduce differences among teachers. Professional development and support can help relatively less effective teachers improve. Policies that include incentives or merit pay can attract and retain high-quality teachers, especially in schools serving at-risk students. On the other hand, policies that evaluate individual teachers in terms of value-added scores encourage competition among teachers and discourage cooperation, which can exacerbate existing differences.

But teachers can also be key resources for one another. As such, teacher networks can distribute expertise and support that can mitigate existing differences in teacher quality. Networks such as NICs or online (e.g., Pinterest) outside of schools can provide teachers and administrators with general knowledge about learning, or ideas for teaching. Networks within schools can provide teachers with local knowledge about how to implement a curriculum within the school context and for a particular student population.

While networks have great potential to mitigate existing differences among teachers, they will likely not realize that potential if they are allowed to emerge without explicit attention to the consequences for equity. Left to their own devices, humans are likely to seek homophilous others with whom the transaction costs of interacting are low (Zeng and Xie 2008; Frank et al. 2013a) or to cultivate interactions with those with whom they can establish an exchange (Blau

1968). These natural tendencies can accentuate baseline differences among teachers.

But deliberate action can mitigate natural tendencies for resources to become concentrated in certain schools or among certain teachers within a school. Formal and informal leaders can provide direct supports for novices or teachers who are struggling. Moreover, formal and informal leaders can cultivate relationships among others that contribute to the even distribution of expertise within and between schools. This might occur through leaders' choices of mentors for novice teachers or those performing inadequately. It may also vary by subject or context, tapping different teachers' expertise in a particular subject or pedagogical technique.

It is likely that effective formal and informal leaders tacitly tap the potential of networks for the creation and distribution of expertise, and for coordinating action among teachers. But here we make the process explicit and link it directly to the underlying distribution of opportunities for education. By doing so we contribute to the language of social capital for describing schools as social organizations, with the ultimate goal of helping all schools cultivate expertise and distribute educational opportunities equitably.

Acknowledgement We acknowledge the work of Zixi Chen, I-chien Chen, Angelo Garcia, Sihua Hu, Qinyun Lin, and Yuqing Liu for helping us identify and summarize literature reviewed.

References

Achinstein, B. (2002). Conflict amid community: The micropolitics of teacher collaboration. *Teachers College Record, 104*(3), 421–455.

Adler, P. S., & Kwon, S. W. (2002). Social capital: Prospects for a new concept. *Academy of Management Review, 27*(1), 17–40.

Atteberry, A., & Bryk, A. S. (2010). Centrality, connection, and commitment: The role of social networks in a school-based literacy initiative. In A. J. Daly (Ed.), *Social network theory and educational change* (pp. 51–76). Cambridge, MA: Harvard Educational Press.

Baerveldt, C., Van Duijn, M. A. J., & van Hemert, D. A. (2004). Ethnic boundaries and personal choice: Assessing the influence of individual inclinations to choose intraethnic relationships on pupils' networks. *Social Networks., 26*(1), 55–74.

Baker-Doyle, K. J. (2015). No teacher is an island: How social networks shape teacher quality. In A. W. Wiseman (Ed.), *Promoting and sustaining a quality teacher workforce* (pp. 367–383). Bingley: Emerald Group Publishing Limited.

Baker-Doyle, K. J., & Yoon, S. A. (2010). Making expertise transparent: Using technology to strengthen social networks in teacher professional development. In A. J. Daly (Ed.), *Social network theory and educational change* (pp. 115–126). Cambridge, MA: Harvard Educational Press.

Bidwell, C. E., & Kasarda, J. D. (1980). Conceptualizing and measuring the effects of school and schooling. *American Journal of Education, 88*(4), 401–430.

Bidwell, C. E., & Kasarda, J. D. (1985). *The organization and its ecosystem: A theory of structuring in organizations* (Vol. 2). Greenwich/London: JAI press.

Bidwell, C. E., & Kasarda, J. D. (1987). *Structuring in organizations: Ecosystem theory evaluated.* Greenwich: JAI Press Inc..

Bidwell, C. E., & Yasumoto, J. Y. (1999). The collegial focus: Teaching fields, collegial relationships, and instructional practice in American high schools. *Sociology of Education, 72*, 234–256.

Blau, P. M. (1968). Social exchange. *International Encyclopedia of the Social Sciences, 7*, 452–457.

Brewer, D. D. (2000). Forgetting in the recall-based elicitation of personal and social networks. *Social Networks, 22*, 29–43.

Bridwell-Mitchell, E. N., & Sherer, D. G. (2017). Institutional complexity and policy implementation: How underlying logics drive teacher interpretations of reform. *Educational Evaluation and Policy Analysis, 39*(2), 223–247.

Bryk, A., & Schneider, B. (2002). *Trust in Schools.* New York: Russell Sage.

Bryk, A., Camburn, E., & Louis, K. (1999). Professional community in Chicago elementary schools: Facilitating factors and organizational consequences. *Educational Administration Quarterly, 35*(5), 751–781.

Bryk, A. S., Gomez, L. M., Grunow, A., & LeMahieu, P. G. (2015). *Learning to improve: How America's schools can get better at getting better.* Cambridge, MA: Harvard Education Press.

Callahan, R. E. (1962). *Education and the cult of efficiency.* Chicago: University of Chicago Press.

Camburn, E., Rowan, B., & Taylor, J. E. (2003). Distributed leadership in schools: The case of elementary schools adopting comprehensive school reform models. *Educational Evaluation and Policy Analysis, 25*, 247–273.

Carolan, B. V. (2013). *Social network analysis and education: Theory, methods & applications.* Thousand Oaks: SAGE Publications.

Cho, V. (2016). Administrators' professional learning via Twitter: The dissonance between beliefs and actions. *Journal of Educational Administration, 54*(3), 340–356.

Cho, V., Ro, J., & Littenberg-Tobias, J. (2013). What Twitter will and will not do: Theorizing about teachers' online professional communities. *Learning Landscapes, 6*(2), 45–62.

Christakis, N., & Fowler, J. (2007). The spread of obesity in a large social network over 32 years. *The New England Journal of Medicine, 357*, 370–379.

Christakis, N., & Fowler, J. (2008). The collective dynamics of smoking in a large social network. *The New England Journal of Medicine, 358*, 249–258.

Cobb, P., & Jackson, K. (2011). Towards an empirically grounded theory of action for improving the quality of mathematics teaching at scale. *Mathematics Teacher Education and Development, 13*(1), 6–33.

Coburn, C. E. (2005). Shaping teacher sensemaking: School leaders and the enactment of reading policy. *Educational Policy, 19*(3), 476–509.

Coburn, C. E., & Russell, J. (2008). District policy and teachers' social networks. *Educational Evaluation and Policy Analysis, 30*(3), 203–235.

Coburn, C. E., & Woulfin, S. L. (2012). Reading coaches and the relationship between policy and practice. *Reading Research Quarterly, 47*(1), 5–30.

Coburn, C. E., Choi, L., & Mata, W. (2010). "I would go to her because her mind is math": Network formation in the context of mathematics reform. In A. J. Daly (Ed.), *Social network theory and educational change* (pp. 33–50). Cambridge, MA: Harvard Educational Press.

Coburn, C. E., Russell, J. L., Kaufman, J., & Stein, M. K. (2012). Supporting sustainability: Teachers' advice networks and ambitious instructional reform. *American Journal of Education, 119*(1), 137–182.

Coburn, C. E., Mata, W., & Choi, L. (2013). The embeddedness of teachers' social networks: Evidence from mathematics reform. *Sociology of Education, 86*(4), 311–342.

Cohen-Cole, E., & Fletcher, J. M. (2008a). Is obesity contagious? Social networks vs environmental factors in the obesity epidemic. *Journal of Health Economics, 27*(5), 1382–1387.

Cohen-Cole, E., & Fletcher, J. M. (2008b). Detecting implausible social network effects in acne, height, and headaches: Longitudinal analysis. *British Medical Journal, 337*(a), 2533.

Cole, R. P., & Weinbaum, E. H. (2010). Changes in attitude: Peer influence in high school reform. In A. J. Daly (Ed.), *Social network theory and educational change* (pp. 77–95). Cambridge, MA: Harvard Educational Press.

Cole, R., & Weiss, M. (2009). Identifying organizational influentials: Methods and application using social network data. *Connections, 29*(2), 45–61.

Coleman, J. S. (1961). *The adolescent society: The social life of teenagers and its impact on education*. Glencoe: Free Press of Glencoe.

Coleman, J. S. (1988). Social capital in the creation of human capital. *American Journal of Sociology, 94*(S), 95–120.

Csermely, P., London, A., Wu, L. Y., & Uzzi, B. (2013). Structure and dynamics of core/periphery networks. *Journal of Complex Networks, 1*(2), 93–123.

Daly, Alan J., Moolenaar, Nienke M., Bolivar, Jose M. & Burke, Peggy (2010, April 13). Relationships in reform—The role of teachers' social networks. *Journal of Educational Administration, 48*(3), 359–391.

Daly, A. J. (Ed.). (2010). *Social network theory and educational change* (Vol. 8). Cambridge, MA: Harvard Education Press.

Daly, A. J. (2012). Data, dyads, and dynamics: Exploring data use and social networks in educational improvement. *Teachers College Record, 114*(11), 1–38.

Daly, A. J., & Finnigan, K. S. (2010). A bridge between worlds: Understanding network structure to understand change strategy. *Journal of Educational Change, 11*(2), 111–138.

Daly, A. J., & Finnigan, K. (2011). The ebb and flow of social network ties between district leaders under high stakes accountability. *American Educational Research Journal, 48*, 39–79.

Daly, A. J., & Finnigan, K. (2016). *Thinking and acting systemically: Improving school districts under pressure*. Washington, DC: American Educational Research Association.

Daly, A. J., Finnigan, K. S., Moolenaar, N. M., & Che, J. (2014a). The critical role of brokers in the access and use of evidence at the school and district level. In K. S. Finnigan & A. J. Daly (Eds.), *Using research evidence in education*. New York: Springer.

Daly, A. J., Finnigan, K., Moolenaar, N., & Jing, C. (2014b). Misalignment and perverse incentives: Examining the role of district leaders as brokers in the use of research evidence. *Educational Policy, 28*(2), 145–174.

Desimone, L. M., Porter, A. C., Garet, M. S., Yoon, K. S., & Birman, B. F. (2002). Effects of professional development on teachers' instruction: Results from a three-year longitudinal study. *Educational Evaluation and Policy Analysis, 24*(2), 81–112.

Dreeben, R., & Barr, R. (1988). Classroom composition and the design of instruction. *Sociology of Education, 61*(3), 129–142.

Finnigan, K. S., & Daly, A. J. (2012). Mind the gap: Organizational learning and improvement in an underperforming urban system. *American Journal of Education, 119*(1), 41–71.

Finnigan, K. S., Daly, A. J., & Che, J. (2013). Systemwide reform in districts under pressure: The role of social networks in defining, acquiring, using, and diffusing research evidence. *Journal of Educational Administration, 51*(4), 476–497.

Frank, K. A. (1995). Identifying cohesive subgroups. *Social Networks, 17*, 27–56.

Frank, K. A. (1996). Mapping interactions within and between cohesive subgroups. *Social Networks, 18*, 93–119.

Frank, K. A. (1998). The social context of schooling: Quantitative methods. *Review of Research in Education, 23*(5), 171–216.

Frank, K. A. (2009). Quasi-ties: Directing resources to members of a collective. *American Behavioral Scientist, 52*, 1613–1645.

Frank, K. A., & Xu, R. (2018). Causal inference. In R. Light & J. Moody (Eds.), *The Oxford Handbook of Social Networks*. Oxford: Oxford University Press.

Frank, K. A., & Zhao, Y. (2005). Subgroups as a meso-level entity in the social organization of schools. In L. Hedges & B. Schneider (Eds.), *Social organization of schools* (pp. 279–318). New York: Sage.

Frank, K. A., Zhao, Y., & Borman, K. (2004). Social capital and the diffusion of innovations within organizations: The case of computer technology in schools. *Sociology of Education, 77*(2), 148–171.

Frank, K. A., Muller, C., Schiller, K. S., Riegle-Crumb, C., Strassman, M. A., Crosnoe, R., & Pearson, J. (2008). The social dynamics of mathematics coursetaking in high school. *American Journal of Sociology, 113*(6), 1645–1696.

Frank, K. A., Kim, C., & Belman, D. (2010). Utility theory, social networks, and teacher decision making. In A. J. Daly (Ed.), *Social network theory and educational change* (pp. 223–242). Cambridge, MA: Harvard University Press.

Frank, K. A., Zhao, Y., Penuel, W. R., Ellefson, N. C., & Porter, S. (2011). Focus, fiddle, and friends: Sources of knowledge to perform the complex task of teaching. *Sociology of Education, 84*(2), 137–156.

Frank, K. A., Muller, C., & Mueller, A. S. (2013a). The embeddedness of adolescent friendship nominations: The formation of social capital in emergent network structures. *American Journal of Sociology, 119*(1), 216–253.

Frank*, K. A., Penuel*, W. R., Sun, M., Kim, C., & Singleton, C. (2013b). The organization as a filter of institutional diffusion. *Teacher's College Record, 115*(1), 306–339. *co-equal authors.

Frank, K. A., Lo, Y., & Sun, M. (2014). Social network analysis of the influences of educational reforms on teachers' practices and interactions. *Zeitschrift für Erziehungswissenschaft, 17*(5 supplement): 117–134.

Frank, K. A., Penuel, W. R., & Krause, A. (2015). What is a "good" social network for policy implementation? The flow of know-how for organizational change. *Journal of Policy Analysis and Management, 34*(2), 378–402.

Freeman, L. C. (1978). Centrality in social networks: Conceptual clarification. *Social Networks, 1*, 215–239.

Friedkin, N. E., & Marsden, P. (1994). Network studies of social influence. In S. Wasserman & J. Galaskiewicz (Eds.), *Advances in social network analysis* (pp. 1–25). Thousand Oaks: Sage.

Friedkin, N. E., & Slater, M. R. (1994). School leadership and performance: A social network approach. *Sociology of Education, 67*, 139–157.

Fullan, M. (1993). *Change forces: Probing the depths of educational reform*. London: Falmer Press.

Gamoran, A., Gunter, R., & Williams, T. (2005). Professional community by design: Building social capital through teacher professional development. *The Social Organization of Schooling*, 111–126.

Garet, M. S., Porter, A. C., Desimone, L., Birman, B. F., & Yoon, K. S. (2001). What makes professional development effective? Results from a national sample of teachers. *American Educational Research Journal, 38*(4), 915–945.

Goddard, Y. L., Goddard, R. D., & Tschannen-Moran, M. (2007). Theoretical and empirical investigation of teacher collaboration for school improvement and student achievement in public elementary schools. *Teachers College Record, 109*(4), 877–896.

Greenfield, T. B. (1975). Theory about organization: A new perspective and its implications for schools. In R. Campbell & R. Gregg (Eds.), *Administrative behavior in education*. London: Athlone.

Henry, A. D., Lubell, M., & McCoy, M. (2012). Survey-based measurement of public management and policy networks. *Journal of Policy Analysis and Management, 31*(2), 432–452.

Hite, J. M., Williams, E. J., & Baugh, S. B. (2005). Multiple networks of public school administrators: An analysis of network content and structure. *International Journal of Leadership in Education, 8*(2), 91–122.

Hoff, P. D. (2005). Bilinear mixed-effects models for dyadic data. *Journal of the American Statistical Association, 100*(469), 286–295.

Hoff, P. D., Raftery, A. E., & Handcock, M. S. (2002). Latent space approaches to social network analysis. *Journal of the American Statistical Association, 97*(460), 1090–1098.

Hong, Q., Youngs, P., & Frank, K. A. (2013). Collective responsibility for learning: Effects on interactions between novice teachers and colleagues. *Journal of Educational Change, 14*(4), 445–464.

Honig, M. I. (2003). Building policy from practice: District central office administrators' roles and capacity for implementing collaborative education policy. *Educational Administration Quarterly, 39*(3), 292–338.

Honig, M. I. (2006). Street-level bureaucracy revisited: Frontline district central office administrators as boundary spanners in education policy implementation. *Educational Evaluation and Policy Analysis, 28*(4), 357–383.

Hopkins, M., & Spillane, J. P. (2014). Schoolhouse teacher educators: Structuring beginning teachers' opportunities to learn about instruction. *Journal of Teacher Education, 65*(4), 327–339.

Hopkins, M., Spillane, J. P., Jakopovic, P., & Heaton, R. M. (2013). Infrastructure redesign and instructional reform in mathematics: Formal structure and teacher leadership. *Elementary School Journal, 114*(2), 200–224.

Hord, S. M. (1997). *Professional learning communities: Communities of continuous inquiry and improve-*

ment. Austin: Southwest Educational Development Laboratory.

Horn, I. S., & Kane, B. D. (2015). Opportunities for professional learning in mathematics teacher workgroup conversations: Relationships to instructional expertise. *Journal of the Learning Sciences, 24*(3), 373–418.

Horn, I. S., Chen, I.-C., Garner, B., & Frank, K. A. (2017). *From conversation to collaboration: How the quality of teacher workgroup meetings influences social networks.* Paper presented at the annual meeting of the American Educational Research Association, San Antonio, Texas.

Hu, S., & Torphy, K. (2016). Teachers' active engagement in social media: Evaluating the nature of mathematical practices within Pinterest (Poster presentation). In *Proceedings of the 38th annual meeting of the North-American chapter of the international group for the Psychology of Mathematics Education (PME-NA 38),* Tucson, Arizona.

Hunter, D. R., Goodreau, S. M., & Handcock, M. S. (2008). Goodness of fit of social network models. *Journal of the American Statistical Association, 103*(481), 248–258.

Kaufman, J. H., Thompson, L. E., & Opfer, V. D. (2016). *Creating a coherent system to support instruction aligned with state standards.* RAND Corporation. Retrieved from: https://www.rand.org/content/dam/rand/pubs/research_reports/RR1600/RR1613/RAND_RR1613.pdf

Kwon, S. W., & Adler, P. S. (2014). Social capital: Maturation of a field of research. *Academy of Management Review, 39*(4), 412–422.

Lave, J., & Wenger, E. (1991). *Situated learning: Legitimate peripheral participation.* Cambridge: Cambridge University Press.

Lazega, E., & van Duijn, M. (1997). Position in formal structure, personal characteristics and choices of advisors in a law firm: A logistic regression model for dyadic network data. *Social Networks, 19,* 375–397.

Leana, C., & Pil, F. (2006). Social capital and organizational performance: Evidence from urban public schools. *Organization Science, 17*(3), 353–366.

Leenders, R. (1995). *Structure and influence: Statistical models for the dynamics of actor attributes, network structure and their interdependence.* Amsterdam: Thesis Publishers.

Lieberman, A. (2000). Networks as learning communities: Shaping the future of teacher development. *Journal of Teacher Education, 51,* 221–227.

Lieberman, A., & Wood, D. R. (2002). The National Writing Project. *Educational Leadership, 59*(6), 40–43.

Lieberman, A., & Wood, D. (2004). The work of the National Writing Project: Social practices in a network context. In F. Hernandez & I. F. Goodson (Eds.), *Social geographies of educational change* (pp. 47–63). Dordrecht: Kluwer.

Lima, J. D. (2010). Studies of networks in education: Methods for collecting and managing high-quality data. In A. J. Daly (Ed.), *Social network theory and educational change* (pp. 243–258). Cambridge, MA: Harvard Educational Press.

Lin, N. (2002). *Social capital: A theory of social structure and action* (Vol. 19). Cambridge: Cambridge University Press.

Little, J. W. (2006). *Professional community and professional development in the learning-centered school.* Arlington: National Education Association.

Louis, K. S., Marks, H. M., & Kruse, S. (1996). Professional community in restructuring schools. *American Educational Research Journal, 33*(4), 757–798.

Lyons, R. (2011). The spread of evidence-poor medicine via flawed social-network analysis. *Statistics, Politics and Policy, 2*(1).

Macià, M., & García, I. (2016). Informal online communities and networks as a source of teacher professional development: A review. *Teaching and Teacher Education, 55,* 291–307.

Marsden, P. V. (2011). Survey methods for network data. In J. Scott & P. Carrington (Eds.), *The SAGE handbook of social network analysis* (pp. 370–388). London: SAGE Publications.

McPherson, M., Smith-Lovin, L., & Cook, J. M. (2001). Birds of a feather: Homophily in social networks. *Annual Review of Sociology, 27,* 415–444.

Meyer, J., & Rowan, B. (1977). Institutionalized organizations: Formal structure as myth and ceremony. *American Journal of Sociology, 30,* 431–450.

Moolenaar, N. M. (2012). A social network perspective on teacher collaboration in schools: Theory, methodology, and applications. *American Journal of Education, 119*(1), 7–39.

Moolenaar, N. M., & Sleegers, P. J. C. (2015). The networked principal: Examining principals' social relationships and transformational leadership in school and district networks. *Journal of Educational Administration, 53*(1), 8–39.

Moolenaar, N., & Sleegers, P. J. C. (2010). Social networks, trust, and innovation. How social relationships support trust and innovative climates in Dutch schools. In A. J. Daly (Ed.), *Social network theory and educational change* (pp. 97–114). Cambridge, MA: Harvard University Press.

Moolenaar, N. M., Daly, A. J., & Sleegers, P. J. C. (2010a). Occupying the principal position: Innovation in schools. *Educational Administration Quarterly, 46,* 623–670.

Moolenaar, N. M., Daly, A. J., & Sleegers, P. J. C. (2010b). Ties with potential: Social network structure and innovation climate in Dutch schools. *Teacher College Record, 113*(9), 1983–2017.

Moolenaar, N. M., Sleegers, P. J., & Daly, A. J. (2012). Teaming up: Linking collaboration networks, collective efficacy, and student achievement. *Teaching and Teacher Education., 28*(2), 251–262.

National Writing Project. (2016). http://www.nwp.org/cs/public/print/doc/nwpsites/summer_institute.csp

Noble, A., McQuillan, P., & Littenberg-Tobias, J. (2016). A lifelong classroom: Social studies educators' engagement with professional learning networks on Twitter. *Journal of Technology and Teacher Education, 24*(2), 187–213.

Nonaka, I. (1994). A dynamic theory of organizational knowledge creation. *Organization Science, 5*(1), 14–37.

Nye, B., Konstantopoulos, S., & Hedges, L. V. (2004). How large are teacher effects? *Educational Evaluation and Policy Analysis, 26*, 237–257.

Penuel, W. R., Riel, M., Krause, A., & Frank, K. A. (2009). Analyzing teachers' professional interactions in a school as social capital: A social network approach. *Teachers College Record, 111*(1), 124–163.

Penuel, W. R., Riel, M., Joshi, A., & Frank, K. A. (2010). The alignment of the informal and formal supports for school reform: Implications for improving teaching in schools. *Educational Administration Quarterly, 46*(1), 57–95.

Penuel, W. R., Sun, M., Frank, K. A., & Gallagher, H. A. (2012). Using social network analysis to study how collegial interactions can augment teacher learning from external professional development. *American Journal of Education, 119*(1), 103–136.

Pil, F. K., & Leana, C. (2009). Applying organizational research to public school reform: The effects of teacher human and social capital on student performance. *Academy of Management Journal, 52*(6), 1101–1124.

Pitts, V., & Spillane, J. P. (2009). Using social network methods to study school leadership. *International Journal of Research and Method in Education, 32*(2), 185–207.

Pogodzinski, B., Youngs, P., Frank, K. A., & Belman, D. (2012). Administrative climate and novices' intent to remain teaching. *Elementary School Journal, 113*(2), 252–275.

Pogodzinski, B., Youngs, P., & Frank, K. A. (2013). Collegial climate and novice teachers' intent to remain teaching. *American Journal of Education, 120*(1), 27–54.

Portes, A. (1998). Social capital: Its origins and applications in modern sociology. *Annual Review of Sociology., 24*(1), 1–24.

Portes, A., & Sensenbrenner, J. (1993). Embeddedness and immigration: Notes on the social determinants of economic action. *American Journal of Sociology, 98*(6), 1320–1350.

Powell, A. G., Farrar, E., & Cohen, D. K. (1985). *The shopping mall high school: Winners and losers in the educational marketplace.* Boston: Houghton Mifflin.

Resnick, L. B., & Scherrer, J. (2012). Social networks in "Nested Learning Organizations": A commentary. *American Journal of Education, 119*(1), 183–192.

Rigby, J. G. (2016). Principals' conceptions of instructional leadership and their informal social networks: An exploration of the mechanisms of the mesolevel. *American Journal of Education, 122*(3), 433–464.

Rigby, J. G., Larson, C., and Chen, I.-C. (2014). *Shifting teacher views of mathematics instruction and student struggle: A mixed-methods analysis.* Paper presented

at the annual meeting of the American Educational Research Association, Philadelphia, PA.

Rigby, J. G., Larson, C., & Chen, I.-C. (Under review). Administrators' influence on teachers' conversations about the problem of teaching mathematics: A longitudinal case study.

Rogers, E. M. (2010). *Diffusion of innovations.* New York: Simon and Schuster.

Ronfeldt, M., Farmer, S. O., McQueen, K., & Grissom, J. A. (2015). Teacher collaboration in instructional teams and student achievement. *American Educational Research Journal, 52*(3), 475–514.

Rowan, B. (1995). The organizational design of schools. In S. B. Bacharach & B. Mundell (Eds.), *Images of schools* (pp. 11–42). Thousand Oaks: Corwin Press, Inc..

Russell, J., Jackson, K., Krumm, A., and Frank, K. (2013). Theories and research methodologies for design-based implementation research: Examples from four cases. In B. J. Fishman, W. R. Penuel, A.-R. Allen, & B. H. Cheng (Eds.), *Design based implementation research: Theories, methods, and exemplars. National Society for the Study of Education Yearbook* (Vol. 112, Issue 2, pp. 157–191). New York: Teachers College.

Schneider, B. (2015). 2014 AERA presidential address: The college ambition program: A realistic transition strategy for traditionally disadvantaged students. *Educational Researcher, 44*(7), 394–403.

Selznick, P. (1948). Foundations of the theory of organization. *American Sociological Review, 13*(1), 25–35.

Spillane, J. P. (1996). School districts matter: Local educational authorities and state instructional policy. *Educational Policy, 10*(1), 63–87.

Spillane, J. P., & Healey, K. (2010). Conceptualizing school leadership and management from a distributed perspective: An exploration of some study operations and measures. *Elementary School Journal, 11*(2), 253–281.

Spillane, J. P., & Kim, C. M. (2012). An exploratory analysis of formal school leaders' positioning in instructional advice and information networks in elementary schools. *American Journal of Education, 119*(1), 73–102.

Spillane, J. P., Shirrell, M., & Sweet, T. M. (2017). The elephant in the schoolhouse: The role of propinquity in school staff interactions about teaching. *Sociology of Education, 90*(2), 149–171.

Spillane, J. P., Halverson, R. R., & Diamond, J. B. (2001). Investigating school leadership practice: A distributed perspective. *Educational Researcher, 30*, 23–27.

Spillane, J. P., Healey, K., & Kim, C. M. (2010). Leading and managing instruction: Formal and informal aspects of the elementary school organization. In A. J. Daly (Ed.), *Social Network Theory and Educational Change* (pp. 129–158). Cambridge, MA: Harvard Educational Press.

Spillane, J. P., Kim, C. M., & Frank, K. A. (2012). Instructional advice and information seeking behavior in elementary schools: Exploring tie formation as a building block in social capital development. *American Educational Research Journal, 49*(6), 1112–1145.

Stoll, L., & Louis, K. (2007). *Professional learning communities: Divergence, depth and dilemmas.* Maidenhead: Open University Press.

Sun, M., Frank, K. A., Penuel, W. R., & Kim, C. (2013a). How external institutions penetrate schools through formal and informal leaders? *Educational Administration Quarterly, 49*(4), 610–644.

Sun, M., Penuel, W. R., Frank, K. A., Gallagher, H. A., & Youngs, P. (2013b). Shaping professional development to promote the diffusion of instructional expertise among teachers. *Educational Evaluation and Policy Analysis, 35*(3), 344–369.

Sun, M., Wilhelm, A. G., Larson, C. J., & Frank, K. A. (2014). Exploring colleagues' professional influence on mathematics teachers' learning. *Teachers College Record, 116*(6).

Supovitz, J. A., Sirinides, P., & May, H. (2010). How principals and peers influence teaching and learning. *Educational Administration Quarterly, 46*, 31–56.

Supovitz, J. A., Fink, R., & Newman, B. (2014). *From the inside in: An examination of common core knowledge and communication in schools* (CPRE Working Paper).

Sweet, T. M., Thomas, A. C., & Junker, B. W. (2013). Hierarchical network models for education research: Hierarchical latent space models. *Journal of Educational and Behavioral Statistics, 38*(3), 295–318.

Thomas, A. (2007). Teacher attrition, social capital, and career advancement: An unwelcome message. *Research and Practice in Social Sciences, 3*(1), 19–47.

Torphy, K. and Hu, S. (2016). Teachers' active engagement in social media: Conceptualizing mathematical practices within Pinterest (Poster presentation). In *Proceedings of the 38th annual meeting of the North-American chapter of the International Group for the Psychology of Mathematics Education (PME-NA 38)*, Tucson, AZ.

Torphy, K., Hu, S., Chen, Z., Liu, Y., & Jurasek, A. (2016a). *Teachers' active engagement in social media: A comparison of network interactions across physical and virtual spaces.* Paper presented at the 36th Sunbelt conference of the International Network for Social Network Analysis. Newport Beach, CA.

Torphy, K., Hu, S., Liu, Y., Chen, Z., & Martin, K. (2016b) *Teacherpreneurial behaviors in social media.* Paper presented at the Second European Conference on Social Networks. Paris, France.

Wilhelm, A. G., Chen, I.-C., Smith, T. M., & Frank, K. A. (2016). Selecting expertise in context: Middle school mathematics teachers' selection of new sources of instructional advice. *American Educational Research Journal, 53*(3), 456–491.

Wood, D. R. (2007). Teachers' learning communities: Catalyst for change or a new infrastructure for the status quo? *Teachers College Record, 109*(3), 699–739.

Yasumoto, J. Y., Uekawa, K., & Bidwell, C. (2001). The collegial focus and student achievement: Consequences of high school faculty social organization for students on achievement in mathematics and science. *Sociology of Education, 74*, 181–209.

Yoon, S., Koehler-Yom, J., Yang, L., & Liu, L. (in press). The effects of teachers' social and human capital on urban science reform initiatives: Considerations for professional development. *Teachers College Record.*

Yoon, S. A., & Baker-Doyle, K. J. (2018). *Networked by design: Interventions for teachers to develop social capital.* New York: Taylor & Francis/Routledge.

Zeng, Z., & Xie, Y. (2008). A preference-opportunity-choice framework with applications to intergroup friendship. *American Journal of Sociology, 114*(3), 615–648.

The Social Contexts of High Schools

Robert Crosnoe, Lilla Pivnick, and Aprile D. Benner

Abstract

In addition to their roles as educational institutions structuring human capital development during a critical period of socioeconomic attainment, high schools organize the peer contexts in which young people come of age during a critical period of development. Consequently, understanding the peer processes that characterize the social contexts of schools sheds light on how schools are operating as formal institutions of teaching and learning. This chapter provides an overview of research from sociologists of education and scholars in other disciplines about the social contexts of high schools and their relevance to curricula, achievement, and other formal processes of schooling. After using three key books in this field to trace the historical evolution of thinking about the social contexts of high schools, we describe key components of these contexts (peer networks, peer crowds, school climate) and then discuss the value of greater attention to them in educational policy and practice.

R. Crosnoe (✉) · L. Pivnick · A. D. Benner
University of Texas, Austin, TX, USA
e-mail: crosnoe@prc.utexas.edu;
abenner@prc.utexas.edu

Of the core subjects within the sociology of education, the social contexts of high schools have arguably been the most prominently featured in popular culture. In hit movies like *The Breakfast Club* and *Mean Girls*, acclaimed television shows like *Glee* and *Freaks and Geeks*, and bestselling novels like *Gossip Girl* and *Pretty Little Liars* can be found earnest depictions, scathing satires, and light-hearted lampooning of how high schools are socially structured. What this popular culture tends to get right is the complex social ecology of high schools—how they are organized around multiple groups with meaningful identities that define the prevailing norms and values to which adolescents entering the school are exposed. What it tends to get wrong is its overemphasis on the negative aspects of this social ecology—how it is enforced by intimidation and bullying, demands conformity and chokes independence, and leaves psychic scars long after graduation. The extensive social science research that both reflects and drives this public fascination with the dark side of high school, however, provides a much more well-rounded view of the social contexts of high schools, including how they develop and are maintained and why they matter to students in the short and long term—neither all bad nor all good but much closer to the everyday reality of going to high school.

In this chapter, we delve into this literature by describing the current state of the field and tracing how we got here. In one common view among sociologists, high school social context refers to the collective structure, organization, and tone of social relations within a school that influence the academic progress and general development of students. This view is conceptually complementary to the idea of the school as an educational context. In this sense, the school is an organizational mechanism of *human capital* development defined by *formal processes*, which refer to the concrete inputs and outputs of the official mission of the educational system to produce a skilled labor force and informed populace. As an educational context, the school is structured by curricula around pedagogical goals and is evaluated by quantifiable metrics of academic progress. Sociologists of education have played a substantial role in constructing the current knowledge base about how schools work as educational contexts and their impact on the socioeconomic attainment of students (Arum 2000). The social contexts of high schools, on the other hand, tap into the interpersonal underpinnings of schools, or what happens when large groups of young people come together for long periods and develop their own social system and how this system shapes their *social and cultural capital* development as well as their *psychological well-being*. As a social context, the school is structured by relationships and relational groupings and is evaluated by often esoteric assessments of what a school is like and what going to a school is like. Sociologists of education have also been a guiding force in building the literature on how schools work as social contexts and their impact on the basic adjustment and functioning of students (Dornbusch et al. 1996). Within the sociology of education, however, the focus on educational contexts has long held primacy over focus on social contexts.

We argue that consideration of the *informal processes* in the social contexts of high schools is fundamental to understanding the *formal processes* in the educational contexts of high schools. The two are clearly related. Although sociological research once largely ignored how formal processes help to organize informal processes, the research that has been done shows that relationship ties in schools are organized in part by the structural and curricular properties of schools (McFarland 2001). Indeed, because propinquity is one of the main drivers of relationship formation and maintenance, formal processes that bring students into the same orbit facilitate friendships and the construction of peer groups, especially when they bring together students of similar academic statuses and family backgrounds (i.e., propinquity x homophily). Examples include the role of course assignments in friendship formation, the link between the more flexible and open instructional programs and greater levels of social integration among students, and the tendency for friendship groups to be more racially segregated in schools that use curricular tracking (McFarland et al. 2014; Kubitschek and Hallinan 1998; see also Epstein and Karweit 1983). Sociological research has also examined the other direction (i.e., how informal processes shape formal processes), and we will cover such research in depth throughout this chapter. For now, we will say that it has shown how school-wide peer cultures and smaller peer networks and cliques can affect—positively or negatively—students' engagement in the formal curricula of schools through value-promotion, modeling, information-sharing, and other mechanisms (Crosnoe 2011; Tyson 2011).

Because of this bidirectionality between the different kinds of contextual processes in schools, research on both—speaking to and learning from each other, even when nominally independent—is necessary to effectively elucidate how schools work in society and the individual life course, perhaps the two major concerns of sociologists of education. In particular, research on the *informal processes* of schooling can inform major *educational policies* and *interventions*, which tend to target the *formal processes* of schooling, by demonstrating how social norms, rituals, and ideologies in a school may undermine seemingly straightforward academic agendas and messages. It also links sociology of education to an array of other sociological traditions (e.g., medical, life course, and cultural sociology) and to an array of other disciplines (e.g., developmental psychology and anthropology), which is important given the value of cross-disciplinary dialogues to good theory and effective *policy* (Crosnoe 2012).

To support this argument, we take a three-fold approach, beginning with a historical review of research on the social contexts of high schools through the lens of three key books published at two-decade-plus intervals, each following a different theoretical tradition. Of course, there have been many other books written on this subject, so the choice of these three is arbitrary. They are key books, not *the* key books. We picked them because we believed that doing so would allow us to cover some of the main concepts, points of discussion, and challenges of this line of research and, more importantly, how thinking about this topic has evolved over the last six decades. Next, we turn to some of the core dimensions of the social contexts of schooling that have organized this field over that same historical period, dimensions that connect the dynamic intimate relations within schools that are most proximate to students' everyday lives to the more stable cultural traditions of the student bodies of schools that are more abstractly understood and experienced. Finally, we end with a discussion of how the contributions of sociologists of education and other social and behavioral scientists to our understanding of the social contexts of high schools have been or could be useful to the development and execution of educational *policy* and practice.

Before getting into these three parts, we should note up front our U.S.-centric focus. We mostly, although not exclusively, cover the literature on U.S. schools for practical purposes. Given the space constraints, we did not think that we could do justice to the rich international literature here (see Buchmann and Dalton 2002; Rohlen 1983; Rutter et al. 1979). We also focus on social relations among students in high schools, even though intergenerational relations within and around schools (e.g., teachers' relationships with each other and with students; parents' relationships with each other, their children, and their children's peers and teachers) are important aspects of the social context of any high school (Frank et al. 2008; Bryk and Schneider 2003; Carbonaro 1998; Lawrence-Lightfoot 1983).

14.1 A History in Three Books

Trying to trace the history of a rich social science literature in a short space is quite a challenge. Too many works could (and probably should) be covered that one never knows where to start or what to include. As already noted, we made the strategic decision to discuss the history of this field through three selected books from three different eras over more than half a century. They were chosen not because they are the most important works in the field but instead because describing them allows us to take readers through the evolution of thinking of scholars of the social contexts of schools—the main concepts that have organized the field and how they have evolved over the years in a cumulative fashion. Importantly, they also cover a range of methods, draw on a variety of disciplinary voices, and have distinctly different tones. Thus, they offer insight into how broad this field is.

Of the three selected books, the first, based on research in the 1950s, was written squarely in the sociology of education tradition, employed a primarily quantitative methodology, and focused on the ways that school social groupings were at cross purposes with the *formal processes* of schooling. The second, based on research in the 1980s, was grounded in linguistics and anthropology, employed a primarily ethnographic methodology, and focused on the dynamic nature of social groupings in high school and how they were shaped by powerful stratification systems in society at large. The third book, based on research in the 2000s, was guided by developmental science, mixed quantitative and qualitative methodologies, and focused on how developing youth adapt to the social groupings of their schools in ways that have implications for the *formal processes* of schooling. Again, these books were selected for strategic reasons, and our focus on them neither negates nor downplays the importance of books that were not selected. Key examples include Willard Waller's pioneering *The Sociology of Teaching* in the 1920s that really marked the beginning of sociological analysis of schools, Paul Willis' *Learning to Labor* in the 1970s that used British schools to show how schools could be sites of counterculture, and, more recently, Murray Milner's *Freaks, Geeks, and Cool Kids* that linked the social worlds of high schools to the broader consumerist youth culture in our new century.

14.1.1 Coleman's *The Adolescent Society*

In 1961, James Coleman published *The Adolescent Society: The Social Life of the Teenager and its Impact on Education*, perhaps the most influential work in the history of research on the *social contexts* of schooling. It was set during the apex of the industrialized economy and the post-World War II political climate in which education became central to national primacy in the new world order. In this setting, schooling had become time-consuming and disconnected from the home environment, leading children to spend less time with parents and more time with their same-age peers so that they ultimately created their own cultures—separate from *adults*—with unique norms of appropriate behavior, *status*, and social rewards.

Studying nine primarily White public and private schools of varying sizes in and around Chicago in the late 1950s, Coleman collected data from observations, interviews with parents and students, surveys, and school records. Perhaps most provocatively and memorably, this work revealed *anti-academic* values in high school *peer cultures* that Coleman characterized as universal. These universal values were out of sync with the educational mission of their schools, as peers devalued *academic achievement* and glorified non-academic pursuits, especially *athletics*, risky (but not too risky) behavior, and attitudes that were oppositional to adults. Gaining *status* in the social hierarchies organized around these values was the primary preoccupation of most students, and success in doing so was a major factor in adolescents' *psychological well-being*. Students who were not successful had to look elsewhere for confirmation and support, especially among deviant peer groups ostracized

by young and old alike. These dynamics, however, were deeply *gendered*.

The story for *boys* was fairly simple. Their *peer networks* were straightforwardly organized and similar from school to school, and the same types of *boys* were socially prominent in every school. Coleman highlighted the strong connection between schools' athletic successes and school identity, which became the focal point for boys' self-assessments as well as how they were assessed by girls and other boys. The centrality of *athletic achievement* in the adolescent society was most clearly evidenced by the proportion of male athletes in leading *crowds*. Some school *peer cultures* that Coleman studied did stress the importance of the "all-around *boy*" who was both academically and athletically successful, but male students in all high schools had better *self-esteem* and were better liked and more admired by their peers when they were athletically successful.

For girls, *peer networks* were far more complex, crossed grade levels, and had a fluid hierarchy, with more groups jockeying for power. Social *status* was predicated on *popularity* with the opposite sex, physical *attractiveness*, and involvement in school activities. Although *academic achievement* had more social value for girls than boys, it was clearly less important than these other considerations for girls. Moreover, girls were forced into a tricky balance of doing well academically without being bookish. Across high schools, girls faced another strong double standard. Unlike boys, they were expected to maintain a good reputation socially and sexually. At the same time, being deemed as attractive to boys was key to their social success, and boys tended to find most attractive the girls who skirted the rules, had a "little fun," and were not too conforming to adult expectations. In the face of the mixed messages, the girls in the study enjoyed school less and had lower *self-esteem* than *boys*.

By shedding light on the consistently problematic values of high school *social contexts*, Coleman hoped to prescribe ways in which schools could positively shift *peer cultures* toward rewarding academic success and realizing school goals. For example, he suggested that educators take advantage of the role of inter-school competition in sports to raise the value of academics by creating academic leagues. He also suggested that schools compete among themselves for students through entrance exams and other requirements so that students might take on the academically competitive personality of the school as their own. In these and other ways, adults could use the extant competitive relationships among schools to frame academic success as a *status* symbol and, in the process, shift student attention back to academics.

In sum, *The Adolescent Society* sketched out the key idea of the interplay between the *informal and formal processes* of schooling and how failure to attend to the former severely undermined efforts to promote the latter. This idea revealed the hidden weakness of many educational *policies*, academic programs, and school goals. In Coleman's rendering, this interplay was nearly always bad in practice (i.e., the *informal* undermining the *formal*) but could be leveraged in more positive ways. Other contributions of this work were Coleman's articulation of how different peer groups within schools were arranged into a social hierarchy, his demonstration of how *gendered* the social contexts of high schools were, his innovative use of school-based data collection techniques geared at giving adolescents their own voices, and his argument that adolescents were agentic architects of their own social worlds and worldviews.

14.1.2   Eckert's *Jocks and Burnouts*

In 1989, the publication of *Jocks and Burnouts: Social Categories and Identity in the High School* by Penelope Eckert was another milestone in the evolution of the field of research on the social contexts of high schools. Eckert essentially dug down into the peer groupings that made up the social contexts of high schools while also expanding her focus to connect the social structure of adolescent society within the school to the social structure of adult society outside the school. In the process, she demonstrated the diversity in norms and values within high schools and articu-lated how *status* could be gained through social systems both aligned with and in opposition to the educational goals institutionalized by schools.

Over the course of two years, Eckert—a linguist—conducted both participatory and non-participatory observations of school activities and interactions as well as group and individual interviews in four high schools in suburban Detroit. Across these diverse schools, she saw a great deal of similarity, much like Coleman did decades before in the Chicago area. Yet, the similar social contexts across schools were organized around two separate poles dominated by different social categories of students with different orientations to academics. Each category encompassed a large group of young people in the school who gravitated together, shared a similar social space in the school, and identified with each other. Moreover, they were generally connected to different *social classes*. The *jocks* were students who had a cooperative relationship with the school and its staff, shared the goals of the school, and centered their lives around school. In other words, they relied on the school to define their personal identities. *Jocks* were primarily from *middle-class* families, and their pursuits were well-aligned with the *middle-class* cultural emphasis on meritocracy and school as an institution for social mobility. On the other hand, *burnouts* had adversarial relationships with school personnel and kept their social identities separate from the school. Primarily from the *working class*, they saw the school institution as a factory for producing college-bound students who would eventually take on *middle-class* jobs, reifying the existing social order that had already marginalized them. Thus, they saw schools as devaluing and disempowering them, and they developed oppositional attitudes. Each of the two categories could be characterized by distinctive tastes in clothing, substance use, school territory, ideas about friendship, and attitudes about adults. Students primarily interacted with and were loyal to people in their same categories, and they developed in-group/out-group distinctions that divided the school along those social lines.

The important points to stress about the *jocks* and *burnouts* are, first, that they demonstrate how not all aspects of high school contexts are *anti-academic* and oppositional to adults and, second, that such attitudes and norms do not emerge from a vacuum. The *jocks* were aligned with adult culture and its academic emphasis due to the socioeconomic stratification within public education and the link between education and future attainment. The school was an adult-facilitated environment in which adolescents had freedom to create their own rules, hierarchies, and ideologies. Students like the *jocks* capitalized on their greater access to teachers' trust and admiration to bargain for special privileges and information. Adhering to the academic priorities of school personnel only helped them, whether they truly cared about those priorities or not, while activities that could interfere with how they were favored *by adults were* avoided. The institution catered to *middle-class* students like them, which they used to get ahead. Students like the *burnouts* considered themselves left out of the educational mission of schools and looked down upon by school personnel, so they rejected schools' academic priorities, saw students who accepted these priorities as adult puppets, and granted social *status* in inverse relation to having *status* in the school at large. Not only did they de-identify with academic success, they identified with *anti-academic* pursuits, such as delinquency and substance use.

In sum, *Jocks and Burnouts* helped to undermine the idea that there was a monolithic *peer culture* that organized the social contexts of high schools, highlighted how social groupings within high schools were connected to larger *class* structures, and emphasized the power of *identity* (both in terms of group identities and how young people worked on their own *identity* development within groups). Eckert's rich description of high school life got us closer to the contemporary notion of schools as contexts of human development—organized by *class* and other stratifying systems—and potentially detrimental to or supportive of the educational missions of schools and the educational prospects of young people. Eckert spent less time articulating specific *policy* implications of this work, enforcing the idea that the social contexts of high schools are important to understand for theoretical reasons and not just

because they can be leveraged to affect the academic bottom line of schools.

14.1.3 Crosnoe's *Fitting In, Standing Out*

The (2011) book, *Fitting in, Standing Out: Navigating the Social Challenges of High School to Get an Education*, was written by the first author of this chapter, Robert Crosnoe, so we apologize if its inclusion in this discussion seems self-aggrandizing. It was conceptualized specifically to build on the work of Coleman and Eckert in an interdisciplinary way that we thought that it would be useful for helping connect past to present in this field. Like *The Adolescent Society*, it is situated in a "new" historical moment with implications for what education represents for individuals and society. Its twenty-first century context is characterized by increased demographic diversity, greater differentiation in course offerings, rapidly developing *social media*, and stronger economic returns to schooling that have made schools bigger, more heterogeneous, more impersonal, more competitive, and less physically bounded. As a result, what happens in the social contexts of high schools can have short-term academic consequences that are then more consequential for the rest of life.

Using both quantitative evidence from a nationally representative sample and qualitative data from in-school interviews and observations in a single public high school in Texas, *Fitting In, Standing Out* sheds light on the importance of social development within the *peer cultures* of a high school during the hyper-social period of adolescence and how it can influence adolescents' academic trajectories with implications long after this period. Crosnoe marshalled this mixed methods evidence to describe a multi-step pathway. Students who felt like they did not "fit in" socially at school—regardless of the actual substance of the values and norms that defined their school social contexts—engaged in counterproductive coping mechanisms that decreased academic engagement in school and, ultimately, lowered their odds of attending *college* after school was over. This pathway was initiated when adolescents gathered and processed information about their own *status* from direct and indirect social feedback, including in face-to-face interactions and on *social media*. If that feedback was negative, it could trigger uncomfortable *identity* discrepancies that students coped with through internalization, self-medication, and disengagement from school. These coping strategies brought relief in the short term but were academically disastrous in the long term, particularly by keeping students from making adequate progress in the highly cumulative curricular sequence that controlled their odds of being accepted to and prepared for *college* when they exited high school. Although the fitting in pathway was particularly relevant to two groups of adolescents at elevated risk for social marginalization, youth who were *obese* and/or *lesbian/gay*, it was generalizable to all adolescents who felt marginalized, whether these perceptions were accurate or not and no matter how academically oriented the peer groups were that they felt alienated from or desired to join.

Importantly, this book did not view the bad side of the social contexts of high schools as inevitable. Crosnoe highlighted several sources of resilience protecting adolescents from feeling marginalized or reacting to such feelings in counterproductive ways, including adult mentoring, activity participation, and religious affiliation. He also used both the vulnerabilities and resources that he identified in the study to discuss possible *policy* avenues for protecting students and more generally ensuring that the *informal processes* of schooling could be harnessed to support rather than undermine the *formal processes*. These avenues included expanding the *extracurriculum*, constraining the range of choices in the academic curriculum, building mentoring relationships in schools, and improving mental health services.

In sum, *Fitting In, Standing Out* reinforced Coleman's messages about the importance of understanding the connection between *informal* and *formal processes* and Eckert's messages about the multi-faceted group structure of high

school social contexts and its links to larger social structures (including *gender* and *sexuality*). It built on both by demonstrating that the risks and rewards of the social contexts of schools go beyond the norms and values of the contexts to encompass all of the work that adolescents have to do to fit into those contexts, meaning that even pro-academic and adult-oriented contexts can undermine academic performance if adolescents' efforts to navigate these contexts distract them from their school pursuits or stress them emotionally. In doing so, it better articulated the mechanisms by which the *identity* development process and academic trajectories influence each other.

14.1.4 Lessons Learned

Across these three books about high school social contexts, we can see a microcosm of the much broader evolution of some basic ideas in the interdisciplinary literature on this subject. These ideas are not solely attributable to these three books, which were part of ongoing dialogues among social and behavioral scientists and should be understood within this diverse field rather than on their own. They include:

- The core unit of these contexts are peer groups with simple but widely recognized identities that are larger than any one student in them, influence students' concrete behaviors, and shape students' self-concepts during a critical developmental period.
- Some of these groups are aligned with conventional adult norms and the academic goals of the educational system, but some are not.
- Regardless, the act of maintaining one's position in these groups can be academically distracting as the work of the social interferes with the work of the academic.
- These influences mean that the *formal* and *informal processes* of schooling are difficult to separate, and educational policies must consider these connections to fully realize their goals.

- How adolescents find themselves in these groups and how they react to them are influenced by their *gender*, *social class*, *sexuality*, and other social and demographic positions, so the social contexts of high schools and their educational importance are part of the intergenerational transmission of inequality.

On this last point about inequality, we should stress that the intergenerational transmission occurs in part because schools tend to be socially organized in ways that reflect and reward some groups over others but also because some groups have more resources and supports to survive the social ups and downs of high school than others, regardless of whether they are favored or not. We should also stress that all three books covered here focused primarily on *gender* and *social class* while paying less attention to *race/ethnicity*, although *race/ethnicity* is clearly a major aspect of the social contexts of high schools and one of the fundamental organizers of schools in the U.S. Other important qualitative and quantitative research on the social contexts of high schools deals with *race/ethnicity* more explicitly (e.g., Harris 2011; Carter 2005; Moody 2001), and we draw on their insights later in this chapter.

14.2   Key Components of High School Social Contexts

During an interview with the first author of this chapter (Crosnoe 2011, p. 38), a 15-year-old boy spoke at length about what going to high school was like for an adolescent and then summed up his thoughts by saying, "The school is just a big building with people in it." His comments captured the lens through which many adolescents perceive and assess their schools—for them, it is all about the people. What matters, however, is not just some *collection* of people but a unique *collective* of people. What turns a number of individual students in a high school into the social context of that high school are the recurring and meaningful patterns of relationships and interactions that unfold over time. Social scientists explore these patterns in different ways on different levels. Below, we highlight some key conceptualizations of the basic components of high school social contexts within sociology of education and related fields, noting up front that they tend to be studied and discussed separately even though they are difficult to disentangle in reality.

14.2.1   Peer Networks

Social network research focuses on the study of the matrix of interpersonal ties within some group or setting. It is grounded in the idea that people in the same shared physical, social, or cultural space tend to become highly interconnected over time. Within that relational matrix, any one person is unlikely to connect to all others, but everyone is likely to be connected to many other people. Even as the matrix changes over time, and as people transition in and out of it, it provides a scaffolding to the social context that is sociologically interesting because of how it is shaped by macro-level forces and how it shapes micro-level processes (Lin et al. 2001; McPherson et al. 2001).

The social network field and the school context field have had a mutually beneficial relationship over the last several decades. As large and often diverse collections of people who remain together over long periods in a concretely bounded space, high schools are ideal settings for network analyses. Indeed, many of the most influential network studies have been in high schools, including the National Longitudinal Study of Adolescent Health, which mapped full networks of over 100 secondary schools in the U.S. (Bearman et al. 1997). In turn, studying how patterns of social relationships in a school evolve over time, are influenced by schools' structural and compositional characteristics, and influence student behavior offers a valuable window into the *informal processes* of schooling at the heart of high school social contexts (Faris and Felmlee 2011). To give a sense of the richness of the literature on high school *peer networks*, we focus on four aspects of networks that illuminate how the social contexts of high schools work:

- Network structure, or the basic topographical features of a network, such as how densely connected people are to each other.
- Network composition, or the individual and collective attributes of the people in a network, such as how racially diverse it is.
- Network norms and values, or the prevailing behavioral and attitudinal patterns in a network that shape the status and integration of individual people, such as the emphasis placed on academic success.
- Network influence, or the degree to which a network shapes the behaviors and attitudes of individual people, such as the higher odds of drinking when surrounded by drinking peers.

As we discuss these four aspects of networks, we will occasionally cross "levels." In the broadest sense, peer networks capture the entire socioemetric "map" of a school—all possible social ties and the aggregate characteristics and patterns that encompass the entire school. In the intermediate sense, peer networks capture specific groupings within the student body, or smaller collections of people who share many ties among themselves. In the narrowest sense, peer networks capture all of the social ties of a single person (i.e., the ego network). For example, if two people attend the same school, any school-level network characteristic will be the same for both of them. They might have different intermediate-level networks, however, because they are in different social spaces of the school that they share. Even if they are in the same intermediate-level peer network in their school, they might have different individual-level peer networks because they each have their own friends within the same general social space.

First, *peer networks* have basic structures that are larger and more stable than any of the relationships (or people) embedded in them, and those structures help to define what a school is like. One structural feature is density, which refers to how interconnected network ties are. In dense school networks, more and more people are tied to the same other people, and the student body is not divided into specific groups that are disconnected from each other. School-level density, however, may subsume many students whose personal networks vary in density. The density of the network in a school or within certain segments of the school population is important in many ways because dense ties facilitate the creation and enforcement of norms (both positive and negative) while also reducing access to diverse resources and stifling innovation, creativity, and non-conformity. In one study, Falci and McNeely (2009) showed that, whereas *boys* suffered more depressive symptomatology when they were embedded in personal networks in their schools that included a large numbers of densely connected peers, girls suffered more when they were embedded in personal networks in their schools that included large numbers of relatively disconnected peers. Boys seemed to be reacting to a sense of being over-controlled, whereas girls were reacting to a reduced sense of belongingness.

Second, the compositional characteristics of networks offer insight into how schools organize diverse populations. They also illuminate how schools reinforce or break down sharp divisions in the larger society among sociodemographic groups, defined by *social class*, immigration, or *race/ethnicity*. Segregation—how the school network is divided into distinct sub-networks according to sociodemographic characteristics—has long been a focus of school network research. Segregated networks represent inequality, and integrated ones represent more fluid social systems that likely facilitate more equitable distributions of opportunities. The level of segregation also signals whether the social context of a school is characterized by trust and community rather than conflict and alienation. Along these lines, Moody (2001) showed that the *racial* segregation of school-level networks increased as school *racial* diversity increased but then eventually declined at high levels of diversity. These findings suggest that students took comfort in homophily when confronted with difference but only up to the point where doing so was feasible and would not unduly constrain their social ties. This work also demonstrated that *extracurricular activities* could be mechanisms of creating more integrated social contexts in diverse schools.

Another study—this one focusing on college students—offered insight into how peer networks can become racially segregated. Partly, segregation occurs because of racial homophily, but it also occurs because of the tendency for people to reciprocate friendships with each other and to become friends with the friends of their friends, regardless of homophily. In other words, network segregation can become self-fulfilling (Wimmer and Lewis 2010).

Third, the prevailing norms and values within a school network can affect the degree to which any one student is socially integrated (i.e., is widely connected with others) and/or popular (i.e., enjoys the esteem of others in the network and has a high status) in a school. Conversely, the average network positions of students and student groups with different behavioral and attitudinal profiles and changes in network positions among students or student groups who change characteristics or behaviors speak to the prevailing norms and values in school social contexts (Ueno 2005; Gest et al. 2001). If students who look or act a certain way are overrepresented among social isolates or among those who are well-connected, researchers can discern what tends to be valued or punished within a school. For example, Kreager and Staff (2009) used network analyses to provide concrete evidence of the oft-discussed *sexual* double standard in some high schools. Specifically, in those schools, the more that girls added sexual partners, the less likely other students in their schools named them as friends. The opposite happened for boys. As another example, Martin-Storey et al. (2015) exploited longitudinal network dynamics to show that *LGBT* students were seemingly more at-risk for being isolated within peer networks in predominantly White schools than in *racially* diverse schools. This pattern likely occurred because *sexuality* was one of the few ways to differentiate and stigmatize in the former but one of many potential dividing lines in the latter. Such research demonstrates how broad school networks are micro-cultures that amp up or downplay youth culture more generally.

Fourth, *peer networks* are a primary channel through which young people are influenced by others. Yes, much of the reason that students' behaviors and attitudes mirror those of the other students in their networks is because they seek out friends and social opportunities that reflect who they are, what they do, and what they want. This strong selection effect, however, does not totally explain that similarity. Peers socialize each other too through modeling, encouragement, and coercion (Dishion et al. 2015; Osgood et al. 2013). As such, carefully studying the links between network characteristics and student behavior can offer a window into how the strong peer influence of adolescence will vary across schools. In some schools, peer networks are characterized by anti-social attitudes. Consequently, transitioning into that school will expose students to negative influences that, over time, could facilitate more problematic developmental trajectories than if they had attended another school. In other schools, peer networks are characterized by pro-social attitudes, and the peer influence that a new student will encounter upon entering that school—relative to another school—will likely facilitate more positive trajectories over time. Consider the case of *drinking*. Although some schools have networks in which *drinking* is widespread, others have networks in which *drinking* is rare. In both cases, smaller and more specific peer networks within the school-level network might have drinking profiles that are discordant with those larger networks in which they are embedded. Not surprisingly, students tend to drink more when they attend schools in which the overall level of drinking among schoolmates is high and when their own personal *peer networks* are consistently high in *drinking*. This influence is not limited to the friends that students have within their own networks. Also important, sometimes even more, are the acquaintances that a student meets through their friends and romantic partners that characterize more intermediate-level networks. At the same time, *drinking* helps students meet new people and gains them entrée into parties and social activities. Thus, the social contexts of schools are a major factor in adolescent behavior, both because students' susceptibility to peer influences and their more agentic socializing are symptoms of their strong drive to become socially integrated during this stage of life (Cheadle et al. 2013; Crosnoe 2011; Kreager and Haynie 2011).

Peer networks, therefore, are multidimensional systems of interpersonal relations and interaction that help to characterize the social contexts of schools and differentiate one school from another. They also shed light on the potential divergence in life course trajectories between students in the same school and in different schools. Students react to their network positions (i.e., stress over being marginalized) and are influenced by those in their networks (i.e., modeling the behaviors of others) in ways that shape their general socioemotional development, affect their academic progress, and moderate the links between the two.

14.2.2 Peer Crowds

Peer networks capture concrete aspects of school social contexts. They are defined by relatively tangible ties, such as self-identification as friends or frequent contact. As such, network positions and features can be quantifiably identified and linked to individual students, such as assessing individual students' *popularity* by the number of fellow students who claimed them as friends. Other research on school social contexts—as exemplified by *Jocks and Burnouts*—strives for a more general sense of the various groups of students who make up the student body, the different venues for socialization that they offer, and how they reflect or undermine the general norms and values of the student body as a whole. They are defined less by concrete ties between specific students and more by shared identities among certain types of students in a school, who may or may not be directly tied to each other.

Such groupings go by many names. We use a single term, *crowds*, here. This term refers to large groupings of students that cut across the student body, loosely linking many smaller *cliques* and friendships into a pool of potential friends and romantic partners. *Crowds* emerge as secondary schooling progresses—as schools become larger, more impersonal, and more diverse just as adolescents' developing brains, pubertal development, and normative individuation from parents increase their need to find supportive and tight-knit niches that enhance their sense of belongingness. Students in the same crowd are viewed by others as a group, tend to interact more with each other than with students outside the crowd, share some common *identity*, and tend to have behavioral and attitudinal similarities. Some *crowds* may be defined by particular activity orientations (such as *jocks*), others by common behaviors (such as partiers), and still others by demographic compositions (such as ethnic groups, like Asian-Americans, within diverse schools). Even though not everyone in a crowd knows each other, they are much more likely to be friends than any two other students randomly chosen from the student body (Brown and Larson 2009; Brown et al. 2008). Importantly, students can and do change their *crowds* over time, often through active strategic behaviors during times of transition, as documented so well in Kinney's (1999) ethnography titled *From Headbangers to Hippies*. Because *crowds* exist somewhat independently of the people in them, however, they are fairly stable over time and eventually replace all members over long periods (Milner 2013; Brown and Larson 2009).

Earlier, we mentioned the 1980s movie, *The Breakfast Club*, which explored some basic high school social archetypes—the *Jock*, Princess, Brain, Basket Case, and Criminal—and how they relate to each other. This movie perfectly illustrates the idea of peer *crowds*, as individual people are perceived and treated according to their group identities rather than their own selves. Indeed, the movie is so closely related to this line of research that a team of educational scholars incorporated it into their large-scale high school data collection. Adolescents were asked to self-identify their school *crowds* and associated identities according to the five *Breakfast Club* archetypes, and they were then followed over time. Not only were the adolescents in the various *crowds* behaviorally more similar to their same-crowd peers than to other peers during the high school years, they remained more similar well after high school was over (incidentally, the *Jocks* and Brains turned out to be the best-adjusted in the long run) (Barber et al. 2001). This research echoed economic research on *identity* groupings in high schools, showing how peer *crowds* cluster liked-minded students together and make them more similar over time (Akerlof and Kranton 2002). Such studies also demonstrate how similar crowd structures are across schools.

Sociologists have argued that the level of peer *crowds*—not *cliques* or individual friends—is where the pressures towards conformity and the bullying that high schools have become famous for are most likely to occur. With longer shared personal histories and stronger affective bonds, friends typically are accepting of each other and are willing to tolerate differences and unconventionality. Absent those factors keeping them connected, students' positions in the peer crowd are much more vulnerable, as unusual or undesirable behaviors, unacceptable attitudes, and stigmatized traits could lead to marginalization and exclusion from the crowd. As such, *crowds* have strong influence over behavior (McFarland and Pals 2005; Giordano 2003). Indeed, one of the major qualitative findings of *Fitting In, Standing Out* was that students tended to view their own *cliques* in highly positive terms but the large peer *crowds* that organized the school in highly negative terms. In their minds, the internal policing of *crowds* and clashes among *crowds* in the school were what fulfilled all of the stereotypes of high schools as miserable places to be. Moreover, students embraced membership in specific friendship groups in their schools but consistently refused to place themselves in a particular crowd. Instead, they saw themselves as bridging multiple *crowds* or above the *crowd* structure altogether, no doubt influenced by the pejorative view of *crowds* as agents of conformity and social oppression in the school (Crosnoe 2011). Because *crowds* are typically defined by single identities related to specific characteristics (e.g., *academic achievement* = Nerds), they may strike adolescents as too narrow and simplistic, even as the everyday reality of high school social life

speaks to how important they are (Milner 2013; Kinney 1999).

Compared to the literature on *peer networks*, the literature on peer *crowds* has paid less attention to the ways in which the structure and organization of a school influence the creation and maintenance of *crowds* in the school. Recent developments in sociology of education, however, have sought to better situate peer *crowds* within particular school and curricular settings. Specifically, instead of drawing on network data or self-reports of crowd membership, Frank and colleagues analyzed thousands of academic transcripts and course schedules across a number of schools to identify students who tended to move through school together—sharing similar academic *statuses* (and all of the background characteristics associated with those *statuses*), populating the same classes from year to year, and participating in the same activities. Conceptualized much like peer *crowds*, these local positions grouped together students who were having a similar experience of attending their high schools, regardless of whether they were friends or not or saw themselves as a group or not. Some were defined by an orientation towards math and science, some were organized by specific activities like band, and some were defined by being on a clear path to dropout. Unlike "*identity*" peer *crowds*, these curricular peer *crowds* varied in both number and nature from high school to high school. The local positions that students were in defined which particular pocket of the social contexts of their high schools that they inhabited, and the configuration of local positions within a school differentiated its social context from other schools. Given their *curricular* nature, this version of peer *crowds* appeared to have particularly strong associations with students' academic progress (Frank et al. 2008; Field et al. 2006).

In many ways, the concept of peer *crowds* better captures how the public thinks about the social contexts of high schools. With recognizable identities and names that divide the student body into a manageable number of smaller groups, peer *crowds* are straightforward, have face validity, and are related to student outcomes in expected ways.

14.2.3 School Climate

Even more abstract than the concept of peer *crowds* is the notion that schools have a general *climate* of social relations among students—from conflictual, oppressive, and toxic to harmonious, affirming, and supportive and everything else in between. When scholars, educators, and parents talk about the *climate* of a school, they are simply trying to get at whether that school is a good place for students, both in terms of their academic prospects but also their general socioemotional development (Crosnoe 2011; Blum et al. 2004).

Beginning with the affective or interpersonal dimensions of school climate, Cohen et al. (2009) saw the concept as connecting a widespread sense of school belonging, perceptions of fairness and safety, and feelings of interpersonal connectedness. Not surprisingly, students tend to do much better academically and otherwise when they attend schools high on these aspects of positive *climate*. They feel comfortable and secure in such schools and encounter fewer stressors and, therefore, are better able to meet the challenges of schooling (Akiba 2010; Hallinan 2008). Contrary to popular opinion, smaller high schools do not necessarily foster more positive *interpersonal climates*, and large high schools are not significantly more likely to have negative *climates* (Gregory et al. 2011; Koth et al. 2008). Another dimension of *climate* is the general *academic climate* of the school. Some schools are defined by a clear push for academic success, where achievement is valued quite broadly, expectations are consistently high, and support is plentiful. That kind of *climate* scaffolds students' navigation of the increasingly differentiated curriculum of high school (including and especially in the face of academic challenges), opens up rather than forecloses academic opportunities more equitably, and facilitates the flow of information and resources more broadly (Smerdon 2002; Lee and Smith 1999; Shouse 1996).

One important theme of research on school *climates* (and related concepts like school culture) concerns the tendency for the *climates of schools* to become *racialized* in often counterproductive ways. For example, one of the strongest school-level influences on the *interpersonal climate* of a school is the *racial/ethnic* composition of the student body. Schools with heterogeneous student bodies tend to have less positive *interpersonal climates* and are especially low on feelings of connectedness among students and their perceptions of schools as fair and safe. Students of all *race/ethnicities* tend to like school less when they are not in a clear majority. As already mentioned, student bodies tend to divide down *racial/ethnic* lines, and, up to a point, the more diversity there is, the less students feel the need to cross those lines. Diversity also provides the opportunity for *racial/ethnic* discrimination and segregation to become apparent to students, and students from *racial/ethnic* minority groups may more fully grasp when they are being mistreated by the system if they are in a heterogeneous setting in which they can make cross-group comparisons (Benner and Graham 2013; Wells et al. 2009; Carter 2005; Johnson et al. 2001; Moody 2001). The fact that diverse schools may struggle building positive *interpersonal climates* does not provide evidence against the value of continuing school desegregation. Instead, it suggests that desegregation efforts need to attend to the special *climate*-related challenges of diverse student bodies in order to fully realize the benefits of desegregation (Crosnoe 2009; Wells et al. 2009).

The large literature concerning the much-debated oppositional culture thesis (see Ogbu 1997) delves deeply into the *racialization* of school climate. One key feature of this multifaceted thesis is the argument that Black and Latino/a peers de-emphasize school achievement and equate it with acting White, which is clearly relevant to the *academic climate* of predominantly *racial/ethnic* minority schools or schools with sizeable pockets of such students within a diverse student body. Sociologists of education have been particularly active in debunking this thesis (e.g., Harris 2011;

Ainsworth-Darnell and Downey 1998). Ethnographers have also used it as a venue for making deeper arguments about *school climate*. For example, Carter (2006, 2005) has argued that the perceptions of an oppositional culture among Black and Latino/a students in schools are manifestations of the historical ways that school personnel have misunderstood minority group culture, including their tendency to imbue non-academic behaviors and attitudes (e.g., acting tough, rejection of White hegemony) with academic significance. As another example, Tyson (2011) has argued that acting White is a *race*-specific illustration of a general phenomenon that crosses *racial/ethnic* lines. Specifically, peers from a broad array of backgrounds denigrate trying too hard academically, if not academic success itself, and contribute to what might seem like academically apathetic or antagonistic *school climates* no matter the *racial/ethnic* composition of the schools. Her work demonstrates that *academic climates* are likely more similar across *racial/ethnic* groups (in separate and *racially/ethnically* homogenous schools or among different *racial/ethnic* groups in the same schools) than the oppositional culture thesis (and the scholarly and public debates on it) imply.

Much like the treatment of *social class* in *Jocks and Burnouts* and the exploration of *gender* and *sexuality* in newer school ethnographies (e.g., Pascoe 2011; Fields 2008), research on the *racialization* of school climate has tethered what is going on culturally in schools among young people to what is going on culturally outside of schools among adults, including their biases, prejudices, and inequities. As such, they illustrate how broader social influences are reworked and reimagined by young people into their own unique *school climates*.

14.3 Policy Challenges and Responses

As we have already argued, understanding the social contexts of high schools is important in its own right because doing so sheds much needed light on the ways schools work that is vital to

theory. It is also important because the social contexts of schools are relevant to many programs aiming to improve the academic functioning of schools in an era of greater accountability. Many of these programmatic efforts have failed to change the *formal processes* of schooling in the desired ways or, at least, underperformed as a result of not taking the *informal processes* of schooling into account when trying to achieve those goals. Moreover, many of the other programmatic efforts aiming to improve the health and wellbeing of young people—rather than promoting academic performance—have also been disappointing because they did not harness the power of the *informal* processes of schooling. In this final section, therefore, we attempt to connect what sociologists of education and other researchers have learned about the social contexts of schools to "action" in the form of *policies* and *interventions*, educational and otherwise.

14.3.1 Changing Social Contexts

If the *peer networks* of a high school transmit anti-social values that deflate students' academic efforts, then reversing the *informal processes* within that school would help it meet academic benchmarks. If the most influential peer *crowds* of a high school are characterized by academic apathy that undermines students' course-taking trajectories, then improving the *informal processes* of that school should enable it to reach a higher level of academic performance. In both cases, the solution seems obvious—create programs to instill and spread more pro-social, academically-oriented attitudes and values among students, who would then influence each other. The problem with this obvious solution, of course, is that conceptualizing and executing such programs is exceedingly difficult.

The social contexts of high schools embody the *policy dilemma*, which refers to the inherent challenges when the factors most associated with desired outcomes are the most difficult to change. Peers powerfully influence students' behaviors, including academic progress, but manipulating peer dynamics from the outside is a tall order (Crosnoe 2011). Past research from sociology of education, public health, and prevention science offers possible ways to overcome this challenge.

Recall Coleman's conclusion in *The Adolescent Society* that schools use academic competitions to harness the social contexts of schools for more academic endeavors. This conclusion speaks to the possibility of changing peer dynamics through indirect means. Time and again, the *extracurricula* of schools have been shown to influence *peer networks*, *crowds*, and other social relations in schools, including across *racial*/ethnic and socioeconomic lines. Also, *extracurricular* activities are much easier to manipulate through *policy* than interpersonal dynamics. Consequently, increasing *extracurricular* offerings, altering requirements for participation, setting standards for the composition of participants, and using *adult* coaches/leaders as well as student leaders within activities to deliver specific messages to students are avenues for changing the *social capital* that is being traded within *peer networks*, the peer crowd structure, and the interplay of the interpersonal and *academic climates* (Mahoney et al. 2005; Moody 2001). Along those same lines, identifying structural and compositional factors of schools with functional social contexts is important. After all, *policy interventions* aiming to change school structure and composition are widely seen as appropriate and doable. If we know what those factors are and can change or implement them in a school, then we may indirectly alter the social context of that school over time.

Lessons for more direct *interventions* into the social contexts of schools can be derived from recent efforts to create and refine programs to increase tolerance among diverse groups of students and to develop *multicultural curricula*. For example, *Gay–Straight Alliances*—which have the goal of fostering greater acceptance of *LGBT* youth in schools through social activities, awareness campaigns, and peer advocacy—have become more common in U.S. high schools in recent years. As another example, ethnic studies programs and associated culturally aware pedagogical practices have received increased attention,

both as a way of broadening the academic scope of what students are taught but also as a means of easing social divisions among students and in society at large. In both cases, schools have rejected the *policy dilemma* and instead actively tried to improve their social contexts for students (Tintiangco-Cubales et al. 2014; Poteat et al. 2013). Whether the observed benefits of such programs are causal, generalize across contexts, and endure remains unclear, as does the degree to which such programs can be implemented outside the realm of social justice issues to improve basic academic norms and attitudes.

Other examples of efforts to directly change school peer cultures include positive behavioral interventions and supports (PBIS) and social and emotional learning (or SEL) efforts. The former is a school-wide approach to reduce the need for disciplinary actions in schools by developing positive social skills among students (Bradshaw et al. 2008). The latter involves incorporating socioemotional skill-building exercises into school curricula and activities as a means of achieving a healthy and supportive school environment for students (Durlak et al. 2001). Both programs are exemplars for altering the peer cultures of schools in positive ways.

14.3.1.1 Other Avenues of Action

Another way to address the *policy dilemma* related to the social contexts of schools is to move beyond attempts to change *informal processes* and instead concentrate on breaking the link between *informal* and *formal processes*. In other words, schools with negative social contexts might not be able to improve those contexts but could develop strategies to protect students from being hurt by them. Consider the ample research by sociologists of education on Catholic schools. Efforts to explain why student performance was much better and socioeconomic disparities in performance much weaker in such schools relative to public schools and other kinds of private schools eventually centered on the benefits of a constrained academic curriculum. Because all students took the same classes and enrolled in the same programs, they had no opportunity to make academic choices that could be undermined by social influences. All students also experienced much greater similarity in the academic norms and expectations to which they were exposed (Hallinan and Kubitschek 2012; Coleman et al. 1982). This constrained curriculum idea has been utilized more recently in *policy* efforts to equalize the math course-taking of public school students in California and other states. Although the academic benefits of this translation of *policy* from the private to the public realm have been disappointing (see Penner et al. 2015; Attewell and Domina 2008), evaluations have not looked at other unintended consequences, such as whether the academic progress or general behavior of students in the most negative school social contexts are protected from further harm.

Finally, understanding the social contexts of schools may help to support the effectiveness of *interventions* in changing students' non-academic behaviors. Because they provide one-stop access to large numbers of adolescents, high schools have long been popular sites for behavioral *interventions*, even those that seem unrelated to academic performance. Examples include efforts to curb *drinking*, improve *sexual* health, and decrease *obesity*. These programs are often doomed to failure when they are implemented with inadequate attention to the specific school contexts in which they are situated. Messages about anti-social behavior could fall flat if they contradict what is valued among peers in a school, programs that group together many students at the same time might double as social activities with diluted impact, and the efficacy of increasingly popular peer educator and peer mentoring techniques in programmatic *interventions* depends on picking the right peers to lead (Crosnoe and McNeely 2008; Bearman and Brückner 2001; Dishion et al. 2001). Indeed, research on the social contexts of schools points to the value of enlisting high-status or well-connected students as agents of norm change for interventions to combat key social problems of childhood and adolescence (e.g., bullying, substance use) in schools (Osgood et al. 2013; Paluck and Shepherd 2012).

The difficulty of dealing with peer influences and the potential value of incorporating them are exacerbated by the strong emphasis on fidelity in *intervention* and prevention (i.e., ensuring that programs are implemented in exactly the same way across different sites), since a "one size fits all" mentality is incompatible with the basic themes of research on the social contexts of schools (Steiker 2008). The point is that the translation of social context research into *policy* action is not just about what can be done about the social contexts of schools. The knowledge derived from this research can improve *policy* and *intervention* far more broadly.

14.4 Conclusion

When magazines and think tanks put out lists of "good" schools and "bad" schools, they are focusing almost solely on the *formal processes* of education. A school is considered "good" if it consistently meets certain academic benchmarks (e.g., high test scores) or consistently produces academically successful students (e.g., National Merit Scholars, enrollees at prestigious *colleges*). These discussions rarely touch on what going to such "good" schools is like. Schools that work well as educational institutions often have positive and healthy social contexts, but this "all good things go together" pattern is not absolute. Some academically successful schools might have toxic social contexts, some academically struggling schools might help students feel safe and develop in healthy ways, and some schools could be doing better or worse academically if not for the attitudes, norms, and behaviors prevalent in their social contexts.

With a significant assist from scholars in other fields and disciplines, sociologists of education have done a great deal to shed light on what a "good" school is and, perhaps more importantly, what a "bad" school is. That research has involved inquiry into the social contexts of schools on their own as well as how the social contexts of schools work at cross-purposes with or in support of the educational mission of schools. Without the insights of this literature, our understanding of schools would be incomplete and our policies to reform schools would be misguided.

By emphasizing the social contexts of schools, therefore, all of those seemingly shallow movies, shows, and books were focusing attention where it was needed.

References

Ainsworth-Darnell, J. W., & Downey, D. B. (1998). Assessing the oppositional culture explanation for racial/ethnic differences in school performance. *American Sociological Review, 63*, 536–553.

Akerlof, G. A., & Kranton, R. E. (2002). Identity and schooling: Some lessons for the economics of education. *Journal of Economic Literature, 40*, 1167–1201.

Akiba, M. (2010). What predicts fear of school violence among U.S. adolescents? *Teachers College Record, 112*, 68–102.

Arum, R. (2000). Schools and communities: Ecological and institutional dimensions. *Annual Review of Sociology, 26*, 395–418.

Attewell, P., & Domina, T. (2008). Raising the bar: Curricular intensity and academic performance. *Educational Evaluation and Policy Analysis, 30*, 51–71.

Barber, B. L., Eccles, J. S., & Stone, M. R. (2001). Whatever happened to the jock, the brain, and the princess? Young adult pathways linked to adolescent activity involvement and social identity. *Journal of Adolescent Research, 16*, 429–455.

Bearman, P. S., & Brückner, H. (2001). Promising the future: Virginity pledges and first intercourse. *American Journal of Sociology, 106*, 859–912.

Bearman, P., Moody, J., & Stovel, K. (1997). *The Add Health network variable codebook*. Chapel Hill: University of North Carolina.

Benner, A. D., & Graham, S. (2013). The antecedents and consequences of discrimination during adolescence: Does the source of discrimination matter? *Developmental Psychology, 49*, 1602–1613.

Blum, R. W., Libbey, H. P., Bishop, J. H., & Bishop, M. (2004). School connectedness—Strengthening health and education outcomes for teenagers. *Journal of School Health, 74*, 231–235.

Bradshaw, C. P., Koth, C. W., Bevans, K. B., Ialongo, N., & Leaf, P. J. (2008). The impact of school-wide positive behavioral interventions and supports (PBIS) on the organizational health of elementary schools. *School Psychology Quarterly, 23*, 462–473.

Brown, B. B., & Larson, J. (2009). Peer relationships in adolescence. In R. Lerner & L. Steinberg (Eds.), *Handbook of adolescent psychology* (pp. 74–103). New York: Wiley.

Brown, B. B., Herman, M., Hamm, J. V., & Heck, D. J. (2008). Ethnicity and image: Correlates of crowd affiliation among ethnic minority youth. *Child Development, 79*, 529–546.

Bryk, A., & Schneider, B. (2003). *Trust in schools: A core resource for improvement*. New York: Russell Sage.

Buchmann, C., & Dalton, B. (2002). Interpersonal influences and educational aspirations in 12 countries: The importance of institutional context. *Sociology of Education, 75*, 99–122.

Carbonaro, W. J. (1998). A little help from my friends' parents: Intergenerational closure and educational outcomes. *Sociology of Education, 71*, 295–313.

Carter, P. L. (2005). *Keepin' it real: School success beyond Black and White*. New York: Oxford University Press.

Carter, P. L. (2006). Straddling boundaries: Identity, culture, and school. *Sociology of Education, 79*, 304–328.

Cheadle, J. E., Stevens, M., Williams, D. T., & Goosby, B. J. (2013). The differential contributions of teen drinking homophily to new and existing friendships: An empirical assessment of assortative and proximity selection mechanisms. *Social Science Research, 42*, 1297–1310.

Cohen, J., McCabe, L., Michelli, N. M., & Pickeral, T. (2009). School climate: Research, policy, practice, and teacher education. *Teachers College Record, 111*, 180–213.

Coleman, J. (1961). *The adolescent society: The social life of the teenager and its impact on education*. New York: Free Press.

Coleman, J. S., Hoffer, T., & Kilgore, S. (1982). *High school achievement: Public, Catholic, and private schools compared*. New York: Basic Books.

Crosnoe, R. (2009). Low-income students and the socioeconomic composition of public high schools. *American Sociological Review, 74*, 709–730.

Crosnoe, R. (2011). *Fitting in, standing out: Navigating the social challenges of high school to get an education*. New York: Cambridge University Press.

Crosnoe, R. (2012). Schools, peers, and the big picture of adolescent development. In E. Amsel & J. Smetana (Eds.), *Adolescent vulnerabilities and opportunities: Developmental and constructivist perspectives* (pp. 182–204). New York: Cambridge University Press.

Crosnoe, R., & McNeely, C. (2008). Peer relations, adolescent behavior, and public health research and practice. *Family & Community Health, 31*, S71–S80.

Dishion, T. J., Poulin, F., & Burraston, B. (2001). Peer goup dynamics associated with iatrogenic effect in group interventions with high-risk young adolescents. *New Directions for Child and Adolescent Development, 2001*(91), 79–92.

Dishion, T. J., Kim, H., & Tein, J. Y. (2015). Friendship and adolescent problem behavior: Deviancy training and coercive joining as dynamic mediators. In T. P. Beauchaine & S. P. Hinshaw (Eds.), *The Oxford handbook of externalizing spectrum disorders* (pp. 303–311). New York: Oxford University.

Dornbusch, S., Glasgow, K., & Lin, I. (1996). The social structure of schooling. *Annual Review of Psychology, 47*, 401–429.

Durlak, J. A., Rubin, L. A., & Kahng, R. D. (2001). Cognitive behavioral therapy for children and adolescents with externalizing problems. *Journal of Cognitive Psychotherapy, 15*, 183.

Eckert, P. (1989). *Jocks and burnouts: Social categories and identity in the high school.* New York: Teachers College Press.

Epstein, J. L., & Karweit, N. (Eds.). (1983). *Friends in school: Patterns of selection and influence in secondary schools.* New York: Elsevier.

Falci, C., & McNeely, C. (2009). Too many friends: Social integration, network cohesion and adolescent depressive symptoms. *Social Forces, 87*, 2031–2061.

Faris, R., & Felmlee, D. (2011). Status struggles network centrality and gender segregation in same-and cross-gender aggression. *American Sociological Review, 76*, 48–73.

Field, S., Frank, K. A., Schiller, K., Riegle-Crumb, C., & Muller, C. (2006). Identifying positions from affiliation networks: Preserving the duality of people and events. *Social Networks, 28*, 97–123.

Fields, J. (2008). *Risky lessons: Sex education and social inequality.* New Brunswick: Rutgers University Press.

Frank, K. A., Muller, C., Schiller, K. S., Riegle-Crumb, C., Mueller, A. S., Crosnoe, R., & Pearson, J. (2008). The social dynamics of mathematics coursetaking in high school. *American Journal of Sociology, 113*, 1645–1696.

Gest, S. D., Graham-Bermann, S. A., & Hartup, W. W. (2001). Peer experience: Common and unique features of number of friendships, social network centrality, and sociometric status. *Social Development, 10*, 23–40.

Giordano, P. C. (2003). Relationships in adolescence. *Annual Review of Sociology, 29*, 257–281.

Gregory, A., Cornell, D., & Fan, X. (2011). The relationship of school structures and support to suspension rates for Black and White high school students. *American Educational Research Journal, 48*, 904–934.

Hallinan, M. T. (2008). Teacher influences on students' attachment to school. *Sociology of Education, 81*, 271–283.

Hallinan, M., & Kubitschek, W. N. (2012). A comparison of academic achievement and adherence to the common school ideal in public and Catholic schools. *Sociology of Education, 85*, 1–22.

Harris, A. L. (2011). *Kids don't want to fail.* Cambridge, MA: Harvard University Press.

Johnson, M. K., Crosnoe, R., & Elder, G. H. (2001). Students' attachment and academic engagement: The role of race and ethnicity. *Sociology of Education, 74*, 318–340.

Kinney, D. A. (1999). From "headbangers" to "hippies": Delineating adolescents' active attempts to form an alternative peer culture. *New Directions for Child and Adolescent Development, 84*, 21–35.

Koth, C. W., Bradshaw, C. P., & Leaf, P. J. (2008). A multilevel study of predictors of student perceptions of school climate: The effect of classroom-level factors. *Journal of Educational Psychology, 100*, 96–104.

Kreager, D. A., & Haynie, D. L. (2011). Dangerous liaisons? Dating and drinking diffusion in adolescent peer networks. *American Sociological Review, 76*, 737–763.

Kreager, D. A., & Staff, J. (2009). The sexual double standard and adolescent peer acceptance. *Social Psychology Quarterly, 72*, 143–164.

Kubitschek, W. N., & Hallinan, M. T. (1998). Tracking and students' friendships. *Social Psychology Quarterly, 61*, 1–15.

Lawrence-Lightfoot, S. (1983). *The good high school: Portraits of character and culture.* New York: Basic Books.

Lee, V., & Smith, J. B. (1999). Social support and achievement for young adolescents in Chicago: The role of school. *American Educational Research Journal, 36*, 907–945.

Lin, N., Cook, K., Burt, R., & Burt, S. (Eds.). (2001). *Social capital: Theory and research.* New Brunswick: Transaction Publishers.

Mahoney, J. L., Larson, R. W., & Eccles, J. S. (Eds.). (2005). *Organized activities as contexts of development: Extracurricular activities, after school and community programs.* New York: Psychology Press.

Martin-Storey, A., Cheadle, J. E., Skalamera, J., & Crosnoe, R. (2015). Exploring the social integration of sexual minority youth across high school contexts. *Child Development, 86*, 965–975.

McFarland, D. A. (2001). Student resistance: How the formal and informal organization of classrooms facilitate everyday forms of student defiance. *American Journal of Sociology, 107*, 612–678.

McFarland, D. A., Moody, J., Diehl, D., Smith, J. A., & Thomas, R. J. (2014). Network ecology and adolescent social structure. *American Sociological Review, 2*, 1088–1121.

McFarland, D., & Pals, H. (2005). Motives and contexts of identity change: A case for network effects. *Social Psychology Quarterly, 68*, 289–315.

McPherson, M., Smith-Lovin, L., & Cook, J. M. (2001). Birds of a feather: Homophily in social networks. *Annual Review of Sociology, 27*, 415–444.

Milner, M. (2013). *Freaks, geeks, and cool kids.* New York: Routledge.

Moody, J. (2001). Race, school integration, and friendship segregation in America. *American Journal of Sociology, 107*, 679–716.

Ogbu, J. U. (1997). African American education: A cultural-ecological perspective. In H. P. McAdoo (Ed.), *Black families* (pp. 234–250). Thousand Oaks: SAGE Publications.

Osgood, D. W., Ragan, D. T., Wallace, L., Gest, S. D., Feinberg, M. E., & Moody, J. (2013). Peers and the emergence of alcohol use: Influence and selection processes in adolescent friendship networks. *Journal of Research on Adolescence, 23*, 500–512.

Paluck, E. L., & Shepherd, H. (2012). The salience of social referents: A field experiment on collective norms and harassment behavior in a school social network. *Journal of Personality and Social Psychology, 103*, 899.

Pascoe, C. J. (2011). *Dude, you're a fag: Masculinity and sexuality in high school*. Berkeley: University of California Press.

Penner, A. M., Domina, T., Penner, E. K., & Conley, A. (2015). Curricular policy as a collective effects problem: A distributional approach. *Social Science Research, 52*, 627–641.

Poteat, V. P., Sinclair, K. O., DiGiovanni, C. D., Koenig, B. W., & Russell, S. T. (2013). Gay–Straight Alliances are associated with student health: A multischool comparison of LGBTQ and heterosexual youth. *Journal of Research on Adolescence, 23*, 319–330.

Rohlen, T. P. (1983). *Japan's high schools*. Berkeley: University of California Press.

Rutter, M., Maughan, B., Mortimer, P., & Ouston, J. (1979). *Fifteen thousand hours: Secondary schools and their effects on children*. Cambridge, MA: Harvard University Press.

Shouse, R. C. (1996). Academic press and sense of community: Conflict, congruence, and implications for student achievement. *Social Psychology of Education, 1*, 47–68.

Smerdon, B. A. (2002). Students' perceptions of membership in their high schools. *Sociology of Education, 75*, 287–305.

Steiker, L. K. H. (2008). Making drug and alcohol prevention relevant: Adapting evidence-based curricula to unique adolescent cultures. *Family & Community Health, 31*, S52–S60.

Tintiangco-Cubales, A., Kohli, R., Sacramento, J., Henning, N., Agarwal-Rangnath, R., & Sleeter, C. (2014). Toward an ethnic studies pedagogy: Implications for K–12 schools from the research. *Urban Review, 47*, 104–125.

Tyson, K. (2011). *Integration interrupted: Tracking, Black students, and acting White after Brown*. New York: Oxford University Press.

Ueno, K. (2005). The effects of friendship networks on adolescent depressive symptoms. *Social Science Research, 34*, 484–510.

Wells, A. S., Jellison Holme, J., Tijerina Revilla, A., & Korantemaa Atanda, A. (2009). *Both sides now: The story of school desegregation's graduates*. Berkeley: University of California Press.

Wimmer, A., & Lewis, K. (2010). Beyond and below racial homophily: ERG models of a friendship network documented on Facebook. *American Journal of Sociology, 116*, 583–642.

Work Intensity and Academic Success

Jeremy Staff, Jeylan T. Mortimer, and Monica Kirkpatrick Johnson

Abstract

In this chapter, we review prior research examining how teenage work intensity, indicated by the average hours of paid work, its quality, and duration, relates to both short- and longer-term success in school. We examine the evidence for three plausible propositions: (1) that work intensity in adolescence has a causal effect on school achievement and educational attainment; (2) that these effects are moderated by gender, race/ethnicity, and family socioeconomic background; and (3) that the relationship between work intensity and academic success is spuriously related to preexisting differences between students. We also highlight shifts in the employment experiences of teenagers over the past 20 years based on cross-sectional data from the Monitoring the Future study, we offer four suggestions for future study, and we discuss implications for policy based upon what we know now about the intensity of teenage work.

J. Staff (✉)
Department of Sociology, Pennsylvania State University, University Park, PA, USA
e-mail: jus25@psu.edu

J. T. Mortimer
Department of Sociology, University of Minnesota, Minneapolis, MN, USA
e-mail: morti002@umn.edu

M. K. Johnson
Department of Sociology, Washington State University, Pullman, WA, USA
e-mail: monicakj@wsu.edu

15.1 Work Intensity and Academic Success

Compared to just 20 years ago, teenagers today are much less likely to be holding a part-time job during the school year. In Table 15.1, we highlight this recent shift in school-year youth employment and average weekly work hours based upon nationally representative data from two cohorts of teenagers in the Monitoring the Future (MTF) study (n = 88,195 students). In 1994, only about one quarter of high school seniors did not work at any point during the school year, and only about one half of 8th and 10th graders avoided employment. By 2014, the percentage of non-working youth had climbed dramatically to 41% of 12th graders, 76% of 10th graders, and 80% of 8th graders. It is also clear from Table 15.1 that employed youth nowadays are less likely to work intensively (i.e., average more than 20 hours per week working during the school year) compared to teenagers in 1994. For instance, the percentage of 12th, 10th, and 8th graders working intensive hours dropped by 36%, 67%, and 75%, respectively, from 1994 to 2014. The percentage of youth working low to moderate hours (i.e., averaging 1–20 h per week) has also declined since 1994, especially among 8th and 10th graders, though the drop was not as steep.

This dramatic decline in youth employment over the past 20 years, especially among teenagers who once devoted substantial time to paid work while attending secondary school, may

© Springer International Publishing AG, part of Springer Nature 2018
B. Schneider (ed.), *Handbook of the Sociology of Education in the 21st Century*, Handbooks of Sociology and Social Research, https://doi.org/10.1007/978-3-319-76694-2_15

Table 15.1 Work intensity during the school year among teenagers in 1994 and 2014

		1994	2014
12th graders	Not working	24%	41%
	Moderate hours (1–20)	46%	40%
	Intensive hours (21 or more)	30%	19%
10th graders	Not working	54%	76%
	Moderate hours (1–20)	37%	21%
	Intensive hours (21 or more)	9%	3%
8th graders	Not working	57%	80%
	Moderate hours (1–20)	39%	19%
	Intensive hours (21 or more)	4%	1%

Source: Monitoring the Future study (sample size = 88,195 students)

come as welcome news to scholars who have long encouraged adolescents to wait to seek a job until after they finish school (Greenberger and Steinberg 1986; Marsh 1991). The central concern surrounding youth employment is that spending time at work detracts from time and effort that teenagers could devote to academic pursuits and school-related activities. Accordingly, the recent drop in employment and work hours should give today's students more time to prepare for exams, complete school assignments, meet with teachers or guidance counselors, spend time in supplemental educational academies (e.g., college test preparation, math enrichment courses, etc.), or participate in a variety of extracurricular activities, such as sports, intramural clubs, or other school-related organizations. In addition, by limiting time teens spend at work, it is sometimes presumed that not only will youth today be better students, they will also minimize the risk of the long list of problem behaviors that have been associated with teenage employment, such as delinquency, substance use, poor mental health, physical injury, school misconduct, negative attitudes toward work, occupational deviance, and precocious family formation behaviors.

Though there are some well-documented academic and developmental risks associated with adolescent employment (Staff et al. 2015), studies have shown how these risks vary depending on several key factors, most notably the "inten-

sity" of the work. While work intensity is usually operationalized by long average weekly hours of work, in this chapter we consider "intense work" as paid employment that is highly engaging temporally or subjects the novice worker to stressful or other low-quality experiences. We also examine risk and protective factors that precede entry into the world of work and that can moderate the impacts of employment. In addition, we review research that has shown that certain workplace experiences can enhance rather than detract from academics and ultimately benefit long-term educational and occupational attainment (Mortimer 2003).

In the first part of the chapter, we highlight some key studies that have documented benefits as well as drawbacks of working while attending secondary school for academic achievement, school engagement, problem behaviors, high school dropout, and long-term educational and occupational attainment. We consider several aspects of these work experiences that can make them more or less intense, such as the average hours spent working each week, the length of the employment, the type of job and the quality of the work, and whether it occurs during the school year or the summer months. We organize this section by examining the evidence for three plausible propositions: that employment intensity influences school achievement and attainment; that these effects are moderated by gender, race/ethnicity, and family socioeconomic background; and, finally, that employment intensity has no effects on school achievement and attainment once selection factors and other sources of spuriousness are accounted for. In the second section of the chapter, we propose four directions researchers might want to explore in the future, and discuss policy implications of what we know now about the intensity of teenage work.

15.2 Prior Research on Teenage Employment

Assessing the impact of early employment on school outcomes is not a frequently studied topic in the sociological study of education. More often, variation in the intensity, duration, and quality of adult employment is considered as a consequence of educational achievement and attainment (Kerckhoff 2000). For instance, in longitudinal models illustrating the process of occupational attainment (Sewell and Hauser 1975), the young person's pay and job status is only measured after the completion of schooling, as educational attainment is considered to be a key mediator linking parental and offspring occupational status. Yet, research shows that these "first" jobs following the completion of schooling often occur long after youth enter the labor market (Entwisle et al. 2000; Staff and Mortimer 2007), and ignoring employment experience gained while young people are still attending school can lead to overestimates of education's positive impact on young adult occupational status and wage attainments (Light 2001).

Among social scientists who do study youth employment, a debate in the literature surrounds whether or not early experiences in the workplace, especially after school or during the weekends while school is in session, impact success in secondary school and long-term educational attainment. Whereas influential committee reports have summarized research documenting the benefits of paid work (National Research Council 1998), and encouraged teenagers to obtain jobs (Coleman et al. 1974), research has also shown how early employment can carry some risk to education as well as health and well-being. As we review below, a sizeable body of evidence suggests that employment during the teenage years does in fact affect educational outcomes, but the direction and strength of the effect depends on the intensity of this experience. Further complicating work–school associations in adolescence are studies that suggest that purported work effects may vary by a diverse set of moderating or spurious influences, such as prior school engagement and academic success, behavioral adjustment problems that emerge long before entering the world of work, the young person's motivation to work and their occupational aspirations, and employment opportunities in the local labor market. We begin with the proposition that work intensity affects educational outcomes.

15.2.1 Proposition 1. Employment Intensity Affects School Success and Long-Term Socioeconomic Attainment

In their now classic studies, D'Amico (1984) and Greenberger and Steinberg (1986) hypothesized that youth employment may have both beneficial and detrimental effects on academic achievement and long-term attainment. On the beneficial side, work in high school may help youth better prepare for adult work roles. Teenagers can learn the skills and effort necessary to obtain a job, such as drafting a résumé, locating a job, and interviewing with potential employers. These early employment experiences can help youth learn what it takes to keep a job (e.g., punctuality, appropriate workplace conduct), teach them specific and more general vocational skills, and push them to think more about the type of work or job conditions (e.g., working with people, high autonomy) they would like after they finish school. Such progress in vocational development may focus teens' attention on the kinds of educational experiences and credentials necessary to obtain the kinds of jobs they are looking for, heightening academic effort and achievement. Working may also contribute to the development of interpersonal skills, as young workers learn how to relate to co-workers and supervisors and come in contact with the public (for example, in commonly held fast food jobs and retail trade). Furthermore, the adult supervisors and coworkers teens meet at work may help them connect with other employers and serve as valuable nonfamilial references as they try to establish themselves in the adult world of work. In short, by providing training, skill development, contacts, and experience about what it takes to be an employee, high school students who have work experience may gain an advantage in the labor market over their peers who have not yet been employed.

On the detrimental side, teenage employment may interfere with educational progress and encourage problem behaviors, ultimately compromising socioeconomic attainment. As mentioned previously, time spent at work may limit time that could be devoted to homework, studying, and extracurricular activities. If working teenagers spend late nights at work they may be exhausted the next morning and unprepared for a day of learning. Work may also increase the risk of problem behaviors through a variety of mechanisms: (1) Exposure to older teens and adults in the workplace may encourage substance use and family formation behaviors; (2) Coworkers and supervisors may emphasize the immediate rewards of work (money, autonomy) at the expense of more long-term rewards that come from education, undermining bonds to school; (3) Parents may grant more freedom and autonomy to their daughters and sons when they work, which in turn increases the time working youth spend in unstructured activities with their peers; and (4) Certain jobs and coworkers may enable workplace misconduct, such as theft or providing friends and family free services, food, and products. Work may also increase the risk of adjustment problems by exposing teenagers to undue stress and demands, noxious or unsafe work environments, and workplace sexual harassment. Mental distress and poor behavioral adjustment could, in turn, lead to immediate declines in school performance and increase the risk of high school dropout and diminished long-term educational attainment.

The majority of research on how youth employment impacts educational outcomes has focused on one dimension of work intensity: the average hours of work youth spend per week in their jobs during the school year. We should note that this focus on work hours is primarily due to survey data limitations, as teenagers rarely are asked about other dimensions of their employment, such as its duration and quality, or their subjective responses to their work. Nonetheless, if work and school have a zero-sum association in adolescence, then school performance should monotonically decline as the hours of work intensify. However, high school students do not necessarily lose 2 h of homework time when they spend 2 h at work, as they could spend that free time doing a variety of more or less academically or developmentally beneficial activities. Shanahan and Flaherty (2001) and Mortimer's

(2003) detailed longitudinal analyses of time use patterns of youth followed through the high school years reveal that teens who worked moderate hours during high school spent similar amounts of time doing homework, participating in extracurricular activities, volunteering, and spending time with friends as those teenagers who did not work. Other researchers have similarly found that employed teenagers do not sacrifice time for leisure reading, studying, doing homework, or hanging out with their families when they spend a moderate amount of time at work (D'Amico 1984; Mihalic and Elliott 1997; Schoenhals et al. 1998; Kalenkoski and Pabilonia 2012). Moderate workers do show an increase in school absences compared to their non-working counterparts (Bachman et al. 2003; Schoenhals et al. 1998), but they also spend less time watching television or in front of a computer screen (Kalenkoski and Pabilonia 2012), and show increases in both school activities (Mihalic and Elliott 1997) and grade point averages (Mortimer and Johnson 1998). Overall, teenagers who work limited hours appear to have sufficient time to pursue a wide range of school, work, family, and leisure activities.

Risks to school progress and positive adjustment do emerge when students average long hours on the job during the school year. For instance, longitudinal studies have documented declines in academic achievement and school performance when teenagers average more than 20 h per week during the school year (Marsh and Kleitman 2005; Marsh 1991; Monahan et al. 2011; Staff et al. 2010b; Tyler 2003). For some teenagers, the decline in school performance that comes with spending long hours on the job may be due to time tradeoff between work and school, as intensive work is associated with a greater frequency of incomplete assignments and truancy as well as low school effort and participation in school activities. In addition, the risks of delinquency, substance use, school misbehavior, truancy, and school suspensions are elevated when youth spend long hours on the job (Johnson 2004; Mortimer et al. 1996a; Staff and Uggen 2003; Staff et al. 2010a), compared to occasions when they do not. These findings suggest that the problem behaviors that coincide with intensive hours of work in adolescence may make it even harder for youth to finish school.

Several studies have shown that youth who average more than 20 h per week increase their risk of leaving high school without a degree (Apel et al. 2008; D'Amico 1984; Lee and Staff 2007; McNeal 1997; Warren and Lee 2003). On average, youth increase their risk of dropout by approximately 40–64% when they work more than 20 h per week during the school year. Importantly, moderate work hours do not carry this same risk. In fact, D'Amico's (1984) seminal study found that moderate work was associated with a reduced risk of high school dropout. Intensive hours of work during adolescence have also been linked to reductions in long-term educational attainment, as intensive workers are less likely to complete four-year college degrees compared to their non-working and moderately employed counterparts (Bachman et al. 2011b; Carr et al. 1996; Mortimer 2003; Staff and Mortimer 2007). Overall, the weight of the evidence indicates a non-linear relationship between work hours and academic success: Intensive hours of work increase the risk of school failure and low educational attainment, whereas moderate hours range from offering some educational benefits to carrying no risk at all.

Given the dramatic decline in teenage employment, and especially the decline in young workers who devote long hours to their jobs, it is important to assess whether high-intensity work still carries a risk. A recent report from the U.S. Department of Education (2015) examined the risk factors for high school dropout among teenagers in the High School Longitudinal Study of 2009 (the HSLS:09). This study included approximately 24,000 ninth graders (ages 14–15) who were first surveyed in the fall of 2009, and then again in the spring of 2012 (ages 16–17). By the spring of the 11th grade, approximately 3% were dropouts (i.e., not enrolled in school or had not earned a high school diploma or an alternative credential), 7% were stopouts (had experienced at least one 4-week spell out of high school but were currently enrolled), and the remaining were continuous students. Of these three groups,

the dropouts were the *least* likely to have previously held a job (33%) compared to 47% of the stopouts and 49% of the continuous students. However, when they did work, dropouts were most likely of the three groups to have worked intensively. For instance, among working youth, 10% of the dropouts had averaged more than 4 h of work on a typical school day, compared to 7% of stopouts and 5% of continuous students. It is also worth noting that the continuous students had the highest percentage who had previously averaged less than 1 h of work per school day (73%), compared to 63% and 60% of the dropouts and stopouts, respectively. These findings suggest that work hours continue to have a curvilinear relationship with school success, despite a substantial drop in the number of youth who are employed and who work intensive hours.

Whereas the majority of studies have focused on work hours, relatively little research has assessed whether the quality of early employment experiences matters for short and long-term achievement. In James Coleman's influential report (Coleman et al. 1974), teenagers in the 1970s were encouraged to find jobs so they could develop vocational skills and gain real world experiences in the workplace that would supplement what they were learning in school. Furthermore, Coleman and his colleagues stressed that employment would force youth to spend valuable time with adult supervisors and coworkers instead of idling about with other teens. In the 1980s, Greenberger and Steinberg (1986) argued, in contrast, that the employment opportunities available to teens had changed over the years as the vast majority of youth were toiling in a low-quality "adolescent workplace" with few opportunities for skill development, low career relevance, and a predominance of supervisors and coworkers who were also teenagers. Studies since then have shown that teenagers work in a diversity of jobs (Hirschman and Voloshin 2007; National Reseach Council 1998) with a wide range of opportunities for learning, skill utilization, career potential, social support, and interaction with adults (Call and Mortimer 2001; Finch et al. 1991; Mortimer 2003; Rauscher et al. 2013; Shanahan et al. 1991).

Yet, as mentioned previously, teenagers today are much less likely to work compared to cohorts of youth from just 20 years ago, which reflects increasing job competition from older workers for entry-level employment (Smith 2011; Staff et al. 2014), the popularity and perceived need for quality internships, and perhaps increasing pressure to do well in school to gain access to selective postsecondary schools (Alon 2009). Has this broad shift in youth employment limited the types of jobs youth could once obtain? Will today's working teenagers be overrepresented in low-quality jobs, with the potential for intense, stressful work experiences, or will they be spared these conditions of work if confined to informal work experiences?

To answer these questions, we turn again to recent survey data from the Monitoring the Future study. Regarding job type, about 64% of 8th graders and 50% of 10th graders in 2014 worked in informal jobs, either doing lawn work or babysitting. By the 12th grade, employed teenagers transition from informal-type work (held by only about 14% of employed seniors) into a wider range of jobs. Most working seniors are currently employed in either restaurants (19%) or in fast food (17%), and about 16% work in sales positions. The percentage of working youth in office jobs also climbs from 1% in 8th grade to 4% in 12th grade. Not surprisingly, less than 5% of teenagers nowadays work on farms, and only 0.5% deliver newspapers. These statistics suggest that youth today still work in a broad range of jobs, despite the overall drop in school-year employment compared to years past. Furthermore, the high number of youth today employed in lawn work and babysitting may be a welcome trend given research suggesting benefits of informal-type work on school success. For instance, McNeal (1997), in his longitudinal analyses of teenagers in the 1980s (i.e., High School and Beyond study), found that students employed in farming, lawn work, and babysitting were less likely to drop out of high school compared to non-working youth. Informal work is often performed in family and neighborhood settings (e.g., lawn mowing and snow shoveling, babysitting), where youth are likely to be exposed to positive adult role models and controls and less likely to be subject to the stresses of more formal employment (Hansen and Jarvis 2000; Hansen et al. 2001). Rural youth still work on family farms (though youth farm workers have relatively high rates of physical injury [National Research Council 1998]).

Regarding the interpersonal contacts in youth's jobs, there is little evidence that employed teenagers mostly work with other teenagers. In fact, less than 4% of MTF high school seniors in 2014 reported working in a job where almost all of their coworkers are the same age and their supervisor is age 25 or younger. In addition, about 42% of the 2014 seniors who were employed also reported being "quite" or "completely" satisfied with their jobs. Despite these positive reports of work for students today (i.e., lack of age-segregation and high levels of job satisfaction), it is clear that their employers continue to have very little contact with teachers and counselors. Among 2014 seniors, 89% of employed youth reported that the teacher did not "at all" help them obtain their job, and even among youth who reported their job was part of a work-study program (only 7% of employed youth), more than half reported that their teacher did not help them acquire their job.

Of course, there are other dimensions of employment that could make it more or less conducive to positive youth adjustment. For instance, research shows that teens report higher levels of school misconduct, class cutting, substance use, poor self-esteem, and depressed mood when they feel that their jobs are incompatible with school, a potentially stressful experience (Barling et al. 1995; Mortimer et al. 2002; Staff and Uggen 2003). Excessive demands and stressors at work have also been linked to poor mental health and problem behaviors in adolescence (Bachman and Schulenberg 1993; Finch et al. 1991; Mortimer and Staff 2004; Shanahan et al. 1991). On the positive side, research shows that jobs that provide learning opportunities and skill development are highly prevalent among teen workers (Mortimer 2003) and that these attributes of work provide both short- and longer-term benefits. In adolescence, these dimensions of youth work have been linked to heightened intrinsic and extrinsic work values (Mortimer et al. 1996b), improved familial relationships (Mortimer and Shanahan 1994), positive mental health (Shanahan et al. 1991), and reduced alcohol and illicit drug use (Staff and Uggen 2003). These work dimensions are also positively associated with success in the labor market (i.e., career relevance, pay) in the years following high school (Mortimer 2003; Stern and Nakata 1989). In addition, Mortimer and Staff (2004) show that work stressors in adolescence can buffer the negative effects of adult work stressors on adult health, suggesting an "inoculation effect" from these early work experiences.

Do teenage workers still find educational relevance and opportunities for vocational development in their work? Unfortunately, little research has assessed work quality among contemporary cohorts. Rauscher and colleagues (2013), using a 2004 sample of students in Massachusetts, found that working teenagers reported high levels of helping opportunities and support from supervisors and coworkers, as well as moderate amounts of learning, skill use, autonomy, and work stress. Similarly, in the 2004 MTF study (the last year these work quality questions were asked), about 30% of employed seniors believed to a "considerable" or "great extent" that: (1) their job allowed them to use their skills and abilities; (2) they would learn new skills that would be useful in future work; and (3) it was an interesting job to do (Bachman et al. 2005). The vast majority of teenagers in the MTF also noted that through their jobs they got to know people from different social backgrounds and adults over the age of 30, experiences that would enhance work-related interpersonal skills. However, the teens were clear that these jobs did not match their long-term career goals. In the MTF, for instance, over 70% of employed 12th graders indicated this job was not at all what they expected to be doing for most of their lives. Similarly, Schneider and Stevenson (1999), in their longitudinal study of teenagers in the 1990s, found variation in the quality of paid work during adolescence, though for most youth these early experiences in the labor market were disconnected from long-term career goals.

In short, these studies suggest that the type of job and the subjective quality of the work (i.e., the degree of learning opportunities, skill utilization, career relevance, and work stress) are important for determining the "intensity" of work, above and beyond the average hours of work. Despite the wealth of studies assessing how these work dimensions among teens in the 1980s and 1990s relate to mental health, problem behaviors, and later success in the labor market, we know little about whether these work dimensions matter for academic outcomes and longer-term educational attainment. Furthermore, we know little about the quality of work among teenagers today, and whether these work dimensions matter for achievement and social development in adolescence and during the transition to adulthood.

A final component of youth employment that garners little attention is the duration of the work. A long-standing critique is that teenagers often work in jobs that are temporary or sporadic in duration, which in turn limits potential opportunities for learning, skill development, adult mentorship, and coworker support. Furthermore, short or sporadic work spells might be especially disruptive to academic pursuits, as teenagers will have little time to develop effective strategies to balance work and school activities. In contrast, those who work over long uninterrupted periods of time during high school may develop effective time management strategies that foster academic success and, since most college students work while attending school, carry over to postsecondary educational pursuits (Staff and Mortimer 2007). Furthermore, youth who hold jobs over a longer duration may be more likely to experience learning opportunities and career potential in their early work (Mortimer 2003). They may be more likely to list these jobs on employment and college applications, or call on former employers for references. Youth with steady work experience might signal to future employers a capacity to be dependable and trustworthy, compared to youth with a more transient employment history. Whereas most studies of youth work focus only on "snapshots" of their work experience, such as the average hours of work at the time of survey administration, the duration of these experiences can shed light on the overall intensity of work.

Using longitudinal data from the Youth Development Study (YDS), Mortimer (2003) identified important patterns in youth work based upon the average hours of work (cumulative hours of work divided by the total weeks work during the school year) and the duration (total months of work during the school year). The most invested workers, who were about 25% of the sample, averaged more than 20 h per week over almost all of the sophomore, junior, and senior years of high school. Sporadic workers (19% of the sample) also averaged more than 20 h per week in their jobs but were employed only half of the months. Steady and occasional workers, encompassing 25% and 18% of the sample, respectively, averaged 20 or fewer hours per week. However, the steady workers were employed nearly all of the months of high school, whereas the occasional workers only worked half of the months. Consistent with the relatively higher rates of employment for this cohort of teens (attending high school during the late 1980s and early 1990s), only 7% of youth in this sample reported no work experience. Mortimer found that teens who averaged moderate work hours over most of the 3 years of high school (i.e., were "steady workers" who were employed on average 22 of the 24 months of observation) were the most likely to receive a BA/BS degree in young adulthood, even after controlling for a variety of background factors (e.g., prior achievements, aspirations, family background). Consistent with proposition 2 (see below), this steady pattern of work was especially advantageous among youth who initially had low educational promise, substantially increasing their likelihood of receiving a 4-year college degree (Mortimer 2003; Staff and Mortimer 2007). The occasional work pattern, which shared low average weekly hours with the steady worker group but with low duration, did not confer this advantage. Vuolo et al. (2014) also report that those who engaged in steady work during high school were less likely to "flounder" during the transition from school to

work, without progressing toward self-identified careers. These findings highlight the importance of examining the duration of employment along with hours of work. Employment at lower intensity work hours may only be beneficial when jobs are held for some duration.

In summary, there is support for the proposition that employment can be risky for secondary students. However, for the most part this risk is confined to students who average long work hours during the school year. Research also shows that work in moderation can benefit academic outcomes, especially if teens follow a steady pattern of work through high school. Furthermore, there is little support for the notion that teenage work experiences are mostly of low quality. Teenagers work in a variety of jobs with some offering ample opportunities for vocational development, work–school balance, and adult mentorship and support. Low-quality work, when it occurs, appears to increase the risk of problem behaviors much like working an intense number of hours, though we know little about whether the quality of work leads to school failure. However, as we review in the next section, early work experiences, both good and bad, are shaped by ascribed characteristics such as gender, race/ethnicity, and family socioeconomic background. Sociodemographic background factors not only predict selection into work, but also influence whether work has beneficial or detrimental effects on school outcomes.

15.2.2 Proposition 2. Employment Intensity Affects School Success and Long-Term Socioeconomic Attainment, But Its Effects Are Moderated by Gender, Race/Ethnicity, and Family Socioeconomic Background

Stratification researchers have well documented how ascribed characteristics such as gender, race/ethnicity, and family background impact academic achievement and adult occupational attainment. Research has also shown how these early life factors shape the timing, intensity, duration, and quality of youths' early experiences in work (National Reseach Council 1998). For instance, girls tend to enter the world of work at slightly younger ages than boys. In these first jobs, girls are more likely to be working in informal or "freelance" jobs, such as babysitting, compared to boys who are more likely to work in "employee" jobs with a more established schedule and pay (U.S. Department of Labor 2000; Apel et al. 2006). In addition, employed girls are less likely than working boys to spend long hours on the job, though gender differences in average work hours tend to disappear by the end of high school.

Research also shows that White youth are more likely than Black and Hispanic youth to hold jobs at younger ages, as well as to hold jobs during the school year. In the 2014 MTF senior year cohort, for instance, about 65% of White youth had worked at some point during the past school year, compared to about half of Black and Hispanic youth. When employed, Black and Hispanic youth were more likely to work intensively during the school year (National Reseach Council 1998; U.S. Department of Labor 2000), though these differences tend to disappear by the senior year of high school (approximately 19% of Black, Hispanic and White youth worked over 20 h per week in the 2014 MTF senior year cohort). Parental education and income are positively linked to the likelihood that teenagers will hold a job during the school year. Youth from families with higher levels of education and income are more likely to hold jobs at younger ages and work limited hours compared to youth from more disadvantaged socioeconomic backgrounds.

Gender, race/ethnicity, and family background also impact the types of jobs teenagers hold. In the 2014 senior year MTF cohort, for instance, girls were more likely than boys to babysit, wait tables, and work in an office. Black and Hispanic youth were more likely than White youth to work in fast food jobs. High school seniors whose mothers had the highest levels of education were most likely to work in office jobs as well as babysitting, whereas those from more disadvantaged

backgrounds were more likely to work in restaurants and especially in fast-food.

Given these sociodemographic differences in the overall "intensity" of early work experiences, an important question is whether work effects on school achievement and dropout are conditioned by gender, race/ethnicity, and socioeconomic background. Such moderation is plausible for several reasons. It could be that intensive work experience exacerbates disadvantages associated with low socioeconomic background and minority status. For example, if parents with lower levels of education do not socialize their children as well for school achievement as those with higher levels of education (Lareau 2003), such youth may experience more difficulty in school and thus be attracted to the diversions of work; they may also be more susceptible to negative influences in the workplace than more advantaged teenagers. Alternatively, if working offers challenges and an arena for the development of time management and related skills, employment may provide greater benefit to disadvantaged youngsters but make less difference for more advantaged teens whose prior experiences have better prepared them to be successful in school. Heller (2014), in a study of over 1600 disadvantaged high school youth in Chicago, found that random assignment to a summer jobs program reduced the likelihood of violence by 43%. We speculate on the bases of subgroup moderation after examining some pertinent evidence.

Regarding average work hours, there is evidence that the effect on dropout varies by population subgroup. D'Amico (1984) found no effect of high average work hours on dropout for minority females and males. Among White youth, the effect of high work hours was inconsistent: Long hours of work in the 10th grade increased the risk of dropout for boys and in the 11th grade for girls. Lee and Staff (2007), using propensity score methods to control for observable differences between students in the National Education Longitudinal Study of 1988, similarly found that the negative impact of long hours on the job on high school dropout was not consistent among all students. In particular, averaging over 20 h per week during the school year was not associated with high school dropout among students who had an especially high probability of long work hours, such as boys, Black and Hispanic students, and youth from disadvantaged backgrounds. Research by Bachman et al. (2013) and Johnson (2004) has also shown null effects of long work hours on educational attainment and substance use among minority students and youth from low socioeconomic backgrounds.

Why are long work hours not as harmful for minority youth or students who come from more disadvantaged backgrounds? Compared to their more advantaged counterparts, minority and low-SES youth may be working for different reasons (i.e., for family expenses or college) or be more likely to need to work more hours (Newman 1999). In 2013, the MTF study asked high school seniors about how they used their earnings, and about half reported saving at least some of their earnings for future education, and about 43% reported using their earnings to help pay family living expenses (groceries, housing, etc.). However, the use of earnings varied by race and ethnicity, as approximately 55% of Black and Hispanic youth used their earnings for family expenses, compared to 37% of White youth. It also varied by parental education: Among teenagers whose parents did not finish high school, approximately 59% used at least some of their earnings for family expenses. Among teenagers whose parents had a college degree, only 37% contributed to family living expenses. Use of earnings in "non-leisure" ways (saving for future education, giving money to parents, or paying for school expenses), instead of just using them for discretionary spending, has been linked to improved relationships with parents (Shanahan et al. 1996). Furthermore, saving at least some earnings for college has been positively linked to participation in extracurricular activities, educational aspirations, grades, and long-term educational attainment (Marsh 1991; Marsh and Kleitman 2005; Ruscoe et al. 1996).

Minority students and teenagers from disadvantaged backgrounds face more obstacles when trying to get a job, such as discrimination, transportation difficulties, and limited jobs in the local labor market (Entwisle et al. 2000). These obstacles, in turn, may explain why the effect of work intensity is moderated by race/ethnicity and family socioeconomic background. In the face of such obstacles, those who manage to get jobs may be a more select group, better poised to make the most of the developmental opportunities of early work experience and less vulnerable to its risks. In addition, the very difficulty of securing employment may shape adolescents' attitudes and behaviors. Whereas White youth and teenagers from high-SES family backgrounds may find it easy to lose and then regain work, disadvantaged youth, especially if they reside in poor neighborhoods, may find that these jobs constitute a rare opportunity to contribute to family expenses and save for college. If jobs are plentiful and easy to obtain, youth may have little stake in their work, fostering nonchalant attitudes and encouraging workplace misbehaviors, such as tardiness, absenteeism, and giving away goods and services for free.

If jobs are harder to come by, these early experiences may instill more positive work orientations and help foster the development of soft skills, increasing the chances of later employment and promoting positive behavioral change. Entwisle et al. (2000), in their analyses of mostly poor youth residing in Baltimore, found that early work involvement increased the skill level of the job held in later adolescence. The authors speculated that early employment (e.g., during middle school) provided poor youth an alternative arena to develop their skills and increase the chances of future employment, especially if they had little interest in school. In fact, these more adult-like experiences reduced the likelihood of high school dropout (Entwisle 2005) and may reduce other problem behaviors. Thus, this greater selectivity into employment might translate into a better job (e.g., more opportunities to work with adults, skill utilization, or vocational development) or being a better worker (i.e., more serious about keeping a job) for disadvantaged students, leading to greater benefits in the long run.

Staff and Mortimer (2007) have argued that early experiences in the labor market can help youth from disadvantaged backgrounds establish strategies of time management that persist in young adulthood and facilitate higher educational attainment. Using data from the Youth Development Study, the authors found that youth from more advantaged backgrounds were likely to pursue a steady pattern of low-intensity and high-duration work during high school, followed by a similar pattern of part-time work combined with schooling in the years immediately following high school graduation. The inclusion of accumulated months of postsecondary "school and part-time work" mediated the benefits of steady high school work on subsequent receipt of a bachelor's degree. By contrast, youth from disadvantaged backgrounds were likely to pursue more intensive work (high average work hours and high employment duration), followed by full-time work immediately after the scheduled date of high school graduation. More intensive workers had little likelihood of acquiring 4-year college degrees, and they were more likely to feel they were in "career" jobs during the years following high school (Mortimer et al. 2008). However, when disadvantaged low-SES youth followed a steady work pattern during high school, their educational attainment and longer term wages were especially enhanced (Staff and Mortimer 2008).

In summary, research shows that gender, race/ethnicity, and family socioeconomic background influence the overall intensity of early experiences in the labor market, such as when youth first enter work, their average hours and duration, the type and quality of the experience, and how the earnings from work are used. Some evidence indicates that the academic and developmental benefits, as well as drawbacks, of work intensity depend on these ascribed characteristics. The most consistent finding is that long work hours are least detrimental for minority youth and teenagers from lower socioeconomic backgrounds. Furthermore, research also shows that early experiences in the workplace can facilitate both educational and occupational attainment for disadvantaged youth, especially when the hours of work are kept low. However, some scholars would argue that these associations are not due to working or the intensity of the job, but instead reflect preexisting differences between students in their motivations and resources. We discuss this idea in the next section.

15.2.3 Proposition 3. Employment Intensity Does Not Affect School Success and Long-Term Socioeconomic Attainment

Almost all of the research we reviewed up to this point is based on observational studies, so causal claims that work "affects" academic achievement and social development must be tempered by the lack of experimental evidence. To test whether employment intensity affects school success, the ideal study would randomly assign jobs of varying intensities to a sample of teens, and then scholars would test for significant differences in their academic achievement and adjustment at a later date. To thoroughly test the time trade-off hypothesis, investigators would want the treatment (i.e., employment) to occur during the school year when work investments would be most likely to interfere with academic pursuits. Scholars would also want to ensure that the employment assignments vary randomly in the hours of work per week as well as other important dimensions, such as the type and quality of the job (the degree of learning opportunities, skill utilization, stressors, etc.). The investigators might want to place restrictions on how the earnings are used (i.e., for discretionary purposes, to help with family expenses, etc.), as well as discourage youth from finding jobs on their own. Ideally, the sample size would be large and diverse so comparisons of treatment effects could be made within population subgroups. Of course, such designs are complicated by the fact that not all teens want to work (though 88% of non-working seniors in the 2014 MTF study wished they could work during the school year), not all teens would agree to work in a high intensity job (especially if they thought it might adversely affect their school performance), not all teens who were assigned jobs would stick with them, and some teens would seek jobs on their own despite the random assignment.

As noted earlier, race/ethnicity and family socioeconomic status shape who works and at what intensities. And despite the lack of experimental evidence (the exception is Heller's (2014) study showing negative effects on violent crime of a summer employment program in Chicago), research clearly shows that prior achievements and orientations also precede early work intensity. Teenagers who have little interest or success in school gravitate earlier to the world of work compared to students who are better students or more invested in school (National Research Council 1998). Teenagers are more likely to spend long hours on the job if they previously had low educational promise (low educational aspirations, poor school performance, little school engagement). Early substance use, school misconduct, delinquency, and arrest also increase the likelihood that teenagers will average intensive hours of work during the school year (Mortimer 2003; Staff and Uggen 2003), and accounting for these preexisting differences between students substantially diminishes the effects of intensive work hours on later problem behaviors (Apel et al. 2007; Paternoster et al. 2003). These findings suggest that problem behaviors, school difficulty, and failure precede rather than follow adolescent work intensity.

Studies using data from the National Education Longitudinal Study of 1988 report little evidence of a relationship between paid work hours and school performance once accounting for prior differences between individuals (Schoenhals et al. 1998; Warren et al. 2000). Rothstein (2007), using data from the National Longitudinal Survey of Youth (1997 cohort), initially show small negative impacts of high school work experiences (measured as the total number of hours worked during the school year divided by the number of weeks in the school year) on grade point average. These effects became statistically non-significant when instrumental variables are used to account for both time-varying and time-stable unobserved factors. However, research by Apel et al. (2008) and Tyler (2003) still find negative impacts of work intensity on academic achievement and high school completion even when instrumental variables are used.

Teenagers who place a stronger emphasis on work than school tend to do poorly in school, even when they are not actually working (Bachman et al. 2003; Warren 2002). Using longitudinal data from three cohorts of 8th graders whose educational progress was tracked until the 12th grade, and within-person analyses to control for unobserved time-stable selection factors, Staff and colleagues (2010b) found that youth performed more poorly in school (i.e., they had low GPA, limited extracurricular involvement, low educational expectations, limited school effort, incomplete assignments, and engaged in more school misbehavior, truancy, and suspension) when they worked more than 20 h per week compared to when they worked fewer hours or not at all. However, youth also had poorer school outcomes when they were not working but wished they could spend long hours on the job. A strong desire to work (measured before youth obtained jobs) also predates both intensive work hours and problem behaviors in later adolescence. Research shows a similar risk of juvenile delinquency when youth actually spend long hours on the job and when they merely wish they could but are not employed (Staff et al. 2010a).

Together, these studies suggest that school disengagement precedes involvement in work and any observed associations between paid work and school success may be spuriously related to preexisting differences between students. A few studies suggest academic risks to working many hours per week, however, even employing some of these more stringent techniques. In contrast to the larger body of research that largely draws on a strategy of controlling for preexisting differences among students, including sociodemographic factors and prior achievement and adjustment, in regression-based models, the research reviewed in this section is still small. It has not examined the range of behavioral, attitudinal and achievement outcomes that we ultimately need to assess to answer the question of how work intensity and academic success are related. It has also not considered the patterns of employment youth engage in over time (i.e. duration and intensity) nor variation in the quality of jobs.

15.2.4 Taking Stock of the Three Propositions

The extensive literature reviewed in this chapter indicates that moderate hours of work involvement during the school year will not hurt students' prospects in school, either in the short- or longer-term. For many youth, work intensity, gauged by long hours on the job, does increase the risk of school failure, though research suggests that these negative effects tend to be weaker or non-existent among disadvantaged, minority, and lower socioeconomic status youth. Moderate hours of employment may actually facilitate better educational outcomes, especially when teens work steadily. Most adolescent work is not concentrated in poor quality or stressful jobs, another form of "intensity," though studies indicate this can lead to problem behaviors when it does occur. While some studies suggest that relationships between youth work hours and school performance may be spurious, more research is needed to examine the dynamic processes through which young people select themselves (and are selected by employers) into work and respond to more or less intense work experiences.

15.3 Unanswered Questions for Future Research

A theme throughout this chapter is that work "intensity" is almost always focused on the average hours of work, but we have stressed that work can be intense in other ways. Research must continue to address the quality of work as well as the duration of these experiences over the high school period. Because of the dramatic decline in teenage employment, there is danger that sociology of education scholars will dismiss work experience as no longer relevant to the academic achievement and educational persistence of high school students. Although contemporary teenagers are less likely to have paid jobs during the school year than prior cohorts, a majority of seniors (59% nationally, see Table 15.1) and a substantial proportion of 10th and 8th graders (24% and 20%, respectively) continue to work at

least some time during the school year. Deteriorating job markets for teenage workers have increased the scarcity of teen work. Under these conditions, work may have assumed even greater importance, accounting for the nearly universal desire of teenagers to have jobs. Moreover, increasing difficulties for young people in acquiring employment after completing their educations provide an altered context of school-to-work transition that may make it all the more imperative for job seekers to have work experience to be competitive in the labor market. Employment of moderate intensity in adolescence, which may facilitate educational pursuits, may then doubly benefit young adults in a labor market increasingly rewarding educational attainment by fostering degree attainment and building an employment history with which to compete well with other degree holders. Though, as noted above, there is some evidence that those who have less salutary employment prospects are less likely to suffer from intensive employment, it is an open question as to whether the heightened precarity of work in general makes it more or less likely that students will benefit from early jobs.

In addition, we see at least four unanswered questions that scholars should consider:

15.3.1 Question 1. Are Teenagers Nowadays Seeking Unpaid Work (i.e., Volunteering, Internships) as a Substitute for Paid Work, and Does This Shift in Type of Work Activity Matter for School Achievement and Dropout?

Given the difficulty of obtaining paid work, some contemporary teenagers may seek unpaid work—volunteering and internships—to obtain work experience. These activities may be seen as functional equivalents to paid work because they get teenagers into a workplace, where they gain exposure to working adults and obtain opportunities to develop the same kinds of work-relevant knowledge and skills that teens acquire in the paid employment setting. Internships can also shape long-term educational and career goals (Schneider and Stevenson 1999). Indeed, there is evidence from the now three-generational Youth Development Study that such work may have become increasingly common. Comparing YDS 11th graders with their 16- to 17-year-old children showed that while only 12% of the 11th graders performed any volunteer work (in 1990), 40% of their same age children did two decades later (in 2009 and 2010). Only 14% of the parents had volunteer jobs when they were in the 9th grade, but a third of their 14- and 15-year-old children held such jobs. (In contrast, 55% of the YDS parent sample held paid jobs back in the 11th grade in 1990, but only 25% of their 16 and 17 year-old children held such jobs in 2009–2010.) MTF cohort data also suggest a similar pattern of declining teenage employment (shown in Table 15.1) coupled with an uptick in teenage volunteering over the past 20 years. For instance, approximately 25% of 8th graders and 27% of 10th and 12th graders volunteered at least monthly in 1994. By 2014, the percentage of youth who engaged in at least monthly volunteering had increased to approximately 28% of 8th graders, 33% of 10th graders, and 38% of 12th graders. Just as scholars turned to the near-universal experience of adolescent paid work in the 1980s, more now needs to be learned about the consequences of unpaid work.

Because volunteer work is more discretionary than paid employment, it is arguably less likely to involve long work hours, that is, more than 20 h per week, and less likely to interfere with schoolwork. However, precisely because of its more discretionary and sporadic character, such work may not be as conducive to the acquisition of time management skills and vocational development. Furthermore, while youth of higher socioeconomic status and White youth have long been more likely to acquire paid jobs, unpaid work may be even more subject to selection processes. Volunteering and internship opportunities may be less visible to disadvantaged teens and access to such jobs may be more dependent on parental and other connections. Selection of volunteers by organizations may also involve less formal procedures than for employment, making it more subject to unconscious bias.

While employed students in the late 1980s and early 1990s had similar patterns of time use as those who did not work, especially if they moderated their work hours (Shanahan and Flaherty 2001), this may no longer be the case in the second decade of the twenty-first century. Do those who are employed exhibit markedly different constellations of time use than their non-employed peers, especially those who are volunteering or working in internships? How does this shift from paid to unpaid work in adolescence relate to academic success and longer-term socioeconomic attainment? Understanding the place of employment in the changing historical context of youth time use will shed light on whether work (both paid and unpaid) has the same meaning and consequences for teenagers today.

15.3.2 Question 2. Does High Intensity Work During the Summer Months Also Compromise School Achievement and Increase the Risk of Dropout?

The controversy surrounding youth employment has been clearly focused on work during the school year, given the potential conflict between working and academic engagement. Rates of employment and the average hours devoted to it among workers are, not surprisingly, higher in the summer months than in the school year (Perreira et al. 2007). Though scholars have linked summer employment to an increase in delinquency and substance use (Apel et al. 2006), to our knowledge, no one has seriously questioned the academic value of working during the summer months, when school is not in session, nor examined the impacts of such employment on school-related outcomes. For many years, American parents have considered the employment of their children beneficial, heightening independence, teaching children the value of money, and developing work-related skills (Aronson et al. 1996; Phillips and Sandstrom 1990), and scholars have not questioned these premises. It would be useful to examine the effects of work of different levels of intensity during the summer on academic outcomes, including consideration of whether summer work is performed in isolation (and not during the school year) or whether it represents a continuation of school-year employment. In this era of diminished employment opportunities, is working during the summer more contingent than in prior periods on already having a job during the school year? What does this mean for the prospects of disadvantaged youth? Are the different kinds of jobs youth hold during the summer and the school year (with summer jobs offering opportunities as life guards, camp counselors, etc.) more or less conducive to vocational development and academic engagement?

15.3.3 Question 3. Does High Intensity Work in College Negatively Impact Achievement and Lead to Dropout?

Whereas most scholarly and public concern focuses on dropout from high school, college dropout, often called attrition, has crucial consequences for students as well as for colleges and the public bodies that often support them. Because of the increasing income payoff for college degrees, both students and their parents recognize the value of graduating from college. Given the increasing skill demands in the labor market, it is widely recognized that a high school diploma is not adequate to secure a well-paying, stable job that provides the wherewithal for economic independence and a satisfactory life style.

In fact, more than 90% of high school seniors plan to go to college (Reynolds et al. 2006), and more than 50% plan to obtain even more education (Bachman et al. 2011a). However, just over half (57%) of students entering 4-year degree programs actually finish their degrees within 6 years (Knapp et al. 2010). Students attending 2-year college programs have even lower rates of completion (Zapata-Gietl et al. 2016). Recent research, using the Youth Development Study panel, documents the difficulties in the labor

market faced by young adults who start, but do not earn any kind of college degree (Vuolo et al. 2016). In fact, on several indicators of quality of work, associate degree recipients fare similarly to 4-year college graduates (but not with respect to income), doing better than college dropouts.

Public sector austerity since the 2008 Great Recession has increased college costs, especially at public colleges where most students attend, and pressures on students to work more hours to finance their educations (Presley 2013). Many college students, in fact, work full-time while taking college coursework, a feat that severely compromises their ability to stay engaged in school and to graduate on time. Zapata-Gietl and colleagues (2016) document the many role conflicts and challenges experienced especially by so-called "non-traditional" students (older, married, parents, first-generation, etc.), who balance families, work, and other obligations as they attend 2-year colleges. Many students at 4-year colleges and universities face similar pressures.

However, college students, like high school students, work for a variety of reasons. Some view work as more of a social experience than a means of financing their educations, blurring the boundaries between work and leisure. Besen-Cassino's study of White college students (2014), mostly from higher socioeconomic status families, found that these students worked not for economic reasons, but as a way to meet people, socialize with friends, and express their identities, all things they found difficult to accomplish at school. And while they highly valued the academic credentials they were pursuing at university, they had little confidence they would develop relevant job skills through schooling. Indeed the strong social ties developed and maintained at work motivated decisions to skip class and otherwise compromise academic work so as to not let friends and co-workers down.

Paralleling findings for high school students, moderate work hours during the school year in college does not increase the risk of drop-out, and may even help students to succeed (Presley 2013). As discussed earlier, Staff and Mortimer (2007), analyzing Youth Development Study data, found that students' work patterns in high school and college were similar. That is, students who had developed a pattern of high duration-low intensity "steady" work during high school pursued a similar pattern in college, and this work pattern contributed to their acquisition of 4-year college degrees. However, working more than 20 h per week during the first year of college increases the likelihood that students will leave early (Bozick 2007). Still, even intensive work during postsecondary education may be conducive to vocational development and success if it is related to fields of study or serves as a steppingstone to occupational goals. Full-time employment does not lower the likelihood of BA completion, though it is associated with lower grades (Hamilton 2013). Some early evidence (Tinto 1987; Ehrenberg and Sherman 1987) suggested that students who held jobs on campus were less likely to drop out than those whose jobs were found off campus, and more recent research (Presley 2013) confirms this observation. On-campus employment, even if not educationally related (e.g., working in a school cafeteria) ties the student to the college in a way that off-campus jobs do not. Especially valuable in integrating the student into academic life is employment that involves interactions between students and faculty. Educationally and vocationally-relevant college student employment is more likely in majors or course sequences that prepare students for a particular type of work, as in community college programs that lead to a vocationally relevant associate degree or occupational certification. More research is needed on how work intensity during college, broadly construed as we have done here, influences college persistence and degree attainment, and the extent to which such effects vary by the type of college or curricular program.

15.3.4 Question 4. How Does Work Intensity Relate to Academic Success Among Immigrant Youth in the United States?

As reviewed previously, research has documented how gender, socioeconomic background, and race/ethnicity moderate the effect of high work intensity on school success, positive youth adjust-

ment, and long-term educational attainment. However, little research has examined whether nativity differences within population groups also influence these short- and longer-term associations.

Nearly two decades ago the National Research Council (1998) concluded in their report on protecting youth at work that "very little data on work among immigrants, in general, and immigrant youth, in particular, have been collected" (p. 52). Since this influential report, some research has shown how nativity shapes early participation in work. For instance, 73% of Hmong parents of refugee children in the Youth Development Study did not want their offspring to do paid work (McNall et al. 1994), while the parents of other YDS children were near unanimous in their approval of their children's employment (Phillips and Sandstrom 1990). Kofman and Bianchi (2012), using data from the 2003 to 2010 American Time Use Survey, found that teenagers ages 15–17 in immigrant households (i.e., who were foreign born or who were residing with at least one parent who was foreign born) from Latin America or Asia spent less time in paid work compared to native-born youths. Oropesa and Landale (2009) similarly showed nativity differences in employment among 16- and 17-year-old Mexican youth in the 2000 census. They found that native-born Mexican teenagers were more likely to be working while in school compared to foreign-born Mexican youth. Perreira et al. (2007), using longitudinal data from the Add Health study, found that adolescents of first- or second-generation immigrant parents spent less time employed while attending high school and during the summer months compared to native born youth.

Why are youth in immigrant households less likely to be employed compared to native-born teenagers? One reason is that informal forms of employment, such as playing music at parties, working as a D.J., or participating in other jobs that are "off the books" may be more common among immigrant youth compared to youth with native-born parents (Kasinitz et al. 2008). Moreover, Kasinitz and colleagues reported that children of immigrants in New York City often viewed work in businesses owned by their family or relatives as something they did to "help out" rather than as more formal paid jobs. Additionally, analyses of time use data from the American Time Use Survey reveals that immigrant youth spend more time studying than their native-born counterparts (50 min per day versus 38 min, respectively), so children in immigrant households may be discouraged from holding a job during the school year out of concern that it could compromise academic pursuits (Kofman and Bianchi 2012). On average, Hmong youth in the Youth Development Study spent 19–26 h per week on homework during the 4 years of high school; other youth spent between 7 and 8 h (McNall et al. 1994). Finally, it is plausible that some youth from immigrant households, especially if any of the family members are undocumented immigrants, may also think their own work is illegal and may be reluctant to report their previous experiences in the labor market to researchers, thus leading to an undercount of actual employment experiences among immigrant youth. However, we are not aware of studies that have considered whether nativity is a moderator of work intensity and academic success in adolescence. Echoing the National Research Council report, we encourage researchers to pursue this line of inquiry in future work.

15.4 Policy Implications

In the absence of causal evidence, recommendations for shifts in policy are hazardous. While mounting evidence suggests that employed teenagers are subject to higher risks of school difficulty and dropout when they work more than 20 h per week, it is a considerable leap to conclude that school-age youth should be discouraged or even prevented from working more than 20 h per week. Uncertain, rapidly changing, and increasingly diverse contexts make such conclusions especially tenuous, and shifts in the regulatory environment may have unforeseen and deleterious consequences. For example, prohibiting high school students from working more than 20 h a week (approximately 20% of seniors

nationally in 2014, see Table 15.1) could lead those who truly need to work, to support themselves or their families, to drop out of school in order to maintain their hours of work. Hours restrictions based on age (for example, applying to all students under 19), meant to encourage students to stay in school and away from employment, could cause widespread hardship for financially independent young people.

Nonetheless, a number of steps could be taken, short of prohibition, which might diminish the likelihood that high school students work intensively and thus jeopardize their academic attainments. First of all, attempts could be made to spread the word—to teachers, counselors, parents, and employers—about the potential dangers of high intensity work. Rather than deflecting students from all employment (a message likely to be widely rejected given the demonstrated, near universal, preference of students to work), those who guide high school students should steer them toward work that will be conducive to their educational and vocational development. That is, moderate work that provides learning opportunities and whose hours, conditions, and task requirements do not interfere with school. To enhance the compatibility of paid work and schoolwork, educators could encourage students to discuss their experiences on the job, the knowledge and skills that enable them to be effective in their jobs, and how curricular offerings in the school might enhance such human capital. Sharing information about work would also serve to spread information to students about opportunities for employment, as well as the most desirable employers in their communities.

Another potentially useful strategy to engage students in the educational enterprise and to reduce dropout is to build connections between school and work. Among modern countries, the United States is distinctive in its lack of institutional bridges from school to jobs. Unlike Germany, Austria, and the Netherlands, with their apprenticeship systems, and Japan, with linkages between high schools and employers, school-leavers in the United States must rely on their own contacts and, if they are among the fortunate who graduate from college, college career services and placement offices. While almost all high school students hope and plan to enter a 2- or 4-year college, approximately a third of contemporary cohorts do not do so. If little is offered with vocational relevance in high schools, the non-college bound may see little reason to invest in, or even stay in, school whether they are employed intensively during high school or not.

In addition to building more and better vocational curricula, high schools might provide other opportunities and services that would enhance students' vocational development. They might offer occupationally-relevant after-school programs, such as the highly successful *After School Matters* program in Chicago (Hirsch 2015), which supports sustained contact and joint projects involving students and professionals in the community; develop connections between employers and teachers (Rosenbaum et al. 1999), who may be able to guide youth toward good jobs that promote work readiness; encourage students to enroll in dual-enrollment courses, which provide opportunities to gain work experience while earning course credits (Schneider et al. 2015); arrange job shadowing experiences for high school students; and promote internships, including monetary supplement for those who would otherwise not be able to participate in these, often unpaid, work experiences. Such innovative methods of steering youth toward high-quality work experiences are becoming ever more popular, perhaps in response to the decline in labor market demand for youth. Work that is connected to, and preferably monitored by, the schools may enable teenagers to have work experiences that are more beneficial to them in the long run than previously typical youth jobs. Such work experiences may convince contemporary teens that staying in high school until completion and pursuing higher education will have substantial payoffs in the labor market.

15.5   Concluding Comments

The possibility that employment during the school year poses academic risks to secondary students has fueled much research on work intensity, particularly the number of hours students spend working for pay each week. To a lesser extent, research has also considered whether alternative ways in which work is "intense," such as working in lower-quality or stressful jobs, undermines educational success. The larger picture that comes out of this research is that employment may have detrimental academic consequences, including lowered performance and higher dropout, but only when students work an excessive number of hours per week or in jobs they report as of problematic quality. Neither of those situations has characterized the majority of teens' work experiences, even at the height of trends in teen employment in the 1980s. Moreover, at least with respect to work hours, a growing body of evidence documents that minority and lower socioeconomic status students do not experience the detrimental academic consequences of working intensely. And finally, recent studies using the most stringent models available cast some doubt on whether there are any consequences to employment and work intensity at all. Whether and how much work teenagers engage in, along with their academic engagement, performance, achievement, and persistence, may both be driven by preexisting differences among students.

As we look to the future, there are excellent opportunities for scholars of education to engage these issues further and deepen our knowledge about the nexus of work and schooling. Recent efforts to address causality are limited in scope to date and have been primarily directed toward examining the impacts of work hours. In addition, assessments of patterns of employment that examine investments in work over time are rare. Strategies of employment over the adolescent years, as well as the balance during school and summer months of the year, need further investigation. In addition, research on employment during tertiary education, including that which attends to continuity and discontinuity compared to the high school years, would be desirable. Finally, we need to understand whether work is related to academic success similarly or differently among immigrant and native born youth.

The fact that participation in paid work during adolescence has declined over the past several decades does not make it any less important to study. Employment remains a key domain of adolescence and critical questions about how it relates to education remain, as noted above. In addition, the nature and context of adolescent employment is changing, and as such, we need to know whether its impact is changing as well. It is important that we learn how paid employment compares to unpaid work experiences so that we can assess the educational implications of this historical shift. The extent to which time spent at work is deemed a threat or complement to educational pursuits may depend on the impacts of alternative uses of time, including volunteering and unpaid interning.

References

Alon, S. (2009). The evolution of class inequality in higher education: Competition, exclusion, and adaptation. *American Sociological Review, 74*, 731–755.

Apel, R., Paternoster, R., Bushway, S. D., & Brame, R. (2006). A job isn't just a job: The differential impact of formal versus informal work on adolescent problem behavior. *Crime & Delinquency, 52*, 333–369.

Apel, R., Bushway, S. D., Brame, R., Haviland, A. M., Nagin, D. S., & Paternoster, R. (2007). Unpacking the relationship between adolescent employment and antisocial behavior: A matched samples comparison. *Criminology, 45*(1), 67–97.

Apel, R., Bushway, S. D., Paternoster, R., Brame, R., & Sweeten, G. (2008). Using state child labor laws to identify the causal effect of youth employment on deviant behavior and academic achievement. *Journal of Quantitative Criminology, 24*, 337–362.

Aronson, P. J., Mortimer, J. T., Zierman, C., & Hacker, M. (1996). Generational differences in early work experiences and evaluations. In J. T. Mortimer & M. D. Finch (Eds.), *Adolescents, work, and family: An intergenerational developmental analysis* (pp. 25–62). Newbury Park: Sage.

Bachman, J. G., & Schulenberg, J. (1993). How part-time work intensity relates to drug use, problem behavior, time use, and satisfaction among high school seniors: Are these consequences or merely correlates? *Developmental Psychology, 29*(2), 220–235.

Bachman, J. G., Saffron, D. J., Sy, S., & Schulenberg, J. (2003). Wishing to work: New perspectives on how adolescents' part-time work intensity is linked to educational disengagement, substance use, and other problem behaviors. *International Journal of Behavioral Development, 27*(4), 301–315.

Bachman, J. G., Johnston, L. D., & O'Malley, P. M. (2005). *Monitoring the future: Questionnaire responses from the nation's high school seniors, 2004.* Ann Arbor: Institute for Social Research.

Bachman, J. G., Johnston, L. D., & O'Malley, P. M. (2011a). *Monitoring the future: Questionnaire responses from the nation's high school seniors, 2010.* Ann Arbor: Institute for Social Research.

Bachman, J. G., Staff, J., O'Malley, P. M., Schulenberg, J. E., & Freedman-Doan, P. (2011b). Twelfth-grade student work intensity linked to later educational attainment and substance use: New longitudinal evidence. *Developmental Psychology, 47*(2), 344–363.

Bachman, J. G., Staff, J., O'Malley, P. M., & Freedman-Doan, P. (2013). Adolescent work intensity, school performance, and substance use: Links vary by race/ethnicity and socioeconomic status. *Developmental Psychology, 49*(11), 2125–2134.

Barling, J., Rogers, K. A., & Kelloway, E. K. (1995). Some effects of teenagers' part-time employment: The quantity and quality of work make the difference. *Journal of Organizational Behavior, 16*, 143–154.

Besen-Cassino, Y. (2014). *Consuming work: Youth labor in America.* Philadelphia: Temple University Press.

Bozick, R. (2007). Making it through the first year of college: The role of students' economic resources, employment, and living arrangements. *Sociology of Education, 80*(3), 261–285.

Call, K. T., & Mortimer, J. T. (2001). *Arenas of comfort in adolescence: A study of adjustment in context.* Mahwah: Erlbaum.

Carr, R., Wright, J. D., & Brody, C. (1996). Effects of high school work experience a decade later: Evidence from the National Longitudinal Survey. *Sociology of Education, 69*(1), 66–82.

Coleman, J. S., Bremner, R. H., Clark, B. R., Davis, J. B., Eichorn, D. H., et al. (1974). *Youth: Transition to adulthood.* Report of the panel on youth of the President's science advisory committee. University of Chicago Press.

D'Amico, R. (1984). Does employment during high school impair academic progress? *Sociology of Education, 57*(3), 152–164.

Ehrenberg, R., & Sherman, D. (1987). Employment while in college, academic achievement, and post college outcomes: A survey of results. *Journal of Human Resources, 22*, 1–21.

Entwisle, D. R. (2005). Urban teenagers: Work and dropout. *Youth & Society, 37*(1), 3–32.

Entwisle, D. R., Alexander, K. L., & Olson, L. S. (2000). Early work histories of urban youth. *American Sociological Review, 65*(2), 279.

Finch, M. D., Shanahan, M. J., Mortimer, J. T., & Ryu, S. (1991). Work experience and control orientation in adolescence. *American Sociological Review, 56*, 597–611.

Greenberger, E., & Steinberg, L. D. (1986). *When teenagers work: The psychological and social costs of teenage employment.* New York: Basic Books.

Hamilton, L. (2013). More is more or more is less: Parental financial investments during college. *American Sociological Review, 78*, 70–95.

Hansen, D. M., & Jarvis, P. A. (2000). Adolescent employment and psychosocial outcomes: A comparison of two employment contexts. *Youth & Society, 31*, 417–436.

Hansen, D. M., Mortimer, J. T., & Kruger, H. (2001). Adolescent part-time employment in the U.S. and Germany: Diverse outcomes, contexts, and pathways. In C. Pole, P. Mizen, & A. Bolton (Eds.), *Hidden hands: International perspectives on children's work and labour* (pp. 121–138). London: Routledge Falmer Press.

Heller, S. B. (2014). Summer jobs reduce violence among disadvantaged youth. *Science, 346*(6214), 1219–1223.

Hirsch, B. J. (2015). *Job skills and minority youth: New program directions*. New York: Cambridge University Press.

Hirschman, C., & Voloshin, I. (2007). The structure of teenage employment: Social background and the jobs held by high school seniors. *Research in Social Stratification and Mobility, 25*(3), 189–203.

Johnson, M. K. (2004). Further evidence on adolescent employment and substance use: Differences by race and ethnicity. *Journal of Health and Social Behavior, 45*, 187–197.

Kalenkoski, C. M., & Pabilonia, S. W. (2012). Time to work or time to play: The effect of student employment on homework, sleep, and screen time. *Labour Economics, 19*, 211–221.

Kasinitz, P., Mollenkopf, J. H., Waters, M. C., & Holdaway, J. (2008). *Inheriting the city: The children of immigrants come of age*. Harvard University Press.

Kerckhoff, A. (2000). Transition from school to work in comparative perspective. In M. T. Hallinan (Ed.), *Handbook of the sociology of education* (pp. 453–474). New York: Kluwer Academic/Plenum Publishers.

Knapp, L. G., Kelly-Reid, J. E., & Ginder, S. A. (2010). *Enrollment in postsecondary institutions, Fall 2008; Graduation rates, 2002 & 2005 cohorts; and financial statistics, fiscal year 2008* (NCES 2010-152). U.S. Department of Education. Washington, DC.: National Center for Education Statistics.

Kofman, Y., & Bianchi, S. M. (2012). Time use of youths by immigrant and native-born parents: ATUS results. *Monthly Labor Review, 135*, 3–24.

Lareau, A. (2003). *Unequal childhoods: Class, race, and family life*. Berkley: University of California Press.

Lee, J. C., & Staff, J. (2007). When work matters: The varying impact of work intensity on high school dropout. *Sociology of Education, 80*(2), 158–178.

Light, A. (2001). In school work experience and the returns to schooling. *Journal of Labor Economics, 19*(1), 65–93.

Marsh, H. W. (1991). Employment during high school: Character building or a subversion of academic goals? *Sociology of Education, 64*, 172–189.

Marsh, H. W., & Kleitman, S. (2005). Consequences of employment during high school: Character build-ing, subversion of academic goals, or a threshold? *American Educational Research Journal, 42*(2), 331–369.

McNall, M., Dunnigan, T., & Mortimer, J. T. (1994). The educational achievement of the St. Paul Hmong. *Anthropology and Education Quarterly, 25*, 44–65.

McNeal, R. B., Jr. (1997). Are students being pulled out of high school? The effect of adolescent employment on dropping out. *Sociology of Education, 70*(3), 206–220.

Mihalic, S. W., & Elliott, D. (1997). Short- and long-term consequences of adolescent work. *Youth & Society, 28*(4), 464–498.

Monahan, K. C., Lee, J. M., & Steinberg, L. (2011). Revisiting the impact of part-time work on adolescent adjustment: Distinguishing between selection and socialization using propensity score matching. *Child Development, 82*(1), 96–112.

Mortimer, J. T. (2003). *Working and growing up in America*. Cambridge: Harvard University Press.

Mortimer, J. T., & Johnson, M. K. (1998). Adolescent part-time work and educational achievement. In K. Borman & B. Schneider (Eds.), *The Adolescent years: Social influences and educational challenges* (pp. 183–206). Chicago: National Society for the Study of Education.

Mortimer, J. T., & Shanahan, M. J. (1994). Adolescent work experience and family relationships. *Work and Occupations, 21*, 369–384.

Mortimer, J. T., & Staff, J. (2004). Early work as a source of developmental discontinuity during the transition to adulthood. *Development and Psychopathology, 16*(4), 1047–1070.

Mortimer, J. T., Finch, M. D., Ryu, S., Shanahan, M. J., & Call, K. T. (1996a). The effect of work intensity on adolescent mental health, achievement, and behavioral adjustment: New evidence from a prospective study. *Child Development, 67*(3), 1243–1261.

Mortimer, J. T., Pimentel, E. E., Ryu, S., Nash, K., & Lee, C. (1996b). Part-time work and occupational value formation in adolescence. *Social Forces, 74*(4), 1404–1418.

Mortimer, J. T., Harley, C., & Staff, J. (2002). The quality of work and youth mental health. *Work and Occupations, 29*(2), 166–197.

Mortimer, J. T., Vuolo, M., Staff, J., Wakefield, S., & Xie, W. (2008). Tracing the timing of "career" acquisition in a contemporary youth cohort. *Work and Occupations, 35*, 44–84.

National Reseach Council. (1998). *Protecting youth at work: Health, safety, and development of working children and adolescents in the United States*. Washington, DC: The National Academies Press.

Newman, K. S. (1999). *No shame in my game*. New York: Knopf and Russell Sage Foundation.

Oropesa, R. S., & Landale, N. S. (2009). Why do immigrant youths who never enroll in U.S. schools matter? School enrollment among Mexicans and non-Hispanic Whites. *Sociology of Education, 82*(3), 240–266.

Paternoster, R., Bushway, S., Brame, R., & Apel, R. (2003). The effect of teenage employment on delinquency and problem behaviors. *Social Forces, 82*(1), 297–335.

Perreira, K. M., Harris, K. M., & Lee, D. (2007). Immigrant youth in the labor market. *Work and Occupations, 34*, 5–34.

Phillips, S., & Sandstrom, K. (1990). Parental attitudes toward "youthwork". *Youth and Society, 22*, 160–183.

Presley, C. (2013). Advising and engaging the "working-class" college student. *The Mentor. An Academic Advising Journal* (available online only). Retrieved January 9, 2016 at https://dus.psu.edu/mentor/2013/11/advising-and-engaging-the-%E2%80%9Cworking-class%E2%80%9D-college-student/

Rauscher, K. J., Wegman, D. H., Wooding, J., Davis, L., & Junkin, R. (2013). Adolescent work quality: A view from today's youth. *Journal of Adolescent Research, 28*(5), 557–590.

Reynolds, J., Stewart, M., Sischo, L., & MacDonald, R. (2006). Have adolescents become too ambitious? High school seniors' educational and occupational plans, 1976 to 2000. *Social Problems, 53*, 186–2006.

Rosenbaum, J. E., DeLuca, S., Miller, S. R., & Roy, K. (1999). Pathways into work: Short- and long-term effects of personal and institutional ties. *Sociology of Education, 72*, 179–196.

Rothstein, D. S. (2007). High school employment and youths' academic achievement. *The Journal of Human Resources, 42*(1), 194–213.

Ruscoe, G., Morgan, J. C., & Peebles, C. (1996). Students who work. *Adolescence, 31*(123), 625–632.

Schneider, B., & Stevenson, D. (1999). *The ambitious generation: America's teenagers, motivated but directionless*. New Haven: Yale University Press.

Schneider, B., Saw, G., & Broda, M. (2015). Work and work migration within and across countries in emerging and young adulthood. In L. A. Jensen (Ed.), *Oxford handbook of human development and culture: An interdisciplinary perspective* (pp. 554–569). Oxford University Press: Oxford.

Schoenhals, M., Tienda, M., & Schneider, B. (1998). The educational and personal consequences of adolescent employment. *Social Forces, 77*(2), 723–761.

Sewell, W. H., & Hauser, R. M. (1975). *Education, occupation, and earnings. Achievement in the early career*. New York: Academic.

Shanahan, M., & Flaherty, B. (2001). Dynamic patterns of time use in adolescence. *Child Development, 72*(2), 385–401.

Shanahan, M. J., Finch, M. D., Mortimer, J. T., & Ryu, S. (1991). Adolescent work experience and depressive affect. *Social Psychology Quarterly, 54*, 299–317.

Shanahan, M. J., Elder, G. H., Jr., Burchinal, M., & Conger, R. D. (1996). Adolescent paid labor and relationships with parents: Early work–family linkages. *Child Development, 67*, 2183–2200.

Smith, C. L. (2011). *Polarization, immigration, education: What's behind the dramatic decline in youth employment? Division of research and statistics and monetary affairs* (Finance and economics discussion series 2011–2041). Washington, DC: Federal Reserve Board.

Staff, J., & Mortimer J.T. (2008). Social class background and the "school to work" transition. *New Directions for Child and Adolescent Development 119*, 55–69.

Staff, J., & Mortimer, J. T. (2007). Educational and work strategies from adolescence to early adulthood: Consequences for educational attainment. *Social Forces, 85*(3), 1169–1194.

Staff, J., & Uggen, C. (2003). The fruits of good work: Early work experiences and adolescent deviance. *Journal of Research in Crime and Delinquency, 40*(3), 263–290.

Staff, J., Osgood, D. W., Schulenberg, J. E., Bachman, J. G., & Messersmith, E. E. (2010a). Explaining the relationship between employment and juvenile delinquency. *Criminology, 48*(4), 1101–1131.

Staff, J., Schulenberg, J. E., & Bachman, J. G. (2010b). Adolescent work intensity, school performance, and academic engagement. *Sociology of Education, 83*(3), 183–200.

Staff, J., Johnson, M. K., Patrick, M., & Schulenberg, J. (2014). The Great Recession and recent employment trends among secondary students in the United States. *Longitudinal and Life Course Studies, 5*(2), 173–188.

Staff, J., Mont'Alvao, A., & Mortimer, J. T. (2015). Children at work. In M. H. Bornstein & T. Leventhal (Eds.), *Handbook of child psychology and developmental science: Ecological settings and processes* (Vol. 4, pp. 345–374). Hoboken: Wiley.

Stern, D., & Nakata, Y. F. (1989). Characteristics of high school students' paid jobs, and employment experience after graduation. In D. Stern & D. Eichorn (Eds.), *Adolescence and work: Influences of social structure, labor markets, and culture* (pp. 189–234). Hillsdale: Lawrence Erlbaum.

Tinto, V. (1987). *Leaving college: Rethinking the causes and cures of student attrition*. Chicago: University of Chicago Press.

Tyler, J. H. (2003). Using state child labor laws to identify the effect of school-year work on high school achievement. *Journal of Labor Economics, 21*(2), 381–408.

U.S. Department of Education. (2015). High school dropouts and stopouts: Demographic backgrounds, academic experiences, engagement, and school characteristics. *National Center for Education Statistics*, 2015–2064.

U.S. Department of Labor. (2000). *Report on the youth labor force*. Washington, DC: U.S. Government Printing Office.

Vuolo, M., Mortimer, J. T., & Staff, J. (2014). Adolescent precursors of pathways from school to work. *Journal of Research on Adolescence, 24*, 145–162.

Vuolo, M., Mortimer, J. T., & Staff, J. (2016). The value of educational degrees in turbulent economic times: Evidence from the Youth Development Study. *Social Science Research, 57*, 233–252.

Warren, J. R. (2002). Reconsidering the relationship between student employment and academic outcomes: A new theory and better data. *Youth & Society, 33*(3), 366–393.

Warren, J. R., & Lee, J. C. (2003). The impact of adolescent employment on high school dropout: Differences by individual and labor-market characteristics. *Social Science Research, 32*, 98–128.

Warren, J. R., LePore, P. C., & Mare, R. D. (2000). Employment during high school: Consequences for students' grades in academic courses. *American Educational Research Journal, 37*, 943–969.

Zapata-Gietl, C., Rosenbaum, J., Ahearn, C., & Becker, K. I. (2016). College for all: New institutional conflicts in the transition to adulthood. In M. J. Shanahan, J. T. Mortimer, & M. K. Johnson (Eds.), *Handbook of the life course, volume 2*. New York: Springer.

Part IV

Educational Opportunities and the Transition into Adulthood

Students' Educational Pathways: Aspirations, Decisions, and Constrained Choices Along the Education Lifecourse

Michal Kurlaender and Jacob Hibel

Abstract

Educational pathways are marked by a series of choices that individuals and their families make that shape students' development and educational destinations. The education attainment model is defined by a notable tension between individual choice and structural constraints that exist throughout the life course. This chapter synthesizes research on the constrained choices that typify educational pathways from early childhood to adulthood in the U.S. We focus on several areas in the literature in which the tension between individual choice and structural constraints plays out, specifically: educational aspirations, curricular differentiation, and informational barriers and opportunities. Within each of these interconnected areas we describe the dominant theories that buttress the individual determinants model, and the structural or institutional forces that shape the educational attainment process. We also review policy trends that have emerged over the past several decades designed to attenuate structural inequalities in students' educational pathways.

We thank Thad Domina and Sherrie Reed for feedback on an earlier draft of this paper, and Elizabeth Zeiger Friedmann and Jake Jackson for research assistance.

M. Kurlaender (✉) · J. Hibel
University of California, Davis, CA, USA
e-mail: jhibel@ucdavis.edu; mkurlaender@ucdavis.edu

Educational pathways are marked by a series of choices that individuals and their families make that shape students' development and educational destinations. Viewed from an individualistic perspective, families invest time and resources in children's educational development early in childhood. These investments are then complemented and augmented by individuals' own decisions about how and where to invest their time and energies as they progress through school. Although this individualistic view of education is represented throughout the sociology of education, it is perhaps more closely associated with cognate disciplines such as economics and psychology. Sociologists, rather, often take a more structural view of education, emphasizing the ways choices are constrained by multiple forces and institutions sorting youth among unequal pathways of educational opportunity, which results in perpetuating social inequalities. The notion of *constrained choice* suggests an important interplay between structural forces and individual decision-making, which we argue ultimately shapes students' educational pathways.

A "pathway" denotes a course individuals embark on; one in which social structures can constrain and define individual choice. Just as pedestrians typically follow pre-defined paths rather than blazing their own trails, students typically move through pre-defined positions in educational institutions. However, students—like pedestrians—can choose among multiple competing paths and these choices have important implications for their developmental, educational, and socioeconomic destinations. Moreover, these choices are made within different types and "levels" of social structures—some more explicit or visible than others (Hays 1994; Sewell 1992).

This chapter synthesizes research on the constrained choices that typify educational pathways from early childhood to adulthood in the U.S. We have organized the review by focusing on several areas in the literature in which the tension between individual choice and structural constraints plays out, specifically: (1) educational aspirations; (2) curricular differentiation; and (3) informational barriers and opportunities. Within each of these interconnected areas we describe the dominant theories that buttress the individual determinants model, and the structural or institutional forces that shape the educational attainment process. Finally, we review policy trends that have emerged over the past several decades designed to attenuate structural inequalities in students' educational pathways.

16.1 Educational Aspirations in a College for All Era

Educational pathways in the U.S. are now defined by a ubiquitous "college for all" ethos that dominates individual students' dialogues about their educational pathways and policy efforts aimed at reducing structural barriers to postsecondary schooling. This is most evident in discussions around a fundamental notion of choice—students' educational aspirations.

Rational choice or human capital perspectives suggest that an individual's decision to invest in education is based on an interaction of tastes, abilities, and resources. With roots in neoclassical economic theory, these perspectives rest on the central assumption that individual actors seek, above all, to maximize their economic interests. According to this line of thought, the knowledge and skills (i.e., human capital) acquired through schooling make workers more

economically productive, creating a positive association between educational attainment and earnings. In light of this well-documented correlation, individuals seek to acquire as much education as they can afford as a means of securing higher earnings and status in adulthood.

Social scientists have produced multiple critiques of the rational choice explanation for the link between educational attainment and earnings, including credentialing theory (e.g., Collins 1979; Labaree 1997), screening or signaling theories (e.g., Rosenbaum and Binder 1997; Spence 1973; Stiglitz 1975), and conflict theories in the Marxian (e.g., Bowles and Gintis 1976), Weberian (e.g., Collins 1971), and Bourdieuian (e.g., Bourdieu and Passeron 1977) traditions. Each of these perspectives suggests that the structure of U.S. society and its central institutions leads individuals onto educational pathways that are determined by factors beyond straightforward cost-benefit analyses of potential educational investments. While other chapters in this volume explore the implications of these theoretical perspectives in greater depth than the present chapter, we note that, regardless of the framework one uses to understand the opportunities and constraints facing students as they navigate formal schooling transitions, a guiding principle of the U.S. schooling structure's design—both explicit through compensatory policies and implicit through the pervasive college for all ethos—is individual choice within open access pathways. Whether wholly realistic or not, this message has clearly been communicated to young people in the U.S. Students perceive that they possess substantial agency with respect to their educational futures, and their reported attainment expectations reveal that they generally intend to exercise this self-determination by obtaining degrees beyond the high school diploma.

Today's youth have registered the college refrain. A majority of middle and high school students, regardless of their academic performance, report that they will attend college (Jacob and Wilder-Linkow 2011; Goyette 2008; Reynolds and Pemberton 2001; Schneider and Stevenson 2000). The nearly universal orientation towards college represents incredible growth in educational expectations (Jacob and Wilder-Linkow 2011; Goyette 2008; Reynolds and Pemberton 2001). Over the past several decades the percentage of 10th graders with college degree expectations has doubled, and has nearly doubled among 12th graders (Fig. 16.1). However, college degree attainment has not kept up with the increased educational expectations present among today's youth (Fig. 16.1).

16.1.1 Aspirations and Expectations as Determinants of Educational Attainment

The role of educational aspirations and expectations in the education and status attainment processes has been intensely debated in recent years. This topic captures one of sociology's longstanding debates over the role of educational aspirations as a mediator of structural determinants of adult status (Sewell et al. 1969; Sewell and Hauser 1975). As educational aspirations have become more uniform over time—a remarkable 93% of all seniors in the most recent large-scale national survey (ELS) report that they planned to continue their education after high school—some sociologists of education have raised questions about the relevance of aspirations as a meaning-

ful predictor of students' ultimate educational attainment (Alexander and Cook 1979; Kao and Tienda 1998; Rosenbaum 2001).

In contrast to earlier periods, academic performance currently accounts for little of the variance in students' *expected* levels of educational attainment. Reynolds et al. (2006) find that between 1976 and 2000, the percentage of high school seniors indicating that they probably or definitely would complete *at least* a baccalaureate degree increased from 50% to 78%. At the same time, the explanatory power of self-reported grades and participation in a college preparatory program for predicting high school students' attainment expectations declined appreciably (Reynolds et al. 2006).

Recent work, however, suggests that educational expectations remain a key determinant of later educational success, and of students' attitudes and behavior in high school (Domina et al. 2011). In their article linking educational expectations to effort, Domina et al. (2011) test whether students' college expectations influence the importance they place on high school mathematics. They find that "educational expectations have a positive causal effect on student perceptions regarding the importance of high school academics for their future success" (p. 101), and that this relationship holds across the achievement

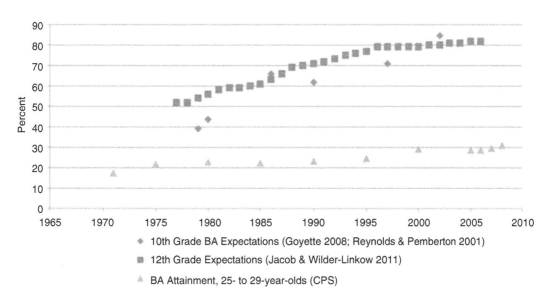

Fig. 16.1 BA expectations and attainment, 1970–2008

distribution, albeit attenuated for students at the lower end. Their findings challenge Rosenbaum's longstanding critique of the false promise of expectations in the college for all ethos, namely, that students believe that college opportunities are available irrespective of their performance in high school, and as such their expectations are a weak predictor of their effort or attainment (Rosenbaum 2001, 2011).

16.1.2 Student Beliefs as Determinants of Educational Attainment

Social psychologists have long demonstrated that students' beliefs about their abilities to succeed are related to their effort (Bandura 1982, 1997; Dweck and Elliott 1983; Schunk 1991). These ideas are related to self-affirmation theory, which suggests that people are inherently motivated to see themselves as competent and in control of their futures and will work to restore their self-worth when it is threatened (Steele 1988; Sherman and Cohen 2006; Yeager and Walton 2011). Relatedly, the belief that people can achieve what they desire through their actions is the foundation of self-efficacy theory (Bandura 1993; Gecas and Schwalbe 1983, 1986; Gecas and Seff 1989, 1990; Marcussen et al. 2004; Owens and Serpe 2003). Self-efficacy is a key component to how students may handle challenging or unpredictable situations and, importantly, how much effort they may decide to expend, or how long they persist in light of challenging or unpredictable situations. Individuals' sense of efficacy can influence actions indirectly by, for example, impacting their goals and aspirations, their effort and commitments to different pursuits, and how they cope with challenging situations (Bandura 1981; Marsh et al. 1991; Murdock et al. 2000; Reyes and Jason 1993).

Experiments from social psychology demonstrate that accentuating positive growth rather than shortfalls enhances self-efficacy, aspirations, and performance (Bandura 1993). This is critical because how students' process early difficulties can influence their educational trajecto-

ries (Cohen et al. 2009). Research on postsecondary STEM pathways illustrates the fundamental importance of self-efficacy for educational success, particularly for sub-groups historically underrepresented in these fields. For example, researchers have established that the under-participation of women in STEM majors is a function of disparities in interest in and affect towards math/science, and not to disparities in preparation or achievement (Mann and Diprete 2013; Morgan et al. 2016; Riegle-Crumb et al. 2012; Buchmann and DiPrete 2006; Xie and Shaumann 2003). Given the importance of students' perceived sense of self-efficacy in their choices and behaviors, researchers have explored how to influence and strengthen this predictor of educational attainment. Information and feedback may play an important role for strengthening students' sense of self-efficacy (a topic we turn to in Sect. 16.3 of this review).

16.1.3 Has Attainment Kept Up with Aspirations?

Educational attainment has changed dramatically over the past century in the U.S. In particular, high school completion rates have substantially improved for all groups. Specifically, from 1990 to 2014, the status dropout rate (representing the percentage of the noninstitutionalized 16- to 24-year-old population who are not enrolled in school and who have not completed a high school program) declined from 13.2% to 7.4% among Blacks and from 32.4% to 10.6% among Hispanics. Both rates, however, remain higher than the rate among non-Hispanic Whites (5.2%)[1] (National Center for Education Statistics 2016b). Although important disparities remain in high school completion, today race and income gaps are notably wider in college degree enrollment and completion (Bailey and Dynarski 2011; Black and Sufi 2002).

---

[1]There has been much discussion in the measurement of high school completion/dropout status (see http://nces.ed.gov/pubs2016/2016007.pdf).

The number of students attending colleges and universities in the U.S. grew to 20.2 million in 2015, an increase of nearly 33% since 2000 (Kena et al. 2015). This increase was due in part to growth in the size of the young adult population of the U.S. as well as increasing rates of postsecondary participation. Approximately 40% of 18- to 24-year-olds (i.e., the traditional college-age population) were enrolled in a postsecondary program in 2013, representing a 12.4% increase over 2000 enrollment levels. However, this increase was not constant across all subgroups. For example, while the percentage of Hispanic 18- to 24-year-olds attending college grew by 56% between 2000 and 2013, the enrollment levels of Black young adults demonstrated virtually no change (NCES 2016a). In 1990, the White–Black gap in college enrollment was 15 percentage points, and the White–Hispanic gap was 12 percentage points. In recent years, the White–Black gap has narrowed to about 7 percentage points and the White–Hispanic gap to about 8 percentage points (NCES 2016a). College enrollment gaps by income have not narrowed nearly as much as race gaps. Since the mid-1970s the high–low income gap in college enrollment has stayed relatively constant at about 30 percentage points (NCES 2016a).

Although more young people are choosing to enroll in college than ever before, the rate of degree completion has not kept up with participation, and disparities in college degree receipt remain pronounced and in some cases are actually growing. Forty-three percent of non-Hispanic Whites aged 25–29 held a bachelor's degree or higher in 2015, compared to 21.3% of Blacks and 16.4% of Hispanics (National Center for Education Statistics 2016b). Gaps by income in degree completion are also pronounced (Bailey and Dynarski 2011). In 2013, less than 10% of young adults from the lowest income quartile earned a college degree, compared to 77% of those from families in the top income quartile (an increase since 1970 of over 30 percentage points among high-income families and only by about 3 percentage points among those in the lowest income bracket (Pell Institute for the Study of Opportunity in Higher Education).

One of the most important determinants of college entrance and completion is prior academic preparation. Given the push for college participation, students' pre-collegiate experiences are a critical part of their educational pathways, and where the notion of constrained choices—individual decision-making amidst forces of structural inequalities—play out through differentiation in schooling experiences from early childhood to high school.

16.2 Curricular Differentiation Along Students' Educational Pathways

Educational pathways are in large part a function of students' schooling experiences, particularly their exposure to high-quality and rigorous curricula. Curricular differentiation, which refers to the process of sorting students into educational settings that differ according to substantive content, pace of instruction, or pedagogical approach, is a key feature of students' educational pathways, starting with preschool environments that promote school readiness, gatekeeping courses in the middle school years, and rigorous high school curricula to facilitate successful transitions to postsecondary schooling. Such curricular differentiation is fraught with tensions of individual choice and structurally constrained access to the opportunities necessary to realize those goals.

There are several plausible mechanisms by which we would expect high-quality and rigorous curricula and instruction through the educational life course to lead to increased educational attainment. First, a rigorous course of study often provides exposure to more advanced material, introducing students to topics they may encounter in subsequent years thereby improving their schooling transitions and supporting greater academic success and confidence (Lee and Ready 2009; Long et al. 2012). Second, high-quality content is often correlated with high-quality instruction. For example, more rigorous courses of study in high school (such as honors and AP) are frequently taught by more skilled teachers (often with additional credentials, more experience, or specialized professional development), than less rigorous courses (Ingersoll 1999; Kalogrides et al. 2013). Third, rigorous schooling environments (across or within schools) attract particular students (and families), often those most socially, financially, or academically able and/or those most motivated (Lareau and Goyette 2014). As such, engagement with these higher-achieving peers (based on ability, social class, motivation, etc.) may positively influence student outcomes.[2] Fourth, enrollment in more intensely rigorous schooling environments can serve as an important, positive signal in future schooling destinations. For example, among kindergarten teachers who often differentiate students based on their pre-schooling environments; or, among college admissions officers who rank high schools on their academic intensity.

Importantly, the relationship between rigorous course of study and student educational destinations may not be causal at all, because, to a large extent, students self-select into rigorous courses in secondary and postsecondary education. Students who take a more rigorous set of courses in high school likely have a host of other attributes that also lead to their success in college and later in life (Domina et al. 2014). For example, such students may simply have better academic skills, more motivation, and a stronger work ethic, or perhaps more academic support and encouragement from their families or teachers. Several studies have also documented the qualitatively different ways parents from different income backgrounds intervene in their children's schooling experiences (Hamilton 2016; Stevens 2007; Lareau 2011, 2000). It is therefore likely that all of these attributes contribute to students' enrollment in more rigorous courses of study in the first place, making it difficult to test whether particular courses or curricular tracks directly *cause* students to succeed in college or later in life. Thus, students' educational outcomes that may appear to vary as a result of differential access to rigorous schools and/or curricula (i.e., a set of structural constraints) are in fact likely the result of much more dynamic interactions between structural barriers and individual selection (i.e. constrained choices).

Nevertheless, students do not enroll in a course of study purely based on their own preferences, nor strictly by chance. Schools serving high concentrations of low-income students often have fewer advanced curricular offerings than do schools serving a more affluent student population (Adelman 1999; Conger et al. 2009). Moreover, canonical studies that account for school differences suggest that, like racial/ethnic and socioeconomic disparities in achievement (Coleman 1966), disparities in course-taking are largely within-school phenomena rather than between-school phenomena (Gamoran 1987). This suggests that curricular disparities are mainly due to tracking or to inequalities in access to more demanding courses among students who are enrolled in the same school (Attewell and Domina 2008). The implications of such inequality suggest that researchers and educators must continue to investigate more closely the processes that contribute to course sorting, particularly when it results in within-school racial/ethnic or socioeconomic segregation (Deil-Amen and DeLuca 2010; Kelly 2009; Riegle-Crumb and Grodsky 2010).

16.2.1 Academic Curriculum in the Pre-schooling Years

For most children in the United States, the pathway through formal schooling begins with participation in center-based pre-kindergarten programming. Most pre-kindergarten programs have the overarching goal of increasing students' "school readiness," the set of intellectual, social, and emotional competencies that foster success in kindergarten and beyond (Duncan et al. 2007). A recent meta-analysis of pre-kindergarten program evaluation studies concluded that, on average, pre-kindergarten participants gained the equivalent of an additional four months of learning compared to children who did not attend preschool, providing them with a stronger foundation as they entered kindergarten (Camilli et al. 2010).

---

[2]See Sacerdote (2001) and Zimmerman (2003) for evidence of peer effects in education.

Moreover, longitudinal studies of pre-kindergarten education's effects demonstrate that short-term improvements in language and mathematics ability are accompanied by positive outcomes in the longer-term as well, including increased educational attainment, higher earnings, and less criminal behavior in early adulthood (Campbell et al. 2002; Heckman et al. 2010).[3]

Researchers studying the effects of pre-kindergarten education on children's academic and socio-emotional development have identified largely positive effects of participation in academically oriented programming (e.g., Gormley et al. 2005). Moreover, these effects demonstrate a compensatory effect: Children from low-SES backgrounds experience greater increases in early achievement and development than do children from middle- or upper-class families. However, because access to academically oriented pre-kindergarten programs is stratified along social class lines, fewer low-income children participate in such programs than do higher-income students. Thus, as the first form of formal education encountered by many U.S. children, structural inequalities in pre-kindergarten programming establish unequal academic pathways that extend into the elementary school years.

Early childhood remains a primary area of compensatory social investments aimed at attenuating inequality prior to formal schooling. Researchers, educators, and policymakers have at turns considered the potential for pre-kindergarten education to improve the education and life course outcomes of children from socioeconomically disadvantaged and ethnic minority backgrounds (e.g., Currie 2001; Duncan et al. 2007;

Heckman et al. 2010). Beginning in the 1960s, findings from a series of now famous experiments began to emerge that demonstrated pre-kindergarten education's ameliorative potential for low-income children (Schweinhart et al. 2005; Campbell and Ramey 2010).[4]

Despite the aforementioned success stories of efforts to improve disadvantaged students' educational outcomes through pre-kindergarten programming, the federal government's preschool programs for children in poverty—Head Start and Early Head Start—have generated a mixed pattern of results. The Head Start Impact Study (Puma et al. 2010) used a randomized control design to estimate the effects of 3- and 4-year-olds' Head Start participation on their cognitive and social-emotional outcomes at the end of first grade. While the study's results indicated that Head Start participants enjoyed benefits during program participation, these advantages "faded out" over a relatively short period of time. Recent findings from a randomized control trial in Head Start programs suggest that this fade-out is attributable to elementary school quality, as program participants who subsequently enrolled in high-performing elementary schools demonstrated continued benefits, while those who attended lower-performing schools experienced fade-out (Zhai et al. 2012). This finding echoed earlier work by Currie and Thomas (2000), who demonstrated that elementary school quality differences explained differential Head Start fade-out effects among White and Black students. Thus,

---

[3]While these outcomes carry clear benefits for individual students, researchers have also performed cost-benefit analyses at aggregate levels, finding that preschool programs provide benefits to society as a whole through cost savings (e.g., reduced spending on expensive special education or juvenile justice programs) and participants' increased economic productivity in adulthood. Estimates of these societal benefits tend to outweigh preschool operating costs by considerable margins, often on the order of $5 or more of economic return for every $1 spent on pre-kindergarten programs (Duncan et al. 2007; Heckman et al. 2010; Reynolds et al. 2011; Yoshikawa et al. 2013).

[4]The Perry project enrolled 58 low-income, Black 3-year-olds in 2.5-h classes that met 5 days per week for the 2 years preceding kindergarten. Members of the treatment group demonstrated multiple advantages relative to the control group in the near-term (e.g., higher IQ scores, increased standardized test performance, better teacher-rated classroom behavior) and in the long-term (e.g., higher high school graduation rates, less involvement in the criminal justice system as adolescents and adults, higher earnings in adulthood) (Schweinhart et al. 2005). Similarly, Abecedarian Project participants, who received pre-kindergarten educational intervention from approximately four months of age until kindergarten entry, experienced improved achievement, attainment, and health outcomes compared to control group members from childhood through adulthood (Campbell and Ramey 2010).

early investments in children's schooling for improving educational and occupational attainment are largely only realized through sustained quality experiences in schooling.

16.2.2 Academic Curriculum in the Elementary Schooling Years

School districts in 46 states are required to offer publicly funded schooling beginning with kindergarten, in which children are typically eligible to enroll at age 5.[5,6] Students proceed through the elementary years along pathways that are differentiated by curricular content, pace of instruction, and pedagogical approach.

Ability grouping in elementary school classrooms has been a frequent subject of sociological research since the 1980s. The term ability grouping refers to the practice of organizing a classroom of students into small groups for the purpose of delivering to each group a modified

---

[5]34 States require districts to offer half-day kindergarten programs and 12 states require full-day kindergarten. Kindergarten attendance is compulsory in 16 of these states. The age at which children must legally begin attending school varies across states, ranging from five to eight years old. (Source: https://nces.ed.gov/programs/statereform/tab5_3.asp)

[6]"Academic redshirting," the practice of voluntarily delaying children's kindergarten enrollment by one year, has received abundant scholarly and popular attention in recent years. While research evidence suggests that the practice is most common among boys, non-Latino Whites, children from high-SES families, and those whose birthdays fall close to kindergarten enrollment cutoff dates (Bassok and Reardon 2013), estimates of academic redshirting's prevalence indicate that it is not as widespread as commonly believed, with between 3.5% and 5.6% of U.S. kindergarteners demonstrating delayed enrollment (Bassok and Reardon 2013; Huang 2015; Snyder and Dillow 2013). Increased age at kindergarten enrollment is associated with a host of short-term positive outcomes, including higher achievement (Datar 2006; Datar and Gottfried 2015), improved social-behavioral skills (Datar and Gottfied 2015), and dramatically reduced odds of being diagnosed with attention deficit/hyperactivity disorder (Dee and Sievertsen 2015), yet evidence for positive long-term effects is scant (Cascio and Schanzenbach 2016; Deming and Dynarski 2008; Lincove and Painter 2006).

curriculum, most often in language arts or mathematics. Classroom teachers make group assignments based on their assessment of students' current knowledge and cognitive ability, with the goal of allowing the teacher to present students with a curriculum that is neither too challenging (which might place students at risk for frustration and discouragement) or too easy (which might lead to developmental stagnation or disruptive behavior).

As a potential solution to the pedagogical challenge of teaching groups of young students with widely varying levels of preparedness and performance, ability grouping offers a compelling logic. Indeed, on the face of things it might even seem irrational to argue that administering a one-size-fits-all curriculum could ever be preferable to presenting students with tailored instruction matched to their specific learning styles and needs. However, research findings from the sociology of education complicate this picture, calling into question ability grouping's educational efficacy, and bringing to light the structural forces that determine students' groupings, which often result in inequities along racial/ethnic and socioeconomic lines (Gamoran et al. 1995; Hallinan 1994; Oakes 2005; Slavin 1987).

The academic pathways constructed through within-class ability grouping are often less visible than those created by, for example, curriculum track placement in high school. Unlike those formal curricular placements, which require parents' and/or students' consent, elementary school ability group decisions generally fall under the classroom teacher's sole purview. Moreover, students' ability group placements are generally not noted in their school records or transcripts. Despite their comparative informality, however, ability group placements have the potential to establish durable academic pathways for young students, and these pathways feed directly into the formally differentiated curricular pathways of middle and high school. The social-psychological consequences of such groupings on students' subsequent choices about curricular tracks (when such choices are at the individual or parental level), however, are not well understood.

Building on the concept of opportunity-to-learn (OTL), sociologists of education have made the straightforward argument that students are more likely to learn material that is presented to them in class than material they never encounter (e.g., Porter 1989; Sørensen and Hallinan 1986). Extending this line of work to research on ability grouping, several researchers have found that the amount of curricular material presented to students in differentiated ability groups exhibits considerable variation across learning groups in the same classroom, with students in high-ability groups being exposed to a greater proportion of the intended curriculum than those in middle- or low-ability groups (Eder 1981; Gamoran 1986; Oakes 1985; Pallas et al. 1994). Thus, ability grouping potentially provides unequal OTL according to teachers' perception of students' ability, leading to further widening of initial achievement gaps over time, a pattern some sociologists refer to as "cumulative advantage" (e.g., DiPrete and Eirich 2006) or "the Matthew effect" (e.g., Kerckhoff and Glennie 1999). To the extent that initially high achieving students cover more curricular ground than initially lower achieving students over the course of each school year, this process tends to be self-reinforcing across the elementary school grades (i.e., the students who finish a given school year having learned the most material are the "high achievers" when the following school year begins, and are therefore placed in high-ability, high-OTL groups once again). This curricular path dependence manifests in the form of unequal educational pathways concealed within what, on the surface, appears to be a singular educational "mainstream."

Research findings suggest that more flexible (i.e., frequently adjusted) and appropriate (i.e., accurate with respect to students' learning abilities) group placements lead to greater equality of academic outcomes experienced by students of varying abilities (Sørensen 1970; Gamoran 1992; Gamoran et al. 1995). In practice, however, ability grouping systems are highly imperfect along these lines. Inappropriate and fairly static group assignments tend to result in students being assigned to differentiated curricular pathways in ways that exacerbate pre-existing achievement inequalities along racial/ethnic, and socioeconomic lines (Gamoran et al. 1995; Hallinan 1994; Oakes 2005; Slavin 1987).

16.2.3 Academic Curriculum in the Middle School Years: The Push for Universal Algebra

Following the publication of *A Nation at Risk* (National Commission on Excellence in Education 1983), American public education took a decided turn toward emphasizing academic achievement, particularly in science and mathematics. This sea change included an expansion of rigorous curricula during the middle school years as a means of ensuring the United States' future economic competitiveness and national security (Schoenfeld 2004). The push for more and earlier student access to advanced mathematics was promoted as a solution to *A Nation at Risk*'s prophesized "rising tide of mediocrity." In response, a contingent of educators and civil rights leaders began to put forth an equity-based argument for curricular reforms, specifically in mathematics, targeting underserved students and schools. Robert Moses, a math educator and an influential activist in the civil rights era of the 1960s, is most closely associated with this movement. Having founded the Algebra Project in 1982 to improve mathematics education among low-income students and students of color, Moses argued that access to advanced mathematics is a requisite for full economic participation and citizenship in an increasingly technological society, and one that is systematically denied to members of marginalized populations (Moses and Cobb 2002). These distinct yet mutually reinforcing arguments—excellence and equity—ushered in an era of intense preoccupation with boosting algebra enrollments nationwide (Gamoran and Hannigan 2000).

The "algebra for everyone" perspective shaped education reform in multiple ways, most notably in the form of heightened course-taking expectations that became part of the emerging standards and accountability reform movement. Reports from the National Research Council (*Everybody Counts* [NRC, 1989]) and National Council of Teachers of Mathematics (*Curriculum and Evaluation Standards* [NCTM, 1989]) codified these new, intensified expectations, leading several states and large school districts to respond accordingly.

These efforts reached a zenith in California, where, in 1997, the state department of education revised its education standards to reflect an expectation that all students be enrolled in algebra, a recommendation that became law with the passage of the *Public School Accountability Act* (PSAA) in 1999 (Domina et al. 2014). Response to this legislative reform was swift: Over half of California eighth graders were enrolled in algebra courses by 2008, up from only 16% at the time of the PSAA's passage. For policymakers concerned with Americans' declining technical expertise, as well as education activists dedicated to equalizing students' pathways to college, this "algebra for everyone" reform represented an encouraging step forward (similarly ambitious reforms in other states and large school districts, such as Chicago Public Schools were also underway (Allensworth et al. 2009; Nomi 2012; Nomi and Allensworth 2013)).

While California made strides toward achieving the near-term goal of increasing access to algebra among middle school students, recent assessments of the algebra for everyone movement's longer-run impacts have been somewhat disappointing. Despite the widely held understanding that algebra operates as a "gatekeeper" for participation in future advanced mathematics coursework (Oakes 1990; Riley 1997; Smith 1996), recent evaluations have revealed that mandatory eighth grade algebra reforms do not lead to increased advanced math course-taking (Liang et al. 2012), nor have mandatory algebra reforms led to increased average mathematics achievement in the high school years (Clotfelter et al. 2015; Domina et al. 2014, 2015; Loveless 2008). Similarly, evaluations of Chicago Public Schools' mandatory ninth grade algebra reforms found that the program was associated with increased failure in subsequent mathematics coursework, as well as

performance declines among initially high-skill students (Nomi 2012; Nomi and Allensworth 2013). Additional research will be necessary to understand the causes of these disappointing outcomes; initial results from quantitative work point toward "peer effects" and the complex set of social relations that result from heterogeneous grouping strategies like universal algebra as key challenges (Hong and Nomi 2012; Domina et al. 2015). Other work, perhaps qualitative in nature, is necessary for understanding why such reforms may not meet desired outcomes.

16.2.4 Academic Curriculum and Rigor in High School

Not surprisingly, students with a more rigorous course of study in high school are more likely to apply and enroll in more selective campuses, and are less likely to require remediation when they enter college (Kurlaender and Howell 2012; Long et al. 2012; Adelman 1999, 2006). Enrolling in a rigorous course of study in high school is not only associated with higher educational attainment, but also with improved labor market outcomes. Several studies find that enrolling in more advanced mathematics courses in high school leads to higher wages once in the workforce (Altonji 1995; Levine and Zimmerman 1995; Rose and Betts 2004).

Researchers have attempted to deal with the complexity of estimating the influence of curricular intensity on future success by using a variety of approaches. When researchers control for as many observable characteristics as are available, they find a consistent positive association between curricular intensity and the following: student test scores (Attewell and Domina 2008), high school graduation (Schneider et al. 1997), college entry (Long et al. 2012), type of college entry (Attewell and Domina 2008), college grades (Klopfenstein and Thomas 2009), college graduation, (Adelman 2006; Attewell and Domina 2008), and wages (Altonji 1995; Rose and Betts 2004).

Using detailed information from students' high school transcripts, Long et al. (2012) find a 7–11 percentage point increase in the likelihood of high school graduation and 4-year college entry between a student who takes no rigorous high school courses and a student taking just one rigorous course during high school. This study finds that the biggest differences in student outcomes are based on math and English course levels, though enrollment in rigorous courses in other subjects also leads to improved outcomes. Long and colleagues also find that, although more rigorous courses are associated with better student outcomes, the differences were greatest between those taking no rigorous course and those taking only one. This result suggests "requiring or encouraging students to enroll in even one rigorous course in their first two years of high school can substantially improve graduation and four-year college enrollment rates" (Long et al. 2012, p. 315).

Improving academic standards in secondary schools has been at the heart of the Common Core State Standards reform efforts, which has emphasized the need to better align K–12 education systems with higher education to ensure a more seamless transition for young adults between high school and college, and between high school and the labor market. The push for more academic rigor is evident in the course-taking trajectories of high school students. Over the last three decades the percentage of students enrolled in precalculus or calculus in U.S. high schools has steadily grown. In 1982, only slightly more than 10% of students graduated high school with precalculus or calculus coursework, by 1992 that figure more than doubled to 21.7%, and in 2004, 33% of high school students were enrolled in at least precalculus coursework.

Efforts to increase the academic intensity of students' high school curricula have also been spurred by an equity agenda that seeks to ensure access to rigorous courses for students from all demographic backgrounds. Data from a nationally representative sample of high school students' course enrollment reveal that White and Asian students are much more likely to be enrolled in a more rigorous set of courses than

are Black or Latino youth (Planty et al. 2006).[7] Data on mathematics course-taking over time reveal that, although increasing numbers of students have been completing precalculus or calculus in high school in recent decades, the rates for Black and Hispanic/Latino students clearly lag behind the rates of White and Asian high school students, and these gaps have actually grown over time (see Table 16.1).

Similarly, students from higher-income families have higher levels of participation in more rigorous academic coursework than do their lower-SES peers. This is consistent with research indicating that lower-SES students, in particular,

Table 16.1 Percentage of high school graduates who completed precalculus or calculus, by race and socioeconomic status: 1982, 1992, and 2004

	1982	1992	2004
Overall	10.7	21.7	33.0
Race/ethnicity			
White	12.2	23.0	36.7
Black	4.0	13.6	19.0
Hispanic/Latino	5.3	12.7	21.9
Asian/PI	30.1	41.6	56.8
Am Indian	2.3	3.1	12.9
Socioeconomic status			
1st quartile (lowest)	2.7	8.0	17.7
2nd quartile	6.7	13.2	22.7
3rd quartile	11.3	21.9	34.0
4th quartile (highest)	2.05	38.5	52.4

Source: U.S. Department of Education, National Center for Education Statistics, High School and Beyond Longitudinal Study of 1980 Sophomores (HS&B-So:80/82), "High School Transcript Study"; National Education Longitudinal Study of 1988 (NELS:88/92), "Second Follow-up, Transcript Survey, 1992"; and Education Longitudinal Study of 2002 (ELS:2002), "First Follow-up, High School Transcript Study, 2004." Available at: http://nces.ed.gov/pubs2007/2007312.pdf

----

[7] Source: U.S. Department of Education, National Center for Education Statistics, Education Longitudinal Study of 2002 (ELS:2002), "High School Transcript Study." Adapted from: Planty, M., Bozick, R., and Ingels, S.J. (2006). *Academic Pathways, Preparation, and Performance — A Descriptive Overview of the Transcripts from the High School Graduating Class of 2003–04* (NCES 2007–316). U.S. Department of Education, National Center for Education Statistics. Washington, DC: U.S. Government Printing Office.

continue to be underrepresented at more selective postsecondary institutions because they have not completed the appropriate coursework (Carnevale and Rose 2003). Importantly, Rose and Betts (2004) find that the type of math courses students take in high school explain 27% of the earnings gap between students from the lowest-income families and those from middle-income families. Similarly, using data on students in Florida public postsecondary institutions, Long and colleagues (2009) find that 28–35% of the gaps (and over three-quarters of the Asian advantage) in college readiness among college-going Black, Hispanic, and low-income students can be explained by the highest math course taken in high school.

There are a host of factors that contribute to students' sorting into various levels of courses in high school: availability of courses, knowledge of offerings at the school, academic ability, interest, motivation, familial involvement, and the influences of teachers, counselors, and/or peers. As such, properly addressing racial/ethnic and socioeconomic differences in analysis of course enrollment patterns requires further inquiry into each of these (and other) possible sources of existing disparities in curricular pathways.

16.2.5 Structural Differences in Academic Preparation for College

Studies that parse out the effects of academic rigor by race/ethnicity and SES find that the return to taking more advanced coursework could vary with the attributes of the school. For example, Long et al. (2012) find that students attending high-poverty schools or those with lower average levels of student achievement experienced larger increases in their high school graduation and college enrollment rates associated with taking more rigorous courses than students attending more affluent high schools. Efforts to ensure opportunities are more equally distributed between schools have focused on addressing disparities in curricular offerings, particularly in college gateway courses such as Advanced Placement (College Board).

In principle, any academically stimulating environment may contribute to academic rigor. In practice, however, evaluating the learning environment for rigor can be difficult. It is common to use measures such as course titles and/or grades as proxies for rigor. But even these do not mean the same thing everywhere. For example, Fig. 16.2 displays a scatterplot of the probability of being college ready (Y-axis) against high school grade point average (X-axis) among students attending one of the 23 campuses of the California State University (CSU) system (the State's primary public BA-granting higher education system and the nation's largest public 4-year postsecondary system). Beyond the obvious positive association between high school GPA and college readiness is the stark difference between School A and School B. In School A, a California public school that serves less than 10% of students on free/reduced price lunch, even a student with a 2.5 GPA enters the CSU system "college ready" (as measured by placement tests); in contrast, in School B, which has an over 90% free/reduced price meal eligibility rate among its students (a great majority of them Latino), even the 4.0 student only has about a 40% likelihood of being "college ready" (i.e., not needing any remediation when she enters college).

In sum, students are not randomly placed into their educational pathways, but rather their curricular pathways are shaped by both the opportunities that they are exposed to (a structural argument) and their choices (an individual agency argument). The result is that it is not only difficult to separate out unobserved motivation, support, or other characteristics that may be associated with both rigorous course-taking and better educational outcomes, but also the many structural dimensions that constrain individual choice. These competing forces often result in educational pathways that self-perpetuate. That is, quality early schooling experiences beget better placement into secondary schooling decisions, and then more intense academic rigor in high school that results in more selective college admissions, and greater likelihood of degree attainment and labor market success. Thus, stu-

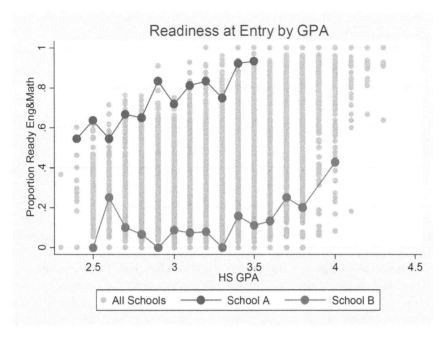

Fig. 16.2 The association between college readiness and high school GPA in California Public Schools

dents do have many choices and self-select (often with the aid of parents, teachers, or counselors) into a course of study; however, they do so within a set of structural constraints or opportunities. A primary way in which educators and policymakers hope to break the self-perpetuating nature of educational pathways and improve mobility between educational destinations is through increased access to information about alternative pathways and opportunities.

16.3 The Role of Information in Navigating Educational Pathways: Barriers and Opportunities

Despite a college for all culture, students often have very limited and only vague information about what college will be like, which is particularly true for students who are the first in their family to attend college (Settersten and Ray 2010). The research on inequality in educational attainment, particularly examinations of pathways to college and college choice, is heavily framed by theories of social and cultural capital,

and the extent to which programs aimed at improving college information can attenuate inequality in postsecondary pathways.

As a set of resources embedded in social relationships that facilitate certain actions (including applying to or enrolling in a particular college), social capital plays a major role in shaping students' educational pathways. It is through their social connections that students learn a normative orientation toward higher education (i.e., the educational expectations to which they will be held by others in their social networks, including their parents, teachers, and peers) and also acquire valuable information from others about the college application and participation processes.

Research on social capital's role in college application and attendance has demonstrated the importance of students' social ties to peers (Perez and McDonough 2008; Perna 2000; Tierney and Venegas 2006), institutional agents such as teachers and counselors (Perna and Titus 2005; Stanton-Salazar 1997, 2001), immediate and extended family members (McDonough 1997; Perna and Titus 2005), college outreach programs (Gonzalez et al. 2003), and the overall school community (Sandefur et al. 2006) for development of college-going attitudes and behaviors. Students who internalize socially constructed norms of college attendance through their social interactions and those whose networks provide access to information about the multifarious details associated with the college choice process enjoy increased probabilities of college attendance and persistence relative to students with fewer social capital resources.

Like social capital, cultural capital's role in the college-going process has also received substantial attention from sociologists. In this context, cultural capital refers to the status-linked sets of skills, knowledge, and preferences that are rewarded by higher education institutions and are transmitted from parents to their children (Lareau and Weininger 2003). In her work on the college choice process, McDonough (1997) describes how middle-class parents' access to first-hand information about college admissions procedures and strategies for maximizing their children's odds of admission (e.g., through the use of private SAT tutors) represent a form of cultural capital—valuable information that is readily available only to children of high-status parents and is not transmitted through schooling. Compared to students who lack dominant cultural capital (particularly in in the form of college admissions information), those who possess institutionally valued cultural capital are more likely to hold high educational aspirations, enroll in college, and reap positive returns to their postsecondary education investments (Aschaffenburg and Maas 1997; Bourdieu and Passeron 1977; DiMaggio and Mohr 1985; Dumais and Ward 2010; Lamont and Lareau 1988; Schneider and Stevenson, 1999). For high-achieving, low-SES youth, this lack of cultural capital also leads them to disproportionately apply to nonselective schools that offer a poor match to their academic skills and to be unsuccessful in navigating the financial aid process (Goldrick-Rab 2006; Hoxby and Avery 2013).

A recent example of sociological research on information qua cultural capital can be found in the work of Holland and DeLuca (2016). Analyzing data from interviews with 150 low-income youth, the authors describe these students as suffering from "information poverty" with respect to the postsecondary school transition and the pathway from college to work. These youths' sense of urgency toward obtaining a solid job led them toward the ill-advised decision to enroll in for-profit trade programs rather than 2- or 4-year nonprofit institutions. As a consequence of their low levels of cultural capital, the students in Holland and DeLuca's study ended up with fewer job prospects and more financial debt than they might have if their postsecondary choices had been better informed.

Like Holland and DeLuca, Harding (2010) uses interviews with low-SES, ethnoracial minority youth to examine the role cultural capital plays in shaping their educational pathways. While the youth in Harding's study overwhelmingly aspired to a college degree, the most effective strategies for reaching this goal were obscured by their lack of cultural capital. Unlike the higher-SES youth who are surrounded by individuals who espouse a "mainstream" model of desirable educational pathways, low-SES youth exist in a context of "cultural heterogeneity," which produces multiple alternative logics of educational success, including alternative credentials (e.g., the GED), attending trade schools, or choosing job training programs over traditional college. Whereas higher-SES youth are presented with a unified cultural front regarding the desirability of a 4-year degree (and the corresponding undesirability of other pathways), lower-SES youths' cultural repertoires include support for multiple educational and occupational pathways, which weakens the relationship between their (almost universally high) postsecondary aspirations and their ultimate educational attainment (Harding 2010, 2011). Along similar lines, Lee and Zhou (2015) attribute children of Asian immigrants' "paradoxically" high levels of educational attainment to a set of culturally grounded "success frames" through which community members establish a narrow definition of academic success as attaining an advanced degree from an elite college or university.

Sociologists often view social and cultural capital resources as intertwined and mutually dependent, with access to one set of resources potentially mitigating low levels of the other. For example, Grodsky and Riegle-Crumb (2010) find that social capital may be especially important to the college choice process for students who do not possess a "college-going habitus." A concept originating in cultural capital theory (Bourdieu and Passeron 1977), habitus refers to the attitudes and dispositions an individual unconsciously develops through repeated interactions with the social world. Grodsky and Riegle-Crumb (2010) identify an individual's taken-for-granted belief that they will attend college as the hallmark of a college-going habitus that is disproportionately possessed by young members of the elite, for whom the postsecondary transition occurs almost as a natural matter of course. Unlike these privileged students, those who do not possess a college-going habitus must develop the knowledge, skills, and attitudes consistent with college attendance via the social capital resources they manage to access over the course of their educational careers (Grodsky and Riegle-Crumb 2010).

Because social and cultural capital, like other valuable resources, are differentially distributed along typical axes of social stratification, inequalities in social and cultural capital tend to magnify existing gaps in college attendance and persistence. Programs designed to facilitate the transfer of college information to all students aim to intervene by interrupting the link between social status and social capital. Programs such as AVID, Upward Bound and Summer Bridge have long focused on providing students (particularly first-generation college students from underrepresented backgrounds) with exposure to not just the academic, human capital skills, but also the social and behavior skills (i.e., cultural capital) required for college success. The evidence about the effectiveness of these programs, however, is mixed and limited (Domina 2009; Barnett et al. 2012).

The most compelling evidence that educational pathways are not seamless for many students is found in the high rates of college remediation present across broad access colleges and universities throughout the U.S. (where the majority of students go to college). Beyond the great financial expense of college remediation (to

the individual and to the public), we also know that students who enter college in need of remediation are less likely to persist and less likely to complete a college degree than those who do not require remedial coursework (Bettinger et al. 2013). Part of the explanation for the large share of students requiring remediation once they arrive in college may be a result of the limited information students possess regarding what they need to do to succeed in college.

An important effort to improve alignment between K–12 and postsecondary systems is to provide high school students with early information about college expectations. High school students use information from many sources to make numerous decisions, such as whether and how to complete high school, and whether and where to attend college. Early information may help students realize that they need additional academic preparation, and motivate students to do well with their remaining time in high school. Moreover, there is evidence that high school students update their college-going trajectories based on information that they receive during secondary school (Jacob and Wilder-Linkow 2011). In fact, students respond to labels assigned to them by standardized tests. Papay et al. (2011) show that the labels assigned to students through state standardized testing impact college-going decisions. A "Needs Improvement" label causes urban, low-income students to be more likely to enroll in college than a "Warning" label. Moreover, Papay et al. (2011) show that urban, low-income students were shown to update their educational attainment expectations based on standardized test result labels as early as eighth grade.

Early information from college assessments, which are intended to motivate students toward their postsecondary goals, could hypothetically be discouraging to lower-performing students. Students taking state assessments who are told that they may require remediation upon entering a particular college may feel that they do not fit well with that college, and decide to enroll elsewhere or not at all. However, research on California's effort to provide students with college readiness information in 11th grade found that the early signal of "not ready" did not dissuade students from applying or enrolling in college, or push them into attending a less academically demanding college, and actually improved overall remediation rates at California's broad access 4-year institutions (Howell et al. 2010; Jackson 2015; Kurlaender et al. 2016).

The literature in education policy is also rich in studies focused on the role of information in college affordability. Despite being eligible, many students do not apply for financial aid for college (King 2004; College Board 2017; Yonezawa 2013). Information plays an important role in financial aid take-up because incomplete or insufficient information can lead students to underestimate benefits or overestimate costs of college, and can preclude students from applying for financial aid (Perna 2007; Scott-Clayton 2012). Household income and parent education are positively correlated with knowledge of college prices; minority and low-income parents are less likely to provide an accurate estimate of college costs when compared to more affluent or White parents (Grodsky and Jones 2007; Horn et al. 2003).

Financing college remains an important structural constraint for many individuals. The primary reason given by a representative sample of youth that did not go to college is because they could not afford to attend (Bozick and DeLuca 2011). Need-based financial aid is designed to provide additional help for low-income students, but complex aid formulas, poor marketing, and complex application procedures can create additional information barriers (Scott-Clayton 2012). Current financial aid barriers include lack of awareness about aid and the complexity of the Free Application for Federal Student Aid (FAFSA) required for all federal and most state need-based aid programs (Long 2010). At five pages and 127 questions, the FAFSA is longer and more complicated than federal tax return forms (Dynarski and Scott-Clayton 2006). This complexity also has significant costs, including the time and resources it takes for individuals to read directions and requirements, collect all needed documents, and actually fill out the application (Dynarski and Scott-Clayton 2006). Low-

income families are also likely to face higher compliance costs because they most likely lack college-going peers and relatives to assist them (Dynarski and Scott-Clayton 2006). If these barriers are larger for disadvantaged students, the primary purpose of federal need-based financial aid may be jeopardized (Scott-Clayton 2012). For students who do attempt the FAFSA, many have difficulty in answering questions, requesting a high school diploma, or having a Social Security number (Yonezawa 2013; McKinney and Roberts 2012).

These information barriers could be especially pronounced for non-traditional age students and students from low-income backgrounds attending broad access institutions, such as community colleges (Bean and Metzner 1985; Taniguchi and Kaufman 2005). Compared to students at 4-year institutions, community college students are more likely to be first-generation college students, to enroll part-time, have discontinuities in terms enrolled, and switch between part-time and full-time enrollment (Crosta 2013; Provasnik and Planty 2008; Bailey et al. 2005; Deil-Amen and Rosenbaum 2003; Dougherty 1994; Brint and Karabel 1989). The current financial aid system is largely designed to assist traditional undergraduates enrolling right after high school (Long 2010). Community college students can also be penalized if financial aid requires full-time attendance, a traditional high school diploma, or a specific goal for a credential or degree (Long 2010; Terriquez and Gurantz 2014). Because need-based financial aid targets students at the margin of choosing whether or not to attend college, the FAFSA's complexity may lead to negative decisions about college enrollment and/or persistence (Scott-Clayton 2012). In effect, the students least likely to be able to afford college are the ones with the least amount of information about college cost (Horn et al. 2003).

In light of these information barriers, some researchers have tested information-based interventions in college financing. Most notably, Bettinger et al. (2012) implemented a randomized field experiment conducted with the tax preparation firm H&R Block to assist families with FAFSA preparation. For dependent students, personal counseling increased FAFSA submission by 16 percentage points (40% increase), Pell Grant receipt by 10 percentage points (36% increase) and college enrollment by 8 percentage points (24% increase) (Bettinger and Long 2009). For independent students with no prior college experience, the intervention increased FAFSA submission by 27 percentage points (168% increase), Pell Grant receipt by 3 percentage points (27% increase) and college enrollment by 1.5 percentage points (16%). There were also longer-term effects. Three years after the intervention, students were more likely to be enrolled for at least two consecutive years.

Even after being admitted and accepting a college offer, 10–22% of students fail to enroll in the following fall semester (Castleman and Page 2014a). This phenomenon—also known as "summer melt"—is particularly high among the lowest-income students (Castleman and Page 2014a, b). This is possibly attributed to the informational barriers imposed during the summer months when students receive a large volume of material from their intended college of enrollment, which can be especially overwhelming for first-generation students and families with lower financial literacy (Arnold et al. 2009). To address such information barriers, low-cost interventions sent via phone, email, social media, and text messages to students periodically throughout the summer, offering counseling and reminding them of enrollment and financial aid deadlines have been tested. These resulted in increases in college enrollment, persistence through freshman year, and persistence into sophomore year (Castleman and Page 2015). Effects were even larger for the lowest-income students, for whom college enrollment increased by 12 percentage points (Castleman and Page 2015).

Finally, information interventions have been used to address "undermatching" in college enrollment. Hoxby and Avery (2013) find that a large majority of high-performing low-income students do not apply to selective colleges despite the fact that their academic performance on the SAT or ACT would make them eligible for admission. In fact, 40% of low-income high-achieving students only send their scores to non-selective schools, while only 8% send them to selective schools for which they are qualified (Hoxby and Avery 2013). These gaps are mainly driven by students' decisions on where to apply to college, instead of college admission decisions (Dillon and Smith 2017; Hoxby and Avery 2013). This is problematic because the persistence and graduation rates at non-selective schools are often lower than more-selective institutions, and also because there are important rewards in the labor market to attending a selective institution (Hoekstra 2009). Undermatching has important consequences; these high-achieving low-income students would actually pay a lower net price at more selective institutions compared to less-selective institutions as a result of selective institutions' more generous financial aid, and would also often qualify for fee waivers to send their SAT/ACT scores to more institutions.

Hoxby and Turner (2015) implemented a low-cost intervention aimed at providing these students with more information and fee waiver applications. Students receiving the intervention submitted more applications, and were 15–19% more likely to apply to multiple peer institutions. As a result, the "maximum" schools students applied to had higher median SAT scores, higher graduation rates, and reported higher spending on students (Hoxby and Turner 2015).

Information is an important determinant of students' educational pathways, and one that is not evenly distributed (by school, by race, or by social class). Today, clear structural barriers to information about successful college navigation pathways and tools endure. However, these information barriers are also the target of some of the most developed and popular areas of interventions among social scientists and policymakers eager to reduce educational attainment gaps between groups from different racial/ethnic or social strata.

16.4 Conclusion

Throughout the twentieth century, the U.S. education system witnessed major expansion, with increasing enrollment of individuals from all backgrounds at all levels of educational attainment (Goldin and Katz 2009). The now ubiquitous college for all ethos permeates much of our discussion of educational pathways. This is perhaps most notable when you ask young people about their educational plans. Today's high school students are nearly universal in their reported choice to attend college.

The sociology of education remains focused on understanding how such expansion in educational attainment has been realized both structurally and among individuals. Although individuals from all backgrounds have experienced increases in educational attainment in the U.S., disparities by race and social background persist. Structural factors create inequalities in students' opportunities to learn in the preschool years, and continue sorting children among unequal pathways throughout primary and secondary schooling. High school dropout rates—albeit much lower in recent decades—remain substantially higher for Hispanics and Blacks than for Whites (Heckman and LaFontaine 2006; Mishel and Roy 2006), and the relative participation and completion rates in college among students of color and those from lower socioeconomic status backgrounds remain low (NCES 2016a, b).

The education attainment model is defined by a notable tension between individual choice and structural constraints that exist throughout the life course. This is evident in the clear schism between students' intended plans and their ultimate destinations. Both academic preparation and information are key brokers in this divide. Much of our theoretical and applied policy discussions focus on how to improve the pathway to college, and, more recently, to improve college degree receipt in particular. For example, recent K–12 school reform efforts, dominated by Common Core implementation, are largely focused on improving college readiness and on better aligning our K–12 and higher education systems. Although it is too soon to tell, this effort may potentially reduce structural barriers along students' pathways to academic preparation for college. Moreover, amidst critiques that college for all has boosted students' college expectations without improving their access to quality infor-

mation about what it takes to succeed in college, a plethora of interventions have surfaced from across the social sciences to aid students along their educational pathways (e.g., in their choice of college, in staying in college, and in believing they can succeed).

In the years to come, fruitful approaches to promoting educational excellence and equity will not necessarily conceive of structure and agency as competing forces—a "structure *versus* agency" approach; rather, they will acknowledge the overlapping, dynamic nature of structure *and* agency in students' educational pathways. Students form their attitudes, orientations, and decisions as they progress along structurally bounded educational pathways, subject to past experiences, opportunities, and information. As such, theoretical models and policy interventions alike that focus solely on structure (e.g., the distribution of opportunities to learn) or agency (e.g., students' choices about course selection) ignore a crucial set of factors that contribute to students' educational trajectories. Sociologists of education are uniquely positioned to develop models of education attainment that connect structure and agency, and, in doing so, to inform future refinements of policy and practice.

References

Adelman, C. (1999). *Answers in the toolbox: Academic intensity, attendance patterns, and bachelor's degree attainment*. Washington, DC: U.S. Department of Education Office of Educational Research and Improvement.

Adelman, C. (2006). *The toolbox revisited*. Washington, DC: U.S. Department of Education Office of Educational Research and Improvement.

Alexander, K. L., & Cook, M. A. (1979). The motivational relevance of educational plans: Questioning the conventional wisdom. *Social Psychology Quarterly, 42*, 202–213.

Allensworth, E., Nomi, T., Montgomery, N., & Lee, V. E. (2009). College preparatory curriculum for all: Academic consequences of requiring algebra and English I for ninth graders in Chicago. *Educational Evaluation and Policy Analysis, 31*(4), 367–391.

Altonji, J. (1995). The effects of high school curriculum on education and labor market outcomes. *Journal of Human Resources, 30*(3), 409–438.

Arnold, K., Fleming, S., DeAnda, M., Castleman, B., & Wartman, K. L. (2009). The summer flood: The invisible gap among low-income students. *Thought & Action, 25,* 23–24.

Aschaffenburg, K., & Maas, I. (1997). Cultural and educational careers: The dynamics of social reproduction. *American Sociological Review, 62,* 573–587.

Attewell, P., & Domina, T. (2008). Raising the bar: Curricular intensity and academic performance. *Educational Evaluation and Policy Analysis, 30*(1), 51–71.

Bailey, M. J., & Dynarski, S. M. (2011). Inequality in postsecondary education. In G. J. Duncan & R. J. Murnane (Eds.), *Whither opportunity? Rising inequality, schools, and Children's life chances* (pp. 117–132). New York: Russell Sage.

Bailey, T., Calcagno, J. C., Jenkins, D., Kienzl, G., & Leinbach, T. (2005). *The effects of institutional factors on the success of community college students.* New York: Community College Research Center.

Bandura, A. (1981). Self-referent thought: A developmental analysis of self-efficacy. In J. H. Flavell & L. Ross (Eds.), *Social cognitive development: Frontiers and possible futures* (pp. 200–239). Cambridge, MA: Cambridge University Press.

Bandura, A. (1982). The psychology of chance encounters and life paths. *American Psychologist, 37*(7), 747–755.

Bandura, A. (1993). Perceived self-efficacy in cognitive development and functioning. *Educational Psychologist, 28*(2), 117–148.

Bandura, A. (1997). *Self-efficacy: The exercise of control.* New York: W.H. Freeman and Company.

Barnett, E. A., Bork, R. H., Mayer, A. K., Pretlow, J., Wathington, H. D., & Weiss, M. J. (2012). *Bridging the gap: An impact study of eight developmental summer bridge programs in Texas.* New York: National Center for Postsecondary Research.

Bassok, D., & Reardon, S. F. (2013). "Academic redshirting" in kindergarten: Prevalence, patterns, and implications. *Educational Evaluation and Policy Analysis, 35*(3), 283–297.

Bean, J. P., & Metzner, B. S. (1985). A conceptual model of nontraditional undergraduate student attrition. *Review of Educational Research, 55*(4), 485–540.

Bettinger, E., & Long, B. (2009). Addressing the needs of underprepared students in higher education: Does college remediation work? *Journal of Human Resources, 44*(3), 736–771.

Bettinger, E. P., Long, B. T., Oreopoulos, P., & Sanbonmatsu, L. (2012). The role of application assistance and information in college decisions: Results from the H&R Block FAFSA experiment. *The Quarterly Journal of Economics, 127*(3), 1205–1242.

Bettinger, E. P., Boatman, A., & Long, B. T. (2013). Student supports: Developmental education and other academic programs. *The Future of Children, 23*(1), 93–115.

Black, S. E., & Sufi, A. (2002). *Who goes to college? Differential enrollment by race and family background* (NBER Working Paper Series: No. w9310). Cambridge, MA: National Bureau of Economic Research.

Bourdieu, P., & Passeron, J. (1977). *Reproduction in education, society and culture.* London: SAGE Publications.

Bowles, S., & Gintis, H. (1976). *Schooling in capitalist America: Educational reform and the contradictions of economic life.* New York: Basic Books.

Bozick, R., & DeLuca, S. (2011). Not making the transition to college: School, work, and opportunities. *Social Science Research, 40,* 1249–1262.

Brint, S., & Karabel, J. (1989). *The diverted dream: Community colleges and the promise of educational opportunity in America, 1900–1985.* Oxford: Oxford University Press.

Buchmann, C., & DiPrete, T. A. (2006). The growing female advantage in college completion: The role of family background and academic achievement. *American Sociological Review, 71*(4), 515–541.

Camilli, G., Vargas, S., Ryan, S., & Barnett, W. S. (2010). Meta-analysis of the effects of early education interventions on cognitive and social development. *Teachers College Record, 112*(3), 579–620.

Campbell, F. A., & Ramey, C. T. (2010). The Abecedarian Project. In A. J. Reynolds, A. Rolnick, M. M. Englund, & J. Temple (Eds.), *Cost effective programs in children's first decade: A human capital integration* (pp. 76–95). New York: Cambridge University Press.

Campbell, F. A., Ramey, C. T., Pungello, E., Sparling, J., & Miller-Johnson, S. (2002). Early childhood education: Young adult outcomes from the Abecedarian Project. *Applied Developmental Science, 6*(1), 42–57.

Carnevale, A. P., & Rose, S. J. (2003). *Socioeconomic status, race/ethnicity, and selective college admissions.* New York: Century Foundation.

Cascio, E., & Schanzenbach, D. (2016). First in the class? Age and the education production function. *Education Finance and Policy, 11*(3), 225–250.

Castleman, B. L., & Page, L. C. (2014a). A trickle or a torrent? Understanding the extent of summer "melt" among college-intending high school graduates. *Social Science Quarterly, 95*(1), 202–220.

Castleman, B. L., & Page, L. C. (2014b). *Summer melt: Supporting low-income students in the transition from high school to college.* Cambridge, MA: Harvard Education Press.

Castleman, B. L., & Page, L. C. (2015). Summer nudging: Can personalized text messages and peer mentor outreach increase college going among low-income high school graduates? *Journal of Economic Behavior & Organization, 115,* 144–160.

Clotfelter, C. T., Ladd, H. F., & Vigdor, J. L. (2015). The aftermath of accelerating algebra: Evidence from district policy initiatives. *Journal of Human Resources, 50*(1), 159–188.

Cohen, G. L., Garcia, J., Purdie-Vaughns, V., Apfel, N., & Brzustoski, P. (2009). Recursive processes in self-affirmation: Intervening to close the minority achievement gap. *Science, 324*(5925), 400–403.

Coleman, J. S. (1966). *The equality of educational opportunity study (EEOS).* Washington, DC: United States Department of Education.

College Board. (2017). *Trends in Student Aid 2017*. Available at: https://trends.collegeboard.org/sites/default/files/2017-trends-student-aid_0.pdf

Collins, R. (1971). Functional and conflict theories of educational stratification. *American Sociological Review, 36*, 1002–1019.

Collins, R. (1979). *The credential society: An historical sociology of education and stratification*. San Diego: Academic Press.

Conger, D., Long, M. C., & Iatarola, P. (2009). Explaining race, poverty, and gender disparities in advanced course-taking. *Journal of Policy Analysis and Management, 28*(4), 555–576.

Crosta, P. (2013). *Intensity and attachment: How the chaotic enrollment patterns of community college students affect educational outcomes*. New York: Community College Research Center, Teachers College, Columbia University.

Currie, J. (2001). Early childhood education programs. *The Journal of Economic Perspectives, 15*(2), 213–238.

Currie, J., & Thomas, D. (2000). School quality and the longer-term effects of Head Start. *Journal of Human Resources, 35*(4), 755–774.

Datar, A. (2006). Does delaying kindergarten entrance give children a Head Start? *Economics of Education Review, 25*(1), 43–62.

Datar, A., & Gottfried, M. (2015). School entry age and children's social-behavioral skills: Evidence from a national longitudinal study of U.S. kindergarteners. *Educational Evaluation and Policy Analysis, 37*(3), 333–353.

Dee, T. S. & Sievertsen, H. (2015). *The gift of time? School starting age and mental health* (NBER Working Paper Series).

Deming, D., & Dynarski, S. (2008). The lengthening of childhood. *Journal of Economic Perspectives, 22*(3), 71–92.

Deil-Amen, R., & DeLuca, S. (2010). The underserved third: How our educational structures populate an educational underclass. *Journal of Education for Students Placed at Risk, 15*, 27–50.

Deil-Amen, R., & Rosenbaum, J. E. (2003). The social prerequisites of success: Can college structure reduce the need for social know-how? *The Annals of the American Academy of Political and Social Science, 586*(1), 120–143.

Dillon, E. W., & Smith, J. A. (2017, January). Determinants of the match between student ability and college quality. *Journal of Labor Economics, 35*(1), 45–66.

DiMaggio, P., & Mohr, J. (1985). Cultural capital, educational attainment, and marital selection. *American Journal of Sociology, 90*(6), 1231–1261.

DiPrete, T. A., & Eirich, G. M. (2006). Cumulative advantage as a mechanism for inequality: A review of theoretical and empirical developments. *Annual Review of Sociology, 32*, 271–297.

Domina, T. (2009). What works in college outreach: Assessing targeted and schoolwide interventions for disadvantaged students. *Educational Evaluation and Policy Analysis, 31*(2), 127–152.

Domina, T., Conley, A., & Farkas, G. (2011). The link between educational expectations and effort in the college-for-all era. *Sociology of Education, 84*(2), 93–112.

Domina, T., Penner, A. M., Penner, E. K., & Conley, A. (2014). Algebra for all: California's eighth-grade algebra initiative as constrained curricula. *Teachers College Record, 116*(8), 1–32.

Domina, T., McEachin, A., Penner, A., & Penner, E. (2015). Aiming high and falling short California's eighth-grade algebra-for-all effort. *Educational Evaluation and Policy Analysis, 37*(3), 275–295.

Dougherty, K. J. (1994). *The contradictory college: The conflicting origins, impacts, and futures of the community college*. Albany: State University of New York Press.

Dumais, S. A., & Ward, A. (2010). Cultural capital and first-generation college success. *Poetics, 38*(3), 245–265.

Duncan, G. J., Dowsett, C. J., Claessens, A., Magnuson, K., Huston, A. C., Klebanov, P., & Sexton, H. (2007). School readiness and later achievement. *Developmental Psychology, 43*(6), 1428–1446.

Dweck, C. S., & Elliott, E. S. (1983). Achievement motivation. In P. H. Mussen (Gen. Ed.) & E. M. Hetherington (Vol. Ed.), *Handbook of child psychology* (pp. 643–691). New York: Wiley.

Dynarski, S., & Scott-Clayton, J. (2006). The cost of complexity in federal student aid: Lessons from optimal tax theory and behavioral economics. *National Tax Journal, 59*(2), 319–356.

Eder, D. (1981). Ability grouping as a self-fulfilling prophecy: A micro-analysis of teacher–student interaction. *Sociology of Education, 54*(3), 151–162.

Gamoran, A. (1986). Instructional and institutional effects of ability grouping. *Sociology of Education, 59*(4), 185–198.

Gamoran, A. (1987). The stratification of high school learning opportunities. *Sociology of Education, 60*(3), 135–155.

Gamoran, A. (1992). Access to excellence: Assignment to honors English classes in the transition from middle to high school. *Educational Evaluation and Policy Analysis, 14*(3), 185–204.

Gamoran, A., & Hannigan, E. C. (2000). Algebra for everyone? Benefits of college-preparatory mathematics for students with diverse abilities in early secondary school. *Educational Evaluation and Policy Analysis, 22*(3), 241–254.

Gamoran, A., Nystrand, M., Berends, M., & LePore, P. C. (1995). An organizational analysis of the effects of ability grouping. *American Educational Research Journal, 32*(4), 687–715.

Gecas, V., & Schwalbe, M. L. (1983). Beyond the looking-glass self: Social structure and efficacy-based self-esteem. *Social Psychology Quarterly, 46*(2), 77–88.

Gecas, V., & Schwalbe, M. L. (1986). Parental behavior and adolescent self-esteem. *Journal of Marriage and the Family, 48*(1), 37–46.

Gecas, V., & Seff, M. A. (1989). Social class, occupational conditions, and self-esteem. *Sociological Perspectives, 32*(3), 353–364.

Gecas, V., & Seff, M. A. (1990). Social class and self-esteem: Psychological centrality, compensation, and the relative effects of work and home. *Social Psychology Quarterly, 53*(2), 165–173.

Goldin, C. D., & Katz, L. F. (2009). *The race between education and technology*. Cambridge, MA: Harvard University Press.

Goldrick-Rab, S. (2006). Following their every move: An investigation of social-class differences in college pathways. *Sociology of Education, 79*(1), 67–79.

Gonzalez, K. P., Stoner, C., & Jovel, J. E. (2003). Examining the role of social capital in access to college for Latinas: Toward a college opportunity framework. *Journal of Hispanic Higher Education, 2*(2), 146–170.

Gormley, W. T., Jr., Gayer, T., Phillips, D., & Dawson, B. (2005). The effects of universal pre-K on cognitive development. *Developmental Psychology, 41*(6), 872.

Goyette, K. A. (2008). College for some to college for all: Social background, occupational expectations, and educational expectations over time. *Social Science Research, 37*(2), 461–484.

Grodsky, E., & Jones, M. T. (2007). Real and imagined barriers to college entry: Perceptions of cost. *Social Science Research, 36*(2), 745–766.

Grodsky, E., & Riegle-Crumb, C. (2010). Those who choose and those who don't: Social background and college orientation. *The Annals of the American Academy of Political and Social Science, 627*(1), 14–35.

Hallinan, M. T. (1994). Tracking: From theory to practice. *Sociology of Education, 67*(2), 79–84.

Hamilton, L. (2016). *Parenting to a degree*. Chicago: The University of Chicago Press.

Harding, D. J. (2010). *Living the drama: Community, conflict, and culture among inner-city boys*. University of Chicago Press.

Harding, D. J. (2011). Rethinking the cultural context of schooling decisions in disadvantaged neighborhoods from deviant subculture to cultural heterogeneity. *Sociology of Education, 84*(4), 322–339.

Hays, S. (1994). Structure and agency and the sticky problem of culture. *Sociological Theory, 12*(1), 57–72.

Heckman, J. J., & LaFontaine, P. (2006). Bias-corrected estimates of GED returns. *Journal of Labor Economics, 24*(3), 661–700.

Heckman, J. J., Moon, S. H., Pinto, R., Savelyev, P. A., & Yavitz, A. (2010). The rate of return to the HighScope Perry Preschool Program. *Journal of Public Economics, 94*(1), 114–128.

Hoekstra, M. (2009). The effect of attending the flagship state university on earnings: A discontinuity-based approach. *The Review of Economics and Statistics, 91*(4), 717–724.

Holland, M. M., & DeLuca, S. (2016). "Why wait years to become something?" Low-income African American youth and the costly career search for-profit trade schools. *Sociology of Education, 89*(4), 261–278.

Hong, G., & Nomi, T. (2012). Weighting methods for assessing policy effects mediated by peer change.

Journal of Research on Educational Effectiveness, 5(3), 261–289.

Horn, L. J., Chen, X., & Chapman, C. (2003). *Getting ready to pay for college: What students and their parents know about the cost of college tuition and what they are doing to find out*. Washington, DC: U.S. Department of Education, Institute of Education Sciences.

Howell, J., Kurlaender, M., & Grodsky, E. (2010). Postsecondary preparation and remediation: Examining the effect of the early assessment program at California State University. *Journal of Policy Analysis and Management, 29*(4), 726–748.

Hoxby, C., & Avery, C. (2013). The missing "one-offs": The hidden supply of high-achieving, low-income students. *Brookings Papers on Economic Activity, 2013*(1), 1–65.

Hoxby, C., & Turner, S. (2015). What high-achieving low-income students know about college. *American Economic Review, 105*(5), 514–517.

Huang, F. L. (2015). Investigating the prevalence of academic redshirting using population-level data. *AERA Open, 1*(2), 1–11.

Ingersoll, R. M. (1999). The problem of underqualified teachers in American secondary schools. *Educational Researcher, 28*(2), 26–37.

Jackson, J. S. (2015). Does an early college readiness signal discourage college application and enrollment? *Journal of Research on Educational Effectiveness, 8*(3), 380–399.

Jacob, B., & Wilder-Linkow, T. (2011). Educational expectations and attainment. In G. J. Duncan & R. J. Murnane (Eds.), *Whither opportunity? Rising inequality and the uncertain life chances of low-income children* (pp. 133–163). New York: Russell Sage Press.

Kalogrides, D., Loeb, S., & Béteille, T. (2013). Systematic sorting teacher characteristics and class assignments. *Sociology of Education, 86*(2), 103–123.

Kao, G., & Tienda, M. (1998). Educational aspirations of minority youth. *American Journal of Education, 106*, 349–384.

Kelly, S. (2009). The Black–White gap in mathematics course taking. *Sociology of Education, 82*(1), 47–69.

Kena, G., Musu-Gillette, L., Robinson, J., Wang, X., Rathbun, A., Zhang, J., & Velez, E. D. V. (2015). *The condition of education 2015. NCES 2015-144*. Washington, DC: National Center for Education Statistics.

Kerckhoff, A., & Glennie, E. (1999). The Matthew effect in American education. *Research in Sociology of Education and Socialization, 12*(1), 35–66.

King, J. E. (2004). *Missed opportunities: Students who do not apply for financial aid*. Washington, DC: American Council on Education.

Klopfenstein, K., & Thomas, M. K. (2009). The link between advanced placement experience and early college success. *Southern Economic Journal, 75*(3), 873–891.

Kurlaender, M., & Howell, J. (2012). *Academic preparation for college: Evidence on the importance of academic rigor in high school*. Report of the College Board. Available at http://advocacy.collegeboard.org/sites/default/files/affinity-network-academic-preparation-college.pdf

Kurlaender, M., Carrell, S., & Jackson, J. (2016). The promises and pitfalls of measuring community college quality. *The Russell Sage Foundation Journal of the Social Sciences, 2*(1), 174–190.

Labaree, D. F. (1997). Public goods, private goods: The American struggle over educational goals. *American Educational Research Journal, 34*(1), 39–81.

Lamont, M., & Lareau, A. (1988). Cultural capital: Allusions, gaps and glissandos in recent theoretical developments. *Sociological Theory, 6*, 153–168.

Lareau, A. (2000). *Home Advantage* (2nd ed.). Lanham: Rowman and Littlefield.

Lareau, A. (2011). *Unequal childhoods: Class, race, and family life* (2nd ed.). Berkeley: University of California Press.

Lareau, A., & Goyette, K. (Eds.). (2014). *Choosing homes, choosing schools*. New York: Russell Sage Foundation.

Lareau, A., & Weininger, E. B. (2003). Cultural capital in educational research: A critical assessment. *Theory and society, 32*(5–6), 567–606.

Lee, V. E., & Ready, D. D. (2009). U.S. high school curriculum: Three phases of contemporary research and reform. *The Future of Children, 19*(1), 135–156.

Lee, J., & Zhou, M. (2015). *The Asian American achievement paradox*. New York: Russell Sage Foundation.

Levine, P. B., & Zimmerman, D. J. (1995). The benefit of additional high-school math and science classes for young men and women. *Journal of Business & Economic Statistics, 13*(2), 137–149.

Liang, J. H., Heckman, P. E., & Abedi, J. (2012). What do the California standards test results reveal about the movement toward eighth-grade algebra for all? *Educational Evaluation and Policy Analysis, 34*(3), 328–343.

Lincove, J., & Painter, G. (2006). Does the age that children start kindergarten matter? Evidence of long-term educational and social outcomes. *Educational Evaluation and Policy Analysis, 28*(2), 153–179.

Long, M., Conger, D., & Iatrola, P. (2009). Explaining gaps in readiness for college-level math: The role of high school courses. *Education Finance and Policy, 4*(1), 1–33.

Long, B. T. (2010). *Financial aid: A key to community college student success*. Paper presented at the White House summit on Community Colleges, Washington, DC.

Long, M. C., Conger, D., & Iatarola, P. (2012). Effects of high school course-taking on secondary and post-secondary success. *American Educational Research Journal, 49*(2), 285–322.

Loveless, T. (2008). *The misplaced math student: Lost in eighth-grade algebra*. The 2008 Brown Center report on American education. Special release. Washington, DC: Brookings Institution.

Mann, A., & Diprete, T. A. (2013). Trends in gender segregation in the choice of science and engineering majors. *Social Science Research, 42*(6), 1519–1541.

Marcussen, K., Ritter, C., & Safron, D. J. (2004). The role of identity salience and commitment in the stress process. *Sociological Perspectives, 47*(3), 289–312.

Marsh, H. W., Walker, R., & Debus, R. (1991). Subject-specific components of academic self-concept and self-efficacy. *Contemporary Educational Psychology, 16*(4), 331–345.

McDonough, P. M. (1997). *Choosing colleges: How social class and schools structure opportunity*. Albany: Suny Press.

McKinney, L., & Roberts, T. (2012). The role of community college financial aid counselors in helping students understand and use financial aid. *Community College Journal of Research & Practice, 36*(10), 761–774.

Mishel, L., & Roy, J. (2006). Accurately assessing high school graduation rates. *Phi Delta Kappan, 88*(4), 287–292.

Morgan, P. L., Farkas, G., Hillemeier, M. M., & Maczuga, S. (2016). Science achievement gaps begin very early, persist, and are largely explained by modifiable factors. *Educational Researcher, 45*(1), 18–35.

Moses, R., & Cobb, C. E. (2002). *Radical equations: Civil rights from Mississippi to the algebra project*. Boston: Beacon Press.

Murdock, T. B., Anderman, L. H., & Hodge, S. A. (2000). Middle-grade predictors of students' motivation and behavior in high school. *Journal of Adolescent Research, 15*(3), 327–351.

National Commission on Excellence in Education. (1983). A nation at risk: The imperative for educational reform. *The Elementary School Journal, 84*(2), 113–130.

National Center for Education Statistics. (2016a). *Digest of Education Statistics 2014 (NCES 2016–006)*. Washington, DC: National Center for Education Statistics, Institute of Education Sciences, U.S. Department of Education.

National Center for Education Statistics. (2016b). *Digest of education statistics 2015 (NCES 2016–014)*. Washington, DC: National Center for Education Statistics, Institute of Education Sciences, U.S. Department of Education.

Nomi, T. (2012). The unintended consequences of an algebra-for-all policy on high-skill students: Effects on instructional organization and students' academic outcomes. *Educational Evaluation and Policy Analysis, 34*(4), 489–505.

Nomi, T., & Allensworth, E. M. (2013). Sorting and supporting: Why double-dose algebra led to better test scores but more course failures. *American Educational Research Journal, 50*(4), 756–788.

Oakes, J. (1985). *Keeping track: How schools structure inequality*. New Haven: Yale University Press.

Oakes, J. (1990). *Multiplying inequalities: The effects of race, social class, and tracking on opportunities to learn mathematics and science.* Santa Monica: RAND Corporation.

Oakes, J. (2005). *Keeping track: How schools structure inequality.* New Haven: Yale University Press.

Owens, T. J., & Serpe, R. T. (2003). The role of self-esteem in family identity salience and commitment among Blacks, Latinos, and Whites. In P. J. Burke, T. J. Owens, R. T. Serpe, & P. A. Thoits (Eds.), *Advances in identity theory and research* (pp. 85–102). New York: Kluwer Academic/Plenum.

Pallas, A. M., Entwisle, D. R., Alexander, K. L., & Stluka, M. F. (1994). Ability-group effects: Instructional, social, or institutional? *Sociology of Education, 67*(1), 27–46.

Papay, J. Murnane, R., & Willett, J. (2011). *How performance information affects human-capital investment decisions: The impact of test-score labels on educational outcomes* (NBER Working Paper Series: No. 17120). Cambridge, MA: National Bureau of Economic Research.

Perez, P. A., & McDonough, P. M. (2008). Understanding Latina and Latino college choice: A social capital and chain migration analysis. *Journal of Hispanic Higher Education, 7*(3), 249–265.

Perna, L. W. (2000). Differences in the decision to attend college among African Americans, Hispanics, and Whites. *Journal of Higher Education, 71*, 117–141.

Perna, L. (2007). Understanding high school students' willingness to borrow to pay college prices. *Research in Higher Education, 49*(7), 589–606.

Perna, L. W., & Titus, M. A. (2005). The relationship between parental involvement as social capital and college enrollment: An examination of racial/ethnic group differences. *Journal of Higher Education, 76*(5), 485–518.

Planty, M., Bozick, R., & Ingels, S. J. (2006). *Academic pathways, preparation, and performance: A descriptive overview of the transcripts from the high school graduating class of 2003-TAB. NCES 2007-316.* Washington, DC: National Center for Education Statistics.

Porter, A. (1989). A curriculum out of balance: The case of elementary school mathematics. *Educational Researcher, 18*(5), 9–15.

Provasnik, S. & Planty, M. (2008). *Community colleges: Special supplement to the condition of education 2008. NCES 2008–033.* National Center for Education Statistics.

Puma, M., Bell, S., Cook, R., Heid, C., Shapiro, G., Broene, P., & Ciarico, J. (2010). *Head start impact study.* Washington, DC: U.S. Department of Health and Human Services: Administration for Children & Families.

Reyes, O., & Jason, L. A. (1993). Pilot study examining factors associated with academic success for Hispanic high school students. *Journal of Youth and Adolescence, 22*(1), 57–71.

Reynolds, A., Temple, J., Ou, S., Arteaga, I., & White, B. (2011). School-based early childhood education and age-28 well-being: Effects by timing, dosage and subgroups. *Science, 333*(6040), 36–364.

Reynolds, J. R., & Pemberton, J. (2001). Rising college expectations among youth in the United States: A comparison of the 1979 and 1997 NLSY. *Journal of Human Resources, 36*(4), 703–726.

Reynolds, J., Stewart, M., MacDonald, R., & Sischo, L. (2006). Have adolescents become too ambitious? High school seniors' educational and occupational plans, 1976 to 2000. *Social Problems, 53*(2), 186–206.

Riegle-Crumb, C., & Grodsky, E. (2010). Racial-ethnic differences at the intersection of math course-taking and achievement. *Sociology of Education, 83*(3), 248–270.

Riegle-Crumb, C., King, B., Grodsky, E., & Muller, C. (2012). The more things change, the more they stay the same? Prior achievement fails to explain gender inequality in entry into STEM college majors over time. *American Educational Research Journal, 49*(6), 1048–1073.

Riley, R. W. (1997). *Mathematics equals opportunity.* Washington, DC: U.S. Department of Education.

Rose, H., & Betts, J. R. (2004). The effect of high school courses on earnings. *Review of Economics and Statistics, 86*(2), 497–513.

Rosenbaum, J. (2001). *Beyond college for all: Career paths for the forgotten half.* New York: Russell Sage Foundation.

Rosenbaum, J. E. (2011). The complexities of college for all: Beyond fairy-tale dreams. *Sociology of Education, 84*(2), 113–117.

Rosenbaum, J. E., & Binder, A. (1997). Do employers really need more educated youth? *Sociology of Education, 70*(1), 68–85.

Sacerdote, B. (2001). Peer effects with random assignment: Results for Dartmouth roommates. *Quarterly Journal of Economics, 116*(2), 681–704.

Sandefur, G. D., Meier, A. M., & Campbell, M. E. (2006). Family resources, social capital, and college attendance. *Social Science Research, 35*(2), 525–553.

Schneider, B., & Stevenson, D. (1999). The ambitious generation. *Educational Leadership, 57*(4), 22–25.

Schneider, B. L., & Stevenson, D. (2000). *The ambitious generation: America's teenagers, motivated but directionless.* New Haven: Yale University Press.

Schneider, B., Swanson, C. B., & Riegle-Crumb, C. (1997). Opportunities for learning: Course sequences and positional advantages. *Social Psychology of Education, 2*(1), 25–53.

Schoenfeld, A. H. (2004). The math wars. *Educational Policy, 18*(1), 253–286.

Schunk, D. H. (1991). Self-efficacy and academic motivation. *Educational Psychologist, 26*(3–4), 207–231.

Schweinhart, L. J., Montie, J., Xiang, Z., Barnett, W. S., Belfield, C. R., & Nores, M. (2005). *Lifetime effects: The High/Scope Perry preschool study through age 40.* Ypsilanti: High/Scope Press.

Scott-Clayton, J. (2012). *Information constraints and financial aid policy* (NBER Working Paper Series: No. 17811). Cambridge, MA: National Bureau of Economic Research.

Settersten, R. A., Jr., & Ray, B. (2010). What's going gn with young people today? The long and twisting path to adulthood. *The Future of Children, 20*(1), 19–41.

Sewell, W. H. (1992). A theory of structure: Duality, agency, and transformation. *American Journal of Sociology, 98*(1), 1–29.

Sewell, W. H., & Hauser, R. M. (1975). *Education, occupation, and earnings: Achievement in the early career.* New York: Academic Press.

Sewell, W. H., Haller, A. O., & Portes, A. (1969). The educational and early occupational attainment process. *American Sociological Review, 34*(1), 82–92.

Sherman, D. K., & Cohen, G. L. (2006). The psychology of self-defense: Self-affirmation theory. In M. P. Zanna (Ed.), *Advances in experimental social psychology* (pp. 183–242). San Diego: Academic Press.

Slavin, R. E. (1987). Ability grouping and student achievement in elementary schools: A best-evidence synthesis. *Review of Educational Research, 57*(3), 293–336.

Smith, J. B. (1996). Does an extra year make any difference? The impact of early access to algebra on long-term gains in mathematics attainment. *Educational Evaluation and Policy Analysis, 18*(2), 141–153.

Snyder, T. & Dillow, S. (2013). *Digest of education statistics.* NCES 2015-011. National Center for Education Statistics.

Sørensen, A. B. (1970). Organizational differentiation of students and educational opportunity. *Sociology of Education, 43*(4), 355–376.

Sørensen, A. B., & Hallinan, M. T. (1986). Effects of ability grouping on growth in academic achievement. *American Educational Research Journal, 23*(4), 519–542.

Spence, M. (1973). Job market signaling. *The Quarterly Journal of Economics, 87*(3), 355–374.

Stanton-Salazar, R. (1997). A social capital framework for understanding the socialization of racial minority children and youths. *Harvard Educational Review, 67*(1), 1–41.

Stanton-Salazar, R. D. (2001). *Manufacturing hope and despair: The school and kin support networks of U.S.-Mexican youth.* New York: Teachers College Press.

Steele, C. M. (1988). The psychology of self-affirmation: Sustaining the integrity of the self. In L. Berkowitz (Ed.), *Advances in experimental social psychology* (pp. 261–302). New York: Academic Press.

Stevens, M. L. (2007). *Creating a class: College admissions and the education of elites.* Cambridge, MA: Harvard University Press.

Stiglitz, J. E. (1975). The theory of "screening," education, and the distribution of income. *The American Economic Review, 65*(3), 283–300.

Taniguchi, H., & Kaufman, G. (2005). Degree completion among nontraditional college students. *Social Science Quarterly, 86*(4), 912–927.

Terriquez, V., & Gurantz, O. (2014). Financial challenges in emerging adulthood and students' decisions to stop out of college. *Emerging Adulthood, 3*(3), 204–214.

Tierney, W. G., & Venegas, K. M. (2006). Fictive kin and social capital: The role of peer groups in applying and paying for college. *American Behavioral Scientist, 49*(12), 1687–1702.

Xie, Y., & Shaumann, S. A. (2003). *Women in science: Career processes and outcomes.* Cambridge, MA: Harvard University Press.

Yeager, D. S., & Walton, G. M. (2011). Social-psychological interventions in education: They're not magic. *Review of Educational Research, 81*(2), 267–301.

Yonezawa, S. (2013). *Increasing federal financial aid access for California community college students.* PATHWAYS to Postsecondary Success.

Yoshikawa, H., Weiland, C., Brooks-Gunn, J., Burchinal, M. R., Espinosa, L. M., Gormley, W. T., & Zaslow, M. J. (2013). *Investing in our future: The evidence base on preschool education.* Ann Arbor: Society for Research in Child Development.

Zhai, F., Raver, C. C., & Jones, S. M. (2012). Academic performance of subsequent schools and impacts of early interventions: Evidence from a randomized controlled trial in Head Start settings. *Children and Youth Services Review, 34*(5), 946–954.

Zimmerman, D. (2003). Peer effects in academic outcomes: Evidence from a natural experiment. *The Review of Economics and Statistics, 85*(1), 9–23.

Richard Arum, Josipa Roksa, Jacqueline Cruz,
and Blake Silver

Abstract

We review research on the "experiential core of college life" for contemporary students at four-year colleges in the United States. We argue that student academic and social experiences need to be understood in the context of broader historical and institutional factors that have structured these organizational settings. As sociologists, we focus attention on variation in college experiences for students from different socioeconomic and racial/ethnic groups, as well as consider issues related to gender, which today include prominent attention to sexuality and sexual violence. We conclude our review by calling for additional research on topics including explicating the relationship between academic and social collegiate experiences, intersectionality, family influences, sexual violence, student political discourse, as well as increased attention to students at two-year colleges and other broad-access institutions.

R. Arum (✉)
University of California, Irvine, CA, USA
e-mail: rarum@uci.edu

J. Roksa
University of Virginia, Charlottesville, VA, USA
e-mail: jroksa@virginia.edu

J. Cruz
New York University, New York, NY, USA
e-mail: Jec538@nyu.edu

B. Silver
George Mason University, Fairfax, VA, USA
e-mail: bsilver@gmu.edu

Student experiences on U.S. four-year college campuses have reemerged, since a relative hiatus from earlier decades, as a subject of considerable public discourse (see e.g., Wong and Green 2016; Gitlin 2015) and increasing sociological analysis. As sociologists we proceed by assuming that students' personal problems should be understood as social issues (Mills 1959). In conducting such an analysis, we argue that student experiences in college must be understood in relationship to historical conditions, variation in institutional contexts, as well as with respect to differences by social class, race/ethnicity, and gender. While student experiences of college vary greatly across these dimensions, there are also commonalities in recent cohorts' collegiate experiences since institutional isomorphism is pronounced in higher education and other developed organizational fields (DiMaggio and Powell 1983).

In order to understand student experiences in college—that is, the "experiential core of college life" (Stevens et al. 2008)—this chapter will begin by highlighting some of the broader historical and institutional factors that have

© Springer International Publishing AG, part of Springer Nature 2018   385
B. Schneider (ed.), *Handbook of the Sociology of Education in the 21st Century*, Handbooks
of Sociology and Social Research, https://doi.org/10.1007/978-3-319-76694-2_17

structured student experiences on campus. We will focus our attention on four-year residential colleges as they represent sites that demand the greatest amount of time investment in college experiences. The chapter will then expand on several dimensions of student experiences related to academic and social engagement and explore variation in college experiences for students from different socioeconomic and racial/ethnic groups. Finally, we will consider issues related to gender, which today include prominent attention to sexuality and sexual violence.

17.1 Higher Education at the Turn of the Twenty-First Century

Student experiences in college occur in the context of larger historical and institutional conditions. Specifically, current cohorts of students face particular structural conditions with respect to: growing economic inequality in society; increasing costs and challenges around financing higher education; the rise of a consumer institutional model (including an emphasis on student services, social amenities, and the promotion of a therapeutic ethic); changes in cultural assumptions around the meaning and timing of adulthood; demographic shifts in students attending higher education; and changing legal regulation of postsecondary institutions operating in the field. Within this context, the structure of academic and social life at universities serves to recreate inequality and stratify students in various ways (Armstrong and Hamilton 2013).

Students experience college today in the shadow of deep and growing economic inequality reminiscent of a period prior to the post-World War II dramatic expansion and massification of higher education. In the U.S. since 1970, income concentration has grown with the top decile of households moving from earning 34% to 48% of total income, and wealth concentration having grown from the top decile controlling 66% to close to three quarters of assets (Piketty and Saez 2014; Stone et al. 2012). This inequality has included greater rewards for privileged occupa-

tional positions associated with elite college education as well as growing consequences for educational and labor market failure (Autor 2014). This growing inequality has also been associated with increasing insecurity about access to elite educational opportunities (Stevens 2009) and a related increase since 1970 in the percentage of young adults who have obtained fewer years of education than their similarly sexed parents (Duncan and Murnane 2011). In addition, there has been dramatic growth in how many colleges one applies to attend—9% of freshmen applied to seven or more colleges in 1991 compared to 32% in 2013 (Clinedinst 2015)—as well as growth in the gap between rich and poor children's access to educational enrichment opportunities (Duncan and Murnane 2011).

In part facilitated by this growth in income and wealth inequality, the cost of higher education has increased at roughly twice the rate of inflation for the past several decades. Simultaneously, state government funding for higher education has stagnated or declined, and federal funding has struggled to keep up with rising costs. Given this economic reality, students and families who are not at the very top of the income and wealth distributions have increasingly had to engage in extensive reliance on a variety of financing mechanisms to fund higher education attainment. These mechanisms have included college savings plans, home refinancing, student loans, and credit card debt. For example, two-thirds of four-year college students who graduated in 2009 had student loan debts two years after finishing college that averaged twenty-seven thousand dollars, and close to half of these graduates had credit card debts averaging an additional two thousand dollars (Arum and Roksa 2014).

Higher education institutions have grown increasingly dependent on student tuition dollars and have relatedly focused on serving students as consumers (Roksa 2016a). Colleges and universities competing to attract adolescents and young adults to their campuses have invested in an expansion of student services and social amenities (such as state-of-the-art dormitories, student centers and athletic facilities) with subsequent declines in instruction provided by full-time faculty. Jacob et al. (2013) have demonstrated that this institutional logic is well aligned with the revealed preferences of the vast majority of students' decision-making about which college to attend.

Young adults are also spending greater amounts of time attending college and residing on or near campus as opposed to commuting from home. Students often spend 5 or 6 years pursuing a bachelor's degree and then increasingly go on to pursue graduate degrees. Increasing time spent in a liminal state in higher education has thus contributed to and legitimized the rise of emerging adulthood or, what we have termed elsewhere (Arum and Roksa 2014), "aspiring adulthood"—an extended period following adolescence in which traditional adult roles (such as leaving home, finishing school, finding a job, financial independence and family formation) are delayed. Higher education institutions have embraced these changes and in an effort to better support students' psychological needs have promoted a therapeutic ethic on campuses (Loss 2012).

Colleges and universities in recent decades have also experienced significant demographic shifts in terms of the characteristics of students attending them. Following the rapid expansion of higher education in the three decades following World War II, growth in enrollments has been less pronounced in recent decades. While this has led to larger portions of students from traditionally underrepresented racial/ethnic groups and socioeconomically disadvantaged family backgrounds entering higher education, class inequality and to a lesser extent racial inequality—i.e., the gap between the more and less advantaged groups—has persisted over time since all groups have increased their access to higher education (Roksa et al. 2007; Bailey and Dynarski 2011). What has changed dramatically, however, is the proportion of men and women attending higher education (DiPrete and Buchmann 2013). At elite institutions, college admissions offices are able to engage in elaborate enrollment management strategies to maintain gender balance on campus

(Stevens 2009). But for the sector as a whole, female students increasingly have become a clear majority of those enrolled on most campuses.

Changes in gender composition in higher education have occurred in the context of changes in the legal environment, which has focused increased attention on sexual harassment and sexual violence on campus. In the last quarter of the twentieth century, colleges and universities have experienced environmental pressures requiring them to abandon their traditional *in loco parentis* role around regulating student behavior and to respect students' due process rights; while in more recent years, the federal government and social movements on campus have demanded the right to a safe campus environment free from sexual harassment and violence.

This broader context provides the foundation for understanding student experiences at the turn of the twenty-first century. It highlights broader cultural forces that affect student experiences, and elucidates the persisting as well as shifting nature of inequality. With the decline of *in loco parentis* and rise of "student consumers," higher education institutions for decades gave students increasing flexibility and choice, catering to their expressed or perceived needs, profoundly shaping student experiences. Demographic shifts and growing inequality in society more broadly placed increasing pressures on higher education to deliver on the American Dream, bringing socioeconomic and racial/ethnic inequalities to the fore. And recent debates about sexual assault shifted both the role of institutions and the conceptions of gender inequality. We begin by highlighting the commonalities of student experiences in residential four-year institutions before turning to inequality by socioeconomic status, race/ethnicity, and gender.

17.2 College Life—The Common Thread

Understanding college life inevitably begins with asking students to reflect on their experiences and considering what they do with their time. Recent college graduates describe college as a time for personal development and learning how to get along with others (Arum and Roksa 2014). Reflecting David Riesman's (1950) description of "other-directed" young adults as focused on getting along with others, rather than being grounded by one's own deeply held "inner-directed" values and motivations, college students place an emphasis on the social realm where sociability and sensitivity to social groups are highly valued. Through interaction with peers, students learn how to become more sociable and how to engage with others. Students emphasize wanting to be "a whole person" and "well rounded." To do so, students do not want to "disappear behind the mountain of books." Instead, they want to have a robust social life that provides opportunities for being socially alive, active, and adept (Arum and Roksa 2014; Grigsby 2009). Such a prominent focus on personal development makes the social aspects of college life indispensable.

Students' time use reflects this focus on their social lives during college. In a recent study at the University of California, Brint and Cantwell (2010) found that each week students spent on average 13 h studying and preparing for class, 14 h working, 17 h watching TV and using computers for fun, as well as 24 h engaged in other forms of entertainment, socializing, student groups, or exercise. College students thus spent over 40 h each week in leisure and social activities, over three times the amount they spent studying. This pattern of limited attention to academic pursuits and substantial allocation of time to social activities is replicated across many different samples from those containing more selective institutions (Charles et al. 2009) to samples more broadly representative of traditional-age students attending four-year institutions (Arum and Roksa 2011).

While spending very little time on academic pursuits, students nonetheless perceive themselves as being academically engaged (Arum and Roksa 2014). The apparent disconnect between the few hours students spend studying and perceptions of academic engagement is reconciled by considering how students describe academic engagement. Arum and Roksa (2014) reported that students overall regarded themselves as being academically engaged if they completed the bare minimum of requirements—such as going to class (most of the time), not missing assignments, or doing enough work not to fail. Under this minimalist definition of academic engagement students can continue to focus on the social, while feeling that they are giving adequate attention to their academics.

Faculty contribute to students' sense of academic engagement by awarding high grades for a limited investment of time and effort. In a study of over 2000 students across a range of four-year institutions, Arum and Roksa (2011) found that on average students studied 12 h a week and earned a 3.2 grade point average. Even the substantial proportion of students who studied alone less than 5 h a week did quite well, having better than a B average. It was possible to get good grades with limited time investment because students were often not asked to do much academically. In a given semester, half of students did not take a class requiring more than 20 pages of writing, and a third of students did not take a class requiring 40 pages of reading per week.

Other studies similarly point to the prevalence of limited academic demands in colleges and universities. For instance, the National Survey of Student Engagement (NSSE) documented that during their senior year, 51% of college students reported they had not written a paper at least 20 pages long (NSSE 2009). Many students also did not take courses that required engagement with complex tasks like analysis and application. Approximately a quarter of college freshmen reported that they had "very little" or only "some" coursework that emphasized analysis of ideas/ theories or applying concepts, and over a third had "very little" or only "some" coursework involving synthesizing ideas or making judgments (NSSE 2007). Many students respond to such modest academic demands by limiting their effort solely to as much time as is necessary to do well in the course and no more (Nathan 2006).

An obvious question following these descriptions of students' limited academic engagement is whether this reflects a new phenomenon. As Horowitz (1987) and Jencks and Riesman (1968) have documented, college life in the U.S. has always had a strong social component. Indeed, college has long been a setting for socializing and networking among elite students (Karabel 2006). But the amount of time students spend on academics has indeed declined over time. In a careful analysis of time use across a number of different surveys, Babcock and Marks (2011) showed that the average number of hours that students spend studying outside of class has decreased notably since the 1960s. Indeed, in the first half of the twentieth century, what it meant to be a full-time college student resembled full-time commitments: 15 h in class and 25 h studying. While students today still spend 15 h in class, they spend only approximately 12–13 h studying. Similarly, measures of general collegiate skills reveal evidence of decreasing learning over time. In an extensive review of the literature, Pascarella and Terenzini (2005) concluded that students' gains on indicators of general collegiate skills are about half of what they were in earlier decades. While the past is not to be romanticized, there are indications that the limited effort expended on academic pursuits by students today is notably different then several decades ago.

Another important change is the increasing role of institutions in supporting the centrality of the social realm in the definition and experience of college. In what Slaughter and Rhoades (2004) term "academic capitalism," universities have become increasingly corporatized, with consequences not only for research and connections with industry but also for interactions with students. The authors argue that universities not only engage students as consumers but also market to them in ways that serve universities' financial interests. Institutions reveal only certain information that directly benefits them and portray colleges as "attractive places in which to live, consume services, and play [rather] than as challenging places in which to learn and become educated" (p. 298).

While higher education institutions operate in a broader cultural context that emphasizes consumerism and the private benefits of education (e.g., Labaree 1997), they facilitate the consumer orientation and emphasis on the social through their policies and practices. Students' social experiences in college are facilitated by an environment that prioritizes socializing in student groups ranging from athletic clubs to student organizations to fraternities and sororities (Stuber 2011; Armstrong and Hamilton 2013) as well as attending and consuming large amounts of alcohol at parties and campus sporting events (Sperber 2000; Harford et al. 2002).

In an in-depth study of a mid-selective flagship state research university, Armstrong and Hamilton (2013) provide insights into how "supports for a social approach to college are built into the university" (p. 50), which enables and even encourages students to follow what they describe as a "robust party pathway." This occurs through a confluence of factors, including the university's support and subsidizing of Greek life, which detracts from students' academic pursuits; the residence hall system that encourages students to join fraternities and sororities and in general "have fun"; as well as the academic schedule (e.g., no classes on Fridays) and presence of "easy majors" that enable students' pursuit of social activities. While there are other approaches to college that diverge from the party pathway—including pathways that emphasize professional development and social mobility—the party pathway is the easiest to locate and hardest to avoid.

Moreover, apart from the party scene, institutions send strong signals to students about college life through their investment of resources. Over time, colleges and universities have increasingly diverted resources toward non-academic functions, and in particular toward a growing category of student services. Rhoades et al. (2007) documented that over the past three decades, non-faculty support professionals were the fastest growing category of professional employment on campus, with the most significant increase occurring in the area of student services. The share of spending on student services increased notably even in a short time period between 2001 and 2011, with private research universities showing the largest increase of 30% (Desrochers and Hurlburt 2014).

Notably, colleges have not only increasingly invested in non-academic aspects of college life; they have also failed to integrate the social/extracurricular aspects with academics. Although some have called for integrating student and academic affairs (Kuh et al. 2011) and conceptualizing learning and student development as inextricably linked (Keeling et al. 2004), the reality speaks to two different worlds. In a joint statement on learning, the National Association of Student Personnel Administrators (NASPA) and the American College Personnel Association (ACPA) noted:

> On many campuses, students may perceive little coherence in the student affairs curriculum, and individual episodes of acquiring knowledge fragments (such as resume writing, developing group living agreements, or alcohol education) or developmental experiences like leadership in student organizations or volunteer service simply orbit the student's world with little sense of their relationship one to another or to academic courses. (Keeling et al. 2004, p. 8)

Historically, student affairs professionals have supported students in planning and executing campus events without connecting these efforts to potential learning that could occur during the process (Keeling et al. 2004). In essence, student services on many college campuses may have little structure, coherence, or intentionality. When this is the case, student affairs programming and resources offer additional avenues to expand student choice and emphasize the social components of the college experience without adding to the cohesiveness or academic rigor of the curriculum.

While these descriptions of college life may appear to be too generic and lacking sensitivity to institutional contexts, institutional isomorphism has produced much similarity across institutions. Indeed, variation in students' experiences is observed primarily within not across institutions. Although there is some evidence that institutional characteristics such as selectivity are related to students' gains in critical thinking skills (Roksa and Arum 2015; Kugelmass and Ready 2011), institutional selectivity is weakly, if at all, related to the quality of instruction and good teaching practices (Pascarella et al. 2006; Kuh and Pascarella 2004; Trolian et al. 2014).

A recent study by Arum and Roksa (2011) documents the extent to which students' college experiences and outcomes vary both across and within institutions. Only a small proportion of variance (between 9% and 13%) in academic rigor (reading and writing requirements) is found across institutions, even in baseline models, without any controls. Similarly, only 10% of the variation in the number of hours students spend studying is found across institutions. When considering gains in critical thinking skills over 4 years of college, only 25% of the variance is observed across institutions (Arum and Roksa 2014). This pattern extends beyond critical thinking—a range of outcomes of college education demonstrate greater variation within institutions than across them (Blaich 2011). Students' experiences and outcomes thus depend less on where they go to college, than what they do once there. There are dedicated students, demanding professors, and rigorous curricula across virtually all institutions. The main challenge is that on average rigorous and engaging academic experiences are in short supply.

The consequences of this overall lack of focus on academics are predictable—students gain relatively little on measures of general collegiate skills such as critical thinking during college. Arum and Roksa (2011) reported that after the first two years of college, students improved on the Collegiate Learning Assessment (CLA) by only 0.18 standard deviations. And even after four years of college, students improved by only 0.47 standard deviations (Arum and Roksa 2014). This represents only an 18-percentile point gain, meaning that freshmen who entered higher education at the 50th percentile would reach the level equivalent to the 68th percentile of the incoming freshman class by the end of their senior year. These patterns of limited learning have been replicated in other data using a different measure of critical thinking and a different sample of students and institutions (Blaich 2011; Pascarella et al. 2011).

What is surprising, however, is that students are not improving substantially even on indicators of development that are more closely aligned with the extracurricular sphere. Out of the 12 outcomes examined in the Wabash National Study of Liberal Arts Education, only one outcome showed greater gains over four years of college than critical thinking: moral reasoning (Blaich

2011). All other outcomes showed substantially lower improvement over time, including openness to diversity and political and social involvement. On some measures students left college worse off than when they entered. For example, students had lower academic motivation at college exit than at college entry. While college is often assumed to improve student learning and development along multiple dimensions, gains in student learning and development have rarely been measured using standardized indicators. When researchers attempt to gauge improvement based on standardized indicators, the gains often appear modest at best.

Moreover, even though students are spending much time socializing, recent research indicates that peer social networks are not particularly helpful for transitioning into the labor market. Following almost a thousand graduates two years after college, Arum and Roksa (2014) reported that only 20% of graduates found their jobs through family or friends, and when they did, those jobs were less desirable than those found through formal means—which was the primary way graduates found employment. Moreover, students who found jobs through internships or through assistance of their colleges were much more likely to avoid unskilled employment. Students who performed well on a measure of critical thinking and complex reasoning were also less likely unemployed, less likely to end up working in an unskilled occupation, and if they had obtained a job, less likely to lose it. Thus, while academic achievement (in the form of complex generic skills) mattered, and social networks provided few occupational benefits, students still invested most of their time and energy on the latter.

17.3   Inequality on College Campuses

Students entering higher education today encounter a particular institutional context, one that we have described as lacking academic rigor and catering to consumer attitudes as opposed to offering a vision for a successful development of knowledge and skills for effective participation in a democratic society and the labor market (Arum and Roksa 2011, 2014). At the same time, higher education remains profoundly unequal. While inequalities in entry and completion are well documented, the more subtle inequalities in student experiences deserve as much attention. We proceed by discussing inequalities in college experiences by socioeconomic status, race/ethnicity, and gender, and conclude by providing suggestions for future research in each of those areas.

17.4   Socioeconomic Inequality in College Experiences

As Stevens et al. (2008) argued, sociologists have tended to focus on inequalities in college entry and completion, dedicating little attention to what happens inside higher education institutions. Activities within higher education institutions have been primarily the purview of higher education scholars and have been embedded in models that emphasize the importance of social and academic integration (e.g., Astin 1993; Tinto 1987; see a review in Pascarella and Terenzini 2005). This literature has been criticized for often interpreting low integration as a failure of the individual as opposed to a shortcoming of the collegiate culture (Hurtado and Carter 1997; Tierney 1992). Moreover, this literature tends to treat students' backgrounds primarily as inputs and statistically adjusts for them, but does not explore or theorize the complex relationships between students' background characteristics and educational institutions.

A few sociological studies, applying Bourdieu's cultural reproduction theory, have aimed to illuminate socioeconomic inequality in students' experiences in college (Bourdieu 1990; Bourdieu and Passeron 1990). These studies show that not all students enter higher education with the same conceptions of college or resources to navigate it. Stuber (2009, 2011) argued that the habitus students bring with them to college leads to variation in their approach to college and their interactions with postsecondary institutions. While more affluent students enter college ready to engage and participate in extracurricular life, working-class students are more inclined to think of college as a time to get good grades and credentials to facilitate transitions into the labor market. Working-class students are thus not eager to engage in extracurricular life and often wait for a direct invitation from someone in their social network, which can be limited. Quantitative studies have similarly shown that students from less advantaged backgrounds are less likely to engage in extracurricular activities (e.g., Pascarella et al. 2004). This differential engagement may be not only cultural, but also practical—students from less advantaged backgrounds are substantially more likely to work, which decreases the amount of time they have for extracurricular engagement (Bozick 2007; Roksa 2011).

Even if considering only students who do get involved, there are notable differences in the types of activities students from various social class backgrounds pursue. Stuber (2011) shows, for instance, that working-class students are more likely employed as resident assistants (or other campus work opportunities) and to become members of groups focusing on specific student populations such as first-generation college students. Upper-middle-class students on the other hand are more often involved in prestigious groups with greater potential to increase one's social network such as student governance, student programming, or Greek life. Other research supports these findings (e.g., Aries and Seider 2005; Salisbury et al. 2009).

Moreover, while students in general prioritize amenities offered by universities in making a decision about where to attend college, this focus on the non-academic aspect of college is greater among more socioeconomically advantaged students (Jacob et al. 2013). An emphasis on tuition, resulting in part from decreasing state support for higher education and the transformation of federal financial aid toward encouraging competition in the educational marketplace, has led colleges and universities to try to recruit a more advantaged student body (Slaughter and Rhoades 2004). The combination of these patterns implies an increasing shift of colleges in ways that would attract socioeconomically advantaged students who are more attentive to social aspects of college life.

For instance, Armstrong and Hamilton (2013) demonstrate that in efforts to draw students with affluent parents who can afford to pay full-tuition, universities try to cater to the interests of upper- and upper-middle-class (often out-of-state) students and, in particular, that institutions are responsive to well-off student preferences for a robust college social experience. As postsecondary institutions compete for these students, they emphasize and shore up the "party pathway" through college, involving extensive partying and minimal studying. The party pathway also lures some less advantaged students, who do not have the knowledge, information, and social networks to navigate this pathway successfully, and thus often experience poor performance or departure. The party pathway also reallocates institutional attention and resources away from other pathways, and in particular the "mobility pathway" that working-class students could utilize to achieve upward mobility. Armstrong and Hamilton describe the mobility pathway as "blocked." Students seeking upward mobility are often isolated and the university support for the party pathway often undermines socioeconomically disadvantaged students' efforts to locate alternative approaches that would facilitate their success.

Moreover, while universities do offer a professional pathway—the pathway often associated with academically driven students on track to professional careers—this pathway is difficult to find and stay on without substantial knowledge and resources (Armstrong and Hamilton 2013). Students from less advantaged backgrounds also face challenges navigating college coursework and understanding faculty expectations (Collier and Morgan 2008). Without receiving guidance from the university, students have to rely on parents to navigate college. In a recent book based on interviews with parents of women at a mid-selective public university, Hamilton (2016) argues that success in higher education necessitates parental involvement, but many parents, especially those from socioeconomically disadvantaged groups, are not able to engage and guide their children toward degree completion. Working-class students depend on institutions to help find the way, making advising services especially important for less advantaged students (e.g., Bahr 2008). Indeed, recent experimental evidence indicates that interventions focused on coaching and advising college students from disadvantaged backgrounds can facilitate persistence (Bettinger and Baker 2013).

While students from socioeconomically disadvantaged backgrounds face challenges across institutional types, sociologists have focused in particular on elite institutions, where socioeconomically disadvantaged students are substantially underrepresented (Oseguera and Astin 2004; Kahlenberg 2010). In their comparative study of a highly-selective liberal arts college, which they refer to as "Little Ivy," and a public institution with a less affluent student body, called "State College," Aries and Seider (2005) found that working-class students in the more elite institution described various difficulties that were not encountered by working-class students at State College. For instance, working-class students at Little Ivy described the ways in which their speech marked their class background, causing other students to look down on them. Such experiences meant that less advantaged students who attended this highly selective liberal arts college often reported feeling intimidated, uncomfortable, inadequate, and even excluded within the institution.

Given the discrepancy between their origins and elite university cultures, low-income or working-class students can experience a sense of pressure to distance themselves from their working-class upbringing, impacting their relationships with friends and family who are not upwardly mobile. Building on Bourdieu's concept of "cleft habitus," Lee and Kramer (2013) have highlighted the experiences of working-class students as they move back and forth between working-class homes and elite postsecondary institutions. Instead of focusing on the social or cultural capital gained through such an experience, this perspective considers the strug-gles experienced by less affluent students as they attempt to maintain relationships with parents, siblings, and friends from home.

Working-class students may also experience what Lehmann (2014)—invoking Sennett (1972)—refers to as, "the hidden injuries of class," as they feel unable to maintain social networks from their communities of origin. Lehmann (2014) claims a loss of "ontological security" may cause working-class students to feel that they do not belong either at home or at their college. Some working-class students also experience "habitus transformation" (Lehmann 2014), whereby they engage in a great deal of self-scrutiny in order to "fashion and refashion" themselves in accordance with the expectations of an elite university environment (Reay et al. 2009, p. 1103). Working-class students who attend preparatory or boarding schools often begin the process of "habitus transformation" before college and thus are more likely to exhibit behaviors such as seeking out interactions with authority figures at college than their working-class peers who attend local high schools (Jack 2016).

17.5   College Experiences of Different Racial/Ethnic Groups

Sociologists have dedicated comparatively less attention to understanding college experiences of students from different racial/ethnic groups (for a review of higher education research, see Pascarella and Terenzini 2005). While some studies have reported that students from traditionally underrepresented racial/ethnic groups may be less likely to engage in activities that are positively associated with academic outcomes (Brint and Cantwell 2010; Charles et al. 2009), others found no differences in the academic experiences of White and Black students net of controls (Roksa et al. 2016a), especially after the first year of college (Roksa 2016b; Trolian et al. 2014). Experiences, however, vary notably by institutional type, especially for Black students attending Historically Black Colleges and Universities compared to those attending other institutions (Bridges et al. 2007; Seifert et al. 2006).

An extensive body of literature in higher education has examined the importance of experiences with diversity on college campuses (see recent reviews by Bowman 2010, 2011). These experiences include interactions with students from different racial or ethnic groups, other countries, different values or political views, religions, etc. (Hu and Kuh 2003). Interaction with diverse others within the college environment has been cited as improving critical thinking (Pascarella et al. 2001), civic engagement (Chang et al. 2004), as well as attitudes and openness to diversity more generally (Whitt et al. 2001). Research on diversity experiences offers conflicting evidence regarding the equity of such experiences. Some studies indicate that all students benefit from such interactions and experiences (Bowman 2013), while others find that White students benefit more on certain dimensions than non-White students (Pascarella et al. 2011; Hu and Kuh 2003; Roksa et al. 2016b). Moreover, non-White students often experience more negative interactions than their White peers (Nora and Cabrera 1996; Laird 2005).

Notwithstanding the potential value of interactions with diverse peers, on many campuses, opportunities for cross-racial interaction and discussions of race may be less common than imagined. For instance, Solorzano et al. (2000) found that staff and students reported that discussions of race were taboo and often avoided. Non-White students in particular saw an inherent contradiction in expectations to interact with diverse groups of their peers, while avoiding discussion of race and ethnicity. Students also often perceive campus spaces as racially segregated (see also Antonio 2004). And while White students on average form more interracial friendships during college than high school, the number of interracial friendships one has either holds steady or declines for non-White students during college (Stearns et al. 2009).

In general, college graduates are more tolerant of a variety of forms of diversity, including racial and ethnic diversity (Campbell and Horowitz 2016), and generally speaking, a college education has been shown to reduce prejudice and increase tolerance (Hout 2012). However, the degree to which these changes—which are often documented with surveys of college students and college graduates—represent a genuine change in attitudes regarding race as opposed to simply acquiring new ways to talk about race is unclear. For instance, in a study of racial attitudes among White college students, Bonilla-Silva and Forman (2000) documented the use of coded racist language to talk about racial and ethnic minorities, while students claimed not to be racist. Further, the identity strategies required of racial and ethnic minorities in college may place pressure on them to avoid acknowledging instances of racism in order to make White students comfortable and combat stereotypes (Wilkins 2012).

Research on campus racial climates more broadly has highlighted the challenges students from traditionally underrepresented racial/ethnic groups face on their journeys through higher education (for recent reviews, see Harper and Hurtado 2007; Hurtado et al. 1998). A diverse student body does not create a supportive and welcoming environment in and of itself (see Roksa et al. 2016b). Diverse campuses can still foster a hostile climate for racial and ethnic minority students, and often non-White students report that the campus climate is less welcoming than White students report (Nora and Cabrera 1996; Rankin and Reason 2005; Roksa et al. 2016a). Notably, such perceptions of a negative campus climate around race and ethnicity have been shown to relate to a diminished sense of belonging for racial and ethnic minority students (Hurtado and Carter 1997). Harper and Hurtado (2007) have thus called on "administrators, faculty, and institutional researchers to audit their campus climates and cultures proactively to determine the need for change" (p. 20) and to encourage positive interactions.

Additionally, Wilkins (2014) found that White, first-generation, male students during the transition into college deployed a strategy of "being normal," using masculine scripts to achieve an adult identity that was useful in achieving success in the college context. Alternatively, the "being cool" identity strategies of Black male students became detrimental to their success as they transitioned from high school to college. In this new environment, the expectations of others narrowed the range of acceptable identities Black men could adopt. Wilkins concluded that Black male students were "stripped of choice over their identities" (p. 185) by their peers, who tended to limit the cultural scripts of masculinity accessible to Black students in the college setting.

Academic performance and self-concept of racial and ethnic minority students are shaped by common racial stereotypes. For instance, Torres and Charles (2004) explain how Black students' understandings of the negative ways in which White students perceive them—which they refer to as "metastereotypes"—encourage Black students to expend significant amounts of energy and time debunking such stereotypes. Similarly, Massey and Fischer (2005) find that racial and ethnic minority students perceive that general negative stereotypes are held by others regarding their academic abilities, which places added pressure on these students in academic settings. The authors refer to this pressure as "academic performance burden," and note that this burden causes students to encounter difficulty performing at the level that they could in the absence of such stereotypes; this phenomenon has been called "stereotype threat" (Steele and Aronson 1995). Further, when some racial and ethnic minority students come to internalize these stereotypes, they may end up withdrawing from engagement with academic material. Stereotypes and perceptions of racial bias even impact Black students' choice of a field of study as they seek to avoid certain majors or academic settings thought to treat minority students unfairly (Chavous et al. 2004). Overall, the literature clearly demonstrates the pervasive influence of race and ethnicity on students' college experiences both academically and socially.

17.6 Gender on College Campuses

While inequalities with respect to race/ethnicity and socioeconomic background have persisted, the shape of gender inequality has changed notably over time. Historically, women faced challenges in gaining access to higher education, but today, they represent a majority of students at nearly all levels of higher education and are not markedly disadvantaged in access to selective institutions. With women's increasing presence in college, inequality has shifted from access to higher education to inequality in educational trajectories and experiences (Jacobs 1996). Much research in this vein has focused on understanding women's choice of and departure from STEM (science, technology, engineering, and math) majors and careers (e.g., see a review in DiPrete and Buchmann 2013). Most recently, a notable legal and cultural shift surrounding romance, gender relations, and institutional responsibility to provide safe environments has focused attention on relationships, sexuality and sexual violence on campus.

Gender, as well as class, structures beliefs around what is appropriate sexual and romantic behavior. Although college is still an important site for long-term relationship formation (Arum and Roksa 2014; Arum et al. 2008), there is an expectation for privileged American men and women to defer family formation until their mid-twenties or early-thirties so that they can focus on investing in their education and careers, or what is called the *self-development imperative* (Hamilton and Armstrong 2009). The self-development imperative makes committed relationships less attractive as the only context for premarital sexuality. Similar to marriage, committed relationships require a lot of time and energy that can detract from self-development. In contrast, casual sexual encounters do not take away from investment in human capital and thus have become accepted as part of appropriate life-stage sexual experimentation. Hamilton and Armstrong (2009) argue that in the case of sexual behavior in college, there is a conflict between gender and class behavior rules. On the one hand, gender beliefs pose that women are not supposed to have casual sexual relationships and should be in committed relationships, while class beliefs say that they should delay relationships while pursuing educational and career goals. The structural conflict means that privileged women are caught between contradictory expectations, while less privileged women are confronted with a foreign sexual culture when they come to college, with both sets of women's experiences in college shaped by gender beliefs (Hamilton and Armstrong 2009).

Recent campus activism, high profile Office of Civil Rights (OCR) sexual assault cases, and private lawsuits have all made salient the experience of sexual violence on college campuses. Sexual violence, which includes rape, sexual assault, sexual harassment, and stalking, is considered sex-based discrimination under Title IX of the Education Amendments of 1972. As a result, universities are required to have an established procedure for handling complaints of sexual assault that ensures students can continue their education free from harassment. However, limited sociological research has examined how universities are creating and implementing their sexual violence policies and how this potentially affects student experiences of college.

Some studies show that university women are at greater risk of sexual violence than women of a comparable age in the general population (Krebs et al. 2010). In recent years, many advocates, legislators, and universities have reported the Department of Justice statistic that one in five women will be sexually assaulted in college (Fisher et al. 2000). Recently, the Association of American Universities (AAU) conducted a campus survey on sexual assault, which drew responses from more than 150,000 students at 27 universities, noting that about 10% of female students reported having experienced sexual assault involving penetration, by force or incapacitation, while in college (Cantor and Fisher 2015). The AAU survey confirmed what researchers have known for the last five decades: Sexual violence is common in higher education and part of many students' college experiences (Fisher et al. 2000; Armstrong et al. 2006). Much additional research is needed on this topic. Scholarship to date has given little attention to variation by race/ethnicity (Krebs et al. 2010) and the incidence of same-sex violence (Scarce 1997).

Scholars interested in understanding why sexual assault is such a common experience in college have looked at the proliferation of "hook-up" culture as a possible factor. In a study on casual sexual activity in college, Paula England and her colleagues surveyed more than 14,000 students from 19 universities and colleges on their hook-up, dating, and relationship experiences and found that around 80% of students hook-up, but on average less than once per semester over the course of college (Armstrong et al. 2010). They also noted that young people today are not having more sex at younger ages than their parents. Even if hook-up culture may not contribute to high rates of casual sexual activity, it can be problematic for girls and women because of pervasive sexual double standards for women and men in society. These double standards stigmatize women's sexual behavior, especially around casual sex, and accept and encourage the same behavior in men. As a result, many female college students find themselves being sexually labeled even when they are not engaging in sexual behavior (Armstrong et al. 2010).

Student experiences of sexual assault are related to specific circumstances and environments. In the vast majority of sexual assaults experienced by college women, the perpetrator and the victim are acquaintances (Krebs et al. 2010). Also, at least half of on-campus sexual assaults involve alcohol consumption, either by the perpetrator, the victim, or both (Abbey 2002). Women who attend schools with medium or high levels of heavy drinking were found more at risk of being raped while intoxicated than women who attended other schools (Mohler-Kuo et al. 2004; Armstrong et al. 2006). While alcohol consumption and sexual assault often co-occur, there is not a direct relationship between drinking and sexual assault. Rather, perpetrators often use alcohol to facilitate a sexual assault (Lisak 2011). For example, some male perpetrators may drink before they assault a woman to help justify their behavior (Abbey et al. 2001). Also, alcohol makes it more difficult for women to resist sexual assault effectively (Abbey 2002).

In terms of specific college contexts, fraternities have garnered much scholarly attention. Multiple studies have shown that the population with the highest likelihood to commit rape is fraternity men (Bannon et al. 2013; Foubert and Durant 2007; Loh et al. 2005). Fraternity men have significantly higher scores on a rape supportive attitude scale (Bleecker and Murnen 2005), and compared with their non-fraternity affiliated male peers, are more likely to believe myths about women, for example, that women enjoy being physically roughed up (Boeringer 1999). Fraternity men are reported to experience pressure to have sex, coerce it from unwilling women through the use of alcohol, and report about it to their brotherhood (Syrett 2011). While sexual violence does occur at fraternities, students also experience sexual violence in other places on campuses, which is not as well researched.

One explanation for the current college climate of sexual violence is that sexual assault is a predictable outcome of the intersection of both gendered and seemingly gender-neutral processes operating at individual, organizational, and interactional levels. Armstrong et al. (2006) describe how organizational practices that are meant to be gender neutral often contribute to gender inequality. For example, enforcement of alcohol policy in dormitories leads many students to find alcohol at fraternities. At most colleges only fraternities, not sororities, are allowed to have parties with alcohol (see also Armstrong and Hamilton 2013). Residential arrangements along with cultural expectations encourage students to party in male-controlled fraternities and drink heavily. Students end up fulfilling the role of a "partier"; they lose control, "have fun," and trust their fellow partiers. These gender-neutral expectations become harmful when interacted with gendered expectations, for instance the idea that women should be "nice" and defer to men. Males, following a heterosexual script, pursue women in an environment where all of their

methods for obtaining sex are seen as being legitimate. These interactions create imbalanced power relationships where female college students are made vulnerable and some male college students exploit this and engage in nonconsensual sex (Armstrong et al. 2006).

Armstrong and colleagues (2006) hypothesize that campuses with similar students and social organizations that create imbalanced power relationships, through gendered and seemingly gender-neutral processes, will have similar rates of sexual assault. In addition, they predict that more racial diversity and integration may lead to lower rates of sexual assault, because of the dilution of upper-middle-class White peer groups. While some studies have shown that White college students are more likely than other racial/ethnic groups to experience alcohol-related sexual assault (Mohler-Kuo et al. 2004; Armstrong et al. 2006), there is little consistency across the literature (Gross et al. 2006). White women's overall higher rates of rape may be due to higher rates of rape while intoxicated (Armstrong et al. 2006). Further research on racial and ethnic differences in the culture and organization of party life and its effects on sexual assault rates is needed.

17.7   Conclusion

Contemporary college students experience college in specific historical and institutional contexts. These conditions structure not only their academic experiences, but also their social interactions. While higher education institutions have benefited from rising demand for college attainment, they face increasing challenges to respond to a larger set of pressures around how effectively to deliver instruction, student guidance, and campus climates that meet the needs of students from diverse backgrounds.

Sociologists, through their attention to structure and culture, are particularly well positioned to explore these patterns. To date, however, they have overwhelmingly focused on the points of entry and completion and dedicated limited attention to understanding complexity and inequality in students' college experiences (Stevens et al. 2008). We highlight a few specific areas that we believe particularly promising in examining inequalities in student experiences by socioeconomic status, race/ethnicity, and gender.

With respect to social class inequality, sociologists have focused overwhelmingly on elite institutions and the processes of cultural reproduction. Expanding investigation to other institutional types is warranted, especially as most students, and students from socioeconomically disadvantaged backgrounds in particular, attend broad-access institutions (Stevens 2015). Moreover, mobility often occurs alongside reproduction, and understanding how college experiences may not only foster reproduction but also facilitate mobility would be valuable. The latter would be particularly instructive in considering how higher education institutions could effectively support students from socioeconomically disadvantaged backgrounds. Finally, future research would benefit from adopting a more nuanced conception of family background. Typically, students' background is defined based on their parents' education (and at times occupation and income), but many students also have siblings who have entered higher education preceding them. Considering the role of siblings, in addition to parents, especially as transmitters of cultural and social capital, would offer a more robust explanation of family influences.

Given the limited extent of sociological research on race in higher education, a myriad of questions remain regarding the experiences and outcomes of different racial/ethnic groups, and especially the relationship between academic and non-academic experiences. Previous studies have for example noted that students' experiences outside of the classroom play a role in understanding racial inequality in GPA (Charles et al. 2009) as well as the development of critical thinking skills (Roksa et al. 2016a). However, these studies tend to focus on a specific set of variables or student populations. Research is needed to link inequalities in students' experiences with inequalities in a range of different outcomes, not just degree completion. This line of research would also facilitate the development of effective policies and practices to support traditionally underrepresented racial/ethnic groups of students on their journeys through higher education.

Sociological literature on gender in higher education has focused most often on inequalities in college major and in particular women's participation in STEM fields (DiPrete and Buchmann 2013). This chapter has illuminated the importance of considering gender inequalities and stereotypes in non-academic aspects of college life. The federal government and the public are currently looking at universities to create substantive change on their campuses by reducing sexual violence and creating policies that maintain a non-hostile equitable educational environment. More research is needed on how universities are creating and implementing these policies, as well as how effective administrative efforts are in creating inclusive campus cultures more generally.

Moreover, to understand fully how students navigate college and to explicate inequalities in students' experiences and how various experiences contribute to inequalities in outcomes, future research would benefit from dedicating more attention to intersectionality (Collins 2000). Given separation of different research traditions and theoretical frameworks within sociology of education, students' experiences tend to be siloed into a specific identity—whether class, race, or gender. Typically, one of those identities takes precedence and considerations of additional dimensions are either non-existent or largely secondary. That, however, leads to a limited understanding of students' experiences as well as potential avenues to reduce observed disparities. Students' experiences in college are classed, raced, and gendered, and the combination of those influences likely produces unique outcomes that will remain elusive unless students' identities are considered jointly. In addition to class, race, and gender, sociologists of higher education would also benefit from considering intersection with other identities, including sexuality and disability.

In addition to the specific questions regarding inequality, more research is needed on the experiences of students in higher education that are not traditional four-year college students. Two-year college students are typically less engaged with and embedded in the institutions they attend than their four-year college peers. They are thus more challenging subjects for longitudinal research. Nevertheless, more sociological research on these students is sorely needed. Increasing numbers of students are also stopping out, transferring from one institution to another and swirling through higher education institutions. Researchers need to focus on the unique experiences of these students as well. Lastly, we argue that student political discourse needs to be understood in the context of students' lived experiences in particular historical and institutional contexts. More work, such as Binder and Wood's (2013) insightful research on college conservatives, is needed on students' political formation in higher education.

Students today often face a bewildering set of unstructured options in college. Core curriculum is often loosely defined, open-ended, and with purposes poorly communicated to students. Too many students are left largely to their own devices in navigating choices of college courses and majors. Extracurricular opportunities are typically even less intentionally designed and structured. For the most-able and motivated students, often with parents in a position to provide knowledgeable counsel, this system can work well. For students without these advantages, college experiences can be considerably less productive (Armstrong and Hamilton 2013). Future research on how students' college experiences vary across sociodemographic groups can help to improve the extent to which higher education delivers its promise to all students.

References

Abbey, A. (2002). Alcohol-related sexual assault: A common problem among college students. *Journal of studies on alcohol. Supplement*(14), 118.

Abbey, A., Zawacki, T., Buck, P. O., Clinton, A. M., & McAuslan, P. (2001). Alcohol and sexual assault. *Alcohol Research and Health, 25*(1), 43–51.

Antonio, A. L. (2004). When does race matter in college friendships? Exploring men's diverse and homogeneous friendship groups. *The Review of Higher Education, 27*(4), 553–575.

Aries, E., & Seider, M. (2005). The interactive relationship between class identity and the college experience: The case of lower income students. *Qualitative Sociology, 28*(4), 419–443.

Armstrong, E., & Hamilton, L. (2013). *Paying for the party: How college maintains inequality*. Cambridge, MA: Harvard University Press.

Armstrong, E. A., Hamilton, L., & Sweeney, B. (2006). Sexual assault on campus: A multilevel, integrative approach to party rape. *Social Problems, 53*(4), 483–499.

Armstrong, E. A., Hamilton, L., & England, P. (2010). Is hooking up bad for young women? *Contexts, 9*(3), 22–27.

Arum, R., & Roksa, J. (2011). *Academically adrift: Limited learning on college campuses*. Chicago: University of Chicago Press.

Arum, R., & Roksa, J. (2014). *Aspiring adults adrift: Tentative transitions of college graduates*. Chicago: University of Chicago Press.

Arum, R., Roksa, J., & Budig, M. J. (2008). The romance of college attendance: Higher education stratification and mate selection. *Research in Social Stratification and Mobility, 26*(2), 107–121.

Astin, A. W. (1993). *What matters in college? Four critical years revisited* (Vol. 1). San Francisco: Jossey-Bass.

Autor, David H. (2014, May 23). Skills, education, and the rise of earnings inequality among the "other 99 percent". *Science, 344*(6186), 843–851.

Babcock, P. S., & Marks, M. (2011). The falling time cost of college: Evidence from half a century of time use data. *Review of economics and statistics, 93*(2), 468–478.

Bahr, P. R. (2008). Cooling out in the community college: What is the effect of academic advising on students' chances of success? *Research in Higher Education, 49*(8), 704–732.

Bailey, M. J., & Dynarski, S. M. (2011). *Whither opportunity? Rising inequality, schools, and children's life chances* (pp. 339–358). New York: Russell Sage Foundation.

Bannon, R. S., Brosi, M. W., & Foubert, J. D. (2013). Sorority women's and fraternity men's rape myth acceptance and bystander intervention attitudes. *Journal of Student Affairs Research and Practice, 50*(1), 72–87.

Bettinger, E. P., & Baker, R. B. (2013). The effects of student coaching: An evaluation of a randomized experiment in student advising. *Educational Evaluation and Policy Analysis, 36*(1), 3–19. https://doi.org/10.3102/0162373713500523.

Binder, A. J., & Wood, K. (2013). *Becoming right: How campuses shape young conservatives*. Princeton: Princeton University Press.

Blaich, C. (2011). *How do students change over four years of college?* Crawford: Center of Inquiry in the Liberal Arts at Wabash College. Retrieved from http://www.liberalarts.wabash.edu/storage/4-year-change-summary-website.pdf

Bleecker, E., & Murnen, S. (2005). Fraternity membership, the display of degrading sexual images of women, and rape myth acceptance. *Sex Roles, 53*, 487–493.

Boeringer, S. B. (1999). Associations of rape-supportive attitudes with fraternal and athletic participation. *Violence Against Women, 5*(1), 81–90.

Bonilla-Silva, E., & Forman, T. A. (2000). "I am not a racist but...": Mapping White college students' racial ideology in the USA. *Discourse & society, 11*(1), 50–85.

Bourdieu, P. (1990). *The logic of practice.* Stanford: Stanford University Press.

Bourdieu, P., & Passeron, J. C. (1990). *Reproduction in education, society and culture* (Vol. 4). Thousand Oaks: SAGE Publications.

Bowman, N. A. (2010). College diversity experiences and cognitive development: A meta-analysis. *Review of Educational Research, 80*(1), 4–33.

Bowman, N. A. (2011). Promoting participation in a diverse democracy: A meta-analysis of college diversity experiences and civic engagement. *Review of Educational Research, 81*(1), 29–68.

Bowman, N. A. (2013). How much diversity is enough? The curvilinear relationship between college diversity interactions and first-year student outcomes. *Research in Higher Education, 54*(8), 874–894.

Bozick, R. (2007). Making it through the first year of college: The role of students' economic resources, employment, and living arrangements. *Sociology of Education, 80*(3), 261–285.

Bridges, B. K., Holmes, M. S., Williams, J. M., Morelon-Quainoo, C. L., & Nelson Laird, T. F. (2007). African American and Hispanic student engagement at minority serving and predominantly White institutions. *Journal of College Student Development, 48*(1), 39–56.

Brint, S., & Cantwell, A. M. (2010). Undergraduate time use and academic outcomes: Results from the University of California Undergraduate Experience Survey 2006. *Teachers College Record, 112*(9), 2441–2470.

Campbell, C., & Horowitz, J. (2016). Does college influence sociopolitical attitudes? *Sociology of Education, 89*(1), 40–58.

Cantor, D., & Fisher, W. B. (2015). *Report on the AAU campus climate survey on sexual assault and sexual misconduct assault and sexual misconduct.* Washington, DC: The Association of American Universities.

Chang, M. J., Astin, A. W., & Kim, D. (2004). Cross-racial interaction among undergraduates: Some consequences, causes, and patterns. *Research in Higher Education, 45*(5), 529–553.

Charles, C. Z., Fischer, M. J., Mooney, M. A., & Massey, D. S. (2009). *Taming the river: Negotiating the academic, financial, and social currents in selective colleges and universities.* Princeton: Princeton University Press.

Chavous, T. M., Harris, A., Rivas, D., Helaire, L., & Green, L. (2004). Racial stereotypes and gender in context: African Americans at predominantly Black and predominantly White colleges. *Sex Roles, 51*(1–2), 1–16.

Clinedinst, M. (2015). *State of college admission 2014.* Washington, DC: National Association for College Admission Counseling.

Collier, P. J., & Morgan, D. L. (2008). "Is that paper really due today?": Differences in first-generation and traditional college students' understandings of faculty expectations. *Higher Education, 55*(4), 425–446.

Collins, P. H. (2000). *Black feminist thought: Knowledge, consciousness, and the politics of empowerment.* New York: Routledge.

Desrochers, D. M., & Hurlburt, S. (2014). *Trends in college spending: 2001–2011.* Washington, DC: American Institutes for Research.

DiMaggio, P., & Powell, W. W. (1983). The iron cage revisited: Collective rationality and institutional isomorphism in organizational fields. *American Sociological Review, 48*(2), 147–160.

DiPrete, T. A., & Buchmann, C. (2013). *The rise of women.* New York: Russell Sage Foundation.

Duncan, G. J., & Murnane, R. J. (Eds.). (2011). *Whither opportunity? Rising inequality, schools, and children's life chances.* New York: Russell Sage Foundation.

Fischer, B. S., Cullen, F. T., & Turner, M. G. (2000). *The sexual victimization of college women.* Washington, DC: U.S. Department of Justice, Office of Justice Programs, National Institute of Justice.

Foubert, J. D., & Durant, D. (2007). Sexual assault survivors' perceptions of campus judicial systems. *Illinois Counseling Association Journal, 155*, 3–18.

Gitlin, T. (2015, November 21). Why are student protesters so fearful? *The New York Times.*

Grigsby, M. (2009). *College life through the eyes of students.* Albany: Suny Press.

Gross, A. M., Winslett, A., Roberts, M., & Gohm, C. L. (2006). An examination of sexual violence against college women. *Violence Against Women, 12*(3), 288–300.

Hamilton, L. (2016). *Parenting to a degree: How family matters for college and beyond.* Chicago: University of Chicago Press.

Hamilton, L., & Armstrong, E. A. (2009). Gendered sexuality in young adulthood: Double binds and flawed options. *Gender & Society, 23*(5), 589–616.

Harford, T. C., Wechsler, H., & Seibring, M. (2002). Attendance and alcohol use at parties and bars in college: A national survey of current drinkers. *Journal of Studies on Alcohol, 63*(6), 726–733.

Harper, S. R., & Hurtado, S. (2007). Nine themes in campus racial climates and implications for institutional transformation. *New Directions for Student Services, 2007*(120), 7–24.

Horowitz, H. L. (1987). *Campus life: Undergraduate cultures from the end of the eighteenth century to the present.* New York: Alfred a Knopf Incorporated.

Hout, M. (2012). Social and economic returns to college education in the United States. *Annual Review of Sociology, 38*, 379–400.

Hu, S., & Kuh, G. D. (2003). Diversity experiences and college student learning and personal development. *Journal of College Student Development, 44*(3), 320–334.

Hurtado, S., & Carter, D. F. (1997). Effects of college transition and perceptions of the campus racial climate on Latino college students' sense of belonging. *Sociology of Education, 70*(4), 324–345.

Hurtado, S., Clayton-Pedersen, A., Allen, W., & Milem, J. (1998). Enhancing campus climates for racial/ethnic diversity: Educational policy and practice. *The Review of Higher Education, 21*(3), 279–302.

Jack, A. A. (2016). (No) harm in asking: Class, acquired cultural capital, and academic engagement at an elite university. *Sociology of Education, 89*(1), 1–19.

Jacob, B., McCall, B., & Stange, K. M. (2013). *College as country club: Do colleges cater to students' preferences for consumption?* (No. w18745). Cambridge, MA: National Bureau of Economic Research.

Jacobs, J. A. (1996). Gender inequality and higher education. *Annual Review of Sociology, 22*, 153–185.

Jencks, C., & Riesman, D. (1968). *The academic revolution*. New York: Transaction Publishers.

Kahlenberg, R. D. (2010). *Rewarding strivers: Helping low-income students succeed in college*. New York: Century Foundation Press.

Karabel, J. (2006). *The chosen: The hidden history of admission and exclusion at Harvard, Yale, and Princeton*. New York: Houghton Mifflin Harcourt.

Keeling, R. P., Day, P., Dungy, G. J., Evans, N., Fried, J., Komives, S., McDonald, W., & Salvador, S. (2004). *Learning reconsidered: A campus-wide focus on the student experience*. Washington, DC: National Association of Student Personnel Administrators/American College Personnel Association.

Krebs, C. P., Lindquist, C. H., & Barrick, K. (2010). *The Historically Black College and University Campus sexual assault (HBCU-CSA) study*. Research Triangle Park: RTI International.

Kugelmass, H., & Ready, D. D. (2011). Racial/ethnic disparities in collegiate cognitive gains: A multilevel analysis of institutional influences on learning and its equitable distribution. *Research in Higher Education, 52*(4), 323–348.

Kuh, G. D., & Pascarella, E. T. (2004). What does institutional selectivity tell us about educational quality? *Change: The Magazine of Higher Learning, 36*(5), 52–59.

Kuh, G. D., Kinzie, J., Schuh, J. H., & Whitt, E. J. (2011). *Student success in college: Creating conditions that matter*. Hoboken: John Wiley & Sons

Labaree, D. F. (1997). Public goods, private goods: The American struggle over educational goals. *American Educational Research Journal, 34*(1), 39–81.

Laird, T. F. N. (2005). College students' experiences with diversity and their effects on academic self-confidence, social agency, and disposition toward critical thinking. *Research in Higher Education, 46*(4), 365–387.

Lee, E. M., & Kramer, R. (2013). Out with the old, in with the new? Habitus and social mobility at selective colleges. *Sociology of Education, 86*(1), 18–35.

Lehmann, W. (2014). Habitus transformation and hidden injuries: Successful working-class university students. *Sociology of Education, 87*(1), 1–15.

Lisak, D. (2011). Understanding the predatory nature of sexual violence. *Criminal Justice Research Review, 12*(6), 105–108.

Loh, C., Gidycz, C. A., Lobo, T. R., & Luthra, R. (2005). A prospective analysis of sexual assault perpetration risk factors related to perpetrator characteristics. *Journal of Interpersonal Violence, 20*(10), 1325–1348.

Loss, C. P. (2012). *Between citizens and the state: The politics of American higher education in the 20th century*. Princeton: Princeton University Press.

Massey, D. S., & Fischer, M. J. (2005). Stereotype threat and academic performance: New findings from a racially diverse sample of college freshmen. *Du Bois Review, 2*(1), 45–67.

Mills, C. W. (1959). *The sociological imagination*. New York: Oxford University Press.

Mohler-Kuo, M., Dowdall, G. W., Koss, M. P., & Wechsler, H. (2004). Correlates of rape while intoxicated in a national sample of college women. *Journal of Studies on Alcohol, 65*(1), 37–45.

Nathan, R. (2006). *My freshman year: What a professor learned by becoming a student*. New York: Penguin.

National Survey of Student Engagement. (2007). *Experiences that matter: Enhancing student learning and success*. Bloomington: Indiana University Center for Postsecondary Research.

National Survey of Student Engagement. (2009). *Assessment for improvement: Tracking student engagement over time: Annual results from 2009*. Bloomington: Indiana University Center for Postsecondary Research.

Nora, A., & Cabrera, A. F. (1996). The role of perceptions of prejudice and discrimination on the adjustment of minority students to college. *The Journal of Higher Education, 67*(2), 119–148.

Oseguera, L., & Astin, A. W. (2004). The declining "equity" of American higher education. *The Review of Higher Education, 27*(3), 321–341.

Pascarella, E. T., & Terenzini, P. T. (2005). In K. A. Feldman (Ed.), *How college affects students* (Vol. 2). San Francisco: Jossey-Bass.

Pascarella, E. T., Palmer, B., Moye, M., & Pierson, C. T. (2001). Do diversity experiences influence the development of critical thinking? *Journal of College Student Development, 42*(3), 257–271.

Pascarella, E. T., Pierson, C. T., Wolniak, G. C., & Terenzini, P. T. (2004). First-generation college students: Additional evidence on college experiences and outcomes. *Journal of Higher Education, 75*(3), 249–284.

Pascarella, E. T., Cruce, T., Umbach, P. D., Wolniak, G. C., Kuh, G. D., Carini, R. M., & Zhao, C. M. (2006). Institutional selectivity and good practices in undergraduate education: How strong is the link? *Journal of Higher Education, 77*(2), 251–285.

Pascarella, E. T., Blaich, C., Martin, G. L., & Hanson, J. M. (2011). How robust are the findings of "Academically Adrift"? *Change: The Magazine of Higher Learning, 43*(3), 20–24.

Piketty, T., & Saez, E. (2014). Inequality in the long run. *Science, 344*(6186), 838–843.

Rankin, S. R., & Reason, R. D. (2005). Differing perceptions: How students of color and White students perceive campus climate for underrepresented groups. *Journal of College Student Development, 46*(1), 43–61.

Reay, D., Crozier, G., & Clayton, J. (2009). "Strangers in paradise"? Working-class students in elite universities. *Sociology, 43*(6), 1103–1121.

Rhoades, G., McCormick, R., Kiyama, J. M., & Quiroz, M. (2007). Local cosmopolitans and cosmopolitan locals: New models of professionals in the academy. *The Review of Higher Education, 31*(2), 209–235.

Riesman, D. (1950). The lonely crowd. In D. Reisman (Ed.), *A study of the changing American character*. New Haven: Yale University Press.

Roksa, J. (2011). Differentiation and work: Inequality in degree attainment in US higher education. *Higher Education, 61*(3), 293–308.

Roksa, J. (2016a). Preparing students for college: Common core and the promises and challenges of convergence. In C. Loss & P. McGuinn (Eds.), *The convergence of K–12 and higher education: Policies and programs in a changing era*. Cambridge, MA: Harvard Education Press.

Roksa, J. (2016b). Structuring opportunity after entry: Inequalities in instructional quality during college. *Teachers College Record, 118*.

Roksa, J., & Arum, R. (2015). Inequality in skill development on college campuses. *Research in Social Stratification and Mobility, 39*, 18–31.

Roksa, J., Grodsky, E., Arum, R., & Gamoran, A. (2007). United States: Changes in higher education and social stratification. *Stratification in Higher Education-A Comparative Study, 2*, 165–191.

Roksa, J., Trolian, T. L., Pascarella, E. T., Kilgo, C. A., Blaich, C., & Wise, K. S. (2016a). Racial inequality in critical thinking skills: The role of academic and diversity experiences. *Research in Higher Education, 58*(2), 119. https://doi.org/10.1007/s11162-016-9423-1.

Roksa, J., Kilgo, C. A., Trolian, T. L., Pascarella, E. T., Blaich, C., & Wise, K. S. (2016b). Engaging with diversity: How positive and negative diversity interactions shape students' cognitive outcomes. *Journal of Higher Education, 88*(3), 297–322.

Salisbury, M. H., Umbach, P. D., Paulsen, M. B., & Pascarella, E. T. (2009). Going global: Understanding the choice process of the intent to study abroad. *Research in Higher Education, 50*(2), 119–143.

Scarce, M. (1997). Same-sex rape of male college students. *Journal of American College Health., 45*(4), 171–173.

Seifert, T. A., Drummond, J., & Pascarella, E. T. (2006). African-American students' experiences of good practices: A comparison of institutional type. *Journal of College Student Development, 47*(2), 185–205.

Sennett, R. (1972). *The hidden injuries of class*. Cambridge: Cambridge University Press Archive.

Slaughter, S., & Rhoades, G. (2004). *Academic capitalism and the new economy: Markets, state, and higher education*. Baltimore: JHU Press.

Solorzano, D., Ceja, M., & Yosso, T. (2000). Critical race theory, racial microaggressions, and campus racial climate: The experiences of African American college students. *Journal of Negro Education, 69*, 60–73.

Sperber, M. (2000). *Beer and circus: How big-time college sports has crippled undergraduate education*. New York, Macmillan.

Steele, C. M., & Aronson, J. (1995). Stereotype threat and the intellectual test performance of African Americans. *Journal of Personality and Social Psychology, 69*(5), 797.

Stearns, E., Buchmann, C., & Bonneau, K. (2009). Interracial friendships in the transition to college: Do birds of a feather flock together once they leave the nest? *Sociology of Education, 82*(2), 173–195.

Stevens, M. L. (2009). *Creating a class: College admissions and the education of elites*. Cambridge, MA: Harvard University Press.

Stevens, M. L. (2015). Introduction: The changing ecology of U.S. higher education. In M. W. Kirst & M. L. Stevens (Eds.), *In Remaking college: The changing ecology of higher education* (pp. 1–15). Stanford: Stanford University Press.

Stevens, M. L., Armstrong, E. A., & Arum, R. (2008). Sieve, incubator, temple, hub: Empirical and theoretical advances in the sociology of higher education. *Annual Review of Sociology, 34*, 127–151.

Stone, C., Trisi, D., Sherman, A., & Chen, W. (2012). *A guide to statistics on historical trends in income inequality*. Washington, DC: Center on Budget and Policy Priorities.

Stuber, J. M. (2009, December). Class, culture, and participation in the collegiate extra-curriculum. *Sociological Forum, 24*(4), 877–900. Blackwell Publishing Ltd.

Stuber, J. M. (2011). *Inside the college gates: How class and culture matter in higher education*. Lanham: Lexington Books.

Syrett, N. (2011). Colleges condone fraternities' sexist behavior. *The New York Times*. Retrieved from http://www.nytimes.com/roomfordebate/2011/05/05/frat-guys-gone-wild-whats-thesolution/colleges-condone-fraternities-sexist-behavior

Tierney, W. G. (1992). An anthropological analysis of student participation in college. *The Journal of Higher Education, 63*(6), 603–618.

Tinto, V. (1987). *Leaving college: Rethinking the causes and cures of student attrition*. Chicago: University of Chicago Press.

Torres, K. C., & Charles, C. Z. (2004). Metastereotypes and the Black–White divide: A qualitative view of race on an elite college campus. *Du Bois Review, 1*(01), 115–149.

Trolian, T., Kilgo, C., Pascarella, E., Roksa, J., Blaich, C., & Wise, K. (2014, November). *Race and exposure to good teaching during college*. Washington, DC: Association for the Study of Higher Education.

Whitt, E. J., Edison, M. I., Pascarella, E. T., Terenzini, P. T., & Nora, A. (2001). Influences on students' openness to diversity and challenge in the second and third years of college. *The Journal of Higher Education, 72*(2), 172–204.

Wilkins, A. (2012). "Not out to start a revolution": Race, gender, and emotional restraint among Black university men. *Journal of Contemporary Ethnography, 41*(1), 34–65.

Wilkins, A. C. (2014). Race, age, and identity transformations in the transition from high school to college for Black and first-generation White men. *Sociology of Education, 87*(3), 171–187.

Wong, A. & Green, A. (2016). Campus politics: A cheat sheet. *The Atlantic*. Retrieved from http://www.theatlantic.com/education/archive/2016/04/campus-protest-roundup/417570/

The Community College Experience and Educational Equality: Theory, Research, and Policy

Lauren Schudde and Eric Grodsky

Abstract

Community colleges serve as the point of entry to higher education for many Americans, but enrollees exhibit high rates of non-completion. A central debate in the sociological research on community colleges concerns whether these institutions enhance opportunity by improving educational access or constrain opportunity by hindering students from achieving their educational aspirations. This chapter lays out the history of community colleges, describes relevant sociological theories, and reviews key developments in research, emphasizing research on the potentially democratizing and diversionary effects of community colleges. Finally, we discuss how sociology can inform the evolving policy discussion over the role community colleges play in education and social mobility.

L. Schudde (✉)
The University of Texas at Austin, Austin, TX, USA
e-mail: schudde@austin.utexas.edu

E. Grodsky
University of Wisconsin-Madison,
Madison, WI, USA
e-mail: egrodsky@ssc.wisc.edu

18.1 Introduction

The higher education system in the United States is structured as a "pyramid of institutions," simultaneously extending opportunity and protecting privilege (Labaree 2013). At the pinnacle of the pyramid, the most prestigious institutions are exclusive, few in number, and offer baccalaureate and perhaps graduate and professional degrees. The base is comprised of the most inclusive institutions, like community colleges, providing broad access, serving a myriad of purposes, and often offering certificates and associate degrees but not baccalaureate degrees. Most students who initially enroll in a community college leave without a degree in hand. The institutions may offer the "possibility of getting ahead" but also the "probability of not getting ahead very far" (Labaree 2013, p. 48).

Sociological and economic research on community colleges has been centrally concerned with the tension between the possibility and probability invoked by Labaree, often framed in terms of whether community colleges enhance opportunity by improving educational access (democratization) or constrain opportunity by hindering students from achieving their baccalaureate and post-baccalaureate educational aspirations (diversion). This chapter lays out the history of community colleges and describes the theories that drive the sociological literature on these complex institutions. We review ongoing

© Springer International Publishing AG, part of Springer Nature 2018
B. Schneider (ed.), *Handbook of the Sociology of Education in the 21st Century*, Handbooks of Sociology and Social Research, https://doi.org/10.1007/978-3-319-76694-2_18

developments in research and consider how sociological research can inform the evolving policy discussion over the role they play in education and social mobility.

18.2 Historical Overview

Community colleges date back to the early twentieth century, increasing in number from 19 colleges in 1915 to 136 in 1925 (Cohen et al. 2014). The growth of the 2-year higher education sector, which traditionally included both public and private colleges, was spurred by a variety of interests: Leaders of baccalaureate colleges hoped that "junior colleges" (as many community colleges were referred to at the time) would relieve universities of the "burden" of educating lower-level undergraduates; business leaders sought publicly supported training for potential employees; elected officials sought to please their constituents by expanding access to postsecondary education and satisfying regional labor needs; administrators engaged in the business of education at the secondary level hoped to enhance their own status by encroaching into the domain of higher education (Cohen et al. 2014; Dougherty 1994). These interests combined to fuel an exponential growth in the community college sector. By 1960, there were over 400 public 2-year colleges; by 1970, there were over 1000—approximately the same number as today (Cohen et al. 2014, p. 17).[1] In fall of 2013, about 6.6 million students enrolled in community colleges (and about 7 million in 2-year colleges more generally) compared to 13.4 million enrolled in 4-year colleges (NCES 2014a, table 311.15).

As a result of these sometimes complementary and sometimes competing interests, the community college is a hybrid institution that seeks to accomplish widely varying and, at times, divergent objectives (Dougherty 1994). It serves as an occupational trainer, a gatekeeper for more selective postsecondary institutions, and a balance wheel for the state budget by offering relatively inexpensive postsecondary education pathways (Dougherty 1994).

18.2.1 Changes in Undergraduate Population

Between 1976 and 2000 the share of students expecting to get some college education rose from about 64% to just over 90% (Reynolds et al. 2006). Many people realize their educational expectations through at least some form of college attendance. Between 1980 and 2000, undergraduate enrollment swelled by 26% (census.gov 2013). During the Great Recession, college enrollment reached an all-time high in 2011, when 16.6 million Americans enrolled in some form of undergraduate education (census.gov 2013).

The undergraduate population in the United States has become increasingly diverse in terms of race, gender, and social class. The proportion of White students steadily declined between 1976 and 2010, dropping from 83% of enrollees to 60%, while the proportion of Hispanic and Asian students nearly quadrupled and the proportion of Black students grew by almost 40% (Snyder and Dillow 2012). As barriers to college entry for women diminished, women became a dominant presence in higher education (DiPrete and Buchmann 2013; Snyder and Dillow 2012). While the link between socioeconomic status and college attendance is still strong, children of parents at all levels of income have become more likely to enroll in college over time (Bailey and Dynarski 2011). Enrollment remains sharply stratified by social origins, however, with low-income students more likely to attend broad access institutions (Haveman and Smeeding 2006).

One of the most controversial issues in American higher education concerns the academic preparation of students. While many perceive the college-going population as increasingly underprepared, that shift is at least partly a function of widening participation. As more

---

[1] While much has been written about the dramatic expansion of community colleges, the rate of growth of baccalaureate colleges appreciably outpaced that of community colleges between the mid-1970s and mid-2000s (Provasnik and Planty 2008).

students from a variety of backgrounds entered college, the average levels of academic preparation declined (similarly, as SAT test taking has become more common, the average score has declined). According to one measure—tested math ability—the proportion of college-goers in the bottom quartile of the distribution increased from 11% to 16% between 1970 and 1990, while the representation of students with scores in the top quartile decreased from 41% to 33% (Bound et al. 2010). Taking these changes into account, it should come as no surprise that 33% of college students report taking at least one remedial course (NCES 2014b). Rates of remediation are high at community colleges, where 41% of students take at least one remedial course. Remedial course-taking is not much lower in public 4-year colleges that do not include doctoral programs, however, at 38% (NCES 2014b). Estimates of the prevalence of remedial course-taking based on transcript data, which are more reliable, show even higher rates. Radford and Horn (2012) estimate that 68% of 2-year and 39% of 4-year students who initially enrolled in college in 2004 took remedial coursework. Estimates from a statewide system of community colleges found that approximately 50% of students attending North Carolina community colleges enrolled in remedial courses (Scott-Clayton et al. 2014).

18.2.2 Expansion of Broad-Access Higher Education

With the compositional transformation of the college-going population, postsecondary institutions evolved, prompting changes in existing colleges and giving rise to new institutions. Like students, colleges are more varied than ever. Between 1976 and 2012, the number of public institutions grew by 25% for 4-year universities, but just 4% for 2-year colleges. Rather than creating new community colleges, growth in enrollment was absorbed by just 13% of the colleges, mostly at large urban community colleges, which now enroll approximately 60% of all 2-year students (Carnegie Foundation for the Advancement of Teaching 2010). In the same time period, the number of private not-for-profit (NFP) 4-year institutions rose by almost 15%, but private NFP 2-year institutions experienced a dramatic decline of 48%; in 1976 there were 188 institutions of this type, but in 2012 only 97 remained (Snyder and Dillow 2012).

More recently, private for-profit institutions began to thrive. In 1976, there were only 55 for-profit institutions in the United States (Snyder and Dillow 2012, p. 443). Forty of these colleges served students seeking associate degrees and short-term certificates, and only 15 offered bachelor's degrees. In 1970, for-profit college accounted for just 0.2% of total enrollment in degree-granting postsecondary institutions. By 2009 that share had risen to 9.1% (Deming et al. 2012). The number of for-profit colleges swelled to 533 two-year and 782 four-year institutions by 2012 and by 2014 there were 1424 proprietary institutions in the U.S. (Cahalan et al. 2016). The private for-profit sector experienced particularly large enrollment gains during the recession, increasing enrollment by approximately 15% from the 2008–2009 to the 2009–2010 academic year alone (Snyder and Dillow 2012, table 230). More recently, the number of proprietary institutions has dropped slightly (Cahalan et al. 2016).

Community colleges and proprietary institutions offer very different educational options. While both proprietary schools and community colleges traditionally provide career-focused education (though both also offer other pathways), the two types of institutions differ in mission, governance, size, cost, and market orientation. They differ in their recruitment techniques, approaches to student services such as job placement, and in how they set tuition and leverage financial aid dollars. Compared with students at public 2-year colleges, students at for-profit institutions are disproportionately women, Black or Hispanic, and single parents (Staklis et al. 2012). Proprietary colleges also have far fewer options in terms of programs and electives, compared with community colleges, and the curricula tend to be more standardized across campuses of the institution (Rosenbaum et al. 2007). While the first-year drop-out rates are slightly lower at proprietary colleges than at community colleges, students at for-profits accumulate more debt, are more likely to default on student loans, have poorer employment outcomes, and are less satisfied with their courses (Deming et al. 2012).

During the 1990s, tighter accreditation standards and federal financial aid policies led proprietary colleges to become more similar to community colleges. While still maintaining their focus on preparing students for careers, these colleges now include general education courses as part of their degree requirements and offer developmental education courses and classes for English-language learners (Bailey et al. 2003). The rapid growth and market orientation of proprietary colleges may have lasting implications for American higher education and particularly for the community college sector. Despite numerous attempts to increase accountability in the private for-profit higher education sector, some scholars argue that reigning in the for-profits requires increasing the capacity of the public sector, particularly 2-year colleges (Rosenbaum et al. 2015; Tierney 2011).

18.3   Whom Do Community Colleges Serve?

Over the course of the twentieth century, community colleges emerged as an inexpensive and geographically proximate alternative to the initial years of baccalaureate college enrollment for students interested in transferring to a baccalaureate institution or earning a sub-baccalaureate credential. Students from low-income families and households in which they are the first to attend college appear more likely to use this alternative, initially entering the postsecondary education system through community colleges. In 2012, 41% of students attending community college were the first in their family to attend college, compared to 27% of students attending public baccalaureate colleges. The average annual income of dependent students attending community college is substantially lower than at 4-year colleges, with a household income of $65,070 compared to $95,675 at private non-profit and $85,418 at public baccalaureate colleges

(Schudde and Goldrick-Rab 2016). Community college students are substantially more likely to work full-time than students in other postsecondary institutions—46% of community college enrollees in 2012 worked 40 or more hours a week, compared to 20% of students at public 4-year, 8% at private 4-year, and 18% at private for-profit colleges (authors' calculations using National Postsecondary Student Aid Study, 2012). Even among traditionally aged college students (23 years of age or younger), this distribution holds. Forty-eight percent of those who attended community colleges worked full-time, compared to 24% at public 4-years, 7% at private 4-years, and 12% at private for-profits.

Public 2-year colleges serve a slightly more racially and ethnically diverse population of students than public 4-year colleges. Where 13% of students attending public 4-year colleges are Black and 14% Hispanic, the comparable shares in community colleges are 17% and 19% respectively (Schudde and Goldrick-Rab 2016). The timing of initial spells of attendance also differ for public baccalaureate and community colleges, with half of community college students transitioning to college immediately after graduating from high school and another 20% of students enrolling within 4 years of graduating (authors' calculations using Beginning Postsecondary Students 2004). Almost 20% of first-time community college attendees enroll 10 or more years after graduating from high school. This stands in comparison to public baccalaureate colleges, where almost 90% of first-time college enrollees transition immediately after high school.

Of course, community colleges also enroll students for whom community college is not their first postsecondary experience. Some students come to the colleges with prior postsecondary experience at a 4-year college where they did not earn a degree (Kalogrides and Grodsky 2011; Shapiro et al. 2015), while others return to college to improve skills or earn a new credential despite having earned one in the past. Community colleges also serve lifelong learners, who attend their local community college for language, literature, and art courses (Pallas 2000).

18.4 Theoretical Overview

Today, more Americans attend college than ever before and one third of all current college enrollees attend community colleges (NCES 2014a, Table 311.15). While community colleges increase educational access, they also "effectively maintain" inequality—they increase opportunity while also preserving a top tier of postsecondary education (elite 4-years) that is out of reach for all but a few (Roksa et al. 2007). Despite improvements in academic preparation among students from low-income families, wealthier students' gains allow them to remain more competitive than their less advantaged peers in the college admissions race; thus youth from low-income families are still concentrated in broad-access institutions (Bastedo and Jaquette 2011). Given low rates of college completion among students who initially enroll at less-prestigious colleges, the sorting of students into different institution types may have important implications for equity.

Several theories seek to account for the role community colleges play in the process of social stratification. One of the most prominent is Clark's (1960a, 1960b) "cooling-out hypothesis" in which he adapts Goffman's (1952) concept of cooling out to argue that diversion from baccalaureate colleges via the management of student aspirations is a central function of community colleges. Drawing from a case study, Clark's research highlights the role of organizations in enabling and constraining the actions of individuals. He interprets the discrepancy between the open-door admission policies of community colleges and the failure of many students to meet their educational aspirations as a structural component of the institution. Community colleges "cool out" high-aspiring, low-ability students through a process of "soft denial" (Clark 1960a, p. 569). Clark suggests that community colleges offer students "substitute avenues" for success (i.e., terminal 2-year degrees) (Clark 1960b, p. 574). The substitute outcome becomes palatable to students over time, after college counselors alter student intentions by accumulating evidence, through grades and recordkeeping, that the student's aspiration for a bachelor's degree aspirations is overly ambitious. In this way, community colleges allow 4-year colleges to concentrate resources on more "able" students, performing the vital function of sorting out students with high aspirations who may lack the skills to handle baccalaureate studies and subsequent career pathways. While Clark is often misread as ascribing an almost sinister exclusionary role to community colleges, he makes the point that the role they play in managing ambitions may actually be much more benign (Clark 1980).

Brint and Karabel (1989) are more critical in their analysis of community colleges. Like Clark, they describe community colleges as agencies for the "management of ambitions" (Brint and Karabel 1989, pp. 7–10, 213). However, they interpret community colleges as a mechanism for reproducing inequality, serving as a buffer to protect baccalaureate colleges from an influx of students seeking a degree. In a field dominated by universities, community colleges found their niche by vocationalizing higher education—they created alternative credentials that were occupation-focused rather than emphasizing pathways toward senior-level institutions. Community colleges reconcile the high demand for and limited supply of college-level education by channeling students away from baccalaureate programs and into vocational programs, despite the fact that many of the professional and managerial opportunities desired by students ultimately required a bachelor's degree. For this reason, Brint and Karabel (1989) argue, the community college diverts students from a higher postsecondary track, resulting in lower educational and economic attainment for students who may have otherwise entered a state university.

Dougherty (1994) suggests that both Clark and Brint and Karabel minimize the role that government officials play in the origins, impacts, and missions of community colleges. Informed by case studies in five states, Dougherty concludes that state governors and legislators promoted community colleges out of self-interest, though the colleges ultimately benefit interest groups (including businesses seeking trained workers, constituents in need of training, and state university officials interested in preserving elite educational institutions). "State relative autonomy" theory adds the pivotal participation of "self-interested, relatively autonomous" government officials in expanding and vocationalizing the community college (Dougherty 1994, p. 35). Dougherty (1994) argues that the contradictory nature of the community college—which democratizes access to higher education, while thwarting the educational aspirations of students—occurred because community colleges are products of many actors with varying interests. The goal diffusion in community colleges, combined with inadequate means to meet concurrent goals, translates to ineffectiveness.

New structural critics, like Rosenbaum et al. (2007), similarly argue that, at the institutional-level, community colleges are overextended and have not found effective means to achieve their many goals (Brint 2003). In contrast to Burton Clark (1960a, b), they suggest that community colleges enroll too many students and employ too few counselors for the systematic institutional "letdown" of student aspirations. Institutional constraints contribute to a structure that ignores the adult responsibilities and realities of the student population. Deil-Amen and Rosenbaum (2003) suggest that cultural capital, which they define as a form of social know-how, is necessary for students to overcome obstacles and successfully navigate the complex postsecondary institution. Students with the appropriate knowledge, perhaps obtained from highly educated parents or academic preparation, are more likely to make it through. Despite serving students with diverse backgrounds and needs, who are often less academically prepared for college, community colleges offer little institutional structure and guidance to support students in navigating bureaucratic hurdles and dealing with conflicting demands. This lack of structure results in long, meandering educational pathways—where the pathway through community college resembles a "shapeless river" (Scott-Clayton 2011). Community college students are more likely to persist and succeed in programs that are tightly and consciously structured, through both institutional policies and procedures, but also "norms and nudges" that influence individuals' decisions throughout their educational trajectory (Scott-Clayton 2011, p. 2).

18.5 Continued Debates Over the Diversionary Effects of Community Colleges

Guided in part by the theories noted above, research continues to explore whether and how community colleges facilitate or thwart student academic progress. Scholars continue to examine "community college effects" (diversion versus democratization) and cooling-out processes. We review the growing literature on diversionary effects before considering research that focuses on mechanisms for community college effects, including barriers that students face at different stages of the college experience. The research covers a wide range of student experiences—including developmental education (also referred to as "remediation") and navigating the college career and transfer process. With increased scholarly attention, narratives about community colleges and the experience of their attendees are becoming more nuanced.

18.5.1 Evidence in Support of Diversionary Effects

In principle, community colleges offer an economical way to complete the first year or two of a baccalaureate degree and to strengthen one's academic skills prior to entering a baccalaureate program. In practice, however, the transfer pathway can be difficult to navigate (Handel and Williams 2012; Monaghan and Attewell 2015; Xu et al. 2016) and the contribution of community colleges to students' academic skills is unclear. Over time, the share of first-time community college entrants that aspires to earning at least a bachelor's degree has risen from just over 70% in 1989 to around 77% in 2003. During the same period, transfer rates have held steady at around one in four (Horn and Skomsvold 2011).

Of course students who begin their postsecondary careers at community college may differ from those who begin at baccalaureate colleges in ways that reduce their chances of earning a baccalaureate degree. On average, those who start at a community college are less advantaged and less academically prepared. This fact has posed a serious challenge to analysts interested in understanding whether, on balance, community colleges are democratizing (increasing total years of schooling) or diversionary (reducing the chances of earning a baccalaureate degree).

Scholars have attempted to address issues of selection into the community college using a variety of methods. Some employ statistical adjustments based on observable measures (covariate adjustment and propensity score matching) while others adopt instrumental variables (IV) strategies. One study employs a regression discontinuity design. Given the different threats to validity and generalizability of these different approaches, we discuss empirical evidence for these models separately.

Early work on the association between community college attendance and baccalaureate completion relied on statistical controls to adjust for differences prior to college entry among those who pursued different postsecondary pathways. These studies show unambiguously negative associations between community college attendance and baccalaureate completion.[2] Using data from the City University of New York (CUNY) system for those who applied to a baccalaureate college, for example, Alba and Lavin (1981) find that students who were denied baccalaureate admission and instead attended a community college experienced steeper rates of college attrition three years after entrance. They were also 35 percentage points less likely to earn a baccalaureate degree than were those who initially attended a baccalaureate college, net of high school achievement. Velez (1985) finds a much more modest, but still appreciable, negative effect of 19 percentage points on baccalaureate completion for those initially enrolling in a community college

after controlling for social origins, high school achievement, and educational aspirations. His analysis focused on students with complete information in the nationally representative National Longitudinal Study of 1972 cohort and examined outcomes seven years after their expected year of high school graduation.

Propensity score matching offers a modest improvement over designs employing a control function approach to the extent that (1) analytic samples are limited to areas of common support[3] and (2) the functional form of the relationship between observable attributes and outcomes operates in a nonlinear fashion through selection into treatment (in this case, initial postsecondary enrollment in a community college). Doyle (2009) evaluates baccalaureate attainment by 2004 among those initially attending college in 1996 using the nationally representative Beginning Postsecondary Students Longitudinal Study. Based on 1:1 matching between those who did and did not start at a community college (n = 818), he finds that beginning at a community college reduces the hazard of earning a baccalaureate degree by 32%. Reynolds (2012) also employs propensity matching, but instead chooses to stratify his sample based on the propensity to initially attend a community college. He restricts his sample of 1992 high school graduates from the National Education Longitudinal Study (1988) to students with baccalaureate aspirations at the time of high school graduation who did not begin their postsecondary careers at elite colleges. Reynolds finds that starting at a community college reduced the probability of earning a bachelor's degree by about 25 percentage points. Finally, employing data from the state of Ohio, Long and Kurlaender (2009) estimate both propensity score models (using propensity stratification) and IV models (instrumenting on distance from high school to college). They further restrict their sample to students 17–20 years

---

[2]For a comprehensive review of this early literature see Dougherty (1992).

[3]By this we mean that analysts exclude observations that differ substantially from the average attributes of those in the opposite (treatment or control) condition. This typically means excluding those virtually certain to get the treatment (initially attend a community college) or not get the treatment (initially attend a baccalaureate college).

of age who took the ACT and expected to earn a bachelor's degree in an effort to insure proper comparison across community college and baccalaureate entrants. They find starting at a community college reduces the chance of earning a baccalaureate degree by 15–20 percentage points, with stronger negative effects for Black than for White students. Estimated effects are similar under IV and propensity matching designs.

IV estimates seek to get around issues of selection by exploiting only the variation in the treatment that is arguably caused by factors otherwise unrelated to the outcome of interest. This reduces the variation in treatment, often quite substantially, and thus increases the magnitude of uncertainty about the relationship between treatment and outcomes. IV estimates also apply only to those whose course of action (in our case, attending a community college) would be influenced by a change in the value of the instrument. In return, however, IV estimators offer estimates of effects that are, for this subpopulation, truly exogenous.

In the literature on effects of community college attendance on baccalaureate completion, the most common albeit somewhat controversial instruments are distance to the closest community and/or baccalaureate college and community college sticker price. Gonzalez and Hilmer (2006), Long and Kurlaender (2009), and Rouse (1995) employ distance to the closest college as instruments. Rouse (1995), the canonical piece in the democratization-or-diversion literature, finds that beginning at a community college reduces the probability of earning a baccalaureate degree by 8–10 percentage points among those graduating high school in 1980 (the High School and Beyond senior cohort). This is much less of a negative effect than most of the estimates from control function and propensity matching studies reviewed above. In terms of years of schooling, Rouse estimates that starting at a community college reduces schooling by half a year to a year compared to starting at a baccalaureate college but increases schooling by a year to a year and a half relative to not attending a community college or 4-year college. We return to the latter

finding below. Gonzalez and Hilmer (2006) replicate Rouse and find that her IV strategy applies to Hispanics students but not to students in other racial/ethnic groups. Consistent with Rouse, Gonzalez and Hilmer (2006) report a diversion effect of half a year.

In contrast to the IV estimates discussed in the preceding paragraph, Denning (2016) leverages an exogenous change in community college tuition and fees, imposed by shifting community college tax districts in the state of Texas. Using the change in sticker price as an instrument, he finds no diversionary effect of community colleges overall and a very modest (3 percentage point) diversionary effect for Black students and economically disadvantaged students. Furthermore, the diversionary effect appears to be temporary. While enrollments of Black and lower-income students in baccalaureate colleges declined, baccalaureate attainment rates for such students did not, and must have been offset by transfer rates later in the postsecondary career.

Finally, we are aware of one study that employs a regression discontinuity (RD) design. Like IV estimators, RD estimators provide estimates of local average treatment effects. While IV estimators pertain to those whose outcomes are influenced by the instrument, RD estimators pertain to those on either side of the assignment criterion. Goodman et al. (2015) evaluate the impact of attending a community college for students in Georgia who took the SAT, exploiting admissions cutoffs imposed by the Georgia State University System based on SAT scores. These cutoffs are fairly low, so the relevant subpopulation includes students with modest levels of academic skills as measured by the SAT. Goodman and colleagues find that enrolling in a public 4-year college instead of a 2-year college increases bachelor's completion rates by 30 percentage points on average and by 50 percentage points for low-income students, relatively few of whom complete if they fail to start at a baccalaureate college (2%).

On the whole, there is substantial evidence to support the theory of diversionary effects. Across samples and methods, most studies find some degree of diversion away from a bachelor's degree. Adjudicating the size of diversionary effect, based on the literature, is a more challenging question than we can address here. Because extant research varies in data, method, and year, a meta-analysis would draw more definitive conclusions. From our synthesis of the literature, it appears (with the exception of Denning's recent work) that the diversionary effect is at least 10 percentage points.

18.5.2   Evidence in Support of Democratization

Through open-access, low costs, and proximity to students' homes, community colleges aim to reduce inequality in educational opportunity by increasing postsecondary access. The hypothesis that community colleges may ultimately increase the years of educational attainment among students who otherwise would not have access to postsecondary education constitute the democratization effect of community college (Leigh and Gill 2003). Despite the large volume of research on diversionary effects of community colleges, relatively few of the studies actually consider democratization. Empirical studies using an IV approach include efforts to observe the impact of attending a community college compared to not attending college at all, but many other studies do not, focusing only on bachelor's completion as an outcome instead of years of schooling.

In her seminal paper, Rouse (1995) estimates that community college attendance increases average years of schooling by about one and a half years, compared to an increase of two to two and a half years for baccalaureate college attendance. Thus the marginal student choosing the community college sacrifices a half to a full year of education. On the other hand, Rouse suggests that "[t]he overall effect of community colleges on educational attainment can be assessed by comparing the magnitudes of the college-type effects weighted by the proportions of students in each group." (p. 222) Taking this approach, she estimates that the democratizing effect of the community college is slightly greater than the

diversionary effect, though the difference fails to attain statistical significance.

Leigh and Gill (2004) extend Rouse (1995) by conditioning on expected years of schooling and, like Rouse, find diversion effects of about a year. However, restricting the analytic sample to only those who aspire to a baccalaureate or graduate degree, Leigh and Gill find that the democratizing effect (1.8 years) exceeds the diversionary effect (−1 year) by eight tenths of a year. Students who initially enroll at community colleges experience a greater reduction in educational aspirations than those that initially start at baccalaureate colleges, but disadvantaged students—particularly those from low-income families earning less than $10,000 per year—see a greater improvement in their educational aspirations from enrolling at a community college than their advantaged counterparts (White students with at least one parents who attended college). Leigh and Gill's (2004) measurement of the diversionary versus democratizing effects of community colleges, which leverages changes in educational aspirations over time, maps onto the sociological literature on the cooling out function of community colleges.

The limited research on this topic leaves us with less empirical evidence supporting the democratizing effect of community college, compared to the diversionary effect. Both studies that compare democratization and diversion at community colleges suggest that the democratizing effects are at least as large (if not larger) than the diversionary effects. However, if the estimates of diversionary effects underestimate the size of the effect—which seems feasible, given that Rouse's (1995) estimates are smaller than most others in the field—then the democratizing effects may not exceed the diversionary effects. Ideally, more studies will evaluate community colleges on multiple outcomes, considering their ability to increase educational attainment overall, rather than focusing solely on their potential to divert students from earning a baccalaureate. The proper question may not be 'are community colleges diversionary' but instead 'for what subpopulations are community colleges diversionary and for what populations are they democratizing?'

18.5.3 Educational Aspirations and Structural Barriers

The "college-for-all" ethos encourages college aspirations among all youth, including those who are poorly prepared and weakly motivated (Rosenbaum 2001; Schneider and Stevenson 2000), even if their optimism is unrealistic (Reynolds et al. 2006). Recent sociological research examines whether the high educational expectations of youth attending community colleges are indeed "cooled out" by attending sub-baccalaureate institutions. Alexander et al. (2008) follow the bachelor's degree aspirations within a predominantly low-income, Black sample of Baltimore youths. While Clark (1960a, 1960b) and Brint and Karabel (1989) emphasize the role of community colleges in rerouting students from their original degree goals, Alexander and colleagues find that the educational expectations of low-resource youths are not cooled out by their experiences at 2-year colleges. Instead, the authors argue that 2-year college attendance is associated with "warming up" (i.e., increasing) educational aspirations rather than with "cooling out." This aligns with Leigh and Gill's (2004) findings that attending community college has a strong "incremental aspirations effect" among disadvantaged subsamples (including low-income youth and racial minorities). Furthermore, Alexander et al. (2008) find that "holding steady"—maintaining expectations—is the modal pattern. However, limited socioeconomic and academic resources are correlated with eventually giving up on bachelor's degree expectations.

Alexander and colleagues recommend a broader framework than Clark's (1960a, 1960b) cooling-out hypothesis allows. They argue that Clark's cooling-out hypothesis is too narrow, primarily blaming institutional actors (i.e., community college counselors) for redirecting students to lower their expectations. Rather than attempting to explain (non-)persistence through "a partial picture of the forces at work," models must capture the multiple forces that influence student persistence (Pascarella and Terenzini 2005, p. 630). A model that considers external pressures, such as financial problems and familial obligations, may better account for post-high school changes in college degree expectations. This research, along with the new structuralist critiques of community colleges, removes the blame from individual actors, instead focusing on the role of external pressures and bureaucratic structures in shifting students' expectations.

The new structuralist perspective, including the work of Deil-Amen and Rosenbaum (2003) and Rosenbaum et al. (2007), provides insight into processes within community colleges that result in low degree attainment and transfer rates for disadvantaged students. Based on the case studies of community colleges and for-profit 2-year colleges, *After Admission* (Rosenbaum et al. 2007) recommends organizational changes to minimize bureaucratic hurdles based largely on the practices in which many proprietary schools engage. The degree completion rates at proprietary 2-year colleges surpass those at community colleges. Their students report less difficulty, on average, navigating the pathway to degree attainment. Rosenbaum et al. (2007) suggest that proprietary colleges, while negative in some regards (see our earlier remarks), may be more successful at helping students satisfy their aspirations because they offer one-on-one assistance for students and simplify processes such as enrollment, course selection, and financial aid application (Deil-Amen and Rosenbaum 2003; Rosenbaum et al. 2007). To achieve similar completion rates, the authors argue that community colleges need to match the prescriptive nature of the proprietary 2-year colleges. While the recommendations from the study are useful in considering structural changes for community colleges, it is important to note that the proprietary colleges in the study are likely not representative of the entire for-profit sector.

18.5.4 Bumps on the Road to Degree Completion: The Role of Remediation

The structuralist explanation for diversionary effects focuses on barriers in navigating college life, including the pathways necessary to meet educational goals. A related literature examines a particularly troubling transition for community college students: making it through remedial coursework early in the college career. "Developmental" education—also referred to as remediation or "dev-ed"—is intended as a means to help underprepared students "catch up" so that they can successfully complete college-level coursework. Developmental education courses are typically required for students whose placement tests indicate they are "not ready" for core college coursework. It often must be completed before students can enroll in coursework that contributes toward a degree.

Estimates of the share of college students that enroll in developmental education vary by source, ranging from around 20% to 30% based on student self-reports (Parsad and Lewis 2003; Sparks and Malkus 2013) to over 50% based on postsecondary transcript data (Radford and Horn 2012; Scott-Clayton et al. 2014). While the discrepancy between sources may seem surprising to some, research suggests that students are often unaware that they are enrolled in developmental courses (Deil-Amen and Rosenbaum 2002; Person et al. 2006). Accumulating credits that do not contribute toward a degree is potentially discouraging to student progress (Deil-Amen and Rosenbaum 2002; Monaghan and Attewell 2015) and many students never complete the sequences intended to catch them up to college level (Bailey et al. 2010). Contentious, also, is the bar at which "college ready" is set—institutions differ in their expectations and in their process for placing students into dev-ed courses and frequently rely on a single assessment to decide whether or not to compel students to complete remedial coursework (Attewell et al. 2006; Scott-Clayton et al. 2014). Scott-Clayton et al.'s (2014) work suggests that relying on a single assessment results in mis-assigning a substantial proportion of students to developmental education—one in four test-takers in math and one in three in English—and recommend using high school grades in addition to and instead of test scores to determine placement. In fact, relying on a single tests for such consequential decisions also violates an ethical guideline of the American Psychological

Association and the American Education Research Association. The latter states quite clearly that "[d]ecisions that affect individual students' life chances or educational opportunities should not be made on the basis of test scores alone" (AERA 2000). It seems clear to us that compulsory remediation, as well as exclusion if remedial courses are not completed in the allotted timeframe, represents a serious constraint on educational opportunity.

The effects of remediation on student postsecondary outcomes are not entirely clear. Our read of this literature, however, is that remediation—at least as practiced in the first decade of the twenty-first century—at best doesn't get in the way. Well-identified studies of the impact of remediation, often using sharp or fuzzy regression discontinuity designs to compare students along the placement cutoff, find nonsignificant effects of remediation on community college transfer or college completion in Florida (Calcagno and Long 2008), Tennessee (Boatman and Long 2010) (null effects for reading and math), and Texas (Martorell and McFarlin 2011). The only exceptions to these at the state level are Bettinger and Long's (2004) positive results in Ohio and Boatman and Long's (2010) positive result for remedial writing in Tennessee.

Studies using nationally representative samples are unable to employ such rigorous methods and instead rely on covariate adjustment (in a control function or propensity score framework) to adjust for potential confounders. Attewell et al. (2006) find that among those who graduate high school in 1992 the impact of remedial courses on graduation net of controls was negligible among 2-year college entrants (though modestly negative among 4-year college entrants). Saw (2016) likewise finds mostly nonsignificant conditional effects of remediation in the National Longitudinal Survey of Youth 1997 data with one important exception. Enrolling in remedial courses in *both* math and English appears to positively affect completion among community college entrants but negatively affect completion among baccalaureate college entrants. Bahr's use of covariate adjustment and data from California community colleges, similarly suggests that, on average, students who successfully complete developmental courses (i.e., reach college-level coursework) achieve similar outcomes as those who were not placed in dev-ed (Bahr 2008b), though there is variation in the effects across race (Bahr 2010). Unfortunately, since this type of study compares those who make it through dev-ed to those who were never in it, the results are unable to speak to whether placement into dev-ed impacts student progress, like making it into college-level courses.

Critics argue that remedial coursework is a structural barrier that serves to divert students from taking college-level coursework, with the greatest negative impact on students who are most prepared (Scott-Clayton and Rodriguez 2014). Scott-Clayton and Rodriguez (2015) argue that placement into remediation may serve three distinct purposes: developing skills for future coursework, discouraging students from continuing their studies, and diverting students onto a separate track. Using administrative data from a large urban community college system, they find that developmental education does not appear to develop students for future college success, nor does it discourage student progress on average. However, it does significantly discourage students who may have been mis-assigned to remedial education, those who passed a more difficult writing test but barely missed the cutoff for testing out of remedial reading education classes. Their findings suggest that the greatest effects appear to be through diverting students from accumulating college-level courses; while students in developmental education may enroll and persist at the same rates as other students, they continue taking remedial coursework instead of coursework toward a degree.

Others argue that the placement into remediation in a "stigma-free" manner implies to students that developmental classes are not different than other classes (Deil-Amen and Rosenbaum 2002). Deil-Amen and Rosenbaum (2002) examined remediation at two community colleges, both of which emphasized the transfer function of community colleges. Many of the students they studied were placed into a remedial class that did not carry credit towards a degree. Yet, the distinction between remedial coursework and coursework that would contribute towards a credential was unclear in catalogues and not emphasized by advisors, feeding into students' unrealistic educational goals. As a result, students enrolled in remedial courses might "go for several months, a full semester, or even a full year" without understanding that the courses were not counting toward a degree (Deil-Amen and Rosenbaum 2002, p. 260). This leads students to assume they are making progress and to maintain or increase educational aspirations, only to experience a letdown once they become aware of the issue. This delayed letdown may contribute to students dropping out of college altogether instead of considering pathways to earn an alternative credential earlier in their college career (p. 264).

Some argue that poor high school preparation, rather than placement into remedial coursework, reduces students' chances of graduating from college (Adelman 1999; Attewell et al. 2006). Attewell et al. (2006) suggest that it is also important to distinguish between the effects remedial coursework has on chances of graduation and on time to degree, showing that it increases the time to degree, but after controlling for student background, does not appear to decrease graduation. However, students who take one or more remedial classes are more likely to leave college with less than 10 credits—they drop out before making much progress toward a degree (Attewell et al. 2006, p. 904). Furthermore, if the remedial coursework is in reading, as opposed to mathematics, there is a negative impact of taking remedial coursework on chance of graduation (p.909). While it is possible that remedial coursework and delayed accumulation of credits toward a degree thwart some students' progress, *completing* remedial coursework may have positive impacts on degree completion (Bettinger and Long 2004). In the case of reading, Adelman (1999) argues that reading is fundamental to making progress in college, so placement into remedial coursework in reading is a signal of poor preparation for the college career.

18.6   Democratization in the Twenty-First Century: Policy Initiatives for Improving Community College Outcomes

In the policy sphere, the "college-for-all" culture is shifting to an emphasis on "credentials-for-all." In his first address to congress in 2009, President Obama set a goal that the United States once again have the highest proportion of college graduates in the world by the year 2020 (Whitehouse.gov 2011). States have created their own initiatives to keep up: Texas's "60X30TX" aims for 60% of 25- to 34-year-old Texans to hold a postsecondary credential or degree by 2030; Tennessee's "Drive to 55" initiative aims to get 55% of Tennesseans to hold a postsecondary credential by 2025; Oregon's "40-40-20" goal aims for 40% of Oregonians to have a baccalaureate, 40% to have an associate degree or certificate in a skilled occupation, and the remaining 20% to have at least a high school diploma or equivalent by 2025 (driveto55.org 2015; Oregonlearns.org 2015; THECB 2015).

In order to achieve these lofty goals, politicians have increasingly turned to community colleges in hopes of finding the appropriate policy levers to rapidly increase degree attainment. Proposals range from local- to national-level improvements. In this section, we discuss some of the most prominent policy changes proposed to improve outcomes among community college students, including strategies for ensuring credits translate to credentials, free tuition at community colleges, improving pathways through community college, and holistic versus targeted interventions to improve student outcomes. We consider how sociological research can inform policy change.

18.6.1   Baccalaureate College Transfer

A growing body of research also shows the inefficiency of the transfer mechanism from community colleges to baccalaureate-granting colleges.

Many policymakers and educational administrators acknowledge that students struggle to navigate the transfer process and devise strategies to overcome these struggles. A common policy response is the creation of a statewide "general education core"—a set of general education courses that all public universities in the state will accept toward a bachelor's degree. Thirty states have adopted this strategy (Jenkins et al. 2014). The rationale is that college advisors often recommend that transfer-intending students take coursework to satisfy lower-division general education requirements, but unless students are guaranteed that they can transfer those credits to a junior standing in a specific major, they are often left with extra credits that do not count toward their degree (Jenkins et al. 2014).

Another common strategy for improving pathways to transfer success is the creation of transfer agreements (also called articulation agreements)—either statewide or between individual institutions. Articulation agreements serve to negotiate the requirements for students to move between institutions, particularly by preventing the loss of credits (Anderson et al. 2006b; Roksa and Keith 2008). While many states have adopted statewide articulation agreements, some, like Texas, still largely rely on "bilateral agreements" (agreements between two institutions outlining transfer rules), leaving students and advisors to navigate specific agreements between colleges and programs (Root 2013). Many scholars advocate for comprehensive statewide transfer agreements, suggesting that they reduce time to degree, cost to student, and cost to the state in terms of excess credit hours (Root 2013).

The only studies evaluating the impact of statewide transfer agreements, to our knowledge, use national data. Roksa and Keith (2008) use data from the National Education Longitudinal Study (NELS), while Anderson and colleagues (Anderson et al. 2006a, b) use data from the Beginning Postsecondary Students Longitudinal Study (BPS). Comparing outcomes for students attending community colleges in states with articulation agreements compared to those without, Anderson et al. (2006a, b) find no evidence that states with statewide articulation experience higher rates of student transfer. However, states were not part of the BPS's sampling frame, biasing the estimates of student outcomes by the state in which a college resides. Furthermore, Roksa and Keith (2008) advocate for examination of outcomes like preservation of credits, time to degree, and bachelor's degree attainment rather than transfer rate. They reason that most transfer agreements ease the process for students who already decided to transfer, which means using rate of transfer as an outcome ignores the goals of the policy (Roksa and Keith 2008, p. 237). Using the NELS, they study the impact of state articulation agreements on bachelor's degree attainment, time to degree, and credits to degree for high school graduates who initially enrolled at a community college and transferred to a public 4-year college in the same state. They find no evidence that students in states with transfer articulation policies have better outcomes than students in states without those policies. However, they acknowledge the limitations of the study, where they are only able to capture the articulation policies "as codified in state statutes," potentially underestimating the role of articulation policies and practices by missing out on the total articulation agreements between 2-and 4-year institutions in a given state (p. 248). Understanding the impact of articulation policies will require a "more careful, contextual, and nuanced analysis" of transfer policies and practices (p. 249).

Sociological theory on community colleges builds a useful scaffolding to interpret the inefficient pathways students take toward a degree. However, these theories, with the exception of Dougherty's (1994) incorporation of political influences, often ignore the policy context and higher education system within which community colleges operate. This places the blame on institutional actors—many of whom are overwhelmed and have little power over the policies they implement—and has the potential to miss important policy levers for improving student success. Finding ways to incorporate more policy analysis into the sociological debates over community college can help move us beyond intra-institutional challenges to consider how larger organizational structures create and constrain students' postsecondary opportunities.

18.6.2 Community College as a Backstop: Transfer in a Credential-For-All Climate

The majority of research on institutional transfer and community colleges focuses on vertical movement from community colleges to baccalaureate-granting institutions. Yet recent sociological research shows that students "swirl" through their college careers, moving laterally to institutions in the same sector, vertically between sectors, and in interrupted spurts of enrollment (Adelman 1999; Goldrick-Rab 2006). As demonstrated throughout this chapter, a large body of work on postsecondary transfer focuses on how initial enrollment at a community college diverts students with bachelor's degree aspirations away from 4-year colleges. Yet much of the movement among college students occurs in much more complex patterns (Andrews et al. 2014; Hossler et al. 2012). One third of college students transfer before earning a degree (Hossler et al. 2012; Shapiro et al. 2015). Community colleges are the most frequent transfer destination for students from all other postsecondary institution types, including students from public 4-year colleges (Hossler et al. 2012). Regardless of the direction of transfer, community colleges play a prominent role in student movement through American higher education, serving as an origin or, perhaps unintentionally, a destination college for many students.

"Reverse transfer" typically describes movement from a 4-year to a 2-year college prior to earning a degree. Shapiro et al. (2015) estimate that, among those initially attending a baccalaureate college in 2008, 38% of students who transferred moved to a community college (though many eventually return to earn a baccalaureate degree). Using the Education Longitudinal Study of 2002, we estimate that 18.4% of students who initially begin their postsecondary education at a baccalaureate college end their postsecondary career at a community college, with 11.8% earning an associate degree or certificate and the remaining 6.6% leaving without a credential. These statistics capture reverse transfer as a *practice*—one that describes the movement of students to a lower degree-granting institution.

But reverse transfer also refers to a set of *policies* aimed at providing lower level degrees to students who have transferred vertically (Friedel and Wilson 2015; Hood et al. 2009). We review the literature on reverse transfer as a practice before describing recent policy changes aimed at facilitating reverse transfer to ensure students with community college credit earn a credential (where student transcripts are sent back to their origin college to offer an associate degree after transfer to a baccalaureate-granting college).

Some scholars view the shift downward from a baccalaureate-granting institution as a setback, and one that serves as a potentially inequitable track for students from low socioeconomic status households. Using the National Education Longitudinal Study of 1988, Goldrick-Rab and Pfeffer (2009) illustrated that, while academic underpreparedness is the strongest predictor of reverse transfer, after controlling for both test scores and prior achievement, students from low-income families are substantially more likely to reverse transfer than their more affluent peers. High-income students who transfer, on the other hand, are more likely to make lateral shifts to a different baccalaureate college. Thus, Goldrick-Rab and Pfeffer (2009) argue that the downward shift of students from low-income families is an underexplored stratification pathway within post-secondary education.

An alternative interpretation suggests that community colleges serve as a safety net for students who would otherwise leave higher education altogether. Kalogrides and Grodsky (2011) examine the causes and consequences of reverse transfer using the same data set. To determine the effects of reverse transfer, they use propensity scores to control for selection on observable measures into a community college among initial enrollees at baccalaureate colleges. Their results suggest that while students who reverse transfer do not fare as well as those with exclusive 4-year enrollment, they have more favorable academic and labor market outcomes than students who drop out. Given the results, community colleges may serve as a safety net, particularly for disadvantaged students who are at greater risk of dropping out of college. This adds complexity to the debate about the diversionary function of community colleges. Community colleges offer additional pathways to social mobility for students who would otherwise leave college without a degree. They also serve as protection against downward mobility for students who earn a bachelor's degree and enroll at community colleges to obtain training for technical jobs in the face of a shifting labor market (Bragg 2001).

More recently, reverse transfer also refers to specific policies that retroactively offer students who transfer from a 2-year college to a 4-year college an associate degree by using credits from the new institution combined with those from their prior institution. The policies are also referred to as a "reverse articulation" (Friedel and Wilson 2015). Several states now promote policies for earning an associate degree after transferring to baccalaureate colleges in order to avoid credit loss and to improve community college completion rates (Friedel and Wilson 2015). For instance, Texas implemented a new mandate for reverse transfer in 2011, which requires that transcripts for transfer students with at least 30 community college credit hours be sent back to their community college once the student accumulates 66 credit hours to allow the community college registrar to determine whether the student is eligible for an associate degree (THECB 2014). While the policy intends to improve attainment—helping transfer students earn a credential even if they fall short of a bachelor's degree—there is some evidence that the policy has been undermined by implementation issues, including inability to process incoming transcripts due to outdated technology and understaffing (Bailey et al. 2016; Reyes et al. 2016). While research suggests that students benefit from earning an associate degree prior to transferring—both for cost efficiency and to avoid leaving college without a credential (Scott-Clayton and Belfield 2015), the reverse transfer pathway to an associate degree allows students to transfer upward while still having the option to earn a degree from their origin college after accumulating more credits. As more states move toward mandating reverse articulation pathways, it's also vital that they recognize the resource constraints at community colleges and provide adequate support to implement new policies.

18.6.3 Free Community College

In early January 2015, President Obama unveiled a proposal, called "America's College Promise" (ACP), for 2 years of free community college. The program would create a partnership between the federal government and states to waive 2 years of resident tuition at community colleges for eligible students by providing a federal match of $3 for every $1 invested by the state (Whitehouse.gov 2015). The benefit would be available for academic programs that are fully transferable to 4-year state colleges or occupational training programs that produce a credential for an in-demand industry.

Our current financial aid system is voucher-based, funding students who in turn make their choice on which institution to attend. The decision to fund students, rather than to fund institutions, contributed to a high-tuition, high-aid model in which grants and loans enable tuition to rise with little accountability for the institutions that set the price of college (Goldrick-Rab and Kendall 2014). As tuition rises, federal aid continues to increase to offset out-of-pocket costs (though the high-tuition high-aid model contributes to rising net tuition, as sticker price has risen more rapidly than financial aid because the two are not forcefully coupled through policy). This cycle has led some scholars to propose that we move away from our voucher-based system and return to funding institutions in order to eliminate or minimize the direct costs for students while offering incentives to public colleges to keep costs down and improve student outcomes (Goldrick-Rab and Kendall 2014; Goldrick-Rab et al. 2014), though such proposals are likely politically untenable as they often require at least partially withdrawing federal funding from private institutions, which have powerful political ties. There is little evidence that a change in funding structure would ultimately reduce costs for students, since there are no examples from which to draw on in the United States. ACP did not go so far as to move away from the voucher-based system, but it moved further toward a free public option, like what we see in America's public K–12 system.

While some states recently adopted a form of "free community college," the implementation is quite different than Obama's proposal due to the funding structure. ACP was proposed as a "first-dollar" program—federal aid would be applied after waiving tuition. This has important implications; it means that students who receive the Pell Grant and other federal grant aid would still be able to receive the aid to cover books, supplies, and other necessary cost-of-living expenses. Other recent programs for free community college—like Tennessee's and Oregon's Promise programs—are "last-dollar" programs. They apply federal grant aid to tuition and fees first, with the state chipping in to cover remaining expenses only after other forms of grant aid. This means the cost to the state for offering free community college to a student who already receives the Pell Grant is quite low (or, possibly, nonexistent), but that the added benefit to the student may be minimal—they may not actually see any extra aid money to offset college costs. Only grant aid that is in excess of tuition and fees will be available for living expenses, which is the same as the status quo.

Some critics of ACP argued that the proposal was regressive in nature—that community college is already free for most students from low-income families, which means affluent students would be the only ones to benefit (Butler 2015; Francis 2015; Tierney 2015). While the program would indeed benefit higher-income students who elected to start at community colleges to get the financial benefit, the first-dollar nature of the program suggests that, in terms of covering the myriad of out-of-pocket costs that come with college education (including living expenses), students from low-income families who face financial hardship would be better off and potentially able to work fewer hours.

It is unclear how many students would have ultimately benefitted from America's College Promise in terms of degree completion. Under ACP, community college students would need to maintain a 2.5 GPA, in addition to remaining enrolled half-time and demonstrating "steady progress" toward a degree, to remain eligible (Whitehouse.gov 2015). These performance standards for renewal were higher than the Satisfactory Academic Progress standards for federal aid (Whitehouse.gov 2015). In 2012, 37% of first-year community college students earned below a 2.5, suggesting that a substantial portion of initial America's College Promise enrollees would quickly lose eligibility (Schudde and Scott-Clayton 2016).

The message of free community college may incentivize students to enroll in college, but it is unlikely to improve graduation rates without significant changes to pathways through community college, especially if over a third of students lose eligibility after one year. Yet the ACP proposal did not build in money for institutions to make the structural changes necessary to improve student outcomes—building in those finances would have reduced the policy's political palatability.

After the 2017 presidential election and the change of administration, the conversation around America's College Promise decreased, though many states and institutions, by that point, had produced their own model of free community college. Recent implementation of "last-dollar" scholarship programs for community colleges give us some insight into expected shifts in enrollment at community colleges as a result of advertising free tuition. The Tennessee Promise program, which offers free community college tuition to graduating high school seniors who meet a number of requirements, including community service, resulted in an initial enrollment boost in Tennessee's public colleges of 10% in its first semester, fall 2015 (Goodman et al. 2015). While community colleges and technical colleges saw, respectively, 25% and 20% increases in enrollment of first-time freshmen, the state's universities are down in freshman enrollment by 8% overall at baccalaureate institutions overseen by the board of regents and almost 5% across University of Tennessee campuses (Goodman et al. 2015).

The impacts of free community college are likely to be complex and will take some time to sort out. On the one hand, free community college may radically democratize higher education. Even though many economically disadvantaged students already attend community college for free, others may fail to enroll due to the perception of cost or to the reality of non-tuition costs that they must bear to attend (including lost wages). On the other hand, the literature on democratization and diversion reviewed above suggests that enrolling in a community college rather than a 4-year college reduces the likelihood of baccalaureate completion and as a result may or may not increase average years of education. Given the fact that economically disadvantaged students and students of color may be more price-sensitive than other students, it may well turn out that free community college reduces baccalaureate attainment rates disproportionately for these subgroups. Our confidence in the impact of free community college is further undermined by recent scholarship suggesting, on the one hand, dramatic diversionary effects of community college attendance at the margin of baccalaureate admission (Goodman et al. 2015) and, on the other, dramatic democratizing effects with virtually no net diversion attributable to a thousand-dollar reduction in community college tuition (Denning 2016).

Additionally, there is increasing debate over the need to incorporate adult learners into plans for offering community college education (Stoltzfus 2015). Many of the recently enacted tuition-free programs focus primarily on younger students—those transitioning directly from high school—like in Oregon and Tennessee Promise programs. But some states are beginning to take steps toward getting more adults into the community college classroom. Alabama, a state stricken with low educational attainment, particularly in high-poverty areas like the Black Belt region, is focusing on the parents of 6th and 7th grade students affiliated with GEAR-UP (Gaining Early Awareness and Readiness for Undergraduate Programs) (Kolodner 2015). While GEAR-UP will offer college preparation and free community college to the 6th and 7th graders, the community college system is funding its own effort to provide free tuition for the students' parents, hoping to increase educational aspirations and attainment for entire families (Kolodner 2015). Tennessee is also attempting to cover tuition for eligible adults in the state's colleges of applied technology, in a program called Tennessee Reconnect (Stoltzfus 2015). Given the diverse student populations traditionally served by community college, many free college proponents argue that the programs need to capture the variety of students who typically pursue degrees at the institutions, not just those who are traditionally "college-aged."

In order to continue moving policy proposals toward improving social mobility in the United States, sociologists should contribute to the careful evaluation of existing initiatives and help to identify possible solutions when unintended consequences arise. In the case of new initiatives, careful attention must be paid to producing programs that improve student outcomes at community colleges, rather than funneling more students into already overwhelmed and resource-constrained colleges. Furthermore, policy proposals that would provide similar funding for students admitted to public 4-year colleges might avoid exacerbating diversionary effects of community colleges on college choice for price-sensitive students from low-income families.

18.6.4 Improving Educational Pathways

18.6.4.1 Dual Enrollment

In dual-enrollment programs, high school students take college courses in which they may potentially earn college credit upon completion of the course (Allen and Dadgar 2012). Because it may offer an inexpensive means of earning college credit while in high school (some states offer free dual enrollment programs (e.g., Florida) and others offer discounted tuition and fees (e.g., Texas and Utah)), dual enrollment is another potential mechanism for increasing college access and completion among students from low-income families (An 2013a; Hoffman et al. 2008). However, high-SES students are more likely to participate in dual enrollment than low-SES students (Museus et al. 2007).

Given SES differences in dual enrollment participation and the potential benefits of these programs for college success, some proponents of

dual enrollment push for equal access to dual enrollment in order to increase its reach to a diverse group of students, arguing that equal access to dual enrollment programs may help mitigate SES gaps in college outcomes (Bragg et al. 2006; Dual enrollment in Texas: State policies that strengthen new pathways to and through college for low-income youth (testimony of Joel Vargas) 2010; Hoffman et al. 2008). Empirical evidence using nationally representative data confirms that dual enrollment participation increases the odds of attaining a postsecondary degree (An 2013a, 2013b). However, evidence using administrative data from Florida to compare students around a threshold of minimum academic standards for participation finds minimal impact of dual enrollment college algebra on high school graduation, college enrollment, or college graduation (Speroni 2011). Thus, the benefits of dual enrollment are not entirely clear, at least in terms of average effects. Furthermore, decomposition techniques suggest that dual enrollment fails to reduce disparities in college degree attainment between first-generation college students and students whose parents attended at least some college (An 2013a). Participation in Advanced Placement courses appears to account for a greater proportion of the parental education gap than dual enrollment (18% of the gap, vs less than 1%), though most of the SES gap in college completion is accounted for by other student background factors.

Still, several states are turning to dual enrollment as a means of providing more cost-effective college coursework by building partnerships between high schools, community colleges, and public universities. One such effort is the "On Ramps" program in Texas, which develops and implements coursework to prepare students for college and offers college-level credit to students at participating high schools. Unknown, however, is the risk that state initiatives like these may inadvertently concentrate opportunities at high-resource schools, which already offer more programming to students to prepare them for college (Reardon and Bischoff 2011; Roderick et al. 2009). For instance, the Texas initiative is currently available on an "opt-in" basis. While many schools likely want to offer the programming, those in low-income communities with a lower tax base may need additional financial support to do so. Thus, the goals that motivate and the means of expanding dual enrollment programs are important. Expansion driven by the goal to improve the quality of the college applicant pool, as opposed to improving college access for underrepresented students, could continue to concentrate opportunities among specific populations. While An's (2013a) research suggests that *equalizing* participation in dual enrollment across the SES divide would not attenuate the SES gap in college completion, the decomposition analysis does not illustrate what would happen if policies were to target low-income students and schools, rather than just equalizing participation. Additionally, there could be unintended consequences of pushing dual enrollment courses at only local community colleges, which could have a potential diversion effect away from baccalaureate-granting institutions. The uneven distribution of dual enrollment programs illustrates the need to study consequences of new policy initiatives and the residential concentration of opportunities that aim to strengthen the K–12 to public higher education pipeline.

18.6.4.2 Guided Pathways

While dual enrollment opportunities focus on increasing college coursework opportunities at the high school level, recent efforts to improve pathways within community colleges consider the roll of existing program offerings within the colleges. Like the new structural critics, recent advocates for "guided pathways" models at community colleges criticize the typical "cafeteria" model employed by community colleges—a term used to illustrate that the colleges operate as largely self-service, allowing students to choose among disconnected courses, programs, and support services (Bailey et al. 2015). As Rosenbaum et al. (2007) argued, despite offering a plethora of options, community colleges often lack one in particular: the option of a "highly structured program" that "curtail[s] choice, but promise[s] timely graduation and an appropriate job" (p. 21).

In this same vein of criticism, Bailey et al. (2015) recommend that community colleges adopt a guided pathways approach, which presents courses in the context of highly structured, educationally coherent program maps that align with students' goals for careers and further education (grouped by "meta-majors"). In this model, incoming students are given support to explore careers, choose a program of study, and develop an academic plan based on program maps created by faculty and advisors, who provide intrusive advising throughout schooling. Whereas much of the advising in the cafeteria approach is "by necessity focused on mechanics of course registration," the guided pathways approach focuses any advising on educational and career goals (Bailey et al. 2015; Scott-Clayton 2011, p. 7). The approach simplifies student decision-making and allows colleges to provide predictable schedules and frequent feedback so students can complete programs more efficiently, aligning with suggestions from Rosenbaum et al. (2007) work.

While the guided pathways model is persuasive, it overlooks some of the key non-academic concerns facing many community college students. As Deil-Amen (2011) points out, the "traditional college student" is increasingly the exception rather than the rule, especially at community colleges. Many students are not transitioning straight from high school, do not live on college campuses (both due to individual constraints and the nature of the institutions they attend), and are from groups traditionally underrepresented in higher education. Yet the guided pathways model is predicated on the expectation that students can invest the time and money into full-time college attendance. Students supporting a family or facing financial obligations that require full-time employment may be unable to comply with the expectations of a guided pathway, which often includes additional class time (sometimes including add-on courses and advising to develop soft skills for college success within students' class sequence). It's unclear how and if the guided pathways model can be effective for part-time students. The model appears most effective for remedying the structural issues at community colleges and helping guide students through academic challenges, but sociological work points to the non-academic pressures faced by the same students (Goldrick-Rab 2016; Goldrick-Rab et al. 2016; Rosenbaum et al. 2007). It's possible that the most effective models for improving student success at community college must deal with the non-academic struggles, in addition to the academic struggles.

18.6.5 Holistic "High-Touch" Interventions

Recent initiatives that appear to drastically improve persistence and completion among students have made headlines in newspapers and waves in the community college sector. One initiative, implemented at the City University of New York, is the Accelerated Study in Associate Programs, also known by its acronym "ASAP." According to a randomized controlled trial testing its efficacy performed by MDRC, the program nearly doubled the share of community college students graduating within 3 years (40% of ASAP students compared to 22% of those in traditional community college programming) (Scrivener et al. 2015). It also showed a measurable increase in vertical transfer, with 25% of ASAP students moving into a 4-year college compared to 17% of those in the control group.

What is the secret of this new intervention? There is no easy answer, as the program is a multipronged intervention with "wraparound" student services. Students in ASAP receive a myriad of extra support services and they also tend to enroll full-time, which speeds up their progress. The services offered to ASAP students include intrusive advising, tutoring, priority registration, free textbooks, a waiver to cover the discrepancy between tuition and fees and financial aid. They also are incentivized to attend meetings with an advisor by being offered a free metrocard, which is quite valuable in the city of New York, where public transit is essential for most.

Ultimately, pinpointing the elements of ASAP that led to such strong results is difficult, if not impossible. Several elements included in the program have been tested individually, with positive but less sizeable results (Bahr 2008a; Cho and Karp 2013; Scrivener and Weiss 2009). That means that scaling up ASAP to use its most effective components is nearly impossible. We also don't know if the program would work in other settings. It seems likely that the "high-touch" intervention—where ASAP students received significantly more attention from their advisors than their non-ASAP counterparts—played a role. ASAP students met with advisors much more frequently than their peers (38 times per year vs 6 times per year), but their advisors also had lower caseloads (600 students instead of 1500), potentially allowing them to provide more individual attention. Students also received substantially more tutoring (34 sessions vs 7) (Scrivener et al. 2015).

Beyond the difficulty of breaking down the program into its core components, a challenge that many interested colleges would likely encounter in implementing a similar set of wraparound services is the financial investment necessary to mimic ASAP. At CUNY, the program required a 60% increase in per pupil spending. While the authors of the report argue that the total cost of a degree through ASAP is less than the cost of a degree through traditional CUNY programming due to greater efficiency (more students earn degrees), running a program like ASAP would require significant funds at the front end. Reducing the student-to-advisor ratio accounts for much of the added costs.

President Obama—like community college leaders across the country—recognized the strength of programs like ASAP. In his proposal for free community college, he highlighted the need for colleges to adopt promising strategies like ASAP, but was vague regarding how colleges should make the large-scale changes necessary to implement a similar approach. Furthermore, it is not clear if ASAP works outside of the CUNY context. Because holistic approaches are expensive, and community colleges are often resource-constrained, colleges rely on targeted interventions, which are more affordable. Without injecting more funding into community colleges, it's likely they will continue to rely on smaller, more targeted interventions.

18.7   Conclusions and Areas of Future Inquiry

Sociological research has contributed substantially to our understanding of the role community colleges play in our educational system and in the process of social stratification. Due to its complex history, the community college has proven to be fertile ground for scholars interested in understanding organizations, students, and pathways into higher education and the labor market. Institutional and organizational analyses are a key contribution of sociology to our understanding of community colleges, with scholars like Clark, Rosenbaum, Brint, and Karabel contributing to our knowledge of the structural barriers within postsecondary organizations. We have to continue driving that focus on higher-level organizational structures, including state higher education systems, to understand the influence of state contexts and broader organizational influences. This will also allow for embracing cross-state comparative work to understand the role of funding and government structures on higher education trajectories.

Shifting the focus to broader state-level and policy questions—including the policy issues reviewed above, which are only investigated by a handful of sociologists—might also move applied sociological research, which appears influential in the academic research sphere (e.g., the "diversionary effects" debate traces its origins back to sociology), into public policy debates. This may help overcome recently highlighted struggles of sociological research to make a dent in public policy, compared to economic research (Patterson 2014; Wolfers 2015). Increasing sociology's presence in the public discourse could inform debates with an understanding of social stratification and the benefits of social mobility, challenging the status quo emphasis on efficiency over equity.

One of the characteristics that make community colleges so interesting is their variability. Given the expansion of access to administrative data, sociologists are better positioned now than in the past to exploit that variability to understand what dimensions of the community college experience—and structure—impact social stratification, under what conditions and for whom. Community colleges may vary in their approach to developmental education, student counseling, scheduling practices, transfer arrangements, and financing in ways that help inform our understanding of their effects on the students they serve. Some may be diversionary, others democratizing, depending on their organizational features and the way they are incorporated into their state's system of higher education.

The same community college may also affect different students in different ways. Gonzalez and Hilmer's (2006) results showing comparatively large democratizing effects for Latino students and Goodman et al.'s (2015) more troubling findings of sharply disproportionate diversionary effects to lower-income students are telling and highlight the urgency of research on heterogeneous treatment effects. Strong research designs are critically important for accurately identifying heterogeneous effects in the presence of unobserved variation in student background attributes, postsecondary preparation, and constraints. Models of selection on observables, including regression adjustment or control function approaches and closely related propensity score techniques, may be ill suited to the task.[4]

Finally, we hope that others will take full advantage of the natural experiments occurring across community college in the United States. Innovations related to remediation, transfer, counseling, and financing, some of which we reviewed earlier in this chapter, are increasingly common. While such natural experiments are often imperfect with respect to causal inference, they can nonetheless inform our understanding regarding whether and how various dimensions of the community college experience affect students.

---

[4] For a recent discussion, see Breen et al. (2015).

Whether one views community colleges as agents of social mobility or reproduction, community colleges are almost certain to remain a critical component of postsecondary education in the United States. Understanding if and how they impact the life chances of the millions of students they serve continues to be of central importance in the fields of education and social stratification.

References

Adelman, C. (1999). *Answers in the tool box: Academic intensity, attendance patterns, and bachelor's degree attainment*. Washington, DC: U.S. Department of Education, Office of Educational Research and Improvement.

AERA. (2000). *Position statement on high-stakes testing* (Vol. 2016). Washington, DC: American Educational Research Association.

Alba, R. D., & Lavin, D. E. (1981). Community colleges and tracking in higher education. *Sociology of Education, 54*(4), 223–237.

Alexander, K., Bozick, R., & Enwisle, D. (2008). Warming up, cooling out, or holding steady? Persistence and change in educational expectations after high school. *Sociology of Education, 81*(4), 371–396. https://doi.org/10.1177/003804070808100403.

Allen, D., & Dadgar, M. (2012). Does dual enrollment increase students' success in college? Evidence from a quasi-experimental analysis of dual enrollment in New York City. *New Directions for Higher Education, 2012*(158), 11–19.

An, B. P. (2013a). The impact of dual enrollment on college degree attainment: Do low-SES students benefit? *Educational Evaluation and Policy Analysis, 35*(1), 57–75.

An, B. P. (2013b). The influence of dual enrollment on academic performance and college readiness: Differences by socioeconomic status. *Research in Higher Education, 54*(4), 407–432.

Anderson, G., Alfonso, M., & Sun, J. (2006a). Rethinking cooling out at public community colleges: An examination of fiscal and demographic trends in higher education and the rise of statewide articulation agreements. *The Teachers College Record, 108*(3), 422–451.

Anderson, G., Sun, J. C., & Alfonso, M. (2006b). Effectiveness of statewide articulation agreements on the probability of transfer: A preliminary policy analysis. *The Review of Higher Education, 29*(3), 261–291.

Andrews, R., Li, J., & Lovenheim, M. F. (2014). Heterogeneous paths through college: Detailed patterns and relationships with graduation and earnings. *Economics of Education Review, 42*, 93–108.

Attewell, P., Lavin, D., Domina, T., & Levey, T. (2006). New evidence on college remediation. *Journal of Higher Education, 77*, 886–924.

Bahr, P. R. (2008a). Cooling out in the community college: What is the effect of academic advising on students' chances of success? *Research in Higher Education, 49*(8), 704–732. https://doi.org/10.1007/s11162-008-9100-0.

Bahr, P. R. (2008b). Does mathematics remediation work?: A comparative analysis of academic attainment among community college students. *Research in Higher Education, 49*(5), 420–450.

Bahr, P. R. (2010). Preparing the underprepared: An analysis of racial disparities in postsecondary mathematics remediation. *The Journal of Higher Education, 81*(2), 209–237.

Bailey, M. J., & Dynarski, S. M. (2011). Gains and gaps: Changing inequality in U.S. college entry and completion. In G. Duncan & R. J. Murnane (Eds.), *Whither opportunity? Rising inequality and the uncertain life chances of low-income children* (pp. 118–131). New York: Russell Sage Foundation.

Bailey, T. R., Badway, N., & Gumport, P. (2003). *For-profit higher education and community colleges*. New York: Columbia University.

Bailey, T. R., Jeong, D. W., & Cho, S.-W. (2010). Referral, enrollment, and completion in developmental education sequences in community colleges. *Economics of Education Review, 29*(2), 255–270.

Bailey, T. R., Jaggars, S. S., & Jenkins, D. (2015). *Redesigning America's community colleges: A clearer path to student success*. Cambridge, MA: Harvard University Press.

Bailey, T. R., Jenkins, D., Fink, J., Cullinane, J., & Schudde, L. (2016). *Policy levers to strengthen community college transfer student success in Texas: Report to the greater Texas foundation*. New York: Community College Research Center.

Bastedo, M., & Jaquette, O. (2011). Running in place: Low-income students and the dynamics of higher education stratification. *Educational Evaluation and Policy Analysis, 33*, 318–339. https://doi.org/10.3102/0162373711406718.

Bettinger, E., & Long, B. T. (2004). *Shape up or ship out: The effect of remediation on underprepared students at four-year colleges* (NBER Working Paper Series, (10369)). Cambridge, MA: National Bureau of Economic Research.

Boatman, A., & Long, B. T. (2010). *Does remediation work for all students? How the effects of postsecondary remedial and developmental courses vary by level of academic preparation* (An NCPR Working Paper). Retrieved from http://files.eric.ed.gov/fulltext/ED512610.pdf

Bound, J., Lovenheim, M., & Turner, S. (2010). Why have college completion rates declined? An analysis of changing student preparation and collegiate resources. *American Economic Journal: Applied Economics, 2*(3), 129–157. https://doi.org/10.1257/app.2.3.129.

Bragg, D. D. (2001). Community college access, mission, and outcomes: Considering intriguing intersections and challenges. *Peabody Journal of Education, 76*(1), 93–116.

Bragg, D. D., Kim, E., & Barnett, E. A. (2006). Creating access and success: Academic pathways reaching underserved students. *New Directions for Community Colleges, 2006*(135), 5–19.

Breen, R., Choi, S., & Holm, A. (2015). Heterogeneous causal effects and sample selection bias. *Sociological Science, 2*, 351–369.

Brint, S. (2003). Few remaining dreams: Community colleges since 1985. *The Annals of the American Academy of Political and Social Science, 586*, 16–37.

Brint, S., & Karabel, J. (1989). *The diverted dream: Community colleges and the promise of educational opportunity in America, 1900–1985*. New York: Oxford University Press.

Butler, S. M. (2015). *Obama's SOTU free college plan is bad for poor Americans*. Retrieved from http://www.brookings.edu/research/opinions/2015/01/20-obama-free-community-college-bad-idea-sotu-butler

Cahalan, M., Perna, L., Yamashita, M., Ruiz, R., & Franklin, K. (2016). *Indicators of higher education equity in the United States: 2016 historical trend report*. Retrieved from http://www.pellinstitute.org/downloads/publications-Indicators_of_Higher_Education_Equity_in_the_US_2016_Historical_Trend_Report.pdf

Calcagno, J. C., & Long, B. T. (2008). *The impact of postsecondary remediation using a regression discontinuity approach: Addressing endogenous sorting and noncompliance* (NBER Working Paper Series, (14194)). Cambridge, MA: National Bureau of Economic Research.

Carnegie Foundation for the Advancement of Teaching. (2010). *Size and setting classification: Distribution of institutions and enrollments by classification category*. Stanford: Carnegie Foundation.

Census.gov. (2013). *Table A-7: College enrollment of students 14 years old and over, by type of college, attendance status, age, and gender; October 1970 to 2013*. Retrieved from http://www.census.gov/hhes/school/data/cps/historical/

Cho, S.-W., & Karp, M. (2013). Student success courses in the community college: Early enrollment and educational outcomes. *Community College Review, 41*(1), 86–103.

Clark, B. (1960a). The cooling-out function in higher education. *The American Journal of Sociology, 65*(6), 569–576. https://doi.org/10.1086/222787.

Clark, B. (1960b). *The open door college: A case study*. New York: McGraw-Hill.

Clark, B. (1980). The "cooling-out" function revisited. *New Directions for Community Colleges, 8*(32), 15.

Cohen, A. M., Brawer, F. B., & Kisker, C. B. (2014). *The American community college* (6th ed.). San Francisco: Jossey-Bass.

Deil-Amen, R. (2011). Socio-academic integrative moments: Rethinking academic and social integration among two-year college students in career-related programs. *The Journal of Higher Education, 82*(1), 54–91.

Deil-Amen, R., & Rosenbaum, J. E. (2002). The unintended consequences of stigma-free remediation. *Sociology of Education, 75*(3), 249–268.

Deil-Amen, R., & Rosenbaum, J. (2003). The social prerequisites of success: Can college structure reduce the need for social know-how? *The Annals of the American Academy of Political and Social Science, 580*, 120–143. https://doi.org/10.1177/0002716202250216.

Deming, D. J., Goldin, C., & Katz, L. F. (2012). The for-profit postsecondary school sector: Nimble critters or agile predators? *Journal of Economic Perspectives, 26*(1), 139–164. https://doi.org/10.1257/jep.26.1.139.

Denning, J. T. (2017). College on the cheap: Consequences of community college tuition reductions. *American Economic Journal: Economic Policy, 9*(2), 155–188.

DiPrete, T. A., & Buchmann, C. (2013). *The rise of women: The growing gender gap in education and what it means for American schools*. New York: Russell Sage Foundation.

Dougherty, K. (1992). Community colleges and baccalaureate attainment. *The Journal of Higher Education, 63*(2), 188–214. https://doi.org/10.2307/1982159.

Dougherty, K. (1994). *The contradictory college: The conflicting origins, impacts, and futures of the community college*. Albany: Suny Press.

Doyle, W. R. (2009). The effect of community college enrollment on bachelor's degree completion. *Economics of Education Review, 28*(2), 199–206.

driveto55.org. (2015). *Tennessee reconnect*. Retrieved from http://driveto55.org/initiatives/tennessee-reconnect/

Dual enrollment in Texas: State policies that strengthen new pathways to and through college for low-income youth (testimony of Joel Vargas). (2010). Joint Interim Hearing before Senate Higher Education Committee and Denate Education Committee on Dual Credit, Austin, TX.

Francis, D. (2015). *Populist, not progressive*. Retrieved from https://www.insidehighered.com/views/2015/09/11/proposals-make-public-college-free-are-regressive-not-progressive-essay

Friedel, J. N., & Wilson, S. L. (2015). The new reverse transfer: A national landscape. *Community College Journal of Research and Practice, 39*(1), 70–86.

Goffman, E. (1952). On cooling the mark out. *Psychiatry, 15*, 451–463.

Goldrick-Rab, S. (2006). Following their every move: An investigation of social-class differences in college pathways. *Sociology of Education, 79*(1), 67–79. https://doi.org/10.1177/003804070607900104.

Goldrick-Rab, S. (2016). *Paying the price: College costs, financial aid, and the betrayal of the American dream*. Chicago: University of Chicago Press.

Goldrick-Rab, S., & Kendall, N. (2014). *Redefining college affordability: Securing America's future with a free two year college option*. Retrieved from http://wihopelab.com/publications/Redefining_College_Affordability.pdf

Goldrick-Rab, S., & Pfeffer, F. T. (2009). Beyond access: Explaining socioeconomic differences in college transfer. *Sociology of Education, 82*(2), 101–125. https://doi.org/10.1177/003804070908200201.

Goldrick-Rab, S., Schudde, L., & Stampen, J. (2014). Making college affordable: Rethinking voucher-driven approaches to federal student aid. In A. Kelly & S. Goldrick-Rab (Eds.), *Reinventing financial aid: Charting a new course to college affordability*. Cambridge, MA: Harvard Education Press.

Goldrick-Rab, S., Kelchen, R., Harris, D. N., & Benson, J. (2016). Reducing income inequality in educational attainment: Experimental evidence on the impact of financial aid on college completion. *American Journal of Sociology, 121*(6), 1762–1817. https://doi.org/10.1086/685442.

Gonzalez, A., & Hilmer, M. J. (2006). The role of 2-year colleges in the improving situation of Hispanic postsecondary education. *Economics of Education Review, 25*(3), 249–257.

Goodman, J., Hurwitz, M., & Smith, J. (2015). *College access, initial college choice and degree completion* (National Bureau of Economic Research, (20996)). Cambridge, MA: National Bureau of Economic Research.

Handel, S. J., & Williams, R. A. (2012). *The promise of the transfer pathway: Opportunity and challenge for community college students seeking the baccalaureate degree*. Retrieved from http://www.jkcf.org/assets/1/7/promise_of_the_transfer_pathway.pdf

Haveman, R. H., & Smeeding, T. M. (2006). The role of higher education in social mobility. *The Future of Children, 16*(2), 125–150.

Hoffman, N., Vargas, J., & Santos, J. (2008). *On ramp to college: A state policymaker's guide to dual enrollment*. Retrieved from http://www.jff.org/publications/ramp-college-state-policymakers-guide-dual-enrollment

Hood, L., Hunt, E., & Haeffele, L. M. (2009). Illinois post-secondary transfer students: Experiences in navigating the higher education transfer system. *Planning and Changing, 40*(1/2), 116.

Horn, L., & Skomsvold, P. (2011). *Web tables: Community college student outcomes, 1994–2009* (NCES publication 2012–253). Washington, DC: National Center for Education Statistics.

Hossler, D., Shapiro, D., Dundar, A., Ziskin, M., Chen, J., Zerquera, D., & Torres, V. (2012). *Transfer & mobility: A national view of pre-degree student movement in postsecondary institutions*. Herndon: National Student Clearinghouse Research Center.

Jenkins, D., Kadlec, A., & Votruba, J. (2014). *Maximizing resources for student success: The business case for regional public universities to strengthen communtiy college transfer pathways*. Retrieved from http://hcmstrategists.com/maximizingresources/images/Transfer_Pathways_Paper.pdf

Kalogrides, D., & Grodsky, E. (2011). Something to fall back on: Community colleges as a safety net. *Social Forces, 89*(3), 853–878.

Kolodner, M. (2015, November 4). *Alabama offers high school students—and their parents—tuition-free community college*. The Hechinger report. Retrieved from http://hechingerreport.org/alabama-offers-high-school-students-and-their-parents-tuition-free-community-college/

Labaree, D. (2013). A system without a plan: Emergence of an American system of higher education in the twentieth century. *Bildungsgeschichte. International Journal for the Historiography of education, 3*(1), 46–59.

Leigh, D. E., & Gill, A. M. (2003). Do community colleges really divert students from earning bachelor's degrees? *Economics of Education Review, 22*(1), 23–30.

Leigh, D. E., & Gill, A. M. (2004). The effect of community colleges on changing students' educational aspirations. *Economics of Education Review, 23*(1), 95–102.

Long, B. T., & Kurlaender, M. (2009). Do community colleges provide a viable pathway to a baccalaureate degree? *Educational Evaluation and Policy Analysis, 31*(1), 30–53.

Martorell, P., & McFarlin, I., Jr. (2011). Help or hindrance? The effects of college remediation on academic and labor market outcomes. *The Review of Economics and Statistics, 93*(2), 436–454.

Monaghan, D. B., & Attewell, P. (2015). The community college route to the bachelor's degree. *Educational Evaluation and Policy Analysis, 37*(1), 70–91.

Museus, S. D., Lutovsky, B. R., & Colbeck, C. L. (2007). Access and equity in dual enrollment programs: Implications for policy formation. *Higher Education in Review, 4*, 1–19.

NCES. (2014a). *Digest of education statistics 2014*. Retrieved from https://nces.ed.gov/pubsearch/pubsinfo.asp?pubid=2016006

NCES. (2014b). *Profile of undergraduate students: 2011–2012*. Retrieved from http://nces.ed.gov/pubs2015/2015167.pdf

Oregonlearns.org. (2015). *Oregon's aspirations for student attainment match the stakes*. Retrieved from http://oregonlearns.org/oregons-challenge/the-40-40-20-goal/

Pallas, A. M. (2000). The effects of schooling on individual lives. In M. Hallinan (Ed.), *Handbook of the sociology of education* (pp. 499–525). New York: Springer.

Parsad, B., & Lewis, L. (2003). *Remedial education at degree-granting postsecondary institutions in fall 2000*. Retrieved from http://nces.ed.gov/pubs2004/2004010.pdf

Pascarella, E. T., & Terenzini, P. T. (2005). *How college affects students: A third decade of research*. San Francisco: Jossey-Bass.

Patterson, O. (2014, December 1). How sociologists made themselves irrelevant. *The Chronical of Higher Education*. Retrieved from http://chronicle.com/article/How-Sociologists-Made/150249

Person, A., Rosenbaum, J., & Deil-Amen, R. (2006). Student planning and information problems in different college structures. *The Teachers College Record, 108*(3), 374–396.

Provasnik, S., & Planty, M. (2008). *Community colleges: Special supplement to the condition of education statistics 2008*. Washington, DC: National Center for Education Statistics.

Radford, A., & Horn, L. (2012). *Web tables: An overview of classes taken and credits earned by beginning postsecondary students*. Washington, DC: National Center for Education Statistics.

Reardon, S. F., & Bischoff, K. (2011). Income inequality and income segregation. *American Journal of Sociology, 116*(4), 1092–1153.

Reyes, P., Alexander, C., & Gu, X. (2016). *Texas reverse transfer initiative*. Paper presented at the Texas Higher Education Symposium, Austin, TX.

Reynolds, C. L. (2012). Where to attend? Estimating the effects of beginning college at a two-year institution. *Economics of Education Review, 31*(4), 345–362.

Reynolds, J., Stewart, M., MacDonald, R., & Sischo, L. (2006). Have adolescents become too ambitious? High school seniors' educational and occupational plans, 1976 to 2000. *Social Problems, 53*(2), 186–206.

Roderick, M., Nagaoka, J., & Coca, V. (2009). College readiness for all: The challenge for urban high schools. *The Future of Children, 19*(1), 185–210.

Roksa, J., & Keith, B. (2008). Credits, time, and attainment: Articulation policies and success after transfer. *Educational Evaluation and Policy Analysis, 30*(3), 236–254.

Roksa, J., Grodsky, E., Arum, R., & Gamoran, A. (2007). Changes in higher education and social stratification in the United States. In Y. Shavit, R. Arum, & A. Gamoran (Eds.), *Stratification in higher education* (pp. 165–191). Palo Alto: Stanford University Press.

Root, M. (2013). *Essential elements of state policy for college completion*. Retrieved from Atlanta, GA: Southern Regional Education Board.

Rosenbaum, J. E. (2001). *Beyond college for all*. New York: Russell Sage Foundation.

Rosenbaum, J. E., Deil-Amen, R., & Person, A. E. (2007). *After admission: From college access to college success*. New York: Russell Sage Foundation.

Rosenbaum, J. E., Ahearn, C., Becker, K., & Rosenbaum, J. (2015). *The new forgotten half and research directions to support them*. New York: William T. Grant Foundation.

Rouse, C. E. (1995). Democratization or diversion? The effect of community colleges on educational attainment. *Journal of Business & Economic Statistics, 13*(2), 217–224.

Saw, G. (2016). *Reducing or reinforcing inequality? Evaluating the impact of postsecondary remediation on college outcomes*. Dissertation, Michigan State University, East Lansing

Schneider, B., & Stevenson, D. (2000). *The ambitious generation America's teenagers, motivated but directionless*. New Haven: Yale University Press.

Schudde, L., & Goldrick-Rab, S. (2016). Extending opportunity, perpetuating privilege: Institutional stratification amid educational expansion. In M. Bastedo, P. G. Altbach, & P. Gumport (Eds.), *American higher education in the 21st century* (4th ed.). Baltimore: Johns Hopkins University Press.

Schudde, L., & Scott-Clayton, J. (2016). Pell grants as performance-based scholarships? An examination of satisfactory academic progress requirements in the nation's largest need-based aid program. *Research in Higher Education, 57*, 1–25.

Scott-Clayton, J. (2011). *The shapeless river: Does a lack of structure inhibit students' progress at Communtiy College?* (CCRC Working Paper). New York: Community College Research Center.

Scott-Clayton, J., & Belfield, C. (2015). *Improving the accuracy of remedial placement*. New York: Community College Research Center.

Scott-Clayton, J., & Rodriguez, O. (2014). Development, discouragement, or diversion? New evidence on the effects of college remediation policy. *Education Finance and Policy, 10*, 4–45.

Scott-Clayton, J., & Rodriguez, O. (2015). Development, discouragement, or diversion: New evidence on the effects of college remediation policy. *Education Finance and Policy, 10*(1), 4–45.

Scott-Clayton, J., Crosta, P. M., & Belfield, C. R. (2014). Improving the targeting of treatment evidence from college remediation. *Educational Evaluation and Policy Analysis, 36*(3), 371–393.

Scrivener, S., & Weiss, M. J. (2009, August). *More guidance, better results? Three-year effects of an enhanced student services program at two community colleges*. New York: MDRC.

Scrivener, S., Weiss, M. J., Ratledge, A., Rudd, T., Sommo, C., & Fresques, H. (2015, February). *Doubling graduation rates: Three-year effects of CUNY's Accelerated Study in Associate Programs (ASAP) for developmental education students*. New York: MDRC.

Shapiro, D., Dundar, A., Wakhungu, P. K., Yuan, X., & Harrell, A. T. (2015). *Transfer and mobility: A national view of student movement in postsecondary institutions, fall 2008 Cohort*. Herndon: National Student Clearinghouse Research Center.

Snyder, T. D., & Dillow, S. A. (2012). *Digest of education statistics 2011*. Washington, DC: National Center for Education Statistics.

Sparks, D., & Malkus, N. (2013). *Table 270: Percentage of first-year undergraduate students who took remedial education courses, by selected student and institution characteristics: 2003–04 and 2007–08 Digest of Education Statistics 2012*. Washington, DC: National Center for Education Statistics, Institute of Education Sciences, U.S. Department of Education.

Speroni, C. (2011). *Determinants of students' success: The role of advanced placement and dual enrollment programs* (An NCPR Working Paper). New York: National Center for Postsecondary Research.

Staklis, S., Bersudskaya, V., & Horn, L. (2012). *Students attending for-profit postsecondary institutions: demographics, enrollment characteristics, and 6-year outcomes*. Washington, DC: National Center for Education Statistics.

Stoltzfus, K. (2015, December 21). *As plans for free community college spread, educators seek to include adult learners*. The Chronicle of Higher Education.

THECB. (2014). *Improving transfer to increase student success*. Austin: The Texas Higher Education Coordinating Board.

THECB. (2015). *Draft of the next higher education strategic plan for Texas*. Austin: The Texas Higher Education Coordinating Board. Retrieved from http://www.thecb.state.tx.us/reports/PDF/6584.PDF?CFID=26748433&CFTOKEN=34632987

Tierney, W. (2011). Too big to fail: The role of for-profit colleges and universities in American higher education. *Change, 43*(6), 27–32.

Tierney, W. (2015). *Why free college tuition is a bad idea: Water and college*. Retrieved from http://21stcenturyscholar.org/2015/01/13/why-free-college-tuition-is-a-bad-idea-water-and-college/

Velez, W. (1985). Finishing college: The effects of college type. *Sociology of Education, 58*(3), 191–200. https://doi.org/10.2307/2112419.

Whitehouse.gov. (2011). *Meeting the nation's 2020 goal: State targets for increasing the number and percentage of college graduates with degrees*. Retrieved from https://www.whitehouse.gov/sites/default/files/completion_state_by_state.pdf

Whitehouse.gov. (2015). *Fact sheet—White House unveils America's college promise proposal: Tuition-free community college for responsible students*. Retrieved from https://www.whitehouse.gov/the-press-office/2015/01/09/fact-sheet-white-house-unveils-america-s-college-promise-proposal-tuitio

Wolfers, J. (2015). How economists came to dominate the conversation. *The New York Times*, p. A3. Retrieved from http://www.nytimes.com/2015/01/24/upshot/how-economists-came-to-dominate-the-conversation.html?_r=0

Xu, D., Jaggars, S. S., & Fletcher, J. (2016, April). *How and why does two-year college entry influence baccalaureate aspirants' academic and labor market outcomes?* New York: Community College Research Center.

College-for-All: Alternative Options and Procedures

19

James E. Rosenbaum, Caitlin Ahearn, and Jennifer Lansing

Abstract

This chapter discusses how the status attainment model has been integral to our understanding of the factors affecting average educational attainment, but it poorly describes institutional procedures and individual strategies that lead to academic success. We pose new issues for understanding the experiences of the growing populations of disadvantaged students in open-admissions 2-year colleges. We describe the experiences of individuals from a small study to provide evidence of how disadvantaged students manage to beat the odds and attain educational success. While we cannot address issues of generalizability, we describe alternative sequences and pathways to educational attainment, institutional supports and procedures, and their self-identified sources of direction, despite the major obstacles and setbacks. We situate our cases in prior extensions of the status attainment model to consider alternative mechanisms to educational attainment. These analyses are crucial if we are to understand the dynamic processes that drive educational attainment despite major obstacles.

J. Lansing · J. E. Rosenbaum (✉)
Northwestern University, Evanston, IL, USA
e-mail: j-rosenbaum@northwestern.edu

C. Ahearn
University of California, Los Angeles, CA, USA
e-mail: cahearn3@ucla.edu

19.1 Introduction

As Durkheim (1961) emphasized, society faces a serious challenge in ensuring the next generation of youth is able to assume productive adult roles. This is obvious, but it doesn't happen automatically. Although stable traditional societies do this easily, it has become problematic in a dynamically changing society where the labor market demands higher skills. Many individuals lack requisite skills; therefore, they get excluded from decent jobs, and social and economic inequality dramatically increases.

In recent decades, our society has made college access a central component of preparing youth for adult roles *and* reducing poverty (Goldrick-Rab 2016, chapter 10). College is seen as the most dependable route to a promising financial future for both individuals and society. The United States has a deep faith in the "education gospel," where college is expected to fulfill a variety of societal needs, including economic prosperity, improved health, and reduced crime (Grubb and Lazerson 2004).

Assuming that high educational plans lead to high educational achievement, reform organizations, educators, and policymakers heavily promote college plans for all students. This college emphasis has reached all corners of society, and students have responded. By the 1990s, over 90% of high school seniors planned to attend college, 80% of high school graduates actually attended

© Springer International Publishing AG, part of Springer Nature 2018
B. Schneider (ed.), *Handbook of the Sociology of Education in the 21st Century*, Handbooks of Sociology and Social Research, https://doi.org/10.1007/978-3-319-76694-2_19

college, and Black, White, and Hispanic high school graduates attended college at similar rates (Adelman 2003). The upward trend in college enrollment has continued, and 90% of the graduating class of 2004 enrolled in college within 8 years (Rosenbaum et al. 2016). If we consider enrollment in this extended window, White, Black, and Hispanic high school graduates continue to enroll at similar rates (ibid.).

Despite high levels of enrollment, large disparities in graduation occur. College degrees are less likely for students who are low-income, belong to a racial minority group, are academically underprepared, or begin in less selective colleges (Ahearn et al. 2016). For those who start at 4-year colleges, one-third of students fail to get BA degrees, including over 50% of students in the bottom third of SES. For those who enter community colleges, success is more rare: only 21% get BA degrees and only 14% of low-SES students do so. As the costs associated with attending college rise, low-income and even middle-income students and their families struggle to make it through (Goldrick-Rab 2016).

Consistent with the status attainment model, research finds that student characteristics (achievement level, socioeconomic status, racial privilege, and age) and student choices (major, college type, work, enrollment intensity, and extracurricular engagement) contribute to completion rates and earnings of community college students (Dougherty 1994; Buchmann and DiPrete 2006; Hout 2012; Goldrick-Rab and Pfeffer 2009; Schudde and Goldrick-Rab 2014; Jacobson and Mokher 2009). Others have studied social, economic, and psychological motivations for "cooling out" (lowering) and "warming up" (increasing) educational plans in 2-year colleges (Clark 1960; Deterding 2015; Alexander et al. 2008). Students with academic or economic disadvantages are especially at risk of dropping out of college (Taniguchi and Kaufman 2005). These various lines of scholarship have been critical to understanding the obstacles to student success in open-access 2-year colleges.

Despite all we know about the predictors of college attainment, community college is the main avenue for opportunity for disadvantaged youth. Yet completion remains low, while aspirations remain high. Many students entering college have vague plans about completing graduate degrees, but very few accomplish that goal (Bailey et al. 2015). In contrast, some students do, in fact, manage to exceed expectations and even complete graduate degrees after enrolling in 2-year programs in open-access colleges. We must wonder: *How do they do it?*

The usual way sociologists analyze these issues, the status attainment model, identifies predictors of educational and occupational status. But, it fails to consider many important alternative options, procedures, and sources of direction, so it conveys a narrow conception of opportunity. To broaden the perspective, our research identifies three alternative processes. First, while the status attainment model focuses on a few credential options and event sequences, we identify *many alternative college options and strategies*. Second, while the status attainment model ignores operational practices in colleges, we identify *alternative institutional procedures* including non-standard programs and practices. Third, although driven by student choices, the status attainment model does not consider *alternative ways to inform direction* about education and career. Students need to see alternative options, alternative procedures, and well-conceived plans to translate vague educational goals into tangible occupational attainments (Schneider and Stevenson 1999). Models that stress "free choice" often ignore how students can make "informed choices" among alternatives that are often unseen. Together, these elements pose new perspectives to improve our understanding of education's role in social mobility, and how youth, especially disadvantaged youth, can succeed despite facing major obstacles.

Going beyond the numbers and correlates, we need to understand what strategies help students in non-selective colleges overcome the usual disadvantages and attain high educational success. This chapter will describe alternative processes that respondents find to have helped them. Instead of blaming students' difficulties on personal deficiencies, we explore how research can identify alternative social contexts that can enable success for disadvantaged students. We are not the first to examine students who beat the odds of educational attainment (Newman and Winston 2016; Attewell and Lavin 2007). While some of these topics have been addressed in prior educational attainment research, we discover alternative options and procedures which extend traditional models and open new avenues for opportunity. Although rarely considered, these alternatives suggest student and school strategies that can reduce or avoid the usual obstacles. We consider these as extensions of the status attainment model. These alternatives are overlooked in the literature, but respondents describe how they support their persistence and degree completion despite obstacles they face as non-traditional students.

We discover these strategies in interviews with non-traditional students who completed an associate degree, and then went on to complete bachelor's and master's degrees. These graduates are taken from a larger sample of 160 associate degree graduates from private and public 2-year colleges. To consider individuals who are clearly educational successes, we focus on a small subsample (11 respondents) who are remarkable for their attainment of a master's degree within 7 years after attaining an associate degree. Despite their small number, we also see similar strategies in the larger group who attained BA degrees (n = 60). Moreover, their experiences provide some insight into the experiences of non-traditional students with the odds against them, and how alternative strategies enable disadvantaged students to succeed. Open-admissions colleges have grown rapidly, and they offer many new credentials and majors. If we wish to understand how low-income individuals manage to succeed in these new contexts, we must study individuals' experiences and strategies. While the status attainment model describes the traditional attainment process, we suspect that these extensions grew out of new college-for-all policies and the new college reality that has emerged.

The chapter begins with an overview of traditional educational attainment research. We emphasize literature that has improved our understanding of non-traditional students and open-access institutions. We then outline three extensions to traditional attainment models that broaden our understanding of how students achieve high educational success despite large challenges. While traditional explanations view students' personal disadvantages as causing their outcomes, we describe features of the college context that shape students' opportunities and outcomes, even for students who face many obstacles.

19.1.1 Poverty Creates Obstacles to Opportunity

A recent study by Jennifer Silva (2013) provides focus on key issues that we must consider. Silva presents a detailed analysis of working-class emerging adults, describing with disheartening clarity the modern obstacles to escaping poverty and the relentless barriers confronting low-wage earners in the United States. Extending and updating an extensive body of prior research (Borman 1991; Sennett and Cobb 1972; Newman 1999, 2006), Silva elaborates how young working-class adults have redefined adulthood as the attainment of traditional markers (marriage, stable employment, and home ownership) have become increasingly elusive. She describes how many young adults have tried and repeatedly failed to gain traction in the labor market or in completing a college degree. She explains that they took initiatives towards self-improvement, made sacrifices, and withstood significant hardships pursuing their goals, but their efforts rarely worked as intended because of powerful social and structural forces working against them. A few isolated cases achieved success, she argues, because they had unusual advantages rarely available to low-income youth, such as social capital in the form of a wealthier or well-connected friend or relative. Silva's study shows the destructiveness of compounded disadvantages, which pose challenges at every turn, and which prevent temporary successes from turning into permanent improvements. Her descriptions are heartbreaking and repeatedly contradict common myths about how initiative and effort are rewarded in U.S. society. From Silva's account, we get an understanding of the reality that working-class young adults cannot always succeed from their own efforts.

Silva's qualitative work and that of others before her reinforces what we know from prior research. It shows the many ways failure occurs, but it says nothing about successes. However, quantitative research using the status attainment model provides a more complicated picture of social mobility. American society is complex and diverse, and quantitative research indicates that, while it is difficult and less common, some low-SES individuals do manage to attain educational and economic success. In fact, quantitative work not only reminds us that such success is possible, but also that disadvantaged students may have more to gain from educational success than their advantaged peers (Hout 2012). Unfortunately, such quantitative studies do not typically consider what allows these unlikely successes to occur, making their replication even more difficult. Moreover, despite her close examination of individuals' experiences, Silva does not examine the options and procedures within colleges which impact students' outcomes. When they fail, she rightly blames the college, but it is not clear what the college is doing that contributes to failures or what alternatives exist that might lead to success. We seek to understand how a sample of working-class individuals achieved educational success.

19.1.2 The Status Attainment Model and Traditional Educational Attainment Models

Created at the University of Wisconsin in the 1960s, the original status attainment model argued that father's education and occupational status, and son's cognitive ability predict the son's educational attainment and subsequently adult occupational prestige (Sewell and Hauser 1975). A simple model, it has nonetheless been important to the sociology of education in providing a framework to explain how socioeconomic background interacts with individual attributes to predict educational and occupational

outcomes (ibid.; Blau and Duncan 1967; Sirin 2005). It has been particularly helpful in a few applications.

First, the status attainment model has allowed researchers to examine differential outcomes based on student attributes and experiences. Gender differences provide a relatively straightforward example. This has been an area of great interest since the 1960s when Sewell and Shah demonstrated that women had lower educational plans and completion than men (1967). That early research described a baseline that permitted later research to see dramatic change. Recent research has demonstrated a dramatic reversal of this trend. Social and political factors have led to female students outperforming their male counterparts in K–12 education, and women now have a greater likelihood of college completion (Buchmann and DiPrete 2006). However, women continue to receive lower earnings, especially after accounting for their higher educational attainment. The model further allows research to analyze racial–gender interactions, and studies have found that Black and Hispanic women are at particular disadvantage in the labor market (Browne and Misra 2003).

Second, the status attainment model has been important for understanding the growing need for higher education to achieve economic success. In the past 12 years, bachelor's degrees have increased by 44% and associate degrees and college-level certificates have increased by 78% (Kena et al. 2014). In addition, all college credentials, including college-level certificates, now have significant economic payoffs relative to a high school diploma (Rosenbaum et al. 2016; Belfield and Bailey 2011). Sociologists and economists have noted that the returns to education have been growing for decades, and there is abundant evidence that society more generally benefits from a more educated population (Oreopoulous and Petronijevic 2013; Hout 2012; Goldin and Katz 2008). A high school diploma, on the other hand, commands low earnings and poor career trajectories (Rosenbaum et al. 2016). Indeed, many high school seniors who planned not to attend college later decide to attend college after a few years in the labor market (ibid.). This line of research has been instrumental in the expansion of college-for-all and emphasized the need to study educational attainment processes.

Finally, and most important for our purposes, the model asserts that more privileged youth (higher parental education and occupational status) attain the most education (Warren 2001). The extent to which this occurs has fluctuated since WWII, with some periods of more opportunity. Recent decades have seen increasing influence of social background on educational attainment (Bills 2004; Gamoran 2014). Even with high college enrollment, first-generation college students and students with working-class parents continue to be thwarted in their attempts to attain college degrees, facing social, financial, and institutional barriers to completion (Rosenbaum et al. 2016; Armstrong and Hamilton 2015; Goldrick-Rab 2016). Disadvantaged high school students who are coming from poor or working-class homes do not receive adequate preparation, advising, and resources to succeed at 4-year bachelor's degrees (Deil-Amen and DeLuca 2010; Lareau 2000).

19.1.3 Non-traditional Students in Non-traditional Pathways

Educational attainment research has also discussed the disadvantage of being a "non-traditional" student. When most Americans picture a college student, they imagine a young person living on a beautiful 4-year university campus, participating in social clubs, attending sporting events, and taking advantage of many educational opportunities. Yet, residential students enrolled full-time at 4-year colleges make up only one quarter of all students enrolled in higher education (Tinto 2012). This means that the vast majority of college students are, in some way, "non-traditional," for whom we must question our traditional assumptions.

Educational attainment models generally conceptualize students as non-traditional if they are older, or take time off between high school and college. However, research has considered many other groups who are non-traditional—enrolled part-time, financially independent, working full-time, raised by single parents, or GED-holders (Horn and Carroll 1996). Non-traditional students, especially those enrolled part-time or who have young children, are much less likely than their peers to reach degree completion (Bean and Metzner 1985; Taniguchi and Kaufman 2005).

Non-traditional students are often low-income and minority students, and, like them, they are more likely to be enrolled in 2-year colleges, making up 45% of public 2-year colleges and 58–65% of private 2-year colleges (Rosenbaum et al. 2016; Kena et al. 2015; Holland and DeLuca 2016). In fact, beginning at a 2-year college has, in and of itself, been called a "non-traditional pathway" (Gerber and Cheung 2008). Although only a minor segment of higher education 50 years ago, open-access colleges (public 2-year colleges, private for-profit colleges, and some not-for-profit 2- and 4-year colleges) have grown in recent decades. These sectors now enroll close to 50% of all undergraduate students (NCES 2015, table 303.70). Although they don't resemble our idyllic vision of college, these colleges are a typical choice for many disadvantaged students. Yet the dramatic growth in non-traditional students raises further questions about how they cope with these 2-year open-access institutions, especially if they use traditional procedures.

Most students in the non-selective college sector are in public community colleges, which enroll 37% of all undergraduates who are recent high school graduates (ibid.). Community colleges were created to provide more accessible and affordable higher educational opportunities, and they have succeeded impressively. Students flock to community colleges for their low tuition, local campuses, flexible schedules, and open admissions. For these reasons, community colleges disproportionately serve non-traditional, low-income, and underrepresented students. Non-traditional students in community colleges may have full-time jobs or dependents, and they appreciate the low-cost, convenience, and low barriers to enrollment at community colleges (Rosenbaum et al. 2006; Stephan and Rosenbaum 2009; Perna 2010). Community colleges serve students with a range of goals, offering both associate degrees and certificates, as well as single-course options for students with no degree goal. Students have a variety of program options, from academic BA-transfer programs to occupational programs. Occupational programs prepare students for immediate employment in a wide range of high-demand fields such as computer technology, business, auto mechanics, and healthcare.

Non-selective private colleges, including both for-profit and non-profit, are a second type of open-access college. The number of students in non-selective private colleges has grown dramatically in the past two decades, from 2% to currently 10% of total undergraduate enrollment (Deming et al. 2012). While they serve a similar population of students as community colleges (Stephan and Rosenbaum 2009), private non-selective colleges serve greater numbers of older and minority students and their students are more likely to be enrolled full-time (Kena et al. 2015; Deming et al. 2012). With aggressive marketing techniques and convenient, often online, courses, private non-selective colleges have attracted students with appealing career promises, which community colleges often don't emphasize.

Although mired in controversy, and some convicted of fraudulent claims, some private non-selective colleges have a strong reputation in the labor market. Prior research indicates that some private non-selective colleges use innovative procedures designed to meet the needs of disadvantaged students (Rosenbaum et al. 2006). These procedures are often "sociologically smart," adjusting demands, schedules, advising, and job search to meet students' needs, not adhering to traditional college norms. Indeed, they focus on expanding students' options, providing supportive procedures, and leading not just to higher earnings but also to rewarding careers (Rosenbaum and Rosenbaum 2013). Private non-selective colleges have higher completion rates for associate degrees and certificates than public community colleges (Deming et al. 2012; Stephan et al. 2009).

The distinctive approaches to student success in these colleges are examples that other colleges and researchers can learn from. While some non-selective private colleges offer 4-year degrees, most primarily offer 1- or 2-year credentials. In this chapter, we refer to these colleges and community colleges collectively as 2-year open-access colleges.

Non-traditional students face many barriers, and non-traditional college pathways are often a common choice because they reduce such barriers. In our interviews with highly successful non-traditional students in 2-year open-access colleges, we discover alternatives to traditional attainment models. All respondents completed degrees at non-selective 2-year colleges, some are older, some have children, none live on campus, and many combine full-time work with full- or part-time college. Most are from working-class families, many did not do well in high school, and many are racial minorities.

However, while we note that their circumstances make it difficult for them to complete traditional higher education, we emphasize that non-traditional is not synonymous with uncommon. The new college-for-all reality is that "non-traditional" students are a majority (Deil-Amen 2016). Their experiences are typical of a major segment of higher education, and their success is critically important to the success of college-for-all. Being a non-traditional student is not a deviant factor that must be overcome, but rather a different student identity that colleges are now serving, although colleges have often had narrow traditional ideas about how to serve these students. Nor is it clear how these students manage to cope with these colleges (Perna 2010). The big question is what alternative processes colleges can use that will better address the needs and capabilities of a new majority of non-traditional college students.

19.1.4 Alternatives to the Traditional Model in Open-Access Institutions

The status attainment model allows researchers to build an understanding of the typical predictors of educational attainment. Quantitative research has advanced the notion of maintained inequality through educational institutions.

Qualitative research has provided valuable insights into the mechanisms that drive educational inequality (Silva 2013; Armstrong and Hamilton 2015; McLeod 2008). Educational attainment research has helped scholars understand who is unlikely to graduate from college, and why.

This research tends to focus on student deficits: What student attributes or choices make it difficult to complete more education? While valuable, this research typically overlooks that some students beat the odds: students who manage to succeed in community college, bachelor's degrees, and even graduate programs (Kena et al. 2014). When they succeed, research tends to credit individuals' personal attributes. These individuals are often characterized as hard-working or lucky, without much further discussion. They are exceptions, and the emphasis is usually on the vast majority who don't make it.

Yet rare events can be very revealing. Qualitative research is particularly useful in understanding what might set the successes apart. These students might have additional assistance in the form of financial support, a highly-educated or connected family member, or membership in a selective college program designed for high-achieving students from low socioeconomic backgrounds (Silva 2013; Armstrong and Hamilton 2015). However, our sample mostly lacks such features, so they demand further study.

Such research can be instrumental for policy reforms. Qualitative research can explore ways that individuals leverage institutions and personal experiences to succeed despite poor odds. This knowledge can lead to policy initiatives to further support disadvantaged students and to diminish the power of the obstacles they face. This is of critical importance as we attempt to "move the needle" on college completion, which has remained stubbornly low for years (Bailey et al. 2015). Studying student deficits alone cannot improve student chances at educational attainment. The options and procedures in the college context must also be examined.

Our sample highlights individuals who beat the odds. Traditional models would predict low odds for this group to achieve even BA degrees,

and indeed they face major obstacles (full-time work, child-care, family emergencies, financial difficulties) that accompany working-class lives. However, their educational success in spite of such obstacles makes their experiences worthy of investigation. We use these cases to bolster prior literature in extending and developing strategies of studying student success. Of course, these individuals were hard-working and dedicated to their studies, but those qualities alone were not sufficient. We noted ways these individuals used alternative options and procedures that they considered important for their successes.

19.2 Three Extensions to Educational Attainment Models

The rest of this chapter is devoted to discussing three extensions to the traditional educational attainment model. Elements of these can be seen in prior literature on educational attainment. However, they remain largely at the margins of prior models. We bring them into the foreground to show that they are strategies students and schools can and do use that enable disadvantaged students to cope with typical college challenges and succeed at completing college credentials. Improving non-traditional student persistence and attainment requires identifying alternative options and procedures that are available but rarely seen, understanding the processes by which non-traditional students can successfully see and use these alternatives, and learning about what institutions can do to support them. We describe three broad strategies that are useful to students who share the constraints and circumstances of non-traditional students. Our sample provides insight into potential strategies that are rarely noticed as important for students' college success. We briefly describe the three extensions here before going into more detail.

First, *alternative options and strategies* can overcome obstacles that prevent progress in the orderly transitions from high school to college to careers. Blau and Duncan (1967) recognized the problems with linear pathways from school to work. Researchers have criticized traditional models' simplification of reality, which excludes rich variation in college options, job outcomes, and life events sequences (Kerckhoff 1995; Pallas 2003; Bills 2004). We discuss alternative options created by non-traditional colleges, and we describe an incremental success strategy that reduces risks and increases degree attainment for non-traditional students.

Second, *alternative institutional procedures* can reduce obstacles and provide support for non-traditional students seeking to cross college transitions. Various types of colleges work differently, and some offer procedures to assist students who are older, work many hours, or have families (Kasworm 2010). Research has increasingly noted the importance of non-traditional college practices as higher education becomes more diverse, and suggests that non-standard programs and structures need to be studied (Rosenbaum et al. 2006; Karp 2011). We provide evidence of the importance of alternative institutional structures and how they shape and support student success at every level of education.

Third, *alternative ways to inform direction for education and careers* can aid in non-traditional students' success. Students must find direction to enter specific programs, remain motivated in those programs, and successfully transition into the workforce. Students must translate vague educational goals into tangible occupational attainments. Research has shown the difficulties students have in finding direction, translating their aspirations into specific goals and actions (Schneider and Stevenson 1999). Our respondents describe how they find direction as they combine college and work, and how direction is crucial for their success.

19.2.1 Alternative Options and Strategies

Perna (2010) notes that the linear college pipeline from high school to BA degrees to careers is no longer the norm of higher education. Moreover, she argues that educational research should not devalue those who deviate from that expectation, but it should better understand those students'

trajectories. Roksa and Velez (2012) assert that the negative outcomes for individuals who follow non-normative sequences of life events occur because students' adult roles inhibit their ability to complete degrees. They argue that with greater access and enrollment in higher education, non-normative decisions should not be dismissed, but rather examined because of their growing prevalence and the possibility that better decisions can have beneficial impact in overcoming obstacles.

We find that respondents specifically address many alternatives—alternative college choices, degree choices, and degree sequencing. We describe the incremental success model that integrates these three aspects, reduces risks of no payoffs, supports smoother transitions and greater success, and promotes further opportunities in education and careers for non-traditional students.

19.2.1.1 Alternative College Choices

Educational attainment literature often considers simply enrolling in an open-access institution as a non-traditional action, and a large body of research has explored the implications of enrolling in various types of colleges (Gerber and Cheung 2008). Generally, students who enroll in community colleges are less likely to complete any degree. Since 80% of entering college students plan to earn BA degrees, it is especially disturbing that few students attain them (Long and Kurlaender 2009; Bailey et al. 2015). Bachelor's degree attainment is further stymied for low-income and underrepresented minority students, who have the least success at making the transition from community colleges to 4-year colleges (Goldrick-Rab and Pfeffer 2009). Private non-selective college students are more likely to complete a credential than community college students, even after comparing matched students (Stephan et al. 2009; Deming et al. 2012).

Educational attainment research has increasingly examined non-normative pathways. Many students transfer not just from community colleges to 4-year colleges (and the reverse), but also laterally between institutions, and research has noted the importance of creating models that account for these moves, sometimes referred to as "swirling" (Andrews et al. 2014; Goldrick-

Rab and Pfeffer 2009). Horn and Carroll (1998) examined the predictors of student decisions to return to higher education after early failure. Calcagno et al. (2007) found that common predictors of success (credit milestones, passing "gatekeeper classes," and avoiding remedial courses) are less important for older students. Prior research by the authors has indicated that among young students, associate degrees and certificates are no less readily attained by students with low test scores and low-SES backgrounds than by average students, and these credentials confer significant labor market payoffs compared to high school, even for students who have low test scores or low-SES backgrounds (Rosenbaum et al. 2016; Wells 2008). Kalogrides and Grodsky (2011) identified the community college as a potential safety net, or a second chance institution, for those who drop out of a 4-year college, although this requires such students to have time and resources to return to college, despite prior failures.

Open-access institutions can provide second chances for students who have previously not been successful, and their low-cost convenience often make them the *only* option for many non-traditional students. Other students are drawn to occupational programs' promises of a quick job payoff despite high costs (Holland and DeLuca 2016). It is therefore important to consider how alternative educational sequences that include open-access institutions might differentially serve students.

19.2.1.2 Alternative Degree Choice and an Incremental Success Strategy

Students who find themselves in non-selective colleges have greater success at completing certificates and associate degrees than bachelor's degrees (Rosenbaum et al. 2016; Deming et al. 2012; Choy 2001). Most studies of status attainment use highest degree attained as the outcome and key educational variable. Students complete a certificate, an associate degree, a bachelor's degree, etc. and that is used to predict their occupational outcomes. This makes analyses simple, and allows models to examine degree attainment or earnings of specific credentials. Attainment

research consistently finds that the higher the degree, the higher the earnings payoffs. A certificate completer has higher average earnings than a high school graduate, an associate degree graduate has higher earnings than a certificate completer, and so on (Rosenbaum et al. 2017; Hout 2012).

However, students can and do combine various credentials. Twenty-five percent of individuals who complete certificates go on to complete higher degrees (Carnevale et al. 2012), and the rate is higher for associate to BA degrees (Rosenbaum 2012). Therefore, the highest degree attained at one point, especially for sub-baccalaureate graduates, may only be one step towards the highest final degree attained. Open-access institutions offer certificates and associate degrees in overlapping fields, which may count towards a bachelor's degree. Of course, we are used to students doing this for graduate degrees; no one can get a master's, a doctorate, or a professional degree without first completing a lower level bachelor's.

When a student completes increasingly ambitious educational goals, beginning with a certificate or associate degree and going on to higher degrees, we call this incremental success. Incremental success allows students at risk of having college interrupted to have higher odds of completing a credential, earn immediate payoffs, and then continue to the next degree, perhaps after an intermission. Essentially, it builds "backup options" into educational plans. It also does not require high ambitions from the start.

"Degree ladders" or "stacking" credentials, are procedures that increase students' options. They permit credits for lower credentials automatically to count towards the higher credential (Rosenbaum et al. 2017; Ganzglass 2014). Goldrick-Rab (2016) urges all public colleges to offer associate degrees, so that students at risk of dropping out can at least get some credential. But students can create incremental success strategies even where degree ladders don't exist, although they are rarely informed how to create such strategies.

To provide insight into the potential process of incremental success for non-traditional students, we turn to our sample of master's degree graduates, all of whom began with a modest goal of associate degree or less, and finished with at least a master's degree. Their circumstances included many complications—children, full-time jobs, returning to school after a long break—all of which made the achievement of a quick credential seem more attainable than a "4-year" degree. After their initial success, these respondents developed increasingly ambitious goals with each educational achievement. Their experiences embody our model of incremental success.

19.2.1.3 An Example of Incremental Success

Like many of their non-traditional peers, the financial pressures of our sample led them to seek occupational programs within their open-access institutions (Laanan 2000; Holland and DeLuca 2016). They were eager for a labor market payoff to support themselves and their families. All respondents but one identified a *specific occupational goal* they had in mind when beginning their degree and their reasons for choosing it. Although they had not previously aspired to a higher degree, after achieving the initial goal, their successes at school and at work gave them confidence to push themselves forward.

Asha, a mother of six, who was 41 at the time of the interview (34 when she graduated with her associate degree 7 years earlier), provides a clear example of how success can be achieved with incremental success. While working in a non-profit center for the homeless with a high school diploma, Asha pursued an associate degree in hopes of receiving more respect from her boss.

Interviewer: When you first entered Midwest Private College, what were your career plans?

Asha: When I first entered Midwest Private College, it was just to obtain that associate degree. I thought that, you know, hey let's just go for the associate to start off.

Interviewer: Right. Did you have a particular career interest?

Asha: I didn't. I just wanted to prove to my boss that I wasn't as dumb as he thought I was.

Asha saw an associate degree as a way of achieving greater workplace status, and was not initially considering a bachelor's or higher degree. While some respondents had differing reasons for entering the associate degree, from specific career goals, to an interest in a field, to more respect at work, all felt that the associate degree was a plausible starting point. Like Asha, many continued to work full-time while pursuing their schooling.

After her associate degree, Asha did earn more respect from her boss, but there was more. Her success in that initial degree gave her confidence to pursue a bachelor's degree and beyond.

Interviewer: Ok, and then how did your plans change while you were at Midwest Private College?

Asha: Well it changed, because I saw that I wasn't dumb. And I was kinda *smart*. And I'm like, "Hey, I can do this!" And so uh after a while I'm like, "Yes, I'm going for my bachelor's" and went for a master's.

Although social science models usually include a variable for "ability," this is regarded as an unchanging attribute that shapes students' success and plans. For Asha, and many other respondents, "ability" is a new discovery, inferred from a new and surprising success in college. While many non-traditional students are channeled into demanding BA-transfer programs at which most fail, Asha and many of our respondents aimed for an associate degree that had lower academic demands at which she succeeded. Although the status attainment model treats "ability" as an individual attribute that precedes college, Asha's experience led her to discover abilities that were unknown prior to college.

With her newfound confidence, she completed her bachelor's degree in business administration, and then she decided to go on to pursue a master's. As she completed each degree, she moved up the ranks of her small non-profit organization, from operations director to human resources director, and finally the chief operating officer.

As streamlined as Asha's trajectory through her programs seems, it does not follow the traditional trajectory through higher education. Using common sociological models and data, her success would not likely be apparent to researchers, since she began college at age 34 (so she wouldn't be in any of the usual surveys that end at age 26–30) and took time off from college between credentials, which might be interpreted as dropout in research that didn't follow her for a longer time. Educational research should seek to learn from, not discount, the positive and reinforcing experience Asha and others like her can achieve by following a model of incremental success. Moreover, newly discovered "ability" is a potentially important process, which may contribute to students' success in the incremental success process.

There are potential downsides to incremental success. Most notably, while it allows students to attain interim credentials and still aspire to higher degrees, it may take longer than following a more traditional pathway. A few respondents discussed the exhaustion they experienced and the sacrifices they had to make in their personal lives in order to attend college for so many years. However, this is the case for many students, even those who begin straight out of high school (Goldrick-Rab 2016). Moreover, there is no guarantee that credits will transfer (Roksa and Keith 2008), and 4-year colleges can be unpredictable in whether they accept specific credits for specific majors (Rosenbaum et al. 2017). Because of this issue, many of our respondents chose to complete their bachelor's degrees in programs that accepted prior credits.

Private occupational colleges often make incremental success strategies the usual model. Although their credits may not count in public 4-year colleges (depending on negotiated agreements), they make all credits count for their own bachelor's degrees. The respondents in our sample often felt these colleges gave them dependable progress and success, where they did not waste their prior coursework. Cindy, a Black mother of two, who had to drop out of college at 18 because she was pregnant with her first son, already had her EMT certificate from a community college.

Interviewer: And was it [the associate degree] as long as you expected?
Cindy: No. Actually I—it was shorter than I expected. That's why I always encourage people to go to Midwest Private College, especially if you are a working adult with a family. And you don't really have time to spend four years at a university. You get the same education with less time and probably less money.

Although we can argue whether she would have saved money by choosing a low-cost community college instead of her pricey private non-selective college, shorter timetables represent fewer opportunity costs (earnings sacrifices) and lower risks of interruptions. Cindy clearly appreciates the quick win she achieved there. Cindy went on to complete her bachelor's degree in healthcare management and a master's in jurisprudence at a semi-selective university. Despite her clear success, she took time off from college so she could work between each of her degrees. Most importantly, she does not believe that she could have completed her degrees had she attempted to complete four straight years.

We cannot know whether Cindy, Asha, and the other respondents would have succeeded at a traditional 4-year program, but we believe it is unlikely, considering their hectic schedules and life demands, and their fair to poor high school achievement. For these respondents, the smaller, more manageable starting point may have been the difference between educational success and educational failure.

19.2.1.4 Studying the Model of Incremental Success

Scholars have noted the restriction imposed by the one-directional sequences in traditional models of educational attainment, i.e., the onset of work signals the end of education. Blau and Duncan's (1967) original conception of the status attainment model was a three-stage process that constrains the variability of pathways within each stage. Most educational attainment research follows this model and emphasizes degree completion as the end point of schooling (Bills 2004). As a result, it dismisses at the outset the possibility that educational sequencing may be tied with experiences in the labor market.

Kerckhoff (1995) has argued that in order to "understand the intergenerational continuity and mobility, we must recognize that the structural locations in the social organizations involved in [educational and occupational attainment] are differentially linked with each other and that those linked locations have cumulative effects on the stratification process" (p. 326). Research must recognize the interrelationships among institutions, such as education and the labor market, because those relationships are relevant to the success of individuals. Pallas (2003), following Elder (1985), similarly asserts that research on educational attainment should expand its focus to include other life events, social roles, and institutional responsibilities, such as work. Moreover, Pallas identifies a general lack of understanding of alternative combinations of school and work, and how transitions among them can shape future achievements. He calls for further research to study individuals' actions and experiences in greater detail as they pursue higher status.

We have provided one possible model of educational attainment, the incremental success model, which allows education and work to interact as students attain higher credentials. The incremental success model maintains the importance of credentials, rather than years of education, for labor market outcomes. Individuals who take four years to get associate degrees do not necessarily get higher earnings than those who take two years for an associate degree, nor do they get as much earnings as individuals who get a BA in four years. But the incremental success model also does not treat any particular credential as an end point. Instead, students use incremental success to complete a sequence of degrees. In this model, these intermediate credentials are steps, rather than the final landing. For students who follow this path, credential attainment may occur simultaneously with career development, and the typical modes of analyzing outcomes would not be sufficient.

Educational attainment research that seeks to capture the true experiences of non-traditional students should broaden its approach to allow for more complex interactions between school and work. More flexible models could address the possibility of incremental success in a systematic way. We know that this is not a rare occurrence (Carnevale et al. 2012). But how this happens and whether it is actually beneficial, as it seemed to be from our cases, remains to be examined.

In an attempt to keep the discussion within the realm of college and degree choices, this chapter does not address other aspects of non-traditional student identities that may also play a role. In particular, dependent versus independent status and family formation can all occur in non-normative ways that have implications for student attainment. We also only briefly address work as it relates to student sequencing choices. For those interested in this topic, Perna (2010) focuses on findings specifically related to students who work.

19.2.2 Alternative Institutional Procedures

After a student has decided on a degree, student learning and degree progress are not equal across institutions. In recent decades, researchers have recognized that institutional differences are likely to impact student outcomes. Some of this research is related to the type of institution (2-year, 4-year, or private non-selective), as discussed above. A large body of sociological literature has also examined other institutional differences. Specifically, scholars have largely emphasized elite institutions, selectivity, and characteristics of the students at an institution (see Gerber and Cheung 2008).

These differences are important, and are a natural extension of the early status attainment models. However, as colleges and the populations they serve have become more complex, education researchers have begun to pay more attention to the impact of institutional procedures. In this chapter, "institutional procedures" is the way a college creates (or doesn't create) transitions, structures, and supports that shape how students move into, through, and out of college, via credential completion and career attainment. Although most colleges merely adopt traditional procedures used in selective colleges, alternative procedures are possible, and colleges can choose procedures around such issues as academic and career advising, course sequencing and scheduling, support services, summer programs, placement testing, transfer agreements, and job placement, to name a few.

Institutional procedures are crucial for student retention, persistence, and graduation. As Tinto (2012) explains, "to improve retention and graduation, the institution must begin by focusing on its own behavior and establishing conditions within its walls that promote those outcomes" (p. 6). In high schools, greater access to school guidance counselors, specialized college success coaches, career entry assistance for vocational students, and an emphasis on being "on track" in the freshman year have all been shown to improve student outcomes (Lapan et al. 1997; Hurwitz and Howell 2014; Stephan and Rosenbaum 2013; Rosenbaum 2001; Roderick et al. 2014).

There have been efforts to determine effective procedures in higher education as well. Research demonstrating the importance of social and academic integration on student retention spurred numerous intervention programs to improve student engagement in and out of the classroom. Although many such programs have been perfunctory, school supports to improve student engagement can have important positive impacts on student retention (Tinto 2007). In community colleges, research has focused on the value of remedial sequences, which are at best diversionary, and at worse active obstructions to student success (Scott-Clayton and Rodriguez 2012; Rosenbaum and Rosenbaum 2013).

College procedures, even in community colleges, are often based on those of traditional 4-year schools and traditional students. The general theme of these procedures is to leave it up to students and their families to make decisions about school. However, non-traditional students might not have the know-how to complete school quickly, or the time and money to support extended years of college if they make mistakes. Moreover, in a 2-year program, this lack of structure can be especially harmful since students inherently have less time to smooth over early

mistakes. With so many students dropping out of college, colleges are starting to reconsider the common practice of placing the burden of figuring out how to "do" college on the student.

In *After Admission: From College Access to College Success*, Rosenbaum et al. (2006) argued that that the procedures used by private open-access colleges can promote student attainment and success. The overarching characteristic of these various procedures is increased structure. While students in community colleges face a bewildering abundance of choices and have little information or help for making decisions, private open-access colleges give students fewer options of majors and course-taking, mandate frequent meetings with advisors, monitor students' progress and difficulties, pose the same dependable class time schedules every semester, and connect students directly to employers. Such structured procedures may be particularly useful for non-traditional students, who do not have time to spend poring over course catalogs, deciphering complex requirements, and coping with accidentally chosen courses that don't meet the program requirements.

There has been some research on the possible value of procedures that lend more structure to the community college experience as well. Hoffman et al. (2007) noted lack of alignment between high schools and colleges, and encouraged these institutions to create procedures that make the transition to community college more accessible to disadvantaged students. These might include summer programs, curricular alignment, and college visits. Similarly, more intensive guidance counseling programs can help students succeed academically (Bahr 2008). The state of Florida mandated a reform which administers the state's community college placement exam to nearly all high school juniors, and then provides a compulsory "college readiness" course in senior year to help students meet expectations (Ahearn et al. 2016).

Despite the influx of interest in procedures in both 2- and 4-year colleges, research on college procedures continues to be relatively rare compared to the study of student and family characteristics. We discuss three procedures that we believe are particularly effective at promoting educational attainment for non-traditional students. While these are just three of many procedures that colleges can implement, they address serious problems that students often confront while seeking sub-BA degrees. In other words, these are relatively general procedures that can help students who do not have time and money to explore. Research must continue to examine such procedures and college practices across the board. Moreover, our master's sample provides insight into how students experience these institutional procedures.

19.2.2.1 Pre-set Course Pathways

If community college students are to succeed, colleges must be innovative in creating procedures to help non-traditional students to cross these transitions. Our earlier research showed that colleges can structure curricula to prevent student mistakes and failures. In 2006, we criticized the "cafeteria" model, which gives students free choices of courses, but often leads to poor progress (Rosenbaum et al. 2006, p.118), and we noted the advantages of "dependable pathways" that give more structure to curricular choices (ibid., p. 16). Curriculum pathways remove some of the difficulty in choosing aligned coursework that will dependably lead to a degree. Since then, leading researchers and reformers have joined in criticizing the cafeteria model and elaborating curriculum pathways (Bailey et al. 2015; Wyner 2014; Venezia et al. 2012). Although curriculum pathways began in community colleges, Richard Arum and Josipa Roksa, two prominent sociologists, have advocated structured pathways in 4-year colleges as well (2012).

Recent research has shown how colleges can combine procedures into a wrap-around pathways model that keeps students' progress on track. These guided pathways provide students with limited curricular choices, clarify an otherwise overwhelmingly complex system, and closely monitor students' progress, frequently advise students' choices, and make mistakes less likely (Rosenbaum and Rosenbaum 2013; Bailey et al. 2015; Complete College America 2013).

Our respondents provide some insight into how students perceive a structured pathway. Those who were offered a pre-set course sequence universally appreciated the structure it provided, just as we found that most current students do (Rosenbaum

et al. 2006). The private school had structured all of its programs so that all students took a pre-set course sequence. While this could feasibly be detrimental for students who are not sure of their occupational plans (Holland and DeLuca 2016), it was highly useful for respondents, who report they were eager to finish quickly and gain occupational skills. Surprisingly, the most valuable aspect of pre-set course pathways for this group appears to have been the lack of "exploration" that was encouraged or even allowed.

Interviewer:	How was your experience at Private Midwest College different from what you expected?
Tanya:	It was more professional. People are more focused there. You're not allowed to get off on the wrong track, take classes that you don't need for your degree.

These structured pathways meant that Tanya's expectations, an associate and a bachelor's degree in three years, were readily met. Respondents in occupational programs in community colleges also sometimes enjoyed the structure of pre-set course sequences. Formal pathway requirements may be weaker in these programs, but students like Lynn (see below) appreciate the focus nonetheless.

Interviewer:	So now did you ever have any problems figuring out like which classes you had to take or anything like that?
Lynn:	No because it was pretty laid-out in the book. And then the teacher, once I got into the track to do the substance abuse [degree program], he was very helpful. I mean like even as when we were ending a class, he was telling us what classes we would be taking next.
Interviewer:	OK, so this was a professor and not an advisor?
Lynn:	Yeah, yeah.
Interviewer:	OK. Now did you have any problems with scheduling, like scheduling conflicts or anything like that?

Lynn: No, I actually lucked out and was able to get things that I needed when I needed them.

Lynn acknowledges that there was an element of uncertainty in the process, but also remembers a specific teacher who helped her plan her coursework. While some community college students flounder in trying to figure out what courses to take (Rosenbaum et al. 2006), her relatively structured program and conscientious professors appear to have alleviated some of that difficulty.

As research and practice continues to examine the benefits of course sequencing, we must consider the potential for differential benefit from these procedures. A student with few external responsibilities and lots of time to devote to scheduling may marginally benefit from pre-set course sequences. Yet, highly structured and dependable offerings might be particularly beneficial for non-traditional students like those in our sample, who want to attain the credential and move on. At the private college, students are encouraged to complete their original degree plan, even if their plans change. The college stresses that the first degree increases their economic value in any job, and the college has ways to do "mid-course corrections" to alternative fields for their next degree.

19.2.2.2 Peer-Cohort Supports

A second procedure colleges can implement to assist non-traditional students is a peer cohort. Persistence is higher if students are socially integrated, that is if they participate in extracurricular activities or live in dormitories (Tinto 2012). However, most students in open-access institutions do not live in dormitories, and most of their interaction with the college occurs in the classroom, so colleges' main opportunity to capitalize on integrating students is through coursework (Rosenbaum et al. 2006). Open-access institutions that serve non-traditional students therefore need to be particularly purposeful about creating opportunities for students to have social interaction with one another.

Schools can actively ensure the creation of cohorts, as Guttman College in New York City has done (Rosenbaum et al. 2016). Students are placed in a cohort from the outset, and they take most courses with their cohort through the entire first year. Peers provide information, support, and even tutoring that many students report are valuable in helping them persist through difficulties.

When students move together through guided course sequences, they will naturally fall into a cohort structure because they take many of their classes together over multiple terms. Some research has shown that a one-semester peer cohort structure improved outcomes for that short time, but did not have discernable impact after it ended (Weissman et al. 2011).

In discussing the social benefits of structured course sequences, our respondents felt that their peers provided a support network. Juliana was in a particularly demanding program for her associate degree, which met four days a week and also required an internship. She had children and was working full-time, and she frequently thought about dropping out because of her demanding schedule. Despite these difficulties, she felt supported by the other students in her cohort, who she connected with in her pre-set course sequences.

Juliana: They told us, we basically went as a cohort. And it was like ok you take this class at this time, you take this class at this time, it was already pre-scheduled, we just knew when to show up, and where basically.

Interviewer: Ok. [What] was so good about that?

Juliana: I'm a big fan of cohorts because you're going with the same group of people, and you're all going through the same thing. You kind of bond with these people. You become like, it's like a family type of situation, when one gets tired, the other one like tries to get you together, you know cause you're all going through the same thing. So, I'm a big fan of cohorts.

Juliana feels that the cohort supports she received were instrumental in her persistence through a demanding program. It is possible that such benefits are more widely felt by non-traditional students in structured occupational programs. The cohort advantages may add to those of pre-set course sequences, but creating a cohort in this way requires little additional efforts by the school.

Educational attainment research should try to identify where cohort procedures exist, and when they might be most useful. It can further attempt to identify whether course sequencing and cohorts lead to compounded advantages, considering the two are likely to co-exist without much additional effort. Colleges can encourage peer cohort support by various activities, like group projects.

19.2.2.3 Degree Ladder Procedures

Our final structured procedure is to streamline the process of attaining multiple degrees in the same educational or occupational field. Transferring from a 2-year institution to a bachelor's degree program is usually a convoluted, uncertain, and bureaucratic process. Many 4-year colleges have arbitrary or highly selective procedures for accepting credit from 2-year colleges, and they often change their requirements without notice, making it difficult to predict transfer chances at college entry. This has been true for a long time (Dougherty 1994), and community college staff report that it remains an issue (Rosenbaum et al. 2017). There are two possible procedures a school can take to combat this issue. One is to create agreements between 2-year colleges (usually community colleges) and bachelor's degree-granting institutions. Although that requires the difficult collaboration of two separate institutions (Roksa and Keith 2008), our recent research has discovered community colleges that have taken on the responsibility to negotiate transfer agreements with 4-year colleges, instead of leaving students at the mercy of complex and ambiguous rules (Rosenbaum et al. 2017).

A second solution is to develop what we call "degree ladders." Sometimes called "stackable credentials," degree ladders have gained attention in recent years as the numbers of sub-BA degrees have increased. These institutional procedures allow students to sequentially and relatively easily combine certificates, associate degrees, and bachelor's degrees in the same field (Rosenbaum et al. 2017; Ganzglass 2014). Degree ladders simplify the typically complex transfer process by guaranteeing credit transfers and clarifying requirements.

We suspect that the process of incremental success described earlier is greatly facilitated by the existence of stackable credentials. We believe it is not a fluke that most of the respondents in our highly successful sample completed degrees in the business and health fields. These fields are more likely to provide opportunities for stackable credentials (Deming et al. 2012). Students can complete one degree or credential and take time to work if they need to, without worrying that transfer requirements will change or their next college will not accept their earned credits. This can facilitate quicker degree completion when they make the decision to return to college.

19.2.3 Alternative Ways to Inform Direction for Education and Careers

19.2.3.1 Educational and Occupational Plans

Student educational expectations, or the highest level of schooling a student expects to attain, is a major consistent predictor of educational attainment research (Sewell and Hauser 1975). However, as students' aspirations have risen (Schneider and Stevenson 1999), this association has declined in recent decades (Jacob and Wilder 2010). In 2002, more than 80% of high school sophomores in 2002 expected a bachelor's degree (Goyette 2008). The ways these expectations are related to SES or academic achievement have declined since the 1970s (Reynolds and Pemberton 2001). Such trends are of special concern because the newly ambitious students are also dropping out of college at high rates. Instead of promoting more success, the increasing educational plans of students have contributed to a larger gap between expectations and reality-more students are expecting to complete a degree than actually graduate (Jacob and Wilder 2010). Moreover, these dropouts lead to enormous costs in time, tuition, and self-confidence, and "some college" with no credentials has no earnings payoffs and minimal nonmonetary rewards (Rosenbaum et al. 2016). In light of these changes, it is important that sociologists continue to examine student plans and their implications.

Despite the significance of plans in educational attainment literature, how students form their educational expectations has remained relatively underexplored (Goyette 2008). Where research does consistently examine the formation of educational expectations, it usually assumes that educational plans are tied to occupational expectations (see Reynolds et al. 2006; Schneider and Stevenson 1999). Occupational outcomes are especially important to low-income students in open-access institutions, for whom the stakes for economic success are higher (Choy 2002). In a study of over 10,000 community college students, Laanan (2000) finds that the majority report that getting better employment is an important reason they are in school. This aligns with the rhetoric of college-for-all, which emphasizes the economic necessity of higher education for all students, as well as the declining returns to a high school diploma (Goldin and Katz 2008).

As with educational expectations, students' occupational expectations have become increasingly optimistic, and decreasingly tied to social and academic background (Goyette 2008). More students have goals for jobs that require bachelor's degrees, but most are highly unlikely to achieve those goals, especially in community colleges (ibid.; Rosenbaum et al. 2016). Schneider and Stevenson (1999) explored in great detail student understandings of the educational requirements of their chosen occupations. In both educational and occupational expectations, youth have become more, some might even say overly, ambitious, with unclear conceptions of their direction. Therefore, it seems that college-for-all has increased student ambitions and even enrollment, but not credential completion rates or career success.

19.2.3.2 Alternative Ways to Inform Direction

Schneider and Stevenson (1999) expanded standard practice of identifying students' goals to also consider the pathways by which students plan to achieve those goals. They found that not only are high school students' expectations misaligned with their career goals, but also that students are often unclear about specific steps they need to take to achieve a goal. Their plans were uninformed and misdirected.

Having direction can be a motivating factor in school (Oyserman et al. 2001), and well-directed students are more likely to meet their expectations when they enter college. As Braxton et al. (1995) explain, "when students' expectations and experiences are appropriately aligned and match the reality they encounter, students are more likely to be satisfied with their college experience and to persist to graduation" (p. 32). It seems that the formation of direction can have a major positive impact on student persistence in college, but the most vulnerable students in our systems lack direction more often than not (Morgan 2012).

Despite the value of direction, research on educational attainment has done little work to understand its formation. Schneider and Stevenson (1999) suggest proper guidance is critical to the formation of direction (see also Mortimer et al. 2002). There are generally two main sources of guidance that research has viewed as having a major impact on student plans: families and schools. Disadvantaged students have been shown to have less access to high-quality guidance from both sources. Their parents often have less experience with college or middle-class workplaces, and their schools have fewer resources for curricula and postsecondary advising (Lareau 2000; Stephan and Rosenbaum 2013; Armstrong and Hamilton 2015).

Non-traditional students and students from disadvantaged backgrounds may have even fewer sources for high-quality guidance. For example, Holland and Deluca (2016) discuss how a group of low-income, Black students in private open-access colleges often choose short-term programs without serious consideration, often because of peer influence. If non-traditional students have been out of school for a long time, they may have families of their own, and they are also unlikely to receive guidance on direction from their parents (Zapata-Gietl et al. 2016). They also no longer have access to the major sources of guidance for forming direction, their high school counselors and teachers. It would follow, then, that non-traditional students are likely to suffer a distinct lack of direction from parents and schools, which might hinder their ability to persist.

If they cannot get direction from high schools or parents, non-traditional students would likely benefit from receiving informed direction and guidance from their colleges. This section explores how both schools and work provide direction for non-traditional students, and whether open-access colleges can more systematically support the formation of direction for this group.

19.2.3.3 How Colleges Can Shape Direction

Some research indicates that student direction is malleable in college. While most educational attainment research considers expectations and plans as relatively fixed traits, this is not a realistic assumption. Jacob and Wilder (2010) found that students readjust educational plans after high school, often in response to their academic achievement in college. There is also growing interest in how students form occupational direction while they are in college, specifically how they choose their major (Morgan et al. 2013; Zafar 2013). However, there is very little evidence of community colleges helping students form educational or occupational direction. This is not surprising, since community college counselors advise over 1000 students, so they can do very little to assist students with direction.

Our sample provides insights to how these students formed direction while in college. Private occupational colleges have more structured course sequences, and their counselors have frequent mandatory meetings with students on how higher education might help them achieve those goals. From the time of admission, students meet with career advisors who explore students' interests and abilities, and suggest occupational programs that match. Students have career direction from the outset, with clear ideas about job tasks and job rewards, and what the college will provide to support their direction. After classes begin, students have frequent mandatory meetings with advisors, often in peer cohort group meetings. These meetings reinforce students'

understanding of their direction, and how they are progressing toward it. These meetings are not very expensive or time-consuming since they are group meetings, and they are often scheduled immediately following a required class to optimize attendance and time-efficiency.

As discussed earlier, community colleges tend to leave most choices up to students, and that includes their degree goals and major choices. While we found little evidence that community college students received formal assistance in developing direction from counselors, they do report receiving informal guidance from professors, who help them construct and revise their educational and occupational plans.

One respondent, Susan, explains how a specific teacher pushed her and her classmates to aspire to a master's degree. She was 36 when she entered Midwest Community College, and, as a recovered addict, aspired to an associate degree that would lead to work in addiction therapy.

Susan:	Well when I first entered, my career plans was to get my associate in addiction, or in substance abuse counseling, and to be certified.
Interviewer:	Were you ever considering any other field? You were talking about social work.
Susan:	Not really. That's what I went in saying that I would do. This community college changed my mind immediately.
Interviewer:	Ok, how did they change your mind?
Susan:	Dr. S. really…encouraged us, especially those of us like me, the older students. That if we were coming in this field that we needed to have a master's degree. They just told us to come into this field and to be able to make a living to take care of your family, you know and to, just to be able to survive at our age with our experience, with our longevity of

already working possibly, you know that we just really need not to just stop at associate degree. So I think, …all of us thank Midwest Community College for that because we really got that word of encouragement, and I know it was like a group of maybe like ten of us that definitely through that have achieved and got our master's.

Susan credits this specific professor and program for giving her and others she knows the motivation to push through two additional degrees, even as she approached middle age. She was open and ready to hear guidance on her educational and occupational direction, and was happy to receive it.

College personnel with occupational expertise can help propel students in the appropriate direction based on their interests and abilities. It is difficult to know how many students would like this type of guidance, or would be open and willing to altering their courses of direction. Schneider and Stevenson (1999) suggest that direction is determined in high school, prior to entering college. However, many students report that they do re-evaluate their goals and pathways while in college, and many report they get faculty help in determining next steps. This is especially the case for students who might be interested in pursuing graduate programs. The area of direction formation is one that researchers should be exploring, despite the difficulty in obtaining accurate information on the process. At the very least, research on community colleges should take note of colleges that are designing programs to help students develop and adjust the paths to their goals.

19.2.3.4 Careers Also Shape Direction

For non-traditional students, school is just one aspect of varied and complex lives (Perna 2010). We cannot expect these students to form and update their direction only in the counseling office or classroom. Most students have spent years working before returning to college, and they continue to work while completing their

degrees. As Bills (2004) writes, "rather than a single 'education–work' relationship in any given biography, there may be many" (p. 135). The labor market experiences that many non-traditional students have may be valuable for the formation of educational and occupational direction. For example, unpleasant labor market experiences may cause students to eliminate certain possibilities for their occupational futures, and thus might influence their educational plans (Mortimer et al. 2002).

Our respondents provide insight into direction formation in the labor market. Although we found little evidence of how careers shape educational plans in prior literature, everyone in this sample had worked prior to enrolling in school, and most continued to work on and off while in school, as well as between degrees. Their interviews reveal that work experiences—successes, failures, or new and interesting opportunities—provided a source of direction for many respondents.

Carol is a Chinese immigrant who began her college career hoping to be a medical secretary, a goal she accomplished soon after her associate degree graduation. While working as a medical secretary, she completed her bachelor's degree and was expecting to be promoted, but she suspects that her accent and poor spoken English limited her chances. Below, she explains why she has returned to a master's program in elementary teaching:

Carol: That is one reason I go for a college education at Midwest Graduate School. Because I had my bachelor's degree in healthcare management, but when I work at Physician Reimbursement Department at the hospital, when they're looking for leader, they never talk about me. None of them had associate degree, none of them had bachelor's degree. I am the only one have those qualification. They never talk about me. I'm thinking it's because my English, my communication skill is what's not that good. That's why they never talk about me. So, I decided to go back to school.

She later decided that she wanted to become a pharmacist, and at the time of the interview was completing pre-requisites for that degree. Carol provides an example of how labor market experiences can drive educational choices. Had she received that promotion, she may not have continued on to her master's degree, and her goals and plans may have changed.

We return to Cindy, the mother of two who had dropped out of her first college after she became pregnant. Below, she describes her trajectory from her medical assisting degree through her bachelor's in healthcare management and into law school.

Interviewer: And what made you decide to move from the medical assisting to the different fields you've gone through?

Cindy: While working at the Community Health Center, it's in a very impoverished area where people were either uninsured or underinsured. And…I felt bad. I couldn't help these people. I could help them from a clinical standpoint. But I couldn't [help] them with regards to understanding their benefits or helping them attain benefits. So I wanted to learn more about the business world and Medicare. So I decided to go back to get my bachelor's.

Interviewer: And then you had a bachelor's of Healthcare Management?

Cindy: Bachelor's in Healthcare Management, yep.

Interviewer: Ok. And then so what made you decide to move to get a law degree?

Cindy: During the bachelor's of Business Administration program, I took a class. It was called Health Law and Administration where I was exposed to torts, medical malpractice and all the legally issues for Medicaid and Medicare. And I realized, "Hey I can do even more with a law degree than I could with a business degree."

In Cindy's case, her experiences at work and her experiences in the classroom helped her continually readjust her goals and reformulate her direction. Time spent working can provide individuals with information on what they like and dislike about certain jobs. If we want to understand how non-traditional students can succeed not only in completing a degree, but also in translating that degree to occupational success, we must consider the formation of their direction. This requires not only research on how colleges can help students form direction, but also how adult students respond to work needs to make decisions about future education.

19.3   Conclusion

While policymakers focus on traditional students in traditional 4-year colleges, the new college-for-all policy has brought new kinds of students into a variety of colleges and programs. We have described students from non-traditional backgrounds, many with modest high school records who are pursuing sub-BA degrees in 2-year non-selective colleges. These students need a different research perspective. The findings of the status attainment model are still relevant and important, and family background and academic achievement are important, but we have proposed extensions and further questions that can raise new questions about the new college students. They face alternative options and procedures, which affect the ways they move through institutional structures and the ways they form their goals and direction.

Students choose from colleges that are public and private, 2-year and 4-year, selective and non-selective. Some students have solid academic skills and an eagerness to learn, and many others are there because they have been told that college is their only chance at success in adulthood. Some have the support of their families and others support parents or children. Some are older or working full-time, and most do not have a good grasp of their options and odds of credential completion. While sociologists who study social stratification using the status attainment model help us understand what prevents success and social mobility, it is also important to see how individuals who do not fit the standard mold of "college student" make the system work for themselves. In order to do this, we must dig deeper than the usual status attainment analyses to examine alternative ways that colleges and work experiences shape students' direction.

While the status attainment model implies that success depends on individuals' choices and actions, we find this is only partially the case for our respondents. Extending prior work critiquing the limitations of the status attainment model, we have described a variety of sequences and combinations of non-traditional credentials, alternative institutional procedures, and sources of direction that working-class individuals experienced in making college fit into their lives.

Educational attainment is far from static, and it is crucial for achieving labor market success. Sub-BA credentials in new fields are instrumental to careers, but they operate by entirely different rules, requirements, and job outcomes. At the same time, education does not necessarily guarantee career advancement, as many college graduates are unable to find steady and reliable employment (Silva 2013; Roksa and Arum 2012). An increasing number of students are choosing non-normative pathways to educational and occupational attainment, via community colleges, returning to school as adults, working while in college, enrolling part-time, and balancing work, school, and family responsibilities. We have shown how some working-class individuals combined work and college in non-normative ways to achieve educational success.

We describe three alternatives that our respondents use to increase their success:

1. Alternative options and strategies.
2. Alternative institutional procedures.

3. Alternative ways to inform direction about education and career.

In contrast with the traditional single-minded pursuit of BA degrees in colleges with traditional procedures, and posing career direction from pre-existing knowledge of careers, these respondents describe how they chose alternative credential options and strategies that combined credential options (often in incremental success sequences), benefitted from non-traditional college procedures, and developed direction from their experiences in college and careers. These alternatives support their persistence and degree completion despite obstacles they face as non-traditional students.

As researchers, we need to include these complexities in our uses of the status attainment model to allow for the inclusion of such pathways and better understand how non-traditional students navigate the attainment of higher education.

If we focus narrowly on the status attainment model, we will fail to account for these difficulties. We often assume that, after students enter college, the only obstacles are their own abilities and determination.

However, the status attainment model does not typically consider institutional procedures as inputs to educational and occupational success. Our respondents report that they benefited from structured programming and peer cohorts, and prior research has indicated that college procedures can help students acquire certifications, industry experience, and good jobs. Students' individual attributes (intelligence, work ethic, and background), choices, and actions are important, but institutional procedures can reduce mistakes and improve progress regardless of individual attributes and choices. The decentralization of our education system leads to dramatically different procedures in every college, and sometimes even between campuses of the same college. Simply controlling for selectivity, sector, and level of the school is not sufficient to capture this variation. Models of status attainment can include information on college procedures, such as cohorts and mandatory advising. As we have noted, the status attainment model rarely measures college procedures, so it only has variation in individual attributes as explanatory variables. We can broaden our research to build alternative options and procedures onto that model.

Finally, we described how individuals find direction to make and plan for educational goals. Like human capital theory in economics, the status attainment model assumes that students make informed choices about occupations, but students rarely make informed choices. Some college procedures may influence the formation of student direction. While there is anecdotal evidence that some colleges and high schools are moving towards policies that promote better planning to provide direction, there is very little information on this topic. Our respondents suggest that they find direction from a variety of sources in their education and careers, but this, as expected, is not systematic. Research can extend the status attainment model to build in processes that include alternative options and procedures, including the formation of direction.

The dismal picture Silva (2013) presented is an accurate description of the many obstacles to opportunity that modern young adults are likely to face. Likewise, our sample faces many of the same obstacles Silva discusses. However, our findings from these working-class individuals identify alternative options and procedures which enabled them to succeed, although they were not noticed by Silva or by the status attainment model. These alternatives help us identify what strategies students and their institutions can take to achieve educational goals. Future research on status attainment must understand how individuals and institutions manage to create success against the high odds described by Silva. Whether others can benefit from the same processes remains to be seen, but to do this, we must expand our models to account for the many facets of today's college reality.

References

Adelman, C. (2003). *Principal indicators of student academic histories in post-secondary education, 1970–2000*. Washington, DC: Department of Education, Institute of Education Sciences.

Ahearn, C., Rosenbaum, J. E., & Rosenbaum, J. (2016). The new college-for-all policy: What educators need to know about community college credentials. *PhiDelta Kappan, 97*(5), 49–53. http://bit.ly/1QwaQZa.

Alexander, K., Bozick, R., & Entwisle, D. (2008). Warming up, cooling out, or holding steady? Persistence and change in educational expectations after high school. *Sociology of Education, 81*, 371–396.

Andrews, R., Li, J., & Lovenheim, M. F. (2014). Heterogeneous paths through college: Detailed patterns and relationships with graduation and earnings. *Economics of Education Review, 42*, 93–108. https://doi.org/10.1016/j.econedurev.2014.07.002.

Armstrong, E. A., & Hamilton, L. T. (2015). *Paying for the party: How college maintains inequality*. Cambridge, MA: Harvard University Press.

Attewell, P., & Lavin, D. (2007). *Passing the torch*. New York: Russell Sage Foundation.

Bahr, P. R. (2008). Cooling out in the community college: What is the effect of academic advising on student chances of success? *Research in Higher Education, 49*, 704–732.

Bailey, T., Jaggars, S. S., & Jenkins, D. (2015). *Redesigning America's community colleges: A clearer path to student success*. Cambridge, MA: Harvard University Press.

Bean, J. P., & Metzner, B. S. (1985). A conceptual model of nontraditional undergraduate student attrition. *Review of Educational Research, 55*(4), 485–540.

Belfield, C. R., & Bailey, T. (2011). The benefits of attending community college: A review of the evidence. *Community College Review, 39*(1), 46–68.

Bills, D. (2004). *The sociology of education and work*. Malden: Blackwell Publishing.

Blau, P. M., & Duncan, O. (1967). *The American occupational structure*. New York: Wiley.

Borman, K. M. (1991). *The first "real" job: A study of young workers*. Albany: State University of New York Press.

Braxton, J. M., Vesper, N., & Hossler, D. (1995). Expectations for college and student persistence. *Research in Higher Education, 36*(5), 595–612.

Browne, I., & Misra, J. (2003). The intersection of gender and race in the labor market. *Annual Review of Sociology, 29*, 487–513.

Buchmann, C., & DiPrete, T. (2006). The growing female advantage in college completion: The role of family background and academic achievement. *American Sociological Review, 71*, 515–541.

Calcagno, J. C., Crosta, P., Bailey, T., & Jenkins, D. (2007). Stepping stones to a degree: The impact of enrollment pathways and milestones on commu nity college student outcomes. *Research in Higher Education, 48*(7), 775–801.

Carnevale, A., Rose, S., & Hanson, A. (2012). *Certificates: Gateway to gainful employment and college degrees.* Washington, DC: Center on Education and the Workforce, Georgetown University.

Choy, S. (2001). *Students whose parents did not go to college: Postsecondary access, persistence, and attainment. Findings from the condition of education* (NCES report 126). Washington, DC: National Center for Education Statistics.

Choy, S. (2002). *Access and persistence: Findings from 10 years of longitudinal research on students.* Washington, DC: ERIC Digest.

Clark, B. R. (1960). The "cooling out" function in higher education. *American Journal of Sociology, 65*(6), 569–576.

Complete College America. (2013). *The game changers.* Washington, DC. https://doi.org/10.1016/j.mnl.2013.01.002.

Deil-Amen, R. (2016). The traditional college student: A smaller and smaller minority and its implications for diversity and access institutions. In M. Kirst & M. Stephens (Eds.), *Remaking college* (pp. 134–168). Stanford: Stanford University Press.

Deil-Amen, R., & DeLuca, S. (2010). The underserved third: How our educational structures populate an educational underclass. *Journal of Education for Students Placed at Risk, 15*, 1–24.

Deming, D. J., Goldin, C., & Katz, L. F. (2012). The for-profit postsecondary school sector: Nimble critters or agile predators? *Journal of Economic Perspectives, 26*(1), 139–164.

Deterding, N. (2015). Incremental and expressive education: College planning in the face of poverty. *Sociology of Education, 88*(4), 284–301.

Dougherty, K. J. (1994). *The contradictory college: The conflicting origins, impacts, and the futures of the community college.* Albany: State University of New York Press.

Durkheim, E. (1961). *Moral education: A study in the theory and application of the sociology of education.* New York/London: The Free Press and Collier-Macmillan.

Elder, G. H. (1985). Perspectives on the life course. In G. H. Elder Jr. (Ed.), *Life course dynamics.* Ithaca: Cornell University Press.

Gamoran, A. (2014). Inequality is the problem: Prioritizing research on reducing inequality. In *William T. Grant Foundaion annual report.* New York: William T. Grant Foundation.

Ganzglass, E. (2014). *Scaling "stackable credentials": Implications for implementation and policy.* Washington, DC: Center for Postsecondary and Economic Success at CLASP.

Gerber, T. P., & Cheung, S. Y. (2008). Horizontal stratification in postsecondary education: Forms, explanations, and implications. *Annual Review of Sociology, 34*, 299–318.

Goldin, C., & Katz, L. F. (2008). *The race between education and technology.* Cambridge, MA: Belknap Press.

Goldrick-Rab, S. (2016). *Paying the price: College costs, financial aid, and the betrayal of the American dream.* Chicago: University of Chicago Press.

Goldrick-Rab, S., & Pfeffer, F. (2009). Beyond access: Explaining social class differences in college transfer. *Sociology of Education, 82*(2), 101–125.

Goyette, K. (2008). College for some to college for all: Social background, occupational expectations, and educational expectations over time. *Social Science Research, 37*, 461–484.

Grubb, W. N., & Lazerson, M. (2004). *The education gospel: The economic power of schooling.* Cambridge, MA: Harvard University Press.

Hoffman, N., Vargas, J., Venezia, A., & Miller, M. (Eds.). (2007). *Minding the gap: Why integrating high school with college makes sense and how to do it.* Cambridge, MA: Harvard Education Press.

Holland, M. M., & DeLuca, S. (2016). "Why wait years to become something?" Low-income African American youth and the costly career search in for-profit trade schools. *Sociology of Education, 89*(4), 261–278.

Horn, L., & Carroll, C. D. (1996). *Nontraditional undergraduates: Trends in enrollment from 1986 to 1992 and persistence and attainment among 1989–90 beginning postsecondary students.* Berkeley: MPR Associates.

Horn, L., & Carroll, C. D. (1998). Stopouts or stayouts? Undergraduates who leave college in their first year. In *NCES report.* Washington, DC: National Center for Education Statistics.

Hout, M. (2012). Social and economic returns to college education in the United States. *Annual Review of Sociology, 38*, 379–400.

Hurwitz, M., & Howell, J. (2014). Estimating causal impacts of school counselors with regression discontinuity designs. *Journal of Counseling and Development, 92*(3), 316–327.

Jacob, B. A., & Wilder, T. (2010). *Educational expectations and attainment* (NBER Working Paper 15683). Cambridge, MA: National Bureau of Economic Research.

Jacobson, L., & Mokher, C. (2009). *Pathways to boosting the earnings of low-income students by increasing their educational attainment.* Washington, DC: Hudson Institute Center for Employment Policy.

Kalogrides, D., & Grodsky, E. (2011). Something to fall back on: Community colleges as a safety net. *Social Forces, 89*(3), 853–877.

Karp, M. M. (2011). *Toward a new understanding of non-academic student support: Four mechanisms encouraging positive student outcomes in the community college* (CCRC paper no. 28). New York: Columbia University, Teachers College, Community College Research Center.

Kasworm, C. (2010). Adult workers as undergraduate students: Significant challenges for higher education policy and practice. In L. W. Perma (Ed.), *Understanding the working college student: New research and its implications for policy and practice* (pp. 23–42). Sterling: Stylus Publishing, LLC.

Kena, G., Aud, S., Johnson, F., Wang, X., Zhang, J., Rathbun, A., Wilkinson-Flicker, S., & Kristapovich, P. (2014). *The condition of education 2014*. Washington, DC: U.S. Department of Education, National Center for Education Statistics. Retrieved from http://nces.ed.gov/pubs2014/2014083.pdf

Kena, G., Musu-Gillette, L., Robinson, J., Wang, X., Rathbun, A., Zhang, J., Wilkinson-Flicker, S., Barmer, A., & Dunlop Velez, E. (2015). *The condition of education 2015* (NCES 2015-144). Washington, DC: U.S. Department of Education. National Center for Education Statistics.

Kerckhoff, A. C. (1995). Institutional arrangements and stratification process in industrial societies. *Annual Review of Sociology, 21*, 323–347.

Laanan, F. S. (2000). Community college students' career and educational goals. *New Direction for Community Colleges, 112*, 19–33.

Lapan, R. T., Gysbers, N. C., & Sun, Y. (1997). The impact of more fully implemented guidance programs on the school experiences of high school students: A statewide evaluation study. *Journal of Counseling and Development, 75*(4), 292–302.

Lareau, A. (2000). Social class and the daily lives of children: A study from the United States. *Childhood, 7*(2), 155–171.

Long, B. T., & Kurlaender, M. (2009). Do community colleges provide a viable pathway to baccalaureate degree? *Educational Evaluation and Policy Analysis, 31*(1), 30–53.

McLeod, J. (2008). Class and the middle: Schooling, subjectivity and social formation. In L. Weiss (Ed.), *The way class works: Readings on school, family and the economy*. New York: Routledge.

Morgan, S. L. (2012). Models of college entry and the challenges of estimating primary and secondary effects. *Sociological Methods of Research, 41*, 17–56.

Morgan, S. L., Gelbgiser, D., & Weeden, K. A. (2013). Feeding the pipeline: Gender, occupational plans, and college major selection. *Social Science Research, 42*, 989–1005.

Mortimer, J., Zimmer, M., Holmes, M., & Shanahan, M. (2002). The process of occupational decision-making. *Journal of Vocational Behavior, 61*, 439–465.

National Center for Educational Statistics (NCES). (2015). *Digest of educational statistics*. Washington, DC: U.S. Department of Education's Institute for Education Sciences.

Newman, K. (1999). *No shame in my game: The working poor in the Inner City*. New York: Knopf/Russell Sage Foundation.

Newman, K. (2006). *Chutes and ladders: Navigating the low wage labor market*. Cambridge: Harvard University Press & Russell Sage Foundation.

Newman, K., & Winston, H. (2016). *Reskilling America: Learning to labor in the twenty-first century*. New York: Metropolitan Books.

Oreopoulous, P., & Petronijevic, U. (2013). Making college worth it: A review of the returns to higher education. *The Future of Children, 23*(1), 41–65.

Oyserman, D., Harrison, K., & Bybee, D. (2001). Can racial identity be promotive of academic efficacy? *International Journal of Behavioral Development, 25*(4), 379–385.

Pallas, A. M. (2003). Educational transitions, trajectories, and pathways. In J. T. Mortimer & M. Shanahan (Eds.), *Handbook of the life course* (pp. 165–184). New York: Plenum.

Perna, L. W. (Ed.) (2010). *Understanding the working college student: New research and its implications for policy and practice*. Sterling: Stylus Publishing, LLC.

Reynolds, J. R., & Pemberton, J. (2001). Rising college expectations among youth in the United States: A comparison of the 1979 and 1997 NLSY. *Journal of Human Resources, 36*(4), 703–726.

Reynolds, J., Stewart, M., Macdonald, R., & Sischo, L. (2006). Have adolescents become too ambitious? High school seniors' educational and occupational plans, 1976 to 2000. *Social Problems, 53*(2), 186–206.

Roderick, M., Kelley-Kemple, T., Johnson, D. W., & Beechum, N. O. (2014). *Preventable failure: Improvements in long-term outcomes when high schools focused on the ninth grade year*. Chicago: University of Chicago Consortium on Chicago School Research.

Roksa, J., & Arum, R. (2012). Life after college: The challenging transitions of the "academically adrift" cohort. *Change Magazine*, July/August: 8–14.

Roksa, J., & Keith, B. (2008). Credits, time, and attainment: Articulation policies and success after transfer. *Educational Evaluation and Policy Analysis, 30*, 236–254.

Roksa, J., & Velez, M. (2012). A late start: Delayed entry, life course transitions, and bachelor's degree attainment. *Social Forces, 90*, 769–794.

Rosenbaum, J. E. (2001). *Beyond college for all: Career paths for the forgotten half*. New York: Russell Sage Foundation Press.

Rosenbaum, J. (2012). Degrees of health disparities: Health status disparities between young adults with high school diplomas, sub-baccalaureate degrees, and baccalaureate degrees. *Health Services and Outcomes Research Methodology, 12*(2–3), 156–168.

Rosenbaum, J., & Rosenbaum, J. (2013). Beyond BA blinders: Lessons from occupational colleges and certificate programs for non-traditional students. *Journal of Economic Perspectives, 27*(2), 153–172.

Rosenbaum, J. E., Deil-Amen, R., & Person, A. E. (2006). *After admission: From college access to college success*. New York: Russell Sage Foundation Press.

Rosenbaum, J. E., Ahearn, C., & Rosenbaum, J. (2016). Remembering the forgotten half: In a college-for-all world, students need to be aware of all their options. *Education Leadership, 73*(6), 48–53.

Rosenbaum, J., Ahearn, C., & Rosenbaum, J. (2017). *Bridging the gaps: College pathways to career success*. New York: Russell Sage Foundation Press.

Schneider, B., & Stevenson, D. (1999). *The ambitious generation*. New Haven: Yale University Press.

Schudde, L., & Goldrick-Rab, S. (2014). On second chances and stratification: How sociologists think about community colleges. *Community College Review, 43*(1), 27–45.

Scott-Clayton, J., & Rodriguez, O. (2012). *Development, discouragement, or diversion? New evidence on the effects of college remediation*. Cambridge, MA: National Bureau of Economic Research.

Sennett, R., & Cobb, J. (1972). *Hidden injuries of class*. New York: Random house.

Sewell, W., & Hauser, R. (1975). *Education, occupation, and earnings: Achievement in the early career*. New York: Academic Press.

Sewell, W., & Shah, V. (1967). Socioeconomic status, intelligence, and the attainment of higher education. *Sociology of Education, 40*(1), 1–23.

Silva, J. (2013). *Coming up short: Working-class adulthood in an age of uncertainty*. New York: Oxford University Press.

Sirin, S. (2005). Socioeconomic status and academic achievement: A meta-analytic review of research. *Review of Educational Research, 75*(3), 417–453.

Stephan, J. L., & Rosenbaum, J. E.. (2009). *Beyond blaming students: How school programs may reduce gaps in the college enrollment process*. Presented at the Annual Meeting of the American Sociological Association, August, San Francisco, CA.

Stephan, J. L., Rosenbaum, J. E., & Person, A. E. (2009). Stratification in college entry and completion. *Social Science Research, 38*(3), 572–593.

Stephan, J. L., & Rosenbaum, J. E. (2013). Can high schools reduce college enrollment gaps with a new counseling model? *Educational Evaluation and Policy Analysis, 35*(2), 200–219.

Taniguchi, H., & Kaufman, G. (2005). "Degree completion among nontraditional college students." *Social Science Quarterly, 86*, 912–927.

Tinto, V. (2007). Research and practice of student retention: What next? *Journal of College Student Retention, 8*(1), 1–18.

Tinto, V. (2012). *Completing college: Rethinking institutional action*. Chicago: University of Chicago Press.

Venezia, A., Bracco, K., & Nodine, T. (2012). *Changing course: A planning tool for increasing student completion in community colleges*. San Francisco: WestEd.

Warren, J. R. (2001). Changes with age in the process of occupational stratification. *Social Science Research, 30*(2), 264–288.

Weissman, E., Butcher, K. F., Schneider, E., Teres, J., Collado, H., Greenberg, D., & Welbeck, R. (2011). *Learning communities for students in developmental math: Impact students at Queensborough and Houston Community Colleges*. New York: National Center for Postsecondary Research (MDRC).

Wells, A. S. (2008). The social context of charter schools: The changing nature of poverty and what it means for American education. In M. G. Springer, H. J. Walberg, M. Berends, & D. Ballou (Eds.), *Handbook of research on school choice*. Philadelphia: Lawrence Erlbaum Associates.

Wyner, J. (2014). *What excellent community colleges do*. Cambridge, MA: Harvard Education Press.

Zafar, B. (2013). College major choice and the gender gap. *Journal of Human Resources, 48*(3), 545–595.

Zapata-Gietl, C., Rosenbaum, J. E., Ahearn, C., & Becker, K. I. (2016). College for all: New institutional conflicts in the transition to adulthood. In *Handbook of the life course* (pp. 201–221). Cham: Springer.

The Future of Higher Education:
What's the Life Course Got to Do
with It?

20

Richard A. Settersten, Jr. and Barbara Schneider

Abstract

Recent decades have brought dramatic changes to both human lives and higher education. This chapter examines what changes in the life course mean for higher education, and vice versa. We address the relevance and vitality of higher education in the contemporary life course, as well as its potential for offsetting the life-course risks and discontinuities faced by the diverse populations it now serves. We describe how higher education can play more significant roles in responding to the vulnerabilities of students, strengthening the transition to adulthood through stable pathways to jobs and careers, fostering relationships and networking opportunities, and refining the boundaries of personal and financial independence from parents. Higher education can also be reimagined by infusing into curricula and learning experiences a broader set of skills than it now does—skills that are less about securing jobs and salaries, and more about finding meaning in and managing the uncertainties and complexities of adult life. It
can also be reimagined by reaching potential students who are in midlife and beyond. These goals are necessary if higher education is to have both stronger effects *on* the life course as well as a bigger place *in* the life course.

The last half century brought dramatic changes to both human lives and higher education. This chapter examines what changes in the life course mean for higher education, and what changes in higher education mean for the life course. We initiate an agenda for the reform of higher education. This vision is built on our research (e.g., Schneider et al. 2016; Settersten 2015a) and that of others, which has raised concerns not only about the relevance and vitality of higher education in the contemporary life course, but also its potential for offsetting the risks and discontinuities faced by the diverse populations it now serves. For young adults, higher education can play more significant roles in creating stable pathways to jobs and careers, in fostering relationships and networking opportunities, and in refining the boundaries of personal and financial independence from parents. Higher education can also do better in nurturing a broader set of skills that are necessary for success in adulthood, and in reaching potential students who are in midlife and beyond.

Before turning to these topics, a few prefatory comments are in order. First, given the complexity

R. A. Settersten, Jr. (✉)
College of Public Health and Human Sciences,
Oregon State University, Corvallis, OR, USA
e-mail: richard.settersten@oregonstate.edu

B. Schneider
College of Education, Department of Sociology,
Michigan State University, East Lansing, MI, USA
e-mail: bschneid@msu.edu

© Springer International Publishing AG, part of Springer Nature 2018   457
B. Schneider (ed.), *Handbook of the Sociology of Education in the 21st Century*, Handbooks
of Sociology and Social Research, https://doi.org/10.1007/978-3-319-76694-2_20

of the ecology of higher education and the life course, we focus on the United States. Many of the issues at stake, however, are equally pressing in other nations. Second, a note on terms: We will often use "universities" to represent four-year institutions (whether colleges or universities), "community colleges" to represent two-year institutions, "colleges" to represent all institutions of higher education, and "broad access schools" to represent those that admit the majority of their applicants (e.g., community colleges, comprehensive public universities, and for-profit enterprises; Stevens 2015).

20.1 The Disconnect Between the Organization of Higher Education and the Lives of Students in the U.S.

The traditional status attainment model (e.g., Blau and Duncan 1967; Sewell et al. 1970), which dominated the sociological literature in the second half of the last century, associated later life success with the acquisition of degree markers: high school diploma; technical, associate, or baccalaureate degrees; and postgraduate and professional degrees. The education trajectory was viewed as occurring fairly early in the life course and, for most individuals, it followed a fairly standard progression (Baum et al. 2013). Additional training and professional development were offered within specific occupations, sometimes in collaboration with colleges and in other instances via independent entities in competition with traditional degree or certificate programs (Butler 2016a).

Yet, many individuals do not follow the conventional degree path of high school to college, often reframing their initial ideas about work and occupations during or after college, or seeking different degrees later on. Some college students leave school without finishing, only to return years later; others start college after working for several years; still others may simultaneously work and attend school, taking many years to complete their degrees (Kena et al. 2016; Dundar

et al. 2011). These vacillating degree paths have dramatically altered the prototypical model of a college student. Although the "inoculation" approach to higher education—get it early in life and you are good for life—may have worked in an earlier time, it seems ill suited to lives today.

The "tripartite" (Kohli 2007) organization of the life course—with education heavily and even exclusively frontloaded, full-time continuous work in the middle, and retirement from work at the end—has for decades been showing signs of disintegration (Angel and Settersten 2012). But it remains a salient cultural frame that affects individuals' choices and how they judge themselves and others. This basic three-box structure is still in place, even though the borders of the boxes have changed. That is, the first box is now longer because of widespread pursuit of higher education, delays in full-time work, and postponement of partnering and parenting (Settersten and Ray 2010a). Similarly, the third box has grown longer because of significant extensions in life expectancy in the last century, and there are steep increases in retirement rates at 62 and 65, which are the current ages for partial and full retirement (National Institute on Aging 2015), but which are gradually rising to the age of 67. Many people are not in a position to retire at these ages, and many choose to work beyond them. For these individuals, the middle box has gotten longer, and the transition to the third box is more often a gradual process that involves reduced or flexible work, or new "bridge jobs" (National Institute on Aging 2015). The instability of the economy during the "Great Recession" exacerbated the need for many people to work longer as retirement resources were lost or undermined (Moen 2016). Work–family dynamics have also strained the conventional middle period of work—such as divorce and remarriage, later fertility, dual careers, child and parent care responsibilities, job relocations or terminations, short-term contracts, and demands for increasing technological expertise (Angel and Settersten 2012; Christensen and Schneider 2015; Schneider and Waite 2005).

The tripartite organization of the life course is reinforced by institutions and policies that were fashioned during and inherited from an earlier age. To the extent that policies and institutions play significant roles in reinforcing it, they can also be actively reformed to better adapt to—and even foster—new life-course patterns. Indeed, major structural changes are challenging the traditional organization of higher education: Tuition costs have risen more than inflation, and student loan levels and policies have burdened young people well into their thirties and forties (Oliff et al. 2013). Market forces have expanded community college systems (Mellow and Heelan 2014), but threatened smaller four-year colleges with possible closures (Ward 2016).

The demand for education and training beyond the young adult years suggests a burgeoning marketplace for learning—one that needs to be more compatible with the great variability in the timing and sequencing of work, family, and retirement statuses today. Perhaps not surprisingly, the for-profit institutional market has been quick to respond to these opportunities and capitalize on virtual learning platforms (Deming et al. 2012).

20.2 Higher Education Has a Crucial Role in Smoothing Discontinuities in the Life Course

The life course has become more discontinuous. Precarious employment, rapid advances in technology, and changes in occupational sectors and positions have created the need to deepen training or freshen skills; seek better paying or more secure jobs; pursue second careers; continue learning, even when family and other responsibilities are a priority; and serve people who bypassed higher education earlier in life or simply seek self-enrichment.

Although contemporary lives have irregular rhythms that interfere with institutional expectations, they *are* longer, and a long life is, in the larger historical picture, a relatively recent reality (National Institute on Aging 2011). When coupled with lower fertility, gains in longevity have resulted in more time in adulthood without active

childrearing. Later ages for partnering and parenting also mean that young adulthood is now a period of life spent without a spouse or children (the median age at first marriage is 29 for men and 27 for women). This, in turn, has created new options for how these years are used, with many young people strategically postponing family formation in order to focus on higher education and career-building (Lundberg and Pollack 2013). There is a sense among young adults that one must finish higher education, gain work experience, and build economic resources *before* marriage and parenthood (Settersten 2011a), which are capstones of the process of becoming adult. In addition, increasing proportions of Americans are or intend to remain permanently single and/or childless (Livingston 2015; Wang and Parker 2014). People in these statuses may be drawn to higher education, as they do not have the same life constraints and may have more disposable time and money to allocate to educational opportunities, such as continuing education or pursuing advanced or different types of degrees, throughout their lives.

Most students in the U.S. expect to enroll in postsecondary school immediately after high school graduation, and the share of students who follow this path has been steadily increasing over the last decades—and is currently around 70% (Settersten et al. 2015). The growth of postsecondary options, including for-profit institutions, has both responded to and created the rapid extension and widespread pursuit of higher education, especially for those who do not follow "traditional" pathways as full-time students (Fain and Lederman 2015). Increasing proportions of students in higher education are now simultaneously enrolled in higher education while they have other major responsibilities. For example, 25% of college students in the United States have dependent children, 40% of whom also work full-time (Knoll et al. 2017). Although higher education is to some extent accommodating students with a somewhat different "age" and "relational" college profile, these multiple obligations can limit financial aid and scholarships, which generally assume full-time student enrollment and only intermittent or part-time paid work.

For those who delay education after high school, there may be a problem in making the assumption that time is plentiful and that there are few risks in waiting. For example, not investing in some form of education or training after high school is likely to seriously limit one's life options and outcomes. Perhaps such education or training can be postponed slightly, and in helpful ways, such as when young people take a year or two off before beginning college to gain experiences that can help clarify life goals and purpose. In some countries, these kinds of experiences are institutionalized in "gap year" opportunities.

The pressures of competing responsibilities often deter students from either starting or continuing their education. Despite the rhetoric of second chances and the perception that time is ample, the reality is that returning to school too much later is difficult both practically and financially, especially alongside work and family roles. Some things in life—higher education among them—probably cannot be postponed for long periods without bringing a host of risks and costs. The rising price tag of college and limited personal and institutional supports (Goldrick-Rab 2016) have also played roles in "de-standardizing" or "de-stabilizing" the transition to adulthood, bringing lasting consequences for adult life. These trends are felt acutely in higher education, especially in broad-access institutions with high concentrations of students whose lives do not match the normative assumptions of four-year universities.

Uncertainty regarding whether, when, and where to attend college is driven by the question of whether a college degree is "worth it." Students and their families have grown more instrumental in their decision-making about what a particular institution, degree, or major will provide them. These trends were exacerbated during the Great Recession, as choices became harder and finances became tighter for many families. Of course, the recession also crippled university budgets and put important programs and services on the chopping block, just as it forced many institutions to reorganize in more efficient ways.

But uncertainty is also something to which higher education *responds*. For example, hard economic times, like a recession, can prompt innovation in the life course. It can create an opening for people to make new kinds of choices, or force them to make choices that are different from those they would otherwise make. Indeed, the Great Recession brought more and different types of students into U.S. college classrooms. Especially in the broad-access sector, institutions were filled with increasing numbers of older students who lost jobs as well as traditional-age students with few employment options or the resources to attend four-year institutions. Two-year college entrants were sometimes greeted with new tuition programs that offered some relief. However, these programs were inconsistent across colleges and nonetheless forced some students into the personal loan market, raising the question of whether institutional responses such as these are meeting the needs of their diverse populations.

Some major employers, such as Fidelity, Aetna, and PricewaterhouseCoopers, have been responding to the problem of student debt by including, as part of their hiring packages, funds to go toward student loans (Friedman 2016). Although only 4% of employers currently do so, all colleges should provide students with information about private sector jobs that can help repay student loan debt. This type of repayment has been part of other occupations with labor shortages. With rising college costs and debt, these types of job "perks" can be a real financial asset for potential applicants. Of course, these arrangements seem likely to further help those who are doing well. Still, employer intervention in paying down existing student loans, coupled with student loan refinancing and consolidation, can help manage some of the financial consequences of college loans. Student loan refinancing is not the same as federal student loan consolidation, and these variations in loan repayment are important options that students of every age need to consider in their postsecondary experience. High schools and colleges must better equip students with this information so that they will be able to make better choices about which institutions to attend and fields to study.

Another strategy of some two- and four-year institutions is to more closely tie educational experiences to occupational opportunities by forming partnerships with businesses in local labor markets in an effort to train and recruit students for specific jobs in which there are labor shortages. Some community colleges, for example, are creating consortia to examine how they can prepare students for local and regional jobs in fields such as science, technology, engineering, and mathematics (STEM). Four-year institutions have long had or required internships in many programs, and these, too, have grown. The point to be underscored here is that these collaborative activities are undertaken to develop clearer pathways out of postsecondary institutions and into subsequent employment—just as was once true of the transition from high school to work in an earlier era when fewer students were college-bound (Rosenbaum et al. 1990).

20.3   Institutional Responses to Differences and Complexities in Students' Lives

How might higher education capitalize on the complexities and constraints of student lives, from those who begin college immediately after high school graduation to older students who were never enrolled or are returning after degrees were disrupted or abandoned? For younger students, too often the assumption is made that parents are both present and involved (even too involved) in getting their students to college and supporting them once they are there. This is not always the case. In addition, colleges walk a fine line of simultaneously drawing in parents and keeping them at bay, whether through recruitment and transition processes, parent weekends, or notices of failing grades or unpaid tuition and fees. For traditional-age students, colleges have realized that they must involve parents, many of whom are as connected to their children as their children are to them, and many of whom do not have the skills or knowledge to help their student navigate college. The latter is especially true in

the broad-access sector and for parents of first-generation college students (see Beattie, Chap. 8, this volume).

For students who are "non-traditional" in age, in direct contrast, parents are often irrelevant to the picture, or at least not as relevant as sources of support as they are to fresh high school graduates. At residential colleges especially, students who are older are acutely aware of the fact that they are "off-time" with respect to university policies, services, and campus life, which are organized around younger students. For these older students, spouses and other adults (including children) may be crucial sources of both support and strain. In contrast to students who are about to graduate high school, colleges do little to engage the relevant relationships that might matter for the success of older students, who may be anywhere from their mid-twenties to retirement age.

Even though parents are recognized as a force to be taken into account, colleges often treat students as if they are autonomous. And yet, students of all ages are embedded in larger networks of family and social relationships that can foster or compete with their success. These complexities only grow with age, and they affect the options students have and choices they make. The notion of an autonomous student, or even an autonomous adult, is therefore somewhat problematic. Adult life is constrained by relationships and responsibilities that are primary sources of meaning. How students relate—or are *able* to relate—to institutions of higher education depends on the relationships they have with other people and the other roles they are juggling.

Rather than design policies and experiences that place such a strong premium on students' autonomy, institutions should recognize the interdependencies that students bring with them. This is especially true of older students and those in broad-access environments, but it is not exclusive to them. Students everywhere, and of all ages, may have financial or caregiving obligations to members of their families. They may be providing emotional support to parents and other family members whose lives have come undone by divorce, illness and death, job loss, or other hardships. A student's welfare and success is compromised by these things. Educators too often assume that the lives of students, especially young students, are carefree and focused on school, when the reality is that students are often carrying significant but invisible burdens of many kinds. Not all students take for granted their presence in college. Many students allocate their time and expenditures carefully and have deep commitments to learning, even as they are balancing financial and family pressures.

20.4 Contradictory Institutional Messages About Students' "Independence"

Traditionally, universities are perceived as places for young people to *get ready* for adulthood. Those who are young and in school (even in graduate and professional schools) are often viewed, and view themselves, as being in a role that sets them *apart* and even *protects* them from adulthood (Settersten et al. 2015). To be fully adult is to be out of school, and to be in school is to be "not quite adult" (Settersten and Ray 2010b). We have even heard administrators and professors use the term "kids" in talking about students, which says something about who we think education is for and perhaps the perceived maturity level of students. An important way to shift dynamics in higher education is to get students to visualize themselves as *adults*—and for parents and those working in higher education to do the same. At the very least, effort in this direction can begin to forge a revised narrative about who a student is and the agency, autonomy, and accountability consistent with that language (Settersten et al. 2015). In contrast, for those who are already well into adulthood, being able to visualize oneself as a *student* seems an important first step in entering or re-entering higher education (Schneider and Stevenson 1999), shedding the idea that being a student means going backward rather than forward in life.

Although the virtues of autonomy and individual responsibility are evident in many university practices and policies, institutions send contradictory signals about the standing of students *as* adults. One of these signals is that four-year residential colleges are designed as if they hold the status of "in loco parentis"—professors, advisors, administrators, and staff track and monitor the academic progress and social life of students. Residential campuses are full-service institutions: one-stop shops for housing, meals, counseling, banking, health care, fitness, social activities, and career planning. This is not to say that these services are not vital to adulthood. But these students have resided under a protective umbrella where access to college, the ability to differentiate quality of service, and payment are largely left up to the institution and parents.

Another example of contradictory signals of adult status is that colleges require that parental income be used to determine financial aid, under the assumption that parents continue to be providers to children well in their 20s. The Affordable Care Act provision for parents to cover their children up to age 26 under their health insurance was a response to the protracted course to adulthood. At the same time, the Family Educational Rights and Privacy Act (FERPA) in higher education gives parents very limited rights to their student's education records. Policies like these convey mixed messages about students and their parents being *legally independent*, even though they are generally *not independent* psychologically, socially, or economically (see also Schneider et al. 2016).

Ironically, the reality of *inter*dependence is especially apparent in the United States, where the government and public place a high premium on personal responsibility and self-reliance. The launching of children into adulthood and the pursuit of higher education are considered "private troubles" to be shouldered by families rather than "public issues" that are shared by many and warrant collective investment, to use C. Wright Mills' (1959) famous phrases. Interestingly, this framing closely parallels the funding debate in higher education and the historic shift in who pays—away from the public and toward students and families. It reveals itself in starkly different political visions from the left and right regarding access to college as well as cost and debt, as was evident in proposals related to college access and financing during the 2016 Presidential election debates in the United States.

Despite the strong master narrative in the United States about the need for independence, the reality is that students of all ages are embedded in matrices of family and social ties that can help them along or hold them back. These relationship interdependencies are part of students' choices and determine how students are able to interface with institutions of higher education. Life-course scholarship repeatedly points to the power of social ties in conditioning individuals' opportunities and outcomes in every period of life (Settersten 2015b). Rather than cling to the cultural myth of independence as the hallmark of adulthood, educators might instead rethink higher education in ways that explicitly recognize the fact that adult lives are deeply constrained by obligations to others.

One of the major sociological contributions to the study of occupational success is the importance of building wide and strong social networks that can be activated as needed to access opportunities and resources (Granovetter 1973; Coleman 1994). For students from more privileged backgrounds, wider and stronger networks of social relationships have been cultivated by parents to ensure their readiness for and access to higher education. After graduation, part of the "value" of a degree from a more elite institution is that it buys a deep and well-connected alumni network, which further extends social connections and opportunities (Alon 2015).

Middle-class parents are more likely to have and to activate people in their networks who can help find opportunities and resources for their children. In addition, middle-class parents expect to support their children through college and beyond, and middle-class students expect to have that support. This is not as true in working-class and low-income families, where there is a stronger emphasis on "independence" and encouragement to achieve it faster (Settersten 2011b). Being an "adult" in these environments often means making it without the help of others. This runs counter to the scenario that advantaged young people take for granted, and it is a poten-

tially detrimental strategy today. These are the very kinds of students who are more likely to be found in families and institutions with limited resources or in families with limited knowledge or guidance in how to access resources.

20.5 Institutions of Higher Education Can Strengthen the Transition to Adulthood

Higher education will seemingly always be focused more on the young, not only because it is a natural continuation of secondary schooling but because young people are more "biographically available" for full-time higher education, to use Doug McAdam's (1988) phrase (that is, they are relatively free of responsibilities). Indeed, colleges are unquestionably the single most important settings in which rising numbers of young adults spend time after they graduate high school (Settersten et al. 2015). Larger proportions of young adults aspire to and are enrolled in higher education—and these pursuits are a major driver of a longer and more variable course to adulthood. Getting education takes time. How higher education plays out in early adult life is also a major driver of inequality as individuals move through and out of their twenties. Life-course studies repeatedly show that early life advantage and disadvantage accumulate in ways that determine options and outcomes in higher education, and that these, in turn, accumulate over the many decades of adult life that follow (Dannefer 2003; DiPrete and Eirich 2006).

In light of the reconfiguration of young adulthood, it is no wonder that higher education is struggling to respond. The massive evolution of the broad access sector, and especially for-profit outfits, has only heightened the sense that higher education is in flux. This sector has moved rapidly to fill this opening in the marketplace, but it often suffers with low graduation rates and low transfer rates for students who intended to obtain baccalaureate degrees (Stevens 2015). The response of two-year environments has in many instances been well designed, with the implementation of stronger advising programs, classes that are labeled as remedial but designed to promote student success, and tutoring and counseling services to keep students on track toward graduation.

Four-year environments are not exempt from having to rethink their mission and impact for whole new generations of students with distinct learning styles, worldviews, and life preferences. Four-year environments represent just one of many types of environments, and efforts to remake college must not be blinded by "traditional" institutions, curricula, and modes of learning. It is problematic that educators continue to see elite institutions as the "gold standard" against which other types of institutions are to be judged, and yet elite institutions comprise only a tiny fraction of the landscape of higher education (Stevens 2015).

Many young people might benefit from delaying higher education for a few years, especially if it means they will enter with a better sense of who they are and what they want, and with a greater commitment to learning. Many also simply do not have the ability, resources, or support to enroll in higher education straightaway. In some countries, such as Norway, Denmark, and Sweden, it is normative for students to take a "gap year" before starting college, especially to travel. In other countries, such as Switzerland and Israel, "civil service" or military requirements force such a delay. In the United States, where students rarely (intentionally) take gap years, even students who enter just a year or two later feel "out of sync" developmentally and socially with their peers. However, growing numbers of institutions, especially elite institutions like Harvard and Princeton, offer deferred admission for a year or even have "bridge year" programs that mimic gap year-type experiences or create travel abroad opportunities for students in their first rather than third or fourth years. In the United States, growing numbers of undergraduate students also seem to have their sights set on immediately enrolling in graduate programs, but again often without a clear sense (or with a misguided sense) of why or of what it will do for them.

Unbridled exploration in higher education is clearly problematic and expensive. But strategic exploration is important in helping students find degrees and majors that are a good match to who they are, how they learn, and where they want to go in the future. Many policies, however, actively discourage and penalize exploration (e.g., time limits in locking into majors, completing degrees, and transferring credits). There are significant and understandable tensions related to having time to explore and being "timely" in degree progress. But students often have underdeveloped (and unrealistic) senses of their futures, and they have been told by personnel and parents that higher education is precisely for figuring that out, especially in the first two years.

When students delay declaring their majors, they also run the risk of being unable to finish their degrees on time, not only because there may not be enough time to meet requirements but because required courses may not be offered with enough regularity. This adds time and therefore cost to getting the degree. The normative time to a "four-year" degree is now five years, and sometimes longer (Bound et al. 2012). But it is not just a problem of money: People who do not finish degrees in a timely manner often are judged as being unfocused and floundering.

There is also the problem of information: whether information is available, helpful, and delivered in the right way or at the right time to help students make decisions. Students often do not know what they want and settle on majors late. But they are also sometimes locked out of courses because of limited offerings or schedule conflicts. Only 19% of students in four-year degrees finish in that time, and institutions of higher education are increasingly being held accountable for graduating students within four years (Akers and Butler 2016). Some, like the College of Liberal Arts at Oregon State, are guaranteeing that students will finish in four years; if not, the university will pay additional tuition costs, as long as certain conditions are met with respect to the timing of major declaration, advising, and staying on track with course load and tuition payments (Oregon State University 2017). Some colleges are even beginning to guarantee minimum degree earnings, with the college paying all or part of the graduate's student loan payments if they do not cross a salary threshold; others are beginning to guarantee job placements, and even jobs in the field of study (Akers and Butler 2016). Indeed, one of the "seismic shifts" in higher education today and in the decade ahead is that the public and policy makers will make ever-stronger demands on institutions to demonstrate returns on student investment (Selingo 2016). This issue of accountability of higher education is raising critical questions about what is learned in college and how to measure it (Arum and Roska 2011, 2014). Higher education is unlikely to be spared the scrutiny and pressure that elementary and secondary schools have encountered in the past two decades.

It is also important to rethink the assumption that students will—or should—finish college where they start it. Particular attention must be paid to a group of students we might call "swirlers." More than one-third (38%) of students attend more than one college, and over one-fifth of students who eventually complete a degree do so at a college other than the one in which they started (Shapiro et al. 2015). How can institutions best serve students when they may only intersect with a small portion of students' pathways? And are they therefore paying for services that students do not need? Institutions naturally want to do what they can to increase retention. In light of the surprisingly high percentages of students who swirl, colleges must work more collaboratively to ease the process as these transitions are being made, and must have a willingness to invest in the wellbeing of students who will not ultimately stay and may even be better served by going elsewhere. This means that something like "learning progress" might need to be advanced as an alternative and appropriate goal for students, rather than to so exclusively interpret transfer and completion rates of degree seekers as the only markers of success.

20.6   Higher Education in the Life Course: Beyond Young Adults

How might higher education be made more meaningful in the life course? It is not only young adulthood that is being transformed, but middle age and old age too. These changes should lead to sizable demand and interest in higher education in all periods of life, if educators can get creative about how to design and deliver it. A greater possibility of getting education after early adulthood hinges on having flexibility in life and whether it meets the person's needs and purposes. Being able to step away from other responsibilities to invest in or reinvent oneself through higher education is easier to do when one has resources. The risks of departing from normative pathways and innovating a life course are also offset when one has resources to fall back on. "Lifelong education" also cannot be primarily for those who are already well educated, or it will simply deepen inequality. It must appeal to those who *need* education throughout life as much as to those who are willing or able to actually take it up. Although colleges continue to cater to traditional-age students, they should begin to think more seriously about how they might be reworked to become more age-integrated, especially at undergraduate levels.

To find a bigger place for education throughout the life course, people in middle and later life must be targets of higher education. Returning to school in midlife, for example, poses unique challenges and demands and different institutional and policy solutions relative to young adulthood. For example, in the U.S. leaving full-time work to pursue study means going without insurance or needing to be partnered with someone who can provide it; leaving full-time continuous work means long-term losses in pensions and Social Security. Stepping into a new career at a later age may not leave adequate time for promotions and may bring age discrimination. The middle of life is also already tightly squeezed by work, parenting, and parent care responsibilities.

Online educational platforms have been crucial to reaching place-bound students who have significant work and family responsibilities. But for these students, education is generally being added onto existing responsibilities, not replacing them. And although online platforms offer a gateway to new educational opportunities, they also require strong self-discipline, goal-directedness, and study habits and skills that may be lacking in the very students these platforms hope to reach.

Similarly, we earlier noted the opportunity in an aging society to intentionally increase the participation of older people in higher education. Later life is embodied with so much possibility, yet it is so contingent on having health, wealth, and other resources, which can quickly undermine the potentials of the later years. This is the difference in what gerontologists call the "third" and "fourth" ages of later life (e.g., Laslett 1989). The third age is a period during which most people no longer have childcare or work responsibilities but are in good health. The fourth age, in contrast, involves major encounters with illnesses and is often followed in short order by death. Any educational programming catered to older individuals must come to terms with the fact that there is an optimal window for designing such programs and outreach because the physical and cognitive challenges of aging can pose challenges for learning (for illustrations, see Findsen and Mormosa 2012; Jovic and McMullin 2011).

Some existing campuses, especially residential campuses, are attempting to become more "age friendly." Along these lines, the Age-Friendly University Global Network has put forward ten principles to foster the inclusion of older adults on campuses (Association for Gerontology in Higher Education 2017). These principles, which have been adopted by a growing network of institutions in Ireland, the U.K., the U.S., Canada, and beyond, include promoting the participation of older people in core activities of the university, personal and career development, intergenerational learning, online learning, health and wellness programs, and arts and cultural activities.

Others are building "universities of the third age" that are explicitly and exclusively meant for retirement-age students in the healthy phase of later life (for example, see u3a.com). This largely European movement is composed of groups that have formal relationships with local universities, while others are groups that rely on the wealth of experience and knowledge of members to create informal learning experiences.

These institutions are a response to a large and growing market niche of "successful agers" who seek personal enrichment and learning communities rather than degrees. The limited time horizons of these students leads them to focus on personal meaning, not labor markets. These initiatives are emerging precisely because four-year settings, in particular, are so focused on the young, which reinforces the segregation of young and old students and misses an important opportunity to create more age-integrated learning opportunities. Lessons for four-year universities can be learned from community colleges, which have long served older students and have had to respond appropriately in designing flexible environments—with student demand for more convenient class times (evenings, weekends, or intensive spurts), formats (online, hybrid or "flipped" classrooms), part-time enrollment, and lower-cost options. For older students, questions about costs of time and money are exacerbated because there is little time to "waste" in school and there is limited time to recoup or reap any economic or other benefits of schooling.

No matter, the term "non-traditional" should be abandoned in an effort to build more age-inclusive campuses. This does not mean that the needs of students of different ages are the same; they are not. But it is being mindful of the ways that such a term, which signals that the presence of students outside of their early 20s is not normal, can be divisive and create dynamics of segregation and stigma. Even if it is not ill-intended, "traditional" becomes a "normative standard against which other kinds of students and colleges are easily viewed as lesser approximations" (Stevens 2015, p. 10). Indeed, the "traditional" college student is an increasingly smaller minority of the student population at large (Deil-Amen 2015). Unlike elementary and secondary schools, which are age-graded, it is important to not exclusively design higher education for students under age 24 when the average remainder of adult life now spans an additional five or six decades. It is also peculiar that the term "non-traditional" is used so exclusively in relation to age rather than to reference other social groups with historically low presence in or access to higher education.

20.7 The Effects of Higher Education *on* the Life Course

Trying to find a bigger place for education throughout the life course is different from the effects that education has *on* the life course—that is, what it does *for* the life course. A common refrain among those who work in higher education is that it is meant to broadly improve the future outcomes of individuals. The outcomes on which educators, parents, and students are focused, however, are immediate and narrow: on degrees and majors that lead to "better" jobs—which usually means higher wages—in the labor market. Of course, these emphases also reflect the growing costs (and debt) of college, as students have become consumers and as colleges and universities have become more corporate. (In the administrative spreadsheets at one university with which we are familiar, the column referring to students was labeled "RGUs"—Revenue Generating Units!) The premium on revenue has also been heightened in the face of shrinking state budgets and diminishing federal research funds. These things are understandable, but they are radically, and dangerously, altering the goals and content of higher education.

Research must interrogate these assumptions from a life-course perspective: Are students really being equipped with skills and capacities that have broad applicability and durability? Are their credentials truly gateways to long-term opportunities? For example, there is growing evidence that college degrees are associated with

effects much broader than employment and salary. Over the life course, higher education has positive effects on health, civic engagement, parent and child outcomes, social relationships, and life satisfaction and self-direction (e.g., Cutler and Lleras-Muney 2014; Goldman and Smith 2011; Hirshorn and Settersten 2013; Hout 2012).

And yet, these positive effects of college are surely much less about what is learned or experienced in a mere handful of years, and much more about where college takes students after they finish—into different patterns of family formation, and into different kinds of professions and workplaces, neighborhoods and networks. For this reason, higher education policy must be recognized as being social, economic, and health policy too. The effects of higher education carry over into other sectors, and are both compounded and underestimated.

In an era where college students and their families focus on the applicability of credentials for the labor market, too much priority is placed on curricula that emphasize narrow skills with a direct link to specific jobs. Many of the goals of higher education seem misaligned with what people need to be successful in adult life. Chief among them are how to (1) adapt and be resilient in the face of change, disappointment, and failure; (2) develop clearer and more differentiated goals; (3) find a sense of purpose (or a "spark," to use the Search Institute's (2017) phrase) that brings meaning and gives shape to plans; and to build capacity for (4) intimacy and close social relationships, (5) intergroup relationships in our diverse and multicultural nations, (6) self-awareness and the ability to take the perspectives of others, and (7) self-regulation, in being able to control one's impulses and emotions in order to live, learn, and work successfully with others (for illustrations, Settersten 2011b). These kinds of "non-cognitive" or "soft skills" have become increasingly important in determining how young people fare in higher education (Walton and Cohen 2007; Yeager and Walton 2011). These skills are important for communicating and finding support in relationships with teachers, administrators, and peers; for accessing resources; and for meeting expectations, handling disappointments, and persisting in the face of setbacks.

Increasingly, researchers are finding these capacities to be predictive of college performance and completion and later personal, social and economic success (e.g., McClelland et al. 2013). Many would argue that these kinds of competencies are prerequisites for entering college. Many students do not have these skills, which are internalized as personal inadequacies and reinforced by others who view them as floundering. But they are also skills that should *result from* experience in higher education. What might higher education look like if curricula were redesigned in ways that prioritized student competencies in these areas? What might it mean if we asked students to, say, declare a *life mission* rather than a major, and design curricula around that mission?

Several colleges have institutionalized these skill sets and are in the process of incorporating them into orientation programs or into the services students seek out or are sent to when they encounter problems. One example of this is the University Innovation Alliance (UIA), which is constituted by a group of public universities dedicated to supporting and improving the social, emotional, and cognitive skills of all students regardless of their racial, ethnic, social and economic backgrounds (see www.theuia.org). The UIA model, which also includes a spate of evaluation strategies, focuses on competencies often not explicitly targeted for higher education classrooms but which, with the life course in mind, should be targeted.

Students from less privileged backgrounds, however, are less likely to have these capacities upon entry, which only exacerbates their risks. This makes the wide array of student services and resources offered in higher education all the more important to successful outcomes for at-risk students so that they are able to "crack the codes" of these environments. In seeking to improve experiences in higher education, it seems crucial to foster these kinds of skills in primary and secondary school students. The model of learning in higher education assumes that these skills are present; success in higher education is dependent

on them, and so many of the challenges in higher education relate to not having them (Yeager et al. 2016). These skills are arguably even *more* important in online platforms, where students are unmoored from the press of formal classrooms and the physical presence of professors and peers.

20.8 Conclusion

Ideas about higher education and jobs are too often in the minds of educators and parents based on the worlds they knew when they were students. Most administrators and faculty are disconnected from the realities of the job market, and most are not knowledgeable about how to navigate careers outside of academia, which very few students will enter. We too often operate as if students need to have their lives planned at the end of high school or in college—yet, the reality is that very few of us are doing the work we imagined ourselves doing when we were 18 or 22. Even with best-laid plans, adult lives are unpredictable, and work trajectories will be characterized by multiple employers and positions, and even spells of unemployment. Educators too often assume a strong and direct link between particular degrees and majors and particular jobs in the market, but the reality is that career dynamics and market forces do not work in a rigid, lock-step fashion.

How then should higher education respond? For one, the curriculum of colleges must accommodate the needs of a changing workforce, and to recognize that the jobs of today are not necessarily the jobs of tomorrow. This means not only producing graduates who have technical knowledge; they must also have strong writing and communication skills and be able to work in teams, make decisions and solve problems, and plan, organize, and prioritize their work. Indeed, these are skills that many bosses say their new college graduates do not have (Strauss 2016), and reports continue to question whether college graduates are prepared for the demands of a creative and innovative workforce (Tierney and Lanford 2016; Obama 2015). Recent evidence reveals a dramatic difference in the views of business leaders and those of chief academic officers of colleges with respect to whether college graduates are properly equipped for the work-force—fully 96% of academic officers believe their graduates are work-ready, and yet only 11% of business leaders think so (Butler 2016b).

There is intense pressure for colleges to inno-vate and reform, and they can expect to see decreased funding, especially in public four-year universities whose budgets are heavily bound to state legislatures and where average operating costs rose by 17% between 2000 to 2012 (U.S. Department of Education 2014). Even though recent attempts in the Obama administra-tion to tie federal financial aid to institutional rat-ings on access, affordability, graduation rates, and earnings of graduates were met with strong resistance and ultimately dropped, we can expect higher education to become increasingly suscep-tible to accountability initiatives, much as it has been in primary and secondary schools.

The issues treated in this chapter point to the need for a bold reimagining of higher educa-tion—of what is learned, of when it should occur and what it is good for, the processes and mecha-nisms through which it affects a wide variety of life outcomes, and how researchers and policy makers should in turn measure the success of students, professors, and institutions. This requires an equally bold agenda of research questions, and methods and data to support it. The future of higher education, and of the human life course, rests on remaking college in revolu-tionary ways.

References

Akers, B., & Butler, S. M. (2016, August 24). *Should col-lege come with a money-back guarantee?* (Brookings Series on Disruptions in Higher Education). Retrieved from https://www.brookings.edu/opinions/should-college-come-with-a-money-back-guarantee/

Alon, S. (2015). *Race, class, and affirmative action*. New York: Russell Sage Foundation.

Angel, J. L., & Settersten, R. A., Jr. (2012). The new realities of aging: Social and economic contexts. In L. Waite (Ed.), *New directions in the sociology of aging* (pp. 95–119). Washington, DC: National Academies Press.

Arum, R., & Roska, J. (2011). *Academically adrift: Limited learning on college campuses*. Chicago: The University of Chicago Press.

Arum, R., & Roska, J. (2014). *Aspiring adults adrift: Tentative transitions of college graduates*. Chicago: The University of Chicago Press.

Association of Gerontology in Higher Education. (2017). *The Age-Friendly University (AFU) global network*. Retrieved from https://www.aghe.org/resources/age-friendly-university-principles

Baum, S., Kurose, C., & McPherson, M. (2013). An overview of American higher education. *Future of Children, 23*(1), 17–39. Retrieved from http://www.jstor.org/stable/23409487

Blau, P., & Duncan, O. D. (1967). *The American occupa-tional structure*. New York: Wiley.

Bound, J., Lovenheim, M. F., & Turner, S. (2012). Increasing time to baccalaureate degree in the United States. *Education Finance and Policy, 7*, 375–424. https://doi.org/10.1162/EDFP_a_00074.

Butler, S. M. (2016a, February 4). *Is business about to disrupt the college accreditation system?* (Brookings Series on Disruptions in Higher Education). Retrieved from https://www.brookings.edu/opinions/is-busi-ness-about-to-disrupt-the-college-accreditation-sys-tem/

Butler, S. M. (2016b, December 20). *Business is likely to reshape higher education* (Brookings Series on Disruptions in Higher Education). Retrieved from https://www.brookings.edu/opinions/business-is-likely-to-reshape-higher-ed/

Christensen, K., & Schneider, B. (Eds.). (2015). *Workplace flexibility: Realigning 20th-century jobs for a 21st-century workforce*. Ithaca: Cornell University Press.

Coleman, J. (1994). *Foundations of social theory*. Boston: Harvard University Press.

Cutler, D., & Lleras-Muney, A. (2014). Education and health. In A. J. Culyer (Ed.), *Encyclopedia of health economics* (Vol. 1, pp. 232–245). San Diego: Elsevier.

Dannefer, D. (2003). Cumulative advantage/disadvan-tage and the life course: Cross-fertilizing age and social science theory. *Journal of Gerontology: Social Sciences, 58B*, S327–S337. https://doi.org/10.1093/geronb/58.6.S327.

Deil-Amen, R. (2015). The "traditional" college student: A smaller and smaller minority and its implications for diversity and access institutions. In M. L. Stevens & M. Kirst (Eds.), *Remaking college: Broad-access higher education for a new era* (pp. 134–165). Palo Alto: Stanford University Press.

Deming, D. J., Goldin, C., & Katz, L. F. (2012). The for-profit postsecondary school sector: Nimble crit-ters or agile predators? *The Journal of Economic Perspectives, 26*(1), 139–164. https://doi.org/10.1257/jep.26.1.139.

DiPrete, T. A., & Eirich, G. M. (2006). Cumulative advan-tage as a mechanism for inequality: A review of theo-retical and empirical developments. *Annual Review of Sociology, 32*, 271–297. https://doi.org/10.1146/annurev.soc.32.061604.123127.

Dundar, A., Hossler, D., Shapiro, D., Chen, J., Martin, S., Torres, V., Zerquera, D., & Ziskin, M. (2011, July). *National postsecondary enrollment trends: Before, during, and after the great recession* (Signature Report No.1). Herndon: National Student Clearinghouse Research Center. Retrieved from https://nscresearch-center.org/signaturereport1/

Fain, P., & Lederman, D. (2015). Boom, regulate, cleanse, and repeat: For-profit colleges' slow but inevitable drive toward acceptability. In M. L. Stevens & M. Kirst (Eds.), *Remaking college: Broad-access higher education for a new era* (pp. 61–83). Palo Alto: Stanford University Press.

Findsen, B., & Mormosa, M. (Eds.). (2012). *Lifelong learning in later life: A handbook on older adult learning.* Rotterdam: Springer.

Friedman, Z. (2016, December 19). Student loan repayment: The hottest employee benefit of 2017. *Forbes Magazine.* Retrieved from https://www.forbes.com/sites/zackfriedman/2016/12/19/student-loan-repayment-benefit/#41fef2c1d6fe

Goldman, D., & Smith, J. P. (2011). The increasing value of education to health. *Social Science & Medicine, 72,* 728–737. https://doi.org/10.1016/j.socscimed.2011.02.047.

Goldrick-Rab, S. (2016). *Paying the price: College costs, financial aid, and the betrayal of the American dream.* Chicago: University of Chicago Press.

Granovetter, M. (1973). The strength of weak ties. *The American Journal of Sociology, 78*(6), 1360–1380. https://doi.org/10.1086/225469.

Hirshorn, B., & Settersten, R. A., Jr. (2013). Civic involvement across the life course: Moving beyond age-based assumptions. *Advances in Life Course Research, 18,* 199–211. https://doi.org/10.1016/j.alcr.2013.05.001.

Hout, M. (2012). Social and economic returns to college education in the United States. *Annual Review of Sociology, 38,* 379–400. https://doi.org/10.1146/annurev.soc.012809.102503.

Jovic, E., & McMullin, J. (2011). Learning and aging. In R. A. Settersten Jr. & J. Angel (Eds.), *Handbook of sociology of aging* (pp. 229–244). New York: Springer.

Kena, G., Hussar, W., de McFarland, J., Brey, C., Musu-Gillette, L., Wang, X., Zhang, J., Rathbun, A., Wilkinson-Flicker, S., Diliberti, M., Barmer, A., Bullock Mann, F., & Dunlop Velez, E. (2016). *The condition of education 2016* (NCES 2016-144). U.S. Department of Education, National Center for Education Statistics. Washington, DC. Retrieved from http://nces.ed.gov/pubsearch

Knoll, E., Gault, B., & Cruse, L. R. (2017, January 30). *College students with children: National and regional profiles.* Washington, DC: Institute for Women's Policy Research. Retrieved from https://iwpr.org/publications/college-students-children-national-regional-profiles/

Kohli, M. (2007). The institutionalization of the life course: Looking back to look ahead. *Research*

in *Human Development, 4,* 253–271. https://doi.org/10.1080/15427600701663122.

Laslett, P. (1989). *A fresh map of life: The emergence of the third age.* London: Weidenfeld and Nicolson.

Livingston, G. (2015, May 7). *Childlessness.* Washington, DC: Pew Research Center. Retrieved from http://www.pewsocialtrends.org/2015/05/07/childlessness/

Lundberg, S., & Pollack, R. A. (2013). *Cohabitation and the uneven retreat from marriage in the U.S., 1950–2010* (NBER Working Paper No. 19413). Cambridge, MA: National Bureau of Economic Research. https://doi.org/10.3386/w19413.

McAdam, D. (1988). *Freedom summer.* New York: Oxford University Press.

McClelland, M. M., Acock, A. C., Piccinin, A., Rhea, S. A., & Stallings, M. C. (2013). Relations between preschool attention span-persistence and age 25 educational outcomes. *Early Childhood Research Quarterly, 28*(2), 314–324. https://doi.org/10.1016/j.ecresq.2012.07.008.

Mellow, G. O., & Heelan, C. M. (2014). *Minding the dream: The process and practice of the American community college.* Lanham: Rowman & Littlefield.

Mills, C. W. (1959). *The sociological imagination.* New York: Oxford University Press.

Moen, P. (2016). *Encore adulthood: Boomers on the edge of risk, renewal, and purpose.* Oxford: Oxford University Press.

National Institute on Aging. (2011). *Global health and aging.* Bethesda: National Institute on Aging, National Institutes of Health, U.S. Department of Health and Human Services, and the World Health Organization. Retrieved from https://www.nia.nih.gov/research/publication/global-health-and-aging/living-longer

National Institute on Aging. (2015). *Growing older in America: The health and retirement study.* Bethesda: National Institute on Aging, National Institutes of Health, U.S. Dept. of Health and Human Services. Retrieved from https://hrs.isr.umich.edu/about/data-book

Obama, B. (2015, September 12). *Weekly address: A new college scorecard.* Retrieved from https://obamawhitehouse.archives.gov/the-press-office/2015/09/12/weekly-address-new-college-scorecard

Oliff, P., Palacios, V., Johnson, I., & Leachman, M. (2013, March 19). *Recent deep state higher education cuts may harm students and the economy for years to come.* Washington, DC: Center on Budget and Policy Priorities. Retrieved from www.cbpp.org/sites/default/files/atoms/files/3-19-13sfp.pdf

Oregon State University. (2017, February 21). *OSU College of Liberal Arts to offer four-year graduation guarantee to incoming students.* Retrieved from http://oregonstate.edu/ua/ncs/archives/2017/feb/osu%E2%80%99s-college-liberal-arts-offer-four-year-graduation-guarantee-incoming-students

Rosenbaum, J. E., Kariya, T., Settersten, R. A., Jr., & Maier, T. (1990). Market and network theories of the high school-to-work transition: Their application to industrialized societies. *Annual Review of Sociology, 16*, 263–299. https://doi.org/10.1146/annurev.so.16.080190.001403.

Schneider, B., & Stevenson, D. (1999). *The ambitious generation: America's teenagers, motivated but directionless*. New Haven: Yale University Press.

Schneider, B., & Waite, L. J. (2005). *Being together, working apart: Dual-career families and the work-life balance*. Cambridge: Cambridge University Press.

Schneider, B., Klager, C., Chen, I. C., & Burns, J. (2016). Transitioning into adulthood: Striking a balance between support and independence. *Policy Insights from Behavioral and Brain Sciences, 3*(1), 106–113. https://doi.org/10.1177/2372732215624932.

Search Institute. (2017). *Sparks and thriving*. Minneapolis. Retrieved from http://www.search-institute.org/sparks

Selingo, J. (2016). *2026 The decade ahead: The seismic shifts transforming the future of higher education*. Washington, DC: The Chronicle of Higher Education.

Settersten, R. A., Jr. (2011a). Becoming adult: Meanings and markers for young Americans. In M. Waters, P. Carr, M. Kefalas, & J. Holdaway (Eds.), *Coming of age in America: The transition to adulthood in the twenty-first century* (pp. 169–190). Berkeley: University of California Press.

Settersten, R. A., Jr. (2011b). The contemporary context of young adulthood in the United States: From demography to development, from private troubles to public issues. In A. Booth, S. Brown, N. Landale, W. Manning, & S. McHale (Eds.), *Early adulthood in a family context* (pp. 3–26). New York: Springer.

Settersten, R. A., Jr. (2015a). The new landscape of early adulthood: Implications for broad-access higher education. In M. L. Stevens & M. Kirst (Eds.), *Remaking college: Broad-access higher education for a new era* (pp. 113–133). Palo Alto: Stanford University Press.

Settersten, R. A., Jr. (2015b). Relationships in time and the life course: The significance of linked lives. *Research in Human Development, 12*(3–4), 217–223. https://doi.org/10.1080/15427609.2015.1071944.

Settersten, R. A., Jr., & Ray, B. (2010a). What's going on with young people today? The long and twisting path to adulthood. *Future of Children, 20*(1), 19–41. http://www.jstor.org/stable/27795058.

Settersten, R. A., Jr., & Ray, B. E. (2010b). *Not quite adults*. New York: Bantam.

Settersten, R. A., Jr., Ottusch, T. M., & Schneider, B. (2015). Becoming adult: Meanings of markers to adulthood. In R. A. Scott & S. M. Kosslyn (Eds.), *Emerging trends in the social and behavioral sciences* (19 pages, published online). Thousands Oaks: SAGE Publications.

Sewell, W. H., Haller, A. O., & Ohlendorf, G. W. (1970). The educational and early occupational status attainment process: Replication and revision. *American Sociological Review, 35*(9), 1014–1027. Retrieved from http://www.jstor.org/stable/2093379

Shapiro, D., Dundar, A., Wakhungu, P. K., Yuan, X., & Harrell, A. (2015, July). *Transfer and mobility: A national view of student movement in postsecondary institutions, Fall 2008 cohort* (Signature Report No. 9). Herndon: National Student Clearinghouse Research Center. Retrieved from https://nscresearch-center.org/signaturereport9/

Stevens, M. L. (2015). Introduction: The changing ecology of U.S. higher education. In M. L. Stevens & M. Kirst (Eds.), *Remaking college: Broad-access higher education for a new era* (pp. 1–15). Palo Alto: Stanford University Press.

Strauss, K. (2016, May 17). *These are the skills bosses say new college grads do not have*. Forbes. Retrieved from https://www.forbes.com/sites/karstenstrauss/2016/05/17/these-are-the-skills-bosses-say-new-college-grads-do-not-have/#7348be985491

Tierney, W., & Lanford, M. (2016). Conceptualizing innovation in higher education. In M. Paulsen (Ed.), *Higher education: Handbook of theory and research* (pp. 1–39). Cham: Springer.

U.S. Department of Education, National Center for Education Statistics. (2014). *Data point: Out-of-pocket net price for college* (NCES Publication No. 2014-902). Retrieved from https://nces.ed.gov/pubs2014/2014902.pdf

Walton, G., & Cohen, G. (2007). A question of belonging: Race, social fit, and achievement. *Journal of Personality and Social Psychology, 92*(1), 82–96. https://doi.org/10.1037/0022-3514.92.1.82.

Wang, W., & Parker, K. (2014). *Record share of Americans have never married*. Washington, DC: Pew Research Center. Retrieved from http://www.pewsocialtrends.org/2014/09/24/record-share-of-americans-have-never-married/

Ward, J. D. (2016). Troubling changes in capital structures at small private colleges. *Journal of Higher Education Management, 31*(1), 57–74. Retrieved from aaua.org/journals/pdfs/JHEM%2031-1%202016.pdf

Yeager, D. S., & Walton, G. M. (2011). Social-psychological interventions in education: They're not magic. *Review of Educational Research, 81*(2), 267–301. https://doi.org/10.3102/0034654311405999.

Yeager, D., Walton, G., Brady, S., Akcinar, E., Paunesku, D., Keane, L., Kamentz, D., Ritter, G., Duckworth, A. L., Urstein, R., Gomez, E. M., Markus, H. R., Cohen, G. L., & Dweck, C. (2016). Teaching a lay theory before college narrows achievement gaps at scale. *Proceedings of the National Academy of Sciences of the United States of America, 113*(24), E3341–E3348. https://doi.org/10.1073/pnas.1524360113.

Part V

Sociological Perspectives on Accountability and Evaluation

Accountability, Achievement, and Inequality in American Public Schools: A Review of the Literature

Joel Mittleman and Jennifer L. Jennings

Abstract

In this chapter, we review the existing social science literature on the impacts of accountability systems in American schools. We begin by providing a brief history of accountability systems in American public education. We then review the impacts of these systems in three domains (*instructional consequences*, *student outcome consequences*, and *policy feedback consequences*), focusing on the literature that has been produced since the implementation of No Child Left Behind. We consider the evidence on alternatives and complements to test-based accountability systems that have been proposed, and close by discussing directions for future research.

21.1 Introduction

In his chapter for Hallinan's *Handbook of the Sociology of Education*, Hoffer (2000, p. 533) concluded that, in most American schools, accountability "consists largely of informal feedback mechanisms whereby…performances are evaluated against commonsense conceptions of appropriate behavior." In reaching this conclu-

sion, Hoffer discussed the incomplete and inconsistent system of accountability governing American education. Surveying the policy landscape, he found that the standards for student outcomes, as well as the consequences for not meeting those standards, varied across states, districts, and even across schools within districts.

In hindsight, the landscape that Hoffer described was on the verge of a seismic shift. The No Child Left Behind Act of 2001 (NCLB) sought to address precisely the inconsistencies that Hoffer identified. The law instituted the first federal mandate that all public schools be judged according to their proficiency rates on annual tests of reading and math. Moreover, the law tied these outcomes to the first national system of sanctions, inaugurating an era of "accountability with teeth" (Stecher et al. 2010). Unlike most state accountability systems that preceded it, NCLB was intended not only to increase achievement in reading and math, but also to close racial and socioeconomic "achievement gaps." The law set the ambitious goal that, by 2014, all students should reach proficiency on state standardized tests, eliminating any remaining difference between advantaged and disadvantaged groups. This goal was not met, but the law nevertheless had profound impacts on students, educators, schools, and the national education policy debate.

In this chapter, we use the term accountability to refer to systems in which federal, state, or local governments set performance criteria that schools

J. Mittleman (✉) · J. L. Jennings
Princeton University, Princeton, NJ, USA
e-mail: jlj@princeton.edu; joeljm@princeton.edu

© Springer International Publishing AG, part of Springer Nature 2018
B. Schneider (ed.), *Handbook of the Sociology of Education in the 21st Century*, Handbooks of Sociology and Social Research, https://doi.org/10.1007/978-3-319-76694-2_21

must meet in order to avoid negative sanctions. In the U.S., these performance criteria have been defined primarily using proficiency rates on state standardized tests. For this reason, we focus most of our attention on the *test-based* accountability systems literature.

We begin by providing a brief history of accountability systems in American public education. We then review the impacts of these systems in three domains (*instructional consequences*, *student outcome consequences*, and *policy feedback consequences*), focusing on the literature that has been produced since the implementation of No Child Left Behind. Next, we consider the evidence on alternatives to test-based accountability systems that have been proposed: market-based accountability, professional accountability, and process-based accountability. We close by discussing directions for future research.

21.2 A Brief History of Accountability in American Education

In many ways, NCLB marked a historic departure in American education policy. At the same time, though, it also built directly upon state accountability policies that had already begun to reshape schools. Indeed, when NCLB was passed, 49 states had already initiated some form of standards-based reform (Mehta 2013). In this regard, the law is better understood as an "evolution" rather than a "revolution" (McDonnell 2005).

In this section, we chart that evolution. We document the steady shift from what Hoffer (2000) called informal accountability to the system of formal accountability we have today. Following Mehta (2013), we highlight the significance of three events: the release of *A Nation At Risk*, the resultant standards-based reform movement, and the passage of NCLB. Then, we extend this history, addressing accountability reforms undertaken by states and districts during the Obama administration. We conclude by providing an overview of the new Every Student Succeeds Act, which overturned many aspects of NCLB and signaled a new era in accountability policy.

As Hoffer explains, American schools have always faced some form of accountability. Schools, as public institutions, rely upon the support of their communities. This dependency requires teachers and administrators to act in ways that are consistent with community expectations. Still, this form of accountability is fundamentally informal. No one is required to measure performance against codified standards and intervene when performance is found to be substandard.

Meyer and Rowan (1977, 1978) offered an influential explanation for this system. They argued that the lack of monitoring in schools was, in fact, essential to their reliable functioning. The outcomes that citizens expected from schools were diverse, contested, and difficult to measure. Moreover, the technology required to produce these outcomes was uncertain and subject to constant local adjustments. Therefore, "to manage the uncertainty, conflict, and inconsistency created by this pluralistic situation," schools buffered their work through "loose coupling" (1978, p. 100). Each level of the system was granted a good deal of autonomy and the system as a whole was held together by a "logic of confidence."

This logic would soon come under sustained pressure. A new period of accountability was ushered in by the release of 1983's *A Nation At Risk*. Coauthored by a panel appointed by Secretary of Education Terence Bell, this 36-page report warned that America's schools faced a "rising tide of mediocrity that threatens our very future as a Nation and a people" (the National Commission on Excellence in Education 1983, p. 5). The report linked economic competitiveness with educational excellence, marshaling an array of statistics to suggest that American schools were failing at the exact moment in history when their success was more crucial than ever. *A Nation At Risk* argued that "learning is the indispensable investment required for success in the 'information age' we are entering" and that America's human capital stock was perilously low (p. 7).

The reaction to the report was "instantaneous and overwhelming" (Mehta 2013, p. 296). Within one year of its release, the U.S. Government Printing Office had distributed more than 6 million copies of it, *The Washington Post* had published an average of two articles a week on it, and more than 250 state task forces had been assembled to discuss it (ibid.). The report's impact was quickly felt in the states. In Utah, for instance, the state's 1982 curriculum plan declared that its schools should promote "the growth of each individual as he searches for meaning and builds competencies" in eight diverse areas of life (Mehta 2013, p. 302). Although intended to remain in place until 1988, this plan was quickly reformulated after *A Nation At Risk*'s release. In 1984, the state issued "action goals" for education that were articulated in a single sentence: "The Utah State Board of Education sets as its primary goals the attainment of excellence in education and the improvement of productivity" (ibid.).

A Nation At Risk did not, in itself, advocate for test-based accountability. Nevertheless, the policy paradigm that it promoted made accountability a natural solution. This paradigm forcefully resolved the plurality of goals identified by Meyer and Rowan, elevating a single goal: educational excellence for economic competitiveness. By narrowing the range of relevant school outputs and shifting the locus of responsibility for their production squarely onto the schools themselves, *A Nation At Risk* also promoted the idea that school productivity could be usefully measured, ranked, and subjected to reward or sanction. With the national crisis in education expressed almost entirely in test score trends, raising test scores became a national imperative.

A movement for test-based accountability was launched. Texas and North Carolina led the way, followed by other states such as Kentucky, Maryland, and California. During the 1980s and early 1990s, these states adopted new curricular standards, designed student tests based on these standards, and instituted incentive systems based on test results (Hamilton et al. 2008). These state initiatives found growing support at the federal level. In 1989, the first President Bush convened the nation's governors for a summit on standards-based reform. The meeting adjourned with a joint statement declaring that "the time has come…to establish clear, national performance goals" backed up by "a system of accountability that focuses on results" (Bush 1989). Bush's voluntary national standards legislation was ultimately rejected by Congress, motivating President Clinton to focus instead on state-level standards. In 1994, Congress passed two pieces of legislation that promoted state standards: The Improving America's Schools Act (IASA), a reauthorization of the Elementary and Secondary Schools Act, conditioned states' receipt of Title I funding on their commitment to establishing state standards and assessments; the Goals 2000 act provided additional money to states working to design such systems.

And so, by the time that Hoffer (2000) was writing, the patchwork system of accountability he described was already on its way to being replaced. He acknowledged as much, noting the emergence of a "significant formal apparatus of student assessments that is increasingly turned to for indications of system, school, and teacher effectiveness" (p. 533). What Hoffer could not anticipate was the magnitude and the rapidity of the shift about to occur. Although IASA had required all states to develop standards-based reform plans, only 17 states actually had their assessment systems in place by 2001 (McDonnell 2005). Moreover, IASA had mandated only that these new tests be administered to Title I students and only once at each level of schooling: elementary, middle, and high (Stecher et al. 2010). Finally, although IASA had required states to take corrective action against schools that persistently failed to meet standards, it granted states great flexibility in how they chose to intervene (McDonnell 2005).

NCLB changed each of these facts. For the first time, NCLB mandated that states test all students in both math and English language arts in grades 3–8 and once again in high school. Beginning in 2007–2008, states also had to administer tests in science at least once in elementary, middle, and high school. The law required states to use students' performance on these tests to determine whether the school was making "adequate yearly progress" (AYP) toward universal proficiency in 2014. To meet AYP, schools had to meet grade-level proficiency targets for their students overall and for each of their numerically significant student subgroups (students in major racial and ethnic groups, low-income students, students with disabilities, and limited English proficient students). The resulting AYP status had to be reported publicly for all schools. For schools receiving Title I funding—about 67% of elementary schools and 29% of secondary schools at the time of the law's passage—failure to make AYP would set off an escalating series of federally defined consequences (U.S. Department of Education 2002).

In later sections, we review the empirical literature assessing the impact of NCLB. For now, we note two tensions within the law itself that have motivated further accountability reform since the time of its passage. First, NCLB followed IASA in avoiding a fight over national standards. Instead, the law allowed each state to define its own standards, exams, proficiency cut points, and schedule for improvement before the 2014 deadline (Davidson et al. 2015). Second, the system of interventions put in place by NCLB largely exempted individual teachers from the threat of sanction, focusing instead on school-level interventions. NCLB prescribed staffing changes only after a school had failed to meet AYP for five consecutive years. Even then, staffing changes were one of six options available to schools and, in practice, they were rarely attempted (Stecher et al. 2010).

These have been the central areas of accountability reform in recent years: the promotion of national standards and the extension of accountability to individual teachers. The push for national standards has taken the form of the Common Core State Standards initiative, a project begun in 2009 by the National Governors Association and the Council of Chief State School Officers. These new "college and career ready" standards are intended to promote rigor and consistency in English language arts and math nationwide. As of 2016, 42 states and the District of Columbia had initially adopted the standards (Common Core State Standards Initiative 2016). However, a rising political backlash drove at least nine states to later repeal their participation (Academic Benchmarks 2016). The effort to extend accountability pressure to teachers has been less centralized and more varied. Across the country, 24 states and 19 of the 25 largest districts have introduced new teacher evaluation systems designed to be more differentiated, consequential, and closely tied to student achievement (Steinberg and Donaldson 2016). As before, both of these efforts were initiated by states and districts but received substantial support at the federal level. Through its Race to the Top competition and selective granting of waivers from certain NCLB mandates, the Obama administration incentivized states to adopt Common Core and reform teacher evaluation.

This status quo was expected to persist indefinitely. With a gridlocked Congress, policy analysts were warning that the prospect for an overhaul of NCLB was "dim" and that a makeshift system of waivers "will be law for at least several years" (Polikoff et al. 2014, p. 45). It came as a surprise, then, when the Every Student Succeeds Act (ESSA) was signed into law on December 10, 2015. Although many details of the act will be worked out in the regulatory process, it is clear that the law is "in many ways a U-turn from its predecessor" (Education Week 2016).

Although ESSA maintained a commitment to standards, testing, and accountability, it also introduced new flexibility and diversity into each of these elements. For instance, although states must still adopt "challenging" standards, they now are allowed to choose their own goals based on those standards. Similarly, although states must still test their students annually in grades 3–8 and once in high school, these tests must now play a smaller role in their system of school ratings. School ratings must now be based on at least four indicators, one of which must be a non-traditional measure of school quality, such as "student engagement" or "school climate and safety" (Education Week 2016). Finally, although the law still requires states to intervene in poorly performing schools, it removes the federally mandated schedule of specified interventions.

Instead, at least once every 3 years, states are required to identify the bottom 5% of schools. These schools will then be subject to a locally-designed, state-monitored turnaround effort.

With all of these changes going into place starting in 2017/18 and a new president who has championed a return to local control of schools, it is clear that we, like Hoffer, are writing on the verge of another major shift in the accountability systems governing American education. To better anticipate the possible consequences of these changes, we now turn to reviewing the existing evidence on the effects of test-based accountability systems.

21.3   Effects of Test-Based Accountability Systems

In this section, we conceive of the effects of accountability systems more broadly than is typical in the public policy literature on this topic. We argue that the direct impact of accountability policies on student test scores can only be understood in the context of a broader evaluation of how accountability affects teachers, students, school systems, and public perceptions of and support for public education. This broader focus not only highlights the tradeoffs associated with test score gains, but also critically investigates the nature of the gains themselves. Specifically, we address three groups of consequences: *instructional consequences* (impacts on teaching practice), *student outcome consequences* (impacts on student achievement, attainment, and identity), and *policy feedback consequences* (impacts on popular understanding of and support for public education).

21.3.1   Instructional Consequences

Understanding how accountability pressure affects teacher practice provides the essential background for any evaluation of student outcomes. Existing evidence suggests that teachers are closely attuned to accountability pressure. Although the introduction of NCLB does not

appear to have affected teachers' job satisfaction or desire to teach until retirement (Grissom et al. 2014), it did lower their sense of job security (Reback et al. 2014). Teachers' fears are not unfounded. Although formal school staffing initiatives were rare under NCLB (Stecher et al. 2010), accountability pressure nevertheless seems to have increased schools' propensity to fire teachers (Sun et al. 2014; Loeb and Cunha 2007). As teachers have sought to respond to this new pressure, there are three areas, in particular, in which they appear to have strategically shifted their practice: Shifts in instructional *time between* subjects, shifts in instructional *emphasis within* subjects, and shifts in instructional attention *between students*.

There is clear evidence that test-based accountability pressure has caused teachers—often at the behest of school leaders—to shift time away from non-tested subjects in order to focus on reading and math. This fact was first reported in nationally representative surveys of district officials (Center on Education Policy 2006, 2007) as well as in surveys of teachers in California, Georgia, and Pennsylvania (Hamilton et al. 2007). Still, one may worry that directly asking how high stakes testing has affected instruction may elicit biased responses. Therefore, two studies (Dee et al. 2013; Reback et al. 2014) address this question indirectly by combining teacher responses on the Schools and Staffing Survey with measures of NCLB pressure. Despite their differing identification methods, both studies reach the same conclusion: Pressure to meet AYP caused teachers to reduce instructional time devoted to social studies and science. Rouse et al. (2013) observe the same effect in their survey of Florida principals: After receiving an "F," these principals reported less instructional time dedicated to science. Other studies have found accountability pressure has caused schools to dedicate less time to other dimensions of schooling like gym, recess, art, and music (Beveridge 2009; Murnane and Papay 2010).

On their own, it is not clear how to evaluate these shifts. One could reasonably argue that tested subjects constitute the core basic skills that students need for future success. If this is true, then reallocating attention toward these subjects is one of the benefits of accountability policy (e.g., Hannaway and Hamilton 2008). A more clearly unintended impact of accountability pressure has been the instructional shifts that have taken place *within* subject areas. Convergent forms of evidence suggest teachers respond to test-based accountability pressure by "teaching to the test": that is, focusing instruction on predictable test features, both in terms of the *content* of questions and in terms of the actual *format* of questions. Moreover, evidence suggests that this response is stronger in schools facing greater accountability pressure.

As with the evidence on between-subject shifts, initial evidence for "teaching to the test" came from teacher surveys. For example, in the RAND study of NCLB implementation in three states, teachers reported that they identified "highly assessed standards" on which to focus their attention (Hamilton and Stecher 2007). Reback et al.'s (2014) study of the same data found that in schools facing substantial accountability pressure (those below the AYP margin), 84% of teachers reported focusing on topics emphasized on the state test, while 69% of those in schools at low-risk of failing AYP did.

An alternate way of assessing the prevalance of test-focused instruction is by decomposing test score gains. If the gains observed on high-stakes tests are narrowly constrained to portions of the tests that are perceived to be easiest to teach or most likely to appear on tests, then we have strong indirect evidence of strategic instruction. Several studies have confirmed this intuition. These studies find that NCLB-era state tests predictably emphasized some state standards while consistently excluding others: Only a small number of standards typically accounted for a substantial fraction of test points (Holcombe et al. 2013; Jennings and Bearak 2014). Analyzing data from three states, Jennings and Bearak (2014) found that students performed better on items testing frequently assessed standards—those that composed a larger fraction of the state test in prior years—suggesting that teachers targeted their

instruction towards these predictably tested skills.

Moreover, many studies suggest that students are unevenly affected by test-specific instruction, with such instruction being used more heavily in schools serving lower-income and non-Asian minority students (Diamond and Spillane 2004; Jacob et al. 2004; Ladd and Zelli 2002; McNeil 2000; Taylor et al. 2002). For example, Shen (2008) identified items that were more or less "teachable" and showed that schools' improvements over time were greatest on teachable items, a trend that was more pronounced in disadvantaged schools. Similarly, Jennings et al. (2011), analyzing data from New York State, show that Black and Hispanic students received more test-specific instruction. As a result, the reduction of racial test score gaps in New York State observed in the post-NCLB period was entirely driven by Black and Hispanic students' improved performance on predictably-tested content. Achievement gaps on less predictable content were left unchanged, and actually grew in some cases. This discouraging pattern may help explain the multiple other studies demonstrating that disadvantaged students' gains on high-stakes tests do not generalize into gains on other assessments (Klein et al. 2000; Jacob 2007; Ho and Haertel 2006).

Finally, a complementary group of studies documents not simply "teaching to the test"—in terms of question content—but also "teaching to the format"—in terms of question design. These studies illustrate how the design of high-stakes tests may lead educators to focus on particular formats in their teaching that parallel those appearing on high-stakes tests (Pedulla et al. 2003; Shepard and Dougherty 1991). The most well-known example of this phenomenon comes from Shepard's (1988) finding that students could effectively add and subtract decimals when they were presented in a vertical format, but struggled when decimals were presented in a horizontal format. While most "teaching to the format" studies pre-date the NCLB era, Reback et al. (2014, p. 223) found that teachers in higher accountability pressure schools reported looking for "particular styles and formats of problems in the state test and emphasize[d] those in [their] instruction." 100% of teachers in schools below the AYP margin reported doing so, while 67% of teachers at lower risk of failing AYP did.

Despite their varying data sources and strategies, these studies are all observational. A more optimal approach to identifying test-based instruction and resultant score inflation is to use "self-monitoring assessments." First introduced by Koretz and Beguin (2010), these assessments incorporate audit items into actual high-stakes tests. These audit items are sufficiently novel that they are not susceptible to test preparation techniques. Only one study has implemented such an approach: In New York State, students received multiple embedded items that attempted to "undo" the predictable features of the test. For example, if a state standard required students to understand positive and negative slopes but consistently only tested positive slopes, an audit item was included to test understanding of negative slopes. Koretz et al. (2016) report the results of this experiment, finding that marginal or "bubble" students—those closest to passing and thus most important to coach—were most likely to perform relatively worse on the audit items. This suggests that these students' test-focused learning did not transfer to other assessments of the same skills.

Qualitative and survey studies have documented similar shifts in attention *between students*. For example, studies document that teachers focus on "bubble" students, those close to the proficiency cut score (Booher-Jennings 2005; Hamilton et al. 2007). All of these instructional shifts have been enabled, in part, by the new forms of testing technology and data that have proliferated in response to accountability pressure. In particular, there has been extensive growth in the use of benchmark assessments designed to help schools track and support students' mastery of standards (Datnow and Hubbard 2015). Although there is no nationally representative data on benchmark assessment use, we can indirectly track their growth over time by considering the changing size of their market. In 2003, districts nationwide spent $212 million on tools related to benchmark assessments (Olson 2005); by 2011, this figure

had risen to $2.2 billion (Lazarín 2014). Reflecting this rapid growth, a 2009 survey found that benchmark assessments were nearly universal among 62 of the country's largest urban districts (Council of the Great City Schools 2011).

Typically administered three or more times a year, these exams have helped to transform school systems into testing and data-intensive environments (Lazarín 2014; Council of the Great City Schools 2015). Both teachers and administrators are now under pressure to practice data-driven decision-making. Large-scale evaluations of benchmark test use have failed to find clear positive or negative effects on state test scores (Konstantopoulos et al. 2013, 2016; Cordray et al. 2012; Slavin et al. 2013). Moreover, certain case studies provide reason to be skeptical of the extent to which teachers have actually embraced district efforts to promote data use (Means et al. 2010). Nevertheless, in some school contexts, benchmark test data and institutional pressure for "data-driven decision making" have reshaped teacher beliefs and behaviors in consequential ways (Booher-Jennings 2005; Marsh et al. 2006). Even so, these shifts have not typically produced "deep" changes in pedagogy. That is, they have not fundamentally changed how teachers engage students around instructional content and didactic instruction continues to dominate classrooms (Diamond 2007). With these findings in mind, we turn to our review of test-based accountability's apparent effects on students.

21.3.2 Student Outcome Consequences

The preceding review of instructional responses suggests that one needs to exercise considerable caution in interpreting any changes in students' high-stakes test scores that are observed under accountability pressure. It is for this reason that we do not review the substantial body of work that concludes that K–12 accountability systems have had positive average effects on high-stakes state test scores (Chakrabarti 2007; Chiang 2009; Lauen and Gaddis 2012; Reback et al. 2014;

Rockoff and Turner 2010; Rouse et al. 2013; Springer 2008; Winters and Cowen 2012). Instead, we focus our review on three broader domains of student outcomes: students' knowledge and skills (as measured by low-stakes tests), students' educational attainment and labor market outcomes (in terms of high school graduation, college enrollment, and earnings), and students' identities (in terms of how social meaning attaches to test-based categorical inequalities).

21.3.2.1 Students' Knowledge and Skills

Compared to the large literature assessing impacts on high-stakes tests, relatively few studies have assesed the impact of NCLB on students' achievement on low-stakes tests. Dee and Jacob's (2009) study of the effects of NCLB on National Assessment of Educational Progress (NAEP) scores found increases in state NAEP scores in 4th and 8th grade math, but no increases in reading for either 4th or 8th grade. Dividing these average effects into subgroups, Dee and Jacob (2009) identified larger positive effects on 4th grade math scores for Black and Hispanic students than for White students; at the same time, in 4th grade reading, only White students gained while Black and Hispanic students did not.

Like Dee and Jacob, Wong et al. (2009) found positive effects on 4th and 8th grade NAEP math scores. They also found evidence for positive effects on 4th grade NAEP reading scores, but only when states had high standards for proficiency. Reback et al. (2014) analyzed data from the Early Childhood Longitudinal Study-Kindergarten (ECLS-K) study, finding small positive effects of NCLB accountability pressure on the ECLS-K reading and science tests, but no effects on the math test.

Taken together, the existing evidence suggests that the positive effects of NCLB identified using high-stakes test scores do translate somewhat into gains on low-stakes tests that are less likely to be corrupted by score inflation. However, the evidence is equivocal: Low-stakes test score gains are found for some students on some subjects under certain circumstances.

Whereas the above studies focused on average effects by subject and student group, others have focused on the *distributional* impacts of accountability systems. That is, they explore the heterogeneous effects of accountability pressure on students across the test score distribution. Such effects are of particular interest because most current accountability systems rely on proficiency rates, a threshold measure of achievement. Since sanctions are a function of the proportion of students brought over the proficiency threshold, slightly increasing the scores of a small number of students—the "bubble" students discussed earlier in this chapter—can positively impact the school's accountability rating.

A large body of evidence addresses this issue, finding mixed results on the extent to which teachers use data to target resources to students. One study found negative effects of accountability pressure on the lowest performing students in Chicago (Neal and Schanzenbach 2007), while another in Texas found positive effects for low-performing students as well as larger gains for marginal students (Reback 2008). In total, four studies identified positive effects on low-performing students (Jacob 2005; Springer 2008; Ladd and Lauen 2010; Dee and Jacob 2009), while another four find negative effects on high-performing students (Krieg 2008, Ladd and Lauen 2010; Dee and Jacob 2009; Reback 2008).

Two more recent studies attempt to make sense of variation in distributional effects across contexts and time periods (Jennings and Sohn 2014; Lauen and Gaddis 2016). These studies suggest that the mixed findings in the literature can be explained by three factors. First, because accountability pressure incentivizes schools to focus attention on students closest to the proficiency standard, the difficulty of the standard itself affects whether lower or higher performing students will gain most. Less difficult proficiency standards appear to decrease inequality in high-stakes achievement, while more difficult ones increase it. Second, when targeting students near proficiency, educators appear to emphasize test-specific skills. Therefore, the effect of accountability-induced targeting should differ across high and low-stakes tests. For example,

Jennings and Sohn (2014) evaluated student scores on high- and low-stakes tests of similar skills administered within the same high standards context. They found an inequality-increasing focus on students close to proficiency on the *high-stakes* tests, but no effects on inequality on the *low-stakes* tests. Finally, it appears that focusing attention on students close to proficiency is most pronounced in the lowest-performing schools. This may help explain why these effects have been identified more in locations with a higher fraction of low-performing schools.

21.3.2.2 Students' Educational and Labor Market Outcomes

One major gap in our knowledge is understanding accountability's effect on students' later life outcomes. From *A Nation at Risk* to the Common Core standards movement, standards and accountability have been justified with appeals to the challenge of success in a knowledge-based economy. Therefore, one of the crucial assumptions motivating test-based accountability systems is that promoting test score gains will ultimately enhance students' ability to succeed after high school. Surprisingly, this assumption remains almost entirely untested.

Deming et al. (2016) offer the first evidence on how accountability pressure impacts students' trajectories up to and after high school graduation. Using longitudinal data from Texas, they compare cohorts within schools that faced different degrees of accountability pressure. The results are mixed. They find that students in high schools facing pressure to avoid a "Low-Performing" rating experienced several positive outcomes: They were more likely to graduate on time, accumulated more high school math credits, were more likely to attend and graduate from a four-year college, and they had higher earnings at age 25. However, the effects of accountability were not uniformly positive. Within those schools on the cusp of a "Recognized" rating, accountability pressure had no effect overall and appeared to cause significant negative long-term effects on poorly performing students. These negative long-term effects appear to be the result of poorly per-

forming students being strategically funneled into special education.

21.3.2.3 Students' Identities

High-stakes test score data divide students into multiple levels of proficiency based on their scores. Students can be labeled as commended, meeting the standard, or not meeting the standard. Teachers and schools use these scores for organizational purposes such as sorting students into advanced courses or remediation opportunities. States sometimes allocate scholarship opportunities based on these scores. Even beyond these institutionalized consequences, however, there is reason to believe that test score labels could come to have broad significance for students. Ever since the Pygmalion study found that providing randomly assigned performance labels to teachers could affect students' subsequent performance on standardized tests (Rosenthal and Jacobsen 1968), research has found that arbitrary performance labels can have real educational consequences. In particular, prior research on students' responses to tracking labels (Oakes 1985) suggests that high-stakes test scores plausibly affect student identities, engagement in school, peer dynamics, teacher and parental expectations, and future educational decisions.

Two quantitative studies have examined the impact of state accountability-based test score labels on students' future achievement and decision-making. Papay et al. (2011) found that students earning an "advanced" label on Massachusetts' exit exam were more likely to attend college than those who scored just below this cut score. Domina et al. (2016) find similar evidence of student responses to performance labels, documenting declines in test scores and grades after a student received a low-status performance label. These results do not directly address student beliefs and attitudes; still, they provide strong, indirect evidence that accountability labels do not go unnoticed by students.

Beyond the test performance labels used in accountability systems, there is evidence that increased state accountability pressure is also associated with a different type of label: ADHD diagnoses. Bokhari and Schneider (2011), for example, determined that demanding state accountability laws increased prescriptions for stimulant drugs. King et al. (2014), contrasting stimulant use in the summer and school year, found the largest use differences for higher-SES children living in states with strict accountability policies. How accountability-induced diagnostic labels affect students over their life course remains an open question. What is clear, however, is that accountability systems have facilitated new forms of categorization, which have the potential to be internalized by students.

21.3.3 Policy Feedback Consequences

Finally, test-based accountability systems do not only impact teachers, students, and schools: They also affect public opinion in ways that may dynamically feed back into the classroom. Because measures themselves play a central role in constructing social problems (Espeland and Stevens 1998), test score data help shape the public understanding of educational achievement and inequality. In this way, the data produced by current accountability systems frame future policy debates, encouraging certain actions while forestalling others.

A growing body of research documents that the school quality indicators disseminated as part of accountability programs could have the unintended effect of reducing public support for schools. Kogan et al. (2015), for example, use data from Ohio tax referenda to demonstrate that voters in school districts that failed to meet AYP were 10% less likely to approve subsequent levies. These votes reduced district revenue by over 13% and disproportionately affected already impoverished districts. Barrows (2014) provides complementary evidence from school board elections in Florida. Applying a regression discontinuity design to the "A–F" letter grades that Florida assigns to local schools, Barrows finds that voters are significantly less likely to vote for school board incumbents in precincts wherein the closest elementary school scored a "B" rather than an "A". Below the "A/B" threshold, school ratings did not have appreciable effects on voting, although there was suggestive evidence for a further penalty at the "D/F" threshold.

These studies suggest that school ratings information—independent of underlying school quality—affects broader support for local schools. Jacobsen et al. (2013) provide direct evidence for this effect. Using parent surveys in New York City before and after a large increase in the city's standards—which caused 71% of the city's schools to fall at least one letter grade on the city's report card—they find significant, albeit small, decreases in reported parent satisfaction. A national survey experiment by the same authors (Jacobsen et al. 2014) revealed that it is not only the *substance* of school ratings that affects attitudes toward schools; the actual style in which ratings are presented (i.e., letter grades vs percent proficient), can accentuate or undermine public approval of schools. Like Barrows (2014), the authors find that these style differences only impacted approval ratings for highly- and poorly-rated schools without any effect on middling schools.

Whereas the above studies focus on the effect of accountability ratings, Rhodes (2015) attempts to assess the impact of accountability systems as a whole. Combining original survey data with summary indicators of the strength of states' accountability systems, Rhodes finds that system strength is associated with significantly lower reports of trust in government, less confidence in government efficacy, and more negative attitudes about schools. Despite her extensive use of individual and state-level controls, however, Rhodes' results are difficult to interpret given the likelihood of reverse causality and omitted variables. Still, in combination with the other studies reviewed, Rhodes provides added cause for concern that efforts to spur school improvement through test-based accountability may have had the unintended consequence of undercutting future attempts at mobilizing broad-based support for reform.

21.4 Research on Alternatives to Test-Based Accountability

The above review suggests that, despite certain positive effects, the national shift toward test-based accountability has also been associated with considerable costs. As such, it is important to evaluate alternative mechanisms that could maintain accountability while avoiding some of the unintended consequences of the current test-based system. In this section, we briefly review research on three proposed alternatives: market-based accountability, professional accountability, and process-based accountability.

21.4.1 Market-Based Accountability

One alternative to regulatory test-based accountability is market-based accountability, by which families can "vote with their feet" and attend schools that better meet their preferences or needs. Such systems are often implemented alongside test-based ratings programs. Indeed, one of the main drivers for school improvement envisioned by NCLB was the coupling of market-based accountability with test-based accountability. In the first year that a school was identified as in need of improvement, the district was required to allow students to transfer out of that school into a better performing school within the district.

The experience of public school choice under NCLB, however, provides reason to be skeptical of the extent to which market-based accountability on its own can deliver on the promise of system-wide improvement. Remarkably, the most recent evidence suggests that only about 1% of eligible students took advantage of NCLB's public school choice provisions (Stecher et al. 2010). Two facts help explain this low take-up rate. First, over a third of districts reported that they simply had no schools available for transfers, often because every school serving the relevant grade level was also failing AYP. Second, survey evidence suggests that school quality reports were not salient enough to parents to warrant action: In eight large districts, only 19% of parents knew that their child's school was designated as needing improvement (Stecher et al. 2010).

These patterns do not appear to be limited only to NCLB. Henderson (2010) found a similar lack of response under Florida's statewide school "A–F" grading system.

Moreover, families' apparent unresponsiveness to NCLB-era school ratings is also consistent with research on other school rating and choice programs that preceded NCLB (Lauen 2007; Rich and Jennings 2015). This research demonstrates that information on school quality, in itself, was not enough to disrupt the socially and contextually constrained process of school enrollment.

An irony of NCLB and its predecessors is that, even though they failed in their intended goal of promoting student mobility, they had the unintended consequence of promoting staff mobility. Numerous studies have demonstrated that the "shock" of a negative accountability rating promotes attrition out of affected schools (Clotfelter et al. 2004; Sims 2009; Hanushek and Rivkin 2010; Feng et al. 2013). This attrition is particularly pronounced among experienced teachers (Sims 2009) and high value-added teachers (Feng et al. 2013). Li (2015) provides similar evidence for principals, showing that the onset of NCLB in North Carolina corresponded with high value-added principals moving to schools less likely to be sanctioned under the new system.

The limited mobility of students but strategic mobility of teachers and principals provides a sobering corrective to the narrative that competition will spur system-wide improvement. In systems marked by residential segregation and inequality in family resources, market-based accountability is unlikely to secure adequate opportunities for all students.

21.4.2 Professional Accountability

Given the risks of relying on families to enforce accountability through school choice, a potentially attractive alternative is to better empower the professionals within school systems through professional accountability. Test-based accountability programs are motivated in part by a perceived need to resolve a principal-agent problem. Confidence in institutions, including public education, has eroded over the last four decades (Lipset and Schneider 1983). The public no longer trusts teachers and administrators to act in the best interests of students without oversight. By providing a way to monitor and incentivize teachers' behavior, test-based accountability programs fill the gap of public distrust. An alternative approach to accountability, therefore, would be to address this distrust itself. One way to do this would be by shoring up teachers' status as professionals: highly qualified, expertly trained in a specialized body of knowledge, and in need of sufficient autonomy to accomplish their work.

Elementary and secondary school teachers in America have fought recurring battles to assert their professional status (Ingersoll and Merrill 2011). As of 2013, only 34% of American teachers agreed that "the teaching profession is valued in society," compared to 59% of teachers in Finland, 67% in Korea, and 84% in Malaysia (OECD 2015). American teachers' perceptions of their poor standing finds apparent validation in international comparisons of teacher salary and working conditions. Compared to 33 other OECD countries, the average salary of American teachers ranks 28th, despite the fact that American teachers rank 6th in terms of the total number of hours that they work (OECD 2014, 2015).

Cross-national comparisons of the teaching profession—and associated student outcomes—is a fraught exercise; disconfirming evidence can be found for nearly any generalization. Nevertheless, Goldhaber (2009, p. 97) suggests that the countries that perform best on international assessments typically train their teachers the way that America trains its doctors. These countries have relatively few training programs, more applicants than available slots, a high degree of standardization across programs, a promise of a relatively high permanent income after certification, and an extended period of post-licensure training under the supervision of more senior doctors. None of these conditions hold in the American teaching profession.

However, even though doctors appear to offer a model for the professionalization of teachers, this arguably reflects a misunderstanding of how professionalization has affected the quality and cost of American medicine. As Starr (1983) has convincingly shown, professional power is often not used to improve practice, but to deflect potential entrants to markets and control price. American physicians' professional control has contributed to a health care system that is more costly than any other country in the world, while still being less effective on almost every quality measure available (Garber and Skinner 2008).

To be sure, professionalization in conjunction with other performance evaluation measures holds promise as a complement or supplement to test-based accountability. However, we are aware of no existing evidence that convincingly indicates that professionalization alone will drive improvements in student outcomes and reductions in cost.

21.4.3 Inspectorate or Process-Based Accountability

Finally, school reformers do not only look abroad for alternate models of selecting, training and compensating teachers; they also point to alternative systems of test-based accountability itself. One feature of accountability systems found in many countries, particularly in Europe, is formal school inspections. Although "the practice of school inspections varies considerably among and within countries," 24 out of the 31 OECD countries surveyed in 2009 reported that school inspections were part of their accountability system (OECD 2011, p. 434). In such a system, trained external evaluators visit schools and assess them on a range of measures. The results of these visits are publicly reported, along with guidance for improvement, and may be tied to reward or sanction.

In theory, because they utilize expert judgment about a holistic range of factors, inspection systems provide accountability without the unintended consequences of a mechanistically test-based system. Under the English system, for example, inspectors determine whether a school is Outstanding, Good, Satisfactory, or Failing based on 27 dimensions, including "the extent of pupils' spiritual, moral, social, and cultural development" (Jerald 2012, p. 7). Despite this holistic approach, student test scores still play a central role in determining schools' overall ratings. Moreover, these ratings still carry consequences: Since 1993, at least 230 schools have been shut down because of failure to improve after multiple inspections (Hussain 2015; Jerald 2012).

Despite their theoretical appeal, there is little evidence on the effect that inspections have on schools and students. Advocates for adopting an English-style inspectorate in America point to the fact that, on average, English schools designated as Failing require only 20 months and 3 or 4 follow-up inspections before they are upgraded to Satisfactory or better (Jerald 2012). This kind of evidence is clearly not sufficient for establishing causal effects. Existing work attempting to estimate the causal effect of inspection on student achievement has come to mixed conclusions. In Denmark, Luginbuhl et al. (2009) find no effect of being inspected. In England, Rosenthal (2004) finds a small negative effect of being inspected at all, whereas Allen and Burgess (2012) and Hussain (2015) find small to moderate positive effects of being inspected and receiving a "Fail" rating.

The mechanisms behind these effects are unclear. Advocates point to the detailed, actionable feedback that schools are supposed to receive after inspection (Jerald 2012). However, Hussain (2015) questions the impact that feedback, in itself, has on student achievement. All schools, Hussain notes, receive feedback, but this feedback apparently has no effect in schools not rated Failing. Nevertheless, Hussain (2015) argues that Fail ratings promote some genuine change in school practice, as he finds no evidence of "gaming" behavior and finds that effects persist even after students leave the Failing school. In another encouraging contrast to the American studies reviewed above, he also finds no evidence that a Failing rating promotes teacher mobility out of the affected school. Given this evidence,

we cautiously conclude that inspectorate-style approaches to accountability could hold promise as schools work to design accountability and improvement efforts for the post-NCLB era.

21.5   Conclusion: The Future of Accountability and Accountability Research

Research on accountability systems has proliferated in the last two decades. Although sociologists have made important contributions to this body of evidence, much of the research reviewed above was conducted outside of our discipline, particularly by economists. With this in mind, we conclude with thoughts for future research, focusing on two areas that would especially benefit from sociological analysis.

An essential area for future research is better understanding how accountability policies are mediated by local context. In schools facing similar pressures and incentives, how do reactions and results differ? What formal and informal characteristics of school communities influence how accountability policies shape practice? These kinds of questions will only increase in salience as accountability under ESSA continues to become more locally differentiated. These are also the kinds of questions that sociologists are particularly well suited to address. Bryk and Schneider's (2002) work on relational trust, for example, provides a model for understanding how and why the effects of reform vary across schools.

A second area for research is examinations of how student performance data comes to shape teacher practice. Understanding the factors that support effective data use would advance school improvement efforts by bolstering a key link in the chain prescribed by policymakers. Data use is more than a technical process, however. The ways in which teachers and school leaders understand and act upon data are also fundamentally social and value-laden processes. For student performance data to become intelligible, teachers and school leaders must engage in a process of commensuration that "changes the terms of what can be talked about, how we value, and how we treat what we value" (Espeland and Stevens 1998, p. 315). Because of this, a sociological perspective has much to contribute to studies of data-driven school improvement efforts.

The new rating systems mandated under ESSA will provide especially interesting case studies of this process. As mentioned above, ESSA requires states to incorporate one nontraditional, nonacademic factor into their ratings: factors like student engagement, grit, and growth mindsets. How will these measures come to be understood and contested on the ground? In what ways will "soft" performance measures reproduce or disrupt the categorical inequalities long observed in "hard" measures? Questions like these call out for sociological analysis.

Since the 1980s, test-based accountability has played an increasingly central role in organizing American education. Despite some difference in emphases across administrations, there has been a clear consensus that government has a duty to hold schools accountable for standardized performance metrics. Even efforts to decentralize accountability—as in school choice programs—have taken for granted the proposition that schools would compete on the basis common performance standards.

The future of this consensus is unclear. The popular backlash against the Common Core Standards movement and the election of a president who campaigned on school vouchers suggest that public support for standards and accountability may be reaching a breaking point. For those who have worked to highlight the limitations and unintended consequences of test-based accountability, the current moment of reevaluation holds great potential. The research reviewed in this chapter suggests a number of areas in which our current accountability system could be improved.

However, the current moment also carries considerable risk. Despite its shortcomings, the test-based accountability movement enshrined the principle that it is unacceptable for any child in America to be left behind by their school system. Accountability was promoted, at least in part, as a tool for equity: a way of identifying a common baseline and ensuring that no student is allowed to remain beneath it. Whatever the future holds for accountability policy in the post-Obama era, we hope that this fundamental tenet of the standards and accountability movement persists.

References

Academic Benchmarks. (2016). Map displaying states' adoption of CCSS. Academic Benchmark's Common Core State Standards Adoption Map. http://academicbenchmarks.com/common-core-state-adoption-map/. Accessed 17 Apr 2017.

Allen, R., & Burgess, S. (2012). How should we treat under-performing schools? A regression discontinuity analysis of school inspections in England. *CMPO Working Paper Number 12/287*, Bristol University.

Barrows, S. (2014). Performance information and retrospective voting: Evidence from a school accountability regime. *Harvard Program on Education Policy and Governance Working Paper Series* (Working Paper PEPG 15-03).

Beveridge, T. (2009). No Child Left Behind and fine arts classes. *Arts Education Policy Review, 111*(1), 4–7.

Bokhari, F., & Schneider, H. (2011). School accountability laws and the consumption of psychostimulants. *Journal of Health Economics, 30*, 355–372.

Booher-Jennings, J. (2005). Below the bubble: "Educational Triage" and the Texas accountability system. *American Educational Research Journal, 42*(2), 231–268.

Bryk, A., & Schneider, B. (2002). *Trust in schools: A core resource for improvement*. New York: Russell Sage Foundation.

Bush, G. (1989, September 28). *Joint statement on the education summit with the Nation's Governors in Charlottesville, Virginia*. Online by Gerhard Peters and John T. Woolley, The American Presidency Project. http://www.presidency.ucsb.edu/ws/?pid=17580. Accessed 2 Mar 2016.

Center on Education Policy. (2006). From the capital to the classroom: Year 4 of the No Child Left Behind Act. http://cep-dc.org/displayDocument.cfm?DocumentID=301. Accessed 2 Mar 2016.

Center on Education Policy. (2007). *NCLB Year 5: Choices, changes, and challenges: Curriculum and instruction in the NCLB era*. http://www.cep-dc.org/displayDocument.cfm?DocumentID=312. Accessed 2 Mar 2016.

Chakrabarti, R. (2007). *Vouchers, public school response, and the role of incentives: Evidence from Florida*. FRB of New York Staff Report, (306).

Chiang, H. (2009). How accountability pressure on failing schools affects student achievement. *Journal of Public Economics, 93*(9), 1045–1057.

Clotfelter, C. T., Ladd, H. F., Vigdor, J. L., & Diaz, R. A. (2004). Do school accountability systems make it more difficult for low-performing schools to attract and retain high-quality teachers? *Journal of Policy Analysis and Management, 23*(2), 251–271.

Common Core State Standards Initiative. (2016) *Standards in your State.* http://www.corestandards.org/standards-in-your-state/. Accessed 2 Mar 2016.

Cordray, D., Pion, G., Brandt, C., Molefe, A., & Toby, M. (2012). *The impact of the Measures Of Academic Progress (MAP) program on student reading achievement: Final Report.* U.S. Department of Education National Center for Education Evaluation and Regional Assistance. http://ies.ed.gov/ncee/edlabs/regions/midwest/pdf/REL_20134000.pdf. Accessed 2 Mar 2016.

Council of the Great City Schools. (2011). *Using data to improve instruction in the great city schools: Documenting current practice.* http://files.eric.ed.gov/fulltext/ED536742.pdf. Accessed 2 Mar 2016.

Council of the Great City Schools. (2015). Student testing in America's great city schools: An inventory and preliminary analysis. http://www.cgcs.org/cms/lib/DC00001581/Centricity/Domain/87/Testing%20Report.pdf. Accessed 2 Mar 2016.

Datnow, A., & Hubbard, L. (2015). Teachers' use of assessment data to inform instruction: Lessons from the past and prospects for the future. *Teachers College Record, 117*(4), 1–26.

Davidson, E., Reback, R., Rockoff, J., & Schwartz, H. L. (2015). Fifty ways to leave a child behind: Idiosyncrasies and discrepancies in states' implementation of NCLB. *Educational Researcher, 44*(6), 347–358.

Dee, T. S., & Jacob, B. (2009). *The impact of No Child Left Behind on student achievement* (NBER Working Paper No. 15531). Cambridge, MA.

Dee, T. S., Jacob, B., & Schwartz, N. L. (2013). The effects of NCLB on school resources and practices. *Educational Evaluation and Policy Analysis, 35*(2), 252–279.

Deming, D. J., Cohodes, S., Jennings, J., & Jencks, C. (2016). School accountability, postsecondary attainment and earnings. *Review of Economics and Statistics, 98*(5), 848–862.

Diamond, J. B. (2007). Where the rubber meets the road: Rethinking the relationship between high-stakes testing policy and classroom instruction. *Sociology of Education, 80*(4), 285–313.

Diamond, J. B., & Spillane, J. P. (2004). High-stakes accountability in urban elementary schools: Challenging or reproducing inequality? *Teachers College Record, 106*(6), 1145–1176.

Domina, T., Penner, A. M., & Penner, E. K. (2016). "Membership has its privileges": Status incentives and categorical inequality in education. *Sociological Science, 3*, 264–295.

Education Week. (2016, January 4). The Every Student Succeeds act: Explained. http://www.edweek.org/ew/articles/2015/12/07/the-every-student-succeeds-act-explained.html. Accessed 2 Mar 2016.

Espeland, W. N., & Stevens, M. L. (1998). Commensuration as a social process. *Annual Review of Sociology, 24*, 313–343.

Feng, L., Figlio, D. & Sass, T. (2013). *School accountability and teacher mobility.* Working Paper. http://www2.gsu.edu/~tsass/pdfs/school%20accountability%20and%20teacher%20mobility%2004-12-2013%20TRS%20Clean.pdf. Accessed 2 Mar 2016.

Garber, A. M., & Skinner, J. (2008). *Is American health care uniquely inefficient?* (NBER Working Paper No. 14257). Cambridge, MA.

Goldhaber, D. (2009). Lessons from abroad: Exploring cross-country differences in teacher development systems and what they mean for U.S. policy. In D. Goldhaber & J. Hannaway (Eds.), *Creating a new teaching profession* (pp. 81–114). Washington, DC: Urban Institute Press.

Grissom, J. A., Nicholson-Crotty, S., & Harrington, J. R. (2014). Estimating the effects of No Child Left Behind on teachers' work environments and job attitudes. *Educational Evaluation and Policy Analysis, 36*(4), 417–436.

Hamilton, L. S., & Stecher, B. M. (2007). *Measuring instructional responses to standards-based accountability.* Santa Monica: RAND Corporation.

Hamilton, L. S., Stecher, B. M., Marsh, J. A., McCombs, J. S., Robyn, A., Russell, J. L., Naftel, S., & Barney, H. (2007). *Implementing standards-based accountability under No Child Left Behind: Responses of superintendents, principals, and teachers in three states.* Santa Monica: RAND Corporation.

Hamilton, L. S., Stecher, B. M., & Yuan, K. (2008). *Standards-based reform in the United States: History, research, and future directions.* RAND Education. http://www.rand.org/pubs/reprints/RP1384.html. Accessed 2 Mar 2016.

Hannaway, J., & Hamilton, L. (2008). *Performance-based accountability policies: Implications for school and classroom practices.* Washington, DC: Urban Institute and RAND Corporation.

Hanushek, E. A., & Rivkin, S. G. (2010). The quality and distribution of teachers under the No Child Left Behind Act. *Journal of Economic Perspectives, 24*(3), 133–150.

Henderson, M. (2010). *Does information help families choose schools? Evidence from a regression discontinuity design.* Unpublished manuscript. Harvard University, Department of Government and Social Policy, Cambridge, MA.

Ho, A. D., & Haertel, E. H. (2006). *Metric-free measures of test score trends and gaps with policy-relevant examples* (CSE Report 665). Los Angeles: National Center for Research on Evaluation, Standards, and Student Testing (CRESST), Center for the Study of Evaluation, University of California, Los Angeles.

Hoffer, T. B. (2000). Accountability in education. In M. T. Hallinan (Ed.), *Handbook of the sociology of education* (pp. 529–543). New York: Springer.

Holcombe, R., Jennings, J. L., & Koretz, D. (2013). The roots of score inflation: An examination of opportunities in two states' tests. In G. Sunderman (Ed.), *Charting reform, achieving equity in a diverse nation* (pp. 163–189). Greenwich: Information Age Publishing.

Hussain, I. (2015). Subjective performance evaluation in the public sector: Evidence from school inspections. *The Journal of Human Resources, 50*(1), 189–221.

Ingersoll, R., & Merrill, E. (2011). The status of teaching as a profession. In J. Ballantine & J. Spade (Eds.), *School and society: A sociological approach to education* (4th ed., pp. 181–189). Thousand Oaks: Pine Forge Press/SAGE Publications.

Jacob, B. A. (2005). Accountability, incentives, and behavior: Evidence from school reform in Chicago. *Journal of Public Economics, 89*, 761–796.

Jacob, B. (2007). *Test-based accountability and student achievement: An investigation of differential performance on NAEP and state assessments* (Working Paper 12817). Cambridge, MA: National Bureau of Economic Research.

Jacob, R. T., Stone, S., & Roderick, M. (2004). *Ending social promotion: The response of teachers and students*. Chicago: Consortium on Chicago School Research. Retrieved March 29, 2011, from http://www.eric.ed.gov/PDFS/ED483823.pdf

Jacobsen, R., Saultz, A., & Snyder, J. W. (2013). When accountability strategies collide: Do policy changes that raise accountability standards also erode public satisfaction? *Educational Policy, 27*(2), 360–389.

Jacobsen, R., Snyder, J. W., & Saultz, A. (2014). Informing or shaping public opinion? The influence of school accountability data format on public perceptions of school quality. *American Journal of Education, 121*(1), 1–27.

Jennings, J. L., & Bearak, J. M. (2014). "Teaching to the Test" in the NCLB Era: How test predictability affects our understanding of student performance. *Educational Researcher, 43*(8), 381–389.

Jennings, J. L., & Sohn, H. (2014). Measure for measure: How proficiency-based accountability systems affect inequality in academic achievement. *Sociology of Education, 87*(2), 125–141.

Jennings, J. L., Bearak, J. M., & Koretz, D. M. (2011). *Accountability and racial inequality in American education*. Paper presented at the annual meetings of the American Sociological Association, Las Vegas, NV.

Jerald, C. D. (2012). *Education sector reports: On Her Majesty's school inspection service*. Washington, DC: Education Sector.

King, M. D., Jennings, J. L., & Fletcher, J. (2014). Medical adaptation to academic pressure: Schooling, stimulant use, and socioeconomic status. *American Sociological Review, 79*(6), 1–28.

Klein, S. P., Hamilton, L. S., McCaffrey, D. F., & Stecher, B. M. (2000). *What do test scores in Texas tell us?* Santa Monica: RAND (Issue Paper IP-202). http://www.rand.org/publications/IP/IP202/. Accessed 4 June 2013.

Kogan, V., Lavertu, S., & Peskowitz, Z. (2015). Performance federalism and local democracy: Theory and evidence from school tax referenda. *American Journal of Political Science, 60*(2), 418–435.

Konstantopoulos, S., Miller, S., & van der Ploeg, A. (2013). The impact of Indiana's system of interim assessments on mathematics and reading achievement. *Educational Evaluation and Policy Analysis, 35*(4), 481–499.

Konstantopoulos, S., Miller, S., van der Ploeg, A., & Li, W. (2016). Effects of interim assessments on student achievement: Evidence from a large-scale experiment. *Journal of Research on Educational Effectiveness, 9*(S1), 188–208.

Koretz, D., & Beguin, A. (2010). Self-monitoring assessments for educational accountability systems. *Measurement, 8*(2–3), 92–109.

Koretz, D., Jennings, J. L., Ng, H. L., Yu, C., Braslow, D., & Langi, M. (2016). Auditing for score inflation using self-monitoring assessments: Findings from three pilot studies. *Educational Assessment, 21*(4), 231–247.

Krieg, J. (2008). Are students left behind? The distributional effects of No Child Left Behind. *Education Finance and Policy, 3*, 250–281.

Ladd, H. F., & Lauen, D. L. (2010). Status versus growth: The distributional effects of accountability policies. *Journal of Policy Analysis and Management, 29*(3), 426–450.

Ladd, H. F., & Zelli, A. (2002). School-based accountability in North Carolina: The responses of school principals. *Educational Administration Quarterly, 38*(4), 494–529. https://doi.org/10.1177/001316102237670.

Lauen, D. L. (2007). Contextual explanations of school choice. *Sociology of Education, 80*(3), 179–209.

Lauen, D. L., & Gaddis, S. M. (2012). Shining a light or fumbling in the dark? The effects of NCLB's subgroup-specific accountability on student achievement. *Educational Evaluation and Policy Analysis, 34*(2), 185–208.

Lauen, D., & Gaddis, M. (2016). Accountability pressure, academic standards, and educational triage. *Educational Evaluation and Policy Analysis, 38*(1), 127–147.

Lazarín, M. (2014). *Testing overload in America's schools*. Center for American Progress. https://www.americanprogress.org/issues/education/report/2014/10/16/99073/testing-overload-in-americas-schools/. Accessed 2 Mar 2016.

Li, D. (2015). *School accountability and principal mobility: How No Child Left Behind affects the allocation of school leaders* (Harvard Business School Working Paper, No. 16-052). http://www.hbs.edu/faculty/Pages/item.aspx?num=50034. Accessed 2 Mar 2016.

Lipset, S. M., & Schneider, W. (1983). *The confidence gap: Business, labor and government in the public mind*. New York: Free Press.

Loeb, S., & Cunha, J. (2007). *Have assessment-based accountability reforms influenced the career decisions of teachers?* A report commissioned by the U.S. Congress as part of Title I, Part E, Section

1503 of the No Child Left Behind Act of 2001. https://cepa.stanford.edu/sites/default/files/Cunha_Accountability_Labor_Decisions.pdf Accessed 2 Mar 2016.

Luginbuhl, R., Webbink, D., & Wolf, I. D. (2009). Do inspections improve primary school performance? *Educational Evaluation and Policy Analysis, 31*(3), 221–237.

Marsh, J. A., Pane, J. F., & Hamilton, L. S. (2006). *Making sense of data-driven decision making in education: Evidence from recent RAND Research* (OP-170). Santa Monica: RAND Corporation.

McDonnell, L. M. (2005). No Child Left Behind and the federal role in education: Evolution or revolution? *Peabody Journal of Education, 80*(2), 19–38.

McNeil, L. M. (2000). *Contradictions of school reform: Educational costs of standardized testing*. New York: Routledge.

Means, B., Padilla, C., & Gallagher, L. (2010). *Use of education data at the local level: From accountability to instructional improvement*. U.S. Department of Education. https://www2.ed.gov/rschstat/eval/tech/use-of-education-data/use-of-education-data.pdf. Accessed 2 Mar 2016.

Mehta, J. (2013). How paradigms create politics: The transformation of American educational policy, 1980–2001. *American Educational Research Journal, 50*(2), 285–324.

Meyer, J. W., & Rowan, B. (1977). Institutionalized organizations: Formal structure as myth and ceremony. *American Journal of Sociology, 83*(2), 340–363.

Meyer, J. W., & Rowan, B. (1978). The structure of educational organizations. In M. W. Meyer (Ed.), *Environments and organizations*. San Francisco: Jossey-Bass.

Murnane, R. J., & Papay, J. P. (2010). Teachers' views on No Child Left Behind: Support for the principles, concerns about the practices. *The Journal of Economic Perspectives, 24*(3), 151–166.

Neal, D., & Schanzenbach, D. W. (2007). *Left behind by design: Proficiency counts and test-based accountability* (NBER Working Paper No. 13293).

Oakes, J. (1985). *Keeping track*. New Haven: Yale University Press.

OECD. (2011). How are schools held accountable? In *Education at a Glance 2011: Highlights*. Paris: OECD Publishing.

OECD. (2014). Indicator D3: How much are teachers paid? In *Education at a Glance 2014: OECD Indicators*. Paris: OECD Publishing.

OECD. (2015). *Country note: United States of America: Key findings from the teaching and learning international survey (TALIS)*. Paris: OECD Publishing.

Olson, L. (2005, November 30). Benchmark assessments offer regular checkups on student achievement. *Education Week*. http://www.edweek.org/ew/articles/2005/11/30/13benchmark.h25.html. Accessed 2 Mar 2016.

Papay, J. P., Murnane, R. J., & Willett, J. B. (2011). *How performance information affects human-capital investment decisions: The impact of test-score labels on educational outcomes* (No. w17120). National Bureau of Economic Research.

Pedulla, J. J., Abrams, L. M., Madaus, G. F., Russell, M. K., Ramos, M. A., & Miao, J. (2003). *Perceived effects of state-mandated testing programs on teaching and learning: Findings from a national survey of teachers*. Boston: Lynch School of Education, Boston College.

Polikoff, M. S., McEachin, A. J., Wrabel, S. L., & Duque, M. (2014). The waive of the future? School accountability in the waiver era. *Educational Researcher, 43*(1), 45–54.

Reback, R. (2008). Teaching to the rating: School accountability and the distribution of student achievement. *Journal of Public Economics, 92*, 1394–1415.

Reback, R., Rockoff, J., & Schwartz, H. L. (2014). Under pressure: Job security, resource allocation, and productivity in schools under No Child Left Behind. *American Economic Journal: Economic Policy, 6*(3), 207–241.

Rhodes, J. H. (2015). Learning citizenship? How state education reforms affect parents' political attitudes and behavior. *Political Behavior, 37*(1), 181–220.

Rich, P. M., & Jennings, J. L. (2015). Choice, information, and constrained options: School transfers in a stratified educational system. *American Sociological Review, 80*(5), 1069–1098.

Rockoff, J., & Turner, L. J. (2010). Short-run impacts of accountability on school quality. *American Economic Journal: Economic Policy, 2*(4), 119–147.

Rosenthal, L. (2004). Do school inspections improve school quality? Ofsted inspections and school examination results in the U.K. *Economics of Education Review, 23*(2), 143–151.

Rosenthal, R., & Jacobson, L. (1968). *Pygmalion in the classroom: Teacher expectation and pupils' intellectual development*. Rinehart and Winston.

Rouse, E. R., Hannaway, J., Goldhaber, D., & Figlio, D. (2013). Feeling the Florida heat? How low-performing schools respond to voucher and accountability pressure. *American Economic Journal: Economic Policy, 5*(2), 251–281.

Shen, X. (2008). *Do unintended effects of high-stakes testing hit disadvantaged schools harder?* Doctoral dissertation, Stanford University.

Shepard, L. A. (1988, April). Should instruction be measurement driven? A debate. In *Meeting of the American Educational Research Association*, New Orleans.

Shepard, L. A., & Dougherty, K. (1991). Effects of high-stakes testing on instruction. In R. L. Linn (Ed.), *The effects of high stakes testing*. Annual meetings of the American Education Research Association and the National Council of Measurement in Education. Chicago, IL.

Sims, D. P. (2009). *Going down with the ship? The effect of school accountability on the distribution of teacher experience in California* (Urban Institute Working Paper). http://www.urban.org/research/publication/going-down-ship-effect-school-accountability-distribution-teacher-experience-california. Accessed 2 March 2016.

Slavin, R. E., Cheung, A., Holmes, G. C., Madden, N. A., & Chamberlain, A. (2013). Effects of a data-driven district reform model on state assessment outcomes. *American Educational Research Journal, 50*(2), 371–396.

Springer, M. G. (2008). The influence of an NCLB accountability plan on the distribution of student test score gains. *Economics of Education Review, 27*(5), 556–563.

Starr, P. (1983). *The social transformation of American medicine: The rise of a sovereign profession and the making of a vast industry*. New York: Basic Books.

Stecher, B. M. Vernez, G., & Steinberg, P. (2010). *Reauthorizing No Child Left Behind: Facts and recommendations*. RAND Education. http://www.rand. org/pubs/monographs/MG977.html. Accessed 2 Mar 2016.

Steinberg, M. P., & Donaldson, M. L. (2016). The new educational accountability: Understanding the landscape of teacher evaluation in the post-NCLB Era. *Education Finance and Policy, 11*(3), 340–359.

Sun, M., Saultz, A., & Ye, Y. (2014). *Federal policy and the teacher labor market: Exploring the effects of NCLB on teacher turnover*. Paper presented at the annual meeting of the Association for Education Finance and Policy, San Antonio, TX.

Taylor, G., Shepard, L., Kinner, F., & Rosenthal, J. (2002). *A survey of teachers' perspectives on high-stakes testing in Colorado: What gets taught, what gets lost* (CSE Technical Report 588). Los Angeles: University of California. Retrieved September 20, 2010, from http://eric.ed.gov/PDFS/ED475139.pdf

The National Commission on Excellence in Education. (1983). *A nation at risk: The imperative for educational reform. An open letter to the American people.* A report to the Nation and the Secretary of Education. http://files.eric.ed.gov/fulltext/ED226006.pdf. Accessed 2 Mar 2016.

U.S. Department of Education. (2002). Fact sheet on title I, Part A. https://www2.ed.gov/rschstat/eval/disadv/title1-factsheet.pdf. Accessed 2 Mar 2016.

Winters, M. A., & Cowen, J. M. (2012). Grading New York accountability and student proficiency in America's largest school district. *Educational Evaluation and Policy Analysis, 34*(3), 313–327.

Wong, M., Cook, T. D., & Steiner, P. M. (2009). *No Child Left Behind: An interim evaluation of its effects on learning using two interrupted time series each with its own non-equivalent comparison series.* Institute for Policy Research (Working Paper 09–11), 18.

Methods for Examining the Effects of School Poverty on Student Test Score Achievement

22

Douglas Lee Lauen, Brian L. Levy, and E. C. Hedberg

Abstract

Measuring school effects has been an important inquiry for sociologists of education for at least 50 years. This chapter summarizes current research on the relationship between school poverty and student achievement, which relies heavily on cross-sectional associations. We then propose that scholars consider longitudinal approaches to estimating school effects in which changes in school outcomes are related to changes in school contexts. We present illustrative examples of both cross-sectional and longitudinal analyses using a census of North Carolina students and schools. Cross-sectional models indicate a significant negative association between school poverty and achievement. Our preferred specification—a three-level model of time within students cross-nested within schools—finds no relationship between school poverty and achievement, which raises important questions about the validity of school poverty effects on student test score growth. This model does, however, suggest that variation in test score growth across schools may be greater than variation in test score growth across students, which opens important avenues for understanding the sources of this variation.

An important mode of sociological inquiry is seeking to understand the effects of groups on individual action. From the earliest days of the discipline, sociologists have investigated this question with many types of evidence, from quantitative counts and rates to interviews and observation. That individual behavior is shaped by social context is a central presumption of sociologists, one that separates our discipline from economics and psychology, which stress the role of individual drives and preferences.

Whether the focus is on schools as organizations, schooling as a set of implicit and explicit practices, or the educational system as a central institution in a system of stratification, sociologists of education have made significant contributions to our understanding of the ways schools affect student's lives, both during the years of formal schooling and thereafter. Focusing on quantitative school effects studies in particular, we have learned that education is a key determinant of status attainment, that family background is a strong predictor of success in school, and that school impacts are

D. L. Lauen (✉)
University of North Carolina, Chapel Hill, NC, USA
e-mail: dlauen@unc.edu

B. L. Levy
Harvard University, Cambridge, MA, USA
e-mail: blevy@fas.harvard

E. C. Hedberg
NORC at the University of Chicago, Chicago, IL, USA

© Springer International Publishing AG, part of Springer Nature 2018   493
B. Schneider (ed.), *Handbook of the Sociology of Education in the 21st Century*, Handbooks of Sociology and Social Research, https://doi.org/10.1007/978-3-319-76694-2_22

relatively small once family background is controlled (Blau and Duncan 1967; Duncan and Hodge 1963; Sewell et al. 1969, 1980).

As James Coleman and colleagues put it in the highly influential 1966 *Equality of Educational Opportunity* report, "schools are remarkably similar in the way they relate to the achievement of their pupils when the socioeconomic background of the students is taken into account. It is known that socioeconomic factors bear a strong relation to academic achievement. When these factors are statistically controlled, however, it appears that differences between schools account for only a small fraction of difference in pupil achievement" (Coleman et al. 1966, pp. 21–22). This claim raised important doubts about the suitability of schools as institutions that could ameliorate social inequality.

However, Coleman's classic work also reported that "children from a given family background, when put in schools of different social composition, will achieve at quite different levels." This finding suggested that proactive efforts to mix students by social background could have beneficial effects. In particular, the report argued that Black student achievement was more strongly related to school inputs than White student achievement: "The principal way in which the school environments of Negroes and Whites differ is in the composition of their student bodies, and it turns out that the composition of the student bodies has a strong relationship to the achievement of Negro and other minority pupils" (ibid., p. 22). This finding became an important rationale for desegregation and busing programs to integrate Black and White students during the 1960s and 1970s.

Fifty years ago and today, there is widespread concern about the performance of segregated minority and high-poverty schools. High-poverty schools tend to have difficulty retaining experienced teachers, who prefer to teach in low-poverty schools with better working conditions (Boyd et al. 2005; Scafidi et al. 2007). Therefore, high-poverty schools tend to have more novice, long-term substitutes, and out-of-field teachers (Clotfelter et al. 2007, 2009; Ingersoll 2002; Lankford et al. 2002). Absences and mobility of students and teachers are usually higher in high-poverty schools, making it more challenging to maintain continuity and coherence in learning across the school year (Allensworth et al. 2009). These factors contribute to diminished instructional capacity and worse curricular coverage (Johnson et al. 2012). In addition, there is the concern of negative classroom spillover effects—that students in these schools learn at slower rates due to the high prevalence of students with low initial achievement and high rates of learning disabilities and disruptive behavior (Hoxby 2000; Sacerdote 2011). Studies report that low-SES or high-poverty schools have lower test scores even once the family background of students is statistically controlled (e.g., Entwisle et al. 1994; Choi et al. 2008; Willms 1986, Battistich et al. 1995).

These concerns have provided a rationale for public policies to mix students by social background. These policies have included busing, school choice, magnet schools, and drawing school boundaries to create more diverse schools. Today, school assignment solely on the basis of race has been ruled unconstitutional, so integration plans that mix students by socioeconomic status are emerging as alternatives and have been implemented in dozens of districts including Wake County, NC; Cambridge, MA; and San Francisco (Kahlenberg 2012). Integrating students by income, however, is becoming harder because neighborhoods are getting more segregated by income (Jargowsky 1996; Watson 2009; Reardon and Bischoff 2011) and within large districts, between-school segregation by free/reduced-price lunch eligibility increased by about 30% between 1990 and 2010 (Owens et al. 2016).

For these reasons, understanding the effects of school poverty on student achievement has been a rich area of research in the sociology of education. In addition, the theoretical and methodological underpinnings of our analysis in this chapter have deep roots in sociological analysis of many phenomena. At its most basic level, we want to understand whether social context has effects on individuals over and above their individual background. In short, whether the setting, or context, in which an individual is embedded has a causal effect on their outcomes.

This chapter aims to both summarize existing work on cross-sectional contextual effects (Blau 1960; Blalock 1984; Iversen 1991; Raudenbush and Bryk 2002) and encourage further development and wider use of longitudinal approaches to estimating contextual effects (Bryk and Raudenbush 1988; Lauen and Gaddis 2013). We begin with the cross-sectional contextual effects case, in which we summarize the large methodological literature on how to examine the effects of school poverty on test score at one point in time. This presentation is made with two caveats. First, we stress in this section that the absence of unobserved confounding is a strong, and likely untenable, assumption for drawing causal inferences from cross-sectional observational studies. In brief, it is difficult to rule out the possibility that adverse selection into high-poverty schools may be driving the residual associations often found from cross-sectional designs. In response to the first caveat, we turn to first two- and then three-level longitudinal contextual effects designs. Our section on longitudinal modeling includes examples of two-level (time within student) and three-level (time within student within school) models. It also covers the complication of the cross-nesting of students in schools over time.

Longitudinal designs examine the association between *changes* in school poverty and *changes* in student test scores. Not without their own complications, longitudinal designs provide a stronger basis for making causal inferences about sociological theories and public policy because (1) one can often establish temporal ordering, an important precondition for estimating causal effects, (2) one can exploit techniques to disentangle fixed confounding factors from the effects of time-varying treatment effects. One can only draw causal conclusions from longitudinal designs with strong assumptions about the absence of time-varying confounding, among others, but arguably the assumptions one must make about the estimates from cross-sectional designs are stronger still (i.e., less likely to hold).

The second caveat is that we assume that our predictor, poverty, is measured without error. Since we are working with state census data (described below), the school-level aggregates of

this variable are also highly reliable. If this second set of assumptions are not met, such that the predictors were some psychometric scale and only a sample of students was available for each school, a multilevel latent variable model would be more appropriate (Lüdtke et al. 2008).

22.1 Data

The data used for this chapter comes from one complete cohort from a statewide database of administrative records compiled by the North Carolina Department of Public Instruction and archived by Duke University's North Carolina Education Records Data Center. We first observe students in third grade in 2006 and retain in the sample only those were promoted to fourth and fifth grade in 2007 and 2008, consecutively. There are more than 216,000 student-year observations over 3 years, with about 72,000 unique students observed in each year. Our measure of student poverty is whether the student is eligible for free or reduced-price lunch, a threshold that is actually 185% of the poverty line, adjusted for family size.[1] About 47% of students fall below this income threshold. The sample is about 55% White, 28% Black, 10% Hispanic, 4% multi-racial, 2% Asian, and 1% Native American. The outcome is a vertically equated math test score

---

[1] Free or reduced-price lunch eligibility is not an ideal measure of family poverty or income, but it is the most widely available one in U.S. administrative data from school districts and states. One might want a continuous income measure from all parents in the school to explore the sensitivity of impacts to different income cutoffs. Unfortunately, family income is generally not available in administrative data. It is also a measure pegged above the poverty line rather than right at the poverty line. In addition, it is a measure that is disappearing. The "community eligibility" standard replaces individual eligibility with schoolwide eligibility for schools that meet the community eligibility threshold. Finally, it does not capture the three aspects of family SES: income, parental education, and parental occupation. In our experience, however, school-level correlations between percent free/reduced-price lunch and average SES or percent college-educated parents are quite high, so even if they mean different things at the individual level, they correlate strongly at the school level.

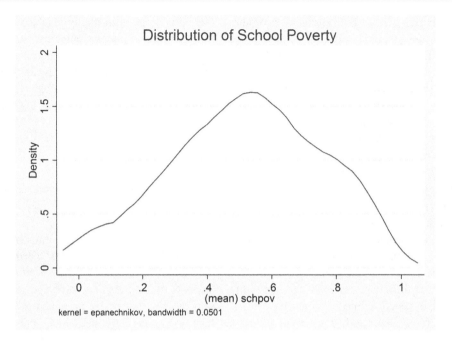

Fig. 22.1 Distribution of school poverty of North Carolina elementary schools with a fifth grade sample, 2008

designed to measure growth across grade levels (mean = 349.6, SD = 10.6). This outcome measure is well suited to longitudinal analysis because it is designed to measure growth in achievement over time. The fifth grade sample includes more than 1300 elementary schools, with an average of 55 students per school. Our focal variable of interest is school poverty rate which is the proportion of students in the school that were eligible for free or reduced-price lunch. Due to the state's economic diversity, the statewide nature of the data, and the sample size, we observe a great deal of variation in school poverty in the sample (mean = .52, SD = .23, interquartile range = .46, 5th percentile = .10 and .95th percentile = .96, see Fig. 22.1) and have plenty of statistical power to reliably estimate contextual effects.

22.2 Cross-Sectional Contextual Effects

Cross-sectional contextual effects models aim to estimate the mean difference in an outcome associated with a change in the group mean of a covariate while holding constant the individual value of the same covariate (Blau 1960; Blalock 1984; Iversen 1991). For example, does the school poverty rate have an effect on test score holding constant student poverty? In this section we consider the cross-sectional contextual effects model, the meaning of the estimated parameters, and how to properly estimate the sampling variances of the effects. We pay special attention to how appropriate estimation procedures either increase or decrease the sampling variances. For the purposes of the exposition, we assume a balanced sample (where each school has the same number of students), but we note that our North Carolina data set is unbalanced.

Consider a hypothetical balanced sample where there are $i = \{1, 2, \ldots n\}$ units (e.g., students) each in $j = \{1, 2, \ldots m\}$ groups (e.g., schools), for a total sample size of $N = n \times m$. Next, assume that an academic student level outcome, y, for unit i in group j is predicted by a student level variable, x, and the average of this variable within each school, $\bar{x}_j$. For simplicity, we will assume that within each school there is the same relationship between x and y. The focus on this section is on three types of relationships

Fig. 22.2 Between, within, and contextual effects

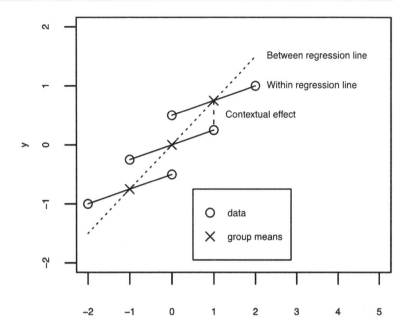

in clustered data: between, within, and contextual. The next section will explore the sampling variance associated with these effects. The contextual effect is derived from two other effects, the between and within effects. We define each of these in turn and then show how they can be used to define the contextual effect.

To fix ideas consider Fig. 22.2, a visual representation of positive between, within, and contextual effects, which plots six observations across three groups, each with a solid line indicating the within-group regression and the between-group regression fit through the group means. In this hypothetical example, the between-group slope is 0.75 and the within-group effect is 0.25. The contextual effect is then 0.5, represented by the long-dashed line that compares the value of the higher value of x in group 2 with the same value of x in the group with the higher mean. That vertical difference is the mean difference in y associated with a single unit change in the group mean. Conceptually, the contextual effect is the predicted difference in test score between two students who share the same individual poverty level, but who attend schools that differ by one unit of school poverty (Raudenbush and Bryk 2002, p. 141).

With this picture in mind, we now define each of the three effects and discuss coefficients gen-

erated from fitting various models to the North Carolina data. The first effect is the *between* effect, which is the effect of the group average of the covariate, $\bar{x}_j$, on the group average of the outcome, $\bar{y}_j$. For example, researchers may be interested in the relationship between a school's average poverty level on school average math achievement. One way to estimate this slope is to calculate the averages of the covariate and outcome for all groups (schools) and then perform a simple OLS regression, $\bar{y}_j = \zeta_0 + \zeta_1\bar{x}_j + v_j$, where the between effect is the estimate of ζ_1.[2] Note that the error term of this model, v_j, is a combination of the between-group error term, u_j, and the average within-group error term, $\bar{e}_j$, so that $v_j = u_j + \bar{e}_j$.

Looking at the example data results in Table 22.1, the first model estimated is the "Between Effects Model." In this model we see that among North Carolina 5th graders, the difference between a school with no poverty (i.e., the mean is 0) and a school that is completely impoverished (i.e., the mean is 100) is about 11

---

[2]With balanced data one can predict unit values the group means $y_{ij} = \kappa_0 + \kappa_1\bar{x}_j + w_{ij}$, where $w_{ij} = u_j + e_{ij}$, and the slope of the group mean from this model is the same as the between model, $\kappa_1 = \zeta_1$.

Table 22.1 Cross-sectional ordinary least squares contextual models, 5th grade mathematics

	1	2	3	4
	OLS between effects model	OLS within effects model	OLS within and between effects model	OLS within and context effects model
Student poverty Indicator		−5.027		−5.027
		(0.067)		(0.072)
Group-mean centered student poverty Indicator			−5.027	
			(0.072)	
School mean poverty	−11.294		−12.781	−7.754
	(0.511)		(0.136)	(0.154)
Intercept	359.617	357.827	361.486	361.486
	(0.296)	(0.043)	(0.071)	(0.071)

Notes: N = 72,252 students nested in 1310 schools. All effects statistically significant at p < 0.001. Standard errors in parentheses. OLS = ordinary least squares

points. We can interpret gradients of this effect by multiplying by the proportion impoverished. For example, the difference between no poverty and 50% poverty is −11.3 * 0.5 = 5.7 points.

The second effect of interest is the *within* effect, which is the effect of the unit level covariate on the outcome with all variance associated with the outcome at the group level removed. This can be accomplished by de-meaning the outcome and predictor's group means from the level-1 values, such as in an econometric fixed effects model, or by entering dummy variables for each group except one. OLS can estimate the within effect with the following model that transforms each variable by subtracting the group means from x and y,

$x_{ij}^{\dagger} = x_{ij} - \bar{x}_j$ and $y_{ij}^{\dagger} = y_{ij} - \bar{y}_j$, to estimate the model $y_{ij}^{\dagger} = \lambda_0 + \lambda_1 x_{ij}^{\dagger} + e_{ij}$, where the within effect is the estimate of λ_1 and the within error

term is e_{ij}.[3] The "Within Effects Model" in Table 22.1 (column 2) shows a within-school poverty gap of five points, less than half as large as the between-school effect of 11.

The between and within effects can be combined in a single model that enters both the group-mean of the unit covariate and the group-mean-centered value of the unit level covariate into the regression $y_{ij} = \beta_0 + \beta_1 \bar{x}_j + \beta_2 (x_{ij} - \bar{x}_j) + w_{ij}$, where $\beta_2 = \lambda_1$ and $\beta_1 = \zeta_1$ if the data are balanced. In Table 22.1, column 3, this model is estimated using OLS and our unbalanced data in the "OLS Within and Between Effects Model."[4] The *contextual* effect is the difference between the *between* effect and the *within* effect. It represents the difference in the outcome when the level-1 value is held constant and the group-mean is increased by one unit. Another way to think of the contextual effect is that it is the between effect net of the within effect. To estimate the contextual effect directly, and compute a standard error of this estimate, we remove the group-mean centered variable, replace it with an uncentered (or grand-mean centered) level-1 variable, $y_{ij} = \gamma_0 + \gamma_1 \bar{x}_j + \gamma_2 x_{ij} + w_{ij}$, which fits the data just as well. The within effect is $\gamma_2 = \beta_2 = \lambda_1$ and the contextual effect is $\gamma_1 = \beta_1 - \beta_2$. This model is represented in the fourth column of Table 22.1, "OLS Within and Context Effects Model," where the effect of the group mean poverty is −7.75 points, the difference between the

---

[3]When estimating the within model through the dummy variable approach, degrees of freedom is calculated correctly because the number of dummies counts toward the number of regressors. When estimating the within model via demeaning, one must adjust the degrees of freedom to account for the number of groups, which increases the residual error variance, which in turn increases the standard errors. This step is taken into account by statistical software. Our estimates were produced by Stata's xtreg be re and fe commands, which compute correct standard errors.

[4]Note that the between effect in Model 3 differs from the one in Model 1 because Model 1 is a regression of the school averages, whereas Model 3 uses the individual level test scores. If the data were balanced, the effects would be the same.

two effects shown in column 3: $-12.781 - (-5.027) = -7.754$.

We note, however, that the OLS model typically underestimates the sampling variance of group-level effects and over estimates the sampling variance of within-group effects. In our example, the standard error on the within effect coefficient is smaller in column 2 than in column 3. While estimating the contextual effect is a straightforward linear combination $(\beta_1 - \beta_2)$, the sampling variance of the effect required for a statistical test, $V\{\beta_1 - \beta_2\} = V\{\beta_1\} + V\{\beta_2\} - 2 \times C$ $V\{\beta_1, \beta_2\}$, is tedious because it requires the sampling covariance of β_1 and β_2, which is usually not reported or easily accessible in many software packages. We turn to this topic in the following section.

22.2.1 Methods to Estimate the Sampling Variance of between, Within, and Contextual Effects

Ordinary least squares (OLS) regression makes the assumption that each observation is independently sampled. The data we use to estimate contextual effects is always clustered into groups. For example, in many surveys and interventions, schools are sampled and then students within the school are selected. This creates two sources of random error: the between-group residual, u_j, which is the difference between the average of the group and the average of group averages, and e_{ij}, which is the difference between each observation and its group average. Therefore, rather than using OLS to estimate context effects, the econometric approach is to represent these two sources of error with a random effects (RE) model estimated through feasible generalized least squares (FGLS), or in psychology, a mixed model, such as a Hierarchical Linear Model (HLM).[5] In essence, these multilevel models use the data to partial out a random intercept, u_j, which generally produce a different parameter estimate of contextual effects than would be produced by an OLS model. Many econometricians express concern over the use of random effects models in lieu of a fixed effects model that carries fewer assumptions. In a fixed effects model, indicators for all but one cluster are included as covariates. However, this model removes *all* the variance associated with the cluster from the model, making the estimation of contextual effects from cross-sectional data impossible.[6]

In an appendix we sketch some important statistical details for FGLS. We show how the estimation relates to the conditional intraclass correlation, how random effects estimates use both between- and within-cluster variation, and thus generally lie between estimates produced by OLS and fixed effects estimates. Perhaps more familiar to sociologists of education are mixed or Hierarchical Linear Models (Raudenbush and Bryk 2002).[7] The statistical details of the estimation are beyond the scope of this chapter, but essentially the estimation of the variance components and design effects are both estimated in a single maximum likelihood step.[8] We refer interested readers to Raudenbush and Bryk (2002) chapters 3, 13, and 14, for an extended treatment of maximum likelihood estimation and Bayesian methods. An advantage of this modeling framework is that it extends naturally into treating both intercepts and slopes as random, as we discuss below.

---

[5] A third option, not outlined here, is to simply estimate OLS coefficients and use cluster-robust standard errors, also known as sandwich estimators. This produces standard errors that take into account clustering, but the coefficient estimate itself is produced from only student-level variation, so will generally differ from one produced by a random or fixed intercept model.

[6] This is due to the transformation of variables in fixed effects models whereby the group mean is subtracted from each variable. In the case of "level-2" variables, this procedure renders the transformed variable into a constant of 0 (because the group mean of a "level-2" variable is the variable itself). This constant of 0 is collinear with the intercept constant of 1 rendering the model impossible to estimate.

[7] Mixed models can be estimated using the HLM software (Raudenbush et al. 2004); proc mixed in SAS; mixed in Stata or SPSS; lme, nlme, and lme4 in R; or other specialized software such as MPlus.

[8] Mixed models are related to, and an extension of, ANOVA procedures (Raudenbush 1993). When restricted maximum likelihood is employed, equivalent estimates are obtained.

The model to estimate the between and within effects for the *ith* student in school *j* is

$$y_{ij} = \beta_0 + \beta_1 \left(x_{ij} - \bar{x}_j \right) + e_{ij}, \text{where}$$

$$\beta_0 = \gamma_{00} + \gamma_{01} \bar{x}_j + u_j, \text{and}$$

$$\beta_1 = \gamma_{10}.$$

Equivalently, in mixed notation, we can write this model as

$$y_{ij} = \gamma_{00} + \gamma_{01} \bar{x}_j + \gamma_{10} \left(x_{ij} - \bar{x}_j \right) + u_j + e_{ij}.$$

In this model, the between effect is noted as γ_{01}, the slope of the group mean of the covariate, and the within effect is noted as, γ_{10}, the slope of the group-mean-centered level-1 value of the covariate. The values of γ_{00}, u_j, and e_{ij}, are the intercept, between-group residual, and within-group residual, respectively.

The "Mixed Within and Between Effects Model" in column 3 of Table 22.2 presents the results using a mixed model estimated with restricted maximum likelihood (REML). We see that the within effect and its standard error is −5.027 (0.067), identical to those produced by the "Random Within and Between Effects Model" estimated with feasible generalized least squares (FGLS) (column 1). The between effects are close, but differ slightly (−11.722 compared to −11.801). In addition, there is a close correspondence between the contextual effects models estimated with FGLS and Mixed models (compare columns 2 and 4 of Table 22.2). In general, we report virtually no differences in the estimates produced by REML and FGLS. We note, however, that the OLS and multilevel model estimates of the contextual effects are not the same as the OLS estimates of the contextual effects (compare columns 2 and 4 of Table 22.2 to column 4 of Table 22.1). This is because the multilevel models take into account both within- and between-school variation in producing the contextual effect estimate, whereas the OLS estimate of the contextual effect is estimated only on student-level variation.

The credibility of these estimates depends on whether students are assigned to schools in a fash-ion that is as good as random. With observational data, we rely on assumptions of "conditional ignorability" or "no omitted confounders." In short, these assumptions mean that once we condition on presumed confounds of treatment assignment and outcome, we can ignore the fact that students were not, in fact, assigned to schools through a random process. If we knew and could measure all confounds related to attending a high-poverty school we could potentially adjust for these confounds and produce a credible estimate.

For example, in Table 22.2, column 5, we control for race/ethnicity, number of absences, and number of school moves. If these variables were sufficient to remove confounding, we could consider these estimates causal. This is not likely the case as there are potentially many more confounds we should include in this model. Two omitted confounds we might wish to include might be the quality of early childhood education and intrinsic motivation to learn math. Nonetheless, it is instructive to examine what happens to the poverty coefficients at the contextual and individual levels once we adjust for race/ethnicity, absences, and school moves: Both decline in absolute value. This suggests that race, absences, and/or school moves are either confounds or mediators depending on the logic of causal ordering, which is challenging to assess with cross-sectional data. To estimate the total effect of school poverty, we should adjust for confounds and should not adjust for mediators through which the school poverty effects operate. Adjusting for a mediator would essentially block a pathway through which school poverty affects the outcome, which is essential for conducting a mediation analysis, but is not appropriate for estimating the total effect of school poverty. By this logic, race/ethnicity is not likely a mediator because it is determined prior to entering school. School move is also measured prior to entering the school in this period since it measures whether a student is new to the school they currently attend, so it also could not be considered a mediator. Absences during the current school year could, however, be viewed as a confound or a mediator: a confound if absences only

Table 22.2 Cross-sectional random effects contextual models, 5th grade mathematics

	1	2	3	4	5
	FGLS random within and between effects model	FGLS random within and context effects	REML mixed within and between effects model	REML mixed within and context effects	REML mixed within and context effects
Student poverty Indicator		−5.027		−5.027	−3.680
		(0.067)		(0.067)	(0.071)
Group-mean centered student poverty Indicator	−5.027		−5.027		
	(0.067)		(0.067)		
School mean poverty	−11.722	−6.694	−11.801	−6.774	−4.353
	(0.513)	(0.519)	(0.454)	(0.459)	(0.454)
American Indian					−3.214
					(0.320)
Asian					−2.827
					(0.206)
Black					−4.811
					(0.087)
Hispanic					−2.013
					(0.115)
Multiracial					−1.711
					(0.162)
Number of absences					−0.017
					(0.002)
School move					−0.912
					(0.105)
Intercept	360.129	360.128	360.228	360.228	360.395
	(0.293)	(0.294)	(0.259)	(0.259)	(0.256)
SD(u)	4.376	4.376	3.790	3.790	3.736
SD(e)	7.974	7.974	7.983	7.983	7.773
Rho	0.231	0.231	0.184	0.184	0.188

Notes: N = 72,252 students nested in 1310 schools. All effects statistically significant at $p < 0.001$. Standard errors in parentheses. *FGLS* feasible generalized least squares, *REML* restricted maximum liklihood, *SD(u)* standard deviation of the between-school error, *SD(e)* standard deviation of the within-school error, *rho* portion of total unexplained variation that lies between schools

reflect family background or health, or a mediator if schools have some control over ensuring students attend school.

22.3   Longitudinal Contextual Effects

Due to the challenges in making causal inferences with cross-sectional data, in this section we consider a different empirical question: whether there is a relationship between *changes* in school poverty and *changes* in test scores. If school poverty has a causal effect on test scores, we would expect that students with higher exposure to high-poverty schools would have slower test score growth. This specification assumes there are changes in school poverty and changes in test score to examine. To conduct this analysis we link students to schools over time and measure student poverty, school poverty rate, and test score at each time point. We have seen in Fig. 22.1

that there is wide variation in school poverty across schools. We call these between-school differences in school poverty rates. A different question is whether student exposure to school poverty varies over time. We call these within-student differences in school poverty rates. These can change very little for students who remain in the same school and quite a bit for students who change schools. Student test scores also have within- and between-student components. Test scores can change due to differences in teacher quality, motivation, family inputs, and changes in context over time. But, achievement test scores are strongly related within the same student over time, suggesting that a student's ability to perform on standardized achievement tests may be largely fixed by the early elementary grades. For example, when we fit an unconditional growth model $y_{ti} = \beta_0 + \beta_1 year + u_{0i} + e_{ti}$, we estimate an ICC (the portion of test score growth that lies between students) of .82, which means that within-student variation around student-specific means is relatively small compared to variation in student-specific means around the grand mean of test scores. This suggests that test scores are fairly stable within the same students over time.

22.3.1 Two Level Growth Model (Time within Student)

We begin our exploration of how test score growth rates vary by school poverty with a two-level random effects linear growth model (time within students) fit to data on students in grades three through five:

$$y_{tij} = \beta_0 + \beta_1 year_t + \beta_2 x_{tij} + \beta_3 x_{tij} year_t \\ + \beta_4 \bar{x}_{tj} + \beta_5 \bar{x}_{tj} year_t + u_{0i} + u_{1i} year_t + e_{ti}$$

Because this model now includes measures of time (year) and interactions with time, we call this a longitudinal contextual effects model. In the cross-sectional model, we had only one contextual effects parameter. Now we have two, β_4 and β_5. Our measure of time, year, is rescaled such that year = calendar year-2006, so that time runs from 0 to 2, in increments of 1. Student and

school poverty are now x_{tij} and $\bar{x}_{tj}$. Both of these variables now have a t subscript to denote that these can vary across time. The intercept is the expected test score for a non-poor student in a school with no poor students at baseline (in 2006). β_2 and β_4 are the estimates of baseline test score gaps between poor and non-poor students and between schools with no and all poor students, respectively. Based on prior research and the results presented above, we expect these to be negative. The primary coefficient of interest is β_5, which measures the annual expected test score growth difference between students in schools with no poor students and students in schools with all poor students. If β_5 is negative, then test score trajectories of students in high-poverty schools are shallower than the trajectories of students in low-poverty schools. Note that we include an interaction with year and x to avoid biasing β_5. We include two random effects, a random intercept specific to each student, u_{0i}, and a random coefficient for time, $u_{1i}y_t$. The random intercept is the student-specific deviation from the grand mean, and the random effect for time is the student-specific deviation from the mean growth rate across all students.

Table 22.3, model 1 presents the results of the two-level contextual growth model with student-level random intercept and growth terms. We include controls for race/ethnicity, absences, and number of school moves and interactions of these controls with year. This model assumes that school poverty is a student-level characteristic and ignores the clustering of students within schools. Although these assumptions may not be tenable, the differences between this model and the cross-sectional models in Table 22.2, model 5 are notable. First, the relationship between school poverty and math test scores declines substantially in magnitude (from −4.3 to −2.1), as does the relationship between student poverty and baseline math test scores (−3.7 to −1.25). It is important to note that the main effects for student poverty and school poverty have different meanings in Tables 22.2 and 22.3. In Table 22.2, for example, the contextual effect of school poverty is a cross-sectional association at grade five, which includes the cumulative effect of school

Table 22.3 Longitudinal random effects contextual models, 3rd through 5th grade mathematics

	1		2		3	
	Two-level longitudinal growth model with student-level random effects		Three-level longitudinal growth model not accounting for partial cross-nesting		Three-level longitudinal growth model that accounts for partial cross-nesting	
Fixed effects						
Year	5.57		5.49		5.55	
	[0.11]	***	[0.16]	***	[0.14]	***
Student poverty indicator	−1.25		−1.51		−1.22	
	[0.05]	***	[0.05]	***	[0.05]	***
Student poverty indicator * year	−0.10		−0.13		−0.13	
	[0.03]	***	[0.03]	***	[0.03]	***
School mean poverty	−2.06		0.18		0.08	
	[0.11]	***	[0.22]		[0.21]	
School mean poverty * year	−0.10		0.20		0.08	
	[0.06]		[0.15]		[0.15]	
Constant	343.58		342.59		342.63	
	[0.27]	***	[0.31]	***	[0.31]	***
Student random effects	x		x		x	
School random effects			x		x	
Accounts for partial cross-nesting					x	
Includes controls and interactions of controls with year	x		x		x	
Random effects						
Student						
Sd(intercept)	7.77		7.28		7.37	
Sd(slope)	1.29		0.53		0.77	
Corr(intercept, slope)	−0.24		−0.36		−0.29	
School						
Sd(intercept)			3.06		2.33	
Sd(slope)			1.24		1.22	
Corr(intercept, slope)			−0.15		−0.27	
Sd(residual)	3.83		3.80		3.79	
Betw school ICC						
Initial status			0.12		0.07	
Growth			0.85		0.72	
N	216,756		216,756		216,756	

Notes: N = 216,756 student-year observations across 3 years cross-nested in 1310 schools. All models include controls for race/ethnicity, absences, and number of school moves and interactions of each control with year. Standard errors in parentheses. ***p < 0.001, ** p<0.01, *p < 0.05

poverty from the past. In Table 22.3, the contextual effect of school poverty is the expected gap in third grade math test scores.

The average annual growth rate is 5.6 test score points. The coefficient on the interaction of school mean poverty and year, −0.10, is not large or statistically significant, which indicates this model would produce test score trajectories for students in high-poverty schools that are quite similar for students in low-poverty schools. Poor students have slightly slower growth rates, a result that is statistically significant due to the large sample size, but one that is nonetheless quite small in magnitude (-0.10, or 2% of a year's growth). The random effects predict that 95% of baseline test scores lie between 328 and 359 ($344 +/- 1.96*7.77$) and that 95% of growth rates lie between 3.0 and 8.1 ($5.57 +/- 1.96*1.29$).

Despite the improvement on a cross-sectional specification that the contextual growth model above offers, the two-level model is not correctly specified and makes assumptions about the structure of the data that are not likely to be valid. Assigning school-level variables as characteristics of the student ignores the clustering of students by demographic, economic, and other characteristics at the school-level. Moreover, treating multiple students within a school as being independent observations is inaccurate and often explicitly contradictory to the structure of data sets such as ours that have repeated observations on students nested within schools.

22.3.2 Three-Level Growth Model (Time Within Student Within School)

A more appropriate specification is a three-level model of student achievement trajectories that treats time as level-1, students as level-2, and schools as level-3 (Bryk and Raudenbush 1988). Continuing the illustrative example using the North Carolina data, at level-1 our measurement model is:

$$y_{tij} = \pi_{0ij} + \pi_{1ij} year_t + \varepsilon_{tij}$$

where Y_{tij} is the achievement score at year t for student i in school j, π_{0ij} is initial status or baseline test score for student i in school j, π_{1ij} is the linear growth rate for student ij, and ε_{tij} is the residual disturbance. Our random coefficient and random slope are the level-2 outcomes of:

$$\pi_{0ij} = \beta_{00j} + \beta_{01j} x_{tij} + r_{0ij}$$

$$\pi_{1ij} = \beta_{10j} + \beta_{11j} x_{tij} + r_{1ij}$$

where β_{00j} is the mean baseline test score within school j, x_{tij} is a student-level time-varying covariate (e.g., poverty status), r_{0ij} is a random intercept effect specific to student ij, β_{10j} is the average growth rate of test scores within school j, and r_{1ij} is a random growth rate effect specific to student ij. Finally, the school-level equation is:

$$\beta_{00j} = \gamma_{000} + \gamma_{001} \bar{x}_{tj} + u_{00j}$$

$$\beta_{10j} = \gamma_{100} + \gamma_{101} \bar{x}_{tj} + u_{10j}$$

where γ_{000} is the mean baseline test score across schools, $\bar{x}_{tj}$ is the time-varying school-level mean of x (e.g., school poverty rate), u_{00j} is a random intercept effect specific to school j, γ_{100} is the average growth rate of test scores across schools, and u_{10j} is a random growth rate effect specific to school j.

Educational research analyzing contextual effects of schools often requires a specific type of multilevel model when using longitudinal data. Cross-sectional data observe students at only one point in time. Quite often in this type of design students appear in only one school, so the data have a hierarchical nesting structure (see Fig. 22.3). This is very rarely the case with longitudinal data as many students change schools from year to year (or even within years). Thus, rather than students nesting perfectly within schools, students are cross-classified into multiple schools (see Fig. 22.4). Cross-classification complicates the estimation of school-level random effects, and to accurately estimate contextual effects with valid significance tests, we must account for the cross-classified structure of the data.

Table 22.4 provides data from a hypothetical sample to illustrate cross-classification. Each row represents a student, and there are four waves of data collected. Whereas some students are perfectly nested into a single school at level-3 (e.g., students 1, 5, 7, and 9), many students change schools at least once during the panel survey. There are two types of cross-classification.

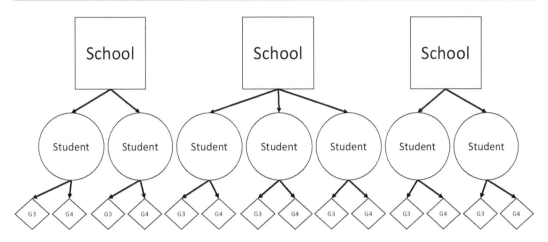

Fig. 22.3 Three-level data structure with perfect nesting

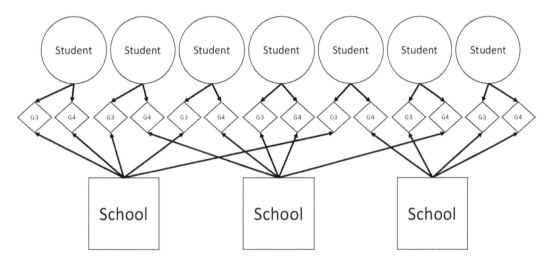

Fig. 22.4 Three-level data structure with partial cross-nesting

Complete cross-classification occurs when there are students in the survey for each permutation of schools by time period. Partial cross-classification, on the other hand, occurs when we observe only some of the potential permutations of schools by time in the data. This is the case in the hypothetical data displayed in Table 22.4, and in longitudinal data sets with several waves and/or multiple geographies in the sampling frame, this is the most common structure of the data. In fact, as the number of schools in the data set rises or number of students observed per school falls, it becomes increasingly likely that the data set is partially cross-classified. Not surprisingly, this is the case with our administrative data on children from North Carolina, which has about 11% of students switching schools between years. For more details about cross classification, readers may consult Raudenbush and Bryk (2002), chapter 12.

Table 22.3, model 2 presents a naïve 3-level model that does not account for the partially cross-nested structure of the data and instead

Table 22.4 Hypothetical panel data set with cross-classification

Student ID	School ID_t1	School ID_t2	School ID_t3	School ID_t4
1	1	1	1	1
2	1	1	1	2
3	1	5	5	5
4	1	2	1	1
5	2	2	2	2
6	2	2	3	3
7	2	2	2	2
8	3	4	4	4
9	3	3	3	3
10	3	10	10	6

assumes perfect nesting.[9] This model, like models 1 and 3, includes controls for race/ethnicity, absences, and number of school moves and interactions of these controls with year. By ignoring the partial cross-nesting, we implicitly assume that every student-school combination represents a unique observation; that is, when a student changes schools, he or she is assumed to be a new student rather than the same student in a different school.

Unlike the 2-level model shown in the first column, this 3-level specification indicates that there is very little relationship between school poverty levels and baseline math scores (.18). We also observe a positive but insignificant coefficient on the interaction of school mean poverty and year, which indicates that students in high-poverty schools have growth rates quite similar to students in low-poverty schools. The coefficients on student poverty and student poverty growth rate differentials are quite similar in models 1 and 2. Turning to the random effects, we find that about 12% of the variation in student third grade test scores lies between schools. While we do not find evidence of strong effects of school poverty on test score growth, we find strong evidence that

schools account for a great deal of the variation in test score growth rates. The standard deviation of *student* growth rates is 0.53; the standard deviation of *school* growth rates is more than twice as large at 1.24. This translates to a between-school ICC of 0.85,[10] which means that 85% of the total test score growth rate is accounted for by schools and only 15% is accounted for by students.

Table 22.3, model 3 presents the results from our 3-level longitudinal growth model of math test scores that accounts for partial cross-nesting. The parameter estimates and standard errors are quite similar to those in model 2, however we observe clear differences in the random effects. In short, accounting for partial cross-nesting increases the portion of variation in initial status and growth due to students relative to that due to schools. Whereas student-specific factors account for only 15% variation in math score growth rates in model 2, they explain 28% of the variation in math score growth in model 3. In addition, schools account for less variation in baseline test scores relative to students: Between-school factors explain 12% of the unexplained variance in baseline math scores in model 2, but they only explain 7% in model 3.

Along with the differences we observe between the 3-level models that do and do not properly account for partial cross-nesting, there are also important differences between the 3-level models (models 2–3) and the 2-level model (model 1). The 3-level results are in clear contrast to those from our 2-level model as we observe sign changes in the fixed coefficients for school poverty on baseline math scores and math score growth. There are also important differences in the random effects, with a small decrease in the standard deviation of the student random intercept and larger declines in the standard deviation of the student random growth coefficient. In fact, whereas less than one-tenth of baseline variance in test scores occurs between schools, over 70% of the variation in growth rates is between schools and potentially attributable to school-level effects rather than student effects (unconditional models yield similar results). Thus, despite the seem-

---

[9]In Table 22.3, models 1 and 3 are estimated with R. Stata's typical coding of multilevel models is strictly hierarchical, with each unit fitting neatly into a single group. It is possible to fit cross-classified data in Stata using a specific notation, but large, unbalanced cross classified data sets pose serious computational problems in this program. Instead, we turned to the lme4 package in R (Bates 2010), which is particularly well suited for computationally efficient analysis of large non-hierarchical data.

---

[10]The between-school ICC for test score growth is calculated as $\dfrac{1.24^2}{.53^2 + .124^2} = .85$

ingly negligible impact of school poverty, the 3-level model reveals a substantial role for school-level effects on math score achievement trajectories. An important implication of these results is that 2-level models can overstate the role of student effects on achievement trajectories when ignoring school-level characteristics and clustering.

The adequacy of this 3-level model rests on a number of assumptions. First, to conclude that our parameter estimates represent mean causal effects, we must assume that, as stated above, we have properly adjusted for all confounds of the school poverty–test score relationship. This is a strong assumption, and it is unlikely to be satisfied in our present example. For instance, parental socioeconomic status (SES) likely affects both school assignment and test score growth (e.g., through investment in non-school educational resources or at-home educational experiences). Student poverty is related to SES, but is most certainly a flawed proxy in the sense that it captures only the bottom end of the income distribution and does not measure either occupation or parental education.

Our estimates of the effect of school poverty on test score growth will be unbiased if all unobserved confounds are fixed and have constant effects on the dependent variable (test scores) and focal independent variable (school poverty). The relationship between school poverty and baseline test scores would incorporate any time-invariant fixed effects. Thus, although baseline effects are sensitive to time-invariant, unobserved confounding, the relationship between school poverty and math score growth should be immune to this type of confounding. Of course, parental SES does vary over time—as do many other unobserved confounders such as marital disruption—and the impacts of school poverty on both baseline math scores and score growth are subject to bias from these omitted time-varying confounds.

A final assumption of the model is that the functional form of the relationship between school poverty and math scores is specified properly. In the present example, we assume that school poverty has only contemporaneous effects; for instance, school poverty at grade 4 affects achievement at grade 4 but not at grade 5. This may not be correct. Increasingly, researchers are examining the cumulative impact of prolonged exposure to contextual disadvantage. For instance, several analyses of the impact of neighborhood disadvantage conclude that sustained exposure to disadvantaged contexts has much more pernicious effects than episodic exposures (e.g., Sharkey and Elwert 2011; Wodtke et al. 2011).

22.4   Conclusion

There are many reasons to expect a strong negative relationship between school poverty and student test scores. As mentioned above, these include differences between high- and low-poverty schools in curriculum, instructional pacing, teacher quality, classroom disruptions, and other factors. On the other hand, it is widely known that there is much more variation in test score achievement levels within than between schools. This suggests that the common narrative of failing high-poverty schools may be overblown. Perhaps U.S. public schools are fairly homogenous in the ways that matter the most for learning. For example, there may be very little variation in instructional time across schools, with instruction organized in age-graded classrooms of the same size, taught by teachers with very similar training, governed by fairly consistent state standards. In short, perhaps over time, schools have become institutionally isomorphic with nationwide expectations about how schooling should be organized (Meyer and Rowan 1977; DiMaggio and Powell 1983).

Our results show that improving model specification reduces the correlation between school poverty and test score. The between-school effect is large, at greater than one standard deviation in test score (the math test score standard deviation is 10.6). But some of this is accounted for by the effect of student poverty on test score and the fact that school poverty is an aggregate property of student poverty. The contextual effect of school poverty, an estimate of the effect of school poverty net of student poverty, is still pretty large at above two-thirds of a standard deviation in test score. Adjusting for race/ethnicity, absences, and number of school moves reduces this cross-sectional association a great deal, to below half a standard deviation. A longitudinal specification is not directly comparable to the cross-sectional model in that the effect of school poverty is now the effect on third grade score rather than fifth grade score. The two-level model reports an even smaller effect of school poverty on baseline (third grade) test scores. The three level model's school poverty effect is indistinguishable from zero. The conclusion we draw from this is that adjustment for student-level confounds and modeling framework (cross-sectional vs longitudinal) matters a great deal to conclusions about the relevance of school poverty to student test scores. The second conclusion we draw from this is that when estimating the effects on student test scores, a three-level specification (time within student within schools) is better than a two-level specification (time within students). The reason for this is that variation in test score growth across schools may be greater than variation in test score growth across students. This perhaps suggests a greater potential to find school correlates of change in test scores rather than student correlates of change in test scores. For this exercise, we only explored one, finding that student growth rates do not vary with the poverty level of their schools. We note that this particular finding does not preclude discovering more promising school correlates of test score change. Third, accounting for partial cross-nesting of students in different schools over time has virtually no impact on fixed parameter estimates, though it does change the size of the random effects. For this reason, this difference could affect standard errors of coefficients. In our study we observe no difference in precision due to a relatively large sample size.

There are some limitations to note. The advantage of using administrative data to estimate contextual effects is that the data contain a census of all students in each school, which reduces standard errors. In addition, students can often be followed over time, and across different schools, which permits longitudinal analysis. A disadvantage is that many important confounds are not measured. National data sets have many more measures of family background, student motivation, and early childhood experiences than does administrative data. Another limitation is that within-student variation in school context is somewhat limited and what variation exists is produced by students who change schools. This itself introduces an endogeneity problem in that the decision to switch schools may be the result of school poverty. If this is the case, then controlling for school mobility may in fact block one of the pathways through which school poverty exerts influence on test scores, which could bias estimates. Methods for proper adjustment of time-dependent confounds are beyond the scope of this chapter, but have been developed by Robins (Robins 1999; Robins et al. 2000) and applied to this question by Lauen and Gaddis (2013). For the sake of ease of exposition, this chapter covers the three time point linear growth case. It is possible that results from a quadratic growth model estimated on grades 3–8 might be more appropriate. Results could vary by state. A national sample with better baseline and time-varying confounds would be a welcome improvement.

Finally, test scores themselves are quite stable within students over time because they are designed to have high reliability. This suggests that estimating correlates of test score changes may be challenging. In addition, test scores are also not the only important outcome of schooling, so examining the cumulative effects of school contexts on non-test score outcomes is an obvious next step for future contextual effects research.

Appendix: The Feasible Generalized Least Squares Method for Random Intercept Models

The first method to estimate within and between effects in a single model was feasible generalized least squares (FGLS), which is a process of transforming the variables to control the error structure and then fitting OLS models to the new data. The procedure outlined here is called the Swamy-Arora (1972)[11] method and is implemented in many software packages. This model requires estimates of conditional variance components.[12] To define conditional variance components, consider that the total conditional variance of the outcome (conditional on the values of fixed predictors and their fixed effects) is a combination of the variances of the error terms from the between and within models, $var(y_{ij}|X_{ij}) = var(u_j) + var(e_{ij})$. These two quantities are called variance components. Variance components can be rescaled to be an estimate of the intraclass correlation (ICC),

defined as $\rho = \dfrac{var(u_j)}{var(u_j) + var(e_{ij})}$, which is the

proportion of the total conditional or unconditional variation that exists between groups is characterized by the intraclass correlation, ICC or ρ.[13] The intraclass correlation is a measure of how much units within the same group resemble

---

[11] See Hill et al. (2008) for a general overview, and Amemiya (1985) for a more advanced treatment and history.

[12] Note that we specify the conditional variance components, since the standard errors are based on the residual variance net of the model. Many other texts on education evaluations employ unconditional variance components because they are performing experiments, where the only impact of interest is the randomized experiments. However, here we are modeling observational data, and thus the standard errors are based on the residuals net of the model specified.

[13] In many cases, such as randomized experiments, the ICC is a measure of how much the population variance occurs between groups. Estimates of these parameters for math and reading are available from Hedges and Hedberg (2007, 2013) and Hedberg and Hedges (2014). However, in contextual analysis, the ICC is a conditional parameter, noting how much of the variance in the outcome, net of predictors, occurs between groups.

each other on their values of an outcome. The larger the ICC, the more correlated (i.e., more similar) two units are within the same group.

The ICC is an important parameter because it is a key contributor to the design effect (Kish 1965) of the variances of the between-group effects, contextual effects, and within effects. Design effects are measures of how much the sampling variance (the square of the standard error) of estimated effects of group level variables (such as between effects) change due to the estimation strategy (i.e., generalized least squares compared to ordinary least squares). The use of OLS naively on the original data produces sampling variances that ignore the design effects, leading to inflated standard errors and false tests of the null hypotheses.

Estimating a contextual effects model with feasible generalized least squares (FGLS) requires transforming the OLS equation with weights defined by a ratio of the variance components. For clustered data, the transformation demeans the value using a weight: For example, a variable z would be transformed by $z_{ij}^* = z_{ij} - \hat{\theta}\,\bar{z}_j$ using the group mean of z and the parameter θ as the weight. The parameter θ is based on the within and between variance components (Cameron and Trivedi 2005):

$$\hat{\theta} = 1 - \sqrt{\frac{var(e_{ij})}{n\left(var(u_j)\right) + var(e_{ij})}}.$$

Thus, a model that estimates both within and between effects can be computed using the following regression,

$$\left(y_{ij} - \hat{\theta}\,\bar{y}_j\right) = \beta_0\left(1 - \hat{\theta}\right) + \beta_1\left(\bar{x}_j - \hat{\theta}\,\bar{x}_j\right) + \beta_2\left(x_{ij} - \bar{x}_j\right) + \left(e_{ij} - \bar{e}_j\right).$$

As between-unit variation increases relative to within-unit variation, then $\hat{\theta}$ approaches 1 and the random effects estimator converges to the fixed effects estimator, which demeans with the entire portion of the group mean. Conversely, as within-unit variation increases relative to between-unit variation, $\hat{\theta}$ approaches 0 and the random effects estimator converges to pooled

OLS, in which group averages are irrelevant. In other words, the random effects estimator uses the information in the data to determine how much of the group mean to include in the estimate, more if between effects are large and less if between effects are small.

The θ parameter is also directly related to how the standard error increases when using the correct model compared to the naïve OLS estimator. For example, if we examine the "Random Within and Between Effects Model" in column 1 of Table 22.2 we see that the standard error of the between effect (0.513) is much larger than the standard error of the between effect from the OLS model in column 3 of Table 22.1 (0.136). The random effects variance is about $0.513^2/0.136^2 = 14$ times higher than the OLS variance. There are about 55 students per school, and the conditional ICC is 0.23, so the expected design effect is about $1 + (55-1)*0.23 = 13$, which is consistent with the observed inflation in the standard error of the between effect coefficient.

References

Allensworth, E., Ponisciak, S., & Mazzeo, C. (2009). *The schools teachers leave: Teacher mobility in Chicago public schools*. Research Report, Consortium on Chicago School Research, University of Chicago. Retrieved from http://files.eric.ed.gov/fulltext/ED505882.pdf

Amemiya, T. (1985). *Advanced econometrics*. Cambridge, MA: Harvard University Press.

Bates, D. M. (2010). *lme4: Mixed-effects modeling with R*. http://lme4.r-forge.r-project.org/book

Battistich, V., Solomon, D., Kim, D., Watson, M., & Schaps, E. (1995). Schools as communities, poverty levels of student populations, and students' attitudes, motives, and performance: A multilevel analysis. *American Educational Research Journal, 32*(3), 627. https://doi.org/10.2307/1163326.

Blalock, H. M. (1984). Contextual-effects models: Theoretical and methodological issues. *Annual Review of Sociology, 10*, 353–372.

Blau, P. M. (1960). Structural effects. *American Sociological Review, 25*, 178–193.

Blau, P. M., & Duncan, O. D. (1967). *The American occupational structure*. New York: Wiley.

Boyd, D., Lankford, H., Loeb, S., & Wyckoff, J. (2005). Explaining the short careers of high-achieving teachers in schools with low-performing students. *American*

Economic Review, Papers and Proceedings, 95(2), 166–171.

Bryk, A. S., & Raudenbush, S. W. (1988). Toward a more appropriate conceptualization of research on school effects: A three-level hierarchical linear model. *American Journal of Education, 97*, 65–108.

Cameron, A. C., & Trivedi, P. K. (2005). *Microeconometrics: Methods and applications*. Cambridge: Cambridge University Press.

Choi, K. H., Raley, R. K., Muller, C., & Riegle-Crumb, C. (2008). Class composition: Socioeconomic characteristics of coursemates and college enrollment. *Social Science Quarterly, 89*(4), 846–866.

Clotfelter, C. T., Ladd, H. F., & Vigdor, J. L. (2009). Are teacher absences worth worrying about in the U.S.? *Education Finance and Policy, 4*, 115–149.

Clotfelter, C. T., Ladd, H. F., Vigdor, J. L., & Wheeler, J. (2007). High-poverty schools and the distribution of teachers and principals. *North Carolina Law Review, 85*, 1345–1379.

Coleman, J. S., Campbell, E. Q., Hobson, C. J., McPartland, J., Mood, A. M., Weinfeld, F. D., & York, R. L. (1966). *Equality of educational opportunity*. Washington, DC: U.S. Government Printing Office.

DiMaggio, P. J., & Powell, W. W. (1983). The iron cage revisited: Institutional isomorphism and collective rationality in organizational fields. *American Sociological Review, 48*(2), 147–160. https://doi.org/10.2307/2095101.

Duncan, O. D., & Hodge, R. W. (1963). Education and occupational mobility: A regression analysis. *American Journal of Sociology, 68*, 629–644.

Entwisle, D. R., Alexander, K. L., & Olson, L. S. (1994). The gender gap in math: Its possible origins in neighborhood effects. *American Sociological Review, 59*(6), 822–838.

Hedberg, E. C., & Hedges, L. V. (2014). Reference values of within-district interclass correlations of academic achievement by district characteristics results from a meta-analysis of district-specific values. *Evaluation Review, 38*(6), 546–582.

Hedges, L. V., & Hedberg, E. C. (2007). Intraclass correlation values for planning group-randomized trials in education. *Educational Evaluation and Policy Analysis, 29*(1), 60–87.

Hedges, L. V., & Hedberg, E. C. (2013). Intraclass correlations and covariate outcome correlations for planning two-and three-level cluster-randomized experiments in education. *Evaluation Review, 37*(6), 445–489.

Hill, R. C., Griffiths, W. E., & Lim, G. C. (2008). *Principles of econometrics*. Hoboken: Wiley.

Hoxby, C. (2000). *Peer effects in the classroom: Learning from gender and race variation* (NBER Working Paper No. 7867). Retrieved from http://www.nber.org/papers/w7867

Ingersoll, R. (2002). Out-of-field teaching, educational inequality, and the organization of schools: An exploratory analysis. CPRE Research Reports. Retrieved from http://repository.upenn.edu/cpre_researchreports/22

Iversen, G. R. (1991). *Contextual analysis*. Newbury Park: SAGE Publications.

Jargowsky, P. A. (1996). Take the money and run: Economic segregation in U.S. metropolitan areas. *American Sociological Review, 61*, 984–998.

Johnson, S. M., Kraft, M. A., & Papay, J. P. (2012). How context matters in high-need schools: The effects of teachers' working conditions on their professional satisfaction and their students' achievement. *Teacher's College Record, 114*(10), 1–39.

Kahlenberg, R. D. (Ed.). (2012). *The future of school integration: Socioeconomic diversity as an education reform strategy*. New York: The Century Foundation.

Kish, L. (1965). *Survey sampling*. New York: Wiley.

Lankford, H., Loeb, S., & Wyckoff, J. (2002). Teacher sorting and the plight of urban schools: A descriptive analysis. *Educational Evaluation and Policy Analysis, 24*(1), 37–62.

Lauen, D. L., & Gaddis, S. M. (2013). Exposure to classroom poverty and test score achievement: Contextual effects or selection? *American Journal of Sociology, 118*(4), 943–979.

Lüdtke, O., Marsh, H. W., Robitzsch, A., Trautwein, U., Asparouhov, T., & Muthén, B. (2008). The multilevel latent covariate model: A new, more reliable approach to group-level effects in contextual studies. *Psychological Methods, 13*(3), 203.

Meyer, J. W., & Rowan, B. (1977). Institutionalized organizations: Formal structure as myth and ceremony. *American Journal of Sociology, 83*, 340–363.

Owens, A., Reardon, S. F., & Jencks, C. (2016). Income segregation between schools and school districts. *American Educational Research Journal, 53*(4), 1159–1197.

Raudenbush, S. W. (1993). Hierarchical linear models and experimental design. *Applied Analysis of Variance in Behavioral Science, 137*, 459.

Raudenbush, S. W., Bryk, A. S., & Congdon, R. (2004). *HLM 6 for windows [Computer software]*. Lincolnwood: Scientific Software International.

Raudenbush, S. W., & Bryk, A. S. (2002). *Hierarchical linear models: Applications and data analysis methods*. SAGE Publications.

Reardon, S. F., & Bischoff, K. (2011). Income inequality and income segregation. *American Journal of Sociology, 116*(4), 1092–1153.

Robins, J. M. (1999). Association, causation, and marginal structural models. *Synthese, 121*(1), 151–179.

Robins, J. M., Hernán, M. Á., & Brumback, B. (2000). Marginal structural models and causal inference in epidemiology. *Epidemiology, 11*(5), 550–560.

Sacerdote, B. (2011). Peer effects in education: How might they work, how big are they and how much do we know thus far? In E. Hanushek, S. Machin, & L. Woessmann, (Eds.), *Handbook of the economics of education*. Amsterdam: Elsevier.

Scafidi, B., Sjoquist, D. L., & Stinebrickner, T. R. (2007). Race, poverty, and teacher mobility. *Economics of Education Review, 26*(2), 145–159.

Sewell, W. H., Haller, A. O., & Portes, A. (1969). The educational and early occupational attainment process. *American Sociological Review, 34*, 82–92.

Sewell, W. H., Hauser, R. M., & Wolf, W. C. (1980). Sex, schooling, and occupational status. *American Journal of Sociology, 86*, 551–583.

Sharkey, P., & Elwert, F. (2011). The legacy of disadvantage: Multigenerational neighborhood effects on cognitive ability. *American Journal of Sociology, 116*(6), 1934–1981.

Swamy, P. A. V. B., & Arora, S. S. (1972). The exact finite sample properties of the estimators of coefficients in the error components regression models. *Econometrica: Journal of the Econometric Society, 40*, 261–275.

Watson, T. (2009). Inequality and the measurement of residential segregation by income in American neighborhoods. *Review of Income and Wealth, 55*(3), 820–844.

Willms, J. D. (1986). Social class segregation and its relationship to pupils' examination results in Scotland. *American Sociological Review, 51*, 224–241.

Wodtke, G. T., Harding, D. J., & Elwert, F. (2011). Neighborhood effects in temporal perspective: The impact of long-term exposure to concentrated disadvantage on high school graduation. *American Sociological Review, 76*(5), 713–736.

Stephen L. Morgan and Daniel T. Shackelford

Abstract

This chapter summarizes the extant sociological literature on the interactive nature of school and teacher effects on student learning. It explains why the most recent literature on teacher sorting demands the attention of more sociologists of education, and it demonstrates what is revealed about patterns of teacher sorting using the type of data most commonly analyzed by sociologists of education. Throughout, the chapter discusses the methodological requirements of research that can and cannot disentangle teacher effects from school effects, and it considers how teacher and school effects may be evolving in the changing landscape of K–12 education in the United States.

For studies of school performance and student learning, the sociology of education has a long history of research on the effects of teachers. Most of the specific literature on these effects predates the push to encourage effective teaching in the United States through accountability policies. In fact, as we will discuss in this chapter, sociologists have contributed very little to the debate on the validity of models and measures that seek to identify effective teachers, including methods that (1) infer effective teaching from growth in pupil test scores or (2) assess teacher performance through systematic classroom observation. Instead, these debates have been dominated by economists and policy researchers who have demonstrated little interest in drawing insight from the extant sociological literature on either teacher effects or school effects.

Although the lack of broad engagement among sociologists in the most recent debate on effective teaching might be considered a failing of the sociology of education, it also reflects a healthy skepticism about the worth of engagement in a debate over methods, such as value-added models (VAMs), thought very likely to fail on their own anyway. Even with this rationalization, now is the time for sociologists to join fellow social scientists and policy researchers in a reconstruction of the literature on teacher effects. Not only is there good reason to expect that the monitoring of effective teaching may have altered the relationships between teachers and other school actors, the debate itself appears to be in a phase of transition to more reasonable modes of analysis and interpretation. More scholars seem to recognize that teacher effects vary fundamentally because of their entanglement with effects generated by school and community differences. These encompassing contextual effects are familiar objects of study for sociologists of education,

S. L. Morgan (✉) · D. T. Shackelford (✉)
Johns Hopkins University, Baltimore, MD, USA
e-mail: stephen.morgan@jhu.edu;
danielshackelford@jhu.edu

© Springer International Publishing AG, part of Springer Nature 2018
B. Schneider (ed.), *Handbook of the Sociology of Education in the 21st Century*, Handbooks of Sociology and Social Research, https://doi.org/10.1007/978-3-319-76694-2_23

and as a result sociologists have an important contribution to offer.

In this chapter, we have several related aims: (1) to convey the contours of the extant sociological literature on teachers, (2) to consider the interactive nature of school effects and teacher effects on student learning, (3) to explain why the most recent literature, largely outside of sociology, on teacher sorting should receive more attention from sociologists of education, (4) to demonstrate what is revealed about patterns of teacher sorting using the type of data most commonly analyzed by sociologists of education (the most recent nationally representative survey of high school students conducted by the U.S. Department of Education), and (5) to offer our perspective on the methodological and measurement requirements of research that can break new ground on unraveling the interrelationships between school and teacher effects.

23.1 Three Themes of Sociological Research on Teachers

In this section, we recount three prominent themes in sociological research on teachers, which can be discussed in a rough chronological order. No review can hope to be comprehensive, and we aim only to offer examples that demonstrate longstanding sociological engagement on three topics—teachers as professionals embedded in communities, teachers as inputs into student achievement models, and teachers as actors in schools with complex organizational structures that are differentially effective.

23.1.1 Teachers As Professionals Embedded in Communities

The most prominent early sociological research on school teachers is easily identified by the work of Willard Waller, whose (1932) book *The Sociology of Teaching* mapped the contours of subsequent scholarship. To align their work with Waller's legacy, contemporary sociologists still frequently adorn their writing with insightful

sentences from Waller's book, most commonly to demonstrate the choppy waters that teachers must navigate when they seek to motivate listless students while accommodating parents and school leaders. Yet, the focus on this single book in the current collective memory often obscures the breadth of related research from early and mid-twentieth-century sociology sociology of education. Consider just three examples of topics of study from this period of scholarship that, as we will explain below, remain important to current debates on teacher effectiveness:

1. *Professionalism*: Teachers should be professionals, and mechanisms for the careful selection and training of teachers need to be further developed (Myers 1934). Teachers differ a great deal in their social origins (Carlson 1961), but they remain valued leaders in their communities (Buck 1960). Teachers retain their community leadership roles partly because their out-of-school behavior is monitored and regulated by the community (Cook et al. 1938; Cook and Greenhoe 1940). Relatedly, teacher satisfaction rests on mutually respectful relations with the community (Roth 1958). In large school systems, teachers move between vacancies in search of students who are easier to teach, typically with the consequence that the schools with students who have the most social disadvantage receive school instruction from the least experienced teachers (Becker 1952a). Fortunately, most teachers remain active readers, including for professional development and the improvement of their own teaching skills (Fisher 1958).

2. *Within-Classroom Performance*: Teachers are most effective when their social distance from the pupils assigned to them is minimized, suggesting that teachers should be trained and sorted in recognition of these challenges (Bogardus 1928). But because of student heterogeneity, and the lack of an effective system that allocates teachers to students with individual-specific needs, it is important for all teachers to tailor their practices to the individual situations of each student (Bogardus

1929; Becker 1952b). Matching effects aside, teachers who maintain a traditional, autocratic mode of instruction teach more content than do teachers who maintain a congenial, democratic mode of instruction (Brookover 1943).

3. *Attitudes Toward School Leadership*: Teachers must navigate conflicting pressures created by students, parents, and principals, and the relationships among teachers reflect their approaches to these pressures (Becker 1953; Gordon 1955). Teacher satisfaction is shaped by whether administrators conform to teachers' expectations of appropriate administrative decision making (Bidwell 1955).

A more comprehensive review of the literature from this period is of limited value, and some of the early research does not meet our current standards of rigor. Nonetheless, some attention is instructive, as these examples demonstrate, to appreciate the provenance of many of the research themes found today in the sociology of education and in debates on teacher effectiveness. Although the three sets of conclusions summarized above range over multiple substantive domains, they are all consistent with the themes set down by Waller: Teachers are professionals, pursuing complicated goals, including their own professional development and career trajectories, which must be pursued within schools and communities with diverse actors and dynamic expectations.

23.1.2 Teachers As Inputs in Educational Production

Research on teacher effectiveness was pushed in a new direction by the 1966 study, *Equality of Educational Opportunity* (EEO), commonly referred to as "the Coleman report" (Coleman et al. 1966). In an attempt to document differences in all schooling "inputs," following on the directive from the Civil Rights Act of 1964 to conduct a national study of educational opportunity, Coleman and his team launched a study of extraordinary importance (see Alexander and Morgan 2016; Gamoran and Long 2007; Sørensen and Morgan 2000).

Possibly because of the attention to resource differences across schools, as well as the compelling case made for the preeminence of family background as a determinant of student achievement, EEO's attention to the study of teacher effects is often forgotten. In fact, it is not clear that EEO's contributions were ever adequately appreciated. Ravitch (1993, p. 130) claims that its findings on teachers were "almost universally ignored by academic researchers and the press" after the report was released and in subsequent decades. In retrospect, and with another couple of decades of reflection, the core findings of EEO on teacher effects must be recognized as one of sociology's most important contributions to the study of teachers.

For their work, Coleman and his team first tabulate differences in teacher characteristics and skills by the racial identities of students, separately by region of the country.[1] The overall goal of EEO was to measure and report on such differences. Through linked surveys of students, teachers, and school administrators, Coleman and his team offer the following summaries of their primary findings on teachers (pp. 148 and 165, respectively):

Compared to teachers of the average White student, teachers of the average [Black student]

- score lower on a test of verbal competence, and the difference is most pronounced in the Southern States.
- are neither more nor less likely to have advanced degrees.
- have slightly more teaching experience, and slightly more tenure in their present school.
- read more professional journals.
- are neither more nor less likely to have majored in an academic subject.
- if they are elementary teachers, were less likely to be trained in teacher's colleges.
- more often are products of colleges that offer no graduate training.

---

[1]For the specific numbers, see Tables 6a and 6b, pages 16–17, Tables 2.31.5 and 2.31.6, pages 124–25, Tables 2.33.1–8, pages 131–40, Tables 2.34.1–14, pages 149–62.

- attended colleges with a much lower percent White in the student body.
- less often rate their college high in academic quality.
- less often are members of academic honorary societies, at least in the South.
- more often participate in teachers' organizations, especially in the South.
- more often have attended institutes for the culturally disadvantaged.

Compared to the average White [pupil], the average [Black] pupil attends a school in which the teachers are

- neither more nor less likely to have high absenteeism rates.
- paid more in some regions and less in others; thus the national averages are about the same.
- more likely to have requested assignment to their particular school and to expect to make a lifelong career of teaching.
- less likely to wish to remain in their present school if given a chance to change, or to declare they would reenter teaching if the decisions could be made again.
- less likely to rate students high on academic motivation and ability.
- less likely to believe that the school has [a] good reputation with other teachers.
- less likely to prefer to teach in an academic high school.
- more likely to spend a substantial amount of time in class preparation.
- more likely to teach large classes.
- more likely to spend time counseling with students.
- somewhat more likely to have taught in the school the prior year.
- more likely to take a teacher's examination as a condition of employment.

Racial differences were, therefore, complex when teacher characteristics are analyzed using all of these measures. The resolution of the complexity for Coleman and his team was to predict student achievement based on teacher characteristics, as part of the larger goal of shifting analy-

sis away from a consideration of equality of inputs toward the capacity of inputs to generate more equality of student outcomes.

Here, the analysis is clear: Teacher characteristics are predictive, and more strongly for Black students than for White students (see Tables 3.25.2 and 3.25.3, p. 318). Perhaps most interesting, teachers' verbal test scores (on a thirty-item vocabulary test) have independent predictive power, above and beyond teachers' levels of education and experience. For this particular effect, Coleman and his colleagues conclude that "the teachers' verbal skills have a strong effect, first showing at the sixth grade, indicating that between grades 3 and 6, the verbal skills of the teacher are especially important" (Coleman et al. 1966, p. 318). Altogether, EEO concludes that teachers are important, that their effects accumulate over years of schooling, and that the achievement of non-White students is especially responsive to teacher quality.

Because of its design, the Coleman report conceptualized teachers as a schooling "input," reflecting the educational production methodology of the time. In this tradition, school environments are nominally additive, even if the subtlety of the writing sometimes implies genuine interactions. Regardless, in this type of teacher effects research, scholars have less use for characterizations of teachers as professionals embedded in communities, struggling to navigate institutional rules and social relations while working with heterogeneous populations of students. They are seen instead as actors with fixed characteristics and capacities, distributed across schools in ways that reflect their own interests as well as the opportunities and constraints in the labor market for teachers.

23.1.3 Teachers As Members of Differentially Effective Schools

With the maturation of the subfield of sociology of education, scholars continued to work on the three subjects from mid-twentieth-century work introduced above: professionalism (e.g., Blase

1986), within-classroom performance (e.g., Sieber and Wilder 1967), and attitudes toward the community and school leadership (e.g., Edgar and Warren 1969; Jessup 1978). Some existing questions received deeper examination, such as studies of student–teacher match advantages that leverage higher-quality data and refined conceptualizations. Alexander et al. (1987), for example, make the case that pupil–teacher background congruence, based on the match of the socioeconomic status of the teacher to that of the pupil's family, promotes higher levels of achievement within the classroom.[2] These studies have also evolved to align with emergent theoretical perspectives and alternative methodologies (e.g., Calarco 2011, 2014).

The major development, however, was the emergence of a developed perspective on schools as complex organizations. From early work, such as Larkin (1973), Bredo (1977), and Barnett (1984), that explored how school organization determines teacher behavior, a whole-school approach to modeling effectiveness developed from the 1980s onward. The emergent model came to see teachers not as learning inputs with fixed capacities for generating achievement, with effects variable only according to match differences across students with differing needs, but rather as vital core workers in schools with variable environments that delimit the range of possible performance. From this perspective, teacher effectiveness varies with administrative structures and the social resources that inhere in work networks (see Gamoran et al. 2000).

This enriched conceptualization of schools emerged from scholarly sources and in response to policy concerns. A preexisting interest in investigating schools as agents of the intergenerational reproduction of inequality was joined to new work on the social organization of schooling (see Hedges and Schneider 2005). The result was increased attention to the unintended and/or

hidden consequences of some prominent educational practices, such as ability grouping and curriculum tracking, as well as new consideration of how organizational constraints can limit school functioning and teacher performance. This work was pursued as efforts to desegregate schooling had stalled, the standards-based reform movement was launched in hopes of preserving the international standing of U.S. educational institutions, and whole-school models of reform were initially crafted (later often relabeled "restructuring" and "school turnaround" models; see, e.g., Lee and Smith 1993, 1995).

Much could be written on the development and general contours of the effective schools literature in sociology from the 1980s through 2000, but we focus only briefly on the subset of this literature that has considered the role of teachers in delivering effective instruction. This literature includes pieces that model teacher commitment, efficacy, and satisfaction as a function of organizational form, leadership structure, and general workplace control (e.g., Bacharach et al. 1990; Bidwell et al. 1997; Ingersoll 1996; Lee et al. 1991; Raudenbush et al. 1992; Rosenholtz and Simpson 1990; Rowan et al. 1997). It also includes research that considers the social relations among teachers, and how these relations can be a resource for supporting a school's mission to generate achievement as a collective project (e.g., Bidwell and Yasumoto 1999; Friedkin and Slater 1994; Yasumoto et al. 2001).

Although much variation exists in the particular arguments of these many studies, most valorize the school community's capacity to develop and support effective teaching, even while the specific analysis of teacher practices is not usually a direct subject of study. A good example of this type of argument is the work on private, and especially Catholic, schools. Bryk et al. (1993) is the exemplar. Here, the notion of "subsidiarity" received particular emphasis as a broad ideological commitment that structures effective Catholic schools. As Bryk et al. (1993, pp. 301–02) write:

> … subsidiarity means that the school rejects a purely bureaucratic conception of an organization. There are advantages to workplace specialization, and it is hard to imagine the conduct of complex work without established organizational procedures.

---

[2]And such studies have continued. Crosnoe et al. (2004), for example, offer evidence of more general achievement gains that result from healthy relationships between students and teachers, which they measure as intergenerational bonding. Now, economists are very much interested in such effects, as we discuss below.

Subsidiarity, however, claims that instrumental considerations about work efficiency and specialization must be mediated by a concern for human dignity. Decentralization of school governance is not chosen purely because it is more efficient, although it does appear to have such consequences. Nor is it primarily favored because it creates organizations that are more client sensitive, although this also appears to be true. Rather, decentralization is predicated on the view that personal dignity and human respect are advanced when work is organized in small communities where dialogue and collegiality may flourish. At root is a belief that the full potential of human beings is realized in the social solidarity that can form around these small group associations.

This sort of writing, and explanatory style, is used to explain why Catholic schools are effective. Teachers are central to the mechanism that generates learning, but it is the organization itself that activates the mechanism.

Following the development of this sociological version of the effective schools literature, sociologists have moved toward more direct assessments of interventions that target teacher performance. In some cases, the connections to the effective schools literature are overt (e.g., Gamoran et al. 2003; Moller et al. 2013) while for others the attention is less direct (e.g., Hallinan 2008; Jennings and DiPrete 2010). Overall, the effective schools literature remains influential within sociology, and it is an important piece of the foundation on which a prevailing consensus would now appear to rest, and which we detail in the next section.

23.2 School Effects and Teacher Effects in Sociology: The Conventional Wisdom in Four Propositions

From the sociological literature on the effects of teachers, we are comfortable asserting that the following propositions are supported by enough convincing evidence to constitute the conventional wisdom of the field:

1. Teacher effects on student learning are real, and these effects vary according to the match of each teacher to each student.[3]
2. Teacher effects are a joint function of teachers' skills and effort, the first of which is strongly shaped by experiences before entering the profession.[4]
3. School environments, which encompass both administrative structures and networks of social relations, shape both student effort and teacher effort.
4. Effective schools align student effort and teacher effort to advance student learning.

The joint implication of these propositions can be expressed as

$$Learning_i = f_i\left(Teacher_j, Environment_s\right) \quad (23.1)$$

where the learning of each student i is an individual-specific function, $f_i(\bullet)$, under exposure to a teacher j in school environment s. The challenge for analysis is that we typically observe a student's achievement, and possibly a student's achievement growth, for a small number of teachers in only one school. We want to know how

---

[3] The recent economics literature, which has leveraged administrative data sources, is also relevant, especially for the claim of match effects. Egalite et al. (2015), for example, show that in Florida the race congruence of student–teacher pairing promotes small but positive effects, even though Winters et al. (2013) argue that gender congruence appears to have no substantial effects. See also Jackson (2013) for a broad treatment of teacher match effects, which demonstrates their importance with empirical results from North Carolina.

[4] The economics literature is also consistent with the skills claim. Ehrenberg and Brewer (1994), analyzing the High School and Beyond data, show that teachers' degrees have positive associations with achievement, perhaps indicating that teacher ability is important. More recently, Clotfelter et al. (2007), through an analysis of North Carolina administrative data, show that teacher experience, test scores, and licensure all have positive associations with achievement, although more for math than for reading. Kukla-Acevedo (2009) show that in a Kentucky school district teachers' math preparation predicted fifth grade math achievement.

learning would differ if each student were exposed to alternative teachers in alternative school environments, after which we could form estimates for groups of individuals of different types, exposed to different types of teachers and in different school environments. Unfortunately, our observational data sets do not permit clean identification of these effects of interest because the institutional structure of schooling restricts individual students' exposure to alternative teachers and schools.

In sociology, it is common to offer estimated regression equations of the form:

$$Y = a + \hat{b}_T\, T + \hat{b}_S\, S + \hat{b}_X\, X + e \qquad (23.2)$$

where Y is a learning outcome measure, T is one or more measures of teacher characteristics, S is one or more measures of school environments, and X is a set of student-level characteristics typically included as "control" variables. The terms such as $\hat{b}_T$ are conformable vectors of estimated slope coefficients for the measures specified by the subscripts. If the analysis considers teacher effects directly, then S is often regarded as a set of school-level controls. If the study is one of school environments, in which it is asserted that teacher effects are part of an unobserved mechanism, then T may be excluded, often because suitable measures are unavailable.

Interpretations of results from estimated regression equations of this form are often developed with language that implies interactive effects, such that, for example, the estimates $\hat{b}_T$ should be interpreted as conditional on values of S, or possibly even $\hat{b}_S$. Such interpretations are usually developed as part of the overall conclusions of a study, when authors use theory and intuition to reason beyond their empirical models that usually have been specified as nominally additive. When reasoning beyond the data, few sociologists discuss their findings with explicit recognition of the individual-specific nature of Eq. 23.1, where the function that generates learning is itself individually variable. Instead, individual variability is usually thought to have been swept away by a lag specification for the outcome Y along with measures in X, even if in some cases

the putative teacher effects in $\hat{b}_T$ are discussed as if they are conditional on S and X. In research where measures in T are unavailable, the reduced form school effects in $\hat{b}_S$ are often discussed as if they encompass complex interactions with latent teacher effects, which could be directly estimated if suitable measures in T were to become available.

Altogether, in sociology it is widely recognized that the effects of schools and the effects of teachers who work within schools cannot be separated easily in an empirical analysis. Outside of sociology, it is less clear that this point is recognized, as we will discuss below. That said, outside of sociology, especially in the work of economists, it is widely recognized that the joint distribution of students, teachers, and schools generates complex matching gains and deficits in the learning process. This recognition has led to a rich literature on teacher assignment, attrition, and sorting, which we present next.

23.3 The Distribution of Teachers Across and Within Schools

Since the Elementary and Secondary Education Act was reauthorized by the No Child Left Behind (NCLB) legislation, we have learned a great deal about teacher assignment and teacher sorting.[5] This research has accumulated progressively, building on templates from the 1980s and 1990s of various types (e.g., how teachers

---

[5]We do not mean to imply that scholars did not study assignment and sorting patterns before the era of accountability arrived in the 1990s. One early careful study in sociology is Becker (1952a), as summarized above. And, in the wake of EEO, and after the U.S. Supreme Court ruled that racial balance in the teaching corps is a measure of unitary status in desegregating school districts, scholars became very much interested in the distribution of teachers across schools in the same area. For example, Greenberg and McCall (1974) show that in the San Diego school system teachers sorted across schools based on the socioeconomic status of students, given that the salaries available did not differ across the district. Studies such as this one led to deeper modeling of teachers' revealed preferences and the possibilities for interventions to change their job search choices (see Antos and Rosen 1975; Levinson 1988).

respond to desegregation remedies, how teachers are laid off as part of "reductions in force" studies). A growing source of motivation is to understand whether the nation's teaching corps is strong enough, and stable enough, to support a schooling system that will allow the U.S. to remain competitive with the surging economies of international peers. More recently, as systems were developed by states to consider whether schools were making the adequate yearly progress (AYP) required for continuation under NCLB, some granular analysis of teacher effects across all schools has become possible. The interests of three groups then dovetailed: (1) those who hoped to develop new formulas for AYP that could replace threshold measures of proficiency with alternatives that recognize school differences in average student achievement growth; (2) those who hoped to develop models of achievement growth that could be used to identify teachers who are deserving of merit bonuses; and (3) those who hoped to use achievement growth models to determine the proportion of teachers who are grossly ineffective, yet protected from dismissal because of teacher tenure.

This literature is important for sociologists to absorb because it has implications for the conventional wisdom on school and teacher effects. Yet, it is impossible to review this vast literature both chronologically and by theme in a piece of this length. We have therefore grouped the studies by primary findings, ordered somewhat chronologically as they have been developed in the literature. With only a few exceptions (e.g., Ingersoll 2005; Kalogrides et al. 2013), this research has accumulated in journals that do not have a sociological focus. The primary findings are:

1. The student composition of schools—percent in poverty, proportion non-White, etc.—predicts both teacher attrition and teacher mobility (see Elfers et al. 2006; Feng 2014; Hanushek et al. 2004; Scafidi et al. 2007). Rates of exit are highest in schools with pupils who have greater social disadvantage, leaving the teaching corps in such schools comparatively young and inexperienced.

2. Across schools in the same geographic region, and frequently the same local education authority, teachers appear to be sorted by the student composition of schools, using standard measures of credentials and experience, and following the pattern first established for teacher attrition (see Allensworth et al. 2009; Boyd et al. 2005; Clotfelter et al. 2005, 2006, 2011; Feng 2010, 2014; Krei 1998; Lankford et al. 2002; Rice 2013).

3. These patterns of teacher attrition, mobility, and sorting may be a response to school management and working conditions, which vary with student composition, rather than a direct response to the greater challenges of teaching students from disadvantaged origins (see Horng 2009; Ingersoll and May 2012; Loeb et al. 2005; Ost and Schiman 2015).

4. Some policy interventions can make between-school sorting even more substantial. These effects have emerged in response to state incentives for hiring certified teachers, merit pay for teachers, class-size reductions, and the passage of accountability legislation (see Clotfelter et al. 2004; Goldhaber et al. 2007; Guarino et al. 2011; Jepsen and Rivkin 2009).

5. Salary inducements have not been effective at eliminating teacher sorting across schools, in part because of patterns of racial segregation (see Clotfelter et al. 2011; Feng 2014; Goldhaber et al. 2010). Nonetheless, there may be some scope for future change, and more results will be needed to examine the range of responses to alternative interventions (see Clotfelter et al. 2008; Fulbeck 2014; Fulbeck and Richards 2015).

6. Sorting may erode the capacity of resource differences across schools to mitigate the learning differences produced by family background (see Bastian et al. 2013; Ladd 2008; Rubenstein et al. 2007; but see also Player 2009).

7. Within schools, sorting is also present, following the same pattern of between-school sorting (see Clotfelter et al. 2005, 2006; Feng 2010; Kalogrides et al. 2013). This finding cannot be surprising to sociologists who know

the literature on the assignment of teachers to curriculum tracks.

8. Recent policy interventions have also generated additional sorting within schools, as school leaders have redistributed teachers to satisfy new challenges. For example, Fuller and Ladd (2013) show that in North Carolina, accountability legislation caused schools to move less credentialed teachers down to untested grades (kindergarten through second grade) and more credentialed teachers up to tested grades (third through fifth grade). For a study in ten Kentucky school districts, Barrett and Toma (2013) show that principals increased the class sizes of teachers they deemed effective based on their own assessments.

9. The most recent literature on sorting has been informed by value-added models of teacher effectiveness. VAMs attempt to identify effective teachers by average gains in their pupils' test scores, not measures of teachers' own characteristics or practices.[6] As of the time of this writing, the implications of the VAM work for teacher sorting results are unclear.

Some studies suggest that teachers with high value-added scores are more likely to remain in their schools (Boyd et al. 2011), although the pattern is stronger in schools with more advantaged students (Goldhaber et al. 2011).[7] Other studies argue that the latter effects dominate (Steele et al. 2015), with effective teachers

more likely to flee schools with larger proportions of students who identify as Black (Jackson 2009). Not inconsistent with this pattern, teachers' value-added scores tend to increase after teachers enter new schools (Jackson 2013). Chingos and West (2011) suggest that, in Florida, VAMs indicate that effective teachers are more likely to be promoted to become principals while less effective teachers are more likely to be reassigned to low-stakes positions, consistent with research that does not utilize VAMs to measure effectiveness (see Fuller and Ladd 2013).

Finally, some of the work on teacher sorting that is informed by VAMs has begun to wrestle with school context effects. Koedel (2009) argues that teachers have spillover effects on achievement in subjects that they do not teach while Jackson and Bruegmann (2009) find evidence of spillover effects through peer learning. Loeb et al. (2012) show that effective schools are able to hire the most effective teachers, as measured by VAMs, while Ferguson and Hirsch (2014) make the case that effective teachers are generated by effective schools.

Overall, the literature on teacher sorting—which now encompasses an older literature on teacher attrition and teacher mobility—raises important questions for sociological research on school and teacher effects. Have we deemphasized the older sociological perspective that conceived of teachers as valuable "inputs" with autonomous capacities to generate learning? Although sociologists have not wavered in their position that "teachers matter," it may be the case that we have been too quick to assume that teachers are broadly similar in their potential, conditional on training, and that variation in any apparent teacher effects is almost entirely attributable to variation in their school environments. Not unrelated to this question, is it possible that schools that appear to be effective because of their administrative structures are instead only effective because they have been better able to attract teachers who are effective because of their own capacities? To begin to address questions

---

[6]For clear, simple, accurate, and balanced summaries of value-added modeling, see Corcoran and Goldhaber (2013) and Corcoran (2016). To understand the required assumptions with more depth, see Reardon and Raudenbush (2009). For studies that have defended and deployed VAMs, see Chetty et al. (2014a, b). For arguments against the use of VAMs, see Rothstein (2009, 2010) and Guarino, Reckase, Wooldridge (2015). For work that compares the results of VAMs to various other types of teacher evaluation systems, see Grissom and Youngs (2016).

[7]Jacob and Lefgren (2007) show that parents disproportionately prefer effective teachers in high poverty schools, perhaps because such teachers are comparatively rare.

such as these, we need to develop a deeper appreciation for the empirics of teacher sorting, and, in the next section, we advance this goal.

23.4 An Example of What a Typical Data Source Reveals About the Distribution of Teachers

Many of the most persuasive studies of teacher assignment and teacher sorting are based on district-level and state-level analyses of administrative data, usually only from states with the most sophisticated data systems that have welcomed academic research. It has been assumed by many researchers that what has been learned in these states is applicable to the nation as a whole, but surely this inference will be evaluated in the future. Furthermore, because of the focus on student testing in grades three through eight, in response to NCLB, most studies of teacher sorting consider only elementary schools; those studies that do consider middle school grades have less clear results.

Sociologists of education most commonly study secondary schools, in part because of their longstanding interest in proximate institutions that shape entry into the adult stratification order. Existing teacher effects research in sociology is therefore dominated by studies of high schools. Because of the mismatch with the teacher sorting literature, it is useful to consider what can be learned about teacher sorting from an analysis using the type of data most commonly analyzed by sociologists of education—a national sample of students nested within high schools, collected by the U.S. Department of Education, following on the template first established by Coleman and his colleagues for EEO.

In this chapter, we offer an analysis of the most recent nationally representative survey, which is the High School Longitudinal Survey of 2009 (HSLS). Still ongoing, the HSLS is a sample of first-year public and private high school students in 2009, which includes linked survey instruments for students, parents, math and science teachers, counselors, and school administrators. In this chapter, we consider the distribution of math and science teachers across students in public high schools in 2009, merging to the HSLS data both funding and school characteristics from the 2009 through 2013 Common Core of Data.[8]

For the HSLS, each sampled first-year high school student is linked, through both an administrative list and a student response, to the teacher of the relevant math and/or science class in which the student was enrolled in fall 2009. These teachers are then asked to complete a questionnaire that assesses their class structure, their attitudes toward their school and its students, and their own qualifications.

The 753 public high schools sampled for the HSLS have student samples that range from 7 to 49 students, with a mode of 24 students. These students are matched to both math and science teachers, so that we have a total of 12,832 students matched to 3172 math teachers and 11,676 students matched to 2362 science teachers.[9] When weighted appropriately, the responses of teachers can be used to estimate the distributional characteristics of the teacher–student match across first-year high school students in 2009 for two linked populations: all students enrolled in math classes in public schools and all students enrolled in science classes in public schools.[10]

---

[8] Our analysis is related to, but distinct from, the most common prior analyses of national distributions of teachers. These prior studies, which have been discussed above, have frequently used the Schools and Staffing Surveys (SASS). Analysis of the SASS surveys allows for the modeling of teacher distributions across schools, but not directly of teacher distributions across students, since only school aggregate measures of student characteristics are available, and typically without detailed measures of the family backgrounds of students.

[9] On average, we have 4.4 sampled students for each math teacher and 5.4 sampled students for each science teacher, with medians of 3 and 4 students, respectively. At the school level, the median number of math teachers is 4 across the 720 schools with sampled math teachers while the median number of science teachers is 3 across the 699 schools with sampled science teachers.

[10] We exclude private schools from this analysis, mostly because the teacher sorting literature is very much focused on public schools. Of course, teachers do sort into private schools as well, and private schools have served as a valuable point of comparison in the effective schools research in sociology. A more comprehensive analysis should consider sorting by sector and type of school as well.

We first offer results on school-level climate, where teachers are the informants on the problems that their schools face, as well as teacher satisfaction with the level of support that is provided to meet their challenges. We consider the relationships that teacher-perceived climate and support have with the characteristics of the student populations of HSLS schools, measured by students' socioeconomic status and performance on a standardized math test. We also consider the relationships that teacher-perceived climate and support have with per-pupil instructional expenditures, measured at the district level. This first portion of the analysis demonstrates that teachers who work in schools with disadvantaged student populations report that the learning climate is more challenging, because of the attitudes and behaviors of students and their parents, as well as available administrative and district support. We then turn toward an analysis of the distribution of teachers, measured by their preparation and experience, and assess the extent to which a pattern of teacher sorting is present among the math and science teachers of ninth graders.

23.4.1 School Climate As Reported by Teachers

Table 23.1 presents 32 partial correlation coefficients, bounded by −1 and 1, between the school-level or student-level variable listed in the first row of each panel and each of the teacher-level variables listed in the row labels of each of the

Table 23.1 Partial correlation coefficients for students' socioeconomic status and algebra test scores in the ninth grade with teachers' reports of resource problems and climate problems

	Math teacher		Science teacher	
	Partial correlation	Standard error	Partial correlation	Standard error
School mean of SES with				
Resources and facilities are a problem	−0.138	0.035	−0.052	0.032
Administrative support is a problem	−0.098	0.029	0.056	0.034
Student attitudes and behavior are a problem	−0.385	0.028	−0.328	0.031
Lack of parent support is a problem	−0.403	0.027	−0.384	0.030
Within-school SES with				
Resources and facilities are a problem	−0.003	0.013	0.003	0.017
Administrative support is a problem	0.007	0.014	−0.002	0.015
Student attitudes and behavior are a problem	−0.020	0.013	−0.015	0.013
Lack of parent support is a problem	−0.030	0.013	−0.033	0.014
School mean of algebra test score with				
Resources and facilities are a problem	−0.163	0.032	−0.091	0.035
Administrative support is a problem	−0.101	0.030	0.014	0.038
Student attitudes and behavior are a problem	−0.380	0.028	−0.352	0.030
Lack of parent support is a problem	−0.360	0.029	−0.382	0.032
Within-school algebra test score with				
Resources and facilities are a problem	−0.010	0.015	−0.001	0.023
Administrative support is a problem	0.024	0.017	0.032	0.023
Student attitudes and behavior are a problem	−0.040	0.015	−0.015	0.018
Lack of parent support is a problem	−0.034	0.016	−0.015	0.016

Notes: The partial correlation coefficients are adjusted for school type (whether the high school is a charter or magnet school), and the data are weighted to the populations of ninth graders enrolled in math and science classes, respectively. The standard errors are heteroskedasticity-consistent and are adjusted for the clustering of students within teachers
Source: High School Longitudinal Study of 2009 (HSLS:09)

subsequent four rows. We offer partial correlation coefficients separately for the reports of math and science teachers, yielding 16 each.

These partial correlation coefficients are estimated by appropriately scaling coefficients from underlying regression models with students as the unit of analysis, and where we adjust the standard errors for the clustering of students within schools and teachers. In addition to specifying each model with one of the two focal variables as the outcome variable and one as a predictor variable (which is arbitrary, given the subsequent scaling of the underlying regression coefficients as partial correlation coefficients), the regression models also include indicator variables for magnet schools and charter schools, with regular public schools as the reference category. The number of magnet and charter schools is too small to permit evaluations of differential associations, and so the indicator variables simply adjust the partial correlation coefficients.

The first panel offers partial correlation coefficients for school mean SES with each of four scales of teacher attitudes about problems at their school. School mean SES is calculated as the mean of the sampled students' SES values; each student's value is a standardized composite of the available information on the "big five" variables: mother's and father's education, mother's and father's occupational prestige, and total family income (and where "mother" and "father" are nominal labels in many cases for those who are listed as parents and guardians). The four scales of problems for each teacher are based on agree/disagree responses for multiple underlying questions, which we group together to form the following scales:

Resources and facilities are a problem

- Lack of teacher resources and materials is a problem at this school
- Teaching is limited by shortage of computer hardware/software
- Teaching is limited by shortage of support for using computers
- Teaching is limited by shortage of textbooks for student use
- Teaching is limited by shortage of instructional equipment for students

- Teaching is limited by shortage of equipment for demonstrations
- Teaching is limited by inadequate physical facilities
- Teaching is limited by high student-to-teacher ratio

Administrative support is a problem

- Teaching is limited by inadequate professional learning opportunities
- Teaching is limited by inadequate administrative support
- Teaching is limited by lack of planning time
- Teaching is limited by lack of autonomy in instructional decisions

Student attitudes and behavior are a problem

- Student tardiness is a problem at this school
- Student absenteeism is a problem at this school
- Student class cutting is a problem at this school
- Students dropping out is a problem at this school
- Student apathy is a problem at this school
- Students coming unprepared to learn is a problem at this school
- Teaching is limited by uninterested students
- Teaching is limited by low morale among students
- Teaching is limited by disruptive students

Lack of parental support is a problem

- Lack of parental involvement is a problem at this school
- Teaching is limited by lack of parent/family support

All scales are factor scored and have acceptable measurement properties (e.g., Cronbach's alpha estimates of reliability between 0.70 and 0.88).

For the first panel of Table 23.1, all partial correlation coefficients are in the expected directions, with slightly stronger relationships for math teachers. Schools with more advantaged student populations (i.e., higher values for school mean of SES) have fewer problems according to the teacher reports, with the associations stronger for student and parent attitudes, behavior, and support than for resources, facilities, and administrative support.

How strong are these associations? Like all product-moment correlations, partial correlations are bounded by −1 and 1. Values for the strongest associations in Table 23.1 have partial correlation coefficients such as −0.4, which we interpret as moderately strong, given attenuation from measurement error for each pair of variables. Most of the other associations are much smaller in magnitude, typically near to −0.1. One might regard these coefficients as too small to be interpreted, but we feel that they are meaningfully negative, usually more than twice the size of their standard errors, and would be larger in magnitude—probably between 25% and 50% larger—in the absence of random measurement error.

By our interpretive standards, values that are smaller in magnitude than their standard errors are the only estimated partial correlation coefficients that we think can be reasonably attributed to sampling error alone. Some partial correlation coefficients of this type are present in the second panel. These partial correlation coefficients are for within-school SES measures of each student with the resource and administrative support scales analyzed for the first panel of Table 23.1. In these cases, individual values for SES are deviated from the school-specific mean, and then all schools are pooled for the analysis. Students with high values for within-school SES are those who are well above their school's mean. Given that the teacher attitudes that compose these two scales reference their entire school, we would not expect these partial correlation coefficients to deviate from zero, except as a result of sampling error. That is precisely what we see.[11]

---

[11] These within-school scales of SES also have more measurement error, and so the correlation coefficients are further attenuated. Notice also that we do have meaningful but very small negative partial correlation coefficients for within-school SES with the student and parent attitude, behavior, and support scales. These coefficients suggest that there is a very slight tendency for teachers who are assigned to lower-SES students within their schools to report more challenges created by the attitudes and behavior of students and parents.

The third and fourth panels of Table 23.1 substitute the available HSLS test score for SES, which in this case is a test of algebra knowledge and skill. The values for these two panels are remarkably similar to the first two panels based on SES. The reason is straightforward: SES is strongly associated with the test score, both at the school level and for within-school variation.

Table 23.2 presents an analogous 32 partial regression coefficients, using the same scales of problems reported by teachers, but using four district-level measure of expenditures. The first panel presents per-pupil instructional expenditures, and the third panel presents per-pupil instructional salary expenditures only. Both measures are drawn from the Common Core of Data, and averaged across the 4 years during which each student was (or would have been) enrolled in their school. The second and fourth panels are cost-adjusted versions of these two expenditure measures, using the same area-cost-adjustment procedure detailed in Morgan and Jung (2016).

Whether cost-adjusted or not, schools with higher levels of expenditures have slightly lower levels of teacher-reported problems. The partial correlation coefficients are close to −0.1 in most cases. But, in relative comparisons to the results from Table 23.1, an interesting difference is present. When considering teacher reports of student and parent attitudes, behavior, and administrative support, the implied associations are substantially weaker than for the school mean of SES and the school mean of test scores. It is unknown whether the relative weakness of these relationships is genuine, or is instead attributable to the necessity of using district-average expenditure measures, rather than school-specific measures. Our interpretation is that the relative weakness of the relationships is genuine, since this is what one would expect based on extant research that demonstrates the weak predictive power of expenditures measures of all types (i.e., from EEO to more recent efforts, such as Morgan and Jung 2016). For the other two problems scales—focused explicitly on resources, facilities, and administrator supports—the associations with resources are comparable to those with the school means of SES and test scores. This is also quite

Table 23.2 Partial correlation coefficients for district-level per pupil expenditures with teachers' reports of resource problems and climate problems

	Math teacher		Science teacher	
	Partial correlation	Standard error	Partial correlation	Standard error
All instructional expenditures (per pupil) with				
Resources and facilities are a problem	−0.104	0.030	−0.035	0.055
Administrative support is a problem	−0.036	0.034	0.049	0.049
Student attitudes and behavior are a problem	−0.077	0.035	−0.088	0.042
Lack of parent support is a problem	−0.078	0.035	−0.081	0.036
All instructional expenditures (per pupil and cost-adjusted) with				
Resources and facilities are a problem	−0.097	0.029	−0.056	0.055
Administrative support is a problem	−0.050	0.034	0.010	0.049
Student attitudes and behavior are a problem	−0.075	0.035	−0.092	0.042
Lack of parent support is a problem	−0.060	0.035	−0.055	0.040
Instructional salary expenditures (per pupil) with				
Resources and facilities are a problem	−0.125	0.031	−0.058	0.049
Administrative support is a problem	−0.054	0.032	0.044	0.047
Student attitudes and behavior are a problem	−0.106	0.033	−0.108	0.039
Lack of parent support is a problem	−0.111	0.033	−0.101	0.035
Instructional salary expenditures (per pupil and cost-adjusted) with				
Resources and facilities are a problem	−0.121	0.028	−0.082	0.050
Administrative support is a problem	−0.071	0.031	0.003	0.046
Student attitudes and behavior are a problem	−0.104	0.034	−0.111	0.040
Lack of parent support is a problem	−0.093	0.033	−0.070	0.037

Notes: See Table 23.1
Source: See Table 23.1

sensible, even if the sizes of the relationships between actual resource expenditures and problems attributable to resources and facilities may be smaller than some readers would expect.

23.4.2 Teacher Sorting Across and Within Schools

The results provided in Tables 23.1 and 23.2 demonstrate that the HSLS generates reasonable results about how teacher reports of the problems faced by their schools are related to measures of expenditures, test scores, and the SES of students. The results suggest that teachers who work with disadvantaged student populations report that the learning climate is more challenging. For some teachers, the challenges may be rewarding, while for others the same challenges may repre-

sent a reason to seek employment in schools with simpler climates.

To assess teacher sorting directly, we now consider teacher characteristics, presenting 24 partial correlation coefficients in each of Tables 23.3 and 23.4, analogous to those already reported in Tables 23.1 and 23.2. Rather than use four scales of teacher-reported problems at their schools, each panel includes three measures of teacher training (whether they have graduate degrees, are certified, and are certified in math or science, respectively) as well as three measures of teacher experience (years since bachelor's degree, years teaching at the current school, and years teaching math or science, respectively, at the high school level).

For Table 23.3, the partial correlation coefficients for the associations with school mean of SES and school mean of test scores are small but

Table 23.3 Partial correlation coefficients for students' socioeconomic status and algebra test scores in the ninth grade with teachers' training and experience

	Math teacher		Science teacher	
	Partial correlation	Standard error	Partial correlation	Standard error
School mean of SES with				
Teacher has a graduate degree	0.095	0.030	0.096	0.031
Teacher is certified	0.070	0.035	0.109	0.033
Teacher is certified in math/science	0.076	0.034	0.105	0.032
Years since bachelor's degree	0.003	0.028	0.048	0.033
Years at current school	0.079	0.029	0.077	0.032
Years teaching math/science in high school	0.051	0.027	0.114	0.030
Within-school SES with				
Teacher has a graduate degree	0.015	0.012	0.025	0.014
Teacher is certified	0.036	0.014	0.015	0.012
Teacher is certified in math/science	0.042	0.014	0.020	0.013
Years since bachelor's degree	0.039	0.012	0.032	0.014
Years at current school	0.032	0.013	0.027	0.013
Years teaching math/science in high school	0.038	0.013	0.030	0.013
School mean of algebra test score with				
Teacher has a graduate degree	0.083	0.029	0.099	0.033
Teacher is certified	0.058	0.037	0.138	0.034
Teacher is certified in math/science	0.065	0.036	0.132	0.034
Years since bachelor's degree	0.003	0.028	0.066	0.037
Years at current school	0.084	0.027	0.073	0.034
Years teaching math/science in high school	0.047	0.025	0.099	0.033
Within-school algebra test score with				
Teacher has a graduate degree	0.051	0.015	0.040	0.015
Teacher is certified	0.060	0.016	0.027	0.022
Teacher is certified in math/science	0.064	0.016	0.036	0.022
Years since bachelor's degree	0.068	0.015	0.023	0.016
Years at current school	0.076	0.016	0.038	0.014
Years teaching math/science in high school	0.085	0.016	0.032	0.015

Notes: See Table 23.1
Source: See Table 23.1

meaningful, and perhaps slightly larger for SES than for test scores. Teachers in high-SES schools and with high test scores are slightly more likely to have graduate degrees, be certified, and have more years of teaching experience. In addition, the partial correlation coefficients for within-school SES and within-school test scores are weak but meaningful because they are generally in the expected direction. Students who have comparatively high SES and high test scores in their schools are very slightly more likely to have teachers with stronger training and more

experience, with the effect perhaps larger for science teachers than for math teachers. This pattern is consistent with the literature on teacher assignments and curriculum tracking, although perhaps weaker in magnitude than that literature would lead one to expect.

Table 23.4 presents evidence that schools situated in districts with higher levels of expenditures are also more likely to have teachers with stronger training, and, to a lesser extent, prior experience. The strongest partial correlation coefficients are for graduate degrees among teachers, which

Table 23.4 Partial correlation coefficients for district-level per pupil expenditures with teachers' training and experience

	Math teacher		Science teacher	
	Partial correlation	Standard error	Partial correlation	Standard error
All instructional expenditures (per pupil) with				
Teacher has a graduate degree	0.151	0.026	0.161	0.037
Teacher is certified	0.056	0.032	0.013	0.043
Teacher is certified in math/science	0.061	0.032	0.018	0.042
Years since bachelor's degree	0.020	0.027	0.038	0.041
Years at current school	0.061	0.035	0.101	0.039
Years teaching math/science in high school	−0.002	0.032	0.028	0.031
All instructional expenditures (per pupil and cost-adjusted) with				
Teacher has a graduate degree	0.115	0.028	0.127	0.040
Teacher is certified	0.065	0.032	0.018	0.047
Teacher is certified in math/science	0.069	0.032	0.021	0.047
Years since bachelor's degree	0.016	0.028	0.028	0.044
Years at current school	0.077	0.036	0.139	0.041
Years teaching math/science in high school	0.012	0.031	0.055	0.033
Instructional salary expenditures (per pupil) with				
Teacher has a graduate degree	0.144	0.025	0.160	0.033
Teacher is certified	0.059	0.033	0.030	0.039
Teacher is certified in math/science	0.066	0.033	0.034	0.039
Years since bachelor's degree	0.006	0.027	0.026	0.036
Years at current school	0.058	0.034	0.083	0.038
Years teaching math/science in high school	0.005	0.028	0.020	0.031
Instructional salary expenditures (per pupil and cost-adjusted) with				
Teacher has a graduate degree	0.110	0.027	0.125	0.036
Teacher is certified	0.071	0.032	0.036	0.045
Teacher is certified in math/science	0.076	0.031	0.039	0.044
Years since bachelor's degree	0.004	0.028	0.015	0.040
Years at current school	0.074	0.035	0.125	0.040
Years teaching math/science in high school	0.020	0.030	0.048	0.032

Notes: See Table 23.1
Source: See Table 23.1

may reflect a type of sorting where teachers with graduate degrees choose to work in, or are hired by, school districts with higher expenditures. We do not have data on individual teacher salaries, but it seems reasonable that the higher instructional expenditures in these school districts reflect higher salary offers to those hired with graduate degrees, or raises awarded to those who acquire graduate degrees during their employment.

Altogether, what have Tables 23.3 and 23.4 shown? On the one hand, the associations are all perhaps weaker than one would expect for this type of analysis, given the established literature on teacher sorting and the strong claims that have been developed based on administrative data, usually for elementary schools in selected states. On the other hand, most of the associations are in the expected direction, suggesting that at the high school level, in a national sample, teacher sorting of the expected pattern is present. Sorting is not confined to elementary schools, nor only detectable in states with comparatively rich administrative data that has been made available to academic researchers.[12]

The implication of these patterns is that schools with the highest performance may well benefit from having the strongest teachers (who themselves benefit from higher levels of resources, more supportive administrative structures, and the opportunity to teach students who present fewer learning challenges and have more supportive home environments). Yet, with partial correlations of this magnitude, it is hard to make the case that we have developed evidence that high school teacher sorting is a powerful source of high school differences.

In this sense, the results can be considered somewhat encouraging for the school effects literature in sociology that has mostly ignored sorting dynamics. The caveat, of course, is that this analysis has only rather limited measures of teacher skill and quality. We cannot eliminate the possibility that a more substantial pattern of teacher sorting exists on the characteristics of teachers not measured by the HSLS instrument. And we cannot establish any connections at all to the most recent teacher sorting literature, which has used VAMs to attempt to identify effective teachers. It is possible that sorting would appear more dramatic if a valid measure of effectiveness were available, rather than simply measures of qualifications and crude measures of experience.

23.5 Conclusions

In this chapter, we first reviewed the long tradition of sociological research on teacher effects and school effects, with particular emphasis on the interaction between the two. We then considered the large literature on teacher attrition, mobility, and sorting, which has matured mostly outside of sociology. To assess the relevance of the sorting literature to the sociological literature, we then offered an empirical analysis of recent data on high school students and their math and science teachers. We showed that sorting dynamics are present in a national sample of ninth graders matched to their teachers, but we also concluded that the pattern of sorting is not so large that it presents a fundamental challenge to the sociological literature on school effects that typically ignores the dynamics teacher sorting.

We conclude, in this section, with some thoughts on how teacher and school effects are likely to evolve, based on our interpretation of the current policy environment. Partly in response to the uncertainty of the value of in-service professional development, as well as the threat of new forms of alternative teacher certification, calls for a more deeply professionalized teaching corps for our public schools are now common. Sociologists will surely study how the teaching profession adapts in the coming decades in response to this new form of teacher mobilization, which seems poised to reshape preservice teacher training and enhance within-classroom autonomy. While it may be comforting to believe that these efforts will protect teachers from future evaluation metrics that are too narrow, this prediction may be too sanguine and is certainly premature. We think it is quite plausible that policymakers, administrative authorities, and parents will remain at least as interested in identifying teacher and school effects with simple output measures that can be used to allocate resources and choose from among competing schools. If so, then a new professionalization movement may not alter the relative distribution of teacher effects, by altering sorting patterns, even if the movement does succeed in

---

[12] In the supplementary appendix, we offer four analogous tables (S1 through S4) for the 10-state saturated sample of schools in the HSLS. For the results reported in these additional tables, we include fixed effects for states in the underlying regression models. The results presented there demonstrate that the average within-state partial correlation coefficients are only slightly smaller in magnitude in nearly all cases of direct comparison to those in Tables 23.1 through 23.4, suggesting that these weak patterns of teacher sorting are characteristic of within-state relationships as well. This result implies, even though it is based on an analysis of only 10 states, that the weakness of the associations is not generated by suppression that is attributable to unspecified state-level differences in the results in Tables 23.1 through 23.4.

boosting teacher salaries and improving working conditions.

Changes in the distribution of teacher effects may, however, arise from other sources. As of this writing, the prospects are uncertain for greater harmonization of curricular standards across states, and across school districts within states. If the move toward more common standards receives a new push from a policy shock or leadership change, then the effects of teachers may become easier to discern in studies that analyze comparable criterion-referenced test scores across schools. If these same test scores are to be used for the evaluation of teacher performance, then there is reason to expect a strengthening of the dynamics that generate teacher sorting across schools. In this scenario, apparent school effects may emerge, which in fact represent the accentuation of the sorting of effective teachers toward schools with students who are easier to teach.

Consider how any such future sorting dynamics may interact with the most common school effect analyzed recently: the effectiveness of charter schooling. A consensus seems to have emerged (or nearly so) that the highest-quality charter schools are no worse than the non-charter alternatives in their vicinity, and frequently substantially better. What has never been effectively determined is how commonly any apparent charter school effects are attributable to (1) their ability to attract higher-quality teachers, (2) their ability to motivate teachers of all types to devote substantially more effort, or (3) features of charter schools that are separable from the effects of their teachers, such as disciplinary policy and targeted curricula. If charter schools increase in number, while the velocity of teacher sorting increases, then estimated charter school effects may increase, as teachers, not just students, are creamed from traditional public schools.

Altogether, it will be essential to devote greater attention to developing study designs that can estimate the interactive nature of teacher and school effects, attuned to the underlying processes that determine the job-seeking behavior of teachers. The sociological literature on school effects has not considered the distribution of teachers with enough care, even if we can take pride in our greater relative attention to both the organizational context of schooling and the advantages and disadvantages conferred by differences in home environments. The greatest immediate need, however, is not a shift in emphasis on the part of researchers, but rather a new and substantial commitment from federal and state data collection agencies to pursue more complete measurement of the features and activities of students, teachers, and schools. Available administrative data, which has effectively opened up many important questions of academic interest and policy importance, does not adequately measure the home environments that strongly shape student performance in school, and offers little granular data on the behavior of students. National data sources, patterned on EEO, are stronger in their measurement of the features of students, their parents, and schools, but they do not include sufficient information on the pedagogy and expertise of teachers or the learning climates within classrooms. Without improvements in available data, nifty new identification strategies from methodologists are unlikely to generate enough insight to enhance our understanding of the complementarities that characterize both school and teacher effects.

References

Alexander, K. L., Entwisle, D. R., & Thompson, M. S. (1987). School performance, status relations, and the structure of sentiment: Bringing the teacher back in. *American Sociological Review, 52*(5), 665–682.

Alexander, K. L., & Morgan, S. L. (2016). The Coleman report at fifty: Its legacy and implications for future research on equality of opportunity. *RSF: The Russell Sage Foundation Journal of the Social Sciences, 2*(5), 1–16.

Allensworth, E., Ponisciak, S., & Mazzeo, C. (2009). *The schools teachers leave: Teacher mobility in Chicago public schools.* Chicago: Consortium on Chicago School Research at the University of Chicago.

Antos, J. R., & Rosen, S. (1975). Discrimination in the market for public school teachers. *Journal of Econometrics, 3*(2), 123–150. https://doi.org/10.1016/0304-4076(75)90042-1.

Bacharach, S., Bamberger, P., & Conley, S. (1990). Professionals and workplace control: Organizational and demographic models of teacher militancy. *Industrial and Labor Relations Review, 43*(5), 570–586. https://doi.org/10.2307/2523329.

Barnett, B. G. (1984). Subordinate teacher power in school organizations. *Sociology of Education, 57*(1), 43–55. https://doi.org/10.2307/2112467.

Barrett, N., & Toma, E. F. (2013). Reward or punishment? Class size and teacher quality. *Economics of Education Review, 35*, 41–52. https://doi.org/10.1016/j.econedurev.2013.03.001.

Bastian, K. C., Henry, G. T., & Thompson, C. L. (2013). Incorporating access to more effective teachers into assessments of educational resource equity. *Education Finance and Policy, 8*(4), 560–580. https://doi.org/10.1162/EDFP_a_00113.

Becker, H. S. (1952a). The career of the Chicago public school teacher. *American Journal of Sociology, 57*(5), 470–477.

Becker, H. S. (1952b). Social-class variations in the teacher–pupil relationship. *The Journal of Educational Sociology, 25*(8), 451–465. https://doi.org/10.2307/2263957.

Becker, H. S. (1953). The teacher in the authority system of the public school. *The Journal of Educational Sociology, 27*(3), 128–141. https://doi.org/10.2307/2263223.

Bidwell, C. E. (1955). The administrative role and satisfaction in teaching. *The Journal of Educational Sociology, 29*(1), 41–47. https://doi.org/10.2307/2263350.

Bidwell, C. E., Frank, K. A., & Quiroz, P. A. (1997). Teacher types, workplace controls, and the organization of schools. *Sociology of Education, 70*(4), 285–307. https://doi.org/10.2307/2673268.

Bidwell, C. E., & Yasumoto, J. Y. (1999). The collegial focus: Teaching fields, collegial relationships, and instructional practice in American high schools. *Sociology of Education, 72*(4), 234–256. https://doi.org/10.2307/2673155.

Blase, J. J. (1986). Socialization as humanization: One side of becoming a teacher. *Sociology of Education, 59*(2), 100–113. https://doi.org/10.2307/2112435.

Bogardus, E. S. (1928). Teaching and social distance. *The Journal of Educational Sociology, 1*(10), 595–598. https://doi.org/10.2307/2961789.

Bogardus, E. S. (1929). Social case analysis and teaching. *The Journal of Educational Sociology, 3*(1), 3–6. https://doi.org/10.2307/2961155.

Boyd, D., Lankford, H., Loeb, S., Ronfeldt, M., & Wyckoff, J. (2011). The role of teacher quality in retention and hiring: Using applications to transfer to uncover preferences of teachers and schools. *Journal of Policy Analysis and Management, 30*(1), 88–110. https://doi.org/10.1002/pam.20545.

Boyd, D., Lankford, H., Loeb, S., & Wyckoff, J. (2005). Explaining the short careers of high-achieving teachers in schools with low-performing students. *The American Economic Review, 95*(2), 166–171.

Bredo, E. (1977). Collaborative relations among elementary school teachers. *Sociology of Education, 50*(4), 300–309. https://doi.org/10.2307/2112502.

Brookover, W. (1943). The social roles of teachers and pupil achievement. *American Sociological Review, 8*(4), 389–393.

Bryk, A. S., Lee, V. E., & Holland, P. B. (1993). *Catholic schools and the common good.* Cambridge, MA: Harvard University Press.

Buck, R. C. (1960). The extent of social participation among public school teachers. *The Journal of Educational Sociology, 33*(8), 311–319. https://doi.org/10.2307/2264408.

Calarco, J. M. (2011). "I need help!" Social class and children's help-seeking in elementary school. *American Sociological Review, 76*(6), 862–882. https://doi.org/10.1177/0003122411427177.

Calarco, J. M. (2014). The inconsistent curriculum. *Social Psychology Quarterly, 77*(2), 185–209. https://doi.org/10.1177/0190272514521438.

Carlson, R. O. (1961). Variation and myth in the social status of teachers. *The Journal of Educational Sociology, 35*(3), 104–118. https://doi.org/10.2307/2264812.

Chetty, R., Friedman, J. N., & Rockoff, J. E. (2014a). Measuring the impacts of teachers I: Evaluating bias in teacher value-added estimates. *American Economic Review, 104*(9), 2593–2632. http://www.aeaweb.org/aer/.

Chetty, R., Friedman, J. N., & Rockoff, J. E. (2014b). Measuring the impacts of teachers II: Teacher value-added and student outcomes in adulthood. *American Economic Review, 104*(9), 2633–2679. http://www.aeaweb.org/aer/.

Chingos, M. M., & West, M. R. (2011). Promotion and reassignment in public school districts: How do schools respond to differences in teacher effectiveness? *Economics of Education Review, 30*(3), 419–433. https://doi.org/10.1016/j.econedurev.2010.12.011.

Clotfelter, C., Glennie, E., Ladd, H., & Vigdor, J. (2008). Would higher salaries keep teachers in high-poverty schools? Evidence from a policy intervention in North Carolina. *Journal of Public Economics, 92*, 1352–1370.

Clotfelter, C. T., Ladd, H. F., & Vigdor, J. (2005). Who teaches whom? Race and the distribution of novice teachers. *Economics of Education Review, 24*(4), 377–392. https://doi.org/10.1016/j.econedurev.2004.06.008.

Clotfelter, C. T., Ladd, H. F., & Vigdor, J. L. (2006). Teacher–student matching and the assessment of teacher effectiveness. *The Journal of Human Resources, 41*(4), 778–820.

Clotfelter, C. T., Ladd, H. F., & Vigdor, J. L. (2007). Teacher credentials and student achievement: Longitudinal analysis with student fixed effects. *Economics of Education Review, 26*(6), 673–682. https://doi.org/10.1016/j.econedurev.2007.10.002.

Clotfelter, C. T., Ladd, H. F., & Vigdor, J. L. (2011). Teacher mobility, school segregation, and pay-based policies to level the playing field. *Education Finance and Policy, 6*(3), 399–438. https://doi.org/10.1162/EDFP_a_00040.

Clotfelter, C. T., Ladd, H. F., Vigdor, J. L., & Diaz, R. A. (2004). Do school accountability systems make it more difficult for low-performing schools to attract and retain high-quality teachers? *Journal of Policy Analysis and Management, 23*(2), 251–271. https://doi.org/10.1002/pam.20003.

Coleman, J. S., Campbell, E. Q., Hobson, C. J., McPartland, J., Mood, A. M., Weinfeld, F. D., & York, R. L. (1966). *Equality of educational opportunity.* Washington, DC: U.S. Department of Health, Education, and Welfare, Office of Education.

Cook, L. A., Almack, R. B., & Greenhoe, F. (1938). Teacher and community relations. *American Sociological Review, 3*(2), 167–174.

Cook, L. A., & Greenhoe, F. (1940). Community contacts of 9,122 teachers. *Social Forces, 19*(1), 63–72. https://doi.org/10.2307/2570843.

Corcoran, S., & Goldhaber, D. (2013). Value added and its uses: Where you stand depends on where you sit. *Education Finance and Policy, 8*(3), 418–434. https://doi.org/10.1162/EDFP_a_00104.

Corcoran, S. P. (2016). Potential pitfalls in the use of teacher value-added data. In J. A. Grissom & P. Youngs (Eds.), *Improving teacher evaluation systems: Making the most of multiple measures* (pp. 51–62). New York: Teachers College Press.

Crosnoe, R., Johnson, M. K., & Elder, G. H. (2004). Intergenerational bonding in school: The behavioral and contextual correlates of student–teacher relationships. *Sociology of Education, 77*(1), 60–81.

Edgar, D. E., & Warren, R. L. (1969). Power and autonomy in teacher socialization. *Sociology of Education, 42*(4), 386–399. https://doi.org/10.2307/2112132.

Egalite, A. J., Kisida, B., & Winters, M. A. (2015). Representation in the classroom: The effect of own-race teachers on student achievement. *Economics of Education Review, 45*, 44–52. https://doi.org/10.1016/j.econedurev.2015.01.007.

Ehrenberg, R. G., & Brewer, D. J. (1994). Do school and teacher characteristics matter? Evidence from high school and beyond. *Economics of Education Review, 13*(1), 1–17. https://doi.org/10.1016/0272-7757(94)90019-1.

Elfers, A. M., Plecki, M. L., & Knapp, M. S. (2006). Teacher mobility: Looking more closely at "the movers" within a state system. *Peabody Journal of Education, 81*(3), 94–127.

Feng, L. (2010). Hire today, gone tomorrow: New teacher classroom assignments and teacher mobility. *Education Finance and Policy, 5*(3), 278–316. https://doi.org/10.1162/EDFP_a_00002.

Feng, L. (2014). Teacher placement, mobility, and occupational choices after teaching. *Education Economics, 22*(1), 24–47. https://doi.org/10.1080/09645292.2010.511841.

Ferguson, R. F., & Hirsch, E. (2014). How working conditions predict teaching quality and student outcomes. In T. J. Kane, K. A. Kerr, & R. C. Pianta (Eds.), *Designing teacher evaluation systems: New guidance from the measures of effective teaching project* (1st ed., pp. 332–380). San Francisco: Jossey-Bass.

Fisher, H. (1958). Teachers reading habits: A sign of professional interest. *The Journal of Educational Sociology, 32*(3), 127–132. https://doi.org/10.2307/2264712.

Friedkin, N. E., & Slater, M. R. (1994). School leadership and performance: A social network approach. *Sociology of Education, 67*(2), 139–157. https://doi.org/10.2307/2112701.

Fulbeck, E. S. (2014). Teacher mobility and financial incentives: A descriptive analysis of Denver's ProComp. *Educational Evaluation and Policy Analysis, 36*(1), 67–82. https://doi.org/10.3102/0162373713503185.

Fulbeck, E. S., & Richards, M. P. (2015, September). The impact of school-based financial incentives on teachers' strategic moves: A descriptive analysis. *Teachers College Record, 117*, 1–36.

Fuller, S. C., & Ladd, H. F. (2013). School-based accountability and the distribution of teacher quality across grades in elementary school. *Education Finance and Policy, 8*(4), 528–559. https://doi.org/10.1162/EDFP_a_00112.

Gamoran, A., Anderson, C. W., Secada, W. G., Williams, T., & Ashmann, S. (2003). *Transforming teaching in math and science: How schools and districts can support change.* New York: Teachers College Press.

Gamoran, A., & Long, D. A. (2007). Equality of educational opportunity: A 40 year retrospective. In R. Teese, S. Lamb, M. Duru-Bellat, & S. Helme (Eds.), *International studies in educational inequality, theory and policy* (pp. 23–47). Dordrecht: Springer.

Gamoran, A., Secada, W. G., & Marrett, C. B. (2000). The organizational context of teaching and learning: Changing theoretical perspectives. In M. T. Hallinan (Ed.), *Handbook of the sociology of education* (pp. 37–63). New York: Kluwer/Plenum.

Goldhaber, D., Choi, H.-J., & Cramer, L. (2007). A descriptive analysis of the distribution of NBPTS-certified teachers in North Carolina. *Economics of Education Review, 26*(2), 160–172. https://doi.org/10.1016/j.econedurev.2005.09.003.

Goldhaber, D., Destler, K., & Player, D. (2010). Teacher labor markets and the perils of using hedonics to estimate compensating differentials in the public sector. *Economics of Education Review, 29*(1), 1–17. https://doi.org/10.1016/j.econedurev.2009.07.010.

Goldhaber, D., Gross, B., & Player, D. (2011). Teacher career paths, teacher quality, and persistence in the classroom: Are public schools keeping their best? *Journal of Policy Analysis and Management, 30*(1), 57–87. https://doi.org/10.1002/pam.20549.

Gordon, C. W. (1955). The role of the teacher in the social structure of the high school. *The Journal of Educational Sociology, 29*(1), 21–29. https://doi.org/10.2307/2263348.

Greenberg, D., & McCall, J. (1974). Teacher mobility and allocation. *The Journal of Human Resources, 9*(4), 480–502. https://doi.org/10.2307/144782.

Grissom, J. A., & Youngs, P. (Eds.). (2016). *Improving teacher evaluation systems: Making the most of multiple measures.* New York: Teachers College Press.

Guarino, C. M., Brown, A. B., & Wyse, A. E. (2011). Can districts keep good teachers in the schools that need them most? *Economics of Education Review, 30*(5), 962–979. https://doi.org/10.1016/j.econedurev.2011.04.001.

Guarino, C. M., Reckase, M. D., & Wooldridge, J. M. (2014). Can value-added measures of teacher performance be trusted? *Education Finance and Policy, 10*(1), 117–156. https://doi.org/10.1162/EDFP_a_00153.

Hallinan, M. T. (2008). Teacher influences on students' attachment to school. *Sociology of Education, 81*(3), 271–283.

Hanushek, E. A., Kain, J. F., & Rivkin, S. G. (2004). Why public schools lose teachers. *The Journal of Human Resources, 39*(2), 326–354. https://doi.org/10.2307/3559017.

Hedges, L. V., & Schneider, B. L. (Eds.). (2005). *The social organization of schooling*. New York: Russell Sage Foundation.

Horng, E. L. (2009). Teacher tradeoffs: Disentangling teachers' preferences for working conditions and student demographics. *American Educational Research Journal, 46*(3), 690–717. https://doi.org/10.3102/0002831208329599.

Ingersoll, R. M. (1996). Teachers' decision-making power and school conflict. *Sociology of Education, 69*(2), 159–176. https://doi.org/10.2307/2112804.

Ingersoll, R. M. (2005). The problem of underqualified teachers: A sociological perspective. *Sociology of Education, 78*(2), 175–178.

Ingersoll, R. M., & May, H. (2012). The magnitude, destinations, and determinants of mathematics and science teacher turnover. *Educational Evaluation and Policy Analysis, 34*(4), 435–464. https://doi.org/10.3102/0162373712454326.

Jackson, C. K. (2009). Student demographics, teacher sorting, and teacher quality: Evidence from the end of school desegregation. *Journal of Labor Economics, 27*(2), 213–256. https://doi.org/10.1086/599334.

Jackson, C. K. (2013). Match quality, worker productivity, and worker mobility: Direct evidence from teachers. *Review of Economics and Statistics, 95*(4), 1096–1116. https://doi.org/10.1162/REST_a_00339.

Jackson, C. K., & Bruegmann, E. (2009). Teaching students and teaching each other: The importance of peer learning for teachers. *American Economic Journal: Applied Economics, 1*(4), 85–108.

Jacob, B. A., & Lefgren, L. (2007). What do parents value in education? An empirical investigation of parents' revealed preferences for teachers. *The Quarterly Journal of Economics, 122*(4), 1603–1637.

Jennings, J. L., & DiPrete, T. A. (2010). Teacher effects on social and behavioral skills in early elementary school. *Sociology of Education, 83*(2), 135–159.

Jepsen, C., & Rivkin, S. (2009). Class size reduction and student achievement: The potential tradeoff between teacher quality and class size. *The Journal of Human Resources, 44*(1), 223–250.

Jessup, D. K. (1978). Teacher unionization: A reassessment of rank and file motivations. *Sociology of Education, 51*(1), 44–55. https://doi.org/10.2307/2112281.

Kalogrides, D., Loeb, S., & Béteille, T. (2013). Systematic sorting: Teacher characteristics and class assignments. *Sociology of Education, 86*(2), 103–123. https://doi.org/10.1177/0038040712456555.

Koedel, C. (2009). An empirical analysis of teacher spillover effects in secondary school. *Economics of Education Review, 28*(6), 682–692. https://doi.org/10.1016/j.econedurev.2009.02.003.

Krei, M. S. (1998). Intensifying the barriers: The problem of inequitable teacher allocation in low-income urban schools. *Urban Education, 33*(1), 71–94. https://doi.org/10.1177/0042085998033001005.

Kukla-Acevedo, S. (2009). Do teacher characteristics matter? New results on the effects of teacher preparation on student achievement. *Economics of Education Review, 28*(1), 49–57. https://doi.org/10.1016/j.econedurev.2007.10.007.

Ladd, H. F. (2008). Reflections on equity, adequacy, and weighted student funding. *Education Finance and Policy, 3*(4), 402–423. https://doi.org/10.1162/edfp.2008.3.4.402.

Lankford, H., Loeb, S., & Wyckoff, J. (2002). Teacher sorting and the plight of urban schools: A descriptive analysis. *Educational Evaluation and Policy Analysis, 24*(1), 37–62. https://doi.org/10.3102/01623737024001037.

Larkin, R. W. (1973). Contextual influences on teacher leadership styles. *Sociology of Education, 46*(4), 471–479. https://doi.org/10.2307/2111900.

Lee, V. E., Dedrick, R. F., & Smith, J. B. (1991). The effect of the social organization of schools on teachers' efficacy and satisfaction. *Sociology of Education, 64*(3), 190–208. https://doi.org/10.2307/2112851.

Lee, V. E., & Smith, J. B. (1993). Effects of school restructuring on the achievement and engagement of middle-grade students. *Sociology of Education, 66*(2), 164–187.

Lee, V. E., & Smith, J. B. (1995). Effects of high school restructuring and size on early gains in achievement and engagement. *Sociology of Education, 68*(1), 241–270.

Levinson, A. M. (1988). Reexamining teacher preferences and compensating wages. *Economics of Education Review, 7*(3), 357–364. https://doi.org/10.1016/0272-7757(88)90007-6.

Loeb, S., Darling-Hammond, L., & Luczak, J. (2005). How teaching conditions predict teacher turnover in California schools. *Peabody Journal of Education, 80*(3), 44–70. https://doi.org/10.1207/s15327930pje8003_4.

Loeb, S., Kalogrides, D., & Béteille, T. (2012). Effective schools: Teacher hiring, assignment, development, and retention. *Education Finance and Policy, 7*(3), 269–304. https://doi.org/10.1162/EDFP_a_00068.

McCaffrey, D. F., Sass, T. R., Lockwood, J. R., & Mihaly, K. (2009). The intertemporal variability of teacher effect estimates. *Education Finance and Policy, 4*(4), 572–606. https://doi.org/10.1162/edfp.2009.4.4.572.

Moller, S., Mickelson, R. A., Stearns, E., Banerjee, N., & Bottia, M. C. (2013). Collective pedagogical teacher culture and mathematics achievement: Differences by race, ethnicity, and socioeconomic status. *Sociology of Education, 86*(2), 174–194.

Morgan, S. L., & Jung, S. B. (2016). Still no effect of resources, even in the new gilded age? *RSF: The Russell Sage Foundation Journal of the Social Sciences, 2*(5), 83–116.

Myers, A. F. (1934). Education of teachers for the schools of tomorrow. *The Journal of Educational Sociology, 7*(9), 569–574. https://doi.org/10.2307/2961057.

Ost, B., & Schiman, J. C. (2015). Grade-specific experience, grade reassignments, and teacher turnover. *Economics of Education Review, 46*, 112–126. https://doi.org/10.1016/j.econedurev.2015.03.004.

Player, D. (2009). Monetary returns to academic ability in the public teacher labor market. *Economics of Education Review, 28*(2), 277–285. https://doi.org/10.1016/j.econedurev.2008.06.002.

Raudenbush, S. W., Rowan, B., & Cheong, Y. F. (1992). Contextual effects on the self-perceived efficacy of high school teachers. *Sociology of Education, 65*(2), 150–167. https://doi.org/10.2307/2112680.

Ravitch, D. (1993). The Coleman reports and American education. In A. B. Sørensen & S. Spilerman (Eds.), *Social theory and social policy: Essays in honor of James S. Coleman* (pp. 129–141). Westport: Praeger.

Reardon, S. F., & Raudenbush, S. W. (2009). Assumptions of value-added models for estimating school effects. *Education Finance and Policy, 4*(4), 492–519. https://doi.org/10.1162/edfp.2009.4.4.492.

Rice, J. K. (2013). Learning from experience? Evidence on the impact and distribution of teacher experience and the implications for teacher policy. *Education Finance and Policy, 8*(3), 332–348. https://doi.org/10.1162/EDFP_a_00099.

Rosenholtz, S. J., & Simpson, C. (1990). Workplace conditions and the rise and fall of teachers' commitment. *Sociology of Education, 63*(4), 241–257. https://doi.org/10.2307/2112873.

Roth, L. J. (1958). Occupational analysis and teacher morale. *The Journal of Educational Sociology, 32*(4), 145–151. https://doi.org/10.2307/2264177.

Rothstein, J. (2009). Student sorting and bias in value-added estimation: Selection on observables and unobservables. *Education Finance and Policy, 4*(4), 537–571. https://doi.org/10.1162/edfp.2009.4.4.537.

Rothstein, J. (2010). Teacher quality in educational production: Tracking, decay, and student achievement. *The Quarterly Journal of Economics, 125*(1), 175–214.

Rowan, B., Chiang, F.-S., & Miller, R. J. (1997). Using research on employees' performance to study the effects of teachers on students' achievement. *Sociology of Education, 70*(4), 256–284. https://doi.org/10.2307/2673267.

Rubenstein, R., Schwartz, A. E., Stiefel, L., & Amor, H. B. H. (2007). From districts to schools: The distribution of resources across schools in big city school districts. *Economics of Education Review, 26*(5), 532–545. https://doi.org/10.1016/j.econedurev.2006.08.002.

Scafidi, B., Sjoquist, D. L., & Stinebrickner, T. R. (2007). Race, poverty, and teacher mobility. *Economics of Education Review, 26*(2), 145–159. https://doi.org/10.1016/j.econedurev.2005.08.006.

Sieber, S. D., & Wilder, D. E. (1967). Teaching styles: Parental preferences and professional role definitions. *Sociology of Education, 40*(4), 302–315. https://doi.org/10.2307/2111938.

Sørensen, A. B., & Morgan, S. L. (2000). School effects: Theoretical and methodological issues. In M. T. Hallinan (Ed.), *Handbook of the sociology of education* (pp. 137–160). New York: Kluwer/Plenum.

Steele, J. L., Pepper, M. J., Springer, M. G., & Lockwood, J. R. (2015). The distribution and mobility of effective teachers: Evidence from a large, urban school district. *Economics of Education Review, 48*, 86–101. https://doi.org/10.1016/j.econedurev.2015.05.009.

Waller, W. (1932). *The sociology of teaching*. New York: Wiley.

Winters, M. A., Haight, R. C., Swaim, T. T., & Pickering, K. A. (2013). The effect of same-gender teacher assignment on student achievement in the elementary and secondary grades: Evidence from panel data. *Economics of Education Review, 34*, 69–75. https://doi.org/10.1016/j.econedurev.2013.01.007.

Yasumoto, J. Y., Uekawa, K., & Bidwell, C. E. (2001). The collegial focus and high school students' achievement. *Sociology of Education, 74*(3), 181–209. https://doi.org/10.2307/2673274.

Experimental Evidence on Interventions to Improve Educational Attainment at Community Colleges

24

David Monaghan, Tammy Kolbe,
and Sara Goldrick-Rab

Abstract

America's community colleges play a major role in increasing access to higher education and, as open access institutions, they are key points of entry to postsecondary education for historically underrepresented populations. However, their students often fall short of completing degrees. Policymakers, scholars, and philanthropists are dedicating unprecedented attention and resources to identifying strategies to improve retention, academic performance, and degree completion among community college students. This chapter reviews experimental evidence on their effectiveness, finding that they often meet with limited success because they typically target just one or two aspects of students' lives, are of short duration, and fail to improve the institutional context. They also rarely address a serious structural constraint: limited resources. We discuss new directions for future interventions, research and evaluation.

D. Monaghan (✉)
Shippensburg University of Pennsylvania,
Shippensburg, PA, USA
e-mail: dbmonaghan@ship.edu

T. Kolbe
University of Vermont, Burlington, VT, USA
e-mail: tammykolbe@uvm.edu

S. Goldrick-Rab
Temple University, Philadelphia, PA, USA
e-mail: SGR@temple.edu

24.1 Introduction

Community colleges play a critical role in higher education. Intended to provide accessible, flexible, and affordable opportunities for postsecondary education and workforce participation, they have contributed to substantial increases in college participation. This is especially true for groups who are historically underrepresented in postsecondary education—including racial and ethnic minority, low-income, part-time, first-generation, and adult students. Today, almost 40% of all undergraduates—more than 6.6 million Americans—attend community colleges (Kena et al. 2015). However, increased college enrollment does not consistently translate into program or degree completion. Completion rates among community college students—as measured by earning a credential or transferring to a four-year institution—are less than 50% after 6 years of enrollment and below 30% for low-income, Black, Latino, and Native American students (Shapiro et al. 2014). Fewer than two in five community college students who enter with the intent to earn some type of a degree do so within six years of initial enrollment (Shapiro et al. 2014) and only three in five enroll in any college one year later (National Student Clearinghouse Research Center 2015).

While even some college education appears to benefit students, degree completion is essential, especially if students must accrue debt along the

© Springer International Publishing AG, part of Springer Nature 2018

B. Schneider (ed.), *Handbook of the Sociology of Education in the 21st Century*, Handbooks
of Sociology and Social Research, https://doi.org/10.1007/978-3-319-76694-2_24

way in order to cover college prices (Goldrick-Rab 2016). Low completion rates coupled with substantial lag times between enrollment and completion levy real economic and social costs (Goldrick-Rab 2016; Bailey et al. 2004). Since they broaden access, community colleges appear to substantially raise the educational attainment of those otherwise unlikely to attend college at all, while doing very little harm to students who might otherwise attend four-year colleges (Leigh and Gill 2003; Brand et al. 2012). Scholars, policymakers, and philanthropic foundations are devoting unprecedented attention and resources to identifying strategies to boost retention and degree completion among community college students (Bailey et al. 2015; Grossman et al. 2015; Sturgis 2014). These interventions address a wide variety of conditions and contexts—at the individual, school, and system levels—believed to pose barriers to student success. Many efforts have been evaluated to assess their effectiveness. In doing so, researchers have increasingly relied upon randomized control trials (RCTs) to generate rigorous estimates of causal effects, providing insights into "what works" to boost attainment among community college students.

This chapter reviews evidence from experimental evaluations of a range of interventions—from financial aid to student advisement to developmental education—with two main goals. First, we examine what the evidence from experimental studies reveals about the most promising interventions. It is evident that while sustained and multi-pronged strategies appear most effective at boosting completion, they are also uncommon. Second, we illustrate the role research and evaluations incorporating experimental design should play in future sociological research, especially when assessing the impact of education and social program interventions targeted at disadvantaged youth, adults, and families. Effectively replicating or scaling programs requires that future studies more carefully document the context in which an intervention succeeded or failed, and the resources and costs involved.

24.2   The Contexts of Community College Education

Unlike other higher education institutions, community colleges were explicitly designed as open entry-points into higher education, emphasizing expanded opportunities for all rather than maximizing outcomes for a few. In the aftermath of World War II, the Truman Commission (1947) called for action to democratize higher education, postsecondary enrollments surged, and higher education leaders sought a means of satisfying popular pressure for access while protecting curricular rigor at existing institutions (Brint and Karabel 1989; Trow 2007). In response, the nation's existing "junior colleges" were rechristened as "community colleges" and their ranks dramatically expanded. Community colleges would serve their purpose as "agents of democracy" by being both *accessible* and *comprehensive*, within the bounds of their *resource constraints*.

Community colleges aim to minimize three barriers to college entry: price, academic requirements, and distance. They are intended to be cheaper than four-year public colleges; open-enrollment, requiring that prospective students complete high school to gain admission; and geographically dispersed so they are within reasonable commuting distance for all Americans. As public higher education institutions, community colleges are primarily funded by state and local revenues. Historically, public funding sources have buoyed costs, keeping tuition non-existent or very low for students. Low-cost educational opportunities reinforced community colleges' missions as open access portals for a broad range of students, including those who could not afford higher education at other public or private institutions. Community colleges are comprehensive in their offerings, reflecting the range of needs and interests of the community they served. They have academic courses for students intending to transfer to four-year colleges, vocational training programs for students looking to upgrade skills or change jobs, and general education courses for community members interested in lifelong learning.

Aspects of the community college context—those related to accessibility and comprehensiveness in particular—may work at cross-purposes with the goal of maximizing completion rates. For example, open enrollment and a relatively low cost of attendance help attract a more heterogeneous mix of students, compared to those who attend four-year colleges and universities. Community college students are disproportionately Black and Latino and are far more likely to be a first-generation college-goer or from a lower-income household. Given open-admissions, community college students have on average lower levels of academic preparation and fewer resources than students attending four-year public and non-profit colleges and universities (Table 24.1). Indeed, despite the constant characterization that they are "diverse" spaces, in fact community colleges are highly segregated (Goldrick-Rab and Kinsley 2013).

Stratification by student composition, and by extension aspirations and outcomes, translates into vastly different educational experiences and, by extension, differences in opportunities and outcomes. Moreover, the effects of segregating students across institutional types may be exacerbated by peer-effects. If having more uniformly poorer, less-prepared peers who are more likely to drop out of college impacts the social and intellectual atmosphere and normalizes non-completion, then community college students may be at a particular disadvantage (Century Foundation 2013).

Because community colleges enroll many students without the skills needed to assimilate college-level material, remedial education has been central to them since their inception (Cohen et al. 2014). Remedial policies effectively bar low-performing students from most classes bestowing credit (Hughes and Scott-Clayton 2011; Perin 2006), and the majority of students never complete the sequences of remedial courses to which they are assigned (Bailey et al. 2010). Assignment to remediation substantially increases the cost of a degree in terms of time and money (Melguizo et al. 2008). Critics allege that remedial regimes permit the colleges to maintain appearance of access, while effectively serving as a holding area for students from the "educational underclass" (Deil-Amen and DeLuca 2010).

Part of accessibility is geographic dispersion. Community colleges are, with few exceptions, commuter campuses. Sociological and education research suggests that students who reside on campus are more likely to remain enrolled and to eventually graduate, as such students spend more time on campus and are far more likely to become socially and academically integrated into the life of the institution (Astin 1984; Pascarella and Terenzini 2005; Schudde 2011; Tinto 1987). In addition, part-time and part-year community college enrollment is the norm—fewer than half of community college students enroll either full-time in both fall and spring semesters (Table 24.1). Indeed, many community college students are on campus only a few hours per week, giving the colleges few opportunities to directly engage them and build institutional loyalty or involvement. The low-intensity student enrollment patterns reflect community college students' "non-traditional" status. Most are older than 23 and, for many, college is negotiated along with full-time work and childcare responsibilities (Table 24.1; Stuart et al. 2014). Students are frequently not exclusively or even primarily oriented towards college-going, and practically speaking completing a degree is often not their top priority. As a result, it is common for community college students to "stop out" for a semester or two to attend to other responsibilities or to transfer when another college is more convenient (Bahr 2009; Crosta 2014).

The effects of more limited opportunities for interaction with faculty are compounded by increasing student–staff ratios. Typically, the ratio of student support and other college staff is double that found at four-year institutions (Baum and Kurose 2013). Staffing shortages are particularly dire for student advisement and counseling; at community colleges, student-to-counselor ratios are frequently higher than 800: or 1000:1 (Park et al. 2013), resulting in inadequate, inconsistent, and often counterproductive academic and career counseling (Deil-Amen and Rosenbaum 2002, 2003; Grubb 2001, 2006; Rosenbaum et al. 2006). Personalized counseling and advisement

Table 24.1 Student characteristics, by sector (2012)

	Community college	Public four-year	Private non-profit four-year	Private for-profit (two- or four-year)
Female	55.7	53.9	56.6	64.1
White	55.8	62.2	65.1	48.5
Black	16.4	12.8	13.4	25.6
Latino/a	18.6	13.8	10.1	18.5
Asian	5.0	6.9	6.9	2.9
First-generation college	46.3	31.7	28.3	58.1
Income < 200% poverty[a]	54.9	34.8	30.3	81.2
HS GPA < 3.0[a]	50.3	27.6	18.7	52.7
HS math: Alg. 2/ less[a]	61.3	26.5	21.3	71.0
Didn't take SAT/ ACT[a]	29.7	3.8	2.0	38.7
Lowest quartile SAT[a]	38.9	16.4	12.9	43.4
Age 24+	50.8	30.4	28.8	68.4
Has children	32.4	15.4	17.0	51.6
Single parent	17.9	7.3	8.1	32.7
Living on-campus	0.9	22.5	45.0	0.9
Enrolled full-time	32.5	59.5	73.5	70.7
Enrolled full-year	46.6	69.6	72.2	42.4
Employed	68.6	65.5	63.7	61.0
Employed full-time	26.2	15.3	14.5	31.2

[a]Among first time freshmen only; Sources: Beginning Postsecondary Students Longitudinal Survey 2012/14; National Postsecondary Student Aid Survey 2012

is crucial to community college student success. Instead, community college counseling offices triage counseling services according to student needs, and devote a limited amount of time to each student during heavy-use periods such as registration.

These challenges are complicated by the role that community colleges play as comprehensive institutions that try to expand college enrollment through a wide range of courses, degree, and certificate programs. However, over time, at many community colleges, "comprehensiveness" has translated into an array of often disconnected courses, programs, and support services that students must navigate with relatively little guidance (Bailey et al. 2015). The immense array of choices can overwhelm students, especially first-generation college students and others with limited experience with postsecondary education (Rosenbaum et al. 2006; Scott-Clayton 2015). Since each program has its own set of required

courses, the diversity of programs also causes problems for coordinating and scheduling courses. This poses challenges for part-time and working students to arrange classes in ways that fit their schedule. For students attending community college as an entry point to a bachelor's degree, the "cafeteria self-service" course-taking model found at many community colleges also can pose challenges for identifying a clear and efficient pathway to a four-year degree. Oftentimes, incoming students do not know to which four-year institutions they will apply, or even the general requirements for transfer to a bachelor's degree-granting institution. The absence of strong articulation policies that link community colleges with four-year institutions—even public ones—means that the four-year colleges often differ in the courses required for transfer and in the courses they will recognize by transferring credit. For community college students who do manage to transfer, substantial loss of credits is a common occurrence (Monaghan and Attewell 2015; Simone 2014).

Recently, researchers and outside experts have suggested that community colleges narrow their program structures in ways that faculty clearly map out academic programs to create coherent pathways that are aligned with requirements for further education and career advancement (Bailey et al. 2015). This involves presenting students with a small number of program options, developing clear course sequences leading to degree completion, arranging the courses so that they are convenient (i.e., scheduled back-to-back), and providing personalized, mandatory counseling services. They contend that community colleges treat their clientele as if they were "traditional college students," equipped with the motivation, knowledge, and skills necessary to negotiate college. Change the community colleges' programs, practices and resources, they argue, and one can improve student outcomes (Bailey et al. 2015; Rosenbaum et al. 2006; Scott-Clayton 2015).

But it is increasingly difficult to maintain both accessibility and comprehensiveness while also increasing completion rates as state governments have reduced support on a per-student basis (Goldrick-Rab 2016). While, on a per-student basis, community colleges receive about as much money from states as do public comprehensives (Baum and Kurose 2013; College Board 2015), they are far more dependent on state funding as a primary source of revenue. On average, community colleges receive about 71% of their revenue from state appropriations, compared to public four-year colleges' 38% (Kena et al. 2015). This makes community colleges particularly vulnerable to state cuts—particularly during recessionary periods, which tend to couple funding reductions with enrollment surges (Betts and McFarland 1995). Community colleges pass some costs on to students. Between 2000 and 2010 the percentage of revenue covered by state appropriations fell from 57% to 47%. At the same time, that met through tuition and fees rose from 19% to 27% (Kirshstein and Hubert 2012). As community colleges' capacity to increase tuition is constrained by their mandate to remain affordable, their principal response to dwindling

resources is to spend less per student. Per-student instructional spending at community colleges fell by 12% between 2001 and 2011; on average, community colleges now spend 78% as much per student on instruction as public bachelor's colleges and 56% as much as public research universities, despite enrolling students with arguably greater academic challenges (Desrochers and Kirshstein 2012).

Lower spending may impact educational quality and output (Jenkins and Belfield 2014). The student–faculty ratio at community colleges was 22:1 in 2009, while at public four-year colleges this ratio was 15:1 (Baum and Kurose 2013). The higher ratio constrains the amount of time faculty can devote to individual students and may affect instructional quality. This is particularly problematic in a commuter setting, where classroom time and faculty are the primary opportunity for "socio-academic integrative moments" (Deil-Amen 2011). The impact of higher faculty–student ratios is further exacerbated by community colleges' other cost-saving strategy: heavy reliance on part-time and contingent faculty. At community colleges, two-thirds of faculty work part time, and only 18% are tenured or tenure-track (Kezar and Maxey 2013). Exposure to part-time and adjunct faculty is negatively associated with degree completion (Eagan and Jaeger 2009). Contingent faculty may not have the institutional knowledge and skills to help students negotiate the institution and contribute to short-term faculty–student relationships that do not last beyond a semester.

Research diligently minimizing selection bias has consistently found negative impacts of initial community college enrollment, relative to four-year college enrollment, on bachelor's degree attainment (Brand et al. 2012; Reynolds 2012; but see Rouse 1995). But the 60% one-year retention rate at community colleges is not appreciably different from that at non-selective public or non-profit four-year colleges (62% and 61% respectively) (Kena et al. 2015). Monaghan and Attewell (2015), comparing community college students with those at non-selective four-year colleges, find that retention differences do not appear until the fifth semester, after adjusting for student characteristics.

In summary, the community college sector arose to accommodate demands to democratize access to higher education and offer a comprehensive battery of general education, vocational, and academic options. The "imperious immediacy of interest" (Merton 1936) in achieving these goals obscured the consideration of whether their resulting organizational features might stymie degree completion. Early critics alleged that community colleges "cooled out" the aspirations of academically disinclined and/or lower-SES youth by tracking them into vocational programs or permitting them to drop out altogether (Brint and Karabel 1989, Clark 1960). But it wasn't until the late 1990s that their low completion rates came to be collectively defined, in Blumer's (1971) sense, as a social problem in need of a solution. In response, policymakers, educational leaders and philanthropists have targeted their efforts at new opportunities to restructure how community colleges deliver education and support services, with an eye towards identifying reforms that improve both the effectiveness and efficiency with which they support not only access to higher education but also completion, for all students.

24.3   Points of Intervention

Efforts to improve outcomes in community colleges are focused on either the student, the institution, or the system (Goldrick-Rab 2010). *Student-focused interventions* reduce financial barriers, provide student support, or improve students' academic skills (e.g., dual enrollment programs, financial aid, advising, or coaching). Financial aid is by far the most popular strategy. Community college tuition is relatively low; yet, many students still struggle with paying for college as well as other living costs incurred while in school. It is hoped that by putting in place programs and resources that alleviate material shortages and reducing stress, financial aid may enable students to focus on academic work and to avoid potentially injurious alternative strategies such as

taking out loans, working long hours, or enrolling part-time. Other interventions seek to improve students' "informational capital"—the knowledge required to select a major, choose the correct classes that will enable them to complete the major, or apply for financial aid (Rosenbaum et al. 2006). Such efforts include informational seminars, orientation courses, and counseling services. Similarly, institutions also intervene to address student academic shortfalls through mandatory remedial courses and through voluntarily-accessed tutoring and writing centers. Finally, given that many community college students enroll part-time, interventions have been developed that encourage full-time attendance or summer course-taking.

School-focused interventions attempt to change how community colleges serve students (e.g., guided pathways, course redesign, or structuring of support services). One frequent leverage point has been the college counseling center: assigning each student to a counselor, making appointments mandatory, lowering student–counselor ratios, and having counselors specialize by degree program. Other interventions include forging social connections among students through linked courses or "learning communities," and by building students' connections to the institution through providing in-class tutors or mentors. Skills assessment and remedial coursework also has been an area for reform. Many community college students enter who are not "college ready," so remediation is widespread; it is estimated that between 60% and 70% take at least one remedial course at some point (Crisp and Delgado 2014; Radford and Horn 2012).

System-level interventions alter community colleges' incentive structures, the financial structures that govern them, or the landscape in which they operate. Statewide policies that provide free or reduced tuition, such as "promise programs" (e.g., Tennessee and Oregon) reorient the nature of community colleges in the higher education system hierarchy (Miller-Adams 2015). Performance-based funding has been used by states to encourage community colleges to orient programs and resources toward specified goals and metrics, oftentimes closely aligned with student outcomes (Dougherty et al. 2016; Hillman et al. 2014). State articulation policies hold the promise of smoothing transfer from community colleges into four-year institutions.

24.4 Evaluating Community College Reforms

Until very recently, social scientists sought to understand the community college through naturalistic observation rather than measuring intervention impacts. However, such approaches are limited in their capacity to provide rigorous estimates of causal effects (Morgan and Winship 2014). When participation in an intervention is voluntary, those who choose to participate tend to differ in measureable and unmeasurable ways from non-participants. As a result, it is difficult to disentangle the intervention's independent impacts from selection bias introduced through these baseline differences. Random assignment to treatment ensures that differences between treated and untreated individuals arise only from chance and are unlikely to be considerable given large enough samples (Rubin 1974). For this reason, randomized experiments permit unbiased, internally valid, and truly *causal* estimates of treatment effects.

But as with all methods, randomized control trials have limitations. Some questions cannot be answered by experimental evaluations, for reasons of feasibility and ethics (Heckman 2005; Lareau 2008). Additionally, unforeseen issues in program implementation and participant behavior after randomization can have substantial impacts on treatment effects (Lareau 2008; Heckman and Smith 1995). Finally, experiments tell us little about *why* causes produce their effects, though additional non-causal evidence on mechanisms can be gathered using mixed-methods approaches (Grissmer et al. 2009; Harris and Goldrick-Rab 2012). They also tell us little about how the context in which an intervention occurred may have impacted its outcomes.

Despite limitations, over the past 15 years, experimental evaluations have increasingly been used to understand the impacts of community college reforms. To a great extent, their application has been in response to efforts on the part of the U.S. Department of Education's Institute of Educational Sciences attention to causal research and the corresponding shift in federal research dollars. At the same time, new institution-level data on student outcomes became readily available, drawing public attention to the considerable gaps in college completion rates between community college students and their peers at other higher education institutions (Bailey et al. 2015). As a result, the "College Completion Agenda" began to coalesce in the early years of the new decade, and philanthropic foundations added their millions of private money to the public money already earmarked for experimental evaluation research.

In this chapter, we catalogue randomized control trials in community college settings. Eligible studies were identified by (1) searching Google Scholar, the Web of Science, EconLit, Social Sciences Full Text, Education Full Text, and the American Economic Association's RCT Registry with combinations of keywords (experiment, randomized control trial, community college, and two-year college); (2) scouring websites of evaluation organizations such as MDRC and Mathematica; (3) searching programs of research conferences such as SREE, APPAM, and AEA; and (4) making inquiries among scholars knowledgeable in the field. Studies that met the following criteria were included:

- Subjects were assigned to intervention or control condition using random assignment;
- Subjects were entering or presently enrolled at community colleges, either exclusively or as a major sub-population; and
- Interventions were aimed at improving academic outcomes such as retention, credit accumulation, academic performance, and degree completion.

Given these criteria, we excluded observational studies, including those employing rigorous quasi-experimental designs, except to provide context for experimental interventions. Interventions where subjects could not be randomized, such as those altering institutional or policy frameworks, were excluded. Also excluded were interventions intending to impact whether or where individuals choose to enroll in college. Given the fiscal constraints under which community colleges operate, knowing the cost of an intervention is crucial for evaluating its realistic potential to be adopted at scale (Belfield et al. 2014; Belfield and Jenkins 2014; Schneider and McDonald 2007a, b). Therefore, wherever possible, a discussion of costs is included alongside the assessment of impacts. However, to a large extent this information is notably *missing* from extant research (Belfield 2015).

In total, we identified 30 studies of community college interventions that met the selection criteria. In addition, we included seven in progress studies to give a sense of the future of this research. Next, the studies are discussed according to their level of intervention.

24.5 Student-Level Interventions

Student-level interventions work principally to augment the resources or change the behavior of individual community college students, while leaving the prevailing institutional environment unchanged. As such, they seek to improve the *capacity* of individuals to navigate an environment which is taken as given. Individual-level interventions are often, but need not necessarily be, prefaced on an assumption that individual deficits are at the root of outcomes deemed unacceptable. We identified 14 such interventions.

24.5.1 Financial Aid

The primary policy effort to raise community college completion rates is financial aid, and nationwide governments spend about $57 billion on grant aid and another $96 billion on loans (College Board 2015). But establishing the causal impact of financial aid on college persistence and completion is not straightforward. Since the same trait—financial need—which renders a student eligible for financial aid also tends to disrupt col-

lege progress, naïve estimations of aid effects tend to be biased. Most research leverages "natural experiments" such as aid cutoffs, program terminations, and tuition reductions in order to identify causal effects (Alon 2011; Bettinger 2004, 2015; Castleman and Long 2013; Denning 2014; Dynarski 2003; Kane 2003; Singell 2004; Van der Klaauw 2002). Such studies have tended to find that an increase in aid of $1000 increases persistence by 2–4 percentage points, and degree completion by between 1.5 and 5 percentage points (for reviews see Bettinger (2012), Deming and Dynarski (2010), Dynarski and Scott-Clayton (2013), and Goldrick-Rab et al. (2009)).

To date there have been seven randomized experiments examining financial aid in community college contexts. Two are evaluations of privately funded, need-based scholarships affecting both four-year and two-year students: Angrist and associates' (2015) evaluation of the Buffett Scholarship, and Goldrick-Rab and associates' investigation of the Wisconsin Scholars Grant (WSG) (N = 2641 and N = 12,722 respectively). Both scholarships targeted low- to moderate-income students, had high school GPA eligibility requirements, and were restricted to residents of a particular state (Nebraska and Wisconsin, respectively) who attended in-state public colleges. The Buffett Scholarship is designed to fully cover tuition and fees; two-year recipients were awarded as much as $5300 per year for up to 5 years. In contrast, the WSG is designed to reduce rather than eliminate tuition expenses; the yearly award was $1800 for two-year students, for up to 5 years. Another crucial difference is the timing of scholarship. The Buffett Scholarship is awarded prior to enrollment, and thus can impact individuals' choice of college, whereas the WSG is awarded towards the end of the recipient's first semester.

Both studies found measurable positive impacts for the full population of recipients, but null or negative results for initial two-year enrollers. Anderson and Goldrick-Rab (2016) estimate that the WSG increased one-year retention by 3.7 percentage points at University of Wisconsin branch campuses and *decreased* it by 1.5 percentage points at Wisconsin Technical

Colleges, but neither result was statistically significant and there were no impacts on other indicators of academic progress. The authors point out that the WSG covered just 28% of the students' unmet financial need at two-year colleges, while it covered 39% at the four-year colleges and universities (and had sizable impacts on degree completion—see Goldrick-Rab et al. 2016). However, offering two-year students the grant did decrease their work hours, and particularly the odds of working the third-shift (Broton et al. 2016). Angrist et al. estimate a statistically non-significant 1.9 percentage point lower one-year retention rate for scholarship recipients who initially enrolled at community colleges. Importantly, Buffet scholarship recipients were 7 percentage points less likely to attend community colleges in the first place than control students, suggesting that the additional aid increased four-year attendance among those who would otherwise have opted for a community college to save money.[1]

In 2004–2005, as part of its larger "Opening Doors" demonstration,[2] MDRC evaluated a "performance-based scholarship"[3] (PBS) for low-income, mostly female parents at two community colleges in the New Orleans area (N = 1019). The scholarship provided $1000 per semester for up to two semesters, awarded incrementally: $250 upon enrollment (at least 6 credits), $250 at midterm contingent on remaining

enrolled at least half-time and earning a "C" average, and the rest at the end of the semester contingent on GPA. At the end of the program year, treated students had earned 2.4 more credits, and were 12 percentage points more likely to be retained into their second year. And one year later, the credit advantage had grown to 3.5 credits[4] (Barrow et al. 2014; Barrow and Rouse 2013; Brock and Ritchburg-Hayes 2006; Ritchburg-Hayes et al. 2009). But Hurricane Katrina brought an end to the experiment. While the program's evaluation points toward potentially promising effects, it also suggested that intervention's costs extended beyond the financial outlay for student scholarships. Program implementation required additional time on the part of counselors who monitored students' enrollment and grades and were available to offer advice and referrals to additional services. The program also required additional personnel time to administer the aid program. That said, the evaluation falls short of identifying the extent of additional time spent by counselors and administrators, and did not estimate the costs associated with implementing the reform.

Encouraged by these results, in 2008 MDRC launched a larger PBS demonstration at community colleges in Ohio, New York City, Arizona, and Florida[5] (N = 2285; N = 1502; N = 1028; N = 1075). The scholarships all targeted low-income populations and made continued receipt of aid contingent upon stipulated enrollment intensity and performance benchmarks (usually part-time enrollment and earning at least a "C"). The scholarships varied in terms of generosity and additional behavioral requirements for parts of the aid. In these RCTs, the experimental group experienced short-term gains of smaller size than in the Louisiana experiment. In only two were

---

[1] Applicants to the Buffett Scholarship needed to specify a "target" college in their initial application, but students were not bound to attend these colleges.

[2] Opening Doors was a multi-site experimental demonstration examining the impact of different sorts of interventions designed to improve college retention and completion among lower-income students. These various interventions included learning communities, college skills courses, intensive counseling, and performance-based scholarships.

[3] This name is something of a misnomer. Most scholarships and grants, need-based or otherwise, have performance and enrollment requirements for continued receipt. Indeed, the specific performance requirements of the PBSs were substantially more lenient than those of the WSG or Buffet scholarship. What distinguishes the PBSs is the incremental disbursal of grants and the tying of these disbursals to the performance of specific behaviors, such as attending tutoring sessions.

[4] We are summarizing results for the first two study cohorts (out of four) only, because four semesters of data are available for these cohorts. Program-semester effects for cohorts 3 and 4 are similar, though of smaller magnitude.

[5] A performance-based scholarship RCT was carried out at the University of New Mexico, and another targeted low-income high school seniors in California (Cash for College), but these results fall outside the purvey of this review.

there impacts on retention: The Arizona scholarship improved one-year retention by between 2 and 5 percentage points, and at one of the New York sites the treatment group was retained at a 9 percentage point higher rate. The scholarships consistently improved credit accumulation over the first year by between 0.9 and 1.7 credits, and modestly improved academic performance, but these effects shrank to insignificance after the end of the scholarship. Completion effects were for the most part not yet available, but in Ohio the treatment group was 3.3 percentage points more likely to have earned an associate degree or certificate at the end of 2 years.

Collectively the five PBS experiments suggest that additional need-based aid can modestly boost retention and credit accumulation, but seems to be more effective when paired with support services such as tutoring and advisement. In all experiments that incorporated such services (Louisiana, Arizona, and Florida) recipients substantially outpaced the control group in meeting program-specified goals. However, in nearly all cases effects were observable only as long as scholarships were still operative (for results of the Arizona RCT, see Patel and Valenzuela 2013; for Florida, Sommo et al. 2014; for New York, Ritchburg-Hayes et al. 2011 and Patel and Rudd 2012; for Ohio, Cha and Patel 2010 and Mayer et al. 2015; for a summary of the demonstration, see Patel et al. 2013). What is unclear, however, is at what cost these gains were achieved. All of the programs involved both financial investments in scholarship payments to students as well as personnel time, particularly at community colleges, to implement. This makes the cost effectiveness of scholarship programs unclear, as well as what might be required of community colleges to implement such programs.

There are at least two ongoing experiments involving either financial aid itself or its method of disbursement. In 2014, the Wisconsin HOPE Lab launched an RCT investigating the impact of need-based scholarships on low-income students who indicate interest in STEM fields. And MDRC is testing a program entitled "Aid Like a Paycheck" that disburses financial aid in small amounts regularly throughout the semester, based on the notion that doing so will temper the "feast or famine" dynamic occurring when aid is distributed in one lump sum. A pilot program was conducted at three community colleges in 2010 (Ware et al. 2013), and a large-scale randomized control trial is presently underway.

24.5.2 Free Computers

Colleges—and even community colleges—tend to assume that their students have access to the Internet. However, in 2010 only 66% of community college students with household incomes below $20,000 per year had home computers with Internet access (Fairlie and Grunberg 2014). In 2006, a randomized control trial at a community college in northern California tested the impact of providing students with free computers. Researchers recruited 286 students for the experiment, and half were given refurbished computers. Treated students were slightly more likely to take courses which would transfer to a state four-year college: Transfer-eligible courses made up 66% of all courses taken by treated students and 61% of courses taken by untreated students. And in the first 2 years, treated students were slightly more likely to take courses for a letter grade. But no impacts were found on passing courses, earning degrees or certificates, or transferring to a four-year college (Fairlie and Grunberg 2014; Fairlie and London 2012).

24.5.3 Financial Aid Information

The financial aid system is complex and requires students to make weighty decisions, and many community college students negotiate it alone. Not surprisingly, this can lead to costly errors. For instance, students who receive Pell grants may not know that they need to reapply for them annually. Nationally, 10% of Pell-eligible students fail to re-apply for financial aid in their second year of college, and the resulting loss of aid is strongly predictive of dropping out (Bird and Castleman 2014).

There are two experiments that identify the impacts of providing students with financial aid information. Castleman and Page (2015) conducted a randomized control trial among low-income first-year college students in the Boston area in which the treatment group was sent text-message reminders to re-file the FAFSA. Among community college students, receipt of text reminders improved retention into the fall and spring semesters of sophomore year by 12 and 14 percentage points, respectively. Impacts were larger among students with lower high school GPAs. Barr et al. (2016) carried out an experiment with new student loan applicants at the Community College of Baltimore in which treated students were sent, over the course of a month, a series of texts with student loan facts. The texts told students that they could borrow less (and sometimes more) than the amount offered by their institution, that monthly repayments depend on the amount borrowed and the repayment plan, and that there are lifetime limits on borrowing. Students receiving the texts borrowed 9% less in Stafford loans and 12% less in unsubsidized Stafford loans, and larger declines in borrowing were witnessed among new enrollees, Blacks, low-income students, and students with lower GPAs.

Turner (2015) is presently conducting an experiment with community college students in three states which randomizes the default option presented to loan applicants. For some, the default option will be to take out a loan, and students will have to take action to opt out, while for the others the opposite will be true. Additionally, the experiment will randomly assign some to be presented with a particular loan amount as a default while others will have to choose a loan amount, and some applicants will be prompted to complete a worksheet helping them take stock of their resources and expenses before making a decision while others will not.

24.5.4 College Skills Classes

College skills classes are one of many interventions that community colleges provide premised on the notion that many students do not have the requisite cultural capital to successfully negotiate higher education. They aim to impact skills in study habits, time management, organization, self-presentation, goal-setting, and negotiating the educational bureaucracy. In this manner, they are analogous to remedial courses, but are lower-stakes as they are usually pass/fail and grant only a credit at most.

College skills courses offered to or required of first-semester freshmen are common, but there is little rigorous research on their effectiveness and most studies are descriptive in nature (Derby and Smith 2004; O'Gara et al. 2009; Zeidenberg et al. 2007). MDRC evaluated the impacts of two college skills course programs for students on academic probation at a community college in the Los Angeles area. In both programs, the treatment consisted of a two-semester college skills course taught by a college counselor, a "Success Center" that provided tutoring services, and a modest voucher to cover the cost of textbooks. In the first program, the skills course was presented to those randomized into treatment as optional; they were merely encouraged to enroll, and participation in tutoring was not enforced. As a result, only half of the treatment group took the first-semester course, very few took the second-semester course, tutoring services were rarely utilized, and treatment effects were nonexistent. In the second iteration, students were told (falsely) that they were *required* to take the first-semester skills course and were strongly encouraged to take the second-semester course, and attendance at tutoring sessions was enforced by instructors. Take-up was much better in this iteration, and the treatment group earned 2.7 additional credits on average over the two semesters of the program and was 7 percentage points more likely to pass all of their classes. At the end of the program year, the experimental group was 10 percentage points less likely to be on academic probation, though this impact did not persist after one additional semester (Scrivener et al. 2009; Weiss et al. 2011). While the programs' evaluations suggest that skills course programs might be a promising strategy, the interventions involve additional resources on the part of community colleges (e.g., services and vouchers). However, existing evaluations do not describe the resources required for implementation, nor the programs' costs.

24.5.5 Social-Psychological Interventions

Social psychologists have recently explored the impacts of teaching individuals that intelligence is not fixed but rather can be augmented through training and effort. Interventions designed to instill a "growth mindset" informed by this incremental theory of intelligence have been found to effectively boost the academic performance of four-year college students and other groups (Blackwell et al. 2007). Building off this work, Paunesku, Yeager, and colleagues developed a 30-min intervention (a webinar and reinforcement activity) that teaches viewers that intellectual skills are learned rather than fixed, and tested it in a community college context. In one field experiment involving mostly Latino students at a Los Angeles-area community college, treated students earned overall GPAs which were 0.18 grade points higher in the following semester. In a second experiment the intervention was tested among students in remedial math courses. In this case, the treated group dropped out of their math class at less than half the rate of the control group (9% vs 20%) (Yeager and Dweck 2012; Yeager et al. 2013).

Other researchers have investigated ways to impact students' motivation and therefore performance in academic contexts. Harackiewicz and colleagues have investigated the impacts of both "utility" interventions and "values" interventions. In the former, students are provided information about the labor market value of science and math skills; in the latter, students complete a brief in-class writing assignment in which they select and explore values (such as spiritual or religious values, career, or belonging to a group) that are important to them. Such interventions have been found to improve outcomes among both high school and university students (Harackiewicz et al. 2014; Harackiewicz et al. 2015). The researchers are currently working

with the Wisconsin HOPE Lab to assess the impacts of similar interventions at six two-year colleges in Wisconsin.

24.5.6 Incentivizing Academic Momentum

The academic momentum perspective suggests that the speed at which a student makes progress towards a degree—through accumulating credits or clearing remedial requirements—has an independent causal impact on their likelihood of completion (Adelman 1999; Attewell et al. 2012; Attewell and Monaghan 2016). This may be because rapid completion minimizes cumulative exposure to the risk of an event that could derail schooling, or because students who spend more time involved in schoolwork will be more academically integrated into the institution. Attewell conducted a pair of randomized control trials at community colleges in the City University of New York to test two applications of this theory. In the first, students who were attending college part-time (fewer than 12 credits) in the fall semester were incentivized to "bump up" to 12 or more credits in the spring. In the second, students who had elected not to sign up for summer courses after their first year in college were incentivized to do so. In both cases, the incentive was a generous $1000. In the experiment involving increased credit load, the treatment group was more likely to be retained into the second year, and at the end of the second year had accumulated six additional credits on average. In the summer coursework experiment, treated students were 8 percentage points more likely to still be enrolled two semesters after treatment, and had accumulated an additional three credits by the end of their second year of college (Attewell and Douglas 2016).

24.6   School-Level Interventions

In contrast to the interventions outlined above, school-level interventions augment or alter the institutional environment that individuals must navigate in order to attain their goals. They may by extension augment students' stock of knowledge or capacities, and they do not necessarily presume that individual deficits do *not* contribute to generating unacceptable outcomes. But they do presuppose that the institutional environment is changeable, and that the status quo may contain unnecessary barriers to goal-attainment. We identified 15 such interventions.

24.6.1 "Enhanced" Student Services

As noted earlier, counseling centers have been singled out for critique by scholars of late. Because of the complexity of community colleges as institutions and students' lack of assistance from knowledgeable family members, effective counseling emerges as utterly crucial to providing the information and guidance necessary for student success (Allen et al. 2013). Effective counseling could also help students feel more connected to the institution by establishing a relationship with at least one trustworthy staff member. But this is simply not present at most community colleges, where counseling services are student-initiated and at which counselors are responsible for a large number of students and provided little training or time to serve them.

One RCT conducted by MDRC at two Ohio community colleges investigated the effect of "enhanced" counseling services. In this evaluation, treatment group students were assigned to a specific counselor, with whom they were expected to meet regularly, and this counselor was assigned a reduced caseload (160:1 rather than the usual 1000:1). Treated students were also assigned a designated contact person in the financial aid office and were given a $150 stipend per semester conditional on meeting with counselors. During the two semesters the program was active, impacts were substantial. Treated students' fall-to-spring retention was 7 percentage points higher than the control group, and treated students accumulated a half credit extra over the course of the year. In surveys, the program group also was more likely to describe their college

experience as "good" or "excellent," report that they had a campus staff member on whom they relied for support, and receive financial aid in the spring semester. After the program year these gains did not persist, but many students continued to seek out the counselor formerly assigned to them (Scrivener and Au 2007; Scrivener and Pi 2007; Scrivener and Weiss 2009).

While the programs' impacts were substantial, replicating this program elsewhere is hampered somewhat by the absence of information on the resources community colleges dedicated to its implementation. It is important to note that these programs required community colleges to potentially dedicate additional personnel hours to carry out the intervention, particularly counselors with whom students met more frequently. However, the study does not describe in detail how community colleges allocated the personnel hours required—either by reallocating or expanding existing counselor time or by adding additional personnel.

24.6.2 Mentoring

MRDC carried out an evaluation of a "light-touch" mentoring program for students taking developmental and early college-level math courses at a community college in McAllen, Texas. In the program, students' math sections were randomly assigned to treatment and control categories. Treated sections were assigned a non-faculty college employee who acted as a mentor for the students in the course and informed them about additional support services, such as the tutoring center. The program succeeded in increasing students' utilization of on-campus services such as the tutoring center, and treated students were more likely to report feeling that they had someone on campus to whom they could turn to for help. However, there were no statistically significant differences in pass rates, GPA, or final exam score. Among part-time students, however, the treatment group was more likely to pass their math course and earned slightly higher scores on the final (Visher et al. 2010).

24.6.3 Testing and Remediation

As previously discussed, remediation is the near-universal institutional compromise strategy community colleges have adopted to resolve the dilemma of being open-door institutions of advanced education. Analogous to the situation with financial aid, the effect of taking a remedial course must be separated empirically from the effects of the academic weaknesses that landed students in the remedial course (Levin and Calcagno 2008). But the matter is even more complicated because though *taking* a remedial course could improve one's skills and odds of completion, being *assigned* to remediation has considerable (likely negative) consequences in its own right. The net impact of a school's testing and remediation policy is the balance of these two opposing effects—something that is typically overlooked in the research literature. In part because of this methodological confusion, scholars have failed to reach consensus on remediation's impacts (Bailey 2009; Melguizo et al. 2011). Observational studies that compare those who take remedial courses and those who do not tend to find only small differences in completion, and their authors have interpreted this as demonstrating that remedial courses are effective (Adelman 1998, 1999; Attewell et al. 2006; Bahr 2008; Fike and Fike 2008). But studies employing more sophisticated quasi-experimental designs have found impacts to be neutral-to-negative (Boatman and Long 2010; Calcagno and Long 2008; Martorell and McFarlin 2011; Scott-Clayton and Rodriguez 2012; for a counter-example, see Bettinger and Long 2009). A recent meta-analysis of this work finds that being placed into remediation has a small, but statistically significant, negative impact on credit accumulation, ever passing the course for which remediation was needed, and degree attainment (Valentine et al. 2016).

There are four randomized control trials that deal with remediation at community colleges in one form or another. Three RCTs investigated the effects of taking remedial courses versus entering directly into college-level work. An early RCT conducted in the late 1960s randomly placed students identified as needing remediation in English either directly into a college-level class or into a remedial course (Sharon 1972). The students assigned to remedial courses were retained at rates similar to control group students, and passed college-level English at similar rates. However, they tended to earn higher grades in this course, suggesting some positive impact of remediation on academic skills. Forty years later, Moss and Yeaton (2013) conducted an experiment in which students immediately below the remedial cutoff on a math placement test were randomly placed into either remedial courses or college-level courses. The authors do not present results for retention or accumulation of college-level credits, but find a positive impact of taking remedial courses on grades in college-level math. Their RCT sample was very small (N = 63), but the authors also conducted supplemental analyses using regression-discontinuity designs and found similar effects. Finally, Logue and others at the City University of New York randomly assigned students identified as requiring remediation into either remedial algebra, remedial algebra with additional tutoring, or college-level statistics with tutoring (Logue et al. 2016). Early results show no difference between the two groups taking developmental algebra, but the group assigned to take statistics passed their assigned course at far higher rates, accumulated more credits in both the program and post-program semesters, and were retained at similar rates. The researchers attribute the gain in credits among the "mainstreamed" group to three factors: They passed their assigned course at higher rates, this course counted for college credit, and it served as a prerequisite for other courses, enabling students to pursue their majors more freely. The costs—to students and institutions—of these remedial course interventions are not well understood. The evaluations did not incorporate direct measures of costs in their analysis.

Another experiment investigated the impacts of alternative methods of remedial placement (Evans and Henry 2015). This project contains two separate experimental groups, both of which take an alternative test called the ALEKS, which provides self-paced personalized learning modules for those who fail the test and allows them to retake it. One of the treatment groups, "ALEKS-2," could only retake the test once, and only after completing all assigned modules. The other, "ALEKS-5," could retake the test up to four times but were not required to complete learning modules. Control students took the standard placement test (the COMPASS, in this case). Only first-semester results are at this point available, but both treatment groups were less likely to be placed into remediation. In addition, the ALEKS-2 group was more likely than the control group to *take* college-level math in their first semester, and the ALEKS-5 group was more likely to *pass* it.

Two more remediation interventions will be evaluated in the near future. In the first study, being conducted by MDRC, the Community College Research Center (CCRC) and CUNY, students placed into remediation will be randomly assigned to complete a one-semester intensive developmental immersion program (entitled CUNYStart) prior to official matriculation. The second, MDRC's "Developmental Education Acceleration Project," evaluates two innovative formats for administering developmental education. The first treatment group will be assigned to developmental courses that are personalized, module-based, and which permit them to enter and exit at their own pace. The second treatment group will take an accelerated program which squeezes two remedial courses into one single semester.

24.6.4 Summer Bridge Courses

"Summer bridge" programs—courses or programs that take place during the summer prior to freshmen year—are widespread in higher education. These programs vary substantially in their content and are nearly always voluntary. At community colleges, bridge courses are oriented nearly exclusively to teaching basic skills to incoming students who scored low enough on placement exams to require remediation, offering such students an opportunity to complete at least some required remedial coursework prior to the first semester. Oftentimes students are not

charged to take these courses. Observational research indicates that these programs effectively boost persistence and even six-year attainment (Douglas and Attewell 2014).

MDRC, in conjunction with the National Center for Postsecondary Research (NCPR), carried out an experimental evaluation of summer bridge programs at eight colleges in Texas, including six community colleges (Barnett et al. 2012; Wathington et al. 2011). Early impacts were encouraging: Treated students were more likely to take and to pass college-level math and English courses in their first year than control-group students, suggesting that the bridge program successfully enabled some students to quickly clear remedial requirements. But there was no impact on one-year retention, and the advantages in college-level course completion and credit accumulation narrowed to statistical insignificance by the fourth semester. Researchers at CUNY carried out another experimental evaluation of summer bridge programs. In this intervention, students who missed the enrollment deadline for bridge courses were recruited into an experimental evaluation, and those selected for treatment were offered $1000 to enroll in sections of these courses reserved for the experiment. Researchers estimated a non-significant *negative* 5 percentage point effect of taking bridge courses on one-year retention, and a non-significant negative effect on credit accumulation (Attewell and Douglas 2016).

24.6.5 Learning Communities

Learning communities are geared towards providing community college students the opportunity to build social connections to other students and to faculty that they typically do not form because of their loose connection to the college. They proceed on the notion that "social and academic integration" into the social world of the college is a key mechanism for retaining students. Social bonds engender a feeling of belonging and an obligation to make good on implicit promises to return and complete degrees. They additionally provide students with information networks and sources of emotional support.

Learning communities seek to cultivate student success through three interconnected mechanisms (Tinto 1997). First, a group of students take multiple courses together, providing opportunities for students to form social bonds and to support each other across courses (Karp 2011). Second, the courses are *linked* in terms of content, allowing for deeper engagement with material. Third, faculty who teach the linked courses collaborate and share information about student progress and engagement. Additionally, many learning communities feature reduced class sizes, block-scheduling, and auxiliary services such as advising and tutoring. Frequently, one of the linked courses is a first-year college skills seminar. Observational research on learning communities almost uniformly finds positive impacts on outcomes such as student engagement, interaction with faculty, relationships with peers, perceptions of institutions, academic performance, and retention (Minkler 2002; Raftery 2005; Tinto et al. 1994).

There have been seven experimental evaluations of learning communities, all by MDRC. In 2003 MDRC evaluated an existing learning community for entering students at Kingsborough Community College in New York City. The treatment group was split into learning communities of roughly 25 students who took three courses together in their first semester: introductory English (mostly remedial), a course in their major, and a college skills course. There were substantial support services: Treated students were assigned an academic advisor (who was granted a smaller caseload), had reduced class sizes, were provided enhanced and often in-class tutoring, and were granted a $150 book voucher for the semester. These supports, and the learning community itself, only lasted a single semester. The program had encouraging early impacts on retention and completion of remedial courses, as well as on non-cognitive outcomes such as self-reported academic engagement and reported feelings of belonging at the school. Positive impacts faded out after four semesters (Bloom and

Sommo 2005; Scrivener et al. 2008; Weiss et al. 2014, 2015).

Subsequently, in conjunction with the NCPR, MDRC carried out experimental evaluations of learning communities at six separate community colleges beginning in fall 2007. These evaluations involved, collectively, more than 6500 students, and the programs evaluated varied from the earlier study in two important respects. First, they for the most part lacked any supplementary services, thus presenting purer tests of learning community impacts. Second, whereas the earlier project evaluated an established learning community at scale, the later evaluations involved either newly-created learning community programs or existing programs which were rapidly scaled up, incorporating faculty with little experience with learning communities and no history of collaborating on linked courses. As was the case previously, all were one-semester interventions. The resources required in order to implement learning communities in community colleges, and their corresponding costs, associated with implementing these learning communities are essentially unknown.

"No frills" learning communities at Merced College in California, Hillsborough Community College in Florida, and the Community College of Baltimore had negligible results. At Merced, the treated group was about a third of a course ahead of the control group in the completion of remedial sequences, and at Hillsborough the treatment group was 5 percentage points more likely to be retained into the second semester. No further impacts were detected on academic performance or credit accumulation, and no effects lasted beyond the first post-program semester (Weiss et al. 2010; Weissman et al. 2012). Learning communities at Houston Community College and Queensborough Community College in New York were slightly more elaborate. The Houston program linked remedial math to a student success course, and tutoring and counseling was inconsistently provided. Treated students completed their first remedial math course at a rate 14 percentage points higher during the program semester, and this advantage persisted for two semesters after the program (Weissman et al.

2011). The Queensborough learning community was supported with a full-time coordinator and a college advisor assigned solely to treatment group students. The treatment group was substantially more likely to pass the first developmental math course in their sequence during the program semester and the second math course in the first post-program semester, and there were modest effects on credit accumulation (Weissman et al. 2011). Finally, researchers returned to Kingsborough Community College to evaluate learning communities aimed at students pursuing particular occupational majors. The program was beset by implementation and recruitment problems, and the school was forced to alter the program repeatedly throughout the evaluation. Not surprisingly, no effects were found on outcomes of interest (Visher and Torres 2011).

24.7 A Comprehensive Support Intervention: CUNY ASAP

In 2007, with support from the City's Center for Economic Opportunity, the City University of New York launched what is likely the single most ambitious program to boost degree completion in a community college setting. The Accelerated Study in Associate Programs (ASAP) initiative does not rely on a single intervention such as financial aid or smaller class sizes. Instead, it builds on prior research, such as the 2003 learning community evaluation at Kingsborough, which suggested that multifaceted programs that address multiple student needs simultaneously tend to have more robust impacts.

ASAP draws on many of the strategies involved in the interventions we have already described and adds a few more. First, there is financial support: Tuition and fees not met through other grants are waived, and students are provided with subway passes and can rent textbooks free of charge. Building on the academic momentum perspective, participating students are required to enroll full-time (at least 12 credits), though they have the alternative of enrolling at slightly less than full-time and using winter and summer intercessions to meet credit require-

ments. There are mandatory support services: Students are assigned an advisor (who has a reduced case-load) and required to meet with them at least twice per month, and they are also required to meet once per semester with a career services and employment counselor (dedicated to ASAP). Students are required to attend tutoring if they are in remedial courses, on academic probation, or are re-taking a course they have previously failed. In each semester ASAP students are required to take a non-credit seminar focused on building and developing college skills. Learning communities are also involved in students' first year, though precisely how these are conducted varies across CUNY campuses. Students are strongly encouraged to take required remedial courses as early as possible, to attend tutoring for courses in which they are struggling, and to make use of winter and summer intercessions to accumulate credits more rapidly. ASAP courses also tend to be somewhat smaller than average courses at CUNY community colleges.

But perhaps most important, in contrast to most interventions reviewed thus far, ASAP is not limited to a single semester or year. Instead, conditional on meeting certain requirements—such as remaining enrolled full-time—students can participate in and access the benefits of ASAP for three full years. Most interventions reviewed above were at least modestly successful during program semesters, but effects faded out rapidly thereafter. One reaction to this is to conclude that the interventions "don't work" because they did not produce "lasting gains." ASAP planners drew the opposite conclusion: In order to be successful, an intervention strategy needs to be not only comprehensive but sustained.

In its first few years, ASAP was open only to "college-ready" students—that is, students with no remedial requirements. Internal evaluations, utilizing propensity-score matching methods, suggested that participation in ASAP was associated with a 28.4 percentage point gain in three-year degree completion and a half-semester's difference in credits accumulated after 3 years (Linderman and Kolenovic 2012). Encouraged by these findings, CUNY contracted with MDRC to carry out a randomized assignment evaluation.

This evaluation began in the spring semester of 2010, and involved just under 900 students at three CUNY community colleges. Instead of limiting eligibility to college-ready students, participation was limited to low-income entering students who demonstrated some, though not deep, remedial need (1 or 2 required courses).

The evaluation found that ASAP generated large early impacts. By the end of the first year, the treatment group was 25 percentage points more likely to have completed all required remedial courses, and had earned 3 more college-level credits on average (Scrivener et al. 2012). These impacts grew, rather than attenuating, over time. After 3 years, treated students had accumulated 7.7 more credits on average than the control group. And whereas only 21.8% of the control group had completed a degree, 40.1% of the treatment group had done so—an 83% gain. Treated students were also 9.4 percentage points more likely to have transferred to a four-year college within 3 years (Scrivener et al. 2015). The ASAP evaluation stands out as one of the few that systematically evaluated program costs, providing some guidance to community colleges seeking to replicate the program. That said, the accompanying cost study shows that ASAP's gains did not come cheaply. The direct costs were estimated to be over $14,000 per student over 3 years. ASAP students also took more classes than control students, and incorporating these costs could raise the per-student total to between $16,000 and $18,500. However, given the large increase in completion, researchers estimated that *per degree*, ASAP spent $13,000 less than was spent on the control group (Scrivener et al. 2015). Despite information on program costs and effects, given the absence of other similar studies it is impossible to evaluate this evidence relative to other interventions, leaving a lingering question—is ASAP a cost-effective alternative relative to other possible interventions?

Efforts to evaluate comprehensive intervention models like ASAP are continuing. MDRC is currently conducting a replication of ASAP at three community colleges in Ohio; the evaluation cohort enrolled in fall 2015 and will be tracked for 3 years. And at Tarrant County College in Fort Worth, Texas, researchers are carrying out an experimental evaluation of a program called Stay the Course. Operated in partnership with a local non-profit, Stay the Course is designed to address non-academic obstacles faced by low-income community college students through provision of comprehensive case management and emergency financial assistance (Evans et al. 2014).

24.8   Discussion and Conclusion

As the vast majority of new jobs require postsecondary training (Carnevale et al. 2013), low rates of degree completion increasingly disadvantage lower-SES and minority youth. Community colleges are positioned to play a central role in expanding educational attainment and narrowing educational disparities. But in order to do so, they must pivot institutionally from guaranteeing access to facilitating degree completion—without compromising on the former. But making community colleges deliver on promises of educational opportunity will require not timid reforms or tinkering, but bold innovation and substantial resources.

Community colleges arose in the era of postwar educational optimism with an explicit set of goals—expanding access to college, providing a broad and comprehensive set of programs, and serving local communities—which they have emphatically achieved. Today, politicians, scholars, and foundations are demanding that community colleges do better in terms of degree completion. The simplest method for community colleges to increase degree completion is to restrict access to those who are "college-ready." Or community colleges could reduce institutional complexity by eliminating scores of occupational programs that serve millions and are valued by employers. However, few policymakers wish to see community colleges abandoning *either* their democratic mission *or* the provision of vocational certifications at low cost. Instead, in an era of withering public support, community colleges are being ordered to do more with less (Jenkins and Belfield 2014).

The new focus on completion has brought unprecedented scholarly attention—supported by unprecedented research funding—to community colleges, leading to a number of promising experimentally-evaluated interventions. Need-based financial aid, particularly when accompanied with supports, has increased retention and credit accumulation. Learning communities do not seem to generate large gains on their own, but have short-run impacts on retention and movement through remedial sequences when coupled with counseling and other supports. "Enhanced" counseling appears to benefit students as long as it remains available. And there is evidence that limiting exposure to remediation and can speed progress toward degrees.

Other interventions should be evaluated experimentally. For example, scholars have proposed developing "guided pathways," clear sequences of courses leading directly to credentials and/or transfer to a four-year college. Others suggest providing housing or food support—campus food pantries or a collegiate equivalent of free and reduced lunch—will provide low-income students greater security and improve educational outcomes (Broton et al. 2014; Goldrick-Rab et al. 2015). Another promising intervention is emergency financial assistance for students facing unexpected crises that endanger their persistence (Dachelet and Goldrick-Rab 2015; Geckler et al. 2008). Single-stop centers, which provide information about and access to a range of benefits and services in a single location, are being established on campuses across the country, and could be evaluated using randomized encouragement (Goldrick-Rab et al. 2014).

The available evidence strongly suggests two tentative conclusions. First, simple interventions do not appear to work as well as multifaceted programs. Complex interventions like ASAP can lead researchers to wonder *which* interventions are most impactful. But this assumes components to have independent, additive effects, when they may interact with and reinforce each other. Second, that many programs impacts are positive while in operation but fade away afterwards suggests that effective interventions must be prolonged. Underlying problems such as resource scarcity or academic weaknesses or slight college knowledge do not vanish when a program closes up shop, but reassert themselves vigorously. Policymakers should not expect short-term programs to have anything other than short-term impacts.

As community colleges operate with limited and unpredictable resources, policymakers and educational leaders considering reforms must attend to the resources required for implementation (Belfield et al. 2014; Belfield and Jenkins 2014). However, as we noted, existing evaluations largely ignore such matters (Belfield 2015). Community college leaders need to know where to invest scarce dollars and how programmatic decisions influence resource requirements. State-level policymakers are also are at a disadvantage. There are few benchmarks for determining at what level community colleges should be funded (Chancellor's Office of the California Community Colleges 2003), and none are explicitly tied to performance (Kahlenberg 2015). Future evaluations should examine interventions' relative cost effectiveness and clearly delineate resources entailed for implementation, or community colleges will risk squandering scarce resources or selecting interventions for which they have insufficient capacity to implement. Research conducted by MDRC, the Wisconsin HOPE Lab, and the Center for Benefit-Cost Studies in Education has begun to incorporate estimates of cost, but more is needed.

The evaluation literature also devotes inadequate attention to the context in which interventions occur. As we discussed, structural features of community colleges work at cross-purposes with efforts to raise completion rates, and recent fiscal developments have further eroded capacity for improvement. Additionally, community college students confront a broader opportunity structure which presents immense obstacles to improving their situation through educational upgrading. If evaluators do not take these structural realities into consideration, unrealistic expectations will be set and improper conclusions reached. Too often, when an intervention has small, short-lived impacts, this is taken as evidence that the strategy *in the abstract* "doesn't work." A more realistic conclusion is likely that the intervention is, by itself, inadequate to overcome the collective weight of countervailing structural forces bearing upon individuals and institutions at the bottom of the educational and social hierarchy.

Failure to take resources and power into account enables the tacit assumption that the only actors that matter in determining community college students' success are the colleges and the students themselves. This conceals the real and pressing need for broader structural reforms to ensure that community colleges are able to provide real educational opportunity to all Americans, regardless of background.

References

Adelman, C. (1998). The kiss of death? An alternative view of college remediation. *National Crosstalk, 6*(3), 11.

Adelman, C. (1999). *Answers in the toolbox: Academic intensity, attendance patterns, and bachelor's degree attainment.* Washington, DC: U.S. Department of Education.

Allen, J. M., Smith, C. L., & Muehleck, J. K. (2013). What kinds of advising are important to community college pre-and post-transfer students? *Community College Review, 41*(4), 330–345.

Alon, S. (2011). Who benefits most from financial aid? The heterogeneous effect of need-based grants on students' college persistence. *Social Science Quarterly, 92*(3), 807–829.

Anderson, D. M., & Goldrick-Rab, S. (2016). *Impact of a private need-based grant on beginning two-year college students* (Working Paper). Madison: Wisconsin HOPE Lab.

Angrist, J. D., Autor, D., Hudson, S., & Pallais, A. (2015, January). *Leveling up: Early results from a randomized evaluation of a post-secondary aid.* Presented at the annual conference of the American Economic Association. Boston.

Astin, A. W. (1984). Student involvement: A developmental theory for higher education. *Journal of College Student Personnel, 25*(4), 297–308.

Attewell, P., & Douglas, D. (2016). *When randomized control trials and observational studies diverge: Evidence from studies of academic momentum* (Working Paper). CUNY Academic Momentum Project.

Attewell, P., & Monaghan, D. B. (2016). How many credits should an undergraduate take? *Research in Higher Education, 57*(6), 682–713.

Attewell, P., Lavin, D., Domina, T., & Levey, T. (2006). New evidence on college remediation. *Journal of Higher Education, 77*(5), 886–924.

Attewell, P., Heil, S., & Reisel, L. (2012). What is academic momentum? And does it matter? *Educational Evaluation and Policy Analysis, 34*(1), 27–44.

Bahr, P. R. (2008). Does mathematics remediation work? A comparative analysis of academic attainment among community college students. *Research in Higher Education, 49*(5), 420–450.

Bahr, P. R. (2009). College hopping: Exploring the occurrence, frequency, and consequences of lateral transfer. *Community College Review, 36*(4), 271–298.

Bailey, T. (2009). Challenge and opportunity: Rethinking the role and function of developmental education in community college. *New Directions for Community Colleges, 2009*(145), 11–30.

Bailey, T. R., Kienzl, G., & Marcotte, D. E. (2004). *The return to a sub-baccalaureate education: The effects of schooling, credentials and program of study on economic outcomes* (Report prepared for the National Assessment of Vocational Education, U.S. Department of Education). New York: Community College Research Center.

Bailey, T., Jeong, D. W., & Cho, S. W. (2010). Referral, enrollment, and completion in developmental education sequences in community colleges. *Economics of Education Review, 29*(2), 255–270.

Bailey, T. R., Jaggars, S. S., & Jenkins, D. (2015). *Redesigning America's community colleges: A clearer path to student success.* Cambridge, MA: Harvard University Press.

Barnett, E. A., Bork, R. H., Mayer, A. K., Pretlow, J., Wathington, H. D., & Weiss, M. J. (2012). *Bridging the gap: An impact study of eight developmental summer bridge programs in Texas.* New York: MDRC.

Barr, A. Bird, K., & Castleman, B. J. (2016). *Prompting active choice among high-risk borrowers: Evidence from a student loan counseling experiment* (EdPolicyWorks Working Paper No. 41). Charlottesville: The Center on Education Policy and Workforce Competitiveness.

Barrow, L., & Rouse, C. E. (2013). *Financial incentives and educational investment: The impact of performance-based scholarships on student time use* (NBER Working Paper w19351). Cambridge, MA: National Bureau of Economic Research.

Barrow, L., Richburg-Hayes, L., Rouse, C. E., & Brock, T. (2014). Paying for performance: The education impacts of a community college scholarship program for low-income adults. *Journal of Labor Economics, 32*(3), 563–599.

Baum, S., & Kurose, C. (2013). Community colleges in context: Exploring financing of two- and four-year institutions. In *Bridging the higher educational divide: Strengthening community colleges and restoring the American dream: The report of the Century Task Force on preventing community colleges from becoming separate and unequal* (pp. 73–108). New York: The Century Foundation Press.

Belfield, C. (2015). *Efficiency gains in community colleges: Two areas for further investigation* (CCRC Working Paper 80). New York: Community College Research Center.

Belfield, C., & Jenkins, D. (2014). *Community college economics for policymakers: The one big fact and the one big myth* (CCRC Working Paper 67). New York: Community College Research Center.

Belfield, C., Crosta, P. M., & Jenkins, D. (2014). Can community colleges afford to improve completion? Measuring the costs and efficiency effects of college reforms. *Educational Evaluation and Policy Analysis, 36*(3), 327–345.

Bettinger, E. (2004). How financial aid affects persistence. In C. M. Hoxby (Ed.), *College choices: The economics of where to go, when to go, and how to pay for it* (pp. 207–238). Chicago: University of Chicago Press.

Bettinger, E. P. (2012). Financial aid: A blunt instrument for increasing degree attainment. In A.P. Kelly & M. Schneider. *Getting to graduation: The completion agenda in higher education* (pp. 157–174). Baltimore: The Johns Hopkins University Press.

Bettinger, E. (2015). Need-based aid and college persistence: The effects of the Ohio College Opportunity Grant. *Educational Evaluation and Policy Analysis, 37*(1 supplementary), 102S–119S.

Bettinger, E. P., & Long, B. T. (2009). Addressing the needs of underprepared students in higher education: Does college remediation work? *Journal of Human Resources, 44*(3), 736–771.

Betts, J. R., & McFarland, L. L. (1995). Safe port in a storm: The impact of labor market conditions on community college enrollments. *Journal of Human Resources, 30*(4), 741–765.

Bird, K., & Castleman, B. L. (2014). Here today, gone tomorrow? Investigating rates and patterns of financial aid renewal among college freshmen. *Research in Higher Education, 57*(4), 395–422.

Blackwell, L. S., Trzesniewski, K. H., & Dweck, C. S. (2007). Implicit theories of intelligence predict achievement across an adolescent transition: A longitudinal study and an intervention. *Child Development, 78*(1), 246–263.

Bloom, D., & Sommo, C. (2005). *Building learning communities: Early results from the Opening Doors Demonstration at Kingsborough community college.* New York: MDRC.

Blumer, H. (1971). Social problems as collective behavior. *Social Problems, 18*(3), 298–306.

Boatman, A., & Long, B. T. (2010). *Does remediation work for all students? How the effects of postsecondary remedial and developmental courses vary by level of academic preparation* (NCPR Working Paper). New York: National Center for Postsecondary Research.

Brand, J. E., Pfeffer, F. T., & Goldrick-Rab, S. (2012). Interpreting community college effects in the pres-

ence of heterogeneity and complex counterfactuals. *Sociological Science, 1*(1), 448–465.

Brint, S., & Karabel, J. (1989). *The diverted dream: Community colleges and the promise of educational opportunity in America, 1900–1985.* New York: Oxford University Press.

Brock, T., & Ritchburg-Hayes, L. (2006). *Paying for persistence: Early results of a Louisiana scholarship program for low-income parents attending community college.* New York: MDRC.

Broton, K., Frank, V., & Goldrick-Rab, S. (2014). *Safety, security, and college attainment: An investigation of undergraduates' basic needs and institutional response* (Wisconsin HOPE Lab Working Paper). Madison: Wisconsin HOPE Lab.

Broton, K., Goldrick-Rab, S., & Benson. (2016). Working for college: The causal impacts of financial grants on undergraduate employment. *Educational Evaluation and Policy Analysis, 38*(3), 477–494.

Calcagno, J. C., & Long, B. T. (2008). *The impact of postsecondary remediation using a regression discontinuity approach: Addressing endogenous sorting and noncompliance* (NBER Working Paper w14194). Cambridge, MA: National Bureau of Economic Research.

Carnevale, A. P., Smith, N., & Strohl, J. (2013). *Recovery: Job growth and education requirements through 2020.* Washington, DC: Center for Education and the Workforce, Georgetown University.

Castleman, B. L., & Long, B. T. (2013). *Looking beyond enrollment: The causal effect of need-based grants on college access, persistence, and graduation* (NBER Working Paper w19306). Cambridge, MA: National Bureau of Economic Research.

Castleman, B. L., & Page, L. C. (2015). Freshman year financial aid nudges: An experiment to increase FAFSA renewal and college persistence. *Journal of Human Resources, 51*(2), 389–415.

Cha, P., & Patel, R. (2010). *Rewarding progress, reducing debt: Early results from Ohio's performance-based scholarship demonstration for low-income parents.* New York: MDRC.

Chancellor's Office of the California Community Colleges. (2003). *The real cost project: Preliminary report.* Sacramento: California Community Colleges. Retrieved from http://www.immagic.com/eLibrary/ARCHIVES/GENERAL/CCC_CAUS/C030929R.pdf

Clark, B. R. (1960). The "cooling-out" function in higher education. *American Journal of Sociology, 65*(6), 569–576.

Cohen, A. M., Brawer, F. B., & Kisker, C. B. (2014). *The American community college* (6th ed.). San Francisco: John Wiley & Sons.

Crisp, G., & Delgado, C. (2014). The impact of developmental education on community college persistence and vertical transfer. *Community College Review, 42*(2), 99–117.

Crosta, P. M. (2014). Intensity and attachment: How the chaotic enrollment patterns of community college students relate to educational outcomes. *Community College Review, 42*(2), 118–142.

Dachelet, K., & Goldrick-Rab, S. (2015). *Investing in student completion: Overcoming financial barriers to retention through small-donor grants and emergency aid programs.* Madison: Wisconsin HOPE Lab.

Deil-Amen, R. (2011). Socio-academic integrative moments: Rethinking academic and social integration among two-year college students in career-related programs. *The Journal of Higher Education, 82*(1), 54–91.

Deil-Amen, R., & DeLuca, S. (2010). The underserved third: How our educational structures populate an educational underclass. *Journal of Education for Students Placed at Risk, 15*(1–2), 27–50.

Deil-Amen, R., & Rosenbaum, J. E. (2002). The unintended consequences of stigma-free remediation. *Sociology of Education, 75*(3), 249–268.

Deil-Amen, R., & Rosenbaum, J. E. (2003). The social prerequisites of success: Can college structure reduce the need for social know-how? *The Annals of the American Academy of Political and Social Science, 586*(1), 120–143.

Deming, D., & Dynarski, S. (2010). College aid. In P. B. Levine & D. J. Zimmerman (Eds.), *Targeting investments in children: Fighting poverty when resources are limited* (pp. 283–302). Chicago: University of Chicago Press.

Denning, J. T. (2014). *College on the cheap: Costs and benefits of community college* (Working Paper). Retrieved from http://www.terry.uga.edu/media/events/documents/Denning_Paper.pdf

Derby, D. C., & Smith, T. (2004). An orientation course and community college retention. *Community College Journal of Research and Practice, 28*(9), 763–773.

Desrochers, D. M., & Kirshstein, R. J. (2012). *College spending in a turbulent decade: Findings from the Delta Cost Project: A delta data update, 2000–2010.* Washington, DC: American Institutes for Research.

Dougherty, K. J., Jones, S. M., Lahr, H., Natow, R. S., Pheatt, L., & Reddy, V. (2016). Looking inside the black box of performance funding for higher education: Policy instruments, organizational obstacles, and intended and unintended impacts. *The Russell Sage Foundation Journal of the Social Sciences, 2*(1), 147–173.

Douglas, D., & Attewell, P. (2014). The bridge and the troll underneath: Summer bridge programs and degree completion. *American Journal of Education, 121*(1), 87–109.

Dynarski, S. M. (2003). Does aid matter? Measuring the effect of student aid on college attendance and completion. *American Economic Review, 93*(1), 279–288.

Dynarski, S. M., & Scott-Clayton, J. (2013). *Financial aid policy: Lessons from research* (NBER Working Paper w18710). Cambridge, MA: National Bureau of Economic Research.

Eagan, M. K., Jr., & Jaeger, A. J. (2009). Effects of exposure to part-time faculty on community college transfer. *Research in Higher Education, 50*(2), 168–188.

Evans, B., & Henry, G. (2015, March). *Self-paced remediation and math placement: A randomized field experiment in a community college.* Presented at the spring conference of the Society for Research on Educational Effectiveness. Washington, DC.

Evans, W., Kearney, M., & Sullivan, J. (2014). *Stay the course: Evaluating an intervention to promote community college persistence and graduation rates* (AEA RCT Registry). https://www.socialscienceregistry.org/trials/223/history/1148

Fairlie, R. W., & Grunberg, S. H. (2014). Access to technology and the transfer function of community colleges: Evidence from a field experiment. *Economic Inquiry, 52*(3), 1040–1059.

Fairlie, R. W., & London, R. A. (2012). The effects of home computers on educational outcomes: Evidence from a field experiment with community college students. *The Economic Journal, 122*(561), 727–753.

Fike, D. S., & Fike, R. (2008). Predictors of first-year student retention in the community college. *Community College Review, 36*(2), 68–88.

Geckler, C., Beach, C., Pih, M., & Yan, L. (2008). *Helping community college students cope with financial emergencies: Lessons from the Dreamkeepers and Angel Fund financial aid programs.* New York: MDRC.

Goldrick-Rab, S. (2010). Challenges and opportunities for improving community college student success. *Review of Educational Research, 80*(3), 437–469.

Goldrick-Rab, S. (2016). *Paying the price: College costs, financial aid, and the betrayal of the American dream.* Chicago: University of Chicago Press.

Goldrick-Rab, S., & Kinsley, P. (2013). School integration and the open-door philosophy: Rethinking the economic and racial composition of community colleges. In *Bridging the higher educational divide: Strengthening community colleges and restoring the American dream: The report of the Century Task Force on preventing community colleges from becoming separate and unequal* (pp. 109–136). New York: The Century Foundation Press.

Goldrick-Rab, S., Harris, D. N., & Trostel, P. A. (2009). Why financial aid matters (or does not) for college success: Toward a new interdisciplinary perspective. In *Higher education: Handbook of theory and research* (pp. 1–45). Dordrecht: Springer.

Goldrick-Rab, S., Broton, K., & Frank, V. M. (2014). *Single Stop USA's Community College Initiative: Implementation assessment.* Madison: Wisconsin HOPE Lab.

Goldrick-Rab, S., Broton, K., & Eisenberg, D. (2015). *Hungry to learn: Addressing food and housing insecurity among undergraduates.* Madison: Wisconsin HOPE Lab.

Goldrick-Rab, S., Kelchen, R., Harris, D. N., & Bensen, J. (2016). Reducing income inequality in educational attainment: Experimental evidence on the impact of financial aid on college completion. *American Sociological Review, 121*(6), 1762–1817.

Grissmer, D. W., Subotnik, R. F., & Orland, M. (2009). *A guide to incorporating multiple methods in ran-*

domized controlled trials to assess intervention effects. Washington, DC: American Psychological Association.

Grossman, J. B., Quint, J., Gingrich, J., Cerna, O., Diamond, J., Levine, A., & Willard, J. (2015). *Changing community colleges: Early lessons from Completion by Design*. New York: MDRC.

Grubb, W. N. (2001). *"Getting into the world": Guidance and counseling in community colleges*. New York: Community College Research Center.

Grubb, W. N. (2006). "Like, what do I do now?" The dilemmas of guidance counseling. In T. Bailey & V. S. Morest (Eds.), *Defending the community college equity agenda* (pp. 195–222). Baltimore: The Johns Hopkins University Press.

Harackiewicz, J. M., Tibbetts, Y., Canning, E., & Hyde, J. S. (2014). Harnessing values to promote motivation in education. *Motivational Interventions, 18*, 71–105.

Harackiewicz, J. M., Canning, E. A., Tibbetts, Y., Priniski, S. J., & Hyde, J. S. (2015). Closing achievement gaps with a utility-value intervention: Disentangling race and social class. *Journal of Personality and Social Psychology, 111*(5), 745–765.

Harris, D. N., & Goldrick-Rab, S. (2012). Improving the productivity of education experiments: Lessons from a randomized study of need-based financial aid. *Education, 7*(2), 143–169.

Heckman, J. J. (2005). The scientific model of causality. *Sociological Methodology, 35*(1), 1–97.

Heckman, J. J., & Smith, J. A. (1995). Assessing the case for social experiments. *The Journal of Economic Perspectives, 9*(2), 85–110.

Hillman, N. W., Tandberg, D. A., & Gross, J. P. (2014). Performance funding in higher education: Do financial incentives impact college completions? *The Journal of Higher Education, 85*(6), 826–857.

Hughes, K. L., & Scott-Clayton, J. (2011). Assessing developmental assessment in community colleges. *Community College Review, 39*(4), 327–351.

Jenkins, D., & Belfield, C. (2014). Can community colleges continue to do more with less? *Change: The Magazine of Higher Learning, 46*(3), 6–13.

Kahlenberg, R. (2015). *How higher education shortchanges community colleges*. Washington, DC: The Century Foundation.

Kane, T. J. (2003). *A quasi-experimental estimate of the impact of financial aid on college-going* (NBER Working Paper w9703). Cambridge, MA: National Bureau of Economic Research.

Karp, M. M. (2011). *Toward a new understanding of non-academic student support: Four mechanisms encouraging positive student outcomes in the community college* (CCRC Working Paper 28). New York: Community College Research Center.

Kena, G., Musu-Gilette, L., Robinson, J., Wang, X., Rathbun, A., Zhang, J., Wilkinson-Flicker, S., Barmer, A., & Velez, E. D. (2015). *The condition of education 2015*. Washington, DC: National Center for Education Statistics, U.S. Department of Education.

Kezar, A., & Maxey, D. (2013, June). The changing academic workforce. *Trusteeship Magazine*. Retrieved from http://agb.org/trusteeship/2013/5/changing-academic-workforce

Kirshstein, R. J., & Hubert, S. (2012). *Revenues: Where does the money come from? A Delta update* (pp. 2000–2010). Washington, DC: American Institutes for Research.

Lareau, A. (2008). Narrow questions, narrow answers: The limited value of randomized control trials for education research. In P. B. Walters, A. Lareau, & S. Rains (Eds.), *Education research on trial: Policy reform and the call for scientific rigor* (pp. 145–162). New York: Routledge.

Leigh, D. E., & Gill, A. M. (2003). Do community colleges really divert students from earning bachelor's degrees? *Economics of Education Review, 22*(1), 23–30.

Linderman, D., & Kolenovic, Z. (2012). *Results this far and the road ahead: A follow-up report on CUNY Accelerated Study in Associate Programs (ASAP)*. New York: The City University of New York.

Logue, A. W., Watanabe-Rose, M., & Douglas, D. (2016). Should students assessed as needing remedial mathematics take college-level quantitative courses instead? *Educational Evaluation and Policy Analysis, 38*(3), 578–598.

Martorell, P., & McFarlin, I., Jr. (2011). Help or hindrance? The effects of college remediation on academic and labor market outcomes. *The Review of Economics and Statistics, 93*(2), 436–454.

Mayer, A. K., Patel, R., & Gutierrez, M. (2015). *Four-year effects on degree receipt and employment outcomes from a performance-based scholarship program in Ohio*. New York: MDRC.

Melguizo, T., Hagedorn, L. S., & Cypers, S. (2008). Remedial/developmental education and the cost of community college transfer: A Los Angeles County sample. *The Review of Higher Education, 31*(4), 401–431.

Melguizo, T., Bos, J., & Prather, G. (2011). Is developmental education helping community college students persist? A critical review of the literature. *American Behavioral Scientist, 55*(2), 173–184.

Merton, R. K. (1936). The unanticipated consequences of purposive social action. *American Sociological Review, 1*(6), 894–904.

Miller-Adams, M. (2015). *Promise nation: Transforming communities through place-based scholarships*. Kalamazoo: W.E. Upjohn Institute for Employment Research.

Minkler, J. E. (2002). ERIC review: Learning communities at the community college. *Community College Review, 30*(3), 46–63.

Monaghan, D. B., & Attewell, P. (2015). The community college route to the bachelor's degree. *Educational Evaluation and Policy Analysis, 37*(1), 70–91.

Morgan, S. L., & Winship, C. (2014). *Counterfactuals and causal inference: Methods and principles for social research*. New York: Cambridge University Press.

Moss, B. G., & Yeaton, W. H. (2013). Evaluating effects of developmental education for college students using a regression discontinuity design. *Evaluation Review, 37*(5), 370–404.

National Student Clearinghouse Research Center. (2015). *Snapshot report: Persistence—Retention.* Herndon: National Student Clearinghouse.

O'Gara, L., Karp, M. M., & Hughes, K. L. (2009). Student success courses in the community college: An exploratory study of student perspectives. *Community College Review, 36*(3), 195–218.

Park, V. C., Nations, J., & Nielsen, K. (2013). *What matters for community college success? Assumptions and realities concerning student supports for low-income women.* Los Angeles: All-Campus Consortium on Research for Diversity.

Pascarella, E. T., & Terenzini, P. T. (2005). *How college affects students: A third decade of research* (Vol. 2). San Francisco: Jossey-Bass.

Patel, R., & Rudd, T. (2012). *Can scholarships alone help students succeed? Lessons from two New York City community colleges.* New York: MDRC.

Patel, R., & Valenzuela, I. (2013). *Moving forward: Early findings from the Performance-Based Scholarship Demonstration in Arizona.* New York: MDRC.

Patel, R., Ritchburg-Hayes, L., de la Campa, E., & Rudd, T. (2013). Performance-based scholarships: What have we learned? In *Interim findings from the PBS demonstration.* New York: MDRC.

Perin, D. (2006). Can community colleges protect both access and standards? The problem of remediation. *Teachers College Record, 108*(3), 339.

Radford, A. W., & Horn, L. (2012). *An overview of classes taken and credits earned by beginning postsecondary students (Web tables).* Washington, DC: National Center for Education Statistics, U.S. Department of Education.

Raftery, S. (2005). Developmental learning communities at metropolitan community college. *New Directions for Community Colleges, 2005*(129), 63–72.

Reynolds, C. L. (2012). Where to attend? Estimating the effects of beginning college at a two-year institution. *Economics of Education Review, 31*(4), 345–362.

Ritchburg-Hayes, L., Brock, T., LeBlanc, A., Paxson, C., Rouse, C. E., & Barrow, L. (2009). *Rewarding persistence: Effects of a performance-based scholarship for low-income parents.* New York: MDRC.

Ritchburg-Hayes, L., Sommo, C., & Welbeck, R. (2011). *Promoting full-time attendance among adults in community college: Early impacts from the Performance-Based Scholarship Demonstration in New York.* New York: MDRC.

Rosenbaum, J. E., Deil-Amen, R., & Person, A. E. (2006). *After admission: From college access to college success.* New York: Russell Sage Foundation.

Rouse, C. E. (1995). Democratization or diversion? The effect of community colleges on educational attainment. *Journal of Business & Economic Statistics, 13*(2), 217–224.

Rubin, D. B. (1974). Estimating causal effects of treatments in randomized and nonrandomized studies. *Journal of Educational Psychology, 66*(5), 688–701.

Schneider, B., & McDonald, S. K. (2007a). *Scale-up in education: Vol. I: Ideas in principle.* Lanham: Rowman and Littlefield Publishers.

Schneider, B., & McDonald, S. K. (2007b). *Scale-up in education: Vol. II: Ideas in practice.* Lanham: Rowman and Littlefield Publishers.

Schudde, L. T. (2011). The causal effect of campus residency on college student retention. *The Review of Higher Education, 34*(4), 581–610.

Scott-Clayton, J. (2015). The shapeless river: Does a lack of structure inhibit students' progress at community colleges? In B. J. Castleman, S. Schwartz, & S. Baum (Eds.), *Decision making for student success: Behavioral insights to improve college access and persistence* (pp. 102–123). New York: Routledge.

Scott-Clayton, J., & Rodriguez, O. (2012). *Development, discouragement, or diversion? New evidence on the effects of college remediation* (NBER Working Paper w18328). Cambridge, MA: National Bureau of Economic Research.

Scrivener, S., & Au, J. (2007). *Enhancing student services at Lorain County Community College: Early results from the Opening Doors Demonstration in Ohio.* New York: MDRC.

Scrivener, S., & Pi, M. (2007). *Enhancing student services at Owens Community College: Early results from the Opening Doors Demonstration in Ohio.* New York: MDRC.

Scrivener, S., & Weiss, M. J. (2009). *More guidance, better results? Three-year effects of an enhanced student services program at two community colleges.* New York: MDRC.

Scrivener, S., Blom, D., LeBlanc, A., Paxton, C., Rouse, C., & Sommo, C. (2008). *A good start: Two-year effects of a learning community program at Kingsborough Community College.* New York: MDRC.

Scrivener, S., Sommo, C., & Collado, H. (2009). *Getting back on track: Effects of a community college program for probationary students.* New York: MDRC.

Scrivener, S., Weiss, M. J., & Sommo, C. (2012). *What can a multifaceted program do for community college students? Early results from an evaluation of Accelerated Study in Associate Programs (ASAP) for developmental education students.* New York: MDRC.

Scrivener, S., Weiss, M. J., Ratledge, A., Rudd, T., Sommo, C., & Fresques, H. (2015). *Doubling graduation rates: Three-year effects of CUNY's Accelerated Study in Associate Programs (ASAP) for developmental education students.* New York: MDRC.

Shapiro, D., Dundar, A., Yuan, X., Harrell, A., & Wakhungu, P. K. (2014). *Completing college: A national view of student attainment rates: Fall 2008 cohort* (Signature report No. 8). Herndon: National Student Clearinghouse Research Center.

Sharon, A. T. (1972). Assessing the effectiveness of remedial college courses. *The Journal of Experimental Education, 41*(2), 60–62.

Simone, S. (2014). *The transferability of postsecondary credit following student transfer or coenrollment.* Washington, DC: National Center for Education Statistics, U.S. Department of Education.

Singell, L. D. (2004). Come and stay a while: Does financial aid effect retention conditioned on enrollment at a large public university? *Economics of Education Review, 23*(5), 459–471.

Sommo, C., Boynton, M., Collado, H., Diamond, J., Gardenhire, A., Ratledge, A., Rudd, T., & Weiss, M. (2014). *Mapping success: Performance-based scholarships, student services, and developmental math at Hillsborough Community College.* New York: MDRC.

Stuart, G. R., Rios-Aguilar, C., & Deil-Amen, R. (2014). "How much economic value does my credential have?" Reformulating Tinto's model to study students' persistence in community colleges. *Community College Review, 42*(4), 327–341.

Sturgis, I. (2014, January 8). Gates foundation invests half-billion in success of community college students. *Diverse Issues in Higher Education.* Retrieved from http://diverseeducation.com/article/59973/

The Century Foundation. (2013). *Bridging the higher educational divide: Strengthening community colleges and restoring the American dream: The report of the Century Task Force on preventing community colleges from becoming separate and unequal.* New York: The Century Foundation Press.

The College Board. (2015). *Trends in student aid 2015.* New York: The College Board.

Tinto, V. (1987). *Leaving college: Rethinking the causes and cures of student attrition.* Chicago: University of Chicago Press.

Tinto, V. (1997). Colleges as communities: Taking research on student persistence seriously. *The Review of Higher Education, 21*(2), 167–177.

Tinto, V., Russo, P., & Kadel, S. (1994). Constructing educational communities: Increasing retention in challenging circumstances. *Community College Journal, 64*(4), 26–29.

Trow, M. (2007). Reflections on the transition from elite to mass to universal access: Forms and phases of higher education in modern societies since WWII. In J. J. F. Forest & P. G. Altbach (Eds.), *International handbook of higher education* (pp. 243–280). Dordrecht: Springer Netherlands.

Turner, L. (2015, November). *Loan nudges: Experimental evidence on the effects of default options on the framing of federal loans.* Presented at the conference of the Association for Public Policy Analysis and Management. Miami.

Valentine, J. C., Konstantopolous, S., & Goldrick-Rab, S. (2016). *A meta-analysis of regression discontinuity studies investigating the effects of placement into remedial education: A working paper.* Madison: Wisconsin HOPE Lab.

Van der Klaauw, W. (2002). Estimating the effect of financial aid offers on college enrollment: A regression–discontinuity approach. *International Economic Review, 43*(4), 1249–1287.

Visher, M. G., & Torres, J. (2011). *Breaking new ground: An impact study of career-focused learning communities at Kingsborough Community College.* New York: National Center for Postsecondary Research.

Visher, M. G., Butcher, K. F., & Cerna, O. S. (2010). *Guiding developmental math students to campus services: An impact evaluation of the Beacon Program at South Texas College.* New York: MDRC.

Ware, M., Weissman, E., & McDermott, D. (2013). *Aid Like a Paycheck: An incremental aid program to promote student success.* New York: MDRC.

Wathington, H. D., Barnett, E. A., Weissman, E., Teres, J., Pretlow, J., & Nakanishi, A. (2011). *Getting ready for college: An implementation and early impacts study of eight Texas developmental summer bridge programs.* New York: MDRC.

Weiss, M. J., Visher, M. G., & Wathington, H. (2010). *Learning communities in developmental reading: An impact study at Hillsborough Community College.* New York: National Center for Postsecondary Research.

Weiss, M. J., Brock, T., Sommo, C., Rudd, T., & Turner, M. C. (2011). *Serving community college students on probation: Four-year findings from Chaffey College's Opening Doors program.* New York: MDRC.

Weiss, M. J., Mayer, A., Cullinan, D., Ratledge, A., Sommo, C., & Diamond, J. (2014). *A random assignment evaluation of learning communities at Kingsborough Community College: Seven years later.* New York: MDRC.

Weiss, M. J., Mayer, A. K., Cullinan, D., Ratledge, A., Sommo, C., & Diamond, J. (2015). A random assignment evaluation of learning communities at Kingsborough Community College—Seven years later. *Journal of Research on Educational Effectiveness, 8*(2), 189–217.

Weissman, E., Butcher, K. F., Schneider, E., Teres, J., Collado, H., & Greenberg, D. (2011). *Learning communities for students in developmental math: Impact studies at Queensborough and Houston Community Colleges.* New York: National Center for Postsecondary Research.

Weissman, E., Cullinan, D., Cerna, O., Safran, S., & Richman, P. (2012). *Learning communities in developmental English: Impact studies at Merced College and the Community College of Baltimore.* New York: National Center for Postsecondary Research.

Yeager, D. S., & Dweck, C. S. (2012). Mindsets that promote resilience: When students believe that personal characteristics can be developed. *Educational Psychologist, 47*(4), 302–314.

Yeager, D. S., Paunesku, D., Romero, C., Brown, R., Muhich, J., & Walton, G. (2013). *Engineering psychological interventions for scale: The case of the "growth mindset" in community colleges* (Working Paper). Austin: University of Texas at Austin.

Zeidenberg, M., Jenkins, P. D., & Calcagno, J. C. (2007). *Do student success courses actually help community college students succeed?* (CCRC Brief No. 36). New York: Community College Research Center.

Research–Practice Partnerships in Education

Paula Arce-Trigatti, Irina Chukhray,
and Ruth N. López Turley

Abstract

The field of education has seen a sharp increase in the formation and participation of research–practice partnerships (RPPs) over the last two decades. Bringing together two parties in education that share a concern for improved student outcomes but differ dramatically in their approaches to that end, RPPs in education have not only grown in number and type, but complementary organizations and efforts have begun to emerge as well. In this contribution, we explore the reasons for these changes, grounding our work in the organizational and institutional theories literature from sociology.

25.1 Introduction

The world of education research–practice partnerships (RPPs) has evolved dramatically over the last two decades. Perhaps most simply understood as collaborative, mutually beneficial relationships between researchers and practitioners that are formal and long-term in nature, there has been a notable recent increase in their formation and persistence in education. In this chapter, we seek to understand why partnerships have been accepted as an important strategy for potentially addressing the long-established education research-to-practice gap using theoretical foundations grounded in sociology. Guiding our work is a key concept from organizational theory: the description of an organization's environment as a field. In particular, knowing how the field is structured or organized, understanding the individual organizations within the field, and defining the challenges faced by organizations are especially useful for gaining an understanding of organizations. To that end, we explore the following three questions: First, have we actually seen an increased presence of RPPs in education? How might we account for the rapid growth in the number of RPPs in the last two decades given that institutional constraints typically slow adoption of new innovations? Second, how can organizational theory help illustrate why we observe multiple models or types of RPPs in education? Finally, we note that in addition to RPPs, complementary organizations and efforts (e.g., those related to RPPs but are not in and of themselves partnerships) have emerged as well. What role do these complementary organizations play within the larger RPP ecosystem?

P. Arce-Trigatti (✉) · I. Chukhray ·
R. N. López Turley
Rice University, Houston, TX, USA
e-mail: parcetrig@rice.edu; Ic11@rice.edu;
turley@rice.edu

© Springer International Publishing AG, part of Springer Nature 2018　　　　561
B. Schneider (ed.), *Handbook of the Sociology of Education in the 21st Century*, Handbooks of Sociology and Social Research, https://doi.org/10.1007/978-3-319-76694-2_25

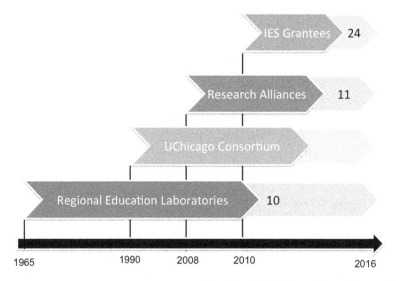

Fig. 25.1 Illustration of the development of research–practice partnerships over time
Notes: This figure helps illustrate the growth in research–practice partnerships in education over time. The numbers to the right of each category indicate how many RPPs of that type emerged starting in a particular year. We note the launch of the UChicago Consortium on School Research separately, to demonstrate that until their arrival, there was a virtual drought of RPPs for an extended time. After their launch, several RPPs modeled after the UChicago Consortium emerged ("research alliances"), as well as a large collection of IES-sponsored RPPs

25.2 Is There an Increase in RPPs? How Can Organizational Theory Help Us Understand the Growth Patterns of RPPs?

We begin our discussion by inquiring if there has indeed been a spike in the number of research–practice partnerships (RPPs) more recently relative to their historical development. Quite simply, data suggest this is the case. Figure 25.1 displays the pattern of growth of several types of RPPs over time. As shown in the figure, the IES-sponsored Regional Education Laboratories were the main type of RPP in the U.S. for multiple decades, before the launch of the UChicago Consortium on School Research in 1990. Following a much shorter dry spell, the next wave of RPPs began in the mid-2000s, with several partnerships modeled after the UChicago Consortium as well as a large collection (over 20 new grantees) of IES-funded RPPs emerging onto the landscape. Related research investigating school district decision-making processes also support the notion of a recent increased presence of RPPs (e.g., Honig and Coburn 2008).

Historically, the research-to-practice model that has been the *modus operandi* of many consisted of a one-way conversation between education practitioners and researchers (see Huberman 1994 for a clear illustration of this model). This simple linear model, where basic research leads to applied research, which then leads to the development of products and/or professional practices, and finally, dissemination to educational practitioners and systems demonstrates the difficulty in changing frameworks once they have been accepted as the norm. How we conceptualize the problem with the research–practice gap in education matters because it influences the policy solutions that are pursued. Because of the linear model assumption, for example, there has been special attention devoted to the role of "linking agents," which are organizations or individuals who transform research findings into understandable material for the public (Hood 1982). Efforts to improve this translational gap led to federal funding for the Regional Education Laboratories, for example, which have been around since the 1960s (Coburn and Stein

2010).[1] Other federal initiatives that have emerged based on this framing include the Education Resources Information Center (ERIC) funded by the Institute of Education Sciences (IES), which is a "nationwide information network that acquires, catalogs, summarizes, and provides access to education information from all sources,"[2] as well as three clearinghouses (e.g., National Clearinghouse for Comprehensive School Reform, National Clearinghouse for Educational Facilities, and the What Works Clearinghouse) that serve solely to disseminate different types of research and information in education. On the research front, there has been a large effort to study how to improve district access to research (e.g., Coburn and Stein 2010).

The linear model in practice, however, is problematic because reality quite often deviates from this clearly structured pathway. Weiss (1980) describes a decidedly *non*-linear way in which policymakers interact with research, suggesting that information gradually filters through multiple channels and "creeps" into thought processes. Simply releasing findings to practitioners is therefore insufficient (Spillane et al. 2002). Fleming (1988) documents the myriad challenges explaining why teachers are so unlikely to use research in their activities. Some examples include the overwhelming amount of time it takes to find research and interpret it (hence the focus on translational linking agents mentioned ear-

lier), the slow research process itself compared to the rapidity with which practitioners need information, and the perception of researchers as outside agents that can provide little usable knowledge for the classroom. Huberman (1989) additionally finds that research use within districts is heavily dependent on the social transactions within that setting, including how leaders relate to the research or which parties are implicated in the policy recommendations, for example. In sum, many of these examples reiterate the dichotomous and distinct environments in which practitioners and researchers operate. Changing accepted ways of doing business, however, is oftentimes a slow process. We next turn to institutional theories to help us reconcile the initial slow growth of RPPs in light of the inadequacies of the linear model.

25.2.1 Initial Slow RPP Growth

Institutional theory can at least partially explain the consistent behavioral patterns of organizations (in our case, districts or schools from the practitioner side and academics from the researcher side) (Zucker 1987; Powell and DiMaggio 1991). In this context, "institutions" may have developed around both sets of parties that have likely contributed to the delayed emergence of RPPs. For example, institutional theorists argue that organizations adopt procedures, formal structures, and vocabularies consistent with expectations of what is "acceptable" and "legitimate" given their operating environment. The importance of institutional legitimacy is underscored by its role in ensuring organizational survival: Adopting innovative practices are often viewed as threatening and incompatible with internal structures of the organization. We next explore how these pressures may have shaped the slow participation of first, researchers and second, practitioners in collaborating within an RPP.

For academics, typical research culture has been notoriously isolated (e.g., "ivory tower"): Building from existing theories, developing new

---

[1] Title IV of ESEA authorized the formation of what eventually came to be known as the "Regional Education Laboratories" (RELs). The motivating ideas behind the introduction of the RELs were first, to facilitate the generation of more useful research in education and second, to somehow encourage practitioners to actually use it (Guthrie 1989). In the years since their inception, the RELs have been reauthorized several times and are currently operating 79 research alliances within ten different RELs across the U.S. They are funded by the Institute of Education Sciences (IES) to conduct research, disseminate findings, and to provide training and technical assistance to link research-proven practices with educational practitioners. In their most recent iteration, there will be greater opportunity to engage with research–practice partnerships (Sparks 2016).

[2] See: http://www2.ed.gov/about/contacts/gen/othersites/eric.html.

ones, testing them out, and so forth are activities that have been carried out in concert with other academics or solo. Additionally, academic researchers are subject to other primary objectives, such as meeting tenure, which directly influences their choices over what types of research activities to engage in. Institutional forces such as peer recognition and the potential to improve one's position in his/her respective field may have led to adherence towards these more traditional research inquiries. Indeed, these influences shape how scientists choose to pursue a particular research problem; innovation, in terms of novel methodologies or questions that divert towards a greater focus on practice for example, is perceived as a gamble (Foster et al. 2015). When academics pursue involvement in developing or contributing to an RPP, they are essentially taking a gamble, given the large time commitment that is required, as well as the distinct shift in the types of research questions that could potentially be examined. Thus, we might predict an initial slow growth of RPPs while such entities remain squarely in a "novel" phase. Consider that after the UChicago Consortium on School Research launched in 1990, more than a decade passed before new RPPs with similar arrangements began to emerge. Further complicating matters, researchers generally operate with much longer timelines relative to practitioners, who commonly need information to make policy decisions very quickly. With a set of organizational norms that differ dramatically from those practitioners face, it is not at all surprising that partnerships in education have taken such a long time to "take off" and instead, simpler solutions of "linking agents" have been adopted.

Financial pressures on the university may have also contributed to slow institutional support for RPPs. In the last few decades, institutions of higher education have experienced massive cuts in federal and state funding, impacting research universities the most (Scott and Biag 2016). In addition to the risk associated with pursuing more innovative research paths, funding challenges may have also presented an obstacle to greater investments in RPPs. In particular,

resource dependence theory suggests that organizations respond to external actors who control the resources upon which the organization depends; this seems to apply to universities (Kraatz and Zajac 2001). We would predict that based on this theory, if grant makers at the federal and private foundational levels increasingly include line items for RPP start-up and persistence costs, this might mitigate the reluctance of universities to invest in such organizations. Indeed, the Spencer Foundation just recently launched a new competitive grant program for partnerships.[3] Greater funding opportunities for academic researchers from outside their universities may thus have helped fuel the growth of RPPs.

Finally, other forces, such as policy pressures, may pull universities in directions opposite to the institutional norms or financial pressures. Institutional theorists argue that changes in the external environment can facilitate new logics to spread within a given organization (Berman and Stivers 2016). For example, Berman (2012) documents how changes in U.S. policies to promote science led universities to increasingly focus on the economic value of science. Furthermore, new resources became available to help support this new focus. Within this framework, we might expect a similar pattern for RPPs, as the U.S. government continues to promote the use of evidence to inform decision making for education policymakers through laws such as No Child Left Behind (NCLB) and the Every Student Succeeds Act (ESSA). NCLB (2002) requires evidence from "scientifically based research," while ESSA (2015) has kept the spirit of the law in tact, but has broadened available research to include "evidence based research." Policy changes in the external environment such as these may present new opportunities for researchers to engage with partnerships that were absent before.

Turning our attention to U.S. schools and districts, we begin by focusing on the influence of institutional norms in shaping these organiza-

---

[3] See: http://www.spencer.org/research-practice-partnership-program.

tions, and the long-lasting effects that can accompany these forces. With roots in rural areas, one-room schoolhouses in the U.S. functioned as efficient transmitters of basic skills essential for societal success. With the arrival of the industrial revolution, however, educators felt pressure to make education more systematic, mimicking the factory-type model common in the business sector (Tyack 1974). The resulting bureaucratization of the educational system in general was, some would argue, necessary to adequately address current needs. A combination of businessmen, university professors and presidents, school superintendents, and middle-class reformers facilitated the shift to a centralized school system with a top-down structure of school management. Post centralization, school boards were comprised mostly of business people and professionals, as it largely remains today. To be clear, schools and districts in the U.S. were not created with the explicit goal of acting as research and development (R&D) centers, which certainly contributes to the lack of research capacity that still pervades the practitioner side today. With the absence of R&D as a primary function within schools, it should not be surprising that successful practitioner interaction with research has been marred by numerous challenges. Work by Rowan (1982) suggests that an institutional environment characterized as contentious and unfocused (which may commonly occur in schools and districts given the multiplicity of objectives that comes with numerous stakeholders) dramatically slows the adoption of innovative structures.

The culture surrounding the use of research evidence, in general, can also mediate how districts and schools interact with research. For example, Honig and Coburn (2008, p. 594) define evidence use as a process that involves "searching for and incorporating evidence" into decision making. Furthermore, evidence use within districts is more likely when district norms, expectations, and routines encourage ongoing engagement with empirical research (Honig 2003; Honig and Coburn 2008; Massell 2001; Corcoran et al. 2001). However, the practice of evidence-based decision making is arguably not yet common or a "norm" for many

district central offices. This means that new models of professional practice that require central office administrators to break some previously held routines may be necessary to enable a new culture of evidence-based decisions (Honig 2006). Absent those, we would expect a slow adoption of RPPs among school districts to generally be the case.

Beyond the cultural factors or norms that may inhibit districts from embracing research, there are other constraints that may contribute to this deterrence as well. Burch and Thiem (2004) and Reichardt (2000) suggest that central office administrators may lack the human capital and technological infrastructure to engage in evidence-based decision making. Additionally, working knowledge also appears to strongly mediate evidence use. For example, some research finds that district central offices are more likely to search and pay attention to evidence that fits in with their conceptions or conforms to their expectations (Birkeland et al. 2005; Spillane 2000). Individual preferences for certain types of evidence can also play a role (Coburn and Talbert 2006). Collectively, these additional constraints may also lessen the likelihood that a district is willing or able to work collaboratively with external researchers in an RPP.

However, despite factors hindering evidence use, district central offices have long used *some* form of evidence in their decision making. For example, practitioner or "local" knowledge, such as input from principals, teachers, parents, and students, is very common (Gonzalez et al. 2005; Datnow et al. 2002). Districts have also been shown to consult with social science research and to incorporate the use of student-level data to inform decisions (Honig and Coburn 2008; Massell 2001; Massell and Goertz 2002). We would expect the culture of evidence use within districts to continue to evolve, even without the presence of RPPs, especially given the recent passage of ESSA. ESSA partially shifts authority back into the hand of the localities, enhancing the role of state and local policymakers that was previously more restrictive under NCLB (Strauss 2015). In particular, states will have a greater say in which standards are adopted, greater control over their accountability systems, and greater flexibility over their teacher certification requirements and evaluation systems (Klein 2016). This flexibility creates a larger role for local policymakers. Second, matching NCLB's previous emphasis of utilizing "evidence-based" research in decision making, ESSA also explicitly defines this term and describes four levels of rigor for research. Taken together, the need for evidenced-based interventions and leeway in standards adoption creates a unique demand appropriate for RPPs to meet. As a result, ESSA contains features that may possibly lead either to a greater number of RPPs or create a larger role for existing RPPs.

25.2.2 Recent Burgeoning RPP Growth

Growing concern over the large gap between research and practice and the failures to address it began to gain traction in the late 1990s and early 2000. Huberman (1994, p. 14) reports on the "state of the art" of knowledge utilization in education and recognizes "the proliferation of centers, laboratories, intermediate units, and collaborative enterprises…is a sign that the process of 'knowledge transfer' is active in several forms." He further describes the importance of "sustained interactivity" between researchers and practitioners in producing research itself, going so far as to describe this interaction as "mutual" in its benefits to both sides. While Huberman critiques and offers changes to the aforementioned linear research-to-practice framework, he stops short of naming this new enterprise a "partnership." In 2003, a major task force from the National Research Council investigating the current approaches to addressing the research-to-practice gap produced "Strategic Education Research Partnership," a report offering an actionable change to business as usual (National Research Council 2003). At this point, the first education research–practice partnership that consisted of a university and school district pairing, the UChicago Consortium on School Research,

had existed for over a decade. Additionally, the reauthorization of ESSA and the NCLB of 2001, led to a greater need for localized capacity to conduct research. The NCLB Act's heavy use of the phrase "evidence-based" for describing what types of education policies should be implemented created further incentives for school districts to invest in research-related skill sets (Feuer et al. 2002). How, then, did the collective efforts on these many fronts influence the growth of partnerships?

First, there was recognition that the current state of affairs was inadequate. The critique of long-held institutional norms led the way for new ideas on the role of practitioners and researchers in the research process. Second, it is likely that the perceived success of the UChicago Consortium led to new definitions for "legitimacy" among these types of institutions. Kramer (1981) describes four key roles that non-profit organizations tend to perform that sets them apart from other sectors: vanguard role, value guardian role, advocacy role, and the service provider role. Of these, the vanguard role, where experimentation with innovative approaches to processes or programs leads to non-profits serving mainly as agents of change best describes early RPPs. If these organizations are proven successful (i.e., the longevity of the UChicago Consortium), other agencies are more likely to adopt them. Universities, which have typically been inflexible with their institutional rules as described earlier, may have shifted their stance somewhat given the reputation of the University of Chicago, for example. Moreover, increased opportunities for funding (i.e., through the Spencer grantee program mentioned earlier, as well as numerous IES-sponsored RPP initiatives separate from the RELs) have accompanied these trends.

Third, changes to the external environment via NCLB likely contributed to the change in institutional norms as well. Tolbert and Zucker (1983), for example, find that when coercive pressures (either direct or indirect pressures to conform to institutional expectations) are large, such as the changes brought in by NCLB, organizations are quick to adopt new structures. More specifically, these accountability policies required districts to invest more heavily in their longitudinal data systems in order to regularly use student performance data as required (Kerr et al. 2005). Other federal grants such as the one provided by IES to help support statewide longitudinal data systems have also contributed to their increased presence. This particular change opens new doors for researchers to interact with practitioners, given the supreme importance of administrative data in conducting research. Taken together, then, these may have influenced the acceptance of and the growing interest in RPPs as a promising mechanism to address the research-to-practice gap.

25.3 What Are the Different RPP Models? Why Are There Multiple Models/Types of Research–Practice Partnerships?

Moving from describing the growth in the sheer number of partnerships that exist today, we next turn to a brief presentation of some of the models that have currently been identified in the literature, and then offer a theoretical exploration into why we might observe multiple types of RPPs.

Currently, to the best of our knowledge, there is only one study that has attempted a typology of the different types of RPPs. A white paper authored by Coburn et al. (2013) and commissioned by the W. T. Grant Foundation identifies three different types of RPPs: research alliances, design-based partnerships, and networked improvement communities. We briefly define each of these:

Research alliances: are partnerships between a school district(s) and a research institution(s) such as a university or non-profit. By their definition, research alliances are long-term commitments where the researchers pursue questions of policy and practice that are relevant to both practitioners and researchers (Coburn et al. 2013). The researchers share the research findings with the district, the community, and other stakeholders and this sharing feature is part and parcel of the alliance commitment. Coburn and colleagues consider both the Regional Education Laboratories (RELs) and partnerships such as the UChicago Consortium on School Research to fit within this category.

Design-based partnerships: are structurally very similar to research alliances, in that they are typically comprised of district and university pairings, such as the Middle-School Mathematics in the Institutional Setting of Teaching (MIST) project at Vanderbilt University. The authors chose to distinguish this type of model based on their scope of work, which departs from that of the research alliances in that it tends to be more narrow (e.g., problems of practice as they relate to curriculum and instruction only). Design-based partnerships feature an iterative research process that focuses on developing as well as testing conjectures; this additional work towards formulating and developing theory is also not commonly part of the research process in alliances (see Barab and Squire 2004 for a more detailed introduction of design-based research).

Networked improvement communities: are networks of districts and researchers that collaborate on one problem of practice with the goals of understanding what works best, where, and in what context (see Bryk et al. 2011 for a more detailed introduction). One of the defining features of this type of RPP is that it involves the collaboration of many districts to exploit differences in contexts in order to improve knowledge surrounding implementation of programs and policies. The concept of "improvement science" is at its core, which is a model adapted from the healthcare industry. The key example of this RPP type is the Carnegie Foundation's Networked Improvement Communities.

This white paper is an excellent first attempt at describing the types of RPPs currently operating in education. Note that there are likely several other models in operation today that have not been captured here since the publishing of the paper, with more likely to develop in the future. To help illustrate the myriad ways a partnership

Table 25.1 This table presents a simplified illustration of the numerous ways research–practice partnerships can differ across a multitude of partnership dimensions

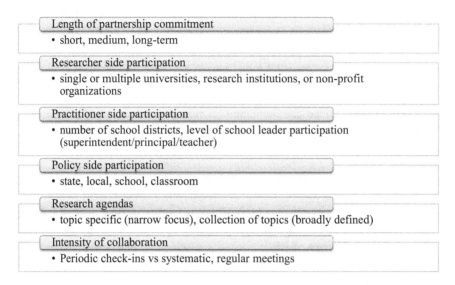

| Length of partnership commitment |
| • short, medium, long-term |

Researcher side participation
• single or multiple universities, research institutions, or non-profit organizations

Practitioner side participation
• number of school districts, level of school leader participation (superintendent/principal/teacher)

Policy side participation
• state, local, school, classroom

Research agendas
• topic specific (narrow focus), collection of topics (broadly defined)

Intensity of collaboration
• Periodic check-ins vs systematic, regular meetings

may be arranged we offer an organized list of individual characteristics that can vary among partnerships in Table 25.1. With a greater number of RPPs emerging and growth in this field likely continuing, a more rigorous typology allowing for additional nuance across models may be possible in the future.

25.3.1 According to Theory, What Might Account for Different Partnership Models?

It might first be instructive to define how research–practice partnerships are similar. They are best considered non-profit organizations, given that their objectives rarely (if ever) focus on maximizing profit: They do not operate in a typical market featuring customers and suppliers, where supply and demand determine price, and efficiency can be measured through clear measurement of production. On the other hand, RPPs also fail to be classified as a pure government agency, where survival is directly linked to satisfying constituent preferences and revenues are generated from a mandated tax base. Structurally speaking, they commonly include representatives from at least two sides of the education realm: those who specialize in researching education (i.e., academics, scholars, and generally, those working either within a university or a research institution) and those who specialize in administering education (i.e., practitioners involved at all levels of education, such as teachers, principals, and district or state leaders). Moving beyond these similarities, we next explore how different social, political, and institutional conditions may give rise to organizational heterogeneity across RPPs.

One can draw from different disciplines to explain organizational heterogeneity; this approach can shed light on the impact various aspects of the organizational form has on strategy or production. For example, in economics, the objectives of the firm can give rise to differences in structural forms, as can the differential costs associated with varying production processes adopted. Similarly, sociologists also recognize the importance of organizational goals in shaping structures and strategies, but they additionally consider how leaders' backgrounds and cultures influence the identity of the organization (Fligstein and Dauter 2007). These basic concepts can help us initially understand the visible differences in how RPPs are arranged and the scope, areas of, or approaches to research they specialize in. For example, the Houston Education

Research Consortium (HERC), a research alliance that is housed at Rice University and features the Houston Independent School District as its practitioner partner, was founded and is currently directed by one of the authors of this work, Ruth López Turley, who is trained in sociology. The research output produced by HERC will thus be framed within the context of sociology and the methodologies utilized throughout the projects will be those commonly found in the field of sociology. On the other hand, MIST (mentioned earlier under the design-based partnership model) is housed in the College of Education at Vanderbilt University. The project's co-PIs are Erin Henrick and Paul Cobb, who are both housed within the Department of Teaching and Learning and are trained specifically in education. The scope of the MIST project is thus much more narrow, focusing on improving the instructional practices of math teachers.[4] Finally, the networked improvement communities of Carnegie arrive at their structural arrangement along a different path altogether. A specific problem of practice is first identified and a network then forms consisting of a variety of parties interested in working on the problem. Organizational goals overall and more specifically, the background and training of the leader, can, at least initially, explain some of the differences in RPP models.

Within organizational theory, we can further identify at least two ways to frame the question of organizational heterogeneity, using either organizational ecology or institutional theory. We explore each in turn.

Organizational or population ecology, an area of research first introduced by Hannan and Freeman (1977, 1984), takes the view that the rational adaptation model popular in economics overemphasizes the role of firm adaptation. Instead, this approach suggests that the environment in which organizations operate presents a fixed constraint; essentially, the environment selects which types of organizations survive and which die. To explain the emergence of heterogeneous organizational forms, Hannan

and Freeman (1977) posited that differential opportunities in the market, in terms of resources available, directly shaped the birth and survival of organizations. Survival is ensured by maintaining good relationships with already-known contacts, predictability in meeting funding targets, and relying on an accepted approach producing output.

The availability of resources deserves special attention in this case. RPPs are strongly dependent on the availability of funding; therefore, the number and types of potential funding sources will have large ramifications on the birth and subsequent survival of RPPs and tracks taken. Because there is external control over resources, RPPs become interdependent on this environment. More generally, what this means is that there is an element of competition among RPPs that may not exist otherwise. The degree of competitive pressure for resources will likely vary widely across localities; how rural or urban a city is, the number of academic institutions that exist, as well as the availability of private foundations serving an area are all examples of how competition may be affected. Greater competitive pressure for funding may lead to larger differences in partnerships (i.e., to stand out from the crowd), while less competitive pressure may allow for imitation of models perceived as successful. Because RPPs are not self-sustaining organizations (and will likely never be, given the absence of a product from which to generate revenues), they are implicitly wedded to the foundations that support their work. The objectives and preferences of the foundations themselves, then, are likely to have a strong influence on the probability of birth and survival.

In addition to the role of resources, we can also highlight the general pressures that arise from the environment as a whole. The number of organizations that can co-exist in an environment is dependent on the *environmental carrying capacity*, which is itself a function of the social, economic, and political conditions and available resources (Anheier 2005). Because many things can affect the environment's carrying capacity, this in turn will affect the dynamics of organizations over time. More precisely, the environment will affect

---

[4]See http://peabody.vanderbilt.edu/departments/tl/teaching_and_learning_research/mist/ for more information.

how organizations choose to allocate resources; this in turn will produce variation across partnership strategies. For example, certain departments within universities may be more amenable to the notion of a partnership than others. If the sociology department is willing to provide support for the creation of a partnership, then the tools of that particular discipline will shape and influence how the research work is approached within the partnership. Furthermore, tenure rules differ across institutions. Qualifying activities, then, could either be limited or numerous, and these environmental constraints will alter features of the partnership. Alternatively, the current research capacity and preferences of a school district will also create pathways to some approaches and not others. Along the practitioner side, there is a greater propensity for leadership turnover, which gives rise to environmental instability. Previous relationships and practices that may have held promise for a partnership may have to change with immediacy. The infinite combinations of these two environmental features could conceivably give rise to multiple types of partnerships. In particular, different environmental characteristics can help describe the shifts in partnership approaches that have occurred more recently (i.e., the introduction of design-based research and the networked improvement communities).

A second way to approach the question of organizational heterogeneity is to use institutional theory, a research area advanced by the work of DiMaggio and Powell (1983), Meyer and Scott (1983), and Meyer and Rowan (1977). In contrast to the assumption in population ecology of a fixed environment, this line of thinking hypothesizes that the environment may be "at least partially a social construction" (Fligstein and Dauter 2007, p. 111). That is, the environment is comprised of other related organizations that could influence the strategic behavior of a particular firm. DiMaggio and Powell (1983) argued that in this context, organizations tend to become more similar over time through three different isomorphic processes: imitative or mimetic, normative, and coercive.

Under the first type, imitative or mimetic isomorphism describes how organizations imitate or copy others that are perceived to be successful. Perhaps one example in the RPP context we can highlight is the recent surge in the number of research alliances that resemble the UChicago Consortium on School Research. Founded in 1990, the UChicago Consortium was the only RPP of its type for approximately 15 years; during that time, it built a strong reputation among many involved in education for producing rigorous, relevant, and timely research that has made important impacts on local decision making. More recently, several RPPs modeled after the UChicago Consortium have emerged: the Baltimore Education Research Consortium (2006), the Research Alliance for New York City Schools (2008), the Los Angeles Education Research Institute (2011), and the Houston Education Research Consortium (2011), just to name a few.

Normative isomorphism describes the process by which firms change due to external pressures initiated by professions or legitimation directed by professional practices. These types of forces lead organizations to conform to accepted ways of practice, given a particular profession or even network of professionals. While new to the RPP ecosystem, the National Network of Education Research–Practice Partnerships, a network connecting several types of RPPs in education, may eventually influence how individual RPPs emerge or change over time.

Finally, coercive isomorphism relates to the changes organizations must undergo due to organizational, political, or social pressures of stakeholders they are dependent upon. RPPs are particularly susceptible to this type of isomorphism, given the previously documented reliance upon foundational dollars. Thus, certain models of RPPs may be more or less common simply due to the financial resources they are dependent upon. For example, several of the design-based research partnerships share a STEM-related focus; unsurprisingly, the National Science Foundation also funds many of these. Coercive isomorphism may also arise from the mere fact that RPPs operate in a new space, where researchers and practitioners must come together in service to solving problems of practice. In this case, relevant stakeholders include not only the practitioners themselves, but local decision makers, students, and communities-at large. Indeed, Roderick et al. (2009, p. 2) describe the founding of the UChicago Consortium as follows:

> Given the magnitude of this experiment, the advocates of reform—largely the foundation community and local reform organizations—believed it was important to establish an independent organization that would be charged with conducting independent, objective evaluations of the progress of reform and engaging in research that would assist local schools in developing their own strategies. Because universities seemed like natural partners in this effort, the Chicago Public Schools (CPS) invited local universities to become involved.

Furthermore, the authors also illustrate the importance of satisfying stakeholder needs through their work:

> This new role—to provide a research-based framework (but not a blueprint) for improvement, to provide critical measures of performance and feedback mechanisms to individual schools, and for researchers to engage in the core questions of what it will take to improve performance—has had a significant impact in shaping the work of CCSR [the UChicago Consortium] and the role of research in the city. CCSR researchers do not just comprise an independent group that does studies on schools and occasionally announces findings. Rather, our studies and products (e.g., individual school reports) are resources that practitioners use to manage their own improvement efforts. (Roderick et al. 2009, p. 2)

Over time, the UChicago Consortium has had to evolve, and as we might expect, they tie these changes explicitly to stakeholder objectives. Moreover, they attribute their success specifically to this type of change:

> Over time, CCSR has evolved into a more complex organization…But key to the success of CCSR has been a consistent focus on these initial themes: (1) research must be closely connected over time to the core problems facing practitioners and decision makers; (2) making an impact means researchers must pay careful attention to the process by which people learn, assimilate new information and ideas, internalize that information, and connect it to their own problems of practice; and (3) building capacity requires that the role of the researcher must shift from outside expert to interactive participant in building knowledge of what matters for students' success. (Roderick et al. 2009, p. 3)

To close this section, we summarize the discussion by reinforcing the notion that many variables can contribute to organizational heterogeneity. Furthermore, these differences can arise at any age of the organization, from birth and over time. More research investigating how RPPs differentiate is needed, especially to further our knowledge of what an "effective" RPP may look like.

25.4 Where Does the Development of the Field Currently Stand?

We have discussed the growth in the number and types of RPPs across the U.S. in the last two decades and provided possible reasons for these trends grounded in organizational theory from sociology. In this next section we widen our focus to examine the field of RPPs as a whole and ask: Where do we currently stand? If we think of RPPs as an "industry," at what stage in the lifecycle do we find ourselves? What can we say about the development of the field given the rise of complementary organizations and, most recently, a formal professional network of education RPPs?

From the larger perspective of the field of RPPs, it is likely that this "industry" is still in its infancy. The number of RPPs (total) across the U.S. suggests they are still relatively uncommon among approaches that connect research and practice.[5] Hannan and Carroll (1992) suggest that the pattern of organizational density over time for several industry types follows a regular path: long, slow growth in the initial phases, followed by an explosive period of growth, and later, stabilization or perhaps even decline. Within this context, RPPs seem to be on the cusp of explosive growth (e.g., Sect. 25.2 of this chapter, which

---

[5]Note: Currently, no resource, such as a directory, exists on the number of RPPs currently in operation. The NNERPP website (nnerpp.rice.edu) contains a list of partnerships that are members of its network (which includes most of the research alliances in operation today), while the R + P Collaboratory website (researchandpractice.org) includes a list of DBIR-type partnerships.

provides an overview of the recent growth in RPPs). Indeed, recent research by Coburn and Penuel (2016, p. 1) on the state of the field describes RPPs as a "promising approach" that is currently witnessing an uptick in interest and funding. Despite a noticeable increase in RPPs as an organizational form, they are arguably not yet a "business as usual" approach. The majority of states and school districts across the U.S. do not participate in RPPs and they are particularly scarce or nonexistent in more rural areas.

25.4.1 What Can We Say About the Development of the Field Given the Rise of Complementary Organizations?

Across the organizational theory literature, there are a few key concepts that can help us better understand the current state of the RPP industry and where it might be headed next. In an industry's infancy, new organizations must develop several innovations—not just the organizational structure itself or the process of work—but also new workplace roles, without having much prior knowledge to build off of and within a larger context that is not quite yet accepting of these ventures (Hannan and Carroll 1992; Stinchcombe 1965). These early challenges may partially explain why the beginning stage of a new industry is characterized by a long, slow build: Moving from innovative, developmental production phases to systematic, efficient processes takes time, while the external environment in which the organization operates may provide additional barriers to acceptance of new norms. To ensure survival, institutional theorists have long suggested the legitimacy of the new organizational form must be expanded and directly addressed (e.g., Meyer and Rowan 1977; Meyer and Scott 1983; DiMaggio and Powell 1991). More recently, Aldrich and Fiol (1994, p. 648) distinguish among two types of legitimacy, especially salient to entrepreneurs: *cognitive legitimation*, describing the knowledge building that must occur around the new organi-

zational form's processes, structure, and services, and *sociopolitical legitimation*, referring to "the process by which key stakeholders, the general public, key opinion leaders, or government officials accept a venture as appropriate and right, given existing norms and laws."

The inception of new ventures may naturally be accompanied by low cognitive legitimacy: "Without widespread knowledge and understanding of their activity, entrepreneurs may have difficulty maintaining the support of key constituencies" (Aldrich and Fiol 1994, p. 649). The authors furthermore suggest that in the absence of developing cognitive legitimacy, especially as it relates to reaching a collective consensus regarding best practices, standards, or procedures, new entrants into the field risk possible failure. This could reflect poorly on the organizational form as a whole, since potential funders or future RPP leaders will be watching closely to see how individual organizations perform. This conceptual framework can help provide some grounding to explain the recent emergence of several peripheral efforts related to RPPs, which we will call "complementary organizations." We define these organizations to be those that support the work of RPPs in some way, but are not in and of themselves partnerships.

With respect to cognitive legitimation, we argue that complementary organizations work to advance the collective knowledge of RPPs that may indeed contribute towards creating conditions where partnerships are more likely to become permanent fixtures in the educational arena. First, the number of individual research studies on RPPs has exploded in the last two decades.[6] This may partly be due to the simple fact that there are more RPPs today relative to 20 years ago, but it could also be argued that those working within RPPs are eager to produce knowledge that helps support their new venture. Second, two new IES-funded research centers

---

[6]Conducting a simple Google Scholar search on "research practice partnerships" + education and restricting the results to the years 1960 through 1989 returns zero results. When changing the yearly range from 1990 to 2000, ten results are listed. Finally, adjusting the yearly range once more, from 2001 to 2016, nearly 300 articles are returned.

focusing on understanding the connections between researchers, practitioners, and policymakers have recently emerged. The National Center for Research in Policy and Practice (NCRPP), housed at the University of Colorado, Boulder and the Center for Research Use in Education (CRUE) at the University of Delaware, are likely to increase knowledge around RPP work into the next decade.[7] Third, three additional resources exist to help develop and support those interested in partnership work. The R + P Collaboratory[8] at the University of Colorado, Boulder, is an organization that helps support STEM-related work within RPPs as well as DBIR-type partnerships, while the William T. Grant Foundation has organized a micro-site[9] of RPP-related information and materials.

The third resource and most recent entrant into this group of complementary organizations and the one most intimately known to the authors is the National Network of Education Research–Practice Partnerships (NNERPP), which aims to construct a connected web of education RPPs across the country to support and develop RPPs.[10] As we will focus on the "network" aspect of this organization shortly, in this section we highlight its role in expanding cognitive legitimacy. Because RPPs require many skills for which education researchers, education agency leaders, and decisionmakers are typically not trained, these collaborations tend to be challenging to set up and maintain. Although researchers often collaborate with other researchers, it is less common for them to collaborate with education agencies in long-term partnerships, as noted earlier. Substantial organizational differences between research institutions and education agencies can lead to a prohibitive working environment.

Members of these different organizational forms may often not be fully aware of the extensive dissimilarities in terms of timelines, communication processes, and internal working structures, to name a few examples. Given these potential barriers to success, NNERPP has made one of its objectives to systematically collect, develop, and share best practices from a variety of RPP models. This is directly in line with raising the cognitive legitimacy of the approach, which may be especially salient at this stage in the industry's development. We hypothesize that collectively, these complementary organizations are likely to directly impact the cognitive legitimacy of the field overall and will more than likely make it easier for new entrants to emerge and develop, given the relatively larger pool of knowledge they will be able to draw from.

Commenting on the state of the field with respect to sociopolitical legitimation is somewhat more challenging. In terms of measurement, Aldrich and Fiol (1994, p. 648) suggest evaluating the degree of this type of legitimacy by "assessing public acceptance of an industry, government subsidies to the industry, or the public prestige of its leader." It is likely that sociopolitical legitimation is still growing among stakeholders. Of the scant evidence we can point to that suggests this may indeed be occurring, we note the increase in opportunities for funding. For example, as mentioned previously, the Spencer Foundation launched their first ever competitive RPP grants award in 2015 while IES has created new initiatives to fund RPPs, in addition to a reorganization of the RELs towards a greater RPP orientation. The founding of NNERPP itself also lends support to the idea that RPPs are gaining sociopolitical legitimacy, especially if we consider that it is financially resourced by five different private foundations. From the governmental perspective, we note the increased demand from policies mandating greater use of evidence-based research. While not explicitly directed at RPPs, the shift towards connecting research and practice could arguably be a form of sociopolitical legitimation. Generally speaking, however, we might expect sociopolitical legitimacy to be

---

[7] Given IES' role in supporting the Regional Education Laboratories, these two centers should come as no surprise, lending support for the notion that advancing cognitive legitimation matters.

[8] See http://researchandpractice.org/ for more information.

[9] See http://rpp.wtgrantfoundation.org/ for more information.

[10] See http://nnerpp.rice.edu for more information.

positively impacted as cognitive legitimacy surrounding RPPs increases.

We next turn our discussion to the "network" aspect of NNERPP: Why does the development of a professional network of RPPs merit attention here? What does it suggest about the state of the field overall or where it might be headed? While the research in the previous part of Sect. 25.3 is more connected to organizational sociology (i.e., institutions), this next subsection relates more closely to economic sociology (i.e., networks). They are often two distinct research areas but share connections, as we will see. By shifting the lens slightly, we hope to further our understanding of the important roles different actors play within the RPP ecosystem overall.

We begin our discussion by exploring the definition of a "network." Podolny and Page (1998, p. 59) broadly define a network as "any collection of actors ($N \geq 2$) that pursue repeated, enduring exchange relations with one another and at the same time, lack a legitimate organizational authority to arbitrate and resolve disputes that may arise during the exchange." These authors distinguish between a market, where exchanges are not necessarily enduring but instead, "episodic," and hierarchies, where there is a clear order to authority, especially regarding the resolution of disputes. Other authors have been more explicit, defining a network as a collection of actors or nodes (in our case, RPPs) that are connected by specific ties (Borgatti and Halgin 2011; Smith-Doerr and Powell 2005). In these cases, ties among nodes are typically descriptive of the relationship between two nodes; for example, in NNERPP's case, the ties may represent a collegial relationship among RPPs. Research in this area has focused on characterizing the structural aspects of a network (e.g., Burt 1992), while others have prioritized an analysis of interorganizational connections and their potential effect on organizational behavior (e.g., Granovetter 1985). A third perspective moves away from previous assumptions that organizations within a network are essentially uninvolved and instead, examines how organizations actively rely on networks as a wellspring of resources (e.g., Gulati et al. 2011). In this subsection, we adopt the third framework,

and consider how a professional network of RPPs, such as NNERPP, might matter for individual RPP behavior or performance.

25.4.2 What Do Networks Provide?

First and foremost, networks establish a clear mechanism through which member organizations can access a wide range of resources (Burt 1992; Gulati et al. 2011; Smith-Doerr and Powell 2005) as well as provide order to an otherwise disconnected collection of related organizations (Burt 2000). Smith-Doerr and Powell (2005, p. 16) suggest "organizations forge connections to other parties to access relevant expertise. Access to centers of knowledge production is essential when knowledge is developing at an unprecedented pace." While knowledge about the internal workings of an RPP is developing, it is not necessarily developing rapidly or systematically but haphazardly. The UChicago Consortium is one example of an RPP that has written about their founding (cf. Roderick et al. 2009) while the R + P Collaboratory, the W. T. Grant Foundation RPP microsite, and NNERPP have created or made available various toolkits to help those interested in pursuing this work. Several additional resources not mentioned here exist across various other websites, but are less known. To access these knowledge centers, however, those interested in launching an RPP would first need to know where to find them and second, may find that the resources, while helpful in their own right, are not quite sufficient. Indeed, the authors have often fielded phone calls, in-person meetings, and online video chats from interested parties seeking "relevant expertise," as Smith-Doerr and Powell describe. Thus, while other, more static resources are available, the dynamic nature of interacting with others may be quite difficult to replace. The network itself becomes a centralized hub, then, that facilitates an arguably more efficient distribution of information and knowledge than individual organizations working alone. This is one reason why we might expect NNERPP to move the field forward more quickly than an RPP ecosystem without it.

Second, in addition to its power of dissemination, other research points to the role networks play in supporting innovation (Bryk et al. 2011; Goldsmith and Eggers 2004; Podolny and Page 1998; Powell 1990). Smith-Doerr and Powell (2005, p. 17) go so far as to characterize the potential for networks to become a "locus of innovation" due to the fostering of meaningful relationships across member organizations that goes beyond a simple knowledge exchange. Furthermore, Smith-Doerr and Powell (2005, p. 25) posit that "[m]uch research has suggested that close interaction among divergent organizations can produce novel recombinations of information leading to greater innovation and learning (Cohen and Levinthal 1990; Powell 1990; March 1991; McEvily and Zaheer 1999; Stuart and Podolny 1999; Ahuja 2000)." In the present case, there are "divergent" organizations along two lines: First, within each individual RPP, there are at least two different institutions involved (i.e., university and school district), and often times, more.[11] Thus, each individual RPP is essentially a mini-network of its own. The close proximity within which each institution works together because of the partnership commitment is very promising for the potential to produce innovations. Second, NNERPP itself consists of a collection of RPPs that differ in terms of arrangements, geographical location, age, size, research approaches, and breadth of topics analyzed.

NNERPP has further indicated that two of its priorities include the facilitation of cross-partnership collaboration and second, the synthesis of research findings produced by RPPs and the building of new knowledge based on RPP research. Education leaders and researchers alike can benefit from other partnerships' research practices and findings. Research produced by RPPs can and should be synthesized in a manner that enables researchers and policymakers from all over the country to strategically build on that knowledge and use it to develop novel solutions to persistent problems of practice. An emerging field of research that studies the relationship between

research and policy for district/state improvement shows evidence that research produced by RPPs is likely to be more beneficial than research produced outside of RPPs, not only because researchers are more likely to produce work that is aligned with district needs but also because district leaders are more likely to view the research as credible and directly applicable to their context (e.g., Coburn et al. 2009; Honig and Venkateswaran 2012). However, there is mixed evidence that districts engaging in RPPs use research in decision making more consistently than districts not engaging in RPPs, and one possible explanation is that it is difficult for researchers and district leaders to learn from one another (Turley and Stevens 2015). Coburn et al. (2013, p. 25) conclude: "What is needed is a more robust dialogue in which district leaders, researchers, policymakers, and funders speak candidly about the strategic trade-offs partnerships face and the resources that are required for success." By organizing these syntheses through a network, greater diffusion of knowledge and ideas that may then spur innovative solutions to current problems of practice may be possible.

To close this section, we circle back to the question of why network analysis may be relevant to the study of RPPs specifically, and to organizational forms, generally. Owen-Smith and Powell (2008, p. 600) suggest that "[n]etworks are essential to fields in at least two senses: they are both a circulatory system and a mechanism for sensemaking. Fields are shaped by networks, which condition the formation of relationships and help establish their consequences." Furthermore, the authors also write that "[w]hile institutions shape structures and condition their effects, networks generate the categories and hierarchies that help define institutions and contribute to their efficacy. Thus, any effort to understand institutional processes must take networks into account, and vice versa" (Owen-Smith and Powell 2008, p. 594). Additionally, complementary partnerships may forge a path for further network establishment. It is possible that networks may feed back into the lifecycle process of RPPs and may help further establish normative culture around RPPs.

---

[11]For example, some RPPs also partner with community non-profit organizations or non-university research institutions.

25.5 Conclusion

We have seen growth both in the number and type of research–practice partnerships (RPPs) in education over the last two decades, as well as the emergence of complementary organizations and even the launch of a professional network of RPPs, all suggesting that the RPP model is gaining traction as a potentially useful way to connect research, policy, and practice in education. We have explored the reasons for these changes using many organizational and institutional theories found in sociology and what they might mean for the future of RPPs. We framed our analysis across multiple levels: At the firm-level, we provided a historical foundation to explain the rise of RPPs and additionally gave a current description of the variety of RPP models in existence. At the industry-level, we have explored how organizations that are not themselves RPPs are situated within the industry and how they may complement the work of partnerships and more broadly, the field. Given limitations in space and scope of work, we aimed to provide the reader foundational knowledge from which one can begin to think more deeply about the evolution of research–practice partnerships and the promises they hold for the future in education. In this final section, we leave the reader with several unanswered questions that will require further analysis and consideration in the coming years, and will likely affect the continued growth and existence of this organizational form.

First, defining the conditions that constitute "best practices" for an RPP is still very much in development. Feedback loops are an essential component to learning more precisely about "what works," but these have been sparse for a couple of reasons. From the perspective of innovation, multiple cycles of success and failure (e.g., closure of the organization) have not yet occurred in this industry, mostly due to the relative newness of the organizational form. Second, and perhaps more importantly, there is currently no consensus about how to define RPP "success" or the features or outcomes that make

an RPP "effective."[12] Because several different models of RPPs exist (with greater variety in structural arrangements likely occurring over time), this also adds complexity to the issue. Should all be judged equally? The literature on RPP failure is equally sparse. What conditions lead an RPP to fail or close, for example? The next stage of the field will require a more explicit definition of organizational performance.

Beyond constructing an accepted definition of success/failure, the interim process of how RPPs evolve over time is not well known, either. For example, how does organizational change occur or what leads to organizational change? There is also, of course, the possibility that RPPs change very little over time. Because there are typically at least two distinct types of institutions that come together to form a research–practice partnership, there are internal and external pressures affecting multiple units within the partnership, which could individually and collectively lead to very different types of changes over time. Analysis of this kind is not straightforward. For those interested in implementing continuous improvement processes as they relate to RPP performance, what types of organizational policies would be most appropriate? Outside of the institutional forms that make up the RPP, there is also the larger external environment to consider. What political contexts or conditions are important for fostering future growth of individual RPPs and the field as a whole? Addressing these questions with rigorous research will likely be important for the overall survival of this organizational form.

Finally, it is important to note the dual roles that collaboration and competition between RPPs can play with respect to individual organizational

---

[12]For example, some have argued that the UChicago Consortium has been a model for RPP success. It is not clear if this accolade refers to its longevity within the industry or due to the strong reputation it has developed over time in being an exemplar for how RPPs can work, or other aspects of the partnership. Although these features may be indicators of success, it should be noted that our general knowledge of RPP effectiveness is still in its infancy.

health and to the larger field. Is it possible for RPPs to continue to learn from one another and remain in a relatively collaborative space? Or will increased competition for funds inhibit the type of knowledge sharing that could provide beneficial growth to the field? Hannan and Carroll (1992, p. 13) suggest that generally speaking, there are "limits to the longevity of firms." One possible explanation for this constraint has to do with the tension between legitimation and competition: To survive initially and to ensure field growth, organizational forms must address legitimation. This often leads to collaboration since systematic knowledge collection around the organization and diffusion of this information is particularly useful for raising legitimation. As a larger number of organizations emerge, however, competition for a variety of limited resources (e.g., financial and human capital related) places greater pressure on the survival of any given organization. This may preclude some organizations that may otherwise have supported others from sharing practices or knowledge.

What, then, can we conclude about the RPP landscape given these important issues? Given the relatively young age of the industry overall, some of these questions will require more time in order to be adequately addressed. Rigorous research examining RPPs of all types is just now commencing (for example, the two IES-funded research centers mentioned in Sect. 25.3). In general, because the interest and momentum in RPPs as a mechanism for connecting research, policy, and practice is currently in an upward trend, we are optimistic that the creation of knowledge around these approaches is likely to grow.

References

Ahuja, G. (2000). Collaboration networks, structural holes, and innovation: A longitudinal study. *Administrative Science Quarterly, 45*, 425–455.

Aldrich, H. E., & Fiol, C. M. (1994). Fools rush in? The institutional context of industry creation. *The Academy of Management Review, 19*(4), 645–670.

Anheier, H. (2005). *Nonprofit organizations: Theory, management, policy*. London/New York: Routledge.

Barab, S., & Squire, K. (2004). Design-based research: Putting a stake in the ground. *Journal of the Learning Sciences, 13*(1), 1–14.

Berman, E. P. (2012). Explaining the move toward the market in U.S. academic science: How institutional logics can change without institutional entrepreneurs. *Theory and Society, 41*(3), 261–299.

Berman, E. P., & Stivers, A. (2016). Student loans as a pressure on U.S. higher education. In Berman & Paradeise, (Eds.), *The university under pressure (Research in the Sociology of Organizations)* (Vol. 46, pp. 129–160).

Birkeland, S., Murphy-Graham, E., & Weiss, C. (2005). Good reasons for ignoring good evaluation: The case of the drug abuse resistance education (DARE) program. *Evaluation and Program Planning, 28*(3), 247–256.

Borgatti, S. P., & Halgin, D. S. (2011). On network theory. *Organization Science*, Articles in Advance, 1–14.

Bryk, A. Gomez, L., & Grunow, A. (2011). Getting ideas into action: Building networked improvement communities in education. In Maureen T. Hallinan (Ed.), *Frontiers in sociology of education*. Dordrecht: Springer.

Burch, P. E., & Thiem, C. (2004). *Private organizations, school districts, and the enterprise of high stakes accountability*. Unpublished manuscript.

Burt, R. (1992). *Structural holes*. Cambridge, MA: Harvard University Press.

Burt, R. (2000). The network structure of social capital. *Research in Organizational Behavior, 22*, 345–423.

Coburn, C. E., & Penuel, W. R. (2016). Research–practice partnerships in education: Outcomes, dynamics, and open questions. *Educational Researcher, 45*(1), 48–54.

Coburn, C., & Stein, M. K. (2010). *Research and practice in education: Building alliances, bridging the divide*. Blue Ridge Summit: Rowman & Littlefield Publishers, Inc.

Coburn, C., & Talbert, J. E. (2006). Conceptions of evidence use in school districts: Mapping the terrain. *American Journal of Education, 112*(4), 469–495.

Coburn, C. E., Honig, M. I., & Stein, M. K. (2009). What's the evidence on districts' use of evidence? In J. D. Bransford, D. J. Stipek, N. J. Vye, L. M. Gomez, & D. Lam (Eds.), *The role of research in educational improvement* (pp. 67–87). Cambridge, MA: Harvard Education Press.

Coburn, C., Penuel, W. R., & Geil, K. E. (2013). *Research–practice partnerships: A strategy for leveraging research for educational improvements in school districts*. Commissioned by the William T. Grant Foundation.

Cohen, W., & Levinthal, D. (1990). Absorptive capacity: A new perspective on learning and innovation. *Administrative Science Quarterly, 35*, 128–152.

Corcoran, T., Fuhrman, S. H., & Belcher, C. L. (2001). The district role in instructional improvement. *The Phi Delta Kappan, 83*(1), 78–84.

Datnow, A., Hubbard, L., & Mehan, H. (2002). *Extending educational reform: From one school to many.* London/New York: Routledge/Falmer.

DiMaggio, P. J., & Powell, W. W. (1983). The iron cage revisited: Institutional isomorphism and collective rationality in organizational fields. *American Sociological Review, 48*, 147–160.

Every Student Succeeds Act, Public Law 95, 114th Cong., 1st Sess. (2015).

Feuer, M. J., Towne, L., & Shavelson, R. J. (2002). Scientific culture and educational research. *Educational Researcher, 31*(8), 4–14.

Fleming, D. S. (1988). The literature on teacher utilization of research: Implications for the school reform movement. In S. D. Castle (Ed.), *Teacher empowerment through knowledge linking research and practice for school reform.* Papers presented at the annual meeting of the American Educational Research Association, New Orleans, April 5–9.

Fligstein, N., & Dauter, L. (2007). The sociology of markets. *Annual Review of Sociology, 33*, 105–128.

Foster, J. G., Rzhetsky, A., & Evans, J. A. (2015). Tradition and innovation in scientists' research strategies. *American Sociological Review, 80*(5), 875–908.

Goldsmith, S., & Eggers, W. D. (2004). *Governing by network: The new shape of the public sector.* Washington, DC: Brookings Institution Press.

Gonzalez, N., Moll, L. C., & Amanti, C. (Eds.). (2005). *Funds of knowledge: Theorizing practices in households, communities and classrooms.* Princeton: Lawrence Erlbaum Associates.

Granovetter, M. (1985). Economic action and social structure: The problem of embeddedness. *American Journal of Sociology, 91*, 481–510.

Gulati, R., Lavie, D., & Madhavan, R. (2011). How do networks matter? The performance effects of interorganizational networks. *Research in Organizational Behavior, 31*, 207–224.

Guthrie, J. W. (1989). *Educational laboratories: History and prospect.* Commissioned by the United States Department of Education.

Hannan, M. T., & Carroll, G. R. (1992). *Dynamics of organizational populations: Density, legitimation, and competition.* New York: Oxford University Press.

Hannan, M., & Freeman, J. (1977). The population ecology of organizations. *American Journal of Sociology, 82*(5), 929–964.

Hannan, M., & Freeman, J. (1984). Structural inertia and organizational change. *American Sociological Review, 49*, 149–164.

Honig, M. I. (2003). Building policy from practice: Central office administrators' roles and capacity in collaborative policy implementation. *Educational Administration Quarterly, 39*(3), 292–338.

Honig, M. I. (2006). Street-level bureaucracy revisited: District central office administrators as boundary spanners in complex policy implementation. *Educational Evaluation and Policy Analysis, 28*, 357–383.

Honig, M. I., & Coburn, C. (2008). Evidence-based decision making in school district central offices: Toward a policy and research agenda. *Educational Policy, 22*(4), 578–608.

Honig, M. I., & Venkateswaran, N. (2012). School–central office relationships in evidence use: Understanding evidence use as a systems problem. *American Journal of Education, 118*, 199–222.

Hood, P. D. (1982). *The role of linking agents in school improvement: A review, analysis, and synthesis of recent major studies.* Far West Lab for Educational Research and Development.

Huberman, M. (1989). Predicting conceptual effects in research utilization: Looking with both eyes. *Knowledge in Society, 2*(3), 6–24.

Huberman, M. (1994). Research utilization: The state of the art. *Knowledge and Policy: The International Journal of Knowledge Transfer and Utilization, 7*(4), 13–33.

Kerr, K. A., Marsh, J. A., Ikemoto, G. S., Darilek, H., & Barney, H. (2005). *Districtwide strategies to promote data use for instructional improvement.* Paper presented at the annual meeting of the American Educational Research Association, Montreal, QC, Canada.

Klein, A. (2016). Under ESSA, states, districts to share more power. *Education Week,* January 5, 2016.

Kraatz, M. S., & Zajac, E. J. (2001). How organizational resources affect strategic change and performance in turbulent environments: Theory and evidence. *Organization Science, 12*(5), 632–657.

Kramer, R. (1981). *Voluntary agencies in the welfare state.* Berkley: University of California Press.

March, J. G. (1991). Exploration and exploitation in organizational learning. *Organization Science, 2*, 71–87.

Massell, D. (2001). The theory and practice of using data to build capacity: State and local strategies and their effects. In S. H. Fuhrman (Ed.), *From the capitol to the classroom: Standards-based reform in the states. One hundredth yearbook of the national society for the study of education* (pp. 148–169). Chicago: National Society for the Study of Education.

Massell, D., & Goertz, M. E. (2002). District strategies for building instructional capacity. In A. M. Hightower, M. S. Knapp, J. A. Marsh, & M. W. McLaughlin (Eds.), *School districts and instructional renewal* (pp. 43–60). New York: Teachers College Press.

McEvily, W. J., & Zaheer, A. (1999). Bridging ties: A source of firm heterogeneity in competitive capabilities. *Strategic Management Journal, 20*, 1133–1156.

Meyer, J. W., & Rowan, B. (1977). Institutionalized organizations: Formal structure as myth and ceremony. *American Journal of Sociology, 83*, 340–363.

Meyer, J. W., & Scott, R. (1983). *Organizational environments: Ritual and rationality.* Beverly Hills: Sage.

National Research Council. (2003). *Strategic education research partnership.* Washington, DC: The National Academies Press.

No Child Left Behind Act of 2001, Public Law 107-110, 20 U.S.C. (2002).

Owen-Smith, J., & Powell, W. (2008). Networks and institutions. In R. Greenwood, C. Oliver, & R.

Suddaby (Eds.), *The SAGE handbook of organizational institutionalism* (pp. 596–623). London: SAGE Publications.

Podolny, J. M., & Page, K. L. (1998). Network forms of organization. *Annual Review of Sociology, 24*, 54–76.

Powell, W. W. (1990). Neither market nor hierarchy: Network forms of organization. *Research in Organizational Behavior, 12*, 295–336.

Powell, W. W., & DiMaggio, P. J. (1991). *The new institutionalism in organizational analysis*. Chicago: University of Chicago Press.

Reichardt, R. E. (2000). *The state's role in supporting data-driven decision-making: A view of Wyoming*. Aurora: Mid-Continent Research for Education and Learning.

Roderick, M., Easton, J. Q., & Sebring, P. B. (2009). *CCSR: A new model for the role of research in supporting urban school reform*. UChicago Consortium on School Research Report. Accessed from https://consortium.uchicago.edu/publications/ccsr-new-model-role-research-supporting-urban-school-reform

Rowan, B. (1982). Organizational structure and the institutional environment: The case of public schools. *Administrative Science Quarterly, 27*(2), 259–279.

Scott, W. R., & Biag, M. (2016). The changing ecology of U.S. higher education: An organizational field perspective. In E. P. Berman & C. Paradeise (Eds.), *University under pressure* (Vol. 46 of Research in the Sociology of Organizations) (pp. 25–51). Bingley: Emerald Group Publishing Limited.

Smith-Doerr, L., & Powell, W. (2005). Networks and economic life. In N. J. Smelser & R. Swedberg (Eds.), *The handbook of economic sociology* (2nd ed., pp. 379–402). New York/Princeton: Russell Sage Foundation & Princeton University Press.

Sparks, S. D. (2016, December 23). New Regional Education Research Labs expand partnerships for ESSA support. Blog post. Retrieved from: http://blogs.edweek.org/edweek/inside-schoolresearch/2016/12/new_regional_research_labs_exp.html

Spillane, J. P. (2000). Cognition and policy implementation: District policymakers and the reform of mathematics education. *Cognition and Instruction, 18*(2), 141–179.

Spillane, J. P., Reiser, B. J., & Reimer, T. (2002). Policy implementation and cognition: Reframing and refocusing implementation research. *Review of Educational Research, 72*, 387–431.

Stinchcombe, A. (1965). Social structure and organizations. In J. G. March (Ed.), *Handbook of organizations* (pp. 142–193). Chicago: Rand McNally.

Strauss, V. (2015). The successor to No Child Left Behind has, it turns out, big problems of its own. *Washington Post*, December 7, 2015.

Stuart, T. E., & Podolny, J. M. (1999). Positional consequences of strategic alliances in the semiconductor industry. In S. Andrews & D. Knoke (Eds.), *Networks in and around organizations* (Vol. 16 of Research in the Sociology of Organizations) (pp. 161–182). Greenwich: JAI Press.

Tolbert, P., & Zucker, L. (1983). Institutional source of change in organizational structure: The diffusion of civil service reform, 1880–1935. *Administrative Science Quarterly, 28*, 22–39.

Turley, R., & Stevens, C. (2015). Lessons from a school district–university research partnership: The Houston Education Research Consortium. *Educational Evaluation and Policy Analysis, 37*(1S), 6S–15S.

Tyack, D. B. (1974). *The one best system: A history of American urban education*. Cambridge, MA: Harvard University Press.

Weiss, C. (1980). Knowledge creep and decision accretion. *Knowledge, 1*(3), 381–404.

Zucker, L. (1987). Institutional theories of organization. *Annual Review of Sociology, 13*, 443–464.

Author Index

A
Abdulkdiroglu, A., 223
Adelman, C., 133, 197, 198, 209, 267, 366, 370, 416, 418, 432, 536, 548
AERA, 415
Ahearn, C., 431–452
Ainsworth-Darnell, J.W., 23, 30, 92, 122, 139, 330
Alba, R.D., 154, 411
Alexander, K.L, 42, 46, 60–63, 65, 110, 111, 121, 254, 256, 259, 363, 414, 432, 515, 517
Allen, D., 422, 487, 547
Allison, K.W., 178
Alon, S., 117, 118, 141, 342, 463, 542
Altenhofen, S., 48, 237, 239
Altonji, J.G., 225, 226, 242, 267, 370
Alvarez, G.A.S., 182
An, B.P., 422
Andreas, R.E., 178
Andrews, R., 418, 438
Angrist, J.D., 33, 222, 225, 227, 241, 242, 542, 543
Apel, R., 341, 345, 348, 350
Aries, E., 180, 186, 392, 393
Armstrong, E.A., 174, 175, 180, 181, 185, 187, 188, 386, 389, 392, 395–397, 399, 435, 437, 447
Aronson, J., 101, 102, 136, 143, 146, 395
Aronson, P.J., 350
Arum, R., 123, 143, 174–176, 185, 186, 228, 229, 266, 267, 318, 385–399, 444, 451, 465
Astin, A., 182, 391, 393, 537
Attewell, P., 332, 336, 370, 410, 415, 416, 433, 539, 546, 548, 549
Austin, M., 221–243
Autor, D.H., 254, 386

B
Bachman, J.G., 78, 340–343, 346, 348, 351
Badway, N., 387
Bahr, P.R., 393, 416, 424, 443, 537, 548
Bailey, M.J., 364, 365, 376, 387, 423
Bailey, T.R, 137, 376, 408, 432, 434, 437, 438, 444, 536–539, 548
Barling, J., 342

Barnett, B.G., 517
Barnett, E.A., 375, 549
Barr, A.B., 236
Barrera, D.B., 177
Bastedo, M., 409
Baum, S., 119, 185, 458, 537, 539
Bean, F.D., 110, 119, 154, 156
Beattie, I.R., 171–188, 461
Becker, K.I., 351, 447
Bednarek, A., 177, 186
Belfield, C., 419, 434, 539, 542, 552, 553
Benson, J., 173, 175, 408
Berends, M., 221–243, 259, 260
Bersudskaya, V., 118, 407
Besen-Cassino, Y., 351
Bettinger, E.P., 223, 224, 229, 375–377, 393, 415, 416, 542, 548
Betts, J.R., 222, 227–229, 267, 284, 370, 372, 539
Bianchi, S.M., 352, 353
Bifulco, R., 229, 235, 236
Billingham, C.M., 237, 238
Birani, A., 183, 188
Bishop, J.H., 267
Black, S.E., 345, 346, 364
Blau, P.M., 73, 173, 175, 304, 310, 434, 437, 441, 458, 494–496
Blumer, H., 540
Boatman, A., 415, 548
Bodovski, K., 3, 13, 23–27
Booker, K., 225, 229
Borman, G., 56
Bound, J., 375, 407, 464
Bourdieu, P., 3–5, 8–10, 12, 14, 15, 19, 33, 45, 56, 91, 98, 138, 174, 179, 182, 287, 362, 374, 375, 391
Bowles, S., 5, 7, 18, 19, 56, 89, 90, 99, 103, 138, 174, 252, 362
Bozick, R., 133, 141, 352, 371, 376, 392
Bradley, C.L., 140
Bradley, K., 31
Bragg, D.D., 419, 422
Brame, R., 341, 345, 348, 350
Brawer, F.B., 406
Bremner, R.H., 339, 341
Brint, S., 376, 388, 393, 409, 414, 425, 536, 540

© Springer International Publishing AG, part of Springer Nature 2018   589
B. Schneider (ed.), *Handbook of the Sociology of Education in the 21st Century*, Handbooks
of Sociology and Social Research, https://doi.org/10.1007/978-3-319-76694-2

CPSIA information can be obtained
at www.ICGtesting.com
Printed in the USA
LVHW061729210620
658633LV00030B/1529

9 783319 766928